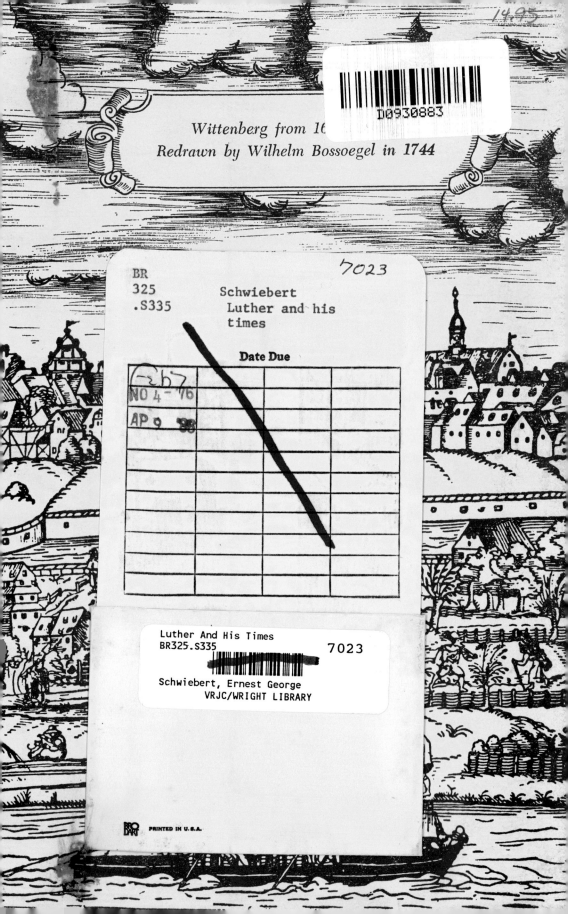

Wittenberg from 16
Redrawn by Wilhelm Bossoegel in 1744

LUTHER
AND HIS TIMES

Martin Luther's wedding picture. Painted in oil by Lucas Cranach the Elder, 1525

PLATE I

Luther and his times

THE REFORMATION FROM
A NEW PERSPECTIVE

by E. G. Schwiebert, Ph. D.

PROFESSOR OF HISTORY
WITTENBERG COLLEGE
SPRINGFIELD, OHIO

《 —— 》

CONCORDIA PUBLISHING HOUSE
SAINT LOUIS, MISSOURI

Publisher's Preface

《　》

THE APPEARANCE of *Luther and His Times* is a book-publishing event the beginnings of which go back to the mid '20's.

At that time Dr. E. G. Schwiebert, studying at Cornell University under the late Prof. Preserved Smith, America's great Reformation scholar, was inspired to embark upon this monumental undertaking.

Following Professor Smith's suggestion that there must have been unexplored influences that vitally affected Luther's life, his teachings, and the subsequent development of the Reformation, Dr. Schwiebert studied the available primary and secondary source materials, both here and in Germany, and as a result of his painstaking and persevering scholarship there emerged a new perspective of the great Reformer.

We believe this historical volume will take its place among the standard works on the life of Luther and the spread of the Reformation.

THE PUBLISHER

Author's Preface

« »

THE WRITING of this volume was undertaken with a feeling of deep humility, if not trepidation; for any attempt to interpret an era which Preserved Smith so ably and comprehensively covered in *The Age of the Reformation* is to tread on hallowed ground. But the twenty-odd years since it was published have seen the steady progress of research in the field and the discovery of much new information. Had Professor Smith lived, he would have undoubtedly issued revisions by this time, for already in the late 1920's he was making copious corrections in the text for the benefit of his students. Since the pursuit of learning is always so much more fascinating than its mere recording, this book would probably never have been written but for the unceasing importunities of my students and colleagues to make available the researches in this area of study by recent European, and particularly German, historians.

To Preserved Smith, kind friend and former professor, the book owes much of its content, for he it was who first kindled the flame that has continued to consume every available hour of time for over two decades. He also suggested that the European universities must have played a hitherto unappraised role in furthering the development of the Reformation. This theme was first approached under his guidance in the doctoral dissertation "The University of Wittenberg and Some Other European Universities in Their Relation to the Reformation." The result of the continued study has been a reorientation of Martin Luther in the sixteenth century with particular

VII

emphasis on the philosophical, theological, and socio-geographical factors that contributed to the molding of the Great Reformer. Too often his doctrines and teachings have been evaluated in terms of the dogmatic seventeenth century, to their resultant misinterpretation. From the study has emerged the towering figure of a man who profoundly influenced his age and the entire course of history.

While the labor has been exacting, the load has been lightened by the helping hands of many friends and colleagues. Among the many American scholars who have lent enlightenment and encouragement are Professor Albert Hyma of the University of Michigan and Professor John T. McNeill of Union Theological Seminary. I am also deeply indebted to the German scholars who discussed with me my findings and made available much new material: the late Dr. Johannes Ficker of Halle-Wittenberg; the late Dr. Walter Friedensburg of Wernigerode; the late Dr. Walther Koehler of Heidelberg; the late Dr. Gottfried Krueger, Dr. Oskar Thulin, Mr. H. Heubner, and Mr. O. H. Heubner, all of Wittenberg. Among my present colleagues at Erlangen University, Dr. Paul Althaus, Dr. Walther von Loewenich, and Dr. Hans Liermann have offered much helpful assistance. In Munich, Landesbischof D. Meiser and Dean Friedrich Langenfass most generously placed their private libraries at my disposal.

Many other individuals gave valuable aid in the collection of material for the book by kindly and generously providing access to valuable book collections, among them Winifred VerNooy, Katharine M. Hall, and Daisy D. Brown of The University of Chicago Libraries; Mrs. Katharine E. Bowden of Valparaiso University Library; Dr. Karl Bruelling and Dr. Theodor Lockemann of the Jena University Library; Dr. Oskar Thulin and Mr. Gerhard Jordan of the *Lutherhalle* in Wittenberg; Mr. Max Senf, the Younger, who graciously permitted use of the rare private collection of his late father in Wittenberg, and Dr. F. Redenbacher and the staff of the Erlangen University Library.

My deepest appreciation is also tendered to those who generously offered special assistance, especially to Dr. Roland Bainton of Yale Divinity School for his many helpful suggestions on the environmental study, to Professor E. Nolte of Northwestern University for his evaluation of the section on the department of music, to Dr. O. P. Kretzmann of Valparaiso University, Dr. J. Pelikan of Concordia Theological Seminary, and the Reverend J. H. Gockel of Wilmette, Illinois, for their assistance in reading portions of the manuscript and their helpful suggestions; and to that host of ministers, teachers, and students whose lively interest in the subject has been my constant inspiration.

The book should be dedicated to my faithful, painstaking co-laborer, my wife, Gayle. To her, I frankly grant, belongs the credit for any literary merit the book may have. The first two drafts were written by the author, the third draft was prepared by her, and the fourth and fifth were joint undertakings. She has devoted countless hours to typing the manuscript, checking and typing footnotes, and compiling the index. My debt to her cannot be measured.

ERNEST G. SCHWIEBERT

Erlangen, Germany
June, 1950

Contents

« »

Publisher's Preface   VII

Author's Preface   IX

PART ONE

The European Scene

1. The Historical Background of the German Reformation

   The Need of a New Perspective   1
   What Was the German Reformation?   7
   The Need for Reform   9
   The Growth of the Papacy   11
   The Medieval Church at Its Height   14
   The Failure of the Reform Councils   20
   The Renaissance Popes   27

2. The Age of Emperor Charles V

   The Holy Roman Empire   32
   Maximilian's Dynastic Ambitions   34
   The Wars over Northern Italy   35
   Charles V and a Polyglot Empire   36
   Charles Becomes King of Spain   37
   The Election of Charles V   39
   Charles Convenes the Diet of Worms   43
   The Spanish Revolution   46
   French and Hapsburg Rivalry   49
   The Problem of the Turks   58

3. The History of Saxony

   The Luther Lands   67
   Old and New Saxony   69
   The Development of Electoral Saxony   72

XI

Saxony Under the Wettin Line   78
Thuringia   79
Meissen   79
The Growth of the New Saxony   81
The Origin of Ernestine and Albertine Saxony   81
The Sixteenth Century Atmosphere   86

PART TWO

THE PROTAGONIST

4. Martin Luther

The Formative Years   99
The Ancestral Heritage   102
His Boyhood   106
The Mansfeld School Days   110
The Year in Magdeburg   117
His Beloved Eisenach   122
The Erfurt Student   128
Luther Enters the Monastery   136

5. The Monastic Struggle

The Reality of the Crisis   145
The Cause of the Conflict   152
The Medieval Plan of Salvation   155
The Contribution of Augustine   158
The Influence of the Schoolmen   162
The Journey to Rome   174
The Promotion to the Doctorate   193

PART THREE

THE UNIVERSITY ENVIRONMENT

6. The Electoral Town of Wittenberg

Medieval Wittenberg   199
The Town of Wittenberg in Luther's Day   201

7. The Physical Plant of the University

The Campus Proper   221
The University Library   244

8. The University of Wittenberg   254
   Academic Organization   256
   The Endowment of the University   257
   The Income of a Wittenberg Professor   262
   The Pre-Lutheran Faculty   268

                      PART FOUR
                 THE EMERGING REFORMER

9. Triumph of Biblical Humanism in the University of
   Wittenberg   275
   The Budding Biblical Humanist   278
   The Tower Discovery   282
   A New Conception of Religion   289
   Luther Wins the Wittenberg Faculty   293

10. Luther Attacks the Indulgence Traffic
   History of Indulgences   303
   The Indulgence Traffic of Albert of Mainz   306
   The Ninety-Five Theses   314
   The Reception of Luther's Theses   321
   The Heidelberg Meeting   326

11. Early Attempts to Silence Luther
   The Sermon on the Ban   331
   The First Attack by John Eck   333
   The Appeal to the Pope   337
   Luther is Summoned to Rome   338
   The Intrigue at the Dresden Banquet   340
   Luther Appears Before Cajetan   344

12. Frederick the Wise in the Hour of Decision   358
   The Diplomacy of Charles von Miltitz   370
   The Death of Emperor Maximilian   379

13. The Leipzig Debate
   Luther is Drawn into the Debate   384
   Luther's Preparation   389
   Rules of Procedure   391

The Debate Begins   393
Luther Accepts the Challenge   397
The Contestants Compared   413
The Selection of Judges   417
The Aftermath   418
The Battle of Words Continues   421
Eck Maneuvers to Prejudice Paris   423
Cologne and Louvain Condemn Luther's Writings   427
The Verdict of the University of Paris   432

14. The Stormy Days Before Worms

The Maturing Reformer   438
Luther's Doctrinal Development   445
Renewed Attacks   459
The Address to the German Nobility   466
The Babylonian Captivity of the Church   473
The Freedom of the Christian   477
The Drafting of the Papal Bull   481
Exsurge, Domine   484
Burning the Canon Law   486

15. The Diet of Worms

Luther Summoned to Worms   493
Luther Before the Diet   501
The Edict of Worms   509

16. In the Land of the Birds

The Wartburg   513
The Luther Room   515
Luther's Labors at the Wartburg   519
The Translation of the New Testament   527

PART FIVE

THE YEARS OF FRUITION

17. Problems in the Early Growth of Lutheranism

The Wittenberg Disturbances   535
Confusion and Consternation   544
The Knights' Uprising   550
The Peasants' Revolt   556

18. Martin Luther the Man
    His Physical Appearance   571
    Other Characteristics   577
    His Handicaps   580
    Katherine von Bora   581
    The Luther Family   594

19. Wittenberg Becomes the Nursery of the German Reformation
    Student Enrollment   603
    The First Lutheran University   608

20. Founding of the Lutheran Church
    The Medieval Heritage   613
    The Church Visitations in Lutheran Lands   615
    The Ordination of the Lutheran Clergy   619
    Ministerial Aids   631
    The German Bible   643
    Liturgical Changes   663
    The Organization of Schools   676

21. Attempts to Unify Christendom
    The Controversy with Erasmus   683
    The Marburg Colloquy   695
    The Augsburg Confession   714
    The Wittenberg Concord   736
    The Schmalkald Articles   740

22. The Close of Life
    The Aging Luther   745
    Luther's Death   747

    Bibliographical Notes   753

    Notes   765

    Index   879

Illustrations

« »

ENGRAVINGS IN THE TEXT

Luther's Correspondence	4
Pope Gregory VII	15
William of Croy, Lord of Chièvres	38
Pope Paul III	56
The Luther Lands	68
Growth of Electoral Saxony	73
Meissen, 1300	80
The Leipzig Settlement, 1485	83
Wittenberg, from the East	88
Eisleben in 1582	105
City Plan of Mansfeld	108
The Augustinian Cloister in Erfurt	139
Plan of Wittenberg, 1623	202
Towers of the Town Church	204
John Cochlaeus	207
Pfarrkirche St. Marien (Town Church)	215
The University of Wittenberg, 1586	222
The Augusteum	231
Towers of Castle Church	236

XVII

The Schlosskirche   237
Casement of a King   239
Other Precious Relics in the Castle Church   241
Conrad Celtis Presents His Amores   276
A Portion of John Reuchlin's Hebrew Grammar   279
Page from Luther's Lecture Notes   284
"Frederick the Wise's Dream"   319
The Pleissenberg, Leipzig   394
Wilibald Pirckheimer   424
Title Page of Luther's "Freedom of the Christian"   479
"Triumph of Truth"   498
Worms, 1560   500
Ground Plan of Knights' House, 1817   517
Title Page of the September New Testament, 1522   530
Illustration, Chapter Six, September Bible   537
Illustration, Chapter Thirteen, September Bible   539
Ulrich von Hutten   553
Town and Castle of Landstuhl   555
"Knight, Death, and the Devil"   557
Peasants at Work   559
"The Sheepfold of Christ"   561
Luther's Second Tract in the Peasants' War   566
Letter on the Harsh Booklet   569
Martin Luther, *by Cranach*   572
Earliest Known Likeness of Martin Luther   574
Martin Luther, 1521   575
Graph of Student Enrollment, University of Wittenberg   605
Martin Behaim's Globe   611
Detail, Martin Behaim's Globe   611
Superintendent and Pastor in Typical Gowns, 1600   628

"The Struggle over the Chorrock"   630

Title Page of Luther's Large Catechism   637

Title Page of Luther's Small Catechism   639

Title Page of Luther's First Complete Bible, 1534   648

Creation of the World, from 1534 Bible   650

Jacob's Ladder   653

Elijah Departing to Heaven   653

Solomon's Decision   657

Solomon's Temple   657

Matthias Flacius   660

Distribution of Lord's Supper, *by Cranach*   670

Marburg, 1582   696

Johannes Oecolampadius   698

HALF-TONE PLATES

  I Martin Luther's Wedding Picture,
     by Cranach the Elder   *Frontispiece*

 II Wittenberg, 1546   *following page 192*

ALBUM OF PHOTOGRAPHS
following page 512

 III The Papal Palace at Avignon

 IV Pope Julius II, *by Raphael*
     Emperor Maximilian I

  V Francis I and Margaret of Navarre

 VI Charles V, 1530, *by Titian*

 VII Commander Frundsberg

VIII Charles V in Middle Age, *by Cranach the Elder*

 IX George Spalatin, *by Cranach the Elder*
     Frederick the Wise, *by Cranach the Elder*

  X John the Constant, *by Lucas Cranach*
     John Frederick, *by Cranach the Elder*

 XI Duke George, Ruler of Albertine Saxony

XII Home of the Luther Family, Moehra, 1618

XIII Luther's Father, *by Cranach the Elder*
Luther's Mother, *by Cranach the Elder*

XIV Luther's Birthplace, modern view from street
SS. Peter and Paul's Church

XV Luther's Birthplace, modern view from rear
Interior View of Luther's Birthplace

XVI The Mansfeld School

XVII Erfurt in the 16th Century

XVIII Erfurt Cathedral, where Luther was ordained as priest

XIX Old University Building at Erfurt
North View of Former Augustinian Library, Erfurt

XX A Page from the Erfurt Matriculation Book

XXI Luther Cell at Erfurt Today

XXII John Staupitz, Augustinian Prior

XXIII Rome in Luther's Day

XXIV Castle San Angelo, Rome

XXV Rome, 16th Century

XXVI Renaissance Porch of Rathaus, *by George Schroeder*

XXVII Bronze Baptismal Font in Use in Town Church

XXVIII Luther Pulpit Formerly in the Town Church

XXIX Luther Preaching, *by Cranach the Elder*

XXX Altar Detail from Town Church, *by Cranach the Elder*

XXXI Augustinian College Building
Courtyard between Collegium Friderici and
Das alte Collegium

XXXII The Melanchthon Study
Luther Study in the Luther House, modern view

XXXIII Katharinen-Portal of Luther House
The Melanchthon House

XXXIV Interior View of Schlosskirche, 1760

XXXV   Fluegelaltar, *by Albrecht Duerer*

XXXVI   Fluegelaltar, *by Cranach the Elder*

XXXVII   Grave-plate of Frederick the Wise,
        cast by Peter Vischer the Younger, 1527
     Grave-plate of John the Constant,
        cast by Hans Vischer in 1534

XXXVIII   John Tetzel
     Doctor John Eck

XXXIX   Erasmus of Rotterdam, *by Albrecht Duerer*

XL   Coat of Arms of Crotus Rubeanus

XLI   Inner Court of the Fugger House in Augsburg, 1515

XLII   Imperial Herald Kaspar Sturm
     Jacob Fugger, *by Hans Holbein the Elder*

XLIII   Emperor Charles V Summons Luther to Worms

XLIV   Luther's Letter of "Safe-conduct" from Charles V

XLV   Cloister of the Carmelite Monastery

XLVI   Small Gate Through Which Luther Departed from
     Worms
     Worms Gateway Through Which Luther Entered
        the City

XLVII   Portion of Luther's Letter to Charles V after Diet
     of Worms

XLVIII   Front Courtyard of the Wartburg with Vogtei,
        16th century
     Lutherstube at Wartburg

XLIX   Windows of the Lutherstube and His View of
     "Land of the Birds"

L   Self-Portrait of Lucas Cranach the Elder

LI   Martin Luther, *by Cranach the Elder*

LII   Katharine von Bora, *by Cranach the Elder*

LIII   Luther's Daughter Magdalena

LIV   Luther's Daughter Margaret, *by Cranach the Younger*
     Luther's Son Paul, *by Johann Georg Menzel*

LV   Martin Luther, *by Cranach the Elder,* 1532
      Luther as "Junker Joerg," *by Cranach the Elder*

LVI   Johannes Bugenhagen, *by Cranach the Elder*
      Ulrich Zwingli

LVII Melchior Lotther, Printer of Wittenberg
      Martin Bucer
      Thomas Muenzer

LVIII Melanchthon, *by Hans Holbein the Younger*
      Melanchthon, 1532, *by Cranach the Elder*

LIX   George Rhau, Printer of Wittenberg
      Johann Froben, Printer of Basle
      Johannes Lufft, Printer of Wittenberg

LX   "Last Supper," *by Cranach the Younger*

LXI   Castle of Landgrave Philip of Hesse

LXII Ruins of the Ebernburg
      Feste Koburg

LXIII Page of Scheurl Copy of the Augsburg Confession

LXIV House of Prince of Anhalt
      Room in Which Luther is Reported to Have Died

LXV   St. Andrew's Church, Eisleben, where Luther
      preached his last sermon

PART ONE

The European Scene

The Historical Background of the German Reformation

THE NEED OF A NEW PERSPECTIVE

MARTIN LUTHER is one of those colossal historical figures over whom the modern world is still sharply divided, even though he died four centuries ago. Evaluations of his life and work range from those which see in him "the evil genius of Germany" to those which would make of him "a plaster saint."

It has been said that no one is really qualified to write on monasticism until he has been a monk; and after he has been a monk, he can no longer write impartially on monasticism. So, too, no one can really understand Martin Luther but a Lutheran; but perhaps no Lutheran can maintain a purely academic approach toward Luther. Yet it is encouraging that such scholars as Holl, Strohl, Scheel, and others have been able to approach Leopold von Ranke's ideal of writing history "as it actually was." [1] This aim is well exemplified in James Harvey Robinson's prefatory remarks to Heinrich Boehmer's *Luther in the Light of Recent Research:* "The author seems to me particularly well qualified by knowledge, temperament and style to give us a fresh and stimulating conception of Luther. He is broadly sympathetic but no hero worshiper. There is no trace of religious partisanship in him. He feels that he can afford to tell all the varied truth without suppression or distortion." To the historian there can be no higher tribute.

Of all the periods in German history none has been more diligently studied than that of the German Reformation. The many sermons, letters, political treatises, and polemical tracts employing German, Latin, and some Greek from Luther's pen appeared in nearly a dozen editions between 1546 and 1883. The related source materials, such as court records, church documents, etc., which have appeared in print are tremendous. Over three thousand biographies and treatises have been written about Martin Luther and his work, and still they continue to roll from the presses. Little wonder that few biographers of Luther have had the time or patience to digest this mass of often apparently contradictory materials before approaching their subject. The result is that all too frequently, both here and abroad, there has been a tendency to oversimplify the German Reformation. A true evaluation of Luther's contributions to the world would require the combined talents and training of a linguist, political scientist, historian, sociologist, and theologian, scarcely to be found in a single individual.

Nor did Martin Luther bring about the German Reformation singlehandedly. At his side labored twenty-two university professors, many of whom were equally zealous to reform the Church.[2] When Luther became convinced that "justification by faith" was God's plan of salvation, he did not rest until he had won the whole faculty of the University of Wittenberg to this point of view. As will be seen in a later chapter, this conversion was accomplished between 1513 and 1518.

When, therefore, Luther nailed his *Ninety-Five Theses* on the door of the Castle Church in Wittenberg, it was not as an isolated individual, but with the firm conviction that the entire university faculty wanted the matter of indulgence abuses clarified so as to establish a common principle of action in their midst. This concerted action by the whole group caused the University of Paris to conclude a few years later that they were dealing not with one "viper, but a whole nest of vipers." The German Reformation was, then, an educational movement centered in the University of Wittenberg.

To be sure, the University was not yet Lutheran in 1517, but remained nominally Roman Catholic until Luther was pronounced a heretic by the Edict of Worms in 1521. After that, all the conservative Catholic princes refused to support a school that kept on its faculty a man condemned by both the Pope and the Emperor. The enrollment dropped tremendously in the next few years, owing to the withdrawal of the Catholic support, leaving only the converts to the reform movement. From this date, therefore, the *Album*, or matriculation book of the University of Wittenberg, became the mirror in which was reflected the spread of Lutheranism in Central Europe.

An examination of this interesting old record in the library at Halle, Germany, reveals that no fewer than 16,292 students enrolled at the University of Wittenberg between 1520 and 1560. Naturally, thousands of them left those halls of learning with their souls on fire for the new reform movement, which they had heard so ably expounded at the feet of Luther and Melanchthon. The location of these students on the map of Europe reveals that, even though most of them came from German lands, many of them came from England, France, Poland, the Scandinavian countries, and the Balkans. Who is to measure the impact of these thousands of Gospel preachers and teachers who returned to their home communities and became apostles of the Lutheran reform? The coming of the Reformation to each region, as reflected in the matriculation at the University of students from that territory, is a fascinating study.

Furthermore, it is significant how intimate was the contact between Luther and important men all over Europe. Any student familiar with his voluminous correspondence will need no further evidence. It is amazing that Luther, a busy professor, town pastor, civic leader, and author, was still able to keep his finger on the pulse of Germany. As for Melanchthon, it is claimed that he knew personally every schoolteacher in Germany who had been trained at Wittenberg.

In the light of these facts the German Reformation must be regarded as a very involved movement, the work not of Martin Luther and a few fellow professors, but of an army of people, some 22,000 students, priests, monks, and laymen carrying the Gospel message to the German people.[3] Each community received the Reformation in its own unique way. In one region the message was brought by a Wittenberg layman; in another by a Catholic priest converted by Luther's writings; in a third by the sermon of some Wittenberg professor; but in every case we find that local conditions varied and the success of the movement in each com-

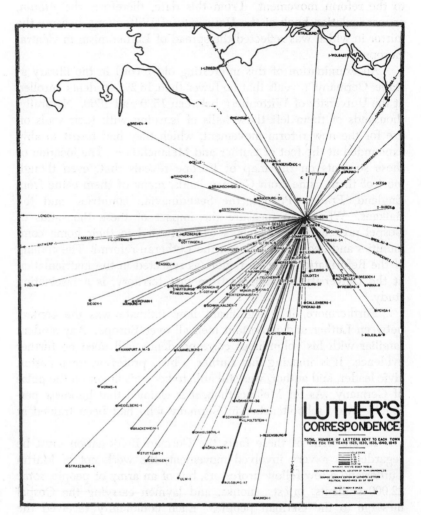

Luther's Correspondence

munity was determined by the ability of its leaders and the attitudes of those people to whom the message was brought. Thus the picture becomes almost kaleidoscopic in its confused complexity.

Nor does this new perspective detract from the glory of Luther; rather, it augments his place in the whole movement. In this setting Luther becomes the commander in chief of a vast army, while Melanchthon, Jonas, Amsdorf, Bugenhagen, and others make up his advisory staff. Fundamentally, then, the German Reformation was possible only because of a well-organized educational program that made Wittenberg the nursery of the whole movement.

The University assumed leadership in the church visitations, which so clearly exposed the deplorable conditions of ignorance and wickedness and the necessity for the organization of all types of schools throughout central Europe. In fact, it was the new Lutheranism produced in the parochial schools, the Latin schools, the boys' schools, the girls' schools, and the people's schools that caused the Reformation to triumph. And it was the counter-educational system of the Catholic Jesuits which rewon southern Germany.

If the work of Martin Luther could be reduced solely to the religious aspects of the German Reformation, the writing of his biography would be infinitely simpler. But Luther did not limit himself to the religious aspects of reform. His principle of "justification by faith" included a participation in civic affairs, which he ably expressed in the famous tracts of 1520. In his *Address to the German Nobility* of that year, Luther really became the voice of the Saxon court, appealing to the newly elected Emperor Charles V to reform the Church, since Rome had neglected its duty. In his *Babylonian Captivity of the Church* he expressed a maturity on the subject of indulgences that gave to men like Ulrich von Hutten a new hope that here was a champion of their common cause to liberate Germany from the economic and political bondage of the Roman See. In his statement of "the priesthood of believers," Luther destroyed the whole medieval concept of the divisions of society. In his tract of 1523, *Concerning Government: to What Extent One is Obligated to Obey It*, Luther defined the borderline between Church and State. One cannot, therefore, correctly evaluate Martin Luther's role in the sixteenth-century society without considering the impact of his advice and opinions on the attitudes and convictions of princes, prelates, and laymen.

To explain Luther's tremendous influence, one must consider also the value of the printing press and especially his use of that new medium, the *Flugschrift*, or tract. This new polemical vehicle had been employed in a lighter vein, but no one had thought of using it in the field of religion. Luther realized its possibilities as an inexpensive means of reaching the common man. Printed in the German language and attractively illustrated with woodcuts, it became an effective organ of reform by which he could reply in a few weeks to the attacks of his Roman opponents, or a medium for sermons, theological treatises, etc., all of which would familiarize the average layman with the Gospel movement. Its extensive use is shown by the fact that between 1517 and 1520 some 370 editions of his writings appeared, selling as many as 300,000 copies.[4] Doubtless this was one of the major reasons why Luther succeeded where Hus had failed. The power of the printing press is shown in the report which Aleander, the papal representative at Worms in 1521, made in his dispatches to Leo X that nine tenths of Germany was shouting "Luther" and the other tenth "Down with Rome!" [5]

This report, however, brings up another aspect of the German Reformation, on which must be sounded a word of warning. Aleander was wrong in assuming that all these enthusiastic supporters of Luther's cause were "Lutheran." It is true that the streets of Worms were crowded to the point where Luther could not pass directly from his quarters to the meetings of the Diet. According to contemporary reports, tremendous crowds greeted the Wittenberg monk on the way to and from Worms. But to assume that all these people held the theological views Luther was teaching at Wittenberg at the time is very wrong. Most of them were only vaguely conscious of the doctrines at stake, but felt that Luther was the champion of a people long bowed under the yoke of Rome. The common impression with laymen was that Martin Luther was the avowed opponent of the indulgence traffic of John Tetzel and the banking house of the Fuggers. Ulrich von Hutten thought he saw in Luther a powerful ally to liberate Germany from the yoke of Roman bondage, but failed completely to understand the deeper implications of Luther's controversy with the Roman Church. All the

German princes, including even his bitter enemy Duke George, agreed with Luther in the belief that it was high time for the Diet to consider and act upon the *Gravamina,* the grievance lists drafted by previous diets from the days of Emperor Maximilian.

In addition, then, to the theological aspects of the Reformation, there were the economic, the political, and the social reforms which Luther's writings seemed to promise. As the reports of Aleander also indicate, many of the princes and even the counselors of the Emperor saw in Luther an opportunity to bring about economic and political changes long since overdue.

WHAT WAS THE GERMAN REFORMATION?

Definitions are never too satisfactory; yet it may avoid considerable confusion to clarify certain accepted terminology. Textbook authors have employed several other terms than the older, more accepted usage, "The German Reformation." Some seem to prefer "The Protestant Revolt," others, "The Protestant Revolution." This is not just a matter of preference. Although perhaps not always aware of it, the writers using this terminology imply a definite basic assumption as to what the Reformation really was, and, therefore, these labels should be used with discrimination.

The term "Reformation" dates to a Cistercian monk, Joachim of Flora (d. 1202),[6] who took the expression from the Latin Vulgate. He predicted that a new age was about to come in the Church, the Age of the Holy Ghost, and he made use of such terms as "New Life" and "Reformation," *nova vita* and *reformatio,* an idea which was continued by Dante and other Humanists. Humanism, then, through the revival of the classical languages, supplied the media for returning to earlier Christian standards. In such Biblical Humanists as Erasmus, Luther, and Melanchthon there developed a *Heimweh,* a longing for the pure forms of early Christianity.

Furthermore, the term "German Reformation" implies a special definition of the Church. In Roman circles the Church was defined as an outward ecclesiastical organization symbolized by the Papacy. In the new reasoning of Lutheranism there was implied something quite different. The Church was not an outward organization, but the *communio sanctorum,* the communion of saints, which had continued to live in the hearts of true believers, even though in outward forms Rome had drifted far from the original course. His many utterances on the subject reflect Luther's deep concern lest a corrupt outward organization create an environment unwholesome for God's elect. Hence, the word "Reformation" meant to Luther a cleansing of the outward Church of the Papacy, the Canon Law, the sacramental system, Scholasticism, saint worship, indulgences, and many other abuses and a restoration of the pure doctrines of the New Testament.

Nor did Martin Luther regard his undertaking as the establishment of a "New Church." Just six years before his death, Luther wrote a lengthy treatise, On Councils and Churches,[7] proving by means of many illustrations from the Church Fathers and the early Ecumenical Councils that he had not founded a new Church, but rather that he had restored the "Early Church," the real Catholic Church, which preceded the Papacy. By comparison he ascertained that it was the Roman Church with its seven sacraments, its pope, and its hairsplitting theology that was new.

The use of the expression "Protestant Revolt," on the other hand, indicates a quite different basic assumption. It implies that the established Roman Catholic Church is the only true Church and that the founding of any other outward organization is a revolt against the divinely instituted authority. In fact, it implies that all those who revolted are now outside the pale of grace. If that is the intent of the historical writer, the use of this term is quite proper.

The expression "Protestant Revolution" has a similar implication, with more of a secular approach toward the whole movement. It implies little interest in, or understanding of, the deeper theological problems which were troubling the sixteenth-century mind. This reasoning places the center of gravity in economic, political, and sociological forces and assumes that they were more influential in shaping the course of events than theological differences.

Because Luther knew better than anyone else his views and objectives, and because he believed, as stated, that he sought only to cleanse and restore the early Christianity in all its purity, the term "Reformation" is most apropos; and because the birthplace of the movement was Germany, it may appropriately be designated the "German" Reformation.

THE NEED FOR REFORM

In the days of Martin Luther it was a common error to consider the Papacy as synonymous with the Catholic Church. In fact, Catholic supporters of Rome, like Eck, Latomus, Emser, and Aleander, tried to identify the two in their polemical writings against Luther. Yet it does not follow that all Catholics of this period were of this opinion. As early as the fourteenth century such men as Wyclif, d'Ailly, Hus, Gerson, and a large body of northern Christians had taken issue with those who overemphasized the importance of the Roman hierarchy. The corruption of the Renaissance popes considerably augmented this number.

Previous to the Council of Trent (1545–1563) the Roman Church had no common system of dogma universally accepted by all the members of that body. In fact, the Roman Church might be compared to a huge edifice under whose roof a number of theological systems flourished. With the establishment of the universities there arose new scholars, capable of thinking independently of Rome, around whom developed distinct and challenging schools of thought. In broad outlines, there were the Scholastics, the Mystics, and the Humanists, but more careful examination reveals that even these were often subdivided into separate schools. The followers of St. Thomas and those of William Occam had little in common; yet both were Scholastics. The Mystics all stressed emotion, but the different schools were not all in agreement with the views of Thomas à Kempis; while the Humanists, although all of them wanted to return to some "Golden Age," were far from agreed on what age this should be. Housed, therefore, under the roof of the Roman Church could be found widely divergent points of view. In some of the most fundamental doctrines these various schools expressed opposite points of view. One group believed in the doctrine of Transubstantiation, another in the Real Presence. In the University of Paris the importance of the Papacy had been minimized ever since the Reform Councils of the fifteenth century. For some time certain Catholic writers had stressed *Sola Scriptura*, the principle of making the Bible the sole guide in matters of faith. Bible reading had been emphasized by the Brethren of the Common Life. Such Biblical Humanists as Erasmus emphasized the need for a revival of Greek, Latin, and Hebrew so that scholars might examine the practices of the Roman Church in the light of early Christianity. There was, then, considerable disagreement among those who regarded themselves as Roman Catholics. In this fact lay one of the fundamental causes of the German Reformation.

It was this world of confusion into which Martin Luther was thrust when he entered the Augustinian monastery at Erfurt in 1505. The result was his tremendous soul struggle over the means of becoming reconciled with an angry and righteous God. After a wider study of the Catholic writings of the Middle Ages, Luther concluded that this was not the Christian Church established by the Apostles. In fact, with Erasmus and others Luther realized that early Christianity had been fundamentally quite different from the existing Roman Church.

The early Christian Church was a perfectly normal growth as the result of the teachings of Jesus and the Apostles. In the footsteps of missionaries like St. Paul and St. Peter, Christian communities sprang up all over the Roman Empire, which extended over an area nearly twice as large as the United States. Since there were no theological seminaries, most of the leaders in these communities were elders, men chosen from among the laymen for their fitness to read and to instruct others. Centers in which were capable leaders naturally lent aid to newer or less-favored communities and gradually assumed leadership of surrounding congregations. To their leader was given the name bishop, or *episcopus*. For some time these bishops were the leaders in this episcopal organization. In the second century, however, the larger communities covering the area of a Roman province were supervised by archbishops, and after the division of the Roman Empire by Emperor Diocletian in the third century the new heads of these vast areas were known as metropolitans. The idea of a papacy is, therefore, not a part of this early simple pattern of the Christian Church.

The simple, informal religion of the early Christians is also reflected in the basilica church, an unpretentious structure which they adapted from the Roman banks to ecclesiastical purposes. In this primitive church there was no railing between the worshipers and the altar, symbolic of the fact that the clergy was not yet regarded as a special order, the custodians of the means of grace.

Nor can the historian find any traces of a papacy before the fourth century, and even then only in embryonic form.

From his studies Luther concluded that the real Christian Church was that *communio sanctorum,* or communion of true believers, which had existed from the first and which existed still in spite of the many human encrustations clinging to it. Others before him had arrived at this same conclusion. Some, like Erasmus, lacked the courage of their convictions. Others, like John Hus, died for their beliefs because the world was not ready. In Martin Luther the propitious moment and the qualities of leadership combined to produce the much-needed Reformation.

THE GROWTH OF THE PAPACY

In the great dome of St. Peter's Church in Rome one reads inscribed in letters of gold the words from Matthew 16:18: *"Tu es Petrus,"* etc. This really is the foundation for the whole papal structure. "Thou art Peter, and upon this rock I will build My Church" is the Latin Vulgate text used as the basis for the "apostolic succession" idea, in the belief that Jesus singled out Peter and made him the head of the Roman Church and that at the end of his term of office he chose Clement, passing on to succeeding popes all the power of binding in heaven and on earth.

But it is very difficult to establish historically that Peter was ever even a bishop in Rome. Three Church Fathers after 96 A. D. mention that Peter visited Rome, but it is not until Dionysius of Corinth in 170 A. D. that the implication appears that Peter and Paul founded the church in Rome. More than likely there is little historical truth in the tradition.

It is peculiar that neither Mark nor Luke mentions this most important congregation of Christendom, even though Mark is the oldest of all the Gospels. The Book of Acts is also strangely silent about Peter as the first pope, even though it is an account of the founding of the Christian Church. There must have been a congregation in Rome as early as 54–55 A. D., because it is fairly well established that Paul wrote his Epistle to the Romans about that time. In all likelihood, however, it was not composed of native Romans, but of African immigrants. If there had been a church with Peter as the first bishop, why would Paul write during his captivity: "I am alone in Rome"? About the only reasonable claim for Peter's founding of the Church of Rome is that he wrote in his Epistle that he was in Babylon. Since that city was then in ruins, supporters of the Petrine tradition claim that he must have meant Rome.

The investigations of James T. Shotwell in *The See of Saint Peter* and Louise R. Loomis' *The Book of the Popes* make still more dubious the claim that Peter founded a church in Rome. Historical evidence shows that the Petrine tradition was the result of an historical growth over three centuries of time. As late as 254 A. D. the great eastern Church Father Origen of Alexandria denied that the Office of the Keys was given to Peter alone, although he mentioned that Peter was crucified in Rome with his head down. After eight additions, between the second and the fourth centuries, the story of Peter as the first pope of Rome emerges full-grown in *The Book of the Popes*, setting forth the exact length of time he was pope and stating that he ordained Clement as his successor. As Loomis' investigations have shown, most of this material was taken from a fifth-century source, Jerome's *De Viris Illustribus*, a part of the same historical tradition.[8]

Therefore, while early tradition seems to show that Peter was at one time in Rome, the claim that he was the founder of a congregation, the first bishop, or even the first pope of western Christendom lacks historical evidence. This weakness explains why later churchmen were so anxious to supply the missing line of popes; it did not even occur to early bishops in the Roman Empire. In fact, there were six great metropolitan centers about the time of the Council of Nicea (325). Jerusalem, Caesarea, Alexandria, Antioch, Constantinople, and Rome. The Council of Constantinople (381) was the first to recognize Rome as equal to the other metropolitan centers, while the Greek text of the Council of Chalcedon (451) still merely states: "The very Holy See of New Rome shall enjoy the same primacy as that of Ancient Rome." It was not until Valentinian III (455) that an edict was issued making all western bishops subject to the Pope of Rome.

There are, of course, a number of reasons why the bishop of Rome became the leading churchman of the western world. When the capital of the Roman Empire was moved from Rome to the East under Constantine, the western part of the Empire was left singularly exposed to the invading barbarian tribes. Pope Leo the Great even went out in person to meet the tribal leader Attila. And Roman missionaries, especially after Gregory the Great (590), by converting the northern countries to Catholicism, united the peoples of western Europe much more closely than the State had ever been able to do. With the rise of Islam (622) the Mohammedan tide swept before it the great metropolitan centers of the East, leaving only Constantinople as the eastern rival of Rome. It became the eastern counterpart in the Byzantine World to the Rome of western Christendom, and it never granted the supremacy of the Pope of Rome.

In fact, the theory of a papacy does not seem to have been the serious concern of the Roman Catholic world until the Carolingian Renaissance, when scholars began to ask some rather embarrassing questions: What was the exact origin of papal power? Could it be proved historically that there had been popes ever since Peter, as the Catholic tradition claimed?

A rather obliging monk of northern France saved the hierarchy much embarrassment. He claimed to have discovered an old document by the Church Father Isidore of Seville, which contained the names of all the popes from Peter to Leo the Great. It is now known that he forged many of the names, freely mixing spurious with genuine historical materials, soaked the document in water to make it look faded and old, and offered it to the Papacy, where it was to rest in the Vatican archives as genuine proof until exposed by the Renaissance scholars of the fifteenth century.

Another equally searching question was asked about this same time: How could an institution like the Christian Church justify the ownership of so much material wealth? Another document was needed, and this appears to have originated either in Germany or in Rome. This document, known as the *Donation of Constantine*,[9] also originated during the Carolingian Renaissance, although it pretends to have been drafted around 325. The story in the latter document briefly is as follows.

Emperor Constantine was struck with leprosy and, after having searched in vain all over Europe for a cure, turned in desperation to

Pope Sylvester. For his alleged recovery he supposedly bequeathed to the Church extensive imperial property in various parts of the world, especially throughout Italy. The gullible medieval mind accepted this forgery, and it was not until Lorenzo Valla (1440) exposed the document that its falsity was made known. Anyone reading Valla's exposé can well appreciate its tremendous effect on Luther's final conclusion in 1520 that the Papacy was only four hundred years old.

THE MEDIEVAL CHURCH AT ITS HEIGHT

After the Carolingian Renaissance in the ninth century the Papacy suffered a noticeable decline, from which it was not to recover until the time of Pope Gregory VII (1073), one of the greatest churchmen that the Roman system produced. Luther made the statement that there was no real papacy before Gregory gave substance and impetus to the papal theory that had been accepted for some time. It was he who established the College of Cardinals to take the papal elections out of the hands of the German emperors and who organized a system of messengers who delivered his letters and decrees directly to the kings and church officials all over western Christendom. These were the papal legates, with power to excommunicate or pardon as the circumstances might demand.

Thompson, in his *Feudal Germany*, says: "The story of Gregory VII is so packed with facts that it would take a whole volume to do him justice." It may be said that the Papacy was the result of four outstanding minds: Leo the Great, Gregory the Great, Gregory VII, and Innocent III. A study of the letters, the papal decrees, and other documentary materials of the last two mentioned clearly indicates that they did more to develop the Papacy into the power it became than any others. If Gregory's fundamental convictions are granted, his subsequent claims as to his responsibility for the souls of kings and emperors are readily understood. Substantiating this line of reasoning, his famous decree the *Dictatus* was issued, containing the following allegations: (1) the Pope is the universal bishop who has been placed by God over all other churchmen; (2) no council can sit in judgment upon a pope, nor

Pope Gregory VII

does it have authority without papal approval; (3) when the Pope speaks from his official chair, *ex cathedra,* he cannot err; and (4) no book is authoritative until it has the official approval of the Pope.[10]

The fact that this reasoning was supported by an able and sincere pope made his claims all the more effective. He believed it was his sacred duty to purge the Medieval Church of its corruption and to keep his house in order by means of dictatorial powers. Disappointing as was his experience with Emperor Henry IV after Canossa, he still laid claim to true greatness in the eyes of Rome for his contribution to the elevation of the Papacy.

From the time of Gregory VII to Innocent III the Papacy reached a hitherto unheard-of authority, for it was the period when

Roman Catholicism had its strongest hold on the western world. It is the period of the building of cathedrals, the founding of universities, the compiling of erudite *summae* in scholasticism, and the undertaking of holy crusades. Walsh rightly calls the thirteenth "the greatest of all centuries"; for, from the viewpoint of a Roman Catholic, it was the Golden Age of Rome.

Innocent III well merited the honor of being considered the greatest of all the medieval pontiffs. Hans Prutz states in his *Weltgeschichte* that Innocent III was a born ruler, more from the clearness of his mind and his sound judgment of men and of things than from the imposing dignity of his character. Pope Innocent III, an Italian by birth, received an excellent education. He was thoroughly grounded in scholastic philosophy at the University of Paris and in canon and civil law at Bologna. This wide educational background stood him in good stead in writing the thousands of letters, decrees, edicts, and bulls which attest to his belief that to rebel against papal authority was to rebel against an order of things ordained in heaven. Like Gregory VII, he sincerely believed that he was God's vicegerent on earth, and the forcefulness and clarity with which he expounded these views helped build the vast ecclesiastical empire which extended from Scotland to Greece. His writings are evidence of the profundity of his scholarship, while his clever maneuverings in his dealings with kings and emperors reveal a diplomacy found only in the greatest statesmen of history. He never attempted the impossible and knew how to create desirable circumstances and when to strike. His clever appointment of his fellow student Stephen Langton to be Archbishop of Canterbury when that metropolitan chair became vacant in 1205 is a good case in point. He had caught King John of England in a moment of weakness, when he dared not risk invasion by King Philip Augustus of France. The rest of the story is well known: on May 13, 1213, John laid down his kingly crown and received it again in the name of the Pope, as a fief of St. Peter, for which he now must pay to Rome an annual thousand pounds sterling by way of feudal rent, a practice that continued until Henry VIII broke the bonds in 1534.

It is readily granted that a pope who could humiliate an arrogant king such as John of England, force a strong king like Philip

Augustus of France to take back his Danish wife, Ingeborg, prevent Peter of Aragon from marrying Bienna of Navarre, and depose the Emperor of the Holy Roman Empire had made papal power a reality.

In order to subdue the last remnants of opposition to the Pope's universal supremacy, Innocent III summoned the Fourth Lateran Council in 1215. At this august gathering there were 70 patriarchs and archbishops from all parts of western Europe, more than 400 bishops, 800 abbots and priors, in addition to representatives of cities and kings from Germany, England, Aragon, Castile, Hungary, Cyprus, and Jerusalem. Historians recognize Innocent's control over, and manipulation of, this august assembly, forcing Church and State to bow to his arbitrary dictation, as the peak of papal authority in the Middle Ages.[11]

An enlightened modern mind can little appreciate the awe and fear displayed by all classes of society for the head of the Church. Ever since Augustine's *City of God* the idea had been developing that we are but pilgrims on earth, with our real home in heaven. The medieval mind was completely saturated with this conception, carefully nurtured by the medieval Papacy. Religion was a strange mixture of superstition and dogma. Among other things, the sacramental system is probably most directly responsible for the fear of bans and interdicts, threats of God's vengeance, and sufferings in purgatory. This sacramental system was controlled and administered through the *sacerdotium*, the system of priesthood.

In the Gothic church architecture of this period an altar railing divided the congregation from the clergy. Only the priests were permitted to go behind this railing. This separation symbolized that the priesthood was a class apart from the laity. They administered the sacraments of the Church and became the connecting link between man and God. Thus no layman could any longer directly approach his God as in the Early Church. Under such circumstances it was of utmost importance that he stood in the good graces of the clergy, for otherwise he might be cut off from the means of grace.

Among the sacraments that stood out as being especially essential was the Holy Eucharist, in which the priest was said to perform the miracle of Transubstantiation. Here in a miraculous way his blessing of the wafer and wine transformed their substance into the actual body and blood of Christ. Since the Fourth Lateran Council had made this miracle the official dogma of the Church and demanded that all Christians confess their sins at least once a year and attend the Lord's Supper at least at Easter, the importance of this sacrament can easily be understood. Also intimately connected with the Holy Eucharist was the Roman Mass. Since Transubstantiation transformed the elements of the sacrament into the body and blood of Christ, it was logical that the Mass, the special worship of the transformed bread that remained, should be instituted. It had by now become a very colorful service with an elaborate ritual, costly vessels, sumptuous vestments, effective lighting, and burning incense, all designed to impress and subdue the common worshiper. Since this was a "good work," in which the Christian again beheld the Savior's suffering and death, it became very important in the life of the Church. Many kinds of masses were said, perhaps mostly in times of peril and to assist the dead in purgatory.

Nor were the sacraments of Baptism, Confirmation, Marriage, and Extreme Unction to be regarded as less important to a Catholic community. Through Baptism the original sin of the child was washed away; in Confirmation the child was made a member of the Church in the sense of taking full responsibility for his life and actions; while in Marriage the union between the couple was blessed and sanctified by God. At the close of life it was essential that the last vestiges of sin be washed away by the sacrament of Extreme Unction. This consisted of anointing with oil the individual who was at the point of death. It is readily understood why no community should want to be deprived of this sacramental system, a monopoly of the clergy.

Closely connected with the sacramental system, then, was the use of those papal weapons, the "interdict" and, in the case of an individual, "excommunication." In excommunication, which might be of major or minor degree, the individual was put under the ban. In the minor form he was deprived of the sacrament of the Holy Eucharist and Mass, and his soul was temporarily condemned to hell. In the case of a major offense he was also exiled from the community and forbidden to attend church services. In some cases the State also pronounced the offender an outlaw. Thus Martin Luther was condemned by both Church and State between 1520 and 1521. If the offender was a king or an emperor, the interdict was more frequently employed. It was delivered in person by the Pope's own legates in the form of a sealed document prepared in the Roman chancery by experts. The seal was usually of lead, and hence the title "Bull," from the Latin *bulla,* meaning seal. When used against an important personage, it implied that a whole geographical or political area was now cut off from the means of grace. Church bells stopped ringing; there were no more Baptisms, marriages, or even burials by the clergy. Everywhere it was evident that the whole land was in God's disfavor. Usually this action brought the offending prince into very bad repute with his subjects, and considerable pressure was put on him by offended Christian opinion. Few rulers or princes dared to defy the interdict for long.

The Papacy by the time of Innocent III had become an international state whose fundamental constitution was the codified canon law. In fact, the peculiar combination of state and papal power is not intelligible without a knowledge of this special legal system by which the whole Church was organized and governed. Through canon law the clergy had their own courts in which they enjoyed the "benefit of clergy." This meant that in case of trouble the clergy were not tried by civil courts, but could be tried only in their own special courts under canon law. Furthermore, the whole papal system and the relationship between the Roman *Curia* and secular princes and kings was all carefully defined to give the Pontiff of Rome a peculiar monopoly in a "Supertheocratic State." Canon Law also fully established the monopoly of the clergy over the sacramental system. Further, the Church claimed the right to try all cases involving marriage, legitimacy, separation, dowries, last wills and testaments. Even contracts made under oath were considered to be under the jurisdiction of the church courts. In short, Canon Law was the codification of all the institutions of the Roman Church, and through this means the popes obtained a firm grip on the medieval man.

The codification of Canon Law began as early as the sixth century, when Dionysius Exiguus made the first collection.[12] It consisted of the decisions of the early church councils, papal decrees, and all other ecclesiastical legislation that had developed through decisions in the church courts. This mass of material was finally connected and harmonized under the abbreviated title *Decretum* by Gratian, the great Italian law professor of Bologna. This code was accepted as the official canon by Pope Gregory IX in 1254. Several other editions followed before the time of Luther. Early in the sixteenth century there appeared a complete *corpus iuris canonici*, which became a textbook at the University of Erfurt. Another abbreviated copy of the Canon Law was compiled under the title *ius canonicum*, the *Law of Canons.*

When Martin Luther became a law student at Erfurt, he studied Canon, rather than Civil, Law under Professor Henning Goede and purchased a copy of the *corpus iuris* mentioned above.[13] When he entered the monastery, Luther abandoned the study of law, but later, as a professor, he found frequent use for the *ius canonicum.* While no expert in law, he yet made ample use of both these collections in his preparation for the Leipzig Debate in 1519. It was through his careful study of the development of canon law that Luther began to believe that the Pope might be the Antichrist. In a letter to Spalatin at this time, Luther clearly shows the trend of his thinking leading to the conclusion that the Papacy and the whole Roman system were entrenched in Canon Law. When Roman officials began the burning of Luther's books in 1520, Luther replied by burning the complete collection of the *corpus iuris canonici* outside the Elster Gate, December 10, 1520.[14] The burning of the papal bull in the same connection was but an afterthought. By this act Luther symbolized the destruction of the very system that gave the Roman hierarchy its power. The teaching of Canon Law was then discontinued at Wittenberg.

THE FAILURE OF THE REFORM COUNCILS

The unparalleled heights to which the Papacy had risen could not be perpetuated. Although outwardly it had the appearance of health and vigor, it was soon to wither, for "a worm was gnawing at its roots." The claim of Innocent III that he was a trifle below God but well above men could not be maintained by weaker successors. He who had been placed above all nations and kingdoms "to root out and pull down and to destroy and to throw down, to build and to plant" was setting a goal that few men could expect to achieve. Although this great medieval Pope was really well-meaning and sincere, so much power concentrated in a less able successor could but lead to tragedy for both the papal office and the body of Christendom. The peak of papal power had been reached, and the inevitable decline was beginning.

Already in Innocent III's day there was evidence that the Church was beginning to emphasize finance, and in the next century this greed was to be the undoing of the Papacy. The contradictions in the spectacle of God's vicar on earth lending his authority to a grasping for worldly power, possessions, and worldly gain were too obvious. In the face of the secularization of society due to the rise of towns, commerce, and the new humanistic outlook on life, the pretentious claims of Rome were soon to be challenged in various parts of Europe. With the evolution of banking and the rise of a new capitalistic class in Italy, the Papacy was rapidly developing into one of the greatest fiscal institutions in western Europe.[15] This development was far from acceptable to the princes, knights, and bourgeoisie of the North.

The widening horizons and emancipation of the minds of the mercantile classes during the Italian Renaissance challenged the naive acceptance of the earlier claims of the Church. As man became more secularized, he became less gullible and less superstitious and, in time, stood less in awe of bans and interdicts. "Man wanted to investigate for himself, to understand the world in its finality without the overrulings of confessions and the sacraments." The time had come when strong personalities were to lift their heads, and the bold claims of popes were to be no longer passively accepted.

Another contributing factor to the breakdown of the papal monopoly was the rise of the universities. In these the study of Roman law was acquainting men like Nogaret of the court of Philip the Fair in France with the ideas of state sovereignty as it had existed in the days of Ancient Rome. The new concept that a state possessed the right to determine its own destiny at home and abroad

was bound to challenge some of the previous papal claims. It was
in France that the first real test of papal power came.

For some time the French monarchs had been attempting to
break down the decentralizing force of feudalism. In time this
process led to the realization that the Church, with its privileges,
its tax exemptions, and its collections of tremendous sums for
the papal treasury, was an octopus impeding the new nationalism.
The king felt that in his struggle at home and abroad he had first
claim to the nation's gold and other resources then being drained
from the country by the Church. He was especially incensed to
learn that there were no taxes to fill the state coffers because of the
demands of Rome. Similar conditions existed throughout Europe.

Shortly before, Boniface VIII had held a tremendous "Jubilee
Festival," in which two men were said to have been kept busy
raking up the money that enthusiastically penitent pilgrims threw
upon St. Peter's tomb. This special festival, which continued for
an entire year, was certainly a financial success. Rome, perhaps
blinded by this fiscal triumph and still gorged with the power
amassed by Innocent III, did not realize that a powerful French
king could become a real challenge. Boniface VIII was soon to
learn, but not until it was too late.

How the crafty Philip sounded out his own people, met all
the papal missives squarely with clever rebuttals, and finally commissioned his lawyer, Nogaret, to meet the Pope's challenge face
to face at Anagni is a matter of common knowledge. The dramatic
episode followed in which the helpless Pontiff, abused and insulted
by the assortment of ruffians the lawyer had picked up in Rome,
was dragged from the "cathedra" and almost annihilated, a humilia-
tion from which he never recovered.

Now began an age which became the undoing of the Papacy.
The French king by clever maneuvering moved the Papacy to
Avignon, where he could observe and supervise its actions. The
period from 1309 to 1377 has become known as the "Babylonian
Captivity" of the Papacy; and it is probable the term was suggested
to Petrarch by the grim Norman architecture of the walls of the
Avignon palace, for certainly it more nearly resembled a prison.

The internal conditions of the new papal headquarters were
hardly as orderly as the average prison, for here the Vicar of

St. Peter mingled freely with the hangers-on and the opportunists of all Europe. Church officials also began to multiply, until the new papal home was a veritable secretariat of notaries, secretaries, and minor officials. It is true that many of the French popes were capable, often well educated in law and finance. Yet, because of the loss of the Papal States they were forced to resort to new varieties of taxation and in time established a pomp, luxury, and extravagance scarcely suitable to the office of the Vicar' of Christ. A new tax was invented, known as *Annates* — already in use locally— which meant that the first year's income from a church position now went to the Papacy. John XXII improved this by adding the system of Translations, which meant that if a churchman at the top passed away, all those below him were moved up one step, each paying a promotional fee. Thus the first year's income of each incumbent could be collected by the Avignon *camera*, which now had matured into the fully organized banking department of the *Curia*. The Church also charged a special sum for Commendments, which was a sort of recommendation for a vacancy. Sometimes this was even paid in advance before a position became vacant, a sort of option, and then it was called an Expectancy. When a churchman wanted to occupy several positions at the same time, he purchased a right of Union, while a church position that had not been filled brought the Papacy "the fruits of the meantime." The legacies of deceased bishops were collected under the Latin title *ius spolii*. Indulgences, too, took on a new popularity during this period, for in 1343 Alexander of Hales advanced the new explanation of how they really functioned. Up in heaven, so he explained, was a treasure chest brimming with the merits of the Christ and the good works of the saints of the Church. When an indulgence priest has heard his confession and forgiven his sins, the penitent sinner can (for a definite sum) bolster the deficit in his own record by drawing upon this treasury for the third part of Penance, the "satisfaction by good works." About this time, too, the uniform indulgence letters developed, making the sale all the more businesslike.

Thus we are not surprised to find that the chancery under John XXII collected four hundred and fifteen different kinds of fees in 1331 and that the average annual income under this pope

amounted to 228,000 florins, a tremendous sum for that day. By
the middle of the fourteenth century it had increased to the sum of
335,000 florins. In view of the gambling, immorality, and vice
which flourished there, it is not surprising that John Wyclif after
his visit should have become all the more vehement in his attacks
upon the Papacy.

In time the practices of the French popes became intolerable
to devout Catholics from all over Europe, and the return of the
Papacy to Rome was advocated that this "Sodom and Gomorrah"
might no longer be tolerated. Finally, in 1377, Pope Gregory XI
was persuaded to move the papal seat back to Rome, but, unfortunately, not all of the cardinals were like-minded. The next year
Gregory died, and the situation became more serious.

When the cardinals met to elect a successor, a large crowd
gathered outside the Vatican, threatening and menacing the already
worried electors. The choice was Pope Urban VI, but disappointment in his regime resulted in the withdrawal of twelve Transalpine
and two Italian cardinals, who now claimed coercion, to the little
suburb of Anagni, where they proceeded to elect Clement VII.
A regular barrage of bans, interdicts, and anathemas followed.
Finally, when neither candidate could convince the other that he
was the true Vicar of Christ, Clement and his cardinals returned
to Avignon, leaving Urban intrenched on the Roman front.

It does not require historical insight to realize the deadly effects
of this Schism on the Roman Church. Not only were there two
heads of Christendom, but there was also a double system of clerical
officials all the way down to the village priest representing the
rival popes, often with much conflict between the two. When we
add to this scene the abusive language in which they referred to
each other, we understand Wyclif's references to them as "monsters," and "limbs of Lucifer," and to some of the lower clergy as
"fiends of hell."

Serious-minded and devout Catholics everywhere began to
criticize this dreadful state of affairs. Many proposals were made
to heal the Schism, which was a serious problem in the face of
generally accepted papal claims. If a pope cannot err when he
speaks *ex cathedra*, as was proclaimed by Gregory VII, who was
to determine which was the impostor, especially since no council

could be summoned without papal approval? Chief among the critics were the university professors of Paris, Oxford, and Prague. At Paris, Pierre d'Ailly, Jean Gerson, and Nicholas of Clemanges boldly suggested a conciliar solution and raised some very penetrating questions as to the real nature of the Christian Church. They concluded that since the true Church was quite independent of the Papacy, a general council could sit in judgment upon the outward head of the Church, the Pope, when he erred. Pierre d'Ailly even pointed out that the Savior had built His Church upon the Bible, not upon the chair of St. Peter. In England, John Wyclif had come to similar conclusions, while in Bohemia, John Hus was adding another powerful voice to the rising chorus. At least a century before Luther sincere and intelligent Catholics were beginning to think for themselves and to arrive at the conclusion that the Bible is the only infallible guide to heaven and that the only true Church is the communion of saints. In the monastery at Erfurt, Martin Luther was to be profoundly influenced by these men, especially the Paris theologians. Certainly, Luther's later break with the Papacy was made much easier by the fact that many educated men all over Europe had come to similar conclusions before his time.

Realizing that inner reforms alone could save the Church, the King of France agreed to be neutral with reference to the proposal of the University of Paris that a general council be summoned. Whereupon a circular was issued by a group of cardinals, who met at Leghorn, summoning a general council at Pisa in the spring of 1409.[16] This body regarded itself as being the official representative of the Church and hence authorized to sit in judgment upon a pope. Thus two popes were summoned before this august body. When they refused to appear, the council brought suit against them and declared them deposed. In their stead it elected Alexander V, who, for the sake of self-preservation, soon found ways and means of disposing of the council. However, since the two existing popes refused to abide by the council's decision, there were now three popes. Alexander died ten months after his election and was succeeded by the warlike John XXIII. Realizing their mistake, the University of Paris, Emperor Sigismund, and other proponents of reform now forced Pope John XXIII to summon a second reform council in southern Swabia on Lake Constance.

Among the reform councils the Council of Constance (1414 to 1418) stands out as the gayest and most colorful of them all.[17] The quiet little city on the lake was so crowded that temporary houses had to be erected all over the neighboring countryside. Ulrich von Richental estimates the guests and visitors as totaling around 72,000. Although this may be an exaggeration, John Hus must have been impressed by the pomp and splendor that paraded daily past the window of his prison cell as 39 dukes, 32 counts and barons of princely rank, 141 lesser counts, 71 minor barons, 1,500 knights, and 20,000 squires joined the passing throng. Added to these were the brilliantly colored robes of 33 cardinals, 350 bishops, 564 abbots, and the somber black gowns of some 2,000 doctors from 37 European universities. Little wonder the natives looked on in awe and amazement. This was the august assembly that had come to heal the Schism, reform the Church, and dispose of the Bohemian heretic, John Hus. Would it do better than Pisa?

The private life of Pope John XXIII would not bear too close inspection. Since he had been a former sea pirate, he did not welcome the council's probing into his former private life. John fled but was captured again, and, singularly enough, he and John Hus were put into the same dungeon. One wonders what subject this corrupt Pope and the saintly Prague professor may have found to discuss.

But the dramatic trial of Pope John XXIII doubtless impressed the other two popes. Gregory XII abdicated July 4, 1415, but Benedict XIII remained defiant in a castle. Even the entreaties of Emperor Sigismund were met with insolence. In time, however, all but a handful of the Pope's supporters deserted him. He was finally deposed on July 26, 1417. Now Martin V was elected as the successor, and the Schism had finally been healed.

As might be expected, the Council of Constance did not present a solid front in matters of reform. It had its liberals and its conservatives, but a number of decrees were passed under the Emperor's leadership. It was agreed that the government of the Church in the future was to be in the hands of representative assemblies meeting at regular intervals. The College of Cardinals was enlarged to avoid the danger of another schism. In matters of reform, however, the council touched but lightly upon some of the worst fiscal abuses. Instead of curbing the greedy fires of Rome, the council's ineffective measures merely fanned the flames. After declaring that its powers were directly from Christ and that it was supreme in matters of faith and in dealing with the Schism, the Council of Constance was finally dissolved, April 22, 1418.

A third reform council was not summoned until 1431 at Basel, but its meeting was like an anticlimax.[18] This body reiterated the claims that had been set forth at Constance, passed a number of laws to limit papal power, and tried to curb the greedy fiscal policy of the Roman *Curia*. For a while it was protected by the governments of France and Germany and was fairly successful in defending its authority. However, in the end the popes won, denouncing through papal bulls the damnable custom of appealing to councils and reasserting the sweeping claims of the previous popes. Rome ignored the rumblings of the earthquake until it was too late.

The Renaissance Popes

Gustav Krueger has characterized the ending of the Council of Basel thus:

> The witches' cauldron ceases to boil, the bubbling stops, the steam clears away, and we see once more the old picture of a triumphant Papacy. But this time the picture had a different frame.[19]

The clever Humanist Aeneas Silvius Piccolomini, later to be a pope himself, devised such an ingenious compromise between the two rival factions that in the end the popes granted little or nothing. And then, when he later assumed the papal throne as Pope Pius II, the crafty schemer put an end to all reforms by proclaiming heretical the doctrine of the supremacy of councils. This unwillingness to undertake reforms was to be no small factor in motivating the German Reformation seventy-five years later.

The period of the Renaissance popes from 1447 to 1527, beginning with Pope Nicholas V and ending with the Medici pope, Clement VII, was a period of extreme secularization of the Papacy. Rome was made into one of the most beautiful centers of Christendom, while the Mausoleum of Hadrian was converted into a regular fortress capable of withstanding any siege. A new Vatican was begun with hundreds of rooms covering acres of ground, and it was in some of these papal chambers that such great Renaissance artists as Raphael painted "The School of Athens," the "Disputata," and other masterpieces. It was also for Pope Julius II that Michelangelo painted his frescoes in the Sistine Chapel. Plans for a nobler St. Peter's were also laid, which later, owing to the combined artistry of Bramante, Michelangelo, and Raphael, became one of the wonders of the western world. The Vatican library, soon to be the best in Europe, also had its inception at this time. Here could be found the most distinguished scholars of the time translating works from Latin and Greek, evaluating questionable documents, and following other literary pursuits. Nicholas V justified this magnificently ostentatious capitol with all its pomp and splendor by claiming that "only through the greatness of what they see can the weak be strengthened in the faith."

However, this outward splendor was but a gilded shell for the corrupt core, the Papacy. Beginning with such men as Calixtus III and Pius II, the degeneration was rapid. The latter had been a secretary at the imperial court, and his private life was far from compatible with the holy office of pope, which fact he admitted by saying: "Let Aeneas be rejected and Pius be received." His successor, Paul II, a greedy Venetian merchant, was entirely self-seeking, with a vulgar love for show. The greatest blot on his pontificate was the persecution of the Platonic Academy, an organization known for its progressive scholarship. Suspicious, selfish, and inhuman, his death from apoplexy following the consumption of two huge watermelons was a fitting climax to his life.

Anyone familiar with the pontificate of Pope Sixtus IV knows that it required only a bloodthirsty, avaricious libertine such as the former Francesco della Rovere to secularize completely the Holy See. Now Italy was to be wasted in desolating wars for worthless favorites. The well-known Pazzi plot of Florence, in which the Pope, the Archbishop of Pisa, and co-conspirators tried to kill Lorenzo the Magnificent in the middle of the Mass, is a case in point. The persecution of the Jews in Spain under the Spanish Inquisition licensed by the Pope in 1478 is one of the most gruesome pages in all Spanish history. None were privileged to escape except those of the tenderest age. Old men and women, young boys and girls of twelve and fourteen, were put on the rack. The whole Mediterranean was covered with famine-stricken and plague-breeding fleets of exiles forbidden to land in any European port, dying by the hundreds like flies.

But the Papacy reached its lowest ebb during the time of Martin Luther, the period of Alexander VI, Julius II, and Leo X. Doubtless, under the first and his depraved son, Caesar Borgia, the lowest depth of all papal history was reached. Alexander would go to any length to help Caesar Borgia accomplish his foul purposes. Contemporary accounts of the latter's crimes are almost beyond credibility. He is said to have been responsible for the death of over a hundred people, including his own brother. He caused his brother-in-law to be strangled in his presence and slew Peroto, Alexander's favorite, in the Pope's own arms, his blood spouting over the papal robes.

Rome's rejoicing at the close of this Borgia period was quickly extinguished by the "Pontificate terrible," under Pope Julius II, the warrior pope. He led his armies in person through the streets of Rome, where the great Erasmus saw him. It may have been this scene that influenced this clever northern Humanist to write his *Julius Excluded*,[20] a play in which he pictures the Pope appearing before the gate of heaven, where St. Peter denies him admission. Erasmus shows by deadly parallelism how far the Papacy had drifted from the days of St. Peter, as the two "popes" do not even understand each other. St. Peter asks Julius to unlock the door with "the key of faith," of which poor Julius admits he has never heard; while, in his anger, Julius threatens Peter with excommunication, which Peter in turn cannot understand, as it was unknown in his day.

Julius has been called "the savior of the Papacy and the curse of Rome." In a sense he was both. He curbed the undisguised outlawry of Alexander's period, and it was his zeal that produced the beautiful Sistine Chapel, Michelangelo's "Moses," and, above all, the beautiful St. Peter's Church. At his death all Rome was in tears, mourning the loss of a national hero. Had he not been in northern Italy, Julius II might have been seen by Luther when, as an obscure monk, he traveled with a companion to Rome.

Leo X, the son of Lorenzo the Magnificent of Florence, next entered upon the papal office amid a scene of pageantry, triumphal arches, allegorical designs and mottoes, never to be equaled. Tradition has it that he said: "Let us enjoy the papacy, since God has given it to us." Although Leo may never have said these exact words, his life was their embodiment.

In the same year that Martin Luther nailed his *Ninety-Five Theses* on the door of the Castle Church in Wittenberg, Leo created 39 cardinals for the neat sum of 500,000 ducats. His annual income was tremendous. Little did Leo realize, amid all the self-gratification and pleasure-seeking of the papal court, the significance of what was happening in northern Germany, where thousands of sincere Catholics began to rally to Martin Luther's cause of reform. Krueger gives us a vivid comparison of the two personalities who were contemporaries in this great drama:

> Leo did not care. He went hunting, amused himself with music, attended very unclerical plays and delighted in rich banquets, boisterous company, and doubtful jests. He did not for a moment realise the tremendous seriousness of what he himself called "monks' squabbles." What a world of difference between Luther and Leo! The one, sprung from the soil of Thuringia, conservative to the core, severs himself, step by step, gasping, with bleeding heart, from the Church to which he is bound by a thousand threads of belief and nationality; he breaks the yoke; erect, carrying his head high, the hero stands there, no saint, a heretic if ever there was one, and yet a man of childlike piety. The other, the son of lighthearted Florence, pampered and weakened from his youth by luxurious pleasures and humanistic trifling, the vicegerent of God, who is yet reported to have said, "It is known on all sides how well the fable of Christ has served us and ours." [21]

The period of the Schism and the Reform Councils, therefore, resulted in a corruption of the Roman See which paved the way for a great catastrophe. Perhaps no better summary of the gravity of the situation may be cited than the words of the Catholic historian Pastor, who writes:

> The approach of great catastrophes is usually heralded by the dark foreshadowing of future events. At that calamitous time prophetic utterances increased, and notes of solemn warning sounded from all quarters. Shortly before the close of the Lateran Council, the noble Gianfrancesco Pico della Mirandola, in the presence of the Pope and the ecclesiastical assembly, delivered a famous oration relating to the reformation of morals in the Church. Nothing can reveal the necessity of reform in a more startling way than the wretched pic-

ture drawn so unflinchingly by this distinguished layman. We have heard a great deal about the making of laws, said he, in apology for his interference, but very little about their observance. Yet nothing could be more urgent. To prove this, he described, by the aid of rhetorical antitheses, a picture, painted in the darkest colors, of the corruption which had made its way into the Church. He emphatically pointed out to the Pope that it was his strict duty to remove the crying abuses in ecclesiastical government. In conclusion, he added these words of warning: "If Leo leaves crime any longer unpunished, if he refuses to heal the wounds, it is to be feared that God Himself will no longer apply a slow remedy, but will cut off and destroy the diseased members with fire and sword." In that very year this oracular prediction was fulfilled.[22]

The Age of Emperor Charles V

THE HOLY ROMAN EMPIRE

T HE PREVIOUS CHAPTER traced the historical background of the German Reformation; but to revivify Martin Luther as a living human being, it is necessary to recapture the atmosphere in which he lived. To appreciate the political conditions of the sixteenth century, imagine yourself a German living in the days of Hans Sachs, Albrecht Duerer, Ulrich von Hutten, Erasmus, and Frederick the Wise. To the modern man the sixteenth century seems almost like a dream world.

These people are now pictured as living in the late Middle Ages at the dawn of modern civilization. They, however, felt quite different about themselves. They regarded themselves, not as citizens of France, Germany, or Spain, but as members of a peculiar political institution, the Holy Roman Empire.[1] Man in that day did not know modern France, England, or Germany, for political states were not yet a part of his pattern of thought. The modern State, as understood today, was still several hundred years in the future. Nor did the modern relationship of Church and State exist in his pattern of thought. Before we can obtain a grasp of the unique political atmosphere in which Martin Luther developed, his point of view must be recreated; and to do this, the background of that mystical institution which embraced all western Christendom, the Holy Roman Empire, must be examined.

In the days of Christ the whole western world, from modern Iraq to northern England, was one huge Roman Empire, with Caesar Augustus at the head. At that time this vast empire, twice the size of the United States, was still pagan. But as the centuries rolled by, the teachings of Jesus of Nazareth transformed this broad domain into a Christian world. In time the Caesars of Rome crumbled to dust, and northern rulers took their place. Although the rule of this vast region had passed to Charlemagne and, later, to the German kaisers, in the minds of the people it was still the same Roman Empire, which had now become "Holy." Was not its population now Christian and its ruler, the Emperor, blessed by the Pope upon the assumption of his office? These devout but naive people concluded on the basis of Daniel 2 that there would be but four world empires. Three of these had passed away, and they were now living in the fourth and last, which would endure to the end of the world. Nor did it seem to particularly bother the people of this period that there were separate rulers in France, England, Spain, and other European countries. In the minds of pious Christians this merely meant that the Emperor was God's divinely appointed secular head of all western Christendom, while the kings governed particular regions with but limited control.

In fact, at one time during the so-called Middle Ages, man believed that all western Christendom was the mystical body of Christ and that in this great Christian commonwealth the Emperor was merely God's divinely established power to curb evil while the godly built His kingdom. That it did not always work out that way could also be easily explained. Satan and evil kept God's elect from working out a perfect state of affairs here on earth. With Augustine, they felt that man on his pilgrim journey to his real home in the City of God was bound to encounter a certain amount of trouble. Emperors and popes were also human, and frequently they, too, became the victims of sin and the forces of evil.

While Martin Luther was growing up in the little country town of Mansfeld near the Harz Mountains in central Germany, he learned about this strange Holy Roman Empire, of which the German lands formed the central nucleus. During his formative years at Eisenach and Erfurt the colorful Hapsburg ruler Emperor Maximilian I was on the throne. Little did Luther realize then the role he was to play in this strange German drama or that it was to be this emperor's grandson, the Emperor Charles V, whom he would meet face to face at Worms in 1521.

Maximilian's Dynastic Ambitions

Like their descendants, the people of the Reformation period
were also very inconsistent. Even though on the one hand they
accepted their medieval heritage of the mystical Holy Roman Empire, on the other, in the hard practical world with its dynastic
ambitions, there was developing a system of power politics that
strangely prophesied many of the evils of modern times. At this
time Cardinal Wolsey in England began to play nation against
nation in his philosophy of the "balance of power," a practice which
was to continue throughout the centuries. It was during Luther's
childhood that these first great European coalitions were being
formed in an attempt to control the wealth of northern Italy. Kings
all over Europe were seeking favorable dynastic marriages.
Henry VII of England tried to arrange suitable matches between
his son Arthur and Catherine, the daughter of Ferdinand and
Isabella of Spain; and between his daughter Margaret and King
James IV of Scotland. The kings of France, Louis XII and
Francis I, were also using every opportunity to cement or enlarge
their territories. Thus Maximilian considered himself fortunate to
secure the hand of Mary of Burgundy, the daughter of Charles the
Bold, for she brought the rich dowry of Franche Comté and the
Seventeen Provinces of the Netherlands. Maximilian continued to
arrange other political marriages for his children to enhance the
Hapsburg power in Europe.[2] His daughter Margaret was given to
Don Juan of Spain; while Philip the Handsome was stupidly
matched with Joanna the Mad, another daughter of Ferdinand and
Isabella and the heiress to the two Spanish crowns of Castile and
Aragon. This mismatched pair were to become the parents of the
Emperor Charles V. Maximilian, often nicknamed the "Dreamer,"
did not quite conform to the concept of God's divinely appointed
ruler. Although not always successful in his military campaigns,
in his dynastic schemes he cleverly laid the foundations for a
powerful Hapsburg state that was to culminate in the age of
Charles V.

Maximilian, although perhaps a little too impetuous at times —
his motto was "Hold yourself in check" — was an extremely gifted

ruler. He spoke no less than seven languages and often displayed a gift for dramatic oratory before the German diets. A daring and enthusiastic hunter, he was considered an expert in the art of war. Perhaps his greatest weakness was the lack of a cool, steady will power which would remain steadfast even though his ambitions were not immediately realized. The passions of his life seem to have been: (1) to outwit and outmaneuver the French kings; (2) to ward off the rising Mohammedan threat from the East; and (3) to obtain permanent control over the rich towns of northern Italy.

The Wars over Northern Italy

War in the Middle Ages was a kind of sport in which the tenets of knighthood demanded certain rules of conduct even during the heat of battle. With the invention of gunpowder, when one no longer met his opponent in personal combat, the modern cannon and the harquebus (the crude forerunner of the musket) turned war into a bloody and serious business.[3] Where formerly sheer physical strength and courage, such as displayed by the Swiss pikesmen, had always triumphed and clever knights were able to win the lasting esteem and admiration of a worthy foe, now a type of warfare developed in northern Italy that made strategy and terrain all-important. Of course, the cannon was not yet perfected — the barrel was held together by straps — but if loaded by an expert who knew just how large a charge to use, it proved demoralizing to a foe depending upon outworn methods of warfare.

The causes of the Italian wars do not interest us here. Suffice it to point out that a not too intelligent French king, Charles VIII, was persuaded by his bribed counselors to invade Italy under the pretext of pressing an old claim to the Kingdom of Naples.[4] Through this perilous adventure he set Europe aflame, where the fires of war were to smolder and break out anew between the years 1495 and 1559 before the rivals became exhausted and the flames of war were finally quenched by the Treaty of Cateau-Cambrésis. This first rather general European war was to outlast Emperor Maximilian and even his grandson, Charles V; and while the German Reformation was developing in Germany, the Emperor was kept from dealing with the Luther question in person partly because of his Italian preoccupation. Strange how history is often shaped by forces far beyond the control of those who happen to be in power at a given moment.

CHARLES V AND A POLYGLOT EMPIRE

As historians frequently point out, it is often very difficult to evaluate the reign of a king or an emperor because of certain intangible aspects of his period. The question may be rightly asked: Did Charles V fail as emperor because of innate lack of ability, or was his failure due to the gigantic problems that he faced during his reign? No doubt, it was due to both, although historians are not agreed on this point.

There are a number of biographies of Charles V presenting wide ranges of opinion as to the gifts of this Hapsburg ruler.[5] Contemporary evidence is confusing and often far from complimentary. To be sure, the most damaging observations of eyewitnesses were by people who did not like Charles; yet there is doubtless some truth to their claims. Certainly it was most unfortunate that Charles, who was destined to become the ruler of a vast polyglot empire embracing almost three fourths of western Europe, should be unable to master languages. He did not even learn to speak his native Flemish fluently, while upon his arrival in Spain his knowledge of Spanish consisted of such phrases as "good morning" and "good-by." This deficiency did not endear him to his Spanish subjects. The capable Cardinal Ximenes, the regent of Spain from the death of Ferdinand in 1516 to the arrival of the young King Charles from the Netherlands, observed: "Charles knows practically nothing of Spain, and most of that is wrong." Little wonder that these people were to give Charles trouble just when he badly needed Spanish support to solve the Luther problem in Germany. He never learned the German language well, and Latin was practically a closed book to Charles, as it was to most princes. Consequently there was a barrier of language between the young Hapsburg and his peoples which must have been a tremendous handicap in understanding the problems of his German subjects at Worms and at Augsburg.

CHARLES BECOMES KING OF SPAIN

Charles had grown up in the Netherlands under an atmosphere not too favorable for a retiring and inarticulate boy. He now and then released his pent-up frustrations by teasing bears and lions in their cages at the zoo. Margaret of Austria, an aunt, whose husband, Don Juan, had died years before, was acting in the capacity of his "foster mother." His father had passed away when Charles was a little boy of six, and his mother was too unbalanced to be trusted with the lad. With Charles in the Netherlands at Malines were three sisters, while his brother Ferdinand and another sister grew up in Spain. He received a good education if tutors and outward advantages can be considered the best means of developing the young prince's abilities.

Sanuto, the Venetian envoy to the Spanish court, saw Charles at the age of sixteen just after the death of his grandfather. Of Charles, Sanuto says:

> He had a good body, thin but well formed, and of medium height. His forehead was broad and clear, but his eyes bulged and stared; they looked, said the Venetian Pasqualigo, as if they were stuck on and did not really belong to him.[6]

The description of Charles by Richard Pace is even less complimentary, for he said that when Charles was absorbed in thought, he looked like an "idiot." Charles had the bad habit of allowing his lower jaw to drop, as it apparently did not quite fit the upper. He must have realized his shortcomings all too well, for he was often hesitant and stammering in speech when faced with a trying situation. Yet he had other compensatory qualities that made him all the more of an enigma to his contemporaries. He was grave and reserved, conscientious and steadfast, with a high degree of loyalty expressed in his devotion to Chièvres, his counselor and grand chamberlain, and other members of his court. Later, he was a tender and affectionate husband.

Charles came to Spain under great handicaps. The country over which he was about to reign was far from unified. Each region had its own Cortes, or parliament, and system of government; and, even though Ferdinand and Isabella had combined the throne in

William of Croy, Lord of Chièvres

a royal marriage between the two leading houses of Castile and Aragon, fundamentally these two regions remained far apart. Charles' hopes for the throne were complicated still further by the natural liking of the aged King Ferdinand for Charles' younger brother. Ferdinand had even considered establishing Joanna the Mad as Queen Regent, hoping a means might be found of legalizing the succession of the young Ferdinand, his namesake; but the old king died before he could complete these arrangements, and Charles, the elder son, succeeded to the throne.

Charles did not improve conditions by bringing with him to Spain from the Netherlands a court of some five hundred Flemish advisers and officials, among whom Chièvres and Adrian of Utrecht, a tutor from the University of Louvain, were the most offensive. Since Cardinal Ximenes, the regent, died before Charles' arrival, the Flemish domination of the scene was all the more complete.

Little wonder that Peter Martyr recorded the following impression shortly after Charles' arrival:

> The Castilians complained that Charles was not king but the subject of Chièvres; that he was led like a muzzled calf, unable to turn his head unless the Flemings willed; that Castilians, the Conquerors of Spain, were treated like born in a sewer by men whose only gods were Bacchus and Cithaera.[7]

Naturally, Charles found it difficult to raise the funds for such a large retinue. In a day when rulers were not allowed a regular budget allowance, but had to depend upon the voting of subsidies, Charles encountered real difficulties in his attempts to raise the money necessary to journey to Aachen to be crowned the successor of his grandfather Maximilian as Emperor of the Holy Roman Empire.

THE ELECTION OF CHARLES V

Charles was en route to Barcelona in 1519 when he received the message that his grandfather had died January 10. Naturally, he was immediately occupied with the thought of becoming his successor. The Spanish people, however, disliked the prospect of their newly established king burdened with additional duties. They feared that Charles as Emperor would make Spain "the tail to a European kite." Charles rushed to the Galician port of Corunna for departure, but not without meeting many difficulties and making many promises. Somewhat unconventionally the Castilian Cortes was hurriedly summoned to Santiago and then moved again to the port of Corunna to make final provisions for the King's departure. In brief speeches before the deputies, the President of the Cortes and Charles pointed out that they were sorry he had to leave but promised that the King would return in three years. Furthermore, the deputies were assured that all foreigners would be kept from governing Spain during the King's absence. After much persuasion the deputies at Corunna reluctantly agreed to permit his departure and voted the necessary subsidies for the trip to Germany. When Charles left, Spain was on the brink of civil war, and his appointment of his former tutor, Adrian of Utrecht, as Governor of Spain during his absence added fuel to the already smoldering fires. There is no question that in his first attempt to govern Spain Charles undoubtedly failed.

The election of the Emperor of the Holy Roman Empire was not just the simple matter of choosing a successor. Since the early Middle Ages there had slowly evolved a complicated system of political election. By the *Golden Bull* of 1356 the number of German electors had been fixed at seven. Three of these electors were the ecclesiastical princes, the Archbishops of Mainz, Cologne, and Trier. The four lay princes were the Margrave of Brandenburg, the Elector of Saxony, the Elector of the Palatinate, and the King of Bohemia. Under the imperial system each of these electors had a special function during an *Interregnum*, or period when there was no emperor.

The seven German electors were but human beings, and in time there developed the usual complicated system of politics and bribery in which political maneuvering and bargaining was forced upon the candidates. To this sorry spectacle the election of 1519 was to prove no exception.[8] As on former occasions, the man who could offer the most substantial bribe was the likely victor, a fact to which the records of the banking house of the Fuggers in Augsburg bear ample testimony.

As early as 1513 Emperor Maximilian became greatly concerned with the problem of a successor. Although at times he did not seem to care particularly whether or not it were Charles, yet by August 7, 1518, all but Trier and Saxony had agreed to support the election of his grandson. Unfortunately, however, the sudden death of the Emperor threw the whole matter into confusion, and the game of bargaining began all over again.

The crown of the Holy Roman Empire must still have had considerable glamour, for the other two candidates were the Kings of England and France, rulers of two rather well-centralized states. The chances of Henry VIII's election were never too promising, but those of Francis I were a real threat to the Hapsburgs. Intense excitement reigned in Germany all through the spring of 1519. French threats of invasion intimidated the near-by Rhenish electors. Leo X played both candidates against Charles and at heart was eager to see Francis I elected. The "war of nerves," however, in the end defeated its own purpose, for it finally became clear to the German electors that the Pope and Francis were working hand in glove, while the subtle diplomatic game played by Cardinal Wolsey in furthering Henry's candidacy was likewise distasteful.

In the meantime Charles' supporters had not been asleep. The Swabian League in southwestern Germany was openly espousing his cause. Even Franz von Sickingen, a powerful Rhenish knight, had been convinced that his bread was buttered on the Hapsburg side.[9]

On the basis of the records of the famous banking house of the Fuggers in Augsburg, Germany, Karl Brandi, in his recent biography of Charles V, claims that the election cost Charles nearly a million gold gulden, of which about half was spent in bribes.[10] The Hapsburgs, with the backing of the Fuggers, had the advantage, as this banking firm had ample resources and could offer better securities than the houses supporting the French King. Translated into American money, Mainz received around $1,500,000; Cologne around $700,000; the Elector of the Palatinate around $2,500,000. Brandi also states that the Fugger records show the sum of $938,000 paid to Electoral Saxony, a considerable part of which was to quiet her claim to Friesland. The allegation that Frederick the Wise accepted such a bribe is in direct contradiction to all evidence from the Saxon court. George Spalatin, Frederick's court chaplain, historian, secretary, and confidential adviser, wrote in his biography of Frederick the Wise one year after the prince's death that the Saxon Elector could not be "bought off through propaganda or gifts" and that he refused to accept "a penny." [11] For this reason, he adds, Charles was uncertain about Frederick's vote to the very last. Brandenburg, perhaps the most greedy of them all, supported the French candidate and went empty-handed.

When the Pope discovered that the candidacy of Francis was losing ground, he tried a clever last-minute maneuver. Charles von Miltitz, a native of Saxony, was sent to the court of Frederick the Wise on a double mission. He was to use his persuasive powers and "crocodile tears" to induce the prince to coerce Martin Luther from his evil ways and to urge Frederick to become a rival candidate for the imperial crown. All kinds of promises were made to the Elector, including the "Golden Rose" and a cardinal's hat, which Frederick might offer to anyone he chose. It is not clear

who was to receive the cardinal's hat, but it is not beyond reason
to infer that it was Luther whom Leo had in mind; for according
to Aleander, the Archbishop of Trier made similar extravagant offers
to Luther at Worms if he would but recant and so heal the breach
in the Church.[12] Frederick, keen and cautious as he was, was also
far too honest to accept these papal overtures, and the whole
scheme collapsed.

A German historian some years ago tried to show that Frederick the Wise was elected for a short time, but historical evidence
seems to make the claim extremely doubtful.[13] Frederick had even
told the French quite frankly that he was not interested in their
proposals as he was already supporting the other side.

Finally, June 28, 1519, the tocsin rang three times in the city
of Frankfurt-am-Main, summoning all God's children to pray for
the election of a good king.[14] Twenty-two trumpeters gave the
signal when the new Emperor had been elected. Charles had
emerged as the unanimous choice. Even the Margrave of Brandenburg had finally decided to cast his vote with the rest for the
young Hapsburg. Charles was now "King of the Romans, elected
Roman Emperor, semper augustus."

After the election, Wolsey and Francis began to draw closer
together. Margaret in the Netherlands became much concerned
about the future, and Charles also feared the *rapprochement*.[15]
It was partly for this reason that young Charles was anxious to
leave Corunna, that he might reach England to cement his relations
with Henry VIII before Francis could successfully undermine their
relationship. On May 27, 1520, Henry and Charles met at Canterbury and again in July on the continent. In the interim, Cardinal
Wolsey had staged a secret meeting between Henry and Francis,
more commonly known as the meeting of the "Field of the Cloth
of Gold," where each ruler tried to impress the other with the pomp
and splendor of his tents and elaborately decorated surroundings.
Promises were made on both sides which neither expected to keep,
and Henry directly contradicted his promises to Francis when he
again met with Charles.

On October 22, 1520, just outside Aachen, Germany, Charles
was welcomed by the German electors. In the colorful procession

were counts, lords, foot soldiers, the town officials of Aachen, all a part of the grand welcoming party; while Charles, accompanied by four hundred cavalrymen, Spanish grandees, and Knights of the Golden Fleece, rode in their midst, dressed in gleaming armor and lavish brocade, his splendor far surpassing the most spectacular of knights. On the following morning the coronation took place, which occasion is well pictured in the following account by Charles' recent biographer, Karl Brandi:

> Very early on the morning of the 23rd the coronation ceremony began in the great cathedral of Charlemagne. In accordance with the *ordines* of past centuries, Charles was first sworn, then anointed, robed, crowned and enthroned. Reiterating the formula *"Volo"* — *"I will,"* the elected Emperor swore in turn to preserve the ancient faith, to protect the Church, to govern justly, to safeguard the imperial rights, to care for widows and orphans, to reverence his Father in God, the Pope. Turning to the congregation, symbolic representatives of the German people, the Archbishop of Cologne put the traditional question — "whether they would be obedient to this prince and lord, after the command of the Apostle?" Loud and jubilant resounded the people's answer — "Fiat, fiat, fiat." After receiving the crown from the hands of the Archbishop, Charles ascended the throne of Charlemagne, created certain knights, and listened to the great Te Deum Laudamus." [16]

At noon followed the coronation banquet and in the evening a grand feast at the *Rathaus*. All Germany was happy and hopeful. Even Martin Luther's *Address to the German Nobility*, written during the summer of the same year, expressed this hopeful note, believing the young prince would correct the abuses in Germany in which Rome had failed. Charles' answer was soon to come in "The Edict of Worms," which has been described as "a white frost" for all the hopes of a reformation within the Church.

CHARLES CONVENES THE DIET OF WORMS

Following his coronation, Charles decided to remain in the northern lands to conduct his first diet at Worms the following year. In the fall the court began to travel by way of Cologne up the Rhine to Worms. On the way Charles held his first official session with the German electors at Cologne. In the meantime the papal representatives, traveling in the retinue of the court, sought every advantage to prejudice the Emperor and his counselors against the Wittenberg monk. However, as Aleander indicated in his official reports to Pope Leo X, it was rather difficult to estimate or control the crosscurrents of propaganda that seemed to emanate from all sides. Aleander had sought to influence Frederick the Wise, but the latter had likewise been in contact with Erasmus and others who earnestly urged that Luther should not be condemned un- heard.[17] Indeed, Erasmus played a major role in the shaping of public opinion from behind the scenes, while Ulrich von Hutten boldly made known the position of the knights should Charles act rashly.

All this was sensed by that seasoned statesman Charles' old Grand Chancellor Gattinara, who felt it was his special duty to shield the young, inexperienced Emperor amid the "kaleidoscopic" diplomacy of central Europe. Chièvres, his former governor, and his father-confessor, Glapion, both sought to advise and guide the young ruler so that he would not make fatal mistakes in meeting his initial German problem. In fact, Glapion even went to the Ebernburg to meet Hutten and Sickingen in an attempt to arrange a private meeting with Luther, hoping thus to avoid a public spectacle.[18]

At this point we are not so much concerned with what hap- pened at Worms in 1521 as with the general background that pre- vented Charles V from taking vigorous action against Martin Luther at the time. Several pressing problems needed Charles' attention at this Diet. Since he was not a full-fledged Emperor until he had been blessed by the Pope, Charles asked the German Estates to vote the necessary subsidy for this trip to Rome. In return for this the German princes requested certain reforms to be made in the German governmental system. In the absence of the Emperor from this part of his realm for long periods of time, the German Estates asked that a permanent administrative body be established. The *Reichsregiment*, an Imperial Council of Regency, was created, which was to have its residence in Nuernberg.[19] This august body was composed of twenty-five members, to function only during the Emperor's absence. Furthermore, the impending war with France necessitated the voting of 24,000 men and a tax of 128,000 gulden, while the disposition of Wuerttemberg was another pressing problem of the Diet. Finally, the matter of the *Gravamina*, or list of grievances drawn up against the Papacy, so closely allied with the case of Martin Luther, seemed to eclipse all others.

The country was seething with rumors. The streets of Worms were filled with anxious faces. Aleander felt helpless. In spite of his many machinations, Charles would not break his coronation oath and condemn a German unheard when it might mean the outbreak of civil war. Contrary to his own wishes, Charles was finally convinced it was wisest to summon Luther to Worms. Upon receiving the official summons and a letter of safe-conduct, Luther left Wittenberg in the company of three traveling companions, escorted by the imperial herald. Their arrival at Worms April 16 almost resembled a triumphal march, with the city gate and streets crowded with excited spectators.

In the next few days Luther was given five hearings, two of which were before the Kaiser and the Estates. Although Luther acted somewhat overawed at his first hearing on April 17, on the following day he gave a speech which took the Emperor by surprise.[20] Unfortunately, young Charles could understand neither Latin nor German, but the content of the Wittenberg monk's dramatic speech could be sensed both by the deep sincerity of its delivery and the reactions of the assembled princes. When Charles learned the full import of the address, he became convinced that Luther was a dangerous heretic and refused him further hearings. All private attempts by the Archbishop of Trier and others likewise failed to move Luther to compromise, and he was dismissed, his safe-conduct having been extended to allow him to reach home safely.

News of Luther's disappearance in the neighborhood of the Wartburg gave rise to a new outburst of rumors, chief of which was that he had fled to Bohemia or Denmark. Whereupon Charles with the advice of his councilors and the churchmen issued the Edict of Worms, which declared Luther a public outlaw. In his first attempt to solve the problem of German reforms the Emperor had failed.

THE SPANISH REVOLUTION

Geographically, Spain is not so much a part of Europe as of Africa. The lofty Pyrenees divide it from the rest of Europe by a barrier far more effective than the Alps; while the narrow straits that separate it from Africa are more like a river. Hence, all through history Spain's contact with the African coast has been very close and the mental outlook of the Spanish peoples very different from that of Europeans.

The early history of the inhabitants of the Iberian peninsula, the Neolithic aborigines and the later Celtic invaders, need not concern us here except to indicate that the Spanish peoples have been very mixed from early times. Carthaginians, Romans, Visigoths, and Moors have all contributed to the peculiar temperament of these peoples. The original Celtiberian strains predominated, while in the northern fringe of Spain, never overcome by the Moors, Christianity was able to survive in the small states of Leon, Castile, Navarre, and Aragon. To the west, Portugal also continued to hold out as a border fief of Leon.

The reclamation of Spain, beginning with these northern Christian states and ending finally in the conquest of Granada in 1492, is indeed a dramatic story. By the close of the fifteenth century Spain was composed of some half dozen states, among which Castile and Aragon attained leadership. With the marriage of Ferdinand of Aragon and Isabella of Castile in 1479 a union was finally effected between these two main states. Under their able rule the feudal forces were further curbed and private warfare forbidden. They also sought to codify older legal practice, to put the army on a scientific basis, and to bring the Church under their control. Judged by sixteenth-century standards, Charles V inherited one of the leading states of Europe when Ferdinand died in 1516.

Like other European states at this date, Spain was far from unified. Many natural barriers prevented intercourse and understanding among its already diverse peoples. It has been seen how Charles V, bringing his Flemish court and making a number of initial mistakes, did not make an auspicious beginning. In fact, when he left Spain, the smoldering fires of a national uprising were already evident. Petty seignorial anarchy had been common in times past. While Charles was in Valladolid, his tutor was very nearly assassinated, and in Toledo there were ominous rumblings of a revolution as the only solution to the problems. The Grand Chancellor, Gattinara, had achieved a respite by promising that no foreigners would be kept in office during Charles' visit to the Germanies and that an acceptable regent would be appointed. But, as noted, after the necessary subsidies had been voted, Charles promptly appointed as regent the hated tutor, Adrian of Utrecht.

In Navarre similar rebellious conditions prevailed. Cardinal Ximenes, former regent of Spain, had quelled by force an attempt on the part of Colonel Cristobal Villalva to recover the Spanish portion of Navarre. His stern repressive measures, the razing of fortresses, and the general mistreatment were but to further the outbreak in 1521.

Six weeks after Charles' departure the revolutionary ideas began to spread. Roger B. Merriman quotes a contemporary description that seems to be the best summary of the situation:

> The Communes of Castile begin their revolt, but after a good start had a bad ending and exalted, beyond what it had previously been, the power of the King whom they desired to abase. They rose in revolt because the King was leaving the realm, because of the *servicio* (Flemish officials), because of the foreign Regent (Adrian), because of the large amounts of money which were being taken out of the realm, and because the chief office of the treasury had been given to Chièvres, the archbishopric of Toledo to Guillaume de Croy, and knighthoods of the Military Orders to foreigners.[21]

Obviously, a variety of grievances brought on the revolts in various parts of Spain. The Spanish uprisings can hardly be termed national, as they had no unity of purpose. The Castilian aristocracy led the way. Here the chief complaints seem to have been the appointment of Adrian, the "procuradores," or royal officials, and the open flouting of the hereditary privileges of the proud nobles. There were a number of individual acts of violence. The hated Adrian had to seek refuge from the wrath of the revolutionary mob, but not all officials fared as well. It was fortunate for Charles that in Navarre the movement was more in the nature of a local feud over Spanish and French claims that dated back to the days of Ferdinand. In Aragon the revolt became a struggle for democratic reforms and a type of early socialism. In the case of the "Brotherhoods," trade guilds rose in the name of democratic rights against the King and the nobles. In Valencia the racial problem was very acute, as the population was heavily Moorish. In the newly acquired Cordova and Granada the population took little interest in furthering the cause of the Castilian nobles and, therefore, furnished a foothold for the counterattacks of the King's army.

When the revolt flared in Castile, the cities and the nobles assumed control, dismissed the King's royal officials, and gathered at Avila to form a *Santa Junta,* or Holy Union. This body proclaimed itself the legal representatives of Spain during the King's absence. The King first tried to conciliate the revolutionaries by letter, but he was finally forced to employ more drastic measures. Adrian, who shrank from violent action, had enabled the uprising to gather momentum. Joanna the Mad was captured by the revolutionaries, but, by a peculiar quirk of her mad mind, at the critical moment she refused to sign the necessary document to dethrone Charles and put herself in power. The claim may be correct that her refusal to sign the necessary papers "marked the zenith of the revolution" in Castile.

The revolution more probably died out because of a lack of co-ordinated action, unity of purpose, and because Charles alleviated the most pressing grievances. In September, 1520, Padilla, the revolutionist leader, had been able to disperse the Regent's Council. By November it was becoming evident that the King's cause was gaining. With the spread of the revolt to the lower classes, as in the French Revolution (1789–1794), it became more radical in nature. The Hidalgos, or country squires, as well as the commercial classes with vested interests, began to fear the mobs more than the King. This fear brought about the rise of a reactionary group that by 1522 joined forces with royalty to stamp out the last vestiges of the revolution. In the end the King had not only won, but even gained in strength because the nobles and conservative classes had made common cause with him.

However, the failure of the revolution cannot be accounted for entirely on these grounds. Charles, too, had changed. He had learned much in Germany, principally that above everything else he would need Spain as the future bulwark of his empire. He resolved, therefore, to be more reasonable with his Spanish subjects, whom he had so completely misunderstood until now. He decided to learn Spanish, to acquaint himself with the life and habits of the people, and to win their confidence. Charles now appointed Spaniards to all important governmental positions, became more conciliatory with the Cortes of Castile and Aragon, and laid the foundations for those mature years in which a new friendship and mutual respect sprang up between King Charles and these people who had disliked him so much in the beginning.

Charles won the loyalty of the Spanish people during the twenties, but from the viewpoint of the German Reformation he paid a high price for his victory in the Spanish uprisings. While Martin Luther was crystallizing his views on doctrine and the reform of the Church after his condemnation by both Church and State, Charles V was busy with the problem of placating and winning the affections of his Spanish people. No doubt, his preoccupation in this respect contributed greatly to the progress of Lutheranism in Germany.

FRENCH AND HAPSBURG RIVALRY

The bitter modern hostility between France and Germany did not exist in the Middle Ages, but had its inception with the marriage between Emperor Maximilian I and Mary of Burgundy.[22] Burgundy had for centuries been a thorn in the side of the French kings, and this diplomatic marriage broadened the feeling to include German soil. The defeat of Francis in the imperial election of 1519 increased the French feeling of resentment, jealousy, and fear of Charles' prestige and power. At the very beginning of his reign, Francis I had proved himself an able commander in the Battle of Marignano, which may have led to overconfidence in his abilities as a soldier. War, therefore, between Francis and Charles seemed inevitable; it was to add another chapter to that longer dynastic rivalry over northern Italy.

Realizing that the war clouds were hanging heavy again over Europe, Charles stopped off in England on his way to the coronation to make a secret alliance with his uncle, Henry VIII. This premonition proved to be correct when, just after Worms in 1521, war broke out with France and Charles won his first victory at Tournai December 3 of that year. Before returning to Spain,

Charles renewed his conversations with Henry's able statesman
Cardinal Wolsey, at Bruges, and the English agreed to invade
France from the north. While in Brussels, Charles also effected
an agreement with his brother, Ferdinand, February 7, 1522, to
take over the Hapsburg crown lands in Austria.

During the summer of 1521 the Papacy was trying very hard
to gain the good graces of Charles' counselors. The Emperor's advisers were just as conscious of the coming war with France and
played an equally clever diplomatic game. Immediately after Luther's trial at Worms, Pope Leo X made a treaty with Charles
offering papal support to the imperial cause in the coming struggle
with France.

When war broke out, Charles had an army in Italy of 20,000
men commanded by the able general Prospero Colonna. Most of
these soldiers were Italians and Germans, though a small group
were Spaniards. In less than two months the French were expelled
from Milan. This, however, was to be but a preliminary skirmish.

In the spring of the following year one of the great battles
of the war was fought at Bicocca.[23] Colonna, in keeping with his
strategy, had selected a walled park for his battleground. In front
of him was the difficult terrain of a marshy field, while immediately
before his troops there ran a deep ditch along the high wall behind
which his soldiers were entrenched. Using the wall as a parapet,
he placed his harquebusiers four deep, supporting them by pikesmen and artillery. Deep in the rear was the cavalry out of range
of the artillery, yet ready to charge. The French attack, which had
to cross the difficult marshy terrain, negotiate the deep ditch, and
scale the wall, proved to be the undoing of the brave but foolish
charging columns of Swiss pikesmen. When the pikesmen finally
retreated, three thousand of their brave comrades were left dead
in the ditch and on the marshy field, while Colonna's lines were
intact. The French paid dearly to learn that the day of frontal
charges against well-entrenched harquebusiers and artillery was
over. This tragic defeat caused Ulrich Zwingli to complain bitterly
against the whole system of Swiss mercenaries. The Sforzas were
now re-established in Milan, and Charles was ready to return to
Spain to deal with the Spanish uprisings.

Further diplomatic maneuverings in European politics proved favorable to the young Emperor. Henry VIII promised to invade Picardy in the summer of 1523. The Venetians now also came over to the Imperialists. France's hope of winning the war was becoming dimmer. Francis, however, who was not lacking in courage, felt certain he could win another Marignano. He was conceited enough to regard his defeats in the meantime as due to exceptional circumstances, and he was certain that sooner or later his generalship would prove superior in the struggle with Charles, a belief strengthened, no doubt, by the death of Prospero Colonna late in 1523.

The Duke of Bourbon, who had rebelled against Francis, was put in command of the imperialist forces. While this imperial army invaded southern France, Francis recrossed the Alps and took Milan without much opposition. Meanwhile, Bourbon had retreated and gathered his forces at Lodi, where he was awaiting the next move of Francis. A part of the imperial army, however, largely Germans, was encamped just a few miles west of there at Pavia.[24] These German troops, encamped on the left bank of the Ticino River and enclosed on the north by the Park of Mirabello, seemed the logical place of attack to Francis. A preliminary test of the enemy lines on October 28, 1524, revealed that a direct attack would be too costly; whereupon, Francis decided to starve out the German army of six thousand men during the winter months. The French threw a walled entrenchment about the town, the first fatal mistake, as it scattered the French army rather thinly in many parts of the line.

When nothing had happened by February of the following year, Bourbon decided to raise the siege. According to Haebler, still the best authority, the two armies were fairly evenly matched, both having about twenty-five thousand troops. In cavalry and artillery the French were probably superior. Since the French were in the Park of Mirabello in one part of the line, Bourbon decided on a surprise attack by breaching the wall at night. The soldiers, dressed in white shirts, were able to effect openings without detection, and at dawn the surprise was complete when the whole army entered somewhere in the neighborhood of the King's camp. Francis' troops were too scattered about the walled en-

trenchments to make a concerted attack. The King charged headlong into the enemy, and even though his charge made a dent,
the imperialist cavalry and harquebusiers were too much for him.
Another charge of the Swiss pikesmen failed, as did one by the
German mercenaries, and when the final assault of the French in-
fantry came, it was too weak to overcome the united imperialist
forces. Finally, Francis, wounded in the arm, surrounded by foes
on all sides, was recognized by a knight who begged him to surrender. So, after seeing that all was lost, he gave his sword to
Lannoy, who was second in command. Surprise was no doubt the
decisive factor in the victory, but it had again proved that the
harquebusiers, well guarded by hedges and copses, were to be regarded as a dangerous factor in future warfare.

Charles received the news of the victory March 10 while in
Madrid. Although it was a dramatic moment for a young man of
twenty-five, perhaps the climax of his military career, he took the
news without "semblance of arrogance," reports Sir Henry Ellis, the
English ambassador, who was with him at the time.

After this decisive victory of Charles over Francis, and with
the French King in captivity in Spain, Europe became frightened.
Northern Italy, Venice, and the Pope were opposed to the im-
perialistic dominance in Italy that followed the victory at Pavia.
Cardinal Wolsey, the original champion of the "balance of power"
politics, now feared the imperial strength and drew closer to
France. Henry VIII began talk of liberating "the Most Christian
King," who was in captivity at Madrid and could not gain an
audience with Charles. Rumors spread that Francis was danger-
ously ill, and yet the Emperor remained inactive.

Finally, after nearly a year of captivity, January 14, 1526, the
Emperor announced the fate of Francis I. The conditions of the
treaty of Madrid would have been regarded as mild under normal
circumstances, but Europe was now sympathetic toward the French
King. No ruler blamed him for making impossible promises just
to obtain his release. That was exactly the way Francis reasoned,
too. Charles feared his perfidy and, therefore, asked that his two
sons be left as hostages as a pledge on the part of Francis to fulfill
his solemn promise, an unreasonable request in terms of modern
standards.

Francis, with his hand on the Holy Book, promised among other things to return the Duchy of Burgundy to Charles, to withdraw his claims to Italy, and to assume Charles' debt to Henry VIII.[25] On March 17, 1526, Francis was escorted by six Spaniards to a boat midstream of the Bidassoa River, where, as agreed, they met the two sons of Francis, accompanied by six Frenchmen. How could Francis rejoice in his escape knowing that his liberty meant the imprisonment of two young boys who were not to be liberated until the Peace of Cambrai in 1529? It was a high price for a father to pay for his own freedom even though a king.

Francis was no more than across the border when he repudiated all his promises made under oath, claiming that since the treaty of Madrid had been signed under duress, it was not binding on his conscience. On May 22, 1526, barely two months later, Francis and Pope Clement VII signed a new agreement, which included Milan, Florence, and Venice, to liberate Italy from the yoke of the Emperor. Since this treaty attempted to re-establish the balance of power, the agreement was to bring in Henry VIII as the protector of the Alliance of Cognac. The situation now seemed to be reversed for young Charles, and at a moment when he could ill afford further wars.

While the tide of diplomacy was shifting abroad, Charles decided to follow the advice of the Castilian Cortes and marry Isabella of Portugal, the sister of the Portuguese king. During the summer of 1526 Charles was spending his honeymoon at Seville in Andalusia. For a while at least, Charles was to find a happy retreat in the South, far removed from the cold world of reality. Although bashful and retiring by nature, he was full of tenderness and consideration for his new bride, whom he was to learn to love deeply and with whom he was to spend many years of happy married life. He enjoyed this little retreat exceedingly, even though he was very much needed in other parts of Europe, and especially in Germany.

In the meantime storms were gathering in the Germanies. Much had been expected of the young Charles V when he was chosen Emperor by the seven German electors, but the experience at Worms had proved a disappointment to both sides. To be sure, a new *Reichsregiment*, the Imperial Council of Regency during

Charles' absence, had been set up with its headquarters in Nuernberg. In its subsequent meetings of 1522, 1523, and 1524 it had
realized that the Edict of Worms could not be enforced. The
demand for "the pure Gospel" was too widespread to risk a condemnation of Luther, which might result in civil war. In fact,
the following year witnessed the outbreak of another peasants'
revolt — these had broken out at periodical intervals for half a
century — which gave the German princes numerous difficulties.
In the fall of 1525 the German Estates were notified that there
would be another diet. It was delayed several times, but finally in
the spring of 1526 it was agreed that the meeting should be held
in the Rhine Valley in the old Imperial town of Speyer. To the
very last the princes had hoped that Charles would be present,
and their disappointment was keen when the *Thronrede,* or opening
address of the Crown, officially opening the Diet, June 25, 1526,
was delivered by his younger brother, Ferdinand.[26]

How decisive the decisions at this Diet were to become for the
progress of the German Reformation is a matter of history. While
Charles was honeymooning with his new bride, the German Estates,
the majority of whose members were in favor of church reforms,
pressed Ferdinand to institute the reforms requested in still another
list of *Gravamina.* Finally, the Diet resolved to send a delegation
to Charles requesting that during his absence from Germany they
be allowed to interpret the Edict of Worms as each prince "would
be ready to answer for before God and His Imperial Majesty."
This principle, commonly known as *cuius regio eius religio,* was not
new in practice.[27] At this time it permitted Luther and his fellow
reformers at the University of Wittenberg to begin their investigations of conditions and to further the establishment of schools and
churches in the territories of John the Constant, who succeeded
Frederick the Wise. This same principle was to be embodied in
the Peace of Augsburg in 1555, thereby becoming a part of legal
agreement between the Emperor and the German territorial princes.
Charles had already failed once at Worms, and now at Speyer he
had missed a second opportunity to settle the Luther problem.

In the afore-mentioned Alliance of Cognac, signed just before
the Diet of Speyer, the Pope and the cities of Milan, Florence, and
Venice had agreed under the blessing of King Henry VIII of Eng-

land to join hands with Francis I of France to expel the imperial forces from northern Italy. More trouble was brewing for Charles, who had hoped to be crowned by the same Pope Clement VII before dealing with the Luther heresy and the menacing Turks. From this quarter he was soon to hear, too, the unpleasant news of the defeat of Hungary by the Turks in the Battle of Mohacs, August 29, 1526. This meant that the last bastion between the East and Vienna had fallen and soon central Europe would be facing the menace of Suleiman's hordes.

In December of that year Charles returned from his honeymoon. After receiving more detailed information on the development of events, he felt that Clement VII was as much to blame for the changed conditions as the French King. Whether or not Charles had anything to do with the sack of Rome the following year cannot be established. He certainly did not prevent the tragedy. Brandi says that Frundsberg and the Prince of Orange, the commanders in charge, tried to stop the troops. Frundsberg drew them into a circle with himself in the center, an old German tradition, and pleaded with them in an attempt to dissuade them. The troops, however, reminded him that they had not been paid and were determined to have a share in the rich spoils of Rome. They even threatened Frundsberg with their spears, and this demonstration of his failure to control his troops is said to have broken his heart and spirit. He was carried to Ferrara, where he died.

On Monday, May 6, 1527, the assault on Rome was made in a dense fog, with terrifying results. A week of horror followed, which shocked a world accustomed to brutality, even though many felt that the Papacy reaped only what it had sown through the years. The officers having been killed in the first part of the assault, the city was at the mercy of a ruthless mob. Merriman adds:

> For more than a week the city of the Caesars was given over to horrors far more awful than those of barbarian days. Lust, drunkenness, greed of spoil, and, in some cases, religious fanaticism, combined in truly hellish fashion to produce the worst outburst of savagery in the annals of the period.[28]

All western Christendom was horrified by such an outrage. Charles was quick to absolve himself of all outward blame. However, considering Francis' repudiation of the treaty of Madrid the

Pope Paul III

previous year and the role of Clement VII in the Alliance of Cognac, Charles cannot have been expected to appear too sorrowful. Most people, of course, blamed Bourbon and Frundsberg. For the Pope it was a bitter hour of reaping the whirlwind he had sown. Doubtless, some such shock was necessary to waken the Papacy to the dire need for improved relations with the Emperor, and this new period began with Clement's successor, Paul III.

The struggle between Francis I and Charles V continued in 1528. It had even been suggested that the two monarchs meet in mortal combat, but the age of feudalism was too remote for either to take such a suggestion seriously. Nor did their subjects consider this a solution.

In the spring of 1528 another French army was in northern Italy. Under the command of Lautrec it first took Milan and by April had re-entered Naples. However, the ranks of the army were being decimated by disease, Lautrec was dying by August, and the campaign did not appear promising. Under the new leader, Count of St. Pol, the next year was even more discouraging, and Francis was looking for a graceful means of terminating the war.

Nor was Charles' condition much more favorable. After the First Diet of Speyer (1526) reports from Germany were increasingly disturbing. Under the protection of the Saxon princes the church visitations had been carried out, and a new school system was being organized. In the northern lands Johannes Bugenhagen was spreading the dangerous heresy of Wittenberg. In Hesse, Philip was making arrangements to bring together the two Protestant leaders, Luther and Zwingli, in an effort to effect a union. In southwestern Germany the evangelical movement was also taking root under the able leadership of Johannes Brenz. Thus the Speyer decision had resulted in a "green light" for the Lutheran cause, and the spiritual condition of Charles' empire was in a sad state of dissension.

Politically, matters were even worse. The Turks were rolling westward in unabated fury. The year 1529 was to be the real test of Ferdinand and the Christian armies, for by fall Vienna was under siege. In Germany, unfortunately, the Christians were split into two hostile camps. The Catholics had formed the League of Dessau in 1525. In reply, John the Constant and Philip of Hesse met at Gotha in February, 1526, and formed the beginnings of the later Schmalkaldic League.[29] The group was enlarged by new signatories from among the princes and towns at Speyer that summer. Since these pressing problems needed Charles V's immediate attention, he, like Francis, felt that peace was most expedient. The French had just suffered two defeats, Aversa and Landriano, and apparently the ideal moment had arrived.

In June, 1529, the Emperor and Pope Clement VII met at Barcelona, and a treaty was signed in which they established peace in Italy and agreed to join in a common front against the Turks. Naples was once more restored to Charles; while the Pope's family, the Medici bankers, were to return to Florence. In the meantime similar negotiations were held at Cambrai between France and the Empire, the two women Louise of Savoy and Margaret of Austria acting as the official representatives. Here Charles agreed to drop

his former claims to Burgundy, and Francis assumed Charles' debt
to Henry VIII. The two unfortunate sons of Francis I were at last
ransomed for a large sum, and the Bidassoa farce of 1526 was re-
enacted. Francis I also married Eleanor of Portugal, the sister of
Charles, a kind of pledge that old rivalries should now have come
to a close. The Peace of Cambrai marked the end of a long and
foolish struggle between two rival monarchs, which was all the
more tragic from the Emperor's point of view since his preoccupation enabled Lutheranism to gain a foothold in central Europe
which could not be dislodged. Charles finally went to Germany in
1530 to settle the Luther problem at Augsburg, but, as will be seen
later, his chance to crush Lutheranism was gone.[30]

THE PROBLEM OF THE TURKS

The seventh century saw the birth of a strange new religion,
which maintained: "There is no God but Allah, and Mohammed is
his prophet." [31] Mohammed, who claimed to have had his revelations directly from God, had many ideas that closely resembled
the faith of the Jewish merchants with whom he had contact on
the caravan routes in and around Arabia. All of these revelations
were recorded by friends and later gathered in the Mohammedan
"Holy Scriptures," the Koran.

Mohammedans believed in spreading their faith by fire and
sword; yet, they practiced an unusual tolerance in conquered lands.
Many discontented peoples in the border lands of Arabia believed
they would prosper under these new landlords, and the faith of
Islam began to spread with unbelievable speed. The lands of the
Fertile Crescent from Palestine to the Persian Gulf, Egypt, and all
North Africa became Mohammedan in a few decades. By the fol-
lowing century Mohammedanism had spread through most of
Spain. In 732 A. D., a memorable battle was fought at Tours,
France, which decided whether the Frankish lands should also fall
prey to Allah's forces. Fortunately, Charles Martel forever dis-
tinguished himself by putting the Arabs to rout.

Spain, however, was not so fortunate; for the Iberian Peninsula
was to be dominated by a flourishing Arab civilization all through
the Middle Ages. After a long, exhausting struggle the Christians,

with the conquest of Granada (1492) under Ferdinand, finally won
back their native land and deprived the Mohammedans of their
foothold in the West. Young Charles V soon added the Turks to
his list of sworn enemies and regarded himself as the defender of
all Christendom.

In the East the Mohammedan tidal wave dashed in vain against
the stone bastion of the Byzantine Empire. All through the Middle
Ages, Constantinople, strategically situated on the "Golden Horn"
at the juncture of two continents, was considered the guardian of
Christendom against the onslaughts of the mighty hordes from the
Orient. What a symbol of strength it was! Its double walls, one
hundred feet in height from the bottom of the moat, towered above
the two land prongs joining the Bosporus Strait, four miles wide
and easy to defend. On two other sides it was guarded by inland
seas. Constantinople, the city of beautiful churches, Roman arches,
parks, and fine forums, rising majestically from its commanding
heights above the neighboring countryside and guarded by its large
fleet, looked well-nigh impregnable. Its population approached
a million souls when London and Paris were sprawling country
towns. The whole western world was awed and amazed by the
stories told by returning Crusaders and travelers from the East.
As long as the Byzantine civilization remained virile, Greece and
the Balkans were protected against the Mohammedan conquests.

After the first burst of Mohammedan missionary zeal the followers of the Prophet began to quarrel among themselves. Perhaps
the decline which set in would have proved fatal had not the
Crusades alarmed the whole Orient. Islam, in danger of being
pushed out of its conquered lands, rallied under the leadership
of the Seljuk Turks to meet the common enemy. The Crusaders
failed to gain their objectives and, in addition, furthered a new
leadership and fervor among the Turks that in the end was to
prove fatal to the Christian Byzantine Empire.

Around 1250 the Seljuk Turks permitted a Bithynian nomadic
tribe to settle in northwestern Asia Minor. Originally they had
roamed the deserts of Turkestan. Their leader was Osman, or
Othman. From this Bithynian clan descended ten generations of
exceptionally gifted sultans. From Osmanli, meaning the "sons of
Osman," derived the English title Ottoman Turks. Since they were

men who had for generations lived on horseback, the use of swift, light cavalry outfits was a natural development. This maneuver was to become one of the secrets of their great success.

The son and grandson of Osman, Orkhan and Murad I, produced a great military machine. In the *Yeni Cheri*, or Janissaries, made up of armed knights, they produced the first disciplined soldiers of the East.[32] Most of these knights were recruited at an early age in the form of tribute children, often Christian. Gathered as infants and reared in military barracks, the Janissaries were regarded as the personal property of the Sultan. At the time of Murad I their number was small; but as the Turks conquered more territory, the Janissaries grew until under Suleiman the Magnificent they numbered 100,000.

Closely allied to this system was the practice of dividing the newly conquered lands into small estates, known as *Timars*. Each member of the Sultan's pet troops had his own small estate on which he could live as a little lord. All *Timars* were held in tenure and reverted back to the Sultan upon the death of the knight. The soldiers were forbidden to marry, but if there should be male offspring, the sons were given new estates elsewhere. Of course, anyone with a good horse and military zeal could aspire to the holding of a *Timar;* the Sultan's pet troops, therefore, were not limited to Christian boys.

The Byzantine Empire had received quite a blow through the Fourth Crusade, whose plunder of Constantinople was a disgrace to western Christendom. Even when restored by the Palaeologus Emperors, the Byzantine Empire was weak and at the mercy of the rising Turkish state. If only the whole Christian world had co-operated at this critical moment! France and England were engaged in the Hundred Years' War. Byzantium had but a weak hold on Greece, Macedonia, Thrace, Albania, and Serbia. The Balkans were torn with rivalry and strife. Beginning with Stephen Nemanya, a strong dynasty of Serbian rulers was established who subdued the Bulgars, Albania, and Macedonia and controlled the Balkans from the Danube to the Aegean. King Louis the Great of Hungary then began his expansion program with no regard for the opportunities it offered the Turks. In fact, he was, perhaps, more responsible for the downfall of the Eastern defenses than any other one person.

In the meantime the Ottoman Turks conquered Asia Minor and were beginning to expand into Europe. Under Murad I, Thrace and Macedonia fell to the Mohammedans. Bulgaria and Albania came next. In the Battle of Kossovo (1389) the forces of the Sultan dealt a deathblow to the Serbian state and converted the region into a Turkish province. Now the Danube was the battle line, and even Hungary was in danger of being conquered. A defending crusading army was badly beaten at Nicopolis, and Constantinople was in grave danger. As if by divine providence, Constantinople was saved by a strange turn of events. Murad I had been murdered, and his successor, Bayezid I, was in the midst of plans for an attack on the great eastern fortress, when a new threat came from an unexpected quarter. From the East swept the mighty forces of the seventy-year-old veteran Timar the Lame, more commonly known as Tamerlane, who had reorganized the scattered hordes of the famous Genghis Khan. After forming an alliance with Constantinople, Tamerlane entered battle with Bayezid's forces at Angora (1402), where he dealt a stunning blow to the whole Mohammedan world. Constantinople was spared for another two generations. Had western Christendom but taken advantage of this moment of weakness, Murad II, who succeeded Bayezid, could not have prepared for the final conquest of the Byzantine Empire.

Later in the fifteenth century Mohammed II (1451–81), one of the ablest sultans of the whole Osman line, came to the throne. Under his able planning a tremendous force was gathered for the siege of Constantinople. The most modern artillery, with guns capable of hurling cannon balls weighing over a thousand pounds, was concentrated on its walls. About seventy ships were moved over land to get control of the neighboring waters of the inland seas. On May 29, 1453, the final assault on Constantinople began in all its fury, the huge cannon tearing big holes in the mighty walls of the fortress. The feeble defenders, of which there were far too few, were in no position to combat this kind of artillery bombardment. Although they fought bravely, their casualties were heavy, and Emperor Constantine VI was numbered among the dead when the city finally capitulated.

The fall of Constantinople struck terror into all Christendom. Everyone feared that the entire West would be overrun by the dreaded infidel. The *Tuerkensteuer* levied during Luther's lifetime testifies to this very real fear in German lands; [33] and Charles V was probably even more deeply aware of the danger due to the course of Mohammedan conquests in the Mediterranean. After the fall of Constantinople, Mohammed II converted this great eastern capital into a powerful naval base. Soon its fleet became a real threat to the trade of the Italian cities and its power a menace in the Balkans.

In 1520 the greatest sultan of them all, Suleiman the Magnificent, became ruler of the Mohammedan world. He was to be leader of the Ottoman Turks for nearly a half century. It is significant that this ablest of military strategists and statesmen ruled over the Ottoman Empire during the lifetime of Martin Luther and Charles V.

In the Mediterranean the Knights of St. John were captured on the island of Rhodes the year after Luther went to Worms, leaving the whole eastern Mediterranean in the hands of the Turks. In the western Mediterranean, Suleiman's commander Khaireddin Barbarossa executed brilliant strategy on the very threshold of Charles' Spanish kingdom. In 1525 Suleiman successfully negotiated an alliance with Francis I, still smarting from his mistreatment under the treaty of Madrid and fearing the future dominance of the Empire. All of these developments heightened Charles' anxiety over the progress of the Turkish menace.

As noted above, between 1520 and 1529 Charles had been too busy with France to wage war against the infidel. As a result, Barbarossa proceeded practically unopposed in North Africa throughout the early twenties. In 1524, when Charles was preparing for Pavia, Santa Cruz, opposite the Canaries, fell prey to the invader. This deprived Spain of the only Atlantic post on the African coast. In time Charles was able to establish the Knights of St. John of Jerusalem at Malta, Gozzo, and Tripoli, following their expulsion from Rhodes in 1522. By 1529 the Spanish lost Peñon d'Algel. Their ammunition ran out during an attack by a fleet of forty-five ships, and most of the defenders were killed. On May 21 Barbarossa entered the fortress and tortured and put to death the twenty-five survivors. This strategic fort, from which the Turkish fleet could be shelled while on the African coast and, especially, in the port of Algiers, was lost at a time when Charles was preoccupied with the Siege of Vienna in 1529 and the meeting at Augsburg in 1530.

In the Mohammedan westward expansion through the Balkans, Hungary's turn had come to fall to the mighty forces of the brilliant Sultan. During the spring of 1526 Suleiman began his campaign with an army of 100,000 men, equipped with the same modern weapons of war which had captured Constantinople in 1453.[34] The young King Louis of Hungary met this formidable force at Mohacs in August with a force not one fourth the size of the Sultan's. The Christians had to rely almost entirely upon cavalry charges, and the result of the battle was a foregone conclusion. Against the Sultan's Janissaries and effective artillery fire the best horseflesh was bound to lose the day. King Louis himself was drowned in the marsh near the Danube while trying to flee from the field of battle. Buda fell next, on September 10, and after terrible devastation and slaughter over 100,000 captives were sold into slavery at Constantinople. Upon the death of the Hungarian king, the Archduke Ferdinand, brother of Charles V, became regent and Louis' sister, Mary, the queen.

Fortunately for Christendom, Suleiman was unable to continue his expansion program the following year, as he had intended. Problems in the Orient demanded his undivided attention. Charles, too, was occupied in fighting his second round with Francis I in Italy after the latter had broken the treaty of Madrid. In the interim, Ferdinand led an army against John Zapolya, the Sultan's Hungarian vassal, and recaptured the capital of Hungary.

In 1529, however, the Sultan returned with an army twice the size of that of 1526, retook the last intervening towns, and marched straight for Vienna.[35] This memorable siege began in the fall of 1529, and all of central Europe awaited the outcome with great anxiety. Charles and Francis signed the Peace of Cambrai, but Charles was unable to muster sufficient forces in time to meet the new threat. Ferdinand's forces took the brunt of the attack, but he, too, felt it prudent to remain in Bohemia while raising an army large enough to rescue the hard-pressed garrison. The Viennese burghers rose valiantly to the occasion. Although the Sultan's devastating artillery blew large holes in the walls, some twenty assaults upon the openings were repulsed. An early, extremely severe winter came to the aid of the defenders and worked extreme hardship upon the exposed Turkish hosts. Many fell ill, morale declined rapidly, and the Sultan decided to abandon the siege.

This was the high-water mark in the westward sweep of the Turkish tidal wave. Never again during the century were the Turks to reach the walls of the Hapsburg capital. A campaign toward Gratz in the following year was also repelled. Perhaps this improvement in the fortunes of the Emperor was the result of the settlement of many of his domestic problems, which left him free to throw all resources into the battle with the Turks.

This improved condition was also reflected in the Mediterranean, where Suleiman's commander Barbarossa had some sixty vessels roving the sea in search of an unprotected spot for an attack on the Spanish coast. In 1529, while Charles was being escorted across the Mediterranean from Spain by most of the navy, one of Barbarossa's captains with fifteen vessels raided Valencia and carried off much loot and some Christians. Charles sent eight galleys to intercept the raiders, but in the encounter Spain suffered a humiliating defeat. Now at last the Emperor began to realize the seriousness of the Mediterranean situation.

Accordingly, in the early months of 1530, when Charles was about to leave for Augsburg, he ordered an expedition against Cherchell, the base of the pirates on the African coast near Algiers. Although the expedition was reasonably successful in that the pirates were taken by surprise, plunder and looting on the part of the Spanish forces exposed them to a counterattack which resulted in heavy losses. The following year the pirates' headquarters at Honeine near Oran were captured, thousands of Moors were slain, and about a thousand taken prisoner. Barbarossa tried to retaliate in 1532 but suffered shipwreck.

It was partly his realization of the need for vigorous action against the Turks which caused Charles to move so cautiously at Augsburg in his dealings with the Lutherans. To gain time, he signed the Truce of Nuernberg in 1532. The situation improved still further when during the same year the Spanish admiral Doria slipped through the Strait of Messina with a fleet of forty-four ships carrying some 12,000 German, Spanish, and Italian soldiers and struck terror into the Turks at Coron on the Greek shore. A year later the same commander defeated a relief fleet that Suleiman sent out to retake Coron, where the Spanish had established a garrison.

Barbarossa, the pirate of Barbary, was now driven out of Tunis in the campaign of 1535, and one of the Emperor's own men was placed in this African position. Charles' campaign in 1541, however, turned into a tragedy due to a storm. In the meantime the Sultan had turned eastward, where he had added Bagdad and all the territory beyond down to the Indian Ocean. From then until 1547 the Emperor and the Sultan were continually at war; but just before the Schmalkaldic War in Germany the Sultan became exhausted and sued for peace. Once more, in 1552, Suleiman sought to take advantage of the fact that Duke Moritz of Saxony had turned traitor to the Emperor, and he even invited Henry II of France to join. France, too, had grown weary of the struggle and signed the treaty of Cateau-Cambrésis in 1559. Further troubles in the Orient frustrated the Sultan's schemes, and the whole war ended in neither side being victorious.

In 1556 Charles, grown weary and exhausted, abdicated, dividing his kingdom between his son Philip and his brother Ferdinand. His closing days were full of disappointment and regret. His mother died in April, 1555, and in that same year the Schmalkaldic War ended in the Peace of Augsburg with terms much too favorable for the Protestants. His beloved Empress had died many years previously, following the premature birth of their seventh child, which also died. Only three living children remained, Philip, Mary, and Joanna. Philip's wife, Mary of England, proved barren, another bitter disappointment to Charles' plans.

On October 22 of the year 1555 Charles resigned his sovereignty of the Order of the Golden Fleece.[36] Just three days later occurred the touching scene of his abdication from the Netherlands, which left the whole audience in tears. Charles, exhausted and pale, sank into his seat, so moved was he by the memory of his last forty years.

To Philip went the Netherlands and Spain, to Ferdinand the empire.

Charles spent his last years in a modest little palace, built adjoining the monastery of San Jeronimo de Yuste in southern Spain. In this peaceful environment Charles enjoyed the sunny terraces, the woods and streams, and especially the company of his father-confessor, Juan de Regla. He passed much of his time in the chapel of the monastery, and he asked to be buried under its high altar beside his Empress. On September 21, 1558, he died with his fingers clasping the same crucifix she had held. As a good Catholic, Charles had left nothing undone for the welfare of his soul. Thirty thousand masses were ordered said and the distribution of 30,000 ducats in alms. The ceremonies with which the Catholic Church consoles the dying were all observed. The Archbishop of Toledo pressed the crucifix into his dying hand with the admonition that his only hope for mercy was in Christ's suffering and death, a doctrine strangely similar to that taught by the Wittenberg monk, whose heresy he had failed to crush at Worms. A few years earlier Martin Luther had closed his eyes in death, steadfastly believing in this same source of all mercy.

« 3 »

The History of Saxony

THE LUTHER LANDS

IN SOME RESPECTS the expression "Luther Lands" is hardly appropriate when limited to a certain area around Wittenberg, for all Germany claims Martin Luther as its native son. The traveler finds "haunts and homes" of Luther all over Germany; yet places like Worms, Augsburg, the Coburg, and the Wartburg have distinct associations with definite experiences in the life of the Reformer. In quite a different sense Wittenberg may properly call itself the *Lutherstadt,* while Eisleben, Mansfeld, Eisenach, and Erfurt all have treasured memories of the great leader much more intimate than those of more remote parts of Germany. Here the Reformer moved in living, daily contact with the people of his home country. In this special sense the "Luther Lands" are those regions in Anhalt and Saxony within a few days' journey of Wittenberg, where Luther lived and labored as a university professor from 1512 to 1546.

The expression "Luther Lands" as here used applies to an area extending from the Harz Mountains in the northwest to the Bohemian Massif in the southeast just below Dresden; while on the other side it began in Electoral Saxony a little above Wittenberg and extended southwest to the Wartburg in Thuringia. No city in this area was more than seventy-five miles from Wittenberg.

The region in which Martin Luther was born, Eisleben, and where he grew up, Mansfeld, in the foothills of the Harz Mountains, was rugged and rolling, similar to that of western Pennsylvania and West Virginia. All of Thuringia is noted for its scenic beauty, and the picturesque ruins along its rivers are nostalgic reminders

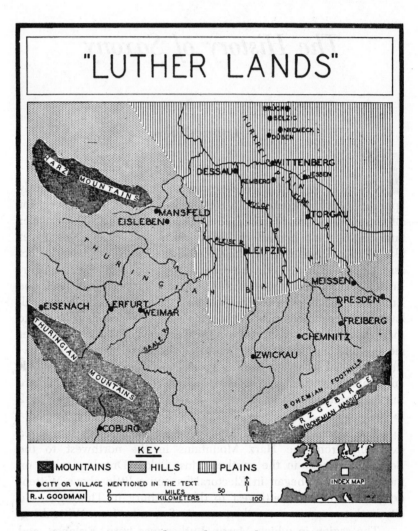

The Luther Lands

of the days when Henry IV had his headquarters in this area and each hilltop was crowned with the storybook castle of one of his colorful knights.

Below the Harz was the "Goldene Aue," a gently rolling plain noted for its fertility; while to the south, in the region around Erfurt and Weimar, Thuringia's largest cities at the time, the land was a little more level. On the southern extremity this area was bounded by a series of mountain ridges ending near Eisenach. At the end of this projection, towering high above Eisenach, was the Wartburg, a fairy-tale castle with a long and colorful history.

The whole region between the Harz Mountains in the north and the projection from Bohemia in the south is known as the Thuringian Basin. [1] In the main this basin is drained by the Saale River, which empties into the Elbe River beyond Wittenberg. The topography of the land east of Thuringia gradually slopes toward the Elbe and becomes more level in the neighborhood of Leipzig. The Mulde River Valley is a fairly level region, especially where the Mulde joins the Elbe, near Dessau; but to the south, around Freiberg and Zwickau, the terrain is quite mountainous. The Elbe Valley is considerably lower than the neighboring lands and very level in the Wittenberg area. Occasionally the landscape is broken by terminal moraines partly covered with small underbrush. As we ascend the Elbe toward Torgau and farther to the south, it, too, enters the hilly regions around Dresden, where it winds through the beautiful land formations of the Saxon Swiss.

Although the climate of the Saxon lands is continental, the temperature of the valleys of the Elbe, Mulde, and Pleisse Rivers is quite mild. In the Erzgebirge and the Bohemian foothills, however, it becomes more severe. The summer mean temperature is around 64° F, while the winter is around 30°. The region about Leipzig has the least rainfall, while that in the Erzgebirge on the Bohemian Massif has the greatest.

OLD AND NEW SAXONY

Students are frequently confused over the use of the two expressions "Old Saxony" and "New Saxony." [2] In the days of Charlemagne, Saxony was located in the northwest corner of Germany. By the time of the Reformation this "Old Saxony" had disappeared, and its name had been transplanted to the eastern frontier, where a "New Saxony" was governed by Frederick the Wise and Duke George.

At the time of the Barbarian Invasions all the Germanic tribes moved westward, leaving a vacuum east of the Elbe River. This region was occupied by Slavic tribes, also moving westward, whom the Germans loosely classified as Wends. In the early Middle Ages the Germanic peoples all lived west of the Elbe, and they were divided into six stem duchies. At this time "Old Saxony" was one of these stem duchies. According to an old medieval chronicler, Adam of Bremen, "Old Saxony" was bounded on the south by the Hessian Highlands and Thuringia, on the east by the Elbe, and on the west by the Netherlands. All sides of this triangle were of equal length, a distance of about eight days' journey, or approximately two hundred miles. The native Saxons were proud, aristocratic, set in their ways, and slow to accept new ideas.

The Germans, however, soon realized their great mistake in permitting the Slavs to occupy the lands east of the Elbe. Already under Henry the Fowler the *Drang nach Osten* began, that systematic reconquest of the Slavland which Lamprecht has termed the "great accomplishment of the whole Middle Ages." [3] Emperor Otto the Great erected chains of *Burgwarde,* or fortifications, along the Elbe and its tributaries. In some respects there is a close parallel between the reconquest of these Slav lands and our own westward movement. Like ours, it, too, had its bitter border warfare and many reverses, especially in the great Wendish uprisings of 983, 1018, and 1066, which obliterated almost every vestige of German colonization. Linguistically and culturally, these regions were not brought into the orbit of German control until the thirteenth century.

The exact nature of this German colonization is not quite clear. Doubtless, many of the settlers came from "Old Saxony" and Thuringia, as they were border states to the Elbe. Some of them, as, for example, the settlers of the "Flaeming" just north of Wittenberg, came from the Netherlands. It is doubtful, however, that their number was large throughout the area. As the *Sachsenspiegel,* an old medieval law book, indicates, there was some intermarriage between the Wends and the German colonists. [4] And the fact that this old code tries to discourage the practice would lead to the conclusion that it was occurring rather frequently. Because of a chain of historic circumstances, the name of "Old Saxony" was transplanted to Electoral Saxony as it was known in the days of Frederick the Wise.

Historians are not agreed on an exact definition of a German duchy or, as it is sometimes called, the "stem duchy." [5] Originally, the regions seem to have been governed by dukes serving as the Emperor's personal officials. Their power over a region rested solely on their relationship to the imperial court. In time, however, the personal representative idea passed into the background, and a kind of territorialism took its place, in which the power of a duke was conditioned by his alodial lands, court rights, and the number of soldiers he could muster. Thus a *Machtpolitik*, or power politics, became the order of the day, with every noble seeking to bolster his own position at the expense of his neighbor. By the time of the Hohenstaufens (1139–1254) this territorialism had become so rampant that not only dukes, but even the Emperors were acquiring all the private property and power possible.[6] Carried to its logical conclusion, this process became a decentralizing force that in time split feudal Germany into hundreds of little garden patches, leaving it weak and divided. Part of this larger story is the birth of the "New Saxony" in the region about Wittenberg.

Before the time of Emperor Frederick Barbarossa the Hohenstaufens and the Welfs had been bitter rivals. Marriage, however, has bridged many a chasm. Frederick Barbarossa and Henry the Lion were cousins and the best of friends. Henry aided the Emperor in all his undertakings, and in turn for this he was made Duke of Saxony and Bavaria. The latter was really a restoration, as the preceding Emperor, Conrad III, had seized this duchy from Henry's father. Apparently Frederick and Henry would remain lifelong friends.

The involved story of their later struggle is not pertinent here except that it explains the disappearance of "Old Saxony" and the formation of the Saxony of central Germany. The rift between the great *Staufen* and his powerful duke may well have begun while the latter was on a visit to the Holy Land. Much of the story of how Henry refused to join Frederick's last Italian campaign and, especially, of the Emperor kneeling before his stubborn prince has proved to be legendary. In all likelihood the source of the trouble lay in Henry's ruthless game of power politics with which he was offending all the neighboring princes as well as causing the Emperor some uneasiness. The neighboring territorial princes were only too glad to support the Emperor in humbling the proud, arrogant Welf.

In 1179 the Emperor began legal proceedings against Henry, and in 1180 he summoned him to stand trial at Gelnhausen, one of Frederick's new castles, a demand which Henry the Lion defiantly ignored. A series of preliminary hearings finally culminated in the *Gelnhauser Urkunde*, by which Henry was deprived of all his feudal possessions and the title of Duke of Saxony.[7] With this historical document, until recently the treasured possession of the *Staatsarchiv* of Duesseldorf, Germany, Frederick Barbarossa destroyed with one bold stroke one of the six original German stem duchies, "Old Saxony." If, as some claim, "Old Saxony" had ceased to exist long before 1180, its dissolution was now made a matter of record, for at Gelnhausen the old duchy was divided between the Archbishop of Cologne and Bernhard, the youngest son of Albert the Bear.[8] However, before they could realize their claims, the neighboring princes quickly seized all possible lands, since even then possession was regarded as nine points of the law. Young Bernhard, who had neither lands nor armies to enforce his territorial claims, was forced to be content with his newly acquired title "Duke of Saxony."

The Development of Electoral Saxony

The early history of Electoral Saxony is shrouded in mystery. Exactly how did it happen that the sandy region about Wittenberg, later known as the *Kurkreis*, became so influential in German history and was one of the seven regions controlling the imperial elections? Although most of the details of the answer to this question have been lost, the broad outlines are fairly distinct.

The history of Henry the Lion's conflict with Emperor Frederick Barbarossa, which ended in the dissolution of "Old Saxony" at Gelnhausen, has been observed. According to the original partition at Gelnhausen, the lands west of the Weser River were given

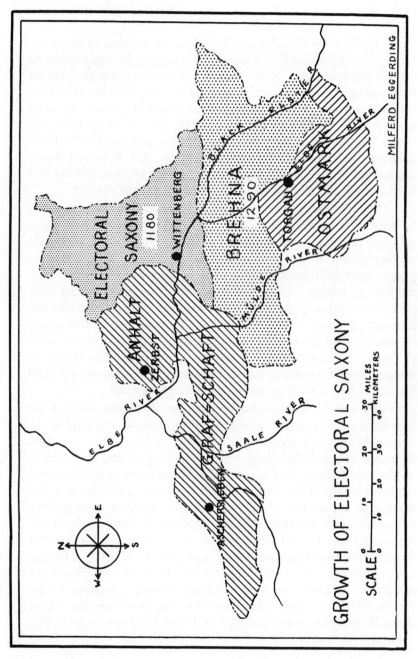

GROWTH OF ELECTORAL SAXONY

SCALE

MILES

KILOMETERS

ELECTORAL SAXONY 1180

ANHALT

GRAF=SCHAFT

BREHNA 1290

OSTMARK

WITTENBERG

ZERBST

ASCHERSLEBEN

TORGAU

ELBE RIVER

SAALE RIVER

MULDE RIVER

ELBE RIVER

BLACK ELSTER R.

ELSTER RIVER

MILFERD EGGERDING

Growth of Electoral Saxony

to the Archbishop of Cologne, while those to the east, in the main, were given to Bernhard of Ascania. The reasons for this settlement are not entirely clear. Some German historians claim that earlier members of Bernhard's family had held the title of Duke of Saxony for short periods of time. The sons of Albert the Bear had spent much time in Frederick's court during the time of his quarrel with Henry and may thus have won his affection and good will. Probably another important factor was the fact that Bernhard was a descendant of the old Billunger family, whose Magnus Billung had been created the first Duke of Saxony by Otto the Great.[9]

Although young Bernhard had been created Duke of Saxony, he was soon to learn that even though he possessed the ducal title and the lands east of the Weser River on paper, it was quite another matter to make his claim an actuality. The neighboring princes gave little heed to the new duke, nor was Henry the Lion the type to submit meekly to this dispensation. After a brief exile Henry returned and made his peace with the increasingly powerful Emperor at Erfurt in 1181. Some have claimed that by this action he won back all the territory that he had lost and his title of Duke of Saxony, but the evidence is not too convincing. The Duchy of Braunschweig-Lueneburg began to emerge from the soil of "Old Saxony," while other fragments passed into new hands.

After several unsuccessful border wars, Bernhard realized the hopelessness of trying to attach his title to these northern lands. A later Wittenberg professor, P. Heynig, writing under the *nom de plume* of Schalscheleth, gave the following version of the birth of Electoral Saxony.[10] In a rather humorous account he compared the breaking up of the Duchy of Old Saxony at Gelnhausen to the shaking of a pear tree with many hungry neighbor boys waiting to pounce upon the fruit. When Frederick Barbarossa shook the Saxon pear tree, the greedy territorial princes were more successful in garnering the fallen fruit than poor Bernhard. Like a beggar carrying his title about with him in a bag, he wandered around the countryside seeking some land to which he might attach his honor. Finally, his father took pity upon him and gave him the region about Wittenberg, a territory which Albert the Bear had recently wrested from the Wends and settled with Flemish settlers. Bernhard attached his title of Duke of Saxony to this undeveloped sandy land east of the Elbe, and by this act "New Saxony" was born.

Unfortunately, the accuracy of the Schalscheleth story cannot be established because of the paucity of sources. Doubtless, the account is highly imaginative; yet history records that a few years later Bernhard made his peace with the descendants of Henry the Lion and that the region about Wittenberg from that date on became known as the *Kurkreis,* or Ducal Saxony, whose rulers from then on helped elect the German emperors.

At the time of Bernhard's death Electoral Saxony was still regarded as relatively unimportant, for his oldest son, Henry, preferred to inherit the home lands and the title of Graf von Ascanien, while Albert I, the younger son, had to be satisfied with Electoral Saxony and the title of Duke. Henry's lands, which began in the lower Harz with Burg Anhalt as the center, were called the Grafschaft Anhalt. Also included was the Grafschaft Aschersleben, extending over the Saale and Mulde Rivers.[11]

Schalscheleth observes that Henry the Lion must have chuckled to see the new Duke of Saxony ruling over a primitive, undeveloped land almost devoid of population. The original Electoral, or Ducal, Saxony was much smaller than at the time of the Reformation. Its boundaries remained fluid for some time. As noted on the map, Ducal Saxony during the thirteenth century lay mostly above the Elbe River, with Wittenberg its principal city. The Grafschaft Brehna, south of the *Kurkreis,* was added to the Electorate in 1290 at the time when the main part of the Grafschaft Wettin went to Magdeburg. By this time the later *Kurkreis* as known from the Reformation was quite well formed.[12]

Under the rule of Bernhard's son, Albert I (1212–1260), the Electoral circle began to assume more importance. Although the Ascaniers did not live in Wittenberg during this early period, they added some buildings to the town. Doubtless, the chancel of the Town Church dates from this period, although at that time it was but a small chapel. Albert's wife, Helena, founded the Franciscan monastery, in which the whole Ascanier family was buried.[13] During the Reformation the twenty-seven oak caskets containing the mortal remains of this family, dating from Helena (d. 1273) to

Barbara (d. 1435), were moved to a vault under the main tower of the Castle Church, where they were still resting in peace in 1936.

When Albert I died, both John, the older son, and his younger brother, Albert II, were minors, and Helena became regent. These two sons were the founders of two Saxon houses. John was head of the Lauenburg line, which continued until 1689; Albert II became the founder of the Sachsen-Wittenberg line, which by a series of fortunate historical accidents was to become the family to carry the Electoral title and the now prized region of the Electoral circle. The line continued until 1419, when their castle at Schweinitz accidentally collapsed upon the sleeping royal family.[14]

The first stroke of fortune for the Sachsen-Wittenberg line was the marriage of Albert II to Agnes, the daughter of Emperor Rudolf of Hapsburg.[15] Not only did Albert spend considerable time at the imperial court, but the Emperor also took a special interest in his grandson and namesake, Rudolf of Saxony. When the Emperor died, the matter of who should cast the Electoral vote arose. John had just died, and his two sons in the Lauenburg line were still minors. Albert II, therefore, was declared eligible to vote in the election of Adolf of Nassau.

These circumstances were repeated in the next imperial election of Albert of Austria in 1298, since the two nephews were still minors. Again, in the election of Henry VII of Luxemburg in 1308, Albert III of the Lauenburg family had just died, and Rudolf of the Sachsen-Wittenberg line participated in the imperial election. When Charles IV finally designated the members of the German Electoral College in that historical document *The Golden Bull* of 1356, there were sixty-five years of historical precedent behind the choice of the Sachsen-Wittenberg family in preference to the Lauenburg line.[16] Unfortunately, too, for the Lauenburg family, they had supported Charles' opponent at the time of his election, while Rudolf of Sachsen-Wittenberg was both his relative and his staunch supporter and the Emperor needed Rudolf's further support in Mark Brandenburg and the Duchy of Braunschweig-Lueneburg. In the Saxon clauses of the *Golden Bull*, Charles IV established Rudolf's family as the sole possessors of the *Kurkreis* and its vote for the imperial crown.[17] Only once more did the Lauenburg descendants claim the Electoral title, when the Sachsen-Wittenberg line ended in the castle crash of 1419; but again they failed.[18]

Thus it is apparent that during the years between Rudolf of Hapsburg and Charles IV (1273–1356) the system of imperial elections became definitely crystallized and the number of electors permanently fixed. By this time, also, their positions in the Empire had been codified and special offices assigned to each elector. In this process it had been to the advantage of the Sachsen-Wittenberg line of German princes that Rudolf I was the grandson of the Emperor. The proud grandfather appointed his grandson and namesake his *Erzmarschall*, which made him Grand Marshal of the imperial stables and private sword-bearer of the Emperor on state occasions.[19] During these years the *Reichsvikariat*, delegating specific duties and powers during the *Interregnum* following the death of the Emperor to two specially appointed vicars over German lands, was also established. These vicars were obligated to preserve the peace of the realm while a new emperor was being chosen. In the *Golden Bull*, the Elector of the Rhenish Palatinate was made *Reichsvikar* of the western half of Germany, while the Duke of Saxony was assigned the eastern half.[20] Through this new office the *Reichsvikars* exercised the following privileges over the other German princes during the interim: (1) the right of trial, (2) the right of Church prebends, or maintenance fee, (3) the right of the collection of certain income dues, (4) the right of the distribution of feudal estates with the exception of those of princes. More specifically stated, the *Reichsvikariat* implied that during an *Interregnum* the Duke of Saxony could exercise the afore-mentioned rights in Brandenburg, Hesse, Westphalia, East Friesland, Bohemia, and Silesia. Subsequent confirmatory letters by later emperors further strengthened the powers of the *Reichsvikars*. In 1328, 1333, and 1334 we see that the dukes, counts, and barons in the lands of Saxon law were all vassals to the *Reichsvikar*. This situation explains why the Elector of Saxony in Luther's day was one of the most powerful of the German electors, wielding considerable influence among his fellow princes.

The reign of Rudolf of Saxony is also closely related to the development of Wittenberg and the *Kurkreis*, as he was the first prince to take a real interest in this region. He erected the original modest Castle Church, founded the endowed Wittenberg *Stift*, which was later to help finance the University of Wittenberg, and made many other improvements in the town. The Sachsen-Wittenberg line was continued under the Ascanier line by Rudolf II, Wenzel, and the latter's son, Rudolf III, the prince who, after a stormy reign, died with his entire family in the tower crash in the castle at Schweinitz, as before noted.[21]

The rule then passed to a distant relative, Albert III, who was also an unfortunate victim of circumstances. While he was on a hunting trip in the vicinity of Wittenberg, the farmhouse at Lochau in which the party was lodged caught fire. Albert rescued his wife from the flames, but died from the effects, ending his brief reign in 1422.

SAXONY UNDER THE WETTIN LINE

So far the story of Saxony has been limited to the region about Wittenberg known as the *Kurkreis,* or the Electorate of Saxony. In the fifteenth century the name was to extend to the lands further south encompassing Meissen and the beautiful hills of Thuringia. To be sure, the natives still continued to use the local names of Thuringia and Meissen, but the entire region became known as Saxony to the European historian. To understand this development it is necessary to pursue the history of Electoral Saxony beyond the tragic end of the Ascanier family.

Under normal circumstances Electoral Saxony should have passed to Erich V of the older Lauenburg line, which in former years had claimed the *Kurkreis.* However, the German Emperor Sigismund bestowed it upon Frederick the Valiant, who had served him well in the defense against the Hussite invasions.[22] Although the Hussite episode has no bearing on this theme, suffice it to point out that after the burning of John Hus at Constance his followers were extremely bitter and expressed their resentment by overrunning the Elbe Valley. The choice of Frederick and the powerful House of Wettin was, perhaps, a wise one, for under his son in 1430 some 70,000 black-shirted Hussites made a foray up the Elbe as far as Magdeburg and burned 400 towns and 1,400 villages, taking enough booty to fill 300 wagons.

THURINGIA

A comparison between the maps of Europe around the date of 1100 and of 1485 at the time of the Leipzig settlement will reveal considerable change. In the early Middle Ages beautiful, green Thuringia did not exist as such, but the territory was the stem duchy of Franconia. Henry IV had crested every important hill with the majestic towers of feudal castles, of which the one at the Wartburg is a splendid example. In the same year that Bernhard received the title of Duke of Saxony at Gelnhausen (1180), a new royal office was created for Erkenbert, the Landgraf of Thuringia.[23] His new title was *Pfalzgraf von Thueringen*. Erkenbert had married Jordana of Saxony, and their descendants founded a line of Thuringian *Pfalzgrafen* that continued until 1247, when the region passed over to Henry of Meissen with the exception of the territory bordering Hesse. In the days of the Reformation this land was to be owned in part by the Electoral house of Saxony. Ever since then it has been a vital part of Saxony although known locally as Thuringia.

MEISSEN

The history of Meissen can be traced as far back as 929, but the *Mark* did not play much of a role in history until 1089, when it passed over to Henry of Eilenburg, a relative of the royal family by that name. Graf Thimo, who had a castle on the Saale by that name, was really the founder of the House of Wettin. After him, Conrad of Wettin built Meissen into a real power.[24] When he died, the Meissen of the sixteenth century had practically taken shape. When the Thuringian line died out in 1247, Henry of Meissen tried to obtain the territory by war and was successful except for the western strip. Now the lands of Meissen stretched from Thuringia into the neighborhood of the Oder River. Frequently the princes of this day undid their life's work by once more dividing the family estates among their sons. However, the Chemnitz partition of 1381 reveals that Thuringia and Mark Meissen were rather well established as two separate states, but the lands in between were not. Margrave William I, a clever territorial prince, did much to build the reputation of the House of Wettin by extending Meissen's hold to the lands beyond the Erzgebirge southward as well as in the regions of the Reisenburg, Vogtland, Colditz, and Eilenburg.

ELECTORAL SAXONY

MULDE RIVER

ELBE RIVER

OSTERLAND

MARK

BAUTZEN

● MEISSEN

ROCHLITZ ●

MEISSEN

● DRESDEN

PLEISSNER-
LAND

● FREIBERG

THURINGIA

BOHEMIA

N
W   E
S

SCALE   10   20   30 MILES
        10 20 30 40 KILOMETERS

MEISSEN – ABOUT 1300

MILFERD EGGERDING

Meissen about 1300

The Growth of the New Saxony

After carefully considering the strength and possessions of the House of Wettin in 1422, Emperor Sigismund selected Frederick the Valiant as the successor to the Electoral title and added to his titles of *Markgraf* of Meissen and *Pfalzgraf* of Thuringia those of *Kurfuerst* and *Reichsvikar* of the whole eastern half of Germany. Slowly the name of the newly acquired lands became associated with the original possessions of the House of Wettin. Gradually all of their possessions were referred to as the Saxon Lands, or Saxony, while the region about Wittenberg was designated as the *Kurkreis*, or the Electoral circle. Thus the name of "Old Saxony" in northwestern Germany was slowly transferred between 1180 and 1450 to the "New Saxony" of modern times.

The Origin of Ernestine and Albertine Saxony

For some sixty years the sons and grandsons of Frederick the Valiant ruled jointly, with but minor instances of land partitions. Finally, however, in 1485 the existing heirs, Ernest and Albert, agreed upon a division of the territories which created the lands of Ernestine and Albertine Saxony, the result of the so-called Leipzig partition.[25]

According to the Saxon clauses of the *Golden Bull,* Ernest, the elder, naturally became Elector. To offset this advantage, it was agreed that Ernest should divide the rest of the Saxon territory as equally as possible and then give Albert first choice as to the part he preferred. To accomplish this, Ernest reorganized the Thuringian basin by dividing it near Erfurt, the region north of Erfurt to the Harz becoming Upper Thuringia and the region to the south Lower Thuringia. The region immediately about Erfurt passed under the ecclesiastical control of the Archbishop of Magdeburg, who was also a member of the House of Wettin. Meissen remained a unit. Franconia, the Vogtland, and the Coburg region were grouped with Lower Thuringia. The results of the settlement proved disappointing to Ernest, for he had hoped that a more natural division could be finally effected.

Ernest had expected his brother to select all of Thuringia and the neighboring regions that were grouped with it; but, instead,

Albert chose Upper Thuringia and Meissen. This left Lower Thuringia and its neighboring lands grouped with the Electoral circle in the northeast. In fact, Ernest could not even pass from one part of his lands to another without crossing the territory of his brother. Therefore, a border region between Upper Thuringia and Meissen was ruled jointly to eliminate difficulties. The new Saxon lands now formed the shape of a letter X, or perhaps, a four-leaf clover. In a general way Albert's territory, which from now on was called Albertine or Ducal Saxony, extended from the Harz in the northwest to the Erzgebirge in the southeast; while the lands of Ernest, or Ernestine Saxony, extended from the *Kurkreis* about Wittenberg in the northeast to Lower Thuringia south of the Wartburg and even the Feste Coburg in the southwest. This arrangement continued in the main through Martin Luther's lifetime, but it was changed during the Schmalkaldic War in 1547, when the Electoral circle passed to the Albertine line.

A year after the Leipzig settlement, Ernest died, leaving the *Kurkreis* and the rest of his land to his oldest son, Frederick. The clever way in which this prince guided the affairs of Saxony during the critical years between 1517 and 1525 won him the appellation of "The Wise." [26] His sense of fairness, instinctive caution, and sound judgment made all attempts to win him over to the side of Rome futile. He founded the University of Wittenberg in 1502 and took a very enlightened interest in its development and influence on German life. The contributions of this farsighted prince to the cause of the German Reformation can hardly be overestimated. After Frederick's death in 1525, Ernestine Saxony passed to his brother John, who, in spite of his gentle bearing, more openly supported the work of Luther and proved himself a warm friend of the University of Wittenberg. Doubtless this support was due in part to the fact that John was the Elector when the Diet of Speyer in 1526 agreed that each ruler would be responsible for the religious conditions in his lands. However, it was not until 1532, when his son John Frederick became the regent of the Ernestine lands, that Lutheranism had a real champion in the Saxon Court. Tutored by such men as George Spalatin and Caspar Lichten, this rugged, enthusiastic prince grew up in a Lutheran atmosphere, and he was the first Elector of Saxony to become an ardent

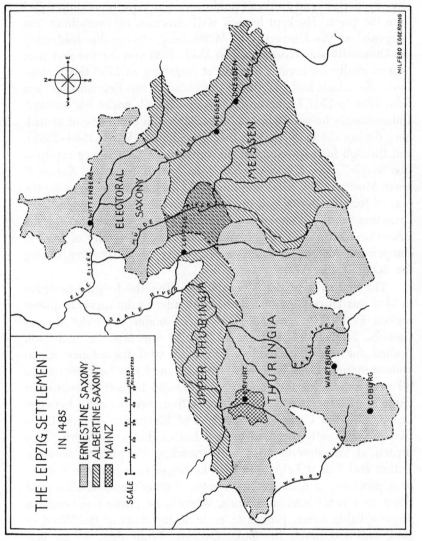

The Leipzig Settlement in 1485

disciple of Martin Luther. As the court correspondence reveals, John Frederick read Luther's publications as rapidly as they rolled from the press. He kept himself well informed on everything that happened at the University of Wittenberg. Under his leadership the University was reorganized in 1535–1536 and for the first time became really Lutheran. Already at Augsburg in 1530 this zealous Lutheran prince had fought for the cause of the Reformation, and from 1532 to 1547 Lutheranism was to triumph under his tutelage. Unfortunately he was defeated and captured in the Battle of Muehlberg during the early part of the Schmalkaldic War (1546–1555), and through his captivity and the subsequent Wittenberg capitulation in 1547, the Electoral circle was lost to Ernestine Saxony.[27] Duke Moritz of the Albertine line obtained the *Kurkreis*, while the sons of John Frederick had to be content with the remainder of the Ernestine lands. Weimar now became the new residence of the Ernestine House, and they founded the new University of Jena to compensate for the loss of the University of Wittenberg during the Schmalkaldic War.

The first ruler of the Albertine line after the Leipzig partition in 1485 was Duke George, who became ruler of the newly acquired regions in 1500.[28] He had been reared under the strict Roman Catholic tutelage of Andrew Proles. At one time he had even studied for the priesthood, a factor of vital importance to an understanding of his later life. He continued just long enough in his preparation for the ministry to consider himself a competent judge of the theological controversies that were to arise between Luther and the Catholic theologians of his court. At first Duke George was kindly disposed toward Luther, but after hearing him preach at Dresden in 1518 and attending the debate between Luther and Eck at Leipzig in 1519 he began to regard the Wittenberg professor as a dangerous heretic. Luther's bold challenge of Rome two years later at Worms, wherein he refused to recant a single syllable unless proved in error on the basis of the Word of God, was too much for Duke George. From then on he was Luther's bitterest enemy among the German princes. Students from his lands were forbidden to attend the University of Wittenberg. His court became the rendezvous for many of Luther's strongest polemical assailants. Obviously, the new evangelical movement could make little progress in Albertine Saxony before the death of Duke George in 1539.

Upon the death of this ardent champion of Roman Catholicism the Albertine lands passed into the hands of his milder brother Henry, who favored the Reformation.[29] As a ruler of Friesland, he had introduced the Reformation into these lands as early as 1536. After Duke George's death the Wittenberg faculty also carried on church visitations in the Albertine lands and soon Lutheranism was taking firm root in this former Catholic stronghold. Since Henry, however, outlived his brother by only three years, the Albertine lands soon passed into the hands of his clever, scheming twenty-year-old son Moritz.[30]

Moritz was an opportunist with no deep religious convictions. He had spent too much of his boyhood in the courts of Albert of Mainz, Duke George, and John Frederick to have been left unaffected. As might be expected, this sparkling-eyed lad turned into a keen, calculating politician, who at the beginning of the Schmalkaldic War joined the forces of the Emperor against the German Protestants until he had gained his objectives, and then turned traitor to Charles V when it was to his advantage to do so. Like most opportunists, Moritz had his little day. He was mortally wounded in the battle of Sievershausen and died on July 11, 1553.

The Elector August, brother and successor to Moritz, was a much nobler type of prince. His generosity and farsightedness were so outstanding that some prefer to call him the second founder of the University of Wittenberg. At the University of Wittenberg a program of expansion was begun during his reign that resulted in the repurchase of the old Black Cloister in which the Luther family had lived. A new structure was erected adjoining *Collegien Gasse* and joined at one end of the quadrangle to the former Luther home by a building moved in from another part of the city, the *Toszen Haus*. The new unit, since it had been undertaken by the Elector, was named in his honor, the *Augusteum*. The refinancing of the University was also necessary since the enrollment of the institution had increased to nearly a thousand students.

The Sixteenth Century Atmosphere

Any student of the German Reformation will be fascinated by the possibility of recapturing the environment of the Luther Lands during the sixteenth century; but this is no simple undertaking. One cannot merely journey to Germany and view the scenes of the present day in Eisleben, Eisenach, Wittenberg, or Worms. One such attempt resulted in a monograph in which Luther visited halls that did not exist in his lifetime, walked down streets which had not been laid out, and passed buildings not yet erected. To restore the exact historical atmosphere requires much painstaking effort. Such an undertaking for all of the Saxon lands lies far beyond the capacity of a single individual.

Unfortunately, few scientific reconstructions of German cities have been undertaken. Until this is done on the basis of such sources as woodcuts, pen sketches, etchings, descriptions, tax records, town chronicles, and other source materials, the historian and the geographer will be at a loss for an accurate conception of the sixteenth-century environment.

The American history student knows what extraordinary changes have come over the Middle West since the opening of the Northwest Territory. Suppose a Mad Anthony Wayne were to revisit the territory around Fort Wayne and other familiar scenes where he fought the Indians. Or imagine Abraham Lincoln returning to the country where he formerly split rails in his boyhood days! That early American environment has changed radically.

Yet, how frequently the tourist who has just returned from abroad assumes that, because a few hours or a day were spent in a German town whose name remains from centuries ago, he, therefore, has seen the buildings and general environment of Luther's day! Martin Luther himself would feel as lost in the modern Erfurt, Leipzig, Dresden, and scores of other German cities as Anthony Wayne or Abraham Lincoln in the Indiana and Illinois of today.

The topography of a country changes little in four hundred years. The Elbe, Mulde, or Saale doubtless follow a course similar to that of the days of the Reformation. This phase has been exhaustively treated by Alfred Hettner's *Grundzuege der Laender-*

kunde (1927), and his study provides much information for the reconstruction of the historical, economic, and political development of the area. Beautiful is Thuringia, "The Land of the Birds," whose heavily wooded hills are crowned with the ruins of castles built during the days of Kaiser Henry IV, famous in song and story! Fortunately for our investigations, some very elaborate maps were produced by the cartographers of the late sixteenth and early seventeenth centuries; and the pen sketches of Wilhelm Dilich and Matthaeum Merian provide very good reproductions of many of the towns of the region.[31]

Wilhelm Dilich was a student at the University of Wittenberg during the late sixteenth century. He majored in art taught by former pupils of the Cranachs and was deeply impressed by the Melanchthonian historical tradition. Doubtless, he received some training in cartography, which was developing at Wittenberg about this time. After a period of apprenticeship in northwestern Germany, Dilich came to the Saxon court in 1624 as court engineer, draftsman, and general architect. One of his first assignments was the interior decoration of the *Riesensaal*, the Enormous Hall of the Electoral Palace in Dresden. He spent the summers of 1626–1629 in the *Kurkreis* and Meissen making pen sketches of the towns and castles of the Saxon lands for illustrative materials for his wall paintings of this *Riesensaal*. Anyone familiar with the towns included in his some one hundred and forty pen sketches will marvel at the remarkable accuracy with which they were done. Among them his four pen sketches of Wittenberg have proved invaluable for the present study. He often drew two or three sketches of such important towns as Dresden, Meissen, Leipzig, Torgau, and Chemnitz. He also reproduced with remarkable fidelity such little villages in Electoral Saxony as Niemeck, Brueck, Belzig, Jessen, Kemberg, Dueben, and scores of others, enabling the historian to obtain a fairly complete picture of all the towns in the *Kurkreis* about Wittenberg. He likewise sketched many of the villages and castles of Meissen.

Matthaeum Merian a little later did a similar type of work in his *Topographia Superioris Saxoniae, Thuringiae, Misniae,* etc. (1650), wherein he reproduced many of these same scenes in beautiful colored etchings. This collection is valuable because of

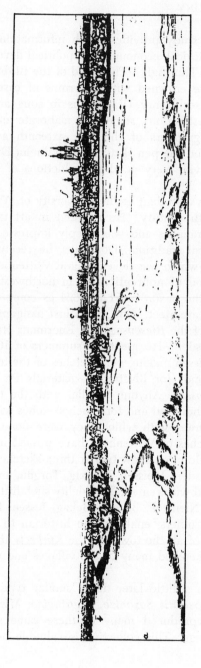

Wittenberg from the east. By Dilich, 1627

a. Elbe
b. Bridge
c. Augustinian Cloister

d. Augustinian College
e. Collegium Fridericianum
f. Castle and Castle Church

g. Town Church
h. Rathaus (City Hall)
i. Mill

its wide scope and because it contains a useful commentary not included in Dilich's studies. As the title implies, Merian also reproduced the towns of Thuringia and the region about the Harz Mountains, adding further materials for a study of the entire territory of the Luther Lands. The Merian etchings are often much smaller than those of Dilich, yet both are invaluable for recapturing the atmosphere in which Martin Luther matured and labored. All of these sketches and etchings are of a somewhat later date than would be preferred, but, since the science of cartography was only coming into flower at this time, the earlier cuts and town plans are so unreal as to be practically worthless. Nor is it likely that the general atmosphere of the German towns changed greatly in the intervening period.

Contemporary descriptions, although rare, add to our knowledge of the general atmosphere. Erasmus, who traveled in the western part of Germany in 1518, described his experiences in his colloquy, *Diversoria,* or *The Inns.*[32] The letters of Christopher Scheurl, who was a Wittenberg professor from the cultured city of Nuernberg, reveal his impressions of the Saxon lands. Fynes Moryson, traveling through Germany at the close of the sixteenth century, also made many unique and revealing observations in his *Itinerary.*[33] Although these sources do not give a complete picture, they provide at least some impression of the conditions in German lands under which the people lived.

From Dilich's series of pen sketches it is evident that most of the people lived in little villages scattered throughout the countryside some four or five miles apart. An excellent example was the *Kurkreis* with Wittenberg as the principal city, while around it clustered the villages of Niemeck, Brueck, Kemberg, Belzig, and Dueben, like a brood of chicks around the mother hen.

In Dilich's day only the larger cities had walls, and a city was considered large when it had a population of four thousand. Niemeck appears to have had a population of possibly seventy-five people; Brueck around one hundred; Kemberg was about the same size; while Belzig was perhaps a little larger. The sketches of Meissen reveal that there were hundreds of these little villages in the Luther Lands ranging from those containing a half dozen houses to such towns as Dresden, Leipzig, Torgau, Meissen, and Weimar with populations of four and five thousand.

An examination of the types of dwellings portrayed in these sketches and etchings by Dilich and Merian reveals that most of the homes were still of the low, thatched-roof type. An actual count of the newer Renaissance type of buildings indicates that many of the larger cities had no more than a half dozen such dwellings. They were constructed of stone or brick with tiled roofs. Since fire was a hazard common to the thatched roofs, the use of slate or tile became increasingly noticeable in centers like Wittenberg, Torgau, Dresden, Leipzig, and Erfurt, even though the general construction remained the typically medieval one-story type.

Although with the passing of men like Ulrich von Hutten and Franz von Sickingen the days of feudalism were over, castles are still surprisingly numerous in Dilich's book. Each prince was likely to have a number of them scattered throughout his lands. Some were very old, like those of Schweinitz or Saaleck; but many had just recently been built or completely renovated. These newer structures, such as those in Torgau, Wittenberg, and Dresden, more nearly resembled the later chateau. As danger lessened from typical feudal sieges and the emphasis on impregnability decreased, the desire for the comforts of living increased. Tile stoves, running water, leaded bull's-eye windows, frescoed walls, and more spacious rooms were to be found, but these modern conveniences were limited to the courts and the homes of the wealthy. Late in his life Philip Melanchthon received a gift of a water pipe near his back door from seven influential citizens [34] who had the line laid to their own homes.

Probably there was considerable similarity between the Luther Lands and other parts of Europe. Albert Hyma in his book *The Youth of Erasmus* gives us the following picture of the Dutch city of Deventer, where Erasmus went to school.

> When one imagines oneself standing about the year 1475 on the right bank of the Yssel opposite the city of Deventer, one notes a striking contrast between the peaceful meadows and the thriving Hansa town across the water. Deventer has become a wealthy center of commerce. Its merchants have enabled the populace to build several stately churches, roomy monasteries, and splendid

homes. . . . Along the bank of the river one sees a busy traffic, and numerous are the ships that are arriving and departing each day. . . .

After crossing the river we enter the city and pass a number of workshops, where in a simple and rather primitive manner . . . all sorts of articles are manufactured. . . . The streets are very narrow, and one must use caution in passing the houses where the bakers have placed their products on "bread benches" in front of their shops, or where the manufacturers of leather goods, of furs, or of textiles have prepared similar exhibitions. . . .

In the center of the city is the market-square, named Brink. Here we can examine at leisure the architecture of the principal buildings. About one-third of them are still of wood, several with the upper story protruding over the lower. The majority have thatched roofs, but some are covered with tiles, and the number of tiled roofs is rapidly increasing, since the magistrates have warned against the danger of fire. There are also a few buildings covered with slate; these belong to the more wealthy burghers, usually merchants who have been eminently successful in various enterprises. Their homes are also distinguished by windows made of glass, but their less favored neighbors have to content themselves with panes of oiled paper, linen, or pigskin. Most houses are very low, leaving but seven or eight feet between the gutter and the street.

It is evident that the knowledge of hygiene is not very widespread in the city, nor is cleanliness deemed a great virtue here. In some places the streets look most unsanitary, for many a burgher keeps a manure pile in his yard, not seldom in front of the house, where pigs, chickens, and children gleefully dig up the filthy dung. Pigs feel quite at home on the streets as well, for generally only a narrow strip in the center has been paved, while the market-square is also largely unpaved. The pavement is not smooth, since it consists of stones of all shapes and sizes. In some of the more narrow streets, named *stegen*, holes in the pavement have been filled with reeds or straw. Most lots have been inclosed by railings or fences, or they are marked off by ditches. Little poles in front of the lots indicate "how wide the street will have to remain"; else greedy burghers might add part of the street to their property. The dirt which collects on the streets is taken away in little carts from time to time by officials, but the men do not come frequently. Many a time it is the rain which has to be relied upon in the cleaning of the streets.

The interior of the homes offers much food for wonder. Chimneys are few, and so are stoves. In the center of each house still re-

mains the time-honored fireplace, above which is seen a large round
hole in the roof to let the smoke escape upward. This opening is
covered when there is no fire, but in cold, rainy weather it is sometimes difficult for the people to keep comfortable. Sleeping quarters
are also rather unsanitary, particularly where beds have been placed
in a room or, rather, a closet, where one sleeps all night behind
closed doors without any ventilation whatsoever. As for bathing,
that is a custom practically unheard of among the adult population.
Children have to be bathed regularly, so the stolid burghers admit,
but grown-ups merely need to change their underwear once in a
fortnight; baths are entirely unnecessary.

And woe to the citizens when perchance a plague should visit the
city! In the previous century such was no rare occurrence, and
who knows that another one is not due again in a few years? We,
who know that in 1483 there will be a visitation which will once
more sweep away hundreds of human lives within this city, feel
duty-bound to warn the heedless burghers. But they reply that
there is no remedy for contagious diseases. Nature must take its
course; man is helpless against plagues and floods and earthquakes,
which are sent by God, who alone knows the value of each human life.[35]

In Erasmus' colloquy, *The Inns*, written in 1518, occurs a
dialogue between Robert and William, which also portrays the
inhospitality and lack of sanitation among the Germans. Robert
extols the hospitality that awaits the traveler in France. Whereupon William describes the cool reception that is given to travelers
in German inns and goes on to describe conditions in the main
living quarters:

> In the stove-room (where the guests all gathered) you take off
> your boots and put on slippers. If you like, you change your shirt;
> you hang your clothes, wet with rain, against the stove; and you
> sit by it yourself in order to get dry. There is water ready if you
> care to wash your hands, but it is generally so dirty that you have
> to seek more water to wash off that ablution.[36]

William explains that "very often between eighty and a hundred persons are assembled in the same stove-room, footmen, horsemen, tradesmen, sailors, coachmen, farmers, boys, women, healthy
people, and sick people." After explaining, "one is combing his
head, another wiping the perspiration from his face, another cleaning his winter shoes or boots," he finally pictures them seated at

the evening meal, which occurs around nine or ten o'clock in the evening.

> Well, after all are seated, the grim servant comes out and counts the company. By and by he returns and sets before each guest a wooden dish and a spoon of the same kind of silver; then a glass and a little piece of bread. Each one polishes up his utensils in a leisurely way while the porridge is cooking. And thus they sit not uncommonly for upward of an hour.[37]

William also complains about the lack of cleanliness in the bedroom. He adds that there you get "just as at dinner; linen washed six months ago, perhaps."

Moryson also made many interesting observations about the customs of the Germans in his *Itinerary*. He mentions that the flies in Saxony were so bad in the summer that horses had to be completely covered with blankets. Nor is this surprising. All sorts of debris and piles of manure were thrown right into the streets. Pigs, chickens, goats, and other livestock were quite at home and unmolested in the easygoing environment of the average German village. University towns like Wittenberg, Erfurt, and Leipzig may have been kept a little cleaner by a system of fining the citizens.[38] Doubtless the desire to attract students prompted this action. The larger cities were made more attractive by the cobblestone paving often found in the main streets and market place.

Many of these towns were enclosed by massive walls, including strong turrets and watchtowers where men were constantly on guard day and night to announce the approach of friend or foe. If the visitor were an important personage, the town trumpeter might be summoned to herald his arrival from the watchtower of the city gate. Many of these towers were high enough to command a good view of the whole surrounding countryside.

At night these towns were dismally dark, as there were no street lights. Because of the dangers in the dark streets most of the citizens retired early. University students were also under regulations which encouraged them to make good use of the available daylight, and thus they retired and rose early. Exceptional persons, such as the mayor and the town pastor, who had to go about the dark streets of their towns, were supplied with "lantern boys" from the city treasury. Private citizens had to furnish their own lanterns in cases of necessity, while university students were required to have special permission from the authorities to be out after night. If this permission was granted for a special occasion, such as a wedding, a lantern could be obtained from his dormitory rector and returned there when the student checked in. Should royalty visit a town or some exceptional celebration take place, *Pechringe,* or tar torches, were placed at the street intersections.[39]

Most German cities were located along streams or at important highway intersections, where the market place for exchange of goods was the early center of activities. In most of the Dilich sketches may be noted the customary *Rathaus,* or City Hall, standing somewhere within this original market place. Every town of any size in Germany had at least one market place; some had several; Butstadt even had a separate cattle market. Since the market was the center of community life, many of the more important buildings faced this open square. The *Rathaus,* often one of the most impressive buildings of the town, usually contained rooms for the use of the city council, the court, and a prison; while on the lower floor were frequently a *Rathskeller,* a number of stores, and storage chambers. Most towns also had *Apotheken,* or drugstores, controlled by the doctors, where spices, wax, wine, paper, paint, and medicines could be purchased.[40] In Wittenberg the *Apotheke* was owned by Lucas Cranach.

The market was the center of all public life. Here weekly and annual markets were held. On weekly market days the people of the whole countryside brought their produce to be sold from the various stalls or booths of the open market. The yearly markets, especially in cities on the important trade routes, such as Dresden, Zwickau, Leipzig, or Erfurt, often were a colorful spectacle. The various national costumes of the merchants from all over Europe and the somber robes of university men, students, monks, and church dignitaries mingled with distinctive peasant garb to compose the kaleidoscopic picture presented by the crowded market. Here silks, woolens, and spices from the Orient, fine leathers, paper, pottery, and every imaginable commodity were for sale. On such occasions the streets were full of pack animals, oxcarts, and other vehicles, which moved slowly, heavily laden with wares from distant lands. Add to the picture the mendicants begging in the crowd, the omnipresent pickpockets and thieves, the bankers busily working out rates of exchange, the emporiums of booksellers and printers, to recapture the cosmopolitan atmosphere of the annual market or fair.

A sixteenth-century traveler would have been especially impressed by the great number of churches appearing on the old pen sketches and etchings, ranging from the impressive cathedral to the small chapel, like the one next to the Black Cloister in Wittenberg, in which Luther preached his first sermon. On one old Erfurt etching fourteen churches are visible, while many small villages of only three or four hundred population have five or six church towers. These were largely due to the many monastic orders, each of which built an impressive chapel next to its premises. And all of these, large and small, added to the colorful sixteenth-century picture of the Saxon lands.

The traveler in those remote times would also have found the guilds still in operation in the Saxon towns and villages, but in the larger cities he would have noted the beginnings of the rise of modern capitalism. In the country the medieval manorial system was still in existence. On the old drawings the fields were still divided into strips and patches like a crazy quilt thrown about the little Saxon villages. In the hilly regions, especially in Meissen, Thuringia, and the foothills of the Harz Mountains, the traveler would have noticed that mining was the important occupation. In the valleys of the Elbe, Muelde, and Saale were productive vineyards.

The Saxon Visitations between 1524 and 1545 reveal that the people in the country were still very backward and almost without culture. Perhaps it was his travels about the *Kurkreis* that led Luther to exclaim as late as 1532 that in Wittenberg they were living "on the very borderland of civilization." As on the Western frontier in American history, the recent colonists of New Saxony had little time or effort to spare from economic pursuits to cultivate the aesthetic or cultural values; and their civilization, only a few centuries old, could hardly be compared with that of the Rhine Valley or of the region around Nuernberg.

PART TWO

The Protagonist

« 4 »

Martin Luther

The Formative Years

Там HERE CAN BE NO DOUBT that many of Martin Luther's
contemporaries realized that he was one of the great men of history.
Almost twenty years before he died, his friends began to collect
the Reformer's letters and writings, while at various times twelve
table companions recorded his conversations with the dinner guests.[1]
The three funeral addresses delivered at the time of Luther's death
in 1546 testify to this same conviction.[2] Since he had died in his
native Eisleben, a service was held there in the *Andreaskirche*, on
which occasion Jonas, who had accompanied Luther on the journey
from Wittenberg, preached the sermon. In this funeral sermon
Jonas spoke of Luther's genius in glowing praise and pointed out
that it had been recognized by all since his early student days.

Three days later, after Luther's body had been returned to
Wittenberg, Johannes Bugenhagen, the town pastor and for many
years his friend and co-worker, spoke of him as the great Gospel
preacher whom all Germany acclaimed and who was esteemed
highly even in many foreign countries. On that same occasion
Philip Melanchthon gave a funeral address on behalf of the University of Wittenberg. This great Humanist, a brilliant man himself, compared his departed friend with the great men of the Bible
and the greatest of the early Church Fathers. Melanchthon regarded Luther as the most penetrating theologian of the Christian
Church since St. Paul.

Yet, strangely, these intimate companions and admirers apparently took Luther's living, dynamic personality for granted, little
realizing that someday he would be lost to them forever. Not one

of his co-workers ever thought of writing a description of him; nor did anyone take the time to write a biography while he was living.

Luther had promised his friends that he would write an auto-biography for the second volume of the *Wittenbergische Ausgabe* of his works. Although it would have been a personal evaluation of his life and work, an autobiography by the Reformer's own pen would have been invaluable to the Luther student, as it would have added insight and understanding impossible of attainment by any other writer. Unfortunately, poor health and overwork de-feated this purpose, and there remain but "a few glances over the shoulder" which the Reformer dashed off for the introduction to the first volume of the Latin edition of his works in 1545.[3] To this may be added a few chance remarks by his fellow professor, Nicho-las Amsdorf.[4] The research student, therefore, is dependent for his information on materials gleaned in the form of indirect refer-ences found in Luther's voluminous writings and on other con-temporary source materials.

Still more to be regretted is the fact that, when Philip Melanch-thon at last undertook to write a biography of the departed leader a few months after Luther's death, he was satisfied to produce a mere sketch.[5] Those ten pages do help to establish some of the disputed dates and facts of Luther's life. Yet, with Philip's gift for writing and his intimate firsthand information about the man who was his friend, colleague, and neighbor for so many years, he could have given us an intimate biography of the central figure of the Reformation.

The first real attempt at writing a longer biography of Luther's life was published in the form of seventeen sermons which M. Jo-hann Mathesius preached to his congregation in Joachimsthal be-tween 1562 and 1564. *Dr. Martin Luthers Leben,* the title which he used in the first edition, 1566, is really not a biography in the literal sense.[6] This series of sermons already incorporates much legendary material of that uncritical age; yet, since he was one of Luther's former table companions and also a reliable and con-scientious observer, it contains invaluable personal observations. A second biographer, Matthaeus Ratzeberger, the court physician of the Count of Mansfeld and later guardian of Luther's children, supplied some new information and personal touches, but must be used with great care because of the legendary embellishments. To this group should be added the biography by Luther's co-worker Friedrich Myconius, *Historia Reformationis,* which was published by Cyprian in 1718 and modernized by the Luther scholar Otto Clemen in 1915.[7]

Martin Luther died in 1546, and shortly after the middle of the century, Melanchthon, Jonas, and Amsdorf also passed from the Reformation stage, leaving a new generation that knew little or nothing of the true spirit of the Reformer. Luther's writings were available in the Wittenberg and Jena editions, but even these had not been too critically edited.[8] If the text did not fit the traditions of the moment, this generation often took the liberty of changing it to satisfy their prejudices. Slowly a new Lutheranism began to emerge that stressed Luther's doctrines but knew little of the evangelical spirit with which the great Wittenberg professor had inspired his students and congregations. Even Luther, whom no one of this period remembered from life, was made a part of the new historical tradition, just as Washington and Lincoln have today been adapted to our twentieth-century thought. A good example of this type of writer was Nicolaus Selnecker, who had heard much about Luther through his father but was now living in the conservative atmosphere of the Dresden court. His *historica narratio et oratio,* 1575, already breathes the spirit which became dominant in the Formula of Concord and makes of Luther a dogmatic personality. Selnecker's materials, however, did not become fully available until the nineteenth century. It was easy for this age to study Luther's Catechism and the Augsburg Confession, but not so simple to recapture the Luther of life. Through Selnecker and other writers of the time an erroneous, one-sided impression was left of the historical, living Luther which required centuries to eradicate among historians and which still prevails in some parts of America.

Another weakness of all the sixteenth-century Luther biographies was that they seemed to take the formative years of the young Luther for granted. The whole emphasis was placed on the period after 1517. Luther's own sketch from the introduction to the Latin edition of his works also stressed the later period; while Melanchthon and Mathesius devoted but a few pages to these

early formative years which were so vital to an understanding of
the real Luther.

By the end of the nineteenth century, after the publication of many heretofore unknown materials, German historians became intensely interested in the young Luther. They assumed that
a careful analysis of Luther's boyhood would explain his whole
later development. Scholarly studies and books appeared by such
able scholars as Scheel, Holl, Ritschl, Koehler, Boehmer, Strohl,
and others, exploring every possible aspect that might shed some
light on Luther's formative years. Among the many studies which
followed, the best are Henri Strohl's *L'Evolution Religieuse de Luther
Jusqu'en 1515* (1922); Karl Holl, *Gesammelte Aufsaetze* (1921);
Heinrich Boehmer, *Der junge Luther* (1925); and Otto Scheel's
Martin Luther (1930).

Following the last seventy-five years of Luther research some
very fundamental changes have been made in our conceptions of
Martin Luther. Catholic historians have been forced to be far more
cautious and less abusive; while Lutheran scholars have discovered
that much of the traditional Luther could not be substantiated, and
the original Luther must be re-established on the basis of sound
historical evidence.

THE ANCESTRAL HERITAGE

All attempts at tracing the ancestral heritage of Martin Luther
have ended in failure because of the scarcity of existing sources.
Early records indicate a variant spelling of the family name — Ludher, Luder, Lueder, Lutter, Lauther — all of which philologists
trace back to the old German name Chlotar. Nothing is known
of the original Luther *Stammhaus*, the old ancestral house in
Moehra, from where the Luthers came, as the building shown to
tourists was not erected until 1618 and belonged to a descendant
of Luther's uncle Klein-Hans.[9]

As far back as historical research has been able to trace the
Luther ancestry, they were living in the Moehra region, just southwest of the Thuringian Forest in the neighborhood of Eisenach.
The family belonged to a rather fortunate economic group known
as *Erbzinsleute*,[10] a family group that held a village and its neighboring lands in a kind of communal ownership. Since the Middle

Ages the family had been free as individuals, for the *Zins,* or tax, which they owed to the Church and to the Elector was on the land rather than on the individuals. Thus the Luthers lived in a German village with fields, meadows, water, and a common woods divided for use but owned by the entire group from generation to generation. To insure continuous succession, the estate always passed to the youngest son. This custom left the older sons free to migrate to other parts if they felt that by so doing they might improve their circumstances.

Luther's ancestors seem to have been of pure German stock. Otto Scheel, who explored this problem rather thoroughly, contends there is no evidence of racial mixture.[11] Since the families of both his father and his mother came from the western part of Germany, where the Wends had not penetrated, and since their ancestral names were German, previous claims of racial mixture seem to be without foundation. The family must have been quite large, for in 1521, when Martin Luther stopped off at Moehra on his way from Worms, he learned that his people occupied the whole region between Eisenach and Rennsteig. In 1536 the Luthers had five *Hoefe,* or small estates, occupied by different branches of the family but considered one under the legal title.[12]

In this beautiful, green, hilly region of western Thuringia, not so far from the Wartburg, lived Heine Luder and his wife, the former Margarethe Lindemann. The four sons of Heine Luder, Gross-Hans, Klein-Hans, Veit, and Heinz, must have loved and enjoyed this old family estate, but historical records are silent on most of this family history. In this respect a biography by Luther himself or by his friend Philip could have been most enlightening. All that we know is that Luther's father, Gross-Hans, married a young lady of the neighborhood, Margarethe Ziegler. Seckendorf, who was fairly reliable as an historian, stated that her family was Franconian, but the statement cannot be proved.[13] Melanchthon spoke of her as a woman of commendable virtues. Hans Luder, Martin Luther's father (also called Gross-Hans, to distinguish him from his younger brother Klein-Hans),[14] was an able, hard-working, ambitious young man who felt that his future would not be too promising in the Moehra region since he could not inherit any of the family estates. Accordingly, he and his young wife decided to go to Eisleben, where the mining industry offered excellent opportunities.

In the southeastern part of Eisleben, on "Long Street," not
more than two blocks from St. Peter's Church, Hans and Margarethe
Luder lived in a two-story house, the foundations of which stand
to this day. The structure built upon the old foundations and now
shown to tourists has little that dates back to the sixteenth century.[15] Here, whether in the exact room on the first floor, as now
claimed, matters little, Martin Luther was born November 10, 1483,
according to the best available evidence. It seems strange that there
should be some uncertainty about the birth of so great an historical
character as Martin Luther; yet Melanchthon tells us in his brief
biography that not even his mother could recall the exact year of
Luther's birth, although she was sure about the hour and day.[16]
Luther's brother, Jacob, claimed that it had been the general impression of the family that the year was 1483, a date also substantiated by the *Liber Decanorum,* the dean's book of the University
of Wittenberg.[17] George Spalatin, a close friend of the Reformer,
wrote in his *Annalen* that it had been in the year 1484. Some modern German historians have tried to prove that Martin Luther was
born December 7, 1482; while one of the later *Tischreden,* a Table
Talk account by Roerer, claims that Hans Luder had already moved
to Mansfeld before Martin was born and that he was the second
son in the family.[18] However, modern historical research has discarded as spurious these legendary aspects told by later biographers,
and the date set by the first biographer, Philip Melanchthon, has
been accepted as the correct one. Nor is the time and place of
much consequence except that it emphasizes the lack of certainty
about most of the story of Luther's boyhood.

As was the custom, on the day following the birth, the young
son was taken to the lower Tower Room of St. Peter's Church, the
only part of the structure then completed, and baptized by Pastor
Bartholomaeus Rennebecher. Since this was on the day of the
Festival of St. Martin, Hans Luder's son was named Martin. The
original baptismal font used on the occasion had been replaced in
1518, but it was restored in 1827 and is still in use in the *Taufkapelle,* or baptismal room, of the present *St. Peter- und Paulskirche.*

Eisleben in 1582

His Boyhood

Early in the summer of 1484, for some unknown reason, the Luders left the town of Eisleben and moved to Mansfeld, a town even closer to the Harz Mountains. Perhaps it was because this town was more in the very heart of the mining region. That it was beloved by the inhabitants is shown by a later sixteenth-century saying: "Whom the Lord cherishes, him He favors with a residence in the Mansfeld region."[19] Mining was the principal occupation, but farming was a very close second.

Mansfeld, a town of about the same size as Eisleben, lay about five miles to the northwest and ten miles from Sangershausen. The general pattern of the region that is pictured in old cuts is one of hills, meadows, woods, and plains, all combined in a complex, colorful picture of rural life. Through the region ran the important highway from Nuernberg to Hamburg, bringing a constant stream of travelers from north and south. Spangenberg, in the *Mansfelder Chronik*,[20] gives us a rough sketch of the town plan from this early period. According to this drawing the town of Mansfeld had one principal street running rather haphazardly through the town. The town was surrounded by a formidable wall with four strong towers, while in the background, on a fairly high, steep cliff, stood the massive castle of the Grafen of Anhalt, an old and distinguished family related to the Ascanier of Wittenberg.

Near the center of the town was the church square. On a slight elevation stood *St. Georgskirche,* and next to the church was the *Ratsschule,* the city school, which was later renamed in honor of the Reformer. To the villagers St. George was the leading patron saint, while Andrew, Simon, Jacob, Thomas, and others were the fourteen assistants. The Virgin Mary, Anna, Elisabeth, Hedwig, and Ursula, as well as the Three Holy Kings, were also called upon in moments of great need.

It was into this environment that Luther's parents moved to seek their fortune in the heart of the copper mining region. That they were very poor seems to be quite evident. One needs but examine the lined faces and toil-worn hands of Luther's parents as painted by Cranach to be convinced that their life was not one of ease, but that they bettered their circumstances only through toil and thrift.[21] Luther later described those early years as *blut-sauer,* or extremely bitter, for the newly arrived couple. However, modern research is convinced that the poverty thesis has been much overemphasized as a contributing factor to Luther's later decision to enter the monastery. True, Luther's mother may have carried wood on her back during those early years, but so did the wives of other German burghers in the fifteenth century.

Hans Luder must have bettered his circumstances considerably by the time his son Martin started to school in Mansfeld. When Martin was about eight, his father was already one of the respected citizens of Mansfeld, for in 1491 he was selected as one of four citizens to protect the right of his fellow burghers in the city council.[22] The complete picture seems to be that of a rather thrifty, steadily rising young couple, respected and accepted by the whole community. Just how early Luther's father became a small cap-italist leasing and operating mines and furnaces is not known, but an old record indicates that he renewed a five-year contract in 1507 and must have been operating since 1502.[23] Thus, by the turn of the century the young man from Moehra had ventured into the mining business for himself. During this time he also purchased a home, on which there was a hundred-gulden mortgage in 1507. He leased one mine and smelter from the Luttichs, the children of his former mining companion, for which he paid 500 gulden rent. Shortly thereafter he was made supervisor of all the property of these minor children. During the same period the records indicate a partnership with a Dr. Dragstedt as well as other interests ex-tending over a rather large area.[24] When Martin became a priest, his father visited the monastery with a company of twenty horse-men and made a gift of 20 gulden to the Augustinians, a handsome sum in a day when one or two gulden was the price of an ox.[25]

Mathesius recognized this prosperity when he wrote "God blessed the mining industry" of Luther's father and that Hans Luder brought up "his son in a respectful atmosphere, using the money he had rightfully acquired as a miner." [26] When Martin later matriculated at the University of Erfurt, the records classified him as being from a family that "had." [27] The pathetic picture of a poverty-stricken lad who sang from door to door to win his daily

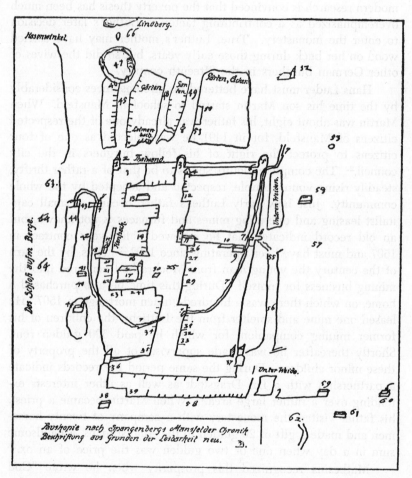

City Plan of Mansfeld

sustenance hardly fits into the frame provided by the historical records of a family that belonged to the better burghers of the town. Even the sons of *Patrizier* families, or the more well-to-do classes, participated in the street serenades. Although Hans Luder never became wealthy in the modern sense, he left a family estate of $18,000.[28]

Likewise, the severity of Luther's childhood has been over-emphasized. Like other parents of that era, Luther's did not believe in sparing the rod and spoiling the child. Parents in the fifteenth century believed in unquestioning obedience; and as the young Luther possessed the indomitable will manifested in his later life, he was, doubtless, a difficult child to handle. Luther said in one of his *Table Talks* that his father once spanked him so hard that he fled from him and for some time was very bitter about this mistreatment.[29] But many will recall similar experiences from their own childhood. This was not an age of child psychology, and Luther's parents, like others, lacked the training and time for insight and self-restraint when they felt the moral integrity of their child was endangered. Again, Luther relates that his mother once flogged him on account of a nut until the blood began to flow.[30] But his account does not give the details of the story, and from the total picture it appears that this was not typical. His father also had his cheerful, jovial moments "over a stein of beer," while his mother often sang to the children.[31] The life of the Luther home was not abnormal.

Severity was common practice in that day, for Luther later advocated a better child psychology for the new Lutheran schools of "placing the apple beside the rod." To be sure, Luther may have received fifteen paddlings in one morning because he did not know his Latin forms; but so did Melanchthon receive daily beatings at Pforzheim some years later.[32] Languages in that day were not taught, they were literally pounded in; and the average student took such treatment for granted and loved his instructors just the same. Furthermore, records show that if these floggings exceeded the point of accepted practice, the parents complained or even withdrew their children from school. Scholars have searched in vain for an explanation of Luther's later soul struggle in the early environmental conditions of his boyhood.[33] In fact, one may safely conclude that the Luther home was ‘that of normal, sincere Catholics who were highly regarded in the Mansfeld community. Luther's parents took a special interest in the promising young Martin, who might someday be one of the leading lawyers of the whole Anhalt community.

The Mansfeld School Days

Even though the sources on the Mansfeld school days are rather meager, there can be little doubt that they have been much misrepresented in many Lutheran circles. Too much emphasis has been placed on a mere reference made to his training here in his tract of 1524, *To the Councilors of all German Cities*.[34] When Luther exclaimed in this call to arms: "We were martyrized there," the occasion demanded strong language, and Luther was a master at creating the desired effect. After Worms the enrollment of the University of Wittenberg rapidly dropped to about a third, and Luther, together with his fellow professors, greatly feared for the whole future of German education. In this document the Reformer sought to shake the indifferent German parents from their lethargy toward higher learning. Since monastic education no longer offered an easy retreat for the youth and the lucrative church positions were not a part of the new Lutheran system, Luther feared that the phlegmatic German might conclude that there was no longer a need for higher education. He was making an appeal for the new humanistic type of learning, and in such a presentation his own Mansfeld school days suffered by comparison. It is true, Mansfeld may not have had as good a Latin school as Eisenach or Nuernberg; yet the fact remains that after Luther had received his early training here, he was able to carry on at Magdeburg and Eisenach without difficulty. Melanchthon praises this later excellent progress which he says was due to Luther's ability but does not imply that his early training had been inferior. As will be seen later, when the new Lutheran school system emerged in the thirties, most of the methodology and school organization already in practice at Mansfeld was retained even though the new evangelical spirit supplanted the old Catholic instruction.[35]

As there is considerable difference of opinion among his contemporaries, it is not exactly certain when young Martin began

his elementary training in the Mansfeld Latin school. Seven was
the customary age; yet there is some evidence which indicates
that he entered school quite early. Melanchthon, the famous school
organizer of the Reformation, was certainly familiar with standard
practice; still he implies that Luther was so young that Nicolaus
Oemler, an old family friend, took him in his arms and carried
him to school.[36] Since the distance to school was but a few blocks,
this would hardly have been necessary for a boy of six or seven.
Nor would Melanchthon have mentioned it had not the incident
been unusual. Mathesius' biography does not add much light when
it states that Luther started in school when "he was old enough
to comprehend" the instruction. Certainly that age would vary
greatly between average and precocious children. In all likelihood,
Luther entered school on St. George's Day, March 12, 1488, when
he was about four and a half years old, an age which might explain
why he had to be carried to school.

The Mansfeld school that Luther attended was a *Trivialschule*,
in which the medieval *Trivium* of Grammar, Logic, and Rhetoric
was taught.[37] This training was· considered essential for all students who were seeking an advanced education. As was common
practice, this school was divided into three *Haufen,* or groups. First
there were the *Tabulisten,* or beginners, who learned the ABC's of
Latin, which was largely a memorization of elementary forms and
the contents of the *Fibel,* or Latin primer. These little youngsters
also learned the *Benedicite,* the prayer before meals, and the *Gratias,*
the giving of thanks after eating. In addition they learned the
Confiteor, or the Confession of Sins, the Creed, the Lord's Prayer,
the Decalog, and the Hail Mary. Three times in the morning and
three times in the afternoon the *Tabulisten* recited; while in the
evening at home they were expected to memorize a few Latin
words with the help of their parents. The second group, often
called the *Donatisten,* was so named after the *Donat,* a medieval
Latin textbook.[38] The *Donat* was published with a German inter-
linear, making possible the study of Grammar by the direct method.
The study of the Latin language in this division became much
more formal. Frequently the assignment was an entire Psalm or
a section from the Latin Vulgate. Doubtless, Luther's later mastery
of the Latin Bible, his ability to quote verbatim almost at will even

late in life, dates back to the Mansfeld days. Thus, by about the completion of the sixth grade, the student was quite familiar with most parts of the Catholic church service and had mastered the elementary grammar of the Latin language.

The upper division group was known as the *Alexandristen*, named after a textbook by Alexander de Ville Dieu, in which the student was given more advanced Latin grammar and syntax.[39] It also had a German introduction and made ample use of this native language in the explanations. These students also began to use a Latin-German dictionary. Obviously the student who had finished a good *Trivialschule*, such as the one in Mansfeld, was ready to attend the university, where all assignments were made and delivered in Latin. Most of these aspects of the medieval Latin schools were retained by the Humanists and the Lutheran Reformers when they established similar institutions. In the upper division, students also served as choir boys and assisted in the Sunday service. That they might participate intelligently, they were taught the hymns, versicles, responses, and Psalms and given an explanation of the Epistle and Gospel readings.

Music naturally played an important role in the curriculum of the *Trivialschule*. The students were taught the Catholic liturgy, processionals, and recessionals as training for the regular and special services held during the church year. Special instruction in all the holy days of the church calendar was given through the *Cisio Janus*.[40] This was not a textbook, but a calendar in verse form, by means of which the students learned to calculate when the church festivals and saints' days would fall. In the *Cisio Janus* every month was treated by two verses. With its abbreviated, hieroglyphic forms the *Cisio Janus* seems somewhat confusing to the modern mind, but in an age during which there were so many saints' days the reckoning of church festivals was a complicated process. Instruction in calculating the church calendar was practical not only for the clergy but also for lawyers, businessmen, and other laymen who could order their daily tasks much more efficiently by avoiding conflict with the church festivals. Nor did the Reformers drop this practice. Melanchthon prepared a revised edition of the *Cisio Janus* for the Lutheran schools.

Students were likewise introduced to the theory of music. They were required to learn the Psalm tones and the rules of harmony. In some schools counterpoint and singing in several voices was practiced. Some years ago there was found in the *Staatsbibliothek* in Berlin an old musical treasure which was a composition and versification by Luther in his student days at Eisenach.[41] In this composition the tenor was the main part, with the bass, alto, and the descant woven around it. This training explains Luther's later enthusiasm for music, a discipline he had mastered during the Mansfeld, Magdeburg, and Eisenach school days.

Rhetoric, even though it was no longer emphasized as in the early Middle Ages, still had a rather respected place in most school systems. According to some old fourteenth-century Luebeck discoveries, the Latin school system was much more practical than would be supposed. Here, according to Warncke, were unearthed all kinds of school materials, wax tablets used by pupils, exercises by students in the lower division, as well as a number of business letters.[42] This seems to testify that much practical instruction was given in these Latin schools. Students were taught how to write letters, proper forms of address, and good manners.

Another aspect of Rhetoric was the literature which was read and memorized by the students. Through this the teacher also imparted much worldly wisdom which Luther late in life still regarded as very valuable. Among the works read were Cato, Aesop, Avian, Boethius, Sedulius, Plautus, and Terence. All of these writers had been carefully edited, and the materials had been selected that seemed most in keeping with the needs of the times. None of this curricular content in the *Trivialschule* was criticized by Luther in his *Weckruf of 1524*. In fact, he later regarded some of this literature as being next in importance to the Bible in the building of morality.[43] He did, however, complain that too little time had been devoted to German history, the poets, and general history.

The Latin schools devoted many hours to an explanation of the Gospels and Epistles, the Lord's Prayer, etc. Even the study of the *Fibel*, the first course of instruction, was in a sense an elementary course in religion. Much of the course in music was also of a religious nature. The cantor was a religious instructor who understood the Latin liturgy and the technique of sacred hymn writing. His work was, therefore, regarded as religious instruction. Nor did the Reformation change this aspect of the music course in the Lutheran schools, although its content became more evangelical.

Since so much has been written about the severe discipline that prevailed in the Mansfeld school system, a few of the details and a general evaluation of it in relationship to other German-Latin schools may be timely. In the Mansfeld Latin school, as was the custom generally, the lower division had a slate at the top of which was a picture of a wolf.[44] Since the Latin word for wolf is *lupus*, every student whose name appeared on this slate became a *lupus*. Every eight days the teacher checked the record, and each offender received one stroke for the number of times his name was on the slate. Although we have no specific information about Mansfeld, in the statutes of some schools the regulations state that students were to be spanked in the place that God had naturally provided. The accepted reasons for flogging were: a lapse into German, failure to decline or conjugate correctly, the use of profanity, or general misbehavior. Thus, when Luther was spanked fifteen times one morning, it must have been for a whole week's accumulation of offenses. Nor does this experience imply that it happened frequently.

Another incentive to study was a method of putting students to shame when they were unable to recite or used German in their recitations. An *asinus*, or wooden donkey, was also used in the Mansfeld school.[45] This was hung around the neck of the lowest student in the division at the end of the recitation period. Every time a student became an *asinus*, a record was made on the slate and added to the total of future whippings. Motivation, therefore, was a combination of fear and shame.

The human factor must doubtless have created a varied condition in different schools. That there were individual cases of student mistreatment cannot be doubted in an age in which corporal punishment was accepted practice. Yet there was a definite limit as to how far punishment could be carried. Neither parents nor the city council permitted much mistreatment. In most schools a definite system had been set up defining the exact punishment that should be meted out for a certain offense. Sometimes there were complaints on the part of parents, but in some instances, as at Stuttgart in 1501, the authorities passed a resolution that if the parents would not permit the punishment of their children, they could not attend school.[46]

The young Luther was no doubt frequently spanked, but so was the gentle Melanchthon and many other boys who were not nearly so gifted. Probably all the boys took the "cleaning of the slate" as a matter of course. And when the Reformer later in life directed the establishment of similar Lutheran schools, the wolf, the donkey, and the rod were retained as essential parts of the psychology of instruction. Since this type of punishment was most effective with youngsters, its application was limited to the lower group. The middle and upper divisions were punished more generally by a system of fines, or Geldbussen, a German system still quite common in modern times.

Anyone interested in Luther's early education is confronted by the problem: Just how good was the Mansfeld Latin school? Walther Koehler and Otto Scheel present opposing viewpoints. Koehler claims that it was not even a fully equipped Trivialschule, that its instruction was poor, and that Luther could not obtain proper training for entry into the University of Erfurt in this school. This, he says, explains why Luther's father sent the young lad away to school at Magdeburg and Eisenach after he had reached his fourteenth year. Otto Scheel, who has investigated this period more thoroughly than anyone else, does not agree with this viewpoint. He evaluates the commonly quoted Luther criticisms of this period in the light of other contemporary evidence and completely recreates the entire Mansfeld atmosphere.

The early Luther biographies do not imply that the Mansfeld school was an inferior institution. Mathesius even says that there Luther learned his materials "with diligence and great speed." Graduates from this school must have been prepared for university work, for the Album of the University of Wittenberg indicates that seven students matriculated there from Mansfeld between 1515 and 1523, several more between 1523 and 1527, while eighteen enrolled between 1530 and 1538.[47] That these students were actually graduates of Mansfeld cannot, of course, be established, as the ex Mansfelde of the Matrikel indicates only the territory or region. But it is reasonable to assume that students did enter the University of Wittenberg directly from this institution. Such evidence leads us to conclude that the Mansfeld school was a full *Trivial-schule,* even though its standing may not have been as high as the Eisenach, Ulm, or Nuernberg type of Latin schools.

The poor *Kirchenlatein,* or Church Latin, which Luther learned here is often cited as evidence that the Mansfeld instruction was inferior. Luther himself later in life vehemently condemned this Church Latin, but a wrong interpretation has sometimes been placed upon his remarks.[48] Those who wish to understand why Mansfeld and other schools instructed students in the late Medieval Latin must examine the objectives of its instructors. At the turn of the century, Scholasticism was still very strong in the German universities. Humanism was just beginning to get a foothold. In such an atmosphere the German students who attended the universities were expected to understand lectures on the works of the various Scholastic writers. To follow university lectures, they had to be familiar with the syllogistic method of reasoning and with the vocabulary of the Schoolmen. When Luther later broke with Rome and changed the University of Wittenberg into an institution in which Biblical Humanism was the accepted method of religious instruction, he naturally was offended with the "donkey manure which the devil had brought into the schools." Had he remained a Catholic, his earlier training would have been as adequate for his daily needs as it was for his Roman critics.[49] It was not the type of Latin but the change in the point of view that occasioned the Reformer's violent reactions to the former Church Latin. Like Erasmus and the Biblical Humanists, he now wanted the Latin of the early Catholic Church and the Greek and Hebrew of the Bible. For his work as the Reformer of the Church his boyhood training was sadly wanting; but for his Roman Catholic contemporaries, who retained the Thomist, Scotist, or some other Scholastic point of view, the Latin of the *Trivialschule* was entirely adequate.

The impression has been left by some Luther biographers that there had been little religious instruction in the Mansfeld school. As has been mentioned, the German *Fibel* used in the lower division was also a *Religionsbuch,* or a book of religion. Although the materials were in Latin, the subject matter aimed to prepare the pupil to be a good Roman Catholic. In the morning the school was opened with prayer and a song, usually "Veni, Sancte Spiritus" or "Veni, Creator." Occasionally the morning session was varied with a few minutes of prayer and a song. The materials to be memorized by the pupils were selected from hymns, prayers, and versicles commonly used in the Catholic church service. In the second and third groups of the school this memorization resulted in the mastery of a considerable body of the *Plenarium,* a full church manual, as we know from Luther's later reaction when he saw the first Latin Bible.[50] He was surprised that the Bible contained much material not found in the *pericopes* with which he was familiar. By the time a student graduated from one of these Latin schools he was well prepared to enter into the spirit of Catholic church services and to participate in the various Masses, which all had their special liturgies. In brief, this training aimed to nurture the children as loyal members of the Church.

THE YEAR IN MAGDEBURG

When young Martin had entered his fourteenth year, doubtless around Easter 1497, he was sent to Magdeburg to school in the company of Johann Reinecke, the son of a quite well-to-do blast furnace superintendent in Mansfeld.[51] The two lads seem to have been close friends, a relationship which continued throughout their lives. The reason for a change in schools is implied by the first two Luther biographers. Melanchthon speaks in one breath of the "blossoming schools of the Saxon lands" and in the next says that Luther's father sent young Martin to Magdeburg. Mathesius claims that the young Luther went there because this school had a reputation "far above many others." It may also be possible that the German custom of attending a number of schools to obtain a diversified education and atmosphere was a factor influencing Luther and the Reinecke boy. Since Luther's father was now in comfortable financial circumstances, he, too, may have felt that Martin should have the advantage of some of the best schools in the land.

Magdeburg at this time had a population of around 12,000. It was a city filled with endowed churches and chapels, which required an unusually large number of clergy to read Masses and hold special services at the various altars. The *Dom,* or Cathedral, was the center of this religious life. Since it was surrounded by a spacious lawn, it offered room for colorful gatherings. Behind and about the *Dom* were many buildings, including the *Mosshaus,* or palace of the archbishop, and the famous Cathedral School. Magdeburg was a storehouse of sacred relics. Weynmann has left us a description of these treasures to be seen on display at stated times. What colorful processions the young Luther must have witnessed on Palm Sunday, Ascension Day, and on September 22, when a great festival was begun in honor of the patron saint of the Cathedral, on which occasion the body of Florentius was placed in the main nave! Great relic processions occurred on Easter Monday and the Monday after Pentecost. That this "miniature Rome" left its impression on the young Luther can hardly be doubted.[52]

Much later in life he once recalled how Prince William of Anhalt, patron of the Franciscan monastery, walked through the streets barefooted, begging alms:

> He had so fasted, neglected, and mortified his body, that he looked like a dead man of sheer skin and bones and died soon after that. . . . Whosoever looked upon him was deeply moved and felt ashamed of his secular way of life.[53]

Doubtless, this sight remained a haunting memory to Luther even in the Erfurt college days and may have influenced him to enter the monastery.

For years historians tried to establish what school in Magdeburg Luther attended. Mathesius took for granted that it was the then famous *Stadtschule,* which the Lutherans had established during the early twenties of the sixteenth century. What Mathesius overlooked was the fact that before the Reformation this town school did not exist and Luther could not have attended it.[54] Melanchthon's reference to the superiority of the Saxon schools is of no value for our problem. Magdeburg had several *Parochialschulen* in the days of Luther's boyhood, of which the parochial school of St. John's was the most distinguished. It was this institution with its established reputation that the city council converted into the Town School. Cruciger became its first rector, or superintendent, and it was his distinguished service that gave the new school its fame. This reorganization of the old school system took place between 1522 and 1524, at which time, upon the advice of Luther and Melanchthon, all the other parochial schools were centralized in the Town School. But research makes it very doubtful that Luther attended the St. John's Parochial School.

Luther gave us a clue to his school when on one occasion he remarked that he had gone to school to the *Nullbrueder,* so named from the low singing, or "lollen," of their devotions.[55] These were the Brethren of the Common Life, an order founded by Gerhard Groote of Deventer, who emphasized Bible reading and the return to simple, pious lives for both the clergy and laity. The chapter in Hildesheim had been invited to found a house in Magdeburg as early as 1482 but encountered considerable opposition from the city authorities. Finally, in 1497, the year of Luther's sojourn there, with the aid of the archbishop they were officially recognized by the city authorities as a fully established order that could no longer be molested. The Brethren of the Common Life did not have a school of their own, but three or four of their number were teaching in the *Domschule,* the Cathedral School, for centuries famous all over northwest Germany. Could it have been here that the young Luther went to school in Magdeburg and could rightly say he had gone to school to the *Nullbrueder?*

Although the school year at Magdeburg was so uneventful that early biographers have nothing to record, yet in all likelihood it was at Magdeburg that Luther made his discovery of the Bible rather than at Erfurt. Nor does it seem unusual that Luther had not seen a Bible before this, since most of his instruction at Mansfeld had been by the blackboard and wax tablets and since students handled few books. Catholic Mass books and *Plenaria* had been used for preparing advanced students to participate in the church service. Luther was apparently well enough acquainted with these to know when he saw the Bible that it contained many more lessons than those selected for the Catholic church postils.

Since Luther's *Table Talks* are the sources for this story of the Bible discovery, a word of caution is in place.[56] Copied by twelve table companions over a period of twenty-some years the *Table*

Talks are often unreliable, of uneven quality, and written at varying periods of time. Certainly, little, if any, of the material was copied in the Reformer's presence. Rather, the copyists later recorded in their rooms their recollections of the evening's conversation. These recordings, purporting to be the exact words of Luther, were often invented and embellished, and additional errors crept in later when the table companions began to copy conversations from each other. In time it was difficult to know by whom and when the original might have been made. Melanchthon on one occasion warned some of the table companions as to the hazardous nature of such practice, realizing that posterity would read meanings into these conversations that Luther had never intended. Furthermore, where every topic imaginable was discussed and the conversation was spontaneous, it is difficult to distinguish jest from serious statement. It is hardly fair, therefore, to hold Luther responsible for all that has come to us in the *Table Talks.* Obviously, a careful checking against evidence from Luther's own writings and additional sources is absolutely essential. By this means scholars have re-examined the story of Luther's discovery of the Bible in the library at Erfurt.

The Erfurt location is rendered questionable by a comparison of older and later editions of the *Tischreden,* which reveals that in one vital place even the textual reading was changed to fit in with this later sixteenth-century tradition. The most frequently quoted accounts from the *Tischreden* reveal considerable variation in the story of the Bible discovery.

Mathesius says:

> When there were no public lectures he spent his time in the university library. On one occasion when he was carefully examining the volumes, one after the other, so that he might learn to know the best among them, he happened on a copy of the Latin Bible, which he had never in his life seen up to this time. Then he noticed with great amazement that it contained many more texts than those that were in the ordinary postils or were ordinarily explained from the pulpits of the churches. As he was looking through the Old Testament, he chanced to see the story of Samuel and his mother, Hannah, which he rapidly read through with great enjoyment and delight, and, because it was all new to him, he began to wish from the bottom of his heart that our good Lord would at some time bestow on him such a book as his own.[57]

Another account is somewhat briefer and gives a slightly different version of the story:

> When I was twenty years old I had not yet seen a Bible. I thought that there were no Gospels and Epistles except those which were written in the Sunday postils. Finally I found a Bible in the library and forthwith I took it with me into the monastery. I began to read, to reread, and to read it over again, to the great astonishment of Dr. Staupitz.[58]

Finally, Veit Dietrich, who seems to be the best informed on this story, gives the following account:

> Once as a boy he happened on a Bible where by chance he read the story concerning the mother of Samuel in the Book of Kings [sic]. The book pleased him greatly and he thought that he would be very fortunate if he should ever be able to possess such a book. Shortly afterwards he bought a postil; this pleased him greatly because it contained more Gospels than it was customary to teach during the course of the year. When he was made a monk he gave up all his books. A short time before he had purchased the Corpus Juris and I do not know what other books. He took none of them with him into the monastery except Plautus and Virgil. There the monks gave him a Bible bound in red leather.[59]

In addition to these three accounts there are several others. Roerer even adds that the striking of the library clock interrupted Luther's reading. Two of the accounts mention Staupitz, whom Luther did not learn to know until much later. Some imply also that he was already a monk.

The Dietrich account, which covers the period from boyhood to the entry into the monastery, appears most consistent with other known facts. Undergraduates at the University of Erfurt could not slip into the library between classes and read.[60] The Erfurt library regulations required that an undergraduate had to be accompanied by an instructor to enter the library, and to use or to withdraw books required a special privilege and the deposit of a forfeit.

It would be interesting to know why the word puer, or boy, was changed to adolescens or baccalaureus in the later Table Talks, implying that Luther was already a young man or bachelor.[61] As Strohl points out, the original reading is much more reasonable, which places the experience in Magdeburg in the Domschule, where the Brethren of the Common Life sought to acquaint their pupils with the Holy Scriptures.

Another aspect of this same tradition has been misconstrued. The older accounts implied that this Bible was chained to prevent its examination, but this error was already corrected by Koestlin-Kawerau in 1903. A glance at medieval library furniture reveals that a *liber catenatus,* or a chained book, merely implies that the book was fastened permanently to a reading desk by a chain.[62] Modern bookcases did not come into being until the second half of the sixteenth century. Before this time there was no means of storing these precious volumes. Sometimes chained Bibles were placed in some suitable location in medieval churches, as, for example, in Leyden, where as early as 1462 a German Bible was placed on a desk in the gallery of St. Peter's Church and fastened with a chain. The practice of chaining books in university libraries continued even through the Reformation. At the University of Wittenberg chains were ordered for additions to the library as late as 1536.[63] As late as 1558 the books at the University of Marburg were still secured with chains.

The old tradition which aimed to prove that the Bible was a closed book is weakened still further by the fact that before Martin Luther made his translation of the German Bible, there were already fourteen High German and four Low German editions in print.[64] Though these Bibles were expensive, there must have been a great number sold to support so many editions. But their number does not imply that the Bible was used as the guide to life that it became when Martin Luther again found the Apostolic principle of *Sola Scriptura* through his struggle in the Erfurt monastery. The Bible before the Reformation could be interpreted only by Masters and Doctors of Divinity, and only then in the light of the Fathers and the Scholastics, in which the University of Paris and the Pope claimed to have a monopoly.

His Beloved Eisenach

Following the year of study in Magdeburg with the Brethren of the Common Life, for some unknown reason Luther's parents decided to send him to school in Eisenach. The explanation given by the early Luther biographies, that young Martin was sent to

Eisenach because his mother had relatives there, is not too convincing. Konrad Hutter, the sexton of St. Nicolaus Pfarrkirche, had married a relative of Martin's mother, Margarethe of Schmalkalden, but Martin did not live with them. Perhaps they were only to supervise him, or he may have lived with them for a while, but later moved to a more favorable location. Luther's later attitude toward these Eisenach relatives does not reveal any sign of resentment or neglect. The final answers to these questions may never be discovered.

Since Melanchthon and Mathesius are too brief, the little information available comes from Luther himself and the few contemporary sources. Ratzeberger embellished the story too much to be trustworthy, yet in a few cases he offers valuable clues.[65] Most of the Eisenach tradition which crept into the later Luther biographies after Walch, came from local historians like Drescher, Rebhan, and Paullinus, who were all too ready to supply from the prevalent stories or their imaginations whatever could not be established in point of fact.[66] A great fire about a hundred years later may also have consumed valuable information. Since Eisenach was Luther's favorite town during his earlier school days, a few words in regard to the environment may be of interest.[67]

The town of Eisenach was one of the principal cities of Thuringia. During one period of the Middle Ages it had been the residence of the Landgrafen. Since it lay at the crossroads of the Frankfurt a. M.-Erfurt-Leipzig highway and the important Hamburg-Bremen and Nuernberg trade route, its future was believed to be quite promising; but it failed to fulfill that promise. Perhaps the steep hills behind the city caused the tradesmen to seek different routes. Hence Eisenach was one of those cities which, at the close of the Middle Ages, had overreached itself by building an expensive wall too large for the town's growth, leaving areas within still undeveloped. The formerly much-frequented Wartburg Castle towering above the city also fell into disuse and decay.

When Martin Luther came to Eisenach, the city was just average size, a little smaller, perhaps, than his native Eisleben. At the turn of the century, according to one estimate, it had 420 houses and a population of 2,100.[68] A few of its streets were partly paved, while in the downtown section it also had sidewalks. In Eisenach were three important churches: the *Pfarrkirche St. Niko-laus* at the northwest wall, the *Pfarrkirche unserer lieben Frau* in the southern part, and the *Pfarrkirche St. Georg* in the market. The latter had a school known as the *Georgenschule*, dedicated to St. George the Dragon Killer. *St. Georgskirche* was without a tower and in such a dilapidated condition that the whole structure was torn down and rebuilt in 1515. Because of the generosity of the princes the clergy had acquired much property in and about Eisenach, which led some of the critical laymen to label the town a regular "Pfaffennest," or "nest of preachers." It has been estimated that about every tenth person was a member of the clergy, who controlled most of the region's resources, income from which flowed into the Church. The situation led to the impoverishment of the town and caused the citizens to make frequent complaints to the princes, asking them to alleviate the conditions. At the foot of the high hill upon which towered the lofty Wartburg stood the little Franciscan monastery which had been founded by a prominent business family in town, the Schalbes. There were other religious orders, but they did not come in contact with the young Luther and are, therefore, not vital to his story.

The *Georgenschule* in Eisenach compared quite favorably with the one Luther had attended in Magdeburg.[69] Although it had not been exceptional in the fifteenth century, it seems that the very time that Luther came there the Eisenach school had acquired some exceptional teachers and was quite good. Perhaps that was what Melanchthon meant when he said that the Saxon schools at that time were "blossoming." The boy Luther was greatly impressed with the school and especially with two of its able teachers. Me-lanchthon tells us: "In Eisenach he heard a teacher who taught grammar more thoroughly and skillfully than it was being taught anywhere else." Ratzeberger says this skillful instructor was Tre-bonius, the rector of the school, "a highly respected, learned man and poet." That Trebonius was a gifted instructor with a good sense of humor cannot be doubted, but Melanchthon's claim that he stood above all the teachers of the land seems a little broad.

The story added by Ratzeberger, that Trebonius always tipped his hat upon entering the classroom out of respect for future distinguished citizens that might be among his students, is probably an embellishment based on Luther's later fame.[70] A second teacher of distinction was Wigand Gueldennapf aus Fritzlar, whom Luther even later in life recalled with pleasure and for whom he tried to get a pension from the Elector in 1526. Ratzeberger implies that there were several other teachers, but such claims are without definite confirmation.

As for Luther's progress in the Eisenach school, Melanchthon says: "Here he rounded out his Latin studies; and since he had a penetrating mind and rich gifts of expression, he soon outstripped his companions in eloquence, languages, and poetic verse." [71] In its general curriculum and methods the Eisenach school was very similar to those previously attended. Here also the wolf, donkey, and rod were used in the lower division, but as Luther was now in the upper division, these unpleasant aspects of the system were not so noticeable. Perhaps better judgment was also exercised by the rector of the school, Trebonius. Those who say "the humanistic spirit" was dominant in Eisenach cannot substantiate their claim. Luther did not come in contact with the classics until at Erfurt and then through teachers who were not real Humanists. From brief comments we gather that he did learn the *artes dicendi* and *poesin;* namely, the spirit of the language in the form of compositions, essays, poems. He still wrestled with the "system of metrics," which was studied in connection with Alexander's *Grammar,* and certain advanced rules of composition which were basic to eloquence and style.[72] Of course in the *Donat* he had already learned some verses from Virgil. Through his former courses he had learned to know the names of many classical authors. But the curriculum of the Eisenach school was that of a typical *Trivialschule,* as Melanchthon's statement also clearly indicates. The art of instruction here was so good, however, that it won Luther's lifelong esteem. Luther was fortunate that immediately preceding his entry into Erfurt he had four years of this high quality of preparatory education.

The young Luther's development in Eisenach was not limited to what he learned in the classroom. Events outside the

classroom have been much confused by the many Eisenach traditions, yet their influence on the later Luther was so vital that their
accuracy must be determined as nearly as possible.

As observed previously, by the time Martin was sent to further
his studies his father was sufficiently prosperous to well afford to
send the lad to school. On the strength of this fact some German
historians have doubted that Luther ever begged for food in the
streets. Begging was an accepted practice, a sort of scholarship,
by means of which the wealthier citizens kept poor students in
school. Since the custom was popular among the boys, the sons
of well-to-do parents often participated. Mathesius observed with
regard to Luther's year at Magdeburg: "Like many a child of respected and wealthy parents, this boy also shouted in the streets
his *Panem propter Deum* [Give us bread for God's sake!]." [73]
Mathesius later adds: ". . . there [in Eisenach] he for a while also
sang for his bread from door to door." Luther himself wrote in his
Sermon on the Duty of Sending Children to School (1530):

> It is true, as is sometimes said, that the Pope was once a student;
> therefore do not despise the boys who beg from door to door "a little
> bread for the love of God"; and when the groups of poor pupils
> sing before your house, remember that you hear, as this Psalm says,
> great princes and lords. I have myself been such a beggar pupil,
> and have eaten bread before houses, especially in the dear town of
> Eisenach, though afterwards my beloved father supported me at the
> University of Erfurt with all love and self-sacrifice, and by the sweat
> of his face helped me to the position I now occupy; but still I was
> for a time a poverty student, and according to this Psalm I have
> risen by the pen to a position which I would not exchange for that
> of the Turkish sultan, taking his wealth and giving up my learning.[74]

From this statement one must conclude that Luther joined in
the custom of begging in the streets. Since Luther's father was by
this time quite well-to-do, it is difficult to accept the above statement that he was "a poverty student." An examination of the purpose of the *Sermon* indicates that Luther was seeking to persuade
parents to send their children to school even though they might not
possess the necessary funds for the student's entire support. He
points out that being a student, even a poverty student, is no disgrace and in support of this statement cites both the Pope and
himself as former students. He further emphasizes the fact that

he was a "beggar pupil," but that such a position is no disgrace
and he would not now exchange places with the sultan. Most
scholars agree that Luther participated in some begging at Magdeburg and at Eisenach with other students from well-to-do families,
but they no longer accept the old Eisenach tradition that Luther
was so poor that he was forced to beg for food in the streets.[75] Nor
do they believe the later embellishment that the young Luther
was about to depart in despair when a distinguished lady, *eine
Matrone*, decided to take him into her own home.

Even though confused, there is likewise some truth in the
Frau Cotta story, which has been traced to a local writer named
Drescher.[76] From him it passed to Rebhan, Paullinus, and Ratzeberger and became the accepted Eisenach tradition. Coupled with
the myth that the Luthers were very poor, the pathetic story of
the hopeless student rescued by the benevolent lady made very
pretty reading. But how all of this came about is not quite certain.

Frau Cotta was the wife of Kunz Cotta, a prosperous businessman whose family had been distinguished in the town for a hundred
years.[77] They lived in a large *Patrizierhaus*, a home that was usually
built of brick or stone and several stories high. It seems to have
been located on *Georgenstrasse* and, according to the Eisenach
tradition, Luther was living at this time in the *Georgenvorstadt*,
the suburb of St. George. Although it cannot be proved, Mathesius
may be correct when he states that the *Matrone* took Luther into
her home because she liked "his singing and devout praying in
the churches." [78] Ursula Cotta was a member of another distinguished family of Eisenach, the Schalbes, and it is rather well
established that Luther tutored little Henry Schalbe and was quite
at home in that family circle. The Cottas and the Schalbes were
very intimate, and there is evidence to support the view that
Luther lived with the Cottas but ate his meals with the Schalbes.[79]
If this view is true, it is highly possible that there is no connection
between Luther's "begging" and his entry into the Cotta home.

In this Cotta and Schalbe circle the young Luther had every
advantage that a young student could desire. Here was a congenial, comfortable atmosphere dominated by strong religious conviction and often the scene of stimulating conversations with dis-

tinguished guests. One of the most frequent of these was the Vicar of *St. Marien,* who was also in charge of the Franciscan monastery at the foot of the Wartburg, the *Barfuesser Kloster,* supported by the Schalbe family.[80] It is entirely possible that some seeds planted by the Vicar in the fertile mind of the young student may have germinated at Erfurt and contributed to Luther's decision to enter the Augustinian monastery there in the fall of 1505. Luther later often recalled his stay in Eisenach as one of the happiest periods of his life. Amidst such a delightful atmosphere of sympathetic friends, and enjoying the stimulation of excellent teachers, it is readily understandable that Luther should later speak of Eisenach as his "beloved town."

THE ERFURT STUDENT

In the spring of 1501, when Martin Luther was not quite eighteen years old, he matriculated at the University of Erfurt. There are perhaps a number of reasons why he went here rather than to Leipzig. It was, of course, near by. Luther states later in life that he also regarded its reputation as far above all other German universities. Trutvetter, who was to become one of his influential professors in college, matriculated him as "Martinus Ludher ex Mansfelt." [81] Luther entered the department of Liberal Arts, from which a well-prepared student from a good *Trivialschule* like Eisenach could graduate in eighteen months. Luther finished the work toward his A. B. degree before the end of 1502, ranking thirtieth in a class of fifty-seven. He immediately began graduate work toward his M. A. degree in Liberal Arts, which he completed in February, 1505, ranking second in a class of seventeen. Now he was fully prepared to teach as the degree implied, provided he taught in a school of Liberal Arts. Yielding to the wishes of his parents, however, he began the study of law in the graduate school the following May. He even bought himself a *Corpus Juris,* as noted earlier, and threw himself into this new work with great earnestness. But he soon found that he did not care for the subject and preferred to devote his time to reading in other fields. This discovery, he knew, would prove a great disappointment to his father. In order to understand more fully the undercurrents of this period in Luther's education, it is necessary to examine closely the conditions under which he labored to determine what factors influenced him to abandon his legal education and to become a monk.

Erfurt lies in a rich, fertile part of the Thuringian basin, where wine gardens, orchards, flax, hemp, and various grains were important sources of wealth.[82] The dyer's weed offered the businessmen another lucrative source of income. Luther was much impressed with the trade and commerce of this community and its evident wealth. The citizens were quite independent even though they were under the ecclesiastical domination of Mainz and the political sovereignty of Albertine Saxony. Since Erfurt was on the main arteries of trade, goods from all over southern Europe could be purchased at its *Kaufhaus,* or merchandise mart. In time Erfurt had also been granted certain monopolies by the state, especially pertaining to commodities from the Orient. Although the city had on several occasions attempted to gain its independence, it never achieved the status of one of the German "free cities."

Exactly how large Erfurt was at the end of the fifteenth century cannot be accurately established. According to Hogel's *Chronik* a great fire in 1472 consumed 2,024 buildings, which he estimated to have been about half of the city. Allowing on the average five persons per house, and granted there were about 4,000 houses, Erfurt's population at this time was around 20,000 people. Others have attempted to arrive at an estimate of Erfurt's population by counting the number of chimneys, but such an approach seems quite unreliable. Tettau holds that the population of Erfurt must have been around 35,000, but Kirchoff doubts that it ever exceeded 20,000 before the Thirty Years' War. When the populations of other German cities are taken into consideration, the estimate of 20,000 seems even a little high. Luther was under the impression that Erfurt was about twice the size of Nuernberg.[83]

The town of Erfurt, though very modern to Luther and his contemporaries, presented the typical medieval picture previously described. The city had no definite street plan, as did few other old German towns. A view for any distance down most of the narrow streets was often obstructed by houses that stood partly in the streets, which were very crooked, many of them resulting in dead ends. Most of the houses in Erfurt still consisted of the light, inflammable materials with thatched roofs, but the city was proud of several stone structures of exceptional beauty. Roofing material consisting of wooden boards was coming into use, and the homes of the wealthier citizens were constructed entirely of stone with roofs of tile or slate.

Street illumination was not introduced until the decade after Luther's student days, and no students were permitted in its crooked streets after dark except with lanterns, since there were many hazardous streams and canals. Many footbridges were used to cross these streams, which also added to the typical medieval atmosphere of its environment. As in other German cities, some of Erfurt's streets were beginning to be paved, and crushed stone was most commonly used for street construction. In this great center of trade various foreigners appeared at the annual markets and in the *Kaufhaus*, adding color to this typical cosmopolitan center. The young Luther was much impressed by Erfurt's pomp and splendor and received the impression that the city was very immoral.[84] Certainly in such a polyglot population there was ample opportunity for debauchery and vice; but it is quite doubtful whether Erfurt and its university deserved the epithets "a beer chamber" or a "house of prostitution," which have been used. Erfurt may have had its *Frauenhaeuser* and its crudities, but so did many other German towns have their houses of ill fame, including Wittenberg, before the Reformation.

Among the ecclesiastical institutions in Erfurt almost every phase of the Roman Catholic Church was represented. Muelverstedt estimated that there were one hundred of these organizations. He lists 2 endowed churches, 22 cloisters, 23 cloister churches, 36 chapels, and 6 hospitals.[85] The most impressive of all the buildings was the Cathedral, around and in which occurred many impressive rituals, such as the election of the university rector each semester and other academic occasions. Luther later recalled with pride these memorable ceremonies and said that he was happy to have had the privilege of being a part of these dignified and majestic rites.[86] With all these churches and other religious houses there certainly was ample opportunity to become acquainted with the complexity of religious life in this "miniature Rome." Doubtless this pageantry impressed him far more than his classes in preparation for the legal profession.

Perhaps the most controversial subject relating to Luther's life in his Erfurt student days, and the question that has been discussed pro and con for some half century by the leading German scholars, is: What kind of life did Martin Luther lead while he was an undergraduate in the University of Erfurt? Was he the immoral, worthless degenerate pictured by Denifle, Grisar, and their followers? [87] Was there a connection, as this group claims, between Luther's immoral life and his decision to enter the monastery? And, finally, was his later discovery of "justification by faith" in the Black Cloister at Wittenberg but an easy escape from his moral degeneration? Impartial scholars such as Scheel, Boehmer, Strohl, and others have critically examined every existing source to ascertain the exact conditions under which Luther lived and matured during his Erfurt days.[88] In an attempt to reconstruct the conditions that prevailed at the University of Erfurt the best evidence is found in the university *Statutes* and regulations.

Erfurt was one of the old, well-established universities of Europe, tracing its beginnings to the early fourteenth century. Its official beginning as a full-fledged university, however, was in 1392, at which time it could already boast of a registration of 523 students.

In Luther's day Erfurt enrolled about 2,000 students. From the very beginning its pattern of organization had avoided the plan of "nations," which had proved a source of continuous trouble at Paris, Prague, Vienna, and Leipzig. The students lived in *Bursen*, or dormitories, patterned to some extent after monasteries.[89] Each was in charge of a rector and his assistants, usually the younger Masters of the faculty. These residences were again subdivided into smaller units of six or eight students with a house master responsible for each unit. The contact between student and professor was naturally very personal in such a small group.

A regulation established by the authorities at the very founding of the university, and still a part of the official university *Statutes*, required every student who wished to take a degree from

Erfurt to live at least one year in a university *Burse* under the close
supervision of a specific faculty member with the rank of Master.
Students were admitted to final examinations only upon permission
of this Master, who also had to assert that he could recommend
the student as to his character. This practice was very important,
since a degree from Erfurt implied not only an academic accomplishment, but moral integrity as well. If a Master misrepresented
an unworthy student, he might be severely punished. Repeated
offense would place his position on the faculty in jeopardy.[90]

Unfortunately, the official regulations of the *Georgenburse,* in
which Luther seems to have lived while he worked on his B. A.
and M. A. degrees, have perished. However, the *Statutes* that regulated the life of several of the other university dormitories exist
today and are doubtless similar to those of the *Georgenburse.*[91]
The general university *Statutes* do not prescribe any particular dormitory in which a candidate had to enroll for his period of supervised undergraduate study. Some claim that Luther lived for a
while in the dormitory named *Himmelspforte,* or, as the students
generally referred to it in Latin, *Porta Coeli.*[92] The *Porta Coeli*
dormitory regulations are still extant as are those of *Das alte Collegium,* the oldest of the dorms, and we may safely assume that
Luther lived under these same regulations.

Erfurt student life for Luther must have been similar to that
of students in a theological seminary. The dormitories had definite
prescriptions as to the kind and number of prayers to be prayed
each day. Since artificial illumination was very inadequate, students were expected to retire at 8 P. M. and to rise at 4 A. M., that
they might make maximum use of daylight.[93] Therefore, a bell
rang announcing the closing of the dormitory a few minutes before the hour for retiring. Required dress for the street was the
Toga, or *Tunic,* in keeping with the dignified, modest tradition of
Erfurt students. The regulations also prescribed specific clothes to
be worn within the dorms. At mealtime, portions of the Bible were
read, as well as selections from the church *Postillen,* for which
Luther may well have served as a reader at times. A student was
expected to make private confession four times a year.

As far as the charge of irregularities with women is concerned,
the university regulations made it very difficult for students to come

in contact with the opposite sex.[94] Under the rules of the *Himmelspforte* students might mingle with women only by permission from the rector, and then only at weddings or other special occasions. No woman was ever permitted to enter this *Burse.* If sewing or laundering was needed, the clothes were taken by a male servant to the proper places. Even to visit a business place off the campus required permission. Nor were students permitted out of the dormitories after closing hours except by special permission. This permission could be obtained only in exceptional cases, and it was necessary for the student to check out a lantern at the rector's office, which he returned later in the evening when re-admitted to the dormitory.[95] The authorities also kept a careful record of the places frequented by students, and a student consistently irregular in his habits would be deemed unworthy of continuing in school.

The students were permitted a prescribed amount of beer. And while there may have been exceptional cases of excesses, as there are in all student bodies, under the Erfurt dormitory rules it would be very difficult for a student to be habitually drunk without the fact becoming known to the authorities.[96] There was even a storage room of beer for the use of a *Burse,* but the Master always had the key to this additional supply.

There is good evidence to believe that Martin Luther lived in such an environment for four years under the careful supervision of a Master, and that, according to the rules of the university *Statutes,* he was given a "good recommendation regarding his life and morals" by his immediate supervisor. Further, Luther received his Bachelor and Master degrees in the minimum of time required, a feat achieved only by the most gifted and diligent students. Surely he must have been held in high esteem by the Erfurt faculty, otherwise he would not have been recommended for appointment at the University of Wittenberg. The Humanist Crotus Rubeanus, his roommate in the *Georgenburse,* also substantiated this belief when he wrote that Luther was regarded as an "erudite philosopher" by his fellow students.[97] In the closely supervised atmosphere in which Luther lived, the habitual drunkard and immoral libertine, as his critics have pictured him, certainly could not have long deceived both his fellow students and a watchful, critical faculty. German scholars have, therefore, concluded that the whole "libido" interpretation was not based on facts, but that Luther's critics willfully misconstrued a few careless remarks made by the Reformer in the presence of some dinner guests later in life by which he meant to show how badly Erfurt was in need of the Gospel before the Reformation.[98]

Just what kind of education did Luther get when he was a student in the Liberal Arts College at Erfurt? Melanchthon implies that Luther's instruction at the university was not the best. In his *Vita* he states that, had Luther been given the opportunity, he could have mastered all the arts and sciences, but unfortunately he became involved in rather "thorny dialects." [99] Yet, he adds that Luther read most of the old Latin authors, such as Cicero, Virgil, Livy, and others in order to gain "patterns of life"; and as he had a very good memory, he retained most of the important materials and drew upon them freely in later life.

One group of German scholars holds the view that while at Erfurt Luther moved in a Humanistic circle, the principal leader of which was Conrad Muth, a great student of the classics, just recently returned from Italy and now settled in the neighboring town of Gotha.[100] Unfortunately, the thesis of this group has not stood the test of research, for the Muthian circle did not penetrate the university until after Luther had entered the monastery. The researches of such scholars as von Schubert, Rommel, Ficker, and Meissinger have definitely shown that Luther did not then know Greek and Hebrew sufficiently well to make his tower discovery of "justification by faith" later at Wittenberg in 1514 on the basis of his knowledge of the Biblical languages.[101] His lectures on the Psalms (1513–1515) and his lectures on Romans (1515–1516) indicate that he leaned heavily on the Latin Vulgate for his exegetical work.

No doubt it is correct to speak of Erfurt as having "Humanistic tendencies." Some of the men on the faculty were traveling Humanistic scholars. Rudolf von Langen had been there years before. Peter Luder, Dietrich Gresemund, Conrad Celtis, Herman von Busche, Jacob Wimpfeling, and Matthias Zell had at various times graced Erfurt's halls, filling the chair of Poetry. Maternus Pistoris and Hieronymus Emser must have lectured there during Luther's college days, but there is no evidence that he heard their lectures.

That the remaining faculty members were influenced by these men is shown in the composition of their publications. Even in the department of philosophy, according to Rommel, there was a kind of "Scholastic Humanism," in which Trutvetter and Usingen, Luther's two leading professors, drew upon the treasures of antiquity "as an arsenal of epigram and proverbs" and frequently quoted the classics to support the points they wished to establish.[102] Doubtless it was through these men that Luther began to read rather widely among the ancient writers, but it is very doubtful whether their spirit permeated the dialectic approach that he was being taught in the regular courses.

Trutvetter, or Doctor Eisenach as he was sometimes called after his native town, was a very able professor who deplored the "hair-splitting type" of Scholasticism. He tried to simplify the dialectics of Occam and Biel. He even used a Humanistic style and poetic verse to make his material more popular and effective. Since the clear line of distinction between the regular Humanists and the late Scholastics does not become very marked until after 1510, men like Trutvetter and Usingen were the transitional link.[103]

Bartholomaeus von Usingen was a second Occamist whom Luther greatly admired and who must have had much influence on him during these years. In theology he distinguished between Aristotle and the Bible as sources of information. In matters of faith he accepted the Scriptures as an unerring guide to truth, while his conception of the Church Fathers and later tradition as evaluated in relation to the revealed Word doubtless influenced Luther in his later discovery of *Sola Scriptura,* or the principle of relying on the Bible alone in determining Biblical doctrines.[104] Usingen's criticism of Aristotle in all theological fields must have had much to do with Luther's rejection of Scholasticism in the Wittenberg curriculum. Usingen was progressive, up-to-date, and quite receptive to new ideas.

The philosophical point of view sought by the Erfurt faculty was called the *Via Moderna,* or the New Way, as distinguished from the former approach of several centuries before, the *Via Antiqua,* or the Old Way.[105] The latter system had flourished in the period of St. Thomas, who taught that human reason could aid the individual in his search for truth even in the realm of faith.

He went so far as to attempt to harmonize pagan philosophy with Christian revelation in his monumental work, the *Sum of Theology*. The followers of William Occam, a Paris professor, and his later disciples d'Ailly and Biel took the opposite approach in the *New Way*, stressing that human reason is of no avail in the realm of faith. They even separated philosophy into two realms. In the realm of faith, revelation could be the only guide; but in matters of this world, human reason should be used to its fullest extent.

Luther studied Aristotle's physics, metaphysics, and ethics for his M. A., and in Trutvetter's lectures in physics he was given the most modern scientific point of view. The progressive Weltanschauung of the school gave him the most up-to-date views in geography, the same views held by his contemporary Christopher Columbus. For example, Trutvetter taught that the earth was a sphere; that thunderstorms were due to natural causes; and that while astrology might have some basis in fact, it did not so affect the lives of human beings that they could not resist its influence, a very modern view for that superstitious age.

As for Luther, in his general scientific outlook he continued to hold this Trutvetter point of view even after he became a Lutheran. All too frequently Luther is considered as being backward in his scientific outlook when, in reality, many scientific theories now commonplace were not even accepted by all the best scientists of that day. For example, in astronomy, when Copernicus developed the heliocentric theory of the universe, he was merely speculating on the veracity of the late Greek astronomic knowledge; while, some half century after Luther's death, the great Danish astronomer Tycho Brahe held to the old geocentric view on the basis of the same scientific data.[106] It was not until the discovery and development of the telescope that the Copernican system could be established with certainty.

LUTHER ENTERS THE MONASTERY

On July 17, 1505, Martin Luther quite unexpectedly applied for admission to the "Black Cloister" in Erfurt, the chapter house of the Hermits of St. Augustine. This action, a great shock to his family and friends, was a commonplace occurrence in the Middle

Ages; but in the gifted young law student it was so unusual that a prodigious literature has arisen attempting to explain why Luther took this step and blighted a very promising future career.

Fortunately, the sources on this subject are ample.[107] There are extant many accounts, several from Luther's table companions, who must have heard the story over and over again from his lips. Crotus Rubeanus, his former roommate, has also given his version of the story. All of these sources seem to have a remarkable consistency with the exception of the one so frequently quoted by Luther's enemies. The two accounts most frequently quoted follow:

> It happened some thirty-two years ago, when Martin was still a young master at Erfurt, before he was a monk, that he went from Erfurt to Gotha, bought some books in jurisprudence wherever he could find them, and returned to Erfurt. On the way between Gotha and Erfurt there appeared a terrible flash [of lightning] from the sky which he at the moment interpreted to mean that he should become a monk. As soon as he arrived at Erfurt, Luther sold all his law books secretly and ordered a grand banquet, an evening repast in Porta Celi (the name of a burse at Erfurt), invited several scholars, some virtuous, chaste young ladies and women, and dined with them in an unusually cheerful spirit, playing on the lute (which he by now was able to do quite well). All were in a happy mood.
>
> When the time for departure had arrived, all thanked him heartily, but they did not know what Luther had in mind, and left in happy spirits. Martin Luther, however, went immediately into the Augustinian monastery at Erfurt during the night, for he had also made arrangements for that, and became a monk.[108]

In a note at the bottom is the following explanation as to the authorship of the above account: "Jonas related this narrative to me [anonymous] in the home of Christopher Seszen, the treasurer of Czerbst, at a light breakfast on January 28, 1538." [109]

The second quotation is one of many from Luther's table companions and was recorded in 1539 when an older Luther at the evening meal began to reminisce about that fateful day:

> "Today is the very date on which I entered the convent at Erfurt," and he began to tell the story of conditions under which he had taken his vow: how nearly fourteen days before, on the road near Stotternheim not far from Erfurt [one mile north] he was so frightened by a thunderbolt that in terror he shouted: "Help, dear Anne, I will become a monk."

"But God understood my vow even in Hebrew, Anne, under Grace
it is no longer binding. Afterwards I regretted my vow, and many
of my friends tried to persuade me not to enter the monastery.
I, however, was determined to go through with it, and the day
before St. Alexius I invited certain of my best men friends to a
farewell party, as on the next day they were to lead me into the
monastery." To those, however, he left behind he said: "Today you
see me for the last time and then no more." In tears they led me
away; and my father was very angry about my vow, yet I persisted
in my determination. It never occurred to me to leave the monastery.
I had died completely to the world until God's proper time and
Junker Tetzel forced me to leave it and Dr. Staupitz incited me
against the Pope." [110]

Luther explained his action on many occasions, though not
always in as great detail as this 1539 story, and the various accounts
fit together rather consistently. Careful examination of the alleged
Jonas story immediately reveals a number of strange additions that
seem to indicate that the story either became confused as it passed
through several hands, or the author himself was not familiar with
the facts.

Assuming that Luther himself knew better than anyone else
the details and circumstances which led to his decision, several
errors are apparent in the anonymous breakfast conversation:
(1) The unknown "me," to whom Jonas is supposed to have related
this story, is wrong on the location of the thunderstorm. From
Luther's account, he was returning from a visit to his parents and
not on the Gotha to Erfurt road. He even stated specifically that
it was at Stotternheim, a mile north of the city. (2) In the authentic sources there is no evidence that Luther had purchased
some law books on this occasion. These had been purchased some
time previously, for he had entered the Law School in May of that
year. He had been home on vacation. (3) No great secrecy surrounded the taking of this step as the Jonas story implies. The
Stotternheim experience had occurred fourteen days before. In the
meantime he had communicated with his friends about his decision,
sold his law books, told his parents, and planned a farewell party
in the *Georgenburse*, where he lived. (4) The date of Luther's
entry was July 17, on St. Alexius' Day, not the evening before as
the Jonas story would have us believe. (5) Nor did Luther slip

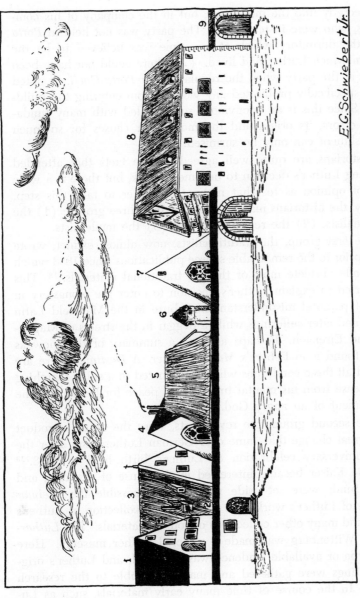

The Augustinian Cloister in Erfurt, south view, showing (1) Granary, (2) Priory, (3) Library, (4) Summer Refectory, (5) Winter Refectory, (6) Kitchen, (7) Sleeping Quarters and Monks' Cells, and (8) Hospital. Redrawn by Ernest G. Schwiebert, Jr. from photograph by W. Lorenz of a re-discovered sketch of 1669

E.G.Schwiebert Jr.

away secretly into the monastery, but in the company of his companions, who were in tears. (6) The party was not held in *Porta Coeli,* the dormitory which at one time was believed to be the *Burse* in which Luther had lived. (7) There could not have been women at the party when the regulations of *Porta Coeli,* as noted above, specifically prohibited any women from entering the building.[111] Since this is an anonymous source filled with many fundamental errors, its origin and the motives or causes for so much embellishment can only be surmised.

Historians are quite well agreed on the facts that attended the young Luther's decision to become a monk, but there is a wide range of opinion as to what motivated Luther to take this step. Roughly, the historians may be classified into three groups: (1) the traditionalists, (2) the revisionists, and (3) the modernists.

The first group, the traditionalists, now almost extinct, wrote mostly prior to the remarkable source publications since 1883 which have made obsolete most of the old traditional materials.[112] This group tried to explain Luther's decision to enter the monastery in terms of parental misunderstanding, abuse in the Mansfeld Latin School, and later sufferings while a beggar in the streets of Magdeburg and Eisenach. Perhaps as good a summary of this view as can be found is in Febvre's *Martin Luther: A Destiny,* where are pictured all these conditions which culminated in a spirit searching for surcease from his mental turmoil and peace for his soul in the appeasement of an angry God.

The second group, the revisionists, were the natural product of the great change that came over German Lutheranism after the 400th-anniversary celebration of Luther's birth held in 1883.[113] Even the Kaiser became interested in the cause of research, and special funds were set aside which made possible the *Weimar Ausgabe* of Luther's works, the *Enders et al.* collection of Luther's letters, and many other collections of source materials. The *Lutherhaus* in Wittenberg was made a national Luther museum. Here every type of available evidence was collected, and Luther's original writings were gathered and made accessible to the research worker. In the course of time many early materials, such as Luther's *Roemerbrief* and other classroom lecture notes, so vital for an understanding of Luther's formative years, were discovered by Johannes Ficker and others and added to these collections. On the basis of these newly acquired materials a new group of historians, such as Kolde, Koestlin, Berger, Buchwald, Hausrath, Loofs, Harnack, etc., began to examine and reconstruct the Luther of history. Perhaps the best spokesmen of this revisionist point of view were Walther Koehler, Johannes Ficker, and Otto Scheel. In many respects Scheel is not strictly one of this group, but belongs rather to the third and last group of writers. However, on this point, the decision to enter the monastery, he must be classified with the revisionists.

This group went to the opposite extreme, making Luther's boyhood no different from that of any other Catholic youth and, therefore, finding no ground in his early experiences for the sudden decision to enter the monastery. They conclude that Luther's decision to enter the monastery was a sudden, spontaneous, unpremeditated act, the direct outgrowth of his great fright in the thunderstorm two weeks before. They base their conclusion upon Luther's *De Votis Monasticis*,[114] or *Treatise on Monasticism*, of 1521, in which he stated that he had decided to become a monk as a result of a "terrifying call from heaven," and upon the statement of Crotus Rubeanus written to Luther in 1519:

> Proceed as you have begun, and leave an example to posterity; for what you do is not without the will of the Gods. Divine Providence intended this when you, returning from your parents, were prostrated to the ground before the town of Erfurt by a bolt of lightning, like another Paul, and compelled to withdraw from our sorrowing company into the wall of the Augustinian monastery.[115]

Furthermore, Luther wrote Melanchthon a letter from the Wartburg in which he again emphasized that he had made his decision in "a moment of terror" and averring that he "was forced rather than drawn gradually into the monastery." Scheel stresses the reference that Luther made to this event in 1539 when he stated in the quotation previously cited, "afterwards I felt sorry that I had made the vow." During the Middle Ages a flash of lightning was identified with the "wrath of God," and it was natural that Luther should so interpret it; therefore, says Scheel, the thunderbolt from heaven forced him into a vow he might otherwise never have taken.[116]

A third group of more recent biographers, Strohl, Boehmer, Holl, Kattenbusch, von Schubert, and others, readily grant that there is much evidence in favor of the revisionist point of view. They concede, too, that Luther's boyhood was that of a normal Catholic youth; but, using the modern psychological approach, they do not believe that the problem of Luther's decision was quite so simple as the "bolt of lightning" thesis accepted by the second school. This third group believes Luther must have been thinking about his relationship to God for some time, otherwise he would not have reacted the way he did in a moment of great emotion.[117] Henri Strohl says: "The stroke of lightning merely made him aware of what was already in his soul." There are some later references to this experience in Luther's writings which imply that he was troubled about his salvation even before he decided to enter the monastery. Luther preached a sermon in 1534 in which he discussed his decision:

> With reference to my previous experience, I was myself a monk for fifteen years and diligently all through these years read and did everything I could. Yet I was never able to console myself regarding my baptism, but always thought: "Oh, when will you once become pious enough and do enough to obtain a gracious God?" Such thoughts drove me into the monastery.[118]

Scheel argues that the Latin text was not intelligible and that the translation into German by Justus Jonas changed the meaning; but George Roerer, one of the table companions, made a similar recording of the same sermon:

> I was a monk for fifteen years, yet I was never able to be consoled with reference to my baptism. Oh, how can you once become pious! Then I became a monk.[119]

As has been implied previously, there were a number of individual experiences in Luther's student days that may have contributed to his later decision. That he recalled much later in life how the Prince of Anhalt walked through the streets of Magdeburg begging for alms, and commented: "Whosoever looked upon him was deeply moved and felt ashamed of his secular way of life," indicates the deep impression that pious man of God left upon the impressionable youth. Again, in Eisenach Luther moved in the pious Schalbe circle, during which time the Vicar of *St. Marien,* John Braun, became his intimate friend and may have consciously or unconsciously influenced the boy toward the monastic life. The fact that Luther, when permitted to hold his *Primiz,* or first Mass, in the Augustinian monastery, invited Vicar Braun and the *Schalbense Collegium* from the foot of the Wartburg to be present, seems to indicate that he had a strong attachment for his former associations.[120]

There were several other experiences during Luther's college days that could have greatly influenced his later decision; or at least have caused him to meditate seriously along the lines of "acquiring the righteousness of God." Veit Dietrich recorded one such experience in his *Tischreden* in 1531:

> When he wished to return to his home country and was on the way, he accidentally slashed his leg with the sword and severed the cephalic vein. He was accompanied by one traveling companion when this occurred as far from Erfurt as Vitsch is from Wittenberg (a half [German] mile). There it bled profusely, nor was he able to stand. When he checked the flow by pressing his finger against the vein, the leg began to swell to unusual proportions. Finally a doctor was brought from the village and stopped the bleeding wound. In the meantime, as he was in danger of his life, he said: "O Mary, help me!" There he would have passed away in the name of Mary, he added. Then, during the night while in bed, the wound broke open again, and when he was beginning to weaken again, once more he called on Mary.[121]

This account is somewhat augmented by the record made by Roerer, another table companion. He adds: "The knife slipped out, and he stuck himself with it." [122] He says that after the accident Luther threw himself on his back and held the leg in the air, pressing the wound with his thumb to stop the flow of blood, while his companion ran to town for a doctor.

Another experience of Luther's college days which left a deep impression upon him was the sudden death of a friend.[123] Melanchthon knew of and mentioned the event but added that he did not know the circumstances of its occurrence. But he considered it of parallel importance with the thunderstorm in its effects upon Luther, "both of which filled him with great terror." Mathesius stated that a "companion was stabbed," which frightened Luther with the wrath of God and eternal judgment. Mathesius, too, believed that the shock of his friend's death and the bolt of lightning near Erfurt were the decisive factors in his determination to become a monk.

Since the first Luther biographers did not mention the name of the friend who was killed, tradition somehow confused him with the saint on whose day Luther entered the monastery. So for centuries the story was repeated that Luther's dear friend Alexius had been killed. His good friend Hieronymus Buntz [124] died of pleurisy during Luther's college days and may have been the individual whom Mathesius confused with the person who was stabbed. There is no historical evidence for any other conclusion.

A good summary of the position of this third school of thought is expressed in Heinrich Boehmer's *Der junge Luther:*

> We may safely conclude that in that moment of great nervous tension a decision, long prepared by the inner battles of recent months but up to then held back by doubt and reflection of various kinds, suddenly broke through. For Luther was one of those men to whom seemingly sudden decisions come only after long bitter struggle and break through abruptly in a moment of tense excitement. We can, therefore, safely claim that inwardly he was already on the road to the monastery when the lightning at Stotternheim crashed down upon him. The hysterical fear that came over him in that moment only hastened the decision; it did not create the attitude of mind out of which the decision was made.[125]

« 5 »

The Monastic Struggle

THE REALITY OF THE CRISIS

During THE YEARS that Luther was a member of the Augustinian Order of Hermits (1505–1524), he said little about his soul's inquietude in the monastery. Denifle claims the real reason for his silence was a lack of any soul struggle, that the whole story was a later invention to justify his breaking of the monastic vow. That there could be no contradiction, says Denifle, Luther waited until all those who knew about his Erfurt monastic years had passed away; then he began to speak of his sufferings during those critical years.[1] Grisar, a disciple of Denifle, granted the reality of the struggle, but he felt that Luther's difficulties grew out of the fact that he was a psychopathic case, a sensitive type not suited for the rigid demands of monastic regulations. Since the sources on this subject are more than ample, let Luther speak for himself. For a clear understanding of the entire circumstances an examination of the life required of a monk may prove helpful.

Details regarding the Augustinian monastery in Erfurt are meager, but it is known that two units were housed within the walls of this chapter. In the front part of the building to the right of the entrance was the *Herberge*, or hospice for guests, which kept all visitors from direct contact with the regular monastic life in the monastery proper at the rear. The Erfurt Chapter belonged to the stricter "Observantine" branch of the Hermits and lived according to the *Constitution by the Brothers of Hermits of St. Augustine* adopted at Nuernberg in 1504.[2] The original order had been founded in Italy under the constitution of 1287, and this new constitution was merely a German adaptation of the original principles.

145

Some thirty chapters composed this reformed group when Luther joined the order the following year. These regulations make it doubtful whether Luther lived in the hospice before he was taken in as a regular novitiate, for according to these rules he could be admitted to the monastery proper for the observation of "the state of his soul." During a probationary period until September, 1505, Luther had to prove that his decision "was of God." He might still contact his parents, although it is doubtful if he did so. His father had been grievously disappointed in him, as Luther related in his treatise *On Monastic Vows* in 1521, and any visit would have called forth the argument from the members of the order: "He who loves father or mother more than Me is not worthy of Me." The prior at the time was Pater Winand von Diedenhofen, who, together with the rest of the monks, determined Luther's suitability for admission to the order.

C. A. Mueller, having had the same experience, described in great detail the ceremony under which Luther was initiated as a novice of the Augustinian Hermits.[3] He was led into the large hall where the first part of the reception took place. There on the steps of the altar sat the prior, before whom Luther prostrated himself. The prior then asked: "What dost thou desire?" Luther replied: "God's grace and mercy." Next the novice was raised from the floor and questioned by the prior as to whether he were single, had any attachments, or any secret disease. Since the answer to all of these questions was "No," there followed a detailed address in which the prior informed him of the severity of the life of the Hermits of St. Augustine and concluded by asking whether he was ready to undergo all these hardships with the help of God in so far as human weakness would permit. The period of his novitiate would last one year. The hymn "Great Father Augustine" was then sung, during which Luther changed his secular attire to that of an Augustinian monk. The ceremony concluded with the words from the prior: "The Lord attire you in the new man, according to which you were created in righteousness and holiness of truth." The new habit that Luther now wore, called *Moenchsgewand*, consisted of a white house dress, over which a black mantle was worn and girded by a leather sash. His hair was clipped and that part of the head shaved which was to be covered by a little black skullcap, the

Kappe. From this somber attire their house, as also the one in Wittenberg, was known as the "Black Cloister." Luther was now a "militant soldier of Jesus Christ."

Just where the little cell, no more than seven by ten feet, in which Luther lived was located cannot be absolutely established.[4] The cell was very plainly furnished; a single table, chair, and straw bed were its only equipment. The rules of the order forbade any decoration of the surroundings. The room had but a single window and was unheated. The monk was not permitted to remove his attire, even at night, and he had to wear his little cap even within the cell. Any noise or conversation in the halls was strictly forbidden. For exercise the brethren walked up and down in the cloister by twos. Unless assigned otherwise, the monks were required to participate in the many prayers that began early in the morning and recurred at regular intervals until the midnight vigils.

The early Luther biographers have no doubt exaggerated the story of Luther's treatment as a novice.[5] There is no good reason to conclude that Luther, more than any other novice, was subjected to many menial tasks which were to train and test him in "the lesson of humility." All novices were taught how to conduct themselves at meals, including how to sit, rise, and eat. They were also taught to walk with downcast eyes while maintaining correct posture and to repeat their "Ave Marias" and other prayers while exercising in the cloister. The monk had to be familiar with the signs of the preceptor and the complicated ritual of the religious services that followed one another from Matins to Vespers.

There is a possibility that Luther was attracted to the Augustinian Order because some of the monks of this order were among the regular professors of the Theological Graduate School at Erfurt. Monks were permitted to listen to the regular lectures in the University and might also attend additional lectures held within the walls of their own order. Since their meditations were not disturbed by worldly distractions, it was commonly believed that a monk could complete his studies toward the doctorate more rapidly than could the regular graduate student.

Luther's theological studies really began before he enrolled in the regular courses toward advanced degrees. After he had made his "profession" for the priesthood, probably at the end of

his novitiate in 1506, Luther was expected to study Gabriel Biel's
Canon of the Mass, which he later in the *Tischreden* evaluated as
having been regarded by him at the time as "the best book." Even
the Bible could not compare with its authority, he thought, for both
John Staupitz and his preceptor, Nathin, a student of Biel at
Tuebingen, had pointed out its significance in interpreting divine
revelation. This book initiated him into the mystery of the Mass,
the very cornerstone of the whole sacramental system, and caused
him rightly to appreciate the priestly vocation, truly a miracle
worker in the sacrament. This book made a fervent disciple of
papalism out of the young monk, for, says Luther in the same conversation: "When I read therein, my heart bled."

In the spring of 1507 Luther was ordained a priest and celebrated his first Mass on May 2, a solemn occasion for him and his
fellow monks.[6] On this occasion his father and other relatives from
Mansfeld were present. Also invited were Vicar Braun and other
friends from Eisenach. Although Luther's father still did not approve of the step his son Martin had taken, he appeared in the
courtyard with twenty horsemen and gave the monastery approximately three hundred dollars toward the expenses of the occasion.[7] Later in the refectory at dinner, Luther took advantage of
the situation by referring to his experience at Stotternheim as a
divine call from heaven. To his great surprise and, doubtless, that
of all the other monks, the father replied: "Would that it may not
have been a mere illusion or deception." [8] Then, a little later, he
added: "Have you not read that you should honor your father and
your mother?" This direct appeal to Scripture in the presence of
all the monks made quite an impression on the young priest. Even
in 1521, in the treatise concerning vows, *On Monastic Vows,*[9] he
recalled it as "God having spoken from afar." No doubt he often
recalled this episode during the dark hours of his soul struggle
which followed.

Shortly after the ordination to the priesthood, under the leadership of Nathin, Luther began the new theological studies which in
time were to make him a Doctor of Theology.[10] In the regular
university there were four steps in the training of a graduate student leading to the Doctor's degree. The Biblical scholar first completed a rather long course of study which gave him the title

Biblicus, or *lector,* for it entitled him to deliver elementary lectures on the Bible. This was followed by a second degree, *Formatus,* which implied that he had now mastered the critical terminology of the medieval dictionaries. The third degree was *Sententiarius,* which entitled the graduate to lecture on the first two books of Peter Lombard's *Sentences.* The final step before the doctorate, *Licentiatus,* granted the candidate the right to become a regular lecturer in theology. The promotion toward the doctorate involved the successful participation in a public debate conducted by one of the leading professors in that graduate school.

It took Luther from 1507 to March 9, 1509, to earn the distinctive title in theology *Baccalaureus Biblicus.* In the meantime, in the fall of 1508, Luther was unexpectedly called to the University of Wittenberg to deliver the lectures on moral philosophy while continuing his studies. With the granting of the *Baccalaureus* degree he was assigned an additional course of lectures on the Biblical books. Luther must have quickly proved his ability as a teacher, for by the fall of 1509 he was already promoted to *Sententiarius.*[11]

Immediately preceding this promotion Luther was called again to Erfurt, perhaps to assist Nathin, his old teacher, in his lectures on the *Sentences.* From November, 1510, to March, 1511, Luther was occupied with the journey to Rome. Upon his return he was recalled to Wittenberg in the summer of 1511. Here Staupitz, Vicar General of the Augustinian Order, suggested that Luther become a doctor and a preacher.[12] Staupitz could appoint him as preacher, but only a University could confer the doctorate, and the necessary fees must be secured. In the fall of 1512 the Elector agreed to supply the funds on condition that Luther be appointed for life to the chair of *lectura in Biblia,* formerly occupied by Staupitz. On October 18, 1512, the degree of Doctor of Theology was conferred upon Luther after five years of graduate work in this most exacting of all disciplines of that day.

Somewhere during the five years of graduate work when Luther was studying the various systems of thought of the Middle Ages, he became very confused in his thinking. The result was a trying soul struggle which was to influence profoundly the future history of the Christian Church. The best introduction to an understanding of this problem is an examination of the principal sources.

In all of Luther's references to these years of his monastic life there runs a general note of sadness and depression. Such expressions as "I was always sad," "I fell into a state of melancholy," "I was the most miserable man on earth," appear over and over again. But let us see why he was so unhappy.

> Being a monk, I wished to omit nothing of the prayers and often overtaxed myself with my courses and written work. I assembled my hours for an entire week and sometimes even two or three. Sometimes I would lock myself up for two or three entire days at a time, with neither food nor drink, until I had completed my breviary. My head became so heavy that I could not close my eyes for five nights. I was in agony and all confused. As soon as I had improved, I tried to work on my courses, but my head began to swim again. I was so imprisoned in this practice that the Lord had to tear me from this self-torture by violence.[13]

In Luther's sermons of 1537 on the Gospel of St. John he again expressed his reactions to those early monastic days:

> I myself was a monk for twenty years and so plagued myself with prayers, fastings, wakings, and freezings that I almost died of cold, which hurt me so much that I would never want to attempt it again even though I were able. What else did I seek through this but God? Who was to see how I observed the rules and lived such a rigid life? [14]

Some six years before, in the absence of Bugenhagen, the town pastor, who was engaged in reorganizing the churches of Bremen, Luther had preached on the same Gospel series of which sermons Roerer and Lauterbach made careful copies. Before the Wittenberg congregation Luther again expressed similar sentiments as to the reality of his soul struggle in the monastery:

> I have been a monk and waked at night, fasting, praying, chastising and tormenting my body, that I might remain obedient and live chastely. I speak of those pious and sincere monks who take their vocation in this world seriously, not of whoremongers and rascals, who live an unchaste, loose life; but those who have made a real effort like myself, who have tried and striven to become like unto Christ that they might be saved. What did they accomplish by all this? Have they discovered Him? Christ says here: "You will remain in your sins and die," that is what they have obtained.[15]

Flacius stated in 1549 that he had met a fellow Augustinian monk six years earlier who had observed that Luther at Erfurt had led a life of "pious observation." The Catholic historian Dungenheim says that Nathin, Luther's superior, in addressing the nuns at Muehlhausen, spoke of Luther at the time as a "new St. Paul converted by Christ Himself."[16] The sources extant today, therefore, reveal beyond doubt that Luther really entered the monastery determined to live the life of a pious monk and in this pursuit taxed his body to the utmost.

The claim has been made that Luther did not refer to his monastic struggle until after 1530.[17] Henri Strohl has gathered the evidence on this point in a rather convincing series of citations. The first reference to the monastic struggle appeared in his lectures at the University of Wittenberg on the Psalms (1513) when he explained the true "compunctio," the despair of one's self that in the case of perfect repentance brings a "sorrow greater than that of the damned." Then he related how he, in former days, had experienced such a soul struggle. In his lectures on Romans (1515 to 1516) he spoke of the devil frightening people into despair of conscience, and he explained to the students that he, too, had had "conflicts, doubts, and troubles of conscience now happily overcome." In a letter to Leiffer in 1516,[18] in which he tried to console his friend in an hour of spiritual unrest, Luther stated that he is sure that Leiffer's difficulties, like his own, were due to too much brooding and advised him to commit himself in such moments to the care of Luther's former teacher Bartholomaeus Usingen. Following these there are frequent references such as: "when I was made a doctor, I did not yet know the light," "the Holy Spirit gave me understanding," and a number of other indirect references.[19]

Strohl says: "Perhaps we should not take too seriously the Reformer's remark made at the table in 1530: 'Ten years ago I felt for the first time the despair and anger.'"[20] Luther, like old soldiers, adds the French historian, could talk about these tragic days only after the wounds were healed; not when the experience was still close to him and he was not yet fully clear in matters that pertained to his salvation. With regard to Luther's integrity, Strohl reaches the following conclusion:

> They are the thoughts of a soul absolutely smitten, profoundly conscientious and humble, refusing all merit; but having also the experience of a living God, who gives a new life by pure grace to those who have faith in Him.[21]

THE CAUSE OF THE CONFLICT

Although there is great diversity of opinion as to the cause of Luther's great soul struggle in the Augustinian monastery, roughly these views fall into two divisions. There are those who take their materials from Luther's enemies, Duke George, Emser, Cochlaeus, Alveld, Eck, Aleander, and others, all of whom are certain the trouble lay with Luther himself. With this group, for whom Denifle and Grisar are the leading modern spokesmen, all that Luther said about his soul problems was either lies or gross exaggerations. Of course, they dare not grant that there could possibly be something wrong with the Roman plan of salvation without destroying themselves. As Duke George and his court pointed out, Luther had failed the Church by breaking his monastic vow. The fault was in the man, not in the teaching of the Roman Catholic Church.

Another group of Reformation students, principally Protestants, holds that any evaluation must begin with Luther's own statements with reference to this period, as he knew more about his struggle in the monastery than could anyone else. Luther may not have always, later in life, described this period in exact detail, but he would certainly have recalled the underlying causes of his difficulties in the monastery. Since Luther repeated over and over again that his problem was a doctrinal one, this group of historians has tried to ascertain exactly what books Luther read while in the monastery at Erfurt to establish the source of his difficulties. In these thorough researches the whole development of the Roman Catholic plan of salvation from Augustine to Luther has been reconstructed, which they believe explains why Luther would have difficulty with such a multiplicity of approaches, many of which varied widely in their basic assumptions.

Luther's statements in later life about this monastic struggle are numerous, yet through them all runs the same common line of thought as to the basis of his problem. Before Luther's entry into the monastery he had been told that "upon entrance into the order a monk would be purified like a child who had just received his baptism." Luther in his last book against Duke George in 1533 complained that all this had been misrepresented, that after he entered the monastery he was deeply disappointed because he did not experience a complete inner transformation of the soul. The peace of mind he felt upon receiving the congratulations of the prior and the monastic brethren when he became a monk turned into bitter doubt as expressed in this later confession:

> But though I was greatly pleased with such fine words and sweet praises, making me out as a "miracle-worker" who had effected his own sanctification with so little effort, as one who could even devour death and the devil, etc., yet I remained so helpless. Every time a little temptation came of sin or death, I was down and out. Neither my baptism nor monastic vow seemed of any avail, as I had lost Christ and my baptism long ago. There in the convent I was the most wretched man on earth, passing whole nights in weeping and feeling that everything was hopeless, which condition no one could alleviate. Thus I was bathed in my monkery and had a real "sweating sickness." Thanks be to God that I was not consumed in my fever, for I would have been in the depths of hell long ago in spite of my monastic baptism. For I no longer knew Christ except as a stern judge from whom I wanted to flee, yet was unable to escape.[22]

Again, on another occasion he expressed a similar disappointment in the fact that the monastery had not completely removed all his evil thoughts and desires:

> When I was a monk, I believed that it was all up with my salvation. Each time I experienced the temptations of the flesh, that is to say, a number of evil desires, such as anger, hatred, jealousy, in regard to a brother, etc., I tried all kinds of remedies. I confessed daily, but it was of no avail; the covetousness always returned. This is the reason why I could find no peace, but was perpetually in torment, thinking: "You have committed such and such a sin. You are still the victim of jealousy and concupiscence; in vain you have joined the order. All your good works are useless." [23]

Denifle thought he had determined the source of Luther's trouble while still in the college at Erfurt and also during his monastic days. The "concupiscence" that he referred to frequently in his early writings was due to sexual problems. The classic quotations are the one cited above and the Jonas breakfast story, which even Grisar repeated without question.[24] The Jonas story, as has been mentioned, is extremely doubtful evidence, although those who would use it seize upon the word "women," completely ignoring the qualification "chaste." In a *Wolfenbuettel Handschrift* there was preserved a series of sermons that Luther preached in the Town Church of Wittenberg from 1537 to 1540. The secretary of the Wolfenbuettel library, Dr. Hoeck, said it had been a part of the unpublished Aurifaber collection and had been purchased from his widow by Duke Julius of Braunschweig-Lueneburg-Wolfenbuettel. Dr. Irmischer reproduced this text in the *Erlanger Ausgabe* of Luther's exegetical writings.[25] In the context Luther told the Wittenberg congregation how the oil of the Papacy had "penetrated to the very marrow of his bones, so that even now he was not able to rid himself of this influence." At the time of his monastic struggle he had been a loyal son of the Pope, and yet he was unhappy. Then he explained the source of his difficulty in the new monastic way of life:

> In the monastery we had enough to eat and to drink, but the heart and conscience suffered pain and martyrdom, and the sufferings of the soul are the most painful. I was often frightened by the name of Christ, and when I looked upon Him and the Cross, He seemed to me like unto a flash of lightning. When His name was mentioned, I would rather have heard the devil mentioned, for I believed that I would have to do good works until Christ was rendered gracious to me through them. In the convent I thought neither of money nor of the wealth of this world nor of women; but my heart trembled and was agitated thinking how I might render God favorable to it. For I had departed from the faith, and I could not make myself believe anything but that I had offended God, whom I would have to make favorable again through my good works. But thank God we again have His Word, which pictures and portrays Christ as our righteousness.[26]

Here Luther plainly states that his problem was not that of "women" nor of the "wealth of this world," but that the basis of his struggle lay in his anxiety to render an angry God gracious unto him.

In the above quotation he asserted that he no longer knew Christ, for he had "departed from the faith." In another sermon he stated:

I always walked around in a dream and real idolatry, for I did not believe in Christ but believed Him to be nothing else than a stern and terrible judge, as one paints Him sitting on a rainbow. For this reason I sought other intercessors, Mary and the saints and my own good deeds and merits of faith. All this I did not do for money or possessions, but for God's own sake; yet, it was all a false religion and idolatry because I did not know Christ and I did not seek to do these things through and in Him.[27]

His critics may not understand why Luther should experience such a soul struggle in the monastery and regard the above statements as the exaggerations and imaginations of an old man; yet, an examination of the actual teachings of the Augustinian Hermits in the light of the Roman Catholic plan of salvation makes the above experience entirely rational.

Denifle points to the medieval "hymns" and "beautiful prayers" and cites from Jordan's *Vie des Freres* the monastic regulations of the members who were to "dominate their flesh by temperance in eating and drinking as much, at least, as their health permits." [28] Any monk could adjust himself to such conditions; no one was asked to do more than he was able. But the aged Dominican Father overlooked the fact that his order was different from that of the Augustinian Hermits. Strohl has pointed out that "as much as their health permits" had no limits to a sensitive, conscientious soul like Luther. Luther had read in the Coridan commentary of Augustinian regulations, published in 1482, that "omission of the slightest part is sin" and the statement by Joseph Calasantius: "Woe unto the monk who loves his health more than holiness!" [29]

THE MEDIEVAL PLAN OF SALVATION

Caspar Schwenckfeld characterized his age in 1528 by the observation: "A new world is emerging, the old one is passing away." [30] There can be little doubt that Martin Luther was born into a world in which powerful forces were at work that had come into being long before him and had paved the way for the great role that he was to play. He, too, like so many others of his day, was deeply influenced by the individualism of the Renaissance, even though its secular spirit never did affect him very deeply. As Jacob Wille has pointed out, many powerful figures were raising their heads.

Man wanted to master his environment, to understand the world
of which he was such a vital part, and even man himself in his
final essence and being.[31]

No doubt this desire to know, this, independence of thought,
was part of the spirit of the age which influenced Luther to examine
the whole Roman plan of salvation and led him to discover that
the Church had drifted far from its original moorings since the
days of the Apostles. Although Luther was trained as a "Modernist," following Occam, Biel, d'Ailly and others, he was far too
critical and original in his thinking to be bound by the thoughts
of any one man or school. Reinhold Seeberg, who has analyzed
the thought of the young Luther in relationship to Occam and the
German Mystics, concluded that there can be no doubt as to the
originality of Luther's thinking.[32] Seeberg, himself thoroughly
familiar with medieval dogma, pointed out that Luther was entirely capable of analyzing the basic assumptions and errors of
medieval theology. May it not be that Luther's monastic struggle
was but a part of the period of confusion and spiritual contradiction then encompassing his entire world?

The students of the "Via Moderna" were taught that in matters
of faith the Bible was the only reliable guide, that theology must
forever be separated from philosophy, that the human mind can
function properly only in the realm of this material world, that
Aristotle must be put out of all Christian thinking; yet they did
not realize that they destroyed the principle of Sola Scriptura by
accepting the Church and the Pope as sole interpreters of the divine
revelation of the Bible.[33] Because they were not ready to drink
from the "fountain of truth," Luther claimed, the Roman Church
continued in its error of insisting upon the sacramental system and
upon the Church as a visible organization on earth. Luther saw
more clearly than any of his contemporaries what had happened
to the Apostolic Church, and he possessed the basic honesty and
necessary courage to follow his convictions. He first became thoroughly confused in the labyrinth of medieval theology; for he was
not satisfied with the rationalizations of the Schoolmen, whose many
inconsistencies seemed to contradict God's divine revelation. Luther
studied not only the "Modernists" but considered also the total picture presented by the medieval Schoolmen. He patiently searched

all the writings of the Scholastics hoping to find light for his troubled soul.

In the ultimate analysis the problem with which Luther wrestled in the monastery was not that of a single individual, but that of the whole Germanic mind. Reinhold Seeberg says that the gulf between the Germanic and Latin minds was never bridged by medieval theology.[34] The German had always regarded religion as a personal and individual experience. The idea of the mystical body of Christ embodied only in the Roman Church and the hierarchy always seemed foreign to Teutonic thought. The Roman mechanization of the whole sacramental system, making it the sole source of the means of grace, seemed strange to a people who felt they could go directly to their God. In the days of Luther, Germany apparently felt a deep inward need for a soul-satisfying religion that went far beyond mere outward reforms. The princes may or may not have realized that the *Gravamina* presented at the German diets were but superficial; there is ample evidence that among the people there was a hunger for the "Bread of Life," the Gospel, which Luther and the German Reformation once more offered them through the "pure Word of God."[35] In its broader implications, the tendency toward "territorialism" in the German lands, making the religion of the prince that of the land, was a revolt against the Latin concept of Rome as the heart of the Church. In a sense Germany's choice was between the "sacramental grace" of Rome and Luther's "priesthood of all believers."

The Reformation was thus not directed solely against the outward abuses in the Roman Church. It, like Luther's own struggle, was concerned with the very core and root of the whole Catholic plan of salvation. Luther began with Gabriel Biel and Peter d'Ailly, who in turn led him to Occam, Scotus, and St. Thomas. Examining the very heart of the Schoolmen, he saw how they in turn had inherited their system from Peter Lombard, Hugo of St. Victor, and others, arriving finally at the writings of St. Augustine and Gregory the Great.

Melanchthon comments that Augustine's book on *The Letter and the Spirit* influenced Luther deeply; and even though Luther remembered Biel and d'Ailly almost word for word, he remembered Augustine best of all.[36] All his unceasing search for truth finally

ended in the Paulinism of the New Testament, which had also
deeply influenced Augustine. In time Luther concluded that *Sola
Scriptura* could be the only sure means of recapturing the spirit of
St. Paul and the other New Testament writers. Now a mature
theologian, Luther was prepared to discard all the Church Fathers
as guides, for even they were like muddy streams when compared
with the pure water flowing from the spring of the New Testament.[37] Since so many pagan streams had emptied their sullied
waters into the river of medieval theology, no traditional interpretation of the Schoolmen or even of the western Fathers was
reliable. Yet, during his formative years, Luther followed Augustine as the best guide out of the labyrinth of doctrinal confusion.
The exact date when Luther began to accept the principle of *Sola
Scriptura* cannot be determined, but it was very probably during
his first year of teaching at the University of Wittenberg, 1508
to 1509.

The Contribution of Augustine

Augustine has been regarded by some as the father of all
medieval thought. This viewpoint may be an exaggeration, yet his
profound influence on all the generations of Schoolmen that followed cannot be doubted. Augustine's theology was essentially
Christian, but his former contacts with Manichaeism and Neo-
Platonism left their imprint on his later doctrinal writings. The
medieval philosophers who did not realize this fact were, therefore, started on lines of thought that were to produce in time a new
plan of salvation quite foreign to that of the early Christians.[38]
Luther later ably evaluated the degree to which Augustine might
be followed as a guide for the Christian theologian, but pointed
out that the medieval edifice was in part constructed of pagan
stones.

The fundamental starting point in Augustinianism is its doctrine of the sovereignty of God.[39] According to him, God in all
eternity had an infinite number of choices as to how He might
create this world and man, a *potentia absoluta*. Yet God, in His infinite wisdom, made this universe according to His final choice, the
potentia ordinata, or the ordained plan which now exists. No
human being, therefore, may question the wisdom of the estab-

lished order of things, since it was ordained in the light of God's infinite number of choices.

As God had originally created the world, man was meant to live in sinless felicity with a will inclined toward the good even though grace was required to maintain man in such a state. The Fall, however, had a far-reaching effect on man. It brought death to both body and soul. Man now became a slave to sin, with self-love, pride, evil desires, and sinful lusts as natural attributes.[40] Since this condition was inherited, original sin had been inherited by the human race ever since. In Adam all men had died, including infants yet unborn. Even though the later Schoolmen modified these views somewhat, all of them built on these foundations. In so far as these ideas are Biblical, even Luther and the Reformers were not left unaffected by them.

After the Fall, according to Augustine, the human race was divided into two classes: (a) The elect and (b) the lost.[41] These members were chosen from all eternity by God according to his divine purpose. Their number was fixed and unalterable regardless of the attitude of the lost. All this had nothing to do with fore-knowledge. Salvation was believed to be entirely a gift of God. God's grace was active only in the elect; it begot in the chosen the will to believe. The fate of all the unfortunate lost souls remained forever hidden in the great ultimate purpose of an all-wise God.

With Augustine, man was in need of preparation by God's divine saving grace. This preliminary work was done by the *gratia praeveniens*, the prevenient grace, which favorably disposed the soul of the elect toward God's saving purpose. After the prevenient grace had paved the way, man was changed in his inner being in that he was now ready to co-operate with God. Now the *gratia co-operans*, the grace of God assisting man, became active in the sinner's soul. If man accepted faith in Christ, he now became the full recipient of God's saving grace. Through all this a change within man's heart had been effected which inclined it toward the good. Now began the process of man's justification.

One of the great weaknesses in Augustine's theology was that he never learned to distinguish in true Pauline fashion between justification and sanctification. In his thinking, justification was not a forensic act, not the declaration of the forgiveness by God of all the sinner's sins and guilt because of faith in Christ's suffering and atoning death; but rather justification was a lifelong process, a gradual reparation of the soul by the inpouring of God's grace.[42] Through Baptism there occurred a remission of original sin, but man was not justified nor certain of his salvation until the end of life. The terrifying aspect of this whole plan of salvation was that it applied only to the elect. For the lost, whose state was already determined, there was no hope whatever.

As has so often been the case in the history of the Church, this great Father, too, emphasized certain teachings because of very practical considerations. At the time, the Donatists would not accept the outward Church as the true one. Their opposition forced Augustine to emphasize that the historic Roman Catholic Church was the guardian of the Truth, the interpreter of the Word, and God's highest revelation. Had it not been for the authority of the Church, says Augustine, not even he would have been a Christian. "Outside the Church there is no salvation" now became the accepted dogma of the Roman Church, for its sacraments were the *media* of the means of grace.[43] This new sacerdotalism, the sanctity of the priesthood, gave the Medieval Church a glamour and atmosphere quite foreign to Apostolic days. Thus the ecclesiastical hierarchy, to whom the sacraments had been committed, developed a monopoly on grace. Now, as Harnack pointed out, in the medieval mind Christ and the historic Roman Church became identified:

> Christ and the Church are really made one, in so far as the same Church which administers the sacraments is also, as the mystical body of Christ, so to speak, *one* mystical person with Him. This is the fundamental thought of Medieval Catholicism, which was adhered to even by the majority of those who opposed themselves to the ruling hierarchy.[44]

For a while the sacramental system remained in a state of flux. The *Verbum*, or Word of the early Church and of Augustine, disappeared in the sacramental sign.[45] Certainty of salvation also disappeared with the change in emphasis on the treasure of the Church; the Word had belonged to everyone in early Christianity, but the sign was reserved for and controlled by the priesthood.

Nor could the disciples of Augustine agree on the number of the sacraments. Bernard of Clairvaux had ten sacraments. Hugo of St. Victor tried to classify them according to their importance, Baptism and the Lord's Supper being given special preference. With Alexander III began the seven sacraments which Peter Lombard also accepted. All the great Schoolmen of the thirteenth century who followed Lombard accepted seven as the number of sacraments. St. Thomas, however, made Baptism and the Holy Eucharist the most important. Finally, in 1439, the Council of Florence definitely fixed the number at seven in the Bull *Exultate Deo*.[46] Now the sacraments became the real treasure of the Church, the all-sufficient media of grace. Harnack also pointed out that this does not imply denial of the meritorious atonement of Christ as being basic:

> That the *grace* springing from the *passio Christi* is the foundation of the Christian religion, and therefore must be the Alpha and Omega of Christian theology — this fundamental Pauline and Augustinian thought was directly denied by no ecclesiastical teacher of the West.

In practice, however, the effect was just the opposite. The Bible was regarded as too obscure for the layman to understand and could be read only in the light of the Fathers and the Schoolmen; interpretation must be reserved for the clergy. This basic principle was well expressed in the syllogistic chain of reasoning published by the Sorbonne of Paris when it condemned Martin Luther's writings in 1521 (see page 436).

What in Augustine had been but a practical matter, a point of emphasis, was gradually magnified by his successors into the accepted dogma of the Church. Slowly a new plan of salvation began to emerge in which the Word had been submerged beneath the all-sufficient grace which the Roman Church was able to offer its members in the sacramental system. The priest had become a miracle worker on whose sacramental sign the whole Church was dependent. How strangely different was this Church with its elaborate ritual, Mass vestments, and colorful processions from the Apostolic simplicity of the services held in the old basilicas! The thorough scholar was bound to encounter and become aware of this change sooner or later, so it was not strange that in all the great northern Humanists there developed the desire to return to that something in the first centuries of Christianity which they felt the human race had lost.

THE INFLUENCE OF THE SCHOOLMEN

The Middle Ages may be regarded as the childhood period of the Teutonic peoples of northern Europe. When they poured their new energy into the remnants of the Roman civilization, a great fusion took place. They little realized that they had fallen heir to a marvelous Graeco-Roman heritage, and, like children, they were not ready to assimilate such mature thought. As H. O. Taylor puts it, "the antique pabulum" had to be prepared for "the medieval stomach" by such men as Gregory the Great, Boethius, Cassiodorus, and Isidore of Seville.[47] Likewise the Christian religion took on a different color in various western countries. Where the Teutonic element predominated, the Gothic temper expressed itself differently in institutions and thought. The Church, for example, in the Mediterranean lands where the Latin element predominated was episcopal in organization and thought. Here the bishop was the central figure, which fact was in time to culminate in the centralization of the Roman hierarchy of Rome. In Germanic lands, however, where Teutonic law was in control, the Church became an *Eigenkirche* in which the ruler retained the land on which the altar stood and the Church became his own private property.[48] It was this situation, very disturbing to the Latin mind, which in part caused Pope Gregory VII to engage in the "Investiture Controversy," which brought Emperor Henry IV to Canossa.

Before and even during the Carolingian Age the Weltanschauung, the philosophy of life, of the Teuton was comparatively simple. In the simple faith of these peoples all life was looked upon as but a "pilgrim journey" toward the real home of the Christian in heaven, the city of God.[49] They could not at the time understand or appreciate the deeper implications of the doctrinal controversies engaging the Church Fathers. They could not know that even these writings were often fused with pagan ideas that had proved useful in the heat of verbal battle. The influence of the Neo-Platonists, who gave the Middle Ages such a distorted, allegorical approach toward all life, including even the Scriptures, is not germane to our story. Suffice it to point out that their ideology caused man to become ashamed of even his own body. They contributed the denial of the body to the rising spirit of monasticism, which all through the Middle Ages was the inner fortress of Romanism. Even men like Athanasius, Augustine, and other Church Fathers were permeated with this type of mystical thinking; and, in their successors, the will of man was placed "in the service of unreason." The Teutonic heritage fused with these new elements produced in a people just emerging from the northern woods such aspects as saint worship, a belief in signs and miracles, the worship of relics, images, etc. No wonder that they stood "in awe" before their "monitors divine and human"; no wonder that they should "rely upon everything except" their own "sin-crushed selves"; no wonder that they in "fleshly joys discerned the devil's lures"; [50] no wonder that they were persuaded to go on fruitless crusades and to kill in the name of Christ; no wonder that they labored like beasts of burden to build the medieval cathedrals, while they existed in mere hovels.

But even though children have a very simple faith which implicitly accepts what they are told, there comes a time when they, too, grow up and begin to weigh, question, and evaluate their heritage. Such was also the case with the western mind. Before the eleventh century these people had not sought to weigh all of the basic assumptions; but now, by way of Spain, even though through an Arabic medium, the translations of Aristotle and other Greek writers were making their impact felt upon the Nordic mind.[51] With the development of trade, the Crusades, and increasingly numerous traveling scholars, the horizon of the western mind began to widen, and the former sheltered philosophy of the cloister came face to face with a new world of reality. Students at the new University of Paris were gathering in the Old Notre Dame in large numbers to listen to the lectures of distinguished professors, such as Peter Abelard, Albertus Magnus, and St. Thomas. In these new crosscurrents of Christian, Aristotelian, Stoic, Jewish, and Arabic thought the simple Christian faith of earlier days needed considerable buttressing if it was to survive. Students in that day learned by the method of disputation, a method of setting up a thesis and

then arguing its validity by the syllogistic method of reasoning.
Often these arguments were continued outside the classroom and
at times became so heated that they resulted in physical combat in
the streets. The students of Paris caused so much confusion in
some of these discussions that they interfered with the business of
the town. Quite naturally, when a problem could not be settled
by the students, it was brought to the professor for a solution. His
title in Latin was *scholasticus*, or lecturer, and from this the schools
of thought which originated with the different professors were
known as Scholasticism. This period is often called the Age of the
Schoolmen. Space will not permit a lengthy study of Scholasticism,
yet a brief analysis of the basic assumptions of the Schoolmen is
essential to understand why they influenced and changed the
Augustinianism, which they had inherited.

Someone has defined Scholasticism as "faith looking for knowledge." This implies that the believer, who until now had without
question accepted his beliefs, was suddenly forced to substantiate
those beliefs when challenged by students of other faiths who
questioned all his basic assumptions. Anselm, one of the earliest
of the Schoolmen, put his problem this way: "I do not seek to know
in order that I may believe; but I believe, that I may know. For
I believe this also, unless I shall have believed, I shall not understand." [52] This is really a paraphrase of Paul, 1 Cor. 2:14: "But the
natural man receiveth not the things of the Spirit of God; for they
are foolishness unto him; neither can he know them, because they
are spiritually discerned." According to the reasoning of the greatest
of the Schoolmen, St. Thomas, there are certain things revealed
unto us which must be regarded as the "superior science." [53]
Reason may, of course, explain and rationalize these truths for the
human mind. Philosophy and science must, therefore, serve as
handmaids to theology.

The great problems that now faced the Schoolmen were in
their essence the same as those that have faced all mankind since
the beginning: the great questions of man's origin, being, and
ultimate destiny, "the whence, whither, and why of life." The early
Scholastics all assumed that a mastery of the fundamentals of
theology presupposed an analysis of ideas. Supplied with the
proper definitions, they believed the human mind could really

understand the nature of all things in heaven and on earth. The Schoolmen were really armchair philosophers who thought that the answer to all problems would come to him who thought long and hard enough.

The Scholastics, however, soon discovered that their conclusions disagreed, not because of their inability to think, but because each school began with a different set of assumptions. In the medieval university, logic, with its syllogism, its reasoning on the basis of a major and a minor premise, became all-important. The veracity of all reasoning thus depended upon the ability of the logician to grasp universal truth. It was all-important that his primary assumptions were correct. As Shaw has pointed out, in their search for an answer as to the nature of ideas the Schoolmen went back to Boethius, who led them to Porphyry, who, in turn, had taken his materials from Aristotle, and he from Plato, the student of Socrates.[54] Scholasticism through these transfusions became a strange mixture of Christian and pagan thought, and, in the days of Luther, Aristotle was still generally regarded as a great assistant to the theologian.

Two schools of thought arose, just as there had been two points of view as to the nature of ideas in antiquity. One group followed Aristotle in their definition of ideas, the other, Plato. Peter Abelard, disciple of the former, claimed that all ideas are the result of experience. For example, the word "cat" has meaning in direct relationship to the experiences the individual has had with cats. A child knows very little about cats, but as its experience increases, new ideas modify the definition. Only the many cats with which the individual has had experience exist in reality. All generalizations of humans about cats are based on reality, but the word "cat" is but a name for the many types of cats the person has known. Since they spoke Latin, the word for this generalization was "nomen," and thus, all who reasoned from a series of particular experiences to a general conclusion were called "Nominalists." The disciples of Plato held just the opposite point of view. They believed that ideas are real, that they exist before the particular illustrations of them are visible to the human mind. A boy building a wagon has a pattern already in mind when he begins, and even though owing to lack of skill his first model only approximates his idea, the real wagon still exists in his mind and will be approached more and more nearly in subsequent models. These Scholastics who held that only the ideas themselves were real were known as "Realists."

Later Schoolmen began to see that both schools of thought were right. In some fields Nominalism was most useful. This was particularly true with reference to this physical universe. On the other hand, Realism seemed much more in harmony with divine revelation in the unseen world of the Spirit. In this realm, as Abelard was to learn with reference to the mystery of the Trinity, the nominalistic approach was tragically inadequate. And during the age of St. Thomas and his *Summa theologica*, the greatest summary of theology during the whole Middle Ages, Realism was to triumph.[55] Its reasoning so aptly explained the mysteries of Transubstantiation in the Holy Eucharist that it became generally accepted. All those who followed either the nominalistic or the realistic points of view were later classified with the *Via Antiqua*, for both schools assumed that reason could be used to solve even the greatest mysteries of theology.

With the English Schoolman Duns Scotus a new school of late Scholasticism was born, the *Via Moderna*, or the New Way.[56] Where St. Thomas had believed in a "prime motor" as the driving force of the world, Scotus restored God's omnipotence and man's freedom of will, hope, and self-respect. His follower William Occam questioned the power of the human mind to penetrate the mysteries of revelation. He held that philosophy and science should be separated from theology and taught as separate disciplines. As was observed above, his later disciples at the University of Erfurt believed that the human mind should be used to its fullest capacity in the realm of nature. Aristotle was regarded as a guide only in physics and its related fields; in the realm of the Spirit the Bible, as interpreted by the Church and the Pope, was the only sure guide to ultimate truth.

Seeberg says it was inevitable that Luther should have come face to face with the searching question "How am I to render God gracious unto me?" All western Christendom had concentrated on the doctrine of penance, for in it all the basic concepts of sin, guilt, punishment, grace, faith and justification, good works, and the authority of the Church are focused.[57] In the Scholastic plan of salvation the sacrament of penance naturally became a focal point. What was this plan?

Peter Lombard was still an Augustinian in his conception of sin, predestination, grace, faith and justification. With Anselm, Abelard, and St. Bernard, however, he could not accept the complete impotence of the human will after the Fall, which made man a complete slave to sin. Lombard held that our will plays a part in preparation for grace; but he was not willing to accept the view that grace is irresistible.

Bonaventura, one of the principal followers of St. Francis, stressed the symbol of light as one of God's main attributes. God's light also enlightens the human mind, making it possible for man to see things in their "transcendental simplicity." In this same class is also God's "Light of Grace," through which man learns to know God. This prominent Franciscan departed even farther from Augustine in claiming that man had a certain power to do good after the Fall. "If man does all within his power, God gives him grace," he wrote. This first winning of God's approval he defined as the *Meritum de Congruo*, which meant congruous to, or in conformity with, his best inner nature.[58] In appreciation of man's earnest effort, God now grants him Augustine's "grace freely given." With the help of this grace, man would be able to rise until he was ready for the second step, the *Meritum de Condigno*, or the merit that is sufficient for receiving Christ's saving grace. With Bonaventura the absolute predestination of Augustine became dependent upon God's foreknowledge of man's future action.

Although St. Thomas in some respects returned to Augustine, especially with reference to irresistible grace and absolute predestination, he also realized that "grace" would have to be harmonized with the "free will" to leave proper place for merit in the Church.[59] Here the influence of Aristotle, who distinguished between the soul and its faculties, became very useful. Thomas taught that the infusion of God's grace created a special, new attitude which he called the "habitus." This newly "informed soul" with its liberated will would now be able to act upon the faculties of the soul. The new man was able to win the *Meritum de Congruo*, for he was no longer a slave to sin. Thomas' conception of justification was a

simultaneous act of God's infused grace, turning man's will toward
God and causing him inwardly to break away from sin. All this
happens through the faith which must perfect itself with God's
co-operating grace. St. Thomas' view of justification has often been
likened to a soul that is inwardly sick and must be slowly healed
through God's infusion of grace until it triumphs in love.

Duns Scotus believed that the dominant thing in this universe
is "will." [60] He thought that God in His ultimate being was also
will. This school, of which Occam, d'Ailly, and Biel were followers,
again stressed the possible choices that God had had in all eternity
and believed that the universe, as we know it, existed because
God had willed it so. Scotus claimed that man through the Fall
merely lost his "supernatural righteousness." Fundamentally, man
remained good, even though there existed in him a tendency toward evil. This natural goodness made it possible for man to love
God because he had retained his free will. But on the question
of predestination his major premise, that God had established all
things, led to the conclusion that the matter of salvation was
God's arbitrary decision. According to this thesis, the historic
Roman Church was also here because God had willed it thus. In
this world order, man had sufficient free will to win the *Meritum
de Congruo,* after which God would grant His "grace freely given,"
with which he could also gain the *Meritum de Condigno.* Therefore, in the final analysis, everything depended upon man's being
able to win God's approval, the *acceptio Dei.* Until man had
proved himself worthy of the "merit freely given," God would not
help him in his difficult upward climb. In such a doctrine of salvation, the human will was a decisive factor.

In William Occam, the pupil of Duns Scotus, the ideas of this
new school reached their maturity. [61] He also stressed the infinite
possibilities that lay at God's disposal in all eternity. He taught that
Christian faith is real only when man holds as true God's divine
revelation in the Bible. This faith God pours into the human soul.
He believed this view to be in harmony with the teachings of the
Church. But here again lay the difficulty, for it was always revelation as interpreted by the Church.

With reference to the doctrine of salvation, Occam also held
that man can definitely prepare the way for God's saving grace.

Since man's will is free, he is capable of doing good by himself, even to the point of achieving a real "contritio," or heartfelt sorrow. Thus, by his own determination, he could win the *Meritum de Congruo*, which would then cause God to come to his assistance and with this co-operating grace enable him to win the second step, the *Meritum de Condigno*. This meant that he had now reached the stage where a "non-imputation of his sins" resulted from God's divine act of forgiveness. Only in the last part, after man had proved his worth, did the sufferings of Christ and His atonement enter into man's salvation. Since this Occamistic approach toward the sacrament of penance stressed so much the will of man during the first two steps in conversion and forgiveness, Luther could never be sure he had finally reached the stage where he was certain that he had been accepted by Christ and had merited God's saving grace.

Luther's teachers at Erfurt had studied with the great Gabriel Biel of Tuebingen, a student of Occam. Biel accepted the Occamist steps of man's role in winning God's saving grace. But in his elaboration of these, he went even further in his claims for man. He added:

> Although Christ's suffering is the principal merit, on account of which grace is conferred, it is, nevertheless, not the sole and total meritorious cause. For it is manifest that there always concurs with the merit of Christ a certain operation of merit on the recipient of grace.[62]

In another connection Biel became even more specific and, since Luther probably knew this passage from memory, it is little wonder that he was worried about the state of his soul:

> The human will can love God above all things through its own natural powers. The sinner is also able to remove the hindrances to grace, because he is able to keep from sinning and committing sinful acts, yea, to hate sin and to will not to sin. By the removal of the impediments and by the good steps toward God made by his own free will he can acquire the merit *de congruo*, the first grace in the turning toward God.[63]

When all this reasoning was carefully analyzed by Martin Luther in the Erfurt monastery, he feared that he was falling short of that perfection which all God's elect must acquire before they were

worthy of the *Meritum de Congruo*. He began to wonder whether
he belonged among the damned. Viewed in this light, God seemed
to him like "an angry judge sitting on a rainbow." [64] Certainly the
medieval doctrine of salvation made it difficult, if not impossible,
for an honestly conscientious soul such as Luther to feel certain of
his salvation.

Philip Melanchthon, who must often have talked to Luther
about this period of his life, stated that Luther threw himself with
great enthusiasm into the study of the doctrines of the Church.
Daily he learned in the university about the teachings of the Schoolmen, and in this connection he pointed out the "inconsistencies" in
the disputations.[65] Yet all this could not quiet his inner unrest, for
his soul was looking for a more satisfying answer. All the while
he was comparing what he learned in the classroom with what he
read in the Bible. He read the "Prophets and the Apostles" to learn
more about God's will and to strengthen his faith. The best evidence
seems to support the idea that Luther retained the "Bible bound in
red leather" which the monks had given him at the time of his entry
into the monastery.[66] Mathesius must have been wrong when he
claimed that the Bible was taken from Luther by the monastic
authorities when he began his theological course in the university.
Luther's reading of the Bible merely intensified his problems, for
the Schoolmen had drifted far from the Biblical plan of salvation,
the doctrine of sin and grace, and Paul's statement of "justification
by faith."

Melanchthon also mentioned that, while in the monastery at
Erfurt, Luther was not without aid in this struggle. Someone
pointed out to him that the confessions taught: "I believe in the
forgiveness of sins." [67] Perhaps he referred to the same experience
that Mathesius related: Luther was very despondent, when God
sent him an *alten Trostvater*, an old priest who consoled him by
recalling the Apostolic Confession and one of the sermons of
St. Bernard; that God must be gracious to offer his "obedient Son"
that He might win the atonement for mankind. Mathesius added
that the meeting became such a living consolation to the disturbed
young monk that Luther often spoke of it later in life and remained
very grateful to the old father. Because of Luther's later statement
"I owe everything to Staupitz" historians have concluded that the

"old father" was Staupitz and place the time of the episode at Wittenberg in 1508 or 1509.[68]

Bernard, the great medieval mystic, stressed Christ and the Cross in his writings, believing that love and mystic union with Christ were the result of pity. Justification he defined as the "non-imputation of sin by a merciful God." There was a remarkable amount of St. Paul in his writings. Melanchthon stated that the following passage in one of Bernard's sermons deeply influenced Luther:

> In addition you must also believe that through Him your sins are forgiven. This is the testimony that the Holy Spirit has put into your heart when He says: "Your sins are forgiven you." For this is the meaning of the Apostle, that man, without merit, is justified through faith.[69]

Melanchthon added that Luther was enlightened and strengthened by this statement; and that it also clarified for him the meaning of the passage in Romans: "The just shall live by faith." Melanchthon continued with the explanation that Luther worked his way to clarity by reading "many explanations," that he began to "see more and more clearly as he meditated, weighed them against one another, and prayed."

The German Mystics also influenced Luther during these dark, critical years.[70] Luther often referred to them and considered their contribution valuable. Of course, it would be easy to exaggerate this influence on the Luther of later years, who was thoroughly grounded in God's Word; but while passing through the valley of the shadow of spiritual death, any rod or staff might comfort him. A soul hungry for the gracious love of the heavenly Father would be moved by statements like these: "His life works itself out in ours." "The Cross separates us from sinful desires and works in us a new life." According to the German Mystics, faith, in the final analysis, is the experience of the supernatural that is already present in this world, the experiencing of that which lies beyond reason. Since all Mystics stressed emotion as the key to religion and the best way of coming in contact with God, the transcendental tendencies of Mysticism seemed to offer an escape from the fine-spun logic of the *Via Moderna* teachings of Occam and his followers.

But how far had Luther progressed in his struggle toward

clarity when he returned to the University of Erfurt and lectured on the *Sentences* of Peter Lombard? Fortunately, the marginal notes which he prepared for these lectures have been preserved and have been reproduced in the *Weimar Ausgabe*, IX, of Luther's works.[71] According to the studies of Herbert Rommel, a student of Scheel, Luther still regarded himself as an Occamist at that time. He still respected Augustine very highly, but had progressed far enough in the principle of *Sola Scriptura* to criticize even him on the basis of the Scriptures. Of course, Luther had been deeply influenced in this principle by his teachers, but in this respect he had advanced even beyond them.

Luther also regarded Peter Lombard rather highly because, among all the Schoolmen, he stressed faith rather than reason.[72] Although he had built his system on Augustine, Lombard regarded him as only human and did not hesitate to point out his mistakes in the light of God's Word. From Luther's notes the following ideas may be gathered: that in his view of "original sin" he was still a modernist, holding the views of Occam and Biel; Aristotle, who was illumined only "by the light of nature," was reliable solely in that field; Augustine knew much more about "eternal bliss" than Aristotle; it was useless to try to harmonize the pagan and Christian ideas of theology. In these notes Luther also revealed that he rejected many of the views of Duns Scotus, especially his theory of conception.

Luther's actual explanation of Lombard to his classes in these lectures revealed him still a thorough Occamist.[73] He discussed the original harmony in man before the Fall in typical Augustinian fashion. Then, after the Fall, following Biel, he held that man's faculties were impaired in three ways: learning, reason, and desire. Man's new "superbia," or haughtiness, was the root of all evil. Luther also distinguished between the act of falling, *Ursuende*, and its effect, the *Erbsuende*. Through the fall of Adam all mankind was robbed of its right to the heritage of eternal life. This original sin resided in the flesh of man. In typical Scholastic fashion Luther still distinguished between four kinds of sins: material, formal, mortal, and venial.

Luther also accepted Occam's doctrine of grace. Man's will was free in so far as it could turn toward good and even fulfill the

Commandments to the point of loving God above all things. Luther accepted the idea that man could win the *Meritum de Congruo* unless God had included him among the "lost." In the marginal notes, strange to say, he still had no doubts of the validity of Biel's reasoning.[74] Once man had won God's approval, however, said Luther, it was impossible to withhold the saving grace. This grace made the soul pleasing to God, and this new *charitas,* or love, became the driving power toward good. This love, which was created in Christ, became man's saving grace, faith, and justification. This, then, saved man from mortal sins, translating him into a state of grace. Now his works also became pleasing to God, for they were born out of this divine grace in Christ.

There is little evidence for the conclusion that Luther by this time was already sufficiently familiar with Greek and Hebrew to draw his ideas from the original text.[75] The marginal notes show little acquaintance with Greek beyond the alphabet and the use of the *Katholikon,* a twelfth-century Greek dictionary. Nor did he know much Hebrew, although he was able to explain words like *Abraham, Sara, elohim hajim.* He probably also used Reuchlin's *Vokabular.* Hans von Schubert, who also made a careful study of this period of Luther's life, has concluded that Humanism had nothing to do with Luther's "tower discovery" in Wittenberg while lecturing on the Psalms.[76] He stated: "It was Luther's genius that penetrated through the medieval maze to the fountainhead of Christianity, the religion of Paul." In the 1508–1509 lectures on Peter Lombard, Luther still used the Latin Vulgate, the Catholic Bible translated by St. Jerome, comparing its text with references from Augustine and the Scholastics. In a letter of 1518, Luther wrote his old teacher Trutvetter of Erfurt that it was he who had taught him to put his trust in the canonical books, but that all other writings must be criticized, as Augustine, Paul, and John had also taught.[77] When Luther started back to Erfurt in 1509 to take over some of the lecturing on the *Sentences* at his old university, he had progressed to the point of criticizing all of the Schoolmen on the basis of the Latin Vulgate, but he had not gone far enough to realize that in time this principle would destroy his whole Catholic plan of salvation.

In the meantime, Luther's personal anxiety was bound to continue, for he feared that he was one of those unfortunate human beings who did not have sufficient will power to rise above sin and to love God so perfectly that he would win the *Meritum de Congruo*.[78] The more he struggled to blot out his own ego, the greater the problem of self-love seemed to become. How could he possibly turn his natural self-love into a perfect love of God, which Bernard had said was the ideal? Perhaps his "tortures of the damned" were, after all, for his own good. Did not Tauler say that you had to suffer such pangs before you could be saved? Might he not, after all, be on the road to heaven? In a swirl of such thoughts his head went round and round until at times he was almost on the point of despair. And all of the time he was testing the medieval plan of salvation and was to find it wanting. Melanchthon implied that the more he thought about it and prayed for light, the more he began to realize that the trouble lay, not with himself, but in the teachings of the Roman Church.[79] Once he was fully prepared to understand just what the Bible did teach on the doctrines of sin, grace, penance, and salvation, he was ready to rebuild the whole system of theology on the basis of his own exegesis and the study of the Bible in the original languages. Luther discovered *Sola Scriptura*, therefore, long before he was prepared to say just what the Bible taught in all matters of doctrine. In the meantime, too, he needed to master the languages through which he, as an exegete, might rebuild the Pauline theology of the New Testament in terms of a sixteenth-century environment. Other events were also shaping Luther's development as a Reformer.

THE JOURNEY TO ROME

No episode of Luther's life is so confused and full of legend as the trip to Rome.[80] Nor is this strange. Luther himself was not always consistent in his recollections of his journey. The first two Luther biographers present widely differing accounts. Catholic contemporaries, although they claimed to have drawn their information from fellow monks, took what was authentic from the Wittenberg group, but added so much legendary material that they only augmented the confusion. Two late-sixteenth-century

Lutheran writers, Dresser and Mylius, assumed that Luther's son Paul, who was living in Leipzig after 1589, knew all about this journey.[81] But Paul Luther was a lad of eleven when his father died and could not be expected to recall much authentic information some forty years later. Their investigations only added new stories, including the one about climbing the *Scala Sancta* and quoting St. Paul's famous verse from Romans, "The just shall live by faith."

It is very difficult to establish how much of what Luther said and wrote about Rome later in life he actually saw. Like other travelers, when he talked about Rome, he combined what he had seen, heard, and read, and out of this compound he commented upon the particular situation under discussion. For example, for a long time it was believed that Luther had learned by personal contact all the specific facts about Rome presented in his famous tract of 1520, *An Address to the German Nobility*. A few years ago the research of Karl Bauer revealed that much of the information had been supplied by the Saxon court.[82] Especially enlightening was the fact that Johann von der Wieck, the special lawyer for John Reuchlin, had visited Luther in Wittenberg for several days and had placed at his disposal all the facts gathered in Rome against the Papacy for the famous humanistic trial so vitally tied up with Hochstraten of Cologne and the *Letters of Obscure Men*.[83] Of course, Luther did journey to Rome, but he was hardly mature enough to see and realize all that tradition has ascribed to this period. As Luther matured and grew away from his earlier papal enthusiasm, he saw more clearly how blind he had been.[84] By 1519 he began to realize that the Pope was the Antichrist, and this conviction grew with the years.

Most of Luther's statements about the Rome trip are found in materials not written until the thirties. Unless the historian is careful, he is apt to read much more into these statements, such as the *Tischreden* accounts, than the trip to Rome actually warrants. The same danger is also attached to the Melanchthon and Mathesius accounts, as they, too, must have based their materials on these impressions from Luther. And since all other accounts are built in the main on these original sources, the statements of Cochlaeus, Oldecop, Milensius, Dresser, and Mylius, each of whom treated this period from his own point of view, must be evaluated with extreme caution.[85]

Melanchthon, the first biographer, wrote but a few hurried lines about the trip to Rome, and he made a number of fundamental mistakes. He evidently did not take time to check the records of the University of Wittenberg. Had he examined the *Akten* and *Rotuli* of the University, he would not have made the mistake of claiming that Luther was teaching Physics at Wittenberg just before leaving for Rome. In reality Luther replaced Wolfgang Ostermayr, who was teaching in *lectura in philosophia morali,* namely, in the *Ethics* and *Dialectics* of Aristotle. Melanchthon did not have Luther return to Erfurt to deliver the lectures on the *Sentences* of Peter Lombard cited above. Melanchthon erred again in stating that Luther lectured on Romans before he lectured on the Psalms after his return from Rome.[86] According to Johannes Ficker, Melanchthon was also wrong in claiming that Luther saw Augustine's book on *The Letter and the Spirit* at Erfurt in 1508. Ficker believes it was in 1515 while Luther was preparing his lectures on Romans at Wittenberg. In the chronology of Melanchthon's account, Luther's trip would have been made either in 1511 or 1512. As to the reason for the journey, Melanchthon mentioned there was "some friction among the monks."

Mathesius, likewise, did not mention that Luther had returned to Erfurt before he made the journey to Rome. Since he wrote later, perhaps he obtained his material from Melanchthon. As to the time of the trip, however, he claimed to be well informed, for he cited as evidence a statement from Luther's own hand that it was in 1510.[87] George Roerer, another table companion and close friend, who apparently had access to the same evidence, agreed with him. As to the reason for the trip, Mathesius stated that the convent sent Luther in the interests of the order. He added that Luther often remarked that he would not take a thousand gulden for what he had seen in Rome along the lines of the "Roman wickedness and idolatry."

The three Catholic contemporaries, Cochlaeus, Duke George of Albertine Saxony, and Johann Oldecop of Hildesheim, merely complicated the problem by copying from Melanchthon and Mathesius and embellishing the stories of the journey to Rome when it suited their purpose. Cochlaeus, who is well known for his many bitter attacks directed against Luther, claimed to have obtained his information from another Augustinian, Anton Kresz. In reality, a close study reveals his entire dependence on Melanchthon. On all vital problems he knew no more than the Lutheran writers from Wittenberg. He knew that seven convents opposed John Staupitz as General Vicar of the order for Germany and that the result was a grave disturbance. About the real cause of the opposition he had no information. As to the time of Luther's journey, he followed Melanchthon in believing it was in 1511.

Duke George's account of the trip to Rome is so biased and childish that it is not worthy of serious attention.[88] This bitter enemy of Luther had attended a Catholic seminary just long enough to feel that he knew all about theology when, in reality, he did not even begin to grasp Luther's fundamental teachings. What he lacked in information he tried to make up by maligning Luther's wife and imputing all kinds of ulterior motives to Luther which are too ridiculous to merit comment.

John Oldecop of Hildesheim had been a student at the University of Wittenberg in 1515. He even attended Luther's famous lectures on Romans.[89] He had a rich and colorful life, traveling all over Europe in the interests of the Church and spending considerable time in Rome. Unfortunately, as so often happens, he kept but a fragmentary record of his experiences. In 1561 he began to write a *Chronik* of the times, which was completed in 1573 and published in 1891 by Karl Euling. Oldecop's *Chronik* has been critically analyzed by Heinrich Boehmer in *Luthers Romfahrt* (1914). His materials, even when checked against the researches of his own fellow-Catholic historians, Paulus, Grisar, Pastor, and Denifle, do not bear close inspection. He was wrong on much that he claimed to have learned in Rome, while on the Luther material his confusion reveals sheer carelessness, if not willful misrepresentation. In some cases not even a poor memory could excuse such flagrant abuses of truth. For example Oldecop related that John Tetzel came to Wittenberg in 1516 and stated that he even assisted Tetzel in collecting indulgences. Nicolaus Paulus, in his book on Tetzel, proved that the indulgence salesman never visited Wittenberg. Grisar claimed that Tetzel did not enter the service of Albert of Mainz until the beginning of 1517; and Oldecop, according to the records, was by that time already in Hildesheim. Yet he wrote: "I was there myself and helped gather indulgences and sang the *Te Deum laudamus* in the Town Church." Obviously, his materials must be scrutinized with great care.

Matthaeus Dresser, a Lutheran writer, attempted to write the first account of Luther's journey to Rome in 1598. He related that Luther set out with another monk as a traveling companion in 1510 and that he received ten goldgulden, about $150, for expenses. The "special business" for the order was to obtain permission with reference to meat on fast days and other monastic regulations. In Padua Luther became quite ill, but was relieved by eating a pomegranate. Before reaching Bologna, Luther had another attack so severe that he began to fear for his life. At that moment, asserted Dresser, the verse from the Prophet Habakkuk flashed through his mind which Paul quoted in his Epistle to the Romans: "The just shall live by faith." He added that when Luther returned to Wittenberg he told Staupitz the whole story. Because of this problem of conscience, the vicar asked him to lecture on the Epistle of Paul to the Romans, which series he completed in three years.

This account, too, says Boehmer, is not too reliable. Staupitz had no authority over Luther after the vicar had left Wittenberg in 1512. Luther did not lecture on Romans until 1515, and his lectures were not of three years' duration, but only for seven months — the fall and spring of the academic year. The story of the passage from St. Paul, "The just shall live by faith," may have come from Paul Luther, but the tale was further confused by Dresser in the Bologna incident. A single cloister, such as Erfurt, could not send Luther and his companion on this mission; concerted action of the entire congregation of the Augustinian convents of Germany was required to make it official. Nor was the problem one of food and fasting regulations. The George Mylius account of three years later compares in reliability with Oldecop and Dresser. These accounts are only significant because they explain why, for the next three centuries, some very strange tales were related regarding Luther's journey to Rome. Many of these tales have been widely disseminated and have become traditional in some modern Lutheran circles.

As to the time of the journey, the sources divided themselves between Melanchthon's date of 1511 and Mathesius' of 1510. Luther himself variously mentioned the years from 1509 to 1511, according to the often unreliable table companions, but the more common date with him was 1510. Boehmer prefers the date of November, 1510, because of the following story told by Luther on one occasion at the table:

> This happened to me in Italy when I was traveling with a brother, that all night until six in the morning we were sleeping with the window wide open, so when we awakened in the morning, our heads were so filled with dullness that throughout the entire following day we were scarcely able to go on a single mile. All the while we were so vexed with thirst, having such a great nausea for wine that we could not even bear to smell it. We were tempted to drink water, which, of course, is deadly. But by the advice of the hospice we were given two pomegranates, and the malady left.[90]

Boehmer believes that Luther would probably remember vividly such an unusual experience, and since this fruit does not ripen in Italy until fall, he concludes that Luther left Wittenberg late in the fall of 1510. The story would not fit into the other alternative, namely, that Luther went in the spring of 1511. Fortunately, a mere pomegranate does not provide the sole evidence. The story of the monastic struggle and subsequent history seem to substantiate the date of 1510.

The historian does not depend upon personal recollection to establish a disputed fact. He approaches the story from the whole pattern, and a number of indirect events must fit into the general picture, for truth is always consistent. An examination of the records and the activities of the General of the order, Egidio, the head of all the Augustinian Hermits in Europe, reveals the difficulties in the Augustinian Order which occasioned the journey to Rome.

Egidio Antonio Canisio was born in Canepina, Italy, about 1465.[91] At the age of eighteen he joined the Augustinian Hermits at Amelia. He studied for a while in Padua under the famous teacher Agostino Nifo, later one of the distinguished professors of Aristotelian philosophy in the University at Rome during the time of Leo X. Egidio became interested in Plato and for a while attended lectures by Ficino in Rome. In 1498 he was called to preach before Pope Alexander VI. He gained such distinction as an eloquent preacher that Julius II and Leo X called upon him on special occasions. Egidio was a master of Latin, Greek, and Hebrew and moved in the circle of some of the leading scholars of the Italian Renaissance. On May 22, 1507, he was signally honored by being elected the General of the Augustinian Hermits, a position which he welcomed, for he realized that the Church was corrupt from head to foot and believed that through his order he could be instrumental in initiating far-reaching monastic reforms throughout all Europe. By reform, of course, he meant something quite different from that achieved by Luther. To him it meant a return to the strict observance of the rules of the order.

In Italy this reform of the order had been instituted for several years before John Staupitz, the Vicar of the German Congregation, visited Rome. During this visit, which lasted from the fall of 1506 to the spring of 1507, Staupitz and General Egidio discovered that they were kindred spirits, both favoring uniform observance of the new constitution, and they made plans to carry out the reform of the German Congregation to include those convents that had not, up to that time, returned to an observance of the rules of 1504. The German Congregation was composed of twenty-nine reformed houses which, because they followed the Nuernberg constitution of 1504, were known as the Observantines; and another twenty-five houses called the Conventuals, who followed the old conventional practice.[92] Rather than use force with the less rigid brothers the officials deemed it wise to unite all the houses with the Observantine group, hoping they would eventually accept the reform. To accomplish this purpose after the union, it was agreed that Staupitz should visit the twenty-five convents within three years and appeal for their support. The leaders thought, too, that by shifting the priors of the houses the desired end might be accomplished.

A bull of December 15, 1507, drafted the whole plan of union and announced that an election was to be held in which a Vicar of the Congregation would be chosen. When the purpose behind this proposed union became known, such violent opposition broke out that the document could not even be published. In Nuernberg,

one of the principal cities of the whole country, the city council was
so hostile that it withheld the drinking water from the Augustinians. Erfurt also was bitter in its opposition. The situation was so
serious that Egidio decided to go to Germany; however, because of
the war between Maximilian and Venice, the proposed visit was
delayed. In the meantime, Vicar Staupitz decided to confer again
with Egidio in Italy. On June 26, 1510, the General reappointed
Staupitz Vicar of the German Congregation and Provincial Head of
the order.

Immediately upon Staupitz's return to Germany, the bull of
1507 was published, making the act of union official as of September 30, 1510.[93] This was a real challenge to the opponents of the
union. Seven of the twenty-nine Observantine convents protested the
action, fearing that union with the lax Conventuals might corrupt
the entire order. Even the district vicar, Simon Kayser of Kulmbach,
supported these dissenting Observantines. Professor Nathin and
Martin Luther were sent to Halle to register their protest with the
Archbishop of Madgeburg through the Provost of Halle, Adolf of
Anhalt, who was to seek the support of Archbishop Ernst of Saxony.
This, then, was the "grave disturbance" which was agitating the
Augustinian Order and necessitated Luther's journey to Rome.

Apparently, Martin Luther and an older monk started for Rome
shortly after that to take up the matter of union in the office of
Egidio. The identity of Luther's fellow monk is uncertain, but it is
highly possible that Cochlaeus was right in naming Anton Kresz of
Nuernberg, who was both experienced in the ways of the Roman
Curia and at the same time a representative from the Nuernberg
convent, which had been so vehement in its protest against the
union. This man, whoever he was, was the *litis procurator,* or the
man in charge of the mission, while Martin Luther was merely his
associate, for Augustinians were required to travel by twos.

The distance from Erfurt to Rome would vary somewhat depending upon the route, and there is no authentic information as to
the exact itinerary the two Augustinians followed. From some of
Luther's shorter trips and other contemporary records it is known
that twenty-five miles was a good day's journey. Since the distance
by the longest route was around 1,400 kilometers, or 850 miles, it
would take at least forty days for them to make that trip on foot.[94]

In all likelihood, Luther and Anton Kresz left Nuernberg a little
before the middle of November, traveling by way of the Ulm
commerce route over upper Swabia and western Switzerland
through the Septimer pass to Milan.[95] From there they traveled
through Florence by way of the old imperial highway through Siena
to Rome. It is not likely that the two came through Bologna on
the way down, for the city was the headquarters of the army of
Pope Julius II until January 2 and would be difficult to pass through.
Besides, this region was blanketed with a heavy snow at this time.
If Luther stopped at the monastery *San Benedetto Po,* he did not
visit Bologna at all.

Travel for monks in that day was considerably lightened by
the fact that there were hundreds of monasteries whose doors were
open to traveling brothers. Doubtless the two monks had been
provided with the customary *litterae testimoniales,* or testimonials
that certified their mission.[96] Later in life Luther mentioned only
a few of the more important places where they stayed. Much of
the evidence is of an indirect nature. In Milan they seem to have
stayed in *Santa Maria dell' Incoronata,* in Florence in the beautiful
Convent of San Gallo built by Lorenzo the Magnificent, while in
Rome their headquarters was *Santa Maria del Popolo.* Luther also
spoke later of staying in a very rich Benedictine monastery on the
Po which had an annual income of 36,000 ducats, around $720,000
in modern money, a third of which was spent annually on guests.[97]
This can have been none other than the well-known *San Benedetto
Po* near Mantua. Of other hospices there is no record. It must have
been about the latter part of December when the two travelers
reached *Via Cassia,* where Luther beheld the Eternal City for the
first time. In his religious zeal, so he said later, "I threw myself
on the ground and said: 'Greeting unto Thee, Holy Rome!'"

Certain things impressed Luther on the journey.[98] In Nuernberg he saw a wonderful clock that even struck the hours. At Ulm,
like most visitors, he was awed by the tremendous size of the
cathedral. He liked the people of Bavaria and Swabia, who were
extremely friendly and tried very hard to make the travelers comfortable. The Swiss Alps seemed to him just a land of mountains
and valleys and, on the whole, not very productive. The Swiss
were a hardy people, sociable, and he ranked them first among the

German peoples. He felt their language was unique in that it had
no diphthongs. Luther says little about Innsbruck, through which
he passed on the way back, nor of the large town of Augsburg.
He also had little to say about Italy, although he liked the country
and its productivity. He remarked that their grapes and figs were
much larger than the German variety. He was impressed by the
lands of Lombardy and the Po.

As for the people of Italy, he thought them more polite, attractive, lively, emotional, and clever than the "barbarous North Germans." [99] They did not drink as heavily, and their clothes were
better fitted. But they had a tendency to laugh at the Germans.
He thought their dancing licentious and disliked their suspicious
natures. The Italian men seemed intensely jealous of the women,
whose faces had to be veiled. They had no respect for the clergy
nor anything sacred and would blaspheme God and the saints without regard to those present, and to regard a fool a "good Christian"
seemed common practice. Luther remarked later in life: "I did not
understand the Italians, and they did not understand me." From
these impressions may be gathered that Luther was only superficially interested in Italian customs and practices and that he did
not experience anything that might be termed unusual.

Luther and his companion arrived in Rome early in January,
1511, and they took up quarters in the Augustinian monastery of
Santa Maria del Popolo.[100] The next day they got in touch with the
Procurator of the order to present the protest of their seven convents
which opposed the union movement. The official could have given
the immediate answer that is later recorded in Egidio's records:
"The appeal denied on the basis of German rules." But the Roman
officials were interested in creating good will among the opposition.
As a result, Egidio delayed the above final answer for four weeks,
taking a personal interest in the matter and discussing the problem
with the two brothers. So, even though their petition was denied
in the end and Egidio continued to support Staupitz, it would be
wrong to conclude that the mission had no effect on the German
Congregation. In the meantime, Luther and his companion were
free to visit places of interest in Rome for a month.

What were Luther's experiences in the Eternal City? Unfortunately, Luther himself never wrote a connected account of his

experiences. All the remarks that he made were suggested by some
specific occasion or reference and occur in sermons, conversations,
and the like. The material is, therefore, not very connected. To
build the complete story necessitates the use of much other contemporary evidence.

Rome at the time Luther visited there was rather quiet. So
quiet, in fact, that it appeared to him like a city of the dead.[101]
Within the tremendous enclosure of the old Aurelian wall were
whole stretches of undeveloped land and a number of fields full of
ruins. The city's population of only 40,000 was spread over a wide
area and apparently seemed rather lifeless in comparison with the
narrow, teeming streets of Erfurt, Nuernberg, or Augsburg. In the
eastern end of the town was even a woods in which deer, rabbits,
and other game provided sport for the cardinals during certain
seasons. Even in the most densely populated sections of old Rome
there were hardly 400 houses totaling about 2,000 inhabitants. Of
this number at least a fifth were monks and nuns. In this section
old cloisters and the basilicas of *S. Giovanni in Laterano, S. Croce
in Jerusalem, S. Maria Maggiore, S. Prassede, S. Pudenziana,* and
S. Clemente were the only impressive structures to be seen rising
amid vineyards, gardens, and fields. But even more neglected was
the center of the city. Here former Forums were now fields of
ruins in which a few cows were grazing. Goats were climbing on
the sides of the Tarpeian peak. The cloister of *S. Bonaventura* was
the only dwelling on the Palatine, while on the Aventine were only
the old ruins of two basilicas. Anyone wishing to visit the various
churches had to find his way through these old ruins, and not without considerable difficulty. The streets, even in the more populated
sections, were mostly narrow and dirty. In every respect Rome had
become a medieval city.

The flowering Rome of Michelangelo and Raphael was only
in the bud. The wonderful St. Peter's Church was largely still on
paper. Part of the old Basilica was still standing, and the foundations of the mighty Michelangelo dome were in completed form,
but there was as yet little evidence of the glory of Bramante's
masterpiece. In the Sistine Chapel the gifted Michelangelo was
leaning backwards painting his tremendous figures into the im-
mortal ceiling. Since 1509 the young Raphael had also been busy

painting the four frescoes on the walls of *Stanza della Signatura*.[102]
Some of his lesser works for the Borgias and the *S. Maria del Popolo*
were already in completed form; but whether the public could view
them is doubtful. The famous steps to the Capitol had not even
been designed.

This, then, was the Rome that Luther saw: old ruins, some
seventy monasteries, endowed churches and hospitals, modern
palaces of cardinals all forming but part of the same picture. The
various trades representing all European countries also added to its
color. The Jews were permitted to live all over the city, but, with
the exception of doctors, they had to wear a yellow-red mantle
marking them from the rest of the population. The German people
were well represented in Rome's business section. They were there
in sufficient numbers to have their own church, guild hall, hospice,
and tavern.[103] In this settlement were tailors, blacksmiths, millers,
printers, and even bankers, such as the famous Fuggers and Welsers
of Augsburg. Johann Zink was in charge of the Fugger business
here during the time of Leo X, and it was he who later arranged
for the John Tetzel indulgence sales in the interests of his firm for
Albert of Mainz in 1514.

Outwardly Rome was certainly a city of many religious institutions. The number of clerics was enormous; yet these various
religious services were sadly neglected. Even the old patriarchical
churches, such as *S. Maria Maggiore, S. Giovanni in Laterano,* and
S. Pietro failed to hold regular services. Preaching was limited to
the seasons of Advent and Lent. Even at Easter time the sacraments
were neglected, and when they were offered to the people, it was
solely by mendicant monks. For a secular clergyman to preach was
an almost unheard-of event. Even more offensive to the serious-
minded suppliant was the manner in which the Roman Mass was
read, since many of the priests did not understand the language of
the Mass. When Admiral Philip of Burgundy visited Rome in 1509,
he wrote: "The heathen live more chastely and innocently than
these people who now draft the ecclesiastical laws for all Christendom." He added that all they cared for was money and things he did
not even dare to mention. Erasmus, who visited Rome about this
same time, stated that he heard with his own ears "abominable
blasphemies against Christ and his Apostles."[104] Often this oc-

curred in the middle of the Mass, and the priests were so callous
that they gave no thought to the possible reactions of the pilgrims.

Monastic life had declined to the same low ebb. Few of the
twenty old Benedictine houses were still operating. The main
cloister of the Olivetane Order, S. *Francesca Romana*, had been the
property of the Congregation of the Holy Justine since 1425. The
nunneries had almost all turned into "houses of joy," to use the
phrase of Contarini in his description of them. Such houses were
for the most part closed by order of the Council of Trent. The
more recent monastic orders had fared better. The Franciscans
and Dominicans were especially well represented. The Augustinians
had two quite large cloisters for men and several smaller ones for
women. The one in which Luther stayed, S. *Maria del Popolo*, had
always had some forty inmates.[105] Several lines of popes had been
especially kind to this order. Although Luther was not well impressed by the religious life among these Hermits, at least they
observed confession and preached.

This was the Rome, the Holy City, that Luther had journeyed
so far to visit — a center of corruption and luxury. The two Augustinians visited many of the religious institutions of Rome and went
about with great zeal during the four weeks of their stay. Is it any
wonder that Luther was shocked more than once by what he saw?
Fortunately, Pope Julius II and all the cardinals except two were
in the Romagna waging a war with the French, so Luther did not
see any of the corruption in high circles.

Although it rained most of that January in Rome, Luther
almost immediately arranged to make the customary pilgrimage to
the seven principal churches of the city, which at that time already
were open all day long. Not only was this pilgrimage a strenuous
task (since the trip was made in a single day), but added to its
rigor was the fact that pilgrims usually fasted during that day, so
that they might receive Communion at the end of the journey.
To prepare himself properly for this sacred journey, Luther made
the customary general confession. Doubtless he now hoped for surcease from his inner turmoil and eagerly anticipated the peace of
mind which was to follow all these holy experiences in Rome, that
city which every Catholic longed to visit at least once during his
lifetime. Perhaps his first and most bitter disappointment was the

routine and indifferent manner in which the priest heard his confession.

The pilgrimage usually began with S. *Paolo fuori le Mura* near the Aurelian wall in the southwestern part of the city, with *San Sebastiano* on the Appian Way following.[106] While in this neighborhood, the catacombs were visited. From here the order was S. *Lorenzo fuori le Mura*, S. *Giovanni in Laterano*, S. *Croce in Jerusalem*, S. *Maria Maggiore*, and finally across the city to S. *Pietro*. Here they received the Holy Eucharist in the evening and drank from the stream which flowed through ground hallowed by the bones of saints before emptying into the papal garden. While Luther was in the Lateran Palace, he, of course, took advantage of the *Scala Sancta* located on the north side of the palace, with its twenty-eight marble steps alleged to be the ones that Christ had ascended to Pilate's *praetorium* in Jerusalem. Here Luther prayed for his grandfather Heine Luder of Moehra, as he related in a sermon on September 15, 1545, while preaching on Col. 1:9 ff.:

> As at Rome I wished to liberate my grandfather from purgatory, I went up the stairway of Pilate, praying a *pater noster* on each step, for I was convinced that he who prayed thus could redeem his soul. But when I came to the top step, the thought kept coming to me: "Who knows whether this is true!" [107]

As Scheel has pointed out, Luther may have derived this skepticism from others in Rome. Similar quotations were already associated with the story of the *Scala Sancta* in the sixteenth century. "Wie weet, of het wel waar is," or "who knows whether it is true," could be read from a verse in the museum at Delft.[108]

Rome was full of altars, at some of which a single Mass could liberate a soul from purgatory. The zealous Luther read a number of these *Seelenmessen* that he might redeem his share. Later, to emphasize what a sincere Catholic he had been, he spoke of the many Masses which he held, admitting he could not even recall the exact number. Nor was he always able to obtain an altar, so occupied were they by the many foreign clergymen visiting the Holy City. In *San Giovanni in Laterano* Luther tried in vain several Saturdays in succession to obtain use of the altar in front of the "Chapel of the Holy of Holies," where were also the two oldest bells in the world.[109] This altar was located between the chapel and the *Scala Sancta*. Luther wrote later that in Rome they said that blessed is that mother whose son can read Mass on Saturdays before this altar of St. John, for a single Mass before this altar would liberate a soul from purgatory.

There were other ways of accomplishing the same goal. Climbing the *Scala Sancta*, praying before the high altar of *S. Giovanni*, or going through the catacombs five times during the reading of a Mass were some of these methods. In fact, Luther, when writing later on Psalm 117, stated that with all these opportunities to win redemption for souls he felt very sorry that his parents were still living, for he would also have liked to liberate them from purgatory through "Masses and other pertinent deeds and prayers."[110] But Luther did not limit himself to the seven principal churches in Rome. As a "madman full of religious zeal" he ran through "all the churches and catacombs that were open." As a result he apparently saw the well-known graveyard near *San Sebastiano* with its 80,000 martyrs and 46 popes buried in narrow aisles.[111] No doubt, he also saw the graves at *S. Lorenzo, San Agnese fuori le Mura*, and the *Pantheon*. Luther specifically mentioned the *deutsche Kirche im Spital*, the *Santa Maria in Aracoeli*, and the *S. Pancrazio on the Monte Gianicolo*. He may have visited others during the four weeks in Rome which were not mentioned in subsequent casual conversations or writings.

Luther did not expect to see or participate in the services of all of Rome's many wonderful churches. To see the *Santo Volto* in St. Peter's, says Pastor, he would have needed the special permission of the Pope; so Luther could not have seen the "holy kerchief of St. Veronica" and the other "relics of Jesus' Passion." What he later wrote about this treasure room came from the above-mentioned Dr. Johann von der Wieck and others.[112] Nor did Luther see the often falsely described "wooden heads" of Peter and Paul which Pope Urban V had discovered in the old Palace Chapel of the *Sancta Sanctorum* in the Lateran on March 1, 1368. These had formerly reposed in two golden busts placed in the ornate *Ciborium* above the main altar of the Lateran Church. They were then displayed only on June 29. Luther once said that he did not see these himself but was acquainted with them only through others.[113] He probably did not see the unusual Virgin Mary of *S. Maria Maggiore*, with the crib, swaddling clothes, and hay from the stable in Bethlehem, which were displayed only on December 25, for it is very doubtful whether he arrived by that time.

So the most treasured relics were not to be seen during Luther's visit to Rome. He did see, however, a number of the minor relics. In *San Paolo* he saw the place where parts of the bodies of Peter and Paul had been placed. He was shown the wall behind which the 300 slain children of Bethlehem lie buried, the crucifix of St. Brigitta that once had spoken, the chain of St. Paul, and the column next to which the great Apostle had once preached. In *San Sebastiano* he was shown St. Sebastian's grave, that of the Samaritan woman, and the well in which the bodies of Peter and Paul had lain for 500 years. He saw the stone with a footprint of Christ and a part of the pillar next to which St. Sebastian was martyred. In *Santa Croce* Luther saw the altar with the rope used to drag Jesus to His Passion. He also saw eleven thorns from Christ's crown of thorns, the sponge used to give Him drink during His Passion, a nail from the Cross, the inscription of Pilate, a large and a small piece from the Cross, another from the cross of one of the malefactors, a sapphire with water and blood from Christ's side, and some milk and some hair of the Virgin Mary.

Even greater than these were the rare treasures of *St. Peter's* and *S. Giovanni in Laterano*.[114] Here was a cross made out of the shining sword with which St. Paul had been beheaded, the grave of the Apostle John, the table at which he read Mass on the Isle of Patmos, the coat with which John once brought two from the dead, two pieces of the five loaves with which Jesus fed the five thousand, a few pieces from the burning bush of Moses, the rod with which Moses struck the rock to give the people of Israel water, and the table on which Jesus instituted the Lord's Supper. Finally, in the entrance of the old St. Peter's itself, was one of the pieces of silver for which Judas betrayed Jesus. Anyone who beheld this relic received 14,000 years of indulgence. To the left was the chapel in which St. Peter held his first Mass in Rome, which gave the pilgrim who beheld it 7,000 years indulgence. In the wall near the Golden Gate was also the stone that had sealed Christ's grave. In the Cathedral was the rope with which Judas had hanged himself. On the wall near the tower were two silver crosses that marked the places of St. Peter's and St. Paul's relics, giving the person who kissed them 17,000 years indulgence. And these are but a few of the many relics referred to in contemporary sources.

In all, St. Peter's had fifty altars, of which seven were main altars adorned with wonderful relics. Add to this number the altars of fifty additional churches which the pilgrim could visit in Rome, and one realizes why Luther described himself as "mad" with religious zeal. How many of these available relics Luther actually saw lies beyond investigation. Years later, when he tried to recall them he probably remembered only the exceptional relics that particularly impressed most visitors, like the heavy rope with which Judas hanged himself or the pictures painted by the Evangelist Luke. Yet all that Luther saw, he later related, he believed at the time to be genuine and did not have the slightest doubt as to its authenticity.[115]

Luther was favorably impressed with the service of the "deutsche Kirche im Spital," the German church known as S. *Maria dell' Anima*, which he described as the best in all Rome, for the Pfarrherr, Heinrich Bode, and some half-dozen chaplains who assisted him had preserved the spirit and form of the old Catholic service. Luther liked this church because there he felt more at home and the clergy seemed to take more of an interest in the service. He could not have met Bode, however, who with some of his men had joined the papal party in Romagna. It may also have been a member of the German Congregation who guided Luther and his associate in their tour of the "Wonders of Rome," as provided by the statutes of the Augustinian Order.

The *Anima*, as the German community was often called in brief, was full of stories and reports about the papal court and its irregularities. Doubtless, much that Luther reported about the visit to Rome he heard later in life through his own countrymen. There is some definite evidence that he learned of the wild escapades and illegitimate children of the preceding pope, Alexander VI.[116] Of him Luther heard that he was not even a Christian, that he believed *plane nihil*, or simply nothing. Luther also heard that Pope Julius had some very strange habits, such as arising at 2 A. M. and working by himself for four or five hours, and then devoting the rest of the day to the pursuits of a secular prince, engaging in war, building construction, coinage, and similar activities.

The *Anima* was frequented by many of the famous Roman courtesans who were clients of the House of Fugger. The Fuggers had even built a new *Muenzhaus,* which handled much of the papal finances. Luther must have heard rumors of some of the rather doubtful financial transactions that were carried out during this time. Aloys Schulte, in *Die Fugger .in Rom,*[117] says that the enormous wealth of Cardinal Meckau was appropriated in the main by Julius II, even though he gave 20,000 gulden to Emperor Maximilian, with whom he was playing politics at the time. Luther may have heard also how Markus Fugger had been favored in church benefices. The church positions given to friends of the *Curia,* the larger number of which were in German lands, were common knowledge. Luther could not have remained ignorant of the lawlessness, murder, and unchastity that were rampant in the highest circles of Rome, even though the Pope and his court were absent. He must have heard much in the *Anima* that shocked his sensitive soul and later lifted the veil from his eyes.

Perhaps the most shocking aspect of the whole Rome experience was the levity of most of his fellow monks in conducting the Mass, rushing through the service without regard to what they were saying, and even ridiculing him for taking the priestly office too seriously.[118] Many of the Italian priests, Luther said later, could not even read the Latin in the Mass correctly. Yet he did not hold this against the Roman Church, but thought them bad priests who had failed to measure up to what the Church professed.

Luther's impressions of Rome were no different from those of most other northern Europeans, such as Erasmus, Schneidewin, Kordatus, Magdeburg, von Schlieben, Monner, and Wierck, all of whom returned with the impression that there was much indifference toward religion and that the corruption of the Eternal City was shameful.[119] Mature men like Erasmus were much better qualified to evaluate what they saw. Luther was but a student whose studies had been interrupted. He went as a sincere and devout Catholic, and even though he saw and heard much that shocked his pious soul, he still believed in the effectiveness of his faith. The antique elements in Rome, its catacombs, saint worship, and relics greatly appealed to his deeply religious nature. As he matured into the Reformer, much of what he had formerly failed to comprehend took on new significance.

Toward the end of January, General Egidio gave his verdict to the two monks in which he denied their appeal. Now the two men started on their homeward journey. It is possible that on the homeward journey they traveled by way of Bologna from Florence and from thence to Verona to take the Brenner Pass through the Alps. It is known that they passed through Innsbruck and arrived in Augsburg toward the beginning of March. Luther says little about the return trip. He remarked once that Innsbruck seemed like a small town.[120] In Augsburg he was amazed by the famed "Wonder Girl, Anna Lamenit," who for ten years had not eaten anything but the host of Holy Communion. But when Luther asked her whether she would not like to die, there came the strange reply: "No, for I am not certain how things are up there, while I know how they are here below." [121] Just as Luther had surmised, in 1512 the miracle-working child was exposed as an impostor.

By the middle of March the two monks had left Augsburg for Nuernberg, where a meeting of the seven Observantine convents took place soon after their arrival. Even though the report of the two monks was that of a "denial of their petition," they believed that in time General Egidio would weaken. It was decided, therefore, to send a new delegation to Rome to request of Egidio the right to appeal to the Pope. This delegation seems to have started for Rome almost immediately. Shortly after this, perhaps early in April, Luther began the return journey to Erfurt. By the time he arrived there, five months had elapsed since his departure. In the meantime a substitute had lectured for him on the *Sentences*, which work Luther resumed upon his return. That same summer he was summoned from Erfurt to Wittenberg, a step that was not only decisive in his own life, but also in all European history.

Following these developments, Staupitz called a meeting of the Augustinians at Jena. Here he explained his situation to the seven opposing convents, stating that he could not renounce his espousal of the union between the entire German Congregation and the convents of the Saxon Province; yet he took such a conciliatory attitude in all other matters that the seven opposing convents agreed

PLATE II

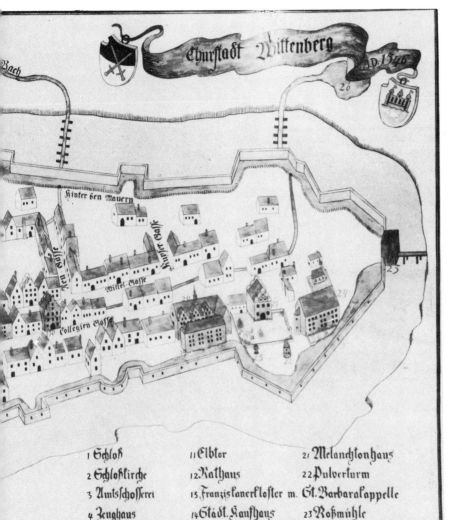

Churstadt Wittenberg A.D. 1546

1 Schloß
2 Schloßkirche
3 Amtsschosserei
4 Zeughaus
5 Churfürstl. Küche
6 Coswiger Tor
7 Amtsmühle
8 Antoniterkappelle
9 Stadt. Marstall
10 Konsistorium

11 Elbtor
12 Rathaus
13 Franziskanerkloster m. St. Barbarakappelle
14 Stadt. Kaufhaus
15 Parrkirche St. Marien
16 Kappelle z. hlg. Leichnam
17 Die Bursa Merkurü
18 Das Rondel
19 Das alte Collegium
20 Collegium Friederici

21 Melanchtonhaus
22 Pulverturm

23 Roßmühle
24 Augustinerkloster und Lutherhaus
25 Elstertor
26 Churfürst. Karpsenteich
27 Cranachhaus
17b Bursa Sophiae

to consider his proposals and to give their answer in two months. The Erfurt officials, however, were not too amenable to conciliation. As a result, Luther and his friend John Lang began to agree with Vicar Staupitz, believing that further opposition was out of order and not wholesome for the Church. Although all the facts are not known, it appears that Lang was forced to leave Erfurt. On August 17, 1511, he matriculated at Wittenberg. Luther also, judging by a letter which he wrote in 1514 to the Erfurt faculty, had some difficulty with the officials because he did not complete his training there. It is highly possible that Staupitz learned through Lang of the conditions in Erfurt and that he decided to move Luther to a more congenial cloister.[122] It is known that Staupitz ordered the change for the two men.

Apparently both Erfurt and Nuernberg refused to abide by the Jena decision, and by September, 1511, Staupitz had concluded that it was useless to continue the struggle. His verdict to drop the plan of union was given at the Chapter of the Congregation in Cologne the following May, 1512. So the peace of the Congregation was once more restored. Staupitz was re-elected General Vicar, and, for a while at least, he visited in the Nuernberg convent which had given him so much opposition.

In 1516 John Lang, who was an able student of the classical languages, was recalled to Erfurt, and Luther, who by this time had been made the District Vicar, appointed him Prior of the Erfurt cloister. The arrangement met with no opposition by the Erfurt brethren; so Luther must have been forgiven. The cloister rallied around Lang's able leadership, and by the time of the Leipzig debate between Luther and John Eck in 1519 Erfurt fully supported its former alumnus and brother.

THE PROMOTION TO THE DOCTORATE

In September, 1511, Vicar John Staupitz had just completed the promotion of four doctoral candidates when he happened to meet Luther under the pear tree in the garden just north of the Black Cloister, where the monks often gathered. Staupitz suggested that Luther also ought to prepare himself for the profession of preaching and become a Doctor of Theology. Luther immediately cited many reasons why this was not a desirable step for him to take. The exact words are not recorded, but the conversation, partially in jest, was somewhat as follows:

> *Staupitz:* O my friend, be not wiser than the whole convent and the Fathers.
>
> *Luther:* Your Honor, Mr. Staupitz, you will deprive me of my life.
>
> *Staupitz:* Do you not know that our Lord hath many great things to be done? Then He needs intelligent people to counsel Him. Should you die, you would become the Lord's counsel in heaven, for He also needs several doctors.[123]

Judging from his rapid rise in responsibility and esteem, Luther had made quite an impression on the Wittenberg faculty even during his first stay as a young graduate student. One of the older and most distinguished professors and founders of the University, Polich von Mellerstadt, expressed this appraisal:

> This monk will confuse all the Doctors. He will start a new religion and reform the whole Roman Church, for he bases his theology on the writings of the Prophets and the Apostles. He stands on the words of Christ, which no philosophy or sophistry can upset or oppose, be it that of the Scotists, Albertists, Thomists, and of the entire Tardaret.[124]

Staupitz, the other founder of the University, was anxious to employ promising young professors. He, too, must have been impressed with the ability of the young monk and, therefore, proposed his further preparation and promotion. The appointment of preachers of the order rested with the General Vicar. Luther could not well refuse the urgent request of his superior and preached the required trial sermon before the monks of the Black Cloister in the *Refectorium,* the dining room of the monks.

Staupitz did not have authority to make Luther a doctor. There were many difficulties to be surmounted, one of which was the payment of a fee of 50 gulden, or about $470.[125] The Elector would hardly supply such a sum unless he was reasonably certain of a direct benefit to his University. It seems that he advanced the sum only after Staupitz had assured him that Luther would fill the chair of *lectura in Biblia* of the theological faculty for the remainder of his life. This was Staupitz's own teaching responsibility, but his duties as General Vicar had forced him to give up his theological lectures for some time. Luther later wrote the jealous Erfurt faculty that he was promoted to the doctorate at Wittenberg quite against his better judgment and will and only because Vicar Staupitz had virtually forced him to take the step.[126]

Following the time of Staupitz's suggestion that Luther be promoted to a Doctor of Theology and before the actual arrangements could be made, almost a year had elapsed. Since the ordination of Luther as a preacher was solely the province of the Black Cloister, Luther was first made preacher of the convent. In the meantime he continued his theological studies. In May, 1512, he attended the meeting in Cologne as a delegate of the Wittenberg chapter, which meeting settled the afore-mentioned Congregational struggle. Here he was promoted to subprior of the Wittenberg cloister, which made him the instructor of the novitiates. As a result of this appointment, Luther was now assigned private office space for the first time, the same room occupied by preceding superiors. This *Stueblein* became the famous "tower room" in which he discovered "justification by faith" in 1514.[127] It has now been established with reasonable certainty that this room was on the second floor of the old tower seen on the southwest corner of the Luther House in etchings of that day. In 1532 Luther was concerned lest the refortification of the town by the Elector would destroy the famous room in which "he had stormed the Pope." After his death his fear was realized.

By the fall of 1512 the final steps had been taken for Luther's promotion to the doctorate.[128] One of these was the granting of the *Licentiatus* in Theology by the Wittenberg theological faculty on October 4, at which time Luther also took an oath of loyalty to the Roman Church. On October 9 he journeyed to Leipzig to receive the necessary funds from the Electoral treasurer. On October 18 the preliminary service for Luther's promotion was held in the Castle Church, Professor Bodenstein von Carlstadt presiding. On the following day at seven o'clock in the morning the actual promotion took place in the Castle Church. On this occasion Luther took a second oath of loyalty. Carlstadt read a number of verses to the candidate during which he presented him first a closed and then an open Bible. He placed on Luther's head a woolen beret and on his finger a silver doctor's ring, which has been preserved in the museum in Braunschweig. The ceremony was followed by a disputation lasting for several hours. By ten o'clock the formal service was over. His fellow students then carried the new doctor through the streets, while the large town bell rang in honor of the newly won distinction. A doctor's title was as treasured by the students of that day as the accomplishments of a football hero on a modern campus. On October 22 Luther was officially received into the Theological Faculty by a special reception of the *Senate*, which consisted of five members of the university faculty.[129] On the following Monday, October 25, Martin Luther began a series of lectures in the Black Cloister which were to resound throughout Christendom, probably on the First Book of Moses.

Luther was now Doctor of Theology, occupying an official chair in the University; but, as he stated May 21, 1537, he had not yet seen "the light."[130] It seems that his old doubts returned in even greater intensity. His trip to Rome had not won surcease from his inner soul struggle. He was still deeply agitated over winning the righteousness acceptable to an angry God. Since Wittenberg was to become the cradle and the nursery of the future Reformation, a little more detailed analysis of the environment and atmosphere will be desirable for an understanding of the development of Luther the Reformer.

PART THREE

The University Environment

« 6 »

The Electoral Town of Wittenberg

Medieval Wittenberg

A S THE ELBE RIVER winds its way in a northwesterly direction through the northern lowlands, it makes a sharp bend to the west in Electoral Saxony. Here the distinguishing feature of the countryside was a large hill of white sand which was a landmark for the travelers who followed the river highway. This point came to be the stopping place for both east and west travelers and gradually developed into a market place where traveling merchants exchanged goods with one another and with the Flemish immigrants and native Wends. Permanent buildings followed as a matter of course, and the nucleus was laid for the town which later occupied this site. The first buildings followed the highway or grouped around the trading center and were designated as *Lange Strasse* and the *Markt*. So Wittenberg was born, receiving its name from the sandy promontory which dominated the scene, the "White Mountain," or "Witten Berg," from the Flemish. Perhaps to the Flemish settlers, recalling the flat lands of their native home, this sandy hill seemed like an actual mountain.

Like most European cities, Wittenberg has a long and colorful history whose earliest beginnings are shrouded in mystery.[1] Recent excavations reveal even the traces of a Roman depot on the sandy promontory on which the town was built. The town itself first emerges above the historical horizon in 1174, when the whole region was still in the possession of the Wends, who had for centuries occupied all the lands east of the Elbe River. This was about the time that Albert the Bear gave the region to his youngest son Bernhard of Ascania, who had been made Duke of Saxony in 1180

199

at Gelnhausen.[2] It was Albert who had wrested the territory from
the Wends and established there the Flemish settlers whose settlement became known as the "Fiaeming," a name which has remained
to this day.

The original population of Wittenberg, however, was not entirely Flemish; for as the town began to grow, its street plan showed
a definite Wendish influence. Most German towns like Jena or Erfurt were simply a network of streets without any definite plan.
The Wittenberg streets were laid out at right angles to the original
market place, the old river highway remaining the southern bound-
ary of the town. As Wittenberg became more important and protection more necessary, it was surrounded by a moat and wall in
a half-moon shape. This wall and moat determined the inner shape
and street plan of Wittenberg until 1873. Although the names of
streets and sections of the town underwent some changes through
the centuries, the general outline has remained the same since
Luther's day.

After several generations the descendants of Bernhard decided
to make Wittenberg their place of residence. In 1266 Albert II
moved to Wittenberg, and the Ascanier family lived there until the
whole family was killed in the unfortunate tower crash of the Castle
of Schweinitz in 1419.[3] This family built the original Castle and
Castle Church, the Franciscan Monastery, and the original Town
Church and was especially interested in the welfare of the citizens.

Perhaps a premonition of impending danger moved the citizens
to further efforts for protection, for between 1323 and 1409 the
town constructed a complete system of fortifications considered excellent for that day. These included a wide moat, a stone wall, and
raised embankments. They were completed just in time, for after
the burning of John Hus, his countrymen mercilessly plundered
and pillaged all open towns and villages. The Ascanier princes gave
the citizens many territorial, fiscal, and legal privileges which made
the town a desirable place of residence, and it soon developed into
the principal city of the entire Electoral Circle.[4]

The House of Wettin, which succeeded the Ascanier, did not
reside in Wittenberg, but selected Torgau as its location. Yet the
town was not neglected. It remained the principal city of Electoral

Saxony, the prized possession of the prince. When Frederick the Wise became the ruler and Elector of Saxony, he began a regular building program to beautify Wittenberg. Between 1490 and 1509 he completely rebuilt the Castle and the Castle Church into a structure of Gothic beauty and employed the best artists of the day to decorate the interior.[5] In the Castle were rooms decorated with all kinds of Graeco-Roman court scenes and used as classrooms for the Law School. Frederick founded the University of Wittenberg in 1502 and launched an extensive remodeling and building program. He rebuilt the Augustinian Monastery to house some of the professors, erected the *Altes Friederici Collegium* (19 on the map) in 1503 and began the first unit of the *Neues Friederici Collegium* (20) in 1509.[6] Other buildings were also improved; the *Rathaus* was rebuilt in a new Renaissance style; homes were built for the more important university professors. This new Wittenberg, just emerging when Luther came there in 1508, is well pictured in an old contemporary source, the *Dialogus of 1507*.[7] From this and other contemporary descriptions a fairly accurate picture may be obtained of Wittenberg as it was to be seen when Luther accepted the position of "lecturer in Bible."

The Town of Wittenberg in Luther's Day

In the archives of the Castle at Wittenberg there is an old town plan, measuring about three and a half by seven feet, well preserved in an old oak case. Even though its authorship is unknown, it is one of the prized possessions of the town archives. According to the accompanying legend, it presents the streets, lots, and principal buildings of Wittenberg as they were around 1623.[8] As shown on the accompanying map, a slightly modified reproduction, Wittenberg at the time was divided into four regions for purposes of taxation: *Coswiger, Jueden, Elster,* and *Markt*. This is the only known real estate plan of Wittenberg on the basis of which the Luther Town can be reproduced, and it was on this background that the buildings and streets were placed in the accompanying reconstruction. For the convenience of the reader, the numbering used on the *Plan of Wittenberg in 1623* and on the

PLAN of WITTENBERG in 1623

1. SCHLOSS
2. SCHLOSSKIRCHE
10. KONSISTORIUM
12. RATHAUS

15. STADTKIRCHE
19. DAS ALTE COLLEGIUM
20. COLLEGIUM FRIEDERICI
21. MELANCHTONHAUS

24. LUTHERHAUS
27. CRANACHHAUS
31. DIE BURSA MERKURÜ
31. BURSA SOPHIAE

Plan of Wittenberg in 1623

"Churstadt Wittenberg A. D. 1546" is interchangeable, and the numbers are inserted in the text for ready identification. See plate II.

To visualize the appearance of a sixteenth-century town, woodcuts and etchings are invaluable. Unfortunately, it is doubtful whether there are any authentic woodcuts of Wittenberg as it appeared during Luther's lifetime. The frequently cited Cranach of 1540 is misdated, and it is very doubtful whether it is even a Cranach.[9] In it the towers of the *Stadtkirche* (15) are already baroque. According to Melanchthon's tower document now in the *Lutherhalle* (24) in Wittenberg, the earlier graceful spires were removed during the Schmalkaldic War in 1546 and not replaced by the later baroque style until 1556. Lucas Cranach the Elder went into voluntary exile with his Elector in 1547 and died at Weimar in 1553. Another old cut reproduced by Max Senf under the title *Altes Wittenberg von 1546* is also of very doubtful origin.[10] In this the towers of the *Schloss* (1) and of the *Schlosskirche* (2) are of a much later period while the *Elbtor* (11) is the same as in cuts of the period of Frederick the Great two centuries later. Since the towers of the *Stadtkirche* (15) are Gothic, the work must be a synthetic reconstruction on the basis of several older cuts. Lucas Cranach the Younger made two pictures of Wittenberg during the Schmalkaldic War, one in 1550 and another in 1553. Both of these woodcuts show the *Stadtkirche* (15), the *Schloss* (1), and *Schlosskirche* (2) with the upper towers removed to provide cannon emplacements.[11] The one of 1550 is very interesting, because it aims to show that Heaven is still pleased with Luther's Gospel reforms even though the town was captured by Duke Moritz and the forces of Emperor Charles V. In the foreground the Electoral family is shown, praying, the large figure of Luther supporting them in the dark hour when they had lost Wittenberg. To the right is portrayed Christ being baptized by John the Baptist, with the dove descending from heaven, while from above God the Father looks with favor upon the whole scene.

The first woodcut of real value for the appearance of Wittenberg is the famous 1611 etching, enlarged by John William Bossoegel in 1744. The two extant originals, measuring about twenty inches by ten feet, are in the Halle University Library and the *Saechsische Landesbibliothek* in Dresden.[12] Useful, too, are the fine pen sketches made by Dilich in 1627, especially the north, west, and east views, approximately four and a quarter by twenty inches in size.[13] These provide the only view from the north and are especially valuable for that reason. There exists also an old cut by F. B. Werner and a colored one by Merian of 1650, which complete the general views of the town of Wittenberg as it appeared to artists between 1546 and 1650.[14]

For a correct impression of the Wittenberg of Luther's lifetime, therefore, these materials must be used very carefully. As mentioned, the oldest usable woodcut presented Wittenberg as it appeared sixty-five years after Luther's death, and although German cities of that day did not change as rapidly as today, wars and other events had taken their usual toll.

For the exact appearance of specific buildings additional information must be gathered from older drawings of individual buildings, such as the Lucas Cranach the Elder of the *Schlosskirche* (2) in his *Wittemberger Heiligthumsbuch of 1509*, or the *Stadtkirche* (15) reproduced by A. Spitzer, and his special studies of the church towers between 1546 and 1558. Evidence from the Melanchthon document found in the south tower of the *Stadtkirche* (15), however, corrects Spitzer's wrong date to 1556.[15] Spitzer's reproduction of the *Lutherhaus* (24), even though made on the basis of old eighteenth-century cuts, is also valuable, for he presents

Towers of the Town Church; left, from 1412 to 1546; right, from 1556 to present. Drawn by A. Spitzer

this building from the inner court including the pear tree where Staupitz persuaded Luther to become a Doctor of Theology in 1511. The tower with its baroque cupola was, of course, not there in Luther's day, for it was not built until 1564 to 1586.[16] In this picture the tower in which Luther discovered St. Paul's doctrine of "justification by faith" is missing. Spitzer's *Markt* and his studies of three types of towers that adorned the different castle churches throughout the last four hundred years are also useful. Finally, in the *Album,* the matriculation book of the University of Wittenberg, now in the Halle-Wittenberg Library, is a fine picture of the inner court of the *Altes* and the *Neues Friederici Collegium* (19 and 20), dated 1644–1645.[17] This view is beautifully colored, showing the students in their customary college garb.

A careful study and comparison of these old sketches will also reveal many changes made in the town fortifications between 1512 and 1650. All of these details were considered in the accompanying reproduction, for the town archivist, H. Heubner, made a special study of the old town walls and fortifications of Luther's day, and his findings were incorporated in this synthesis.[18]

No one can recapture by old woodcuts and other illustrative materials alone the atmosphere in which Luther moved. Fortunately, there are nine eyewitness descriptions of Wittenberg as it appeared between 1507 and 1650 which augment considerably the knowledge gained from pictures. As might be expected, these materials are not all of equal value. Some were made by warm friends of the town and the University, three by very bitter Luther enemies. One, the *Dialogus of 1507,* is a sixty-six page imaginary conversation between a professor and a student in which the Town of Wittenberg of 1507 is pictured in great detail.[19] Although written for the purpose of attracting students, it nevertheless supplies much valuable information.

All of these descriptions must be carefully evaluated and the underlying motives considered, for even Luther at times extolled the town's attractions and sometimes criticized it severely. Christopher Scheurl came from the cultured town of Nuernberg and definitely agreed with Luther that Wittenberg was "on the very borderland of civilization." [20]

Frederick Myconius, a close friend of Luther, wrote in his *Historia Reformationis* (1517–1542) that Luther and Melanchthon had a profound effect upon the old Wittenberg to which they came:

> Wittenberg up to that time was a poor, unattractive town with small, old, ugly, low, wooden houses, more like an old village than a town.[21]

Even more disparaging was the description of the town by the afore-mentioned Cochlaeus, who wrote the following description to his friend Dietenberg in 1524:

> A miserable, poor, dirty village in comparison with Prague, hardly worth three farthings; yes, in fact, it is not worthy to be called a town in Germany. It has an unhealthy, disagreeable climate, is without vineyards, orchards, or fruit-bearing trees of any kind; a regular beer chamber; on account of its cold and smoke it is not an enjoyable place; it is very dirty; in fact, what would there be in Wittenberg were it not for the castle, the Stift and the University? One sees there nothing else but Lutheran, that is, dirty homes, unclean alleys; all roads, paths, and streets are full of filth. It has a barbarous people that make their living from breweries and saloons; and a body of merchants not worth three cents. Its market place is empty, its town is without better citizens. The people dress as those of a lower middle class. There is great poverty in all the homes of the town.[22]

From the venom in this well-known quotation may be gathered the impression that its author might be slightly biased. The author, who was really Dr. Dobeneck from Wendelstein, was a bitter Luther enemy from the court of Duke George and produced at least one attack a year against the Reformer after 1517, including the well-known *Septiceps Lutherus,*[23] the Luther with the seven heads. The recipient was none other than the Chief Inquisitor of Mainz and Cologne during the John Reuchlin trial. How much of Wittenberg he actually saw when he visited it in 1524 cannot be established, but his patron agreed with his opinion, for Duke George once remarked: "That a single monk, out of such a hole, should undertake a reformation is not to be tolerated." [24] There is no evidence that Duke George was ever in Wittenberg.

Statements by less biased individuals indicate that there was some basis for these unflattering remarks. Valentin von Mellerstadt son of one of the founders of the University, once remarked that he

felt as though he were sitting on top of a flaying ground.[25] No doubt
the wind that day was from an easterly direction, for the stock-
yards were located east of the town near the Elbe River. It was on
this slaughtering ground that Luther burned the papal bull, December 10, 1520. Philip Melanchthon once referred to Wittenberg
in a letter to Camerarius as "a spot which has no houses, but only

John Cochlaeus

tiny cottages, mere huts built of clay and covered with hay and
straw." [26] Luther, too, once remarked that "even among the people
of the *Kurkreis* he failed to find honor, culture, hospitality, and
religion." But another time from the pulpit he pointed out to the
people of Wittenberg:

> Our land is very sandy, in fact none other than mere stones, for it is
> not a fertile soil; yet God gives us daily from these stones good wine,
> delicious cereals; but because this miracle happens constantly, we
> fail to appreciate it.[27]

The antithesis of the Cochlaeus description appears in the *Dialogus of 1507* and presents quite a different picture.[28] Discounting the fact that it was written by a Professor Meinhardus of the University of Wittenberg upon the request of its Rector, Polich von Mellerstadt, and that it was to be a *Lockschrift* to draw students to the new university, it contains much useful material. When checked against records in the *Rathaus* and other sources, it proves to be a gold mine of information for reconstructing the atmosphere of the town at the time Luther came to the University as a young Bachelor of Divinity. According to this old source the town had three public baths and a drugstore, and fairly bristled with new structures in the process of erection. The account is useful for locating many buildings and streets, and for the general atmosphere, university customs, and typical scenes of that day which the professor described to the prospective student. For an exposition of the purpose of All Saints' Day and a description of the Castle Church, this old source is without a parallel.

Professor Meinhardus and John Cochlaeus paint the two extremes in their pictures of the city on the Elbe, and the reader must choose the middle ground between the two to form a correct conception of the environment in which Luther moved. The details of the picture can be filled in by much additional evidence from existing source materials in the town records.

In the private collection of the late Max Senf, a former director of the *Lutherhalle*, is an old manuscript by M. D. Andreas Charitius, the former Superintendent of Merseburg. He did a monumental piece of research c. 1741 on conditions in the Wittenberg of Luther's day which he apparently intended to publish in a series of volumes. All of this material has disappeared except 316 handwritten pages which seem to be a kind of introductory summary. Much of the material either pictured conditions in Wittenberg as they then existed or was based on old sources now either very rare or altogether lost. The work is made more valuable because Charitius critically evaluated all of his materials, presented under the title *Chronik des Wittenberger Archidiakonus.*[29]

Another old work by Samuel P. Schalscheleth, *Historisch-geographische Beschreibung Wittenbergs und seiner Universitaet*

(1795), contains much valuable information.[30] The author, P. Heynig, a former Wittenberg professor, used the above nom de plume in order to write more frankly. Included in his valuable history of the town is a comprehensive discussion of the origin of the name Wittenberg.

Contemporary research students of Wittenberg, Dr. Gottfried Krueger, Lic. Oskar Thulin, and Dr. Edith Eschenhagen, have supplemented the history of Wittenberg by special studies. Dr. Krueger, the director of the museum of the *Verein fuer Heimatskunde* since 1910, has devoted much time to the investigation of the environment of Wittenberg in Luther's day. His findings are ably summarized in a publication in 1933, *How Did Wittenberg Look During Luther's Lifetime?* [31] Lic. Oskar Thulin is the present director of the *Lutherhalle* in Wittenberg, where all Luther materials are being collected by the Luther Society organized in 1883. Dr. Edith Eschenhagen, niece of Dr. Johannes Ficker, dean of the theological faculty of the Halle-Wittenberg University, wrote her doctor's thesis on *Wittenberger Studien,* in which she used the town records, tax lists, and other available materials to reconstruct the economic and social life of sixteenth-century Wittenberg.[32] From these materials and the findings of H. Heubner in his *The Building of the Electoral Castle* (1937)[33] the environment in which Luther lived from 1512 to 1546 may be quite accurately reconstructed.

In size Wittenberg compares quite favorably with other sixteenth-century cities of Germany. Miss Eschenhagen has published the following comparative study.

Muehlhausen (1504–52)	7,750–8,500
Freiberg (1474)	5,000
Leipzig (1474)	4,000
Dresden (1474)	3,200
Chemnitz (1474)	2,000–3,000
Meissen (1481)	2,000
Eisleben (1433–1595)	4,000–9,500
Torgau (1505–1535)	2,462–3,500
Wittenberg (1500–1550)	2,146–2,453
Naumburg (1517)	5,000 [34]

These statistics and the woodcuts and pen sketches of Merian and Dilich of this period indicate that Wittenberg compared quite favorably in size with Dresden, Meissen, and Torgau. Wittenberg was larger than the average German walled town in the Luther Lands, but was smaller than Leipzig, Erfurt, Muehlhausen, or Magdeburg. The town records show that in 1500 there were 392 houses and a population of 2,146, while by 1550 it had grown to 446 houses, and the population had increased to 2,453.[35] Wittenberg was an average town for the sixteenth century and was far from the "dirty hole" that it sometimes was pictured. From the "Churstadt Wittenberg A. D. 1546" can be obtained specific impressions of the main buildings and streets.

Wittenberg at that time was about 3,280 feet long, or about eight city blocks.[36] Even today the distance is a leisurely walk of ten minutes from the *Elstertor* (25) to the *Coswiger Tor* (6). The distance from the *Elbtor* (11) to the *Franziskanerkloster* (13) was about four city blocks. Against attack the city was protected by an outer breastwork, a kind of embankment, behind which was a covered path, the *Bedeckter Weg*.[37] Then came the moat about a block wide and some seventy feet deep, the wall, and inner breastworks. Day and night the city was guarded by ten men on watch at the three town gates and at regular intervals in special places provided for them in the walls. By 1546 the town wall was provided with a number of small openings through which the defending citizens could fire upon the enemy. The guards had their headquarters in the town gates.

To provide water and flour during a siege, the city turned two streams from the neighboring region through the town. The little trout stream, the *Rische Bach*, was led by means of an aqueduct over wooden pontoon bridges across the moat through the north wall into the *Jueden Viertel* and down *Coswiger Gasse* to the *Amtsmuehle* (7). A second stream, the *Faule Bach*, was led from the *Churfuerstliche Karpfenteich* (26) into the eastern part of the city by a similar aqueduct down *Mittel Gasse* past the Market Place and along the *Schloss Gasse*, joining the *Rische Bach* just before entering the mill.[38] Beyond the mill the streams emptied their water into the town moat, keeping it supplied with fresh, flowing water. At the western end of the moat, not shown in the drawing, there was an overflow to the Elbe River, which at the time was just a few hundred yards south of the town. It is interesting to know that these two streams still flow under the paved streets of modern Wittenberg, and the fishwives keep their wares fresh in traps in the *Rische Bach* behind the *Rathaus* (12).

Wittenberg had really only one principal street, the old river highway from Torgau to Magdeburg.[39] It crossed the town from the *Elstertor* (25) in the east to the *Coswiger Tor* (6), the western gate near the Castle (1). This street was formerly known as *Lange Gasse,* but by Luther's time the eastern part had been renamed *Collegien Gasse,* or College Street, from the University, while the western end beyond the *Markt* was now called *Schloss Gasse* from the Castle at that end. Just north of *Collegien Gasse* was *Mittel Gasse.* At the time Luther first came to the city this area was still entirely undeveloped and was largely a meadow through which flowed the *Faule Bach* almost entirely exposed. Only two or three university dormitories stood on the north side of *Collegien Gasse* between the University and the *Markt.* Toward the end of Luther's life, however, this northern section had been fairly well built up, making *Mittel Gasse* and *Collegien Gasse* two separate streets. The other important street was *Coswiger Gasse,* which ran from the *Coswiger Tor* (6) to the *Rathaus* (12), where it became the *Jueden Gasse.* By Luther's time, however, according to the conversation in the *Dialogus of 1507,* Jews were no longer living in Wittenberg.[40] Other sources indicate that under the Elector John Frederick, Jews were even forbidden to visit Wittenberg after 1532. As may be seen in the old *Plan of Wittenberg in 1623,* the street next to the west wall was known as *Pfaffen Gasse* or *Ritter Gasse,* perhaps because a few knights once lived there, but farther on the street was called *Hinter den Mauern.* Along the northeastern part of the town this wall street became *Fleischer Gasse.* The cross streets from west to east were *Marstall Gasse,* named after the city stables, *Juristen Gasse,* after the Law College building called the *Konsistorium* (10), the *Buergermeister Gasse* and *Toepfer Gasse,* named from the potters on that street, while *Neu Gasse* and *Kupfer Gasse* were the last two streets in the undeveloped parts of the town.

What did Luther see when he approached from the Elbe River bridge the Wittenberg which was to be his home? How different was this scene from the modern "Linden City" with its 25,000 population, its walls removed, its parks, pools, and flower gardens! To Luther, the town looked like a fortress with its strong walls, heavy breastworks, and guards standing on the walls and above the well-fortified gates, each of which served as a regular observation tower. In Luther's day, especially when he came there in 1512, he would also have noted the many newly erected buildings. To the left towered the impressive new Gothic *Schloss* (1) and the *Schlosskirche* (2), just completed three years before. On the eastern end of the town the *Lutherhaus* (24) was only partially rebuilt, but the new university structures, the *Altes Friederici Collegium* (19), and the just completed *Neues Friederici Collegium* (20) were very impressive.[41] Many houses were also being erected.

Entering the city by way of the *Elbtor* (11) and passing along the *Elb Gasse*, attention is drawn to the large, attractive house at the corner, the *Cranachhaus* (27).[42] This home was just completed and was the property of Judge Kaspar Treuschel, the town judge. However, Treuschel died in 1513, and the home became the property of the famous artist Lucas Cranach the Elder, who converted the center into an art studio where at one time forty students studied. Here Luther spent many happy evenings visiting with that eminent citizen and true gentleman and probably sitting for the only authentic portraits in existence. In the inner court of this building may still be seen a massive unfinished sculpture of Elector John Frederick, the completion of which was interrupted by the tragic events of the Schmalkaldic War.

Facing the *Markt*, a large dwelling stood at No. 4 just three lots from the corner of *Elb Gasse*. This home was erected for Polich von Mellerstadt,[43] the former court physician and one of the founders of the University of Wittenberg. It was referred to by the students as the "Electoral Palace," a reference that implied that it was both attractive and imposing and that it was a gift from Elector Frederick the Wise.

A little farther to the north on the corner of *Elb* and *Coswiger Gassen* and facing the *Markt* (lot No. 10) was located another impressive building, the drugstore. Some local color is added from the conversation between the professor and student in the *Dialogus of 1507* (Sec. XVI):

Reinhardus: Whence that unusual odor?

Meinhardus: From the drugstore.

Reinhardus: Where is there a drugstore?

Meinhardus: In that building.

Reinhardus: That new building was constructed recently.

Meinhardus: The drugstore was erected in the same year as the college.

Reinhardus: An elaborate drugstore, indeed, no less decorated than a home.[44]

Lucas Cranach owned considerable property in the town, including the drugstore in which spices, wax, paint, and paper were sold in addition to drugs. The town records show that by 1528 the elder Cranach owned four houses and a number of gardens and fields. He was so respected by his fellow citizens that between 1535 and 1544 he was mayor of the town. After the defeat and capture of Elector John Frederick at Muehlberg in 1547, Cranach went personally into the camp of Charles V to plead for his release. When his petition was refused, this faithful citizen chose to remain with his prince in voluntary captivity.[45] He died in Weimar shortly after his release in 1553.

The open Market Place was the center of a colorful and diversified activity. Several times a week the farmers from the neighboring countryside held open-air markets, and twice a year this event reached the proportions of a medieval fair.[46] Some of the guilds presented plays on a specially built platform. Sometimes game was released in other parts of the city for the purposes of a hunt that culminated at the *Markt*. Since public executions were not permitted outside the town, several took place in the town square during Luther's period. The present-day statues of Martin Luther and Melanchthon to be seen in the square were not placed there until the nineteenth century. The town well was added in 1540.

The town records reveal that most of the *Markt* and some of the principal streets of Wittenberg were paved and that these pavements were frequently repaired. Furthermore, they were kept quite clean, for Baltizar Heyns was fined for not keeping the area in front of his house swept.[47] At night the town square was rather dark, and great care would have to be exercised not to fall into the streams flowing partially exposed on either side. On important occasions, however, tar candles would illumine the *Markt* from the four corners, making the approach to the *Rathaus* (12) and the *Stadtkirche* (15) much easier for the stranger. Citizens who had to be out after nightfall carried lanterns, but these were provided at the city's expense for the Mayor and Town Pastor together with a lantern boy to carry them.[48]

Luther would have seen the plain old *Rathaus* built by the Ascanier in 1317, for it continued to serve the town until the early twenties, when the improved structure shown in the reproduction of 1546 (12) was erected. The old building was partially razed in 1523, and a larger structure was erected, considerably roomier than the old building. This new *Rathaus*,[49] completed in 1526, was large enough to provide space for a council chamber, courtroom, and a number of clerks' offices upstairs, while the ground floor could be used for stores, a prison, a *Ratskeller*, and the town scales. The impressive Renaissance-style *Rathaus* seen today with the artistic porch designed by George Schroeder of Torgau was not erected until the time of Elector August in 1573.

To the east of the *Markt* the *Pfarrkirche St. Marien*, or *Stadtkirche* (15), with its old pointed Gothic towers and the beautiful Claus Huling painting of the Virgin Mary between them presented a spectacle of ethereal beauty.[50] This church, which was very old, was not built as a unit. The chancel was the original chapel used by the early Flemish settlers almost from the very beginning of the founding of Wittenberg. The main nave was added in 1360, while the two Gothic towers were erected in 1412. The beautiful painting of the Virgin was made in 1483. The little circular stairway now on the north side was designed by the same George Schroeder of Torgau in 1570. As today, the outside of the church was already adorned with many sculptured figures and inscriptions. For example, the stone relief *Die Sau*, on the southeast corner, commemorated the expulsion of the Jews from the town in 1304 and is testimony of the anti-Semitic feeling existing at that early date.

Pfarrkirche St. Marien (Town Church) before 1547, by A. Spitzer

Inside the church the artistic bronze baptismal font cast in 1457 by Hermann Vischer the Elder of Nuernberg was already in use as was the small, quaint-looking pulpit made in 1490, now a museum piece in the *Lutherhalle*.[51] Its exact location is not known, and the only clue to its installation is the picture by Cranach the Elder in the now famous *Fluegelaltar*. According to Mentzius, however, this altar with its paintings was not completed until the time of the Schmalkaldic War.[52] Just off the chancel to the left is a room in which the first candidates for the Lutheran ministry were examined and ordained. The upper story, however, now a treasure house of records from bygone days, was not built until 1571.

An old source, written in 1655 by Sennert, a former librarian of the University, contains a description of the *Stadtkirche* (15). In it he describes the towers, the bells, and their uses.[53] A watchman lived in rooms atop the north tower whose duties included striking the hours, keeping a lookout against fires, and sounding an alarm in case of approaching enemies, as was done upon the approach of the army of Charles V in 1547. Upon this signal the watchmen at the gates blew their bugles and closed the gates. One of these bugles may be seen in the Town Museum housed in the Castle.

There were three bells in the main towers, a small, a medium, and a huge bell. These bells were used for funerals, depending upon the economic and social status of the deceased. The large bell was rung only for the most impressive occasions, such as the funeral of a distinguished personage, for special celebrations, and for the solemn processions announcing the conferral of a master's or doctor's degree. Doubtless this same bell was rung for Luther's promotion to the Doctorate in 1519 and for his funeral procession in 1546. There was a small bell in the little bell tower near the rear of the church roof which was used as a school bell to call the children to their classes.

In 1936 a very old woman lived in the watchman's rooms in the north tower and confirmed the earlier accounts.[54] Most of those duties were still performed by her, and she had not set foot on the ground for forty years. The metal railing now guarding the apartment was placed there only after the child of some former watchman fell from the tower to the churchyard below. Under the cobblestones of the churchyard rest the remains of many of Wittenberg's well-known citizens. One of these graves is that of Melanchthon's wife, who died while her famous husband was absent from the city attending a disputation at Worms at the request of the state.

In the south churchyard stands one of the most interesting buildings of Wittenberg, the *Kapelle zum heiligen Leichnam* (16).[55] Its age can no longer be determined, but it must have stood there in 1308. Only the Fransciscan monks could perform the burial rites prior to its establishment; so Elector Wenceslaus equipped the little chapel with an altar and renovated it for funeral services. It was richly endowed and in 1507 was incorporated by Pope Julius II as part of the *Stift*, which included also the *Schlosskirche* (2) and its possessions. Funds from the income of the little chapel helped to defray the pastor's salary. In Luther's time it fell into disuse, and it is now a museum.

To the north of the *Stadtkirche* (15) was a building which housed the girls' school, and to the west of the chapel was the boys' school. After 1564 the boys were transferred to the Melanchthon School newly erected near *Juden Gasse*, and the girls were moved into the former boys' building.[56] At the northeast corner of the churchyard on *Juden Gasse* stood a large dwelling, the former home of Simon Heins, brother of the famous Chancellor (Heins) Brueck of the court of Frederick the Wise. In 1525 this residence was renovated and remodeled as a home for the Town Pastor, Johannes Bugenhagen.

Along *Buergermeister Gasse*, leading north from the churchyard, was the home of Hans Lufft, the famous printer of Luther's Bibles. Also on this street is a house pointed out to modern visitors as the home of the Widow Reichenbach, where Luther and Katharina von Bora became engaged in 1525. Dr. Krueger has established the fact that the Reichenbach home in 1525 was on the corner of *Kloster Gasse* and that his widow moved to the *Buergermeister Gasse* after the professor's death.[57] Dr. Krueger also mentioned that some Catholic residents claim still another house as the Reichenbach home and realize a tidy sum in admission fees from gullible tourists.

In this vicinity was one of three city bathhouses, the "Bath of Minors," according to Meinhardt. In this section was located the town *Frauenhaus*, which was supervised by the *Marktmeister*. Only single persons were permitted here, for the town records show that Erasmus Kersten, a married man, was fined in 1504 for visiting the place. It appears that Luther was instrumental in having this house closed in 1521; but that Wittenberg, like other German cities, continued to have its problems along this line may be gathered from the Reformer's sermons.[58]

As also indicated by his sermons, Luther was disturbed by the coarse language and unseemly action which he heard and saw about him. A careful comparison of his sermons, as made by Werdermann, reveals that the youth were admonished and the congregation reproved much the same as is done today. Wittenberg was no different from other German towns, for Luther once mentioned that a certain town in Saxony had three *Frauenhaeuser*.[59] Nor does the presence of this institution indicate general immorality, for again he stated that Wittenberg had a large number of people who lived up to their Christian beliefs. The general subject matter of Luther's sermons indicates the normal congregation with the usual tares among the wheat as experienced also by Calvin and Zwingli in their work.

Westward along the *Kloster Gasse* stood the imposing *Franziskaner Kloster* (13), occupying all the western part of the block and facing on *Brueder Gasse*, later renamed *Juristen Gasse* when the *Konsistorium* was built opposite the monastery. The Franciscan Order had been established here in 1238, and Helen, the wife of Albert I, provided the large cloister church, which became the burial place of the Ascanier family.[60] During the Reformation the monastery became vacant, and Elector John Frederick acted upon Luther's suggestion that it be converted into an infirmary. Before doing this, he ordered all the twenty-seven coffins of the Ascaniers moved into a subterranean chamber of the Castle tower, where they have been well preserved to the present day. A large memorial tablet in the rear of the *Schlosskirche* denotes their presence. The monastery proper became a hospital, but the church and other rooms were used as a "food magazine" in case of siege.

Near the wall on *Juristen Gasse* the *Konsistorium* (10) was located. A clue to its establishment is to be found in the *Dialogus of 1507:*

Reinhardus: What lot is that?

Meinhardus: If the rumor is correct, a law school may be built on that spot.

Reinhardus: If I am any judge, it will be a convenient place, since it will be free from disturbance.

Meinhardus: You have judged the case correctly.[61]

Since the name of the street later became *Juristen Gasse* and on the old woodcuts a *Konsistorium* (10) was shown, the *Dialogus* rumor apparently became a reality. The law professors of the University were housed here, but there were no classrooms in this building, for the whole first floor of the Castle was available for this purpose. In 1539, after the Saxon visitations, a consistory was established in this building to decide upon the merits of incumbent priests; the first real church supervision under Lutheranism had begun. In this system the Elector was the *summus Episcopus* as long as it concerned property and all external features of Church government, but the theological faculty of Wittenberg reserved the right to solve theological problems in Saxon lands. The Augsburg Confession now became the new standard of judgment.[62] There were also two auxiliary consistories, one in Zeitz and the other in Zwickau; but the one in Wittenberg served as the court of final appeal. Its influence on the action of the Elector of Saxony can well be imagined by the number of *Gutachten* issued by the theological faculty of the University during these formative years.

Beyond the *Konsistorium* (10) toward the *Schlosskirche* (2) were two more unusual buildings. On *Marstall Gasse* was the *Staedtischer Marstall* (9), which housed the horses and carriages for the knights. These town stables, like those of other cities of that day, contained war equipment, wagons, chariots, and the usual supplies of an armory and provided additional storage space for supplies from the *Rathaus*. It is highly possible that Duering, who lived at No. 4 *Schloss Gasse*, kept the wagon here in which Luther and his companions rode to Worms in 1521.[63] A little farther along *Ritter Gasse*, also called *Pfaffen Gasse*, was a beautiful little Gothic chapel, the *Antoniterkappelle* (8).[64] These monks were not permanently established in Wittenberg, but made periodic visits from Lichtenburg to take care of the sick. Meinhardt pointed out its Gothic vaulted chapel and its beautiful altar. Even today, though used as a blacksmith shop, the architectural beauty of this little chapel is still discernible.

At the junction of *Coswiger* and *Schloss Gassen* stood the old three-story mill, which a century later fell victim to a large fire. Next to the *Coswiger Tor* (6) and along the wall, not shown on the reconstruction, but noted on the Town Plan, stood a group of buildings, the *Probstei*, where the provost of the *Schloss* lived, the *Decan Haus*, and the *Choraley*.

Somewhere in this section of the town was also the "Bath of Jove," as may be surmised from the following conversation from the *Dialogus:*

> *Reinhardus:* What is the name of this bathing place?
> *Meinhardus:* It is the Bath of Jove.
> *Reinhardus:* Why have they named it after Jove?
> *Meinhardus:* Because it is next to the Castle of Jove as you note by the location.[65]

The further conversation indicates that the third bath was "Elster Bath" near the gate. These public bathing houses were open to the public only certain days of the week, at which time a wash basin was hung outside the door.[66]

Since the *Schloss* (1) and the *Schlosskirche* (2) were a part of the University of Wittenberg's physical plant, their description will be included with the buildings of the University proper. This completes the survey of the western portion of the town.

The first building east of the *Markt* on the north side of *Collegien Gasse* was the Hamlet House, or as it is called in the *Dialogus of 1507, Merkurue* (17).[67] It was one of the university dormitories where, according to tradition, the tragic Shakespearian character Hamlet once lived while attending the University. Farther along the street was a second dormitory, *Bursa Sophiae* (17 b), named in honor of the wife of an earlier Elector.[68] The remaining eastern portion of the town was largely open meadow and gardens in Luther's time except for the University buildings.

« 7 »

The
Physical Plant of the University

THE CAMPUS PROPER

To THE AMERICAN COLLEGE STUDENT accustomed to spacious, artistically landscaped campuses, a visit to a sixteenth-century German university would be quite disappointing. In fact, in the case of Wittenberg one cannot even speak of a campus in the American sense of the term. As at old Leipzig, Jena, and Heidelberg, also in Wittenberg the university buildings were all intermingled with the residential dwellings. Nor were the university buildings all in one part of the town. There was quite a concentration of them in the eastern end near *Elstertor*, as we note in the accompanying cut, "The University of Wittenberg in 1586." [1] This date was chosen because by that time the unit of six buildings shown on the etching had been completed by Elector August. However, the Augustinian College (5) and the Toszen House (6) were not there in Luther's day; so a reconstruction of the environment around the University in which Luther moved must be based on the period prior to their construction.

On the map of the "Churstadt Wittenberg A. D. 1546" may be noted the buildings which were a part of the physical plant during Luther's lifetime.[2] When Martin Luther came to Wittenberg in 1508, the *Augustinerkloster* (24) was used as one of the university buildings, even though it was not entirely completed. *Das alte Collegium* (19), completed in 1503, served as one of the main buildings, but between the time that Luther returned to Erfurt in 1509 and his return from Rome in 1511, the *Collegium Friederici*

221

The University of Wittenberg in 1586. Drawn by Wilbert Seidel on the basis of the author's reconstruction. (1) Luther House, (2) Old Friederici College, (3) New Friederici College, (4) Melanchthon House, (5) Augustinian College, (6) Toszen House

(20) had also been added to the university plant.[3] In the meantime the *Schloss* (1) and *Schlosskirche* (2) were completed and were being used by the University.[4] This Castle provided quarters for the Law College and, after 1512, the new University Library was located on the second floor.[5] The Castle Church served as the university church. All convocations and academic promotions were held here. Its north door was also the university bulletin board. As has been noted, the dormitories were scattered along the street between the main college buildings and the Castle. The *Bursa Merkurue* (17) and *Bursa Sophiae* (17 b) have been located.[6] Some old references mention a *Bursa ad fontem* which cannot be located with certainty but was probably on *Mittel Gasse* just behind the other two dorms, for here was formerly an old well which may have given the building its name. The *Konsistorium* (10) was also included in the university plant. To the picture must be added the *Melanchthonhaus* (21), built between 1536 and 1541, in which Melanchthon met many of his smaller classes and where several students were housed.[7]

This, then, was the physical plant of the University which was to change the course of European history between 1512 and 1560, and a more detailed examination of these various buildings is of value for an understanding of their historical significance.

The *Augustinerkloster* (24) is the first in importance because of its close relationship to Luther. As was usually the custom with monasteries, the whole area was enclosed with a board fence. A gate led from *Collegien Gasse* into the courtyard, where grew several trees, among them the pear tree under which Staupitz persuaded Luther to become a doctor. To the east, near the wall, stood the little chapel described by Luther's friend Myconius, as it appeared in 1508:

> At Wittenberg the Augustinian Cloister was just begun to be erected, and no more than the sleeping room, in which Martin is still living, was completed. The foundations of the church had been laid up to where they were level with the ground. In the middle of this foundation stood an old chapel made of wood which was braced on all sides. It was in the neighborhood of from twenty feet by thirty feet long as I recall. It had an old, crude gallery on which scarcely twenty men could stand. On the wall to the south

was a pulpit made of old, unfinished boards, one and a half yards from the ground.[8]

Myconius adds that from this pulpit Luther delivered his first Gospel sermons and that here also he attacked the indulgence trade of John Tetzel. Luther's fame as a preacher spread until the little chapel could no longer accommodate the crowds that wanted to attend, whereupon arrangements were made for him to preach in the *Stadtkirche*.

The Augustinian Order had a long and colorful history in Wittenberg. Since 1365, when Elector Rudolf II had erected a *Terminierhaus*, or overnight stopping place, for this order, the monks had come from Herzburg to Wittenberg to collect alms.[9] Just where this original structure stood cannot be established, but it is doubtful whether it was in the extreme eastern part of the town. According to the *Urbarium III*, an old town record, a hospital had stood in this corner since 1300, of which the little chapel described by Myconius was a part. The hospital had to be torn down before the new *Augustinerkloster* (24) could be built on that location.[10]

When Frederick the Wise decided to found the University of Wittenberg in 1502, the Prior of the Augustinians, John Staupitz, was asked to supervise the building of a new cloister and church in order to house adequately the members of the order teaching in the University. Records of 1504 show that construction was impeded because of a shortage of funds, which accounts for the fact that by 1508 only the sleeping quarters were ready. When the building was finally completed in 1518, it was a moderately sized structure, forty-five feet in width, forty feet in height, and one hundred and sixty-five feet in length.

According to Hermann Stein, there was, on the north side of the monastery on the second floor, the *Kreuzgang*, where the monks could walk up and down by twos for exercise.[11] Their sleeping rooms were on the south side lower floor. Early in the morning a bell gave the signal which called the monks to the little chapel described by Myconius.[12] They maintained absolute silence while leaving the cloister by means of a little winding stairway on the east end. At the morning meal following the early service the

Benediction was spoken, and while the monks ate, a part of the Bible or a selection from an edifying book was read. At the end of the meal the Prior gave the *Gratias,* or thanks, after which all retired quietly to their cells. In the evening the monks were summoned to the *Nachtmette,* an evening devotion, where on bended knees all prayed the prescribed prayers and made the responses in a low tone, whereupon they were all dismissed with the blessing from the Prior. This routine was followed daily except on festival days.[13] The novices also spent considerable time collecting *Almosen,* gifts that in part supported the monastery.

Under the able leadership of John Staupitz, many capable men were brought to the Wittenberg cloister in compliance with the request of the Elector. Among them were John Gruenenberg, who printed Luther's *Roemerbrief* with the wide marginal notes, John Lang, the able Humanist from whom Luther learned Greek, and Wenceslaus Link, a later Vicar of the order. Yet, amid such able men, Luther soon was made subprior, as noted before, was advanced to district vicar, and by 1515 was in charge of the theological studies of the monks. Professor John Lang assisted Luther, while Professor Bodenstein von Carlstadt gave a course in Canon Law. The records show that by 1516 a total of 41 students were enrolled in the theological courses of the monastery.[14]

The year 1517 wrought an epochal change in the life of the Black Cloister, as it came to be known, for in that year Luther began to oppose the indulgence trade of John Tetzel. The monasteries all over Germany were also feeling the repercussions of the John Reuchlin trial and of such books as the well-known *Letters of Obscure Men,* in which Crotus Rubeanus and his Erfurt circle made Ortwin Gratius and other apologists for the monastic system the laughingstock of all Germany.[15] The work raised a veritable shout of laughter in the universities, and the monks of the Augustinian Order in Wittenberg were not unaffected. Everywhere the monks were ridiculed, and they were not even safe in the streets against a shower of eggs or vegetables. The Prior of the order asked Luther to refrain from further writing against Rome, but Luther felt constrained to defend the cause of the Gospel. The situation became really serious after Luther's condemnation at Worms and his subsequent stay at the Wartburg. When in November, 1521, the Zwickau

Prophets stirred up the student body of the University of Wittenberg, thirteen Augustinian monks joined the movement, departing from the monastery amid considerable commotion. Soon others followed, for it was no longer respectable to be a monk. As a result, early in 1522 the Vicar Wenceslaus Link called a general meeting at the convent on which occasion the monks were given the choice of (1) leaving the monastery as quietly as possible, or (2) remaining but providing for their own living without begging and no longer receiving fees for conducting Masses.[16] Under these conditions it was very difficult, if not impossible, for the monks to remain. By 1523 the only monks left were the former Prior Eberhard Brisger, Luther, and a few guests. Strangely enough, Luther was still delivering his exegetical lectures to this little group, which at the time was studying the Pentateuch.

In October, 1524, Luther had reached a point in his "New Theology" which moved him to demonstrate that he no longer believed in monasticism. He put aside his "black Augustinian frock" and in its place put on the new "black preacher's robe" for which the Elector furnished the cloth.[17] Since Brother Brisger had also decided to abandon monasticism, Luther feared that the former property of the order might be appropriated by the town. Accordingly, he wrote a letter to the Elector in December asking Frederick to take over the Wittenberg convent; but, since he had no other place to live, he asked for the Elector's permission to live quietly in the *Spitalraum*, a little place which the cloister had recently purchased for nine gulden.[18]

The Elector's reply has been lost as has the document which gave the Cloister to Luther, but the document of Elector John which reaffirmed the gift in 1532 warrants certain conclusions. When the Elector heard that Martin Luther was to marry Katharine von Bora in 1525, he decided to give the couple all the monastic property as a wedding gift. Hermann Stein writes: "In addition to the spacious yard in front, he gave him the cloister itself and the garden next to it, all as a free gift." [19]

In 1532 Elector John confirmed this grant in a letter, the essential part of which states:

> To the afore-mentioned Doctor Martin Luther, Katharina, his lawful wife, and their joint heirs, sons and daughters, we have given as

a lawful, free property, the new dwelling in our town of Wittenberg, known as the Black Cloister, in which Doctor Luther lived
for a while and which is still in his possession, which includes the
surrounding property, the garden and courtyard, nothing being
excepted, and insofar as he still holds this property in his possession
and uses the same, we therefore grant and confirm them in this as
the lawful owners.[20]

The letter does contain a clause stating that the property was
given on the condition that it was not to be sold during the lifetime
of either Luther or his wife without first notifying the Elector, that
the University might have an option on repurchasing the property
for its use. While in the possession of the Luther family, however,
this property was to be exempt from city taxes. In the *Urkundenbuch* of the University is a document dated September 27, 1564,
stating that the "University purchased the *Kloster* near the *Elbtor*
from the sons of Dr. Martin Luther for 3,700 gulden." [21]

In the same transaction the Elector gave Prior Brisger a lot
near the Town Gate, where he built a little house. When Brisger
later went to Altenburg as a preacher, it was left in the care of
Bruno Brauer for a while, from whom Luther purchased it in 1542.[22]
Luther then owned all the property between the Cloister and
the street.

On June 13, 1525, Martin Luther became engaged to Katharine
von Bora, and on June 27, fourteen days later, a public celebration
was held in honor of the event, following which the couple began keeping house in the newly prepared rooms of the Cloister.[23]
The town records show that two tons of plaster were required for
the necessary remodeling. The Elector also gave 100 gulden for
"new home necessities." But there is no definite information as to
the exact changes made to convert the Black Cloister into a home.
It undoubtedly underwent further changes when purchased from
Luther's heirs in 1564 and together with the *Augusteum* provided
living quarters for some 150 scholarship students.[24] Again in the
nineteenth century, when Stueler reorganized and renovated the
old cloister, quite fundamental and drastic changes were made.
In the meantime the north tower seen today had come into
existence, while the original Luther tower on the southwest end,
where he had discovered that "the just shall live by faith," had

disappeared.[25] With the exception of the *Lutherstube,* the room
in which Luther worked as a scholar, translated the Bible, and
visited with the table companions, there is little evidence of the
remaining family rooms or their location.

The *Katharinenportal,* prepared out of Pirna sandstone in 1540
for Katharine's birthday gift to her husband, still provides an impressive entrance from the north courtyard. Above the seats on
either side can still be read: *Vivit,* or "He lives," and: *Etatis sue 57,
in silentio et spe erit fortitudo mea,* or "you are fifty-seven, in
silence and in hope shall my strength be." [26] To the right of the
entrance were the old monastic supply rooms and kitchen, which
arrangement seems to have remained the same. Doubtless, the old
monks' sleeping room was left unchanged, but during Elector
August's priod it became a dining hall serving several hundred
students.[27]

Of particular interest is the second floor, for it was here that
Luther lived with his family, relatives, table companions, and many
friends. Stein remarks on the change that had come over the old
monastery. Where formerly the monks had walked in absolute
silence, the voices of children now replaced the absolute quiet of
the order. The Old Catholic world had passed away; in its place
had come the happy life of faith that expressed itself in normal
family relationships.

Since the former cloister walk was on this floor along the north
side, great changes must have been made to accommodate the
Luther family with proper living quarters. Today as the visitor
ascends to the second story by way of the winding tower stairway,
he enters a fair-sized hallway. From this a door leads off to the
right into a kind of reception room about 12 by 24 feet. It is uncertain whether this room was the same in 1525. The adjoining
room overlooking the inner court was the *Lutherstube,* the room
most famous for its vital connection with the Reformation.

According to Jordan, the *Lutherstube* was immediately converted into a museum; and to preserve the hallowed memory of
Luther, it has been retained comparatively unchanged throughout
the centuries.[28] It was 24 feet square with frescoed walls divided
into panels and decorated by a frieze of flowers at the top. The
beamed ceiling was also divided into squares that were likewise

profusely decorated. Quite early the Reformation was commemorated by a brief service in this room held by the members of the Wittenberg faculty. In fact, these gatherings were the beginning of our present-day observation of the Reformation Festival. During subsequent centuries visitors from all over Europe came to the *Lutherstube,* many of whom left descriptions of the room from 1748 to 1802.[29] These sources also speak of the thousands of names that were written all over the walls, including that of Peter the Great of Russia above the west door. The first reference to the furniture in the room is in a *Tagebuch* by a Strassburg professor in 1775. At that time the room contained the old worm-eaten oak table so frequently shown, a chest, a tile stove, and a bench in front of the deeply recessed window, whose small bull's-eye glasses overlooked the court. Another description about twenty years later by Schalscheleth speaks of a number of wooden chairs and benches built into the walls. When the Berlin architect A. Stueler was given the assignment to renovate and restore the *Lutherhaus,* as it was now called, he decided to restore the original appearance of this room as nearly as possible. The names were removed from the walls and the panels redecorated to resemble the sixteenth-century originals. The worn-out floor was relaid over a new subfloor. Thus, in its renovated form the *Lutherstube* with its old windows, the old oak table, benches, and tile stove is a fairly accurate restoration of Luther's main living room as it appeared during the years from 1525 to 1546. The entire room was new at the time Luther and Katherine began housekeeping and was doubtless much more cheerful and homelike than its present dark, gloomy appearance would indicate. The tile stove in the *Lutherstube* today is undoubtedly of a later date, perhaps from the seventeenth century. Recent renovations in 1932 of the *Lutherhalle,* as the present occupants have named it, have left the building comparatively unchanged because of the appreciation of its historic value.

Of the authenticity of the remaining rooms there is no information. Under Elector August the building was remodeled to house scholarship students, but definite details are lacking. Beyond the *Lutherstube* is another room now designated as the former family living room. Its dimensions are about 12 by 24 feet. Next to the west wall, just beyond this living room, was another chamber measuring about 15 by 15 feet. South of this room are two chambers that may have served as bedrooms. In all probability the niche now seen in the wall of this southwest chamber led to the famed tower room, for excavations have shown that the tower was located at this end of the Black Cloister.

On the basis of these assumptions the newly married couple had the following rooms in their living quarters, beginning with the hallway on the north side: (1) the reception room, (2) the Luther study, (3) the Luther living room, (4) the northwest bedroom, (5) the central bedroom, (6) the southwest bedroom, and (7) the little Tower Room "in which Luther had stormed the Pope."

But as the Luther family grew and a number of relatives moved in with them, other rooms had to be prepared, doubtless on the third floor. Where these were located and how many there were, no one is in a position to state. Numerous children of relatives were raised in the Luther home in addition to providing for a number of aunts and several table companions, and additional accommodations were a necessity.

Luther did most of his teaching in the Black Cloister, and two rooms on the east side of the second story are also of special interest. The *Grosse Hoersaal*,[30] or large lecture room, just above the former sleeping quarters of the monks is the room in which Luther is supposed to have delivered his famous lectures on the Psalms and on Romans. It was in this room, whose present dimensions are almost 25 by 70 feet, that George Spalatin heard Luther lecture to 400 students in 1520. The *Grosse Hoersaal* today has five windows. Even though it is quite doubtful that Luther ever ascended the *Katheder*, or lecture stand, shown there today, he probably used one quite similar, now disappeared. If a class was too large for this room, Luther lectured in a larger room of the *Collegium Friederici* (20) some 500 yards away. Luther may also have preached his *Hauspostille* in this *Grosse Hoersaal* before his family and numerous inmates of the Luther home, or in a smaller room in the west end of the hall, now known as the *Kleine Hoersaal*, or small lecture room. Whether this room is the same as in former years cannot be established, nor whether Luther used it in his university work.

When the Luther House was purchased by the University, the plans were to build the new Augustinian College next to *Collegien Gasse* (No. 5 on "The University of Wittenberg in 1586"). These two buildings were then joined by moving in another building from another part of the city, the Toszen House (6). The completed unit was named the *Augusteum* in honor of Elector Augustus, who financed the building program.[31]

The *Statutes* of the University in 1508, 1536, 1548, and 1569 all indicate that from the very beginning poor students were given every opportunity here to obtain an education. But now this Lutheran University instituted something unique for that day. The *Augusteum* was the home of 150 scholarship students who were furnished with food, lodging, and fuel at the Elector's expense.[32]

The Augusteum, composed of the Luther House (left), the Augustinian College (right), joined at center rear by the Toszen House. Redrawn by Ernest Schwiebert, Jr., from Dilich and other sketches

In the time of Merian (1650) 300 students were eating in the refectory of the first floor, the former sleeping quarters of the monks. The old vaulted ceiling may be seen in this room today, and it now serves as a lecture room. This room was probably a dining hall already in Luther's day, otherwise Katharine would not have complained that the students came up in too large numbers to visit with Luther after meals.

A few hundred yards west along *Collegien Gasse* stood *Das alte Collegium* (19),[33] or the Old Friederici College, which was the first college building erected by Elector Frederick the Wise in 1503. Before Konrad Pflueger began the erection of the structure, three old buildings had to be cleared away. As mentioned earlier, a very clear, old etching in the University *Matrikel* of W-S, 1644 to 1645, presents a view of the inner court between this building and the *Collegium Friederici* (20), or the New Friederici College. From available evidence it appears that the lower floor of this building was used for classrooms, while the upper stories served as a student dormitory. That there were some 20 rooms on the top floor may be surmised from the dormer windows. Whether meals were served here in Luther's day is not certain, but it is quite likely. Later two types of tables were maintained, one served twice a day for a sum of four groschen per week, while the other, for seven groschen, served as good meals as could be had anywhere in town. Each table had a faculty *Vorsitzer* whose duty was to supervise the student etiquette at meals and the payment of the cook each week. No women were permitted in the university dormitories, not even in the kitchen. Merian relates that the Medical and Philosophical departments of the College held their classes in the Old Friederici College. At that time the anatomical museum was also located in this building. But since Merian wrote in 1650, those arrangements may not have existed in Luther's day.

Next to the Old Friederici College was *Collegium Friederici* (20), or the New Friederici College.[34] This building was begun in 1509, when the university enrollment was rising rapidly. The New Friederici College was larger and roomier than the old one. According to the picture in the Matriculation Book, this building also had a *Dachreiter*, or little tower, artistically decorated with an attractive little clock. The gables and general plan of this building show a definite Renaissance influence, as may be noted in the Melanchthon home built some two decades later. General references also indicate that this building had the largest lecture rooms on the campus. It, too, was a combination of recitation halls and dormitory, but the arrangement was more hygienic. Of the 32 rooms in the two colleges, 6 were used by the supervisors. According to the old Wittenberg statutes (1569) there was also a beer and wine tavern in the New Friederici College. At the time of Merian's visit to Wittenberg the theology and philosophy classes were held in this building.

Students were also accommodated in three other university dormitories, as has been noted. These were not as large as the two main college buildings, and little is known about them beyond their location and names, but it is safe to assume that the university dormitories were all controlled by the same university regulations. The housing of students of varying races and territories was a real problem in the medieval university. Younger professors were required to live with the students in the different dormitories. They saw to it that the students spoke only Latin, carried no weapons, and in other respects conducted themselves properly. The Rector, who was chosen each semester by the faculty from its ranking members, inspected the *Bursen* regularly.[35] The relationship between professor and student was very close at Wittenberg.

Another famous memorial of the Wittenberg of the past is the home of that distinguished professor, Philip Melanchthon. The *Melanchthonhaus* (21) was completed only five years before Luther's death and, while well known to Luther, who spent many pleasant hours in its garden, can hardly be considered as having contributed to the major part of the Reformation.[36] This long, high, narrow structure with its typical Renaissance roof and gables faces *Collegien Gasse*, from which it is entered by an attractive sandstone portal, similar to the one Katharine gave Martin. This door is so constructed that the upper part can be opened separately. Beyond this opening the vaulted hallway along the west side runs the entire length of the building to the court in the rear. Doors opening into this hallway lead into the respective servants' rooms and storerooms. A winding stairway leads to the family rooms on the second floor. From a central hall a north door gives access to the Melanchthon study, which is well preserved and was partially restored in 1897 for the 400th anniversary of his birth.

The peace and quiet of this room, so far removed from the busy world, immediately makes itself felt. The ancient bull's-eye window panes admitting the light but barring the confusion of the street, the table at which was probably written the biography of Luther, the old chairs and couch, the coats of arms of Melanchthon, Bugenhagen, Camerarius, Luther, Jonas, and Peucer embellishing the walls, all of these are somehow permeated with the spirit of the man who so profoundly influenced the Reformation as the bosom friend of Luther.

On the second floor at the rear were the family kitchen and the children's playroom. On the southern end of the third floor was a classroom where Melanchthon formerly instructed some of his *pension* students. It contains an old stove decorated with pictures and numerous student coats of arms on the walls. The rest of the third floor seems to have been used for bedrooms and student rooms.

At the rear of the house was a garden which today is quite shady and enclosed on all sides. In the east wall was a portal through which Melanchthon could pass to the Luther home some two hundred feet away. In the garden was a fountain shaded by four taxus trees. This flowing water was quite a distinction in the sixteenth century. In 1556 seven distinguished citizens of the town installed the first pipe line providing for flowing water into their homes, and they included Melanchthon's home as a gift. An old stone table may still be seen under the two remaining trees bearing the inscription "P. Melanchthon 1551." Whether it stood here in Luther's lifetime cannot be determined, but Luther and Melanchthon did meet here frequently in the closing years of life to sit companionably together and perhaps to discuss the weighty problems facing Wittenberg and the rest of Germany. Luther, particularly, was often disappointed and depressed with the progress of events; perhaps partly because he was old and ill, or because he saw the gathering of the war clouds of the Schmalkaldic War. It must have been a real relief to unburden his tired soul to the gentle, good-natured Philip in moments when he felt particularly disturbed. The survey of the campus proper is now complete, but there remain the *Schloss* (1) and the *Schlosskirche* (2) at the opposite end of the town, which were also used by the University.

As early as the period of Otto the Great the whole eastern frontier bristled with a chain of forts. It is not unlikely that in this very dawn of German history one of these old *Burgwaerde* stood at the bend in the Elbe where the later Wittenberg was located. There is evidence of the existence of such a fort, for when Elector Albert II constructed a castle in this place around 1260, he salvaged some building materials from an earlier structure.[37] According to Lucas Cranach's introduction to the *Wittemberger Heiligthumsbuch,* in the days of Elector Rudolf I, in reward for his distinguished service as a warrior and in honor of his wife Kunigunda, King Philip VI of France presented Rudolf with a very special gift: "a holy thorn from the sacred crown of our Lord and Savior in a special, golden casement of a king, together with a special written history of the same." [38] As a suitable repository for this precious treasure, Rudolf decided in 1353 to build a chapel to house adequately his princely gift. This first Gothic structure was dedicated to the Virgin Mary and all the saints. There was also a special altar dedicated to the Blessed Anne, where Mass was said every Tuesday.

The *Schlosskirche* (2) has had many names. Charitius says it was originally called a *Basilica* by Rudolf; other names were the Cathedral Church, All Saints' Church, the Castle Church, and the Collegiate Church.[39] Rudolf endowed this chapel richly, and its annual revenues were sufficient to support six canons. It also enjoyed the distinction of being under the direct control of the Pope. Rudolf's successors emulated the founder's worthy example, enriching the *Stift* with many additional grants. In fact, the *Stift's* annual income was so great that Frederick the Wise was able to endow the University of Wittenberg from its surplus when he incorporated them together in 1507.

Shortly before 1490 Elector Frederick the Wise decided to build a new Castle and Castle Church in Wittenberg, for which he employed Konrad Pflueger, the ablest architect in central Germany, who had also built the Old Friederici College.[40] As a model for the new structure the architect used the Castle he had built for Duke George in Meissen. The construction of the new edifice

lasted from 1490 to 1509.[41] The Castle was laid out according
to the usual rectangular plan, with the Castle Church forming the
north wing, the Castle the south wing, while the re-enforced city
wall joined the towers of the two and formed the west side of the
rectangle. The east wing apparently housed the horses, carriages,
and other princely equipage. This wing is now missing, but the
inner courtyard partially remains.

As seen in the Dilich sketch of the town from the west side,
the completed structure was one of harmonious beauty.[42] Spalatin's
records indicate that the princely sum of 200,000 florins or $2,500,000
was spent on the Castle Church alone.[43] From the Weimar Archives

Towers of the Castle Church, 1499, 1548, 1778, and since 1892
Drawn by A. Spitzer

we learn that six major artists contributed to the decorations.
Krueger commented on the contrast between the former and the
present Castle when he wrote: "He who sees the Castle in its present
pitiful, neglected condition can hardly imagine its former glory,
which was given it by men like Konrad Pflueger as the architect
and Lucas Cranach, Albrecht Duerer, and other artists of high
quality." [44]

The appearance of the Castle Church in the Cranach etching
of 1509 was the same as that which Luther saw during his entire
stay in Wittenberg. But in 1546 these towers were cut off, as were
those of the *Stadtkirche*, to provide emplacements for cannon.[45]
There is in existence one old etching showing the interior appear-

ance of the Castle Church before its destruction during the Seven Years' War in 1760. Meinhardt's *Dialogus of 1507* also adds to our information, and Charitius described it as it looked before it so tragically burned to the ground.[46]

The Cranach picture of the *Schlosskirche* in the *Wittemberger Heiligthumsbuch* is very clear and distinct, but it gives the impression that the Castle Church was a very small chapel. The Dilich

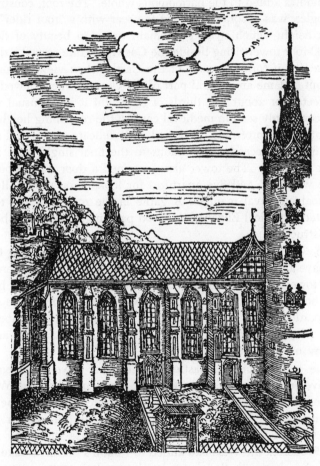

The Schlosskirche from the "Wittemberger Heiligthumsbuch," by Lucas Cranach, the Elder, in 1509

pen sketch of 1627 is more useful, for it presents the same view of
the Church and the Castle in proper proportion to the surrounding
buildings.[47] As the tall tower indicates, the church itself was large
and gracefully proportioned. Its nave was nearly a hundred feet
in height, forty-five feet in width, and one hundred sixty feet in
length. On either side six large Gothic windows, ten by forty feet,
gave ample illumination to the interior. The buttressing between
the windows added to the harmonious whole. The roof, constructed
of shingles, was decorated toward the rear with a "roof rider" sixty
feet in height which rivaled the main tower in beauty of design.
The 200-foot tower rising beside the Coswiger Gate served a double
purpose, for it formed a part of the Castle when viewed from the
west, but became an integral part of the Church when viewed from
the street. For about two thirds of its height it is the usual round
tower commonly seen in medieval castles; the remaining height was
elaborately and profusely decorated with delicate arches and spires
rising in two successive gradations to the final single spire about
60 feet in height. The tower also contained a door, four groups of
double windows, and five apertures for lookout purposes, all built
in typical medieval manner. A gable in the roof near the tower,
decorated in typical Elizabethan wood paneling, gave added beauty
to the structure.

The Castle Church had two north entrances, one leading to the
main nave and another to the *emporiums*.[48] Besides these there was
also a tower entrance. Both main doors were approached by inclined boardwalks, and the structure was separated from the street
by a boarded fence, with roofed arches covering the two gateways.
In the whole design the architect produced an edifice of artistic
harmony of which the Elector could be justifiably proud.

The interior of the Castle Church must have been equally
attractive, judged by the descriptions of Meinhardt, Sennert, Wernsdorf, and Charitius.[49] No doubt a considerable amount of the total
cost must have gone into the beautification of the interior. The
Castle Church was especially designed to house the many relics
which Frederick the Wise had added to Rudolf's thorn. Unlike most
Gothic churches with their naves, aisles, and short transept which
included a choir for the clergy and an apse for the altar, this

church had but one main nave or, rather, an extended choir. This design was introduced into Germany by Arnold of Westphalia, a former teacher of the architect. There were two other examples of these Indulgence Churches, the afore-mentioned Meissen Castle built for Duke George, and the Moritzburg, a similar treasure house of Albert of Brandenburg.[50] In this type of church, galleries, or

Casement of a king containing "one thorn which wounded the sacred head of the Lord Jesus." The Castle Church was built especially to house this sacred relic. Drawing by Lucas Cranach, the Elder

balconies, were built all the way along the sides of the church on
which the precious relics could be displayed. The Castle Church
had three of these *emporiums*. The ingenious manner in which
these were incorporated into the architecture of the walls can be
ascertained from the drawing of the interior of the Castle Church
by Michael Adolf Siebenhaar in 1730, now in the *Lutherhalle* at
Wittenberg.[51] The typical Gothic vaulting can also be seen. The
windows in this old drawing do not show the Gothic design of the
Cranach of 1509, but rather a slightly rounded Roman arch. The
panes are the same small bull's-eye type found in the Melanchthon
study and in the Luther room. The interior view also shows the
seating arrangement for academic purposes. Unfortunately, this
drawing is the only one known, and it fails to portray the inward
beauty of the Castle Church as described by visitors in that day.

The interior must have been very beautiful, judged from Reinhardt's account.[52] Old court records contain evidence that Albrecht
Duerer worked on the Castle Church in 1503 as well as a Welsh
painter, Meister Jacob, between 1503 and 1505, and the Elder
Cranach. It is also highly possible that the prominent Dutch artist
Jan Mabuse may have been the "Meister Hans" from the Netherlands mentioned in the sources of 1491. Mention is also made of
a Venetian painter, Jacopo dei Barbari, a former teacher of Duerer.
From the afore-mentioned 1730 woodcut of the interior a number
of wall statues can be noted. Matthaeus Faber stated that Rudolf I,
the founder of the Church, and his wife are the two Ascanier to be
seen. The other statues were the bronze reliefs of Frederick the
Wise and John the Constant, made by Peter Vischer the Younger in
1527 and Hans Vischer in 1534, respectively, which compared favorably with the remarkable work of this family in the Nuernberg
churches. No doubt the interior was carefully planned by the architect and the artists to combine the stone masonry, wood carvings,
paintings, and statuary into a structure of beautiful symmetry.
Gurlitt concludes his description of the Castle Church with the following observation:

> The new connections that were being spun between Wittenberg and
> Nuernberg resulted in a new type of art. The city of the Reforma-
> tion was also the nursery town of the Renaissance, perhaps even the
> most important [in Saxony].[53]

dis heiligthumbs

Zum.xj. ein kleyn silberē vnubergult Monstrantz

Von Sant Cecilia
xix . partickel

Zum.xij.
Ein Berlin mutter mit silber vberguldt oben ein lawen

Von sant Felicola ein partickel
Von sant Fidentia ein partickel
Von sant Eugenia ein partickel
Von sant Gasilla ein partickel
Vom gebein sant Anastasie .xxij. partick.
Ein zahn von sant.Anastasia
Vom gebein sant Agathe .iiij. partickel
Von dem gebein sant Apolonie .vij. ptic.
Von einem zahn sant Apolonie .j. pticfel
Zwen Zehn von sant Apolonia
Von dem Sarck sant Agnetis ein partic.
Jungkfraw vnd merterin
Vom Klaydt Agnetis ein partic.   Von yrem heiligen gebein.xv.ptl.
Ein zahn sant Agnetis   Von yrem Hirnschedel ein partickel
Von yrem heiligen haupt ein ptic.   Vom gebein sant Lucie.vij.ptic.
Ein Zahn von sant Lucia   Suma .lxix. pticfel   6 ij

*Other precious relics in their bejeweled containers in the Castle
Church*

The most detailed description of the interior of the edifice is in the *Dialogus of 1507*, for it describes, together with the many interesting observations on the town, a visit to the Castle Church on All Saints' Day. The two dialogists had supposedly reached Wittenberg on the evening of October 31, just a decade before the time of Luther's famous theses. Meinhardt informed Reinhardt that they must attend the six o'clock Mass, for this happened to be the most fortunate of all days, the Sunday of *Misericordias Domini*.[54] Wax candles were purchased at the drugstore and sent in advance by carrier to the Castle Church. When the travelers arrived at the door, the *Propst* of the Castle Church, Friedrich Kitzscher, received them in most hospitable fashion and assigned them to a chaplain who had a register of the relics displayed in the six aisles of the *emporiums*. This list was so detailed that in Meinhardt's account it filled six pages of the *Dialogus*.

Exactly how many relics there were in the Castle Church at any given time is impossible to establish, for the Elector was increasing their number daily. At the time that Lucas Cranach the Elder prepared the guide for the Festival of All Saints' Day, the *Wittemberger Heiligthumsbuch*, there were eight aisles containing 5,005 particles. By 1518 there were 17,443 relics, requiring twelve aisles for their display.[55] Meinhardt stated that the Castle Church relics were the most distinguished in all Germany, which explains the pride of the Elector in his treasure house and the vast throngs of people who sought to expiate their sins by praying before these sacred shrines.

Although there were many minor celebrations in the Castle Church throughout the year, since the days of Rudolf I it had been the practice of the Electors to place the "thorn of Christ" on a special altar on All Saints' Day, while all the other relics were placed in special display cases in the three *emporiums* of the Castle Church.[56] A visit to a similar present-day treasure chamber, such as those in Aachen or Cologne, impresses the visitor with the psychological effect of the worship that took place in the Castle Church in this era. As the Cranach illustrations show, it is not so much the relics themselves that impressed the visitor, but the beautiful gold and silver casements which left him speechless and overawed by the priceless treasures before him. Add to this the fact that the prayer of a contrite sinner before each relic earned for the petitioner 100 days' indulgence, or a grand total of 127,709 years, 116 days, which might be acquired for thus viewing all of them, and the eagerness of the pilgrims to view the display can be appreciated.[57] Doubtless, the devout visitors likewise contributed to the church revenues.

The *Wittemberger Heiligthumsbuch* illustrates the following more impressive relics from the Castle Church: a part of John the Baptist's garb; a part of the rock on which Jesus stood when He wept over Jerusalem; another piece from the Mount of Calvary; another from the spot where Jesus ascended into heaven; the gown of the Virgin Mary and some of the milk of her breast; a piece from the burning bush of Moses; 35 particles from the Cross; some hay and straw from the manger; the swaddling clothes; hair, a shirt, a coat, and a girdle of Christ; and 204 particles and one entire skeleton of the poor innocent babes of Bethlehem; all artistically housed in their containers of silver, gold, marble, and other precious materials made by Paul Moeller, the court goldsmith.[58] The conversation in the *Dialogus* shows that the sacristy also, with its sacred vessel for the Mass adorned with gold, silver, and precious gems, was a place of exceptional beauty.[59]

The lavish splendor of the Church was equaled by that of the Castle itself. Again the visitors of the *Dialogus* describe the scenes before their astonished eyes. The first room they entered was called the "Hall of Colors." [60] It contained many scenes from Roman history, which Meinhardt explained to the student. On one wall was the scene of a Roman youth waiting for a senator, on another Scipio cleaning out his camp, while on a third were scenes from the lives of Roman Emperors, and on the last wall was the slave Marcus Antonius dying in the defense of his master. The visitors agreed that this room must deeply impress the law students whose classes met here. The next room they entered was embellished with trial scenes.[61] They were symbolical paintings, such as the man with his mouth tied, indicating that the Elector preferred councilors who knew when to remain silent. On the walls of a third room were depicted scenes from Greek mythology such as the "Liberation of Andromeda by Perseus," "Hercules Taking the

Golden Apples from the Hesperides," and "Scenes from the Argonauts," indicating that the Elector was also a patron of poetry. In the room of John the Constant were scenes from Ovid's *Metamorphoses* portraying the fable of "Pyramus and Thisbe" and their tragic death. Scenes of "Absalom's Death" and "David and Bathsheba" were also portrayed.[62] From here the party passed to the Cabinet Chamber, in which were seen such pictures as the "Destruction of Jerusalem," the "Verdict of the First Consul Brutus Against His Sons," the "Verdict of Manlius Fulvius Against His Son," and the "Punishment of an Unjust Judge." [63]

The *Dialogus* reveals that the Castle was almost completed, only the two towers remaining unfinished. Although 1509 is usually listed as the date of completion of the Castle and the Castle Church and they were used by the University at that time, H. Heubner has concluded that the entire structure was not completed until 1525.[64] The *Rechbuch des Schloss Bawes zu Wittenberg A. d. 1516* shows that the northeast corner of the Castle joining the Church was completed between 1515 and 1517. In 1517 Niemegk was still working on the roof, for he reported that there was not enough lead to finish his task. In 1523 Lucas Cranach was decorating the *Ziergiebel des Schlosses.* In 1525 the building was completed, but the ground for the inner court still had to be leveled. In its finished form the Castle and its Church must have been quite an impressive Gothic structure, replete with artistic paintings, statues, wood carving, and the marvelous images and relics of the Castle Church.

THE UNIVERSITY LIBRARY

In addition to the law classes the Castle provided quarters for another important branch of the University, the Library, which was housed on the second floor. The information on the origin and nature of the University Library is quite scanty. There are references to a monastic collection which the Elector had inherited from Thomas Loesser, a canon in Meissen, as early as the year 1504.[65] Whether other collections were added during these early years is not certain. An entry in his *Annalen* by the court chronicler, Johann Sebastian Mueller, based on the Weimar court records, stated that in the year 1514 "an excellent library was founded by Elector

Frederick the Wise in Wittenberg." [66] M. J. C. Mylius, who actually handled the books in 1746, also assumed that the University Library had come into existence in 1514, but he was aware that the Thomas Loesser collection had been stored somewhere in the Castle. For him the word *gestifftet* meant that the library in 1514 was set aside for "public use." [67]

Fortunately, George Spalatin, the court preacher of Frederick the Wise and special librarian for the Elector, kept rather careful records. His *Annals, Diary,* and other materials prove extremely enlightening for this phase of university history. In his *Ephemerides* of the year 1512 he recorded that the Elector of Saxony had founded a library in the Castle at Wittenberg and had made him the librarian.[68] This statement is corroborated by a letter from Frederick the Wise to Aldus Manucius, a Venetian printer and bookseller: "We are engaged in establishing a library in our Castle in Wittenberg, Saxony." [69] Spalatin also wrote Aldus for book lists, while Christopher Scheurl jested that Spalatin was so extremely busy collecting books that he could "scarcely breathe between sweatings." [70] Finally, the old pigskin-covered account book from Spalatin's personal library, now in the *Landesbibliothek* in Gotha, shows that he, as librarian, purchased 151 works between July 28, 1512, and Easter, 1513, at a cost of about $3,000.[71] From this evidence it seems safe to conclude that the Wittenberg University Library came into existence the same summer that Martin Luther was promoted to a Doctor of Theology and accepted the position in the University of *Lectura in Biblia.*

None of the contemporary sources bothered to describe the internal appearance of the Castle Library, assuming that all were acquainted with its appointments. For information on its equipment and practices, then, it is necessary to examine the customs in general of the western European libraries of the sixteenth century.

As is generally known, the modern library grew out of the need for preserving the books of the medieval monasteries. The practice of preserving precious manuscripts in the monks' cells, or even in the *armarium,* or in carrells, was hardly satisfactory in the rigorous climatic conditions of northern Europe. The earliest known provision for a special room for the library was made by the monks at Fleury in the ninth century, but as a general practice it did not emerge throughout Europe before the period from 1373 to 1387.[72] During the Renaissance the more enlightened princes began acquiring private collections. The practice of chaining books to reading desks was a necessary preservative during the Middle Ages and continued until the forerunner of the modern bookcase came into use during the second half of the sixteenth century.[73]

The old Canon Loesser collection in the Castle may just have been piled into some upper room, but it seems reasonable on the basis of general practice to assume that the real ducal library when founded in 1512 was housed in a special room. An old source mentions moving the library in 1536 to the *alte Hofstube*, or Old Court Chamber, on the second floor and states that this would be "in a more convenient place." [74] From this statement may be inferred that the original library (1512–1536) was located in one of the rooms of the upper stories of the Castle. When Spalatin made his semiannual visits to Wittenberg as superintendent of the ducal library, he occupied a guest chamber on the fourth floor. May not the library also have been near here? Perhaps it was housed in the large room on the north side, readily accessible from the stairway, where is now located the museum of the *Verein fuer Heimatskunde*. The appearance of this room in that day is impossible to establish. It is clear, however, from the type of books ordered and other references that the library was used by the professors and especially by the poor students of the University. The location of the library may have had a natural connection with the use of the church door for announcements.

Although today it is extremely difficult to establish the arrangement of the inner rooms of the Castle, yet it seems reasonable that the second library room as of 1536 was located on the second floor immediately above the room referred to in the *Dialogus of 1507* as the *Aestuarium commune*, which today contains the *Stadtarchiv* under the direction of H. Heubner. A source cited by Heubner shows that the weight of the University Library caused the ceiling to sag considerably, which made necessary the installation of two additional pillars in the large room below "which again helped carry the weight of the library." [75]

The size of the library rooms is pure speculation; yet a room of considerable size would be required to house the entire ducal collection. Mylius, who handled the actual books, lists them as follows:

Theological	1,040
Legal	562
Medical	545
Philosophical	964
Musical	21 [76]

Summary of all the books in the Electoral Library — 3,132. In another tabulation, Mylius adds that 1,756 of these volumes were of folio size, 626 quarto, 607 octavo, and 22 duodecimo, which indicates that over half of the Wittenberg collection was large folio volumes. Many of these rare manuscripts required a special bench and chain, as may be learned from the *Urkundenbuch* of the University.[77] Other references and the accounts of the sums expended indicate that many of these rare volumes were ordered at the special request of the professors for their research.

Descriptions of some other libraries may prove helpful in visualizing the Wittenberg collection and facilities.

> At Canterbury the library, built, as I have said, over the Prior's Chapel, was 60 feet long by 22 feet broad; and we know from some memoranda written in 1508, when a number of books were sent to be bound or repaired, that it contained sixteen bookcases, each of which had four shelves. I have calculated that this library could have contained about 2,000 volumes.[78]

The library at Clairvaux was described by the Queen of Sicily on July 13, 1517, as follows:

> This library is 189 feet long by 17 feet wide. In it are 48 seats *(bancs)* and in each seat 4 shelves *(poulpitres)* furnished with books on all subjects, but chiefly theology; the greater number of the said books are of vellum and written by hand, richly storied and illuminated. The building that contains the said library is magnificent, built of stone and excellently lighted on both sides with fine large windows, well glazed, looking out on the said cloister. . . . The said library is paved throughout with small tiles adorned with various designs.[79]

Similarly, a library of 3,132 volumes, 1,756 of which were large old manuscripts, could be housed in a room 60 by 35 feet. The *alte*

Hofstube, then, from 1536 to 1547, must have provided comparable space, conveniently located on the second floor of the south wing of the Castle, well lighted by the five large Gothic windows which may be seen in the woodcut of 1611.[80] Probably the windows were the same "bull's-eye glass" as in the Melanchthon and Luther studies, for the Elector provided the materials for all of these structures.

Although no descriptions of this library are extant, a number of references infer that it was quite as attractive as the other rooms of the Castle. Spalatin in a letter to Aldus Manucius in Venice in 1512 wrote that the Elector was "adorning" his new "University at Wittenberg with a fine library replete in all fields." [81] Conrad Mutianus Rufus, who had formerly studied in Italy and was now the canon at Gotha, even used the superlative *ornatissime* in describing the new humanistic library which the Elector had just opened in Wittenberg.[82] In a letter found in the Kolde collection of *Analecta Lutherana* Spalatin proposed to the Elector that portraits of a number of prominent educators be hung in the University Library.[83] Although there is no evidence that the project was undertaken, it indicates the probable environment of the University Library. Other correspondence of the time speaks of a large globe to be installed in the University Library.[84]

As for the library furniture, there are occasional references to "desks and benches as well as chains for the valuable works." A general reference to library furnishings is implied in a letter from Elector John Frederick to George Spalatin, October 12, 1536:

> It is correct that the 100 gulden for the buying of books for the University Library are to be taken from the foundation funds. In the future someone is to be employed who will look after the library, opening and closing it daily, as soon as it has been moved into the *alte Hofstube.* Spalatin is still to be the superintendent buying the books for the 100 gulden set aside annually and send them there. He is also to visit Wittenberg twice a year to look things over. Furthermore, in case the ordered rods and chains have arrived from Nuernberg, he is to see that the library is equipped with them. Before doing this, however, he is to take the route by way of Torgau and discuss the matter with the Elector of other things needed.[85]

Even though this reference is not very specific, the fact that Spalatin was to stop off in Torgau before purchasing additional supplies implies purchases of major proportions. The "other things needed" probably refers to furniture. This reference likewise indicates that Elector John Frederick was genuinely interested in equipping his library with the most modern furnishings from the cultured center of Nuernberg. In order that the library might be managed in an orderly way, the Elector insisted that a record be kept of all "incomes and expenditures." Two old catalogs of books, prepared by the new librarian, Christopher Nicolas, under George Spalatin's direction, are still preserved in Jena.[86] All the references to the library, therefore, seem to indicate that it was well equipped and suitably housed in a spacious, artistically decorated room.

The confusion of names by which the library was known obscures the exact ownership of the volumes. Sometimes it was called the "Ducal Library," again the "Library in the Castle at Wittenberg," or the "University Library," implying several different kinds of ownership. When Elector John Frederick was defeated at Muehlberg in 1547, he claimed the collection as his own private property.[87] From his captivity he ordered Edenberger, the librarian, to take the 3,132 books from Wittenberg to the cloister library in Weimar. This was done, but they were never unpacked. In 1549 the Elector ordered the books taken to Jena to form the nucleus of a library for the new university which he had decided to found there, since he had lost the one in Wittenberg through the Wittenberg Capitulation, May 19, 1547.[88]

Time and space will not permit a detailed exploration of this question. Suffice it to point out that the Electors had not always taken this position. In the *Fundationsurkunde fuer die Universitaet* (1536), by which Elector John Frederick reorganized the whole University into a real Lutheran institution, the library was regarded as university property.[89] The 100 gulden set aside for the purchase of new books was from the university budget. A university professor served as librarian and was paid a regular salary by the University. But the whole University of Wittenberg was the Elector's private institution. Perhaps the best answer to the question is found in Mylius' discussion of the purpose of the founding of the Castle Library:

> Elector Frederick III, rightfully and deservedly called "The Wise," laid the foundation for this library. After the Elector had founded

the University of Wittenberg in 1502 with great liberality of spirit and at great expense, having received expert advice, and had put distinguished and excellent doctors on its faculty, he was further solicitous that a fine collection of books be purchased, which could not only be of service to the Elector privately but would also be useful to the scholars of the University whose private supply of books was curtailed or at any rate insufficient.[90]

The Wittenberg faculty had considerable influence in building up the new ducal library. Melanchthon, especially, was frequently consulted in the selection of new books and recommended many worth-while purchases. It is highly possible that he discussed these purchases with Luther and other professors. In 1533 Melanchthon wrote a letter to George Spalatin urging the purchase of more research materials:

> Oh, that our plan for buying a variety of books would seem worth while to the Prince! For I have heard that the Prince wishes that only theological and native works be purchased, yet I recall in discussing this matter in correspondence with the Prince to have read this remark that a variety of all kinds of Latin and German works should be bought.[91]

The request must have been granted, for many rare and unusual volumes were purchased. Not even the annual fairs at Leipzig and Frankfurt am Main could supply the need. On February 11, 1533, Spalatin wrote his Prince that the books desired by the Wittenberg faculty were not to be found in German lands.[92] In 1539, at the Elector's request, Spalatin went to Venice to buy Hebrew and Greek manuscripts. Mylius says Spalatin made a number of trips to Venice to buy additional manuscripts.[93] It is quite possible that this need for manuscripts was made necessary by Luther's translation of the German Bible and subsequent editions. It may be gathered from some of the remarks by Spalatin that the Castle Library was much frequented by both the students and the faculty.

In conclusion, it seems evident that the Castle Library was regarded as the property of the Electors as were the college buildings; but it was also the University Library, an integral part of the institution and available to student and faculty. The type and content of the many volumes purchased show that the Prince intended them for the use of the University.

Professor Walter Friedensburg, after analyzing the Gotha records of Spalatin's early purchases as the superintendent of the library, made the following observation:

> More remarkable than the number of books purchased (153), or the price ($3,000), is their content. Here we search in vain for Aristotle, and only now and then we encounter a Scholastic. They disappear almost entirely amid the number of editions of the Church Fathers. There is also a Bible with a common glossary. A long list of classical authors also appears in the list, as well as some works during the first Christian centuries. Nor is there a lack of grammars and dictionaries. In the collection were also writings by the Humanist Marsilius Ficinus, Aeneas Sylvius, Angelus Politianus, Leo Aretinus, Picus of Mirandula, Laurentius Valla, Reuchlin, and Erasmus. Finally, among them are also legal, historical, medical, and astronomical works. There was also an itinerary to the Holy Land. With these works a solid foundation had been laid for the library, on which Spalatin could build, aided by others through the coming years.[94]

The Renaissance influence, with its stress on the Humanistic languages, Latin, Greek, and Hebrew, became increasingly evident in the future purchases. But who advised the young institution in this choice of books? According to Dr. Georg Berbig this guiding spirit was Mutian, the leader of the Erfurt circle at Gotha. It was he who made the contact for Spalatin with Aldus Manucius, the famous printer of Venice.[95] Christoph Scheurl of Nuernberg, a former Wittenberg professor, also informed Spalatin in 1512 where the works of the great astronomer John Regiomontanus could be purchased, then valued at a thousand Hungarian gulden.[96] The aged Polich von Mellerstadt, one of the afore-mentioned founders of the University of Wittenberg, located a work by Ptolemy. Correspondence between Spalatin and Hans von Dolzig indicates that the latter had searched the New Year's Leipzig Fair for certain volumes that the University needed.[97] Additional correspondence in 1515 with Aldus Manucius of Venice resulted in the purchase of additional Latin and Greek books.

It is an interesting coincidence that Martin Luther became a regular professor of the Wittenberg faculty the same year that the Elector founded the library in the Castle. A parallel analysis of the growth of the library and the development of the University of Wittenberg under his leadership is very interesting. Luther's study of Greek and Hebrew after 1514 caused him to mature very rapidly into a great Biblical exegete and by 1516 was beginning to affect Spalatin quite profoundly. As the University of Wittenberg was being transformed into a school in which Biblical Humanism was the key to theology, this change is reflected in the materials added to the Castle Library.

There is little information on the purchases made by Spalatin during the twenties. Mylius says that John the Constant, the successor of Frederick the Wise, was little interested in the library. In all likelihood the real reason was that the student enrollment had dropped so much after Worms in 1521, that the primary concern of the authorities was the perpetuation of the University. To this end the University was fully incorporated with the Castle Church in 1526 in order that there might be a stable source of income to meet the annual budget. In this connection Spalatin requested that surplus funds from the endowment be used to buy books at the three annual Leipzig fairs for the "library in the Castle at Wittenberg." [98]

In 1532, when John Frederick became the Elector, he displayed renewed enthusiasm for the University of Wittenberg. This Prince had formerly been tutored by Spalatin and had been reared in a Lutheran environment. True to his boyhood vows, he so completely reorganized the whole University between 1535 and 1536 that he might rightly be called the second founder. He was not satisfied to buy books occasionally as had been the former practice, but allocated one hundred gulden in the university budget annually for the improvement of the library. Additional libraries, such as those of the Franciscan Monastery and of All Saints' Church, were added to the already rich collection of the Ducal Library, and the entire library moved to better quarters in the *alte Hofstube*.

That the range of reading materials was considerably diversified may be surmised from scattered and vague references in the sources. All kinds of books were picked up in Frankfurt am Main and at Nuernberg, according to Spalatin's report in 1537. [99] On March 3, 1538, John Frederick suggested to Spalatin that the Augustinian Library in Grimma be added to the one at Wittenberg.[100] Upon the death of Duke George, May 23, 1539, Spalatin sought to obtain all of his collection, knowing it would contain the many treatises written by enemies of Luther. For this purpose the Court Preacher of the Duke's heir, Prince Henry, was commissioned to make the necessary contacts.[101] In 1541 there is reference to a Talmud which was not purchased because the price was considered exorbitant. Two years later the librarian requested that the Elector examine the libraries of Christof von Pappenheim and of the Margrave von Brandenburg while attending the Diet of Speyer to learn if they contained any desirable Hebrew volumes, and in that same connection there is reference to a rare globe measuring four yards wide with the 12 signs of the zodiac depicted thereon.[102] The Elector, however, considered the globe impractical for general library use and suggested that it be purchased by the mathematics department, where it would be of greater service.

The many casual references in the correspondence of the period indicates that Spalatin, Melanchthon, Chancellor Brueck, and possibly several professors were constantly on the alert for new collections, such as those of Duke George, Aurogallus, and Hassenstein, and that a close supervision was kept over the fairs at Leipzig and Nuernberg in the search for choice volumes. Spalatin even made several trips to Venice.

This, then, was the library which must have played a vital part in the whole Reform movement. Its contributions to that movement are difficult to measure; but when John Frederick removed these rare volumes from Wittenberg, as indicated by his instructions of July 13, 1547, from his camp in Bamberg, one of the most powerful factors of the movement was lost. The preceding year the University had lost Luther, now it was also to lose much of the literature which had been so vital to the whole Wittenberg movement. Although the University continued to grow in numbers, the motivating spirit began to decline rapidly, especially after Melanchthon also passed from the stage in 1560, and the whole Reform movement fell prey in many parts of Germany to the Catholic Counter Reformation.

« 8 »

The University of Wittenberg

IT WAS IN THE ENVIRONMENT pictured in the previous chapter that the Elector of Saxony, Frederick the Wise, located his new University in 1502.[1] The exact reasons for the foundation are not altogether certain, but certain factors seem to have influenced the Elector in his decision to found another German university. Emperor Maximilian I had made an appeal to the German princes at the Diet of Worms in 1495 in the interests of higher education. Southwestern Germany could already boast of the five universities of Mainz, Heidelberg, Tuebingen, Freiburg, and Basel. Bavaria had its Ingolstadt, and Albertine Saxony took pride in two universities, Leipzig and Erfurt.[2] Frederick the Wise, Elector, *Erzmarschall*, and *Reichsvikar*, on the other hand, could claim no institution of higher learning in his lands, and it seems perfectly natural that the political and cultural center of the Elector's own *Kurkreis* should be chosen as the site for the new University.

As indicated in the letter of foundation from Emperor Maximilian I, the University of Wittenberg was to be a typical medieval institution modeled after such schools as Paris, Prague, Tuebingen, and Leipzig, with similar privileges, honors, immunities, favors, and concessions.[3] Like other similar institutions, the University of Wittenberg was also to be a separate corporation subject only to the Elector of Saxony. The University was granted complete control over the life of its students, and only in criminal cases, after conviction by a grand jury trial, could a case of student discipline be taken over by the State. The local police were not permitted to enter any of the university dormitories without the special permission of the Rector of the University. The faculty members were

254

classified as *potentia cives*, potential citizens exempt from most civil obligations. Only in very exceptional cases were they taxed. The university corporation also had certain hunting, fishing, and sportsmen's rights. As will be shown later, the faculty was well paid, lived on a scale comparable to that of the wealthy businessmen, and was held in high esteem by the whole community.

As shown by the *Album Academiae Vitebergensis*, the record of the university matriculations, the University of Wittenberg during the first half of the sixteenth century was not a large school.[4] Since students registered only once, the university record does not reveal exactly how many students were in the University in a given year. The first few semesters show a heavy enrollment: 416, 258, 132, and 158, respectively.[5] The majority of these students came from the Saxon lands from an area of about a hundred miles radius, but there were students from all over Germany and even a few from foreign countries. By 1507 the faculty was becoming concerned about the drop in student enrollment; but as Martin Luther's reputation as a reformer began to spread from 1517 to 1521, the enrollment increased rapidly. The peak was reached when 552 students registered at the University.[6] When Luther made his courageous stand at Worms and was subsequently condemned by both the Emperor and the Catholic princes of Germany, the enrollment quickly fell. In a few years it had fallen to around a hundred students, and it was not until a Lutheran Church had been organized with its own instruction of the youth that the University recovered from the blow. Again from 1535 to 1536, when Elector John Frederick reorganized the University of Wittenberg into a Lutheran university, the matriculations increased. During the last decade of Luther's life the enrollment had climbed from less than four hundred to a peak of eight hundred. After Luther's death there was a gradual but steady decline. The University in Luther's day, therefore, was never very large. George Spalatin, who visited the University in 1520, reported that he had seen 400 students in one of Luther's lectures, while some 600 attended the lectures of Philip Melanchthon in the College of Liberal Arts.[7]

Academic Organization

The University of Wittenberg, modeled after Paris and the German universities, was composed of an undergraduate College of Liberal Arts and the three graduate schools of Theology, Law, and Medicine.[8] At the head of the institution was a Rector, who was elected each semester by the faculty from its ranking members. According to the university records, of the 84 rectors who served during the years from 1502 to 1546, 62 were selected from the ranking professors, the Masters and Doctors of the four colleges. The rotation was also somewhat, regular; for during this period 21 were from the field of Theology, 21 from Law, 17 from Medicine, and 17 from Liberal Arts. Although many of the other rectors remain unidentified, there is occasional mention of a young instructor like Bernhardi, who was Rector when the problem with Rome became unusually acute in 1518. The real authorities in the University were the four deans of the respective colleges. These, although re-elected from time to time, often served for a number of years. As the *Liber Decanorum* shows, Luther was dean of the Theological Seminary from the time of its reorganization in 1535 to his death in 1546.[9] It is strange to note that Luther never served as Rector of the University. Perhaps the explanation lies in the fact that the faculty wished to spare him from this post for other more important duties, which by 1536 had become so arduous that the Elector did not even require of him a specific teaching program, but gave him special permission to arrange his courses to suit his own convenience and interest.

The University of Wittenberg had a small teaching staff. The *Rotulus of 1507*, prepared under Rector Christoph Scheurl of Nuernberg, names 37 members on the faculty: 21 in Liberal Arts, 8 in Canon and Civil Law, 3 in Medicine, and 5 in Theology.[10] But of this teaching staff, especially after it became reorganized under Luther's leadership in 1518, only 22 were regular faculty members; the rest were graduate students serving as instructors and assistants while completing advanced degrees, as Martin Luther had done between 1508 and 1509 while working on his Bachelor's degree in Theology. In a general way this arrangement continued until 1536, when the University was again completely reorganized. These new regulations provided for 22 professional chairs: 4 in Theology, 3 of which were Doctors and one a Licentiate; 3 in Medicine, 2 Doctors and 1 instructor; 4 in Law, 2 Doctors and 2 instructors; and 11 in Liberal Arts, the ranking of which was not stated.[11]

Whether this arrangement continued after the Wittenberg transfer to the Albertine line under Elector Moritz is impossible to establish because of lack of sources. Grohmann seems to think that Luther was not replaced in Theology and that Hebrew was taught by one of the theology professors.[12] Under August, in 1580, the Theology Department of the University was again enlarged to four regular faculty members, while an additional professor was employed to teach Hebrew and considered a part of the Theology Department.[13] The College of Medicine was also given a faculty of four, for this branch of graduate work had been placed on a very scientific basis providing courses in anatomy and actual dissection of human bodies.[14]

THE ENDOWMENT OF THE UNIVERSITY

Usually there is a very close correlation between the financial resources of an educational institution and its standard of excellence as an institution of higher learning. Casual mention has been made of the financing of the University of Wittenberg, and a more detailed examination will add further information on the high achievement of the institution. On the basis of the financial reports and fiscal regulations of the University, preserved in the archives of the Saxon princes, the manner in which the Castle endowment was converted into a source of income for the University of Wittenberg may be established. There were three acts of incorporation, in 1507, 1526, and the final one in 1536, which influenced most deeply the organization of the University.[15]

Before such a study can be appreciated, the relative buying power of sixteenth-century money must be ascertained. Naturally, there is a wide variance of opinion as to the value of different *media* of exchange. A good introduction to this problem may be found in Preserved Smith's *Age of the Reformation* in the chapter on "Wealth and Prices." [16] He points out that the total wealth of

Europe increased 128 times between 1514 and 1914, and goes on
to say:

> It is impossible to say which is the harder task, to compare the total
> wealth of the world at two given periods, or to compare the
> value of money at different times. Even the mechanical dif-
> ficulties in the comparison of prices are enormous. When we read
> that wheat at Wittenberg sold at one gulden the scheffel, it is
> necessary to determine in the first place how much a gulden and
> how much a scheffel represented in terms of dollars and bushels.
> When we discover that there were half a dozen different guldens
> and half a dozen separate measures known as scheffels, varying
> from province to province and from time to time, and varying
> widely, it is evident that great caution is necessary in ascertaining
> exactly which gulden and exactly which scheffel is meant.[17]

After this preliminary precaution, considering such problems
as quality of goods, fluctuations of coinage, and other factors,
Smith concludes that

> an ounce of gold was, in 1563, let us say, expected to do about ten
> times as much work as the same weight of precious metal per-
> formed in 1913.[18]

This is probably a conservative estimate, as some writers regard
the relative buying power of money in Luther's day to have been
twenty-five times that of our period.

When Professor Friedensburg published the *Urkundenbuch*,
he introduced the monetary references with a footnote stating that
all references in the university records were to Rhenish gulden,
subdivided into twenty-one groschen.[19] The intrinsic gold would
make content of this coin $1.34 as of 1563, with a buying power of
about $13.40 in terms of 1913 values.[20] But, in the evaluation of the
university finances the problem of fluctuation must also be taken
into consideration. Before evaluating a professor's salary or a
budget expenditure, the specific year must be considered, 1507,
1526, or 1536, the three years in which basic changes were made
in the institutional finances. To simplify this problem, all future
references will be based on the Rhenish gulden of 1536 with a
buying power of $13.40, the most nearly accurate valuation. These
sums compare very conservatively with similar costs today: poor
students could attend the University of Wittenberg an entire year

for 25 gulden, or $335; ministers' sons for 30 gulden, or $402; while the nobles paid 40 gulden, or $536.[21] Luther in recording his property in 1542, evaluated his pigs at one gulden each and cows at 3 gulden per head. A price of $13.40 does not seem exorbitant for a full-grown hog, and a cow was certainly worth $40.[22] (This standard of values of 1913 is used throughout the book.)

When the University of Wittenberg was finally completely reorganized into a Lutheran university in 1536, a definite budget was established. Salaries of seven of the faculty were still paid from the funds of the highly endowed Castle Church, and an additional budget of $47,220 was set aside to meet the remaining expenses. According to the statutes the grand total of the annual budget was $55,440.[23]

Wittenberg was a medieval institution financed in a manner quite strange to us today. In the begining the faculty was paid largely from Frederick's own income, but when finally organized, the enormous reserves of the Castle Church provided a source of stable income. This unique arrangement merits closer observation.

When the first Castle Church was built to house the famous "thorn of Christ," Electors Rudolf I and Rudolf II set aside an adequate endowment to provide for the remuneration of a number of clergy serving the *Stift* in various capacities. According to Grohmann, this Wittenberg *Stift* had under its control 18 villages, 2 woods, and 3 priories, each of which was obligated to make a definite annual payment in money or kind to the church.[24] Elector Wenceslaus made further additions, the total properties of the *Stift* being 30 villages, 3 priories, 2 woods, and 1 chapel.[25] At one time the number of vicars, chaplains, canons, choir boys, and other retainers supported through these rich endowments totaled 81.[26] Under Wenceslaus the feudal document of the *Stift* stated exactly how much rye, chickens, meat, or coin each of the pieces of property or villages was obligated to pay annually to the endowment of the Castle Church. The following examples from Grohmann will serve as an illustration:

1. Nymik: 12 bushels of rye and 12 bushels of barley.
2. Bergzow: A tax of one-half Neuschock, about $19.20.

3. Swisiko: Tax of one-half Neuschock, 4 gute groschen, total of $21.66; two houses donating one tenth meat; five farms with a tax of 16 gute groschen ($10.24); and two young chickens.

4. Bomolau: 24 bushels of rye.

5. Bietegast: 13½ bushels of rye; 13½ bushels of wheat; and 27 bushels of oats.[27]

At the time the University of Wittenberg was founded in 1502, thirty towns were paying similar annual dues in money or kind. To these Frederick the Wise added seven parishes at the time of the incorporation with the University in 1507, and this arrangement continued throughout Luther's lifetime. In 1567 Elector August enlarged the endowment by adding three more towns, making the grand total of 33 villages, 7 parishes, 3 priories, 2 woods, and 1 chapel.[28] In reality, the secularization of these endowments was a slow process. Changes were made in 1526 and again in 1536, but even at that late date seven members of the Wittenberg faculty were still on the payroll of the Castle Church.[29] The 1536 statutes stipulated that as these men passed on, their incomes were to be diverted into the university treasury.

The university income, therefore, was both in money and in kind. One of the provisions reads: "All the incomes, whether in money or in kind, grains, geese, woods, and other necessities, usable or salable, which up to this time belonged to the University, shall remain incorporated in that way, with no exceptions."[30] This statement indicates that the former obligations of the towns, parishes, etc., continued after their incorporation with the University.

The annual income from these sources available to the University amounted to $34,318, which, together with the $8,220 paid the seven professors directly from the church funds, still lacked $12,902 of equaling the total university budget of $55,440.[31] The Elector wisely provided for the deficit by asking that certain cloisters in the regions of Saxony, Thuringia, and Meissen raise annually 500 gulden, 700 gulden, and 700 gulden, respectively.[32] When the finances had been completely reorganized, the annual income from all sources was $59,073 against an annual budget of $55,440.[33] This left a few thousand dollars surplus that might be kept in reserve for an emergency.

Since the officials of the Castle were not replaced upon their deaths, these sums were gradually added to the university treasury. As the amount thus increased, it was arranged that the income from the cloisters be proportionately decreased. In order that the income might be perpetually insured, the Elector further provided that in case of the possible loss of the Electoral circle and Wittenberg, the ruling prince should be obligated to continue the regulations whether of Frederick's own descendants or those of the Albertine line.

In 1547 his forebodings proved well founded, for the Electoral circle passed to Moritz, victor over John Frederick. Moritz, however, drew up new statutes the next year governing the university funds. From these new articles, drawn up at Torgau on January 7, 1548, may be noted that the incomes from the Castle Church endowment fund had risen to $36,722.[34] Nor do the additional sums provided for in the Statutes of John Frederick seem to have been met in the prescribed manner. The two cloisters of Pfiffl and Nauendorf formerly paid 800 gulden together, but an additional 861 gulden was coming out of the Electoral treasury. Moritz provided that the 861 additional gulden be paid by the *Stift* at Altenburg. The total provisions of Duke Moritz provided for a sum of $58,979, slightly less than that arranged by John Frederick in 1536.[35]

The new Elector, Moritz, was mortally wounded in the Battle of Sievershausen and died July 10, 1555. His successor, August (sometimes called "the Second Founder"), virtually re-established the University by reorganizing the whole plant and building the *Augusteum* with its accommodations for the 150 scholarship students.[36]

In Dresden, October 23, 1555, August the Benevolent gave the University a new set of Statutes. In these the incomes of the Castle Church were still the same, but the 861 gulden required of Altenburg in the Statutes of Moritz had shrunk to 600 gulden. The 800 gulden furnished by Pfiffl and Nauendorf was shifted to the cloister of Brehna. The new total amounted to but 4,132 gulden, 9½ groschen, 4 pfennige, or a total of $55,370 in modern money.[37] No doubt the difference lies in the fact that Luther's chair was not filled after his death. The Statutes specifically state that only two men are to teach Theology in addition to the Town Pastor. This arrangement of 1555 seems to have been effective until a new reorganization of the University in 1569.

Elector August then gave the University of Wittenberg a second set of Statutes, which made the additional provision for the 150 scholarship students soon to be housed in the new *Augusteum.* Though these new Statutes are not specific in many of their clauses, the university records of the year immediately following (1569–70) indicate that a total income of $79,274 was provided, while the disbursements for the year were $75,745, leaving a surplus of $3,529.[38] Since the date for the 1-to-10 ratio of the relative buying power of 16th century and modern money is 1563, the figures in the 1569 Statutes should be used for all comparisons.

THE INCOME OF A WITTENBERG PROFESSOR

There is no specific information on the faculty salaries and incomes at the University of Wittenberg during the formative years. By 1536, however, the records are fairly complete. The Electoral *Statutes of 1536* provided for the following faculty salaries when translated into American monetary values:

I. *Theology:*

Luther	$4,020
Melanchthon	4,020
Jonas (from university funds)	1,350
Cruciger	2,680
Bugenhagen (plus pastor's salary)	804

II. *Medicine:*

C. Lyndeman	1,720
A. Schurpf	2,010
Instructor (S. N.)	1,072

III. *Law:*

H. Schurpf	3,350
Embden	4,020
Instructor (S. N.)	1,876
Instructor (S. N.)	1,340

IV. *Liberal Arts:*

Greek	1,340
Hebrew	1,340
Latin	1,073
Mathematics (2 each)	1,073
Physics	1,073
Rhetoric	1,073
Albertus Magnus (Lesen)	1,073
Pedagogi (2 each)	536

V. *Other Officials:*

Notary	670
Business Manager	804
Beadles (2 each)	268
Speiser	536
Preacher of Castle Church	1,073
Famulo Collegii	201
Reader at Table	134 [39]

In addition to the faculty salaries, the university budget also provided for a few scholarship students who served as *Koraulles,* or choristers, in the Castle Church. There is also the mention of two janitors and an organ blower. Some 120 gulden of the budget each year was paid to poor students.

For a study of the incomes and living conditions in a 16th-century university an examination of the university budget and the salaries of the faculty is not sufficient. Other factors, such as tax exemptions, gifts from royalty and friends, including gardens, farms, building materials, and other tokens of appreciation must be considered.

Grohmann classifies the Wittenberg professors as *potentia cives,* potential citizens, exempt from all but a few of the taxes and duties of the active citizens, *actu cives.*[40] An Electoral communication of Oct. 15, 1525, confirms this observation, for it exempts the Wittenberg faculty from all forms of city taxes except "fishing, table, and watchman" taxes, unless the professor had more than one home, in which case he paid the regular tax on his additional property.[41] Faculty members were required to keep themselves and their villages in constant readiness for war, a common 16th-century practice. The customary tenth tax on drink was exempted in the case

of faculty members, as long as such beverages were used exclusively
for the home. Only in exceptional cases were faculty members
asked to contribute to the National Tax, or *Landessteuer*, such as
the Turkish taxes of 1523, 1542, and 1565.[42] A letter to the *Rath*
of the University of Wittenberg, March 21, 1542, exempts Luther
from this general tax, though the Reformer's property was assessed
and the report sent to the Elector.[43] This exemption may later have
been extended to the rest of the faculty, for the Wittenberg records
of this same year give the names of 26 faculty members with a note:
"Exempt; university members are not taxed." [44] In that event,
however, there would have been no necessity for a special letter
regarding Luther. The sources are not clear on this point. Perhaps
somewhere an unpublished letter holds the key to this question.

The Electors were especially benevolent toward their favorite
professors. The old court physician of Frederick the Wise, Polich
von Mellerstadt, was given a nice house on the *Markt*, referred to
in a previous connection. Luther and Kathie were presented with
the Black Cloister as a wedding gift, which, when one learns that
it sold for 3,700 gulden when the University bought it back from the
heirs in 1564, was no mean present.[45] This was probably a bargain
price, as Luther himself evaluated it at 6,000 gulden for the *Tuerkensteuer* of 1542.[46] An old Weimar record (June 6, 1535) shows that
Melanchthon's house was remodeled by the Elector at his own
expense and that a garden at the rear was presented in addition
to this beloved professor. When Luther bought the Zulsdorf farm
from Kathie's brother in 1540 for 610 gulden, the Elector paid 600
of the amount from the Electoral treasury and, in addition, furnished Luther the building materials for improving the farm buildings.[47] It was customary for the Wittenberg professors to send
copies of newly printed books to the neighboring Protestant princes,
who in turn presented handsome gifts as tokens of appreciation.
Doubtless, many of the "rings, chains, gift coins," referred to in
Luther's second will originated in this way. Many of these are now
on display in the Luther House, and the visitor will be impressed
by their number. Then there were also minor gifts, such as table
cloths, wine, wild boars, deer, and other gifts, provided by the
Elector for festive occasions, of which there is frequent mention
in the Luther correspondence. The court apparently furnished the

Wildpret, wild game, for the weddings of Agricola, Melanchthon, Jonas, Bugenhagen, Luther, and other professors, as well as for many a doctor's promotion. Then, too, appreciative princes favored Luther and other Wittenberg professors with special gifts of money. In 1520 Luther received 100 gulden as a legacy from Henry Schmidberg, the Bishop of Naumburg. Henry VIII of England gave him 50 gulden in 1535, and the King of Denmark gave Luther a 50-gulden-per-year pension in 1546, following, perhaps, the precedent set by Luther's own Elector in 1541, when John Frederick set aside 1,000 gulden as an endowment fund from which Luther received a pension of 50 gulden per year. Another letter to the Wittenberg tax collector, January 26, 1536, shows that Luther was given 100 cords of wood per year and 150 bushels of grain as well as "two malts." [48]

Another source of faculty income was from disputations and declamations in which faculty members were asked to participate. An examination of Paragraph 191 in the *Urkundenbuch* will reveal that the Elector set aside 3,695 gulden for this purpose alone.[49] From this fund Luther received 19 gulden 13 groschen for presiding over some 50 debates during the academic year of 1538–39. Small sums from student matriculations added to the incomes of certain faculty members. A third went to the Rector of the University, another third to the two beadles, and the remainder into the university treasury. The total matriculation fee was $3.27, making each portion $1.09. Student rents for housing added to the incomes of the *Reformatores* in charge of the dormitories as did the fines for absences from class or disputations. The Rector also received 5 groschen for each signature on an official document and some of the money received for the granting of degrees. These fees, which added considerably to the income of the University, were as follows:

Theology			*Medicine*	*Law*
Biblicus	$ 79.80	Bachelor	$116.16	$147.06
Sententiarius	81.04	Licentiatus	186.36	220.16
Formatus	13.40	Doctor	194.00	194.00
Licentiatus	160.20			
Master or Doctor	214.40			
Total	$548.84		$496.52	$561.22 [50]

These figures explain why Luther as a struggling student had to accept the 50 gulden from the Elector before he could receive the Doctorate.[51] According to Melchior von Osse's *Testament*, students also paid their instructors small fees for lectures until 1562, after which date they were gratis.[52] The law professors augmented their salaries somewhat by serving in the Electoral court, to which cases were submitted from all over Electoral Saxony.

It is interesting to ascertain the total income of one of these professors such as Luther. Information may be drawn from his correspondence, his two wills, a tax assessment of his real estate and livestock made by his own hand in 1542, as well as a "household account." On the basis of these materials Luther's yearly income and the total value of his estate shortly before his death can be established fairly accurately.

Luther's hospitality is a fact too well known to require mention here. The *Table Talks* and numerous letters in which he pleads the case of poor unfortunates are convincing evidence of his extreme liberality. Fortunately, Luther's generosity was well balanced by his thrifty and industrious Kathie, who took efficient charge of the gardens and farms, considering it not beneath her dignity to keep pigs, goats, cows, and even a fish pond. She also supervised the *Brauhaus*, though Luther seems to have preferred other beverages to Kathie's brew.[53] That Luther was not entirely impervious to personal gain may be gathered, however, by this letter to Spalatin of July 13, 1542, in which he writes:

> Although I, my Spalatin, care little (as Paul) for the necessities and delicacies of this life, as far as it concerns myself, yet I am married and, as Paul says, am a debtor to my family, for whoever neglects those of his own household has denied the faith and is worse than an infidel. I pray you, therefore, that you assert yourself in my behalf as you would rightly expect of me, so that I am not deceived, cheated or defrauded in the Elector's gifts (as I now suspect).[54]

In another letter the Reformer complains that his wood has been reduced from 100 cords to 60, which mistake was immediately corrected by an order from the Elector.[55]

Luther's regular income from the University varied. In 1525 he was receiving $2,680; in 1536, $4,020; in 1541, $4,690; and in the last year of his life his income, including the above-mentioned pensions, totaled $5,360. When the tax exemptions, the 150 bushels of wheat, the 100 cords of wood, and numerous other emoluments are added, his income in the later years of his life must have averaged five to six thousand dollars.[56] Whether because of his open-handedness or the heavy expenses of his ever large household, Luther's income was usually spent by the time the year was ended. Realizing this, the Princes, especially John Frederick, took care that Luther should have holdings in real estate that would amply provide for his old age. Luther's life is an exemplification of the Biblical passage "Seek ye first the Kingdom of God and His righteousness, and all these things shall be added unto you." Most of Luther's property, and he died a comparatively wealthy man, was received in the form of donations and gifts from the Princes and his many friends. In 1542, when his property was assessed for the *Tuerkensteuer*, Luther evaluated his real estate at 9,000 gulden, less a debt against it of 450 gulden.[57] In his second will he evaluates his books and jewels, including rings, chains, and silver and gold gift coins, at approximately 1,000 gulden.[58] Thus, the grand total of Luther's possessions must have been around 10,000 gulden or, roughly, $134,000.[59]

The largest donation that Luther received from the Elector was the Black Cloister, which alone Luther evaluated at 6,000 gulden. The next piece of property was the Zulsdorf farm, which Luther bought from Kathie's brother for 610 gulden, of which the Elector paid 600. The third was the *Brauer Haus*, which Luther bought for 430 gulden from a neighbor who left town. This house was but partly paid for at the time of the assessment and formed a portion of the 450-gulden debt. Luther expected his hired man, Wolf Sieberger, to live in this house until such a time as Kathie might require it if she outlived her husband. He probably surmised that the University would purchase the Black Cloister, as it would be much too spacious for Kathie alone. Another piece of property was the garden with its buildings just north of the Luther House and worth about 500 gulden. Here Kathie had her fish pond and kept the livestock when they were not on the Boos farm, which was rented from the Elector. Luther owned another small garden which he had turned over to his hired man and, hence, frequently referred to as *Wolfs Garten*. In 1544 Luther bought a hop garden for 375 gulden.

The following is a brief summary of Luther's possessions on the basis of his second will and the *Tuerkensteuer*.

1. Zulsdorf property with improvements (610 gulden) [$8,174].
2. Books and jewels, such as rings, chains, gift coins, etc. (1,000 gulden) [$13,400].
3. The Black Cloister (6,000 florin °) [$80,400].
4. Brauer Haus, "Brisger Cottage" (420 florin) [$5,628].
5. Wolf's Garden (20 florin) [$268].
6. The garden on the Swine Market where Kathie had the fish pond (cost 900 florin, valued at 500 florin) [$6,700].
7. A little farm and garden (90 florin) [$1,206].
8. 5 cows (15 florin) [$40.20 each].
9. 9 large calves (2 florin each) [$26.80 each].
10. A goat with two kids (2 florin) [$26.80].
11. 8 pigs (8 florin) [$13.40 each].
12. 2 "mother pigs" (5 florin) [$33.50 each].
13. 3 little pigs (1 florin) [$13.40].
14. 50 *Adde* (50 florin) [$13.40 each].[60]

The Pre-Lutheran Faculty

There has perhaps never been a body of men that varied more widely in line of thought or philosophy of life than a university faculty. Therefore, it is both dangerous and misleading to speak of the pre-Lutheran University of Wittenberg as being "dominated by a strong Humanistic flavor," or of its teaching staff as permeated by the *Via Antiqua*. The men who taught at Wittenberg were from all over Europe and represented every shade of thought from that of the most liberal poets to the most conservative theologians. Since only a decade is involved, the period before 1512 may well be characterized as a formative period in which no definite philosophy of life had yet been crystallized which dominated all the four colleges of the school. Perhaps it was for this reason that in this new environment Martin Luther was to find his opportunity to become the leader of the German Reformation.[61]

° The florin and the gulden were here used interchangeably.

In the *Rotulus of 1507* five men were listed as teaching in Theology, with one, John Staupitz, inactive because of outside monastic duties.[62] Yet, other information shows that no less than nine different men taught in Theology during the decade from 1502 to 1512 of whom very little is known except their names. Mantel, Herrgott, and Link are three of these, the latter was the dean of Theology at the time of Luther's promotion to the Doctorate.[63] Three others are directly associated with the Luther story: Polich von Mellerstadt, John Staupitz, and Jodocus Trutvetter.

Polich von Mellerstadt had been the former court physician of Frederick the Wise. He had gained quite a reputation in medicine as an expert on the deadly disease of syphilis, which was spreading rapidly through Europe because of the use of public baths.[64] Later he had turned to the study of theology, in which field he became a conservative, dyed-in-the-wool Thomist.[65] Although popular with the students, Mellerstadt does not seem to have been too congenial with the faculty, who may have resented his favors at the Court. Whatever the cause, during his incumbency, many able liberal, Humanistic spirits, such as Herman von Busche, Nicolaus Marschalk, and Petrus of Ravenna, remained but a short time at Wittenberg. These men with their strong Humanistic leanings could not harmonize their thought with Mellerstadt's narrow-minded, bigoted views.[66] In addition, his continued bitter personal quarrel with Wimpina of Frankfurt an der Oder was thoroughly disgusting to these more tolerant men.[67] One after another they withdrew from Wittenberg.

Another important member who was to serve on the Wittenberg Theological faculty for a brief time was Luther's old Erfurt teacher, Jodocus Trutvetter, also called "Doctor Eisenach" by the students after his home town.[68] He was widely read, a creative thinker and an able lecturer, but he was the only representative of the *Via Moderna* on the Wittenberg faculty. Since there were nine Thomists and Scotists, who represented the *Via Antiqua*, Trutvetter was rather a lone wolf.[69] Rector Christoph Scheurl, an equally liberal spirit from Nuernberg, was much impressed with the Erfurt professor.[70] But conditions at the new University were not in keeping with Trutvetter's scholarly interests, and he soon decided to return to Erfurt. With his departure the University of Wittenberg suffered a heavy loss; but, although it seemed as if the liberal cause in theology were lost, the seeds sown during these formative years were to bear fruit later on, for they paved the way for the later triumph of "Biblical Humanism" under Martin Luther around 1517.

John Staupitz, who became Vicar of the Augustinians in 1503, wielded a great influence upon the University and the whole German Congregation, as has been noted.[71] Upon the Elector's request, Staupitz brought many able students and teachers to the Wittenberg faculty, one of whom, Martin Luther, was to play a decisive role in the German Reformation. Upon his retirement from Wittenberg to devote his full time to the Augustinian Order, Staupitz's chair was filled by his more famous Saxon successor, Martin Luther.

The School of Law during this period had six regular professors, some of whom stayed but a brief time, such as Ambrosius Volland and his successor, Petrus of Ravenna.[72] The remaining four, all able men, served throughout the period and three of these for many years to come. Of these, Wolfgang Stehelin remained for 18 years, serving the University several times in the capacities of Rector and Dean.[73] The chair vacated by Volland and Petrus of Ravenna was finally filled by the well-known Reformation character Jerome Schurff. Staupitz was instrumental in bringing Schurff from Tuebingen to Wittenberg, where he served for 45 years and acted as Luther's legal adviser during the troublesome days of the Reformation. Friedensburg describes him as a "fluent and penetrating individual of great acumen."[74]

Another distinguished and highly interesting member of the Law faculty from 1507 to 1512 was the afore-mentioned Christoph Scheurl, a member of a wealthy *Kaufmannsfamilie* with considerable background and culture.[75] A capable organizer with original ideas, Scheurl published the *Rotulus of 1507*[76] during his term as Rector, patterned after the Italian custom of publishing the names of the teaching staff and courses offered during the semester. He also started the interesting old book recently photostated by Johannes Ficker of Halle and known as the *Liber Decanorum*, or *Book of the Deans*.[77] The University lost a capable member when

Scheurl left to take an important legal position in Nuernberg. The remaining member of the Law faculty was Henning Goede, a former Erfurt legal light who was faithful to Wittenberg from 1510 until his death in 1521.[78]

The Medical School does not seem to have been very successful during these formative years. In 1511 there were no candidates for promotion to the Doctorate, and students of the graduate school served as instructors. Mellerstadt also taught some courses in this school. He is listed in the *Rotulus* under *medicina extraordinarie*, with Symon Steyn and Thomas Eschaus under him, while Johannes Schwob is the only professor listed as *medicina ordinarie*. Two others, Johannes Schwabe and Dietrich Bloch, stayed but short periods.[79] The Medical School at that time did not compare very favorably with the later school, whose candidates were required to dissect human bodies before graduating as doctors.

The Liberal Arts College is more difficult to evaluate. Changes here were very frequent, with a number of young poets serving as instructors. Both schools of the *Via Antiqua* were well represented, Bodenstein von Carlstadt and three others under him representing the Thomists, Nicholas von Amsdorf and three others representing the Scotists.[80] On the other hand there were an equal number of Humanists. These included Herman von Busche, who had crossed the Alps with Langen to study in Italy.[81] But, as noted above, this liberal Humanist could not endure Mellerstadt's petty struggle with Wimpina and soon left in disgust. Another name which attracts our attention is that of Nicolaus Marschalk, one of the foremost Greek scholars of northern Germany.[82] In spite of much unpleasant opposition, Marschalk stayed at Wittenberg until 1505 and introduced the study of Greek. His commencement address in 1503 made a distinct impression on the student body by its Humanistic tone and frequent quotations from the classics. Unfortunately, "the standard-bearer of Hellenism" did not remain to see the result of his work. Marschalk did not have a competent successor until the versatile Melanchthon came to Wittenberg in 1518. In addition to those mentioned, there were a number of enthusiastic young poets, viz., George Sibutus, Ricardus Sbrulius, and Otto Beckmann.[83] It was to Beckmann that Melanchthon later dedicated his inaugural address, which left an impression similar to that of his predecessor, Marschalk.[84]

Humanism, then, received its first impetus in the school from von Busche, Marschalk, and Petrus of Ravenna and was ably championed after them by Scheurl, Trutvetter, Beckmann, and a number of the poets.[85] At no time was the student body minus this liberal influence. The very election of the liberal, progressive Scheurl, the epitome of the spirit of Italy, shows the strong influence of Humanism. Even the more conservative members of the faculty were being affected by the new spirit as evidenced by Carlstadt's *Distinctiones*.[86] The students looked upon the lecturer who quoted frequently from the classics as using the new polished Italian method, and many of the conservative Scholastics were beginning their addresses and publications with a quotation from some great writer among the Ancients. All of this shows the extent to which the new leaven was working.

Another index to the changed attitude of the pre-Lutheran faculty was the introduction of the newer Humanistic textbooks. Trebelius' *New Greek Reader* was introduced for the benefit of budding theologians, and Veranus' *New Grammar* was added upon Scheurl's suggestion to replace an older out-of-date medieval one.[87] In 1509 the poet Sibutus ordered the new edition of Aristotle's *de Anima*, just published by Johannes Argyropulos.[88] The demand for textbooks was so great that John Gruenenberg, who had set up a press in Wittenberg, could not supply them, and books were still printed at Leipzig and Erfurt.

It thus becomes evident that the faculty which had at first been extremely conservative was undergoing an evolution. The liberal-minded Modernists were joining forces with the Humanists to break the strangle hold of the *Via Antiqua*.

PART FOUR

The Emerging Reformer

« 9 »

Triumph of Biblical Humanism in the University of Wittenberg

MUCH HAS BEEN WRITTEN on the role which Humanism played in the German Reformation, but emphasis varies with the viewpoints of the expositors. Scholars have discovered that there were no less than a half dozen different kinds of Humanism, the common denominator of each being a *Heimweh,* or homesickness, for something in ages past.[1] In some cases the search was for some standard in classical antiquity or for certain Roman political virtues. In Conrad Celtis the return to the age of the *Urdeutschen* was very marked. Erasmus, Reuchlin, Luther, and Melanchthon, on the other hand, saw in the classical languages the *media* for the rebirth of primitive Christianity in all its pristine purity. For want of a better term they have often been called the "Biblical" Humanists. All those who sought for this truth contributed to the main stream of events, although their interests and motives may have varied widely. As good a summary of Humanism as has been written may be found in Huizinga's *Wege der Kulturgeschichte:*

> For us, who look back and judge things in terms of their later development, the gulf between the literary and Biblical Humanists seems much larger than it really was. The ideas which motivated both carry the same token even if the spirit of the one is less religious than the other. All their ideas are permeated with a homesickness for the old, original purity, for a striving for renovation through their activity. Whether this longing is directed to the old Christianity, or towards the superior, well-governed Rome of Cato or Scipio, or a purified Latinity, a perfected poetry, a rediscovered art, it is always striving for things of the past, a renovation, a restitution, and a restoration.[2]

275

QVI MALEDICT PRINCPI SVO MORTE MORIATVR EX.xxi

Conrad Celtis Presents His Amores to Emperor Maximilian

While Martin Luther was still a confused and bewildered monk in the Black Cloister at Wittenberg, Biblical Humanism was paving the way for his work as a Reformer. The writings of Erasmus, such as *Julius Excluded, The Praise of Folly,* and the Commentary to his *Latin Vulgate,* were all well-aimed blasts at the very foundations of Scholasticism and Aristotelianism, the bulwarks of an indifferent Catholic world. They also supplied a new measure of Christian values which the world had not possessed. The well-known *Letters of Obscure Men* made the whole institution of Monasticism the laughingstock of Europe and led to the gradual abandonment of many monasteries.[3]

Humanism also supplied the scholars of northern Europe with the necessary tools to rebuild the Christian Church. In 1509 the French Humanist Lefèvre d'Etaples published his *Psalterium Quintuplex,* which not only supplied the student a textual basis for exegetical lectures, but also offered them the most up-to-date commentary on the Psalms.[4] Lefèvre's commentary severely censured all those who trusted in human merits. He weighed critically the sacramental system of the Roman Church and also attacked the mere *Plappern* of the priests, a rote recitation of Latin prayers without regard to their meaning. Although Lefèvre always remained a good Catholic, as did Erasmus, the grace of God holds high place in all of his writings, which proved to be quite a stimulus toward Bible reading. Martin Luther, the young theological professor at the University of Wittenberg, used the Lefèvre *Psalterium Quintuplex* as the guide to his lectures on the Psalms. At Luther's request, Magister Johann Decker von Grunenberg, a fellow monk, reprinted the Latin Vulgate in a special student edition with wide margins and space between the lines for student notes.[5]

An even greater tool for the work of Martin Luther and the Wittenberg faculty was Erasmus' Greek New Testament.[6] The great Dutch Humanist became interested in this field after examining Lorenzo Valla's notes on the Latin Vulgate and observing how corrupt the Latin text had become. Following Lefèvre's publication of his works on the writings of Paul, Erasmus felt it was safe to publish the New Testament on the basis of the best avail-

able Greek manuscripts. In 1515 Erasmus arrived in Basel with a
whole collection of manuscripts to be used as the basis for the
new edition. The undertaking was given added impetus when
Froben, the great Basel printer, heard that Cardinal Ximenes of
Spain was also preparing a Greek New Testament for publication
in the spring of 1516.

Almost immediately upon its publication, Martin Luther used
Erasmus' new edition for his lectures on Romans.[7] In 1519 Erasmus
published a second edition of the Greek New Testament, as he had
discovered four additional manuscripts, on the basis of which he
made four hundred corrections in textual readings. It was this edition which Martin Luther used at the Wartburg in 1521 and 1522
for his translation of the Greek New Testament into German.[8] The
publication of Erasmus' Greek New Testament, therefore, became
the very foundation stone of Lutheran reforms. Without this tool
the work of the German Reformation would doubtless have been
greatly retarded if not frustrated. Paul Wernle sensed Erasmus'
contribution when he wrote:

> There can be no doubt but that something great and new had hap-
> pened, which declared war on Scholasticism and occasioned its fall;
> for Christianity was taken back more than a thousand years to the
> very time of the first expositors of the New Testament, yes, even to
> the building of the canon itself.[9]

What Erasmus had done for the New Testament, John Reuchlin, the greatest Hebrew scholar of his day, did for the Old Testament. Although a lawyer by profession, his study of the classical
languages, especially Hebrew, made him eminently well qualified
to publish his *De Rudimentis Hebraicis*, a combined grammar and
dictionary, which was invaluable for the Old Testament studies of
the Reformers.[10] This grammatical dictionary greatly simplified
the study of the Old Testament and provided a new scientific approach. The publications of Reuchlin were also of immeasurable
value to Luther in his exegetical work.

THE BUDDING BIBLICAL HUMANIST

Thus it is evident that, as with most great historical movements,
many minds and hands in various parts of Europe paved the way
for the work of Martin Luther. Biblical Humanism not only criti-

nis literulis tibi pingam ut et illo scribendi modo nõ careas. Oportet igitur omnium primum alphabeti uersum proponere sic.

th ſ r q z z p p a ſ n m m l ch c i t h z v h d g b a

ﬡ ﬣ ﬤ ﬥ ﬦ ﬧ ﬨ ﬩

Nunc constructionis uerborum exorsa pertexere studebimus.

פֶּרֶק vndecim habet uariationes.

פֶּרֶק־דֵם habet decem uariationes.

A Portion of John Reuchlin's Hebrew Grammar, De rudimentis Hebraicis, 1506

cized the abuses in Roman Catholicism, but also prepared the tools
with which the Wittenberg faculty began its work of reform. The
time was ripe for a Reformation when Luther began his lectures on
the Psalms. Martin Luther, the man, met the challenge of the time
and provided effective, albeit unwilling, leadership; and therein
lies his greatness. Hans von Schubert claims that Biblical Humanism had nothing to do with Luther's discovery of "justification by
faith"; that it was Luther's genius which penetrated the maze of
medieval theology to rediscover Paul's meaning of "justification." [11]
But it is likewise true, as Luther stated later in life, that in this
remarkable discovery he had but the "first inklings" of what Paul
really meant by his *justitia Dei*.[12] Luther did not fully understand
St. Paul until 1520; and in the meantime he wrestled with the problem of developing a whole new perspective of religion in which
justification, Christ, and Him Crucified, would occupy the central
place.

Those who would understand and appreciate Luther's theological evolution during these critical years from 1512 to 1520,
must bear in mind that he was brought up as a Roman Catholic.
Both of his parents were staunch, loyal supporters of the Roman
Church. Luther had been educated in Catholic schools; not for
just a few years, but all the way through the entire system to the
Doctor's degree in Theology.[13] Further, he had lived the life of
an Augustinian monk since 1505. No wonder he mentioned later
in life the difficulty of forgetting all this, for his Catholic training
had penetrated to the very marrow of his bones. True, his teachers,
especially at Erfurt, had been critical of Aristotle and had aided
him along the path to *Sola Scriptura;* but all of them had accepted
the fundamental assumptions of medieval theology.[14] The Gospel
of St. Paul was quite foreign to their thinking. None of them could
be called Biblical Humanists. From here on Luther had to travel
alone. In rediscovering the God of the Bible, Luther had to evolve
a whole new theology. It is not exaggeration to say that Luther
virtually "lifted himself by his own bootstraps" from one world
to another. He soon discovered that even Augustine was not a
safe guide.[15] Nor did Erasmus, Lefèvre, or their Italian contemporaries understand the great Apostle Paul, and, therefore, none
of them could help him.[16] It was one thing to establish the Bible

as the guide to the new religion; it was quite another to determine the currents which had swept the Roman Church from its original moorings. The rediscovery of the world of St. Paul and the spirit of early Christianity was a long and painful undertaking, for it required a mastery of Greek and Hebrew, the languages in which the original Bible had been written.

As has been observed before, Rommel's studies of Luther's marginal notes on the *Sentences* reveal that Luther knew but little Greek or Hebrew by 1511. As Meissinger, the student of Luther's early lectures on the Psalms and Romans, has shown, Luther was not even an accomplished exegete when he began to lecture in 1512 and 1513.[17] He followed the old medieval method of breaking down the text, giving first a crude word-for-word explanation of the Latin text called *Glossae,* and then a more detailed interpretation called *Scholia.* In these early lectures before 1517, Meissinger found little evidence of an improved methodology.

Luther probably did not begin to study Greek seriously until 1514.[18] No doubt he was aided by John Lang's knowledge of Greek and his rich classical library. In 1516, when Luther began to use Erasmus' Greek New Testament, he was still a novice; but as he matured through 1517 and 1518, his mastery of Greek and Hebrew became more apparent and with it, also, his understanding of the Bible. By 1520 Luther was developing into an able linguist, and this maturity is well reflected in the three major tracts written in 1520 and in his second lectures on the Psalms, which undertaking was interrupted by the summons of Charles V to appear before the Diet of Worms in 1521. Luther now felt ready to begin the translation of the Bible into German. The translation of the New Testament, *Das Newe Testament Deutzsch,* the first evidence of the mature scholar, was completed during his short stay at the Wartburg from the summer of 1521 to the spring of 1522.[19] Luther next began to translate the Old Testament, a colossal undertaking, finally completed in 1534.

As Luther thus matured into a Biblical Humanist, he rediscovered and recaptured the spirit of early Christianity. He was now capable of supplying the exegetical interpretations to determine in what respects the Roman Church had departed from the faith of the Fathers. Remembering his Roman Catholic background and training, his complete saturation with the teachings of the Roman Church, Luther's slow progress toward Lutheranism is readily understandable. He had begun to drift from the pale of the Roman Church as early as 1506, but he did not realize the full extent of his departure until the Leipzig Debate in 1519.[20] After this date Luther developed rapidly, yet it was not until the late twenties that he had matured fully as a Lutheran. Following the Marburg Colloquy and the Augsburg Confession, Luther realized that the building of a new Evangelical Christianity was the only solution to the problem of reforms.[21] Rome could not be persuaded from the error of her ways.

THE TOWER DISCOVERY

Although there is no longer any positive evidence, in all likelihood Luther began his work at the University of Wittenberg with a series of lectures on Genesis, 1512–1513.[22] This was the first of a series of sixteen lectures which he delivered during his professorship at the University from 1512 to 1546.[23] During this entire period he covered but thirteen books of the Bible. Usually he lectured only twice a week because of his many other additional duties. Already in 1511 he was appointed the official preacher for the Black Cloister. Soon after that he became subprior and the supervisor of the education of young monks as *regens studii*.[24] In 1514 he also began to preach in the Town Church, often several times a week. In one year alone he preached 170 sermons. In 1515 John Staupitz, as Vicar of the Augustinian Congregation of Germany, selected Luther as district vicar, in which capacity he was responsible for the welfare of ten or eleven convents in Meissen and Thuringia. How he found time to lecture at all is a mystery; in fact, he himself related later that he was so busy during the week that he had to neglect his *Breviary*, which forced him to lock himself up on Saturdays to make up the lost time.

In the summer of 1513 Luther was preparing his materials for the famous series of lectures on the Psalms.[25] For these lectures, which began August 16, 1513, and ended October 21, 1515, Luther used the best commentaries available. The *Psalterium Quintuplex* of the French Humanist Lefèvre d'Etaples, which Luther used with his own marginal notes, is still extant. The commentaries of Nicolaus of Lyra and Paul of Burges, and John Reuchlin's *De Rudimentis Hebraicis* also proved useful aids for the young theologian, although the latter work was still a little difficult for him to use at this time.[26] As already mentioned, Luther's methodology in these lectures was still typically medieval in form. All but two leaves of his *Glossae* has been preserved in the *Wolfenbuettler Psalter* and reproduced by Kawerau in the *Weimar Ausgabe*, III, of Luther's works. Likewise, two thirds of his *Scholia* was discovered by Franc Schnorr in what is now known as the *Dresden Psalter* and also reproduced in the *Weimar Ausgabe*, IV. His *Praeparationen*, or summaries of materials, are also still extant.[27]

As Meissinger has pointed out, however, it is perhaps impossible to recover the lectures which Luther actually delivered.[28] He doubts whether scholars have deciphered Luther's fine handwriting between the lines and on the margins correctly; and the student notes that have been preserved on Romans, Galatians, and Hebrews point to the conclusion that the *Glossae* and *Scholia* were not too closely followed by the versatile Luther when he began to lecture. He seems to have assumed that these notes were but mental aids in the presentation of his materials. The problem is further complicated in these early lectures by the fact that Luther apparently did not prepare the *Glossae* and *Scholia* to the various Psalms simultaneously. Rather, he seems to have worked out the *Glossae* to some thirty Psalms before beginning his interpretation in the *Scholia*.[29] This procedure makes it difficult to trace his development in doctrinal problems. The greatest care must therefore be used in tracing Luther's unfolding on "justification" in the Weimar text, remembering that Luther's materials were not meant for publication; rather, they were just a collection of notes for private use.

From the viewpoint of methodology, these lectures were very similar to those of other Wittenberg professors. In typical scholastic fashion Luther used the "chopping-up method," which left the students often completely confused. The text was presented as having a fourfold meaning: the literal, allegorical, tropological, and anagogical.[30] Luther, however, soon began to use contemporary illustrations and anecdotes to liven up the subject.

In the lectures on Romans, from November 3, 1515, to September 7, 1516, the *Glossae* and *Scholia* still remained, but their

Page from Luther's Lecture Notes on Romans 3:1-9, with marginal notes in Luther's handwriting. Presented to the author by Johannes Ficker of Halle, Germany

use was greatly changed.[31] The text was expounded largely on the basis of the grammatical historical method, while the interpretation became almost entirely spiritual. Allegory left the Luther classroom, even though it remained with him for a while in the pulpit. The emphasis on the original text as the only canonical one also became stronger. Luther did not hesitate to question the Spanish journey of St. Paul, or to evaluate Erasmus, Lefèvre, Reuchlin, and the Church Fathers on the basis of their own merit. In a public disputation with Carlstadt, Luther even questioned the authenticity of a commonly accepted book by Augustine on *True and False Penance,* even though Peter Lombard and Canon Law had accepted it as genuine.[32]

In the lectures on Galatians, delivered from October 27, 1516, to March 10, 1517, although Luther's own notes have not been discovered, the available student copies show some drastic changes in methodology.[33] The *Glossae* and *Scholia* had now been discarded. The four senses of Scripture were displaced by the literal and spiritual. Luther believed that neither the Fathers nor St. Paul used any other interpretation. The grammatical-historical method was now the accepted practice in his classes. The presentation also was much clearer, while at the end of each section there always appeared a kind of summary. The lectures on Hebrews, delivered from March 27, 1517, to April, 1518, reveal that Luther had developed still further.[34]

An even greater change than that of Luther's methodology was the content. When he began the series of lectures on the Psalms, his spirit was still quite medieval, but in 1514 and 1515 a great change came over him through what has been commonly called the great *Turmerlebnis,* or Tower Discovery. Luther wrote an account of this experience in his preface to the Latin edition of his works, the *Opera Latina I,* published in 1545, and this is his own story:

> In the meantime in the same year (1519) I had begun again to lecture on the Psalter, believing that with my classroom experience in lecturing on the Psalms and the Letters of Paul to the Romans, Galatians, and Hebrews, I was now better prepared. All the while I was absorbed with the passionate desire to get better acquainted with the author of Romans. Not that I did not succeed, as I had

resolved, in penetrating more deeply into the subject in my investigation, but I stumbled over the words (chapter 1:17) concerning "the righteousness of God revealed in the Gospel." For the concept "God's righteousness" was repulsive to me, as I was accustomed to interpret it according to scholastic philosophy, namely, as the "formal or active" righteousness, in which God proves Himself righteous in that He punishes the sinner as an unrighteous person . . . until, after days and nights of wrestling with the problem, God finally took pity on me, so that I was able to comprehend the inner connection between the two expressions, "The righteousness of God is revealed in the Gospel" and "The just shall live by faith."

Then I began to comprehend the "righteousness of God" through which the righteous are saved by God's grace, namely, through faith; that the "righteousness of God" which is revealed through the Gospel was to be understood in a passive sense in which God through mercy justifies man by faith, as it is written, "The just shall live by faith." Now I felt exactly as though I had been born again, and I believed that I had entered Paradise through widely opened doors. I then went through the Holy Scriptures as far as I could recall them from memory, and I found in other parts the same sense: the "work of God" is that which He works in us, the "strength of God" is that through which He makes us strong, the "wisdom of God" that through which He makes us wise, and so the "power of God," the "blessing of God," and the "honor of God," are likewise to be interpreted.

As violently as I had formerly hated the expression "righteousness of God," so I was now as violently compelled to embrace the new conception of grace and, thus, for me, the expression of the Apostle really opened the Gates of Paradise.[35]

This was the historic experience that changed Luther's whole life and profoundly influenced western Christendom. As early as 1516–17, while giving his lectures on Galatians, Luther referred to this as "a wonderful experience." [36] Again in 1519, when he published his *Commentary on Galatians*, he spoke of this same discovery as a "wonderful new definition of righteousness" for which he felt deeply obligated to St. Paul, who had given him new insight. Later, in the thirties, Luther told his table companions more details about the discovery of the meaning of *justitia Dei* which had given him the key to the whole Bible.

When and where did this unusual experience occur? When the Elector was having the walls and breastworks of Wittenberg strengthened in 1541, Luther became fearful that they would destroy his "*Stuebchen* in which he had stormed the Pope." [37] In the remodelings of the *Lutherhaus* of 1546 and 1586, on the southwest corner may be noted a square tower which has since been removed. In the wall of the southwest corner room on the second floor is evidence of a filled-in doorway which led to this room. Recent excavations by the keepers of the *Lutherhalle* (as it is called today) have established that the foundations of this former tower still remain at that corner.[38] This location also conforms to other evidence. Luther mentioned overlooking the Elbe River from this study. There is evidence that the room could have been heated, and Luther in a letter to Jonas, November 11, 1527, refers to his study as a *hypocaustum,* meaning a heated room.[39] In one of the *Tischreden* accounts this word is also used to refer to the place of the Tower Discovery. Luther was assigned this room when he was made a subprior of the Black Cloister, and scholars, therefore, feel almost certain that here was made the remarkable discovery which for him opened the "Gates of Paradise."

As to the time of the discovery, historians are not quite agreed. The afore-mentioned preparation of the *Glossae* and *Scholia* at different periods makes it difficult to establish the time with absolute certainty. When Luther talked with his table companions in the three accounts which have come down to us, his story differed slightly with reference to the details, but in substance he told the same facts. Luther was working on a Psalm in which there appears the expression "deliver me in Thy righteousness," which he says struck him with terrific impact. But this expression appears in both the 31st and the 71st Psalms and does not shed light on the problem of chronology. Boehmer, who tries to establish that the event occurred some time in 1513, believes Luther was working on the 31st Psalm at the time.[40] Vogelsang, however, feels that the content does not substantiate this interpretation. There is little evidence in the *Scholia* of the 31st or the following Psalms that any fundamental change had happened to Luther. But by the 71st Psalm a definite change was evident. And subsequent *Scholia* show that Luther had discovered the light, that Paul's message, "The just shall live by faith," had taken on a new meaning.[41]

Luther describes his experience in the *Tischreden* story of his Tower Discovery. He says he was weighing such expressions as "The just shall live by faith," "the justice of God," etc., when the thought flashed through his mind:

> If, through justification, we live by faith, and that justification is for all those who believe, then justification must be the result of faith, and eternal life must grow out of this justification.[42]

He then realized for the first time that justification did not presuppose some inner change in man, an inner healing, as had been formerly taught; now he knew it was something outside of man, the belief in Christ's atoning death, that liberated man from the bondage of sin and death. If this new light burst upon Luther when he was working on the 71st Psalm, as seems most probable, then the *Turmerlebnis* occurred some time in the fall of 1514.[43]

The question has been asked: What was so challenging about the lectures which followed the Tower Discovery? Luther threw light upon this query when he made the following observation in 1546:

> No one can hope to understand Virgil with his *Bucolics* (Shepherd Life) and *Georgics* (Husbandry) who has not been a shepherd or farmer for at least five years; no one can hope to understand Cicero unless he has participated in the activities of a large city for at least twenty years; and the Holy Scriptures no one has sufficiently studied who has not associated with the Prophets for at least a hundred years.[44]

In brief, Luther believes that one can understand a subject only when he is familiar with the field from personal experience. No one can understand the Bible unless he has had considerable religious experience. Intelligence and education may even sometimes be a hindrance. A simple-minded person who has experienced a great religious conflict may have a much better grasp of God's ways than the person who has never undergone any soul suffering or spiritual conflict. Luther did not mean to imply that the grammatical-historical method was not essential; but rather, that even after the text is fully explained, the real grasp of the inner message depends upon the individual's capacity to understand what the Bible writer is discussing. In this respect Luther had already far outstripped Lyra, Lefèvre, or even Erasmus. It was the spiritual conflict he had experienced from 1505 to 1514 that made it possible for Luther to grasp Paul's message even before he fully understood the key to Romans' "justification by faith."

In the Tower Discovery, Luther had obtained the key to the Scriptures. After 1514 there shines from his lectures the rich soul experience through which he understood St. Paul better than had been the case for a thousand years. The God of the New Testament, who had been lost in the maze of medieval fusion of pagan and Christian elements, was once more brought to the light of day. The Bible once more became Christo-centric, and Luther's lectures breathed the atmosphere of first-century Christianity.

A New Conception of Religion

While Luther's discovery of "justification by faith" was in one sense a sudden awakening, crystallized in his *Turmerlebnis,* the actual change which came over Luther was much deeper and involved a long period of time. Karl Holl states that Luther first had to undergo a complete change in his conception of God.[45] As he points out, the earliest manifestation of this change was Luther's dissatisfaction with his spiritual progress in the Erfurt monastery in 1507. The result was a complete re-evaluation of the Catholic conception of God examined in the light of the Church Fathers and of the New Testament, and a completely new orientation of religion in the light of the Gospel and the Epistles of St. Paul. The Tower Discovery, then, was not just an isolated experience, but the climax of a slow spiritual growth which in time developed Martin Luther into a Lutheran.

In New Testament Christianity, the Final Judgment is emphasized always in the light of God's mercy and grace; that He desires all sinners to come to the truth and finally to be saved. Jesus preached the same interpretation, namely, that the Son of Man did not wish that men should perish, but that they might have everlasting life. During the Middle Ages the idea of the Final Judgment was overemphasized until fear became the principal motif of the Church. It was no mere accident that Luther had thought of God as a "stern Judge sitting on a rainbow," for He was actually presented as such.[46] During the early centuries another idea from the Old Testament was fused with the concept of the stern Judge. The Jewish conception of God as a spiritual Being far removed from the ordinary mundane problems of man made Him seem even more remote; and it made the problem of rendering Him favorable to man all the more difficult.[47] This conception made the average man more dependent upon the magic of the sacramental system with its miracle-working priests. The ideas of "merit" and "satisfaction" date as far back as Tertullian, but the medieval Scholastics developed them to the full in a complete system of "work righteousness." [48]

As Luther, however, read the Church Fathers and examined the teachings of the Apostolic Church, he began to see that the answers to all his problems were found in God's Holy Word. Seeking to understand the God and the religion of St. Paul while preparing his lectures on the Psalms and Romans, a fundamental change gradually came over him. The God he found in the Bible seemed strangely new to him and very different from the God he had learned to know through Occam, Biel, and other Scholastic writers. As he slowly recaptured the spirit of the great Apostle Paul, a whole new viewpoint of religion began to emerge. The God of the New Testament was not a stern Judge; rather, He was a merciful heavenly Father whose innermost being was love, a God who loved the world with an infinite love that was beyond all human understanding.[49] The God of St. Paul did not wait for man to prove himself worthy of grace; He came and sought man even before man realized that he was a condemned and a lost sinner. This God sought to lift all men from their lost condition that they might live unto Him in righteousness. Even evil, according to the Bible, was under God's control, and ultimately it was made to serve His divine purpose. Nor was this God of the Bible far removed. Christ had spoken of making men's bodies His living temple. Paul spoke of a mystical union with Christ, He living in man and man in Him. Only after Christians became the temples of God, were they numbered among those who had been justified.

In Paul's Gospel of love there was no room for fear. God had built a bridge through which man could escape from sin and be saved. The key to the Gospel was God's promise of forgiveness to all those who believed in Christ's redemptive grace. Even God's wrath contained the ultimate purpose of turning men from their evil ways. Confession of one's sins was self-judgment, which brought men to the right, saving relationship to God.[50] Of course, God's forgiveness as revealed in the Scriptures was an incomprehensible mystery. Thus, in the place of the medieval concept of the Mass, with Luther there evolved an individual religion of the personal conscience, a *Gewissensreligion*,[51] in which the Christian lived in direct personal relationship with his God. It was out of this new understanding that Martin Luther finally grasped what Paul meant by the expression in Romans 1:17, "The just shall live by faith."

By the summer of 1515, when the series of lectures on the Psalms was drawing to a close, Luther rejoiced in his progress toward being able to understand the Bible. He retained the Catholic terminology of grace, faith, good works, justification, original sin, etc., but he was already giving them new life. Their meaning was beginning to change for him in the light of the Scriptures. When asked how man's sins are forgiven, he still answered in Scholastic language: Through the grace of God being poured into his heart. He was not yet clear on the *how*, but grace was no longer a supernatural medicine effecting a healing of the soul. Grace had become something spiritual and living, "the living, active Spirit of God." What does this work in man? Again Luther answered as a Scholastic: Makes man righteous, or justifies him. He no longer held the medieval conception, but believed a psychological mystery took place in man. In this justification there is a personal union with God, an ethical regeneration which expresses itself in a life of thankful service to one's fellow man.[52] Faith then becomes a trusting in God's favor, a trusting, waiting, hoping, in happy childlike certainty that God loves man and is well disposed toward him. What brought all this about? Luther answered: God's Word, the Gospel, which is with and under the Holy Spirit, effects this change in the soul. Luther regarded the soul as passive in all this until the effect of God's love brought about an inner change. It now becomes clear how in Luther's "New Theology" the Gospel took the central place, where in the former Scholastic theology the sacramental system had occupied first place.[53]

The Scholastic definition of "good works" had been: "Love the Lord, your God, with your whole heart and your neighbor as yourself." This was rationalized by a fine-spun line of reasoning which tried to justify self-love on the basis of God's own commandment. The word "neighbor" was explained in a clever gradation beginning with "self-love," and continuing with relatives, unknown people in need, and one's enemies. Luther now threw this whole interpretation overboard as not having a Scriptural foundation. "Loving your neighbor," Luther interpreted as meaning all men without exception, good or bad, friend or enemy. He would have nothing of the learned Scholastic rationalization of "Love." In fact, claimed Luther, the road to God began with a repudiation of oneself; and, in God's sight, of greatest import was the motive which prompted this love toward one's fellow man.

As Luther matured, he also began to understand that monasticism received no special recognition over other professions. A farmer or a businessman who does his work faithfully and lives up to his *Beruf*, or high calling from God, is equal to the priest in God's sight.[54] Each man, peasant or cleric, who helps his fellow man in Christian charity, is equally regarded by God's standards. In this Luther had far surpassed Tauler, Gerson, and other Mystics in their conception of man's *Stand*, or *Beruf*, the calling in which God had placed him in this world. Already in Luther there appeared much of the spirit of the later tract of 1520: *The Freedom of the Christian*. Already he believed that the Christian is a free lord over all things through faith, and a servant of all his fellow men through love. This latter servitude is of the highest freedom in that it owes nothing, receives nothing, yet always gives freely.

Luther's definition of the Church was also beginning to change. He saw it now as a spiritual body, even though the medium of the Gospel was still the Roman hierarchy. The Gospel now became its crowning glory, for only through the Gospel could the message of the Cross grow and flourish. Conversion was the key to membership in this invisible body. The fundamental conceptions of Luther's later definition of the Christian Church were already forming then, during his lectures on the Psalms and on Romans, but it took the trying years of 1517 to 1521 to bring him to the realization that the Roman hierarchy would have to be discarded as the vessel in which God's grace was brought to man.[55] As will be seen, this realization became one of the great driving forces of Luther as the Reformer.

LUTHER WINS THE WITTENBERG FACULTY

In the summer of 1514 a Benedictine monk, Paul Lange, was visiting the universities in central Germany to gather material for Trittenheim's *Schriftstellerlexikon,* a kind of *Who's Who* among German university professors.[56] That it might be all-inclusive, he even inquired about any *vir inluster,* or promising young instructors who might be expected to make important literary contributions. Strange to relate, even though Polich von Mellerstadt, according to Mathesius, had observed several years before that Luther would someday effect a Reformation of the whole Roman Church, Lange passed by Luther's door. In spite of Mellerstadt's evaluation, the fact that Lange did not even contact Martin Luther indicates that he was still regarded as a novice in academic circles. But according to the somewhat unreliable John Oldekopf, Luther's classes were already quite popular with the Wittenberg students as early as 1515. German university students were not required to attend specific classes, and, as a result, the lectures of the most popular professors were always best attended. Melanchthon says that even prominent citizens attended Luther's lectures. For example, the father of Chancellor Brueck, who happened to be living in Wittenberg at this time, walked several blocks, even though old and feeble, just to hear Luther's "consoling message on the Son of God." [57] Already by 1515 Luther's "New Theology" had made quite an impression on the Wittenberg student body.

Though still a young professor, Luther's dynamic personality must have attracted the attention and admiration of the older, more experienced professors. Luther was one of those individuals who just cannot restrain their enthusiasm when they have a mission to fulfill. According to Walther Koehler, after Martin Luther discovered justification by faith, he did nothing less than effect a Reformation of the entire University of Wittenberg.[58] The first evidence of Luther's unusual ability to draw others to him may be noticed in the reactions of a person of no less importance than the Vicar of the whole German Congregation of Augustinian Hermits. Luther had opposed John Staupitz in his attempted reforms of the Augustinian Order; yet, in 1511, when the Vicar vacated his Wittenberg professorship, he nominated Luther as his successor; and he continued to promote him in the Augustinian Order. There are, doubtless, many reasons why Staupitz did not follow Luther in his path as Reformer. It is likely that he chose the path of least resistance; or that, like Erasmus, he did not feel himself fitted for a martyr's role.

Luther's new Biblical Humanism was soon receiving attention from the Wittenberg faculty. John Lang, Luther's tutor in Greek, was drawn into theology by his contact with Luther. An intimate friendship sprang up between the two men, attested by their later voluminous correspondence after Lang's transfer to the Erfurt convent. Spalatin, Lang, and Luther became the triumvirate against Scholastic theology.[59] There was no important problem which Luther did not discuss with these intimate friends, and both Lang and Spalatin did all within their power to further the German Reformation, for their souls had been set on fire for the cause of the Gospel.

Like all German universities of the time, Wittenberg had a very strong Scholastic representation. Eight professors taught the *Via Antiqua* in 1505, four of whom were Thomists and four Scotists. After Trutvetter's return to Erfurt the *Via Moderna* was not represented. At the head of the Thomist group was Bodenstein von Carlstadt, with Lupinus, Reuter, and Beskau supporting him.[60] At the head of the Scotist group was the conservative noble Nicholas von Amsdorf, supported by Kannegiesser, Kuechenmeister, and Koenig.[61]

On September 25, 1516, Luther's pupil Bartholomaeus Bernhardi defended a set of theses opposing Scholasticism in a public disputation for the degree of *Sententiarius,* in which Professor Carlstadt and Lupinus provided the opposition.[62] Luther, who presided over the disputation, supported his candidate, while Amsdorf was inclined to agree with the opposition. Bernhardi had been so well trained by Luther in the Scriptural teaching on sin and grace that his attack made a very deep impression on the faculty. Lupinus was soon won to the new point of view, but convincing the head of the Thomists was quite another matter. On January 13, 1517, Carlstadt journeyed to Leipzig, where he purchased the complete works of Augustine so that he might gather additional evidence for his Scholastic position.[63] His subsequent discussions with Luther finally satisfied him that the *Via Antiqua* had misrepresented the theology of Augustine and was actually dangerous for the youth. Carlstadt now became an ardent exponent of the new approach, and in April, 1517, he posted 151 theses on the door of the Castle Church to expound the cause of the Gospel further with the rest of the faculty.

On September 4, 1517, Luther had a second student, Francis Guenther of Nordhausen, arraign Scholastic theology in a public debate.[64] Augustine's teachings on free will and grace were used to disprove the views of Scotus, Occam, D'Ailly, and Biel. The Scholastics were presented as false teachers holding views based on the heretic of Augustine's day, Pelagius. All the way through the discussion Luther's pupil stressed the importance of a correct inner attitude of heart in relationship to God.

In the meantime Nicholas von Amsdorf became attracted by Luther's Biblical Humanism, and before long the two became warm friends.[65] Amsdorf also became a warm supporter of the German Reformation. Although he had been an ardent champion of the Scotists, he now turned into a conservative Gospel preacher who did all within his power to further the cause of Luther's reforms. At Worms, Amsdorf was at Luther's side; and he was one of the traveling companions when Luther was suddenly taken from the carriage and spirited away to the Wartburg. It was in his *Probstei* next to the Coswiger Gate that Luther stayed during his brief visit to Wittenberg in 1521, at which time Lucas Cranach painted Luther in his disguise as *Junker Georg*. Upon Luther's request, Amsdorf became the pastor of Magdeburg in 1525 and, later in life, the Bishop of Naumburg. Even after Luther's death Amsdorf continued to defend Luther's theology. In Amsdorf Luther had won a real friend whose support meant much to the growth of later Lutheranism.

The two professors of the Law School, Schurff and Stahelin, were next won to Luther's point of view, as was Thiloninus Philymnus, a Greek and Hebrew instructor.[66] In 1516 his new convictions were published in *The Triumph of the Christian*.[67] The progress made by Luther and his supporters in the University is evident from Luther's correspondence with John Lang, who followed the movement closely after the Bernhardi debate. On February 8, 1517, Luther wrote:

> Nothing so inflames my feelings as that actor (Aristotle) who with his Greek mask mimics the Church. If there were but time, I should like to expose him and show his ignominy to the entire world.[68]

Luther was beginning to see that Scholastic confusion was in part due to the fact that Aristotle had been accorded such an important place in Catholic theology. In the September 4 debate Francis Guenther had included the thesis:

> It is false to say that without Aristotle one cannot become a theologian. The opposite is true, no one becomes a theologian unless it be without Aristotle, for the whole of Aristotle is related to theology as darkness is to light, and his *Ethics* is the worst enemy of grace.[69]

Now that most of the influential faculty members had been won to Luther's point of view, the University was undergoing an enormous inner change. By May 18, 1517, Luther could already rejoice to his friend Lang in Erfurt:

> Our theology and St. Augustine are continuing to prosper and reign in our University through the hand of God. Aristotle is declining daily and is inclining toward a fall which will end him forever. It is remarkable how lectures in the *Sentences* are despised; no one can hope for an audience unless he proposes to lecture on this theology; that is, the Bible, or St. Augustine, or some other doctor of ecclesiastical authority. Farewell, and pray for me.[70]

George Spalatin had been interested in the University of Wittenberg since he organized the library in 1512. His friendship with Luther became very strong after 1514, when they met through John Lang. This friendship with the court preacher, secretary, and confidential adviser to Frederick the Wise proved very valuable when the Saxon court was called upon to investigate the University in 1516, as shown in the records of the *Urkundenbuch* of April 9, 1516, and following.[71] Apparently Frederick asked his lawyers, Fabian von Feilitzsch and Hans von Taubenheim, to make a complete survey of the situation. A letter to Spalatin of March 11, 1518, indicates that Luther was the guiding spirit in the investigation and that he proposed some definite reforms:

> Yet, that it may be sufficient and in keeping with your desires, I am sending for your contemplation this proposal in which is presented the curriculum which, it seems to us, you should now be able to institute. Thus, if it were possible to institute this plan to the honor of the everlasting God, along the lines I have suggested, how great would then our glory be, as well as that of the Prince, and of learning! At the same time it would be an opportunity to reform all the universities of the country; yes, to eliminate universal barbarism and to further the cause of learning everywhere.[72]

Evidently under Luther's leadership the Wittenberg faculty convinced the court that Biblical Humanism should be introduced into the university curriculum; for on March 21, 1518, Luther again wrote to Lang with reference to the recent progress in the curriculum changes in the University.

> Our University is getting ahead. We expect before long to have lectures in two or three languages. New courses are to be given in Pliny, Quintilian, mathematics, and other subjects. The old courses in Petrus Hispanus, Tartaretus, and Aristotle are to be dropped. The Prince has already given his consent, and the plans are before his council.[73]

Between the lines may be read the triumph of Luther's new Biblical Humanism; for now, only subjects useful for a Humanistic background were to be taught in the University, while all courses related to the Scholastic background were to be dropped from the curriculum. An entry in the *Urkundenbuch* reveals that two instructors were to be provided to teach Latin, Greek, and Hebrew.[74]

The progress made by the new movement is well illustrated in a rather unusual occurrence in Wittenberg. Some Wittenberg students went there en masse to heckle an indulgence salesman sent from Halle by John Tetzel. Some bought copies, while others tore the theses of Wimpina, a strong opponent of Wittenberg, from the indulgence agent by main force and burned them boldly in the

Market Place to the great dismay of the agent and the Roman
authorities. In a letter to Lang, March 21, 1518, Luther explained
that the students lost control of themselves because they could no
longer stomach the old Scholastic ways and wanted to hear nothing
but the pure Word of God.[75] In other words, the Humanistic
Gospel movement had progressed so far that not even the students
of the University would tolerate anything which pertained to the
old system.

In the spring of 1518 the proposed fundamental changes in
the faculty and curriculum were finally completed. The philosophical lectures on Aristotle were presented strictly according to the
new Humanistic methods using only the best up-to-date original
texts.[76] Master Bartolomeus von Feltkyrchen gave the courses in
Aristotle's *Physics* and *Metaphysics*. Another Biblical Humanist,
Master Augustin Schurff, the brother of law professor Jerome
Schurff, taught Aristotle's *Logic*. The courses on Pliny, Quintilian,
and Priscian were all taught by men who had studied in Italy
and who, therefore, had the true approach to the Classics. Even
more interesting is the fact that plans were also afoot to procure
adequate teachers in Greek and Hebrew. Soon Luther's request to
Spalatin "not to forget to send them a real teacher in Greek and
Hebrew" was answered in the person of Master Philip Melanchthon.

The Elector had hoped to secure John Reuchlin himself, Melanchthon's great-uncle, but at the time he was too occupied in
the struggle with the Scholastics of Cologne and the repercussions
from the *Letters of Obscure Men*.[77] Furthermore, Reuchlin felt he
was not the professorial type, and he, therefore, proposed his
nephew as his substitute. Perhaps he was biased, but he stated
that he regarded young Philip as the best Greek scholar in all
Europe, excepting the great Erasmus.[78] The young lad was without doubt a prodigy. He matriculated at Heidelberg at twelve,
completed the A. B. degree at fifteen, entered Tuebingen, and received the Master's degree at seventeen. He had published a Greek
grammar and was the author of a text on Terence by the time he
was called to Wittenberg in the year 1518.

Philip's inaugural address on August 29, delivered before a
capacity audience in the Castle Church, on "How to Improve the

Course of Study for the Youth," made a deep and lasting impression.[79] In this address he reviewed the progress of education from the Roman civilization to that day, pointing out how it had been corrupted during the age of the Scholastics and averring that the classical languages were the only keys to true learning, providing the real background for the study of the Scriptures. The same day Luther sat down and wrote enthusiastic praise to Spalatin of the new Greek professor: "As long as we have Melanchthon, I care for no other Greek instructor." [80] To Lang in Erfurt he wrote: "He seems like a boy when one considers his age, but a man of our own age [35] when one considers the versatility of the man and his knowledge of books." [81]

The attraction between these two men must have been mutual, for Melanchthon, who also knew John Lang, likewise wrote him the observation: "If there is anything on earth I love, it is Martin and his pious writings; but, above everything else, I love Martin himself." And after he learned to know Luther still better, he wrote again: "Never was there a greater man on the face of the earth; I would rather die than sever myself from that man." [82]

For Luther and Melanchthon, who from then on were to make an excellent team, the past reforms in the University had not been adequate. Already on September 2, 1518, Luther wrote Spalatin again asking for further changes:

> We offer the most useful courses, and the young people are very enthusiastic in regard to the Holy Scriptures and real theology; but they cannot follow their real inclinations without interruption because the old courses are still required for their examinations. We beg you, therefore, that Aristotle's *Ethics*, which is as hostile toward theology as the wolf toward the lamb, be taken from the list of required subjects.[83]

Accordingly a plan was drawn up for further revision of the university curriculum in 1520, in which Aristotle's *Physics, Metaphysics,* and *Ethics* were all to be dropped, but his *Logic, Rhetoric,* and *Poetry,* so useful for eloquence to the clergy, were to be retained. Canon Law was also to be dropped, and only Civil Law to be taught. Latin, Greek, and Hebrew were to be stressed in undergraduate study; while, in Theology, the Bible was to be the sole guide. However, this plan was not fully realized until 1523.[84]

The *Urkundenbuch* shows that Biblical Humanism was then flourishing in the University. George Spalatin, who visited Wittenberg between December 3 and 7, 1520, reported that he found around 500–600 students attending the very interesting lectures of young Philip Melanchthon; that some 400 were in Luther's more advanced classes; while the Town Church had become far too small for the throngs eager to hear Luther's Gospel sermons.[85] He particularly noted the enthusiasm of the student body.

By this time Martin Luther had become the central figure of the University of Wittenberg. Students and faculty alike had recognized his gifted leadership. John Hornberg regretted his wasted time at other schools, for he wrote: "Here I began to learn all over again." To Thomas Blaurer from Constance, Luther was a great herald of God, for he said:

> I consider myself fortunate, that under God's guidance I have come to a place where, it seems to me, one can learn the Christian religion right; and where the only man is living who really understands the Bible, which fact I can daily witness here.[86]

And finally, Felix Ulscenius, one of Capito's protégés, writing home his impressions, stated that in Luther he had found a powerful interpreter of the Word of God and that he considered himself fortunate to be Luther's contemporary.[87]

As has been pointed out, in the decade previous to Luther's entry into the University of Wittenberg, the faculty could not have been said to represent any one definite philosophy of life; yet, the *Via Antiqua* was so strongly entrenched that neither the Humanists nor the followers of the *Via Moderna* felt the atmosphere congenial. In all, there were eight regular men in philosophy, but many of the professors in other departments also accepted the approach of the Old Way. It is, therefore, almost miraculous that Martin Luther, who was passed by unnoticed when Paul Lange was gathering material for his *Who's Who* in 1514, should in the course of four years have changed the philosophy of life of the entire institution. By the time Martin Luther nailed his Ninety-Five Theses on the door of the Castle Church, he had the complete support of the whole University. The act was, therefore, not a step taken by a single individual, but the concerted action of the entire institution in opposition to the disgraceful indulgence traffic of the

Dominican monk John Tetzel. Nothing more convincing of this fact may be cited than the comparatively recent discovery with a reference to a letter reproduced in *Die Deutsche Bibel*, IV, of the *Weimar Ausgabe*, 1923.[88] Although this story is in the main an integral part of the later indulgence struggle which Luther waged with Rome, it is also an excellent illustration of how warmly Luther's cause was espoused in the University. The story, in brief, is as follows.

After Martin Luther became very much involved with Rome in 1518 over the matter of indulgences and when Cajetan and Miltitz had both exerted every means to induce Frederick the Wise to turn Luther over for trial, the entire Wittenberg faculty became much disturbed. The incumbent Rector was Bartholomaeus Bernhardi, the same young Master who in 1516 had debated against Scholastic theology and roused his hearers from their lethargy. When the faculty was asked to write a letter to the Elector in Luther's behalf, Bernhardi, sensing the gravity of the situation and knowing the disposition of the Wittenberg faculty, suggested that Luther write his own defense in the name of the faculty, who would sign it. H. Degering discovered this original document some twenty years ago still well preserved.[89] Although some phrases in the letter are crossed out and additions are written on the margin by another hand, handwriting experts are agreed that the letter was composed in Luther's own hand. The only additions to the letter which the faculty made were a few superlatives, such as "noble and most revered professor in our midst." The letter presented Luther's case clearly, stating that he was most anxious to have his errors pointed out to him on the basis of God's Word and the Church Fathers. But the letter makes it quite clear that Luther's views are entirely in harmony with those of the faculty on such questions as the original teachings of the Catholic Church; for, they add, were this not the case, they would be the first to ask that Luther be surrendered to Rome. Frederick was, therefore, asked to intercede for Luther and not to reject the "petitions of a just man," but to "bring this matter straightway before the Holy See and the Pope."

Imagine the situation. Luther was under a cloud of doubt with both the Roman Church and the Electoral court. In such an hour, an entire university faculty willingly jeopardized its reputation and position with both the Elector of Saxony and the Roman *Curia* to uphold its colleague Martin Luther. Had they not agreed wholeheartedly with his New Theology, they would certainly not have been willing to harbor and uphold an archheretic, and, above all, to permit him to draft a letter to the Elector to which their individual signatures were appended. That this heretical uprising was not just the case of one man was sensed by the Sorbonne a few years later, when, in condemning Luther's writings, this distinguished faculty pointed out that in Wittenberg there was not just one viper in the bosom of Mother Church, but a whole nest of vipers.

This incident is the best kind of evidence that Biblical Humanism was flourishing in the University of Wittenberg by 1518; and it is also ample testimony to Luther's unusual gifts for leadership; for in four years he had risen from a comparatively unknown young professor to the spiritual leader of the whole institution.

« 10 »

Luther Attacks
the Indulgence Traffic

HISTORY OF INDULGENCES

WHILE HISTORIANS TRIED to understand the theory and practices of medieval indulgences from the viewpoint of the people who purchased them, little progress was made. However, when Adolf Gottlob investigated the problem from the viewpoint of those who issued them, at once a new understanding of their evolution began to develop.[1] It became apparent that the theory of the indulgence traffic could be traced to the wars between the Mohammedans and the Christians. The Mohammedans taught that when a soldier died in battle, his soul immediately went to heaven. This was not the case with the Christian; unless he had performed sufficient penance for his sins, he might still belong among the lost. To meet this special need, and to augment the Christian armies, the popes of the eleventh century began to grant absolution for all their transgressions to Christian warriors who died in battle. During the Crusades a new indulgence was invented whereby the complete remission of the penitential punishment was granted to all who fought in battle against the forces of Allah.[2] The next step was the indulgence as a substitute for the penalties of souls in purgatory. Thus, all who participated in a crusade were freed from both temporal punishment and the suffering in purgatory after death.[3] But not all men were physically fit to participate in a holy war, and a means was sought whereby this group might also make a contribution. The idea developed in the Roman *Curia* whereby the individual who contributed the amount required for

303

sending a soldier on a crusade might regard the payment of this sum as the equivalent of actual participation in the crusade itself. By the time of Innocent III the mere payment of money was sufficient to receive the advantages of a crusading indulgence.[4]

By the end of the thirteenth century the Crusades had lost most of their glamour, and with their decline the Papacy began to feel the loss of a lucrative source of income. Consequently, the *Curia* during the time of Boniface VIII sought new sources of raising money through indulgences.[5] After searching through the Old Testament, the idea was conceived of instituting a Jubilee Indulgence which would be celebrated every one hundred years. Originally, the plan was to have Christians from all over Christendom make a pilgrimage to Rome and to leave their gifts on St. Peter's tomb. The first Jubilee Indulgence in 1300 proved to be a huge success from the viewpoint of the Roman *Curia*. Throughout its celebration two men were busy raking together the money which pious pilgrims deposited upon the tomb of the sainted Apostle. This success only whetted the insatiable appetite of the popes. The period of time was variously reduced from 100 to 50, to 33, to 25 years, each decrease being accompanied by various rationalizations to explain why the change had been made.[6] Finally, in 1393 Pope Boniface IX made the purchase of indulgences much easier and more systematic. All Europe was covered by agents fully empowered to absolve the sins of the penitent according to the pocketbook of the sinner.

Alexander of Hales contributed a plausible explanation of how indulgences really worked, which was officially sanctioned by Pope Clement VI in 1343. According to Canon Law, Roman penance consisted of three steps: (1) sincere contrition of heart, (2) the oral confession to a priest and his absolution from sins and eternal damnation, and finally, (3) the satisfaction by good works which proved that the confession had been really sincere. Satisfaction by good works in the Early Church had taken the form of actually performing some good deed, such as erecting a church, building a bridge, engaging in poor relief, making a pilgrimage, etc. Alexander of Hales claimed that when a Christian bought indulgences, he satisfied the requirement for good works. Up in heaven, explained Hales, is a treasury filled with the merits of Christ and all the saints. Suppose a man's record was bad all his life and he suddenly becomes aware of the certainty of death. His total of good works in the sight of God would certainly be deficient. As a result, when he dies, this man would have to suffer grievously in purgatory; but by purchasing indulgences his deficit in good works could be met from the *Thesaurus Meritorum,* or heavenly treasury.[7] The purchase of an indulgence would relieve this man from both the temporal punishment for sin and the suffering in purgatory.

Around the turn of the century another feature was added which greatly facilitated the sale of indulgences. An impressive document was drawn up, the Indulgence Letter, elaborately ornamented with both papal signatures and seals. The purchaser now had tangible evidence of heavenly forgiveness, and sales of the "sacred commodity" increased accordingly. The final step in the development of indulgences was taken by Pope Sixtus IV, who in 1476 established indulgences for the dead in purgatory.[8] Soon available was an indulgence known as plenary, meaning complete coverage of every possible requirement, which made forgiveness available for all contingencies. Unfortunately, the Canon Law of the Roman Church did not legalize this latest bold innovation of providing indulgences even for the dead. Many able Catholic theologians were dubious as to its validity. They were willing to grant the Pope power to relieve the penitent of Church-imposed papal penalties, but they were very doubtful of the papal power to remove souls from purgatory and to transmit them to the realm of heavenly bliss just because their relatives had funds to purchase indulgences.

The Roman *Curia* found many means of augmenting the salability of their product. Among the wares offered by the indulgence salesmen was a *Butterbrief*[9] which exempted its purchaser from some of the inconveniences of the Roman Church regulations. Such a letter permitted the owner to eat the otherwise prohibited butter, eggs, cheese, and other milk products on prescribed fast days. Also offered were dispensations from certain vows, excepting those of chastity and monasticism, provided they were expiated in other types of good works. Even a grant of pardon could be purchased for the unlawful possession of property, provided the rightful owner was no longer living or known. These many features made Tetzel's enterprise extremely lucrative, for he had been amply provided with all these sacred wares offered by the Roman *Curia.*

This nefarious trafficking in human souls and preying upon the gullibility of a simple-minded and superstitious public was severely criticized and opposed by sincere and thoughtful Catholics long before Luther. The critics of indulgences had questioned their validity ever since Peter Abelard. In the long list of opponents of the practice appeared such names as John Wyclif, John Wesel, Pedro Martinez, Wessel Gansfort, Jean Laillier, and Jean Vitrier.[10] Nor had the Church ever definitely defined in Canon Law the exact scope of indulgences; yet, with the whole institution having developed from the top down on the basis of a number of papal decrees, it required a bold person, indeed, to assail the validity of indulgences.

THE INDULGENCE TRAFFIC OF ALBERT OF MAINZ

In the year 1513 three important church positions became vacant in northern Germany. These were the Archbishopric of Magdeburg, the Bishopric of Halberstadt, and the important Archbishopric of Mainz. The death of the incumbent Uriel von Gemmingen was a serious blow to this latter archbishopric, for it was the fourth vacancy in a decade, and the election of a new archbishop was expensive business by the time of the sixteenth century.[11] To the ambitious Hohenzollern Elector Joachim of Brandenburg the moment seemed auspicious for the rise of that house; so he plotted to capture the unprecedented prize of three simultaneous church positions for his young brother Albert, cost what it may. However, to hold more than one church position at a time was illegal, and Albert was only twenty-three, which was below the canonical age required for an archbishop. These natural obstacles only increased the amount which the Hohenzollerns would have to raise for the purchase of the necessary papal dispensations.

The offices of Archbishop of Magdeburg and Bishop of Halberstadt did not prove difficult to obtain. By August 13, 1513, young Albert had been chosen for the two offices and by December 16, 1513, Pope Leo had granted the necessary dispensations in consideration of a fee of 1,079 ducats, or about $25,000.[12] To secure

the appointment to the Archbishopric of Mainz, the leading ecclesiastical position and the Primacy of all Germany, for one who
already held two other church positions was a different matter.
There were, as a matter of course, other candidates for this
lucrative office. Joachim's chief opposition came from Matthaeus
Lang, Emperor Maximilian's adviser, who had private ambitions.
Hohenzollern interests were ably represented in Rome by Dr. Blankenfeld, a former university professor, who was thoroughly acquainted there.[13] For years he had moved in the German circle
in Rome and in the *Anima*, where he learned to know the man in
charge of the Fugger Bank in Rome, Johannes Zink. He also knew
personally Pope Leo X, who spoke highly of the talented German.
Although not all the details are known, most of the later strategy
of Albert of Mainz was concocted by Dr. Blankenfeld and his
associates. Pope Leo X and the other officials involved insisted that
their sole interest was in the suitability of the candidates, but in
reality they fully realized the opportunity to augment the papal
treasury and were holding out for the highest possible figure and
the candidate considered most solvent. Albert finally secured the
prize and was permitted to become the Archbishop of Mainz, provided he paid the *Curia* 10,000 ducats in addition to the customary
fees of 12,300 ducats. To finance this big-business venture, the
Curia proposed that the transaction be handled through the House
of Fugger in Augsburg, which had been handling most of the papal
indulgence loans since the days of Pope Alexander VI.[14]

The House of Fugger, as noted before, had also financed the
election of Emperor Charles V. For over 150 years this family, by
pooling its resources and securing monopolies in various fields of
business, had steadily risen to the position of the wealthiest banking
house in all Europe.[15] Popes, emperors, and kings were dependent
upon its favor, and through its financial power it virtually ordered
wars to begin or cease. Cold, hard-headed businessmen, the Fuggers knew how to drive a bargain, and even in handling the indulgence trade they worked with great efficiency. They had an
ironclad agreement with Rome that no indulgence chests could be
opened except in the presence of one of their officials and a notary.
Regular price schedules had been established according to which

the indulgence agents were to charge.[16] At stated intervals the moneys were officially counted and delivered to the proper Fugger officials.

Why would such astute financial wizards be willing to finance young Albert for the huge sum of better than a quarter of a million dollars? Not without good sound collateral and ample assurance from the *Curia* as to the security of the loan. The arrangement was made for Rome to issue a bull authorizing the sale of a plenary indulgence in Mainz, Magdeburg, Halberstadt, and the Brandenburg lands. Leo X demanded a payment in cash of $120,000,[17] while the remainder was to be paid as the money was raised from the sale of indulgences. After the expenses were deducted, the money was to be divided half and half. On paper, one half went for the building of St. Peter's Church in Rome, and there can be no doubt that some of the money was spent for this. Most of it probably went into Leo X's lavish entertainment. The other half was to repay the enormous Fugger loan and its substantial interest rates.[18]

The papal bull issued by Leo X for Albert's benefit offered the greatest possible advantages. Sadoletus, who drew up the document, missed no opportunity by the use of apt pious phrases to raise the highest possible revenue for the *Curia*. Sins, no matter how "grave or enormous," with but few exceptions, were to be fully remitted upon confession. The sinner also had his choice of confessor. Those guilty of simony, of uncanonical marriage, of the acquisition of property through usury, or of perjury were offered full remission for their past sins. The document named Albert as the chief commissary with power to appoint his assistants.[19]

A complete procedure for all salesmen was also given in the Archbishop's *Instructions*. The indulgence agents were particularly to stress the four "graces" offered by the Pope in this plenary indulgence, covering every possible aspect of forgiveness for both the living and the dead: (1) the plenary forgiveness, even for those already in purgatory; (2) the choice of a confessor fully empowered to absolve even the gravest of offenses; (3) the availability of an indulgence ticket permitting even the dead to participate in the prayers, alms, fasts, pilgrimages, and Masses of the Church here on earth; (4) the remission of all good works required of the souls in purgatory without confession or contrition, except in the case of extreme offenses while here on earth. A careful study of this document reveals that it was simply a pious fraud and an unblushing scheme to raise funds.[20]

Empowered by the papal bull, Albert employed a number of subcommissaries, of whom the most notorious was John Tetzel, an unscrupulous Dominican monk from St. Paul's Convent in Leipzig.[21] Perhaps the others were equally infamous, but Tetzel has become the better known because it was he who was peddling the sacred wares in Jueterbock and Zerbst, about 20 miles from Wittenberg, when Luther's attention was drawn to his pursuits. The exact details of his procedure no longer exist, but a number of general reports have made it possible to reconstruct somewhat the type of service he generally held.

Tetzel had sold indulgences for the Fuggers and Rome since 1504 and, therefore, regarded himself as being an extremely successful salesman. According to Myconius, who heard him preach, Tetzel boasted that he had saved more souls through indulgences than had St. Peter himself through the Gospel.[22] His regular salary was $1,070 a month plus living and travel expenses. The Fuggers also frequently gave Tetzel a "large bonus" to keep up his interest. Even his servant was paid a yearly salary 20 guldens higher than that of the best-paid official in Leipzig. That Tetzel became rich in the service of the Fuggers cannot be doubted.[23]

Personally, he was a rather large man, of eloquent speech, quick to sense and take advantage of a situation, and on the whole quite well educated. By nature he was easily excited, and when aroused, his language became rather coarse. Nor was it below his dignity to resort publicly to all sorts of threats. One of his favorite means to impress the common man was to build a fire in the town square and then to point out that he was also a *Ketzermeister*,[24] or heresy hunter. Even people of considerable education were afraid of the man.

Myconius heard Tetzel preach in 1512 in Annaberg, the young but rich mining town, in an effort to raise funds for the erection of the *Pfarrkirche zu St. Anna*. Apparently he had already developed quite a sales psychology. After a description of Tetzel's boastful manner of preaching, Myconius gives an interesting account of his arrival at Annaberg:

> In those days indulgences were so much respected that when an indulgence agent was brought to town, the papal bull was carried on a velvet or gold cloth, while all the priests, monks, councilmen, teachers, students, men, women, girls, and children met him carrying flags and candles and singing while they marched in procession. Meanwhile all the bells in town rang, and as the procession entered the church, the organ played. A red cross was placed in the middle of the church on which the papal papers were hung, etc.; in brief, one could not have received and entertained God in a more impressive fashion than this.[25]

Although it is doubtful whether Tetzel used the slogan attributed to him: "As soon as the money clinks in the chest, the soul flits into heavenly rest," he may have used some similar catch phrase. According to Myconius, in 1512 he was saying: "As soon as the groschen rings in the bowl, the soul of him for whom it was given rises from the mouth directly into heaven." [26]

Tetzel may not have always pursued the same methods and sales psychology, but in general his procedure was similar to the publicity campaign of a present-day circus.[27] His arrival was announced some weeks before his visit to a town or city. His advance agents would have a special directory prepared classifying the citizens as to pecuniary resources. When he finally arrived, the whole town was prepared to celebrate a festive occasion. The agent was met at the town gate by a procession which proceeded to the town square. Here the first service was held that a record crowd might be attracted. In the town square Tetzel was at his best, for here he gave his sermon on "Hell," in which he pictured the place of the damned in language made vivid with fire and brimstone. For the second service the procession continued to the largest church or cathedral. Its highlight was Tetzel's sermon on "Purgatory," in which he pictured the sufferings of the poor parents of many of those in the audience. He asked in dramatic fashion if they could not hear them wailing there, while their children were calmly enjoying their inheritance here on earth. Tetzel's third sermon was on "Heaven," in which he pictured with equal eloquence the contrast between the saved and the eternally damned. How sweet and peaceful were the souls in heaven in contrast to the sufferings of the poor souls in hell! Now the audience was fully conditioned for the sale of the "sacred wares."

If the sale was conducted in a church, Tetzel stood behind the altar railing, while the people lined up to buy. As they approached, their names were checked in the directory for their classification. As shown by the Fugger records, the following table of charges had been compiled:

Kings, Archbishops and Bishops	25 gulden, or $335.00	
Counts	10 gulden, or $134.00	
Businessmen	3 to 6 gulden, or $40.20 to $80.40	
Guild members	1 gulden, or $13.40	
Poor	½ gulden, or $6.70	
Destitute	Free of charge [28]	

However, there were those who could not understand such a classification. A wealthy lady in Magdeburg asked her father confessor to explain why Tetzel had asked her to pay 100 gulden instead of the customary 25 paid by the nobility.[29] The monk was fearful lest Tetzel would have him burned; but, after swearing her to secrecy, he exposed the whole fraud and pointed out why indulgences could not take the place of true penance. This incident happened several years before Luther nailed his theses on the door of the Castle Church in Wittenberg.

Martin Luther, like many of his contemporaries, early criticized the abuses connected with the sale of indulgences; and by 1515 his classroom lectures indicate that he was much concerned about the religious and ethical effects of the Roman traffic. Where originally the indulgence plan applied only to the third step in penance, namely, to the penalties imposed by the Church, now Luther felt that the infamous Tetzel was dragging the whole Sacrament of Penance into the questionable proceedings.[30] When Luther obtained a copy of Albert's instructions to his salesmen, he was deeply shocked. In excitement he exclaimed: "As certainly as Christ has redeemed me, I, just as other people, did not realize what indulgences were like."[31] Now he was convinced that even Albert the Archbishop was misrepresenting indulgences, ascribing to them the power of complete forgiveness of sins, and that the former sincere contrition of heart and confession to a priest had been pushed into the background; only the mere volume of sales interested the unscrupulous Archbishop.

Luther was still more shocked when his own congregational members boldly displayed their indulgence letters and refused to change their evil lives. In the confessional Luther severely took them to task, refusing them absolution and Communion unless they sincerely repented and mended their ways.[32] Offended and puzzled, they went back to Tetzel and demanded an explanation. Tetzel became furious at the audacity of the Wittenberg monk.[33] Since John Tetzel also had the power to excommunicate his critics, the general public feared his wrath and was cautious in its remarks. Luther's challenge, therefore, of Tetzel's sweeping indulgence claims and his refusal to grant absolution without true repentance endangered the whole community. Yet his action was born of a deep conviction and the belief that, as a Doctor of Theology, he could no longer remain silent.

The Castle Church in Wittenberg had, ever since its original dedication to all the saints, achieved the distinction of *jus patronatus*,[34] or independent control, directly under the jurisdiction of the Pope, and enjoyed special privileges and immunities. As early as 1343 Bishop Otto of Magdeburg had granted a special forty-day indulgence to those who prayed before its altars. Under Pope Boniface IX (1389–1404), according to Matthaeus Faber (1717), it received the special right to grant indulgences.[35] Though there were many special services throughout the year, the principal celebration was always the festival of All Saints' Day on November 1. As described in Lucas Cranach's *Wittemberger Heiligthumsbuch of 1509*, the various relics collected by the Elector were placed in eight aisles readily accessible to visitors.[36] Dr. Hausleiter estimates that by 1518 there were 12 rows of relics displaying a total of 17,443 pieces. Those who viewed these relics and prayed before them might gain the equivalent of "127,709 years, 116 days of indulgences."[37] Thus, annually an indulgence traffic very similar to Tetzel's was carried on in the Castle Church the week following the festival of All Saints' Day. This practice provided the special occasion for Luther's second sermon on indulgences, delivered on All Saints' Eve, October 31, 1516, just one year before the nailing of the *Ninety-Five Theses*.[38] This sermon was an explanation of the correct use of indulgences rather than a criticism of any existing practice. Luther warned against the very real danger of pushing true penance into the background. He pointed out that true, heart-felt contrition lasts throughout the Christian's entire life, and the sincere penitent welcomes rather than evades punishment.

Martin Luther became even more outspoken in a sermon preached February 24, 1517, for he had by now noted the effect of Tetzel's preaching on his Wittenberg congregation.[39] In this sermon Luther deplored the fact that people were regarding sin so lightly and that they seemed to have so little fear of punishment. He added that indulgences should perhaps be called an *Ablass*, because they permitted people to sin. In reality, asserted Luther, the indulgence sales kept many from really finding Christ. Now he was definitely convinced of the dangers that lurked in this kind of Christianity; that man by man-made means could assure his salvation. Although Tetzel had somewhat exaggerated indulgences, his claims were basically in keeping with the medieval Catholic conception of salvation. The whole tendency had been to create machinery by which the people could be made to feel safe as long as they conformed to the outward regulations of the medieval hierarchy. Luther's sermon, then, touched the inner nerve of the whole Catholic system. His new *Gewissensreligion*,[40] or religion of conscience, knew no other certainty than that of the transformed soul which has acquired God's righteousness through Christ and entered upon a living partnership with God.

When Luther preached this February sermon, John Tetzel was active in the neighboring Brandenburg lands. Throughout the summer Luther continued to be much concerned with the effect that these sales might have throughout Germany. The more returns the indulgence traffic promised, the more extravagant and misleading Tetzel's preaching became. It was not until October, after Tetzel had left the region, that Luther obtained the afore-mentioned copy of Albert's official instructions to his salesmen bound in a book beautifully decorated with his coat of arms. This book and the experiences related by his students caused Luther to resolve that this problem should be discussed with his fellow professors that the faculty might agree upon some concerted action in the matter.

Therefore, on October 31, 1517, Luther had his 95 propositions ready for discussion and was prepared to post them on the university bulletin board, the door of the Castle Church.[41] The time was, indeed, propitious, for the city was thronged with pilgrims for the celebration of the festival of All Saints.

THE NINETY-FIVE THESES

Let us imagine the scene as it must have appeared on that long-ago day. A spirit of excitement and tension pervades the air, for last year Luther had preached a rather critical sermon on that evening. Since then the Tetzel indulgences have roused the populace. What will happen this year? In the university section, students are gathering here and there in groups or engaging some professor in earnest conversation.

Now a young monk in professor's garb enters the street from the Black Cloister and walks purposefully toward the Market Place, accompanied by his *famulus*.[42] Passing among the loitering groups, he is greeted with deference and respect by students and faculty alike. As he passes, the cause of his evident popularity and influence can easily be ascertained. He is a man apparently in his middle thirties, although the deep lines and sharply chiseled features of his thin face indicate that he has endured much mental and physical suffering. His walk is rapid and his carriage very erect; so erect, in fact, that he appears to bend slightly backwards. Who would not be drawn by his large, deep, penetrating, brown eyes, so expressive of deep feeling and sincere purpose? His firm features convey a strength of purpose not easily swayed, an indomitable courage, and high conviction. He is Martin Luther, and his companion is Johann Schneider.

The two men pass the *Markt,* whose open square is filled with the vast crowds who expect to receive healing and blessing from worshiping before the thousands of relics which the Elector will display in the Castle Church on the morrow. Some are prepared to purchase the special indulgences to be offered during the coming week. Beyond the homes of Mellerstadt and Cranach the companions enter the *Schloss Gasse,* which rises gradually to the Castle Church. Reaching this beautiful Gothic edifice, the men pass through the quaint, covered gateway pictured in the Cranach woodcut in the *Heiligthumsbuch* and ascend the boarded walk leading to the main north door of the Church.

Now the young professor draws from beneath his gown and nails to the *Schwartze Brett* a document, freshly printed by his fellow monk Johann Gruenenberg.[43] This act in itself was not unusual, for this sturdy wooden door, ever since famous in history, served as the medium for announcing both university and public events. The document was none other than Luther's *Ninety-Five Theses*, on which he summoned his fellow professors to debate. To the passer-by there is nothing particularly startling in the opening words:

> Out of love and zeal for the elucidation of truth, the following theses will be debated at Wittenberg, the Reverend Father Martin Luther, Master of Arts and Sacred Theology, presiding. He begs that those who cannot be present at the oral discussion will communicate their views in writing. In the name of our Lord Jesus Christ. Amen.[44]

What, then, was the unusual content of the document which, according to Myconius, spread throughout all Germany in fourteen days and in a month had put all Christendom on fire?[45] Perhaps no other document in history has been more carefully scrutinized than Luther's *Ninety-Five Theses*, with reactions as varied as the backgrounds of the respective critics. One aspect is quite certain. When Luther announced his *Theses*, his motive was exactly as stated in the introduction, "love and zeal for the elucidation of truth." If he had not been perfectly honest in his intentions, he would not have scattered copies of his *Theses* so freely in the camp of the opposition; and on the same day they were posted he sent a copy of the document to Albert of Mainz, whose agent was being attacked.[46] Luther firmly believed that Tetzel was misrepresenting indulgences without the knowledge of the officials of the Church and that these officials need only be informed of the practice and the evil abuses would be corrected.

There was much more to the *Theses* than a mere attack. Already apparent was an undertone of the later Reformer of which Luther himself was completely unconscious. His new revelations from the study of Romans had changed his whole conception of religion. In reality his teachings no longer fitted into the old accepted Scholastic pattern, yet he still believed that his new outlook merely made him a better Catholic. In Luther's *Ninety-Five Theses* was reflected the great progress he had made by that time as a Biblical student. Although still clinging to the Catholic framework with the medieval system of Canon Law and its definition of penance, the content of the *Theses* revealed a new spiritual meaning.[47]

As Walther Koehler has pointed out, the whole viewpoint of Luther is summarized in the first thesis, wherein he states that penance is not an outward mechanical performance, but an inner attitude of mind which continues throughout life.[48] This new conception of religion made it impossible for Luther to harmonize Tetzel's teachings on indulgences with the Scriptures. Partly for his own clarification, then, he announced a disputation at Wittenberg, hoping that other universities would also debate the propositions in their faculties and that a clearer comprehension might be gained of these pernicious and dangerous tendencies in the Church. The following year, when Luther elaborated on the Theses in his *Resolutions* (1518), he still assumed that Tetzel's abuses were without the knowledge and approval of the Roman *Curia* and, especially, of the Pope.[49]

Two years later, in the famous tract *The Babylonian Captivity of the Church* (1520), Luther first spoke of how much his Roman opponents had taught him in the meantime, and then he added:

> Some two years ago I wrote a little book on indulgences [*Resolutions*, 1518], which I now deeply regret having published; for at the time I was still sunk in a mighty superstitious veneration for the Roman tyranny and held that indulgences should not be altogether rejected, seeing that they were approved by the common consent of men. Nor was this to be wondered at, for I was then engaged singlehanded in my Sisyphean task. Since then, however, through the kindness of Sylvester and the friars, who so strenuously defended indulgences, I have come to see that they are nothing but an imposture of the Roman sycophants by which they play havoc with men's faith and fortunes. Would to God I might prevail upon the booksellers and upon all my readers to burn up the whole of my writings on indulgences and to substitute for them this proposition: *Indulgences are a knavish trick of the Roman sycophants.*[50]

While Luther's intentions were entirely sincere, a careful study of the Theses clearly shows that his propositions were full of potential dynamite for the indulgence traffic. Not only did they criticize the abuses of John Tetzel rather severely; but they likewise presented some questions based upon a wholly new viewpoint of religion which opened the eyes of the layman. His new realization of the meaning of penance has been noted. Now the real counterpart of penance for Luther was forgiveness, which rests solely with God.[51] Only he who has been truly humbled before God and is sincerely penitent can receive God's forgiveness. Every Christian who feels this inner contrition has already God's forgiveness, the perfect remission of guilt and pain, without the purchase of letters of indulgence; for every Christian is the recipient of Christ's benefits and those of the Christian Church whether living or dead. The Pope and the clergy have their power only as vicars of Christ. Consequently, neither the Pope nor any other mortal can remit punishment except that which has been imposed on the sinner through the man-made canons of the Church.

As for purgatory, Luther still accepted the Catholic teaching of its existence, but he was very dubious about the boastful claims of the indulgence preachers.[52] He doubted that a priest could remove canonical penalties of those already in purgatory; rather, Luther suspected that the whole indulgence traffic was a grand humbug, introduced into the Church while the bishops were asleep, and believed that, once man has passed from this life, the Church Militant can do no more for him, for all canonical regulations apply solely to the living.[53] Luther also criticized the extravagant claims made by the indulgence agents for papal power.[54] The Pope's indulgences cannot exempt sinners from all punishment in purgatory and guarantee automatically their salvation.

The real danger about the whole indulgence trade, according to Luther's Theses, lay in the tendency of the gullible masses to put their complete trust in the saving merit of indulgence letters.[55] By surrounding indulgences with so much pomp and ceremony people began to value them above true charity. Luther stated that it would be far better if indulgence moneys were used to help the poor and needy, for this would tend to improve the state of man.

In the Ninety-Five Theses the Pope was still held in high

esteem.[56] Yet many questions were causing Luther great perplexity. Why did the Pope not deliver poor souls from purgatory for the sake of "holy love"? Why for money? Why did the Pope not build a church out of his own funds, for he was richer than Croesus? Why did the penitent have to pay money before they were forgiven? But Luther still concluded that the Pope must be innocent and his intentions above reproach.

As Luther emphasized the nature of true penance and forgiveness, he made the Gospel the real treasure of the Church. The Office of the Keys he believed to be God's means of redemption. The Gospel was the good news that all men have pardon for their sins if they are but truly contrite. Men, therefore, should not rely on the treasury of indulgences, but upon the real treasury of God's wonderful grace, the holy Gospel.[57]

The *Ninety-Five Theses* were cast in a typical Catholic mold, for they still accepted at least fifteen fundamentally Roman teachings.[58] Yet it can be readily understood why they aroused the opposition of Tetzel and those who were interested in the returns from the indulgences. Perhaps the best illustration of the immediate effect of Luther's *Theses* is a contemporary *Spottbild*, or cartoon, labeled "Frederick the Wise's Dream." [59] It is possible but highly improbable that Frederick had such a dream; yet it so well illustrates the circumstances in which the Papacy found itself that it was widely circulated and is cited here as an illustration of the temper of the times.

The time is October 31, 1517, the very evening on which Luther's historic theses appeared on the door of the Castle Church. At the right of the picture the slumber of Frederick the Wise has been disturbed by the unusual vision spread before him. In the middle appears the city of Rome, with the Pope and his cardinals presiding over the Eternal City. On the left the tremendous fire kindled by the Council of Constance is consuming its unfortunate victims, John Hus and Jerome of Prague. Below that on the left is Luther busily searching the Scriptures, while contact with the Holy Ghost guides Luther and Frederick in their lifework as reformer and protector. Immediately in the foreground on the left is the door of the Castle Church in Wittenberg, at which stands Martin Luther writing with an enormous pen whose other ex-

"Frederick the Wise's Dream"

tremity extends to Rome and knocks off the Pope's triple crown. The writing on the door reads: "The 31st of October, 1517, concerning indulgences."

This is but one of the many examples of contemporary feeling which were published during the Reformation, and it amply illustrates why Tetzel and his supporters might well be concerned over the reception of Luther's *Theses*. A few years later, when Frederick the Wise in a private interview with Erasmus in Cologne asked the great Humanist his opinion of Luther, the reply was: "Luther sinned in two respects, namely, that he attacked the crown of the Pope and the bellies of the monks." [60]

In summary, Luther's *Theses* stated that even the Pope had no special powers beyond those declaratory powers given to all the priesthood. God was placed once more into the foreground as "the Lord over life and death." Once the soul had left this life, asserted Luther, no Catholic canon controlled it any longer. Religion was once more restored to a personal relationship between man and God, a spiritual inner attitude in man known only to God, between which the clergy with their sacerdotal system could not intervene. The Gospel with its wonderful message of Jesus Christ was restored to the foreground, while the heretofore miracle-working clergy became but God's mouthpiece even in the administration of the Office of the Keys.

Luther's *Theses* affected even more than the Pope's prestige by making forgiveness a personal matter between the Christian and his God; far greater was the effect on the revenue of indulgence agents. As the news of Luther's challenge of Tetzel's indulgence claims reached the common man, he, too, began to question the whole matter. The receipts in the Brandenburg region were only one fifth of the expected amount.[61] It can well be imagined how Jacob Fugger, who was, after all, not in this business for reasons of conscience, reacted when he learned of the drop in sales. His first thought would be to protect his loan to Albert. In Rome, too, where it was first regarded as just another monks' squabble, Leo X became really concerned when he realized that the rich returns promised by their real estate investment in the ecclesiastical lands of Albert of Mainz were being seriously threatened.

The Reception of Luther's Theses

The same evening that Luther had nailed the *Theses* on the door of the Castle Church in Wittenberg, he wrote his first letter to Albert of Mainz, the original of which is still in the state archives in Stockholm, and with which he included a copy of his *Ninety-Five Theses*.[62] This was the first copy of the *Theses* to be circulated in Germany. Luther's letter to Albert of Mainz was respectful and humble, yet through the polite language radiated a deep concern over what has been going on in the Archbishop's ecclesiastical domains. Luther advised Albert to recall the instructions given to Tetzel and his subcommissaries, for he was certain that they were being misconstrued and might even expose Albert to attack. Had Albert had no further interest in the indulgence traffic, Luther's warning might have been heeded. Also, on that same day Luther sent another copy of his *Theses* to Bishop Jerome Schulze of Brandenburg that he, too, might be alert to the dangers in Tetzel's preaching.[63] Part of the Saxon lands were also under the ecclesiastical jurisdiction of Albert, but Frederick the Wise would not permit the indulgence salesmen in his lands, as he felt previous abuses had "sucked the land dry." [64] Luther, therefore, did not need to warn his own Prince. Furthermore, Luther had anticipated the possible assumption of the opposition that the motive behind the *Theses* was the desire of the Saxon Court to curb the rising power of Brandenburg. For this reason it seemed wise not to involve Frederick. In a letter to Spalatin in early November Luther wrote:

> I do not wish my *Theses* to come into the hands of the illustrious Elector or of any of the courtiers before they are received by those who believe that they are branded by them, lest perchance it be thought that I had published them at the instigation of the Elector against the Bishop of Magdeburg, as I already hear some persons dream. But now, we can even swear that they were published without the knowledge of Frederick.[65]

In spite of Luther's attempts to keep the *Theses* from spreading until they had been properly evaluated in a public disputation, a disputation which for some unknown reason was never held, the opposition was quick to seize upon them to prejudice the public against the Wittenberg professor. Tetzel threatened publicly to have Luther burned and his ashes scattered on the waters.[66] During November Luther's supporters in Magdeburg and Leipzig prepared reprints of the *Theses*, while in December a German translation appeared in Basel. Now the *Theses* were displayed all over Germany on street corners, public buildings, and even on trees. Myconius, a personal friend of Luther in his *Historia Reformationis* written between 1517 and 1542, claimed that the news of the *Ninety-Five Theses* spread with unbelievable rapidity:

> Before fourteen days had passed, these *Propositiones* had spread throughout all Germany and in four weeks throughout all Christendom. It was as though the angels themselves were the messengers carrying the news to all peoples.[67]

It is highly possible that Myconius got his information through a conversation with Luther, for the Reformer himself made a similar statement in his treatise *Wider Hans Worst* (1541), in which he mentioned that in just two weeks the news had spread throughout Germany.[68] Doubtless, Luther's impression was based on contemporary reports and letters from various parts of the country showing how rapidly people in all the distant parts of Germany learned of the event. As for the actual reprinting of the *Theses* and their circulation, research has shown that at least fourteen weeks were required.

When Albert of Mainz received the *Ninety-Five Theses*, not being trained in theology, he turned to the leader of the Aschaffenburg Council, Jodocus Lorcher, for expert advice.[69] He also sent a copy of the *Theses* to the theological faculty of the University of Mainz, requesting their opinion.[70] It was upon the combined advice of these bodies that Albert turned to Rome and urged the initiation of the well-known *processus inhibitorius*, the Church's method of silencing her critics, by means of which an attempt was made between 1517 and 1520 to quiet Luther.

Fortunately, the original communications of the Archbishop and the subsequent replies have been preserved in the *Bodmannschen Papiere* of the *Stadtbibliothek* of Mainz.[71] In the official university *Opinions* the theological faculty after a careful examination of Luther's *Theses* noted among other things "how they limit the power of the Pope and the Apostolic See, and that they disagree with the generally accepted writings of the blessed and venerable doctors of the Roman Church." They made the following recommendations: (1) that they deemed it far wiser and safer to exalt the power and authority of the Pope than to uphold the opinions of a single individual; (2) that they owed it out of gratitude to God to elevate the powers of the Papacy, for God had bestowed the highest possible powers on the person of the Pope; and (3) that, since Pope Nicholas had prohibited by Canon Law either to "judge or debate concerning the powers and judgments of the Pope," it seemed neither expedient nor wise to deny or approve the *Theses* themselves. Therefore, the faculty concluded, it would be far wiser to take this matter to the very font of wisdom and power, the Papacy itself, where it could be examined strictly in the light of Canon Law by the proper authority, the Roman *Curia*.[72] It is interesting to note that in the meantime the Council of Halle had given Albert similar advice.

Meanwhile, John Tetzel, who was not informed of Albert's communications with the papal *Curia*, did all within his power to silence Luther through the Dominican Order. An abbot was even sent to Wittenberg who visited the Black Cloister and tried to intimidate the members of the Augustinian convent; but Luther was not to be frightened so easily.[73] In January, 1518, the Saxon Chapter of the Dominicans met at Frankfurt an der Oder to consider this special problem.[74] On this august occasion John Tetzel was elevated to a Doctor of Theology. Since it was customary on such occasions to hold a disputation, John Tetzel disputed a set of 106 countertheses to Luther's, performing nobly before the 300 members of the Dominican Order present. The countertheses had been specially drafted by Dr. Konrad Koch, commonly known as Wimpina, who was mentioned earlier and who, as an ancient enemy of the University of Wittenberg, hoped that through them Luther's case might be weakened.

Tetzel further instructed a Halle bookdealer to deliver a number of printed copies of Wimpina's theses in Wittenberg, where they were to be sold among the students of the University; but when delivery was made, the unexpected happened. Some of the students bought or seized the copies by force and burned them in the *Markt* without informing Luther. Luther wrote the following about this incident in a letter to his friend John Lang, March 21, 1518:

> If rumor has perhaps told you anything about the burning of Tetzel's *Theses*, lest anyone should add anything to the truth, as is usually the case, let me tell you the whole story. The students are remarkably tired of sophistical and antiquated studies and are truly desirous of the Holy Bible; for this reason, and perchance also because they favored my opinion, when they heard of the arrival of a man sent from Halle by Tetzel, the author of the *Theses*, they threatened the man for daring to bring such things here; then some students bought copies of the *Theses*, and some simply seized them, and, having given notice to all who wished to be present at the spectacle to come to the market place at two o'clock, they burned them without the knowledge of the Elector, the town council, or the rector of the university, or of any of us. Certainly we were all displeased by this grave injury done to the man by our students. I am not guilty, but I fear that the whole thing will be imputed to me. They make a great story out of it and are not unjustly indignant.[75]

Luther added that he had no idea what would come of the whole matter, for he had heard that Wimpina was the real author of these *Theses*.

There is good reason to believe that Luther was not as displeased as he inferred about the student action, for just a few days before he had written a letter to Spalatin in which he was unusually cheerful concerning his difficulties with the indulgence struggle. On the preceding day Lord Abbot of Lehnin had visited the Black Cloister as a special representative of Bishop Schulze of Brandenburg in an attempt at conciliation.[76] Luther said that he "was overcome with confusion to think that so great a bishop had sent so great an abbot" to establish better relations between them. Luther had already prepared a set of *Resolutions*, in which he enlarged upon the more controversial aspects of his *Ninety-Five Theses*, but the Lord Abbot kindly asked him to hold his peace at least for a while. Not that there were any objections to the *Theses*, "yet, for fear of scandal, he judged it better to be silent and patient a little while." The Abbot stated that he was sorry Luther had already published the *Sermon on Indulgences and Grace* in the vernacular and asked that in the future no more copies be printed and sold. Now, just when the Bishop of Brandenburg had been

willing to overlook Luther's former offenses and had made a very
conciliatory move by sending Lord Abbot of Lehnin to Wittenberg,
the students had unwittingly added fuel to the dying fire and
aroused the Dominicans anew.[77]

The Dominicans, at their meeting in Frankfurt an der Oder,
had not been satisfied with words, but had insisted that Rome be
informed that Luther was spreading new doctrines and was guilty
of heresy. So certain were they of action that many were already
preaching from their pulpits throughout the Saxon lands that within
a month at most Luther would be burned at the stake.[78] Even
Frederick became alarmed for the safety of his able professor, of
whose new theology he had heard a great deal through his court
preacher, George Spalatin. Nor was the Dominican threat mere
words! Their influence in Rome was far-reaching, for most of the
officials of the Roman *Curia* who would handle Luther's case were
Dominicans. There was Nicholas von Schoenberg, secretary of
Julian de Medici, cousin of the Pope and papal vice-chancellor,
a Saxon and a Dominican. Through this contact their case would
be well received in the highest circles of the *Curia*.[79] Besides, Cardinal Cajetan, the greatest theologian in Rome, was not only a
Dominican, but even the General of that order.[80] Naturally, any
report as to "new doctrines" or accusation of "heresy" was of great
interest to him, as this was his special business. Unfortunately, the
records of the Dominican report from Frankfurt are no longer
extant, and the exact time when the Roman officials were notified
as to the official action of the Frankfurt an der Oder meeting can
no longer be ascertained; but it is evident that the Dominicans
made much more of an impression than did Albert of Mainz in his
report in December of the previous year.

The Roman *Curia*, however, did not immediately show its
hand. Before taking any official action, an attempt was made to
silence the Wittenberg monk through the General of the Augustinian Order. To accomplish this, Leo X, through Cardinal Julian
de Medici, contacted the General of the Augustinian Hermits,
Gabriel della Volta, also called *Venetus*, who was in turn to contact Vicar John Staupitz of the German Congregation to see if they
could not solve this problem within their own group.[81] The story

that Volta wrote Staupitz, requesting that Luther be made to recant
at the next General Chapter meeting at Heidelberg in the spring
of 1518 is based on mere supposition. It seems reasonable to believe from Luther's letter of March 31, 1518, to Vicar Staupitz that
Luther had kept him fully informed on the Wittenberg problem
and that Luther knew that Staupitz sympathized with the Wittenberg point of view.[82] Luther mentioned that the Vicar doubtless
knew his name had been placed in bad repute; but also stated that
he taught "that men should trust in nothing save in Jesus Christ
only, not in their own prayers, or merits, or works, for we are not
saved by our own exertions, but by the mercy of God." He said
he was certain that Staupitz approved of his position and added:
"But as I did not begin for the sake of fame, I shall not stop for
infamy." In fact, Luther pointed out that he merely attacked the
Scholastics, which was a very common practice. If the Scotists
were permitted to attack the Thomists, and the Thomists were
granted the right to question the position of all other schools, why
should not they, too, be open to question? He was only following
the advice of St. Paul, "Prove all things, hold fast to that which is
good," and added, "Truly I have followed the theology of Tauler
and the book which you recently gave to Christian Doering to
print," namely, *The Love of God*.[83] Since this letter was sent just
before the Heidelberg meeting, it was no doubt meant to aid
Staupitz in handling the heresy problem which was certain to be
raised.

THE HEIDELBERG MEETING

Luther wrote to his close friend John Lang at Erfurt on
March 21, 1518, telling him that, although advised on every hand
against the trip to Heidelberg, still would he remain true to his
vow of obedience and travel there on foot; however, since he might
be delayed until as late as April 13, he advised the Erfurt brethren
to go on without him.[84] He assured his friend that he would be
safe, since his Prince, unasked, had taken every possible precaution
for both himself and Carlstadt in order that his enemies could
not accomplish against him by guile that which they were unable
to do by force. Frederick the Wise has done everything within
his power to protect and shield Luther on the arduous journey.

He amply provided Luther with letters of introduction, and he wrote special communications to those princes through whose lands the party would pass. He also asked Vicar Staupitz to expedite the business as quickly as possible that Luther might be exposed no longer than necessary.

Luther in company with Brother Leonhard Beier as traveling companion left Wittenberg April 11, going by way of Bitterfeld to Leipzig, and from there following the Weissenfels-Saalfeld-Graefenthal-Judenbach route, arriving finally at Coburg, tired and worn, on April 15, having walked all the way. In a letter of that date from Coburg, Luther wrote Spalatin about the trip in jocular vein in spite of his great fatigue. He spoke of having been entertained in Judenbach by their mutual "friend Pfeffinger," who no doubt had been asked by the Elector to watch over them in that region, and confessed "that I sinned by coming on foot. Since my contrition for this sin is perfect and full penance has been imposed for it, I do not need an indulgence." [85] From this letter may be inferred that the Elector had arranged for Luther to be passed from hand to hand in order to complete his journey safely.

The journey was resumed the next day, and they arrived in Wuerzburg on Sunday evening, April 18, and presented their letter of introduction to Prince-Bishop Lorenz.[86] Here again they were received with cordial hospitality and entertained in the Castle Marienburg, which looms high above the city. Bishop Lorenz was so impressed with Luther that he offered to provide him with special transportation, which Luther declined, as Lang and his party were also in Wuerzburg at the Augustinian monastery and they had offered Luther and Beier a ride the remainder of the way. The Bishop never forgot the interview, for in 1519 shortly before his death he urged the Elector of Saxony to continue to provide special protection for his good professor so that he might remain unharmed. Finally, on April 21 or 22 the group arrived in Heidelberg and took up their quarters at the Augustinian convent, where the meeting was held.

On April 25 the Augustinian Vicar John Staupitz opened the Chapter in the large hall of the cloister. Just what transpired between Luther and the officials of the Hermits is not known, but John Staupitz asked Luther and his associate Beier to hold a

disputation to acquaint the members of the order with the New
Theology of the University of Wittenberg.[87] The Vicar's anxiety
to have Luther appear in a favorable light was reflected in the
theses chosen for debate. In these materials there appeared no
reference to indulgences or to the abuses of John Tetzel. Rather,
they were asked to debate less controversial theses relative to
original sin, grace, free will, and faith. Most of the debate was
thus directed against Aristotle and the Scholastics, as had been
the case in the *Ninety-Seven Theses Against Scholasticism* debated
by Francis Guenther, Luther's candidate for Bachelor of Theology,
at Wittenberg in 1517.[88] Usingen, Luther's former Scholastic professor at Erfurt, submitted twelve countertheses defending the *Via
Moderna* against Luther's attack.

The professors of the University of Heidelberg, although somewhat surprised by this new theological approach, were, on the
whole, polite and respectful. However, one young instructor, Georg
Schwarz von Loewenstein, not being able to restrain his feeling
any longer, burst forth: "If the peasants heard that, they would
stone you." [89] The Count Palatinate of the Rhine, Wolfgang, wrote
his reactions to the debate in a letter to the Elector of Saxony,
May 1, 1518:

> He [Luther] has acquitted himself so well here with his disputation
> that he has won no small praise for your Grace's University and was
> greatly lauded by many learned persons. This we would not with-
> hold from your Grace, for we are always ready to serve you.[90]

Even more impressed were the younger generation, who were
naturally drawn toward the new Biblical Humanism.[91] Among
them was a certain Martin Bucer of Schlettstadt, a devoted follower
of Erasmus. This was Bucer's first contact with Luther, and he
became and remained an admirer of the great Saxon. On May 1,
1518, he, likewise, communicated his impression of Luther's debate
at Heidelberg to Beatus Rhenanus of Basel:

> . . . I will oppose to you a certain theologian, not, indeed, one of
> our number [Heidelberg], but one who has been heard by us in the
> last few days, one who has got so far away from the bonds of the
> sophists and the trifling of Aristotle, one who is so devoted to the
> Bible, and is so suspicious of antiquated theologians of our school,
> . . . that he appears to be diametrically opposed to our teachers.

Jerome, Augustine and authors of that stamp are as familiar to him as Scotus or Tartaretus could be to us. He is Martin Luther, that abuser of indulgences, on which we have hitherto relied too much. At the general chapter of his order celebrated here, according to the custom, he presided over a debate, and propounded some paradoxes, which not only went farther than most could follow him, but appeared to some heretical. . . .

To return to Martin Luther: although our chief men refuted him with all their might, their wiles were not able to make him move an inch from his propositions. His sweetness in answering is remarkable, his patience in listening is incomparable, in his explanations you would recognize the acumen of Paul, not of Scotus; his answers, so brief, so wise, and drawn from the Holy Scriptures, easily made all his hearers his admirers.

On the next day I had a familiar and friendly conference with the man alone, and a supper rich with doctrine rather than with dainties. He lucidly explained whatever I might ask. He agrees with Erasmus in all things, but with this difference in his favor, that what Erasmus only insinuates he teaches openly and freely. Would that I had time to write you more of this. He has brought it about that at Wittenberg the ordinary textbooks have all been abolished, while the Greeks and Jerome, Augustine and Paul, are publicly taught.[92]

The above-mentioned Count Palatinate, Pfalzgraf Wolfgang Wilhelm, had been a former student of the University of Wittenberg, and he invited Staupitz, Luther, Lang, and a few friends for a repast and a tour of his still famous Heidelberg Castle.[93]

There is very little specific information on what official action was taken at Heidelberg with reference to Luther's attack on indulgences. A sharp communication from General Volta addressed to Staupitz was read to the Chapter, but it seems that no official legislation was passed.[94] Luther was asked to prepare for publication the *Resolutions,* on which he had been working for months, and to forward this exposition of the *Theses,* together with a special letter of apology, to Staupitz for transmission to the Pope.[95] To this Luther agreed.

The return trip for Luther and his companion proved much more pleasant, for they were provided with transportation.[96] The first day from Heidelberg to Wuerzburg Luther rode with his Nuernberg friends, while from there to Erfurt he rode in the wagon with Lang and the Erfurt chapter members. The latter

journey proved quite entertaining, as much of the time was consumed in theological discussion between Luther and his former
Erfurt professor Usingen.[97] Even though the learned champion of
the *Via Moderna* was too old and fixed in his beliefs to be convinced, yet Luther argued so effectively from the fund of his new
Biblical knowledge that the old man was left confused and bewildered.

On May 8, 1518, Luther tried to call on his beloved old Professor Trutvetter in Erfurt, but was told that he could not be admitted as the ailing old man was too weak to receive visitors.[98]
Luther believed that this was merely an excuse, for Trutvetter was
also opposed to his New Theology and wished to avoid a heated
argument. Therefore, Luther wrote Trutvetter a letter on May 9,
1518, in which he sought to make his peace with the old man; but
in an interview, which was finally granted, the rift between the
two was widened still more. Trutvetter had no understanding of
Luther's Biblical Humanism, and Luther became convinced that
he, like Usingen, was beyond hope of conversion. When the aged
professor passed away May 9, 1519, Luther felt depressed lest their
differences had hastened his death because of the old man's grief
for his brilliant student, who had departed from the faith.[99] With
such men as his former Prior Nathin at Erfurt, an arch-conservative,
Luther had even less success. It was experiences such as these
which tortured Luther with doubts, as he often later confessed to
his table companions, as to whether his reforms were of God.[100]
The cumulative effect of such experiences was the conviction that
the only hope for reforms within the Roman Church lay with the
younger generation.

Around May 12 Luther continued the journey homeward in
company with friends from Eisleben, leaving there two days later
in a wagon furnished by the Eisleben brethren. So, finally, on
May 15, 1518, Luther again arrived at the Black Cloister in Wittenberg quite safe from the Dominican wrath.[101] According to his correspondence, Luther's health following his return was very good,
for the journey had offered a badly needed respite from the arduous
routine of writing and teaching in Wittenberg.[102]

« 11 »

Early Attempts to Silence Luther

THE SERMON ON THE BAN

TOWARD THE CLOSE of the Middle Ages the Roman *Curia* had developed into one of the leading fiscal institutions in western Europe, with its channels of revenue carefully guarded through threats of bans, excommunications, and interdicts.[1] Where formerly these agencies of the Roman Church served as disciplinary measures against incorrigible sinners, they now became a bold instrument for the collection of papal revenues. Luther said that bans and interdicts flew about like so many bats every fall when the time for the collection of the tithe tax had arrived. All individuals who failed to meet their annual fiscal obligations were put under the ban, which not only affected them, but all their immediate relatives as well. On occasion, a whole community might even be put under an interdict. A person or community thus afflicted was outwardly cut off from grace. All the sacraments of the Church except Baptism and Extreme Unction were denied, and in case of death, members of the family would see their loved ones interred without the rites of the Church. Others were forbidden to associate with the condemned for fear of also being banned. The terror of the ban was enhanced by the teaching that anyone who passed away in such relationship to God was certain of eternal damnation. This terror became the chief weapon of the *Curia* in its collection of revenues.

Although Martin Luther may not have had any definite information on the action being planned in Rome, Wittenberg was buzzing with rumors. Doubtless Luther was warned over and over again, as in the letter from Count Albert of Mansfeld to John

331

Lang, not to leave Wittenberg under any circumstances.[2] He was, however, familiar enough with Roman *Curia* practices to realize that no person could cause Tetzel to fall behind in his indulgence traffic without putting himself in jeopardy of retaliation. The Heidelberg meeting had failed to bring the desired recantation for Rome. More drastic measures were certain to be forthcoming. Perhaps Luther thought that by anticipating and exposing Rome's action he might weaken its effect. Whatever his reasoning, he took another very drastic step, the decision to preach on the papal ban.

Shortly after his return from Heidelberg, early the Sunday morning of May 16, Luther preached in the Wittenberg *Stadtkirche* on the subject "Concerning the Validity of Excommunication," [3] a message that must have left his already excited parishioners breathless. Apparently some of Tetzel's fellow Dominicans were represented in the audience on this unusual occasion. Luther doubtless realized that stormy days were ahead, and his people would have to be informed fully on the true meaning of excommunication.

In this sermon Luther classified the Christian's relationship to the Church as twofold: external and internal. The external relationship, that of participation in the sacraments and outward activities of the Roman Church, was the only one affected by the ban. It had no effect on his relationship to God, for this he had already broken before the ban declared it to the world at large. His internal relationship to the Church was based on faith, hope, and charity, and those no human could touch. Only God could change this relationship between Himself and the individual believer. No papal ban could affect this inner relationship between the Christian believer and his God.

Following this reasoning, Luther also believed there were two kinds of excommunication: the just and the unjust. Excommunication was just only when an incorrigible sinner had refused the normal means of grace and would not mend his evil ways. When the Church placed such a sinner under the ban, it did not cut him off from God's divine grace, but merely declared to the world what had already taken place. Such a sinner should be excluded from the holy things of God, for that act might cause him to repent and reform his evil ways. On the other hand, the unjust excommunication, of which there were many, could effect only an external separation. In fact, he who was excommunicated for any other reason than that of having fallen from grace, was thereby asked to bear an unjust burden which God would recognize as a real test of his faith. Mistreatment did not harm the soul; rather it promoted its spiritual growth. The following excerpt from the sermon must have shocked the whole congregation:

> Should you be undeservedly excommunicated even though you are persevering in righteousness and truth, you must continue in those pursuits even though you might die without the Sacrament of the Eucharist, the rights of burial, the grave, etc. For these are insignificant by comparison with that righteousness on account of which they are being endured. For he who dies as a just man in excommunication will not be damned, unless perchance he should die without contrition or in contempt of excommunication. True contrition and humility satisfy everything and are acceptable even though his body were exhumed and thrown into the water. Blessed, however, and fortunate is he who has died under an unjust excommunication; because of the righteousness which he has not deserved, even though he received such a blow of the whip, he will be crowned in eternity.[4]

The sermon is reported to have made a memorable impression on the people of Wittenberg. But even more impressed were the professors of Canon Law and Tetzel's fellow Dominicans. Luther had spoken quite openly and further endangered his position with Rome. His Wittenberg congregation was prepared for the worst. But they had heard an able theological exposition on fiscal abuses and the misuse of the ban which prepared them to judge their leader's cause in the dark hours which were to follow.

The First Attack by John Eck

Although Luther well knew he must expect reverberations and recriminations from his activities, he still was not prepared for the source from whence they first came nor the violence of the attack. From his good friend Wenzel Link in Nuernberg came a copy of John Eck's *Obelisks* containing a vitriolic attack on both the *Theses* of Luther and his person. The attack was all the more astonishing because this well-known Ingolstadt professor was reported to be sympathetic to the Wittenberg reforms and to Humanism generally. He had taken his title, *Obelisks*, meaning "dagger points," from Origen's use of these signs to denote questionable statements in contemporary literature.[5]

Luther's astonishment is reflected in the letter he penned to John Sylvius Egranus at Zwickau on March 24, 1518:

> A man of signal and talented learning and of learned talent, has recently written a book called *Obelisks* against my *Theses*. I mean John Eck, Doctor of Theology, chancellor of the University of Ingolstadt, canon of Eichstaett, and now, at length, preacher at Augsburg, a man already famous and widely known by his books. What cuts me most is that we had recently formed a great friendship. Did I not already know the machinations of Satan, I should be astonished at the fury with which Eck has broken that sweet amity without warning and with no letter to bid me farewell.

> In his *Obelisks* he calls me a fanatic Hussite, heretical, seditious, insolent and rash, not to speak of such slight abuse as that I am dreaming, clumsy, unlearned, and that I despise the Pope. In short, the book is nothing but the foulest abuse, expressly mentioning my name and directed against my *Theses*. It is nothing less than the malice and envy of a maniac. I would have swallowed this sop for Cerberus, but my friends compelled me to answer it. Blessed be the Lord Jesus, and may he alone be glorified while we are confounded for our sins. Rejoice, brother, rejoice, and be not terrified by these whirling leaves, nor stop teaching as you have begun, but rather be like the palm tree which grows better when weights are hung on it.

> The more they rage, the more cause I give them. I leave the doctrine they barked at yesterday for one they will bark at more fiercely tomorrow. . . .[6]

Luther replied to John Eck's "little daggers" one by one in a document titled *Asterisks*, another term borrowed from Origen, who had used it to denote explanatory notes to passages in his own writings.[7] Luther wrote a letter to Link, who was to transmit the reply to John Eck, in which he stated that the purpose of the *Asterisks* was to make Eck realize how rashly he had condemned an unsuspecting friend. With the *Asterisks* Luther also enclosed a letter on May 19, 1518, to John Eck himself in which he repaid the Ingolstadt professor in kind. The following lines are illustrative:

> Certain *Obelisks* have come to me, by which you have tried to refute my *Theses* on indulgences; this is a witness of the friendship which you offered me unasked, and also of your spirit of evan-

gelic charity according to which we are bidden to warn a brother before we accuse him. How could I, a simple man, believe or suspect that you who were so smooth-tongued before my face, would attack me behind my back? Thus you have fulfilled the saying of Scripture: "Which speak peace to their neighbors, but mischief is in their hearts." I know that you will not admit that you have done this, but you did what you could; see what your conscience tells you. I am astonished that you have the effrontery alone to judge my opinions before you know and understand them. This rashness of yours is sufficient proof that you think yourself the only theologian alive, and so unique that not only do you prefer your own opinions to all others, but even think that what you condemn, though you do not understand it, is to be condemned because it does not please Eck. Pray let God live and reign over us.

But to cut the matter short, as you are so furious against me, I have sent some *Asterisks* against your *Obelisks,* that you may see and recognize your ignorance and rashness; I consult your reputation by not publishing them, but by sending them to you privately so as not to render evil for evil as you did to me. I wrote them only for him from whom I received your *Obelisks,* and sent them to him to give you. Had I wished to publish anything against you, I should have written more carefully and calmly, though also more strongly. If your confidence in your foolish *Obelisks* is still unshaken, pray write me; I will meet you with equal confidence. . . .

You have your choice; I will remain your friend if you wish, or I will gladly meet your attack, for as far as I can see, you know nothing in theology except the husks of scholasticism. You will find out how much you can do against me when you begin to prefer war to peace and fury to friendship.[8]

This appears like rather strong language from a professor of theology, but considered in the light of Eck's caustic comments and treacherous attack, it becomes righteous indignation.

Subsequent research seems to substantiate Eck's claim that he had not intended to harm Luther with the *Obelisks*.[9] He had visited the Bishop of Eichstaedt with regard to quite another matter, but the conversation gradually led to Luther's *Ninety-Five Theses*. The bishop seemed quite favorably inclined toward Luther's point of view; and Eck, who was ambitious and eager to rise, sought to impress the bishop with his criticism. As a result the bishop asked for his opinions in writing. A copy of the *Obelisks* fell into the hands of one of Eck's enemies, Bernhard Adelmann, who was the bishop's nephew and the Canon of Augsburg.[10] Bernhard seems to have felt that he would settle a score with Eck by seeing that the document reached Luther by way of his friend Link in Nuernberg. Luther, of course, did not know the story behind the scenes.

Carlstadt, without Luther's knowledge, published 406 Theses against the *Obelisks* after Luther had shown them to him sometime in the spring. He attacked Eck quite vehemently. When Luther learned of the episode, he again wrote to Eck, suggesting that he temper his reply, for after all it was he who had started the controversy, not Wittenberg. Eck accepted Luther's advice and on May 28, 1518, wrote Carlstadt a very conciliatory letter in which he stated:

> Truly, if I may presume upon my recently formed friendship, I shall consider it a friendly act if you will let whatever you meditate against innocent Eck fall into oblivion. For it was not my intention to hurt Luther.[11]

To this Carlstadt replied June 11, in a letter that began somewhat gruffly, justifying his publication against the *Obelisks*, but he ended by inviting Eck to join their group, for, "I believe that from Saul you will be made Paul." After expressing his desire to keep Eck's friendship, Carlstadt added: "Long live our Luther, who gives us a chance to extract the kernel of the law of God. Long live Eck, as his friend." [12] To all appearances the feud between Wittenberg and Ingolstadt had been amicably settled.

During this period Luther's amazing powers of productivity were becoming apparent. Instead of being completely preoccupied with the indulgence struggle, as might have been expected, Luther demonstrated a remarkable ability to retire to his cell and to lose himself somehow in divine contemplation. Some of the most inspiring and consoling lines flowed from Luther's pen during the period of his greatest trials. On June 4, Luther's second edition of the *German Theology* with the famous introduction ascribing the work to a Frankfurt Anonymous came from the press, and a Latin edition of Luther's *Sermons on the Ten Commandments* was published July 20.[13]

THE APPEAL TO THE POPE

After his return from the Heidelberg meeting, Luther completed his *Resolutions Concerning the Virtue of Indulgences* [14] and forwarded the manuscript to Staupitz for transmission to Pope Leo X, as had been agreed. In the accompanying letter to Vicar Staupitz, a grateful and tender communication, Luther expressed his indebtedness to his Wittenberg superior, who had helped him to grasp the real meaning of "penitence." [15]

There still exists a part of the Ms copy of Luther's *Resolutions*, in which Luther sought to prove to Tetzel and his boisterous crowd that he was not afraid to bring his case directly before the Roman *Curia*. The *Resolutions* were written to amplify and clarify those portions of the *Ninety-Five Theses* which his enemies had so twisted and misrepresented that the questions which he had raised for purposes of academic discussion were made to appear as bold, defiant charges against the accepted teachings of the Roman Church. The whole approach of the document was that of a humble, pious Christian, who sincerely believed the Pope would understand that he sought only to bring to the attention of the Papacy certain malicious abuses within the Church. Luther emphasized that he did not hold any views contrary to the Scriptures, the Fathers, and the Roman Church. He believed himself still a good Roman Catholic, whose real friend was the Pope.[16]

Yet a careful study of the *Resolutions* would reveal to a sharp-eyed Thomist like Prierias, official theological adviser to the Pope, that Luther had drifted even farther from the pale of the Church than in the *Ninety-Five Theses*. Luther insisted that he would accept no other authority than the Bible and that he had learned to follow Paul's advice: "Prove all things." Here he expressed the belief, not found in the *Theses*, that even popes and councils could err, and he concluded that a Reformation of the Church was God's work and should be done through a universal council.[17] The Pope's power over purgatory, he asserted, was no greater than that of every bishop or pastor. As for Sixtus IV's claims of power over the souls of the dead, Luther said in effect: "Holy Father, prove what you claim." [18] In the *Resolutions*, Luther's emphasis on the Gospel as the most precious treasure of the Church became much stronger. The

whole document breathed an atmosphere of bewilderment that so
much ado was being made about his *Ninety-Five Theses*; the right
of academic disputation to dispute theological problems had been
granted the universities for centuries.[19] Others had dared to criticize Aquinas, the Thomists had not hesitated to criticize everything
and everybody; whether Luther's situation were different, he would
leave to the Roman See:

> Wherefore, most blessed Father, I prostrate myself at your feet
> with all that I am and possess. Make alive, kill, call, recall, ap-
> prove, condemn, I will acknowledge thy voice as the voice of Christ,
> presiding and speaking in thee. If I have merited death, I shall not
> refuse to die.[20]

LUTHER IS SUMMONED TO ROME

While Luther was completing his humble *Resolutions*, through
which he hoped to invoke once more the "blessing of the Pope,"
events were happening behind the scenes which were to make his
case infinitely worse. During the week from May 23 to May 31,
1518, the Dominicans held their Chapter in *Santa Maria sopra
Minerva* in Rome, where Tetzel was ably represented by the Saxon
Provincial Hermann Rab of Bamberg.[21] Rab used all his influence
with the fiscal Procurator Perusco to have Luther's case opened in
the usual manner of "suspicion of heresy." [22] The preliminary investigation was made by the chief judge of the Roman *Curia*,
Auditor General Jerome Ghinucci; but since Ghinucci was not a
theologian, he was not qualified to appraise the *Theses*. He turned
to the sixty-two-year-old experienced Master of the Sacred Palace,
Silvester Prierias. This Dominican theological expert boasted that
it took him only three days to evaluate Luther's *Theses* in the form
of a *Streitschrift*, a dialogue attacking Luther's position.[23] That he
did not penetrate the wealth of theological thought behind the
Theses in that length of time is quite obvious. In his dignified
position of official theological adviser to the Pope and in view of
the experience gained from the recent John Reuchlin trial, Prierias
felt that he needed only to write "in error," "false," and Luther
would be sufficiently cowed. In a letter to Luther, Prierias spoke
of the *Dialogue Concerning the Powers of the Pope*, the full title

of his reply, as a wrestling match in which he was obligated to defend "the truth and the Apostolic See." [24]

Chief Judge Ghinucci took no exception to the acrimonious style of the document; and on the basis of this superficial diagnosis of Luther's early writings he summoned Luther to appear in Rome within sixty days after the notice reached Wittenberg.[25] Both Prierias' *Dialogue* and the summons reached Cardinal Cajetan in Augsburg, where the papal legate was staying in the beautiful home of the Fuggers while attending the Diet of Augsburg. Additional copies reached Luther via their *Filiale* in Leipzig on August 7.[26] Immediately upon the arrival of the *Dialogue* Luther prepared a hurried reply.[27] In two days his eighty-page manuscript was in the hands of Printer Melchior Lotther in Leipzig. The Wittenberg printers were already occupied with previous documents and could not keep pace with his productivity.

Rome's theological expert, Prierias, had made the mistake of underestimating the rugged Saxon wrestler, whom he proposed to engage in a match as Entellus did Dares in Virgil's *Aeneid*. He was soon to learn that Luther was not to be intimidated so easily by Rome; nor was he incapable of analyzing the superficiality of Prierias' *Dialogue*, as is shown by his introductory letter of August 10, 1518:

> That supercilious *Dialogue* of yours, very reverend Father, written in the usual style of an Italian and a Thomist, has reached me. You boast in it that you, an old man, done with fighting, are impelled anew by my words to the combat, but nevertheless, you say you will get the victory over me in the unequal contest, as Entellus did over Dares, but by this alone you show that you are vainglorious Dares rather than Entellus, because you boast before you are safe and ask for praise before victory. Pray do what you can; the Lord's will be done. . . .
>
> Behold, reverend Father, I am sending your treatise back quickly, because your refutation seems trifling; therefore, I have answered it *ex tempore* with whatever came uppermost in my mind. If, after that, you wish to hit back, be careful to bring your Aquinas better armed into the arena, lest perchance you be not treated as gently again as you are in this encounter. I have forborne to render evil for evil.
>
> Farewell! [28]

Luther's reply may not have contributed to the Roman case against him, but it certainly contained additional evidence that Luther was drifting farther and farther from the way of accepted Roman thought. No longer did he identify the true Church with the Catholic Church and the Roman hierarchy. As Karl Holl has shown, Luther's conception of the Invisible Church of Jesus Christ had changed before this, though he still believed that the true Church was within the pale of Roman Catholicism.[29] In the fall of 1518, after his experiences with Rome, Luther did some very serious thinking while searching the New Testament for light. The Church is really present only in Christ, said Luther in his reply to the *Dialogue* of Prierias, and it cannot be represented in any group other than a universal council. Luther's study of the history of the Catholic Church led him to the conclusion that in the past both councils and the Pope had erred, and he advanced as a counter-argument to the Master of the Sacred Palace, who made some very bold claims for the Papacy, that only the Holy Scriptures were without error. Luther even became so bold as to assert that though the Roman Church had never formally denied the true faith, there were many in the hierarchy who were no longer real believers. Again he repeated the question asked in his former documents and letters: Why should it be heretical to debate theological questions upon which there had been no official doctrinal agreement? His criticism, he declared, was not directed against the Catholic faith, but against the lack of faith and the abuse and misinterpretation of the beliefs of the early Roman Church.

The Intrigue at the Dresden Banquet

Luther little realized how active his enemies had been or the means to which they would stoop until reports reached him from the Augsburg Diet in September, 1518. Everything possible was being done to prejudice princes and even the Emperor against the Wittenberg professor. According to the reports the opposition had concocted and was circulating a forged set of theses.[30]

When Luther preached his sermon on the ban, John Tetzel and his group had spies in the audience. On the basis of what they heard that morning and other writings of Luther, the Dominicans forged a set of theses on the papal ban which they claimed were by Luther. The document as it appeared in print was usually accompanied by a violent attack, also purported to be by Luther, against the insatiable hunger of the Roman *Curia* for gold.

Luther innocently accepted an invitation to preach in the Castle Church in Dresden on July 25,[31] which occasion was followed by a banquet given by Duke George's secretary and the court chaplain, Jerome Emser.[32] During the meal Luther became involved in an argument with a Leipzig Thomist, Magister Weissestadt,[33] whom Luther later characterized as a man who "thought he knew everything." The conversation revolved around Luther's favorite topics of indulgences, excommunication, and the worth of Aristotle and St. Thomas to theology. The discussion became quite heated, and Luther said many things on which normally he might have restrained himself, such as the statement that the papal ban did not worry him, that he was prepared to die quietly; for he believed himself to be among friends. Too late he realized that he had been led into a trap of which the banquet was the bait.

Luther wrote to Spalatin: "All the while there stood outside, without my knowing it, a Dominican preacher, listening to all I said." Through the Dresden prior Luther learned how his statements and his sermon had been twisted and misrepresented whenever possible. "In short," he added, "I found them a generation of vipers, wishing to do everything and able to do nothing, and considering it a spot on their glory if they leave a single word of mine unblamed." [34] Emser, the host, claimed that he knew nothing of the whole affair, but his later record makes his assertion rather doubtful.

Then came the report from Augsburg that the same spurious theses which Weissestadt was quoting were also being circulated in the Augsburg Diet of the Emperor. Even Spalatin was misled as to their genuineness and wrote Luther, begging him to exercise more restraint.[35] Luther now published his *Sermon on the Ban* as he recalled it from memory, but it was too late; the forged documents had left an indelible impression.[36] Cajetan had used them to good effect with the Emperor, who on August 5 wrote the well-known letter to Pope Leo X in which he expressed great concern for the activities of Martin Luther and the danger that his ideas on the papal power of excommunication, in which he obstinately persisted, might spread and infect others. He urged that action be taken, and he closed with the following promise:

> [Because] of our singular reverence for the Apostolic See, we have signified this to your Holiness, so that simple Christianity may not be injured and scandalized by these rash disputes and captious arguments. Whatever may be righteously decided upon in this our Empire, we will make all our subjects obey for the praise and honor of God Almighty and the salvation of Christians.[37]

This letter, together with the two forged documents, the pseudo-theses of Luther against the papal ban and the forged diatribe against the Roman *Curia,* made a deep impression in Rome. If even Emperor Maximilian I was so disturbed about the Luther problem, Luther must be a far more dangerous heretic than had heretofore been realized in Rome. Even the Auditor General Ghinucci agreed that the situation was grave. Not knowing the authorship of the forged documents, Ghinucci declared Luther a "notorious heretic" on the basis of this new evidence and asked Pope Leo X to proceed against him according to the well-established practice of Canon Law.

When the original papal summons had reached Luther in Wittenberg on August 7, his natural reaction was to appeal to the court of Frederick the Wise, whose lawyers were familiar with the steps in a trial for "suspicion of heresy." [38] Luther hoped that Frederick might have enough influence in the Diet of Augsburg to persuade Emperor Maximilian I to intercede with the Pope in his behalf that he might be tried before a neutral German tribunal. However, the Wittenberg professor little realized the nefarious business which had been going on behind the scenes through the circulation of the bogus theses and forged diatribe against the avarice of the Roman *Curia.* Luther's pamphlet giving his true position had come too late to correct the false impression which the Emperor and many of the princes now had of Martin Luther. The papal legate, Cajetan, immediately disapproved of a neutral tribunal and proposed that Luther could just as well appear before him.

Upon receipt of the Maximilian letter and the false Cajetan report, Rome suddenly reversed its previous intention of calling

Luther all the way to Italy. On August 23, 1518, Pope Leo X dispatched an official communication which empowered Cajetan to deal with the German heretic in summary fashion.[39] The danger of infection of others by the heresies of this bold and dangerous man had become so great that there was no time for delay. Cajetan was asked to arrest Luther, using all powers at his disposal, calling, if necessary, upon the Emperor and the German princes; and the message added: "When you have Martin in your power, keep him under a safe guard until you hear further from us." If Luther recanted, Cajetan was to absolve him of all his sins and receive him into the Holy Mother Church; but should he persist in his evil ways, he was to remain in custody, his devoted followers likewise arrested, and the ban and interdict employed as deemed advisable. The same day Pope Leo X also sent an appeal to Frederick the Wise, reminding him of his obligations to the Catholic faith and asking him to do all within his power to aid in the apprehension of

> a certain son of iniquity, Friar Martin Luther . . . forgetting his cloth and profession . . . sinfully vaunts himself in the Church of God, and, as though relying on your protection, fears the authority or rebuke of no one.[40]

In addition to the letters to Cajetan and Frederick the Wise, the Augustinian Order was also called upon to take action against its brother. Gabriel della Volta,[41] the new General of the Augustinian Hermits, had been elected at the request of Leo X earlier in the year, because Leo believed Volta would "quiet that man, for newly kindled flames are easily quenched, but a great fire is hard to put out." Volta realized he would get nowhere through the Vicar of the German Congregation, John Staupitz, who had proved to be a warm friend of the heretic. Therefore, the Augustinian General and the Pope conceived the idea of vesting Gerard Hecker,[42] the Provincial of Saxony representing the group which opposed Staupitz at the time of the proposed union in 1510, with powers to go over the head of his spiritual superior and to arrest Luther in spite of all his supporters.

Volta wrote to Hecker, deploring the "most damnable heresy" being practiced by this "schismatic heretic" and urging the neces-

sity of applying "remedies to this contagious pestilence . . . lest
he should infect and ruin others." He then charged Hecker:

> Therefore we command you under pain of losing all your pro-
> motions, dignities and offices, when you receive this letter, to
> proceed to capture the said Brother Martin Luther, have him bound
> in chains, fetters and handcuffs, and detained under strict guard
> in prison at the instance of our Supreme Lord Leo X. And as he
> belongs to that Congregation which thinks itself free from your
> government, that he may have no way of escape, we give you in
> this matter all our authority, and we inform you that our Supreme
> Lord, the Pope, has delegated to you plenary apostolic authority
> to imprison, bind and detain this man, notwithstanding anything
> done to the contrary, all of which, in as far as concerns this business,
> his Holiness expressly waives. Furthermore, he grants you power
> of putting the interdict on all places, and of excommunicating all
> persons by the apostolic authority, as you will see further in the
> apostolic breve, and of doing all things which seem to you needful
> for imprisoning this scoundrel; all of this in the name of the Father,
> and of the Son, and of the Holy Ghost. Amen.[43]

With Cajetan and Hecker both empowered to arrest Luther and
the Emperor and many German princes supporting the papal position, Luther had good reason to feel that his days were numbered.
Yet, at such moments the deep spiritual convictions which had
grown out of his monastic struggle came to the fore. In a letter to
Link in Nuernberg he wrote that he had now become like Jeremiah,
a "man of strife and contention" to the whole earth.[44] Yet he added:
"The more they threaten the bolder I am." With Reuchlin, he was
glad that he was poor, for he had nothing to lose. At best, no matter
what they did to his weak and worn body, they could but deprive
him of a few hours of this life. Like the Apostles of old, he expected
death at any moment.[45] The many letters he received from faithful
friends and even comparative strangers offering support and sympathy must have been a very real comfort.

Luther Appears Before Cajetan

The forgeries and the reports from Cajetan and the Emperor
received from Augsburg had left a false impression in Rome. Luther's cause was far more generally supported than the Pope had
been led to believe. Many people were ready to support any

movement which held hope of far-reaching reforms, though many different types of reform were sought. The German Humanists were watching Luther's case with great interest, while many of the knights and princes were anxious to escape the yoke of Roman tyranny.[46] Though the Emperor had promised all aid to the papal action against Luther, he was, after all, only a figurehead in German lands who could do little without the support of the German Diet.

One factor which both the Emperor and the Pope had failed to evaluate fully was the role which the Elector of Saxony was to play in the *processus inhibitorius,* the attempt to silence his Wittenberg professor. True, Frederick was a cautious, tactful prince, but he fully merited his title of "the Wise." [47] Frederick had never met Luther, but he knew a great deal about him and his work through the court preacher Spalatin and the Saxon Court lawyers, most of whom were enthusiastic champions of the Wittenberg reform movement. Furthermore, it must be remembered that Frederick was not only one of the seven German Electors who would choose the Emperor upon the death of Maximilian I; he was also the *Reichsvikar* who would rule all eastern German lands during the interim.[48] Without the co-operation of Frederick, those who sought to arrest Luther were assuming quite an assignment.

The Diet of Augsburg had been called because the Pope was in need of a German subsidy to wage the war against the Turks. But the old Emperor realized that his days were numbered, and he was anxious to arrange for the election of his grandson, Charles I of Spain and Naples. By August 27, Maximilian had secured the support of five of the German Electors, but the Archbishop of Trier and the Elector of Saxony were not well disposed toward his imperial plans. Frederick apparently realized that he had more power than a mere pawn on the imperial chessboard, and he began to use this new advantage in behalf of Luther.

The Luther problem immediately gathered political significance, for Rome feared the election of the young king of Spain and Naples would destroy the European balance of power. When Frederick the Wise agreed to support the Papacy in its war with the Turks, it seemed advisable to soften the demand for the prose-cution of the Luther heresy. Cajetan had heard much contradictory evidence and was not altogether certain of his ground. He feared that the Tetzel faction had overplayed the case. So when Frederick the Wise proposed a fair hearing before a neutral German tribunal, Cajetan wisely countered with the proposal of hearing Luther himself, with the assurance that the interview should not be under duress or threat. On the 5th of September Spalatin already optimistically reported that the Elector would be able to arrange for a fair trial.[49] He stated also that both he and the Elector had received the impression that Cajetan was not nearly so prejudiced against Luther as they had been led to believe.

Accordingly, Cajetan offered to give Luther a "fatherly" hearing. He sent a letter to Rome advising a more conciliatory attitude toward Luther in the light of subsequent developments. The revision of opinion on the part of Cajetan and his recommendation for the treatment of Luther had an immediate effect upon the politically minded Roman *Curia.*   The Pope had already thought out a plan whereby he hoped to win the shrewd Elector of Saxony over to the papal cause. He planned to send Miltitz with two special favors to Frederick. One was a new grant of indulgences for the Castle Church in Wittenberg; the other was the much coveted "Golden Rose." [51] When Cajetan's new proposal arrived, Rome immediately decided to postpone the Miltitz mission. On September 11, the Pope suspended the former summons to Rome and empowered Cajetan to hold the proposed Luther audience in Augsburg with the special provision that he refuse to engage the Wittenberg professor in any disputation.[52] Should Luther recant, the former authorization for his reinstatement in the Church still held; but if he refused, the right of condemnation was not to be followed by an arrest. Frederick was apparently not too certain of the good faith behind the proposal, for he insisted upon an imperial safe-conduct before Luther should submit himself to such a hearing.

When Luther finally set out on September 26 from Wittenberg,[53] in the company of the same Leonhard Beier who had accompanied him to Heidelberg, he had been assured of safe-conduct by both his Prince and the Emperor; but he did not know of the Elector's secret diplomacy, nor that the Pope's summons of August 7 had been changed. He stopped in Weimar to preach before the Elector on September 29, but his interested patron did not arrange for an interview. Luther was given the Electoral letter of safe-conduct and other documents, but he had no idea what the future held for him at Augsburg.[54] Spalatin's optimistic letter had led him to believe that there would be a trial before neutral judges, during which he would probably engage in a disputation in defense of his former teachings and writings. Luther mentioned in the *Table Talks* that during the long foot journey he more than once said to himself: "Now you must die." Various thoughts flashed through his mind. In sorrow and regret he mourned: "Oh, what a disgrace I shall bring to my parents!"[55] In imagination he beheld the funeral pyre and admitted that his flesh shrank from the idea. Luther felt certain he had no more than three months to live, and he reproached himself for being so foolish as to leave Wittenberg without the imperial safe-conduct.[56] Added to his own doubts were those of his friends, many of whom sought to persuade Luther to turn back. The Augustinian prior at Weimar declared Luther was walking right into a trap. Myconius, who related the story, added that the prior told Luther: "They will burn you at Augsburg."[57] From Nuernberg Luther wrote to his Wittenberg friends that he had found many fainthearted Christians who were trying to dissuade him from appearing before Cajetan. But Luther, convinced that he was obeying the Lord's will, resolved to face his trial, come what might. That conviction dominated his thoughts through all his trials and vicissitudes.

> Let the Lord's will be done. Even at Augsburg, yea in the midst of His enemies Jesus Christ rules. Let Christ live, let Martin die and every sinner, as it is written, God will be exalted to my salvation. It is needful that we be rejected either by men or by God. God is true though every man be a liar.[58]

Finally, on October 7, Luther arrived in Augsburg, tired from the arduous journey and ill from a stomach disorder.[59] He was immediately taken to the Carmelite Cloister, where he was cordially received by Prior Johannes Frosch, for the Augustinians had no convent in Augbsurg.[60] Luther was surprised to find himself the center of attraction among the common citizens, while many influential friends, such as Conrad Peutinger, looked after his well-being.

In Augsburg Luther was able to penetrate for the first time the true nature of his situation. Those who knew the inside politics warned him not to rely too much on Cajetan's promises, that in spite of all his seeming "fatherly" attitude he was a bitter enemy at heart and not to be trusted. Accordingly, Luther reported his arrival to Cajetan through his friend Link, but he followed the advice of his Elector not to appear before the Cardinal before the arrival of the imperial safe-conduct.[61] During the three days of waiting Cajetan became offended that Luther had not trusted in his promise to receive him in a "fatherly manner," and he later reproached Luther for this act of bad faith.

Luther was disappointed to learn through Serralonga, the legate's representative, that he would not be granted the right of disputation. Serralonga visited Luther several times before the safe-conduct arrived and tried to persuade him to recant, stating that only the six letters "Revoco" were necessary to settle the whole problem.[62] Luther replied that he was approaching the coming interview with an open mind and was ready to be instructed. Should the Cardinal be able to show him his errors, he would be the first to pronounce judgment upon himself. In these conversations Luther for the first time discovered that Tetzel's actions were approved by the *Curia*, for Serralonga justified Tetzel by the statement that it was quite permissible for indulgence preachers to stretch the truth in order to increase the papal revenues.[63] Luther described the interviews for his Table Companions and in his introduction to the 1545 edition of his Latin works *Martin Luther to the Pious Reader.*[64]

On the third day the Emperor's court council informed Cajetan that the safe-conduct had been granted and that no acts of violence against Luther's person should be perpetrated.[65] Luther stated that the Cardinal added: "Good, I will nevertheless do my duty according to my office." With this new uncertainty, Luther was still wavering between fear and hope; and he wrote Spalatin that at the time his fear seemed to overpower his hope. To Melanchthon he wrote that he would perish rather than revoke what he had so long been teaching.[66]

Finally, on October 12, Luther, in the accepted custom, prostrated himself in all humility at the Cardinal's feet.[67] He first apologized for not having appeared earlier, pleading that he had been advised by the Elector and his friends not to appear before the "very reverend lord legate" until the promised safe-conduct had arrived.[68] Luther also begged pardon for any rash action of his in the past and stated that he had come to be instructed in regard to the errors of his ways. The Canon of Augsburg, Conrad Adelmann, reported in a letter to Spalatin on October 18 that "Dr. Luther acquitted himself before the legate as beseems a Christian man." He summarized Luther's plea as follows:

> First he offered to leave everything to our Holy Father the Pope, to support what pleased his Holiness and to root out what did not. Secondly, he said that he had debated questions before the universities, according to their custom, and if they desired he would debate further. And if anyone came with good reasons and arguments from Scripture he would abandon his opinion and embrace a better one. Further, that if the Christian Church desired to take exception to a single saying of his he would at once submit to her. It was not his intention and never had been to write or say anything against the holy see or against the honor or dignity of the Pope.[69]

As Cajetan had promised the Elector, from the very beginning he adopted a fatherly tone in the hope of persuading Luther through kindness that he was wrong. Luther stated in the *Acta Augustana*, which he later drew up of the meeting with Cajetan, that it was difficult for him to understand this almost deferential treatment after the accustomed violence of others in the order.[70] Cajetan was doubtless sincere in this, for as a confirmed believer in the *Via Antiqua* he was no doubt eager to win Luther back into the Catholic fold; and if that could be accomplished by gentle and peaceful means, the reactions of the Elector of Saxony would be all the more desirable. But Cajetan's boundaries had been fixed for him by the papal *Breve* of September 11: he had been specifically instructed not to engage Luther in a disputation and to secure from Luther a recantation of his previous statements and writings.[71] Luther, on the other hand, was just as anxious to clarify what seemed to him just a misunderstanding.

It is not strange that these two men could not find common ground. They began with two entirely different points of view. On the one hand, Cajetan, a Thomist through and through, was clinging with the Roman Church to a way of life quite foreign to that held by the original Catholic Church. Luther, on the other hand, as a Biblical Humanist basing his New Theology on the Gospels and the Epistles of St. Paul, was teaching a religion which these men simply could not understand. In fact, as the meeting at Heidelberg had shown, none of the contemporary Catholic theologians could meet Luther on the ground of Biblical exegesis; and it was, therefore, dangerous to engage him in public debate on church doctrines.[72] Cajetan, then, had no choice but to proclaim: "You have erred, because Rome says you teach new doctrines." As Luther reported to Carlstadt on October 14, 1518: "He will hear nothing from me except 'I recant, I revoke, I confess that I erred,' which I would not say." [73]

Cajetan began the interview with a demand for a recantation, which Luther's conscience would not permit him to make unless apprised and convinced of his errors. When he asked to discuss the matter, the Cardinal replied that no discussions would be permitted.[74] When Luther asked wherein he had erred, Cajetan cited as an illustration Luther's teachings on the Treasure of the Church and on the Sacrament of Penance. As sufficient and generally accepted proof the legate cited the papal bull of Pope Clement VI of 1343, *Unigenitus*,[75] which clearly asserted that Christ's suffering and death had acquired an infinite treasure for the Church in heaven, to which the Virgin Mary and the saints had been adding ever since; all of which treasures had been committed to Peter and his successors for the benefit of the faithful. He further cited Luther's teaching that faith was essential to the Sacrament of Penance as being not only against Scripture and the teachings of the Holy Church, but also placing the sinner in such a position of uncertainty that he could never be sure of its efficacy. All this was presented in such a confident, patronizing tone that it was offensive to the searching, serious-minded monk who was earnestly seeking for light.[76]

Cajetan was soon to learn that Luther was far better informed in Canon Law than he had assumed. The questions raised in his

struggle for spiritual comfort had caused Luther to examine carefully the Scriptures and the writings of the Fathers. He had not
come to Augsburg just to be told that he was wrong, but to be
shown wherein his error lay. In raising the question of the true
treasure of the Church, the Gospel, Cajetan had touched the very
heart of Luther's New Theology, the doctrine of justification by
faith alone. Luther had no intention of being refuted on the evidence of a papal bull when his whole teaching had been painfully
rediscovered on the basis of the New Testament.[77] With Luther
this was a matter so vital that he would die rather than deny his
new understanding of the Scriptures unless convinced of error.

Aroused by Luther's contradictions and rebuttal, Cajetan soon
found himself involved in a heated argument with an opponent
who was easily his equal. Although a Thomist specialist, Cajetan
found himself face to face with a man who was questioning his
whole approach and assailing the foundations of his argument; for
the bull of Clement VI concerning the Treasure of the Church
could not counterbalance the Scriptures, from which Luther drew
his sole authority.[78] The more Cajetan insisted on the absolute
and inerrant power of the Papacy, which he pictured as being above
councils or even the Bible, the more apparent became the utter
irreconcilability of the two views.[79] Luther stoutly refuted this extreme interpretation of papal power and cited the University of
Paris, whose theological faculty ranked as the leading one in Europe, in support of his view. On the doctrine of sacramental grace
they were equally deadlocked, because each did not admit the
opponent's basic assumptions. When Cajetan asserted that the Bible
supported the doctrine of the efficacy of sacramental grace without
faith, Luther was in his own field of specialization. He cited
copiously from Scripture and asked Cajetan to meet his arguments
from the same source.[80] Luther maintained that, while he might
accept the Thomist view of indulgences, he would never concede
that true penance was possible without faith in Christ's atoning
death.

Following the stormy sessions of the first day, Luther's friends
accompanied him to the meeting on the second day. Vicar Staupitz
had come to Augsburg especially on his behalf and was joined

by a notary and four imperial councilors.[81] Luther was still not
fully conscious of the gulf which already existed between him and
accepted Catholic teaching, and believed that he had taught
nothing contrary to the Bible, the Fathers, and Canon Law.[82] Yet,
there was a possibility that he was in error, which could be most
easily determined by a public disputation. Were this petition
denied, Luther proposed to reply to the objections to his writings
raised by the Cardinal and to submit the written statement to
the expert opinion of the Universities of Freiburg, Louvain, or
even Paris.[83]

Cajetan had no choice but to follow Rome's instructions, and
he continued to plead with Luther to be reasonable and not
vainly persist in obstinacy.[84] It must be said to the credit of Cajetan
that he continued to maintain a fatherly attitude; but Luther, firm
in his belief that to recant without being convinced of error was
a violation of his conscience, maintained his determination to
present a written statement. At first Cajetan was inclined not to
consider Luther's request, but when Staupitz also intervened in
his behalf, consent was finally given.[85]

Accompanied by Feilitzsch and Ruehel, the lawyers of the
Elector, Luther on October 14 presented a thorough exposition of
the two problems which Cajetan had raised.[86] In unmistakable
language Luther here asserted that the Pope not only *could* err,
but *had* erred in the past, and that all papal decrees must be
evaluated in the light of Holy Writ; he supported the view of the
Council of Basel that a general council was superior to the Pope;
that even the opinion of a Christian supported by the Scriptures
and the Fathers was to be considered of more value than an unsupported papal decree: "justification by faith" was a fundamental
teaching of the Bible, supported by many passages from God's
Holy Word; the Sacrament of Penance without faith was of no
avail, and its recipient was on the road to eternal perdition; since
the individual conscience was really the supreme guide and authority, Luther had no other choice, he concluded, but to obey
God rather than men.[87] Therefore, he pleaded that Cajetan might
ask "our lord," Pope Leo X, to be clement with him and to consider him an humble penitent, not proud and arrogant, earnestly
seeking the truth as found in God's holy Word.

This presentation was too much for the sorely tried patience of the legate. He treated the document with contempt, but he agreed to forward it to Rome with ample refutation. When Luther tried to add further extenuations, both men began to shout, and finally the Cardinal completely lost his temper and ordered Luther out of his presence with the words: "Begone, either revoke or come not again into my presence." [88] Luther then realized that all further attempts to persuade Cajetan were hopeless.

After Luther and Staupitz had departed, Cajetan thought of one last-minute means of obtaining the result required by Rome. He summoned Staupitz and begged him to use all his influence to make Martin recant.[89] He had even worked out a special plan; but Staupitz, who knew all too well how deeply Luther felt about the matter, declined to employ force if he could not be persuaded from God's Word. Myconius, who was *not* there, claimed that at this time Staupitz turned to Cajetan and asked him why he did not persuade Luther himself; whereupon the Cardinal replied that he would have nothing further to do with that beast with the dark piercing eyes and the strange fantasies flitting through his head.[90] Link, who had been with Luther all the while, agreed with Staupitz that it was no use to ask Luther to violate his conscience; that he was, in fact, even then preparing an appeal from the Cardinal to the Pope.

After discussing the problem with Staupitz and Link, Luther wrote an apologetic letter to Cajetan for having spoken irreverently and indiscreetly during the heat of discussion and begged forgiveness.[91] He promised to refrain from further discussion of the subject of indulgences, provided his opponents also agreed to remain silent. Luther stated, too, that because of his very deep regard for Vicar Staupitz he would be willing to revoke his former position as far as his conscience permitted; but he made it clear that mere arguments from St. Thomas were not sufficient to convince him of error. Luther informed Cajetan that he was appealing directly to the Pope in order that the points of issue raised in this series of interviews might be settled by the Church.

In the meantime, because the rumor had been circulating that Cajetan planned to arrest both Luther and Staupitz, the vicar and Link left Augsburg rather unexpectedly without paying their farewell respects to the legate. Before leaving, however, Staupitz absolved Luther from his former monastic vow, thus liberating him from obedience to the order.[92]

Luther remained behind to complete the letter of October 17 which Staupitz had advised him to write. On the next day Luther prepared a second letter to Cajetan in which he bade him farewell, explaining that since he could not recant, there seemed no further object for remaining in Augsburg.[93] He asked that the legate might graciously receive his appeal to the Pope. There was no reply from Cajetan. The latter, when he heard of Staupitz's unexpected departure, was rather puzzled as to what to do about Luther. On the other hand, when the legate did not reply for several days, the court lawyers and all of Luther's advisers became very uneasy. They concluded that Luther should leave at once. Accordingly, on October 20, Luther was awakened and spirited by the prior of the Cathedral, Langenmantel, through a little gate in the city wall, where a rider awaited him with an extra horse. The whole scheme was effected so rapidly that Luther found himself riding to Monheim as he was, in his knee breeches and stockings; and as the horse provided was rather unmanageable, it proved to be a wild ride which Luther never forgot.[94]

Before leaving Augsburg, Luther completed his appeal to Pope Leo X, in which he restated and explained his former *Theses*, charging Cajetan with being biased and in sympathy with his opponents; but he repeated that he was open to conviction to well-reasoned arguments from the Scriptures. Luther's fellow monk, Leonhard Beier, was asked to take the document to Cajetan in person; but he, badly frightened, gave the assignment to a notary who, rather than face the legate, fastened it to the Cathedral door.[95]

Luther spent the night and the next day in Monheim and on October 22 hurried on to Nuernberg, where he was graciously received by Willibald Pirckheimer, Staupitz, and the rest of his friends.[96] Here he saw for the first time the papal *Breve* of August 23 in which the Pope had instructed Cajetan how to conduct the Luther interview. On October 24, Luther continued his journey home and on the second day was the guest of Albert of Mansfeld. On October 31, the first anniversary of the *Ninety-Five Theses*, he paused in the little town of Kemberg just outside of Wittenberg to conduct Sunday morning Mass. In the afternoon he arrived at the Augustinian Monastery in Wittenberg. That very night he sat down and wrote a letter to Spalatin in which he rejoiced that he was back safe and sound and included a good summary of the Augsburg interview:

> I appealed to the badly informed most supreme Pontiff, about to be better informed, and thus I departed, having left behind a brother who, accompanied by a notary and witnesses, is to give the appeal to the Cardinal. In the meantime here I shall prepare another appeal to a future council, in accordance with the practice of Paris, should the Pope refuse, on the basis of his power or rather his tyranny, my first appeal. I am so full of joy and peace that I wonder that many strong men should regard my trial as severe. Benevolence and clemency were copiously shown to me, as the Cardinal legate had promised our illustrious Elector; but we did not understand him thus. He offered to do all paternally, very paternally, and doubtless would have done so, had I only been willing to recant. For in this difficulty rested the whole cause, for I would not, and he demanded it (nor do I believe he had any other instruction than to condemn); I was forced to appeal.[97]

The repercussions of the Augsburg interviews were twofold. Luther had begun his indulgence struggle against Tetzel with the assumption that Rome was innocent in the whole matter and that the Pope and the Roman *Curia* need only be properly informed to curb the awful abuses of the indulgence preachers. His interviews with Cajetan, on the other hand, had all begun with the assumption that Luther was in error rather than the indulgence salesmen. When he saw the papal *Breve* of August 23, his faith was rather badly shaken by the "diabolic" document, but he still could not believe that the Pope himself had had anything to do with this last example of Roman perfidy. "It is incredible," he wrote Spalatin from Wittenberg on October 31, "that such a monster should come from a pope, especially from Leo X." [98] Luther still believed the Pope was ignorant of the actions of the Roman *Curia;* but since the Dominicans so thoroughly dominated the situation in Rome, Luther had little hope of receiving an impartial hearing from that quarter, and falsely believed that his only hope lay with a future council. He, therefore, prepared the appeal he had mentioned in the letter to Spalatin. This document, which was drawn up with the aid of the Wittenberg faculty lawyers, was completed November 28 and appeared in print December 11.[99] Shortly thereafter Melanchthon sent a copy to George Spalatin and stated that "Luther clears himself so entirely that they cannot pretend that he is guilty of a new crime."

Cajetan, on the other hand, realized that such a gifted professor as Luther, thoroughly familiar with the canons of the Roman Church and the Scholastics, would not be satisfied with mere arguments. He was convinced that Luther was right in claiming that the Church had never officially spoken on the matter of Tetzel's indulgence claims, and so he resolved to remedy the deficiency. On October 25 he enclosed with his official reports on Luther's heresy an opinion on indulgences. Rome transformed this document into a decretal, dated November 9, 1518, and designated *Cum postquam,* and included it with the many bulls and breves carried by Charles Miltitz to Germany.[100] This document officially confirmed the claims made by Cajetan in his arguments with Luther at Augsburg: (1) that the Pope had the power to remit temporal punishments for actual sins through the superabundant merits of Christ and the saints; (2) that the Pope can through specific indulgences draw on this heavenly treasury for the benefit of the dead as well as the living; (3) that these indulgences may be partial or plenary, depending, at least in part, on the purchase price as well as the spiritual condition of the purchaser; (4) that this doctrine must be taught by all under pain of excommunication. All ecclesiastical authorities of Germany and elsewhere were officially to publicize, support, and teach this new Catholic truth under threat of excommunication. Martin Luther, therefore, was now informed in no uncertain terms from the Holy See itself that his claims of the true meaning of the bull *Unigenitus* had been unmistakably refuted. Furthermore, the decretal, since it was drafted by Cajetan, also legitimatized the whole Dominican approach to indulgences and papal power. Luther's entire appeal to Holy Writ had been pushed aside, and Roman authority had been used to silence Luther as the spokesman of many pious Catholics who wished to see the indulgence scandal destroyed. These developments left little hope for an impartial hearing for Luther's New Theology. His position at that time was well summarized in the first Froben edition of Luther's *Works* printed in Basel in October, 1518.[101] Wolfgang Capito wrote the following anonymous introduction, which well illustrates why the Thomist Cajetan could find no common ground with Luther when discussing his writings at Augsburg:

> Here you have the theological works of the Reverend Father Martin Luther, whom many consider a Daniel sent at length in mercy by Christ to correct abuses and restore the evangelic and •Pauline divinity to theologians who have forgotten the ancient commentaries and occupy themselves with the merest logical and verbal trifles. And would that he might arouse all theologians from their lethargy, and get them to leave their somnolent summaries of divinity and choose the gospel rather than Aristotle, Paul rather than Scotus, or even Jerome, Augustine, Ambrose, Cyprian, Athanasius, Hilary, Basil, Chrysostom, Theophylact rather than Lyra, Aquinas, Scotus and the rest of the Schoolmen. May they no longer drag Christ to the earth, as Thomas Aquinas always does, but may they instruct the earth in the doctrine of Christ. May they cease saying one thing in their farcical universities, another at home, another before the people and something else to their friends; and may they cease calling good men who refuse to fool with them heretics as they now do for small cause or for no cause at all. . . .[102]

Fortunately Spalatin and the Elector both realized that the mere statement of Cajetan and his friends that Luther was a heretic did not carry much weight. They also realized that something progressive and important was developing at their new University, as may be gathered from a postscript to a letter sent by Spalatin to Guy Bild of Augsburg, December 10, 1518:

> That most holy, true and German theology, not fouled by the dregs of metaphysics and dialectics, not polluted by human traditions, not burdened with old wives' tales, but such as the primitive theologians knew, praised and extolled to heaven, this theology, I say, is taught (praise be to God!) in the University of my Elector at Wittenberg with such success that those learned doctors of theology, Martin Luther and Carlstadt have full lecture rooms and disciples not only eager to learn, but already proficient, who do not fear even the greatest of the sophists. Philip Melanchthon teaches Greek there to about four hundred pupils. There are also not a few scholars of Dr. John Boesschenstein, who teaches Hebrew. In short, the best studies are so successfully taught at Wittenberg that you would call it another Athens.[103]

« 12 »

Frederick the Wise
in the Hour of Decision

T HE AUGSBURG INTERVIEW and its precipitous ending
with the sudden disappearance, first of Staupitz and Link, then
a few days later of Luther himself, left a very bad impression on
the papal legate and, through him, in Rome. Cajetan, who had really
tried hard to treat Luther in a fatherly spirit, as he had promised
the Elector, felt deeply hurt by this last act of apparent bad faith
and distrust.[1] Luther, on the other hand, who had been told in
the final interview to remain out of Cajetan's sight unless he was
ready to recant, had waited from Friday until Tuesday for further
instructions, while constant rumors circulated even among men in
high circles that Cajetan was about to disregard the imperial safe-
conduct and cause Luther's arrest.

The aftermath of the Augsburg interview was dreaded both
in Wittenberg and the Electoral court. A barrage of epistles now
began to fly fast and furiously from Rome to the Saxon lands,
to which the archheretic had fled.[2] Cajetan wrote to Frederick the
Wise on October 25, giving the Elector his personal impressions
of the Augsburg interview, pointing out the lengths to which he
had gone to give Luther the promised fatherly hearings, showing
him every consideration; but how, in spite of the best of intentions,
all hope for conciliation had been frustrated by the unwarranted
flight of Luther and his associates. He complained bitterly that the
whole affair had been turned into a mockery and was indignant
at what he termed the "deception and treachery" which revealed
so little appreciation for his genuine, fatherly interest in Luther's

358

problem. After having sufficiently proved that the interview had failed because of Luther's bad faith, he gave his real evaluation of Luther's heresy. In the closing paragraphs of the letter, Cajetan granted Luther's point that his *Ninety-Five Theses* were drafted for purposes of debate and should not be interpreted as his own opinions; but he maintained that Luther's subsequent sermons and writings were certainly filled with positive assertions which were his own doctrinal teachings, heresies that were certain to mislead the masses. Accordingly, since it was a self-evident fact that Luther was guilty of heresy, he exhorted and begged his Illustrious Majesty either to turn Luther over to Rome or at least to expel him from his lands.[3]

It is impossible to prove that the Elector of Saxony was already in full agreement with Luther's "New Theology"; but he was far too cautious and careful a prince to act rashly upon Cajetan's advice.[4] The whole Wittenberg faculty seemed to be supporting the Augustinian monk, and Frederick was not ready to surrender one of his ablest professors to Cajetan, whom he himself did not trust too far. He fully realized that sending Luther to Rome was sending him to certain death. All the court councilors and the chaplain concurred in the opinion that the Elector should refuse the legate's request. Frederick, therefore, sent a copy of the Cajetan letter to Luther, asking him to answer the charges which had been made against him.[5] After hearing both sides, Frederick the Wise would be better qualified to decide the question fairly and to make his reply to the infuriated Cajetan.

Cajetan's letter reached the Saxon court on November 19, and by November 21 Luther sent his reply to the Elector, giving a detailed account of his reactions to the Augsburg interview.[6] The letter contained a remarkable summary of his appearance before Cajetan, making quite clear the points of issue upon which they had failed to agree. Luther's chief complaint was Cajetan's use of Tetzel's afore-mentioned forged *Theses* against him. He also explained the two points of doctrine raised by Cajetan the first day. Luther again asserted that he could not accept as final evidence a papal bull, as Cajetan had demanded, which was contrary to Holy Writ.[7] In refuting this claim Luther developed the

Scriptural view of the *Priestertum,* or priesthood, which he asserted was not given to Peter alone, but was Christ's own eternal
institution in the Church. Luther even questioned the Canon
Law, in which these unscriptural doctrines propounded by Cajetan
were strongly entrenched; and he certainly could not grant the
extravagant claims of Tetzel with reference to the priestly power
of the indulgence salesmen even over the souls in purgatory on
the strength of a papal bull which empowered them with these
prerogatives. On the second point, that faith was essential to the
efficacy of the sacraments, Luther maintained that he would have
to be convinced of his error on the basis of the Scriptures, from
which he had supported his view, while Cajetan had not cited
a single passage from the Bible to defend his Scholastic position.[8]
Luther again pointed out that he was not attacking an established
precept which had already been accepted by the Church, but had
simply questioned the highly debatable assertions of a few papal
bulls and indulgence preachers.

With reference to the charge of his sudden departure, Luther
offered quite a reasonable answer. On the second day he had
proposed to resolve their difficulties by submitting his position in
writing to the universities of Freiburg, Basel, Louvain, or even
Paris.[9] On the third day he had presented his reply to the two
disputed points. He had then been summarily dismissed with the
understanding that unless he changed his mind and offered to
recant, the legate would have nothing more to do with him.[10] What
further business was there for him? After waiting from Friday to
Tuesday without further word from the Cardinal, it seemed useless to remain longer.

To Cajetan's claim that Luther's initial *Theses* might have
been debatable, but that his later assertions were undoubtedly false
doctrines, Luther made no satisfactory reply. He probably began
to realize that there was no answer if Cajetan's theological views
were to be accepted as the standard of judgment; for, from the
Thomist point of view, Luther's writings were full of heresy. An
examination of the Froben edition of his works just off the press
would convince anyone that Luther was teaching a "New Theology."
But Luther did not yet realize how far he had drifted from the

pale of the Roman Church.[11] He did not yet understand that the support of the Scriptures and of the Fathers, namely, the doctrines of the Early Christian Church, did not make him acceptable in a day when tradition and Canon Law were the determinative factors. Luther honestly believed his teachings were in keeping with early Christianity and that he was a good Catholic by wishing to eradicate those innovations and impurities which had crept into the Mother Church. Hence, Luther again spoke with a blind optimism about appealing his case to a neutral university or judge; Leipzig, Erfurt, Halle, and Magdeburg were cited as choices where he might be given a fair hearing, for he believed that Cajetan had been too much influenced by Dominican bias to judge his case impartially. Apparently, after reading this letter, the Elector, too, decided that the Luther problem was far too delicate and involved for his decision but should be given a fair hearing before some neutral body which was competent to judge the case.

The Wittenberg faculty also had followed the cause of their colleague with great concern. Rumors had reached Wittenberg that the Pope was planning to commission Charles von Miltitz, a fellow Saxon, to go to Germany to persuade the Elector to surrender Luther to Rome or to expel him from the Saxon lands so that he might be taken into custody. The nuncius was to be the bearer of the prized "Golden Rose," blessed by the Pope in person during the Fourth Sunday in Lent and offered only once annually to some Christian king or prince. The faculty was much concerned lest this clever technique of temptation and flattery be successful with the Elector, and they resolved to write Miltitz before he arrived at the Saxon court. In a communication of September 25, 1518, the faculty spoke of Luther as a "magnificent and generous man," a "most illustrious member" of the Wittenberg faculty who had been summoned to the Holy See; but they expressed their misgivings about bringing Luther to trial anywhere except in Germany before a body of impartial judges. They added that had Luther really been guilty of the "awful and unchristian errors" with which he was being charged, neither the faculty nor the Elector would have retained him in their midst, but, rather, they would have expelled him at once, as was their clear duty as good

Roman Catholics. They suggested that perhaps Miltitz, who had great influence with the Pope as private chamberlain, could intercede with the easy-going and reasonable Pontiff, Leo X. Finally, with great psychological acumen, the faculty made the following appeal to Miltitz's nationality:

> Grant this, therefore, we pray, to your fatherland, that a German may not be deserted by a German, and especially, when laboring under such a calamity; for we should feel much better about the future if the Pope knew about this man's integrity, piety, and erudition.[12]

The same day the Wittenberg faculty dispatched a special letter to Pope Leo X, asking that Luther be excused for not having appeared in Rome "because of illness and the perils on the way."[13] The Pope might rest assured, they wrote, that Luther had "written nothing contrary to the Roman Church," though they were willing to concede that Luther, a very fluent debater, might have made assertions which were offensive to his enemies. Nor were they making this plea on Luther's behalf because they were not faithful patrons of the Roman *Curia*, but because they were certain that Luther's cause was right.

Neither of these letters seems to have had any appreciable effect on the "Process of Inhibition" or upon the attitude held by the Roman *Curia*. The events taking place in the meantime at Augsburg between Luther and Cajetan have already been related. The Augsburg interview having failed, Rome decided to revive the former Miltitz mission. He was to be sent to Germany with a sack full of bulls and special concessions which might prove useful in bribing the Elector of Saxony and others necessary to effect the arrest of the Wittenberg monk. Although Miltitz carried the title of "Nuncius," he was not a fully empowered emissary (commissarius); for the instructions show that his mission was to be strictly subordinated to Cardinal Cajetan, to whom he was to deliver the "Golden Rose" and other documents upon arrival and who was to decide on the final course of action.[14] In no event were concessions to be made to the Elector unless he was willing to co-operate fully with the Roman *Curia*.

To prepare the ground for a favorable reception of Miltitz, seven letters were dispatched to the Saxon lands. On October 24 the Pope wrote Duke George of Albertine Saxony that Charles Miltitz was being sent to the court of the Elector to deal with Martin Luther, that "son of perdition." [15] Duke George was to help him "extirpate this tare and cockle from the fertile field of the Lord." The Pope tried to impress Duke George, the Elector's cousin, with the gravity of the Luther problem in order to enlist his sympathy in helping Miltitz carry out his commission. On the same day the Pope also dispatched a special letter to Frederick's confidential adviser and court chaplain, George Spalatin, who was likewise asked to use his influence to bring the Elector around to the proper course of action. Speaking of the special gift which the Pope was sending to Frederick the Wise through his nuncius, he wrote:

> . . . we have decided, with much affection and paternal love, to send him the most sacred golden rose, annually consecrated with mysterious rites on the fourth Sunday of Lent, and sent to some powerful Christian king or prince. We send it by our beloved son, Charles von Miltitz, our chamberlain and servant.[16]

This was followed by the flattering statement that they knew how much influence and favor his "wholesome and prudent counsel" had with the Elector in helping to silence "that only son of Satan, Friar Martin Luther," so that his "notorious heresy" might not "blacken the name and fame of the great Elector and his ancestors." A similar communication was directed to the Elector himself, announcing the departure of Miltitz with the Golden Rose, "our noblest gift, a thing of secret meaning and a splendid decoration for the noble House of Saxony this year." [17] Luther again was pictured as the revelation of Satan himself, who even dared to preach against the Pope and criticize the holy Roman See in the Elector's own lands. In rather strong language the Pope expressed his concern about Luther's dangerous preaching before a credulous people:

> It becomes us not to tolerate this any longer, both because of our honor and that of the papal see, and because the credulous people may be hereby led to evil doctrine with great scandal. In order,

therefore, that this infected, scrofulous sheep may not grow strong
in the healthy sheepfold of the Lord, and in order that the boldness
of this wicked Martin may stop, and not send his root too deep and
firm to be rooted out of the field of the Lord given to our charge,
and as we know and have no doubt that this troubles your conscience not a little, for the reputation and honor of yourself and of
your famous ancestors, who were always the hottest opponents of
heresy, we have commanded the said Charles, our nuncio and
chamberlain, in another letter and breve, to take cognizance of this
affair and to act against the said Martin and against his followers,
who support his scandalous opinions.[18]

In addition to these letters, the Pope and Cardinal Julius de Medici,
the later Pope Clement VII, also communicated with the Elector's
most influential lawyer, Degenhard Pfeffinger,[19] whom they tried
to influence with similar flattering praise to induce his Prince to
support the Miltitz assignment. Two breves were dispatched
with Leo's signature to Naumburg and Wittenberg.[20] Donat Gros-
sen, the *Domherr* of Naumburg and one of Frederick's confidential
advisers, was asked to lend his influence in the interests of Rome;
while the Mayor and the Council of Wittenberg were also asked to
assist Miltitz in his attempt to deal with the heretical professor
at their local University.

Long before Miltitz's arrival at the Electoral court, reports had
reached the Wittenberg faculty which convinced them that Rome
this time really meant to arrest their fellow professor. Luther,
too, was now fully aware of the danger in which he had placed
himself by refusing to recant at Augsburg. He really did not know
what course to follow.[21] Advice and counsel were offered freely
from all quarters. Sometimes it seemed wisest to leave Germany
for some distant land like France or Bohemia; again he considered delivering himself to the Elector, who then could deal with
him as he saw fit. He was deeply concerned lest his Elector become involved on account of his personal doctrinal difficulties; yet
he was equally convinced that only through the influence of the
Elector could he hope to receive a fair and impartial examination
of his case.

When Luther had completed his reply to Cajetan's letter of
October 25 to the Elector, he decided to ask the Wittenberg faculty to write an official communication to the Elector in his behalf,

for he realized that such a letter would have considerable influence at court. This interesting document was published in *Die Deutsche Bibel* IV and included the entire story in documentary form.[22] Since this letter was of such vital importance in Frederick's hour of decision and really set the framework for the Elector's future attitude toward Rome, it merits translation in full. Dated November 22, 1518, it reads as follows:

Jesus. Grace and peace from our Lord and Master with his guidance. Most illustrious and clement Prince, Venerable Sir. Martin Luther, (Master of Arts and Theology, regular lecturer, noble and most reverend) member from our midst, has informed us how Cajetan, Cardinal Presbyter of the Church of St. Thomas the Apostle, plans on either having this same Martin Luther sent to Rome or driven from the country because of certain *Theses* which have long been in the hands of the Pope, with reference to which you doubtless have been informed by this time. He has also informed us that he had answered all summons to public debate in person, and to private disputations by letter. Besides, he had expected that the errors in his writings would be pointed out to him on the grounds of the Scriptures and the sainted Fathers, on which basis the illustrious man might discover and recognize his mistakes; yet to date he was unable to obtain any answer, but was rudely asked to recant the errors in his writings. And still, should he not have been granted that pastoral courtesy through which he might have been brought back to the fold, for it is commanded to instruct both the willing and the unwilling alike, in season and out of season.

Wherefore, he has come and asked, a request which was granted, that we intercede with your Illustrious Lordship and humbly pray that, as far as your Highness may see fit, to write the same highest legate or the Pope himself and graciously intervene in his behalf, in order that the articles and errors in his writings may be pointed out to him, giving the reasons and citing the authorities by which he may correct himself and thus recant. Nor does he know what sentences should be gathered for condemnation before he knows which ones deserve condemnation.

Moreover, the practice of the Early Church and the example of the Fathers should furnish ample criteria for judgment, for after having advanced the reasons and cited authorities, Rome would be in a position to demand a recantation. Mere assertions or human power cannot condemn the contentions of anyone.

And therefore, O Illustrious Prince, believing his story to be true and not being in a position to reject the petitions of a just man, we

would be much pleased in case your Illustrious Majesty were to
bring this matter straightway before the Holy See and the Pope.
Nor would it be wise to pursue any other course.

In conclusion, may we add that should we discover that this man
has been teaching heretical views, we would be the first to regard
him as an outcast, for we look upon nothing as more authoritative
than a verdict by the Roman Church. Therefore, by God's grace
and your consideration, O most Illustrious Prince, we come to you
with this one petition of supreme worth, as your Highness may not
wish to be bothered further. And especially do we ask this favor
because of the very humble and devout way in which he has shown
his reverence for the Roman Church (without supervision on our
part, as we know full well). Furthermore, this man's petition must
not be disregarded because of the revelation of the truth in his
writings, but rather it should be considered worth while to appeal
to the light in the man, which according to them is clouded in darkness, especially since he does not deny that he may be in error. In
truth, he only prays for a worthy and just consideration of his
position, that having found the light and given testimony to the
truth, he may then be led from this darkness and not be pushed
down into greater confusion. Nor does he take this position because
of fear of what his Holiness, Pope Leo X, may be about to do.
Rather he fears the pursuit of wickedness and especially when it is
done under the name of the Holy Church, which doctrinal teaching
he would entirely reject in case he recognized in what respect he
had erred in the name of the Church. May the Lord Jesus protect
us and His entire Church through Your Majesty for a long time to
come. Amen. Dated Wittenberg, the twenty-second of November,
in the year 1518. Your Electoral Grace, humbly,

The Rector, Masters and Doctors of the
University of Wittenberg [23]

Interesting as the contents of the letter may be, its history is
even more fascinating; for the letter was not drawn up by some
obscure member of the Wittenberg faculty, but by Luther himself.[24] The Rector of the faculty at the time was Bartholomaeus
Bernhardi, one of Luther's former graduate students. When Luther approached him with the special request that the faculty
write a letter to the Elector in his behalf, the young Rector felt
that no one was better qualified to present his case than Luther
himself. He, therefore, invited Luther to compose the important
document which the faculty would then sign.

This remarkable discovery as to its authorship was made by H. Degering, who published his findings for the first time in the Weimar text, *Die Deutsche Bibel*, 1923.[25] It seems strange that the original owner of the document should not have recognized Luther's handwriting when he gathered the text for his *Sammelbande Ms. germ. fol. 715*. George Mentz's collection of Luther's handwriting corroborated Degering's conclusions in the *Handschriften der Reformationszeit* (1912), Bl. 4; and two of the greatest Luther handwriting experts, Professor Johann Luther and the Reverend D. A. Freitag, have further substantiated the discovery. In fact, Luther's writing stands out so plainly that each addition by a strange hand among the faculty can be clearly distinguished. That it was the original draft is further supported by the fact that it contains many marginal corrections, some words of the text have been crossed out and others entered by a strange hand, all of which were very faithfully reproduced in the Weimar publication.. The insertions, probably by the Rector Bernhardi,[26] were chiefly in the nature of superlatives about Luther personally. A few changes were also made with reference to the Pope and the Elector and have been indicated in the text by parentheses, but the original phraseology by Luther was left practically unchanged.

The official letter, therefore, of the University of Wittenberg which greatly influenced the Elector in the critical hour of decision was written by Luther's own pen; or, in brief, Martin Luther really helped determine his own status with Rome by seeking the protection of Frederick the Wise through the official letter which the university faculty requested him to write.

In spite of these developments Luther expected the worst. On November 25, and again on the 28th, Luther prepared the Wittenberg congregation for his sudden departure.[27] Although, as Luther later wrote Spalatin, he did not bid the congregation a final farewell, they fully realized that the situation was indeed grave, and many were in tears.[28] On November 28, a letter finally arrived from the court in which the Elector agreed to the plan that Luther should leave Wittenberg immediately. Accordingly, on the evening of December 1, Luther and his colleagues held a farewell dinner at the Black Cloister, and it was planned that Luther should slip quietly away during the night.[29] Naturally, much excitement pervaded the gathering, and everyone tried to give him some last-minute advice. During the meal a letter was delivered to Luther from Spalatin in which he expressed his surprise that Luther had not left town.[30] Luther was more disturbed than frightened, for he firmly believed that the Lord would take care of him. Strangely enough, before they had finished eating, a second letter arrived from the Elector, revoking his first request.[31] He now asked Luther to bide his time until they might discuss the situation. This turn of events threw the group into confusion as to the proper course of action.

What had prompted this sudden change of mind? During those days of Luther's uncertainty, culminating in the farewell dinner, the Elector realized that he would have to decide upon a definite policy. Early in December he called a meeting of his court to discuss the problem from every angle. Doubtless, a number of factors influenced the total picture in this critical hour. The weight of a letter from John Staupitz and the influence of the advice of men like Spalatin and Pfeffinger are beyond evaluation.[32] A careful study of the whole case reveals that all were most deeply impressed by Luther's letter to Cajetan and the letter received from the faculty of the University of Wittenberg. After wrestling with the problem for days, the Elector requested that Luther come to the Castle of Lichtenberg near Pretzsch for an interview. This was the message received at the farewell dinner, and the meeting occurred some time between December third and sixth. Here Luther was fully informed of all recent developments. It was now agreed that he remain in Wittenberg and await excommunication, at which time he would suddenly disappear.

During the period of waiting, Luther continued his literary activities. For some time he had wished to publish his *Acta Augustana* so that the people might know what had actually happened in Augsburg; but the Elector feared that the action might give further offense. When the document was completed on December 8, the Elector granted its circulation rather reluctantly and only upon condition that the part referring to the forgery of the papal breve of August 23 be covered with printer's ink.[33] Already on November 28, in the presence of a notary and two witnesses, Luther had perfected his *Appeal to a General Council,* which came from the press on December 11.[34] Luther had assumed that the printer would not circulate any copies of the *Appeal,* but that they would be ready in the event he was placed under the ban. He failed to realize the printer's eagerness to reap the profit from what he knew would be an enormous sale. This action further complicated the Luther problem, for, as Mueller has shown, in the case of a notorious heresy an appeal to Canon Law was invalid. In fact, ever since Pope Pius II on January 18, 1460, had published his bull *Execrabilis,* such an appeal was, in itself, regarded as heretical.[35]

Frederick the Wise was one of those careful, cautious individuals who take ample time to weigh a problem from every angle; but he was also capable of independent action after having considered the counsel of his lawyers and friends.[36] In him was also a very strong sense of fairness, a sincere conviction of right and wrong which did not permit him to act lightly. After he had once thought a matter through and made a decision, he was not easily turned from that course of action which his conclusions warranted. It is doubtful whether he ever became a Lutheran or acted purely from religious conviction.[37] In the funeral sermon at his grave Luther expressed the hope that he had received sufficient light from the Gospel to save his soul.[38] His convictions were those of an evangelical Catholic who was convinced that the Church was in dire need of reforms and believed that Martin Luther could provide the remedy.[39]

Frederick, then, after long deliberation and careful consideration of all evidence completed his reply to the Cardinal on December 8.[40] Boehmer says it required some twenty readings and rewritings before he was completely satisfied with the final draft prepared by his chancellery.[41] Although the reply was phrased in very flattering and diplomatic language, it left no room for misunderstanding as to Frederick's final conclusions. It stated that in accordance with their previous agreements Luther had already appeared before the legate, and his promises had, therefore, been kept. In it Frederick repeated the former university argument that

the case had been far from sufficiently discussed and that, therefore, Luther had no way of knowing in what respects he was in
error. Furthermore, argued the Elector, there were a great number of learned men in his lands, in the court, at the university, and
elsewhere, who were not convinced that "the impious doctrines
of Martin are unchristian and heretical"; that those who have set
themselves up as his opponents did not arrive at this charge of
heresy on the basis of their learning, but because of "private business and pecuniary advantages." The Elector assured the Cardinal
that it was his solemn wish to act in this whole matter as seemed
most fitting to a Christian prince and that with God's help he
desired to counsel his subjects according to the dictates of his own
conscience. He stated that he hoped Rome would not use threats
against him for this reason should he not agree to surrender Luther
or to exile him from his lands. Furthermore, continued Frederick,
had Luther really been guilty of heresy, he would have been expelled from the University long ago, for it was a fine Christian
institution on whose faculty many erudite teachers and good
doctors were serving. Since Martin had offered to submit his case
to other universities, or to engage others in public disputation
in some neutral place that he might discover his errors and be
taught and guided in the truth, a hearing could hardly be denied.
In fact, added the Elector, it was not even right to speak of Luther as a heretic until he had been proved such by some impartial
and competent body. He was, therefore, not ready to be drawn
into the same error by surrendering Luther to Rome or expelling
him from his lands.

THE DIPLOMACY OF CHARLES VON MILTITZ

Charles von Miltitz, a native of Rabenau near Dresden, was
a descendant of the Saxon nobility.[42] He was seven years younger
than Luther. After a preparatory education the young noble had
matriculated at Cologne in 1508 and continued his studies at
Bologna in 1510. Since he had studied law, he decided to try his
fortune in Rome, where he spent the years 1513–1518. His intellectual gifts were but moderate, and he sought to improve his
circumstances through clever diplomacy. His fellow countryman

the Dominican Nicolaus von Schoenberg assisted him in making the proper contacts, so that by April 22, 1514, he was an understudy of the papal chamberlain, or as Paul Kalkoff puts it, *cubicularius extra cameram*.[43] On November 5, shortly before his departure for Saxony, he was promoted to papal secretary. Miltitz, therefore, was well acquainted in the inner circle of the papal *Curia*.

But Miltitz's assignment was such that he could not act independently in his dealing with the Wittenberg professor. He was instructed to deliver the Golden Rose and the papal breves and bulls to his superior, Cardinal Cajetan, without whose permission he was not empowered to act.[44] Perhaps the *Curia* knew too well that Miltitz was given to heavy drinking, at which times he was not altogether reliable, that he was inclined to boast, with little regard for truth, of his importance and influence in Rome.[45] He may have been chosen originally for the visit to the Saxon court because the Pope believed that a fellow Saxon might have more success with Frederick than a foreigner like Cajetan. No doubt the clever Miltitz encouraged this belief, for he was very eager to try his fortune. How far Miltitz's plan had really developed before he arrived in Augsburg is impossible to establish, but he must have hoped that the visit to Germany would bring advancement in the papal court.

For reasons already noted Miltitz's trip to Germany was delayed until the middle of November.[46] By the end of November he had arrived at the Fuggers in Augsburg and delivered his collection of seventy papal papers.[47] Cajetan, who was short of funds by that time, decided to accompany the Kaiser to Linz, and Miltitz was permitted to join them. He, however, told Cajetan nothing of his future course of action. On the way to Linz he met the Saxon lawyer Degenhard Pfeffinger, who was returning to the Elector's court at Altenburg.[48] Now Miltitz decided to leave Cajetan and the Kaiser and to join Pfeffinger on his return journey.

On the way to Saxony, Miltitz talked far too freely. His acumen was not too great, and it is highly possible that he did not clearly understand the nature of his original assignment, for he boasted to Pfeffinger about the number of documents he had brought from Rome to Augsburg. He represented conditions in

Rome as being much more favorable than Cajetan had led the
Elector to believe. He became very confidential, claiming that Leo
was not so well disposed toward the Dominicans as had been supposed, and even stated that when the Pope learned about Tetzel's
extravagant claims for the powers of indulgences, he had exclaimed: "Der Schweinehund!" (the filthy rascal).[49] All this confidential information was to establish the importance of his mission to harmonize the relations between Luther and the *Curia* and
to weaken the bad influences of the Dominicans. All the while
Pfeffinger was obtaining information which would be useful to the
Elector in preparing for their arrival. As the journey progressed,
he anticipated that Miltitz might be playing a clever game of
his own.

Luther was kept well informed on the progress of the Miltitz journey to the Electoral court by friends along the way. On
December 9, 1518, Luther wrote Spalatin that he had just heard
from Nuernberg that Miltitz was on the way north, bringing three
papal bulls, which, according to a trustworthy friend, empowered
him to deliver Luther bound to Rome.[50] Similar reports had
reached Wittenberg from other parts of Germany from friends
who believed that Luther was still in grave danger even though
the Elector had refused to turn him over to Cajetan. On December 19 or 20 Luther's friend Christopher Scheurl,[51] who had
just been visited by Miltitz, informed Luther that Miltitz's exact
assignment was to work as "a simple commissioner, with instructions to act on the legate's advice." Yet, he had learned that Miltitz had sent more than forty breves from Augsburg to the powers
of Germany, asking their assistance in the arrest of Luther.[52] He
also had gathered the impression during the visits that Miltitz had
his private ambitions and intended to act quite independently of
the papal legate Cajetan, under whom he served.

Scheurl also assured Luther that he did not need to fear "the
[papal] thunders, nor rashly believe everything." [53] Scheurl, of
course, had reference to the promised future meeting of the Emperor to be held at Worms or Frankfurt am Main the following
year, but his remarks also paved the way for the actual meeting
between Miltitz and Luther at Altenburg in January, 1519. He

even implied that he favored that Luther "get a hearing in Germany." [54] Miltitz had also suggested that the university and town councilors aid Luther in bringing about such a hearing.

On December 25, 1518, Miltitz wrote Spalatin from Gera that he might expect him in Altenburg December 27, but he was forced to remain there an extra day because of illness.[55] Pfeffinger went on to Altenburg, arriving two days ahead of Miltitz.[56] This allowed sufficient time to prepare for the meeting with the papal nuncius, who, when he arrived on December 28, immediately requested an audience with the Elector.

Although his understanding of the situation in Germany was not too profound, Miltitz had learned enough on the journey to realize that it would be wise to proceed with caution.[57] Instead of perfunctorily demanding that the Elector expel the Wittenberg professor from his lands, he merely explored the subject sufficiently to determine the Prince's convictions. He very delicately hinted that otherwise he doubted whether the Golden Rose would be delivered to the Elector. Frederick, who was equally aware that his adversary was merely sparring for advantage, as cleverly intimated that he doubted the wisdom of driving Luther into Bohemia, and he made it evident that he did not intend to take such action.

When Miltitz realized that Frederick had no intention of surrendering Luther to Rome, he turned to an entirely new psychological approach.[58] Perhaps it was because he had already learned something of Luther's widespread popularity in the Saxon lands. First, he tried to impress Frederick with his official capacity by claiming that Pope Leo X had now begun to realize that Luther's case had been entirely misrepresented in the Roman *Curia*. Tetzel and his Dominican friends had blackened Luther's name unjustly with the Holy See, while even Cajetan had given a prejudiced report on Augsburg because of his affiliation with the opposition. Thus, as he had already revealed to Pfeffinger, he had been specially selected to bring about a reconciliation between Luther and the Roman *Curia*. To impress Frederick and his advisers further with his importance and the seriousness of his intentions, he summoned John Tetzel to Altenburg. Tetzel's failure as an indulgence salesman and his subsequent retreat to St. Paul's Convent in Leipzig for fear of his life made Miltitz's action reasonably secure against offense to the Roman *Curia*. Thus, Miltitz sought to convince Frederick of his authority by "butchering the black sheep," but Tetzel refused to come.[59] Miltitz sent for him a second time, whereupon the former indulgence salesman excused himself on the ground that Luther had made the people so hostile toward him that it was not safe for him to appear in public. Tetzel, undoubtedly, realized that Rome was through with him and had no intention of being made its scapegoat.

Frederick, sufficiently impressed with Miltitz's good intentions, arranged an interview for him with Martin Luther in Spalatin's house in the Schlossberg at Lochau (now Annaberg).[60] Here in the presence of Spalatin, the able lawyer Fabian von Feilitzsch, and other officials of the Electoral court, Luther and the papal chamberlain engaged for two days in a colloquy over the indulgence problem, which had caused so much difficulty.

The Altenburg interviews must have provided a strange spectacle for those who were present at this meeting. On the one hand there was the Roman nuncius, a shallow, boastful, unscrupulous politician, who had neither the training nor the depth to comprehend the real issues at stake between Luther and Rome; while on the other hand was one of the ablest theologians and research professors of the sixteenth century, who had for years searched the Scholastic writings and Canon Law for the answers to the problems of sin and salvation, only to find the answer in God's Holy Word, especially in the Epistles of St. Paul. Luther soon realized the futility of their discussion, yet he wished to treat the nuncius with respect as a representative of the Roman *Curia* and also because he earnestly desired to conclude a struggle that had engaged him for five months.[61] Outwardly, therefore, the colloquy had the appearance of a very friendly discussion.

Early on January 5 or 6 Luther wrote the Elector his impressions of the interview of the first day, the original of which is still in the Gotha folio collection.[62] After expressing his regrets for involving the Elector in his personal affairs, he stated that, after Miltitz had requested that he humbly recant out of honor for the Roman Church, the following suggestions were agreed upon, three of which had been advanced by Luther, while the fourth came from the Elector's lawyer, Fabian von Feilitzsch: (1) that Luther remain silent and permit the issues to die a natural death, provided, of course, his enemies promised to do likewise; (2) that Luther would write his Papal Majesty, prostrating himself in all humility, admitting that he had been too excited and harsh; that while he had meant no harm to the Roman Church in his attack upon the blasphemous indulgence preachers, yet his action had been detrimental, for it had turned the people against the Holy Roman Church; (3) that Luther would publish a Zettel,[63] a kind of public apology, in which he would urge the people to remain devoted to the Roman Church, to be obedient subjects, and to regard his writings as meant to honor the Church, though they might have been a little untimely and perhaps too severe; and, finally, (4) that the whole question be submitted to the honorable Archbishop of Salzburg, who, with other learned, impartial men, would render a verdict in the case.[64] All of which Luther agreed to accept to the extent his conscience would permit or to await a future council.

In the course of the discussion Luther tried to show Miltitz that the scandalous indulgence traffic with its shameful deception and misrepresentation had been only the ground for his attack; that, ultimately, the cause was far deeper.[65] The final blame would have to rest with the Roman Curia, which had permitted the connivance of the Archbishop of Mainz in securing several ecclesiastical Sees requiring such enormous fees that their payment necessitated this shameful abuse. These practices, which swindled and bled the pious people, had caused Luther to preach against the whole nefarious financial system of the Roman Curia. Had the guilty rectified these abuses, this fearful storm would not have arisen over one who was really trying to protect the honor of the Church.

Miltitz now began to realize that the problem was not as one-sided as it had been pictured in Rome. He agreed that Luther should be given a neutral hearing, although he was not sure that the concession would be acceptable to the Roman Curia. However, he was ready to give the matter further consideration on the morrow. Luther had made considerable effort to accommodate himself to Miltitz to effect a settlement, but added at the close of the letter to the Elector his belief that "nothing will come of the recantation." [66]

Before the meeting scheduled for the following day, Luther drafted his letter to the Pope as promised under the second point of the previous day's agreement. The letter was never sent, as its content made it seem inadvisable to the calculating Miltitz, but the original is still in the Gotha collection.[67] From it may be determined Luther's true position in the controversy and the extent of Miltitz's misrepresentations in his account of the interviews written a few days later. Luther expressed his sorrow over the fact that his earnest intention to preserve the honor of the Church had been so misinterpreted as to cause only mistrust and suspicion in the mind of the Pope. He added that a revocation of his writings, now so widely circulated throughout Germany, would not only be impossible, but, since there were so many learned men in the country, a revocation might even harm rather than honor the Roman Church. For it was not he, but his opponents who had made the Church hideous in the evil light of avarice and greed. Being concerned only with personal gain, they had brought upon the Church the reproach of "Egypt." He also asserted that he had no intention of attacking the power of the Roman Church, as his opponents had so audaciously asserted, but fully acknowledged the power of the Roman Church over all things save Jesus Christ, who is the Lord of all. If his opponents agreed to remain silent, he would not only do likewise, but would also instruct the people sincerely to reverence the Roman Church. However, the Pope must defend the Church from pollution by greed and avarice, as has been practiced in the indulgence traffic.

Little wonder that Miltitz did not wish to send this document to Leo X, who, contrary to the impression created by Miltitz, had previously addressed Luther as the "son of perdition." Certainly, Luther's letter was anything but an apology; it was, in fact, a "scathing indictment" of all the filth and corruption which had made his attack necessary. Since such a letter would only frustrate his own plans and schemes, Miltitz decided to drop the matter entirely.[68] He had already represented in overly optimistic language the willingness of Leo X to become reconciled to Luther, and it was necessary to persuade Leo of a similar willingness to recant on the part of Luther, if he was to succeed in effecting the reconciliation that would make him forever famous.

After the meeting on the second day some revisions had to be made in the proposed agreements, but the following points were accepted as to the future course of action: (1) that the indulgence problem would be permitted to "bleed to death" and that Luther would refrain from treating the indulgence problem by preaching, writing, or in any other form of communication, provided the opposition also abided by this agreement; (2) that Miltitz would communicate his impressions of Luther's case to the Pope and ask him to appoint a learned German bishop to examine Luther's materials and cite the errors in his writings which Luther would be asked to recant, so that all might result to the honor and power of the Roman Church.[69]

That evening Miltitz invited Luther to a private dinner in the castle. This was, doubtless, the confidential interview which Luther later so vividly recalled in the *Table Talks*.[70] Miltitz confided that he had come to Germany with the idea of arresting Luther, but that on the way he had inquired about Luther everywhere and that of "every five men to whom he had spoken . . . scarcely two favored the Roman side." [71] He expressed surprise that Luther was a young, vigorous professor, in the prime of life. In the conversation, Miltitz admitted that Rome was much concerned about the Luther problem, the like of which had not been witnessed by the Papacy in a hundred years, and that Rome would rather lose 10,000 ducats ($250,000) than have this state of affairs continue. Moreover, he added that Luther's following was so strong in Germany that, had he 25,000 Swiss soldiers at his disposal, he would still not risk taking Luther out of Germany. In a letter to his friend John Sylvius Egranus of Zwickau, February 2, 1519, Luther described how Miltitz used every trick of flattery and cajolery to persuade him to recant for the honor of the Roman Church. The final touch is depicted in Luther's description of the dramatic parting from the erring brother:

> We finally agreed to leave the matter to the arbitration of either the Bishop of Salzburg or the Bishop of Trier, and thus we separated amicably, with a kiss (a Judas kiss!) and tears — I pretended that I did not know they were crocodile tears. Thus far we got; I know not what they will do at Rome.[72]

At the conclusion of the meeting Luther felt relieved and encouraged. The Elector and the court were apparently convinced of the righteousness of his cause. The Elector had approved his willingness to accept the decision of a neutral German bishop, assisted by several capable theologians acceptable to both factions. But the Prince had resolved to have a hand in the choice of men himself and asked Luther to suggest several people. Among those named was the Archbishop of Trier, Richard Greiffenklau, and through the influence of the Elector he was contacted by Miltitz.

On his return journey Miltitz stopped in Leipzig to question Tetzel personally. In the presence of the Fugger official the ailing old man was rudely questioned and severely reprimanded.[73] In a letter to Pfeffinger, Miltitz boasted that his investigation of Tetzel's indulgence practices and shameful private life had furnished him with the necessary evidence to blacken his name with the Roman *Curia*. Whether he actually employed this means is not a matter of record. But, as so often happens, Tetzel had been made the scapegoat for Albert of Mainz, the Fuggers, and the Roman *Curia*. He was even deserted by the members of his own order and lived the last months of his life in misery and despair. When Luther learned of his pitiable circumstances, he penned a word of consolation to the dying old man. In this communication Luther urged him to take heart and not to brood over the situation, for, after all, it was not really he who "set the ball a-rolling. This child had quite another father." [74] Tetzel, however, was unable to withstand the blow and passed away on July 4, 1519, the same day that Martin Luther stepped into the arena at Leipzig to face an even more formidable opponent in his new antagonist, John Eck.

The report which Miltitz made to his superiors in Rome is no longer extant, but judging by the letter Leo X wrote to Luther on March 29, 1519, the Pope had been given an entirely false impression of the situation.[75] Leo's letter indicates he had been led to believe that Luther was very sorry for his offenses against the Roman *Curia* through his rash and bitter attack on the indulgence traffic of John Tetzel and that he was now ready to recant. Moreover, the Pope stated he had learned that Luther would have recanted before Cajetan had the latter taken a less partisan view because of his membership in the same monastic order as Tetzel. The Pope had now been assured that Luther had no intention of attacking or harming the Apostolic See or the Roman Church, but that he merely wished to protect its honor against the greedy, grasping indulgence salesmen of Albert of Mainz. Realizing this, and that his action was taken in the heat of anger, the Roman See was ready to receive him once more into its fold. In closing, Leo X not only invited Luther to Rome, where he was assured a friendly reception, but even offered to defray the traveling expenses of the journey.

THE DEATH OF EMPEROR MAXIMILIAN

What would have happened had the real truth become known is difficult to estimate. Miltitz would probably have been in trouble for abusing his commission once he reported back to his superior, Cardinal Cajetan, but he was saved by a singular stroke of fortune. On January 12, 1519, Emperor Maximilian suddenly passed away at Wels in Upper Austria, and with his death the scramble of candidates in a new imperial election occupied the whole papal horizon.[76] As has been observed, Pope Leo X did not favor a strong candidate for the imperial throne, especially not the young King of Spain, King Charles I. After due consideration the Pope decided to push the candidacy of the Elector of Saxony. In the light of this new turn of events, Miltitz's favorable report was particularly welcome to the Pope. With the imperial election the all-absorbing interest of the moment, the Lutheran heresy was not merely pushed into the background, but it provided further pawns on the chessboard of European diplomacy. This new light adds illumination to the breve of March 29, the afore-mentioned letter of Leo X to Luther, which addressed him as his "Beloved Son" and assured him every fatherly kindness when he arrived in Rome to recant.

> Wherefore we, who are the vicegerent on earth of Him who desireth not the death of a sinner, but that he shall turn from his wickedness and live, with paternal love accept your excuses, and because of the benevolence with which we regard all learned men, especially those learned in divinity, desire to hear and see you personally, so that you may be able safely and freely to make before us, the vicar of Christ, that recantation which you feared to make before our legate. Wherefore on receipt of this letter prepare for

a journey and come straight to us. We hope, moreover, that you will lay aside hatred and reconcile your mind to us, that you will be filled with no passion, but with the Holy Spirit alone, and armed with charity, so that you will care for those things which make for the glory of Almighty God, that we may thus rejoice in you as an obedient child and that you may be happy to find in us a kind and merciful father.[77]

This letter arrived some time in April at the Electoral court, but Frederick the Wise with his usual insight decided not to deliver it to Luther. Knowing the heart of Luther far better than Miltitz, the Elector felt that Luther had no choice but to decline the offer of the misinformed Pope, a step which could only result in further complications.

After several months of futile waiting in Augsburg for his expected reward from Rome, Miltitz finally decided to join his superior in Coblenz. He succeeded in persuading the wily Cajetan by clever misrepresentations to agree that the Archbishop of Trier examine the Luther case in his presence. Miltitz even deceived himself to some degree and invited Luther to come to Coblenz at once, where he assured him every consideration.[78] On May 17, 1519, Luther rejected Miltitz's summons rather bluntly, giving five reasons why he did not care to make such a worthless trip: [79] (1) because they had agreed at Altenburg that his presence would not be necessary while the Archbishop of Trier, or some other neutral judge, examined his writings in order to point out the errors which he must recant; (2) since no mandate had yet arrived from the Pope authorizing the Archbishop to act in this capacity, the summons was without authorization; (3) since this was an *interregnum*, a period between two rulers, it would be impossible to obtain a letter of safe-conduct; [80] (4) a debate had already been scheduled with John Eck at Leipzig in the presence of many learned men, which would afford a much better opportunity for fair and impartial consideration than could be offered by the Archbishop or the Cardinal; and, finally, (5) there was no point in again presenting his case before Cajetan, a man whom he did not even regard as a "Catholic Christian," whose "rank errors" he would have exposed in writing to the Pope if he could have found time.

How utterly the Miltitz diplomacy had failed was indicated by Luther's reaction when he received the invitation to come to Coblenz for an interview. On that occasion he remarked: "Are these people in their right mind? No mandate has arrived from Rome, yet this ludicrous Miltitz invites me without consulting the Archbishop of Trier and summons me for an interview with Cajetan!" [81] The Saxon court was equally distrustful of Miltitz, but the Elector felt it would be unwise to break completely with him, as he might then be replaced by someone who would be far more dangerous. Thus, as late as May 27, 1519, Miltitz met the Elector at Weimar, in which interview he was still trying to secure a recantation from Luther, urging that following the papal decretal of November 9, 1518 (*Cum postquam*), Luther had no legal ground for refusing to admit his errors.

While Miltitz was engaged in his own little game of diplomacy in Germany, the papal legate Orsini made a new proposal to the Elector through Miltitz which outdid anything that the former chamberlain might have conceived in his wildest imagination. On June 21, 1519, Frederick was informed at Frankfurt am Main that the Pope was ready to offer a cardinal's hat to any person chosen by the Elector, provided, of course, that the Elector would cooperate and help to elect the King of France.[82] Could the Pope have had anyone else in mind but Luther? Furthermore, the legate reported that the Papacy was ready not only to give this protégé a cardinal's hat, but he would also be granted an important archbishopric.[83] Nothing came of the offer. By the middle of June, Leo X had been informed that nothing could stop the young Hapsburg from being elected, and before Orsini had made the offer, it was already too late, for the Pope now believed it expedient to appear as though Rome had favored the election of Charles I of Spain.[84] Yet the record shows that in the spring of 1519 Pope Leo X was prepared to do everything within his power to defeat Charles,[85] even to the extent of adding the heretic, Martin Luther, to the College of Cardinals.

Luther adhered to the Altenburg agreement very rigidly.[86] When Prierias published a diatribe against him, Luther allowed it to be reprinted with a mere remark on the title page. In a rather detailed report to the Elector on the entire Altenburg interview he reaffirmed his willingness to recant anything in his writings which had been proved false, but again stated emphatically that he would never recant indiscriminately all that he had written.[87] Further, Luther stated that he was more than ready to stop preaching and teaching, but that he could not consider only his own choice, but would be submissive to God's commands. Luther again proposed the Archbishop of Trier as his first choice for an impartial judge and named the Bishop of Naumburg and the Archbishop of Salzburg as second and third choices.

He felt obliged to remind the Emperor of the extreme temporal power of the Pope and recalled that Pope Julius II (1511) had not only humiliated both King Louis XII of France and Emperor Maximilian, but that he had even broken up the Council of Pisa by deposing four out of nine cardinals. Yet, Luther concluded, he was certain Rome had learned the true circumstances of the Tetzel indulgence abuses and that it would not tolerate such preaching in the future.

As for the often cited "new decretal" (*Cum postquam*), Luther stated that it was a most unusual document. It seemed contradictory in parts, for it did not repeal other papal laws and was particularly unique since it contained no citations from the Scriptures, Canon Law, or the Fathers. In fact, it did not give valid reasons in support of claims, but was merely a collection of words. He felt, therefore, that the decretal offered no solution to his problem with Rome and that he was unable to accept its unsupported claims as the doctrines of the Roman Church. Yet, he assured the Elector he would neither accept nor completely reject the document. Although point number two of the agreement with Miltitz had been dropped on the second day, upon the advice of the Elector, Luther's *apologia vernacula*, the public apology, appeared late in February, 1519.[88] This *Zettel* is divided into six brief divisions treating Saint Worship, Purgatory, Indulgences, Commandments of the Church, Good Works, and the Roman Church. Luther's position is briefly as follows: As to the reality of miracles at the graves of saints there can be no doubt, but saints are mere intercessors with no power of their own, and all honor must be given to God for such miracles. As for indulgences and their relationship to purgatory, Luther accepted that souls were suffering there and had to be helped through prayers, fasting, and alms, but the exact nature of their suffering and the effect of any action by the priests to hasten God's judgment were extremely doubtful. The common man should know that indulgences were purely voluntary, that they had not been commanded, and that they were far less important than the good works which God had commanded. As for the commands of the Church, such as fasting and the observance of saints' days, these outward observances were less important than true inward piety. Luther stated that he had no objection to the veneration of the Pope, provided it did not imply a disregard of God's Commandments. Good works, said Luther, are impossible except in a regenerated man. Just as Jesus in Matthew 7:18 speaks of a tree bearing good fruit, so also good works had to flow from grace, for God regards not the outward action but the inner attitude of heart. In his treatment of the Roman Church, Luther made a strong plea for loyalty regardless of how corrupt it might appear outwardly. Of the honor of the Roman Church there could be no doubt. It claimed Peter and Paul, 46 popes, and thousands of martyrs who gave their lives for its life. Momentary corruption should not be cause for disunity. In fact, when the conditions were worst, the greatest loyalty would be demanded. Love should be the all-unifying force. Luther ended by stating that he hoped it was clear from this apology that he never intended to detract from the honor of the Roman Church. He wished only to oppose those who would hypocritically use it to cloak their own nefarious enterprises.

« 13 »

The Leipzig Debate

LUTHER IS DRAWN INTO THE DEBATE

THE STRATEGY of Charles von Miltitz had ended in a second failure on the part of Rome to silence the fearless Saxon monk. Through the Altenburg interview, Frederick the Wise was all the more certain of the wisdom of insisting upon a fair and impartial trial for Martin Luther. Officials of the Roman *Curia*, who had followed the steps in the *Processus Inhibitorius* with a discerning eye, were convinced that Luther was, indeed, guilty of heresy, but that there was, as yet, no definite evidence which might be used against him in a trial. The bold Wittenberg professor had repeatedly stated his willingness to recant any time that the Roman *Curia* or other churchmen would establish the errors in his teachings on the basis of the Scriptures or evidence from the history of the Church Fathers.[1] Here was a real opportunity for someone to distinguish himself and to win the everlasting gratitude of the Roman Church.

Such a candidate was Johann Maier of Eck in Swabia, more familiarly known as John Eck, a distinguished debater from the University of Ingolstadt.[2] Three years Luther's junior, John Eck had made an enviable record during his whole academic career. He had matriculated at the University of Heidelberg as a mere child of twelve and, like most German scholars, completed his education at various other universities, including Tuebingen, Cologne, and Freiburg, studying with some of the leading scholars of his day. Completing his Master's degree in Liberal Arts at the first three institutions, he began his theological studies at Freiburg and here completed the Doctorate in Theology in 1510 at the age

384

of twenty-four. Eck was well known in academic circles as a facile, versatile public speaker, while in public disputation he was greatly feared both for his erudition and for the venom of his tongue.

It is clear from the correspondence between Eck and his friends in Paris and Rome that he did everything within his power before the debate to prejudice influential individuals in his favor.[3] Contemporary evidence also indicates that he wanted to debate with Luther himself rather than with Carlstadt, though he pretended to be reluctant to grant Luther this permission. Eck believed such a debate would offer him a double advantage. He was confident that by a cleverly framed set of theses and skillful maneuvering in the public debate he could expose Martin Luther as a heretic and secure for Rome the much-needed evidence to obtain conviction. Such an exposal would bring no end of glory and fame to him as champion of the cause of the Roman *Curia* and would, doubtless, result in the advancement so much coveted by the ambitious Eck. Even though he had posed as a friend of Martin Luther during the Augsburg meeting in 1518, he did not mind sacrificing this friendship, provided he benefited by the exchange. Recent research has shown that he was even financed during the period of the Leipzig Debate by the Fuggers, whose financial interest in restoring the indulgence trade has been noted.[4]

That Eck had followed the Luther problem rather closely is shown by his previously mentioned attack on his *Obelisks*. Since they were published while Luther was appearing before the Heidelberg Chapter, Bodenstein von Carlstadt had taken it upon himself to reply to Eck. Later Luther had become reconciled with the Ingolstadt professor, but the battle between Carlstadt and Eck continued, culminating in the challenge from Eck to a public debate.[5] Luther now tried to arrange for the debate and proposed to Eck that it be held either at Leipzig or Erfurt.[6] Accordingly, on December 4, 1518, John Eck communicated with Duke George of Albertine Saxony, in whose lands the University of Leipzig was located. Duke George was extremely flattered and immediately notified his University and also expressed his gratitude to Eck. He encountered much more opposition, however, than he had expected. The Leipzig faculty, fearing to become involved in the

Luther heresy, stated that they believed such a debate would only make the situation worse, and since it was really no concern of theirs, they proposed that Duke George summon a synod, composed of bishops and university representatives from surrounding schools, to sit in judgment on the problem. On January 11, 1519, Bishop Adolf of Merseburg, the ecclesiastical head of the bishopric where the University was located, wrote the Leipzig faculty that he was also opposed to holding the debate within his territory on the grounds that a disputation on such matters had been forbidden by Rome and that it would do much harm among the laity. Four days later the Leipzig faculty sent this communication to Duke George, requesting his final decision.[7]

Duke George now became insistent and brought pressure to bear upon both the University and the Bishop of Merseburg. After several months of correspondence, the Prince asserted his authority as head of the land, and the faculty finally acquiesced and agreed to serve as host for the debate. Upon securing this permission on February 15, 1519, Eck wrote the faculty four days later asking that the debate be scheduled for June 27, 1519.[8]

So certain was Eck that Duke George would secure permission from the University that he had already published some of the preliminary materials for the debate. On December 29, 1518, he had published *Twelve Theses* in a letter to Bishop Lang of Salzburg.[9] An analysis of these statements reveals that they were directed more against Luther than Carlstadt, for Eck's whole struggle with the latter had been over the "freedom of the will and grace," while the *Twelve Theses* were concerned with penance, indulgence, good works, purgatory, and papal power, all of them related to Luther's "New Theology." What made the new attack on Luther all the more obvious was that Thesis Twelve was apparently meant to be the key to the whole debate, and it struck at the very core of Luther's controversy with Rome, the question of the origin and power of the Papacy:

> We deny that the Roman Church was not over other churches before the time of Sylvester, but, on the contrary, we assert that he who possessed the seat and the faith of St. Peter was always regarded as the successor of Peter and the general Vicar of Christ.[10]

The clever Ingolstadt debater had discovered a vulnerable statement made by Luther while defending his *Ninety-Five Theses.* In Article 22 of his *Resolutions,* Luther had made the assertion that "the Roman Church in the days of Gregory the Great had not ruled over the Greek World"; [11] and later in his *Acta Augustana,* Luther made a similar assertion, stating "the Christians during the first eight centuries after Christ were not under the Pope, yet they had been members of the Christian Church." In these two statements Eck saw his opportunity to expose the false teachings of Luther on the power and origin of the Papacy.[12]

The *Twelve Theses* were clearly meant to draw Martin Luther into the arena. Luther smarted within when he recalled that just two months earlier he had met Eck at Augsburg and had been led to believe that their differences had been resolved and that the desire to continue the former friendship was mutual. Luther was not the person to accept such a public challenge without retaliation. Early in February, 1519, he replied to "the vain-glorious, presumptuous, double-dealing sophist" in the form of an open letter to Carlstadt at Wittenberg.[13] Although Luther had promised Miltitz that he would remain silent, he regarded the agreement as having been first broken by his opponents. Luther met Eck's *Twelve Theses* one by one with a set of countertheses, but he trumped the twelfth by an even stronger statement than he had made in any previous publication. His twelfth thesis read:

> The claim that the Roman Church stands above all others rests merely on the weak papal decretals of the last 400 years; while over against this claim there are 1,100 years of church history, the texts from the Holy Scriptures, and the decrees of the Sacred Council of Nicaea.[14]

In this first public writing against John Eck, Luther pointed out that none of the twelve articles were concerned with the "freedom of the will and grace" being disputed by Eck and Carlstadt, but were devoted wholly to the questions between Luther and Rome.[15] Eck now admitted that he had had Luther in mind rather than Carlstadt, for the latter's heresies were Luther's rather than his own, and Luther was really the principal cause of all the disturbance. Luther sent a copy of his countertheses to Spalatin by February 7, 1519.[16]

Eck now felt free to come into the open. He set to work re-drafting his theses, adding an additional one, Number Seven, on the freedom of the will and making the crucial Number Twelve now Number Thirteen. On March 14, 1519, the new theses were printed with a letter addressed to the churchmen Abbot Caspar von Wessobrunn and Provost Johann Zinngiesser von Polling, under the title: *A Disputation and Excusation of the Dominican John Eck Against the Accusations of Brother Martin Luther of the Order of Hermits.*[17] It is significant to note that these theses omit the name of Carlstadt entirely.

On April 26 Carlstadt published seventeen theses of his own, which he expected to dispute with Eck at Leipzig, entitled *The Conclusions of Carlstadt Against Dr. John Eck to be Presented at Leipzig on June 27.* Luther also replied to Eck's most recent set of *Thirteen Theses* under the similar title: *The Disputation and Ex-cusation of Brother Martin Luther Against the Accusations of Dr. John Eck,* which he published on May 16, 1519, with an introduc-tion filled with sharp ridicule.[18] With Luther's thirteen counter-theses the ground for the Leipzig Debate had been thoroughly prepared.

Although Eck had admitted in letters and theses that he meant Luther to be his principal opponent, it was not until Luther ac-tually reached Leipzig that he knew he would be permitted to debate. Luther had made a grave mistake. Even though Eck had publicly attacked him, he should have requested permission before stating that the debate between Eck and Carlstadt was canceled and that he would engage Eck. In a letter to Duke George, the University of Leipzig protested Luther's announcement that at Leipzig he would "cross swords with Eck." They informed the Prince that they would not consider announcements of unauthorized debates without the permission of either Duke George or of the faculty.[19]

His hasty action caused Luther considerable trouble. To mend the harm he had done and to receive the coveted permission to participate in the debate, Luther forwarded a humble apology to the Leipzig faculty, which mollified that body. On March 9, 1519, the faculty wrote Duke George for Luther's permission to participate.[20] But the haughty Duke, who had long been an enemy of Luther, was not inclined to overlook what he regarded as proud arrogance on the part of the Wittenberg professor. Even though Luther wrote him three successive letters in which he apologized profusely, Duke George kept putting him off. Each reply from the Prince stated that Luther would first have to come to terms with Eck, but every communication to Eck was left unanswered by the wily Ingolstadt professor.[21] Evidently Eck took keen delight in keeping Luther in suspense for months, even though he had himself announced his new set of *Theses* against Luther on March 14. Even to Luther's third and final request on May 16, 1519, Duke George replied that he could not understand Luther's insistence on participation in the debate when neither the Leipzig faculty nor Eck seemed to approve. Luther was not even granted the courtesy of a reply from Eck, who perhaps hoped that Luther would not be well prepared for the disputation; nor did Luther receive the Duke's permission to debate with Eck at Leipzig until the contest had been in progress a whole week.[22] Nor was Luther granted a safe-conduct, but had to make the journey, as he later humorously put it, "under the wings of Carlstadt," for the latter was granted blanket protection for himself and those who might accompany him. Luther appeared in the upper chamber of the *Pleissenburg*, therefore, only as a spectator.[23] His only opportunity to defend himself would be through the medium of Carlstadt in a battle of wits with one of the most famous debaters in all Germany.

LUTHER'S PREPARATION

Even though Luther had no assurance when he went to Leipzig that he would participate in the debate with Eck, he was not unprepared. Realizing that the thirteenth thesis would be the principal issue, he had prepared a treatise entitled *Resolutio Lutheriana super propositione sua decima tertia de potestate papae,* which he intended to distribute should Duke George or John Eck prohibit his entry.[24] If he were permitted to debate with Eck, it would provide excellent reference material to refute Eck's thirteenth thesis on the basis of exegetical, historical, and dogmatic

evidence gleaned from the Catholic Church since the days of
Christ.

An analysis of this treatise reveals again Luther's amazing
capacity to digest materials in a few months, which would have
required years for the average scholar. The document shows his
complete familiarity with the commonly cited texts from Canon
Law on the origin of papal power; but he had not been content
to accept merely the traditional interpretation of the sixteenth-
century Roman Church. He had further analyzed such passages as
"Thou art Peter" (Matthew 16:18) in the light of their Biblical
context, interpreting them in their exegetical-grammatical sense,
and then tracing the historic growth of their traditional interpretation through the Church Fathers into later medieval history. As
Ernst Schaefer has shown in his book *Luther als Kirchenhistoriker*,[25]
Luther made considerable progress during the winter and spring
of 1519 in his fundamental grasp of the origin and the slow historic
growth of papal claims to power by a *iure divino*, or divine sanction
in the Scriptures. He reviewed the *corpus juris canonici*, which he
had begun to study at Erfurt as a law student, and also studied
Gratian's *Decretum*, Cassiodorus' *Historia ecclesiastica tripartita*;
Platina's *De Vitis Pontificium Romanorum*, Sabellicus' *Rhapsodiae
historiarum*, Jacobus Forestus' *Supplementum chronicarum,* and
Johann Nauclerus' *Chronicon*.[26] Although the problem of the
origin of papal power was essentially an exegetical one, based on
the New Testament, Luther also realized the value of other historical sources in support of his claim that the arguments of contemporary Romanists were not based on historic truth, but on the
"cold decretals of the last four hundred years." Luther in his paper
analyzed the problem much like any modern scholar. Were it
not for the references to contemporary situations, this paper might
well have been written by a well-informed modern Protestant
theologian. In addition to his mastery of the Church Fathers and
Canon Law, Luther had also read Erasmus' deadly exposal of the
corruption of the Papacy in the *Dialogue Between Julius and Peter,*
and had even considered translating it in the spring of 1519.[27] He
dropped the idea because he feared his translation would not do
justice to its clever style.

Luther was, therefore, well qualified on the basis of his research to defend his assertion that the Catholic Church had not even claimed superiority over all other churches before the days of Gregory the Great (590), while its present *de facto,* or actual, power was the product of the past 400 years. He was still willing to state publicly, though inwardly he was not so certain, that the existence of the Papacy in the present world order implied that God had permitted its coming into existence. He had begun to believe that the Christian Church founded in the days of the Apostles was an invisible body, the "Communion of Saints," of which Christ was the Head. The Papacy was, therefore, merely a form of monarchy in the outward Roman Church; and Luther told Spalatin confidentially that he was even beginning to wonder whether the Papacy might not be the "Antichrist or his apostle." [28]

RULES OF PROCEDURE

John Eck arrived in Leipzig a few days in advance of the Wittenberg group to prepare the ground for himself.[29] As might be expected, most of the Leipzig faculty and city officials regarded the Ingolstadt professor as the champion of the orthodox Roman faith. He was accorded every honor and courtesy, including a place in all religious services, and was provided with a special riding horse and riding companion. Eck made good use of his popularity by insisting on the most favorable terms for the debate with Carlstadt.

Two days later, on Friday, June 24, 1519, the Wittenberg party arrived.[30] The cavalcade consisted of two open wagons, the first occupied by Carlstadt with books piled all around him; the second by the Rector of the University of Wittenberg, Duke Barnim of Pomerania, Luther, and Melanchthon. The two carriages were surrounded by nearly two hundred students and friends armed with spears and other weapons with which they meant to guard the honored men in their train. Just as they reached the churchyard of St. Paul's, one of the wheels of Carlstadt's carriage broke, and the debater with all his reference materials was dashed into the mud. Some of the more superstitious in the party thought the unfortunate accident might be an ominous foreboding of what was about to happen to their professor in the forthcoming debate. But no one was seriously injured, and the party proceeded to the home of the printer Melchior Lotther, who had been printing Luther's publications since 1518, and here they found lodging.[31]

On Sunday, June 26, the final agreement as to the conditions of the debate was reached between Carlstadt and Eck.[32] Eck hoped to persuade Carlstadt to use the "free Italian method," which meant a free, unrestricted give-and-take repartee, in which he believed his facile tongue would give him an easy advantage. He also opposed the proposal to publish the speeches of the debaters. A compromise was reached wherein Carlstadt refused to grant Eck the first point, but Eck had his way in limiting the latter. The speeches of the debaters were to alternate. Eck would first attack Carlstadt's position, while the latter defended his propositions, then the situation would be reversed. Four secretaries were to record all the arguments. After the debate an official text was to be prepared on the basis of the notes taken by all the four secretaries. The contestants, however, insisted that the official text should contain no materials on which there had not been unanimous agreement by the four scribes. After the debate these notes were to be submitted to some neutral universities for an official verdict. The selection of these institutions was, however, postponed until after the debate.

Luther was not present when the conditions of debating were first agreed upon. On the second day, however, he was also summoned, for Eck had really come prepared to debate with him. Now Luther appeared reluctant to accept such a belated invitation to participate in the debate and gave as the reason for his hesitation his apprehension lest certain evidence from the debate might be submitted to the Pope and might further jeopardize his chances for a favorable reply to his appeal for a general council.[33] Luther's friends urged him to accept the invitation, otherwise the already proud, overbearing Eck would gain a psychological victory which would enable him to claim that Luther was afraid of him. Their contest was postponed, however, for it seems that the clever champion of orthodoxy first wanted to distinguish himself by scoring a decisive victory over Carlstadt. After thus winning the audience in his favor, he also hoped to slay that "monster" from Wittenberg.

The Debate Begins

As was customary, the Leipzig debate opened with much pomp and ceremony on June 27, 1519.[34] Simon Pistoris, a professor from the department of Jurisprudence, delivered the address of welcome in the large auditorium of the principal college building located on *Ritterstrasse*. The group then attended Mass in the *Thomaskirche*, for which occasion Cantor George Rhau had prepared special choir music for twelve voices. The remainder of the opening exercises were held in the *Hofstube*, the elaborately decorated Hall of Princes in the Ducal Castle, the *Pleissenburg*, where Mosellanus, professor of Poetry, delivered a two-hour address on *De ratione disputandi, praesertim in re theologica*.[35] This lecture was meant to instruct both the debaters and the audience, as the title implied, in "the Art and Method of Debating, Especially in Theological Matters." The address portrayed an unusual sympathy for Luther's "New Theology," which some in the audience must have detected, especially Luther. The speaker made it quite clear that all sound arguments would have to be based on the Scriptures, and he also lauded St. Paul as an authority far above the Fathers. He warned the audience against putting too much faith in the Fathers, for they, too, had read and were greatly influenced by pagan writers. He cited the Eastern Fathers, Origen, Basil, Athanasius, and Chrysostom as being more trustworthy with reference to this problem than the later Western Fathers, including Jerome and Augustine. Mosellanus went on to point out that Peter and Paul, as well as the Eastern and the Western Fathers, had disagreed at times on points of interpretation; yet, they had remained friendly and kindly disposed toward each other. Mosellanus urged that the debate should be conducted on this same high plane. No doubt, on this point the speaker had Eck in mind, whose reputation as a rough and bold antagonist, a master of satire and invective, was known throughout Germany. To close the preliminary service, the St. Thomas Choir sang and the town band played the familiar hymn *Veni, sancte Spiritus,* while the whole audience knelt.

In addition to his participation in the opening ceremonies, Mosellanus also took the time to describe the three debaters at

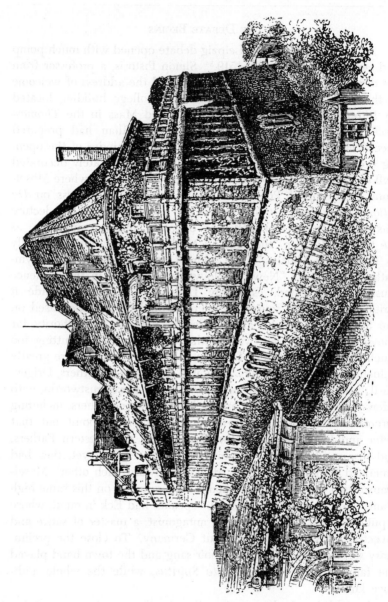

The Pleissenburg in Leipzig, where the famous debate was held

Leipzig in a letter to Justin von Pflug.[36] His description of Luther's appearance will be incorporated in a more detailed treatment in a later chapter.[37] His impression of Bodenstein von Carlstadt was not too flattering, for he described him as a small man having a dark-brown, sunburnt complexion and a weak and unpleasant voice for debate, combined with a poor memory that forced him to consult piles of reference books and practically to dictate from his notes. Perhaps in fairness to Carlstadt it might be added that the accident he had experienced and a subsequent bloodletting by a doctor had possibly further weakened his memory. He also had a quick and irascible temper, which, when played upon by a somewhat aggressive debater, did not add to his "audience appeal."

Eck, by contrast, was a large man with heavy limbs and broad chest, though he looked somewhat flabby and bloated, frequently the sign of the heavy drinker.[38] This weakness may also have accounted for his coarse features, which did not give him the appearance of a theologian. His voice was loud, though indistinct, resembling that of a town crier more than a professor. All were impressed by his remarkable memory, which, had it been combined with an equally discerning, penetrating intellect, would have made him a formidable opponent indeed. As it was, he frequently piled up a mass of irrelevant evidence, which impressed the masses, but not those who followed his arguments with discernment. Boehmer, after examining his some seventy-five publications, concluded that in originality of mind Eck did not even compare favorably with Carlstadt; for in none of them did he find a single original idea which had not been expressed before and often better by someone else.[39] But as a debater, Eck was feared and respected. He knew and practiced all the arts of deception. When advantageous to his argument, he would adopt his opponent's position, making it appear as though he had always held that view; again he might cleverly change the subject, but so gradually that the uninformed would not notice the transition; and worst of all, he was a master at twisting his opponent's presentation to convey meanings which the adversary had never meant and which, though refuted, gained for him a psychological advantage with a prejudiced audience. He spoke rapidly, jumping about in a diversity of materials, which gave the impression of great learning and made it difficult for an average debater, such as Carlstadt, to follow him.[40]

In the afternoon of June 27, following the elaborate opening ceremonies, Eck and Carlstadt opened the first week of the Leipzig Debate. Immediately, the inequality between the two men was very apparent. The debate began over the problem of free will and grace, with Eck attacking Carlstadt's position in the opening statement. Carlstadt was busy leafing through the pile of books and papers before him.[41] The audience, composed of many distinguished personages, listened to Eck's free, easy delivery with interest and admiration. In contrast, Carlstadt, surrounded by his pile of books and notes, frequently dictated laboriously to the secretaries in a slow, methodical fashion that lulled most of the audience to sleep, especially the Leipzig University professors, who slept so frequently and profoundly that they had to be awakened at the end of each session.[42] However, there may have been more method in their madness than generally realized, for, having opposed the disputation from the very beginning, they probably chose the easiest means to avoid becoming involved. The students from both schools expressed a lively interest in the proceedings and demonstrated vociferously their pleasure or disappointment with each point and rebuttal scored in the progress of the debate.

As the disputation progressed into the second day, however, Eck began to realize that Carlstadt's careful, precise method might not provide dramatic listening, but he was slowly dictating much valuable evidence into the official record which could not have been reproduced from memory, and the future judges would not consider the method of presentation, merely the evidence. Eck knew, therefore, that he must gain a revision of the previous agreement and lodged a protest. To support his point he again requested the "Italian method," which permitted no references to books or notes, but forced each contestant to rely directly upon his memory. Eck, knowing that the majority were his supporters, asked for the opinion of the audience. The majority approved his request for a change in the procedure of the debate. Carlstadt protested; the Wittenberg students were furious; but Eck won his point. Carlstadt was permitted to finish reading his statement which he had begun on the 28th, but when the debate would be resumed on July 1, the 29th and the 30th being special church festival days, he was to come prepared to debate without the aid of his books and notes.[43]

When the debate was resumed on Saturday morning, Carlstadt found himself at a great disadvantage. Bereft of his support, poor Carlstadt was soon confused and bewildered by the sarcasm of his opponent. On several occasions his friends even tried to prompt Carlstadt, which did not add to his popularity with the audience. The record shows that from then on his replies were short and often consisted of a few counterquestions.

Yet, Eck was not entirely victorious. Carlstadt had made the claim that man's unregenerated will is entirely impotent in performing good works, for, without grace, God still regarded man's good works as sinful and worthless. Eck, on the other hand, had claimed that the will is capable of doing some good works. Under Carlstadt's searching questions based on the Scriptures, Eck finally granted the point that, in comparison to grace and God, man's will is no more than a "slave and a servant." Immediately, Carlstadt claimed that this was equal to an admission of his main thesis, whereupon Eck struggled to get out of the dilemma by a clever distinction between the Latin words *totum* and *totaliter*.[44] Again Eck's supporters were impressed with the skill of their man, but men like Melanchthon and Luther felt that Carlstadt had really won the point and that Eck's reply was no more than wordsplitting sophistry. Judged by outward polish and facility of debate, the two could well be classified by Mosellanus as "indeed an unequal pair"; yet, from the point of actual truth based on the Scriptures, Carlstadt had often proved himself the superior.

The debate between Carlstadt and Eck was then temporarily interrupted, for Eck and Duke George had finally completed arrangements for Eck to engage Luther on the basis of the *Thirteen Theses* previously drawn up for their consideration.

Luther Accepts the Challenge

Although Martin Luther had written Duke George three times for permission to enter the Leipzig Debate, he had been snubbed and ignored and went to Leipzig without a safe-conduct or any assurance that he would be permitted to take part in the great event. Eck had been planning to debate with Luther from the very beginning, but he wanted to wait until the opportune moment had arrived. After a week of debate with Carlstadt he had won the wholehearted support of the audience and was regarded as a peerless debater by his friends. He was now confident of victory over Luther, and after final arrangements had been made with Duke George, the agreement was completed for Luther to enter the arena with Eck on July 4.[45]

Though Eck had tried to keep Martin Luther in the background by refusing him the right to enter the Leipzig Debate and by publicizing Carlstadt as the principal figure, the Augustinian monk was already well known to the people through his writings. As early as June 29 the Rector had yielded to the pressure from all sides and had asked Luther to preach on Matthew 16:13, the text for the day. Such a crowd gathered for the service that the Castle Church was not large enough to accommodate them, and Luther finally preached the sermon in the same hall in which the debate was being held. Immediately, John Eck replied with two sermons in St. Nicolai before equally packed houses and tried to prejudice the populace against Luther.[46]

When Luther and his companions arrived shortly before 7 A.M. on July 4, they found the Ducal Chamber in the Castle even more crowded than on the opening day. In this disputation both debaters spoke from opposite *katheders*, or somewhat elevated lecture chairs (compare with Luther's *katheder* in the *Lutherhalle*, before cited). The patron saint portrayed above Luther was St. Martin, according to Froeschel's report, while that over Eck was St. George.[47] Beside Eck sat the Leipzig theological faculty, led by their senior member and former Luther opponent, Hieronymus Dungersheim. On his side, also, were the leading abbots and preachers of the region. Even the former indulgence preacher Baumgartner was there. But the Dominicans were conspicuously absent. John Tetzel was dying in the Dominican Monastery not many blocks away. Miltitz and Cajetan were likewise absent. Whether Duke George attended that morning is not established. Near Luther's *katheder* sat Duke Barnim, Rector of the University of Wittenberg, who never missed a session, Melanchthon, Amsdorf, Eisermann, and Fach. In the group were also Luther's friends Lang, Adam Krafft, Prior Hitz-schold von Posa, Doctor Auerbach, the Electoral court lawyer John Ruehel, and the court official Hans von der Planitz. Again there were the four secretaries who kept the official record, while thirty other individuals kept personal notes.

There was great tension and anxiety in the audience that morning of July 4, 1519, when finally the two greatest debaters of Germany were to meet. Not the slightest detail escaped the atten-tion of the spectators. Some reported that Luther had brought a carnation that morning, which he calmly smelled while Eck was attacking his position. Others said that Luther wore a silver ring instead of the customary gold one. One even noticed that the ring had a capsule and, upon wondering what it contained, was assured by his neighbors in the audience that it held "the devil." All man-ner of stories and rumors began to float about Leipzig. The carna-tion grew into a whole carnation crown, which Luther was sup-posed to have worn later as he rode out of the city gates on the way home.

The extremely partisan students in the audience were not too quiet either, but they had been a problem from the very beginning. After Eck had forced Carlstadt to surrender his reference materials, brawls and demonstrations had been so numerous in the taverns and around the Eck quarters that 34 special guards were placed in that section of town by the authorities.[48] Even Emser approached Luther just before the debate, pretending to be disinterested, and expressed the wish that the debate might be conducted on a level that would keep these emotions under control. Since the episode of the Dresden dinner, Luther probably doubted the sincerity of Emser, whom he regarded as a double-dealer.

Luther well understood the gravity of the moment. He realized that this was one of the vital hours of his life, one he would have preferred to avoid. For in entering the arena against John Eck he would be opposing the established orthodoxy of the Roman Church; and the champion of change is always vigorously opposed by the complacent mediocrity of the champions of the *status quo*.[49] It was not a question of how much truth Luther had on his side, but the fact that he dared to attack the accepted way of thinking which roused the cry of heresy from the established officialdom as

a matter of self-defense. All of the varying emotions would be all
the more intensified when the problem under consideration was as
crucial as the origin of papal primacy.

John Eck had purposely framed Thesis Thirteen to place the
Wittenberg professor in an embarrassing position. To dare to question the divinity of the Papacy and the supremacy of the Roman
over all other churches required extreme courage and profound
conviction. The more ably Luther defended the statement that the
papal primacy was the result of slow historic growth, the more the
audience would turn against him. Even the history of the University of Leipzig, founded as a result of the withdrawal of the
German students and faculty from the old University of Prague at
the time of the John Hus heresy in 1409, prejudiced faculty and
students against any challenge to the established order.[50] Thus, it
was not merely a question of debating skill, nor the ascertainment
of the degree of historic and dogmatic truth on each side, that
would decide the victor. Also to be considered were the reactions
of the audience to clever insinuations designed to appeal to the
entrenched prejudice of the defenders of Rome. Although he was
known to favor Eck's position, it must be said to Duke George's
credit that he tried to create an atmosphere of fairness and neutrality at Leipzig in which the two contestants might establish the
truth on its own merits.

Luther and Eck agreed to follow the same method which had
been used by Eck and Carlstadt. According to this "German
method" one contestant spoke for a half hour, while the other
listened in silence.[51] The debate opened that early July morning
with a brief address of acceptance by Luther. He stated that
though he was accepting Eck's invitation to enter the debate, he
would have preferred to avoid the subject under discussion out of
respect for the Pope and the Roman Church. He added that a
discussion of these issues could only generate feeling and odium,
but that he had no choice in the matter since Eck had involved
him by his Theses. Luther also added that he was disappointed
to observe that those who had been attacking him in the past and
had sullied his name were now absent when he was finally about
to defend himself publicly. No doubt Luther was thinking of John

Tetzel and the other Dominicans who had not come to the debate. He could not know that Tetzel lay dying in St. Paul's Cloister near by. After this brief speech of acceptance Luther sat down. Eck now began the initial attack.

Eck in the opening sentences revealed his real intention by stating that he was submitting his assertions to the judgment of the Papacy and others whose duty it was to correct those who had erred from the truth.[52] He was playing the role of defender of the faith for all it was worth. To Luther's claim that he did not welcome a debate on this issue, Eck replied that Luther had no one to blame but himself. He pointed out that the Wittenberg professor had made statements in his *Resolutions* and other writings which asserted that before the time of Pope Sylvester the Roman Pontiff had not been supreme over all the other bishops of Christendom.

Eck began his arguments by claiming that the Scriptures and the Fathers had distinguished between the Church Militant and the Church Triumphant. He cited John 5, Dionysius the Areopagite, Gregory Nazianzen, and letters from St. Cyprian in defense of his position that the Roman hierarchy was a monarchy modeled by God after the heavenly pattern in the Church Triumphant that there might be unity and truth in the Church Militant instead of confusion and heresy. According to Eck the Pope was God's vicar in the Church Militant to preserve the unity of the Church.

Luther's reply to Eck was brief. Perhaps he had not fully grasped Eck's strategy, or perhaps he wanted to hear Eck's further argument before giving a detailed answer. He merely observed that Eck had presented well his claim for a universal head of the Roman Church, and should anyone wish to defend the opposite point of view, let him step forth. He closed with the observation: "This argument does not concern me." [53]

Before proceeding further, Eck complimented Luther for granting a monarchy in the Church Militant established by divine right, *de iure divino*. Now his arguments became much more definite.[54] Such a monarchy, he asserted, could never have been under any other control than the Roman Pontiff. In support, he cited a letter by Cyprian to Pope Cornelius which implied that the Chair of

Peter had been the original cause of sacerdotal unity of all Catholic Christendom; that Jerome in his writings against the Luciferians had also expressed the same truth by pointing to the Supreme Priest as the chief cause of avoiding schisms; while in two letters to Pope Damasus, Cyprian had spoken of Peter as being the rock on which the Christian Church was founded. Therefore, Eck concluded that the sacerdotal unity of the Church flowed from the Roman Pontiff, who had always occupied the principal seat of all Christendom.

Luther, in reply, granted that the Church Militant was a monarchy; but its Head was not a man, it was Christ Himself.[55] In support of his claim that Christ was the Head of the monarchy, Luther cited 1 Corinthians 15:24-25, which stated that Christ would rule until all His enemies were put under His feet and that only at the end of the world shall He deliver the kingdom to God the Father and give up all power. To prove that this view was accepted by the Early Christian Church, Luther cited the book of Augustine *De Trinitate* I, in which Augustine interpreted this passage as referring to Christ's kingdom in the present world. Furthermore, added Luther, Christ in the Great Commission had promised the Apostles that He would be with them until the end of the world. And the story of Paul's conversion also implied Christ's rule in the Church Militant when the voice from heaven said: "Saul, Saul, why persecutest thou Me?"

Luther then discussed Eck's distinction between the Church Militant and the Church Triumphant. Eck had stated that Christ had withdrawn from the Church Militant to place it under his vicar, the Pope. Ephesians 4, asserted Luther, implied plainly that Jesus was still the Head of the Church Militant.[56] Again in 1 Corinthians 3:22-23, where factions aligning themselves with Apollos, Cephas, and Paul were all criticized, Paul states that Christ alone is the Head of the Church Militant. Eck's citation of John 5, said Luther, was of no value to this discussion, for it did not refer to the Church, but was concerned solely with the equality between the Father and the Son. The references from Dionysius and Gregory of Nazianzen Luther dismissed as irrelevant since the point at issue was not that the Church needs a head, but rather, who was the head, Christ or the Pope.

Luther then raised some questions of his own: What happens when the pope dies? Who is then in charge of the Church Militant during the interim? Or does Eck claim Christ steps in and takes the place of a dead pope? Why is it worse to claim that Christ takes the place of the living pope? Luther attacked Eck's citation of Cyprian, by which Eck claimed the contemporary pope had tried to put aside all heretics who attempted to destroy the head-ship in the Church, as a misrepresentation of historical facts. Rather, said Luther, Cyprian's reference was to the head of a diocese, not to the Roman bishop in particular. He never saluted the Roman Pontiff in any other form than "dearest Brother." Also in his descriptions of the episcopal elections and confirmations treated in his many letters, Cyprian plainly showed that the epis-copal power of election was exercised by the people, aided by two or three neighboring bishops. This popular method of election was also sanctioned by the Council of Nicaea, the holiest of the councils. Augustine in his *De Baptismo* II asserted that "every bishop, in the privilege of his liberty and authority, is his own master; for as he cannot be judged by any other, he likewise is not able to judge another." [57]

Luther next examined Eck's claim that sacerdotal unity had originated in Rome. That sacerdotal unity had been established for Western Christendom through *Petri cathedra,* or the Chair of Peter, Luther was ready to grant.[58] Had this authority of Rome been universally obeyed, Eck's claims might have had firmer support, but history proved that this had not been the case. When one considered the Church as a whole, primacy might more reasonably be claimed for the Jerusalem church, the mother of all churches. Further, Luther asserted, Eck's logic might easily be reversed, making Jerusalem the original source of sacerdotal unity.[59] Nor had Eck quoted Jerome correctly in this connection. What Jerome had tried to prove was that the episcopal office, whether in Eugu-bium, Rome, Constantinople, Rhegium, Alexandria, or Thanae, everywhere had the same authority for all these episcopal centers and began with the Apostles. In Number 93 of the *Decretals* no distinction was made between a presbyter and a bishop. Since then bishops were placed over presbyters as a result of practice; and custom, therefore, rather than divine institution, determined the practice. Luther further cited the African Council, Distinction Number 99, in support of his claim:

> The bishop of the first seat shall not be called the chief of all the bishops, nor the highest bishop, or any other like title, but only the bishop of the first seat. Moreover, he shall not be called the Universal Roman Pontiff.[60]

Luther added that, had the Roman monarchy come into being by divine right, this assertion by the African Council would have been the rankest kind of heresy. Luther closed with the citation of Luke 22:26: "But he that is greatest among you, let him be as the younger; and he that is chief, as he that doth serve." This had been Jesus' advice to the Apostles and was a guiding precept of the early Christian Church.

Eck, who for a week had been debating with Carlstadt, was impressed. He began his rebuttal with a pseudo-apology. He asked the audience to forgive him if his materials were not quite as well organized as Luther's. The Father had just written a book and had, therefore, come to the debate "quite well informed." [61] He hoped their illustrious lordships and excellencies would pardon him, for he had been much engrossed with other business and had come there, after all, to debate, not to publish a book. This fact explained why he was not able to gather such well-rounded, accurately phrased generalizations as the Reverend Father had already presented. Following this hypocritical introduction, he turned to the materials which Luther had presented and began a speech which lasted the remainder of the forenoon.

Eck began his rebuttal with an evasion of the main point Luther had tried to establish, namely, that Christ was the Head of both the Church Militant and the Church Triumphant, resorting to his favorite weapon of sarcasm. He stated that certainly no one would deny that Christ was the Head of the Church except the Antichrist. But that was exactly what he had earlier denied when he had explained why Christ was only in charge of the Church Triumphant and had tried to prove that the Pope, as Christ's vicar, was in charge of the Church Militant. He hastily abandoned that point and began to analyze Luther's material.

The quotation from 1 Corinthians 3, which Luther had cited to establish that Paul wanted all the followers of Christ to regard themselves, not as members of some faction in the Church, but as Christians, Eck interpreted according to Jerome, who, he claimed, had accepted that Peter was the chosen head of the Church. He again pointed to John 5 stating that it should be interpreted according to St. Bernard, who in his book to Eugenius, *De consideratione* III, had found in John 5 a parallel between the organization of the Church Triumphant in heaven and the Roman hierarchy in the Church Militant. Luther's embarrassing question as to who would be the head of the Church Militant in case the pope died, Eck dismissed as not even worthy of the attention of such a distinguished audience.

The Cyprian citation, claimed Eck, had been misunderstood by Luther. Cyprian chided those who had fallen away from Pope Cornelius. As for the use of the word "Brother," this would have been the common form of addressing a pope, for even the Apostles used the same appellation. Luther's citation of the method of the election of bishops in the Early Church, Eck also brushed aside as irrelevant. Eck then appealed to national feeling and attempted to prejudice the audience by asking that Luther refrain from citing the Greeks and Orientals, as they were really exiles from the Christian Church.[62] He then turned once more to Luther, asking why he was willing to accord the Pope the highest dignity, yet base this distinction on human rights only. Jerome had regarded the Pope as the successor of the fisherman, the "Rock" in Matthew 16 upon which Christ had built his Church. Bernard had taken the same view, supported by the fact that all the metropolitan centers of the East had disappeared, therefore, the Roman center must be the true Church, since Christ had said that the gates of hell would not prevail against it. To Luther's citation of the decision of the African Council in its Distinction 99, Eck replied by stating that this was only natural, for the Lord had bidden His Apostles to be humble.[63] The Council had merely forbidden the proud name "universal bishop," but had not denied the title of first bishop of Rome. Pope Gregory the Great had spoken in this spirit when he called himself the "servant of servants."

In summary, he claimed that Cyprian, Dionysius, and Jerome all supported his view that the Papacy had been in existence from the beginning of the Church and that they regarded it as being of divine origin. With this ended the first forenoon discussions.

The debate on papal primacy continued along these lines for the next five days, but its pattern was already determined the first forenoon. Eck was a typical traditionalist who interpreted the Scriptures and the Fathers in conformity with established practices and to the benefit of contemporary vested interests. Luther, on the contrary, claimed that the Bible was clear in itself and should be interpreted on the basis of its own hermeneutical principles through the grammatical-historical method. He also drew freely upon the Church Fathers and Canonical writings to support the idea that papal primacy was the result of an historic evolution.[64] Luther's claim that the papal primacy was only 400 years old had to be modified somewhat when Eck cited the writings of St. Bernard as already holding this same interpretation. Luther then placed particular emphasis on that aspect of his thesis which denied that papal primacy was tenable on the basis of the Scriptures. He added that he, too, venerated Bernard, but that he regarded the clear texts in the Bible as invincible authority. He asserted that a study of the New Testament revealed that Jesus had based His episcopacy upon all the Apostles; that while Peter might have been accorded a special rank, The Acts clearly show that Jesus had given the Great Commission to all of his Apostles equally.

In the course of the debate Luther questioned Eck's claim that the Roman Church had always been the champion of orthodoxy. One Roman pope, according to Jerome, had even been ordained by an Arian bishop at the order of Emperor Constantine. Eck ignored this historic citation by claiming that no bad Roman Pontiff had ever officially established Christian doctrine.[65] To prove that the Roman Church could not claim universal supremacy, Luther cited the Greek and Oriental Church, which had never been under Rome's control. When Eck claimed that the Eastern Church was regarded as schismatic, Luther censured him on the ground that the Orient had produced many Christian saints and Fathers. Furthermore, how could it be regarded as schismatic when its founding preceded that of Rome?[66] The debate then turned to the interpretation of Matthew 16:18, "Thou art Peter," etc. Eck tried to show that the Fathers and the *corpus iuris canonici* supported his view. While citing Augustine, Jerome, Ambrose, Chrysostom, and Cyprian, he kept reminding Luther of his claim that the papal primacy was only 400 years old.[67] To Eck's citation of the "rock" which was to be the foundation of Christ's Church, Luther insisted that this section be interpreted according to its context. All Scriptural passages, said he, must be interpreted in the light of the context and of the entire Gospel. When examined in that light, it becomes clear that Christ referred to Peter's confession made just previously: "Thou art the Christ, the Son of the living God." This confession was the *petra*, or the rock, upon which He would build His Church. Luther asserted that the entire New Testament supported this interpretation.[68] He pointed out further clarification of the point by both Peter and Paul. Paul, in 1 Corinthians 3:11, clearly stated: "For other foundation can no man lay than that is laid, which is Jesus Christ"; while Peter spoke of Christ in 1 Peter 2:4-5, "as unto a living Stone" upon whom was built "a spiritual house, an holy priesthood." Furthermore, added Luther, the facts of history supported this view. Neither the Early Church nor the Eastern Christian Church had ever acknowledged the divine origin and supremacy of the Roman See. Were the Greeks, who had produced so many saints and martyrs, to be regarded as heretics? Was Gregory Nazianzen a schismatic and a Bohemian?

Eck was in a corner, and he knew it; were this same high plane of questioning to continue, his cause would be lost. The word Bohemian flashed into his mind. If he could cloud the issue by accusing Luther of being a Bohemian, he could weaken the effect of Luther's argument. Now he spoke of the strange resemblance between Luther's teachings and those of the Bohemian Reformer John Hus and pointed out that the present followers of Hus were now aligning themselves with Luther. In fact, he added, Luther could be classified with Marsiglio of Padua, John Wyclif, and John Hus, all of whom had denied the primacy of Rome and all of whom had been condemned by the Church. In the Leipzig environment it was a nasty insinuation, for it roused the old flames of prejudice and national pride.

Luther first brushed aside Eck's charge with rightful indignation as irrelevant to the debate. He declared that it was unfair to

classify Greek martyrs and saints with Bohemian schismatics.[69]
He re-emphasized that the Roman Church had not been founded
until several decades after that of the East. He also pointed out
that Eck's citations had erroneously interpreted the Fathers, for
they had not supported Eck's view of papal primacy. At the close
of his address, Luther expressed surprise that Eck, with all his
concern for the Bohemians, did not use his talents to enlighten
them. Why did not someone in brotherly love show them the error
of their ways and win them again for the Church?[70]

Luther stated that he neither could, nor cared to, defend the
Bohemian schism, but that he had merely tried to point out that
a large number of Christian saints in the Greek Church, who had
never been under Rome, had gone to heaven. Then, just as an
afterthought, he added that certainly not all the articles of John
Hus had been heretical, for some of them had been fundamentally
Christian and evangelical.

These words, according to an eyewitness, Sebastian Froeschel,
fell like a stone into the hall.[71] Fortunately, this observer, who was
sitting right in front of Duke George, left the following impression
of this crucial moment:

> One thing I shall have to report which I heard myself at the dis-
> putation. It happened in the presence of Duke George, who often
> attended the meetings and listened intently, that all at once Doctor
> Martin Luther, the saint, when pressed hard by Eck with reference
> to John Hus, said to Doctor Eck: "My dear Doctor, not all the
> articles of Hus are heretical." Whereupon Duke George shouted
> loudly so it could be heard in the whole auditorium: "May the
> plague take him," at the same time shaking his head and putting
> his hands into his side. I heard and saw the whole thing, for I sat
> between his feet and those of Duke Barnim of Pomerania, who at
> that time was Rector of the University of Wittenberg.[72]

After the audience had quieted down, Luther proceeded to
prove that not all the Hus articles had been heretical; for example,
the one that claimed it was not essential to salvation to believe
that the Roman Church was superior to all other churches. In support he cited Basil the Great, Gregory of Nazianzen, Epiphanius of
Cyprus, and many Greek bishops, all of whom were saved without

this belief.[73] Luther asserted that no Roman pontiff, nor any inquisitor or council could create new articles of faith. The Pope had power only to pass judgment on the teachings of others on the basis of accepted Christian truth found only in the Scriptures. This was nothing new; Gerson and Augustine had said this long ago. However, Luther was ready to give the Papacy all honor and reverence that schisms might be avoided throughout Christendom.

Eck was not one to drop an advantage however questionable and continued his clever incriminations. He charged Luther with merely using the pious Greek saints as a cover for his heretical perfidy. Arius, the heretic at the time of Nicaea, had also quoted Scripture. He insisted that Luther was either unable or unwilling to grasp the arguments of the Church on Matthew 16:18. Certainly, Bernard's position was invincible. He charged Luther with the typical attitude of the Bohemian schismatics toward the Scriptures. They, too, had claimed to understand the Bible better than the Pope, the councils, and all the doctors of the universities, even though the Holy Spirit guided these authorities of the Christian Church. Luther's position, he charged, swept away all authority of councils, popes, and juristic faculties, and, in fact, made the whole of Canon Law worthless.[74]

Twice during the address Luther protested against the false charge that he was the "patron of the Hussites." [75] He complained that Eck had set himself as his judge rather than his opponent in debate. He added that he wondered whether in this the safe-conduct had not already been violated. Hans von der Planitz, the Elector's lawyer, now intervened and asked that Caesar Pflug, the official in charge, make an announcement requesting that the debaters refrain from making personal charges and the use of incriminating language. Luther later stated that this action rescued the debate from the low level to which it was descending.

When the debate was resumed, Luther re-emphasized his former arguments against the divine origin of Roman primacy. Who had enjoyed primacy during the twenty years that the Jerusalem church existed before the one in Rome was even founded? [76] Augustine had also conceded that *Petrus* (masculine) was not the *petra* (feminine), the rock upon which Christ was to build His

Church. Ambrose had gone even further in interpreting *super hanc petram*, "on this rock," when he added:

> In this passage I understand the Lord to have meant nothing else than the words which Peter had just spoken to Him: "Thou art the Christ, the Son of the living God." For it was on this article of faith that the Church was founded. Therefore, Christ founded the Church upon Himself.[77]

Certainly in the face of such plain evidence, Eck could not claim the support of the Fathers.[78] Eck's charge that Luther put himself above councils, popes, and the university doctors in his interpretation of the Scriptures, Luther dismissed as malicious insinuation designed to discredit him before the audience. Eck's presentation of the position of the Council of Constance, Luther branded as misleading. The council had not condemned all the articles of John Hus, but had variously classified them as erroneous, rebellious, confused, or offensive to pious ears. Eck's citation of Augustine's warning against questioning the inerrancy of a council had also been misquoted.[79] Luther pointed out that in the cited connection Augustine was not even concerned with councils. He was speaking of the inerrancy of the Scriptures. To place a church council on an equal plane with the revealed Word only harmed the latter. Popes and councils were only men, asserted Luther, against whom Paul's admonition must always be applied: "Prove all things; hold fast that which is good."

Although Luther's position seems perfectly tenable to the modern Christian Church, to make such a claim at Leipzig at that time was extremely hazardous. In reality, he had questioned all authority in the Roman Church and challenged its right to interpret God's revealed Word. To Eck, arch-Romanist and self-appointed defender of the faith, this presented an ideal opportunity to expose the Wittenberg professor. Duke George and Chancellor Pflug also realized the dangerous turn the debate was taking. Pflug once more warned the contestants against making rash assertions on such themes as the Church and councils.[80]

Eck now took Luther to task for his last assertion that church councils were not infallible. A church council was not just a body of men. Such a universal council, legitimately called and authorized, was guided by the Holy Spirit and, therefore, was infallible.[81] Eck talked along this line most of the afternoon, leaving little time for Luther to defend himself against the new charges of heresy. Since Duke George had previously announced that the debate on papal primacy must close that day, Luther briefly stated that, for lack of time, he would answer Eck on this point in writing. It may have been for this reason that Duke George decided to extend the time.

On the morning of July 7 Eck again attacked Luther in the same vein. Luther asked permission to give a few words of explanation in German, for he had noted that Eck was succeeding in turning the audience against him.[82] He pointed out that Eck had falsely charged him with Hussite heresies, which he flatly denied. Nor had he questioned the *de facto,* or real, power of the Papacy. The point at issue was not one of papal power, but of its origin. No one questioned the imperial power in Germany, even though it had not been established by divine right. Likewise, even though papal power could not be established by the Scriptures, it must be obeyed. After this explanation the debate continued in Latin, but no change was effected either in arguments or in the position of the debaters.

Finally, in the afternoon of July 8 the two debaters briefly summarized their positions.[83] As a parting shot Eck remarked that he hoped Luther would join the representative of the Greek Church who at the Council of Florence (1439) had acknowledged the Pope of Rome as the "true vicar of Christ." This closed the debate on papal primacy. After a brief intermission the debate continued with a discussion of purgatory, indulgences, and penance.

The debate on those subjects was exceedingly dull for the spectators in comparison with that on papal primacy. Friday afternoon, Saturday, and Monday morning were devoted to the debate on purgatory. No marked difference of opinion developed, for Luther had not yet progressed to the point in his theological development where he rejected this belief of the Roman Church, but he did doubt that it was supported by the Scriptures. As for the Book of Maccabees on which Eck's evidence rested, Luther regarded it as spurious and rejected by the Early Christian Church.

The discussion then turned to indulgences, on which Eck gave much more ground.[84] He realized, as he stated later, that it was useless to attempt to defend the abuses of the indulgence preachers when pious Catholics everywhere disapproved of the flagrant misuse of the sacred wares. In fact, Eck practically admitted that Luther was justified in criticizing those abuses. Nor did Eck regard indulgences as essential to salvation; but he disputed Luther's claim that in them the papal power was limited to the remission only of those penitential satisfactions previously imposed by the Papacy. Luther wrote later to Spalatin that there was not such a great difference between their views:

> On the subject of indulgences we were almost in agreement. If this doctrine had been preached by the indulgence sellers, the name of Martin would today have been unknown and the indulgence commissaries would have died of hunger if the people had been taught not to rely on this wretched system.[85]

From July 12 to 14 the subject of penance was debated, and again the sharp distinction between Luther's new approach to theology and Eck's traditional interpretation became very apparent.[86] Eck, who relied mostly upon the accepted four-sense interpretation of Holy Writ, disgusted Luther with his quibbling exegesis which never read into passages what the context and grammar indicated. Finally, on Thursday morning Luther became so wearied of Eck's practice of pulling Scriptural texts out of their natural connection and reading into them all kinds of new meanings that he closed his part of the debate with the sarcastic observation:

> I grieve that the Holy Doctor penetrates the Scriptures as profoundly as a water spider the water; in fact, he flees from them as the devil from the Cross. Therefore, with all reverence for the Fathers, I prefer the authority of the Scriptures, which I commend to the future judges.[87]

In his final speech Eck was equally sarcastic when he turned to the audience and made the observation:

> The impatient monk is more scurrilous than becomes the gravity of a theologian. He prefers the authority of Scripture to the Fathers and sets himself up as a second Delphic oracle who alone has an understanding of the Scriptures superior to that of any Father.[88]

So ended the debate between Luther and Eck, which had begun a full two weeks previously. After a brief intermission the debate between Eck and Carlstadt continued for the rest of that day and until Friday afternoon on the subject of "free will and grace." Finally, at two o'clock on Friday afternoon, the farewell service for the debate began.[89] Master John Lange of Lemberg delivered the farewell address. Once more George Rhau's choir and the city fife and drum corps joined the audience in the *Te Deum Laudamus.* One of the greatest debates in European history had come to a close.

The Contestants Compared

After four centuries there is far from unanimous opinion on the nature and importance of the Leipzig Debate. Naturally, the contemporary reactions varied according to the interests and prejudices of each individual. Even a modern evaluation depends entirely upon the standards of judgment employed.

Evidence from the spectators and from contemporary correspondence furnishes the basis for an evaluation of the debate. Both men were extremely able, but there was a wide gulf between their views because of their basic assumptions and techniques. John Eck, primarily a Scholastic and traditionalist, tried to adjust all his reasoning to fit into the pattern accepted by the Roman Church.[90] The Scriptures occupied a secondary position; and by means of the four-sense method he managed to interpret all evidence cited by Luther so that it appeared to support his point of view. His carefully selected quotations from the Fathers also seemed to support his position; but a careful examination reveals that historically his quotations were neither representative nor authentic. Luther, who had developed into a Biblical Humanist, had rejected this medieval method of interpretation. He accepted the Bible as the Christian's supreme guide to be understood in only one sense, that established by the context. Furthermore, Luther believed that the Scriptures explain themselves by means of the grammatical-historical method and the examination of a passage in the light of its context and its relationship to the entire book.[91] He believed this method produced a better principle of

Scriptural authority than the official verdict of a general council which rested only upon the judgments of men. Luther turned to the Fathers principally for proof of the historical development of the concept of papal primacy and to show that the Christian Church in the East antedated the Church of Rome by at least two decades.

As might be expected, the debate revealed that Eck was more of an authority in Scholastic theology and on the period of the Reform Councils than was Luther; but he was no match for Luther in the early history of the Christian Church either in his familiarity with the sources or in their critical evaluation.[92] But the superiority of Luther over Eck was even more pronounced in knowledge and interpretation of the Scriptures. Both men revealed an unusual acquaintance with Canon Law. Eck was perhaps a little more widely read in this discipline, but he was far less critical in its use and historical evaluation.[93]

Eck made quite an impression on the masses. But some of the more critical observers, such as the Humanistic Leipzig professor Peter Mosellanus, were more discriminating in evaluating Eck's materials and method of debating. This professor wrote his impression of Eck in a letter to his friend Julius Pflug, December 7, 1519:

> He has a fine memory; were his understanding only equal to it he would possess all nature's gifts. The man cannot grasp a thing quickly nor judge it acutely, so that his other talents are vain. This is the reason why in debate he brings together all his arguments and texts of Scripture and quotations from authors without any selection, not considering that many of them are inept and impertinent to the subject, and that some are *apocryphal* or mere sophistry. He only tries to discharge a copious mass of matter, thus deceiving his audience, most of whom are stupid, and from whom he thus wins the opinion that he is victor. Add to this incredible audacity covered by admirable craft. If he thinks he is falling into the snares of his adversary, he turns the debate into another channel, sometimes embracing his opponent's opinion, clothed in other words, as his own, and, with equal guile, imputing his own absurdities to his antagonist. . . .[94]

Some of the spectators were not even too much impressed with Eck's knowledge of Scholasticism. Nicholas von Amsdorf, the head of the Scotists at the University of Wittenberg and an able and independent thinker in his own right, made the following observations in a letter to Spalatin at the court:

> Eck is entirely unversed in the Holy Scriptures. And, what is more, he does not even know as much sophistry [Scholastic philosophy] as a man who wants to be thought so great a debater ought, for he boasts and claims to be a father and patron of sophistry. For I have smelled about a little, and understand the affair rightly (although I have neither reason nor discrimination), namely, that Eck speaks all that is in his mind and memory without reason, judgment or discrimination, although he can utter the words he has learned with great pomp and proper gesture. He does not seek the truth, but only to show off his memory and to defend the teachers of his school.[95]

Philip Melanchthon wrote a restrained report of the debate in a letter to John Oecolampadius immediately after the event and also spoke of Eck's bitter and discourteous charges through which he tried to incite feeling against Luther.[96]

But the critical reader today may rightly conclude that he would expect adverse criticisms against Eck from Luther's friends and great praise for their colleague. On the whole, this was true and quite natural. But there were also a number of learned and discriminating scholars among the opposition who were much impressed by Luther's new theological approach and his ability.[97] Many were even won over to his point of view, and the enrollment of the University of Wittenberg the following two years reflected the growth of interest in the Reformation. One of the secretaries at the debate, John Graumann, the former Rector of the St. Thomas School in Leipzig and better known as Poliander, later entered the University of Wittenberg and became the "Evangelist of Prussia." [98] He then used his abilities in the service of the Reformation, copying Luther's sermons verbatim as he preached. George Rhau also later entered Wittenberg.[99]

Among those from the ranks of the opposition impressed by Luther's role in the debate was a member of the College of Princes, Heinrich Stromer, Duke George's own court physician, who wrote to Spalatin on July 19, 1519:

> It is indeed remarkable how modest the holy theological learning of Martin has remained. The man, believe me, is worthy of being immortalized. He stressed nothing except the vital, wholesome

truths, omitting all the extraneous materials and being satisfied with the majestic Gospel and the writings of the Fathers.[100]

Simon Pistoris, who had opened the Leipzig Debate with an address of welcome, wrote his father on July 23, 1519: "Luther was the most learned of the debaters, and he overcame Eck." [101] Mosellanus, in the same letter which criticized Eck, made this observation about Luther's ability as a debater:

> He is so wonderfully learned in the Bible that he has almost all the texts in memory. He has learned enough Greek and Hebrew to form a judgment of the translations. He has no lack of matter in speaking, for an immense stock of ideas and words are at his command.[102]

Melanchthon, Amsdorf, and other Wittenberg friends were proud of Luther for the manner in which he conducted himself in spite of Eck's unfair charges of being a Bohemian and a schismatic.[103] True, there had been moments in the debate when both lost their tempers. But Luther had tried to achieve and hold a high plane in the controversy and had confined his remarks to the subject under discussion.

The Leipzig Debate greatly accelerated Luther's theological development. Since the beginning of his spiritual struggle in the monastery at Erfurt, Luther had been steadily drifting from the Catholic fold, but the change was so gradual that not even he was fully aware of its magnitude. During all of his conflict with the Roman critics over the *Ninety-Five Theses* and his other polemical writings he had insisted that he was a good Roman Catholic. In the Leipzig Debate he came face to face with the orthodox Roman position on sin, grace, justification, the Church, and papal power, and he began to realize how far he had really drifted. Eck's blind, fanatical acceptance of a position that seemed untenable on the basis of the clearly revealed Word of God made Luther realize that the whole Roman hierarchy rested on a very flimsy foundation. He determined that the principle of *Sola Scriptura* would have to be the basis for testing all decisions of church councils and the official decrees of the Papacy as recorded in Canon Law. Eck, in his determination to defend the *status quo*, had insisted that a church council was guided by the Holy Spirit and that its decisions were as infallible as the revealed Word of God. Luther maintained that a council was composed of human beings and was subject to error. Following his return from Leipzig, Luther after additional reflection expressed himself in even stronger and clearer language on the subject of councils. He questioned the assertion that a council had the power and authority to condemn clear statements of Scripture or the errors of heretics. On that basis, Luther thought, the whole Bible could be condemned, for it was the source of all heresies. Luther pointed out that it was a most dangerous assertion to claim that councils were infallible, for the various decrees of those bodies were so contradictory that the individual could not know whom to believe: popes, councils, or the Church.

As an aftermath of the debate, Luther's convictions were all the clearer on the following points: (1) the Word of God must be the Christian's sole guide in matters of faith and doctrine; (2) the Church which Jesus Christ had founded was not founded upon St. Peter, nor was it an outward, corporate body, as Eck had claimed; it was the invisible body of Jesus Christ, the communion of saints in existence since Jesus' day in spite of all the errors and corruption which had crept into the outward Roman Church; (3) that the Papacy, in fact the whole Roman hierarchy, was a human governing body that had slowly risen to power throughout the centuries; and that it was to be obeyed, not in the sense of being the divinely instituted authority by Christ, but as any human ruler is obeyed for the sake of unity and peace; (4) that it was his divine mission to point out the human weaknesses and errors in the Roman Church by the preaching of the Gospel and by once more restoring the Scriptures to their rightful central place. Privately, Luther was now beginning to wonder whether Rome, by its insistence on opposing this Gospel reform, might not even be the Antichrist or at least his apostle.[104]

THE SELECTION OF JUDGES

When the debate between Luther and Eck closed on the morning of July 14, 1519, Caesar Pflug summoned the contestants to arrange for the judges.[105] Both Luther and Eck agreed that the

Universities of Erfurt and Paris should act as judges of the debate. But immediately a difficulty arose over the question: Should the entire faculties sit in judgment or just the Doctors of Theology and the Canonists? After some discussion, Chancellor Pflug proposed that the question be submitted to Duke George for his decision.[106] In the meantime Eck and Luther were to draft a brief statement of their reasons for their respective positions.[107]

Both of these original papers are still in existence.[108] Luther stated briefly that he preferred to include the younger faculty members in the verdict, because they were more open to new ideas; that many of the so-called Doctors of Theology were not really theologians and would be opposed to any new theological ideas. Eck wrote in considerable detail. He said he could not understand why Luther was requesting that young Bachelors of Arts sit in judgment on this case when he had complained that Sylvester Prierias, a distinguished doctor of the papal court, was not well enough informed. Eck was sure a distinguished faculty such as that of Paris would not agree to the arrangement, nor would Eck consent to be judged by a man less learned than himself. He hoped that Duke George would be of the same opinion.

Duke George did not require much time for reflection. His chancellor announced the verdict of his Prince on the following day.[109] Duke George, as might have been expected, agreed with Eck that under no circumstances should the entire faculties of the two institutions participate in the judgment. In Erfurt, both the Doctors of Theology and the Canonists were to be included as judges; but in Paris, since there were no Canonists, only the Doctors of Theology were to participate. It was ruled further that neither Augustinians nor Dominicans might participate in the official verdict, since the two contestants represented these orders of monks. Before the official text reached the two universities, however, much history had been made in central Germany.

The Aftermath

There can be little doubt that Eck was now hailed as the champion of the Church. Not only had he won the plaudits of the masses, but many of the Leipzig faculty members and Duke

George were also much impressed. On August 26 Eck wrote Christoph Tengler of Ingolstadt that he had remained in Leipzig for eleven days after the debate, being entertained by the leading citizens.[110] The town council showed its appreciation by giving Eck a coat and jacket of camel's and goat's hair.[111] Duke George indicated his special approval by inviting him to a private dinner in addition to the earlier one when Luther and Carlstadt had been present. As special tokens of his appreciation, he gave Eck a mounted deer, paid his entire hotel expenses of 18 gulden (about $250),[112] and introduced Eck to his special guests, the Elector Joachim of Brandenburg and the Bishop Schulze of Brandenburg, who had honored the Duke by stopping in Leipzig on their return from Frankfurt am Main, where they had attended the election of Charles V.[113] While visiting with the Bishop of Brandenburg, Eck took occasion to warn him against Luther and Carlstadt. Since Eck now posed as the great authority in matters of doctrine, the Bishop of Brandenburg also consulted him with regard to the Franciscans at Jueterbock. It seems that one of Luther's former students, Francis Guenther, was now preaching at St. Nicolai in that region and encountering considerable opposition from the Franciscans there. Luther had previously defended Guenther; so Eck now dashed off his *Gutachten*,[114] or official reply, in two hours. The Bishop rewarded him with 15 kronen and his deep gratitude. Eck's reply was then officially circulated throughout the Bishop's diocese.

Following such honors and recognition, it was only human for Eck to regard himself as invincible. Duke George and the Bishop of Brandenburg had been easy conquests. He now decided to make a hurried visit to Altenburg on horseback to see whether he could not also win Frederick the Wise. On July 22 he wrote to the Elector, requesting an interview.[115] He summarized the story of the Leipzig Debate as it could appear only to Eck. He asserted that Luther had repudiated all the Fathers and claimed to know more about interpreting the Bible than they. He pointed out that Luther had upheld as "most Christian and evangelic" many articles condemned by the Council of Constance. Eck added that he would be willing to debate Luther further at Cologne, Louvain, or Paris, and requested that the Elector have Luther's forthcoming *Resolutions* burned. But Eck was also to discover that the Elector was far too cautious and wise to be easily misled, and his strategy failed completely with Frederick.[116]

Finally, on July 26, Eck began his homeward journey, which seems to have assumed the appearance of a triumphal march by way of Erfurt, Bamberg, Nuernberg, and Regensburg.[117] He arrived in Ingolstadt on August 23 and was received as a conquering hero by the faculty of the school, who expressed their regard by presenting him with a nice gift of money.

What was accomplished by the debate? What were the objectives sought by the authorities and the participants? If Eck's basic objective was to expose Luther as a real schismatic and Bohemian, and to win thereby the everlasting gratitude of the Pope and the Roman *Curia,* he had reason to believe that he had won the victory, and he boasted that he had routed the two "monsters" from Wittenberg. Although Eck was to be disappointed in his expectations of a verdict in his favor from the Universities of Erfurt and Paris on the debate, a letter of Crotus Rubeanus to Luther, October 31, 1519, reveals that Eck had been duly rewarded in Rome by being appointed chief inquisitor over three dioceses. Subsequent history shows that Eck did realize his ambitions. Through the prominence gained in the Leipzig Debate he became well known throughout Europe and played an important role in shaping the future strategy of the Roman *Curia* in its attempt to stem the rising tide of the German Reformation.

Nor is it surprising that Luther should be disappointed with the course of events at Leipzig.[118] He had hoped that the controversy which had been agitating the Church might be resolved once and for all; that he might be shown his error or succeed in convincing others of the righteousness of his new viewpoint. It is significant to note that on the question of indulgences, which had begun the whole struggle, Luther had gained the victory.[119] What he and his contemporaries had not realized was that, in his search for truth in support of his stand on indulgences, he had discovered equally disturbing issues which were now leading the controversy between Luther and Rome into new and more dangerous channels.

Luther had sought at Leipzig to restore the Scriptures to their rightful pre-eminence in the teachings of the Church and to strip from them the shrouds of medieval interpretations with which they were clouded. It appeared to him, therefore, that Eck was not interested in the search for truth, but sought only to defend the entrenched, orthodox position of late medieval Scholasticism.

If the officials of the Church had hoped the debate would silence Luther and scatter his followers, they, too, were doomed to disappointment.

THE BATTLE OF WORDS CONTINUES

Eck's blatant boasting of how he had vanquished the monsters from Wittenberg was not to continue for long. He was soon to learn that the debate was not nearly so conclusive as he had believed. An epistolary and pamphlet warfare followed the debate which involved many of the leading figures of Germany. At Leipzig the opponents had agreed not to publish the official text of the debate, but no agreement had been made to maintain silence during the interim in which Europe awaited the official decision from Erfurt and Paris. As a result both sides took to the pen and expressed themselves freely in both their correspondence with friends and in the publication of pamphlets. Luther summarized the situation in a letter to John Lang at Erfurt:

> In the meantime, while we await the judgment, we mutually judge one another; both learned and unlearned are everywhere writing tracts about one another.[120]

While at Leipzig, Eck had learned of Philip Melanchthon's letter to his friend Oecolampadius at Augsburg and wrote a sharp reply on July 25.[121] Melanchthon, by nature a gentle and peace-loving man, replied with a scholarly rebuttal that threw Eck's scholarship into unfavorable contrast. The classical scholar made quite clear his opinion of Eck's sophistry and his questionable methods of interpreting the Scriptures and the Church Fathers.[122] Melanchthon supported Luther's earlier contention that the Bible must be interpreted in its own light and maintained that the Church Fathers were no sure guide in matters of faith. In fact, he claimed, the patristic writings were full of error because of their faulty prin-

ciples of interpretation. The proud and vain Eck must have chafed
under such scholarly criticism. But this was only the beginning.

Shortly after his return to Ingolstadt, Eck visited Augsburg.
He expected to be received as a conquering hero, but, instead, he
found little enthusiasm. Here he saw a pamphlet by the Prior
Hitzschold of Posa which contained an evangelical note so similar
to publications emanating from Wittenberg that he felt constrained to answer it immediately. Another battle of words was
raging between Eck's friend Professor Rubeus of Leipzig (Pol-
linger) and a Wittenberg professor Eisermann which reached a new
level of satire and sarcasm.[123] By the middle of August, Luther's
pen had produced a revised edition of his *Resolutions*.[124] In this
enlarged work he further supported his position at Leipzig with
ample citations from the Scrpitures, and all the world might now
see that Eck had not refuted his claims. In these *Resolutions* further
progress in Luther's theological development can be noted. In the
debate Luther had questioned the Books of the Maccabees. Now he
also questioned the authenticity of the Epistle of James. But
Luther's criticism of the Biblical canon was not fully developed
until his publication of the New Testament in 1522.[125] In this work
he included a general introduction and individual introductions to
each of the books of the New Testament. He compared James
with the other books of the New Testament, such as Romans, the
Gospel of John, the First Epistle of Peter, and concluded that
James seemed like "a straw epistle." As his knowledge of the entire Bible matured, he modified this position somewhat, but he
was still doubtful about the authorship of James, Hebrews, and
Revelation.[126]

The publication of Luther's *Resolutions* inspired Eck to write
his *magnum opus*,[127] his great work *On the Primacy of Peter Against
Luther*. In 1520 Eck took this with him to Rome to convince the
Pope of his supreme worth to the Roman *Curia*. Modern scholars
have pointed out that this strange compilation of facts and fiction
reveals Eck's inferior scholarship more than any other of his writings. In it he still accepted the fictitious Dionysius, the forged
Isidorian Decretals, the later interpolations in the canons of the
Council of Nicaea, and other fallacious accounts of the popes, most

of which Luther before the debate had already diagnosed as spurious.[128] As further evidence against Luther, Eck also took a Latin translation of the first edition of Luther's works compiled in 1518.[129]

Toward the end of August two more tracts appeared from Luther's pen. The first was a commentary on the thirteenth thesis, over which most of the controversy had raged at Leipzig.[130] The second was a reply to Eck's hasty condemnation of Luther's defense of his pupil Francis Guenther, which Eck had produced for the Bishop of Brandenburg. In his reply, entitled *Against the Malicious Judgment of Eck*,[131] Luther attacked Eck's faulty judgment and pointed out the correct Scriptural views on the issue. He closed the reply with a list of forty errors found in the writings of Eck and the Franciscans. The Franciscans do not seem to have replied, but Eck composed a hurried, superficial answer filled with bitter invective against Luther, which the latter did not deem worthy of notice.

The conflict began to assume monumental proportions. On the one battle line were Emser, Dungersheim, and Alveld from Leipzig, who were supported by Hochstraten from Cologne and Latomus from Louvain. On the other side were Oecolampadius, Spengler, Pirckheimer, Pellican, Bucer, Capito, Montanus, Rubeanus, and Hutten, mostly Humanists from the larger cities. These men saw in Luther a rising national hero and rallied to his support. Soon Eck was referred to as "Jeck," or fool, and, following the publication of Pirckheimer's tract, *The Planed-Down Eck*,[132] the pompous Doctor became the laughingstock of all Germany. The reaction was very similar to that against the monks and monasticism following the publication of the *Letters of Obscure Men*. More ammunition was contributed by Johann Oecolampadius in his *Answer to Unlearned Canons*.[133] The rallying of so many men to Luther's support, especially among the leading Humanists, must have been rather alarming to Eck and his supporters.

Eck Maneuvers to Prejudice Paris

Duke George seems to have been in no hurry to send the official text of the Leipzig Debate to the University of Paris.[134] The reason for this delay is not fully clear, but Eck made good use

Wilibald Pirckheimer. Etching by Albrecht
Duerer in 1524

of the interim in an attempt to assure a favorable verdict. He wrote
Hochstraten from Leipzig, asking him to use his influence with the
Sorbonne.[135] Knowing that King Francis I was a good Roman
Catholic, Eck addressed a letter to the King, asking him to use his
influence with the Paris faculty in Eck's behalf.[136] He also induced
Duke George to enclose with the official report Luther's former
reply to Prierias. This action violated the Leipzig pledge, but that
was of small account if it was of value in obtaining a favorable
verdict.

When Luther entered the Leipzig Debate, it had been with
the understanding that nothing which he said would be used
against him at Rome.[137] The temptation, however, was too great.
Rome was also in a position to wield much influence with the
Paris theologians. Eck, therefore, wrote to his old college friend

Paul de Citdainis, the recent bishop of Milan.[138] As secretary to Lorenzo Pucci, the Cardinal of the Four Sacred Crowns, Citdainis was very close to Pope Leo X himself. Eck requested his friend Citdainis to write Etienne Poncher, the Archbishop of Sens, asking him to write or to contact personally the Paris faculty.

Eck was not the person to leave a stone unturned to induce the Sorbonne to issue a "prompt and exact judgment" in his favor. He also sent a letter directly to the Pope which, according to a letter written by Crotus Rubeanus to Luther on October 31, 1519, was seen by very few persons besides the Pope and two theologians.[139] Rubeanus reported the reading of the letter as overheard by a friend of his. Eck informed the Pope of Luther's Hussite tendencies and the peril which he, Hutten, and others were creating in the Roman Church and urged Leo X to take quick action. Rubeanus went on to say:

> As an additional proof of the immediate peril of the Church, the new and daily increasing study of Latin and Greek is cited. Then the Pope is diligently admonished in this dangerous state of affairs to lose no time, but to force the University of Paris and ours at Erfurt to pronounce sentence; for if he delays, it is said that he will soon lose Thuringia, Meissen and the Mark [Brandenburg], and soon after that, other regions in which the people are embracing with all their heart your "heresy" as Eck calls it.[140]

In fairness to Eck, however, it should be pointed out that he had every reason to be concerned over the outcome of the debate. Luther was an alumnus of Erfurt, and Paris was far from sympathetic toward Rome. Ever since the Pragmatic Sanction of Bourges in 1438 relations between the University and Rome had been strained.[141] In that famous declaration the Gallican Church had tried to eliminate the control of the Pope in France. Later, according to the Concordat of Bologna in 1516, Francis I had persuaded Pope Leo X to renounce in favor of the King his rights in the nomination of French bishops and abbots.[142] Further, the Sorbonne had always been the champion of the conciliar movement, advocating the position that a universal council was above the pope, and had appealed to such a council in 1518.[143] The University had also publicly condemned the bold claims of certain indulgence preachers in Paris, May 6, 1518, as "false, scandalous, and exceeding the bounds of the Bull for the Crusade." [144] Eck had ample reason, therefore, to fear that the faculty of Paris might sympathize with Martin Luther.

The prestige of the Sorbonne was such that not even the Papacy could risk its negative decision. Its masters and doctors could teach throughout Europe without an examination.[145] Louis XII and Francis I had felt themselves obliged to renew the ancient privileges of the Sorbonne. All Paris paid silent respect when its distinguished professors marched in solemn procession. Moreover, at commencement time, all the pulpits of Paris were silenced, while their incumbents honored the baccalaureate preacher with their presence.[146] No wonder that the decision of the Sorbonne was awaited with anxiety by the most important of personages. Feret, the authority on the history of Paris, says that Frederick the Wise addressed a special letter to the University in the spring of 1520.[147] Aleander, a papal nuncius at the time of Worms, supplied the Sorbonne with Luther's most recent publications, in the hope that additional evidence might help render a favorable judgment for Rome.[148] Indeed, the Roman *Curia* put forth every effort to have the decision in the debate redound to the glory of John Eck and of Rome.

But if Eck and his supporters had hoped for an early verdict from the universities, they were to be disappointed. Months passed, and there was no word. The Sorbonne was in no hurry to reply; too much was at stake. A letter of December 26, 1519, by Thomas Gramye to Duke George mentioned that a committee of 24 members had been selected to prepare a decision.[149] Frederick the Wise did not even receive an answer to his letter' addressed to the Sorbonne. Some construed the silence as a victory for Luther.

Erfurt refused to give an opinion in the case. Just when Duke George sent the official text to Erfurt cannot be established, but on December 29, 1519, the faculty wrote Duke George that after repeated consultations they had decided to decline giving a verdict.[150] They were not sure the disputants wanted their opinion, and the faculty was not satisfied with the decision to exclude

Dominicans and Augustinians from the eligible judges. Another attempt on the part of Duke George in a letter of January 9, 1520, to persuade the Erfurt faculty to participate was without result.[151] Erfurt had decided to remain silent.

COLOGNE AND LOUVAIN CONDEMN LUTHER'S WRITINGS

While Paris and Erfurt maintained their silence, a reaction to the Leipzig Debate came from an unexpected quarter. The Universities of Louvain and Cologne issued a public proclamation condemning certain teachings in Luther's writings. Owing to the great demand for Luther's various treatises in all parts of Germany, the Basel printer John Froben published the first collection of all his writings to October, 1518.[152] A copy of this first edition was preserved by the Amerbach family, to which Froben was related through marriage, and may now be seen in the library of Cornell University. So successful was this publication that by February, 1519, a second edition appeared, to be followed by a third in August, 1519, and a fourth in March, 1520. As Froben indicated in a letter to Luther, February 14, 1519, these editions had been distributed all over Europe.[153] English records show that Cardinal Wolsey's officials found copies enclosed in bales of cotton as early as 1519.[154] From the Netherlands, France, and Italy there were similar reports. Doubtless, the sale of these editions in German lands was enormous, and copies must also have come into the hands of the professors of Cologne and Louvain. Professor George Lincoln Burr, who purchased the 1518 edition of Luther's works for Cornell University, believed that Lutheranism did not gain a real foothold in southwestern Germany before this edition appeared.[155]

This little volume dedicated to Pope Leo X contains an interesting introduction by Capito, in which the writer compares Luther with Daniel, whose mission it is to "arouse all theologians from their lethargy" and to persuade them to leave their "somnolent summaries of divinity and choose the gospel rather than Aristotle, Paul rather than Scotus, or even Jerome, Augustine, Ambrose, etc." It adds: "May they no longer drag Christ to the earth, as Thomas Aquinas always does, but may they instruct the earth in the doctrine of Christ." [156] Imagine Latomus or Tapperus of the Louvain faculty reading this introduction.

An examination of the articles of condemnation issued by Louvain and Cologne reveals that both groups used the second Froben edition, which contained a section on Luther's *Ninety-Five Theses* and a reprint of Franz Guenther's September 4, 1517, debate at Wittenberg on Scholasticism, neither of which was included in the first edition.[157] Doubtless, it was also this second edition which was burned in the Low Countries.

The claim has been made that the condemnation from Louvain came as a result of a struggle between the Dominicans and the Augustinians on the faculty. Such a claim is not supported by the facts. The authority in this field, H. de Jongh,[158] has pointed out that few of the fifteen members present at the meeting of November 9, 1519, were Dominicans; while of the six ringleaders, only two, Vincent de Harlem and Eustache de Sichem, were of that order. As for the rest, Niceolas d' Egmont was a Carmelite, Dorpius a wavering Humanist, and the last two, Latomus and Tapperus, were secular priests.[159] Moreover, among the four chief writers of the Netherlands against Luther, only one, the aforementioned Eustache de Sichem, was a Dominican; while the chief instigator of all the opposition was Tapperus, the young secular priest. Louvain as a center of orthodoxy was eager to do all within its power to further the cause of conservatism. Although outwardly humanistically inclined as far as the techniques of theology were concerned, inwardly they were champions of Scholasticism. That these men should draw up articles of condemnation, November 9, 1519, is not difficult to understand.

Others have claimed that the Louvain and Cologne articles of condemnation grew directly out of the John Reuchlin struggle of a few years earlier.[160] The claim was supported by the belief that Jacob Hochstraten, the chief inquisitor of heresy in northwestern Germany, came to the Low Countries with the intention of inciting the Louvain faculty. This confusion has grown out of the fact that an anonymous pamphlet, *Acts of the University of Louvain Against Luther*, was somehow falsely associated with the official verdict of Louvain.[161] The facts in the case do not substantiate that conclusion. The above-mentioned tract referred to Aleander's arrival in the Netherlands in 1520 and to the publication of the papal condemnation of Luther in the papal bull *Exsurge, Domine.*

The German Reformation had made its impact felt in the Low Countries long before the appearance of the Froben editions of Luther's works. Other writers, the Wittenberg graduates, numerous converts among the clergy, all these constituted a problem for the champions of orthodoxy.[162] The Froben edition was a new menace in that it presented Luther's teachings in a readily accessible unit. After several meetings, the Louvain professors decided to take more drastic action than mere suppresion of Luther's writings, but they were not willing to take such a stand alone. Accordingly, the faculty resolved to send Jodocus van den Hove,[163] one of the university beadles, with a copy of the Froben edition to the University of Cologne to consult with them in the matter. Naturally, the Cologne faculty, under the leadership of Hochstraten, whom Eck had kept well informed of developmer.ts, found this edition full of errors. Accordingly, on August 29, 1519, the University of Cologne published eight articles condemning the Froben publication.[164]

These articles began with the customary greeting and an introductory explanation of why they were drawn up by the faculty. As part of the reason for their publication the faculty mentioned that the University of Louvain had sent one of its Bachelors of Arts with a copy of the Froben publication, requesting the Cologne faculty to examine it carefully and to render an official verdict. Accordingly, upon finding it full of rank heresies not in keeping with the Holy Writers and the teachings of the Fathers, they were submitting the said articles. The articles condemned Luther's position on good works, his method of interpreting the Scriptures, the misrepresentation of the Sacrament of Penance, the Universal Church, denial of the treasury of the Church, the condition of souls in purgatory, and the denial of papal supremacy. In conclusion, the articles stated that the faculty had discovered many more errors; in fact, the book was found so full of errors that it not only deserved to be condemned, suppressed, and prohibited, but it should even be burned together with its supporters, while its author should be summoned to a public recantation.

After giving its official verdict, the Cologne faculty commissioned one of its ranking members, the same Hochstraten, to deliver it in person to the Louvain faculty.[165] In this way developed the original confusion that Hochstraten had started the whole proceedings. The Cologne articles were delivered to the Louvain faculty on October 12, 1519, and the Louvain professors completed their judgment on November 9, 1519. But although the Cologne articles appeared first, they were not the originators of the condemnation. As de Jongh has pointed out, Cologne acted upon the reguest of the Louvain faculty.[166]

The matter had further complications. Five universities had become involved in the Reuchlin struggle without first obtaining the necessary papal sanction, and the Bishop of Liege warned them to be cautious. He advised that they also contact Adrian of Utrecht before the publication of the articles of condemnation.[167] Thus, after months of meditation and a consultation with the Cologne faculty, the Louvain doctors finally met in St. Peter's to pass the official sentence against Luther's collected writings. Their resolution contained a very similar introduction to that of the Cologne document, giving as its ground for the condemnation the many heresies found in the recently published Froben edition, which had influenced many heretical defenders to arise in their midst. They added that they had already prohibited its further sale and had suppressed the publication.

The number of articles condemned by the Louvain faculty was fifteen, where Cologne had condemned only eight.[168] In a brief summary of the entire book which preceded the articles, mention was made of Luther's *Ninety-Five Theses* and other documents, indicating that they used the second edition of the Froben publications. After condemning Luther's views on good works, merits of the saints, indulgences, the Holy Eucharist, confession, the authority of a council, original sin, etc., they added that Luther made many other stupid and false assertions. For these many reasons the faculty condemned Martin Luther's recent work, which it considered harmful to the congregation of believers as well as to the teachings of salvation. Moreover, this volume should be committed to the flames and its author summoned to a recantation of his errors. It was officially notarized in the College Church of St. Peter by Jodocus van den Hove, on November 9, 1519. Modern scholarship has, therefore, established that the condemnation of Martin Luther was not the work of a small group of radicals, but that the entire faculty was present and cast not one dissenting vote.[169]

Acting upon the advice of the Bishop of Liege, the articles were sent before publication to Adrian, Cardinal of Tortosa, for official approval. The cardinal replied on December 4, 1519, giving his hearty approval but correcting an accidental error in the manuscript. According to Paul Kalkoff, the faculty sent an enlarged version of the articles to Adrian that he might be more fully informed of the grounds for their condemnation.[170] Since these finer points were understood only by those trained in theology, it was not thought suitable or necessary to include them in the subsequent publication.

How much influence the Louvain articles had in the Low Countries cannot be determined. There seems to be some direct connection between the more detailed copy prepared for Cardinal Adrian and the 41 articles of the famous papal bull *Exsurge, Domine*,[171] directed against Luther in 1520. Following the Louvain articles, Professor Latomus wrote a tract against Luther in 1521; after that the curtain fell for twenty-three years, and it was not until 1544 that the Louvain doctors felt themselves constrained to compose a set of orthodox doctrines to guide simple souls in a confused and heretical age.[172] The aged Luther apparently felt obliged to answer the Louvain faculty, for a copy of his unfinished reply was found on his person at the time of his death.

The official action taken by the fifteen members of the Louvain faculty in 1520 probably had its greatest influence on the official Catholic world and upon the Emperor. Later the Council of Trent (1545–63) gave much consideration to the list of 1544 in drafting the *Index* of prohibited books.[173] The Louvain professors had done their part; no one could hold them accountable on Judgment Day should souls be lost as a result of Luther's perverse doctrines.

THE VERDICT OF THE UNIVERSITY OF PARIS

Meanwhile, all Europe was anxiously awaiting the final verdict of the Sorbonne.[174] The faculty consistently refused to give out any information until the official announcement was ready. The many inquiries, however, forced the faculty to hold more frequent meetings and to hurry the reply.[175] As the verdict shows, the Paris faculty decided not to limit its official findings to the Leipzig Debate. It considered all of Luther's writings to date and tried to evaluate them in the light of historic truth. The verdict of Paris, therefore, was based on much more material than that considered by the Cologne and Louvain articles.[176] Had it confined its deliberations to the notes of the debate, the problem of papal primacy would have been the dominant note; but Paris had been too much involved with this question ever since the Pragmatic Sanction of 1438 to risk further censure. Nearly a fourth of the material considered in the verdict was drawn from Luther's famous tract of the summer of 1520, *The Babylonian Captivity of the Church*.[177] Perhaps the papal bull against Luther, *Exsurge, Domine,* also wielded considerable influence toward making the Paris verdict more conservative.[178]

On the same morning that Luther entered Worms in 1521 great excitement pervaded the University of Paris.[179] It was the morning on which the committee was to give its official report. The faculty marched in solemn procession to Mass at St. Maturinus, where the entire body, led by the fanatical Syndicus Beda, was to hear the official verdict pronounced on the writings of a certain Wittenberg monk, Martin Luther. This august body designated 104 articles which they officially proclaimed heretical.[180] The news of this condemnation was to be kept secret until the King of France, Emperor Charles V, and Duke George had been officially informed of the faculty decision; but such secrecy was impossible in a college faculty. In ten days the verdict was known all over Paris.[181]

The document began with a brief introduction naming a long list of men who had strayed from the Mother Church, all of them bad children of a good mother. Luther, the last of these, was saturated with old heresies and thought himself wiser than all the universities. He regarded himself as one called by God to lead the Church out of darkness to the light.[182] Like the Manichaeans of old, he claimed divine guidance through the Holy Spirit when in reality the devil had made him mad. The author of these heresies was certainly an indisputable archheretic and a dangerous rejuvenator of old heresies.

A list of parallel teachings comparing Luther with the Manichaeans, the Hussites, the Wycliffites, the Begards, the Cathari, the Waldensians, and the Bohemians was then presented. All his teachings, they asserted, were based upon Luther's own philosophy rather than upon the Holy Scriptures. In addition to his general attack upon the Church, Luther even published a special book under the title *The Babylonian Captivity of the Church*.[183] He blasphemously revived old heresies and was a pernicious enemy of the Church of Christ. They deemed it necessary, therefore, to draw up a list of condemnation of the errors in his writings. Not only should these writings be committed to the vengeful flames, but their author should also be forced to a public recantation by every lawful means.

An *Index* of materials was compiled from Luther's tract *The Babylonian Captivity of the Church*, and the materials condemned by the faculty.[184] The *Index* was divided into five main divisions dealing with (1) the sacraments; (2) ecclesiastical constitutions; (3) good works; (4) vows; and (5) the divine essence. This section was followed by another main division of eighteen citations from other writings of Martin Luther. These touched upon almost every aspect of Catholic doctrine; among them the cardinal points of difference between Luther's "New Theology" and the accepted Scholasticism, in which the Doctors were thoroughly steeped: confession, absolution, satisfaction, sin, purgatory, freedom of will, the Eucharist, and Scholastic philosophy.

There then followed page after page of citations from Luther, accompanied by the position taken by the Paris doctors, of which the following are samples:

> *Luther:* The invention of sacraments is of recent origin.
>
> *Paris:* This article, in that he claims sacraments were recently invented by man, not instituted by Christ, is indiscreet, unchristian, and openly heretical.
>
> *Luther:* It is unchristian and tyrannical to forbid the distribution of Communion in both kinds.

Paris: This article is false, schismatic, unchristian and drawn from the damned heresy of the Bohemians.

Luther: The whole efficacy of the Sacrament is dependent on faith.

Paris: This article breaks away from the sacraments of the New Testament and is heretical.

Luther: Christ never yet forced sinners to penance through fear.

Paris: This article, in case "force" is used in the sense of "constraint," as it often is regarded in the Holy Scripture, is heretical.

Luther: God always forgives and pardons sins without money and demands nothing save a godly life.

Paris: This article is foreign to the teachings of the sacred Doctors and encourages believers to have faith in empty, foolish trust of having done enough for their sins and is heretical.[185]

In conclusion the Paris doctors mentioned the series of meetings which they had held from time to time, ending with the final meeting in St. Maturinus, and the careful study by which the Sorbonne had compared Martin Luther's writings with the sacred Doctors, the decisions of the church councils, and the teachings of the Holy Scriptures.[186] The document was officially completed under oath on April 15, 1521, the entire faculty participating, and properly sealed by the official seal of the University. The original was locked in the Paris University vault, and copies were sent to all parts of Europe.[187]

The feelings of John Eck and his friends and supporters were considerably mixed when they learned the nature of the official verdict of Paris. Although they rejoiced in the condemnation of Luther and his writings, they were much chagrined to find that in the entire document there was not a single reference to the Leipzig Debate and not one syllable on its principal issue, the problem of papal primacy.[188] So hurt were Eck's feelings that he prepared a special paper for print in which he cited fifty-four heresies discussed at the Leipzig Debate and condemned by the Paris doctors, which proved he had won the debate.[189] Aleander, the papal nuncius at Worms, was also disappointed that Paris had avoided the problem of papal primacy.[190] Rome, however, was satisfied that Paris had, at least in general, supported its cause.

As has been noted, Luther was occupied at Worms when Paris released its decision, and news of the verdict did not reach him until he was already in hiding at the Wartburg.[191] Around July 13, 1521, he issued a violent, satirical reply. Who are these Paris theologians, said he, that they should compare themselves with the Apostles? He observed sarcastically that King Francis was certainly to be congratulated upon the distinguished faculty of the Sorbonne. Paris might be called the "mother of the universities"; in reality, it was the "mother of heresies." He ended by saying that now that they had the Paris verdict, "you sophists, papists, Cologne, Louvain, and Leipzig, now dance and make merry over it." [192]

In October, 1521, Philip Melanchthon also issued a reply to Paris which, though outwardly polished and scholarly, was inwardly full of subtle, biting satire.[193] He expressed his disappointment that such a distinguished faculty failed to grasp their opportunity to render a real service to the Church.[194] He was amazed that, with their reputation for scholarship, they did not turn away from the authority of men and return to the original source of truth, the Bible. How, observed Melanchthon, could the Paris theologians condemn Luther without so much as citing a single line of Scripture or definite quotations from the church councils or the patristic writings in support of their position? He condemned their lack of familiarity with the Fathers and the heresies of the Early Church and bitterly assailed their unscholarly procedure. On such a basis anything could be condemned as false! "Who do the Paris doctors think they are," he asked, "the embodiment of the Church of Christ?" [195] As copies of Melanchthon's reply began to be circulated in and about Paris, they were ordered burned and their publishers threatened with imprisonment. The King also issued a mandate forbidding the circulation of future publications unless they had passed the censors of the Sorbonne.

Melanchthon's polished, clever defense of Martin Luther was far too powerful to be left unanswered. Under the leadership of Beda the faculty prepared a reply which appeared in 1523.[196] They professed to be deeply hurt by Melanchthon's document and cited twenty points through which they were offended by the "boy." [197] They even took the trouble to explain in detail what Melanchthon had left to inference. Melanchthon had stated that the Sorbonne derived its name from the word *sorba,* a fruit from the Dead Sea region which when ripe crumbled into dust.[198] The parallel between it and the Paris faculty was obviously clear enough without dwelling further on the implications of the insult. They claimed disrespect for their dignity and for that of distinguished men all over Europe who supported their views. Melanchthon, they said, was a mere lad of twenty-four, "a married man, of small stature," and a layman besides. It was preposterous and presumptuous for a small boy to dare to challenge the whole Sorbonne. How Charles V and Frederick the Wise could tolerate a mere child as "Bachelor of the Bible" in the University of Wittenberg lecturing to a group of ordained priests surpassed their comprehension. They doubted not that before long the University of Wittenberg would be permitting women on their faculty as Masters of Theology. In despair they cried out: "Oh, thou erring Wittenberg, thou art perverting everything, thou wilt turn the Church into a veritable Babel!" [199]

As the final clinching argument the doctors of the Sorbonne set forth the basic principles of Biblical interpretation:

1. The Scriptures are obscure.
2. The Scriptures cannot be used by themselves.
3. The Scriptures must be interpreted by Masters, and especially by the Masters of Paris.
4. The Fathers are obscure.
5. The Fathers cannot be interpreted by themselves.
6. The Fathers must be interpreted by Masters, and especially by the Masters of Paris.
7. The Sentences are obscure.
8. The Sentences cannot be used by themselves.
9. The Sentences must only be interpreted by Masters, and especially by the Masters of Paris.
10. Therefore, the University of Paris is the chief guide in matters of Scriptural interpretation, for its decrees against Luther and Melanchthon are clear and can be understood by everyone.[200]

This shows, as nothing else could, how root-bound and blind the devotees of Scholasticism had become even on the famous faculty of the Sorbonne. To the twentieth-century mind it seems incredible that such syllogistic reasoning could have been drafted by the Paris faculty. How the Wittenberg faculty, by now saturated with

Luther's modern grammatical-historical method of interpretation, must have chuckled when they read the Paris decree! With this reply the curtain of Paris fell, too, as had those of its two sister institutions two years previously. It was not until the close of the Reformer's life that Paris once more spoke, and Luther again replied.[201]

The appeal of Duke George and John Eck to the universities had proved a great disappointment. Erfurt had declined to become involved. Paris had waited for two years, and when it finally spoke made not one reference to the Leipzig Debate. In its effect on the course of the Reformation or in silencing the Wittenberg monk, Paris might as well have followed Erfurt's example and also remained silent.

With this episode ended the medieval chapter of collectivism and an appeal to authority, and a new age of individualism was ushered in wherein such progressive thinkers as Martin Luther and Philip Melanchthon were to be the pioneers of individual freedom and liberty of conscience.[202]

The Stormy Days Before Worms

THE MATURING REFORMER

NEVER DID LUTHER PERMIT the stormy days between 1517 and 1521 to obscure his life's mission. He enthusiastically loved the good, and as passionately abhorred all evil. God was very close and very real to him; but he was also equally aware of the power of the forces of darkness which were constantly at work in the world. For him God was truly a mighty Fortress, an ever-present Help. In the midst of the storms of controversy raging and crashing around him, Luther could calmly compose consoling tracts for the weary and afflicted, the halt and the lame. Many of his tracts reflect a calm quietness and certainty which reveal no trace of the environment in which they were written. They are thoughts from heaven, whose message is as eternal as the Scriptures from which they were taken. One Caspar Hedion was so moved by their content that he wrote Luther on June 23, 1520:

> I perceive that your teachings are of God, O dearest man. They cannot be destroyed, rather they are growing day by day. Daily they are winning many souls for Christ, leading them from wickedness to true Christian piety. But why do I speak of them as your teachings when in reality they are not Luther's, but Christ's? I perceive nothing in your theology which has not been basically and completely supported by the Scriptures. There is nothing in them which is not firmly anchored in the Word of God and is, therefore, fundamental.[1]

Luther's productivity from the Leipzig Debate to Worms in 1521 is phenomenal. In the nineteenth century a manuscript was discovered in the *Stadtbibliothek* in Koenigsberg which contained 116 sermons transcribed by the afore-mentioned Leipzig secretary

Poliander [2] from October 30, 1519, to April 2, 1521, less than 19 months. During this time Luther preached in the Town Church on Sundays and festival days, while every afternoon he preached for the monks in the little Augustinian chapel of the Black Cloister.[3] In the six months following the Leipzig Debate, Luther wrote sixteen treatises, not counting his *Commentary on Galatians*, filling more than four hundred pages in print of octavo size.[4] In addition, then, to the quarrel with Rome, his daily classroom work as professor, and his preaching, he prepared an average of sixteen pages of material for the press each week. Boehmer says that material literally flowed from Luther's pen. He never rewrote his tracts and made but few corrections in the proofs. Luther explained his facility by saying:

> I have a fast hand and rapid memory. As I write the thoughts just naturally come to me, so I do not have to force myself or ponder over my materials.[5]

The rapid spread of his ideas through the power of the printing press has been noted, and the force of their impact cannot be overestimated.[6] When the critical moment came, Luther's fate was, therefore, quite different from that of his forerunners, who had not the use of such a powerful means of expression and potent weapon of defense as the printing press. Even Luther was astonished by the number of those who rallied to his support and offered him their protection.

An examination of these popular pamphlets explains their wide dissemination. They were printed on inexpensive paper with no special binding. Woodcuts usually adorned the covers. By this method of printing and use of materials these tracts could be sold for a few cents, especially since Luther asked no material returns on his publications.

Luther's style was lively, full of figurative language and effective illustrations. In a tract of his own, such as the *Sermon on Good Works* (1520), his treatment remained the typical thesis form, with points arranged in numerical order.[7] In his tracts offering rebuttals against the arguments of Emser, Dungersheim, Latomus, etc., Luther followed the line of thought of his opponents. The materials were sent to the printer as fast as he dashed them off, even before

the entire tract was completed. This fact explains why Luther
sometimes repeated himself. Like Edison of our day, Luther had
the habit of working on a subject for days practically without rest;
and even when the task was completed, he did not allow his body
sufficient time to recover by then sleeping the necessary hours or
days, as did the modern scientist. This practice accounts, in part,
for his poor health later in life. Space will not permit a detailed
discussion of Luther's many writings; but a brief analysis of a
few of the more important writings which appeared following
the Leipzig Debate will reveal remarkable progress in Luther as
the developing Reformer of all Germany.

The first important publication from the pen of the Wittenberg professor was the long-awaited *Commentary on the Epistle
of Paul to the Galatians*,[8] which came from the press on September 3,
1519, not to be confused with the 1535 publication under the same
title. Luther had begun this work as early as October 27, 1516.
Its completion was delayed by the plague and the fact that Luther
decided to revise some of the materials in the spring of 1519. From
the preface, written in the form of a letter to two Wittenberg professors, Lupinus and Carlstadt,[9] it appears that Luther clearly realized
that such publications would help to turn the people from the worship of Baal. This publication was the first glimpse of the "New
Theology" to be made available to the public, which makes the
Commentary on Galatians all the more significant. The theology
of St. Paul, heretofore not even available to the scholarly world,
was now in the hands of the layman.

Most of Luther's creative writing between 1519 and 1521 was
done in response to special requests from the Saxon court or
private individuals.[10] Perhaps the Elector realized that Luther's
forte lay in exposition rather than polemics, where he so often
became too vehement for his own good. When the fifty-six-year-old
Frederick the Wise returned from the strenuous imperial election
at Frankfurt am Main, he was so exhausted that he was ill for
eight weeks and fear was felt for his life.[11] Spalatin turned to
Luther and asked him to write a consoling pamphlet for the Prince.
The pious Catholic of the late Middle Ages was accustomed to
turning at such moments to the fourteen patron saints often por-

trayed on the altars of the churches, as was the case in Torgau. Perhaps for this reason Luther composed the beautiful fourteen consolations which he called in Latin *Tessaradecas consolatoria*.[12] Instead of the fourteen patron saints, Luther created a spiritual altar panel of fourteen images. The Prince was to reflect on seven evil and seven good images. Such meditation would help him to realize how small is the outward evil in comparison with the evil within, sin; or, again, how little is our suffering in this life when compared with others, and especially with the Passion of our Savior.[13] Likewise, a meditation upon the seven images of good would reveal that all outward blessings were small when compared with the great blessing within, faith; and, especially, when compared with life's supreme blessing, the risen and glorified Christ.[14] Both the Elector and Spalatin were delighted by the little pamphlet, and the latter suggested that Luther have the manuscript published. It became so popular that it ran through a number of editions in both Latin and German.[15]

When the Elector had recovered from his illness, he expressed the wish that Luther would prepare a book of sermons for the Sundays and festival days of the church year.[16] He was especially anxious to obtain that portion of the sermons suitable for his meditations during Lent. This request was the motivation for Luther's *Church Postil;* but his pressing duties as professor and preacher, not to mention the many polemical tracts which he felt obliged to write in answer to renewed attacks by his enemies, delayed the new assignment. By March, 1521, he had prepared but a sample copy for one of the Sundays in Lent.[17] At the Wartburg he found time to resume his work on the *Postil* in addition to his strenuous work of translating the New Testament into German and the completion of his Psalter for publication.[18]

As Luther mentioned in his introduction to the first volume of the Latin edition of his works in 1545, he had in 1519 acceded to the request of friends and agreed to give a second series of lectures on the Psalms.[19] Although better prepared for the task because of his previous experience as a lecturer on the Psalms, on Romans, Hebrews, and Galatians, before he had completed the first twenty-one books, he again felt himself inadequate for the undertaking. In a later translation of this Psalter, Luther wrote:

> There is still an immature theology in the work, even though it may be admitted that the section on justification and against the Pope was faithfully treated. But the Hebrew grammar is still not entirely developed in the work.[20]

That his contemporaries did not share his modest opinion of his work was evidenced by its reception. Melanchthon and Erasmus thought very highly of Luther's Psalter,[21] and when Ulrich Hugwald wrote an introduction for a Basel reprint, he committed the study to his fellow Germans with highest words of praise. A fellow professor, Justus Jonas, said of the Psalter: "It is the work of the Holy Spirit; it pleases me."

Scholars cannot establish the exact date when Luther began this second series of lectures on the Psalms, which are so important for an understanding of the growth and development of the professor during the stormy days of Worms. By April 3, 1519, Melanchthon had sent the first portion to John Lang.[22] The printing shows that by the end of 1519 Luther had completed the 199 pages reproduced in the Weimar Edition, V. In the spring of 1521, just before his departure for Worms, he began his lectures on the Twenty-First Psalm.[23] The work was interrupted by his journey and the events transpiring at Worms and was only resumed after he was safe in hiding at the Wartburg. By June 10, 1521, Luther informed his friend Spalatin that the work was complete and in the hands of the printer.

In addition to the sermons from 1519 to 1521 contained in the Poliander manuscript, Luther wrote a number of outstanding sermons in response to special requests. At the request of his friend Otto Beckmann,[24] Luther also composed a series of three sermons on the sacraments which he still accepted, Penance, Baptism, and the Eucharist. By November 9, 1519, Luther had completed his *Sermon on the Sacrament of Penance* and the *Sermon on the Holy Sacrament of Baptism*. By December, 1519, the final document, a *Sermon on the Holy Eucharist and Fraternities*, was completed. The three were sent to Duchess Margaret of Brunswick. During this same period Luther also wrote a *Sermon on the Preparation for Death*, which had been especially requested by Marx Schart.[25]

Another burning problem of the day was *usury*.[26] With the development of the Renaissance, Christian businessmen and merchants complained about the restrictions under which they had been placed by Canon Law, while Jews could charge rates of interest which at times amounted to sixty per cent. Shakespeare emphasized this resentment in his comedy *The Merchant of Venice*, wherein a pound of flesh was demanded as security. Risks were, of course, very high on loans, and large banking houses were extremely cautious. The Roman Church was keenly aware of the problem. Ever since 1514 John Eck and several other clergymen had been employed by the Fuggers to engage in public debates through which they tried to justify the charging of interest. It is interesting to note that in Bologna, Vienna, and Leipzig, where Eck debated, the Fuggers furnished the contestants for both sides.[27]

How much Martin Luther knew of these inner manipulations in the debates on usury has not been determined. But judging from Luther's later remarks about the great banking firm, he probably suspected that the debates were arranged to influence public opinion in favor of usury. It is significant that Luther's writings on the subject directly parallel Eck's activities. He first criticized the practice in the series of sermons preached in 1516 and 1517 on the Ten Commandments, in which he spoke of the charging of high rates of interest as a form of clever theft eating into normal business as a "worm eating within the apple." [28] In the fall of 1519, when Eck renewed his activities in the interest of the Fuggers, Luther again preached on the subject in his *Short Sermon on Usury*.[29] This he enlarged for a sermon in Kemberg at Christmas time of the same year and later published under the title *Long Sermon on Usury*.[30] In June of 1520, in his famous *Address to the German Nobility*, Luther once more spoke out against usury. All of these former ideas were combined in his tract of 1524 under the title *On Trade and Usury*.[31] Late in life Luther again raised his voice against "money robbers" in his *Exhortation to the Pastors to Preach Against Usury*.[32]

During this same period Luther published a number of other short tracts and sermons. Among them is a beautiful little pamphlet on how to pray and to understand the Lord's Prayer. The tract

begins with an introduction to the whole prayer and follows with
a brief commentary on each of the petitions. In subsequent publications of Luther's writings this little treatise usually appeared
third in a series of three pamphlets often called the "Catechism
of 1520," [33] which were arranged as (1) A *Short Form of the Ten
Commandments,* (2) A *Short Form of the Creed,* and (3) A *Short
Form of the Lord's Prayer.* In some of Luther's later publications
a brief supplement was also added.

During the month of December, 1519, Luther also prepared
another *Sermon on the Ban.*[34] Luther had preached on this subject just after his return from Heidelberg in 1518, when he believed that he was about to be excommunicated. After the death
of Emperor Maximilian, pressure from Rome had eased, but rumors
were now circulating that the old threat might be renewed. As in
his earlier sermon on excommunication, the *Sermon on the Ban*
made the same distinction between the inner communion of saints
and outward church affiliation as did his sermon on the Eucharist.
In the New Testament Church, souls were united in an outward
and an inner communion. Excommunication meant a separation of
the inner or outer relationships, or both, but it could not be accomplished by mere human action. This sermon of twelve pages
is divided into twenty-one parts. This clear distinction between
the former conception of the Catholic Church and the real inner
communion of saints must have had a far-reaching effect on the
average pious layman in Germany. Certainly, after this sermon
Luther's followers were prepared for the forthcoming papal bull
Exsurge, Domine of June 15, 1520.

The first two months of 1520 were mainly devoted to polemical replies to those enemies who had attacked his *Sermon on the
Eucharist.*[35] Perhaps it was for this reason that Spalatin and his
other friends sought to occupy Luther once more along creative
pursuits. Previously Luther had promised his congregation that
he would write a treatise on good works.[36] At first he was somewhat hesitant to begin this publication, but the more he meditated
on the subject, the clearer his convictions became. As Luther
worked on this tract, he became more and more enthusiastic and

began to speak of it as the finest work from his pen to that time. By March 25 he was already commenting on the size of the new publication. No doubt the suggestion that the book should be dedicated to Duke John, the brother of the Elector, came from the Saxon court. Piecemeal it now went to the press, and by the end of May the work was done.[37] By June 8, Philip Melanchthon had a copy of this famous sermon in his possession. The work became so popular that eight editions had to be printed before the end of the year. Melanchthon praised it as the "best of Martin's writings on faith and good works," [38] and in 1521 he wrote a special preface to a translation into Latin because he believed its Gospel spirit should be made available to men in all languages. Many modern Luther scholars regard this work as superior to the three major tracts which Luther wrote shortly thereafter during the summer of 1520, the *Address to the German Nobility*, *The Babylonian Captivity of the Church*, and *The Freedom of the Christian*. Both in spirit and in style Luther reached a lofty height in the *Sermon on Good Works* unsurpassed in his whole literary career.

All of these activities left a profound effect upon the developing Reformer. Often he was forced to engage in disputatious writing in defense of his convictions. But in spite of repeated attacks upon his position and threatened attacks upon his person, Luther still found time and opportunity to develop and to deepen his knowledge of the Bible and its truths.

LUTHER'S DOCTRINAL DEVELOPMENT

When Martin Luther nailed his *Ninety-Five Theses* to the Castle Church, there was already stirring within him the new evangelical spirit which came to its fruition in the sermons and tracts of 1519 and 1520. As Reinhold Seeberg has shown, Luther concludes a long line of writers who began to question the basic assumptions of the Catholic sacramental system.[39] In 1517 Luther presented the conception of a whole life of contrition and repentance, as opposed to the Catholic conception of penance with its three parts, contrition, absolution, and satisfaction, and in one sweep changed the whole manner of Christian living.[40] Luther's sermons and tracts during the years before Worms reveal a maturity that already expresses the essential framework around which his "New Theology" was to be built. These were the creative years, the years in which he changed from a Catholic into a Lutheran, for he now clarified his views on sin, grace, justification, sanctification, the sacraments, good works, and usury. He also began to redefine his position on the relationship between Church and State. An analysis of these theological views places the forthcoming papal bull of June 15, 1520, the famous *Exsurge, Domine*, into its proper historical perspective.

Luther had been brought up to believe that there were seven sacraments through which the priest administers the means of divine grace. Even the architecture of the later medieval churches, with the altar railing between the altar and the laity, symbolized the belief that the priesthood formed the connecting link between God and man. Luther's Biblical research led to the conclusion that many of the existing sacraments were of human invention, originating since the period of Early Christianity. By 1520 Luther had rejected all sacraments except Penance, Baptism, and the Holy Eucharist;[41] and he was already doubtful about the first. Luther did not yet insist that a sacrament had to be instituted by Christ. Two aspects were essential to his definition of a sacrament: (1) an outward sign, such as bread and wine, comprehensible to the senses, and (2) a divine promise of certain inward gifts to all who received the sacraments in true faith. On the basis of these two essentials, Luther rejected the remaining four sacraments.[42] Further study of the Gospel led Luther to still greater clarity and changed his views of the sacraments entirely. Penance,[43] he saw, is not a mere routine of performing the confessional, partaking of the Holy Eucharist, and attending Mass. The emphasis is placed on the faith of the believer,[44] the proper attitude of heart through which he appropriates those gifts which God promises him in the outward signs. Luther did not teach that the efficacy of the sacrament is determined by the believer, but rather that only the believing, contrite heart can appropriate the divine gifts.

The distinction between *culpa*,[45] or guilt, which God alone forgives, and those canonical punishments imposed by the Church,

Luther entirely eliminated. All sins were alike guilty in the sight of God. The Office of the Keys had been entrusted to the entire Church and was a brotherly service rather than a papal power.[46] Luther was crystallizing his understanding of the "priesthood of all believers" [47] fully six months before the famous *Address to the German Nobility* and held that every believing Christian was a priest before God and had the power to forgive the sins of a brother.

The confessional was also given a new interpretation.[48] As the art of the Middle Ages shows, during this period the emphasis was on eternal damnation. God was pictured as an angry judge sitting on a rainbow without mercy or pity. Even for baptized Christians the approach to the confessional was negative and could produce, at best, only a sorrow which grew out of the imperfect motives of shame or fear of punishment. Luther now asserted that Penance should have a positive orientation.[49] When a baptized Christian came to the priest in the confessional, his attitude should be one of love toward God, for through Christ he had already been made a child of God. As Staupitz had taught, the Christian should find his sorrow for sin in the wounds of Christ.[50] His repentance should not be momentary, but constant, because he is still daily falling short of God's standards. The driving spring in such inward sorrow is love, a deep realization of the sweetness of the Gospel. Absolution followed this sorrow as a matter of course even without the priest; while satisfaction, the third step in the old Penance, now became the Christian's continuing acceptance of Christ's Cross and the determination and desire to follow Him.

The outward effects of this new approach toward Penance are obvious. The placing of any faith in human merit, such as prescribed in the satisfaction of the Catholic confessional, ignored Christ and denied the Office of the Keys. The whole confessional was converted into a personal relationship between God and the sinner. Private and public confession alike were judged by God alone and were dependent entirely upon the faith of the believer.

Although Luther touched upon the subject of Baptism frequently, the first detailed treatment of this sacrament appeared in the sermon of 1519. Luther concluded that the word "baptism" meant to immerse completely and became, therefore, a perfect symbol of the drowning of sin.[51] As he matured, he realized that the outward form was not essential, since Baptism simply symbolized the washing away of the sins of the sinner. Luther again stressed the two characteristics which make of Baptism a sacrament.

Baptism was a testament, a binding agreement between God and sinful man, through which God promises forgiveness of sins and continued grace, while man promises Him a life of penitent gratitude. It is, then, a sacred act in which sinful man dies in the Lord and is reborn as a child of God. This child of God now lives in a constant state of penitent forgiveness. Sinful though man remains in the flesh, the "old Adam" through daily dying becomes ever weaker, while the new life grows in strength because of the constant struggle between the flesh and the inner child of God. The Sacrament of Penance continues the good work which was begun in man at the time of his Baptism.

The mature Luther further clarified the views expressed in the years just before Worms, but the basic concepts expressed here remained unchanged. The later Luther emphasized that the water used in Baptism was not just ordinary water, but when combined with the words of institution it became a "godly, blessed, fruitful water full of grace." [52] It became a bath of the soul through which the Holy Trinity recreated the natural man's soul. In this rebirth man's soul was washed clean and his nature so transformed that he now desired a life of righteousness even though the "old Adam" still dwelt in his members.[53] Daily the sinner drowned the sinful man within him by the renewal of his baptismal vow to live a life of godliness, and since God's spirit is ever active within his soul, there is a constant growth in the ethics of Christian living.

In the sermon of 1519 Luther did not refer to Infant Baptism, yet from this period on he defended it as being Scriptural.[54] Since Baptism had been instituted by Christ and was used by the early Christians regardless of age, Luther felt that it was not a matter for human decision whether or not a child should be baptized. Luther did not attempt to explain the how and the why; he merely accepted that Christ had commanded the Apostles to go and baptize "all nations," for only in that way could they become children of God and heirs of eternal life. This conviction is well expressed in these lines:

> We bring the child with the conviction and the hope that it will come to faith, and we pray that God will give it faith; but we do not baptize on the strength of this belief, but wholly on the fact that God has commanded it.[55]

Luther never wavered on this point even when the Anabaptists insisted on a second Baptism. It was not a matter of reason being essential to the sacrament. He was willing to leave the problem involved to God and trust wholly in His promise.[56]

When Luther wrote his *Sermon on the Holy Eucharist* in 1519, he was far from mature on this subject. In fact, he did not devote serious consideration to every aspect of the Scriptural teaching on this sacrament until his struggle with the "Heavenly Prophets" in 1524 and the discussion with Zwingli at Marburg in 1529; but his new Gospel approach had not left this field untouched. Perhaps the most significant change in Luther's conception of the Lord's Supper was the beginning of the doctrine of the "real presence" of Christ in the sacrament.[57] Luther was not quite clear on some of the details, but he was certain that the historic Christ, who had dined with the Apostles at the first Lord's Supper, reappeared and participated in the Communion. In the famous tract of 1520, *The Babylonian Captivity of the Church*, Luther definitely rejected the Thomist views of transubstantiation, which taught that during the Communion the substance of the bread and wine actually became the body and blood of Christ. In a sense Luther had merely accepted that view, developed by a line of Schoolmen in the Catholic Church beginning with Duns Scotus and continuing through Occam and d'Ailly to Luther,[58] who had taught that there was no essential change in the bread and wine during the Lord's Supper, yet Christ was really present during the sacrament. In the sermon of 1519 Luther already expressed this concept of the "real presence":

> There are those who practice their arts and subtleties to such an extent that they ask where the bread remains when it is changed into Christ's flesh, and the wine when it is changed into His blood; also in what manner the whole Christ, His flesh and His blood, can be comprehended in so small a portion of bread and wine. What

does it matter? It is enough to know that it is a divine sign, in
which Christ's flesh and blood are truly present — how and where,
we leave to Him.[59]

Luther later frequently used the expression "in, with, and under"
to convey that the *how* was an inexplicable mystery.[60] In 1520 he
used the illustration of fire and iron, in which, when combined, the
former communicates its heat and light to the latter without either
losing its original identity. This explanation was the forerunner of
the later *communicatio idiomatum,* or the communication of Christ's
divine attributes to the human nature, making the mystery of the
"real presence" possible. In the meantime Luther accepted the
simple explanation that the real historic Christ with all the merits
of the Cross communed with the sinner and all the saints in a real
life-giving fellowship. Yet as time went on, the point of emphasis
changed. Where in 1519 the emphasis had been on fellowship with
Christ and the saints, when he treated the subject again in 1520
in his *Sermon on the New Testament,* Luther placed the emphasis
on the words of institution.[61] He now held that unless the believer
accepts in implicit faith Christ's original words of institution, the
sacrament becomes an empty symbol like "an empty pocket without money." [62]

Luther criticized another abuse in the Catholic Eucharist,
whereby the clergy withheld the cup from the laity and offered
them only the bread in Communion. As could be anticipated, this
view roused much opposition among the conservative Catholics,
and Luther's enemies were quick to use it against him.[63] This
criticism was the beginning of a renewed attack starting in the
court of Duke George. In 1520 Luther still regarded the withholding of the cup of negligible importance, but he doubted the
papal right to have made this liturgical change. By 1522 he was
convinced that the practice of offering the communicant both the
bread and the wine should be reintroduced in the Christian Church;
but he also realized that it would have to be done gradually for
fear of giving offense.[64] The wisdom of gradual change was clearly
demonstrated when new congregations were organized in the middle twenties as a result of the Reformation. Luther set a good
example in this respect when he gradually changed the liturgy in
the Wittenberg Town Church between 1523 and 1535.[65]

Luther's *Sermon on Usury* reflects his growth in an understanding of the ethical implications of "justification by faith." Faith with Luther was something dynamic, an active force in society which could not passively tolerate injustice in the world. The Christian was, therefore, concerned about abuses in the world of trade and business. When Luther wrote about these problems, he wrote not as an economist, but as a theologian who was concerned only with the ethical implications of property and money.[66]

During this same period Luther also rejected the medieval conception of a *Beruf*, or calling.[67] He rejected the distinction between the clergy and the laity, the recognition of a special calling on the part of the former. Every calling, he believed, even that of the simplest folk, was of God. In the *Long Sermon on Usury*, preached on Christmas Day, 1520, Luther for the first time stated his view of the "priesthood of all believers," which wiped out with one stroke any special merit in the work of a regular or secular clergyman.[68] Rosaries, masses, and other good works meant nothing if they resulted in the neglect of one's daily duty in his calling. God had called each man to a *Beruf*, and this was a trust held in stewardship which man was expected to fulfill on the highest possible plane.[69]

"Usury" to Luther did not mean merely an exorbitant rate of interest on money that had been loaned, but rather the taking of unfair advantage of a specific situation. He did not even prescribe a specific charge, as he felt that it should vary according to the situation. When making a loan to the poor or to needy relatives, it was sinful to charge interest. If the loan was to a businessman who expected to use the money as an investment, a charge of five or six per cent interest seemed reasonable. All transactions should be entered upon in a Christian spirit, and the creditor should always consider the ability to pay on the part of the debtor. Luther even proposed an annual adjustment of the rate of interest for farmers dependent upon how well God had blessed their crops. In the case of a crop failure, he recommended a re-evaluation of their capacity to pay.[70]

In later years Luther never departed from the basic principle expressed in this sermon of 1519. He was unusually fair and open-minded on loans in normal channels of business. Perhaps as good an illustration as may be cited is found in Luther's later sermon on Matthew 23:25:

> Some time ago people would sing: "The merchant has become a nobleman." But now the nobles and princes have become traders. It is not yet twenty years ago that one would say that to take ten guilders on a hundred was usury. Now the big fellows exact twenty or thirty per cent, and some of them get from forty to sixty per cent a year. The devil is in that game. Consequently, when one asks the Emperor and the princes for help, they can do nothing, for they themselves are immersed in the whole scheme. The law has been violated and corrupted. We should be glad to approve of the rate of six per cent, and we would be satisfied even if seven or eight per cent interest were charged on loans. For prices are higher now. We would, however, require that there be security given in the form of a mortgage, and that the debtor may be permitted to redeem the mortgage.[71]

Some two decades ago Max Weber and Ernst Troeltsch presented the view that Martin Luther, as a peasant's son, was extremely backward in his views of commerce and business. In recent years Albert Hyma in his *Christianity, Capitalism, and Communism* has capably analyzed this viewpoint and found it both uninformed and historically unsound. He concludes that John Calvin could hardly be credited with being chiefly responsible for the rise of modern business and capitalism and that Luther was the more progressive thinker in his analysis of the Christian's attitude toward business and trade.[72]

True, Luther's views on capitalism are both naive and simple to twentieth-century readers, but the student must never forget that Europe in the sixteenth century was just emerging from the medieval guild system into capitalistic production.[73] The Fuggers have been called the first modern businessmen, but they were the exception rather than the rule. Luther's understanding of their business was no doubt incomplete, but he had observed that all too frequently the common man was swindled through high rates of interest and foreclosures. Luther even advocated that the poor be provided for through a common treasury, and he set an example by helping to establish such an institution in the Franciscan monastery at Wittenberg in 1527.[74] Since all property belonged to

God, Luther felt it his duty to protest against financial manipulations which brought about the need for such poor relief. Nor was his censure too severe. He granted that the laborer was worthy of his hire, and a fair return on money loaned in normal channels of business he did not criticize. But to live on the interest from wealth earned by a previous generation meant to Luther to become a parasite in society.

Even though Luther's "New Theology" profoundly affected his sermons on the sacraments and usury, the new evangelical spirit is even more pronounced in his *Sermon on Good Works*.[75] To his Catholic contemporaries it must have seemed like a book from another world. Even though there are still some traces of his earlier training, the sermon presented a wholly new interpretation of Christian ethics, which normally flowed from his doctrine of justification by faith.

Religion for Luther had by now (1520) become something entirely spiritual, a personal relationship with God. In this relationship the supreme good work is faith, an implicit acceptance of the Gospel that Christ died for the individual sinner and that there is no further need for human effort to effect a reconciliation with God.[76] All the accepted good works in the former Catholic system, such as pilgrimages, fastings, and special masses, were thus rendered superfluous and even positively sinful. Luther now realized that such an approach to religion as he had held before assumed that God must become reconciled through human effort; for the first two steps in Penance do not suffice. Rather, implicit faith in the Gospel converts the life of the reborn Christian into a life of constant good works.[77] Whatever the Christian does, eating, sleeping, working, performing his daily tasks in all faithfulness, all these are accepted by God as good works when flowing from a life of faith. But only those who have this faith are capable of good works acceptable to God. The Christian's highest task is, therefore, his daily duty. The greatest sin is to doubt the Gospel, relying on human effort to save man rather than on Christ's supreme sacrifice for him on the Cross. Reliance upon human effort rejects Christ by denying the efficacy of His atonement.

Such a message had not been heard in the Christian Church for over a thousand years. By removing the distinction between the sacred and the secular, at one stroke the whole system of Christian ethics was altered.[78] All the previous forms of satisfaction, expressed through monasticism, ritualism, pilgrimages, and other outward symbols of worship, were now discarded by the rising tide of Lutheranism. By making one's daily duty God-pleasing when flowing from faith,[79] a new dynamic system of Christian ethics was born which, when adhered to, made the believer the "light of the world" and the "salt of the earth." In Lutheranism, therefore, his *calling* required that the Christian render daily faithful service in his divinely appointed place in the social structure. No matter how humble his position in life, by living in close companionship with Christ, the lowliest Christian transformed his daily service into good works pleasing to God.

During these critical years Luther also reached a new understanding of, and carefully redefined his conception of, the Christian Church. His views in this field were closely linked with his changing views of God, justification, the sacraments, and good works. As has been pointed out, Luther's conception of the Roman Church had been gradually changing for a number of years. Catholic historians have tried to prove that Luther's new definition of the Church was the direct result of his break with Catholicism; on the contrary, Luther's new understanding of the true Church inevitably led to a rejection of the Roman Church.[80] There can be no doubt that the Leipzig Debate and some of the extravagant claims made by his opponents caused Luther to reflect seriously upon the true nature of the Christian Church.[81]

Recent research into Luther's teachings with reference to the Church has substantiated Karl Holl's earlier claim that the new definition of the Christian Church was the direct outgrowth of the Reformer's *Rechtfertigungslehre,*[82] or teaching of justification. Therefore, Holl asserted that Luther's basic definition had nothing to do with his struggle against Rome between 1518 and 1521. In the Roman Church the sacraments had occupied the central position, but in Luther's "New Theology" the Gospel was once more moved to this important place.[83] Luther's doctrine of justification by faith required a vital, inner transformation in the sinner, bringing him into living fellowship with Jesus Christ; and the Chris-

tian Church, therefore, is composed of those true believers that
Christ has gathered unto Himself through the power of the Gospel.[84]
Luther already possessed the nucleus of this understanding as soon
as he had made his great tower discovery, but its development
was retarded by his earlier teaching that the Papacy and the Roman
Church were the outward embodiment of this true Invisible Church.
It was not easy for Luther to face alone the opposition of cen-
turies. He wrote later that he kept saying to himself:

> Do you mean to say that all the previous teachers knew nothing?
> Do you regard all our Fathers as fools? Are you alone the nest egg
> of the Holy Ghost in these last times? Could God have permitted
> all these years that His people should be in error? [85]

When his opponents began to emphasize the point that he was
alone in his thinking, opposing the Pope and all the clergy and
claiming that all the Schoolmen were in error, Luther stated later
that he was in great mental anguish:

> Oh, with what great effort and work, even though I had the Scrip-
> tures on my side, did I labor to justify my own conscience to think
> that I alone should rise up against the Pope and consider him the
> Antichrist, the bishops his apostles, and the institutions of higher
> learning houses of ill fame. How often did my heart pound and
> punish me by confronting me with the very powerful argument: Are
> you alone wise? Are you certain that all the rest are in error and
> that they have been in error for so long a time? What if you should
> be in error and through this lead so many people astray who would
> then all be eternally damned? This lasted until Christ with His only
> certain Word reassured and supported me so that my heart no
> longer continued to pound, but was like a cliff on the shore which
> laughs at the waves of papal argument that dash against it, threaten-
> ing and storming its existence.[86]

By the time of the Leipzig Debate, Luther concluded that the
Papacy was not of divine origin, but merely an essential of government to preserve unity in the outward Roman Church. During
the coming winter, however, he finally reached a conclusion which
he dreaded to accept, that the Pope was the Antichrist.[87] By this
Luther did not designate any particular Pope, but rather the institution, which now appeared to him as the worst enemy of the
Gospel. This deduction also contributed to the logical conclusion
that there was no vital connection between the outward Roman
Church and the real Christian Church founded by Jesus Christ,

which had lived on in the hearts of true believers regardless of
where they had dwelt on earth throughout the passing centuries.
Viewed in this light, the Papacy was but a human monstrosity
surrounded by a pagan priesthood. Luther was not yet ready
to divorce the true Church from the Roman hierarchy and all other
outward organizations, making it purely a *Christusgemeinde*, or
congregation of Jesus Christ, governed by His Spirit and Word.

Luther's first clear statement of this later view of the Christian
Church appears in his tract of 1520 directed against the Franciscan
monk Alveld,[88] who had previously attacked him and gone to
great extremes in support of the Papacy and in his attempts to
prove that the Roman Church was the true visible Church on earth.
In his reply, *Concerning the Papacy in Rome,* Luther first criticized
Alveld's reasoning and then presented his own views as to the true
nature of the Christian Church.[89] In this tract Luther pointed out
that the word *church* has been used in at least three senses:
(a) an outward building, (b) the Roman organization or some
other outward physical body, such as the Greek Church, and
(c) the inward body of Jesus Christ. He discards the first two,
claiming that in the presence of God no outward forms are dignified
by that title. The Christian Church is an assembly of souls, those
true Christians whom Christ has gathered unto Himself and who
are now united by His unifying Spirit even though physically they
may live a thousand miles apart.[90] Luther now and later always
stressed that this *Gemeinde,*[91] the union of souls, was not the result
of human decisions, but that it was created entirely by the will of
Christ. Luther also pointed out that the Church had to be made
up of human beings and that the Church dwells in these as the
soul dwells in the human body. But he made it clear to Alveld that
it was not outward membership, the body, which determined membership in Christ's Church.[92] Those who do not have faith are
dead as far as Christ is concerned and only outward symbols.
Luther clearly stated his position thus:

> Whosoever would not go astray should, therefore, hold fast to this,
> that the Church is a spiritual assembly of souls in one faith, and
> that no one is reckoned a Christian for his body's sake; in order
> that he may know that the true, real, right, essential Church is

a spiritual thing, and not anything external or outward, by whatever name it may be called.[93]

There have been those who claimed that Luther emphasized the spiritual aspect of the Church merely as an argument against Alveld because he had championed the outward Roman Church; but that when Luther later organized his own congregations he changed his point of view. That he later had to face this administrative problem is, of course, recognized; for when Luther's followers were regarded as being outside the pale of the Roman Church, the various groups naturally formed into congregations. In many parts of Germany the German *Landeskirche* [94] was substituted for the former Roman Church, but did Luther regard this outward organization as now fulfilling the requirements of the true Christian Church?

A number of schools of thought have arisen over this difficult problem in the German Reformation, and an enormous volume of literature has been acquired. An older German school, the extreme champions of which were Stahl, Vilmar, Loehe, and Kliefoth, went to the same extreme as had the Roman Church in insisting that the Lutheran Church was now the true visible Church on earth.[95] This view has been modified by Holl, Althaus, Walther, Kattenbusch, Holstein, Elert, Rietschel, and Reinhold Seeberg.[96] These men are but a few of the many who have thoroughly reexamined Luther's teachings on the Christian Church from every possible angle. Even though there are differences in details, a considerable body of information is now available which is quite generally accepted.

One of the most controversial points has been the relationship between an outwardly visible and the true invisible Church in Luther's thinking.[97] Many of the conflicting opinions grew out of different interpretations of Luther's tract against Alveld. Some claimed, because Luther used the illustration of a body and a soul, that in this he already presupposed there were two churches. Others insisted that the tract still reflected some traces of the Catholic Luther, which were later discarded completely. Space will not permit a detailed treatment.

Ferdinand Kattenbusch wrote a whole volume trying to prove that Luther had thought of the Church at two different levels, a *Doppelschichtigkeit*,[98] an outward body composed of true and nominal Christians, and an inward body composed only of true Christians, the communion of saints. To prove his point, Kattenbusch cited Luther's words to Ambrosius Catharinus in a tract of 1521: "Without an outward location there can be no church." [99] In 1932 Ernst Rietschel replied to this in a thorough and searching study, entitled *The Problem of the Invisible-Visible Church According to Luther*.[100] He seems to prove his point that Luther knew of only one type of Church worthy of that name, The Invisible Church of Jesus Christ. He cites Luther's *Ansbacher Ratschlag* of 1524 as an explanation of what Luther meant by invisible:

> This Church is spiritual and invisible, not in the sense that we cannot see its members, but rather in that no one knows who really belongs to the Christian Church.[101]

Reinhold Seeberg claims that Luther's conception of the Church in the years that he broke away from Rome did swing farther toward an invisible body than he was willing to hold after he faced the problem of reorganizing the new Lutheran communities into Christian congregations.[102] This is hardly tenable in the light of all the evidence brought forth by Rietschel. The statement of Luther, "the Church is to be my fortress, my castle, and my chamber," seems to be more typical. Luther stressed that the Church is found wherever there are praying Christians, wherever a Christian is in contact with the Word. The Church is the body of believers whom Christ has gathered unto Himself, that "priesthood of believers" who are living in vital, life-giving personal relationship with their Lord.[103] Rudolf Sohm was one of the first to grasp this deep undercurrent of Luther's view of the Church when he wrote:

> The Church in the Lutheran sense of the term is not an institution, but rather a holy people . . . also not a people which belong to a definite, fixed group, but rather a people the members of which are determined by a spiritual stream which works on them in common.[104]

This theme is very strong in Luther's many references to the Christian Church. Luther was never willing to regard the Church as a *Sammelbegriff*,[105] or group concept, but as an invisible group of Christians, scattered far and wide, who all experience the heavenly reality of being in contact with Jesus Christ. He strongly believed that the true Christian could actually feel the sympathy, fellowship, and life-giving power of the whole body of the communion of saints.

Karl Holl has ably proved that Luther's conception of the Christian Church did not come into being as a result of necessity when he found himself excluded from the pale of Roman Catholicism:

> The concept of the Church with which Martin Luther attacked the Roman Catholic Church, grew . . . not out of opposition but out of the faithful following of Luther's basic religious concepts; for again in this case one is led into the very center of Luther's world of thought. His doctrine of "justification by faith" also immediately brought to the fore his new conception of the Church.[106]

The Middle Ages had laid much stress on the outward Roman Church as the visible Church on earth. Even though Luther recognized the need for a German *Landeskirche,* or territorial Church, which had to provide the outward organization for his followers, he was never willing to dignify this body with the title of Church. In Luther's writings there is a continuing emphasis on the Invisible Church. He did not wish that his followers should name themselves after him, for who was Luther that a Church should bear his name? Paul had not said his followers should call themselves "Paulinians." [107] Melanchthon, however, already in the Augsburg Confession days (1530) and in the Apology began to stress once more the outward organization of Lutheranism. Finally, in 1543, when he published another edition of his *Loci,* he, for the first time, identified the Lutheran Church with the true visible Church on earth.[108] After Luther's death the dogmaticians developed Melanchthon's view, and from them it has passed into the Lutheran tradition.

RENEWED ATTACKS

As was to be expected, many powerful voices were raised in answer to Luther's new doctrines, which challenged so many of the existing practices of Roman Catholicism. One was that of Luther's traditional enemy, Duke George. This conservative Prince took issue with Luther's *Sermon on the Sacrament of Christ's Body,* etc.,[109] which had expressed the hope that a church council might reinstitute the distribution of both the bread and the wine to the laity. At the instigation of the Prince the Bishop of Meissen published an edict against Luther; but since the document had appeared only in the name of the Bishop, Luther assumed that it was published by some official in Stolpen, where the episcopal chancery was located.[110] In a letter to Spalatin, February 5, 1520, Luther expressed his doubt that the "Honorable Father in God and Lord of Meissen" could be so ignorant as to be the author of such an "unfounded, shameful, wicked" document.[111] In a half day Luther dashed off a reply in German, and by February 11 it was off the press.

When the Reformer's reply reached the Bishop's seat on February 16, Charles von Miltitz happened to be present, and he repeated the following impression in a letter to the Elector of Saxony:

> After dinner we were relaxing and drinking, when the secretary (of Albert of Mainz) Licentiate Reisch of Pirna arrived at nine in the evening and delivered Doctor Martin's reply. Accordingly, his Grace (the Bishop) read the response forthwith in the presence of the official and myself, which was very displeasing to the official (Christoph Betzschitz), and the more he swore, the more I laughed.[112]

Miltitz stated that the Bishop later showed Luther's reply to Duke George, who was likewise much amused and laughed heartily over Luther's humorous reply.[113] This report of the unreliable Miltitz seems highly unlikely. To Duke George this was no laughing matter, and he now suggested that the Bishop reveal to Luther that he, the Duke, was the author of the edict.[114]

Apparently, many other clergymen agreed with Luther's request for a change in Communion. When the Duke's edict was posted at Oschatz, some brother (monk) of Waldheim who evidently favored the reform wrote on the mandate:

> Behold the bishops of this age post up their ignorance even on church doors! Alas, Bishop, reread the Gospel! [115]

Spalatin, who knew how impetuous Luther was, warned him not to write a reply to the Bishop's edict, but his warning arrived too late.[116] Luther's reply in German was already in print. Frederick the Wise, who also was under pressure from his cousin, Duke George, now counseled moderation. Luther was to write letters to both Albert of Mainz and the Bishop of Merseburg.

How excited the court of the Elector of Saxony had become over the edict is made clear from Luther's letter of February 16, 1520:

> Greeting. Good Heavens! Spalatin, how excited you are! More than I or anyone else. I wrote you before not to assume that this affair was begun or is carried on by your judgment or mine or that of any man. If it is of God, it will be completed contrary to, outside of, above and below, your or my understanding.[117]

Luther made the observation that the ground for the Stolpen boldness was the "five or six wagonloads of Emser's and Eck's curses" which had gone unanswered. Luther was not angry at the attack upon himself, but at what he considered blasphemy against the Gospel truth.[118] Moreover, Luther told Spalatin that he must not suppose that the Gospel can be advanced "without tumult, offense, and sedition." The Christian must also wage a war against sin. "The Word of God is a sword, it is war and ruin and offense and perdition and poison." Nor did Luther consider abandoning his preaching. If the bishops had forgotten the dignity of the episcopal office, he was ready to make them conscious of its meaning by citations from Holy Writ. Luther admitted that he was by nature far "more vehement" than he should be and that he was "naturally warm" and wrote with a "pen which is not at all blunt." He was sometimes carried "beyond the bounds of moderation by these monsters."

After reflecting two days over the matter, Luther wrote Spalatin that he was ready to write another reply to the Bishop of Meissen. But this time he would write in Latin, and he would permit Spalatin and his friends to see the copy before it appeared in print. Luther added that even though he was willing to be personally quite apologetic in this matter, he would not permit the Gospel to be misused and blasphemed:

> I will not suffer a condemned error to be assumed in God's Gospel even by all the angels of heaven, much less by the idols of one terrestrial church.[119]

By February 24 Luther had sent the letters to the Archbishop of Mainz and the Bishop of Merseburg, as he had promised the Court, and he was awaiting an answer. The next day the Bishop of Merseburg wrote a reply to Luther's former letter of February 4, but which was not received by Luther until February 29.[120] The Bishop expressed his regret over the fact that Luther's *Sermon on the Sacrament of the Body of Christ,* etc., had aroused the common people in his diocese. He also asked that in the future Luther refrain from further attacks on the Pope. On February 26 Albert of Mainz also wrote Luther and expressed his gratification that Luther was willing to be instructed further and, if properly taught, willing to give up his own position. The lamentable part of the situation, however, was that he, even as the highest-ranking churchman in all Germany, admitted that he had no more than a passing acquaintance with Luther's problem and was not qualified to inform him as to his errors. He further expressed the wish that Luther would "treat sacred things reverently, piously, modestly, without tumult, hatred, and contumely," trying to defend his own opinions in such matters as "whether the power of the Roman Pontiff is divine or human, and of free will, and many other similar trifles, which do not concern true Christianity." [121] He also objected to the dissemination of Luther's teachings "among the fickle crowd and the unlearned people" in which he suggested many practices contrary to the "long-established customs of the Church of Christ." Especially did Albert deplore the proposal that the "venerable sacrament of Communion should be indiscriminately distributed in both kinds to all assembled, laymen as well as clergy." He likewise expressed his disapproval of the suggestion that the authority of a general council be invoked in order to "uphold and defend" Luther's personal opinions.[122] Luther later complained to Albert from the Wartburg on December 1, 1521:

> . . . I wrote you a second time, humbly asking for information. To this I got a hard, improper, unepiscopal, unchristian answer, referring me to higher powers for information.[123]

In another letter to Spalatin, February 29, 1520, Luther also acknowledged that he had received a reply from the Bishop of Merseburg to his recent letter, who admitted that his action against

Luther's *Sermon on the Eucharist* had been on the basis of "the letters and reports of others." [124] The whole question of the Stolpen edict had been incited by men who were poorly informed as to Luther's actual writings and who were in no position to clarify the problems which they labeled as heresy.

It was at this point, as has been noted, that Spalatin and others sought to dissuade Luther from wasting his efforts in argumentation, but to turn his abilities into creative and constructive channels.[125] The result was Luther's remarkable *Sermon on Good Works*, the first copy of which was in Melanchthon's hands early in June.

His opponents, however, were far from willing to live and let live. While he was busily engaged in the above tract, another coarse, bitter attack was hurled against him in which he was called a "heretic, a blind, senseless fool, one possessed with the devil, a serpent, a poisonous reptile," and similar complimentary titles. The author was a certain Franciscan friar in Leipzig, the aforementioned Augustin von Alveld, who twice before this had written against the Reformer. This tract regurgitated the old theme of Leipzig: Is the Papacy of divine origin? Alveld was really a spokesman for Prierias, Eck, Cajetan, and Emser.[126] His tract contained nothing essentially new, but merely defended the theme that the Roman Church was visible Christendom. At first Luther was inclined to ignore this crude, vulgar tract as not worthy of his attention. But when he learned that it was making an impression on the common people and even on some Wittenberg professors, he felt constrained to reply.[127] The reply was the afore-mentioned *Vom Papsttum zu Rom*, etc., in which Luther not only evaluated the Papacy, but the Roman teachings on the Church. In his tract, which he dashed off in two weeks, Luther began to remove the glamour from the Papacy and to expose its basic corruptions. The Church he defined as an invisible body of which Christ alone is the Head; and, therefore, the Papacy or the outward Roman hierarchy were not essential to its existence.

Another writing which moved Luther to rebuttal was the *Epitome* of Prierias' reply to Luther's thirteenth thesis at the Leipzig Debate.[128] This document defended papal absolutism in such sweeping terms that Luther regarded it as the hellish manifesta-

tions of the Antichrist.[129] Where formerly he had merely wondered
whether Rome might not be the seat of the Antichrist, he was now
convinced. The fact that Luther had by now in his possession a
copy of Lorenzo Valla's exposal of the *Donation of Constantine*,[130]
the forged document by means of which the temporal claims of the
Papacy had been defended throughout the Middle Ages, may have
added to this conviction.

Before the *Epitome*, Luther had held the view that as a human
institution the Papacy was fallible, yet he regarded its existence
as essential to unity in the Church. Now he was certain that the
Papacy as an institution was the Babylon of the Scriptures.[131] But
his reasoning did not follow that of other medieval reformers before
his time who essentially cited the following reasons: (1) the striving after worldly power and splendor, (2) the lust for gold and
riches, and (3) the immorality of the papal court. With penetration
equal to his former discernment of Roman abuses, Luther laid his
finger on the crux of the whole problem. The Papacy as an institution — not a single pope, not Pope Leo X, whom Luther misjudged
and regarded as the innocent victim of a wicked system — was the
Antichrist because it claimed for the Pope an infallibility that placed
him above even the Word of God, yes, even God Himself.[132] This
was the cardinal sin which caused all the perversions in doctrine
and practice.

Melanchthon, who probably knew Luther more intimately than
any of his contemporaries, spoke of his use of violent language at
the Reformer's grave.[133] Melanchthon pointed out how zealous
Luther had been in the defense of the Gospel, asserting that Luther
had never been violent for personal reasons. Only when someone
exalted the Papacy above God or made light of the precious Gospel,
had he raised his voice in righteous indignation. The tract by
Prierias in Luther's estimation did this very thing. By misrepresenting God's Word and enslaving unlettered consciences, whole nations were being led to the devil. Feeling that the final judgment
was perhaps near and that the Antichrist was sitting on the throne
in the very temple of God, Luther replied to Prierias in the following, often quoted, strange language:

> If the Romanists continue in their madness, nothing else remains
> but that the Emperor, kings, and princes proceed with arms against

this pest of the land and no longer try to settle the matter with words, but actually use the sword. Since we punish thieves with the gallows, robbers with the sword, heretics with fire, why should we hesitate to use arms against these teachers of perdition, the cardinals, popes, and the whole Roman Sodom, which corrupts the Church of God without end, and wash our hands in their blood? [134]

It was to be expected that both Luther's contemporary opponents and modern critics would emphasize this passage. There is no doubt that here Luther used language which was far from becoming to a theologian.[135] But to argue on the basis of this one passage that Luther actually favored an attack by armies on Rome is hardly in keeping with good historical criticism. Considering the total of Luther's references to the use of arms in the interest of reform, this outburst cannot be upheld as typical. When Hutten eagerly offered the services of the knights in western Germany, Luther definitely declined the use of force.[136] Proof positive was the refusal of the Protestant princes even to prepare for a war with the Emperor in 1529.[137] Luther always denied that the cause of the Gospel could be furthered by force even in the case of persecution. Over and over again he emphasized that the Gospel, and it alone, would have to change human hearts. Like the early Christians, Christ's own would have to suffer in silence. Koehler and Boehmer seem justified, therefore, in their interpretation that Luther was merely elaborating upon the language of the Latin Vulgate on Psalm 58:10-11, when he used the phrase "wash our hands in their blood." [138] Luther felt sure the final judgment was near and that this would be the fate of the blasphemous city of Rome. Thus, Luther merely applied the language of the Psalm to the condition of his time.

There is one note in the reply to Prierias that had been growing as a slow conviction in Luther. It already appeared in the *Commentary on Galatians,* delivered during the year 1516 to 1517 and appearing in revised form in September, 1519. This new conviction was that, since Rome had become so corrupt, the only hope for a Reformation lay with the German princes.[139] In the *Sermon on Good Works* in the spring of 1520 the thought appeared once more.[140] In the face of further developments it is not strange that

Luther should have resolved to face this problem squarely in the summer of 1520. Thus, the tract of Prierias formed part of the psychological background of the famous *Address to the German Nobility*, which immediately followed.[141]

THE ADDRESS TO THE GERMAN NOBILITY

The exact circumstances which induced Martin Luther to write his famous tract *An Address to the German Nobility*, etc., in the summer of 1520 are still as obscure today as when Eduard Schneider deplored their lack a half centurgy ago.[142] Otto Clemen first pointed out that he doubted that the famous tract was a unit.[143] Since then the researches of Koehler, Kohlmeyer, and especially Karl Bauer have thrown much additional light on the subject of the origin of this powerful tract, which so well expressed the feeling of the German princes and nobility.[144] Recent research also reveals that the tract was originally meant to be but a brief pamphlet, but grew into a veritable book. Luther's remark that he owed it to God to play "the court fool" is likewise revealing. Historians now believe that this tract was the product of a joint undertaking of the Saxon court, Reuchlin's lawyer, Johann von der Wieck, and some of Luther's fellow Wittenberg professors, especially Melanchthon.[145] The story, so far as it is known, is most interesting.

Luther had decided, perhaps as a result of a request from the Elector of Saxony, to appeal to the newly elected Charles V and the German Nobility to call a general council which was to effect the necessary reforms in the Roman Church which its clergy had failed to initiate.[146] During the preparation of the document, some of the lawyers from the Saxon court discussed certain aspects of the problems involved with the professors of the Wittenberg faculty. Melanchthon spoke of "distinguished friends" having influenced Luther. It is doubtful whether either Hutten or Sickingen exercised much influence.[147]

At one time scholars believed that Luther's very specific refernces to conditions in Rome in the tract were made from his own ,bservations when he visited there in 1510 and 1511. But Karl ,auer has pointed out that Wieck, who had gathered a whole brief ·ase full of information about the exact conditions in the Roman

capital, served as Luther's informant on that point.[148] He visited
Luther in person and made his materials available. Hans von
Taubenheim from the Saxon court, with whom Luther corresponded
during this period, also supplied information.[149] Lauterbach in his
Diary speaks of Luther discussing technical points with respect to
Canon Law with Jerome Schurff of the Wittenberg law faculty.[150]
All of this would also explain why Luther referred to the tract as
"our treatise." [151] Yet, in all fairness it must be said that, even
though others contributed valuable information, the tract had
passed through Luther's being and become a vital part of his own
convictions.[152] Theodore Kolde also came to this conclusion when
he wrote: "It had become his own, flowing anew from the depths
of his own thinking and convictions." [153]

Obviously, the *Address to the German Nobility* was far more
than just another tract from the pen of Luther. Much research
and thought had gone into this brochure, in which were expressed
the thoughts of distinguished members of the Christian nobility
of Germany. Frederick the Wise was much pleased and wrote his
brother John, August 25, 1520: "In it you will find many unusual
things." [154] William of Bavaria reported that the Roman nuncio
Contarini had expressed the conviction that, had Luther not attacked the doctrines of the Church, he would have had all Germany at his feet.[155] Hutten and Schaumburg were in wholehearted
agreement and offered Luther a refuge should he be forced to flee
from Saxony.[156] At Worms the German princes studied the document for guidance in that hour of national crisis, and it deeply
influenced the new *Gravamina* [157] which were presented to the
young Kaiser, grievances which had been often presented but never
corrected.

The address swept like a hurricane over a corrupt and de-
caying system. In the powerful style of which he was a master,
Luther unloosed the torrents which were to lash further at the
foundations of the Roman hierarchy. All the knowledge gathered
from ancient or contemporary writers which he had used at the
Leipzig Debate was focused upon the corruption of the Roman
Curia. Erasmus' *Julius Exclusus* and *The Praise of Folly*, Valla's
exposal of *The Donation of Constantine*, the writings of D'Ailly,

Gerson, Nicolas de Tudesco, all these materials lay in the background and furthered Luther's convictions for the need of reforms.[158] But these are not the vital and new features of the *Address to the German Nobility.* The new and life-giving aspect of this tract lies in its basic principle of an escape from the "tyranny and wickedness of Rome." It is the previously announced belief in the New Testament teaching that there is a priesthood of all believers.

Karl Bauer says that in this tract Luther enunciated for the first time the principle of *ius reformandi,*[159] which later gave the territorial princes the right to effect religious reform in their respective regions. On this principle were based the church visitations of 1524 to 1545 and the reorganization of whole regions of Germany into the Lutheran *Landeskirche.* At the Peace of Augsburg in 1555 this principle became part of the law of the land.

The monograph is divided into three parts.[160] (1) An exposal and refutation of the foundations for the three walls behind which the Papacy was entrenched. (2) An exposal of the wickedness and corruption in the Roman system. (3) The presentation of a series of reforms for the abuses in the Church and in the nation. The first two parts seem to have been conceived as a unit, while the third part appears as an afterthought, and there is, therefore, a certain amount of overlapping of Parts Two and Three.

In Part One, Luther began by a refutation of the theological grounds for the claim that the Papacy was above any temporal power and that the latter had no jurisdiction in matters of reform. Immediately recognizable in this tract was the fact that Luther still accepted the idea that all western Europe was a Christian commonwealth.[161] In this commonwealth were two divinely appointed agencies: (1) the Church, which was Christ's divine institution consisting of the souls which He had gathered unto Himself from the world, and (2) the State, the divinely appointed power within the commonwealth to curb evil so that God's elect might not be hindered in their work to further Christ's kingdom nor in their journey to the yonder world. On the basis of Romans 13, 1 Corinthians 12, and 1 Peter 2 Luther accepted the idea of the Christian commonwealth, which was the body of Christ.[162] He had no conception of the later eighteenth-century idea of the

State. His contributions to the accepted pattern were his new definitions of the functions of the two institutions.

Another new idea is expressed in Luther's statement of the "priesthood of believers." [163] In the Middle Ages the Roman Church claimed that the clergy belonged to the "spiritual estate," while the State belonged to the "secular estate." Luther in this tract for the first time developed the idea that the medieval distinction was basically unscriptural. All baptized Christians were by virtue of their Baptism members of the "priesthood of believers." Through this sacrament they all became a "spiritual and Christian people." The elaborate dress, complicated rituals, spiritual offices, and other outward displays did not make the clergy a class unto themselves. It was, therefore, not the *Stand*, or class, but the *Amt*, or office, which distinguished a clergyman from a layman.[164] This office was conferred upon him by the rest of the priests, and he remained a clergyman only as long as he held that office. Should he be removed by the "Christian people" who put him into that office, he automatically again became a layman. Potentially, then, all baptized Christians were priests, even though not all might be qualified by fitness and training to serve. Nor did the power to preach and to administer the sacraments rest upon an episcopal succession and the sacrament of ordination. The right belonged essentially to every baptized Christian by virtue of his Baptism. It was only to obtain competent and orderly procedure that the body of the "royal priesthood" assigned the office of the ministry to certain of their number. As observed before, this new conception of the Christian Church was entirely spiritual, and only God knew the true members of the "priesthood of believers."

With this interpretation, the whole medieval distinction between the clergy and the laity had been removed. The Emperor and the German nobility might have limited power in the realm of government, but as baptized Christians they had each equal responsibility in the Christian commonwealth. The rulers and the German Diet, therefore, were responsible for the moral conditions within their respective realms. Furthermore, laymen had a duty and the power to call a general council which would correct the *Gravamina* of such long standing.[165] Likewise, it was the duty of

young Charles V and the German princes to curb evil no matter
where it appeared. Whether the offenders be the Pope, cardinals,
bishops, abbots, or lower churchmen, it was the duty of the State
to act regardless of who the culprit might be. This new understanding, by wiping out the distinction between the clergy and the
laity, automatically widened the function of the State, since its
heads were also Christian princes and, hence, priests before God.

It is, however, entirely wrong to reason that through this
interpretation the German State Church was created by Luther.
Ever since the days of Charlemagne there had existed in German
lands an institution known as the *Eigenkirche*,[166] or prince's church.
It dated back to early Germanic law when the princes had insisted
on owning the land on which the altar stood. Through this means
they had always controlled the officiating clergyman and, in time,
had effectively converted the churches into territorial institutions.
The adoption by the First Diet of Speyer in 1526 of *cuius regio eius
religio*, that the prince should determine the religion of his region,
was essentially nothing new in German lands.[167] It merely confirmed a principle which had been practiced by the German princes
for centuries. In setting forth the doctrine of the "priesthood of
believers," Luther merely applied the New Testament teaching to
sixteenth-century conditions and pointed out the duty of a prince
to supervise the religious conditions in his lands.

The second wall behind which the Papacy was firmly entrenched, according to the tract, was the claim that the Pope was
the final and infallible interpreter of Holy Scriptures.[168] The recent
tracts of Alveld and Prierias had made much of this doctrine. How
could an ungodly pope, asks Luther, motivated by the basest of
personal interests, be the instrument of the Holy Ghost? How
could a pope, a human being, speaking *ex cathedra,* or from his
official chair, be immune to error? By what teaching in the Scriptures could he be made the equal or even the superior of God,
as his fanatical champions had recently claimed? Luther called
upon every Christian to be a judge. All Christians, who permitted
the Holy Spirit to work in their hearts, could discern whether or
not the immoral conditions in the Roman "Sodom" were of God.
Through this, Luther re-established the basic principle of Protestantism that each Christian, be he a layman or a clergyman, is

potentially able to determine what God wishes to say to him in His Word. This does not mean that Luther considered all human beings equally competent to interpret the Bible.[169] He later insisted that ministerial students learn Greek and Hebrew in the new Lutheran schools so that, when entering the theological seminary, they would have the necessary tools to become able, scholarly interpreters of the Word. To these tools he advocated the addition of a knowledge of history and archaeology as essential to Biblical interpretation. When the Anabaptists and the Carlstadt group went to the other extreme and advocated that simple laymen were as capable of interpreting the Word as the most educated theologians, Luther rightly protested.

The third and final wall behind which the Papacy was entrenched was the assertion that no one could call a general council except a pope.[170] Pope Gregory VII in his *Dictatus* had asserted that no council was authoritative unless it had the official sanction of the Pope.[171] In this field Luther could draw upon ample historical tradition for guidance. The University of Paris during the time of the Reform Councils (1409—1450) had constantly championed the view that the papal claims were not in keeping with the practices of the Early Church.[172] Luther also pointed out that the first universal council was summoned by the Apostles and that the Council of Nicea, the most distinguished of them all, was summoned by Emperor Constantine. Why, then, should the Papacy in recent centuries set forth the doctrine that no council is authoritative without the approval of Rome? When a pope uses his powers to prevent reform, he becomes an instrument of the devil and the Antichrist.[173]

The second part of the *Address* contained a vehement denunciation of the official and moral corruption in the Roman *Curia*.[174] Luther, the prophet, invoked God's wrath upon the modern Sodom and Gomorrah, Rome, the Babylon of the New Testament. Imagine contemporary Germany reading the following scorching indictment:

> At Rome there is such a state of things that baffles description. There is a buying, selling, exchanging, cheating, roaring, lying, deceiving, robbing, stealing, luxury, debauchery, villainy, and every sort of contempt of God that Antichrist himself could not possibly rule more abominably. Venice, Antwerp, Cairo are nothing com-

pared to this fair and market at Rome, except that things are done there with some reason and justice, whilst here they are done as the devil himself wills. And out of this ocean flows a like virtue into the whole world. Is it not natural that such people should dread a reformation and a free Council and rather set all kings and princes by the ears than that, by their unity, they should bring about a Council? Which of them would like to have such villainy exposed? Finally, the Pope has constructed a special shop for this fine traffic, that is, the house of the *Datarius* at Rome. Hither all must come who bargain in this way for prebends and benefices, etc. . . . If you bring money to this house, you can get all the things that I have mentioned, and not only these, but any sort of usury is here made legitimate for money. What has been stolen, robbed, is here legalized. Here vows are annulled. Here the monk may buy freedom to quit his order. Here the clergy can purchase the marriage state, the children of harlots obtain legitimacy, dishonor and shame be made respectable, evil repute and crime be knighted and ennobled. Here marriage is allowed that is within the forbidden degree, or is otherwise defective. Oh what oppressing and plunder rule here! So that it seems as if the whole canon law were only established in order to snare as much money as possible, from which everyone who would be a Christian must deliver himself. Here the devil becomes a saint and a god to boot. What heaven and earth may not do, this house can do.[175]

These are strong words, but well deserved by the Rome of the Borgias, della Rovias, and Medicis. Gregorovius and Pastor, eminent Catholic historians, amply support these indictments which may seem exaggerated to the modern reader. Even Duke George reluctantly admitted that the need for reform was great. The indictment of Pope Hadrian VI and the findings of the Contarini Commission under Pope Paul III fully confirmed Luther's charges.[176]

In the third part, Luther further elaborated the charges made in Part Two and frequently recommended some definite reforms, such as: the Pope's triple crown must be taken from him; all the pomp and luxury of the Roman court must go; the Pope must once more become the simple servant of Christ; there must also be a drastic reduction of the College of Cardinals and in the swarm of officialdom in the Roman *Curia*.[177] As for the papal chair, from which the pope uttered his pronouncements *ex cathedra*, Luther wished that God would hurl it into the lowest "abyss of hell." [178] The episcopal system in existence in the days of the Council of

Nicaea should be restored and papal power limited to mere spiritual oversight.[179] Nor should the Pope be longer regarded as above the Emperor in political matters. Luther even questioned the medieval teaching of the *translatio imperii*,[180] the theory that the Roman Empire had never passed away; that during the Middle Ages the imperial power had merely passed to the Carolingians and the Saxon Emperors and, because they were blessed by the Pope from Charlemagne's time on, it had become the Holy Roman Empire. No doubt in this part of the tract Luther was influenced by Philip Melanchthon. Other abuses, such as pilgrimages, monasticism, celibacy, etc., were also censured heavily and pictured as badly needing reform.

One other new thought was advocated in the tract. As early as 1302 the Occamists had proposed that in case of an emergency the problems facing the Christian world could be solved by a congress of princes who, as baptized Christians, were to exercise this act of love. In this tract religion was once more assigned its rightful role in the Christian commonwealth. Here were also the beginnings of Luther's tract of 1523, *Concerning Government, to What Extent One is Obligated to Obey It,* in which Luther assigned government control over man's body, his outward possessions, and human life in general; but his soul, spirit, and inner spiritual freedom belonged only to God.[181] In it may be noted also in embryonic form the later conception of the separation of Church and State. By dignifying man's calling in life as being of God, secular life was once more placed on an equal plane with the Christian ministry.[182] The influence of this tract on the German nobility is difficult to overemphasize, for in its "priesthood of believers" it offered a solution for the *Gravamina* which had been so far disregarded.

THE BABYLONIAN CAPTIVITY OF THE CHURCH

In the previous tract Luther had destroyed the three walls that formed the bulwark behind which Rome was entrenched. Now, after reading Prierias' and Alveld's tracts, Luther was ready to attack the citadel of the Antichrist himself to expose the yoke of bondage which had been placed upon poor Christian souls.[183] As noted in the previous development of Luther in his sermons on

Penance, Baptism, the Lord's Supper, Good Works, and the Mass, the ideas expressed in this tract had been forming in Luther's mind for the last year.[184] As early as December, 1519, Luther had questioned the whole sacramental system of Rome.[185] In his letter to Spalatin he had also promised to write on this subject. Luther informed Spalatin that Alveld's boastful claims with reference to papal power were the immediate cause of his writing the tract.[186] He discussed the subject with Melanchthon at great length and was finally ready to give substance to his thoughts, especially with reference to the clergy and its relationship to the "priesthood of believers."

The *Babylonian Captivity* was fundamentally very different from the first of the famous tracts written during the summer of 1520.[187] The *Address* had been written for the laity and was in German, but the new tract was definitely addressed to the clergy alone and was written in a heavy Latin style. It was aimed at the very heart of the Roman sacerdotal system which had been built around the seven sacraments.

Although Luther jested that Prierias, Eck, Emser, and Alveld had been his theological professors ever since he had nailed his theses on the door of the Wittenberg Castle Church, there is more truth in the statement than is generally realized. These men had forced him to search the Scriptures, and the effort had born abundant fruit. Now he wrote that he wished all that he had written on indulgences in the past two years might be burned. At that time he was too much steeped in the superstitions surrounding the Pope to realize what was behind the movement. Now he recognized the papal institution as being the "wicked deceivers" and at the bottom of the whole graft.[188] What Prierias taught Luther on indulgences, Emser and Eck taught him with reference to the Papacy. He now believed "the Papacy is the mighty hunting ground of the bishop of Rome." [189] After this brief introduction as to how his eyes had been opened, Luther turned to the main theme of his tract, the attack on the whole sacramental system through which Rome had enslaved the souls of Christendom.[190] The tract took its title from the fact that the souls of the German people were in bondage in a foreign land, in spiritual slavery in a modern Babylon.

Considering the length and content of these two tracts, the speed with which Luther worked is amazing. The *Address* was begun June 8 and had been published, enlarged, and reprinted by August 18.[191] The *Babylonian Captivity* was begun by August 5 and was completed and published by October 6.[192]

In the main body of the latter tract Luther immediately raised the question of the distribution of both the bread and the wine. The sixth chapter of John, he felt, had been misinterpreted on this point. He asserted that it was really impious to withhold the cup, for in 1 Corinthians 11 and in the Gospels the Scripture reads: "Drink ye all of it." [193] Luther questioned by what authority the Church could withhold part of a sacrament. He then defined three errors in the teachings of the Church relative to this sacrament: (1) the denial of half of the Lord's Supper to the believer, (2) the teaching of Transubstantiation, and (3) the metamorphosis of the Mass into a sacrifice.[194] Luther pointed out that he followed the Bishop of Cambrai in the belief that there was no change in the substance, that real bread and wine remained on the altar, while Christ appeared truly in Communion.[195] Certainly the glorified Christ could appear in the Lord's Supper without the necessity of a change in the substance in the Holy Eucharist. He cited the fact that Christ used the pronoun *hoc* rather than *hic,* indicating reference to the bread and wine.[196] With reference to the actual administering of the sacrament, so much had the original Holy Eucharist changed that it had been converted into a huckstering, money-making proposition. As a solution, he proposed changes in the liturgical forms associated with the Holy Eucharist which were not instituted in some Lutheran communities until two decades later.

> . . . We must take the utmost care to put aside all that has been added by the zeal or the notions of men to the primitive and simple institution such as vestments, ornaments, hymns, prayers, musical instruments, lamps, and all the pomp of visible things; and must turn our eyes and our attention only to the pure institution of Christ.[197]

Luther re-emphasizes what he had pointed out in previous sermons, that the Lord had granted us the merits of Christ's suffering and death, the promise of the forgiveness of all our sins,

sealed in His own blood. All that was required of us was faith in
this promise and love in return. There was no place in this divine
gift for the sacrament of the Mass, an *opus operatum*,[198] where,
through the efforts of a priest, man tried to earn grace before God.
Luther thought that Infant Baptism best expressed the true relationship of the sinner to God in the matter of salvation. The helpless
child symbolized how the grace of God alone saves man; and once
saved through this washing, the effect was permanent unless man
interrupted the blessed relationship. Scholastic theology had also
perverted this sacrament by requiring human effort to secure man's
salvation after Baptism. Since Luther believed that man, in matters of faith, was absolutely helpless even as an adult, that it was
a divine miracle which God worked in him through His grace, it
was not difficult for him to accept Infant Baptism. But Luther
never held that the efficacy of the sacrament depended upon its
intrinsic power, but rather upon the faith wrought in the human
heart. Luther never tried to fathom the mystery of how a child
could have this faith, but he firmly believed that faith was essential.

Luther pointed out that the sacrament of Holy Eucharist had
been obscured by added laws and regulations which nullified the
rights of Christian liberty. He defined the attributes of which
Christian liberty should be composed:

> I say, then, that neither Pope, nor bishop, nor any man has the
> right of constituting a single regulation over the Christian man un-
> less it is done by his own consent. Whatever is done otherwise is
> done in a tyrannical spirit. Therefore prayers, fasts, contributions,
> and whatever of this kind the Pope statutes and exacts in his
> decrees — as numerous as they are iniquitous — he statutes and
> exacts by no right, and he sins against the liberty of the Church
> as often as he has attempted anything of this kind.[199]

In the section following, Luther elaborated his point further,
namely, that the Papacy and the Roman hierarchy had prescribed
all kinds of human regulations which had no Scriptural foundation,
yet were made obligatory because the Pope demanded that they
be observed. In this confusion of human regulations many souls
were led astray for which the kingdom of Babylon was responsible.

The sacrament of Penance, which Luther no longer regarded
as a real sacrament, had been even more perverted. The Pope had

abused the power of loosing and binding of Matthew 16:19 and John 20:23, until a complete tyranny had resulted. Instead of stressing true contrition and a desire for absolution, the sacrament had degenerated into mere outward formalities.[200]

As for the rest of the Roman sacramental system, Luther pointed out that it had no Scriptural foundation.[201] The Word of God, not the servant of the Church, but rather its Creator, must always be regarded as the guide in such matters. Once more he reminded the priesthood of believers of their responsibility for the preaching of the Word and the administering of the sacraments of Baptism and the Lord's Supper.

An evaluation of this bold, yet, judged by later developments, conservative, tract is very difficult. Luther himself later in life regarded his views of this period as very immature. Yet, recalling his strict Catholic background and his thorough saturation with the whole tradition of Scholasticism, the originality of his thinking is most remarkable. For him religion had become a matter of the spirit, but he was not yet ready to translate all of his convictions into action. It was not until all hope of a restoration of the pure Christianity of the Acts had to be abandoned that Luther relinquished his plan for reforming the Roman Church. When he finally realized that vested interests and personal advantages rendered impotent all hope of reform from within the Roman hierarchy, granted even the most willing leadership in both Church and State, Luther finally accepted the challenge of a clean break with tradition and a new beginning. Only then did he give active motivation to the convictions which had slowly developed.

THE FREEDOM OF THE CHRISTIAN

When Charles von Miltitz learned that John Eck was on his way to Germany carrying the papal bull threatening to excommunicate Luther, he realized that all of his efforts to effect a reconciliation between Luther and the Pope would be in vain unless something could be salvaged at the last moment. It happened that John Staupitz had summoned a Chapter of the Augustinians at Eisleben for August 28, 1520.[202] Miltitz resolved to attend. At this official meeting, Staupitz retired from his office as the General Vicar of the German Congregation of Augustinians, and Wenceslaus Link was chosen for the position. Miltitz persuaded these two men to visit Luther at Wittenberg in an attempt to induce him to write a conciliatory letter assuring Leo X that there was nothing personal in his attacks on the Papacy.[203] Accompanied by several fellow monks, Staupitz and Link conferred with Luther on September 6. Luther agreed to their request, but he was very dubious as to its advisability or its probable result, since Eck was already on his way with the bull *Exsurge, Domine*.[204]

Miltitz, however, wanted personal information as to the content of this communication. Accordingly, through the Electoral official, Fabian von Feilitzsch, a meeting was arranged between Luther and Miltitz at Lichtenberg, October 12, 1520.[205] After discussing the problem, Luther agreed to write the letter to Pope Leo X, to be accompanied by a booklet written in Latin. The result was Luther's tract *The Freedom of the Christian*. Toward the end of the month Luther had completed the letter to Leo under the title *A Letter to Pope Leo X*.[206] Just when the accompanying tract came from the Gruenenberg press at Wittenberg cannot be established. An original copy, perhaps the very copy which Luther sent to Hermann Muelpfort in Zwickau, containing his own dedicatory note, has been rediscovered in Budapest. Miltitz had sent a copy to his friend Willibald Pirckheimer in Nuernberg, by November 16.[207] This was the third of the Wittenberg tracts of 1520, all completed in a period of six months, which were to make Luther famous in German history and literature.

Where the first two tracts had been of a revolutionary nature, the third was calm and conciliatory.[208] As the title indicated, Luther discussed that freedom which comes to the Christian who has been truly justified by faith. Luther had by now fully grasped the inner implications of his earlier teaching in Psalms and Romans. In the tract Luther developed two thoughts: (1) A Christian through faith is a free lord and subject to no one. (2) A Christian is the most dutiful servant of all and subject to everyone. In simple language Luther explained the first theme, showing how God's justifying grace liberates the sinner who has been a slave. God, in justification, not only has declared man free from all sin and

Von der Freyhayt
Aines Christen
menschen.

Martinus Luther

Vuittenbergae

Anno domini.

1520

Title page of Luther's famous tract of 1520, "Freedom of the Christian"

guilt for Christ's sake through faith; He has also effected an inward
regeneration of man's soul which in turn affects his whole inner
life. No longer is he a slave to his own passions and desires, for
Christ now reigns in his new life of grace. He no longer lives under
the Law, but by the Gospel. This inward liberation means freedom from those outward regulations with which Rome sought to
strangle Christendom.

This is but one aspect of the doctrine of justification, the establishment of the right relationship to God and the liberation from
sin. The reborn sinner looks at the world through the eyes of love.
His actions are motivated, not by what someone tells him he *ought*
to do, but by what he *wants* to do as a result of his regeneration.[209]
A Christian cannot help but have compassion for his fellow man;
but his motive is not a veneer of humanitarianism, but a deeper love
that sees in lost mankind potential sons of God. Out of this love
he will seek to improve the lot of his fellow man.

The German mysticism to which Luther had been exposed in
his study of Tauler is evident in the tract. The Christian is mys-
tically united with Christ through faith. Sin, death, and condemnation are no longer imputed to him; instead, he enjoys God's grace,
life, and salvation. While the Christian is in the world, he strives
to serve his fellow men to the honor and glory of God. Sixteenth-
century Lutheranism, therefore, actively participated in business,
trade, and the professions.[210] Yet, although in the world, it was
not a part of this world, but held itself above the accepted practices
and standards of the times.

This treatise of Luther's clearly stated his position with reference to the Christian's participation in the community life in which
he found himself, and as clearly refuted the claims of those who
sought to connect Luther with the indifferentism of modern German
Lutheranism.[211] All through the tract, faith is pictured as something
vital, alive, dynamic, expressing itself in a social consciousness and
a striving toward its improvement. Typical of Luther's thoughts on
Christian social responsibility is the following passage:

> Lastly we shall speak of those works which we are to exercise to-
> ward our neighbor. For man lives not for himself alone in the
> works which he does in this mortal life, but for all men on earth,
> yea he lives only for others and not for himself. For to this end he

subjects his body in order that he may be able the more freely and wholeheartedly to serve others, as Paul says in Romans 14: "For none of us liveth to himself, and none [sic] dieth to himself. For whether we live, we live unto the Lord, or [sic] whether we die, we die unto the Lord." It is not possible, therefore, to take his ease in this life and abstain from works toward his neighbor. For, as has been said, he must perforce live and have converse with men, as Christ, made in the likeness of men and found in fashion as a man, lived among and had intercourse with men.[212]

The Drafting of the Papal Bull

The death of Emperor Maximilian and the ensuing political maneuvering afforded Luther a respite from the *Processus Inhibitorius* which had been gathering momentum ever since he first nailed the *Ninety-Five Theses* on the door of the Castle Church. It has been noted how, during the election, both Frederick the Wise and Luther were important pieces on the chessboard of imperial and papal diplomacy, the highlights of which were the near election of Frederick himself as emperor, the tentative offer of a cardinal's hat as a bribe to silence Luther, the promise to Frederick of an ecclesiastical estate, and even the tempting Golden Rose to bribe the evasive prince.[213] But with the election decided, the Luther question assumed greater importance than before. Something had to be done. Knowledge of the situation was too widespread to permit further delay. Reports of the Leipzig Debate, the condemnation of many fundamental doctrines in Luther's works by the important theological faculties of Cologne and Louvain, all pointed toward the gravity with which the situation was viewed.

Rome may have become dubious by now of the reliability of the reports of Miltitz's activities in Germany. Miltitz, however, still insisted that he could bring Luther around, and since Cajetan's mission had failed, there was no other resource but to give Miltitz one last chance. He it was who was now empowered to offer again the Golden Rose on September 25, 1519.[214] So certain was he that this would win the Elector's alliance that he wrote "Doctor Martin is in my hands." But the meeting between Luther and Miltitz on October 9 accomplished nothing. Frederick heard the report from both sides and then quietly informed Miltitz that he had already made arrangements at Frankfurt am Main to take Luther to the

next German diet, where his problem could be discussed with the
Archbishop of Trier in person.[215]

Pope Leo X seems to have been at last impressed with the importance of Luther's case, for in November, 1519, he asked Eck to
come to Rome.[216] No doubt he felt that Eck's personal knowledge
of Luther might prove useful. Paul Kalkoff, who has perhaps made
the most thorough study of the origin of the papal bull *Exsurge*,
Domine, asserted that Eck's report aroused Leo to the gravity of
the situation in Germany. Miltitz was again commissioned to contact Frederick the Wise, informing him that unless he co-operated,
his lands would be put under the interdict and Martin Luther
would be placed under the ban.[217] Walch reports that Spalatin
served as the intermediary in Torgau, but the Elector feigned innocence in the whole matter. He pretended to have misunderstood
Miltitz and inferred that Miltitz had bungled the papal mission
which had been entrusted to him. Furthermore, the case was now
under advisement pending an interview with the Archbishop of
Trier at the forthcoming German Diet at Worms.

On January 9, 1520, the Roman consistory officially reopened
the former case against Luther under the customary legal title,
"suspicion of heresy." Two days later, at an official reception held
for Cardinal Bibiena, Luther was pictured as the German "hydra,"
the instigator of revolt in German lands, while Frederick the Wise
was regarded as the enemy of the true faith.[218] Perhaps it was this
pointed reminder which caused Leo X to appoint a commission to
examine the problem. The two leaders were Cajetan and Accolti.
The former, it will be remembered, was the official expert in
Thomist theology, while the latter was a distinguished jurist in
Canon Law. Cajetan had learned much in Germany; he had actually told the members of his order that caution should be used
in the Luther case, for he might be guilty of error but hardly of
heresy. He even told his fellow Dominicans that Luther had attacked none of the fundamental doctrines of salvation.[219] May it
have been that he, also, realized that Luther had revived the original teachings of the Roman Church and was more in harmony with
the spirit of the true Church which Jesus had founded? But as
a high church official, he lacked the courage to choose any other
course.

Kalkoff's research as to the composition of Pope Leo X's Sacred College is rather revealing.[220] Only seven members remained of the original group prior to Leo's pontificate. He had created twenty-seven new cardinals, twenty-four of them since 1517. It was no secret that the Sacred College was the political football of prominent Roman families. The Orsini and Colonna families as leaders of *condottieri* armies played the dominant roles. How much these new members were under Leo's control is not difficult to gauge. These men discussed Luther's fate and in the end were successful in tempering the papal bull. But after a preliminary discussion it seemed expedient to appoint a commission to do the actual drafting of the document. The work began on February 1, 1520. Much discussion revolved about the questions: Should Luther's writings be re-examined and the errors actually pointed out to him? Would it perhaps be sufficient to take the Louvain list? Should the errors be condemned separately or en masse? The papal Vice-Chancellor, Giulio de Medici, realized that the commission was too unwieldy for efficient operation and needed to be revamped.[221] Under Cajetan's leadership a smaller, abler, second commission was organized which favored giving Luther another chance. Still later a third commission of four was created composed of two cardinals, Eck, and a Spanish doctor.[222]

According to Kalkoff, who has traced the origin of each article in the bull, the small commission drew heavily on the Cologne and Louvain articles of condemnation, but it was also influenced by Eck's report.[223] Had he not been one of the group which drafted the 41 articles of condemnation in the bull, their tone might have been much milder. Before the finished draft of the document was presented to the papal consistory, Leo also met with the group.

Between May 21 and June 1, 1520, the consistory met four times to consider and to polish the final draft which was to become the famous bull *Exsurge, Domine*.[224] The politicians now had their hearing. They naturally considered the expediency of the bull from the perspective of the total picture. They insisted that Luther's writings alone were not sufficient bases for such drastic action. They urged the Papacy to consider the effect of the bull upon Luther's entire homeland.[225] Other questions arose. Should he be condemned forthwith, or should he be given a period of

grace in which to recant? It was finally agreed that Luther should
be given sixty days from the date of the bull's official proclamation
as a period of grace. Furthermore, it was decided not to cite specific heretical teachings but merely to follow the precedent set by
the Louvain and Cologne faculties. A pope, so they said, should
not lower himself to a discussion of the details in the false doctrines of a heretic. After all the preceding events and developments,
Rome was still too blind to see or too obstinate to admit that this
course was the only solution to the Luther problem.

EXSURGE, DOMINE

On June 15, 1520, the papal chancery signed the papal bull
Exsurge, Domine, and it was publicly proclaimed together with the
burning of Luther's books in *Piazza Navona*.[226] On July 18, 1520,
John Eck, who had now realized his reward for the Leipzig Debate,
started north with the papal document, accompanied by the former
Paris professor Aleander, now secretary to the Pope's brother,
Giulio de Medici, Vice-Chancellor of the Roman *Curia*.[227] As
Aleander's later dispatches from Worms indicated, the choice of
messengers was not a happy one. The German people at Worms
eyed him with suspicion and distrust, while regarding Luther as
a national hero. As for Eck, his connection with the Leipzig Debate
had made him thoroughly disliked by many Germans; nor had the
subsequent pamphlet warfare improved his reputation. In Rome,
however, his stock had risen considerably, and in grateful appreciation for his services the Roman *Curia* had granted him the distinction of carrying to Germany the document which was finally to
convince Luther of the enormity of his error.[228] Many Germans of
influence, especially among the nobility, the knights, and the
burghers of the larger cities, were definitely antagonistic to the
strutting, ambitious Ingolstadt professor, who was ready to sell
out his fellow Germans for his own advancement and glory. Such
German princes as Frederick the Wise, who had seen in connection
with the recent imperial election just how far Rome was willing to
stoop, must have smiled as they read the pious, lofty phrases of
the papal bull as it sought to protect the faith from the gross errors
of a poor monk of the Augustinian Hermits, Martin Luther, who

in all charity was to be granted sixty days to recant the errors cited in the document.[229]

All papal bulls take their title from their initial words. The bull which Eck brought to Germany was named *Exsurge, Domine* from the Psalmist's words "Arise, O God, judge Thine own cause."[230] Then followed a most solemn introduction with the customary use of the phrase "Bishop Leo, servant of servants of God, to the perpetual memory of the occasion." The document called upon the Lord to consider the foolish insults which men have heaped upon Him; upon Peter to be mindful of the pastoral office which God has entrusted to him and to be "solicitous of the Holy Roman Church"; upon Paul, the great light of the Church, to arise; let all the saints arise, all the members of the Universal Church, lest their true interpretation of the Holy Scriptures be trampled under foot.

This introduction was followed by forty-one articles that had been condemned from Luther's writings.[231] Luther was in error on original sin, concupiscence, penance, justification by faith, the Lord's Supper, the true treasures of the Church, indulgences, excommunication, the power of the Pope, general councils, good works, free will, purgatory, etc., which if not recanted, exposed both him and his protectors to the dangers of excommunication and the interdict.[232]

The fear of the Roman officials of adverse reactions to the bull in German lands, where Luther was fast becoming a national hero, was reflected in the next section. With much psychological adroitness, the Pope was pictured as the essence of clemency, but all of his gracious offers had been spurned. Worse, Luther had boldly asked for a general council when both Pope Pius II and Julius II had declared such an appeal heretical. Yet, in spite of all that the errant and prodigal son had done, he still was welcome to return to the arms of the Mother Church. Hence, sixty days grace would be extended Luther after the bull was publicly nailed to the doors of the Lateran, the apostolic chancery, and the cathedral churches of Brandenburg, Meissen, and Merseburg. Should Luther fail to recant, then the "withered branches" were to be cut off. That there might be no future memory of this heretic, all his writings from which the 41 heretical articles were drawn were to be burnt everywhere publicly in the presence of the clergy and the people. Those who protected and harbored the heretic were in like condemnation. The German nation was reminded that at one time it had been among the most zealous to defend the faith, extirpating heresy throughout the realm. The penalties of medieval Canon Law were awaiting those who failed to expel Luther from their lands; excommunication and anathema would be theirs regardless of rank or class. The clergy were to be responsible for making the clauses of the bull effective in their lands. At the expiration of the sixty days of grace a proclamation was to be issued declaring Luther a heretic, and all those who abetted his perversion were, likewise, to be avoided as condemned heretics. The bull was to be read and posted everywhere, a decree which was more easily declared than enforced.

BURNING THE CANON LAW

As has been noted in a previous connection, the proclamation of the bull *Exsurge, Domine* was not unexpected in Germany. As early as March, Luther had heard rumors of the drafting of the document.[233] Naturally, much hearsay also spread concerning its content. Hutten prematurely announced in a letter to Luther that he was already excommunicated, while Melanchthon heard that the commission was deadlocked on its draft of the bull.[234] Luther, with his characteristic faith in God, consoled his friends Lang, Spalatin, and Jonas during the spring of 1520 in three successive letters assuring them that God was still running the world and that even Rome was subject to Him.[235] In the letter to Jonas he added that though "the miserable Romanists rage against me and seek my life" he was ready to die for the Gospel if death should be required of him.

Luther would not have been human had he not taken a certain satisfaction in the rallying of the German nation about him in spite of the Louvain and Cologne condemnation of his books and the issuance of the papal bull. Leading Humanists like Erasmus, Hutten, Crotus Rubeanus, Bucer, Capito, Pellican, and others were supporting his cause.[236] Silvester von Schaumburg, a professed follower of Luther, assured him the protection of one hundred Franconian nobles should the Elector of Saxony weaken under the threat of a papal interdict.[237] Franz von Sickingen also offered Luther a haven should he find it necessary to flee Saxony.[238] His was no idle promise, for this knight had wielded more influence on Hochstraten in the Reuchlin trial than had all the decrees of the Emperor and the Pope combined. As Holborn has shown, Hutten was very much impressed with Luther's bold defiance of all Roman threats and hailed him as a potential leader in liberating Germany from the Roman menace.[239] As has been mentioned, he thought chiefly of the political and economic implications of Luther's work and had neither the inclination nor the training to understand the basic theological issues at stake in the struggle with Rome. Luther gently refused Hutten's proposal on the ground that the Gospel must not be furthered by use of force.[240] He preferred to trust wholly in God, realizing that God works out the destiny of mankind through human instruments. His position was stated in a letter to Spalatin, July 17, 1520:

> Remember that it behoves [sic] us to suffer for the Word of God. For now that Silvester von Schaumburg and Franz von Sickingen have made me secure from the fear of man, the fury of the demons must needs break forth. It shall be a struggle to a finish with this diabolic power. Such is the will of God.[241]

Luther was aware of the pressure being placed, meanwhile, on Frederick through Cardinal Riario and Tetleben to withdraw his support.[242] The Elector had forwarded their letters to Luther asking for arguments in reply.[243] Luther's replies indicate that he was somewhat irritated by the evasive tactics being used by Frederick. As far as Luther was concerned, the die was cast; and he chafed under further restraint and uncertainty. He stated his position clearly in the following:

> But for my part the die has now been cast. . . . I hold in contempt alike the fury and favor of Rome. I will not be reconciled to them; I will nevermore hold communion with them. Let them condemn and burn my books. I will return the compliment and wherever I can get fire, I will condemn and burn the whole papal law, that brood of heresies, and will make an end of the humility so long and vainly exhibited by me, and no longer puff up with this profession of obedience to the enemies of the Gospel.[244]

There was no room for doubt as to Luther's future action regardless of what course the Elector followed in further dealings with Rome. Should the Elector choose to abandon Luther, Schaumburg and Sickingen would offer him protection. The letters also carried a warning to Rome. The new Gospel movement had been so warmly embraced in Germany that any application of force would convert Germany into a second Bohemia.[245] On the basis of these communications the Elector once more gave a typical evasive answer, professing innocence, promising obedience, asking that Luther's case be settled by a neutral tribunal, and pointing out that Luther was awaiting an interview with the Archbishop of Trier.[246]

Everywhere the Pope's minions were seeing further evidence of the extent of Luther's support. They had urged the burning of Luther's books in an effort to demonstrate his guilt to the populace. Tempers on both sides were at a high pitch. In Mainz the official hangman refused to burn Luther's books. He turned to the crowd and asked if these books had been properly condemned? The crowd shouted "No!" Then the official replied that he would burn only what had been condemned according to the law of the land. That night he was almost stoned to death, and an insulting poem was put on his door. Albert of Mainz, who bore the initial responsibility for the whole controversy, announced that the books would be condemned with the blast of trumpets the next day. During the night a crowd also gathered outside his quarters, and he barely escaped with his life.[247]

Into this same period falls the frequently quoted story, related in George Spalatin's *Annales Reformationis*, of the meeting between the Elector of Saxony and Erasmus in Cologne while waiting for the young Emperor, Charles V, to arrive from Aachen. Since the Elector could not speak Latin, he asked Spalatin to sit in as the interpreter. Frederick asked Erasmus many questions about Luther's teachings and sermons. Although somewhat evasive at first, when the Elector cornered him for a direct answer, Erasmus gave the following clever reply:

> Luther sinned in two respects; namely, that he knocked off the crown of the Pope and attacked the bellies of the monks.[248]

Spalatin added that Erasmus did not have the courage to uphold his beliefs before Aleander. This lack of stamina was typical of

Erasmus, who had earlier signed some *axiomata,* short statements
in his own hand, which he later retrieved after considerable effort
for fear Aleander might use them as evidence against him.[249]

Eck was soon to experience the same opposition wherever he
went to proclaim the bull. In Leipzig, the very town in which he
claimed to have won the debate the previous year, he was insulted
with satirical verses. St. Paul's Monastery was the only place where
he felt reasonably safe. Finally, after some Wittenberg students
had also threatened him, he fled by night to Freiberg.[250] The
Leipzig faculty would not publish the bull until requested to do so
by Duke George; and when it was posted, it was here, as elsewhere,
smeared with mud and defaced.[251] Many of the bishops of Germany refused to publish it, but perhaps their action was not so
much the result of their convictions as of their fear of violent disturbances among the people. When Caracciolus and Aleander reproved the Elector for his delay in carrying out the provisions of
the bull, he also used for an excuse the threat of a popular uprising.[252] There was also a provision in Eck's instructions authorizing him to name any of Luther's adherents which should be summoned. Now he foolishly named Carlstadt, Pirckheimer, Spengler,
Egranus, Feldkirch, and Adelmann, which action only increased
the fury of men like Hutten and Sickingen.[253]

Luther, on the other hand, treated the whole proceeding with
contempt. He had decided to fight to the finish. Two tracts came
from his pen in October: the one, *Eck's New Bulls and Lies;* the
other, *Against the Execrable Bull of the Antichrist.*[254] The language in these was most violent. He pretended that the document
which Eck was promulgating was not genuine, even though he admitted in a letter to Spalatin that it was authentic. He stated that
his appeal to a general council and his hearing before the Archbishop of Trier were still pending and that under such circumstances the Pope would not send Eck on such a mission. In the
second treatise he censured Leo X if he had permitted this bull to
go out in his name. There followed some rather strong, direct
language with reference to the seat of the Antichrist:

> Unless you do this, know that I, with all who worship Christ, will
> esteem your seat possessed and oppressed by Satan, the damned
> seat of Antichrist, to which we will not render obedience or be

subject, or be united, but will detest and execrate as the chief and
supreme enemy of Christ. We are prepared in behalf of this conviction not only to bear your censures, but even to ask that you
may never absolve us and may fulfill your cruel tyranny. For the
sake of this conviction we offer ourselves to death and by these
writings we proclaim that, if you persist in your fury, we condemn
and deliver you, along with your Bull and all your Satanic decretals,
to the destruction of the flesh in order that your spirit may be delivered with us in the day of the Lord.[255]

Luther apparently was reluctant still to admit that the Pope
had actually taken such a step. He still hoped that the Pope and
the Roman Church might somehow find another solution. On November 17, 1520, he once more appealed to a general council,
calling upon the secular authorities named in his former *Address*
to force the calling of a council.[256]

Early in the morning of December 10, 1520, Philip Melanchthon nailed a significant document on the *Schwarze Brett,* the university bulletin board, announcing the long-awaited reaction on the
part of Luther to the burning of his books all over Germany. The
announcement invited the doctors and masters of the University
and the student body to assemble at Holy Cross Chapel at 9 A. M.
just outside the east gate of the city.[257] A pile of wood had been
gathered at the spot near the Elbe where the town burned the
clothing of those infected with pest and where cattle were butchered.
The occasion was the burning of certain books by means of which
the Papacy and the Roman hierarchy were particularly entrenched.

After the gathering had assembled, one of the masters, probably Agricola, started the fire. From one of Luther's letters, written
around 10 A. M. that morning to Spalatin, it is clear that the
Decretum of Gratian, the papal decretals, *Sextus Clementinae
Extravagantes,* the *Summa Angelica,* and some of Eck's and of
Emser's books were included in the list.[258] But the principal collection of writings which Luther wished to destroy was the *corpus
iuris canonici,* that body of Canon Law which gave the Pope all
the extravagant powers which Eck, Emser, and others tried to defend.[259] One after the other the various tomes were consigned to
the flames. Finally, Luther unexpectedly drew a printed copy of
the bull *Exsurge, Domine* from his gown and threw it into the

flames with the remark: "Because thou hast destroyed the truth of God, may the Lord consume thee in these flames."[260] Since historical research has proved that he did not utter the oft-repeated traditional phrase: "Because thou hast offended the Holy One of God," the criticism directed against him by those critics who claimed he was referring to himself falls by the wayside. Luther may have talked before about burning the bull *Exsurge, Domine*, yet Boehmer maintains that all 16th-century evidence points to the idea that burning Pope Leo's bull was just sudden impulse of the moment.[261] Luther, therefore, on this occasion impulsively burned the papal bull which threatened him with excommunication, but he intentionally destroyed the whole basic framework upon which the Roman Church had been built. After the burning of these books and the bull the audience sang the *Te Deum* and the *De profundis*, whereupon the faculty returned to the college.

The students, however, did not seem to realize the serious implications of the occasion and turned the rest of the day into a frolic festival. More shingles were added to the flames and robust jeering at the Papacy and general buffoonery lasted well into the afternoon. When one student appeared in the attire of the Pope wearing the triple crown, it was immediately consigned to the flames.[262] Later a parade was organized through the streets of the town. Four students singing a funeral dirge in Hebrew preceded a farm wagon occupied by several other students, one of whom held a copy of the papal bull six feet long.[263]

The next day Luther began his lecture to his students with an explanation of the necessity for eradicating all traces of homage to the Papacy from their hearts if they were to be saved. Luther meant that his "New Theology" required a complete rejection of the Canon Law and the whole outward Roman system.[264] But the students proceeded to illustrate his remarks. A second parade took place that day. One student in the guise of the Pope, accompanied by others in masks portraying the cardinals, was followed through the streets by a crowd of remaining students. The "pope" put on such lofty airs that the students began to chase him. The demonstration became so boisterous that the town authorities finally stopped the revelry.

It was, perhaps, significant that the burning of the bull took place at exactly the end of the sixty days of grace allowed Luther.[265] Now the threatened ban was inevitable. On January 3 the final bull of excommunication appeared, known to history as *Decet*.[266] Symbolic of this excommunication and in keeping with tradition, Luther's works and a wooden statue of him were publicly burned on the *Piazza Navona* on June 12. But the German church authorities paid little or no attention to the bull; and many practical considerations, such as the strong feeling against Eck personally, vested interests, the many German grievances, and other causes, made it seem advisable not to push the case against the Saxon monk too earnestly.[267]

« 15 »

The Diet of Worms

Luther Summoned to Worms

IN A PREVIOUS CONNECTION the kaleidoscopic diplomacy
during the period of the imperial coronation of Charles V at
Aachen and Luther's condemnation by the new Kaiser in the Edict
of Worms has been observed from the viewpoint of the Emperor
and his officials.[1] But before the complete picture of Worms can be
grasped, it must also be viewed from the perspective of the background of Martin Luther and his following among the German
princes, burghers, knights, and the people. Events at Worms were
especially typical of the complex interplay of the many opposing
forces in the background, of which Luther was almost wholly
unaware as he appeared before the Kaiser and the Estates.

Rome was represented at Worms by two nuncios, Caracciolus
and Aleander.[2] Unfortunately, the dispatches of the former have
been lost, which makes Aleander appear to have been the principal
figure in Roman diplomacy at the imperial court. Rome hoped
that the Emperor would issue a mandate against Luther in Germany similar to that of the Netherlands, but the German constitution stood in the way.[3] It stated, and Charles had agreed to uphold
it in his coronation oath, that no German should be condemned
unless his case was heard before an impartial panel of judges.
This legal point favored the position of Frederick the Wise and
the German princes, and it was deemed inadvisable by Charles'
seasoned counselors to go contrary to the will of the German
Estates.

As the drama unfolded, the leading puppets were some of the
most important figures in European history. Erasmus was busy

behind the scenes; [4] Hutten and Sickingen, men of action with trained knights at their command, formed a silent but potent threat; [5] Glapion and Chièvres wisely counseled the inexperienced young ruler; [6] while Frederick the Wise and his able Chancellor Brueck tried to outmaneuver Aleander and Caracciolus in winning the approval of the court. [7] That no possible advantage might be overlooked, Caracciolus, who represented Rome in secular politics, and Aleander, in the ecclesiastical realm, were at the imperial court in the Netherlands before the Emperor's arrival in the German lands. [8] For the Emperor there were three possible choices of action: (1) to yield to Rome and condemn Luther summarily by imperial mandate since he was already under the ban; (2) to follow a middle-of-the-road policy by arranging a meeting with Luther privately in a further attempt to persuade him to bow to Rome; and, finally, (3) to permit Luther to appear before the Diet of Worms and to have a neutral, competent body investigate the points at issue between Luther and the Roman *Curia*. [9]

Though Aleander succeeded in getting certain of Luther's books burned in Louvain, the students made light of the affair by also including Roman books. [10] Erasmus had been very active in this region in an attempt to defeat the bull *Exsurge, Domine* in the fall of 1520. He had ridiculed the idea of burning books without first pointing out the errors on the basis of which the books were condemned. It was shortly after these events that the meeting was arranged between Frederick and Erasmus to discuss the Luther problem. Just at this time Aleander was putting considerable pressure on the Elector. Rudely he had interrupted Frederick's worship at Mass at a local monastery. [11] Aleander's tactics may have contributed to Frederick's determination to oppose the papal nuncios with all his power, and for the time being it seemed as though he was gaining ground with the Emperor. He succeeded in getting an audience with Charles V in Cologne and presented Luther's protest to the bull *Exsurge, Domine*. [12] He asked the imperial protection and reminded Charles of his promise not to condemn a German untried. [13] Charles renewed his promise that Luther would not be condemned unheard, for he realized that Luther's case supplied a counterweight to Roman diplomatic maneuvering.

When on November 14 Charles began the journey to Worms, the Elector started for Lochau, where he arrived on November 29.[14]

When Aleander, in the retinue of the Kaiser, arrived in Worms, he met with anything but a friendly reception. Sarcastic poems ridiculing him were to be seen everywhere. Even with his liberal supply of money he was unable to get anything but a small, unheated room in Worms.[15] As they passed the papal nuncio in the streets, various people gestured as though reaching for their swords and gnashed their teeth. In contrast, all the bookstores displayed Luther's writings and pictures for sale. These actions explain why Aleander wrote the Pope: "Nine tenths of the people are shouting 'Luther,' and the other tenth shouts: 'Down with Rome!'" [16]

Aleander made good use of his opportunities during Frederick's absence. The day before the Elector arrived at Lochau, the Kaiser had issued written confirmation of his request that Luther be brought to Worms.[17] But the report of the burning of the Canon Law and the papal bull on December 10, 1520, and a copy of Luther's *Babylonian Captivity of the Church* reached Charles at about the same time. They had a decidedly unfortunate effect on the Kaiser and supplied Aleander with his most potent ammunition. Charles now consulted with Glapion and decided on December 17 to revoke the permission for Luther to accompany the Elector to Worms.[18] With the burning of the bull, Luther became a condemned heretic; and the Kaiser was unwilling to grant him an audience even if he recanted. Should he recant, however, an audience might be granted him at Frankfurt am Main or elsewhere.[19]

Aleander now also urged the Emperor to issue a sharp mandate against Luther.[20] By the beginning of February the mandate had been drawn up, but its enforcement without the support of the Estates seemed doubtful. Aleander reported to the Pope his famous speech of February 13, 1521, when he talked for three hours against Luther, stressing that the bull *Decet Romanum pontificem* of January 3, 1521, altered the whole situation.[21] He asked that the Kaiser, Electors, princes, and the Estates burn Luther's books and pronounce a general edict that henceforth his books should no longer be published, bought, or sold.

In the meantime the Elector had decided to fight the Aleander program with vigor. In this situation the Glapion group thought it best to follow the middle road, but this plan was opposed by Frederick's Chancellor Brueck, for he wanted Luther to appear at Worms.[22] The next session, held February 15, proved to be a stormy one. The normally cautious, easy-going Frederick became so violent that he almost came to blows with the Margrave of Brandenburg.[23] The result was the decision on February 19 to follow a compromise:

> Luther is summoned to Worms through a safe-conduct, and there he is to be heard through learned specialists, that is, he is to be asked whether he will abide with his writings and their content or not. Beyond that, nothing. There is to be no disputation. If he recants, he shall be treated with grace; if he remains obstinate, then the Kaiser's mandate against him will be executed.[24]

Charles V was now forced against his will to summon Luther on March 6, a copy of which summons is still extant.[25] Aleander had failed in his attempt to push through a mandate ordering Luther's writings burned. Just at this critical juncture, the *condottiere* leader, Robert of the Mark, invaded the Kaiser's lands in Belgium, a move behind which the hand of the Papacy could be detected.[26] Luther's summons was, in a sense, another blow aimed at the Papacy in the complicated game of international politics. Martin Luther was now officially asked to appear at Worms before the Kaiser, Electors, Princes, and the Estates.

On March 26, 1521, the imperial herald, Kaspar Sturm, arrived in Wittenberg.[27] On his arm blazoned the imperial golden eagle symbolic of his office, and he was empowered to provide both a safe-conduct and himself as guide for Luther to Worms. Frederick had also arranged for safe-conduct through his lands. On March 29 Luther wrote his friend Lang in Erfurt that he would be spending April 5 and 6 with him.[28] The Wittenberg magistrates gave Luther 20 gulden, about $260, for expense money which was to provide food and lodging for the Luther party consisting of Amsdorf, his fellow professor, Petzensteiner, a fellow Augustinian, and Peter Suaven, a young student.[29] According to available evidence, the carriage, a sort of surrey, was provided by a man named Duering, who lived at No. 4 *Schloss Gasse* just west of the Cranach House.[30] Leaving Wittenberg on April 2, the group proceeded over

the Dueben-Leipzig-Naumburg-Erfurt-Gotha-Eisenach route to
Frankfurt am Main and from there via Oppenheim to Worms.

As the travelers proceeded, the simple journey began to assume
the appearance of a triumphal march with the imperial herald
leading the way, followed by the carriage drawn by three horses
and surrounded by crowds of admiring and curious spectators.

In Leipzig and Naumburg the customary wines were offered
to welcome the guests. Upon their arrival in Weimar, a messenger
informed them that Luther and his works had already been condemned by the Kaiser. The herald then asked Luther: "Doctor, do
you still wish to continue?" To which Luther replied: "Yes, regardless of the fact that I have been placed under the ban and that it
has been publicized in all the towns, I shall proceed and trust in
the Kaiser's safe-conduct." [31] The Kaiser had actually published
a mandate against Luther in spite of the German diet probably
because he shrank from the meeting and hoped to frighten Luther
into returning to Wittenberg. Many friends and admirers pleaded
with Luther not to make the journey, but he would not be turned
from his purpose. Duke John donated additional money for the
expenses of the expedition. Outside Erfurt the party was met by
Justus Jonas and forty horsemen who escorted the guest of honor
into the city. Nearer the city they were joined by members of the
university faculty, members of the town council, and other prominent citizens ready to receive the Wittenberg group. Luther went
to the Augustinian cloister, which he had left only a little over
a decade before. Since it was Saturday evening, the party remained
over Sunday. On Sunday morning Luther preached in the cloister
church of the Augustinian monastery. The place was so crowded
that the balcony began to creak and Luther had to interrupt
his sermon to reassure the audience regarding the safety of the
building. During the visit Luther was feasted and honored as a
distinguished son of the University and of the Augustinian Hermits.
In Eisenach Luther again preached. Then the strain of the journey
began to exact its toll of his physical strength, and he did not feel
well when they arrived at Frankfurt am Main on April 14.[32]

In the meantime Spalatin, and no doubt Frederick, had become much alarmed for Luther's safety following the turn of events.
Not knowing whether Luther had received warning of his danger,

"Triumph of Truth," a popular cartoon portraying Hutten's support of Luther's Gospel reforms

Spalatin wrote to him. There is some confusion regarding the reply made by Luther. The *Tischreden* reports the following, and is supported by Spalatin's *Annales Reformationis*:

> When I came into the neighborhood of Worms, I was warned by Spalatin lest I throw myself into grave danger. At the same time I wrote back: "Even though there should be as many devils in Worms as shingles on the roof, I would still enter." [33]

What he actually wrote to Spalatin from Frankfurt was, "Indeed, Christ is alive, and I shall enter Worms in spite of the gates of hell and the powers of darkness." In a similar vein he had written to Melanchthon earlier from Gotha: "I shall enter Worms under Christ's leadership in spite of the gates of hell." [34] When Luther decided to leave the Wartburg and return to Wittenberg against the wishes of his Prince, he wrote to Frederick an explanation of why he was taking such a step, and it was in that letter that he made the famous statement quoted above:

> I have obeyed your Grace this year to please you. The devil knows I did not hide from cowardice, for he saw my heart when I entered Worms. Had I then believed that there were as many devils as tiles on the roofs, I should have leaped into their midst with joy.[35]

At Oppenheim another conspiracy came to light. Glapion, who represented the middle party and wished to keep Luther away from Worms at all costs, had worked out a clever scheme with Sickingen and Hutten, for whose aid Sickingen was to be rewarded with a command under the Kaiser and Hutten with a suitable gift. Luther was to be brought to the Ebernburg, where Sickingen and his friend had earlier offered him protection, and here Glapion hoped to solve the problem without allowing a public hearing. But the imperial father confessor had not counted upon Luther's courage and basic honesty. When Bucer, the court chaplain at the Ebernburg, and also in on the plot, approached Luther with the proposal, the Wittenberg monk replied: "I will continue on my journey. If the Kaiser's father confessor has something to discuss with me, he can do it at Worms." [36]

Finally, on April 16 at ten o'clock in the morning the town watchman of Worms announced with his trumpet from the cathedral spire that distinguished visitors were approaching the city.[37]

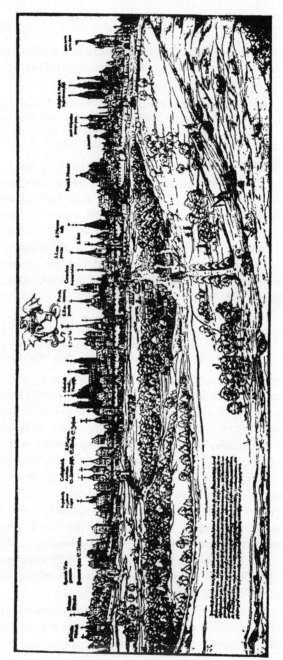

Worms in 1560

A group of 100 horsemen immediately set out to provide a triumphal escort. When the cavalcade arrived around eleven o'clock, such a crowd had gathered about the city gate that the vehicles could scarcely enter. The streets, walls, windows, and trees were all filled with more than 2,000 interested spectators. Aleander, who reported the entry in detail on the basis of the observations of one of his men, added that some obscure monk embraced Luther as he emerged from the carriage in front of the *Johanniterhof*, the residence of The Knights of St. John, where Luther was to be quartered.[38] After the embrace he touched the hem of his robe as though Luther were some miracle-working saint. The nuncio added that Luther eyed the crowd with his "demoniac eyes" and remarked: "God will be with me." [39] After he had entered the hostel, many distinguished persons gathered about him. Some dozen had lunch with him, and all through the day many others tried to see the distinguished Wittenberg professor if only for a moment.

LUTHER BEFORE THE DIET

The *Pfalz* near the Cathedral of Worms in which the Emperor was quartered and which served as the seat of the bishop has long since fallen victim to the ravages of war. Here in a narrow upper chamber sat Charles V, the Electors, and distinguished prelates of the Empire, while around them were gathered the counts, nobles, knights, and burghers who composed the German Diet. At the time of Luther's first appearance this small upper room was so crowded that officials with pikes and halberds had to control the crowd. An exact reconstruction of the scene is no longer possible.[40] Such pictures as that by Werner in the Museum of Fine Arts in Stuttgart are entirely from imagination.

On the morning of April 17 the *Reichsmarschall* Ulrich von Pappenheim came to Luther's room announcing that he was to appear before the Diet at four o'clock in the afternoon. Meanwhile, Luther, Spalatin, and the court lawyers had discussed the procedure and agreed that Dr. Jerome Schurff, a Wittenberg professor in Canon Law, was to act as Luther's lawyer before the Diet.[41]

At four in the afternoon imperial herald Sturm and *Reichsmarschall* Pappenheim called for Luther. Since the streets were full

of people, the two officials led Luther through a garden and into
the *Pfalz* by a back door.[42] Here he was surprised to see Dr. Peutinger. If the highly improbable story of a conversation with
Frundsberg has any historical truth (contemporary sources do not
support the story), it must have occurred while Luther was waiting
downstairs for official summons from the Kaiser that he was to appear. The later leader of the troops that were to win the Battle
of Pavia in 1524 and to storm Rome in 1527 is reported to have
encouraged Luther to stand his ground in this critical hour, and
God would not forsake him.[43] This was no doubt a tense moment
for a man who had never before faced such an august assembly,
knowing that both his life and his cause were at stake.

When Luther was finally called upstairs, there was much excited tension in the crowded room.[44] The *Reichsmarschall* reminded
Luther that he was not to speak except in answer to direct questions from the presiding officer, Johann von Eck, an official from
the court of the Archbishop of Trier (not to be confused with the
Ingolstadt professor, who had opposed Luther in the Leipzig
Debate).[45] After the customary opening remarks honoring all the
dignitaries present with the proper forms of address, the presiding
officer tried to impress Luther with the gravity of the moment. The
preliminaries once completed, the official turned to Luther. On
a bench near by was a pile of books which Aleander had graciously
gathered for the occasion. Pointing to the volumes, Eck asked
Luther a double question: Was he ready to acknowledge authorship of the volumes lying before him, and was he ready to revoke
the heresies they contained? Luther, who may have been somewhat
overawed by all the pomp and dignity before him, was about to
answer when his lawyer, Dr. Schurff, interposed: "Please have the
titles read." [46] After the reading of twenty-five titles of books which
he had written, Luther was quite ready to acknowledge that they
were his.[47] But the second question was an entirely different matter.
Since it was a question "concerning faith and the salvation of the
soul" and one that directly affirmed or denied "God's Word,"
Luther felt he should have more time to consider a proper answer.
This request was granted with the condition that Luther give his
reply the next day at four o'clock in the afternoon.[48] The Roman

officials were furious. Why should Luther be given time to answer such a question? Why did he come to Worms if he was not ready to answer?

After his return to his quarters, Luther gave much serious thought to his address for the next day. The notes which he prepared for the world-famous reply are still extant in the Weimar archives.[49] A number of eyewitnesses have also left accounts of the famous Worms session on April 18, when Luther gave the speech that shook the world. At four in the afternoon the imperial official again called for Martin Luther. Once more he was obliged to wait in an anteroom. By the time he was finally summoned it was six o'clock and candles had to be lit. This time the session was held in a larger but even more crowded hall than that of the previous day.[50] The Emperor and all the dignitaries were in their official positions except for the papal nuncios, who had refused to attend. As on the previous day, the presiding officer addressed Luther with the question he had left unanswered the day before.[51] But on the second day Martin Luther was a changed man. Gone was any awe or timidity. On his face there was an expression of confidence and supreme faith in God, which made his friends and even his Elector proud. Luther delivered his address in Latin and in German. Considering his excellent memory, there is reason to believe that he knew the speech verbatim. Unfortunately, the exact text has not been preserved, but from the Weimar notes, the reports of Spalatin, Aleander, and others, the whole session can be accurately pieced together.[52]

Luther began his reply by addressing "The Most Serene Lord Emperor, Illustrious Princes, most clement Lords, etc." He pointed out that he had not been reared in the etiquette of princes and the court but as a simple monk and, therefore, begged the pardon of anyone whom he might not address with the proper title. He then turned to his inquisitor, Eck, and began to analyze the question. In a clear and distinct tone Luther pointed out to his hushed and expectant listeners that not all the books before him fell into one class.[53] One group dealt with practical, Christian morality, which he had expressed in a simple, evangelical way that not even his enemies could criticize. To condemn such materials would mean the condemnation of simple Christian truth. Another part of his writings was directed against the Papacy, which he proceeded to denounce in such clear fashion that even Charles V objected. The Papacy and the Roman *Curia*, he said, had destroyed Christendom in both body and soul. Through Canon Law it had enslaved the lives of men. If he recanted these truths, he would open not only the windows, but even the doors for a further oppression of his fellow countrymen. And, finally, another portion of his writings had been directed against the enemies of the Gospel, the defenders of this Roman tyranny. He was quite ready to grant that at times he had become too vehement in his attacks upon these individuals; yet, it should be remembered that it was never in defense of himself, but of the teachings of Christ that he wrote. To reject these writings would merely help to entrench further the papal power. Thus, as he had told his friends on the previous day, Luther was not ready to withdraw from his position.

The Emperor and the court advisers now left the chamber for a little consultation. When they returned, Eck, who had been well coached in his strategy by Aleander,[54] presented a rather lengthy exposition as to why he and the other Catholics assembled were not interested in Luther's personal interpretation of the Scriptures. Had he not supported Hus and through this denied the validity of general councils? The Emperor now wanted a direct answer, one "without horns or any evasion."[55] Was he ready to recant his errors?

Luther realized that the time had come when he would have to make a complete break with Rome; there was no middle road. Either he would deny all of his convictions as to the teachings of Scripture, gathered through years of painful struggle, and bow to the accepted traditional Roman hierarchical system with all of its corruption; or he would make a clear, unmistakable declaration of the faith that was within him. Luther spoke but a single sentence, but its reverberations still resound throughout Christendom. Since a simple answer had been requested, he would give a simple answer. Turning his piercing black eyes upon his questioner, Luther replied:

> Unless I am convinced by the testimonies of the Holy Scriptures or evident reason (for I believe neither in the Pope nor councils alone, since it has been established that they have often erred and con-

tradicted themselves), I am bound by the Scriptures adduced by me, and my conscience has been taken captive by the Word of God, and I am neither able nor willing to recant, since it is neither safe nor right to act against conscience. God help me. Amen.[56]

The hall was thrown into pandemonium. Peutinger reported: "There was a great noise." [57] Amid the commotion the interrogator tried to control the situation by telling Luther his conscience could not be used as a guide in such matters, that general councils were far safer guides than the individual conscience. An argument followed. The Emperor, excited and angry, rose to his feet and exclaimed he had had enough of such talk.[58] With the Emperor's retirement the meeting broke up. Luther's friends were overjoyed with his courageous stand in the presence of both Rome and the Empire. The Spaniards, however, amid hissing and jeering, shouted: "To the fire with him!" [59] Once outside, in the midst of friends, Luther raised his arms like a victorious knight at a tournament and shouted: "I am through; I am through!"

Luther had made a profound impression upon the Diet. For once a German had had the courage to face these foreigners and to give expression to the newly emerging self-reliance of these northern people. He had held firm to his belief that an individual thoroughly grounded in God's Word must follow the dictates of his own conscience until he is proved in error on the basis of that same infallible source. The Elector was so impressed that Spalatin recorded a visit with him that evening in which he enthusiastically said: "Doctor Martin has spoken right well in both Latin and German in the presence of the Emperor, the Princes, and the Estates. He is far too bold for me." [60] Philip of Hesse also personally expressed his approval; while the Catholic prince Duke Eric of Braunschweig is reported to have expressed his approval with the gift of a pitcher of *Eimbecker* beer.[61] Nobles, knights, and prominent citizens all professed their admiration and vowed their support should he be in danger as a result of his bold confession.

Charles V would have preferred to yield to the importunities of Aleander and to condemn Luther without further ado; but the problem was not that simple. He had no real power in Germany according to the constitution of the Holy Roman Empire; and he needed money for his Italian campaigns. There were other reforms which he hoped to effect in Germany but for which he needed the good will of the German Diet. Then there were still those who asserted that were Luther approached privately in a less offensive manner, his case might still be brought to a reasonable solution.

The next day Charles summoned the Electors and some of the more powerful princes to discuss what should be done with the Wittenberg monk. When the group expressed the opinion that the Diet should not rush to a conclusion, the Emperor presented his own personal views in no uncertain terms.[62] He could not see how a single monk could be right and the testimony of a thousand years of Christendom be wrong. He cared not for the opinions of others; as for himself, he was ready to abide by the faith of the fathers. Although he was willing to honor the safe-conduct, he had resolved to give Luther no further audience and would take the necessary measures to suppress this heresy.

The Electors and the remaining members of the Diet were not as convinced as the Emperor that this was the proper course of action. After all, there were the people to consider. No one wanted a recurrence of the Bohemian problem after Constance! And the temper of the people was all too evident. Placards appeared on the *Rathaus* doors.[63] Four hundred nobles pledged themselves to Luther's support. The *"Bundschuh,"* symbolical of Sickingen and his group, threatened the Emperor with an uprising should Luther not receive fair treatment. True, the Emperor laughed at this empty threat behind which was Herman von Busche, who had formerly taught at Wittenberg. Yet, he must have sensed the inflammable qualities of the situation. On Charles' own door appeared the note: "Woe unto the land whose king is a child!" Not to be outdone, the Catholics put up countersigns. Johann Cochlaeus, now a canon in Frankfurt and a bitter enemy, posted the notice: "Luther! Pope and Kaiser have condemned you. Now Frederick will not keep your safe-conduct, for in your madness you have merely brought up again the old heresies and presented nothing new." It was true that Sickingen had gathered troops in the neighborhood of Worms, but it is not at all certain that Charles V could not as easily have used them against Luther's followers. No one was quite certain what might happen.

Under the leadership of Albert of Mainz, in whose lands the Diet was being held, the Elector of Saxony, and others a plan was finally evolved to give Luther an opportunity to discuss his differences with a select group composed of three or four learned theologians to see whether a reconciliation could be effected.[64] The Emperor and his officials would have no part in these unofficial discussions. Rather reluctantly Charles now granted that Luther should be given three more days, from April 22 to 24, in which these private hearings might be conducted.

The first of these meetings took place on Wednesday, April 24, in the quarters of the Archbishop of Trier, who presided over the deliberations.[65] Those invited were the Elector of Brandenburg, the Bishop of Augsburg, Dr. Peutinger of Augsburg, Duke George of Albertine Saxony, the Bishop of Brandenburg, Count George of Wertheim, Representative Bock of Strassburg, and Dr. Vehus, Chancellor of the Margrave of Baden. Luther was accompanied by three Wittenberg professors, Schurff, Jonas, and Amsdorf. Dr. Vehus was chosen to discuss the issues with Luther, and since he was an easygoing, amiable personality, his substitution for the more offensive Dr. Eck was a good choice. There were really no theologians in the group commissioned to weigh Luther's problems, a fact granted by Dr. Vehus in his introductory speech when he disclaimed all knowledge of theology, but in a very friendly tone tried to impress upon Luther that Catholicism could not grant an individual an opinion in matters of faith and doctrine where a general council had already spoken. Luther replied in the same friendly manner, saying that it was not his intention to belittle a general council; but he pointed out to the assembled group that councils had frequently erred when they did not judge problems of the Church in the light of God's holy Word. Then he was asked if he were willing to let his writings be judged by the Emperor or the Diet. Luther gave his assent and even added his willingness to submit them to a general council, provided it was guided by the Bible and not by human tradition. The Elector of Brandenburg then asked: "Do you mean that you will not submit unless convinced by Holy Scriptures?" To which Luther replied: "Yes, most Gracious Lord, or by clear and evident reason."[66]

Now the Archbishop of Trier invited Luther to luncheon and an afternoon session.[67] He also invited Cochlaeus, and Luther was asked to bring Amsdorf and Schurff. This meeting, too, broke down on the same grounds as the morning session. In the middle of the afternoon Cochlaeus visited Luther in his quarters, and in a lively conversation between him and Luther's friends he even challenged Luther to a debate provided that his safe-conduct were revoked.[68] As the day did not seem entirely fruitless, the Archbishop asked the Emperor to extend Luther's time two more days.[69] That evening Luther was notified that discussions would continue on Thursday morning.

The next morning between seven and eight o'clock Chancellor Vehus of Baden and Doctor Peutinger arrived at the *Johanniterhof*.[70] After a morning and an afternoon session they finally persuaded Luther to agree to a future council under well-guarded conditions. Upon the favorable report of Vehus, the Archbishop summoned Luther once more to a private conference, to which Spalatin was later admitted.[71] After all proposals had failed, which Aleander claimed included even the offer of a rich priory and complete protection in one of his castles, the Archbishop turned to Luther with the question: "My dear Doctor, what else can we do?" Whereupon Luther replied that he knew no better advice than that given by Gamaliel in The Acts (5:38-39): "If this counsel or this work be of men, it will come to nought: But if it be of God, ye cannot overthrow it; lest haply ye be found even to fight against God." [72]

By this time Luther's patience was becoming rather exhausted. There seemed to be no thought in the minds of any of the men who tried to bring him around that he might possibly be right; their only concern was a desire to maintain and uphold the *status quo*. It never occurred to men like Eck, Cochlaeus, Vehus, and others that Roman Catholicism might have drifted far from its original position; that it had lost its way in the swamp of medieval Scholasticism; and that the church councils merely reflected the traditional development of the times. When Luther spoke against this *Zeitgeist* and insisted that the problem must be solved on the basis of the Scriptures, they simply could not follow his reasoning. So he turned to the Archbishop and pointed out that he had now been there ten days and nothing had been accomplished. He, therefore, begged his Electoral Grace to ask the Kaiser's permission to return home.[73] The request was granted immediately, and that same evening Luther was given another safe-conduct for twenty-one days on the condition that on his return he would not preach, speak, or otherwise do anything to inflame the people further. But the Emperor's request to stop preaching seemed to Luther beyond the boundaries of the state's authority, and he refused to abide by this command.[74]

That same evening Luther wrote a communication to the Emperor and the Estates, thanking them for every consideration shown him and especially for honoring the safe-conduct.[75] Recalling the experience of John Hus, it is doubtful if Luther believed he would live through the Worms experience. He regretted, however, that the interviews had been fruitless:

> I have sought nothing beyond reforming the Church in conformity with the Holy Scriptures. I would suffer death and infamy, give up life and reputation for His Imperial Majesty and the Empire. I wish to reserve nothing but the liberty to confess and bear witness to the Word of God alone.[76]

The next morning, April 26, about ten o'clock the imperial herald Kaspar Sturm escorted the Luther carriage through the city gates on its homeward journey.[77]

THE EDICT OF WORMS

As early as April 30, 1521, four days after Luther's departure, Charles V announced to the German Diet his intention of placing Luther and his supporters under the ban. In the discussion which followed it was evident that the German Estates would assert their constitutional right and refuse to permit a fellow German to be condemned without their approval and consent.[78]

The normal procedure would have been to appoint a German commission, presided over by the Archbishop of Salzburg, to draft the Edict of Worms, but the Archbishop was no longer in the good graces of the Emperor. Furthermore, it seemed doubtful whether the type of edict the Emperor desired could be obtained through the normal channels.[79] The same evening Gattinara commissioned

Aleander to draft the Edict of Worms, which he prepared that same night in Latin and presented to the German Privy Council the next day.[80] Aleander was deeply disappointed when this body hesitated to accept his draft. Discussion and revisions followed more in language than in substance, and by May 8 it had been translated into German. But when Aleander presented the two drafts of the Edict of Worms neatly copied on parchment on May 12, Charles was not ready to sign.[81] He was waiting for a more opportune moment.

Many factors helped to determine the attitude of the Emperor during the early days of May, 1521.[82] French troops had just crossed the border of Charles' realm both in the Netherlands and in Spain. Sickingen's troops were on the outskirts of Worms, a contributing factor to the early departure of both Philip of Hesse and Albert of Mainz from the Diet. A treaty with the Pope was hanging in the balance. Much important business was still unsettled for which Charles needed the German Estates. The bargaining over the *Reichsregiment*, the body to rule Germany in the Emperor's absence, was in full swing. The Estates were also debating the nature of the new *Kammergericht*, or court of law for the German nation. In the coming war with France, Charles was asking both for subsidies and for an army of 4,000 horsemen and 20,000 foot soldiers. All of these things Charles and Gattinara hoped to accomplish before bringing the Edict of Worms into the open.

There may have been another contributing factor to Charles' reluctance to sign Aleander's edict on May 12. About this time the report of Luther's capture near Eisenach had reached Worms. The followers of Herman von Busche became alarmed. The ensuing disturbances in the streets made the publication of an edict just at that time hardly advisable.[83] Charles probably intended to dismiss the Diet first and then proclaim the ban against Luther. On May 25, 1521, the Diet of Worms officially closed.[84]

On the evening of the same day, Charles V, to give his edict some semblance of having the official sanction of the German nation, called together the remaining four Electors, princes, and bishops in the palace where the Diet had met.[85] The Elector of Saxony, who had been deathly sick from food poisoning, had already gone home. Albert of Mainz was also gone, as was the Elector of the Palatinate.[86] Gattinara read a papal brief to the Emperor, praising his excellent work against the Lutheran heresy. Similar briefs were also distributed by the clever Aleander to the others in the group. Then the Emperor, speaking in French, called upon Dr. Spiegel, one of the translators, to read the German version of the Edict of Worms.[87] Naturally, this rump session of conservative Catholics approved of the edict, even though they did not sanction its violent language.

At the close of the reading in this mock session of the German Diet, the Archbishop of Brandenburg expressed his enthusiastic approval of the edict and assured the gathering that the Estates would not wish to see "a single jot" changed.[88] The following day, May 26, after attending High Mass in the Worms Cathedral, the Emperor signed the original Latin Edict of Worms and its German translation with all solemnity.[89] In a public proclamation he sought to create the impression that the Edict of Worms had been drawn up with the "consent and will of the Estates."

The edict first presented a history of Luther's case in the most unfair and biased fashion.[90] Unmentioned were the abuses of which even the most conservative princes had complained. Luther's teachings were pictured as subversive in government, religion, and morality. With his dirty mouth he had made light of the Council of Constance. He was the very devil himself, dressed as a monk. Thus, the Emperor, in duty bound to protect the faith of the fathers, placed him under the imperial ban. All of the Emperor's subjects were forbidden to have any dealings with the man. It, therefore, became the duty of every loyal subject to seize him, if possible, and to deliver him to the imperial authorities. His followers and supporters were to be treated in the same manner and their property confiscated. The buying, selling, printing, reading, or even possession of any of Luther's writings was placed under penalty. Further, any books to be written in the future against the Roman faith, the Pope, the Roman Church, the clergy, the Scholastic theology were expressly prohibited. Anyone guilty of these acts might be arrested, put to death, and his property taken by the faithful soul who executed the edict. In brief, in the future, episcopal approval

was to be required of creative authors in all fields. The *Index* of
the Council of Trent was certainly in the making. As for Luther,
he was now declared *"vogelfrei"* and could be killed on sight.

The Emperor had reason to fear the reception of the Edict of
Worms. Aleander rejoiced, but his rejoicing was not to be long-
lived. Safe behind the walls of the Wartburg was the man whom
they had declared an outlaw. As subsequent sessions of the German
Reichsregiment were to show, the Edict of Worms was too unreasonable to be enforced.[91] Too many Germans, even such enemies
of Luther as Duke George of Meissen, were too fair-minded to fall
in line with the Latin fanaticism. As Paul Kalkoff has shown, in
the end it was to mean the victory of the German spirit. Even
the Catholic princes realized that Aleander had misrepresented
Luther's case. They knew that any attempt to enforce the fanatical
edict would result in civil war and the destruction of the German
nation.[92]

There can be little doubt that the Edict of Worms was a perfect illustration of what Luther was opposing in his courageous
stand at Worms. The edict reflected the spirit which meant to
crush all claim to the right of individual liberty of thought and
conscience, the very cornerstone of modern Protestantism and of
democracy.

Album of Photographs

The Papal Palace at Avignon

PLATE III

Pope Julius II. Painted by Raphael

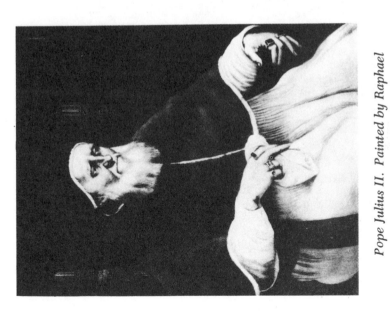

Emperor Maximilian I

PLATE IV

Francis I and Margaret of Navarre

PLATE V

Charles V in 1530. Painted by Titian.

PLATE VI

Commander Frundsberg

PLATE VII

Charles V in middle age. Painted by Lucas Cranach the Elder

PLATE VIII

Frederick the Wise, Elector of Saxony. Painted by Lucas Cranach the Elder.

George Spalatin, 1482–1545, court chaplain of Frederick the Wise. Painted by Lucas Cranach the Elder

PLATE IX

John Frederick, Elector of Saxony. Painted by Lucas Cranach the Elder.

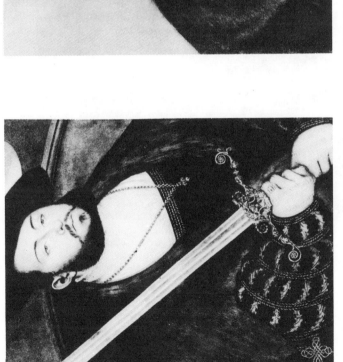

John the Constant, successor to Frederick. Painted by Cranach the Elder.

PLATE X

Duke George, ruler of Albertine Saxony

PLATE XI

Home of the Luther family at Moehra, built in 1618

PLATE XII

Luther's father. Painted by Lucas Cranach the Elder

Luther's Mother. Painted by Lucas Cranach the Elder

PLATE XIII

*Luther's birthplace.
Modern view from
street*

*SS. Peter and Paul's
Church, where Luther
was baptized*

PLATE XIV

Luther's birthplace. Modern view from rear

Interior view of Luther's birthplace

PLATE XV

The Mansfeld School

PLATE XVI

Cyriax
Castle

Small Gate

Carthusian
Monastery

Loeber Gate

Bruehl Gate Tower

Mountain Stream

Cathedral and
Severi Chapter

St. Peter's Monastery

St. Andrew's Gate

St. John's
Gate

Kraempfer
Gate

Servite Monastery

Schmidtstadt Gate

Erfurt in the 16th century

PLATE XVII

Erfurt Cathedral (left), where Luther was ordained as priest

PLATE XVIII

The Old University Building at Erfurt

North view of former Augustinian Library at Erfurt, begun in 1501. Lower floor contained summer refectory; upper floor housed library and lecture room

PLATE XIX

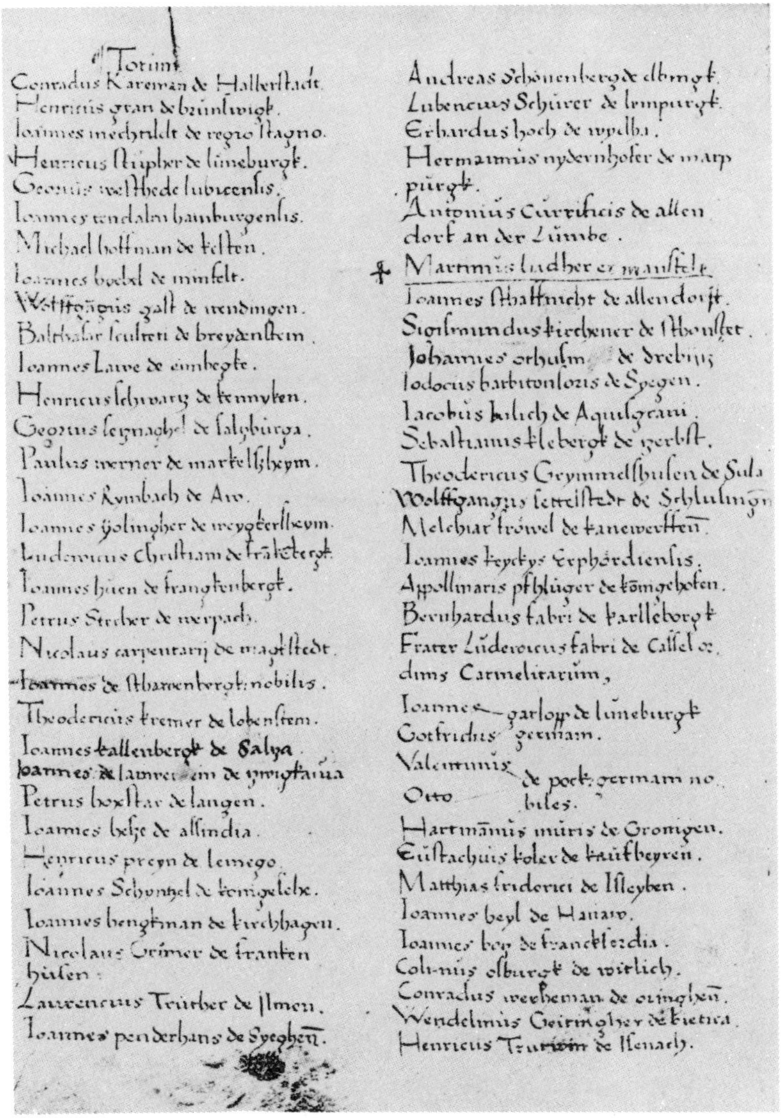

A page from the Erfurt Matriculation Book, containing the registration of Martin Luther

PLATE XX

The Luther Cell at Erfurt today

PLATE XXI

John Staupitz as Augustinian Prior

PLATE XXII

Scene in Rome in Luther's day

PLATE XXIII

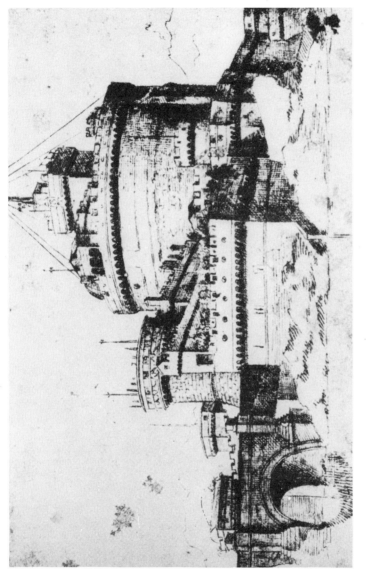

Castle San Angelo, Rome

PLATE XXIV

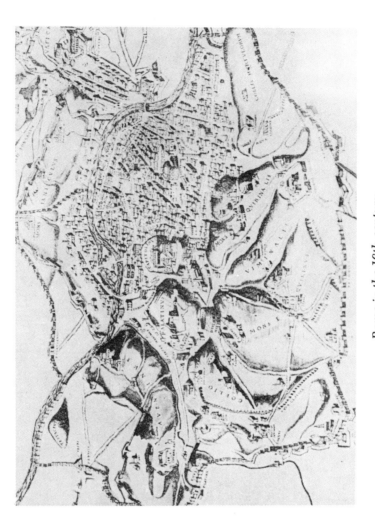

Rome in the 16th century

PLATE XXV

Renaissance porch of Rathaus designed by Schroeder
PLATE XXVI

*Bronze baptismal font in use in the Town Church, made in 1457
by Herman Vischer the Elder, of Nuernberg*

PLATE XXVII

Luther pulpit formerly in the Town Church

PLATE XXVIII

Luther preaching. Detail from "Fluegelaltar" in Town Church painted by Lucas Cranach the Elder

PLATE XXIX

Altar detail from Town Church, Luther's congregation. Catharine von Bora in center foreground, Lucas Cranach center background. Painted by Lucas Cranach the Elder

PLATE XXX

The Augustinian College Building erected by Elector August
1564–1586

Courtyard between "Collegium Friderici and "Das alte Colle-
gium" from the university "Matrikel," 1644–1645

PLATE XXXI

The Melanchthon Study

The Luther Study in the Luther House. Modern view

PLATE XXXII

The Melanchthon House, built for him by the Elector in 1541

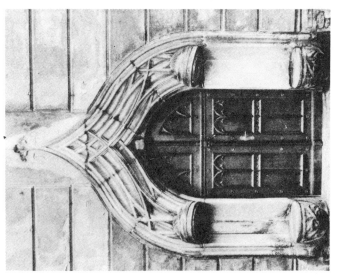

"Katharinen-Portal" of Luther House

PLATE XXXIII

Interior view of "Schlosskirche" before 1760

PLATE XXXIV

"Fluegelaltar" painted by Albrecht Duerer for the Castle Church

PLATE XXXV

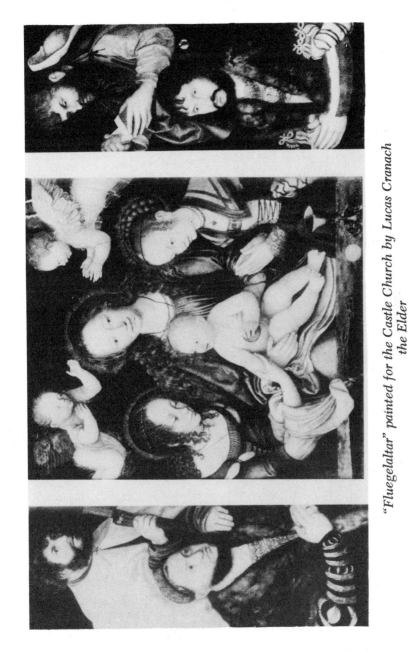

"Fluegelaltar" painted for the Castle Church by Lucas Cranach the Elder

PLATE XXXVI

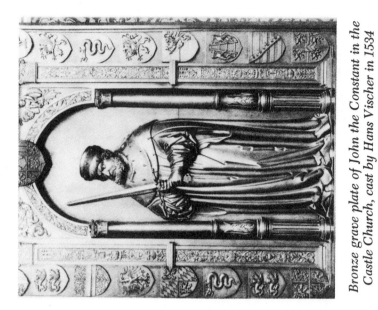

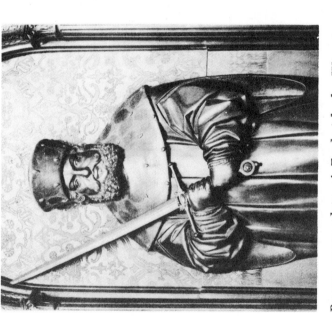

Bronze grave plate of Frederick the Wise in Castle Church, cast by Peter Vischer the Younger in 1527

Bronze grave plate of John the Constant in the Castle Church, cast by Hans Vischer in 1534

PLATE XXXVII

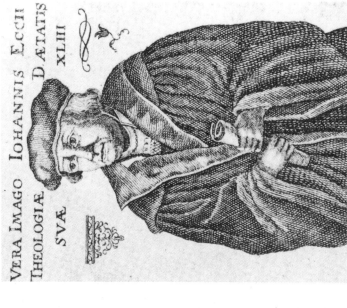

Dr. John Eck

John Tetzel

PLATE XXXVIII

Erasmus of Rotterdam. Etching by Albrecht Duerer

PLATE XXXIX

Coat of arms of Crotus Rubeanus, surrounded by those of other contemporary Humanists. Note Martin Luther's at upper left. They were roommates at Erfurt

PLATE XL

Inner Court of the Fugger House in Augsburg in 1515

PLATE XLI

Imperial Herald Kaspar Sturm.

Jacob Fugger. Painted by Hans Holbein
the Elder

PLATE XLII

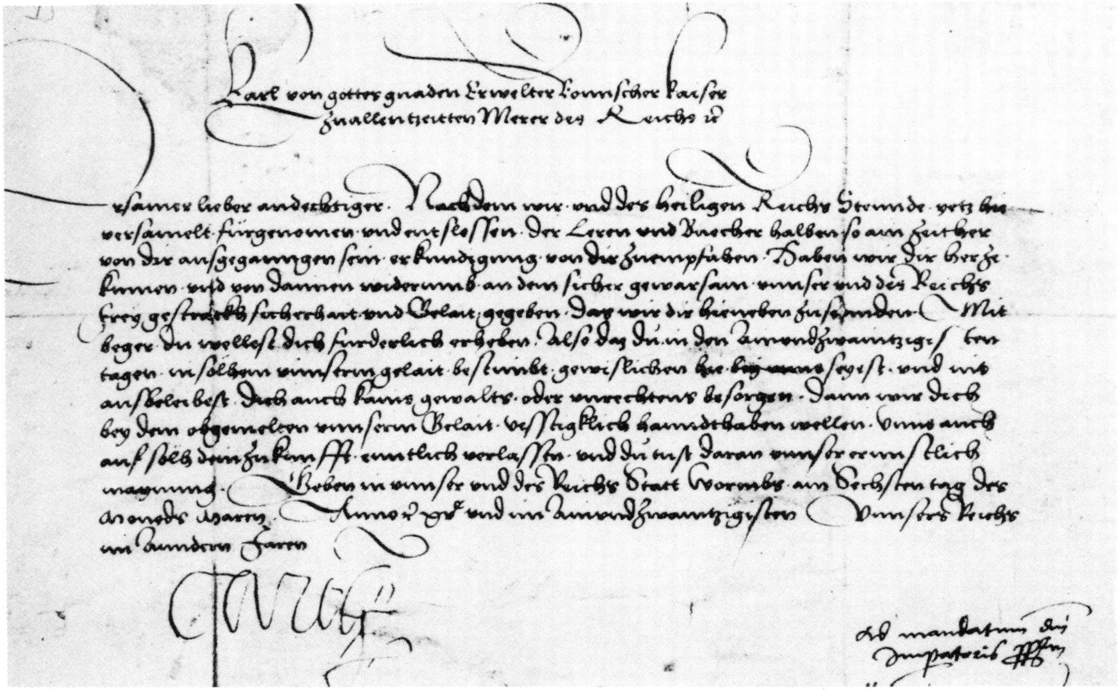

Emperor Charles V summons Luther to Worms, March 6, 1521.

PLATE XLIII

Luther's letter of "safe-conduct" from Emperor Charles V, March 6, 1521.

PLATE XLIV

*Cloister of the Carmelite Monastery, where Luther stayed in Augs-
burg in 1518 (above); the courtyard of the monastery (below)*

PLATE XLV

*Small gate through which
Luther departed from
Worms*

Worms gateway through which Luther entered the city in 1521

PLATE XLVI

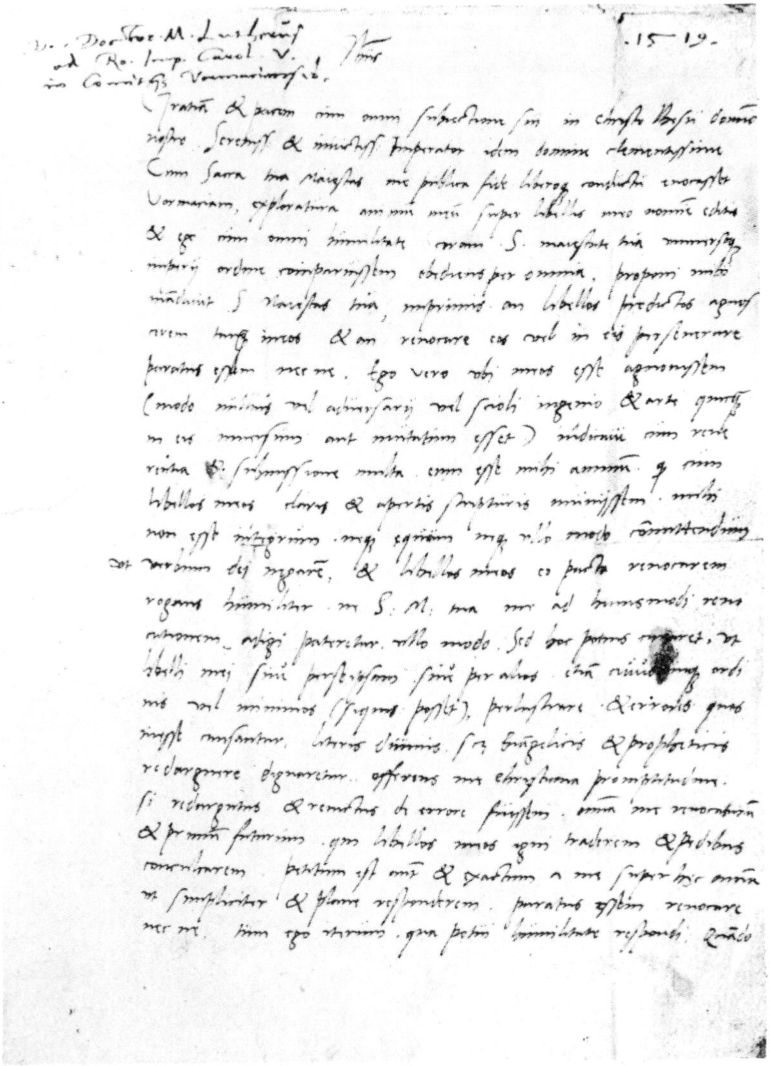

Portion of Luther's letter to Charles V after the Diet of Worms, 1521

PLATE XLVII

Front courtyard of the Wartburg with the "Vogtei" in the 16th century

"Lutherstube" at Wartburg showing bedroom door

PLATE XLVIII

Windows of the "Lutherstube" and his view of "The Land of the Birds"

PLATE XLIX

Self-portrait of Lucas Cranach the Elder

PLATE L

Martin Luther. By Lucas Cranach the Elder, 1532

PLATE LI

Katherine von Bora. By Lucas Cranach the Elder, 1526

PLATE LII

Luther's daughter Magdalena (1529–1542)

PLATE LIII

Luther's daughter Margaret. By Lucas Cranach the Younger, 1557

Luther's son Paul. By Johann Georg Menzel

PLATE LIV

*Martin Luther. By Lucas
Cranach the Elder, 1526*

*Luther as "Junker
Joerg." By Lucas
Cranach the Elder,
1521*

PLATE LV

*Johannes Bugenhagen. By
Lucas Cranach the Elder.*

Ulrich Zwingli

PLATE LVI

Melchior Lotther, printer of Wittenberg

Martin Bucer

Thomas Muenzer

PLATE LVII

*Melanchthon. Painted by Hans Holbein
the Younger*

*Melanchthon in 1532. Painted by Lucas Cranach
the Elder*

PLATE LVIII

George Rhau, printer of Wittenberg

Johann Froben, printer of Basle

Johannes Lufft, printer of Wittenberg

PLATE LIX

"The Last Supper." Painted by Lucas Cranach the Younger, 1565.
To the left of Christ in the center are Prince George III of Anhalt,
Luther, Bugenhagen, Jonas, and Cruciger. At the right of Christ
are Melanchthon, Bernhardi, Pfeffinger, Forster, and Major. Judas
in the center foreground is an unknown person. Joachim, Prince
of Anhalt, kneels at front left. Cranach, the painter, is serving the
wine at front right. In the background stand Prince Wolfgang
and Johann II of Anhalt with their sons, Carl, Joachim, Ernst, and
Bernhard.

PLATE LX

*Castle of Landgrave Philip of Hesse, scene of Marburg
Colloquy, 1529.*

PLATE LXI

Ruins of the Ebernburg

The "Feste Koburg"

PLATE LXII

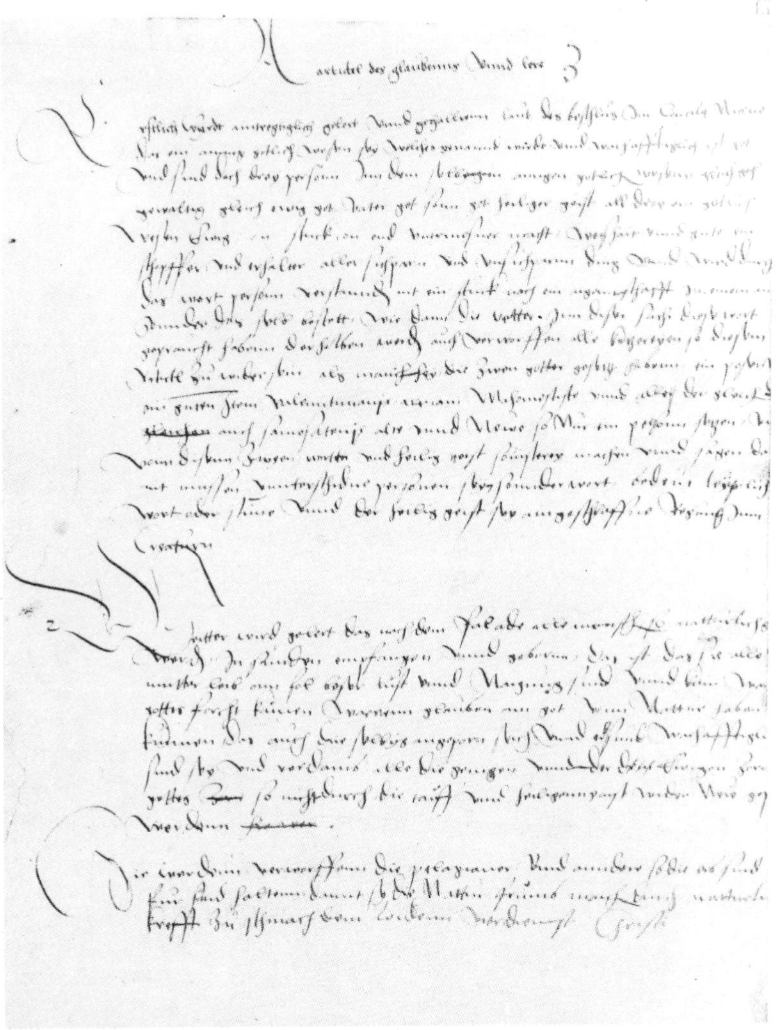

*The first page of the Scheurl copy of the Augsburg Confession.
The original, read at Augsburg and presented to Charles V,
has been lost*

PLATE LXIII

House now occupying the site of the former home of the Prince of Anhalt in which Luther died. Only the foundations of the original building remain

Room shown to tourists in which Luther is reported to have died. Original house no longer exists

PLATE LXIV

*St. Andrew's Church in Eisleben, from whose pulpit
Luther preached his last sermon. Here also a funeral
service was held*

PLATE LXV

« 16 »

In the Land of the Birds

The Wartburg

WHEN THE ELECTOR OF SAXONY saw how cleverly Aleander had maneuvered Luther's trial before the Diet of Worms and realized that it was only a matter of days before the safe-conduct would expire and Luther placed in danger of his very life, Frederick decided to take matters into his own hands. The evening before Luther's departure George Spalatin informed him that the Elector had made arrangements to take him to a safe hiding place, but that the details mut be kept a complete secret. Because of the necessity for absolute secrecy only a very few trusted agents were used in the plan.[1] Neither Luther nor the Elector knew the details. That Amsdorf knew something of what was to transpire may be gathered from a letter Luther wrote to Spalatin on May 14, in which he says:

> Amsdorf knew, of course, that I was to be captured by somebody, but does not know the place of my captivity.[2]

Hans von Berlepsch, a guard from the Wartburg, and Burkhard von Wenkheim, a worthy knight from Altenstein and custodian of the Castle, who with a few trusted assistants was to intercept Luther in the Thuringian Forest, were advised of the plan.[3] To circumvent the Emperor's herald, who would be leading the Luther party on its homeward journey, Spalatin suggested that Luther write a letter to the Emperor and the Estates which the *Reichsherold* would deliver.[4]

On the return journey the Luther party traveled over the Frankfurt-Friedberg-Gruenberg-Hersfeld-Eisenach road.[5] They ar-

513

rived in Friedberg on April 28. Here Luther wrote a Latin letter to
the Emperor and the German Estates, once more assuring them
that in all matters temporal he was more than ready to obey them,
but that in the realm which pertained to the salvation of the soul
he must obey God rather than men.[6] The following day Luther
sent Sturm back with the letter. It was to be delivered to Spalatin
first for translation into German. It is doubtful whether the Kaiser
ever saw the original communication, but the German translation
was referred to the Estates on April 30 and was printed by the
Wittenberg press a little later.[7]

From Friedberg the journey continued on April 29 to Gruen-
berg, where the group spent the night.[8] In Hersfeld the next day
the local abbot had prepared a pompous reception. Even though
warned by Luther of the dangers involved, the enthusiastic abbot
insisted that Luther preach.[9] On May 2 at Eisenach the two groups
decided to part and to travel different roads.[10] Jonas, Schurff, and
Student Peter Suaven followed the main Gotha-Erfurt-Wittenberg
road home. Luther, Amsdorf, and the monk Petzensteiner made a
slight detour to visit Moehra, where lived Luther's grandmother
and the family of his uncle Heinz. Their route lay through the
Thuringian Forest, a perfect setting for an ambush.

Luther spent the night with his relatives and preached in the
village the next morning before proceeding on the journey home.[11]
A relative supplied them with fresh horses. To return to the Gotha
highway from Moehra, they had to travel over the Schweina road
past the Castle Altenstein and through the forest of Waltershausen.
Some of the relatives accompanied the party until nearly nightfall,
by which time they had reached the neighborhood of the Castle
Altenstein. Here Luther bade his relatives good-by and continued
the journey. His friends were scarcely out of sight when four or five
armed horsemen rushed from the woods near the chapel and surrounded the helpless travelers at the spot which today is called
Lutherbuche. The monk Petzensteiner leaped from the wagon and
ran through the woods toward Waltershausen, but Luther whispered
to Amsdorf: "Do not become excited. We are among friends."[12] One
of the ruffians stopped the horses and struck the driver such a blow

that he fell under the wagon. Another demanded the identity of the travelers, and when Luther announced his name, the bully pointed the crossbow at him as though he were a criminal and demanded his surrender. Luther was then jerked from the carriage with a feigned roughness and hurried into the woods.[13] Amsdorf and the driver were allowed to continue their journey, and Amsdorf's anger, whether real or assumed, was so convincing that the driver had no suspicion of a prearranged plot.

Once out of sight in the woods, Luther was dressed as a knight, placed on a horse, and led by all manner of devious byways to the Wartburg, where he arrived completely exhausted around eleven o'clock.[14] Here again his captors roughly threw Luther into a locked cell as though he were a dangerous criminal so that the guard might not suspect his true identity. Myconius, who later heard the details of the story, wrote:

> Never has a case been reported in which a plot like this was kept so secret as to who did capture Luther and lead him away. Many people at the Diet also believed that it was a real captivity, so well was the secret kept.[15]

The outside world knew only that he had been captured by knights somewhere in the Thuringian Forest near Waltershausen and had disappeared.

There was still a chance that Luther might be recognized by some inmate or visitor to the castle. Therefore the professor and monk was transformed into the knight "Junker Joerg," whom Lucas Cranach preserved in the excellent oil painting of 1521.[16] He was confined to his room until both beard and tonsure had grown sufficiently to hide his identity. Meanwhile he was thoroughly instructed in all the forms and manners of knighthood.

THE LUTHER ROOM

Heinrich Boehmer in his *Der Junge Luther* seriously questioned the authenticity of much of the information given the general public about the *Lutherstube* in the Wartburg. His chief reason for doubting that the room now shown was the room in which Luther stayed while at the castle was the apparent discrepancies between the room shown and the quotation from Luther describing the room to his friends in Eisleben:

> As I·in the year 1521 . . . at the Castle of the Wartburg sat in my Patmos, I was far removed from people in a room, and no one could come to me except two nobles' sons who twice daily brought me something to eat and to drink. Once they brought me a sack of hazelnuts which I at times ate but the rest of the time kept locked in my chest. When I wished to retire, I undressed in my living room, put out the light, went into the little sleeping room and went to bed.[17]

Boehmer had carefully examined the modern *Lutherstube* and could find no evidence of such a bedroom connected with the living room by a door.

Herman Nebe in an article "Die Lutherstube auf der Wartburg" (Eisenach, 1929), presented further and most enlightening evidence.[18] He pointed out the remarkable changes undergone by the various parts of the castle throughout the centuries which did not leave the inner rooms unaffected. The *Vogtei,* the section in which Luther lived, was originally built on Roman foundations in Gothic style. In its present form it probably came into existence about 1480.[19] There still exists an old plan, dated 1574, on which someone has written: "Dr. Martin Luther's Room." [20] When this room was restored in the 19th century, names and dates were found on the walls as far back as 1580. It is difficult to believe that the residents of the Castle would have forgotten where their distinguished visitor stayed so few decades after his death.

Nebe's reconstruction of the part of the *Vogtei* in which Luther lived was aided by the discovery of an old "Ground Plan of the Knights' House at the Wartburg, 1817," [21] which throws much light upon the problem which Boehmer could not solve. In the plan of 1817 the difficulties are removed. The present stairway did not exist, and Luther's room was reached only by a back stairs connected with the room of the keeper "well protected with iron and chains." [22] Therefore Luther might well say that he was "far removed from people" in his "Patmos." [23] The old plan also shows a little narrow chamber running parallel to the *Lutherstube* all along the north side.[24] Another old picture shows a connecting door opening into this bedroom in the northwest corner of the room

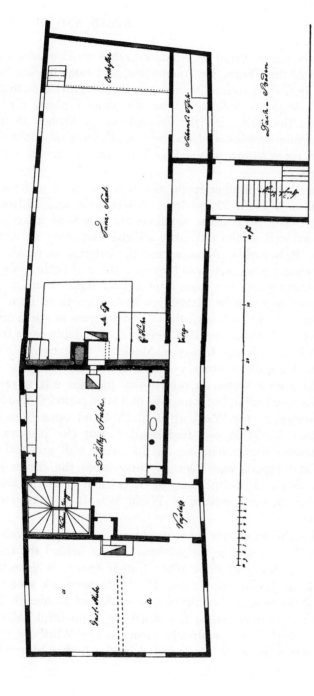

Ground plan of Knight's House at the Wartburg in 1817

next to the window. From his window Luther could overlook the rolling hills of the Thuringian countryside, and since he was high above the ground, it seemed to him like dwelling in "the land of the birds." With the evidence from the ground plans, the inscriptions on the walls, and the descriptions by Luther all supporting the same conclusion, Nebe believed there is no doubt that the present room shown in the Wartburg was the one in which Luther lived.

The size of the Luther room, although not quite uniform in its dimensions, is about 20 feet long, 15 feet wide, and 12 feet to the ceiling.[25] The worm-eaten, weatherworn boards of the ceiling and walls as well as the old floor, all give testimony of its extreme age. It is highly probable that the original materials are still in the floor, ceiling, and wall that were there in Luther's day.[26] The door leading into the room is of a later date. None of the interior furnishings can be claimed to have been there from the days of "Junker Joerg," although they probably were in use in other parts of Germany during the 16th century.[27] The table came from one of the Luther family homes in Moehra.[28] The carved chair is doubtless of the 16th century, but its origin is unknown. The old stove in the corner shown in present-day pictures was salvaged from the Wartburg ruins, but it must be of a later period.[29] The bed was not brought to the Wartburg until 1854 and came from the *Gasthof Zum Stiefel* in old Rudolstadt.[30] But the pictures of Luther's parents shown hanging on the north wall are genuine Cranachs, and experts have recently pronounced the corner pictures of Luther and Melanchthon to be original Cranachs also.[31] (The fate of all these articles in World War II is unknown to the author.)

The description of this room would not be complete without mentioning the ink spot in the northeast corner behind the stove. Its origin, like those in three other Luther towns, is uncertain. Professor J. D. Jordan relates that the Wittenberg ink spot was put there at the time of the visit of Charles XII of Sweden.[32] The claim that it later traveled to the Wartburg is doubtful. Merian in his 16-century etchings already mentions the Wartburg spot. In all likelihood the story was invented by the Luther biographer

Ratzeberger, the medical doctor who wrote toward the end of the 16th century, plentifully embellishing the Reformer's life with many stories from tradition or his own imagination.[33] Nowhere in Luther's writings, not even in the *Table Talks*, is there a reference to throwing an inkwell at the devil.[34] The place on the wall at the Wartburg has often been replastered and the spot renewed, but the spot continues to disappear as tourists testify to the tenacity and longevity of the legend.[35]

LUTHER'S LABORS AT THE WARTBURG

Luther loved the quiet peace of his mountain aerie. He enjoyed long walks through the fields and woods.[36] On one occasion he went hunting, but he does not seem to have enjoyed that diversion.

> Last week I hunted two days to see what that *bitter-sweet* pleasure of heroes was like. We took two hares and a few poor partridges — a worthy occupation indeed for men with nothing to do. I even moralized among the snares and dogs, and the superficial pleasure I may have derived from the hunt was equaled by the pity and the pain which are a necessary part of it. It is an image of the devil hunting innocent little creatures with his gins [sic] and his hounds, the impious magistrates, bishops and theologians. I deeply felt this parable of the simple and faithful soul. A still more cruel parable followed. With great pains I saved a little live rabbit, and rolled it up in the sleeve of my cloak, but when I left it and went a little way off the dogs found the poor rabbit and killed it by biting its right leg and throat through the cloth. Thus do the Pope and Satan rage to kill souls and are not stopped by my labor. I am sick of this kind of hunting, and prefer to chase bears, wolves, foxes, and that sort of wicked magistrate with spear and arrow.[37]

Like Sir Thomas More, Luther was tenderhearted and kind toward the animal world about him.

The most disturbing element in his idyllic retreat was the uncertainty and unrest among his Wittenberg supporters.[38] He tried to reassure them by an exposition of the 68th Psalm and its theme, "Let the Lord arise, and let His enemies be scattered," which may have been suggested by the Pope's theme in his bull excommunicating Luther. Luther next wrote an exposition of the 37th Psalm,[39] which breathes the assurance of one who was certain that his cause was righteous and that the Gospel would triumph. He was now sure that there was no hope for reform from Rome, which had been turned into the seat of perdition. Let its satellites rage and storm against the Gospel. As long as the little Wittenberg group held steadfast to God's Word, it might defy Louvain, Paris, Leipzig, and even Rome.

No man with the tremendous vitality of Martin Luther would rest for long without chafing at his inactivity.[40] He recalled his second series of lectures on the Psalms,[41] the unfinished *Postille*,[42] and his study of the Magnificat, which he had only begun. He requested books and materials from his friends at Wittenberg that he might resume his work. By June 10, 1521, the Magnificat was completed and the manuscript sent to Spalatin for publication.[43]

"Junker Joerg" in his knightly dress and far removed from his enemies could view the panorama of past events and his entire relationship to the Church in a much more detached light. Here he was able to think things through and to evaluate truly the prophetic mission of his life with a clarity that was essential for the leader of the budding German Reformation.[44] During the ten months at the Wartburg, all alone with his God, Luther the Reformer of later years was born. His new realization that a Reformation of the Christian Church demanded a complete break with the outward Roman Church caused him reluctantly to accept the role of leader in building anew on the foundations which he had been rediscovering ever since he had accepted the professorship in the theological faculty of the University of Wittenberg nearly a decade before.

He must also have realized that he would become the target of even more bitter calumny and recriminations. The pens of his enemies were flying feverishly. The first of these attacks came from the University of Louvain. As observed in connection with the Leipzig Debate, this university had condemned 41 articles in Luther's writings in 1520, which had served as the basis for the papal bull *Exsurge, Domine*.[45] Luther had replied to this condemnation, and one of the Louvain professors, Latomus, now felt obliged to defend his university.[46] In a tract which sought to justify the action of the university Latomus criticized bitterly

Luther's whole attack on the Roman *Curia* and in his defense placed the Pope even above Jesus Christ. As always, Luther would not permit any besmirching of his Lord and rose to the challenge. In strong and forceful language he excoriated the man who had belittled his Christ just to elevate the Pope and to defend the graft and greedy fiscal practices of the Roman *Curia*.

Now, too, the Paris verdict, released, as has been noted, on the day Luther entered Worms and condemning 104 errors in Luther's writings, reached Luther at the Wartburg. Luther was much pleased with the clever *Apology* of Melanchthon and decided to prepare a reply himself.[47] He translated the Paris verdict into German, introducing it with a preface and an epilogue.[48] With ironic humor he poked fun at the unbelievable arrogance of a faculty that simply labeled his articles as "false, foolish, sacrilegious, unchristian, presumptuous, erroneous, heretical," without citing a single reason. The modern reader of the Paris verdict will readily note the attitude of the Paris faculty, frequently encountered in modern academic circles, of expecting others to accept their pronouncements solely because they had spoken. In theological depth they were certainly no match for the new progressive Wittenberg faculty.

These first few months also brought forth a reply to Ambrosius Catharinus,[49] another defender of the papal system, whose article had been especially directed against Luther's *Resolution Concerning the Power of the Pope* of 1519. On the basis of Daniel 8 [50] Luther tried to show that the Pope was really the Antichrist of the Scriptures. In the customary Maundy Thursday ceremony in Rome the Pope publicly named those who had been banned during the year. Luther translated the Pope's address into German and, in typical Hutten fashion, prepared copious marginal notes for the people. This document was given to Melchior Lotther for printing with a dedicatory letter to the Pope and an exposition of the 10th Psalm, which Luther felt pictured the Pope in his true light.

Fortunately, Luther did not spend all of his time in argument and discussion. For some time he had felt that the subject of auricular confession was a cause of much confusion. He believed

the confession as demanded by Rome was a perversion not supported by Holy Writ and a means for the enslavement of the
individual's private life.[51] Through this practice the priests, bishops,
etc., had obtained a talon-grip on the people's conscience which
gave them power to practice religious blackmail. The confession
had become a rite of dead formalism, a routine through which
every Roman Catholic in good standing was required to pass.
The decisions of the Fourth Lateran Council made general confession obligatory at least once a year.[52] In a tract which appeared
in September, *Concerning Confession, Whether the Pope Has
Power to Order It*,[53] Luther had severely criticized the whole
foundations upon which penance was built. Now he pointed out
with the clarity so pronounced in his later writings and so devastating to his enemies that a general council can create no new
doctrines.[54] Its only function must be to elucidate truth on the
basis of the revealed Word; but as soon as it permitted human
rationalization, as so many of the councils had done, its authority
was only human. Never could human reasoning be used as an
argument from Christ and the Apostles. Furthermore, the Scripture cited must be germane both as to content and meaning to
the problem in question. Real repentance, then, could not be
forced, but rather must become the fruit of the true Gospel; it must
be voluntary, genuine, and entirely devoid of human regulation.[55]
True repentance can be found only at the foot of the Cross, and
he who confesses to Christ in true contrition in his chamber is
more worthy in the sight of God than he who performs the dead
formalism of confessing his sins to a priest. With Luther the emphasis was always upon the inner attitude of heart known only
to God and to the repentant sinner.

The renewed indulgence traffic of Albert of Mainz brought
another blast from Luther's pen. When this worldly ecclesiastical
prince learned of Luther's disappearance, it occurred to him that
now was the time to replenish his empty treasury by reviving the
indulgence sales in Halle, where many relics were also collected
similar to those in the Castle Church in Wittenberg. Luther first
intended to write a tract against Albert, but this was discouraged
by the Saxon court.[56] On December 1, 1521, he wrote to Albert

personally and severely criticized him for having "again erected at Halle that idol which robs poor simple Christians of their money and their souls." [57] He recalled that he had formerly thought that the Tetzel affair had been carried on without the Archbishop's knowledge but that he was now convinced that "your ignorance is willful, as long as the things ignored bring you money." He added the further warning:

> And let not your Grace think Luther is dead. He will gladly and joyfully put his trust in God and will start such a game with the Cardinal of Mayence as few people expect. Get together, dear Bishops; you may be fighting men, but you will not put this Spirit to silence or deafen Him. If you unexpectedly become a laughing-stock, remember that I have warned you.[58]

Luther ended by pointing out that if his Grace did not answer within a fortnight, he would publish his tract *Against the Idol of Halle*.[59] Nor would the withholding of his letter from the Archbishop by his secretaries excuse him. The tract would appear just the same. Albert was duly impressed by the warnings from the mighty knight of the Wartburg. In a letter of December 21, 1521, he replied:

> My dear Doctor. I have received your letter, and I take it in good part and graciously, and will see to it that the thing that so moves you be done away, and I will act, God willing, as becomes a pious, spiritual and Christian prince, as far as God gives me grace and strength, for which I earnestly pray and have prayers said for me, for I can do nothing of myself and know well that without God's grace there is no good in me, but that I am as much foul mud as any other, if not more. I do not wish to conceal this, for I am more than willing to show you grace and favor for Christ's sake, and I can well bear fraternal and Christian punishment. I hope the merciful, kind God will give me herein more grace, strength and patience to live in this matter and in others according to His will.[60]

In the light of the complete picture such an "abject capitulation" on the part of Albert seems forced and insincere. Luther also received it with considerable reservation, for he knew that Capito, Albert's secretary, had visited Melanchthon in the hope of quieting the angry Luther.[61] Capito had also sent a conciliatory note with Albert's reply which, when combined with the Wittenberg visit, made Luther all the more suspicious. The Electoral court had also tried to silence Luther for political reasons. Luther could not bear to see human expediency placed above true religion. Hypocrisy and insincerity he loathed with all his soul. But the tract *Against the Idol of Halle* was never published.[62]

While Luther was at the Wartburg, another problem developed within the Wittenberg faculty. Carlstadt, who was not a very profound theologian nor too well-balanced as an individual, had even anticipated Luther with proposed reforms.[63] On June 21, 1521, he proposed an academic disputation on celibacy. By his own exegesis he claimed on the basis of 1 Timothy 3:2 that all priests should be married men and that those who were then living with concubines should be forced to marry. On the basis of 1 Timothy 5:9 Carlstadt further declared that young persons below the age of sixty should not enter a monastery, while monks and nuns below sixty were to be given freedom to live in wedlock together in the monastery.[64]

Luther was both shocked and disturbed by these proposals, for he had not yet given any thought to what were to him the minor problems of celibacy and monastic vows.[65] He no longer believed that celibacy of the priests was based on Scriptural teaching, but felt that Paul had permitted Christians to exercise liberty in this regard.[66] He was not yet ready to grant that a monk who had taken his vows in good faith could reject them at will. Nor did he accept Melanchthon's arguments against the monastic vows on the basis of human weakness and inability to keep them.[67]

The discussions set Luther to thinking, and he began to search the Scriptures for light on this pressing question. On September 9, 1521, he sent the faculty a set of theses entitled *Themata de votis,* or Topics Concerning Vows.[68] Beginning with the basic assumption that jusification comes only by faith in Christ Jesus, Luther drew the conclusion that the determinative factor in monasticism was the spirit in which it was performed.[69] If the Gospel were to be displaced by a life of work-righteousness, then the purpose was wrong. If, however, a monk took his vows in the spirit of St. Bernard, trusting solely in Christ's merits, monasticism was not wrong. As for the vow itself, claimed Luther, in a second communication, that should not be perpetual and binding.[70] Christian liberty should permit both the taking and the revoking of such a vow.

When the first series of theses reached Wittenberg, Peter Suaven, Melanchthon, and Bugenhagen were dining together.[71] After reading them carefully, Bugenhagen expressed the belief that they would effect a revolution in monasticism, and Melanchthon agreed that they would result in the liberation of the monks.[72] By early October both sets were in print and provided the foundation for Luther's famous study of November 21, 1521, *De votis monasticis,* or *On Monastic Vows,* which he dedicated in a special, touching letter to his aged father.[73] By this time he had clarified his thinking on monasticism and believed the practice only stifled true Christian liberty. He told his father that Christ had absolved him from his monastic vows, by which he meant that for Christ's redeemed such a vow was no longer essential.

There have been those who questioned Luther's reasons for writing *On Monastic Vows,* ascribing to him even such base motives as his inability to control his emotions. Only a consuming desire to discredit the man and a complete disregard for historical evidence could deduce such a claim. Luther had not at this time, nor for several years following, any thought of marriage for himself.[74] He realized, however, that there were those who were really vexed by the problem. Now he felt obliged to focus the clear light of God's Word on the question which had been so perverted through human reason. In this tract, which he regarded as one of the best-substantiated of any he had written, Luther made it quite evident that the monastic ideal was directly opposed to justification by faith.[75] Monks who sought to save their souls through their own good works really denied Christ's promises through Baptism.[76] Basically, such action implied that Christ's crucifixion and death were not sufficient. Luther pointed out that a life lived in the world could be more holy than that of monastic seclusion, for in reality monasticism was a perversion of the Gospel and God's grace.[77] Although formerly Luther had made a distinction between the regular and the secular clergy, he now rejected all such differences. He also criticized the triple vow of poverty, obedience, and chastity as not being drawn from the Scriptures.

This mighty attack on the whole monastic system and its potential far-reaching effects frightened the Elector and other members of the court.[78] Spalatin tried to delay its publication, but yielded to Luther, and it appeared in February, 1522. In its doctrinal progress this new tract could take its place beside Romans or the major tracts of 1520. It was a veritable bombshell in the camp of the enemy.[79] Luther was not alone in challenging the problem of monasticism, which had been awaiting a solution for some time. The Reuchlin struggle and *The Letters of Obscure Men,* satirizing the whole system, had drawn public attention to the many absurdities in monastic practices. Now Luther had made it clear that monasticism and its vows were not essential nor necessarily helpful in achieving Christian piety, but might rather directly undermine and obscure true religion.

Luther had not specifically stated that monks and nuns must leave the monasteries; he had left the question to individual choice. Those who wished to remain in the cloisters should be permitted to do so and should be provided for through life. And those who wished to leave their seclusion to take up new lives in the world should be permitted to do so without prejudice.[80] Luther recommended that the abandoned monasteries be closed or converted to other uses, such as hospitals, and that others be consolidated. Under the leadership of the monk Zwilling the Augustinians of the Black Cloister in Wittenberg had renounced their vows and had become rather destructive in their enjoyment of their new freedom.[81] In this case, Luther, as in all others, deplored their lack of self-discipline and censured their excesses. Luther's hope for an orderly solution of the problem is well expressed in a communication which he sent to the Vicar of the German Congregation of the Augustinians, Wenceslaus Link:

> Certain I am that you will not do or suffer anything to be done against the Gospel even if all monasteries are to go under. I do not think you can prevent the departure of those who wish to go, and the best plan to adopt at the forthcoming Chapter is, following the example of Cyrus in the case of the Jews, to issue a public declaration granting liberty to go or stay, expelling no one and retaining no one by force.[82]

The Translation of the New Testament

Luther's translation of the Bible into German has been regarded by many as the greatest of his contributions to the German people and to Christendom; yet his opponents have tried hard to prove that the work was not original.[83] A large accumulation of literature has been written and much detailed research devoted to minute comparisons of his translation with those of its fourteen high German predecessors dating from 1462 to his day.[84] But the more careful the research, the more Luther's true greatness has emerged through the detailed studies of Walther, Pietsch, Thulin, Freitag, and the Hans Vollmer students.[85]

Three schools of thought have arisen over this question of Luther's originality. (1) One has claimed that the Luther translation was an independent undertaking and constituted a complete break from all previous translations.[86] (2) Another holds that the Luther translation was but the utilization of the vast body of materials, usages, and arrangement previously developed by Catholic scholars.[87] (3) The third and most widely accepted concept is that there was a large accumulation of materials at Luther's disposal of which he made good use; yet, his gift of languages and his fine memory for little distinctions in diction developed an entirely new synthesis, original, poetical, and expressive of the "New Theology." [88]

Luther was a great master of the German language. Melanchthon once wrote:

> Bugenhagen is a grammarian, I am a dialectician, Jonas is an orator; but Luther is all in one; no one can be compared with him.[89]

Erasmus Alber observed:

> Our Lord also illumined the German language through Doctor Martin, so that, as long as the world has stood, no human has written or spoken the German language as well as he.[90]

The German poet Klopstock said of him:

> No one who knows the nature of a language dares to appear in the presence of Luther without reverence. Among no people has one man done so much to help create their language.[91]

Other eminent Germans, including Goethe, Grimm, Wagner, and Treitschke, have added their corroboration to this appreciation of Luther's command of the German language.

Just when Luther realized that he should translate the Bible into German is impossible to establish.[92] He was hardly ready for the task before his stay at the Wartburg. A letter to John Lang of December 18, 1521, shows that he had by then decided to use his leisure time to complete the above-mentioned unfinished works and to translate the New Testament:

> I will remain hidden here until Easter. In the meantime I intend to prepare the *Postils* and translate the New Testament into the language of the people. Our friends demand it. I hear that you are engaged in the same task. Continue as you have begun. Oh, that every single city had its own translator and that this Book were translated into all languages, by hands, eyes, ears, and hearts! [93]

He had been engaged in some translations at Wittenberg. He had begun with the seven Penitential Psalms in 1517, followed by a translation of the Lord's Prayer, and of the 110th Psalm in 1518 and the 37th, 68th, and 118th Psalms and the Magnificat in 1521.[94]

As observed in connection with Luther's earlier development, he did not know much Greek before 1514 and practically no Hebrew. Under the guidance of Lang and Melanchthon he had made considerable progress in Greek, but in Hebrew he still felt inadequate, for he wrote to Amsdorf in January, 1522: "I will not be able to touch the Old Testament without your presence and assistance." [95] He considered returning to Wittenberg secretly to live in the neighborhood of the faculty to have the expert advice of Melanchthon and other linguists.[96] In fact, only Melanchthon's encouragement and promise to help with the finished product decided Luther on the undertaking.

The Italian Renaissance, and more specifically Humanism, had paved the way for Luther's translation of the Bible. Although primarily a theologian little interested in the secular aspects of life, Luther was a child of the Renaissance.[97] This whole struggle with Rome manifested the individualistic spirit so characteristic of that age. His insistence on sound reasoning, sound scholarship, and proof on the basis of evidence exemplified the spirit of the

Italian Renaissance. Unconsciously perhaps, Luther voiced the spirit of the age. And the Renaissance supplied the foundation for his work. The Biblical Humanists Erasmus and Reuchlin had furnished the tools with which the Reformers, Luther, Zwingli, and Calvin, were to do their work. Erasmus had provided a Greek text which could serve as the basis for Luther's translation.[98] Using ten manuscripts dating as far back as the 10th century, he prepared a restored Greek edition in 1516 and a revised and improved edition in 1519, incorporating four additional manuscripts. Although no older than the tenth century, Dr. Hort has pointed out that many of these manuscripts were copied from an original even antedating the oldest manuscripts extant today.[99] There has been debate as to whether Luther actually used the 1519 edition, the best available in that day, but the detailed study of Freitag in the Weimar publication of *Die Deutsche Bibel*, VII, has removed all doubt.[100]

What Erasmus had done for the Greek translation, Reuchlin duplicated in Hebrew. His lexicon, *Rudimenta linguae Hebraicae* of 1506, was extremely useful for a translation of certain passages in the New Testament quoted from the Hebrew original.[101] Alexander's *Lexicon Graeco-Latinum* of 1512 was also used by Luther, and he may even have had the recent Basel edition of 1519, *Dictionarium Graecum*.[102] There were also Latin-German dictionaries, Zainer's *plenarium*, Lyra's *Postilla in Biblia*, all of which were useful for the translator.[103] Those who claim that Luther followed only a single work in his translation are not in accord with the most recent conclusions. Amazing as it may seem, Luther completed the work of translation in the original draft in exactly eleven weeks.[104] Granting his phenomenal grasp of the Scriptures, the accomplishment once more demonstrated the unbelievable speed with which he worked. Even his friends were astounded.[105] And Luther was an exacting taskmaster.

The actual task of printing the *September Bibel*, as it later came to be known, was assigned to Melchior Lotther. By July three presses were in operation. The exact date of the completion of the printing is unknown, but a letter from Luther to Freiherr von Schwarzenberg of September 21, 1522, indicates that it was

Vuittemberg.

1

2

Title page of the September New Testament, 1522

completed by that date.[106] The book was of folio size of 222 pages. The title page consisted of a simple woodcut with neither the name of the translator nor the date given, but the place of publication was *Vuittemberg*.[107] Quite a detailed introduction was included in order to prepare the reader for an understanding of the "New Theology." The book was adorned with beautifully illuminated initial letters, pictures of the Evangelists, and twenty-one woodcuts embellishing the Apocalypse of a style which seems indicative of the Cranach studio.

The book, *Das Newe Testament Deutzsch,* sold in huge numbers. Erich Zimmermann estimates that a total of 5,000 copies was sold in two months. The price is difficult to evaluate. One entry states: "I bought the New Testament for 1 gulden," while another person mentions paying two gulden for four copies. Since Germany had many different types of gulden, it seems reasonable to estimate that the book sold for ten or fifteen dollars in modern values. The first printing was followed by numerous reprints. Zimmermann says:

> Until the year 1534 eighty-seven High German and nineteen Low German editions of the New Testament appeared, twenty-four in 1524 alone. If one takes an average of 2,000 copies per edition, then it follows that in the twelve years between 1522 and 1534, over 200,000 New Testaments were disseminated among the German people.[108]

PART FIVE

The Years of Fruition

« 17 »

Problems in the Early Growth
of Lutheranism

The Wittenberg Disturbances

BEFORE WORMS, "Lutheranism" cannot be said to have existed in the German lands. As has been shown, Luther himself had far from crystallized his thinking and could not, therefore, be called a "Lutheran." [1] His enormous following at Worms and elsewhere was largely motivated by political, economic, and other human considerations. While doubtless many agreed upon the necessity for correcting the existing abuses in the practices of the Roman Church, the organization of a new Church was far from their thoughts. Luther expressed the same idea when he wrote to his followers from the Wartburg that they should not call themselves "Lutherans." Who was Luther that they should name themselves after him? St. Paul's followers did not call themselves "Paulinians." [2] They were simply Christians.

But Martin Luther had written too many tracts, sermons, and commentaries for his influence to be quickly or easily forgotten. *The Address to the German Nobility, The Babylonian Captivity of the Church* and *The Freedom of the Christian* had awakened in the layman an entirely new conception of his obligations with reference to the existing order. As members of the "priesthood of believers," princes, nobles, and simple laymen could not sit idly by while Christendom was held in bondage. As priests before God they were required to act to correct the abuses. Nor did the fact that Martin Luther had been condemned at Worms remove his impact upon the public mind. His banishment from the scene of action merely roused others to carry on the struggle. The up-

535

risings among the Erfurt students upon receiving the news of the Edict of Worms indicated what the future might have in store.[3]

As is often the case, the new movement suffered from the over-enthusiasm of its followers who substituted vigorous action for their lack of understanding and levelheaded thinking. The men who now felt in duty bound to carry on the struggle in Luther's absence were not very clear on either Luther's objectives or the methods which as Christians they might employ. The result was a radicalism and mob rule, which often result from impulsive action not based on clear thinking.

As has been noted, Carlstadt considered himself the interpreter and champion of the new Gospel movement.[4] Through disputations, sermons, and the press he aroused the laity of Wittenberg. Carlstadt's sincerity was unquestionable, and much of his preaching was in accord with the new movement, but he tried to introduce too drastic changes too rapidly.[5] To a people still steeped in Catholic forms and doctrines he made such statements as: "Who partakes only of the bread, sins"; "Organs belong only to theatrical exhibitions and princes' palaces"; "Images in churches are wrong"; "Painted idols standing on altars are even more harmful and devilish." [6] All of these pronouncements he sought to prove by citations based largely on the Old Testament.

Another disciple who almost outdid Carlstadt in fiery zeal was the afore-mentioned monk Zwilling, whose enthusiasm for the cause earned for him the title of "the second Luther" from the citizens of Wittenberg.[7] He proclaimed that no one should henceforth attend Masses, for they were an atrocious sin against the divine Majesty. As was to be expected, Carlstadt, Zwilling, and their cohorts joined forces to put their words into action. On January 6 the Augustinians had held their Chapter in Wittenberg and decreed that those who wished to leave the monastery might do so.[8] Five days later, under Zwilling's leadership, the monks destroyed the side altars of the old convent church, in which Luther had preached his first sermon and burned the oil used for the Extreme Unction. All images were burned in their fanatical zeal. The Town Council feared similar unrestrained action at the Town Church under their control and in a joint meeting with the University passed A Worthy Ordinance for the Princely City of Wittenberg.[9] In this ordinance

Illustration from Chapter Six of Revelation in the September Bible

a day was set upon which the images would be removed from the Town Church. But Carlstadt and the clamoring mob could not be restrained. They visited the church, despoiling gravestones and destroying images inside and out. Marks of their vandalism can still be seen on the old structure.[10]

The Castle Church was under the direct control of the Elector, but Carlstadt was Archdeacon. The Elector was already much disturbed by the service which Carlstadt had conducted on Christmas Eve, when he had officiated in the Holy Eucharist without Mass vestments and had encouraged the laity to help themselves to the bread and the wine directly from the altar.[11] After this service there had occurred further demonstrations at both the Castle and Town Churches.

The situation was given added impetus with the arrival in town late in December, 1521, of a group often referred to as the Zwickau prophets. Zwickau had been a hotbed of religious revolt since twenty-seven Waldensians were tried there in 1462.[12] Most of the group arriving in Wittenberg were simple peasants or artisans; but one Markus Stuebner, a former Wittenberg student, had become quite well versed in the Scriptures and claimed to have held "familiar conversations with God." [13] Even Melanchthon was confused by his bold claims and apparent learning and longed for Luther's advice and guidance. He was convinced that in the "prophets" there were "certain spirits," but he could not tell whether they were of God or of the devil. Felix Ulscenius evaluated the situation in a letter to Capito in Mainz:

> There has come to us a certain man with a great deal of the Spirit and so exceedingly well versed in Holy Scripture that even Melanchthon cannot satisfy him. He adduces such weighty passages of Scripture that he has got the Wittenbergers badly frightened. Melanchthon has written the Elector to have Luther sent hither, or else to let this man go to Luther. You would find him a man otherwise very simple. Melanchthon continually clings to his side, listens to him, wonders at him and venerates him. He is deeply disturbed at not being able to satisfy that man in any way.[14]

When Luther in his mountain retreat first heard vague rumors of the activities of Carlstadt in Wittenberg, he was well pleased that the struggle was being furthered actively. He wrote to Spalatin

Illustration from Chapter Thirteen of Revelation in the September Bible

in September, 1521: "I am glad that Wittenberg is flourishing, and especially that it is flourishing when I am away." [15] Luther had expressed ideas similar to those of Carlstadt in his *On Monastic Vows* and *Concerning the Abrogation of the Private Mass.* But continued reports of disturbances in Wittenberg were partly responsible for Luther's secret visit there in December. [16] Even on the journey he noted a restlessness among the people. In Thuringia it bordered close on open rebellion. He was more disturbed by this fact than by what he actually encountered in Wittenberg, where matters had not yet reached their later excesses. Later in December he wrote *A Faithful Exhortation for all Christians to Shun Riot and Rebellion,* [17] whose theme was that Christians must never resort to force, but allow the Word to prepare the hearts of men for the true faith, being ever mindful of the weak in faith lest they be offended.

Even after the unrestrained acts of the followers of Carlstadt, the Elector was unwilling to risk Luther's return to the town. [18] Not even Melanchthon's plea that Luther see Stuebner fully convinced the Elector of the advisability of Luther leaving his protective custody. [19] But when Luther learned of the course events were taking and that even Melanchthon was confused and bewildered by the *Bilderstuermer,* as these fanatics were sometimes called, he decided to go to Wittenberg at once regardless of the danger. [20]

In the famous letter written from Borna on March 5, 1521, Luther informed the Elector that he would have gone even to Leipzig had duty called him even though it had "rained Duke Georges nine days and every duke nine times as furious as this one." He made it quite clear that he did not expect the Elector to protect him:

> I am going to Wittenberg under a far higher protection than that of the Elector. I do not intend to ask your Grace's protection. . . .
> If I thought your Grace could and would defend me by force, I should not come. The sword ought not and cannot decide a matter of this kind. God alone must rule it without human care and co-operation. [21]

In explaining to his Elector why he felt he must make the journey, Luther revealed his acceptance of the role he was to play in the forthcoming Reformation.

Your Grace knows (or, if you do not, I now inform you of the fact) that I have received my Gospel not from men but from Heaven only, by our Lord Jesus Christ, so that I might well be able to boast and call myself a minister and evangelist, as I shall do in the future.[22]

On Friday, March 6, 1522, Luther arrived in Wittenberg as a *Junker*, wearing a sword, and accompanied by several knights.[23] The following Sunday he ascended the pulpit of the Town Church to begin a series of eight sermons which continued through the following week.[24] One can well imagine the tense excitement of his audience. Here was the man who had boldly defied the Pope and the Emperor, the condemned outlaw, now returned to further champion his faith and lead his people. In the sermon series he treated many of the problems which were confounding his followers. Again he emphasized that the Christian cannot resort to force, that the Word alone must accomplish the needed reforms. He cited the position of Paul in Athens among heathen altars, temples, and idols, wherein he pleaded with the people to forsake them but did not advocate their destruction by force. Citing his own experiences Luther said:

> I will preach it, teach it, write it, but I will constrain no man by force, for faith must come freely without compulsion. . . . I have opposed the indulgences and all the papists, but never by force. I simply taught, preached, wrote God's Word; otherwise I did nothing . . . the Word did it all. Had I desired to foment trouble, I could have brought great bloodshed upon Germany. Yea, I could have started such a little game at Worms that even the Emperor would not have been safe. But what would it have been? A fool's play. I did nothing; I left it to the Word.[25]

Luther defined the fundamentals of religion, faith, love, and other basic doctrines as a matter of revelation and absolutely essential. But he pointed out that religion had also many *adiaphora* concerning which man is allowed free choice.[26] Marriage, burial, monastic vows, liturgical forms, language are all in this category. The same applied to the presence of images which do not affect all people alike. If they are regarded as mere symbols, their presence is not wrong. Their destruction accomplishes nothing; it is the spirit which matters. Some worship the sun, the moon, and the stars; still we do not tear them from the heavens. Luther treated the Sacrament of the Holy Eucharist, and while granting it was not wrong to give the bread and the wine into the hands of the laity, he urged moderation and restraint.[27] Nor should such changes be made compulsory. The important attribute in the Lord's Supper was the proper spiritual preparation and attitude for its reception. Furthermore, if the Eucharist were properly given and received, love would naturally flow from its reception, of which result he had noticed little evidence in Wittenberg so far.[28]

The effect of Luther's preaching upon the troubled Wittenberg scene may be gathered from a communication which Professor Jerome Schurff wrote to the Elector:

> I humbly wish your Grace to know that there is great gladness and rejoicing here, both among the learned and the unlearned, over Doctor Martin's return and over the sermons with which, by God's help, he is daily pointing us poor deluded men back again to the way of truth, showing us incontrovertibly the pitiful errors into which we have been led by the preachers who forced their way among us. It is plain as day that the Spirit of God is in him and works through him, and I have no doubt that it is by the special providence of the Almighty that he has come to Wittenberg just at this time. Even Gabriel (Zwilling) has confessed that he has erred and gone too far.[29]

Albert Burer, a student who also heard these sermons, wrote his impression to Beatus Rhenanus in Switzerland as follows:

> On March 6 Martin Luther returned to Wittenberg in equestrian habit, accompanied by several horsemen. He came to settle the trouble stirred up by the extremely violent sermons of Carlstadt and Zwilling. For they had no regard for weak consciences, whom Luther, no less than Paul, would feed on milk until they grew strong. He preaches daily on the Ten Commandments. As far as one can tell from his face the man is kind, gentle and cheerful. His voice is sweet and sonorous, so that I wonder at the sweet speaking of the man. Whatever he does, teaches and says is most pious, even though his impious enemies say the opposite. Everyone, even though not Saxon, who hears him once, desires to hear him again and again, such tenacious hooks does he fix in the minds of his auditors.[30]

But Carlstadt remained "unreconstructed." He left Wittenberg, as did the Zwickau prophets, and all was once more tranquil in the little city.[31] Luther continued to stress toleration and patience. His eight sermons appeared in summary in April, 1522, under the title *On Partaking the Sacrament in Both Forms.*[32] Luther also went on a preaching tour, visiting Borna, Altenburg, Zwickau, Eilenburg, and Torgau.[33] In Altenburg Luther encountered his first opposition when he proposed Zwilling, now quite a changed man, for the post of preacher of the local parish church.[34] The "old guard" provost and canons insisted upon their right to appointment rather than the town council. Luther appealed to the Elector, claiming that the town council was right in opposing the conservative enemies of the Gospel. Luther even requested the Elector to use his power as a Christian prince throughout his dominions to see that the Gospel flourished. The Catholic-minded clergy objected, but the Elector agreed with Luther that he should take the matter in hand. Still Frederick was dubious about Zwilling and requested Wenceslaus Link to fill the Altenburg pulpit.[35] Link resigned his position as the Vicar General of the Augustinians and accepted the new post.

The next test of Luther's policy of tolerance and forbearance came in Erfurt, where he had gone to school and entered the Augustinian Order. Bitter strife had broken out between the followers of John Lang and those of Usingen.[36] By aggressive preaching and rather tactless remarks Lang and his supporters had aroused the citizens. Luther again remonstrated with those monks who were carrying their new freedom to excess and wrote a letter on July 10, 1522, entitled *Epistle to the Church of Erfurt,*[37] in which he discussed the burning issue of the "intercession of saints" and pleaded for moderation and tolerance, but his plea had little effect on the situation. Finally, in spite of his personal danger, Luther decided to visit Erfurt in the hope of reconciling the opposing groups.[38] In the company of Melanchthon and Agricola, Luther arrived there on October 20 and was greeted with enthusiastic acclaim. He tried to resolve the differences by several evangelical sermons, but Usingen still wrangled and refused to be reconciled.[39]

Even more embarrassing to Luther and his policy of patient tolerance and reliance on the Gospel was the situation existing in the local Castle Church. This *Stift* had become heavily endowed

as successive Electors had added to its incomes since its founding.
Here Frederick the Wise also housed more than 18,000 relics, and
the elderly, conservative, Catholic element among its canons still
preserved the old forms, singing Masses for the dead, and defending the old order.[40] It was further well known that their private
morals would not bear too close scrutiny. By the end of the year,
Luther's patience with these supporters of Rome in the very center
of the new Gospel movement was about exhausted. The aging
Elector was loath to part with this rich treasure house and was
made further hesitant by the two Diets of Nuernberg in 1522 and
1524.[41] Luther became increasingly irritated by the dilatory tactics
of the Elector and was becoming almost as aggressive as Carlstadt in his demands that this "idolatry" be suppressed.[42] Jonas, as
provost of the *Stift*, rendered considerable aid, but even after the
opposition had dwindled to a mere handful, the Elector sought to
retain the *status quo* by reminding Luther of his former policy of
winning the opposition through the Gospel alone.[43] Luther granted
that the former principle still applied, but he had begun to realize
that not all men can be converted and won to the faith. There
were obstinate Catholics who refused even to listen to his preaching.
On November 27, 1524, Luther preached an aggressive sermon
against the Silent Mass, appealing to the princes to use their
authority to put aside this evil.[44] Faced by the town council, the
University, and the majority of the citizens all supporting Luther,
the dean of the Castle Church finally acquiesced. On December 2,
1524, Luther wrote to Amsdorf in Magdeburg: "We have at last
compelled the canons to agree to abolish the Mass." [45]

Confusion and Consternation

The intense longing of the German people for the Gospel led
them to rush headlong into the interpretation and use of the Bible
before their new leaders had time to clarify its meaning. Luther
was soon beset with further problems. For a number of years he
had preached a return to the Bible; but before his own thinking
had become crystallized on the many aspects of the problem, his
self-styled followers began their own interpretations. Now they
charged Luther with failure to go far enough in his restoration of

the customs and institutions of the early Christian Church. Many of them insisted that they were more Biblical in their views than he. What was he to answer to such simple folk who thoroughly believed that they were more in harmony with Christ's teachings than their leader? Carlstadt, for instance, had gathered quite a following in Orlamuende which drew its inspiration and framework largely from the Old Testament. Before the stream of the pure Gospel could become established in its new bed, it was being hindered and obstructed by eddies and whirlpools made by the hands of men. Numerous pressing questions had to be solved. What was the relationship between the Old and New Testaments and of both to the Christian? What was the importance of the Sermon on the Mount? Should all of the *adiaphora* of the early Church be preserved along with its doctrines, including habits of dress, eating, drinking, etc.?

Luther gave long hours of thought to these troublesome questions. When he had finally thought them through, he concluded that the Old Testament had ceased to exist as a pattern of life for the Christian. Its laws and precepts had been satisfied by Christ's atonement, and thereafter the New Testament became the guide to Christian conduct. Nor did Luther believe that all of the social institutions, customs, and practices of the New Testament times were applicable to peoples of other ages and environments. Again and again his thinking brought Luther to the realization that the heart of the Gospel was the spiritual message, and the important object of its application was the heart of the believer. The Gospel has power to work a miracle in the heart of sinful man, causing him to be as one reborn. If the Gospel was admitted to his heart and he was actually reborn, his every act flowed from love of Christ as transformed into love of his fellow man. All other outward forms and practices were essential only if they enhanced the preaching of the Gospel. Unless they actually obstructed the Gospel message, they need not be rejected. The Sermon on the Mount became for Luther the ideal pattern for the Christian, the exemplification of the soul truly reborn and transformed through justification by faith. In all other non-essentials the Christian was given freedom of choice, but in the reborn man that choice would be governed by his desire to do good and not to give offense to his fellow man. Always man must be led through love and persuasion along the right path and never compelled or coerced. Essentially, then, Luther's religion was conservative, which explains why men like Sickingen and some of the more impulsive princes were disappointed in Luther's leadership. This difference also explains in part the basic misunderstanding between him and the masses during the Peasants' Revolt. The *forcible* overthrow of the Feudal System and its existing tyranny was not possible within the framework of Luther's conception of religion.

In recent years considerable investigation has been made regarding the religious and social teachings of the radical groups which Luther described as the "*Schwaermer.*" [46] These studies reveal that many of them were laymen, simple uneducated folk, and that Luther judged them superficially and unfairly. There were wide variances of interpretation and action among the various groups. Carlstadt and Thomas Muenzer may be said to have represented the two extreme wings of radicalism, but there were dozens of other leaders, among them Schappler, Wehe, Hubmaier, Waibel, Storch, each with his following. [47] Each group presented its own peculiar problem to the Wittenberg theologians, and their solution is reflected in the many *Gutachten* prepared for the Elector of Saxony and other princes. [48]

Thomas Muenzer was the leader of the extreme left wing of those religious fanatics who thought it their duty to inaugurate the Kingdom of God by force and social revolution rather than waiting for the tedious process of conversion. This revolution, if need be, was to be "blood red," and he believed himself to be the divinely commissioned emissary of the Holy Spirit to inaugurate such a social transformation. [49] Muenzer was a university-trained man who had studied at both Leipzig and Frankfurt an der Oder. He was a sincere, if misguided, seeker after truth. [50] Both Muenzer and Carlstadt had been influenced by German mysticism. [51] Muenzer and his followers claimed that their religion was based on direct revelation from God like that of the prophets of the Old Testament. [52] They said that God was constantly talking to them and revealing their path both in teaching and in action. Luther they rejected in favor of this new authority. Muenzer dreamed of a communistic society in which all class distinctions were removed and all property owned communally.[53] This new order was to be maintained for the "Elect of God" by the merciless expulsion of unbelievers. Muenzer's religion also contained a note of asceticism, a denial of the world, which formed a part of the individual's growth in Christ, whose Passion formed an example of "perfect composure." [54] His following was composed of laymen who likewise claimed enlightenment by the inner light through visions, dreams, and other revelations.

Muenzer had met Luther at the Leipzig Debate and had become a minister in Zwickau through Luther's influence.[55] Here he began to manifest his radical tendencies and was forced to leave by the town council. He went to Prague, where on May 26, 1521, he publicly proclaimed himself as God's prophet of the "living Word," whose mission it was to restore the Church of the Elect.[56] The town council of Prague proved unreceptive to his mission, and he moved to Thuringia, where he became the self-appointed minister of Allstedt. Here he introduced the German liturgy and made other innovations in the church service. He preached that the most untutored layman might know more of God through his inner light than could the most learned scholar. He further proclaimed that the "ungodly have no right to live farther than the elect shall accord them." His fiery fanaticism led to an attack on a local chapel. When the government tried to arrest some of the "spirits," they summoned an armed band to offer resistance.

Luther now published his *Letter to the Princes of Saxony on the Revolutionary Spirit*, in which he rejected Muenzer's claim to special revelation and pointed out that his preaching of the sword and the establishment of God's kingdom through murder, fire, and pillage could emanate only from the devil.[57] In August, 1524, Muenzer was summoned before the town council in Weimar and humiliated. He fled to Muehlhausen to the protection of Pfeiffer, who was preaching a similar gospel.[58] Later he traveled to Nuernberg and thence to southwestern Germany. His preaching had its effect in the outbursts of banditry and brigandage which char-

acterized the Peasants' Revolt. It was also Luther's experience with
Muenzer and his fellows which contributed to his bitter denunciation of the peasants.

Representing a quite different, yet equally misguided interpretation of religion was Andreas Bodenstein von Carlstadt, who
had been for years a close friend of Luther.[59] A former professor
of philosophy and champion of Scholasticism, his conversion to
Luther's Biblical Humanism has already been described; but his
persuasion seems to have been rather superficial. What considerations motivated his later acts cannot be determined. Was it jealousy
of Luther's prominence? Was it a deep desire to gain recognition
for himself? [60] Whatever the reasons, he became a changed man.
As has been mentioned, he rushed into print with statements which
exceeded anything yet dreamed of by the other reformers. Himself the holder of several academic degrees, he renounced all such
ranks and honors. Calling himself a "new layman," he married a
local girl and moved to a small country estate, neglecting his duties
at the University.[61] He affected the manners and dress of the
peasants and sought to identify himself with them, claiming, like
Muenzer, that they knew more Gospel than the professors, for
God had revealed His Word to "babes and sucklings." He preached
and distributed Communion in his rough peasant dress, and the
results of his fiery exhortations have already been observed.

Shortly before his departure from Wittenberg, Carlstadt had
managed to obtain an appointment as minister in Orlamuende,[62]
but he had neglected to relinquish his position as archdeacon of
the Castle Church or on the university faculty. He completely
neglected to fulfill the duties of either office. After repeated attempts to bring him to his senses had ended in failure, the University and town authorities lost patience, and Carlstadt lost both
positions as well as his post in Orlamuende.[63] However, the damage
had been done. Carlstadt had introduced many radical innovations,
and his preaching had already resulted in some destruction of
property. The congregation did not receive his dismissal passively,
but insisted upon their right to call any pastor they might choose.
The town council asked Luther to visit the city to calm the troubled
situation.

Luther apparently thought this problem could be resolved as easily as had been the one in Wittenberg, and he set out in the middle of August.[64] On the way he heard of Muenzer's flight from Allstedt, and when asked to preach in Jena on August 22, 1524, he launched an attack against the radicals. Carlstadt happened to be in the audience and bitterly resented being considered one with Muenzer and his followers, since he had never advocated a revolution as a means of attaining a new society. Friends of the two men hoped to undo the damage by arranging a personal meeting, which took place that same afternoon in the Hotel of the Black Bear.[65] Although Luther related later that he gave Carlstadt a gulden as a token of liberty of speech, subsequent events seem to deny any permanent reconciliation between the two.

On August 24 Luther arrived in Orlamuende, but since he had been expected on the previous day, the people were all working at their various tasks and had to be summoned.[66] During the discussions which followed, Carlstadt unexpectedly appeared, but Luther refused him permission to remain. This attitude on the part of Luther only further aggravated the situation, and the meeting ended in complete failure. Luther left amid shouted curses and hostile gestures. He returned by way of Weimar and informed the Prince of the events.[67] In September Carlstadt was ordered to leave the Saxon lands.

Carlstadt was not silenced, however. He published his views on the Lord's Supper and other doctrines.[68] Spiritual growth, he said, meant growing in likeness unto Christ through denial and reflection. Man would have to become thoroughly permeated with God's will before he could attain the "heavenly composure," the Christian's ultimate virtue. Like Muenzer, he believed in his prophetic mission, but did not preach bloodshed and confusion. He believed that the Lord's Supper helped man to grow in likeness to Christ by reflection on the Lord's supreme example of "spiritual composure." [69] But, Carlstadt taught, Christ was not actually present in the sacrament, and, hence, it could not bestow forgiveness of sin. To him it was a commemoration of Christ's death. He claimed that Christ had pointed at Himself when He said: "This is My body." Man's free will enabled him to develop the perfect composure and to pattern his life more and more after that of the Savior. Carlstadt, therefore, developed again a sort of work-righteousness very similar to that of the Catholic Church, which he had renounced. He had obtained many of his earlier ideas from Luther and Erasmus, but had become considerably influenced by German mysticism. His religion was not the result of an inner soul-struggle such as Luther's, but was based on a haphazard collection of ideas gathered from many parts of the Bible as support for his proposed religious and social reforms.

Carlstadt's ideas, particularly on the Lord's Supper, created considerable confusion, which later found echoes in southwestern Germany. Strassburg even sent Martin Bucer to Wittenberg to clarify the problem.[70] Luther sent a letter to the Strassburg brethren and replied to Carlstadt with his tract *Against the Heavenly Prophets*.[71] His own views of the Lord's Supper were beginning to take definite form.[72] He insisted that the bodily presence of Jesus is absolutely essential, the very point on which he and Zwingli later could not find common ground. Luther's irritation and keen disappointment in his old friend Carlstadt made the language of his tract much too bitter, a trend which was to become even more apparent with the aging Luther.[73] He realized further the very evident damage being done to the cause of the New Gospel by teachings such as Carlstadt's which rejected the inspired Word of God and relied on personal revelation. But it required the Peasants' Revolt to bring Carlstadt to the realization of the havoc he had helped to create. His followers fell away, and he was treated everywhere as an outcast, finally finding refuge and Christian forgiveness in Luther's own home.

The Knights' Uprising

Two tragic events in the political history of the era have long been laid at Luther's door because of their theological implications without due consideration being given to the many other forces contributing to the total scene.

The serious student of the age will bear in mind that Europe during these same years was experiencing a revolutionary commercial and economic transformation. Until about 1200 European society was almost exclusively agrarian; but with the growth of trade and towns a new age dawned.[74] Some economic historians regard the period from 1450 to 1750 as the first phase of a vast capitalistic revolution which reached its maturity in the nineteenth century. Certainly the age produced the first large concentrations of capital with the rise of such powerful families as the Bardi, Medici, Fugger, Welser, Hochstetter, and Coeur houses.[75] Expanding travel and commerce likewise brought about the development of many of the modern business practices, such as bills of exchange, sea loans, double entry bookkeeping, partnerships, etc., all of which were puzzling innovations to a people just emerging from the guild system.[76] All that the poor peasant understood was that his already miserable existence grew steadily worse as prices increased. He naturally looked to his lord or others in authority for succor. But even the educated were at a loss to explain the circumstances in which their economic system was floundering. The following quotation expresses the same views repeated in Luther's writings and those of his contemporaries:

> Writers, politicians, officials, and churchmen in Spain, for example, sought to explain the rise in prices as the result of one or more of the following causes: bad crops, too heavy exports, monopolies and frauds of foreigners, speculation, high taxes, high wages, decrease in population, excessive luxury, debasement of coinage, laziness and idleness of the workers, manipulation of the markets.[77]

It was not until 1568 that Jean Bodin advanced the thesis that the vast imports of gold and silver from the Aztec and Inca Empires into Europe were causing the increase in prices. Recent studies by Earl J. Hamilton have shown that during the first century and a half after the discovery of the New World about 18,600 tons of fine silver and 200 tons of gold found their way into Europe to add to the metal already in circulation.[78] It was the now well-known story of more money in circulation than available goods for purchase which was causing a drastic rise in prices.

The knights were no better able to cope with the situation than were their contemporaries.[79] Like their humbler brethren, the peasants, they knew only that their familiar pattern of life was changing, and they sought some means by which it might be maintained. Again, like the peasants, they blamed those in authority,

both state and ecclesiastical. Holborn has made a detailed and
fascinating study of the complex motives which underlay the violent
measures which they adopted.[80] Doubtless they were sincere in
their intention to further the Gospel; yet, as is so often true of
human action, they were also moved by political and economic considerations. It was probably expecting too much of them to separate religious freedom from economic freedom.

Northern Germany had already witnessed the rise of the new
Junkers who had acquired their wealth through the flourishing
trade of the towns and were now buying up large estates. Sensing
that the rise of the towns and the burgher class were a threat to
their existence, the knights began to prey upon the merchant wagon
trains in the hope of acquiring rich booty.[81] Because of their ruthless tactics they earned the fear and hatred of peasant, burgher,
and prince. Ulrich von Hutten is a typical example of the age;
a knight who should have lived in the thirteenth rather than the
sixteenth century and who simply could not accept the fact that he
belonged to a dying aristocracy.[82] He tried vainly to rally the
Franconian knights to united action, but they were content merely
to draft new lists of grievances to be presented to the *Reichsregiment.*[83] The knights of the Upper Rhineland were united in their
proposed war against the princes and elected Sickingen as their
captain for the planned attack on the Archbishop of Trier.

Sickingen's role in the Reformation drama has been debated
furiously. That he was influenced by Luther cannot be doubted,
for one of the first Lutheran congregations flourished in his lands
under the leadership of Martin Bucer.[84] Before the Diet of Worms,
Hutten and Sickingen believed that the whole German nation would
rise in defense of the Gospel and liberate the country from the
tyranny of Rome.[85] After the Diet and the Emperor had condemned
Luther by issuing the Edict of Worms, the cause looked hopeless.
When Luther from the Wartburg pleaded for peaceful means of
spreading the Gospel and denied the use of the sword, his remarks
seemed to the knights to be directed at them, and they realized
that they could not expect help from "Junker Joerg."

Their limited resources made them ill-prepared to carry out
their campaign.[86] The attack on the Archbishop of Trier failed,

Ulrich von Hutten

and the aroused princes rallied to his support. Philip of Hesse
and the Elector Ludwig of the Palatinate met with the Archbishop,
and all agreed to furnish foot soldiers, cavalry, and equipment, including siege guns. Added to a shortage of ammunition and ineffective weapons was a questionable strategy on the part of the
knights. Their best-fortified castle was the Ebernburg; but instead
of taking refuge there, Sickingen proposed to scatter his forces in
an attempt to protect all of the castles, he himself taking a position
in the Castle of Landstuhl.[87] The opposing forces made a feint in
the direction of the Ebernburg, where Sickingen hoped to attack
them from the rear. But without warning the enemy appeared and
blocked all roads to Landstuhl and laid siege to the castle. Although
surrounded by a wall, its location on the side of a hill left its
southern flank vulnerable. Sickingen's son and his secretary managed to escape and were to send reinforcements, but events moved
too rapidly. Surrounded by the three armies, the castle was subjected to a terrific bombardment. The southeast tower was the
first to crumble. A lucky hit struck a pile of lumber near Sickingen's position and a flying timber tore a gaping hole in his side,
exposing his lungs and liver. He was moved to the underground
passageways, where with the aid of candlelight he wrote two letters
in which he admitted that the castle could not hold out without aid.
Both letters were intercepted by the enemy. Finally, a capitulation
was arranged providing that the nobles should be held captive but
unharmed, while the infantrymen might return to their homes after
being disarmed. With much pomp and ceremony the victors entered the ruined castle to find their adversary dying. Offered the
last rites of the Church, Sickingen refused saying that he had
already made his peace with God.

After the destruction of Landstuhl the princes resolved to complete the total defeat of the knights. They marched against each
remaining fortification, most of which offered no resistance. After
thoroughly plundering each castle, they set it on fire. The Ebernburg, however, proudly perched on a high hill and guarded by
Sickingen's bold friend Schenk Ernst von Tautenberg, resolved to
try its strength against the new weapons of war.[88] After a fierce
bombardment lasting five days it, too, was made to realize that the

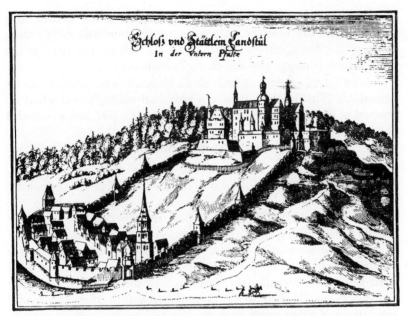

Town and Castle of Landstuhl

day of the castle as an effective instrument of warfare was over. It, too, capitulated, its defenders were taken captive, its booty divided among the victors, and the castle was burned. The fate of the captives is a story in itself.

Hutten meanwhile had fled to Switzerland, where Ulrich Zwingli gave refuge to the dying man.[89] Holborn has thrown some light upon his life also, claiming that he was really not so bad as he had been pictured, although his life was certainly not commendable.[90] With the deaths of Sickingen and Hutten a proud order died. The knights were never again strong enough to menace either the towns or the princes, and had not the Peasants' War made their remnant useful as a bulwark against the peasants, they might have been exterminated entirely.

Sickingen has been severely criticized for his cruel and inhumane methods of warfare, but the impartial student will discern that the methods of both adversaries differed little. Nor were their records of pillage and plunder much different. Again, these acts must be judged in the perspective of their historical setting and evaluated on the basis of sixteenth-century standards rather than those of the twentieth century. And God will be the final Judge as to which century was the more "inhumane."

When Luther first heard of Sickingen's wild campaign, he remarked: "This affair will have a very bad ending"; and when he learned of Sickingen's death, he said: "God is a just and wonderful Judge."[91]

The Peasants' Revolt

At the beginning of the twelfth century the relationship between the peasant and his lord was still rather intimate. Agriculture was regarded as an honorable profession or calling supplying one of man's basic needs. The peasant performed his daily work under the direction of his lord and depended upon the lord to make available the necessities of life. But the lot of the peasant grew steadily worse until by the sixteenth century two systems of land control were in operation in Germany. In southwestern Germany the system was known as the *Grundherrschaft*.[92] Here the feudal regulations of tithes, rents, and services had become almost entirely a part of land tenure which had even been codified in Roman Law.[93] Since the duties were attached to the land and passed from father to son generation after generation, there was little hope for the peasant to better his lot. Often those over him were harsh and unreasonable in their treatment and sometimes, through control of the courts, even exercised authority over the body of the peasant. Naturally, the ignorant peasant credited his lord with his miseries or his benefits. He gave no consideration to crop failures, destruction by storms, or other misfortunes which might befall his lord and affect his economic circumstances.

In northern Germany from Holstein to East Prussia the system known as *Gutsherrschaft* was practiced.[94] Here the relationship between lord and peasant bordered on serfdom. There were instances of the landlord driving the peasants at their work with a whip. Often the services on the lord's land were so long that the peasant could till his own meager plot only by moonlight. In some instances he needed the lord's approval to marry. Surely the life of the peasant was not a pleasant or desirable one. Had he any

"*Knight, Death, and the Devil.*" *By Albrecht Duerer*

inclination for self-improvement, neither the opportunity nor the materials were available. Gradually, he became the laughingstock of the remainder of society.

Kurt Uhrig has made a study of the peasant as he was reflected in contemporary art and literature through the period.[95] In poetry, play, and song he was pictured as stupid, obscene, nasty, scheming, stubborn, gluttonous, and hard-drinking, little above the level of an animal. The minnesingers loved to ridicule him in court entertainments. The burghers of the town made him the butt of their coarse jokes. Contemporary artists treated him more kindly, portraying him as he really was, not the degraded, depraved individual presented in literature. However, Bartels concludes that there was a definite peasant type.

> One need but examine the poorly shaped forms and the coarse faces in these pictures (1500) to realize that there was a definite peasant type which cannot be denied.[96]

His conclusions were based on an examination of some 400 woodcuts, etchings, and pictures extant of this period.[97] The peasants were themselves aware of the position they occupied in the esteem of their contemporaries, and by the middle of the fifteenth century they had little self-respect left, only a bitter resentment toward all those whom they considered their tormentors.

With the development of the printing press an entirely new peasant emerged in contemporary literature.[98] A specific type of literature was created aimed at this mass audience which frankly propagandized the peasants' lot. Luther's writings were drawn upon and given an appeal directed to the peasants. There was *The Address to the German Nobility* and *The Freedom of the Christian*, whose themes were elaborated upon by other writers. There was particularly the principle of the "priesthood of believers," which the peasants were led to believe applied especially to them.[99] Were not the Apostles humble folk like themselves? [100] Gradually a new type of peasant emerged in literature which went to the opposite extreme. Now he was portrayed as the noble son of the soil whose simple mind was best fitted to absorb the teachings of the Bible.[101] He was even presented as capable of discussing the writings of Erasmus, Murner, and Luther or of entering into dis-

Peasants at work, dated 1504

Peasants at work, dated 1504

putations with the best minds of his day[102] His work of *Ackerbau* was now presented as far above all other professions and very pleasing to God.[103] Art also contributed to this peasant portrayal. A good example was Sebald Beham's picture of "The Sheepfold of Christ," in which Christ was inviting his true lambs to enter.[104] Here the peasants gained uninhibited entrance, while priests, monks, and nuns used ladders and staves in a vain attempt to enter. Hans Sachs, the famous bard of Nuernberg, prepared the poetic legend for this picture which made the monks, nuns, and clerics the thieves and robbers of the parable, while the peasant, entering the sheepfold, with his ax on his back, was "Christ's own." All of this was very flattering to the peasant but, unfortunately, was not a true picture. Such a peasant did not exist, but the psychological effect on his brothers was immeasurable. They readily believed that they were destined to perform an important role in furthering the Gospel and, incidentally, inaugurating much-needed social and economic reforms.

To this already smoldering tinder was needed only the spark of such preaching as that of Carlstadt and Muenzer to kindle a conflagration which might well envelop all Germany. Ever since the Hussite Wars of the fifteenth century, Germany had been troubled with peasant uprisings.[105] There had been one in Wuerttemberg as late as 1514, before Luther emerged on the national scene. Tragically, his writings which were to influence men in all walks of life so profoundly were misunderstood and misinterpreted. His *Theologia pauperum* was written for the encouragement of all laymen; but the peasants believed it was a special assignment for them to effect a reformation of the Roman Church.[106] The doctrine of *The Freedom of the Christian* was changed from Luther's meaning of an inner freedom of the reborn man to mean freedom from the economic bondage of feudalism.[107] Although Luther's doctrine of the "priesthood of believers" originated with the New Testament and was not meant to favor any particular class, it became potential dynamite in the hands of the unrestrained masses. It was this gross misinterpretation of his doctrines which caused Luther to modify his views on lay control when the Church in Germany was reorganized after the Peasants' War.

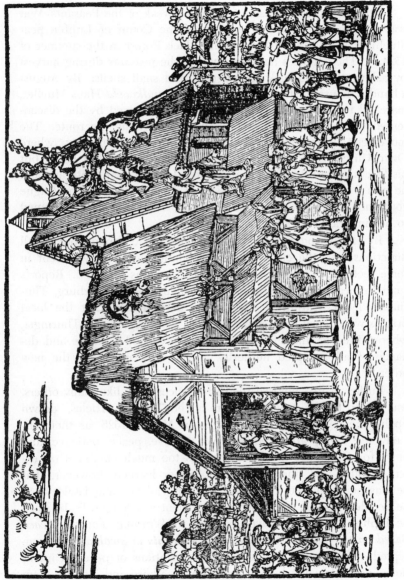

"The Sheepfold of Christ." By H. S. Beham

The immediate occasion for the outbreak of the Peasants' War was a disturbance in the territory of the Count of Lupfen near Stuehlingen on the outskirts of the Black Forest in the summer of 1524.[108] The countess had antagonized the peasants during harvest by asking them to pick strawberries and snail shells. By August a band a thousand strong, led by former *Landknecht* Hans Mueller, marched to the Austrian town of Waldshut, joined by the discontented elements from several small villages along the route. The movement spread to Upper Swabia and Wuerttemberg, where Duke Ulrich tried to use the peasants to regain his lost lands, but his forces were routed by the Swabian League near Stuttgart, and he was forced to flee to the Castle of Hohentwiel.[109] The league could not cope with the entire situation, however, as there seemed to be simultaneous outbursts everywhere.

By the spring of 1525 the movement had fanned out in all directions, and the clashes were becoming increasingly violent in some sections. Virtually the whole Empire was inflamed. Reports from Franconia, Hesse, Brunswick, Baden, Treves, Salzburg, Thuringia, Tyrol, Carinthia, and Styria all indicated that the local princes were faced with civil war. The worst region was Thuringia, where Muenzer and his followers had preached violence and defiance of all accepted authority as the only means to the new order.[110]

Luther at first ignored the disturbances. He, like many others, was misled by the peaceful nature of the "Twelve Articles," drawn up by the peasants at Memmingen in March, 1525, as their objectives.[111] They appeared to advocate love, peace, patience, and unity for Germany, though there was too much emphasis on external rights and liberties. When Luther learned, however, that he was being quoted in support of their violence and lawlessness, he decided that he could not remain silent any longer.[112] In April he replied to the "Twelve Articles" in *Warning Toward Peace Based on the Twelve Articles of the Peasants in Swabia.*[113] He accepted at face value the peasants' protestations of peaceful intentions and believed it his pastoral duty to advise and instruct them on the basis of the Word of God. He had not yet learned of the reported "Bloodbath of Weinsberg," the murder of the Count of

Helfenstein, and other acts of violence in southwestern Germany.[114] In his tract he spoke only as a theologian, clearly with no particular partiality for any special group. As he had denied the use of the sword to Sickingen and Hutten, so he now believed that the same violence must be curbed in the peasants.[115]

Two concepts are clearly discernible in this tract and form the frame of reference for all three tracts of 1525. Religion to Luther, as has been noted again and again, was something inward and spiritual, a personal relationship between the individual and his God. God is a God of love, and the whole panorama of history is steadily unfolding according to his omnipotent and ultimate purpose.[116] Evil may have its little day, but in the end even it must become subservient to God's will. Governments which had been legally established were certainly in the world by God's good will and had been instituted to preserve God's kingdom. Hence, rebellion against God's established institutions was a grievous sin. Only political changes which developed peacefully as the result of the work of the Gospel in men's hearts could be supported by Christians.[117] Anyone who resorted to force to correct the social order was not worthy to be called a follower of Christ.[118]

The second concept was the relationship of Church and State. Luther accepted the medieval theory of this relationship which assumed that all western Europe was made up of a Christian commonwealth in which God had placed two powers: the Church and the State.[119] Both were divinely instituted and had an inner relationship which was very vital. The Church, which to Luther was an invisible body, looked after the souls of men. The State had been instituted to curb evil and to control the wicked so that God's kingdom might flourish. In a tract of the year 1523, *Concerning Government, to What Extent One is Obligated to Obey It*, Luther also defined the borderline between these two divinely instituted powers in the Christian commonwealth.[120] The Church, claimed he, was obligated to provide for man's spiritual life and his soul; the State had control of his body and other outward possessions.[121] Thus, in the case of a revolution, especially when it seemed to endanger the Church, it was the duty of the State to curb this evil.[122] Luther did not argue in favor of any particular form of

government, but assumed that the legally established institutions
have the right, the power, and the duty to restore peace and order.

In the article *Warning Toward Peace* Luther pointed out to
his "dear brothers," the peasants, that those who would be followers
of Christ cannot resort to force.[123] He pointed out that he had not
used force in opposing the Kaiser or the Pope, yet the Gospel had
flourished. The whole theme of the tract was similar to that of his
letters and sermons in the Wittenberg disturbances and the language very mild. But before the article could come from the press
the whole situation had changed. Everywhere violence and destruction were increasing. The princes were hesitant as to their
exact role in the drama, especially since Luther had intimated in
his tract that the princes were now being punished for having
formerly opposed the Gospel. Knowing that they were prepon-
derant in numbers, the defiant peasants, led by Muenzer and
Pfeiffer, roamed over the Harz and northern Thuringia, plundering
castle and cloister at will and holding the whole region terrorized.[124]

On April 16, 1525, Luther, accompanied by Melanchthon and
Agricola, journeyed to Eisleben to establish a new Christian school
at the request of Count Albert of Mansfeld.[125] While in the region,
Luther visited his parents and other relatives, including a brother-
in-law, Ruehel, one of the court councilors. Apparently from these
visits, Luther received much firsthand information as to the depre-
dations being committed by the peasants. Likewise, Ruehel sought
Luther's advice as to the course which his prince should pursue.
Luther decided to make a trip through the region in an effort to
restore peace. Now he saw for himself the evidences of unrestrained
violence by the peasants. His preaching, too, fell on deaf ears. In
Nordhausen he was rudely interrupted in the middle of his sermon
by "hecklers" in the audience.[126] He became increasingly aware
of the fact that the situation was completely out of hand. Others,
too, realized that his influence would not solve the problem. One
tax collector wrote the Duke: "Dr. Luther cannot stop such uprisings." Arriving in Weimar, Luther again preached. And now
the court learned the conclusions which he had reached. He was
convinced that the troublemakers would stop at nothing less than
a complete overthrow of the government and was certain that the

devil was behind the whole rebellion. He promised to write another tract treating the disturbances as soon as he arrived home. On the way he wrote to Ruehel advising firmness in dealing with the "murderers and robbers." He reached home on May 6 and immediately plunged into the writing of the tract *Against the Murderous and Plundering Bands Among the Peasants*,[127] for which he has been severely criticized to this day.

Granted that the language of the tract was unbecoming to a clergyman and that Luther would have been wiser to wait until he could view his recent experiences with more detachment. Yet he had seen for himself the excesses of the peasants, and he feared even worse events to come. The tract reflects one of Luther's greatest weaknesses, a tendency to biting, bitter vituperation when in the heat of anger.[128]

However, in all fairness, his severest critics would grant that Luther had extreme provocation. It should be further recognized that to take the stand which Luther took required quite as much courage as to stand alone before Worms.[129] He knew that the peasants who had heretofore regarded him as their hero would now view him as a mortal enemy. There was even a chance that the peasants might be the victors, in which case Luther's own life would not be safe. The easiest path and the one indicated by his own interests would have been to favor the peasants. But Luther had always boldly championed his convictions regardless of personal interests, and he did so again:

> A Christian preacher does not consider whether he has a following or keeps it, but only that he preaches the Word of God.[130]

He indicted the peasants on three counts: (1) they had broken their oath to the government and, hence, were subject to arrest and trial; (2) they had robbed and murdered and were subject to death in body and soul; and (3) they had covered all their sins in the name of Christian brotherhood; thus, they blasphemed God and disgraced His Holy name.[131] Luther likened them to a mad dog which must be destroyed lest it contaminate a whole community. He called upon the government to use its divinely appointed power to curb the evil, for the prince is God's *Amptmann* entrusted with the sword for just such emergencies.[132] Those who

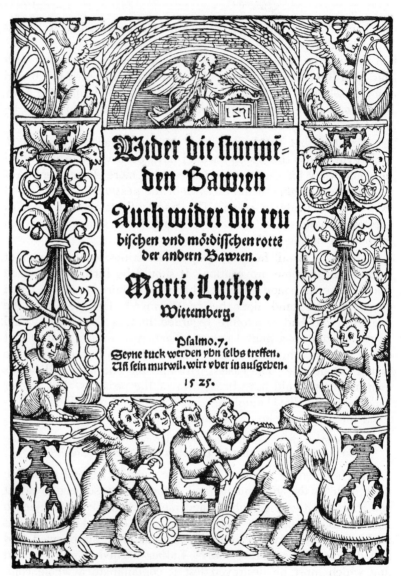

Luther's second tract in the Peasants' War, 1525

might lose their lives in preserving justice and order would be true martyrs in the cause of the Gospel.

There was no new idea contained in this tract which Luther had not previously expressed; its only offense was the abusive language which was employed.[133] Probably its principal contribution was the appeal to the Christian princes to stand firm according to Romans 13:1-4:

> Let every soul be subject unto the higher powers. For there is no power but of God; the powers that be are ordained of God. Whosoever therefore resisteth the power, resisteth the ordinance of God; and they that resist shall receive to themselves damnation. For rulers are not a terror to good works, but to the evil. Wilt thou, then, not be afraid of the power? Do that which is good, and thou shalt have praise of the same; For he is the minister of God to thee for good. But if thou do that which is evil, be afraid; for he beareth not the sword in vain; for he is the minister of God, a revenger to execute wrath upon him that doeth evil.[134]

Again, due to the time lag between composition and publication, the situation had radically shifted before Luther's tract reached the public. On May 15 the peasants were defeated at the battle of Frankenhausen and were routed in the south.[135] A terrible bloodbath followed, for the princes had determined to teach the peasants a final lesson. Just when news of the abuse and mistreatment of the vanquished began to spread throughout the country, Luthers' tract appeared.[136] Its theme, which would have been welcomed by a terrorized and apprehensive countryside a few weeks earlier, now seemed like striking a man who had already fallen.

The peasants had reached the peak of their power with Muenzer's march through Eichsfeld at the end of April, 1525, and continued their triumphant and defiant progress until the defeat at Frankenhausen.[137] By the end of June they were completely overcome. Just when Luther's tract appeared from the press has not been established, but it was read from a pulpit on June 21.[138] Catholic writers, such as Emser and Cochlaeus, were quick to seize upon it as the cause of the "bloodbath." They forgot•to point out that the damage had been done before it reached the public or to mention the part devout Catholic princes, such as Duke George, had taken in the reprisals. They declared that Luther showed inconsistency, a desire to shed blood, and had now given evidence of his true spirit, etc.[139]

His friends were much dismayed at the avalanche of criticism directed at Luther and begged him to make some public retraction.[140] This Luther could not do.

> Tell me, dear friend, what kind of an excuse is it when someone strangles your father and mother, rapes your wife and child, burns your house, steals your money and goods, and says afterward he had to do it, he was forced to such action? [141]

He denied responsibility for those princes who carried things to extremes, and there are several instances of letters which he wrote in individual cases asking for clemency in the treatment of the vanquished.[142] He viewed the whole unfortunate event as a righteous judgment of God on the peasants, but far from a justification of the princes. Paul Althaus adds that Luther's attitude was that of a true servant of God's Word, looking neither to the right nor to the left.

In response to the entreaties of his friends, Luther issued *A Letter on the Harsh Booklet Against the Peasants* in which he reaffirmed his basic position on the Biblical foundation of Romans 13.[143] He thought it useless to try to convince the peasants on the basis of reason, since they, as rebels, were not capable of reasoning, but understood only force. He believed that an apology or retraction from him at that point would only further confuse the situation.[144]

Many of the peasants were bitterly disillusioned by Luther's denunciation and were hopelessly alienated from the new Gospel movement. Whether they had ever been sincere converts to its doctrines cannot be established. Many others remained faithful. The impartial historian would hardly base his conclusions as to Luther's attitude toward the whole peasant class on the basis of one tract. Rather, his numerous tracts on business and trade, his attacks on usury because of its effects on the common man, the total picture of his views must be considered. In sermon and *Table Talk* he constantly revealed his love and sympathy for the lowly and downtrodden. That they loved him in return cannot be doubted. They gathered about him on his preaching trips and

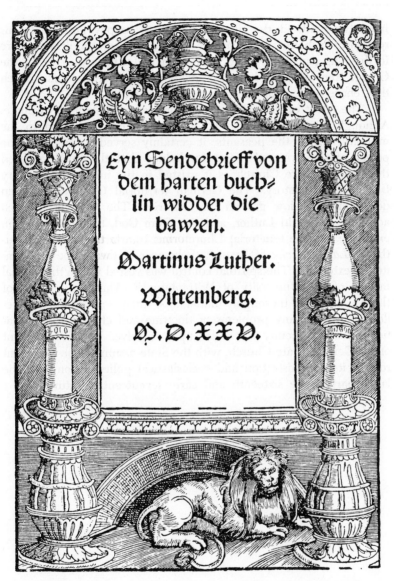

Eyn Sendebꝛieff von
dem harten buch-
lin widder die
bawꝛen.

Martinus Luther.

Wittemberg.

M.D.XXV.

Letter on the harsh booklet against the peasants, 1525

lined the roads at the time of his death to pay homage to his remains. Probably the peasants would have accomplished more in the long run if they had hearkened to Luther's plea to let the Gospel transform the hearts of men. Certainly the course which they chose only made their circumstances worse.

The effect of the revolt on the princes is difficult to evaluate. Although it may have resulted in some social awakening to the miserable lot of the peasants, it certainly served to augment the power of the princes.[145] But to deduce that the revolt created the German State Church as it existed in the nineteenth century is to misread history. The German territorial Church had been developing by slow growth for centuries. The Catholic Church accepted it, as did Luther, as being from God, because it was in existence. As the territorial Church was transformed into the Lutheran *Landeskirche* of Saxony, the power of the prince was limited to externals. The spiritual control was vested in the theological faculty of the University of Wittenberg.[146] That the princes of the Saxon lands thoroughly understood their responsibilty is reflected in the many problems of doctrine and church administration which the faculty was called upon to solve. The development of the German State Church, with the State assuming the dominant role in its administration and ecclesiastical polity, belongs to the latter part of the sixteenth and early seventeenth centuries.

« 18 »

Martin Luther the Man

His Physical Appearance

UNFORTUNATELY, LUTHER LIVED BEFORE the age of photography, and the only sources of information concerning his general appearance are descriptions by his friends or enemies and the portraits made of him by Lucas Cranach the elder, a local artist of Wittenberg, whose zeal in reproducing the Reformer outstripped his talent. It is most regrettable that the life's ambition of Duerer to paint Luther was never realized, or that no portrait of him was ever done by Holbein the younger, who so faithfully portrayed Henry VIII, Erasmus, Melanchthon, and other contemporaries of Luther.[1] The differences in ability between Cranach and Holbein can best be seen by comparing their portraits of Melanchthon. Probably no likeness in history has been reproduced more often than Luther's, for in his day he was as well known to every school child and citizen of Germany as is a modern president of our country. His likeness appeared in hundreds of paintings, etchings, woodcuts, on china, in leather, and every possible medium.[2]

All available reproductions of the Reformer have been carefully collected and preserved by the scholars of Germany. At the Halle Exposition of 1931 all of these were displayed and grouped into periods.[3] German critics are unable to find any likenesses done from life in the period before 1520, and only one woodcut, very small and indistinct, was displayed prior to that date. The remaining pictures have been classified as follows: (1) Luther, the Monk and Professor of Theology during the period of Worms (1520–1524), all of them copied from Cranach's three etchings of this period discovered in Munich (1520 as a Monk), Vienna (1520 as a Monk), and the Feste Coburg (1521 as Professor of Theology);

AETHERNA IPSE SVAE MENTIS SIMVLACHRA VTHERVS
EXPRIMIT·AT VVLTVS CERA LVCAE OCODVOS
·M·D·X·X·

Martin Luther. Etching by Lucas Cranach the Elder, 1520

(2) Luther as "Junker Joerg" at the Wartburg, the first painting done in oil (1521);[4] (3) Luther, the Bridegroom (1525), the attractive little "round picture" (frontispiece), painted in oil, and a second (1526), the companion picture to the one of Katharine von Bora, his wife; (4) Luther, the Preacher (1528); and (5) Luther, the Professor (1532) in black gown with white collar and black beret; (6) Luther, the Church Father (1537), the authenticity of which has been questioned by Boehmer and others; and (7) the death mask prepared at Halle by a local artist.[5] Using the very poor Cranachs, innumerable artists drew their own interpretations of the leading figure of Germany, and as might be expected, there gradually emerged an idealized Luther, bearing very faint resemblance to the Luther of life.

Luther's contemporaries, those who were closest to him and knew him best, apparently just took him for granted, little realizing that someday the Luther of life would be lost. Most descriptions of him, therefore, come from outsiders: Mosellanus, a Leipzig professor; Kessler, a Swiss student; Aleander, the papal nuncio at Worms; Cajetan, Luther's inquisitor at Augsburg; Erasmus Alber, one of the table companions; Thomas Blaurer, a student; Philip Melanchthon, his bosom friend and fellow professor; and others.[6] None of them are very detailed in their descriptions; many of them are quite biased in one extreme or the other; yet all evidence must be combined with the impressions left by Cranach to determine the true likeness of Luther.

In reconstructing Luther's general appearance, the element of time is very important. During the first thirty-eight years of his life he was extremely thin. Mosellanus, who gave the opening address for the Leipzig Debate, mentioned that Luther was so thin that every bone in his body could be counted.[7] A coin of this period with his image reflects his emaciated condition.[8] By 1520 and 1521, when Cranach made the afore-mentioned etchings, Luther had begun to eat more regularly and to assume a "befitting plumpness."[9] Vergerio, the papal nuncio, noted that Luther had a heavy, well-developed bone structure and strong shoulders, a fact not discernible from the Cranachs.[10] The Swiss student Kessler accidentally met Luther at the Hotel of the Black Bear in Jena

Earliest known likeness of Martin Luther

when Luther was returning to Wittenberg from the Wartburg, still dressed as a knight. Kessler wrote in his *Sabbata* that Luther walked very "erect, bending backwards rather than forwards, with face raised toward heaven." [11] Erasmus Alber, the table companion, described Luther as well-proportioned and spoke of his general appearance in highest praise.[12] No doubt, as the portraits show by 1532, the Luther of later life was somewhat inclined to corpulency. Due allowance must, however, be made for the loose, flowing gown, and it is doubtful whether Luther ever weighed over two hundred pounds, which was not excessive for a man of his height.

One important aspect of his general appearance, noted by every observer, was Luther's unusual eyes. Melanchthon made

Martin Luther. Woodcut, 1521

a casual remark that Luther's eyes were brown and compared them
to the eyes of a lion or falcon.[13] Kessler, when he became Luther's
pupil, observed that his professor had "deep black eyes and brows,
sparkling and burning like stars, so that one could hardly bear
looking at them." [14] Erasmus Alber also likened them to falcon's
eyes.[15] Melanchthon added the observation that the eyes were
brown, with golden rings around the edges, as in the case of eagles
or men of genius.[16] Nikolaus Selnecker also compared Luther's
eyes to those of a hawk, falcon, fox, and eagle, having a fiery, burning sparkle.[17] There can be little doubt that Luthers' eyes were
an unusual factor in his influence over men. Members of his congregation said that when Luther preached it seemed as though
he could look right through them. They feared he could see everything they had done during the week.

Catholics, on the other hand, saw in these eyes diabolic
powers. After the first meeting with Luther at Augsburg, Cajetan
would have no more to do with this man, the "beast with the
deep-seated eyes," because "strange ideas were flitting through his
head." [18] Aleander wrote in his dispatches to the Pope that when
Luther left his carriage at Worms, he looked over the crowd with
"demoniac eyes." [19] Johannes Dantiscus, later a Catholic bishop,
visited Wittenberg in 1523 and noticed that Luther's eyes were
"unusually penetrating and unbelievably sparkling as one finds
them now and then in those that are possessed." [20] His enemies
also commonly compared him to a basilisk, that fabulous reptile
which hypnotizes and slowly crawls upon its helpless prey. They
asserted that Luther used this same power to hypnotize people
and turn them to Lutheranism.

Another attribute which greatly enhanced Luther's physical
qualifications as a preacher and professor was his voice. It was
clear, penetrating, and of pleasing timbre, which, added to its
sonorous, baritone resonance, contributed much to his effectiveness
as a public speaker.[21] Without modern amplifiers, such a voice
was a decided asset in a large church or cathedral. Luther's students enjoyed his classroom lectures because of the pleasing qualities of his delivery. Erasmus Alber added that he never shouted,
yet his clear, ringing voice could easily be heard.[22]

Other Characteristics

Not the least of Luther's many remarkable gifts was a warm and magnetic personality. When the court preacher George Spalatin visited Wittenberg in 1520, he reported that there were 400 students attending Luther's theological lectures, which was exceptional for a graduate department.[23] Soon after Luther began his sermons to the brethren in the little cloister church, the services had to be transferred to the Town Church to accommodate the crowds.[24] Kathie also had her problems with the students who loved to gather in Luther's study after the evening meal to enjoy his company further. On preaching trips he was surrounded by the common folk, entertaining them with stories and engaging them in sprightly conversation. His warm sympathy and understanding for the class from which his parents had sprung was felt by them all. He was one of those truly great men who are equally at ease with the great or the lowly. As has been observed, in this way he also familiarized himself with the German language which he later used to translate the Bible into the vocabulary of the common folk. He was equally well loved by the great men who had been won by his reforms. Philip Melanchthon, shortly after he came to Wittenberg, wrote: "If there is anything on earth that I love, it is the studies of Martin and his pious writings; but above everything else I love Martin himself." [25] On another occasion he added: "Never was there a greater man on the face of the earth; I would rather die than separate myself from this man." [26] Nor were those empty words. The gifted Philip had many opportunities for positions in more famous institutions, but he declined them all to stay in Wittenberg. The attitude of Luther's students, who were usually very critical, gave added testimony to his attraction and charm. Johannes Hornberg said that in Wittenberg he was beginning to learn all over again; Thomas Blaurer stated that he was sitting at the feet of "the only man living who really understands the Bible";[27] and Felix Ulscenius recognized in Luther a "powerful interpreter of the Word of God," [28] of whose sermons he and his roommate would not miss one, for they felt extremely privileged to be Luther's contemporaries.

An outstanding mental quality of Martin Luther was his phenomenal memory. No one in German history has known the Bible in greater detail than he, for he could quote verbatim from both the Old and the New Testament at will. Seldom did he make a mistake. Equally well could he recall the classics, the writings of the Church Fathers, and other materials which he had covered in his earlier reading, as has been noted in the story of the Leipzig Debate.[29] As a result of this vast storehouse of information being constantly at his disposal, Luther could write with unbelievable speed, which added to the timeliness of his tracts. When an enemy attacked him, a reply was off the press in a few weeks. He never rewrote, seldom polished, yet the richness and diversity of thought that came from his productive brain are truly amazing.

Equally remarkable was the originality and penetrating quality of his creative mind.[30] He had been trained along traditional Roman Catholic lines and thoroughly saturated with their dogma. His doctrine of "justification by faith" was an entirely new synthesis of the teaching of Scripture.[31] In the beginning he followed Occam, Augustine, and others, but he soon discovered that they, too, were unreliable guides. He read the works of Tauler, which fascinated him for a while, but always he weighed everything by the absolute standard of divine revelation.[32] As the result of this humanistic approach, he returned to the original sources. In theology, he asserted, the original thinker will drink from the fountainhead of truth, the Bible itself. In time a new Paulinism emerged from his thought, based upon the New Testament and breathing an atmosphere unknown for a thousand years.[33]

Luther dashed off with amazing speed an essay, *The Bondage of the Will,* in which he examined the freedom of the human will. In this document he praised and evaluated the contributions of Erasmus with remarkable clarity and insight. In his own homely way he pointed out how much he had learned from the great Dutch scholar, to whom God had given remarkable gifts.[34] Without the help of Erasmus his own work would have been impossible. But, said Luther, Erasmus had one principal fault: he wished to walk on eggs and not break any.[35] How clearly he recognized both

Erasmus' true worth and his greatest failing! Not even his bitterest enemy could accuse Martin Luther of lack of courage. His every action was that of a man having complete disregard for his personal safety and the "courage of his convictions." [36] Never was he governed by considerations of political expediency, and he deplored such considerations in others.

Luther also possessed considerable dramatic ability. In his lecturing and preaching he made use of it with great effectiveness. Even in private conversation the dramatic element played a large part in his skillful wit and ready charm and, combined with his love of poetry and his musical ability, made him a popular figure in all circles. In this respect he resembled Bernard of Clairvaux and George Whitefield, both of whom charmed their audiences with clever gestures and dramatic speech.[37]

Valuable as were all of these attributes to Luther, they do not explain why he became a great man of God. Combined with all his genius was the simple, trusting faith of a child. This faith greatly impressed Urbanus Rhegius, the Humanist, who spent a day with Luther at the Coburg.[38] When he happened to overhear Luther engaged in prayer for the success of the Lutheran cause at Augsburg, he thought there was another person with Luther in the room. Said Erasmus Alber: "No one could more energetically and earnestly pray than he, no one could more genuinely console the afflicted." [39] Luther implicitly believed in God's providential protection. He had no fear for the future. On several occasions he bade his Wittenberg congregation good-by, and he was disappointed when God did not consider him worthy of martyrdom.[40] It was not his desire to hide at the Wartburg, and the correspondence with his Elector when he decided to return to Wittenberg displayed his complete faith in the protection of Providence. His life was an exemplification of that faith described by Christ as necessary to enter the kingdom of heaven. According to Alber, God knew what He was doing when He wished to attack the Antichrist and once more "reveal the Gospel to the world; for then He chose a man after His own heart and assigned him this great task, the like of which since the days of the Apostles has not been seen, a man with all these wonderful gifts." [41]

His Handicaps

One of Luther's principal handicaps was his poor health.[42] That he suffered physically from his rigorous monastic disciplines and fastings was evidenced by his emaciated condition as late as middle age. The tremendous pressure under which he labored, the many demands upon his time as professor and pastor, the nervous tension attendant upon anyone so constantly in the public eye, all of these combined to take further toll from his physical stamina. In 1537 he suffered a severe gall bladder attack.[43] No doubt all of these factors contributed to a growing irascibility, increasingly evident as Luther grew older. This tendency was further aggravated by his disappointments in such men as Carlstadt and Muenzer and the seemingly slow progress of the Gospel.

Added to his growing shortness of temper was a gradual increase in his intolerance of the viewpoints and convictions of others which differed from his own. In the writings of his later years he revealed a growing tendency to assert that his contentions were right without bothering to show why he believed them to be right.[44] Perhaps he was weary of the struggle and conflict which had surrounded him constantly and simply chose the easier path. This tendency was most unfortunate for the cause of the Gospel, for it alienated many followers who had been drawn by his former "sweet reasonableness." [45]

Perhaps his sense of the dramatic was a contributing factor in Luther's proneness to overemphasis. He has likewise often been criticized for the coarseness of the language which he sometimes employed. But that must again be considered against the background of his age.[46] An examination of the literature of the era will find such coarseness the rule rather than the exception. It has been estimated that in the total picture not more than a small percentage of Luther's writings is subject to this criticism. Shakespeare, on the other hand, would indicate a much larger percentage.

Luther would not have made a successful diplomat, for he lacked the necessary tact and circumlocution. He was probably too blunt and outspoken.[47] The point has been argued that Luther would have achieved greater success in dealing with Rome had he been less stubborn and forthright. Perhaps; but he might also have suffered the fate of John Hus.

All of these traits combine to make a man loved by his friends, respected by his colleagues, feared by his enemies, human in his weaknesses, strong in the faith of the Apostles. This, then, was the leader of the German Reformation. He was also the gentle, kindly husband of Katharine von Bora and the father of six children.

KATHARINE VON BORA

As Luther matured in his understanding of the Holy Scriptures, his view of marriage also changed, and the celibacy demanded by the Roman Church seemed to him another human imposition. Already in 1519 in his *Sermon on the Institution of Marriage* this new conviction was expressed:

> Oh, truly a noble, great, holy estate is the estate of matrimony, provided it is rightly observed! Oh, what a truly miserable, frightful, dangerous estate the estate of matrimony can be when it is not observed in all faithfulness! And he who were to meditate upon these things would soon lose his fleshly desires and would as much grasp for the estate of virginity as marriage.[48]

In *The Address to the Christian Nobility* in 1520 he suggested that priests should have the choice of wedlock, but the monks should continue their self-imposed burden.[49] By 1521 in his treatise *On Monastic Vows* he began to grant freedom to monks.[50] A vow taken under the old Catholic system was no longer binding on him who had been enlightened through the Gospel. Since the members of the orders were already redeemed through Christ, there was no need for a life of celibacy to gain work-righteousness. Forced chastity was not the work of Christ; true chastity was a gift of God and was possible only in the redeemed, not a meritorious work as claimed by the Catholic Church. In 1522 Luther further elaborated these convictions in the treatise *Concerning Married Life.*[51] Whether a person wished to marry or to remain single was a question of individual choice, but neither state should ever be cited as being the more holy or meritorious.

This new approach to the problem of wedlock was certain to be reflected among his followers. His former pupil Bartholo-

maeus Bernhardi, now the *Propst* at Kemberg, had taken a wife
the previous year. This was a very bold and dangerous step, for
two other priests had been arrested by Duke George and Albert
of Mainz for similar action.[52] On December 1, 1521, Luther wrote
Albert in rather forceful language in behalf of the priests who
had married, reminding Albert that he was living with a mistress,
Ursula Riedinger.[53] But when the impetuous Carlstadt married
fifteen-year-old Anna von Mochau, Luther was much displeased,
for he feared unworthy desires had motivated the step.[54] On October 13, 1522, Bugenhagen married Walpurga.[55] Early in 1523
Link, successor to Staupitz as Vicar of the Augustinian Congregation in Germany and now minister at Altenburg, married the daughter of an Altenburg advocate.[56] The ceremony was performed by
Luther personally on April 14 and 15 in Bartholomaeus Church of
Altenburg in the presence of Melanchthon, Jonas, Schurff, Bugenhagen, Brisger, Camerarius, Crappe, and Cranach. Luther's sermon praised the institution of marriage. The local canons of the
cathedral were so enraged that armed guards were necessary to
escort the newly married couple to safety.

Everywhere the marriage of priests, monks, and nuns was
occurring with increasing tempo. In a letter to Capito in May,
1524, Luther wrote: "I am exceptionally pleased with the marriages of the priests, monks, and nuns in your community." [57] Eight
had recently married in the face of Bishop Wilhelm von Hohen-
stein's excommunication. On August 1, 1524, Capito himself married.[58] In November, 1523, Luther advised Albert of Brandenburg-
Ansbach to marry and to secularize his lands. Albert followed
Luther's advice on both points. On April 10, 1525, he took the
title "Duke of Prussia," and on June 1, 1526, he married Dorothea,
the daughter of the King of Denmark.[59]

Luther received so many requests for advice in the matter
of marriage that he decided to print a letter addressed to Wolfgang
Reissenbusch, which appeared April 12, 1525.[60] Luther stated
the reasons why celibacy did not apply to the Christian: (1) It was
not within the power of man to be chaste; chastity was a gift from
God, and celibacy, therefore, was not a holy estate in God's sight;
(2) the institution of celibacy was in opposition to God and the

Christian faith because it was built upon human merit rather than upon God's grace. On April 26, 1525, Reissenbusch married Hanna Herzog, the daughter of a poor tailor's widow in Torgau.

In the summer of 1525 Rome became really alarmed, for the pressure of the Peasants' War was about to force the Archbishop of Mainz, the same Albert who had earlier arrested the priests, to marry and to secularize his lands. Would he follow the example of his cousin in Prussia? Dr. Ruehel, the Mansfeld and Magdeburg councilor, asked Luther to use his influence. On June 2, 1525, Luther wrote Albert, urging him to live a more chaste life by embracing matrimony.[61] But with the defeat of the peasants the political expediency was removed, and Albert saw no further reason why he should take the step. Like many others, he much preferred to continue with his mistress and thereby remain an archbishop with full sanction of the Roman Church.

During this time the light of the Gospel was beginning to penetrate the German nunneries. On April 10, 1523, Luther wrote Spalatin that nine nuns, all of noble lineage, had been brought to Wittenberg by a burgher of Torgau, Leonhard Koppe, who had helped them to escape from the cloister of Marienthron in Nimbschen near Grimma.[62] Twelve had originally escaped, three of whom found refuge immediately in their former homes. Of the remaining nine, three names held peculiar significance. One was the sister of John Staupitz, one an aunt of Katharine von Bora, and Katharine herself.[63]

Continuous research has shed some light on the origin and childhood of Katharine von Bora, but much of her early life is still unknown. If the inscription in a locket given her by Martin in later years may be accepted, Katharine was born on January 29, 1499, probably in the little village of Lippendorf three miles south of Leipzig.[64] Her father, Hans von Bora, owned two pieces of property in this region, one in Lippendorf, the other a little farm on the Saale, later known as the Zulsdorf farm, which Luther bought from Kathie's brother in 1540 for 610 gulden.[65] As far as the father's family history has been traced, it seems that his ancestors were knights in western Germany, for the family possessed its own coat of arms. Some hundred years before, they with other knights had settled in the region upon the invitation of the prince. Since these lands had formerly been occupied by the Wends, the villages and towns often had Wendish names such as Wendishbora and Deutschenbora. The word *bora* used for both persons and places was a Wendish word meaning "fir trees." [66]

Even less is known about Kathie's mother, but it is likely that she was Katharine von Haubitz.[67] Her mother's sister was abbess of the nunnery where Katharine took her vows, but the aunt who escaped with Kathie was a sister of her father. It has also been established that the second wife of Philip of Hesse, Margarete von der Saale, was related to Katharine.[68]

According to Kroker, Katharine had three brothers and possibly a sister.[69] Her first education was received in the Benedictine school at Brehna, where another relative was in charge. About this time her mother died, and in 1505 her father remarried. Katharine seemed to be in her stepmother's way, and in 1508 or 1509 she was placed in the rich Cistercian nunnery, Marienthron, where she was to be trained for the Holy Order.[70]

This Nimbschen cloister was situated in a beautiful sunny valley, with shady woods, rolling fields, silvery streams, and lovely gardens surrounding the walled enclosure, part of which is standing today.[71] Most of its novitiates and nuns were of noble extraction. The massive buildings of the convent were artistically built of stone. The cloister church contained twelve altars and many highly treasured relics similar to those of the Castle Church in Wittenberg, which enabled it also to offer indulgences. On October 8, 1515, the sixteen-year-old novitiate Katharine von Bora was taken into the Cistercian Order and vowed to live according to the precepts of Bernard of Clairvaux, the second father. Margarete von Haubitz, her aunt and the abbess, was a kindly, understanding soul, and Kathie, who had known no other life, was probably happy as she performed her duties and prayers in a manner similar to that of Martin in the monastery in Erfurt.

Nimbschen was close to the border of Electoral Saxony, although actually located in the lands of Duke George.[72] The abandonment of so many cloisters in near-by Saxony, including the one in Wittenberg, was sure to have echoes in neighboring lands. In 1522 the prior of the Augustinian Hermits in Grimma left that monastery with a number of the monks.[73] Since he was related to two of the nuns in Nimbschen, the news must have reached this convent soon afterwards. Possibly Luther's tracts and sermons had been smuggled to its inmates.[74] Accepting the new Gospel that salvation was a gift from God which could not be earned by monastic observances, that true service must be motivated by love of Christ, not by formal observance of monastic rites, nuns and monks alike prepared to abandon their former way of life.

A group of nuns in Marienthron appealed to Luther to aid them in escaping from the cloister.[75] It was a dangerous undertaking to liberate nuns. According to both Canon and Civil Law the offender might expect the death penalty. The true story of the liberation of Katharine is difficult to re-establish, for the details were a well-kept secret, which tradition has embellished and confused beyond restoration. Even in its barest outlines the story is a fascinating one. Leonhard Koppe was a respected elderly citizen of Torgau, a member of the town council and at one time tax collector for the Elector, who made Torgau his home.[76] Koppe held a contract for the delivery of various supplies to the Nimbschen cloister, including numerous barrels of herring. These he was accustomed to carry in a canvas-covered wagon, and he would return the empty barrels on the homeward trip. Details of the escape are missing.[77] Some claim the nuns were hidden in the wagon and covered by the empty barrels. No one seemed to know just how the nuns made their escape from the cloister walls and eluded the vigilance of their keepers. The whole affair must have been well-planned, and it is most remarkable that with so many persons involved in the secret there should not have been some leak in the plans. The authorities had no means of stopping the vehicle once it was under way, for it could quickly cross the border into Saxony. The trip to Torgau through the lands of the Elector was comparatively safe. They arrived in Torgau on Easter Sunday and remained there on Monday before going on to Wittenberg, accompanied by Gabriel Zwilling, where they arrived Tuesday evening.[78]

Luther accepted his responsibility for their future, and in his letter to Spalatin he asked for funds to provide for them until homes could be found.[79] Soon all were located, some in their former homes, some as governesses, and in time many of them married.[80] But Katharine's father apparently had just died, and her stepmother and brothers were in poor circumstances and were not able to add Katharine to their burdens. Just where she lived is debatable. Kroker says she first lived with the Wittenberg professor Reichenbach and his wife. Boehmer believed she lived in the Lucas Cranach home, where the two Schoenfeld girls, who escaped with her, were staying.[81] In either event she spent considerable time in the Cranach home, and it must have been there that the King of Denmark, when he visited Wittenberg, gave her the ring which she later treasured so highly. It is interesting to note that among the small group invited to witness Kathie's engagement to Luther the Cranachs were included.

Kathie at this time was 24 years old. Was she an attractive young lady? This cannot be established on the basis of the few Cranach paintings in existence. But a medallion of 1540, while portraying a Kathie considerably more plump, shows mouth and nostrils delicately molded, with wide-set, intelligent eyes, broad brow, and well-proportioned face.[82] That she possessed a lively spirit is evidenced by her escape and subsequent events.[83] Erasmus, who must have obtained his information through Wittenberg acquaintances, spoke of her as "a young lady remarkably gracious." [84] But it cannot be assumed that Luther married her because of her beauty. At one time he mentioned that had he been inclined to choose one of the nuns, he would have chosen Ave Schoenfeld.[85]

Katharine was something of a problem, because she was too proud and too particular in her choice of a husband, not being satisfied with any of the suitors found for her. Although already past the marriageable age of girls in that day, she was immediately popular with the younger Wittenberg crowd, which often gathered in the home of Philip Melanchthon, himself only 25, where they formed a special Latin class and also presented plays. One of the star performers was Camerarius, who later located in Bamberg

and was a lifelong friend of Philip.[86] Another was Jerome Baumgaertner, son of a distinguished patrician family in Nuernberg, who
studied at Wittenberg from 1518 to 1521. In 1523 he revisited Wittenberg and met Kathie. The two immediately fell in love.[87] The
affair made such progress that by the time Baumgaertner left
arrangements had been made for his return, when he would take
Kathie to Nuernberg as his bride. But in his youthful enthusiasm
he had forgotten to consider the position of his parents. This proud
family would hardly approve of a runaway nun as daughter-in-
law. Baumgaertner did not return. This was a severe blow to the
proud Katharine; in fact, she became ill. At least one Wittenberg
student wrote to him in her behalf. Finally, on October 12, 1524,
Luther himself wrote to the young man:

> If you still wish to hold your Kathie von Bora, you had better act
> fast before she is given to another who is at hand (Dr. Kaspar
> Glatz). She still has not conquered her love for you. I would cer-
> tainly be happy to see you two married. Farewell.[88]

The man whom Luther had in mind was the present pastor
at Orlamuende and a former Rector of the University of Wittenberg.[89] He was not popular with his colleagues, who regarded him
as somewhat miserly. He was not popular with Katharine either,
who had not yet given up hope of Baumgaertner, nor did she until
she received the report that he was marrying a southern girl.[90]
Perhaps he was more faithful than she knew, for it was not until
after Katharine's marriage that he married the fifteen-year-old
daughter of Dichtel von Tutzing, a high-ranking official of Bavaria.
Luther continued to promote Glatz with Katharine until in desperation she decided upon bold strategy. A notation by Nicholas
von Amsdorf recently discovered in Abraham Scultetus' library
reveals that Katharine visited him and protested that Luther was
trying to force her to marry Glatz, whom she detested. She knew
that Luther and Amsdorf were close friends, and she boldly added
that if Luther or Amsdorf were willing, she would readily arrange an
honorable marriage with either, but with Glatz, never. Amsdorf
undoubtedly relayed the message to Luther.

There are many reasons to believe that up to this time Luther
had given the question of his own marriage little thought. When

at the Wartburg Luther first heard reports of monks taking wives, he wrote Spalatin August 6, 1521, "They will never force a wife upon me." [91] Later he pointed out that he was in danger of losing his life as a condemned heretic and should not expose a wife to such hazards. Furthermore, such a step might retard his reforms. In 1524 he was of the same opinion. Spalatin forwarded to him an inquiry from a pious woman of the Upper Palatinate who had heard a rumor that Luther was already married. In reply Luther wrote:

> I thank Argula for what she wrote me about marrying, nor do I wonder at such gossip when so many other things are said about me; please give her my thanks and say that I am in the hand of God, a creature whose heart he may change and rechange, may kill and make alive, at any hour or minute, but that hitherto I have not been, and am not now inclined to take a wife. Not that I lack the feelings of a man (for I am neither wood nor stone), but my mind is averse to marriage because I daily expect the death decreed to the heretic. However, I shall not ask God to bring my labors to an end, nor shall I strive in my heart, but I hope He will not let me live long. [92]

What caused Luther to change his mind in the spring of 1525 cannot be determined. No doubt, the fact that Kathie had expressed her willingness to marry him was a factor. [93] He visited his parents in April, on which occasion his father expressed his happiness over the fact that he had left the monastery and suggested that he should now marry, as he had urged him to do years ago. [94] Luther also took the problem to his Lord in earnest prayer, and the more he considered the matter, the more inclined he was to take the step. Nothing is known now about the details of Luther's courtship of Katharine. He admitted later in life that at the time he was not in love with her. Nor can it be assumed that Kathie was in love with him in the light of her regard for Baumgaertner and the fact that she had told Amsdorf that she would marry either of them.

Theodore Knolle has made a thorough study of the contemporary evidence and concluded: "Luther's marriage cannot be explained on personal grounds; it can only be understood in connection with his work as Reformer." [95] Luther probably realized that his teachings would lose some of their force unless he, too, practiced them. It was not sufficient to write against celibacy and to extol marriage as a divinely established institution unless he actually practiced what he believed. There were other contributing factors. Luther badly needed someone to look after him. His bed in the Black Cloister had not been made for years. He did not observe regular hours of eating and sleeping and neglected his health generally. Many of his associates had married, and he could observe their well-ordered home life and general well-being. Furthermore, he was responsible for Katharine's present circumstances, for it was due to his encouragement that she had left the nunnery. He felt sorry for her, too, because of the unfortunate love affair with Baumgaertner, and pity has often led to a deeper emotion.

There is reason to believe that once Luther had decided to take the step the final arrangements were made very quickly, for he later remarked:

> It is very dangerous to put off your wedding, for Satan gladly interferes and makes great trouble through evil talkers, slanderers, and friends of both parties. If I had not married quickly and secretly and taken few into my confidence, everyone would have done what he could to hinder me; for all my best friends cried: "Not this one, but another." [96]

The wedding was held on the evening of June 13, 1525, in the Black Cloister, whose second floor had been converted into living quarters. Only a small circle of close friends was invited. Lucas Cranach and his wife took the place of Luther's parents, and the former also represented the town as a member of the town council. Three other persons were present: Jonas, Prior of the Castle Church, Apel, law professor from the University, and Bugenhagen, town pastor and officiating clergyman. [97] No mention is made of the Reichenbachs, nor was Melanchthon present. The engagement formalities and the marriage ceremony followed in quick succession on the same evening. The following morning the guests assembled for a special breakfast. Jonas was deeply moved by this step which his friend Martin had taken, for on the following day he wrote thus to Spalatin:

Our Luther has married Catherine von Bora . . . yesterday. Seeing
that sight I had to give way to my feelings and could not refrain
from tears. Now that is has happened and is the will of God,
I wish this good and true man and beloved father in the Lord
much happiness. God is wonderful in His works and ways.[98]

What reason Luther may have had for not inviting Melanchthon to the wedding is today obscure, but Philip was deeply
offended. He wrote a letter to Camerarius which he later bitterly
regretted. Apparently, he wrote two letters, the first of which,
written on June 16, was not sent.[99] When, however, he received an
inquiry from Camerarius concerning the rumor that Luther had
married, he wrote the second letter, dated July 24, evidently with
the first letter before him. Both letters have been preserved, and
since much has been made of Melanchthon's remarks, the letter is
quoted as translated by Dr. Henry E. Jacob from the Greek:

Greetings. Since dissimilar reports concerning the marriage of Luther will reach you, I have thought it well to give you my opinion
of him. On June 13 Luther unexpectedly and without informing
in advance any of his friends of what he was doing, married Bora;
but in the evening, after having invited to supper none but Pome-
ranus and Lucas the painter, and Apel, observed the customary
marriage rites. You might be amazed that at this unfortunate time,
when good and excellent men everywhere are in distress, he not
only does not sympathize with them, but, as it seems, rather waxes
wanton and diminishes his reputation, just when Germany has es-
pecial need of his judgment and authority.

These things have occurred, I think, somewhat in this way: The
man is certainly pliable; and the nuns have used their arts against
him most successfully; thus probably society with the nuns has
softened or even inflamed this noble and high-spirited man. In
this way he seems to have fallen into this untimely change of life.
The rumor, however, that he had previously dishonored her is mani-
festly a lie. Now that the deed is done, we must not take it too
hard, or reproach him; for I think, indeed, that he was compelled
by nature to marry. The mode of life, too, while, indeed, humble,
is, nevertheless, holy and more pleasing to God than celibacy.

When I see Luther in low spirits and disturbed about his change of
life, I make my best efforts to console him kindly, since he has done
nothing that seems to me worthy of censure or incapable of defense.
Besides this, I have unmistakable evidences of his godliness, so that
for me to condemn him is impossible. I would pray rather that he
should be humbled than exalted and lifted up, as this is perilous

not only for those in the priesthood, but also for all men. For success affords occasion for the malevolence not only, as the orator says, of the senseless, but even of the wise. Besides, I have hopes that this state of life may sober him down, so that he will discard the low buffoonery which we have often censured. As the proverb runs: "A new state of life, a new mode of living."

I have enlarged on this subject that you may not be excessively disturbed by this unfortunate occurrence, for I know that you are concerned about Luther's reputation, which is imperiled. I exhort you to bear it meekly, since marriage is said in the Scriptures to be an honorable mode of life. It is likely that he was actually compelled to marry. God has shown us many falls of His saints of old because He wants us, pondering upon His Word, to be bound neither by the reputation nor the face of man. That person, too, is most godless who, because of the errors of a teacher, condemns the truth of the teaching.

The company of Michael (Roeting) is a very great comfort to me in the midst of this turmoil; I wonder that you allowed him to leave you. I am awaiting a letter from you concerning things in Franconia. Farewell. The day after Corpus Christi.

The courier who delivers this letter is to return to us immediately.[100]

Philippos

That Philip was occasionally inconsistent is shown by the letter he wrote to Link on June 20:

Doctor Martin has married. May it bring him good fortune and blessing. The guests are being invited to a wedding dinner on Tuesday after the day of John the Baptist. He did not wish to invite you that you might not have to make expenditures on his account. I, however, pray you on account of our friendship, come, for Doctor Hieronymus has further materials for discussion.[101]

Philip soon overcame his resentment, was promptly forgiven by Luther and Kathie, and became a frequent visitor in their home, where he learned to admire her fine qualities.

The wedding of Martin Luther was certain to have reverberations among both friends and foes. The couple became the target of much criticism and malicious gossip. It may have been that Luther wished to keep the event rather quiet in the hope of creating as little disturbance as possible in the already troubled times. But when his friends realized the damaging construction being placed upon the lack of publicity, they advised him to hold a public celebration. Bugenhagen wrote an explanatory letter to Spalatin, who was invited:

> Malicious talk has brought it to pass that Dr. Martin has unexpectedly become a husband. After a few days we have thought these sacred nuptials should be celebrated before all the world by public ceremony, to which you also without doubt will be invited.[102]

In the next few days Luther sent invitations to many friends and relatives, including the Mansfeld officials, Dr. John Ruehel, John Thuer, and Caspar Mueller, who were to bring his aged parents.

> Tuesday week, June 27, it is my intention to have a little celebration and housewarming, to which I beg that you will come and give your blessings. The land is in such a state that I hardly dare ask you to undertake the journey; however, if you can do so, pray come, along with my dear father and mother, for it would be a special pleasure to me.[103]

Many other well-known names were on the guest list, including Wenceslaus Link, Nicholas von Amsdorf, and other Wittenberg friends.[104] Marshall Hans von Dolzig and Spalatin from the Electoral Court were to bring some wild game for the wedding feast.[105] Leonhard Koppe was invited to bring a keg of "the best Torgau beer" instead of herring! [106] The city also contributed some liquid refreshment to the celebration.[107]

A special service in the Town Church began the day's festivities on June 27, when Martin Luther and Katharine von Bora publicly proclaimed to all the world that they had been married.[108] Whether there was an exchange of rings at this time is not certain. The ceremony was followed by a special wedding dinner at the Black Cloister and an *Ehrentanz,* a kind of square dance, held at the *Rathaus.* After this celebration the distinguished couple set up housekeeping in the newly renovated Black Cloister. Among the many gifts showered upon them was a silver pitcher decorated in gold, now the prized possession of the University of Greifswald.[109]

The reactions of his friends, colleagues, and others were extremely varied and may have elicited Luther's comment upon the undesirability of long engagements. Jerome Schurff, a colleague, was certain that Luther had now undone all that he had hitherto accomplished. Some were convinced that Katharine was a poor choice; Luther should have married a more distinguished woman. Still others pointed out that the time was far from opportune. Frederick the Wise had died just the preceding month. The Peasants' War was not yet over. The future of Germany looked very dark indeed. These critics felt that Luther could ill afford to add to the country's burden by weakening his leadership. Luther, however, was not affected by criticism whether of friend or foe. He was sure in his own heart that the step he had taken was right. Perhaps it is well that Luther did not give too much consideration to the reactions of others to his reforms or personal decisions. Had his leadership been as discreet and diplomatic as his critics wished, most of his bold tracts would never have been written, and the Reformation would not have been possible.

Although Luther was perfectly honest in admitting that he was not motivated by love in marrying Katharine, it was not long before he grew very fond of her.[110] A year later he already wrote to a friend:

> Kathie sends greetings, and thanks you for thinking her worthy of such a letter. She is well, by the grace of God, and is in all things more compliant, obedient and obliging than I had dared to hope, — thanks be to God! — so that I would not exchange my poverty for the wealth of Croesus.[111]

Kathie was no doubt just the type of wife Luther needed. She was a conscientious mother, an efficient housekeeper, a wise manager of the farms, gardens, cattle, and other livestock, for which Luther had so little time. After 1540 he occasionally called her the "boss of Zulsdorf," for sometimes she made lengthy visits to the farm which Luther had purchased when her brother was about to lose it through foreclosure.[112] Kathie's management must have added considerably to Luther's income, making it easier to provide for his family and some dozen nieces, nephews, aunts, and needy relatives, and also freed Luther from many family details and responsibilities. Luther, who had little time from his labors to help rear obedient, God-fearing children, often thanked God for such a "pious and true wife on whom the husband's heart can rely."

The Luther Family

Unfortunately, the many changes undergone in its subsequent
history by the Black Cloister, or Luther House, as it came to be
known, make it impossible to determine with certainty the exact
living conditions of the Luther family. Scholars have pointed out
that only the *Lutherzimmer* has been preserved in its original
size and appearance. This famous room was the heart of family
life and also the center from which Luther's leadership radiated
to all parts of Germany. The other living quarters were grouped
about this room, except the kitchen, which was on the ground floor.
Hermann Stein tried to reconstruct the general environment in his
now rare study *Geschichte des Lutherhauses.*[113] The property was
fenced off from the street and entered by means of a gate with
two small houses on either side.[114] A garden of flowers and shrubs
lay between the gate and the house itself. To the right of the
garden was a small stable and on the left the little chapel in which
Luther had first preached to the monks.[115] Behind the house next
to the city wall was a small vegetable garden, in which Luther ex-
perimented with all kinds of plants, flowers, and vegetables sent
to him by friends from all over Germany.[116] Here he raised melons,
cucumbers, cabbages, radishes, and other garden crops for the
family table. Just west of the Luther House stood a small building, the *Brauhaus,* or brewery, in which Kathie prepared the
family brew from the barley sent annually by the Elector.[117]

The contrast in the life of the Black Cloister must have been
extremely noticeable to its neighbors. Where formerly sedate monks
had walked about by twos with bowed heads and sober mien,
dressed in the somber black robes of the order, the halls now echoed
the laughter and chatter of children's voices, the hustle and bustle
of a busy household, the vitality and exuberance of youth.[118]
When Luther married Katharine, he was forty-two years of age;
she was twenty-six. During their two decades of married life God
blessed them with six children. When little Hans, the eldest,
arrived on June 7, 1526, it was a day of great rejoicing for Luther's
friends all over Germany.[119] On the same day the child was baptized in the Town Church by George Roerer.[120] Bugenhagen, for
whom he was named, was the sponsor, who had the distinction

of lifting him from the famous Vischer font after the immersion.
Jonas, Cranach, and the *Buergermeister's* wife were other local
sponsors, while by proxy Vice Chancellor Christian Baier of the
Saxon court, the Mansfeld Chancellor Mueller, and Nicolaus Gerbel
served in the same capacity.[121] After eight days Hans already began to correspond with his father's friends and received many
greetings. Presents arrived from all over Germany. Jonas sent a
coin engraved with the likeness of the Elector John; Hausmann sent
a rattle from Zwickau; when Hans was about a year old, Jacob
Wildeck sent him a little wagon.[122] His parents were pushed into
the background; the arrival of the first tooth at six months was
a national event.[123]

But Luther and Katharine were soon to experience the anguish
of parents who suffer the loss of a little one. Their second child,
Elizabeth, born December 10, 1527, lived less than a year, for
she died August 3, 1528.[124] The parents were deeply grieved by
her passing, and Luther confessed that she had left him a "very
sick, effeminate heart, so much do I grieve over her." The following May 4, 1529, their grief was assuaged with the arrival of little
Magdalena, and on November 9, 1531, the parents welcomed their
second son, who almost duplicated his father's birthday and was
named Martin.[125] Luther once looked upon the little lad and said:

> My little Martin, my dear treasure, needs my care more than John,
> my dear son, or my daughter Magdalena, who can already talk and
> ask for things which they need. For this reason one does not need
> to look after them so much any longer.[126]

On January 29, 1533, a third son was born, whom they named
Paul.[127] Their youngest child, Margarethe, was born on December 17, 1534.[128]

In his educational writings Luther had pointed out that the
schools in previous generations had placed too much emphasis on
physical punishment. He believed that the apple should always
lie beside the rod. His genuine understanding of child psychology
is reflected in the famous letter he wrote to little Hans, a lad of
four, while at the Feste Coburg in 1530:

> Grace and peace in. Christ, my dear little son. I am happy to see
> that you are studying well and saying your prayers faithfully. Con-

tinue, my dear son. When I come home, I will bring you a nice present.

I know an attractive, pleasant garden full of little children who wear golden jackets and gather nice apples under the trees, and pears, cherries, purple and yellow plums. They sing and skip and are happy and have pretty little ponies with golden reins and silver saddles. Then I asked the owner of the garden whose children they were, to which he replied, "Dear man, they are the children who like to pray, enjoy studying, and are good." I said to the man, "Dear sir, I also have a son, whose name is Hans Luther. Could he not also come into this garden that he might eat such nice apples and pears, and ride such pretty ponies, and play with the children?" The man replied, "He can, provided he likes to pray, studies hard, and is very good. Phil and Justy may come with him, and they will have whistles, drums, and fifes, and dance and shoot with little bows and arrows."

Next the man showed me a nice lawn in the garden all equipped for dancing, where golden whistles, fifes, and drums, and nice silver cross bows hang from the trees all over. But it was still early in the day when the children had not yet eaten, and I just could not wait to see them dance, so I said to the man, "My dear sir, I must immediately go and write my dear Hans about all this that he may pray, study, and be a good boy, so he may also come into this garden. But he also has an Aunt Lena, whom he must bring with him." The man replied, "Very well. Go and tell him about it." So, my little lad Hans, study and pray well and tell Phil and Justy to repeat their prayers and study also, for then you will enter the garden together. May God bless you. Give Aunt Lena my love and a kiss for me.[129]

Herein is revealed the tender love of Luther, the father, and his ability to enter the realm of childish fancy and imagination. That he had a sterner side is evidenced by his remark that he would prefer to have a "dead rather than a disobedient son." That Hans might fully realize the seriousness of his misbehavior, he was once forbidden to see his father for three days, a punishment which was carried out in spite of the entreaties of Kathie and other friends.[130]

Contrary to what might have been expected, Luther did find time for attention to the small deeds of his children, for his sermons and table talks are profusely illustrated with his observations of their activities. Again Katharine's efficient home management must have played a large part in arranging for the children to enjoy intimate companionship with their father while at the same time providing the necessary hours of quiet and solitude for his prodigious labors. Her burden was eased somewhat by the aid of the numerous aunts and other relatives who made their home with the Luthers. But even the commodious living quarters on the second floor of the Luther House must have been sometimes inadequate for such a large household.[131] Sometimes the presence of these numerous "guests" must have added many problems to the complicated family life.

The following letter of advice to Prince George of Anhalt, who was considering a visit to Wittenberg, gives some insight into the circumstances of the Luther home:

> The home of Luther is occupied by a motley crowd of boys, students, girls, widows, old women, and youngsters. For this reason there is much disturbance in the place, and many regret it for the sake of the good man, the honorable father. If but the spirit of Doctor Luther lived in all of these, his house would offer you an agreeable, friendly quarter for a few days so that your Grace would be able to enjoy the hospitality of that man. But as the situation now stands and as circumstances exist in the household of Luther, I would not advise that your Grace stop there.[132]

Included in the "motley crowd" were two daughters and four sons of a sister of Luther; Hans Polner, son of another sister; and another nephew, the son of his brother; a great-niece, Anna Strauss; a lady teacher, Margarethe von Mochau; other tutors of the Luther children, at one time numbering six; and Aunt Lena, mentioned in the letter to Hans, the same aunt who had escaped with Kathie from the nunnery and who faithfully cared for the children until her death in 1537.[133] To these more or less permanent members of the family must be added numerous nuns and monks who found themselves without occupation, the twelve table companions who spent varying lengths of time under the Luther roof, a steady flow of guests, and indigent pastors without pulpits.[134] All who for any length of time took up their abode in the Luther House were considered members of the family and were expected to conform to the family customs. They were expected to study the Catechism, pray, and attend the family devotions, which included the reading from the *Hauspostille* on Sundays.[135] Luther was in every sense the bishop of his own household.

There was also provision for wholesome recreation in the Luther family life. There was a bowling lane in Luther's garden, much enjoyed by the young people and friends of the family. Sometimes Luther himself found time to roll a few balls.[136] The children had ample space for play in the roomy grounds of the Luther House. Music and singing held a favored place in family amusements, and chess was a game much enjoyed by Luther. His delight in these family pastimes was expressed following a particularly enjoyable hour of singing.[137]

> If the Lord God has given us such noble gifts already in this life, which is, after all, a storeroom, what will happen in yonder eternal life, where everything is entirely perfect and most lovely? In this world we have everything only in the rough.[138]

At times the demands of the family life and Luther's labors must have strained the capacity of the *Lutherzimmer* and Kathie's nerves to the utmost. When Luther became extremely busy, chairs, wall boards, window ledges, and even the floor were covered with accumulated correspondence, manuscripts, reference works, dictionaries, and other books until it must have been one mad jumble.[139] His work table was so loaded down that no one but he could find his way through the materials. Kathie fully appreciated the importance of her husband's work and did not dare to disturb his tools. She frequently sat by the window, quietly spinning or sewing, while her husband was deeply engrossed in some tract or problem. Often some discussion begun at the evening meal by the table companions would be continued in this family living room, or other student groups would drop in to engage their distinguished professor in conversation. In this same room the commission of professors which assisted Luther in the translation of the Bible after 1531 held their sessions. Consisting of Melanchthon, Aurogallus, Cruciger, Jonas, and Bugenhagen, the members of the commission were the most intimate friends of the Luther family, and no doubt they frequently visited in the home on other occasions.[140] As important personages came through Wittenberg, they usually called upon its most famous citizen. Katharine was fully conscious of the fact that God had made her the wife of one of the great men of history, and she nobly fulfilled the role of wife, mother, and hostess.

Included in its many joys, the Luther home also experienced its measure of earthly sorrow. Luther suffered a severe illness in the summer of 1527, and it was the following summer when little Elizabeth passed away.[141] In the winter of 1530 Luther's father became seriously ill, and he died May 29, while Luther was at the Coburg.[142] On June 30, 1531, his mother also departed this life.[143] Luther experienced numerous minor illnesses, but in 1537 he had a severe gallstone attack, so serious that fear was felt for his life, and Bugenhagen assisted him in making his will.[144] In the summer of 1542 the uncertainty of human life was again demonstrated when little Magdalena became seriously ill. Her brother Hans had just gone to Torgau with his teacher, and he was called home immediately, for little Lena was much attached to her big brother. Those were anxious and sorrowful days. Although his own heart was sorely grieved, Luther tried to comfort Kathie by saying: "Dear Kathie, remember where she came from. She is faring well." On September 20 she passed away in her father's arms just after he had asked her if she was willing to go to her Father above and she had answered: "Yes, dear father, just as God wills." [145]

A really staggering blow was struck the little family with the sudden death of Martin Luther on February 18, 1546, in his native town of Eisleben.[146] Added to their deep sorrow was the necessity for providing means of livelihood. Luther had received a generous salary, but it had been consumed in the large expenses of the household. He had accumulated some property, but it did not provide ready revenue. Now Kathie needed her gifts for management as never before. Fortunately, the princes of Anhalt and the Electoral Court considered her plight. Elector John Frederick honored the agreement whereby Kathie was allowed possession of the Luther House during her lifetime, and he placed an additional 1,000 gulden at interest for the Luther children.[147] The Princes of Mansfeld also promised to pay 2,000 gulden, but payment was delayed, and only half of the sum had been received by Kathie's death. The Elector also enabled her to procure a new farm for the children, the *Gut Wachsdorf*, for 2,200 gulden.[148]

But even more disturbing to Katharine than her financial circumstances was the insistence of Chancellor Brueck that the boys should be taken from her in order to receive proper training.[149] By every means at her command, Kathie fought to keep the family together. Enlisting the aid of Melanchthon and Cruciger, she finally persuaded the chancellor that Hans had no talent for the law and that the two professors were quite capable of instructing the two younger boys.

Further trials were to come. When the Ratisbon meeting with the Kaiser on June 16, 1546, failed, the Schmalkaldic War burst over Germany. The Protestants were strong in numbers, but they lacked leadership. During the fall and early winter the opposing armies faced each other across the Danube without a major engagement.[150] Then Moritz, the Elector John Frederick's cousin, turned traitor, bribed by the promise of the Electoral title. In the middle of winter Kathie and her children fled to Magdeburg.[151] Others from the University took refuge in various cities. Kathie's only means of sustenance was gifts from friends and princes.[152] As Moritz withdrew to the south, the townspeople gradually returned to their homes, among them the Luthers.

In the spring of 1547 the forces of Charles V, his brother Ferdinand, and Duke Moritz joined and moved down the east bank of the Elbe River.[153] John Frederick was encamped on the opposite bank near Muehlberg. Under cover of a fog the combined imperial forces crossed the river unexpectedly, defeated the surprised troops, and made John Frederick a prisoner.[154] When this news reached Wittenberg, panic struck the town. In the few days' delay before the victorious troops could surround the town there was a second exodus. Kathie and her family, accompanied by Bugenhagen's wife, again fled to Magdeburg.[155] Plans were made through Melanchthon to continue to Denmark, whose king had shown his sympathy for Luther's widow by sending 50 thaler per year for her maintenance.[156] But the Duke of Lueneburg advised against the journey as the country was full of troops. With the Wittenberg capitulation on May 19, 1547, Moritz as the new

Elector of the region promised security and peace to the town and University.[157] Gradually the faculty returned, and in the latter part of June, Kathie also felt obliged to return, as her faithful servant, Sieberger, had just died and there was no one to care for her property.

The war had meant considerable loss to Kathie.[158] Her farms lay right along the highways that both armies had used. Her livestock had disappeared, barns and sheds had been pillaged and burned. To rebuild the farms, she borrowed a thousand gulden and resumed the boarding of students. Many unscrupulous persons were quick to take advantage of the helpless widow. The defection of Moritz caused the politically minded Protestants to scramble for his favor. Many of the former friends of Luther deserted Kathie now, but Jonas, Melanchthon, Cruciger, the King of Denmark, and the Duke of Prussia, among others, stood faithfully by her side.[159] The King of Denmark continued his annual gift of 50 thaler, while the Duke of Prussia even educated Hans in the University of Koenigsberg.[160]

In the summer of 1552 the plague again broke out in Wittenberg, and the University was moved to Torgau. By fall Kathie decided to leave also. On the way the horses became frightened and bolted, and Kathie jumped from the carriage. Added to her many misfortunes, the accident and shock were more than even her gallant spirit could endure.[161] For months she lay between life and death and finally passed away on December 20, 1552, aged 53 years, 11 months. Perhaps owing to the unsettled conditions Kathie was buried in the near-by *Pfarrkirche* at Torgau instead of near her famous husband, to whose faith she had remained faithful unto death.[162]

At the time they were left orphans, Hans, the eldest of the Luther children, had reached the age of 26 years. Martin was 21, Paul 19, and Margarethe 18 years old. When his third son, Paul, was born, Luther had remarked that Hans should become a theologian, Martin might become a jurist, while the sturdy Paul showed the characteristics of a warrior; but like the plans of so many fond parents, the future held a different story. Following his father's death, Hans studied law and, more from respect for his father's memory than recognition of any ability on his part, was subsequently employed in the Weimar chancellory as adviser. Martin studied theology, but never occupied a pulpit.[163] Paul became an able physician and served in several courts with distinction. He first served in the Ernestine court as the family physician of the three sons of John Frederick. Later he was the physician of Duke John Frederick of Gotha. Next he went to the court of Elector Joachim II of Brandenburg, whom he served until the Elector's death in 1571.[164] The same year Paul Luther was called to the court of Elector August of the Albertine Saxon family in Dresden and, when August died, continued under his successor, Christian I. But this court had become too liberal for his religious views, and he settled down in the more orthodox Leipzig in 1590. He finally passed away March 8, 1593.[165] Paul Luther, the father of six children, had a son, John Ernest, in whom the male line continued. When his descendant, the Dresden advocate Martin Gottlob Luther, died in 1759, the male line of the Luther family died out.[166]

Luthers' youngest daughter, Margarethe, married a Wittenberg student, Georg von Kunheim.[167] He was of a rich Prussian noble family. Their wedding on August 5, 1555, was well attended by representatives from the nobility and university professors and was performed with great pomp and ceremony. The marriage was a very happy one, but unfortunately Margarethe passed away at the early age of 36 in 1570.[168] Her descendants on the maternal side have lived on to the present time.

Wittenberg Becomes the Nursery
of the German Reformation

A S HAS BEEN OBSERVED in a previous chapter, Martin Luther was supported by the entire faculty of the University when he nailed his *Ninety-Five Theses* on the door of the Castle Church in Wittenberg. From that time on the school was the nursery of the German Reformation. Luther became the chief of a whole army of reformers, while Melanchthon, Jonas, Bugenhagen, Amsdorf, and other members of the Wittenberg faculty formed the general staff. To understand Luther, one must consider him in this university environment, together with the thousands of other contributors to this involved historical movement. After the early twenties Luther's life became inextricably interwoven with that of the University. Therefore, an examination of the transformation which took place in the University of Wittenberg between 1521 and 1560 is essential.

STUDENT ENROLLMENT

All students enrolled at the University of Wittenberg were recorded in a book known as the university *Album*.[1] The earlier entries gave the German town from which they came, but later only the region was mentioned. These entries make it possible for the research student to locate the regions from which the students came each year, and in this manner the spread of Lutheranism can be determined. Before the year 1520 the records are not particularly significant, as students naturally came from all over Germany to the University on the Elbe.[2] Many came out of curiosity, because the institution was new. After 1517 the enrollment increased rapidly, as the fame of Martin Luther spread and many students were eager to meet this man who was firing the minds and souls of all Germany. After 1521, however, a great change occurred. After Luther's condemnation by the Edict of Worms, conservative Catholics were no longer willing to expose the faith of their youth to such heretics as Luther, Melanchthon, and the "whole nest of vipers." [3] Wittenberg then became a Lutheran school in fact, for only parents who accepted Luther's reforms would knowingly enroll their children there. From this time on the matriculation book, the original of which is still in Halle, Germany, became the mirror in which the growth of the German Reformation was reflected.[4]

Between the years 1520 and 1560 approximately 16,000 students matriculated at the University of Wittenberg.[5] Judging by later centuries, historians always believed that the Reformation had spread mainly to northern Germany, but a plotting of student enrollment reveals that the movement had gained as many converts in southern as in northern Germany, each of them contributing approximately one third of the total registration. From northern Germany came 5,685, and from southern Germany 5,750.[6] After 1560, when Luther and Melanchthon had both passed from the scene, Lutheranism began to coast on the reputation of the founders. The Church lost most of its former dynamic evangelical spirit and was content to maintain the *status quo* and to dissipate its strength in a new type of scholastic dogmatism which quibbled over what the Reformer had or had not actually taught. Then it was that southern Germany was lost to the cause through the activities of the Jesuits and the Counter Reformation.[7]

An examination of the detailed information to be drawn from the university *Album* throws much light upon heretofore little-understood situations. The withdrawal of the Catholic support had an immediate effect on the University, a fact disclosed by the accompanying graph.[8] In 1520 the student matriculation had reached a new peak when 552 registered in the University.[9] In two years that enrollment had dropped to about 200 and was still going down. Historians previously blamed the decline on the disturbances caused by Carlstadt and the Zwickau prophets. No doubt they

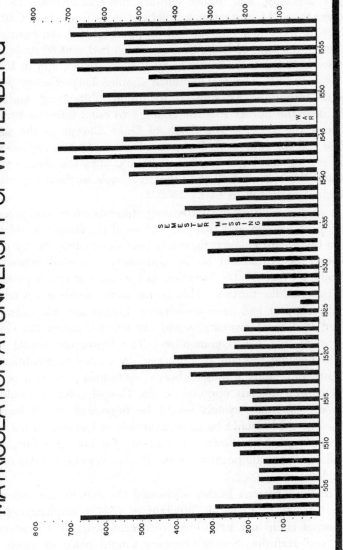

Graph of student enrollment at the University of Wittenberg, 1502 to 1560. By the author

were a factor; but a plotting of the students from Meissen, Bamberg, Wuerzburg, and Mainz supplies the real answer. In 1520 no fewer than 214 student matriculations were from these Catholic lands;[10] by 1530 their number had dropped to 24.[11] An example is Meissen in the land of Duke George, which had sent 83 students in 1520; by 1530 the number was 8; by 1540 it was 43; and in 1550 it was back to 84.[12] The explanation is simple. Duke George posted placards forbidding his subjects to attend Wittenberg, and only a few near the border had the courage to cross into the lands of Frederick the Wise.[13] The death of Duke George in the spring of 1539 and the rule of his Protestant brother, Henry, are reflected in the rise in enrollment to 43 in 1540, and after the church visitations and the organization of Lutheran schools in these regions the enrollment increased to 84 by 1550.[14]

A similar plotting of Wittenberg students every ten years on the map of Europe and the study of local conditions in relationship to these matriculation figures is very significant. As the graph indicates, the enrollment of the University remained around the 200 mark all through the twenties, and it did not rise appreciably until the middle thirties. This is no mere accident. After the Catholic support had been withdrawn, Luther and his colleagues realized that the University would not survive unless the Gospel was spread into new communities. The University would itself have to become thoroughly Lutheran. A survey of conditions in the Lutheran lands through church visitations was a necessity. Those church officials opposed to the Gospel reforms would be removed. Christian schools would be organized at all learning levels. The Bible would be made available in German to the laity. The people must be shown the necessity for lay education, since clerical and monastic positions in the Roman system were no longer available.

For these reasons Luther addressed the mayors and aldermen of the German cities in his *Weckruf of 1524*,[15] emphasizing that the Gospel could not have been recovered without a mastery of Greek and Hebrew. Surely Germany should place as much emphasis on education as had the pagans of the Graeco-Roman world. Germany should have educated lawyers, bankers, doctors, and others to provide leadership. Only by the establishment of schools and the training of the necessary teachers could this aim be realized. The same viewpoint was reiterated in 1530 in his *Sermon on the Duty of Sending Children to School.*[16] He now knew the tragic religious conditions in the Saxon lands from the visitations carried out in the late twenties. The pressing need was vividly portrayed in the following citation:

> Consider for yourselves how many pastorates, schools, and other offices are daily becoming vacant. That fact assures your son of a support before he needs it or has earned it. When I was a young student, I heard it said that in Saxony, if I mistake not, there were about eighteen hundred parishes. If that is true, and if with each parish two persons, a pastor and a sexton, are connected (not counting the preachers, chaplains, assistants, and teachers in the cities), it follows that about four thousand learned persons belong to such a principality, of whom one third die in ten years. Now I would wager that there are not four thousand students in the half of Germany. I venture the assertion also that there are scarcely eight hundred pastors in Saxony; — how many must be wanting in all Germany? [17]

Luther added that the situation would indeed be desperate in a few years when there would be but one pastor for three or four cities and a single chaplain for ten villages. He pointed out that Erfurt, Leipzig, and other schools were deserted, leaving the whole task of meeting the need for Gospel preachers, teachers, and consecrated laymen to Wittenberg alone with its pitiful enrollment of only 200 students.

The response to Luther's pleas and the organization of schools and churches supplied with Lutheran teachers and pastors bore fruit in the middle thirties, when the Wittenberg enrollment rose to around 400 and by 1540 topped the 500 mark.[18] Melanchthon, Bugenhagen, Jonas, Amsdorf, Spengler, Brenz, Hesz, and dozens of others had pioneered in the development of new Lutheran communities, and students were now graduating from these schools and beginning to fill the lecture rooms of the University of Wittenberg.[19] In this whole movement Luther was still the central figure, but was assisted in the enormous task of reconstruction and reorganization by the entire University and hundreds of enthusiastic and loyal outside supporters.

The First Lutheran University

Before the University of Wittenberg could perform such an important role in the German Reformation, it, too, needed to be reorganized. This was done under the leadership of Luther and Melanchthon with the help of the new Elector, John Frederick. With the new set of statutes given the University from 1533 to 1536 the first real Lutheran university came into being.[20] In many respects this new institution of higher learning was remarkable for its day.

When the University of Wittenberg was founded by Frederick the Wise in 1502, he expected it to differ little from other universities of Germany. Until Luther's discovery of "justification by faith" and his conversion of the faculty to his point of view, Scholasticism had flourished in Wittenberg as elsewhere. But as has been shown, after 1517 many changes were made, and the new Biblical Humanism championed by Luther and Melanchthon had finally triumphed. In the statutes drafted by Melanchthon for the University in 1523 he pointed out that "disputations in philosophy have become dull," and henceforth they would be devoted twice a month to "rhetoric and grammar." [21] But as the Reformation progressed, the University outgrew its framework, and basic changes were again made in the statutes of 1533 to 1536.

Melanchthon, who was undoubtedly the spokesman for the whole faculty, prefaced the statutes of 1533 for the theological faculty with the following statement:

> As in the churches and boys' schools throughout our territories, so in the University, which should be the chief guide and censor of doctrine, we wish to have taught the pure doctrine of the Gospel in accordance with the confession which was presented to Emperor Charles in August, 1530, which doctrine we assert with certainty to be the true and eternal teaching of the Catholic Church of God, to be piously and faithfully proclaimed, preserved, and propagated.[22]

These statutes assert that there shall be four members composing the theological faculty of the University, all of whom must have the title of Doctor granted by Wittenberg or some other well-qualified school.[23] Should a candidate for a theological position be a graduate of another institution, the statutes require that he first be examined in a public disputation. Although other books of the Bible were to be studied and interpreted, the statutes provided that special emphasis must be placed on Romans, the Gospel of St. John, the Psalms, Genesis, and Isaiah, for they best emphasize Christian doctrine.[24] Augustine's book on *The Spirit and the Letter* was also to be expounded before the students.[25] The annual courses in the theological curriculum were to be arranged by the dean and one other ranking member of the faculty and constantly adjusted to the need of the times. The theological faculty was to engage in public disputations four times a year.[26] Lest there might be a possibility of giving offense, the materials for the debate were first to be examined by the dean of the University. Should there be any doubt, the Rector of the University and the dean might defer the disputation until the entire faculty had examined the subject. Should a problem of heresy or disagreement arise, the statutes provided for the appointment of judges to deal with the problem.[27]

Theological students were required to be graduates from the Liberal Arts College with an emphasis on Latin, Greek, and Hebrew. The candidate for the first theological degree, *Biblicus,* had to be conversant with Romans and the Gospel of St. John.[28] For the second degree in the Lutheran Seminary, *Sententiarius,* the student was versed in exegesis and dogmatics, thoroughly imbued with the writings of St. Paul, and possibly the Psalms or Prophets.[29] The former reading of Peter Lombard's *Sentences* was now completely discontinued. The next degree, *Formatus,* was granted only after the candidate had shown his theological comprehension in a public disputation.[30] Finally, after six years of intensive study and undeniable proof that the candidate was filled "with the pure doctrine of the Gospel," he was granted the degree of Doctor of Theology.[31] The 1533 statutes state that great care must be exercised in selecting candidates for these higher degrees both as to ability and consecration.

Elector John Frederick incorporated these provisions in refounding the University under the *Fundationsurkunde* given the University in 1536.[32] The basic provisions of the original statutes remained, and the organization of the first Lutheran university was as follows. At the head of the school was a Rector, who was selected each semester by the faculty from among its ranking members.[33] Under the Rector were four deans, representing the College of Liberal Arts and the graduate schools of Theology, Law, and Medicine.[34] The total membership of the faculty was still twenty-two regular staff members and fifteen graduate assistants.[35]

In the graduate school of Theology, Luther, Jonas, Cruciger, and Bugenhagen were named as regular professors.[36] In the school of Law were listed Schurff, Emden, and two unfilled chairs; in Medicine Lindemann, Schurpf, and an unfilled chair; and in Liberal Arts Melanchthon is mentioned, while the incumbents of the chairs of Greek, Hebrew, Latin, Mathematics, Physics, Rhetoric, Pedagogy, and several others are not specifically named.[37] This was not a large group of men, but contained in the faculty were some of the ablest minds of the day. Melanchthon wrote textbooks in a number of fields, some of which were used in the universities of Europe for over a hundred years.[38] He even wrote a textbook in *Seelenlehre,* a book in psychology, which took most of its material from the ancients. Bugenhagen engaged in translating and other writing. Cruciger was as well known for his botanical studies as for his linguistic accomplishments.[39] Jonas, too, was extremely helpful to Luther in the work of translation.[40] The faculty was reasonably well paid for that day and the Wittenberg staff was never lacking in capable men.[41]

The first Lutheran university was also equipped with a very fine library, which has been described in detail in previous pages.[42] This ample and up-to-date library collection added greatly to the efficiency of the institution both in student preparation and in the private research of the professors. Classroom instruction seems also to have been of high quality. After 1560 students in Medicine actually dissected human bodies, a practice rare in other universities of that day, and were required to know the human anatomy in detail before graduating from the medical school.[43] Students received instruction in Geography very similar to that of Columbus. The University had purchased a large globe, which certainly acquainted students with the viewpoint that the earth was round.[44] That Luther, Melanchthon, and others still held to the geocentric

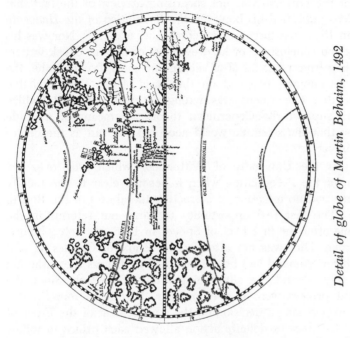

Detail of globe of Martin Behaim, 1492

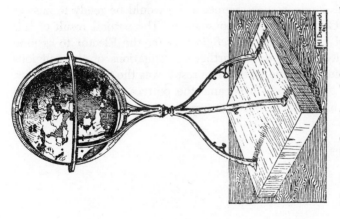

Martin Behaim's globe as used in various German universities. Drawn from an original by Denemarck

theory of the universe was not surprising in view of the fact that Copernicus published his book *On the Revolution of the Heavenly Bodies* in 1543, just three years before Luther died.[45] Nor was his evidence too conclusive, for he drew most of it from Greek writers rather than from personal observation, and even Tycho Brahe, the Danish astronomer, believed on the basis of the then available evidence that Copernicus was wrong. It was not until Galileo began to support the Copernican theory by means of a crude telescope that the scientific world accepted the sun as the center of the universe.[46]

It was the University of Wittenberg which took over the direction of the Reformation when it became clear to the faculty that Rome had no intention of correcting the abuses of the Roman Church. The first real opportunity to carry out reforms in the field came after the first Diet of Speyer in 1526. As noted before, this German Diet was not attended by Emperor Charles V, and his brother Ferdinand had been instructed to dismiss the gathering immediately, should the situation get out of control. Since the Protestant princes were in the majority, Ferdinand found it expedient to postpone a decision on the enforcement of the Edict of Worms. This lack of definite action allowed each prince to follow a practice already centuries old, that of conducting the religious affairs of his lands in such manner as he would be ready to answer for before God and his own conscience. The natural result of this principle of *cuius regio eius religio* was for the Elector to assume responsibility and to order further investigations of the religious conditions in Ernestine lands. The result was the Saxon Visitations, carried on to 1545, which became the pattern for an inquiry into conditions in the lands of all evangelical princes.

« 20 »

Founding of the Lutheran Church

THE MEDIEVAL HERITAGE

EARLY CHRISTIANITY in the Mediterranean lands had been episcopal in form, an ecclesiastical organization centered about a bishop.[1] When Christianity spread to the north, Germanic law forced it to undergo a basic metamorphosis. The German princes and kings insisted that they owned and controlled the land on which the altar stood. As Ulrich Stutz has shown, from this day there began to develop the German *Eigenkirche,* or Proprietary Church.[2] Being the proprietor, the prince could engage the clergy as he would hire his own personal servants. He owned the altar, and all other appurtenances were regarded as adjunct property, which could be increased but not diminished.[3] By the time of Charlemagne this system of church organization was generally recognized throughout Germanic lands.

Basically, the medieval investiture controversy continuing from the time of Pope Gregory VII (1073) to the Concordat of Worms (1122) revolved about this fundamental organization, which had almost completely secularized the Roman Church in Germanic lands. To engage both the Emperor and the princes simultaneously seemed inadvisable; hence, Gregory VII began his campaign against the Emperor, seeking the support of the princes.[4] But by making common cause with the medieval princes, both the Papacy and the medieval Empire were ruined in the end, and the German princes emerged as the real victors in the Concordat of Worms. Therefore, instead of being crushed, the German *Eigenkirche* lived on in the territorial Church and became an integral part of the new movement of the late Middle Ages known as Territorialism.[5]

613

By the time of the Hohenstaufens (1139–1254) this new force in the German states was definitely apparent, seeming to have its greatest vigor in the new East. Before this time dukes and princes had been proud to hold offices in the medieval Empire. As Territorialism emerged, the emphasis shifted to fiefs, castles, rights of coinage, local diets, justice, anything which augmented the real power of the territorial prince.[6] Nor did strong territorial princes regard the lands of the Church as inviolate. By every means in their power these princes sought to gain control of local church officials by granting them special privileges and protection, relief from taxation, and offering them posts in the government to win them from the control of the Church.[7]

The period of the Babylonian Captivity (1305–1377) and the Schism (1378–1417) did not enhance the power and prestige of the Roman Church in these territories. Its lack of spirituality and general decline was transmitted to its German clergy and served to aid further the growth in power of the territorial prince. A letter from Aeneas Silvius Piccolomini to King Charles VII of France in 1443 may be exaggerated, but it gives considerable insight into the changing attitudes of the formerly arrogant clergy:

> I see no ecclesiastic who for this or that party would court martyrdom. We all have the same faith as our princes. If they pray to idolatrous pictures, so do we, and not only deny the Pope, but even Christ, should the secular power force us to that position.[8]

This decentralizing force continued during the second half of the fifteenth century. By the time of Emperor Maximilian (1493 to 1519) the power of the Holy Roman Emperor had practically disappeared in German lands. In his stead, it was common practice to look upon the territorial prince as sovereign and to regard his estates as his private property.

After Luther had been condemned by the Imperial Edict at Worms, a Council of Regency was formed to deal with the enforcement of the Edict and other German problems arising during the absence of the Emperor; but the German Estates refused to act in subsequent diets held in Nuernberg in 1522 and 1524, and papal pressure was of little avail.[9] Even among the most conservative princes there were those who, like Duke George, felt that there was great need for reform and that the people were justified in demanding the preaching of the "pure Gospel."[10] As for the problem of Luther, the princes were uncertain of the course they should pursue, especially since he had been a restraining influence during the Wittenberg disturbances and the subsequent Peasants' Revolt.[11] They were convinced that any violence to Luther would provoke further bloodshed.

With the lack of decisive action the situation grew rapidly worse. In parts of Germany two opposing leagues were beginning to raise their heads. The Catholics had organized at Dessau in 1525, and the evangelical princes held an embryonic meeting at Gotha the following spring.[12] Under pressure of events, Charles agreed to meet a German diet at Speyer in the summer of 1526. When the Diet of Speyer, therefore, gave legal sanction to the principle of *cuius regio eius religio*, it merely recognized a principle which had been practiced for centuries.[13]

THE CHURCH VISITATIONS IN LUTHERAN LANDS

As the Roman Church lost its hold over the clergy in the lands of evangelical princes, new problems presented themselves, which the princes felt obliged to solve. The disturbances caused by Carlstadt and Muenzer added to this conviction.[14] Out of this need grew the idea of church visitations, and Ernestine Saxony led the way toward the organization of the Lutheran *Landeskirche*.[15] Jacob Strauss of Eisenach had visited the charges in the vicinity of the Wartburg, and the conditions he found caused him to appeal to John Frederick, the Prince of that region. Nicholas Hausmann urged a similar survey in Zwickau, where the "prophets" had worked havoc among the people.[16] Luther was still reluctant, fearing the results of allowing the secular authority to assume control of orthodoxy and reforms, but in time he saw no other solution.[17] The Peasants' War and the subsequent pitiful condition of the Saxon clergy convinced him that the problem could best be approached by conducting a general visitation.[18] The Diet of Speyer had placed the responsibility squarely upon the shoulders of John the Constant, and Luther now urged the Prince to conduct such an investigation throughout his lands.[19]

Under Luther's direction a rather detailed set of instructions was prepared by June 16, 1527.[20] These had been enlarged and revised by the time the visitations actually began in 1528.[21] The Ernestine lands were divided into five regions, each of which was to be visited by a special commission composed of members of the Wittenberg faculty, representatives from the Saxon court, and some of the prominent clergymen of the land.[22] The instructions for the various visitations and the reports have been preserved. Since these were not intended for publication, but only for the private use of these committees, they provide considerable insight into the actual religious conditions. They also served as the basis for the organization of the new Lutheran *Landeskirche* and the establishment of new schools.

The first visit to each region surveyed the problem and made the necessary recommendations. Between 1529 and 1545 each region was visited a number of times to see what progress had been made.[23] In the early instructions it is clear that the visitors were expected to exercise much patience, especially with pastors who had but recently renounced the Roman Church. In the early thirties there was increasing emphasis on "pure doctrine," but not yet in the dogmatic sense of the second half of the sixteenth century.[24] The Catechism became the standard of judgment rather than the Augsburg Confession, but even that requirement was too high for many of the country parsons.

The death of Duke George and the succession of his brother Henry added the Albertine lands to the territory covered by the visitations.[25] This Prince, the brother-in-law of Philip of Hesse, had joined the Schmalkaldic League. He accepted responsibility for religious conditions in his lands and requested that these formerly conservative Catholic regions be visited.[26] Nor was the rest of Germany left untouched. Johannes Bugenhagen spent many years in the north organizing church communities and establishing new schools.[27] In southwestern Germany Johannes Brenz carried out the Saxon pattern.[28] Around Nuernberg Lazarus Spengler was active in establishing the new Lutheran Church.[29] The example of Ernestine Saxony, therefore, became the guide for many other lands.[30]

While the Roman Church was being displaced by the new evangelical Lutheran Church in Saxon lands, many new problems confronted the clergy. Few of them favored retaining the bishops of the Roman system; yet the new Church needed some means of centralized control.[31] For a period the visitors served in an advisory capacity. But there were problems of marriage, divorce, inheritance, legal claims, etc., with which they could not deal adequately. During the thirties there was much discussion about the establishment of ecclesiastical courts. Finally, in 1539 Elector John Frederick proposed setting up a system of consistories.[32] Two preparatory courts were located at Zeitz and Zwickau and a kind of supreme court, the *Consistorium*, at Wittenberg. A special constitution was drafted in 1542, which reveals the status of Lutheranism a few years before Luther's death.[33] This court was administered by several theologians and two law professors from the Wittenberg faculty. There is no record of the preparatory courts ever being used, but the court in Wittenberg functioned for several decades.[34] This legal system was adopted in some other Lutheran lands.

The instructions of the visitors and their reports reveal that the Lutheran *Landeskirche* grew very slowly.[35] How could it be otherwise? Some of the former Catholic clergy were enthusiastic followers of Luther from the beginning. Others were very indifferent to his teachings.[36] Still others were unfit to serve in the new capacity. The first task of the visitors was to determine the worthiness of each individual and to remove the incompetent.[37] This examination involved both time and complicated problems.[38] As the instructions indicate, the chief concern of the visitors was twofold. First, the new clergy should have an elementary grasp of the differences between Lutheranism and Catholicism. They should understand why Carlstadt, Muenzer, and the Anabaptists were in error. *Sola Scriptura*, the Scripture alone, must be accepted as a guide in matters of faith with a thorough understanding of the implications of the doctrine of "justification by faith" and of the insistence on preaching the Gospel in all its purity.[39] In brief, the pastors and laity were to be familiarized with the teachings contained in Luther's Catechism, which would be regarded as suf-

ficient for the country pastor.[40] Secondly, the Lutheran clergy were
to make it clear that the Christian must lead a godly life. The instructions specifically defined the sins which would exclude members from the Christian congregations. When the life of a Christian
belied his protestations of faith, the pastor was to give him several
"brotherly warnings." Should the sinner, however, continue in his
ungodly ways, he would be placed under the minor ban.[41] This
act implied that he was excluded from Communion and other Christian fellowship. He could attend the church services in the hope
that through the sermons he might be reconverted. In some cases
he was even forbidden to practice his trade.[42] If the offender was
a clergyman, he was removed from office. Should the offense be a
public one, such as excessive drunkenness, he might even be thrown
into a special cell provided for the clergy.[43] Excommunication deprived the individual of the right of Christian burial and interment
in the people's cemetery.[44] He was forbidden to act as a sponsor
in Baptism. Early Lutheranism insisted that the clergy preach the
"pure doctrine," but the dogmatism of the age which was to follow
was not yet apparent.

It is significant that there is no mention of the Augsburg Confession in the constitution of the Wittenberg *Konsistorium*.[45] This
omission is consistent with Luther's fundamental convictions. Luther never became a systematic theologian. He always remained
primarily a Biblical exegete. To prove a position on the basis of the
Augsburg Confession or other man-made dogma was foreign to his
thinking, for it denied his fundamental principle of *Sola Scriptura*.[46]
That is why Luther's theology was ever so dynamic, so relevant,
so forceful. During the age of the dogmaticians this vitality was
lost in the effort to reduce Luther's thinking to a dogmatic system.

Although the church visitors expected to find conditions deplorable, the actual situation was appalling, even to Luther. In
many regions the clergy had opportunely left the Roman Church
and called themselves Lutheran, but when questioned as to their
beliefs, they were colossally ignorant concerning Luther's writings.
Many could not repeat the Ten Commandments or the Lord's
Prayer and knew little or nothing of the Bible.[47] Some of the congregations complained that their preachers spent their time during

the week making beer and malt and on Sundays explained the art to the congregations.[48] In many regions at least a third of the avowedly celibate clergy lived in "wild wedlock." Others were married for a time, only to desert their wives and families.[49] In one region in the lands of the former Duke George, Menius reported the conditions so dreadful that out of 200 clergymen all but ten lived in open fornication.[50] It was not unusual to find pastors in gambling places and beer chambers, and distinguishable from the laity only by the title of clergyman.[51] Little wonder that their admonitions, if made, were unheeded by their flocks. Throughout the regions visited there were very few schools, and those few were taught by very poorly qualified teachers.[52]

Not all of the incompetent clergymen could be removed at once, for the young Church had no ministers to replace them until new ones could be trained. This training would require years of time; therefore, only the worst offenders could be removed immediately. In some regions congregations could be consolidated, and *Notprediger*,[53] or emergency pastors, were placed in some pulpits. This urgent need explains why Luther hurriedly prepared his two Catechisms in 1529 and increased the supply of practical sermons in the *Kirchenpostillen*, which these ministers read from the pulpits if they could not memorize and deliver them orally.[54]

The Ordination of the Lutheran Clergy

As early as 1520 Luther had given the evangelical body in the Roman Church a new conception of the meaning of ordination. In his *Address to the German Nobility* (1520) he first developed the idea of the "priesthood of believers." [55] It had been customary to classify the Pope, bishops, priests, and monks as members of one order, the "spiritual estate," and the princes, nobles, professional people, and farmers as another order, the "secular estate." [56] This classification Luther regarded as unscriptural. In reality all belonged to the same estate, though some might have a special office. All who had been baptized, said Luther, were automatically members of a "spiritual and Christian people." [57] The outward dress of the clergy mattered little; inwardly they were one with the laymen in the Baptism in Christ. Thus all baptized Christians were regarded as priests before God, whether they had an office in the Church or not.

> For that which has emerged from Baptism may boast itself already to be consecrated priest, bishop, and pope, even though it may not be becoming to everyone to serve in the office.[58]

This was a radical departure from the concept of the Roman Church, where ordination had become one of the seven sacraments. In Rome, to "ordain" meant to carry out the divinely instituted act of designating a trained candidate for the priesthood, making him a member of that select body to whom God had entrusted the seven sacraments and the right to loose and to bind the sins of Christendom.[59] With Luther, ordination meant that a group of Christians, all of whom were already priests before God, selected a fellow Christian and delegated to him the responsibility for conducting the rites of the Church in dignified and orderly manner.[60] Luther later wrote: "Ordaining means calling and committing to the ministry." [61] Jonas added: "Indeed, the sacrament of ordination means a real ordination and vocation for pastoral care." [62] On one occasion Luther cited Acts 13:3, the calling of Saul and Barnabas to the ministry by the Holy Ghost: "And when they had fasted and prayed and laid their hands on them, they sent them away." [63] This, insisted Luther, was the nature of ordination in the Early Church.

> This was the custom of ordaining ministers, etc. They did not call them, but rather the Holy Spirit. They only confirmed this call. Our bishops have followed this practice, and, however badly, the clergy should again be installed, so that prayer is offered for them in the presence of the whole congregation and they are commended to preach the Word of God.[64]

On another occasion Luther discussed this new principle of the "priesthood of believers" and pointed out more clearly how he understood this principle in action.

> We shall preach and ordain differently from those (Roman) bishops. However, we who already have ministerial offices shall refrain from being again ordained. To ordain does not mean to consecrate. If, therefore, we know of a pious man, we select him; and, on the basis of the Word which we possess, we give him the full authority of preaching the Word and administering the Sacraments. This is

what ordination means. They themselves take the term "appoint" which has come down to us from Apostolic times and give it the meaning of "ordain," a meaning which we are not willing to accept. For we, who are assembled in the name of Christ, also possess the Word. If, therefore, we agree among ourselves that this or that man should be put into office, certainly he is ordained. But this idea is going to be opposed because it is new. In ordination the office is regulated through selection lest everyone should wish to preach. Thus, the ones ordained are to perform the duties of their office, but not necessarily for the rest of their lives; for today we may appoint a man to an office and dismiss him tomorrow.[65]

There seems to have been some difference of opinion as to the type of service which was to be held when new members of the clergy were set aside for the ministry. It is doubtful that Luther had in mind any kind of public service. Very few details are known of the ordination of Roerer in 1525, who claimed later that he was the first clergyman in the German Lutheran *Landeskirche* to receive ordination.[66] Bugenhagen, the Wittenberg town pastor, seems to have objected to a public laying on of hands, for he thought the congregation might be confused thereby.[67] In his unprinted sermons between 1524 and 1529 he made the observation: "Anyone who has been called and accepted by a congregation has been ordained." [68] It seems apparent that he practiced this conviction when he made his church visitations in the northern lands. In Braunschweig, the evening before Ascension in 1528, Bugenhagen summoned the local clergy in the *Andreaskirche* and consecrated them in the new manner by prayer and laying on of hands, but not in the presence of any congregation.[69]

During the early twenties the matter of ordination was not important. Perhaps in some peasant and Anabaptist circles the principle of the "priesthood of believers" was practiced, but Luther had no occasion to ordain any clergy. The question did not apply to the Roman clergy who entered the evangelical fold.[70] With the church visitations, however, many of the clergy were found unfit and incompetent, and new ones had to be chosen to fill their positions. The determination of clerical fitness was first left to the visitors to the different regions and later to the superintendents.[71] By 1530 the removal of the many unqualified priests had created such a shortage of clergymen that Luther mentioned the problem in a letter. He also began to recognize that there was need for some kind of outward ritual to satisfy the common man who, accustomed to the elaborate Catholic ceremonial, was rather dubious whether Lutheran clergymen without public ordination were duly empowered to preach the Word and administer the Sacraments.[72] Luther indicated by a letter of 1530 that he felt constrained to return to some kind of ritual for ordaining the Lutheran clergy.

> There is such a shortage of faithful pastors everywhere that the time may be near when we will be compelled to ordain with some appropriate ritual; however, it will be without shaving, anointing, priest's fillet, chirothesia, staff, incense, and other forms of bishops.[73]

The papal nuncio Vergerio, who visited Wittenberg during this time and discussed ordination with Luther and Bugenhagen, also received the impression that the new ritual was to be introduced, not for doctrinal, but for human considerations.[74] The Roman nuncio added that Roman clergymen looked down upon the Lutheran clergymen who had not been ordained.[75] These developments led Elector John Frederick to authorize the University of Wittenberg and the Town Church to provide for regularly ordained clergymen.[76] Luther first drafted the form for this ceremony in 1537, but it was later modified.[77] Kolde and Rietschel have debated the question whether Luther's ritual of 1537 was the oldest or whether it had been revised from earlier forms used by Bugenhagen. The point is not really important. Luther had examined and fully approved several forms, and he did not regard the exact wording as essential. His test for liturgical forms was always whether they added to, or detracted from, the Gospel; beyond that norm the question became a problem in *adiaphora*.

When so many clergymen had to be removed and there were not enough trained clergymen to fill the vacancies, the intervening period became one of "emergency preachers." These were consecrated laymen selected largely from among the professions. How many of these were admitted to the ministry before the official form of ordination began is impossible to establish. The *Wittenberger Ordiniertenbuch* shows that in 1537 a large percentage of these preachers were still of the emergency class. According to this record only 8 pastors were ordained in 1537; in 1538 there were 22;

but by 1539 the number had risen to 110.[78] The number of annual candidates remained near that figure until Luther's death. A recapitulation of the distribution among the professions in 1539 will illustrate how few candidates had theological training.

Pastors ordained in the Town Church, Wittenberg, 1539:

Merchants	1	Councilmen	1
Town secretaries	2	Clothiers	1
Burghers	10	Village teachers	3
Stonemasons	1	Printers	11 [79]
Sextons	6		

Of the total of 110 ordained in that year the emergency preachers numbered approximately one third. As the University was able to prepare additional candidates, the number of untrained clergymen decreased; in 1542 there were but 27 out of 103; and in 1546 only 15 out of 102.[80] In time only regularly trained clergymen with a theological background were ordained.

In the meantime the immediate problem confronting Luther and his fellow reformers was to determine the fitness of an incumbent for the office of the ministry.[81] During the days of the early visitations the requirements do not seem to have been too severe. In Electoral Saxony, for example, in 1529 the visitors pronounced 94 out of 154 as satisfactory; [82] in Meissen and the Vogtland 25 per cent were regarded as satisfactory, 37 as fair, 11 as poor, and 21 as worthless.[83] In the region around Jena and Neustadt 33 per cent were regarded as unfit for the ministry.[84] All types of questions were asked in each congregation. When the clergy practiced habitual drunkenness, "wild wedlock," [85] or other evident sins, it was, of course, easy to determine ministerial fitness. Theological qualifications were not so easily measured. The requirements in this respect were superficial during the first years. In the thirties, however, regular agencies to check the qualifications of candidates were established. In Prussia the bishops of Samland and Riesenburg were assigned the task of determining clerical fitness; in Pomerania this duty fell upon certain ministers in Stettin, Greifswald, and Kolberg; while in Hanover and Saxony the superintendents were responsible.[86] After 1535 the regular procedure was followed at the request of Elector John Frederick, wherein the

University formally examined the candidates, who were then ordained by Bugenhagen and his assistants in the Town Church.[87]

Since the original examinations were later referred to as *Scheinexamina*,[88] or examinations of mere form, it appears that the later ones instituted in 1535 were more rigid. Again, in the years 1549 to 1555 they were given more definite form by Melanchthon and were probably made even more severe.[89] In these later examinations the candidate had to be familiar with the fundamental Lutheran teaching and how it differed from that of the Roman Church. Melanchthon's questionnaire also presupposed an elementary knowledge of church history and the fundamentals of Christian ethics. The examination, which was generally conducted in Latin, lasted about an hour. The form drawn up by Melanchthon in 1552 under the title *Examen ordinandorum*, examination of those to be ordained, was written to serve both the candidate and the examiner.[90] The records show that provisions were made in some regions for candidates not quite ready to receive the office. In Stettin they were permitted to live in the *Armenhaus*, a poorhouse, until they could become more fully instructed.[91] In some regions preparation for the ministry could be made by serving as the understudy of an older clergyman.

As has been indicated, the procedure in ordination varied in the early Lutheran *Landeskirche*. In the beginning the calling and consecrating to office was very simple. After the formal liturgy was formulated, ordination was made a part of the regular service.[92] Since the examination and call to the ministry had been conducted privately beforehand, the actual ceremony of ordination was considerably simplified. The ordination was a part of the regular Sunday service and commonly followed the sermon, which prepared the congregation for participation in the ceremony. Several pastors usually assisted.[93]

The order followed in Wittenberg has been preserved in the Rietschel text and, according to Roerer, was the form drawn up by Luther himself.[94] It underwent some changes between 1537 and 1539, but, in general, ordination in Wittenberg must have been conducted as follows. After the sermon the candidate and the visiting clergymen approached the altar. The ritual began with some rubrics relative to the previous examination of the candidate, whereupon the choir sang *Veni, Sancte Spiritus,* while the candidate and the regular pastor knelt before the altar.[95] Then followed a versicle addressed to the congregation and a response. A prayer by the pastor "Of the Holy Spirit" followed. To this point the ritual was all conducted in Latin, but the vernacular was used for the remainder. The minister conducting the ordination read a lesson addressed to the candidate, an "Apostolic summary" of the duties of the office, and an exhortation to faithfulness. After the ordinand had vowed his intention of fulfilling the Apostolic commission, the assisting ministers gathered about him and laid their hands on his head, while the officiant prayed the Lord's Prayer. The regular pastor then delivered a brief address to the ordinand, followed by the blessing and the sign of the cross. The congregation sang "Now Pray We All God, the Comforter." The visiting ministers withdrew from the altar, while the candidate remained to partake of Holy Communion.

The Reformation brought about other changes, which considerably affected the relationship of the clergyman to the community. In the Roman Catholic system he had been a part of a closely woven hierarchical system of Pope, bishop, and priest. In fact, the country and the city pastor was but a representative of the bishop and responsible to him.[96] In the new Lutheran Church the *Pfarrer* became the leader of a self-governing, independent congregation, of which he was the spiritual head, but to which he was also responsible.[97] In a large community the *Pfarrer* might require several assistants, who held such titles as deacon, subdeacon, chaplain, or preacher, the last-named being permitted to preach only, and possibly a ministerial student. The office of pastor was not based on ordination, but upon Baptism, and the individual chosen was minister and servant of the community only as long as he was in office. In this new interpretation he had a personal responsibility and a spiritual mission. Since he was permitted to marry, his whole social status was likewise changed.[98] High ideals were absolutely essential to such a system. The Reformation could succeed only with an able and consecrated clergy.[99]

In the old Roman system there had been private Masses, festival days, vigils, and many other sources of private priestly income, which the Reformation had swept away.[100] Even with these additional sources of income the remuneration in some of the country districts was so low that some of the Roman clergy had been forced into secular trades, which were not always becoming to a man of the cloth. In the young Lutheran Church the financing of the clergy became a real problem. Peasants and burghers were not yet educated to assume responsibility for their clergymen. Even though specific sums might be set aside, their collection was something else. In Pomerania some clergymen received scarcely 50 marks a year.[101] In Thuringia it was quite usual to receive 15 gulden, less than $200 a year.[102] In Prussia the country pastor's salary ranged from 20 to 30 marks annually.[103] These facts explain Luther's comment in 1531 that the country clergy had been reduced to begging. Their need was well expressed in one of Luther's letters to the Saxon court in 1525:

> Two pressing situations present themselves, which demand investigation and correction by your Electoral Grace. The first is that the pastorates are in dire need as no one gives them anything, no one pays his dues. The sacrificial and soul pennies have been dropped; taxes are not levied, or at least seldom; and the common man is concerned neither with the preacher nor the pastor. Unless a rigid system of support of the pastorates is undertaken by your Electoral Grace in a short time, there will be neither pastorates nor schools nor pupils, and God's Word and service will fall to the ground.[104]

The church visitors tried to correct the situation by determining the sources of income, combining pastorates, fixing rents and taxes, and naming specific seasons when they were to be paid. The *Beichtpfennig*, or Communion penny, was introduced and was to be paid four times a year, beginning at the age of 12, when the individual first attended Communion.[105] These efforts did not entirely relieve the situation, and many of the emergency preachers continued to practice their former professions during the week. In 1544 John Frederick turned his attention to the lot of the common pastor. He thought it unseemly for the pastors to till the land and raise pigs and cows like the peasants in order to eke out a living, but it was not until after Luther's death that the income of the country pastors was sufficient in itself.

The clergy of the Lutheran *Landeskirche* fell naturally into two classes, the city and the country clergy.[106] Most of the city clergy were well-educated, college-trained men of considerable culture. Many of them married into the better middle-class families and became financially quite comfortable. They commanded the respect of their congregations and were better paid than their country brethren. In Wittenberg by 1529 Bugenhagen's salary from the Town Church was 200 gulden, with an additional 60 gulden as university professor and 40 *scheffels* of grain. This amount was equivalent to a $4,000 salary based on money values of 1913.[107] Generally, the salary of the ministers in cities of similar size ranged from $3,000 to $3,500. Among this group could be found such theologians as Hesz in Breslau, Amsdorf in Magdeburg, Jonas in Halle, Brenz in Schwaebisch-Hall, and Hausmann in Zwickau; all were men who supplied Wittenberg with leadership and who wielded a powerful influence on the surrounding territory. They wrote their own sermons, had considerable knowledge of Latin, had acquired quite adequate personal libraries, and were generally admired and respected by both the burghers and the nobility.[108] The salaries of the assistants in the larger congregations were proportionately less, but, added to the cost of maintaining a school, required a considerable budget.

The clergy of the villages and in the country parishes were of a much poorer type on the whole.[109] In their ranks were included the emergency preachers, many of whom had no advanced college training. They knew no Latin and little theology. It was for this group that Luther wrote the *Postils,* so they might read these sermons from the pulpit instead of preparing their own.[110] These clergymen were unable to marry into the more influential families. Many of them were unable to command the respect of their congregations and were looked down upon by both the nobles and the peasants. It was not unusual for the peasants to talk or even to walk around outside the church in the graveyard during the service.[111] Because of lack of funds and poor taste these preachers often conducted their services in unseemly attire. They gave the broadest possible interpretation to their new "freedom" from Rome and wore "multicolored coats," "baggy knee breeches," and "shoes with pointed toes" during the services.[112]

*Superintendent and pastor in typical gowns of
about 1600*

The problem of what constituted the proper attire of a clergyman aroused much controversy. The Roman Church had prescribed
specific attire for each rank. Monastic orders each had their own
distinctive dress. Luther characteristically believed that the matter
of dress was unimportant except that it should not detract from
the message of the Gospel. He even wrote to one inquirer that it
mattered not if he wore three robes so long as he preached the
pure Gospel.[113] Three types of thinking emerged from the discussions. There were those who approved the continued use of the
Catholic vestments, since many pastors already owned them. The
principal controversy arose over the use of the elaborate em-
broidered white *Chorrock,* worn over the cassock.[114] Another group
sought to displace the white *Chorrock* with a plain black robe
called the *Schaube,* "an additional black mantle which reached

below the knees and had wide sleeves." [115] Zwingli introduced this garment in the fall of 1523, and Luther first wore a similar gown at a service on the afternoon of October 9, 1524.[116] That same morning he had preached in his customary monks' attire. The example of these two leaders influenced others, particularly in southwestern Germany, but the use of the *Schaube* did not become widespread. The third group which has been mentioned were those who, partly from conviction and partly due to financial circumstances, approved full freedom in pulpit attire and the complete discard of Roman customs. Principal opposition to the use of the *Chorrock* developed in southwestern Germany, but in Wittenberg both the *Chorrock* and Mass vestments continued in use for some time, and occasionally the chasuble was added.[117] By the time of Luther's death the controversy was far from settled. During the first four decades of the growing Lutheran Church there was a wide diversity of practice, but, in general, the trend was away from the elaborate ceremonialism of the Roman Church, associated with Mass vestments, chasuble, and stole to the simple, plain black gown.

The duties of the clergy in a city congregation in the new Lutheran *Landeskirche* were manifold. The Wittenberg charge included the Town Church and 13 villages and required the services of a head clergyman, the *Pfarrer*, and three or four deacons, or assistant pastors.[118] No less than 500 sermons had to be preached during the year in such a parish, as many services were held during the week.[119] The minister's first duty was the preaching of the Gospel. In addition he conducted private confessions and confessions for Communion, visited the sick, instructed the children for confirmation, and kept a financial record of the congregation. Then there were weddings and funerals, which required additional sermons. The seriously ill were to be visited every three days and given Communion frequently. Twice a year a series of sermons on the Catechism was preached, continuing for two weeks at a time.[120] Parts of the Catechism were read in unison by the pastor and the congregation. In the larger communities much of the burden could be borne by the assistant pastors. They conducted many of the weekly services, made sick calls, and baptized the children. For this rite, immersion was the preferred practice though not con-

"The Struggle over the Chorrock," 1550

sidered essential. In the villages, in addition to the above duties, the minister frequently also conducted the school, since teachers were difficult to obtain, but his labors were lightened somewhat by fewer church services.

It is interesting to note that the Reformation succeeded or failed almost in direct relationship to its spiritual leadership. Men like the afore-mentioned Amsdorf, Hesz, Brenz, and Hausmann are illustrations of the high type of new Lutheran clergymen, who supplied the *esprit de corps* of the new order.[121] Luther naturally occupied the center of the picture. That all the followers should have equal ability or success could hardly be expected. Many clergymen had renounced the Roman Church without properly informing themselves as to the new ideal. Some even seem to have been Catholic and Lutheran at the same time, conducting services in the two forms in the same congregations.[122] Many had adopted the new Lutheranism merely for the sake of their stomachs. One odd individual carried a can of beer into the pulpit and refreshed himself occasionally during his preaching.[123] Some of the emergency preachers did quite well, others lost the respect of the laymen because of their limited education. Luther would have preferred that all the clergymen in the new Lutheran Church be seminary graduates of the University of Wittenberg. He and his fellow reformers stressed the need of highly trained, consecrated men who could provide leadership for autonomous congregations; but this ideal could not be realized until the men could be trained and new schools established preparing a second generation of Lutherans trained from childhood in the Gospel spirit.

MINISTERIAL AIDS

The Postils

No one more clearly realized than Luther how poorly prepared many of the Lutheran ministers were to lead their flocks from Catholicism to the new faith. The reports of the church visitors confirmed his personal observations, which he recorded in the introduction to the Small Catechism:

> The deplorable, wretched conditions which I recently experienced as a visitor constrained and forced me to put this Catechism of Christian teachings in this small, common, simple form. Dear Lord, how much misery I did observe everywhere! The common man knows practically nothing about Christian teaching, especially in the villages. A good many of the ministers are almost wholly unprepared or else unfit to teach. Yet they are all to be regarded as Christian; they are supposed to be baptized; and they receive the Lord's Supper. Still they do not even know the Lord's Prayer, the Creed, and the Ten Commandments. They live like veritable cattle and act like swine without conscience. And now that the Gospel has come, they have also learned how to abuse all their Christian liberties in masterful fashion.[124]

These sad conditions caused Luther and his fellow reformers to begin the preparation of ministerial aids and practical teaching materials, among which the *Church Postils, House Postils,* the Catechism, and the German Bible are the most important.

Perhaps the greatest need of the clergy of the new Lutheran Church was sermon material, for the "New Theology" which Luther had begun to preach was not to be found in a book on dogmatics.

The clergy were to preach the Gospel, but what Gospel? The medieval theologians of the Roman Church also claimed to be preaching the Gospel. The clergy were to rely on *Sola Scriptura* as their guide in matters of preaching and teaching, but what theology had been preached by the Apostles? The individual minister would need to master Greek and Hebrew before he could determine the original teachings of the Scriptures. Luther had been applying the principle of *Sola Scriptura* ever since he had begun his teaching at Wittenberg; yet in 1521 he was still groping his way to theological clarity.[125] Though he had made much progress toward an understanding of the New Testament teachings, he had not yet completely discarded his past Roman Catholic training. If this was true of the leading theologian of the age and the leader of the new evangelical movement, how much more was it true of his followers! If the members of the new clergy trained in Roman Catholic schools could not preach from the Bible without guidance, what of the emergency preachers who had practically no theological training? It was readily apparent to Luther, Melanchthon, Amsdorf, and other Wittenberg faculty members that the ministers would have to be supplied with sermon materials and other help until a new generation of thoroughly trained theologians could be prepared in the Lutheran school system.

For this task no one was better qualified than Luther. Although Luther had been reluctant to enter the ministry, he proved to be a naturally gifted preacher. Without exaggeration he may be called one of the greatest preachers of all time. His mastery of the Bible, his originality and depth of thought, his dramatic yet simple form of expression, all enabled him to hold a congregation in the hollow of his hand. Throughout his lifetime people journeyed for miles to hear him preach. He seems to have possessed the unusual ability to express the most profound truths in an original and yet very simple manner so that even the man in the street grasped their meaning. His physical features, intellect, memory, voice, easy manner, and sincerity all contributed to the effectiveness of his preaching.[126] At Wittenberg he might preach as many as three or four times a day, and each time the audiences crowded into the *Stadtkirche* to hear his powerful exposition of the Word of God.

After Worms his reputation spread to all Germany, and clergymen everywhere were anxious to preach like Luther. That his sermon material was regarded with respect and widely used was shown by the many publications of his *Postillen*.[127] These volumes contained sermonets with text ready to be read to the congregation. Luther expected them to be used only by those ministers unable to prepare their own sermons. In his *Deutsche Messe* of 1526 he wrote:

> It seems to me if one had the German *Postillen* for the entire church year it would be best that it be required that the *Postille* for the day, or at least a part of it, be read to the people. Not only should this be done for the sake of the preachers who can do no better, but also for the protection of the congregation against *Schwaermer* and other sects as has been observed and experienced in the homilies during Matins, where something similar was done. Otherwise, when preachers lack spiritual insight and the spirit speaks through the minister — which I do not wish to set as a goal, for the spirit learns how to express itself better than all the *Postillen* and homilies — it ultimately results in a situation where everyone preaches as he pleases, what he pleases, and the ministers again preach about "blue ducks" rather than the Gospel and its lessons.[128]

And again in 1542, when the Reformation had become rather well established and the ministry much better trained, Luther wrote in his introduction to Spangenberg's *Postille:*

> But again several indolent preachers and ministers are not good parsons in that they depart from such (*Postillen*) and other good books, failing to make sermons from such materials. They do not pray, study, or read anything. They have no desire to learn anything from the Bible, acting as though it were not to be read. They use such books as a mere formality and according to the calendar to earn their yearly keep. They are mere conductors and drain pipes repeating everything without any understanding even though it is our purpose in these works and those of other theologians to guide them in the Scriptures and to admonish them of their duty also to defend our Christian faith against the devil, the world, and the flesh after we have passed away.[129]

Before Luther went to Worms, he had begun the preparation of a *Postille* for the benefit of those ministers not fully prepared to preach Gospel sermons. This work was undertaken at the request of Frederick the Wise, who was much impressed with Luther's ability as a preacher. While at the Wartburg, Luther completed the first series of sermons, the *Weihnachtsteil* relating to the Christmas season, which came from the press in March, 1522.[130] A month later the *Adventpostille* for the Advent season was published.[131]

After his return from the Wartburg the Carlstadt and other disturbances interrupted the preparation of the postils for other seasons of the church year, but the work was resumed in 1524, for Luther wrote his friend Nicholas Hausmann in Zwickau: "I am working on the *Postille*. which is in the press." [132] By 1525 the *Fastenpostille* for Lent was completed.[133] His work again ceased, but his student Roth took copious notes on Luther's sermons when he preached each Sunday on the pericopes for the day. These sermons Roth published in 1526 and 1527.[134] Although these two postils were much inferior to Luther's own work, they filled in the gaps in the church calendar for which preachers still did not have sermons.

In the later twenties there was a trend toward combining the *Postillen* in general editions, such as the Lotther publication of the *Advent* and *Christmas Postils* of 1525, taken from Grunenberg's first general work in the *Winterpostille* of 1525.[135] Then Lotther published a general edition in folio form in 1526, and Grunenberg followed with a folio edition in 1527.[136] Luther was not satisfied with all the many reprints, as the work had not been of an even quality and many mistakes had occurred. Perhaps for this reason he turned to the famous Lufft for his 1528 edition, which was followed by printings in 1530, 1532, 1535, 1540, and 1543.[137] Lotther added his seventh and eighth editions in 1533 and 1535.[138] Wolf Koepfel in Strassburg printed general editions of Luther's *Postillen* in 1529, 1531, and 1542, and Wolf Wolrab of Leipzig reprinted a general edition in 1544, using Lufft's edition of the previous year as his model.[139] Each succeeding edition had to be closely allied to the Bible translations, which were appearing concurrently, to maintain agreement both in the textual renderings and in their theological exposition.[140]

When Luther began preaching in his home on Sunday evenings in 1532, another series known as the *Hauspostille* was begun. Veit Dietrich and George Roerer took notes on these sermons until the series ended in 1534. The Dietrich *Hauspostille* appeared in

1544, but the Roerer was not printed until 1559, after Luther's death.[141] Other writers contributed postils, among them Melanchthon, Antonius Corvinus, and Spangenberg being the best known.[142] Thus, by the time of Luther's death there were ample postils for the use of the clergy. In fact, the first two general editions of Luther's works, the *Wittenbergische* and the *Jena Ausgaben*, did not include either *Kirchen-* or *Hauspostillen* as the supply seemed adequate, and it was not until the days of Walch that a republication of the postils was undertaken.[143]

A study of the content of Luther's postils makes the reason for their popularity with cleric and laymen readily apparent. Walther Koehler has determined the foundations for the high quality of Luther's work.[144] The texts are based on the Greek and Hebrew Bible, which Luther had. He did not have the Septuagint, but he consulted the Latin Vulgate. He used Lefèvre's *Quintuplex Psalterium*, Nicholas von Lyra's *Glossa interlinearis*, the *Interpretationes nominum Hebraicorum* and Aleander's *Lexicon Graeco-Latinum*. There is evidence that he used Reuchlin's *De rudimentis Hebraicis*, Adam Petri's *Predigten Taulers*, Erasmus' *Adagia*, and a number of the classics. He may have used Augustine's *Tractatus* and the *Vitae patrum*.[145]

It has been claimed that the medieval *Plenarien*, the Roman forerunner of the *Postille*, influenced Luther as to form. Drews has shown that the influence was very negligible, if any, and that after 1521 the demand for the *Plenarien* ceased entirely and no more were printed.[146] In content Luther's *Postillen* were something distinctly new, which accounts for their popularity and far-reaching influence during the formative years of the German Reformation. Again Luther demonstrated his gift for making the most scholarly treatment readily understandable and adaptable to both the trained theologian and the unlettered layman.

The *Postillen* reflect Luther's growth in theology. They are not just cold homilies of Scriptural texts. In them Luther expressed many of his convictions treating the vital problems confronting the rising new Lutheran *Landeskirche*. The stormy days of Worms, the Wittenberg disturbances, the battles with opponents in the Roman Church, and the bull *Coenae Domini* are illustrations of the contemporary problems reflected in the *Winterpostille*, which was available to Lutheranism at the beginning of the church visitations. The *Postillen*, however, offer much more positive material. Luther's own personal, dynamic concept of religion became available to a much wider following, for in the *Postillen* he expounded the dynamics of Christian ethics in Christ's redeemed, the inner relationship between Law and Gospel. Of what good to you are a thousand deaths of Christ if He did not die for you personally? Even such brief sermonets enabled preachers with little background to catch the spark and to preach a vital message to their backward congregations eager for light.

Luther's *Postillen* did far more than supply poorly prepared clergymen with easy sermon materials. Though simple in form, their scholarly foundation and sound doctrine caused the best scholars of the day to consult them eagerly, and they were particularly useful to the leaders of the new Protestantism. Johannes Adelphi, city physician of Schaffhausen, wrote in a letter August 5, 1522: "Today I saw Luther's treatise on the Epistles and Gospels, printed in Basel, an exceptional piece of work," and added that it contained all the essentials to salvation.[147] Zwingli and Oecolampadius in Switzerland were soon using the *Postillen* in their work.[148] Walther Koehler says that it was the study of one of Luther's postil sermonets which first caused Zwingli to disagree with Luther on the Lord's Supper.[149] Among the long list of those influenced by these practical sermons were Caspar Schwenckfeld, Sebastian Franck, Andreas Osiander, Philip Melanchthon, Eberlin von Guenzburg, Johann Sonnentaller, Sebastian Lotzer, and Andreas Keller.[150] In fact, it may be said that no single source was more effective in planting the seeds of Lutheranism so widely throughout German lands in the early twenties than were the enlarged editions of the *Winterpostille*.

The Catechism

Another ministerial aid prepared by Luther for the Lutheran Church was the Catechism of 1529. This proved to be particularly useful to the emergency preachers, to the improperly indoctrinated Roman clergy who had joined the evangelicals, and to the teachers of the parochial schools. In fact, all aspects considered, it was probably the most useful and the most unique of his original

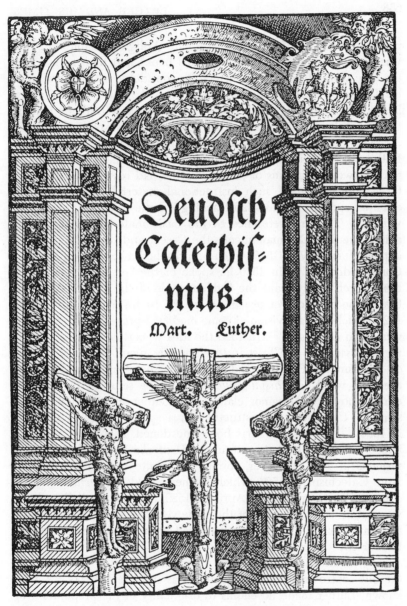

Deudsch Catechismus

Mart. Luther.

Title page of Luther's Large Catechism, printed by George Rhau, Wittenberg, 1529

publications. In 1537 Luther wrote to Wolfgang Capito that he was very indifferent to the fate of his books and then added that the only works from his pen which he considered satisfactory were his *De servo arbitrio* and the Catechism.[151] One German writer has pointed out that, exclusive of the Bible and Luther's hymns, the Catechism is his only writing still in common use.

The Saxon visitations, as noted previously, deeply touched Luther and convinced him of the immediate and urgent necessity for the two Catechisms of 1529. That he had recognized the need for a compilation of such instructional material to serve as the essential epitome of Christian teaching is quite evident in his earlier writings. The first reference to the basic materials of the Catechism, the Ten Commandments, the Creed, and the Lord's Prayer, appeared as early as 1516, when he preached a sermon on the Ten Commandments.[152] In 1520 he spoke of the "precious treasure of the Church" and meant the fundamentals of the Catechism, even though he did not yet use the word.[153] In his *Prayer Booklet* of 1522, which was a revision of some medieval prayer books, the idea was again expressed.[154] In 1525 the idea of certain materials forming the essentials of Christian teaching was mentioned in a sermon on Baptism and Penance, and in that year he also for the first time used the word *catechismus puerorum* in the sense of the instruction of boys.[155] Althamer claims that Luther first used it in the sense of *Unterricht*, or instruction, in a specific body of material in 1528. This viewpoint has been questioned, as Luther seems to have used it also in that sense in the *Deutsche Messe* of 1525. The sermons of 1528, however, formed a definite background for the large Catechism of 1529, which Luther called the *Deudsch Catechismus*.[156] It appeared on April 23, 1529, and the Small Catechism was published on May 16 of the same year.[157] As the Weimar editors have pointed out, Luther prepared both books simultaneously, but for two different purposes.

As in the hymns and much other material from Luther's pen, the old controversy as to originality has been raised. As far as is known, Luther made no claims to originality in the preparation of the Catechism. He was very familiar with the early history of the Church, and almost from its very beginning the Church had recognized the need for certain fundamental instruction in preparation

Der kleine
Catechismus fur
die gemeine Pfar;
herr vnd Pre;
diger.
Mart. Luther.
Wittemberg.

Title page of Luther's Small Catechism, printed by Conrad Treffer,
Erfurt, s. d.

for Baptism. Especially were the Creed and the Lord's Prayer regarded as sacred treasures.[158] To them had been added the Ten
Commandments in the 13th century, and from that time on the
three were grouped together.[159] Luther believed that they expressed all the knowledge essential to the Christian and must be
preserved in Lutheranism. He, therefore, regarded them as the
basic groundwork of the Catechism.

A variety of arrangements had been used in the Roman Church
of the Middle Ages. St. Thomas had used the order of Creed,
Lord's Prayer, and Ten Commandments.[160] Johann Herolt in his
Discipulus de eruditione Christi fidelium arranged a very elaborate
grouping, containing the Ten Commandments, the nine strange
sins, the seven deadly sins, the six works of mercy, the Lord's
Prayer, the Ave Maria, the Creed, the Seven Sacraments, and the
seven gifts of the Spirit.[161] Lanzkranna in his *Hymelstrasz,* or *Road
to Heaven,* included five components: the Ten Commandments, the
Sacraments, the Lord's Prayer, the Ave Maria, and the Articles of
Faith.[162] The most common usage included the Lord's Prayer, the
Ave Maria, the Creed, and the Ten Commandments. This arrangement was accepted by the synods of Wuerzburg (1453), Passau
(1466), Mainz (1493), Basel (1503), Speyer (1509), and Regensburg (1512) and must have been quite generally known in Luther's
day.[163] In addition to these compilations there was also the Geffcken
Picture Catechism of the fifteenth century.[164] As noted in connection with Luther's Mansfeld education, the medieval primers contained materials which Luther later added to his Catechism: the
blessing at meals, the giving of thanks, the morning and evening
prayers. Therefore, even though the word *catechism* was not used
as a title for any of the medieval instructional books, the basic
idea of a body of instructional material did exist in the Christian
Church from earliest times to Luther's day.[165] K. Knoke in his
*D. M. Luthers Kleiner Katechismus nach den aeltesten Ausga-
ben* etc. (1904) has made the following summary of Luther's Catechism:

> It came into existence in connection with more than a thousand
> years of teaching and training in the Church. It grew from the
> struggle of the Reformers to establish the Church according to the
> basic principles of the Gospel. It was the ripe fruit of Luther's

catechetical experience, in which he had schooled and exercised himself for over a decade by 1529.[166]

It does not follow, however, that because there were catechisms all through the centuries, Luther's work was not original. Then Shakespeare should not have credit for his plays because he reworked old plots; rather, it is this very faculty which reveals his genius. Luther regarded the Ten Commandments, the Creed, and the Lord's Prayer as a sacred trust handed down through the ages through the Roman Church.[167] His "New Theology," or rather the theology of the New Testament, which he considered the "old church," led him to omit the Ave Maria and all but two of the Sacraments, Baptism and the Lord's Supper. Penance and the prayers were never considered as an integral part of the Catechism. The originality of Luther's Catechism is not in the skeletal form, but in the innate richness of its evangelical spirit.[168] It might well be called the Bible in miniature. Its epigrammatical, terse explanations of the Commandments, Creed, and Lord's Prayer have been so useful to the teacher and the preacher that it has lived for four centuries. The Large Catechism lent itself so well to sermon material and for oral reading that it became very popular in Lutheranism.[169] The Small Catechism with its questions and answers and its supply of Bible passages was so readily understandable that every father could use it for instruction in his home and the parochial teacher found it invaluable in the newly organized Lutheran schools.[170]

The word *catechism* is used in a number of senses in sixteenth-century sources, which raises the question of what Luther meant when he used the word. Kawerau in his treatise on this subject has made the observation:

> On the one hand the word *catechism* is used to describe a definite body of material . . . the essentials of which were the Decalogue, the Apostles' Creed, and the Lord's Prayer; on the other, the word is used as describing the presentation of materials to its followers in Christendom by means of oral instruction.[171]

That Luther used the word *catechism* to describe a body of material is shown by the fact that he never distinguished between the Large and the Small Catechisms, both were just the "Catechism." [172] To the three essential parts mentioned by Kawerau, he added the two divisions on Baptism and the Lord's Supper. These were included for the enlightenment of the *Schwaermer* and the Anabaptists.[173] Later the Confessional and Prayer sections were added as practical appendages. While in 1520 he had been willing to regard the Ten Commandments, the Creed, and the Lord's Prayer as all that man needed to know to be saved, he later considered it necessary to include instruction in the Sacraments and the proper sphere of penance.[174]

The word *catechism* was also used in an instructional sense. Such references as "time set aside for catechism" implied instruction in Christian fundamentals.[175] Augustine had used the word in the sense of oral instruction of baptismal candidates.[176] It could also be found in the New Testament, where it is used in the instructional sense. Such passages as Luke 1:4, Acts 18:25, Romans 2:18, and Galatians 6:6 in the original Greek probably supplied the precedent for Luther's use of the word *catechism* for his layman's book of instruction. He once observed:

> Catechism is a form of instruction in which persons are questioned and asked to recite just as a school teacher has her pupils recite their lessons to determine whether they know them.[177]

As has been noted, the Catechism became an integral part of the new Lutheran Church.[178] Parts of the Large Catechism were read regularly to the congregation, which may be what Luther had in mind when he prepared it in that form. Pastors likewise used it to prepare their sermons.[179] Froeschel stated that in Wittenberg it was used quarterly in the instruction of the young people, which may have been the forerunner of the later confirmation instruction.[180] The Catechism was also essential to Holy Communion, since Luther believed that unless the communicant could recite the Catechism he should not attend the Holy Supper.[181] The Confessional was reintroduced in this sense, as is shown by Luther's opinion in the matter:

> Such confession is not only proper so that they may give an account of their sins, but it also affords an opportunity to ascertain whether they still know the Lord's Prayer, the Creed, and the Ten Commandments and other contents of the Catechism. For as we have well experienced, the masses and the youth learn little from the sermons when they are not specifically questioned and examined.

On what occasion can this be done more properly, and when is it more essential than when they want to partake of the Sacrament? [182]

Nor did Luther apply this practice only to the congregational members. All through his life he recited parts of the Catechism daily.[183] He required the same of Katharine and his children.[184] In pondering its simple truths, he insisted, even the most profound theologians learned daily and continued to grow in grace.[185]

The German Bible

Although Luther's Postils and Catechisms played an important role during the formative years of the emerging Lutheran Church, they pale into insignificance when compared with his translation of the Bible into German. Oskar Thulin has stated that the translation of the Bible was the "crowning accomplishment" of Luther's whole life's work.[186] True, as noted before, there were many German translations before Luther's day.[187] Even in the Middle Ages there were illustrated Bibles which reached the people in some degree; but when compared with the excellent Bible produced by Luther and his fellow professors in 1546, all these faded into the background and were forgotten.[188] Even the Old Testament was rendered so well into the German idiom that Job seemed to be speaking in their sixteenth-century tongue rather than in remote Hebrew.[189] The German Bible now became the center of the service and its message the daily spiritual food for many a devout German home.[190] It is impossible to evaluate its role in the furthering of the Reformation, for its assistance in spreading the Gospel to the common man was immeasurable.

It has been noted that Luther began his work by translating the New Testament into German while at the Wartburg. When he returned to Wittenberg in the spring of 1522, he carried the finished manuscript.[191] After a careful rechecking with Philip Melanchthon, the New Testament was published in September, 1522. From this time on the translation of the Bible into German was to occupy Luther continuously until his death in 1546.[192] The first complete translation, which appeared in 1534, did not satisfy his high standards, and with the help of his fellow professors he carefully prepared two additional complete revisions. The last did not appear in print until after Luther had passed to his reward.

That the translation of the New Testament was entirely the work of Luther was shown by a letter from Melanchthon to Spalatin dated March 30, 1522, and stating that he and Luther were busy checking the New Testament, "which he has translated in its entirety into our language." [193] Other letters were addressed during the checking to Spalatin, Mutian, and Sturtz, seeking technical information as to the value of certain New Testament coins in German money.[194] This meticulous attention to details reveals Luther's unceasing efforts to achieve an accurate rendition. It will be recalled that he undertook the translation only upon Melanchthon's promise to help, and that Luther had stated earlier that he could not attempt the Old Testament without Amsdorf.[195] In the meantime Amsdorf had become pastor at Magdeburg, and in his stead Luther relied upon the able Hebrew professor Aurogallus for consultation on doubtful points.[196] In the introduction to the first part in 1523 he stated his difficulty:

> I acknowledge openly that I undertook too great a problem especially in attempting to translate the Old Testament, for the Hebrew language is in such a neglected state that even the Jews know little about it, and the glossaries and the commentaries are not to be trusted. . . . Even though all of us should co-operate, there would be sufficient work for all in the reconstruction of the Bible and bringing it once more to the light. Some might assist with their ability to reason; others through their mastery of languages. Nor did I labor alone in this undertaking, but I utilized the services of others where it might assist me in mastering a problem.[197]

Almost immediately after the New Testament had appeared, Luther began translating the Old Testament. As his correspondence during these months reveals, he completed the first two books of Moses by November and had finished the Pentateuch by December, 1522.[198] Realizing that the complete translation would consume a great deal of time, Luther decided to publish the various sections as they were completed. Accordingly, the Pentateuch appeared in the summer of 1523 under the title *Das Alte Testament deutsch*, M. Luther, Vvittemberg.[199] No date was given on the title page, which was adorned with an attractive woodcut of a Roman archway with ornate pillars. Eight angels ornamented the top of the arch and two more the supporting pillars. At the bottom of the woodcut was the crucifix surrounded by nine additional angels. The title appeared within this ornate framework. The printer must have been Melchior Lotther, judging by the insignia of the snake on the cross at the end of the introduction. Eleven plain but effective woodcuts by an unknown artist were included.

The second part of the Old Testament from Joshua to Esther appeared without date or authorship on the title page under the title *Das Ander teyl des alten testaments*,[200] but at the end there appeared for the first time the two shields of Luther. On the left was the shield with the lamb and flag of the cross, on the right Luther's coat of arms, the rose with the heart and cross marked M. L. Beneath the shields was the inscription:

> May this symbol be proof that these books have passed through my hands, for many are today engaged in falsifying publications and ruining books.[201]

An armed warrior decorated the title page, perhaps in honor of Joshua, while the section contained 23 additional attractive woodcuts, several of which were full-page illustrations. The story of Samson was particularly well illustrated, but the story of David and Goliath was less effective. This portion was published by the Cranach press, with Melchior Lotther as printer.[202]

Luther was already working on the next part, in which he planned to include the didactic and prophetic books, but in Job he encountered real difficulty. On February 23, 1524, he wrote to Spalatin:

> All is well with us. Only we have had hard work with the translation of Job because of the sublimity of its exceedingly grand style, so that he seems to be much more impatient with our translation than with the consolation of his friends; or he will certainly persist in sitting upon his ash heap, if it was not perhaps the desire of the author of this book that it should never be translated. This situation is delaying the printing of the third part of the Bible.[203]

In the preface to this book Luther further explained his great difficulty. Its lofty and majestic language did not permit a literal translation, as had been attempted in the past by Jews and other foolish people:

> The language of this book is more lofty and splendid than that of any other book in all the Scriptures, and if it were translated everywhere word for word (as the Jews and foolish translators would have done), and not, for the most part, according to the sense, no one would understand it; as, for example, when he says: "The thirsty will drink up his goods," meaning: "Robbers shall take them from him"; or "the children of pride have not gone therein," i. e., "the young lions, that stalk proudly"; and similar cases. Again, by "light" he means "good fortune," by "darkness" "misfortune," etc.[204]

Because of the delay in translating Job, Luther decided to publish the third section without the Prophets. In September or October, 1524, this part appeared under the title *Das Dritte teyl des allten Testaments*, Wittenberg, 1524.[205] Like Luther's earlier printings, this was also in folio form. The woodcut adorning the title page pictured twelve men assembled about an opened book, among whom David could be recognized on the left and Moses on the right. This drawing enclosed the title from the top, while at the bottom was a crucifixion scene. Only one other woodcut was included in this part, portraying Job after he had been struck with leprosy.

After the third printing, Luther became preoccupied with the Peasants' War and the preparation of the new liturgy and hymnal. He completed the Psalms, which he had begun before Worms, and they were printed in small octavo volume by Lotther in 1524.[206] The church visitations were planned and carried out between 1524 and 1529, and the controversies with Erasmus over the freedom of the will and with Bucer, Zwingli, and Oecolampadius over the Lord's Supper continued until after the Marburg Colloquy in 1529.[207] That year Luther prepared the two Catechisms, and in 1530 he and Melanchthon were deeply involved with the preparation of a document which could be presented to the Emperor at Augsburg. Since this Augsburg Confession, as it was later called, was to be a statement of the faith of the new Lutheran Church, its preparation involved much careful thought.

During these intervening years, Luther lectured in the University on Deuteronomy, the Minor Prophets, and the book of

Isaiah.[208] He also worked intermittently on his translations. Habakkuk appeared in 1526, followed by Zechariah and Isaiah in 1528.[209] Something of the labor which went into the translations was reflected in a letter to Link, June 14, 1528:

> We are now sweating over the translation of the Prophets into German. O God, what a great and hard toil it requires to compel the writers against their will to speak German! They do not want to give up their Hebrew and imitate the barbaric German. Just as though a nightingale should be compelled to imitate a cuckoo and give up her glorious melody, even though she hates a song in monotone.[210]

In 1529 the Wisdom of Solomon appeared, followed by Daniel early in 1530.[211] During Luther's stay at the Coburg in 1530 he continued his labors with the Prophets.[212] By the end of June Jeremiah was completed, and Ezekiel appeared after Luther had again returned to Wittenberg.[213] According to a letter written to Spalatin in October, 1531, Luther was working two hours each day, completing the final work on the Prophets, which were published in February, 1532, under the title *Die Propheten alle Deudsch. D. Mart. Luther. Wittemberg, MDXXXII.*[214] This section was printed by Lufft and was without illustrations other than the title page adorned with an arch, columns, and eight angels.

Luther now turned his attention to the Apocryphal Books, since he had decided to include them in his complete Bible, even though he did not regard these books as a part of the Canon. Ecclesiasticus and Maccabees appeared in 1533, but the remainder were reserved for the complete Bible in 1534.[215] Detailed information on the final checking has been lost, but the existing copies of this beautiful Lufft edition reveal the infinite care which had been given to this volume. As the accompanying cut shows, its title read: *Biblia/das ist/die gantze Heilige Schrifft Deudsch.* Mart. Luth. Wittemberg. M. D. XXXIIII.[216] In addition to the beautifully illuminated initials with which the books began there were 124 woodcuts, of which 117 were new. Some, like Adam and Eve in the Garden, were done in attractive colors in full-page size. What specific artist or series of artists contributed these illustrations remains unknown, but they represent the very highest artistry in Bible illustrations of this time.

Title page of Luther's first complete Bible in 1534

The Lutheran Church now had the first complete Bible, but Martin Luther was far from satisfied with the work. In fact, he regarded the Bible of 1534 as only a beginning. Mathesius in his sermons on Luther's life included this interesting description of the work of revision undertaken by Luther and his fellow professors of Wittenberg:

> When the entire German Bible had been published, as each day, besides its trials, teaches the next, Dr. M. Luther again took the Bible and reviewed it from the very beginning, with great zeal, industry and prayer, and because the Son of God had promised that wherever two or three are gathered together in His name and prayed in His spirit He would be present, Dr. M. Luther at once gathered his own Sanhedrim of the best persons available, which assembled weekly, several hours before supper in the doctor's cloister, namely, D. Johann Bugenhagen, D. Justus Jonas, D. Creuziger, M. Philippum, Mattheum Aurogallum; Magister Georg Roerer, the *Korrektor* was also present. Frequently other friends, doctors and learned men came to take part in this important work, such as Bernhard Ziegler and D. Forstemius.
>
> Then, when D. (Luther) had reviewed the previously published Bible and had also gained information from Jews and friends with linguistic talents, and had inquired of old Germans about appropriate words, as when he had several rams slaughtered in his presence, so that a German butcher could tell him the proper name for each part of the sheep, he came into the assembly (*Konsistorium*) with his old Latin and a new German Bible, and always brought the Hebrew text with him. M. Philipp brought the Greek text with him. D. Creuziger a Chaldean Bible in addition to the Hebrew. The professors had their rabbinical commentaries. D. Pommer also had the Latin text, with which he was very familiar. Each one had studied the text which was to be discussed and had examined Greek and Latin as well as Hebrew commentators.
>
> Thereupon the president submitted a text and permitted each to speak in turn and listened to what each had to say about the characteristics of the language or about the expositions of the ancient doctors. Wonderful and instructive discussions are said to have taken place in connection with this work, some of which M. Georg (Roerer) recorded, which were afterwards printed as little glosses and annotations on the margin.[217]

This description by Mathesius was the only information available to the scholarly world until the late 19th century, when George Buchwald found in the library at the University of Jena the protocol

The Creation of the World, from the 1534 Bible

of a consistory that had met in 1531.[218] Since then other protocols
and additional materials have come to light, which provide a faïrly
complete picture of the work of the Bible revision. The introduction to the Bible protocols of the Weimar Edition, *Die Deutsche
Bibel,* especially those by Paul Pietsch and O. Reichert in Volumes III and IV, provide a comprehensive treatment of the subject.[219] From letters and other statements may be gathered that
the most difficult translations of the Old Testament were Job, the
Psalms, and the Prophets.

In his famous letter of 1530 on the art of translating, Luther
revealed that with Melanchthon and Aurogallus he sometimes
labored three or four days on but a few lines of Job.[220] His dissatisfaction with the 1524 Psalms may be learned from its frequent
revisions, the first in 1528. He carried a copy of this *New Deutsch
Psalter* and wrote notes on the margin for future use. In 1529
it was republished in Latin under the title *Psalterium translationis
veteris, correctum,* Vuittembergae, 1529.[221] In this volume he also
made notes for future revision and then had the two bound together. This dual volume has been preserved in the Breslau
Stadtbibliothek and is known as the *Kunheim Psalter* from a later
owner.[222] That Luther used it at the Coburg is revealed in the
materials which he dictated to Veit Dietrich on the Twenty-Fifth
Psalm. It was also Luther's reference work after his return to
Wittenberg in preparing further revisions of the Psalter, which
appeared in 1531, 1534, 1535, 1538, 1542, and 1544.[223] These
volumes are invaluable as a reflection of the evolution of the
translation as it progressed and the development of the rendition
of the Hebrew tongue. Luther's approach to translating the
Psalms is revealed in the closing words of the Psalter:

> In case there should be those who wish to criticize and claim the
> Psalter has gone too far from the meaning of the original, let them
> be wise not to touch the Psalter. For we engaged in this work with
> our eyes open. In fact, every word was weighed in golden scales
> and translated with all care and fidelity. And there were a sufficient
> number of scholars present. Still we should keep our previous
> German Psalter for those who would like to trace our footsteps to
> learn how in the art of translating one approaches nearer and nearer
> to the goal. The former German Psalter in many places was nearer
> the original Hebrew, but it was farther removed from the German;

this translation is closer to the German and father removed from the Hebrew.[224]

Luther first summoned the consistory or commission of several faculty members in 1531 to assist him with the revision of the Psalter.[225] From the above-mentioned protocol the method of procedure may be discerned. The group met sixteen times from mid-January to mid-March, 1531. The official secretary of the meetings was the faithful recorder of Luther's sermons since 1523, George Roerer.[226] The document was never bound, and some of the leaves were lost before Johann Stols had them printed in 1552 and they found their way into the Jena collection.[227] The notes are detailed enough to provide an intimate acquaintance with the problems confronting the group as well as the usage of the German language at the time. Here is revealed Luther the linguist, the innovator of German expressions, the patient searcher for just the right word to express the Hebrew text. It is clear that Luther always attempted to grasp the meaning of the original and then to recast it into the clearest possible German expression.[228]

From the Jena manuscript may be learned that there were three sets of notes, the protocols of 1531, 1534, and 1539.[229] Recent research has uncovered two more devoted exclusively to the New Testament.[230] One contained the notes made in rechecking the New Testament in 1541, and a final check in 1544.[231] Nothing seems to have been done to the Old Testament text after 1539–40. After Roerer's death the Protocols were in the possession of Master Albertus Christian, a former Wittenberg student and later a preacher at Coethen.[232] Since quite a lengthy controversy has raged over the later revisions, an analysis of the work in chronological order will clarify this issue.

A supplement to Roerer's notes printed in 1552 makes it clear that Luther again assembled the consistory of Wittenberg professors before publishing the complete Bible of 1534.

II. On January 24, 1534, certain invited men started to revise the Bible anew and in many places it was rendered into more distinct and clear German than before. They particularly had trouble with the section of the Prophets from Jeremiah on as it was difficult to render into good German. Isaiah and Daniel had been printed in German several years earlier. The words of Jesus gave the com-

Jacob's Ladder, from the 1534 Bible

Elijah Departing to Heaven, from the 1534 Bible

> missions great concern to render them into clear German as may be gathered in detail from the book signed in B and printed in quarto size.[233]

Unfortunately this old source "signed in B," to which several references were made, has been lost.[234] In 1562, during the controversy over the pure doctrine between the Universities of Wittenberg and Jena, this book was requested for a special edition of the Bible published by Jena in 1564.[235] It may, however, have been lost earlier, for there is no evidence in the text of this edition that the "book signed in B" was used.[236] Since many other sources believed to have been lost have been discovered, it is to be hoped that this protocol may likewise be found by some future scholar.

Even though the notes were lost, there is other evidence that Luther and a commission revised the translation of the Bible before putting it into print in 1534.[237] Veit Dietrich mentioned it in a letter to John Fasel at the Coburg and implied that the checking was largely in the Old Testament.[238] Luther himself mentioned the work in a letter to Amsdorf in March, 1534.[239] An examination of the text also reveals changes in many parts already covered by the consistory of 1531. Comparison of earlier translations of other books of the Bible reveal further changes. In Isaiah, the Song of Solomon, and the books of Maccabees additional progress is apparent, but following Jeremiah the text shows little departure from the 1532 edition of *Die Propheten alle Deudsch*.[240] The little evidence available seems to imply that the first months of 1534 were devoted to a final rapid recheck of the complete Luther Bible. A few parts were revised quite carefully. Most of the work was devoted to the Old Testament. By June, 1534, the typesetting was in progress. On August 6 the Elector of Saxony granted Lufft permission to publish the first complete Luther Bible.[241] Exactly when it came from the press is not known, but by October 17, 1534, Levin Metzsch had a copy in his possession.[242]

The 1534 Bible was not reprinted in revised form until 1541. Meanwhile, however, Luther was making additional notations in his *Handexemplar*,[243] his personal copy of the Bible still preserved in the Jena Library containing his marginal corrections. When Mathesius mentioned "a new German Bible" which Luther always brought to the meetings of the consistory, he referred to the *Handexemplar,* which consisted of the five books of the Pentateuch reprinted in 1539 and the books from Joshua to Malachi of 1538.[244] These were the newest reprints of the Old Testament, and Luther had written many notes on the margins in preparation for later revisions. That it was bound later is shown by the fact that some of the marginal notes are now gone.[245] These notes seem to indicate that Luther continued to correct and improve the Old Testament in these two parts even after the 1541 revision.

Fortunately, Roerer's protocol of the second revision of the complete Bible of 1541 has also been preserved in the Jena collection.[246] Where the 1534 work of the commission is shrouded in darkness, the information on the meetings of the "Sanhedrin" is very complete. From this protocol it is quite clear that the Mathesius description of the work of revision referred to the commission of 1539—41.[247] This Roerer protocol of the second revision of the Bible fills nearly 300 pages in the Weimar edition of *Die Deutsche Bibel,* III and IV, and reveals at close range the actual deliberations of the group.[248] Sometimes Roerer entered the dates of the sessions. On other occasions the different color of the ink reveals the beginning and ending of meetings. The notes contain numerous passages struck out and other additions written between the lines, which indicate the fluid nature of the discussions.[249] The earliest date which appears is July 3, 1539, but it was struck out and July 17 written in.[250] From this correction it would appear that the sessions began on the latter date and continued for nearly a year and a half. German scholars have concluded that between 60 and 70 sessions must have been held.[251]

A study of the protocol brings the student very close to the nature and spirit of the work of this commission. Roerer was a rapid and accurate writer, yet he could not record the entire conversations.[252] He did, however, get the main points and much detailed information. In the notes are epigrams, humor, ridicule, satire, and argument flowing from the give and take of the conversation. Also revealed is a patient, conscientious, scientific methodology. The word-for-word searching in an attempt at a literal translation of the Greek and Hebrew texts had been replaced by a spirit of freedom, an attempt to render the exact meaning of the original in the idiom of the 16th-century German.[253] Reu has stated that these notes bring the reader closer to the real Luther than the *Tischreden*.[254] They reveal that he was the master and leader of the group, not just the organizer of a commission of experts, as some critics have claimed. Both in his command of the original languages and in an acquaintance with the German tongue he had no equal in the group.[255] His colleagues recognized Luther's preparation for the task, for he had lived closely with the work of Bible translation for twenty years.

Though there were some Lufft Bible reprints of 1540 and 1541, they were too early to incorporate the results of the second revision of the Old Testament.[256] The work of the commission was first reflected in the September Bible of 1541.[257] After that date no systematic revision of the Old Testament was undertaken by Luther. Changes were made in later printings, however, on the basis of Luther's marginal notes in his *Handexemplar*. Roerer inherited this document and used these later Luther entries on the Old Testament as his guide in later changes in the Bible, particularly for the Bible of 1546.[258] This must be what Mathesius had in mind when he observed:

> Afterward when Luther wrote against the Jews, his understanding grew from day to day, and many a quotation from the Bible was put into clearer and plainer form, which Roerer with the knowledge and advice of the scholars at Wittenberg entered into the last Bibles after Luther's death.[259]

Walther, one of the Lufft printers, added further light on the subject in reply to an attack by Aurifaber, one of Luther's table companions:

> That such *Scholien* (Commentaries on 1 Moses 8:21) are not on the Bible in which Luther often wrote in his own hand, I know much better than Aurifaber, for I did often have these Bibles in my hand and more than ten times I read them to Master Georg Roerer while in the process of printing.[260]

The notes remained in Roerer's personal possession until his death in 1557, after which they passed into the Jena collection.[261]

The 1539–41 commission did not neglect the New Testament. In the Jena Library a companion volume to the one on the Old

Solomon's Decision, from the 1534 Bible

Solomon's Temple, from the 1534 Bible

Testament was rediscovered by George Coelestin on May 8, 1578, which proved to be Luther's copy of the New Testament text also with marginal notes.[262] To distinguish between these two documents, the Old Testament volume has been named *J. A.* and the New Testament *J. N.*, the equivalents of the German titles, *Jena Altes* and *Jena Neues*.[263]

The work on the Old Testament was completed on February 8, 1541.[264] On the first of February Melanchthon and Cruciger returned from a meeting at Worms,[265] but from March to August they were in Regensburg.[266] The Enders editors claim that the work of revising was done between May 23 and August, 1541, which would imply that Cruciger and Melanchthon were present only toward the end, when the actual printing must have been well along, since the complete Bible with a new set of woodcuts appeared in September.[267] This was to be the final textual rendition of the Old Testament; but Luther was not at all satisfied with the New Testament treatment, perhaps partly because of the fact that the services of the greatest Greek scholar of the age, Melanchthon, had been available for such a brief period, or he may have felt the work on the New Testament had been too hurriedly done. Therefore, though tired and worn with exhaustive years of productive effort, Luther felt constrained to assemble once more the "Sanhedrin" in his *Lutherstube* in 1544 for a final revision of the New Testament.[268]

The 1545 Lufft Bible, though for centuries regarded as the final Luther Bible, could not have utilized any of these final textual corrections.[269] Comparisons will reveal that it is mainly a reprint. The work of the group, evidenced in the changes in the section from Romans to 2 Corinthians 3, did not appear until the final 1546 edition. Luther had guided part of it through the press before his death in February, and Roerer and Melanchthon completed the task on the basis of Luther's *Handexemplar* then in Roerer's possession.[270]

As has been noted in the political history of Electoral Saxony treated previously, Elector John Frederick was captured by the Emperor's troops during the Schmalkaldic War at the Battle of Muehlberg in 1547. With his capture the Electoral title and lands with the University of Wittenberg passed to Moritz of the Albertine line. The library, however, had been moved to Jena in the flight from Wittenberg, and the Elector claimed it as his personal property. It later became a part of the University of Jena founded by his sons.

Not long after these tragic events the controversy broke out among his followers over Luther's teaching. On the one hand were the theologians of Jena, led by Flacius, as opposed to the Wittenberg group, led by Melanchthon.[271] Some of the bitterness was, no doubt, due to the aftermath of the Schmalkaldic War with the loss of the Electoral title and the University of Wittenberg. In ten years' time the son of John Frederick, called John Frederick the Medium, was engaged in bitter controversy with Elector August of Albertine Saxony, who had inherited the *Kurkreis* after Moritz's death and, with it, the Wittenberg theologians. The Jena group insisted that Luther had been much more dogmatic in his teaching than granted by the Wittenberg men. In 1555 they began the collection of their own edition of Luther's works to counteract the Wittenberg edition published from 1539 to 1558, which they claimed was not reliable.[272] They, likewise, insisted on publishing their own Bible, charging that Roerer, under Melanchthon's influence, had falsified the Luther text to prove the interpretation of the Wittenberg group.[273] It is most regrettable that the bitter personal rivalries of the two courts should have spread to the college faculties and even into the ranks of modern Lutheranism.

Though the editors stated in their introduction that they had carefully re-edited the Bible on the basis of the "Honorable Doctor Martin Luther" as "corrected by his own hand," there is no internal evidence to show that they used any later material than that found in the 1545 Lufft reprint. This 1545 Bible they regarded as the final Bible, containing Luther's own corrections, and they transmitted their opinion to the "Age of the Dogmaticians." All through the 16th, 18th, and 19th centuries it was generally assumed that the 1545 edition was the *textus receptus* of Lutheranism.[274] In 1549 Polycarp Leyser stated this position regarding the 1545 Bible as the "authentic" Bible of the Lutheran Church when he wrote:

Matthias Flacius, from a woodcut, 1587

Still the 1545 edition alone can be regarded as the last Bible published under Luther's supervision, and it is the authority with which all German Bibles must agree if they are to bear the title of genuinely Lutheran.[275]

As indicated earlier, modern research has established that Flacius and the Jena group were in error with reference to the last Luther Bible.[276] It has likewise confirmed that Roerer had been authorized to supervise changes in the 1546 Bible and that Luther had given him his personal Bible with the marginal corrections for that very purpose.[277] Roerer and Melanchthon had used both the *Handexemplar* and the 1544 protocol to complete the publication of the 1546 final Luther Bible. An examination of the finished work with the two documents shows clearly that they were faithful to Luther's notations. There can be no doubt, therefore, that the 1546 edition of the complete Bible was the final bequest to Lutheranism by its founder.[278]

In translating the Bible, Luther began with several fundamental presuppositions. He regarded the entire Bible as a unit and translated the meaning of the more obscure passages in the light of the clear Gospel.[279] He believed that the Gospel message was contained in both the Old and New Testament, even though not so clearly expressed in the former. The story of the Cross, Christ and Him crucified, was the central theme of the entire Bible, and this fact the translator must keep ever in mind.[280] Luther also believed that the translator must penetrate beyond the external linguistic peculiarities, that he must study the grammar carefully, attempt to grasp the exact meaning, and then forget all about the original language.[281] In some cases the peculiarities of the Greek or Hebrew were impossible to translate into German. It was this fact which had prevented the Jewish rabbis in Germany from perceiving the divine message, and it likewise obscured much of the work of Jerome.[282] God spoke through the media of human language to the soul, and the message must be in a language comprehended by the common man. Once at the table Luther told his companions:

> One must not ask the letters in Latin how to express the idea in German . . . but the mother in the home, the children in the street, and the common man in the market place and inquire of them how it should be expressed, and then translate it accordingly. Then they understand it and notice that someone is speaking to them in German.[283]

It was the task of the translator to understand thoroughly the divine message in the original language and then to express the same thoughts in the language of the people. The final Luther Bible, therefore, was not, nor was it meant to be, a literal translation; rather, Biblical values had been translated into 16th-century German values.[284]

Like his Postils and the Catechism, the contribution of the Luther Bible to the cause of the Reformation cannot be measured. However, Erich Zimmermann's comparatively recent study, "The Spread of the Luther Bible during the Reformation," does throw some light on its reception and circulation in central Europe.[285] It is, of course, impossible to establish a relationship between the number of copies sold and their probable influence upon the people; yet, the fact that so many Bibles were sold indicates the eagerness of the people for the new translation. Sales of the New Testament between its publication in 1522 and that of the complete Bible in 1534 probably reached 200,000, as noted earlier.[286] The complete Bible was also printed in many forms. No less than 19 High German and 4 Low German editions were printed in Wittenberg, and these were reprinted 83 times in High German and 19 times in Low German in Wittenberg alone during Luther's lifetime.[287] Printers in other cities were quick to join in the publication of Luther's translations. There were many reprintings of the separate sections of the Old Testament, the New Testament, and the complete Bible. Between 1522 and 1546 a total of 430 complete or partial Bibles was published by various printing establishments throughout Germany.[288] The Augsburg and Magdeburg printers led with 55 reprints each, closely followed by 42 in Strassburg, 37 in Nuernberg, 26 in Erfurt, 18 in Leipzig, and many others both in High and Low German.[289] If Zimmermann's earlier figure of 2,000 copies per edition is accepted, the total number of copies available to the people is readily computed.[290] Oskar Thulin, present director of the *Lutherhalle* in Wittenberg, which houses the largest collection of Luther Bibles, estimates that approximately 500 woodcuts were prepared for the various printings, which totaled 104 issued during Luther's lifetime.[291] Included among the contributing artists were some of the most famous names of the day, including Burgkmair, Schaeufelain, Waiditz, and Satrapitanus in the Augsburg editions; Hans Holbein d. J. in Basel; Springinklee, Schoens, and Beham in Nuernberg.

Luther's own evaluation of the importance of this work of translation is evidenced by the years of his life which he devoted to the task still unfinished at his death. In his own words its importance was thus expressed:

The need of the Bible in German is so great that no one can imagine it. No one realizes the insight which it has offered to our world today. What we once tried to accomplish through continual lecturing and great industry and still could not attain, this text now offers clearly by iself; for none of us realized in what darkness we were living because of the former translations.[292]

LITURGICAL CHANGES

Much controversy has arisen over Luther's contribution to the music of the sixteenth century.[293] Some would deprive him of all originality, including the credit for having composed the battle hymn of the Reformation, "A Mighty Fortress"; others would have him the "Palestrina of the Reformation." The fact remains that he must have had considerable appreciation of music and some talent for the art of composition.[294] A recently discovered musical composition by Luther dating to his Eisenach days reveals a fair mastery of polyphonic composition.[295] Luther corresponded with such musicians as Isaac, Josquin, Senfl, Rupff, and Walther, indicating that he held the respect of these capable artists.[296] Some of them even called him "our hymn master" and, like Walther, recalled their former association with Luther with great pride. Praetorius in his *Syntagma Musicum* records Walther's words of 1565:

> When Luther, forty years ago, wanted to prepare his German Mass, he requested of the Elector of Saxony and Duke John . . . that Conrad Rupff and I be summoned to Wittenberg, where he might discuss music and the nature of the eight Gregorian Psalm tones with us. He himself selected finally the eighth tone for the Epistle and the sixth for the Gospel, saying at the same time that Christ is a friendly and charming Lord, hence we shall take the sixth tone for the Gospel. Since St. Paul is a very serious-minded apostle, we shall use the eighth tone for the Epistle. He (Luther) prepared the music for the Epistles and Gospels, likewise for the Words of Institution of the true body and blood of Christ; he chanted these for me and asked me to express my opinion of his efforts. At that time he kept me in Wittenberg for three weeks; we discussed how the Epistles and Gospels might be set properly. I was in Wittenberg with Luther until the first German Mass had been presented (October 29, 1525). I had been asked to listen to this first performance and then take a copy with me to Torgau and report, at the command of the Doctor, my impression to His Grace, the Elector. . . . I know and hereby truthfully testify that . . . Luther

. . . found great delight in the chorale as well as in figurate music
(i. e., solo or unison music as well as part music). I spent many
a pleasant hour singing music with him and often experienced that
he seemingly could not weary of singing or even get enough of it;
in addition, he was able to discuss music eloquently.[297]

In a day when the cathedral organist in Zurich wept because
the fanaticism of Calvin had caused his fine instrument to be
destroyed, and when the Berne organist lost both his organ and his
home because the new Protestants there saw in music mere "popish
conceit," it was remarkable that Luther should encourage music
and musicians that the Gospel might also be spread through song.[298]
In an unfinished thesis *Concerning Music* he wrote briefly what he
often expressed in greater detail:

> He who despises music, as do all the fanatics, does not please me.
> For music is a gift and largess of God, not a gift of men. Music
> drives away the devil and makes people happy; it induces one to
> forget all wrath, unchastity, arrogance, and other vices. After
> theology I accord to music the highest place and the greatest
> honor.[299]

And again, how different his attitude toward music was from that
of the stern Calvin may be seen in the following observation:

> God has His Gospel preached also through the medium of music;
> this may be seen from the compositions of Josquin, all of whose
> works are cheerful, gentle, mild, and lovely; they flow and move
> along and are neither forced nor coerced and bound by rigid and
> stringent rules, but, on the contrary, are like the song of the finch.[300]

Luther's writings are full of tender thoughts about the beauties
of music in family and social relationships.[301] That he was very
fond of playing and singing is well established. He may not have
been one of the outstanding musicians of the sixteenth century, yet
his place in early Protestantism is well defined by Professor Paul
Henry Lang of Columbia University in his recent volume *Music
in Western Civilization* (1941):

> In the center of the new musical movement which accompanied the
> Reformation stands the great figure of Martin Luther. He does not
> occupy this position because of his generalship of the Protestant
> movement, and nothing is more unjust than to consider him a sort of
> enthusiastic and good-natured dilettante.[302]

Luther soon realized that his new evangelical teachings could not leave the Roman liturgy unaffected; yet he loved the old Gregorian hymns and chants and approached the problem of revising the forms of service with great reverence.[303] He further realized that to a people who were but lately Roman Catholic much of the symbolism of the old Church seemed sacred. In order that sensitive souls might not be offended, it would be far better if the Gospel slowly paved the way for whatever changes were introduced.[304] As the experience in different Lutheran lands was later to prove, the transition from the Roman Mass to the Lutheran Communion could only be made gradually. Sometimes the change was entirely impossible because of the pressure of circumstances. In any event it was a problem that required careful judgment, tact, and patience.

In the development of the Roman Church during the Middle Ages the center of emphasis had shifted from the preaching of the Gospel to the celebration of the Roman Mass.[305] As noted earlier, the clergy had become the medium between the people and their God. The Mass was an *opus operatum,* or work of acquiring merits, for the sinner by a clergy that was offering Christ again as a sacrifice in behalf of the congregation. The more colorful and impressive the service became, the more effective its psychology. In a beautiful cathedral setting a Mass conducted by clergymen robed in gorgeous Mass vestments and surrounded by candles, incense, and gold and silver Communion vessels was a breathtaking spectacle. The picture was completed by the addition of the rich Gregorian music, intercessory chants, introits, and Psalm versicles. Luther, like others, was impressed by its sheer artistry, for he had an aesthetic soul, and he hesitated to discard all this beauty when he transformed the Roman Mass into the Lutheran Communion.[306] But those parts of the Mass which made of it an *opus operatum* would have to be removed, since justification by faith left no room for a second sacrifice of Christ on the Cross.[307] As for the embellishments, many of them might be included in a new service in which the sermon was placed into the central position.[308] The early part of the Mass would be made introductory to the sermon, followed by a Communion service. The entire service would be in German, and the congregation could participate in it from beginning to end. The two most striking features would be the sermon and the hymn singing by the congregation. This gradual transformation involved the greater part of the next two decades in Saxon lands.[309] Other Lutheran lands witnessed similar changes, and the speed of transformation varied with local leadership and other circumstances.

As Luther's emphasis on the Gospel began to permeate the clergy in German lands, it became necessary to create new orders of service to frame this "New Theology." Changes in the German Mass, which eliminated the objectionable features of the old Roman Mass, appear as early as 1522.[310] In Kemberg, just a few miles from Wittenberg, where one of Luther's former students, Bartholomaeus Bernhardi, was pastor, changes in the Roman Mass suggested by Luther were tried before being introduced into the larger Town Church in Wittenberg.[311] The early experiments by various pastors in different parts of Germany paved the way for some definite liturgical changes. The result was the preparation of the *Formula missae et communionis* of 1523, in which Luther removed the canon of the Roman Mass.[312] Luther's fundamental principle of purifying the Communion service was expressed in the following section of the *Formula missae:*

> We assert, it is not now, nor has it ever been in our mind to abolish entirely the whole formal cultus of God, but to cleanse that which is in use, which had been vitiated by most abominable additions, and to point out a pious use.[313]

His principle was Christo-centric, meaning that those aspects of the Mass which stressed His redemptive work should be kept, while all those which emphasized the offerings and accomplishments of man should be swept away.[314] Luther's primary concern was not the creation of a new liturgy for the Lutheran *Landeskirche,* but rather a return to the simple, pure forms of the Early Church.[315] He was fully aware that this first Lutheran Communion service was far more elaborate than in the days of the Apostles. He even stated the order in which the various embellishments were added. He was too much of an artist not to appreciate the beauty of many of the later additions, and he fully realized that the people were not ready for so abrupt a change. As long as the additions emphasized the Gospel and glorified Christ, they might well remain. For the same reason the "abhorred canon," the sacrificial elements teaching work-righteousness, would have to be removed lest the people be misled.[316]

Essentially, then, the *Formula missae* introduced the later Communion service, and for this reason it becomes extremely important. Paul Strodach in his introduction to the *Formula missae* regards it as the most important of Luther's liturgical writings.[317] Its influence extended even beyond the day when the *Deutsche Messe* of 1526 had been quite generally accepted.[318] Certainly, this liturgy for Communion was a significant step in the development of a Lutheran service in harmony with the new teaching of the Reformer.

Luther, however, was not satisfied with the *Formula missae*, as it still excluded the people from the service. This defect was partly remedied by Speratus' translation of the Mass into German in Wittenberg.[319] In Nuernberg another translation appeared. The addition of several German hymns by Luther made it more suited to congregational participation.[320] Still, at best, it was but a makeshift, an alteration. Luther's ideal was a transformation of the Roman Mass into German, with even the Gregorian music changed in measure and accent to fit the German words,[321] but recalling the unfortunate episode of the impetuous Carlstadt, he felt it advisable to proceed slowly.

In the meantime German Masses were introduced in a number of places. Nicolaus Hausmann, who had eagerly awaited the new Communion service, used it for the first time in the Latin in the *Marienkirche* at Zwickau for the Christmas service in 1523.[322] Altenburg, Leisnig, Borna, Hirtzberg, and Schweinitz all were celebrating Communion in new forms.[323] In Schwaebisch-Hall Johannes Brenz introduced a German Communion service, as did Zwingli in Zurich and Oecolampadius in Basel.[324] Encouraged by this reception and yielding to the importunities of friends, Luther decided to rearrange the Mass into German, including the Gregorian music. Realizing the magnitude of the problems involved, Luther requested that the two court musicians, Conrad Rupff and Johann

Walther, come to Wittenberg to assist him as technical advisers.[325] To transform the old Gregorian music to fit the text of the German translation was a courageous and enormous undertaking, and modern music critics are amazed at the skill with which the new arrangement was set to the German words.

On October 29, 1525, the *Deutsche Messe* was celebrated for the first time in Wittenberg in the presence of the two court musicians.[326] Walther then took it to Torgau upon his return for the reactions of the Elector and other competent judges. When it was officially introduced in the Town Church on Christmas, 1525, Luther briefly explained its content and purpose to the congregation.[327] The *Deutsche Messe* was regarded by Luther as a kind of colorful Sunday dress for those not yet strong enough in the faith. In time he hoped to dispense with the outward glitter and display of vestments, incense, candles, etc., and to provide more mature congregations with simple preaching, prayers, and hymn singing; but, unfortunately, he did not yet have a congregation ready for the removal of such props.[328] By 1526 the Elector made the new form of service official throughout his lands with the proviso that those who felt obliged to deviate had the freedom of choice in the matter.[329] The instructions to the visitors of 1528 indicate that there were still congregations following the old form. Nor was the Latin *Formula missae* of 1523 to be discarded entirely, for it was instructive for the ministerial students.

In both the *Formula missae* and the *Deutsche Messe* the word Mass is misleading when used instead of Communion. Yet, in a sense, it is even more fitting, for Luther meant to emphasize that he had not created a new Communion, but merely restored the original Catholic Mass of Apostolic days. This form of service with its old sixteenth-century square notes looks quite strange to modern Lutherans; yet, allowing for the Mass vestments and other outward forms, a closer examination will find it remarkably similar to the Lutheran Communion service of later centuries, and of the early Lutheran Church in America.[330] All communicants had to announce themselves in advance.[331] The church ordinances and even contemporary woodcuts show that great care was exercised lest anyone attend Communion improperly prepared. One such woodcut pictures even high-ranking princes and nobles sitting in the *Beicht-stuhl*, or confessional chair, while being examined by Luther or some other well-known clergyman as to their moral conduct and familiarity with the words of institution and significance of the Holy Supper.[332] Each individual should be examined at least once a year, Luther thought, to determine whether he still remembered the Catechism, the Creed, and the Lord's Prayer.

In form the *Deutsche Messe* was very similar to the *Formula missae*. The service began with a selection from one of the Psalms, chanted by the pastor in *primo tono* of the Gregorian mode, followed by the Kyrie, Eleison on the same tone.[333] The latter Luther reduced from nine to three, as used in the later Lutheran Church. Then followed the Collect and Epistle chanted in *octavo tono*.[334] The arrangement still preserved in the old square notation shows that Luther prepared a more flexible and expressive arrangement than that of the former Roman Mass. The congregation and the choir then sang some hymn suitable to the period of the church year. The Gospel was chanted in *quinto tono*, the pastor facing the congregation as he did for the Epistle. During the collects and prayers the minister faced the altar. After the Gospel the congregation sang the confession in German.[335] All the preceding liturgy was preparatory to the sermon, the high point in the service. In the case of the "emergency preachers" the sermon might be read from Luther's *Kirchenpostille*.[336]

The Communion service, which followed the sermon, was begun with a sermonet on the Lord's Prayer and the words of institution, reminding the communicants of the seriousness of the Holy Supper.[337] After the sermonet the pastor turned to the altar and began the Communion service. The words of institution were practically the same as those of later centuries.[338] The host and the wine were still elevated as was done in the Catholic Mass, a practice which was not dropped in Wittenberg until 1542. The old German custom of all the men first partaking of Communion and then the women was also followed in this service. The bread was distributed first to the entire group if only one clergyman officiated; but if there were two, the wine could immediately follow the bread. While part of the congregation was receiving Communion, the remainder sang an appropriate Communion hymn. At the close of

Interpretation by the Cranach School of the distribution of the Lord's Supper to the Protestant Saxon princes. Note John Frederick confessing to Luther at upper left. Painted about 1560

the Communion a hymn written by Luther for this service, "the German Sanctus," was sung, followed by the customary collects and, later, the customary blessing. Luther also prepared a *bet-buchlin*, or prayer book, for use of the communicants in preparing themselves for participation in Communion.[339]

The *Brandenburg-Nuernberger Kirchenordnung* of 1533 has this to say about the new form of service:

> As for other outward features, the external physical aspects, such as Mass vestments, altar cloths, silver and gold containers, lights, etc., these are in all respects optional and are not important to the faith and conscience. Therefore, since they have been previously in use and are there, they are to be used; especially the clothes, so that they do not wear their daily attire and the congregation may be served properly and respectfully.[340]

In certain other aspects, however, this ordinance reveals that by the thirties the Communion service was becoming somewhat fixed in pattern. No one could receive Communion any longer unless he accepted both the bread and the wine, nor could pastors commune themselves. The order and method of confession was generally established, but the use of the common cup was not always practiced, as the following quotation also from the *Kirchenordnung* shows:

> Here in Koenigsberg we use in each congregation three cups, two for the sick because several are unclean and some have infected lips, and the third cup is used on Sundays for the communicants.[341]

The same source adds that on special occasions an extra large cup was used apparently to serve a larger than usual number of communicants.

Owing to the diversities in practice it is impossible to state exactly when the transition from the older Roman Church to the Lutheran pattern was complete. As has been stated, each locality differed in the ability of its leaders and the capacities of the laity to grasp the fundamental differences in the two systems. In Breslau, John Hesz required a period of two decades to effect the change, while in Magdeburg the change was comparatively rapid.[342] It is interesting to note that Bugenhagen wrote to Bucer in 1536 that for the first time in Wittenberg the Lord's Supper had been

celebrated "without lights, Mass vestments, and the elevation of
the host," but in all simplicity.[343] This service must have been
an experiment, for the elevation of the host was not entirely dropped
in Wittenberg until 1542, a few years before Luther's death.[344]

Not the least in importance among all of these innovations was
the hymn singing introduced into the congregation, and this contribution has provided another fertile field for claim and counter-
claim. Two particular schools of thought emerge from the conflicting theories.[345] The one, represented by Marburger, Spitta, and
others, advances the viewpoint that Luther must have been writing
hymns all through his life, that it is illogical to suppose that he
would have remained silent through his early years, then all at once
burst forth in song. They believe that "A Mighty Fortress" was
the result of the period of stress culminating in the appearance at
Worms and the retreat in the Wartburg.[346] This group believes
that Luther began writing hymns as early as 1511 and was very
proficient by 1524, when the first four hymnals appeared in Lutheran lands.

The opponents of this theory, whose chief spokesman was
Bachmann, point out that the Wartburg period is probably one of
the best known in Luther's life, and had he written the battle
hymn while in seclusion there, some mention would have been
made of it. They advance the view that Luther's first attempt at
hymnology was inspired by the martyrdom of two young students
in Brussels in 1523, whose death at the stake moved Luther to
write "By Help of God I Fain would Tell." [347] Two other hymns
must have followed closely upon the first, for in 1524 an aged
linen weaver in Magdeburg was arrested for publicly singing in
the street Luther's hymns "May God Bestow on Us His Grace"
and "Out of the Depths I Cry to Thee." [348] Encouraged by the
success of his early efforts, so says the second school, Luther must
have written some twenty hymns in a short time, for the Walther
Gesangbuechlein appeared in the summer of 1524, containing
24 hymns credited to Luther.[349]

Wackernagel supported the view that Walther prepared both
the music and the text arrangements for the 37 hymns in the *Gesangbuechlein*, but Bachmann challenged that belief.[350] He believed that Walther supervised the musical part of the publication,

but since Luther wrote the introduction, he was certainly consulted. Bachmann's view is supported by Walther's later acknowledgment of Luther's contribution. The fact that Luther later issued an edition of his own in 1529, the "lost" *Klugischen,* testifies to his qualifications to assist in the preparation of the first hymnal.[351] The editor of the *Weimar Ausgabe* has the following opinion:

> It was compiled by Luther according to a definite arrangement. Not only original manuscripts, but also individual printed compositions were used. After the beginning of the printing, which was begun before Pentecost of 1524, the five compositions which had appeared earlier were placed at the head of the rest. The work appeared in the late summer of 1524. . . . In it were 24 of Luther's own songs.[352]

In the same year Jobst Gutknecht in Nuernberg prepared an *Achtliederbuch,* a hymnal of eight songs, probably a collection of the single compositions published by that time.[353] This book seems to have been reprinted in Augsburg the same year. In Erfurt two editions of a similar *Achtliederbuch* came from the press of the *Schwarzes Horn.*[354] Two years later the Lufft press in Wittenberg produced the *Lufftschen Enchiridion von 1526,* an adaptation for congregational singing of the Walther *Gesangbuechlein,* which had been written principally for the choir.[355]

In the late twenties other hymnals appeared. Professor Knaake owned an undated *Enchiridion* which contained "A Mighty Fortress." [356] Scholars are not agreed as to its date and origin. Knaake ascribed it to Michael Blum of Leipzig in 1528 and cited a letter by George Rhau of Wittenberg to Stephan Roth, dated February 10, 1528, in which Rhau mentioned the various enterprises engaging the attention of other printers and stated: "Hans Weiss is printing a songbook." [357] Knaake believed this was the "lost" Wittenberg hymnal of 1528, on which the Blum hymnal was based.[358] Wackernagel has pointed out its similarities to both the Lufft hymnal of 1526 and the earlier Walther hymnal of 1524, including the introduction by Luther written for the latter.[359] The Blum hymnal also contained the German Litany first mentioned in the "lost" *Klugischen* hymnal of 1529.[360] Correspondence between Luther and Hausmann, however, reveals that the Litany was being sung in both Latin and German in the Town Church early in 1529. Kawerau has pointed out that the choir boys of the Town Church must have had the Litany in printed form even earlier.[361] The obvious conclusion would seem to place the Blum hymnal between the "lost" Weiss publication of 1528 and Luther's collection of 1529, likewise "lost." Both of these contained "A Mighty Fortress." [362]

The *Weimar Ausgabe* of Luther's works has devoted some forty pages to a discussion of the mighty Battle Hymn of the Reformation. Numerous scholars have made detailed studies of its origin and the date of its composition.[363] Their conclusions have been as varied as their numbers. The inspiration and date for its composition have been variously found in the stormy days of Worms around 1521, in the preparation of the *Deutsche Messe* in 1526, in the martyr's death of one Leonhard Kaiser of 1527, in the visitation of the pest in that same year, in 1528, when the Pack incident raised the threat of war with Charles V, in the rebuff given the evangelical princes at the second Diet of Speyer in 1529, in the spiritual solitude of the Coburg in 1530, and in Luther's first reference to the hymn in 1531.[364] About all that can be said with certainty is that "A Mighty Fortress" appeared before 1529 in a hymnal printed around that date.[365] Since it did not appear in the Lufft hymnal of 1526, it is reasonable to suppose that it had not been composed at that time and to conclude that its date lies somewhere between the summer of 1527 and the spring of 1528, but no definite date can be cited with certainty.[366]

Another question which has been widely studied and debated, with opinion sharply divided, is that of Luther's originality. That he loved music and had considerable technical knowledge of its composition is indisputable. Reliable evidence shows, as concluded by Winterfeld, that Luther was the composer of three original hymns: "We All Believe in One True God," "Isaiah, Mighty Seer, in Days of Old," and "A Mighty Fortress Is Our God." [367] Three more he classified as rearrangements of older materials, and three others he considered as "probable" compositions by Luther. Of the 36 hymn texts credited to Luther, the remainder were set to older medieval melodies or even to popular tunes of his day.

Baeumker disagreed violently with Winterfeld's viewpoint. He questioned any originality on the part of Luther or even his ability to set his texts to familiar melodies. He interpreted Walther's statement to mean that Luther had required Walther's help with the entire musical arrangement of the *Deutsche Messe*.[368] He advanced the theory that the German Sanctus, written by Luther for the 1526 Communion service, had been taken from a Sanctus, *De angelis*, found in the Roman Gradual.[369] Baeumker asserted that "A Mighty Fortress" had been patched together out of parts of the Roman liturgy, and he claimed to have found an earlier hymn by Hugo von Reutlingen, printed in Strassburg in 1488, which contained a parallel note arrangement to the melody for the words "a trusty shield and weapon." [370] He also claimed to have discovered the fifteenth-century source of the melody for "We All Believe in One True God." [371]

Naumann and others challenged Baeumker's evidence, showing that the *De angelis* cited by him did not come into existence before the seventeenth century.[372] Many students of the problem have pointed out that Luther was deeply steeped in the Gregorian tradition, which would explain any similarity in feeling and tone sequence. Speaking of "A Mighty Fortress," Zahn says:

> A student of music can hardly accept the thesis that Luther took this beautiful melody from the debris of medieval compositions and pieced it together mosaiclike in this form.[373]

Music critics have often pointed out that no musical composition can be entirely original, for the inspiration is due to contact with the music of the past. Regardless of the source of its inspiration, the Battle Hymn of the Reformation forms such a unity of composition and is so distinctive of Luther that it can hardly reasonably be labeled a "patchwork" of other compositions.[374]

Luther's distinction in the field of music lies not so much in the degree of his originality as in the fact that he encouraged and even increased the use of music in the Church.[375] In his treatment of the musical heritage of the Church he remained consistent with his practices in other fields, always retaining the good, discarding the untenable, creating where necessary. In such a picture it is not essential that Luther be an original composer. For that undertaking he called freely upon contemporary musicians. Storck has stated the generally accepted viewpoint of impartial critics regarding Luther's role as a hymn writer and composer thus:

> The selection and reworking of old melodies of the Gregorian hymnody and the spiritual and secular folk songs and their adaptation to the evangelical church hymns. . . .[376]

Luther's belief that music should also serve the Gospel gave to Lutheranism that distinctive feature which earned for it the title of "the Singing Church." [377] Under his encouragement musicians composed, reclaimed, and transmitted the rich treasure of the Church in an unbroken line of musical development from Luther to Bach.

Before Luther's death German hymnody was fairly well established, for by that time a large variety of hymns was available in numerous editions of hymnals. Among these was one printed by Joseph Klug at Wittenberg in 1535, of which a copy may still be seen in Munich.[378] In 1537 Johann Walther issued the "corrected, enlarged, and improved" Wittenberg *Gesangbuechlein,* a copy of which is still in Augsburg.[379] A Valten Schumann edition of 1539 was in Wernigerode.[380] The forties produced several additional hymnals, including another by Klug, prepared in 1543, for which Luther wrote the introduction; Johann Walther's choir hymnal in 1544 for four and five voices, also printed in Wittenberg; and the final edition before Luther's death printed by Valentin Bapst in Leipzig in 1545, for which Luther likewise wrote the introduction.[381] By 1546, therefore, when Luther passed from the scene, Lutheranism was well supplied with hymnals and hymns for every occasion.

THE ORGANIZATION OF SCHOOLS

In a time when all education was in the hands of the Church, there can be little doubt that the new schools established throughout German lands between 1525 and 1546 contributed greatly to the success of the German Reformation. As has been remarked again and again, Luther and his co-workers realized that the complete success of the Reformation would be reached only with a second generation of Lutherans having little or none of the old Roman background and trained from childhood in the new evangelical tradition. The Reformation in no small measure ebbed and flowed with the quality of school instruction received by the German youth. The Lutheran schools of the forties and fifties reached a high level of efficiency; but with the passing of Luther and Melanchthon the leadership waned. By 1560 a decline had begun in education. During the Age of Dogmatism the Lutheran Church lost the vital, dynamic, creative energy of its founders and began to stagnate.[382] Large sections of Lutheran Germany were rewon to Catholicism by the Jesuits, who established excellent schools following the Council of Trent.[383]

As noted in connection with Luther's education, centers like Nuernberg, Ulm, Augsburg, and Vienna had excellent Humanistic schools.[384] Luther and Melanchthon adopted almost bodily the curriculums and techniques of these Humanistic schools, yet they made many innovations and adaptations to fit specific needs. Scheel may be correct in claiming that the Reformers did not think in terms of the later German *Gymnasium* when they established schools preparatory for the university, nor of the *Volksschule* when they established schools which had their terminal at the age of sixteen.

Luther probably wrote the *Weckruf of 1524* to the mayors and aldermen of Germany in response to the pressure of events.[385] The monasteries were being emptied. The enrollment of the University of Wittenberg had dropped to a new low. Carlstadt had discouraged the pursuit of higher learning and the attainment of degrees. The Anabaptists were also belittling education. Following the reports on the Saxon visitations of 1528—29, Luther became vehement in the *Sermon on the Duty of Sending Children to School.*[386] The visitors had reported that, in general, the educational facilities for the youth were tragically inadequate. In all Electoral Saxony there was but one Humanistic school, at Torgau, where the youth could obtain some measure of efficient instruction.[387] From then on instructions to the visitors and the various church ordinances emphasized the need of an effective school system. The *Hallische Kirchenordnung* in 1526 already contained a section under the title "Concerning the Schools," in which it stressed the need for a proper training of the youth.[388] The "Instruction to Visitors" in Saxon lands contained a very specific section on the schools, recommending the typical Humanistic division into three sections, as noted in the Mansfeld school attended by Luther.[389] While this was not to become the universal pattern, it is interesting to note that Latin alone was to be taught, Greek and Hebrew being reserved for the University. In the *Braunschweig'sche Kirchenordnung*, which Bugenhagen introduced in the north in 1528, there was a section providing for Latin Boys' Schools and Girls' Schools.[390] A similar provision was made in the *Hamburger Kirchenordnung* of 1529.[391]

Luther's views on education are partially reflected in the aforementioned *Weckruf* and *Sermon*, but they do not provide a comprehensive view of his contributions to the developments in education. An examination of his correspondence with Bugenhagen, Amsdorf, Jonas, Brenz, Hesz, and other church organizers in all parts of the German lands reveals that they were constantly seeking his advice. The several organizers kept in close touch with the Wittenberg faculty, sharing ideas and experiences and finally evolving as a group the general pattern of Lutheran education. The first Lutheran school was founded in Magdeburg by Nicholas Amsdorf in 1524, but it did not as nearly approach the educational ideal of the Reformers as did the school established by Luther and Melanchthon in Eisleben in 1525 at the request of the *Grafen* of Mansfeld.[392] The educational program introduced into the Saxon lands by the *Kursaechsische Schulordnung* of 1528 was patterned on the Eisleben school.[393] The church visitations by Bugenhagen in Halberstadt, Brunswick, Luebeck, Hamburg, Bremen, Pomerania, Denmark, and Norway resulted in the introduction of all kinds of schools varying widely with local conditions, established with the knowledge of, and upon consultation with, Luther.[394] He was also in close touch with the Reformation carried on by John Hess in the Breslau region, which changed it into a flourishing Lutheran community with dozens of churches and schools.[395]

Another school which closely approached the ideal of the Reformers was that established in Nuernberg. When that community, under the leadership of the town secretary Lazarus Spengler and the pastors of its principal churches, St. Sebald and St. Lorenz, freed itself from the control of Bishop Wiegand of Bamberg, a call went out to the University of Wittenberg for aid in organizing the community along Lutheran lines. Spengler journeyed to Wittenberg in person to seek the advice of Luther and Melanchthon, and the latter gave every assistance in establishing the famous Nuernberg school in 1525.[396] Two teachers were called from Wittenberg, Joachim Camerarius and M. Rothing, and the faculty was completed by the addition of Eobanus of Erfurt and J. Schoner.[397] These teachers were fairly well compensated for their labors for that day, as Camerarius and Eobanus each received $2,010, while Rothing and Schoner received $1,340 each.[398] The success of the undertaking was attested later when Luther in speaking of this fine school said: "It shines like the sun, moon, and stars in all Germany." [399] Before the publication of the *Brandenburg-Nuernberger Kirchenordnung* of 1533 the Wittenberg theologians were again consulted.

The educational pattern of the emerging Lutheran Church can best be understood by examining the schools which it organized. Luther followed the Humanistic approach to learning, believing that the three classical languages, Latin, Greek, and Hebrew, were absolutely essential to college and advanced work.[400] For this reason he believed the educational program should be a unit, with the study of these languages begun in the Latin schools. Melanchthon held the same viewpoint, as did Bugenhagen, but the latter found it necessary to modify his approach in some of the forty communities where he established schools. In general, Latin was stressed at the lower levels, while in the highest division some Greek and Hebrew were taught, especially in the schools of northern Germany. Students who followed this course were prepared for entrance to the University of Wittenberg and would have mastered Greek and Hebrew by the time they entered the seminary classes with their emphasis on Biblical Humanism.

Probably the best example of the new schools established under Lutheran supervision was the Wittenberg Latin School, founded in 1533 under the direction of Luther and Melanchthon.[401] It was located just south of the Town Church near the small *Kapelle* and was for boys only.[402] Like earlier schools mentioned, it was divided into three groups or grades, the *elementarien*, the *secunda*, and the *summa*. The school building was very plain in both architecture and furnishings. The students sat on wooden benches, facing the teacher on a slightly elevated platform at the front of the room. The smaller children sat in front, the second division in the middle, and the older boys in the rear. Magister More was the *Supremus* in charge of the school, assisted by the *Schulmeister*, the *Cantor*, and the *Tertius*.[403]

At the front of the room was a blackboard, and in evidence also were the "wolf" and the "donkey," reminiscent of the Mansfeld school days of Luther.[404] Also on the blackboard was a record of the week's accumulation of misdemeanors to be balanced with a specific number of strokes by the teacher's rod, but there were careful restrictions limiting this form of punishment.[405] The ringing of the small bell in the bell tower toward the rear of the Town Church was the signal for the beginning of school at 5.30 A. M. in the summer time and 6:30 A. M. in the winter.[406] The students assembled, and the director offered prayer, followed by the singing of the hymn *Veni, Creator Spiritus* under the direction of the *Cantor*. All instruction and assignments were in Latin. The beginners memorized the Ten Commandments, the Lord's Prayer, the Creed, and a number of Psalms during their first three years. Their textbook was Melanchthon's primer. They were not given formal instruction in grammar, but were expected to become proficient in reading and writing Latin. They also received some instruction in music, for they would become choir boys upon entering the next division.[407]

In the *secunda* the students studied Cato and other Latin authors. They had considerable exercise in grammar, including composition of prose and verse.[408] In the upper division the emphasis on composition continued, and there might even be an oratorical competition each week. The boys from these two groups composed the church choir and, therefore, devoted considerable time to learning the hymn and liturgy.[409]

That there would be much time given to religious instruction was to be expected. After two hours of schoolroom study and recitation the morning was interrupted for chapel exercises, for which the students marched into the Town Church.[410] The service consisted of hymns and a brief address. Similarly, the students attended a vesper service in mid-afternoon. Once each week the pupils were drilled in the Catechism in both Latin and German and might be called upon to recite prayers in either language.[411] On Saturday the upper divisions were instructed in the Gospel for the Sunday service. There were no regular classes on Wednesday or Saturday afternoons, but the boys were expected to attend vespers. Each student was required to learn the *Cisio Janus,* or church calendar, for in an age when so much activity revolved around the church a knowledge of the various special days was most useful in any business or profession.[412]

Education for the girls was not neglected in Wittenberg. The *Kirchenordnung* for 1533 included provisions for a *Jungfrauen,* or girls', school.[413] The introduction states that the school was organized because of "the pleading of Martin and the preacher." This ideal had been voiced by Luther as early as 1520, for in his *Address to the Christian Nobility* he said:

> Above all, in schools of all kinds the chief and most common lesson should be the Scriptures, and for young boys the Gospel; and would to God each town had also a girls' school, in which girls might be taught the Gospel. . . . Should not every Christian be expected by his ninth or tenth year to know all the holy Gospels, containing as they do his very name and life? [414]

The Wittenberg Girls' School was north of the Town Church until 1564, when a new building was built for the boys, and the girls were moved into their former building.[415] The girls were taught to read and write and were given some instruction in music and mathematics. They memorized short prayers, Bible verses, and Psalms and were regularly instructed in the Catechism. The town pastor was to be consulted in disciplinary problems, and the ordinance specifically stated that punishment of the girls must be light and their treatment polite and wholesome.

In addition to the schools for the youth established by the Reformers there were also established *Lectorien,* or adult lecture courses.[416] These were usually in the larger cities, where demand was greatest, and were not received with similar enthusiasm everywhere. In Luebeck they were frowned upon by the local guild. In Hamburg the Cathedral chapter of the Roman clergy gave continuing opposition. In Stettin, however, the lectures, delivered by local lawyers, physicians, and clergymen, were received with favor and flourished. Under the Lutheran school system, then, education was provided from "the cradle to the grave," and for those in all walks of life, not just for prospective clergymen.[417] The core of the curriculum was the teaching of the Gospel, although the necessary tools of learning were not neglected.[418] Another innovation introduced in Nuernberg was a provision for poor but gifted students from town funds. So unheard-of were these scholarships that they drew from the now embittered Erasmus the satirical remark that in Lutheran circles it was necessary to pay both the teachers and the pupils.[419]

The impact of the excellent school system was immediately noticeable in the growth of the Reformation movement. Enrollment at the University of Wittenberg doubled, then tripled.[420] The leadership of an educated laity as well as clergy resulted in strong, well-rooted congregations everywhere. The fruits of their labors must have been immensely satisfactory to those founders who had struggled against almost insuperable odds of ignorance and indifference to bring learning to the common man.

« 21 »

Attempts to Unify Christendom

The Controversy with Erasmus

IT WAS TO BE EXPECTED that the Reformation in various parts of Europe should have varied according to the pattern of its leadership. Product of the resurgent intellect of the Renaissance, off-spring of the rising tide of Humanism and individualism, the movement was an expression of the new appreciation of the importance of the individual. Once the principle of ecclesiastical authority in all things had been rejected and that of individual conscience substituted, varying interpretations were bound to result. The several Reformers differed in their fundamental assumptions and points of emphasis.[1] All of them were deeply affected by Biblical Humanism, but they could not agree on what to stress or where to begin in their interpretation of the Bible. They agreed that the Church should return to its early purity and practice, but they could not agree on its original nature.

Erasmus believed in a simplified, rationalized interpretation of the Scriptures beginning with the Sermon on the Mount.[2] He was partially supported by Zwingli, Bucer, Oecolampadius, and Calvin. The Anabaptists sought to restore literally the social and economic institutions of Apostolic times.[3] Luther and the Wittenberg theologians stressed *Sola Scriptura*, the Bible alone, as the guide in matters of faith and morals and believed that the key to the Bible, Christ and Him crucified, was to be found in the Pauline Epistle to the Romans.[4] From this point they progressed to the Sermon on the Mount as the pattern of sanctification for Christ's redeemed. These differences in assumptions and emphases were to divide early Protestantism, even though the Reformers would have

683

preferred to preserve a solid front against the Roman Church, with which they had broken.

In the early stages of the Reformation, Luther received an almost universal support in his challenge to Rome and its indulgence traffic; but as he matured as a Reformer and his convictions crystallized, he began to encounter disagreement and opposition. The first of such groups were the *Schwaermer,* among whom Luther roughly classified Carlstadt, Muenzer, and the Anabaptists and contemptuously labeled the "drifters" as unworthy of serious consideration.[5] Little attempt was made to reconcile them after the series of Wittenberg disturbances. The later treatment of individual Anabaptists may be clearly followed in the many *Gutachten* issued by the Wittenberg theologians advising the princes in their treatment of these erring children.[6] Often these acts strongly resembled the religious intolerance of the Church they sought to reform and certainly contributed to the age of intolerance and religious persecution which was yet to come.

Probably the sharpest differences arose between Luther and Erasmus, first a supporter and powerful friend of the Reformation, later a deserter and bitter opponent. The climax of their struggle was reached in the early twenties, when they debated the question of the nature of the human will after the fall of Adam, a point fundamental to Luther's whole theology.

Erasmus first noticed Luther when his name was heard throughout Germany after the appearance of the *Ninety-Five Theses.*[7] Erasmus accepted him as a fellow worker for the reform of the Roman Church and, like Rubeanus, Hutten, Lang, Pirckheimer, Oecolampadius, Bucer, and others, regarded Luther as the champion of the Gospel and the deliverer of Germany from the bondage of Rome.[8] At the time he posted his Theses, Luther had never met Erasmus nor corresponded with him, but was quite familiar with his writings. Already in 1516 he had misgivings about Erasmus as a theologian, and in 1517 he expressed himself pointedly in a letter to John Lang:

> I am reading our Erasmus, and my opinion of him becomes daily worse. He pleases me, indeed, for boldly and learnedly convicting and condemning monks and priests of inveterate ignorance, but I

fear he does not sufficiently advance the cause of Christ and God's grace, in which he is much more ignorant than Lefèvre d'Etaples, for human considerations weigh with him more than divine.[9]

Erasmus at first considered it beneath the dignity of a famous scholar with a European reputation to become too concerned with this obscure Wittenberg monk; but as the Roman plot against Luther began to thicken, Erasmus' sympathy grew. During the critical years from 1518 to 1521 Erasmus exerted a powerful influence behind the scenes in Luther's behalf and was especially insistent that he be given a fair hearing.[10] Erasmus took care, however, that he should not become personally involved.[11] He once said that he had not a drop of martyr's blood. He admired Luther's courage at Worms, but his personal feelings he expressed in a letter to Richard Pace in which he said:

> Not all have sufficient strength to face martyrdom. I fear I should act the part of Peter over again. I follow the Pope and the Emperor when they decide well, because it is pious to do so; I bear their bad decisions, because it is safe to do so.[12]

What Erasmus failed to realize was that a scholar with his reputation could not remain on the sidelines; he must be either for Luther or against him. When he did not openly condemn Luther, he was accused of being the brains behind the whole Lutheran movement. His fellow Louvain professors added further pressure upon him to declare his position.[13] Since Louvain and Cologne had both been active opponents of Luther, it was not expedient to support Luther, particularly after he had been condemned by the papal bull and the Edict of Worms. Hochstraten of Cologne, Egmond, Aleander, and other stanch Romanists constantly taunted Erasmus with the accusation that were he not a Lutheran at heart he would publicly rebuke the heretic.[14] It was not enough that he sought to placate both sides and remain neutral when he wrote:

> There are many things in Luther's books which are worthy of being known; some things which had better have been omitted and all things too violently, not to say seditiously, written. For if he had said what was necessary more moderately, even if he had accused the intolerable vices of the Roman Curia, he would have had the support of all.[15]

Erasmus tried to escape the issue by going to Basel in November, 1521, but the clamor only increased. He had told Aleander that it mattered not to him whether Luther were "roasted or boiled," [16] and the Luther enemies rejoiced. New voices were added to those demanding a positive attack. Duke George of Albertine Saxony, King Henry VIII, and even a special nuncius from Pope Adrian VI all urged him to enter the lists against Luther.[17] Before such powerful proponents a stronger spirit than Erasmus might have quailed.

The issue was finally joined by an attack from an unexpected quarter. After the tragic failure of the knights' uprising, Hutten had sought sanctuary in Basel with Erasmus, whom he had long admired, but who now refused shelter and succor to the ailing knight.[18] This bitter disappointment was the final straw which drew from Hutten the vitriolic attack upon Erasmus called *An Expostulation,* in which he accused Erasmus of being a turncoat, a coward, and a betrayer of the true religion.[19] Hutten tried to sell the unpublished manuscript to Erasmus, but failing that, published the attack.[20] There was just enough truth in the accusations to sting Erasmus to retaliation. He first protested to the town council and succeeded in having Hutten expelled from Basel in the middle of January, 1523. In addition he hastily wrote a reply, *A Sponge to Wipe Off Hutten's Aspersions,* distinctly an attempt at personal apology.[21] To excuse his failure to take a stand on the issue, he rather feebly alleged that Christ had apparently dissembled the truth on occasion or even suppressed it as inconvenient to be spoken at all times. In the meantime the dying Hutten had found asylum in Zuerich with Zwingli. Not content with his previous success, Erasmus also wrote to the town council of Zuerich, urging that Hutten be refused shelter there.[22] By the time Erasmus' reply appeared in print Hutten was dead, and public opinion at once reacted in his favor. Realizing this fact, Erasmus issued another apology, which did more harm than good. He pointed out that he had not reproached his enemy with "his military life, not to use a worse term, nor with his debts, nor with his vices, which even his shameful disease could never make him stop." [23] The dead Hutten was to gain more allies than the living Hutten had enjoyed. Otto Brunsfels wrote a reply to the *Sponge,* and the battle of words began in full force.[24] Its reverberations were certain to embroil the two leaders.

To Luther's earlier opinion of Erasmus' weaknesses were now added scorn for his seeming cowardice and the conviction that Erasmus was incompetent to deal with theological questions. This opinion Luther expressed in a letter to Oecolampadius in June, 1523:

> He has done what he was called to do; he has brought us from godless studies to a knowledge of the languages; perhaps he will die with Moses in the plains of Moab, for he does not go forward to the better studies — those that pertain to godliness. I greatly wish he would stop commenting on the Holy Scriptures and writing his *Paraphrases,* for he is not equal to this task; he takes up the time of his readers to no purpose, and delays them in their study of the Scriptures. He has done enough in showing us the evil; to show us the good and to lead us into the promised land, he is, I see, unable.[25]

As was to be expected, Oecolampadius showed the letter to Erasmus, who expressed his reactions in a letter to Zwingli, in which he revealed his complete misunderstanding of Luther's doctrines.

> Luther proposes some riddles that are absurd on the face of them: all the works of the saints are sins, which are forgiven by the undeserved mercy of God; free will is an empty name; a man is justified by faith alone, and works have nothing to do with it. I do not see that it does any good to dispute about the way Luther wishes these things to be understood. . . . Luther has written Oecolampadius that not much attention must be paid me in those things that are of the Spirit. I should like to learn of you, my learned Zwingli, who that "Spirit" is, for I think I have taught almost everything that Luther teaches, only I have not done it so fiercely and have abstained from certain riddles and paradoxes. I hope, indeed, that much fruit may someday come from them, but I prefer present fruit. . . .[26]

Several months later, having heard that Erasmus was writing against him, Luther addressed a letter directly to Erasmus in which he stated that he had waited for Erasmus to speak first "as the greater and elder man," but that he now believed "charity itself" compelled him to begin. Luther pointed out that he did not hold against Erasmus his desertion from the cause, realizing that he had not the fortitude to face the issue.

> For since we see that the Lord has not given you courage or sense to assail those monsters openly and confidently with us, we are not the men to exact what is beyond your power and measure. Rather we have tolerated and even respected the mediocrity of God's gift in you. The whole world knows your services to letters and how you have made them flourish and thus prepared a path for the direct study of the Bible. For this glorious and splendid gift in you we ought to thank God. I for one have never wished you to leave your little sphere to join our camp, for although you might have profited the cause much by your ability, genius and eloquence, yet as you had not the courage it was safer for you to work at home. . . . Even if you cannot and dare not declare for us, yet at least you might leave us alone and mind your own business. . . .[27]

If Erasmus had been undecided before, he was now determined to join the fray against Luther, and he chose a most vital spot for his attack.[28] In August, 1524, the Froben press published his *De libero arbitrio,* and its author immediately sent copies to his distinguished patrons, Cardinal Wolsey, Pope Clement VII, Duke George of Albertine Saxony, Henry VIII, and others.[29] In a letter to the King he said:

> The die is cast. My book on Free Will has seen the light. An audacious villainy, as things now stand in Germany! I expect to be stoned.[30]

Luther himself admitted that Erasmus had "seized him by the throat." [31] Were his thesis granted, Luther's whole doctrinal system would crumble.[32] Erasmus' viewpoint was the exact opposite of "justification by faith."

Keeping his dissertation on a seemingly high academic plane, Erasmus modestly admitted his inadequacy to treat all of the problem. He granted that he might have misunderstood some of Luther's writings and asserted his willingness to be converted. He believed that the layman should not be exposed to these theological speculations which could lead only to further confusion, but that Luther, who had freely taken issue with Rome, should not object to an academic discussion.[33]

Throwing in an occasional pointed barb for good measure, Erasmus repeated the old and well-worn argument that Luther assumed a great deal to claim to know more than the Greek and Latin Fathers and that it was difficult to believe that for 1,300 years the Holy Ghost had permitted error to be taught on the doctrine in question.[34] Following Lombard, Erasmus claimed the fall of Adam had merely dulled man's moral faculties, but that he could refrain from evil and choose those things which led to his salvation.

His exposition revealed what Luther had already intimated, that Erasmus was no theologian. He had completely failed to grasp Luther's new *Gottesbegriff* and the distinction in the "New Theology" between justification and sanctification.[35] Erasmus in his thinking still accepted the medieval theology of *meritum de congruo* and *meritum de condigno,* believing that man by the efforts of his will achieved those changes in his life which finally made him worthy of God's saving grace.[36] Erasmus followed the concept of man's whole life as a continuing struggle to earn enough merit to render himself finally worthy of God's salvation. This view Luther had already rejected by 1514 on the basis of Romans. Luther divided mankind into two groups: those who had never heard of God's mercy and saving grace and those who had a knowledge of God and His plan of salvation. In speaking of the slavery of the human will, Luther referred to the "natural man" before conversion who knows nothing of sin or of Christ's suffering and death on the Cross for him.

Erasmus argued that man's will must have the power to choose between good and evil, otherwise God would not have asked him in the Scriptures to choose the good.[37] He cited many Old Testament passages with reference to the moral degeneration of Israel and God's constant urging to mend their ways, all of which he thought implied freedom of choice.[38] Jesus, too, by weeping over Jerusalem, indicated that the people might have chosen a different way of life. Paul's Epistles, speaking of a striving for the crown of life, implied a series of choices. Erasmus pointed out the danger of "moral laxity" should man claim no responsibility for his own acts. He granted, however, that the final work of salvation must be due to God's saving grace wrought through Jesus Christ; but he could not find a place for prayer in a world of absolute determinism, where every action was foreknown and foreordained and man could only accept his fate. In a sense, therefore, Erasmus stood somewhere between Luther's position and that of the Romanists. The fact that Erasmus was thinking of man's whole life, while Luther meant only the period before man had been brought to faith, led to much confusion; and it is doubtful that Erasmus ever realized that he had completely misunderstood Luther.

Whatever may have been its theological shortcomings, Erasmus' work was hailed with rejoicing by Luther's opponents.[39] They felt sure their hero had laid the heretic low. *The Freedom of the Will* was a most remarkable document written in a clear, penetrating style and couched in academic phrases which greatly impressed his followers. Duke George immediately asked Emser and Cochlaeus to translate the Latin tract into German that it might be more widely read.[40] In Lutheran circles there was outward calm but inward misgiving. Luther was too occupied with other pressing problems to make an immediate reply. His correspondence of the period is full of references to the Peasants' Revolt, the Carlstadt attacks, the revision of the Lutheran church service, but little mention of Erasmus. His close friends, however, were certain that Luther would not allow the attack to pass unanswered.[41] Melanchthon especially feared the results of the blast when it would come and took it upon himself to write to Erasmus counseling moderation. He chided Erasmus for the "pepper" with which he had spiced his remarks and pointed out that it was most unfair to identify Luther with the excesses of Carlstadt and Muenzer and the revolts of the knights and peasants.[42] He expressed the hope that Luther, if he should reply, would refrain from bitterness and that Erasmus, too, would practice self-restraint. Erasmus replied to Melanchthon in December, 1524, further explaining his position and requesting that Melanchthon not interfere with, or try to influence, Luther's reply, as he wished Luther to express himself quite frankly. He was not to be disappointed.

It was not until a year later that Luther wrote his *De servo arbitrio*, or *The Bondage of the Will*,[43] but the length of the finished article and the speed with which it was written indicated that he had given considerable previous thought to the subject. In this work Luther reached his peak as an able and well-balanced controversialist. Though thoroughly exasperated by the sly pin pricks practiced by his adversary, his respect for the ability of his opponent may have cautioned him to restraint. He willingly granted that in style, in literary skill, and facile expression he was no match for the famous Dutchman.[44] But his work revealed that in theological depth, comprehensiveness, and grasp of the problem Erasmus was far from his equal. Luther later remarked that he would be willing to have all of his works perish except the *Catechisms* and *The Bondage of the Will*.[45] The document was widely read, for seven Latin and two German editions were printed within a year. Preserved Smith evaluated it as "one of the most important of sixteenth-century works," principally because of its influence on Calvin.[46]

Perhaps the chief difference in the disputants was that to Erasmus the entire subject was essentially a rhetorical exercise in curious and superfluous speculation; to Luther it was the very essence of the Christian faith.[47] Without the dogma of the impotence of the will in the unconverted man "neither God, nor Christ, nor the Gospel, nor faith, nor anything is left us." [48] He pointed out the contradiction in Erasmus' conclusion that without grace the will is powerless, but that, nevertheless, it still has the means of choice.[49] Luther disagreed with the viewpoint that the common man should not be exposed to such discussions, asking why the truth of Scripture should be withheld from him; and, if Erasmus believed his statement, why write a book on the subject? [50] "For if I am ignorant as to what, how far, and how much I can do in relation to God, I shall remain equally ignorant and uncertain as to what, how far, and how much God can do and does in relation to me."

To the argument that the Church could not have been in error for 1,300 years, Luther replied that the Church was not the Pope, Fathers, priests, and monks, but that body of true believers in existence since Adam, the few whom He has chosen, not the many.[51] To the plea that he should cease from stirring up dissension and strife in the Church, Luther replied that Christ had said He came not to bring peace, but the sword, and that the preaching of the true Word was ever bound to raise disagreement with the cohorts of Satan.[52] In raising the question of the danger of "moral laxity" among those who believe that they have no power of choice, Erasmus displayed his utter misconception of Luther's doctrine of justification and the reborn man.

In the positive presentation of this theme, Luther focused his attention on Romans 3. Here Paul pictured mankind as being completely lost in trespasses and sins: "There is none that doeth good, no, not one." [53] Fallen man knows only destruction and misery; all have sinned and fallen far short of the glory of God. The natural man prior to his rebirth is a slave to sin. If this were not true, why did God sacrifice His only Son for man's redemption, of what purpose the death on the Cross? Augustine had compared fallen man to an animal which is directed by its rider. Should God be the rider, he moves in the direction of "good"; but should Satan be in control, he would move toward "evil." [54] The helpless animal has no choice, but is caught in a constant rivalry between two masters. Luther drew a careful distinction between inward and outward freedom, explaining that the natural man has the choice of external actions, such as what to eat or drink, whether to marry, his selection of a profession or calling, and other outward choices; but in the realm of his soul's salvation his only hope lies in the mercy of an all-wise, all-loving God. Erasmus' references to the Children of Israel, therefore, were not pertinent to the subject, for they belonged to the second group who knew God and His mercy, yet deliberately fell away from Him.

As indicated earlier, the core of Luther's doctrine of the servitude of the will was his *Gottesbegriff*, or conception of God, and His relationship to sinful man.[55] As Holl, Seeberg, and other dogmaticians have shown, Luther perceived this new *Gottesbegriff* as early as his Erfurt days, and in his early exegetical lectures on Romans and Galatians he rejected entirely the medieval Roman Catholic God.[56] His later exegetical studies reveal that he consistently held this view in which *The Bondage of the Will* was firmly anchored. Luther believed that God is a "hidden God" whom natural man can only faintly detect through his five senses.[57] What he determines on the basis of reason is almost wholly wrong. Only by divine revelation does the "hidden God" become the "revealed God," a revelation which reached its peak in Jesus Christ.[58] Beyond this revelation a human being cannot know God. According to this revelation, God is the only free, independent agent in the

universe.[59] This revealed God was not just the outward, ultimate
cause of the drama of human life; He was the ubiquitous, life-
generating will according to whose plan the universe unfolds. Not
one hair falls from our head nor a sparrow from the roof unless
it be God's will. Even evil, in Luther's universe, was only relatively
free; it has its little day, but it, too, must eventually work out to
the unfolding of God's ultimate purpose.[60] For God to be God,
claimed Luther, there could be no other force directing His action.
He alone could be completely free in the universe. As Luther expressed it:

> God is a being whose will has neither cause nor norm which serves
> as a rule or measure that has been prescribed to Him, as nothing
> is His equal or superior, but He Himself is the rule of all. For, if
> it were true that any rule or measure or cause or norm were His
> equal, then it would no longer be the will of God. For not because
> He ought or ought not to have willed a certain thing is the same right
> which He wills; but, on the contrary, because He Himself wills it,
> thus the same is right which He wills.[61]

Thus, Luther finds in the universe a divine determinism: the panorama of human life unfolding according to a divine pattern. The
God of heaven and earth is not the "stern judge sitting on a rainbow" of the Erfurt days, but a kind heavenly Father guiding our
footsteps in love and in wisdom seeking the salvation of our souls,
but punishing those who deliberately and knowingly reject His
saving grace.[62]

Luther explained to Erasmus the difference between *necessitas*
and its opposite, *coactio*, the distinction between "necessity" and
"force." [63] Judas was not forced to betray Christ, but his act was
necessary in the eternal unfolding of the plan of redemption. Here
God's foreknowledge had seen what Judas would do, and prophecy
could predict the later divine necessity. Man is not forced by God
to act a certain way, but as he chooses to act according to his normal
inclinations, he fulfills God's ultimate purposes.[64] The Babylonians,
for instance, when they led Israel into capivity, were instruments
in God's hand to punish the erring Children of Israel. The wicked
Nebuchadnezzar, although in the power of Satan, probably believed he was acting as a free agent. In the end he, too, received

his just reward. Luther granted that God, therefore, at times made use of evil, even of Satan himself, to the ultimate triumph of good.[65]

On the basis of this divine revelation, Luther believed that man before his conversion was a slave to sin and not a free agent. Without the light of God, how could he find his way to the Cross? He was still in the kingdom of darkness, ruled only by God's omnipotence. After his conversion he was in the Kingdom of Grace, ruled by the Holy Spirit. To pagans God could only be a God of force; to Christians He became a God of love, as revealed through Jesus Christ. For the redeemed, God's ultimate power was a great comfort and consolation, for He had promised that even the gates of hell should not prevail against them. To think that mere man walking in darkness might be able to achieve his own salvation ignored and belittled the redemptive sacrifice of Christ, who said: "No man cometh unto the Father but by Me." When Christ said: "It is finished," man no longer needed partially to redeem himself, as Erasmus claimed. To Luther any other interpretation was rank blasphemy.

Erasmus professed to be deeply hurt by the vehemence of Luther's reply to his comparatively mild and courteous dissertation.[66] The letter which accompanied a copy of the treatise from Luther to Erasmus has been lost, but, judging from his earlier epistles and from Erasmus' reply, one may conclude that its contents must have been far from conciliatory. In part Erasmus said:

> The same admirable ferocity which you formerly used against Cochlaeus and against Fisher, who provoked you to it by reviling, you now use against my book in spite of its courtesy. . . . It terribly pains me, as it must all good men, that your arrogant, insolent, rebellious nature has set the world in arms . . . as if it were your chief aim to prevent the tempest from ever becoming calm, while it is my greatest desire that it should die down. . . . I should wish you a better disposition were you not so marvelously satisfied with the one you have. . . .[67]

Erasmus rushed into print with a reply, his *Hyperaspistes*,[68] purporting to be a defense of his earlier work but chiefly concerned with the doctrine of the Evangelicals, which he held as doomed to failure because of the personality of its leader, on whom he centered his attack. Luther did not bother to reply to this latest effort of Erasmus, but the gulf between the two had widened irreparably.

THE MARBURG COLLOQUY

Regrettable as was the break between Erasmus and Luther, its schismatic effect on the Reformation movement was mild compared with that of the disagreement within the fold of Protestantism between Luther and Carlstadt and, finally, between the Lutherans and the Zwinglians, culminating in the Marburg Colloquy of 1529 and the Wittenberg Concord of 1536. The controversy arose between two theological systems that sooner or later were certain to come into conflict.[69] Basically, the approach of Zwingli, Oecolampadius, and Bucer followed Erasmus with a strong Humanistic leaning which sought to rationalize Biblical exegesis: any passage which was not clear to human reason should be interpreted to harmonize with human understanding.[70] Luther's doctrine of the "real presence" was oriented in his Christology of the God-Man, revealed in time and space through Jesus Christ, for his exegetical principle of *Sola Scriptura* permitted no other explanation.[71] The conflict, therefore, was unavoidable, but it was most unfortunate that it could not have been conducted in a more brotherly and seemly manner by both parties.[72] The sixteenth-century man was not noted for his emotional control, especially in affairs of religion, and the resulting bitterness did great harm to the cause of the Reformation. It may even have been a contributing factor to the successful rise of the Jesuits and the Counter Reformation in central Europe.

The dispute over the doctrine of the "real presence" first began at the very core of the movement, the University of Wittenberg, when one of the faculty members, Bodenstein von Carlstadt, began to set forth his own symbolical interpretation of the Lord's Supper.[73] No doubt Carlstadt was sincere in his views, but he was one of those unfortunate human beings whose ambition far outstripped his ability. He wanted to be a leader like Luther, but he was never quite clear on what or where to lead and only created a muddle wherever he went. After Luther's return from the Wartburg, public reaction forced Carlstadt to leave Wittenberg and, later, Orlamuende. The embittered man tried to establish a following in Strassburg, where he preached his interpretation of the Gospel. Bucer and other Strassburg clergymen viewed his efforts with considerable alarm, and when he published a book entitled

Marburg, Etching of 1582

Interpretation of These Words of Christ, the council expelled Carlstadt from the city.[74] He next sought to join Zwingli in Zuerich, but was not welcomed. After the Peasants' War, Carlstadt was permitted to return to Wittenberg on the condition that he remain silent, but the harm had been done. As revealed in Luther's tract of 1524 *Against the Heavenly Prophets,*[75] the struggle between the leader and Carlstadt had developed into a bitter feud.

Unfortunately, the seeds Carlstadt had sown in his wanderings in southern Germany and, especially, in Strassburg began to bear strange fruit. Although the Strassburg preachers refused him entry into their midst, they began to speculate about his interpretation. Bucer was particularly anxious to clarify the problem, for he had received a book by Christopher Honius of the Netherlands expounding an interpretation of the Lord's Supper very similar to that of Carlstadt.[76] Essentially, Honius claimed that the *est* in the words of institution, *Hoc est corpus meum,* must be interpreted as *significat,* or symbolizing Christ's body and blood. So disturbed were the Strassburg theologians by this new approach that they sent Gregory Cassel in person to interview Luther. He evidently did not present the case very successfully, or Luther failed to realize its importance, for he replied too briefly in an *ex cathedra* manner, offering little clarification of their problem.[77] Perhaps Luther was not yet entirely clear as to his own position. Following Luther's reply, Bucer made a parallel study of all the pertinent passages in the New Testament and concluded that the symbolical view was the only tenable one on the basis of the Scriptures.[78] Soon after that, Zwingli, Oecolampadius, and Capito joined Bucer in a common front against the Wittenbergers in a wordy battle which was to grow exceedingly bitter.[79]

Urged on by their friends, Zwingli and Oecolampadius decided to reply to Luther's tract of 1524 aimed at Carlstadt, *Against the Heavenly Prophets.* In March, 1525, Zwingli's first attack appeared in the tract *On True and False Religion,* in which he asserted that both the Roman and Luther's views of the Lord's Supper were false.[80] In September Oecolampadius at Basel added his ammunition in *True and Real Explanation of the Words of the Lord, This Is My Body,* with which he hoped to win the Swabians to the

Zwinglian point of view.[81] This volley was answered by the Swabian Lutheran Johannes Brenz, who both by letters and a tract, the *Swabian Syngramma,* tried to hold the line in southwestern Germany for Luther.[82] Oecolampadius added his *Antisyngramma* and Bucer his *Apologia* as reinforcements, and the battle raged unabated.[83] Meanwhile the general was studying the campaign and the issue involved.

Luther's views on the Lord's Supper may be divided into two

periods: (1) those he held before the struggle with Carlstadt and the Zwinglian attack on the "real presence," and (2) those after 1527, when he had fully clarified his position in the dispute with the Sacramentarians.[84] The former view has been examined in connection with Luther's theological development from 1519 to 1520.[85] During this period the emphasis was on the actual presence of the historical Christ of the first Lord's Supper in the Holy Eucharist. The challenge of the Sacramentarians shifted the emphasis to the nature of this "real presence." When the warfare with the *Schwaermer* and the Sacramentarians began to assume alarming proportions, Luther re-examined the Scriptures in support of his former position.[86] He also studied the Honius thesis of a mere symbolical interpretation, but two factors made it impossible for him to accept such a view. The one was exegetical; the other his Christology.[87] These ideas he clearly set forth in three tracts, which were published in 1526, 1527, and 1528.[88] The first was a group of three sermons which Luther had preached on the Lord's Supper in the Town Church in the spring of 1526.[89] When the publication reached

Johannes Oecolampadius

Switzerland in the fall, Zwingli thought it necessary to reply in person and prepared his answer during the winter months so it would be ready for sale at the spring fair at Frankfurt am Main. The reply was available under the Latin title *Amica exegesis* or in German, titled *Fruentlich Verglimpfung und ableynung*.[90] Luther heard from a number of quarters that the Zwinglians were boasting that Zwingli would win all of Luther's supporters in a short while. Urged by his friends, Luther also prepared a treatise on the Lord's Supper for the Frankfurt am Main book fair of 1527. In characteristic scholarly and thorough fashion he had reviewed the twenty-three tracts now available among the opposition and replied to them all, basing his remarks principally on Zwingli's first tract and that of Oecolampadius.[91] The impressive theological depth of his work was tarnished by the personal acrimony which he could not refrain from including.[92] His tract *That These Words of Christ "This Is My Body" Still Firmly Stand Against the Schwaermer*, reflects his growing exegetical maturity on the Lord's Supper and was available side by side on the bookshelves with Zwingli's *Amica exegesis*.[93] It is not difficult to imagine the interest which these two tracts aroused throughout central Europe. By early summer Oecolampadius and Zwingli had issued replies.[94]

Luther and his wife both suffered illnesses during the following months, which delayed any reply from that source, but the supporters of both disputants maintained a steady epistolary barrage, which kept the tempers of all concerned at fever heat.[95] At the turn of the year Luther wrote Hausmann and Probst that he was engaged in another reply to the Zwinglians which was to be his final word on the subject.[96] His greatest work on the Lord's Supper, therefore, was not meant so much as a reply to the Sacramentarians as a final word to his followers as to his understanding of the Sacrament. The document, *Concerning the Lord's Supper, a Confession*, was printed in time for the Frankfurt am Main fair in 1528.[97]

As before, the personal references and sarcastic satire obscured the admirable theology of his tract.[98] Both Capito and Oecolampadius urged Zwingli to answer Luther, treating him as an erring brother but being careful not to offend the princes with whom Luther was quite popular.[99] Bucer alone was impressed with the theological arguments of the last tract and felt that up to now he had misunderstood Luther. He now began to understand that by "real presence" Luther did not mean an outward physical presence in the realm of space, but rather a "sacramental union." [100] He now wrote his friends about his new discovery and in his *Homilies* pointed out that Luther did not really mean "bodily presence" by "real presence." In his treatise *Comparison of the Position of Luther and His Opponents Concerning the Lord's Supper,* Bucer pointed out that the Lutherans and Zwinglians were not so far apart.[101] He now saw himself in the role of peacemaker and planned to bring the opposing groups together in an attempt to settle their differences.

Philip of Hesse had had a similar idea since 1527, but had been unable to make any real progress.[102] In the early part of 1529 at the Diet of Speyer a Catholic majority of princes had succeeded in revoking the principle of *cuius regio eius religio,* making the prince no longer responsible for the religious faith of his state. The evangelical princes had protested and on April 22, 1529, formed an embryonic union to protect the Gospel, in which the princes of Saxony, Hesse, Nuernberg, Strassburg, and Ulm were included.[103] It now seemed expedient that steps be taken to eliminate the doctrinal differences which stood in the way of a united political front. The Wittenberg theologians were not too eager for such a meeting. Other princes, such as Margrave George of Brandenburg-Ansbach, felt there should be some preliminary basis drawn up for discussion. Accordingly, the Schwabach Articles were prepared in the summer of 1529 by some of the Wittenberg theologians, court lawyers, and princes, their efforts being surrounded by the utmost secrecy.[104] This set of articles was the basis on which the Lutherans were to discuss doctrinal differences with the Zwinglians.

Philip of Hesse invited the groups to meet at the Marburg Castle.[105] Although hesitating at first because of the distance, the Swiss leaders and the Strassburg delegates arrived on September 27. The principal men in the delegation were Zwingli, Oecolampadius, Bucer, Capito, and Sturm, all of whom participated in the colloquy.[106] On Thursday morning, September 30, the Wittenberg delegation arrived, composed of Luther, Melanchthon, Myconius, Jonas, Menius, Cruciger, and George Roerer. Later they were joined by Johannes Brenz of Schwaebisch-Hall and Osiander of

Nuernberg, who also attended some of the sessions.[107] The two princes present were Philip of Hesse and Duke Ulrich of Wuerttemberg. The meetings took place in the quarters of the prince rather than in the *Rittersaal* of the Marburg Castle, as has been claimed.[108] Osiander referred to the *Fuerstengemach,* and Jonas reported that the meeting took place *in interiore hypocausto ad cubiculum principis,* an inner heated room of the castle.[109]

For an understanding of the course followed by the Marburg Colloquy, a brief analysis of the differences between the two Protestant groups may be helpful. When Luther re-examined the New Testament in his quest of support for the literal interpretation of the words of institution "This is My body," he found the clearest exposition in 1 Corinthians 10:16:

> The cup of blessing which we bless, is it not the communion of the blood of Christ? The bread which we break, is it not the communion of the body of Christ? [110]

Were there no other passages, this one would be sufficient to persuade all his opponents, thought Luther. In his *Confession* of 1528 Luther emphasized the importance of this passage, which he considered the key to the words of institution themselves:

> This text I have praised and still praise as the joy and crown of my life, for it not only says that it is Christ's body, as stated in the text of the Lord's Supper, but even cites the bread which is broken and says that the bread is Christ's own body, yes, not only Christ's body, but the distribution of Christ's body. Here is once and for all a text as distinct and plain as the *Schwaermer* and all the world could wish for and demand.[111]

Once convinced that the New Testament corroborated the "real presence" of Christ in the Holy Eucharist, Luther preferred to defend his view in the simple words of institution, "This is My body." [112] The fact that the Lord who raised Lazarus from the dead, stilled the unruly sea, and Himself rose from the grave had said these words made them all-sufficient for Luther. Paul Althaus, Seeberg, and others who have examined Luther's theology have pointed out that it was natural for Luther to find proof and certainty in these texts because they harmonized so well with his Christology and his whole theology, which had been slowly forming since his Erfurt struggle.[113] He rejected the sacrament in the Roman sense as having been converted into an *opus operatum* or good work of man. Instead, he thought that, in reality, the sinner's role in the Lord's Supper was passive. He merely accepts in faith what God freely offers.[114] In the doctrine of the "real presence" man is not only promised a gift from God, but actually receives the flesh and blood of His only-begotten Son. The historic Christ of the first supper comes again to sinful man.[115] In this understanding Luther found enduring comfort.

There were even deeper implications accompanying Luther's view, for it revealed a vital part of God's divine plan of revelation in Christ Jesus. For Luther there could be no God outside of the one revealed in the God-Man, Christ Jesus Himself. Where Christ was present, there existed the entire Divinity. Thus, the Christ who gives Himself in the Lord's Supper cannot be separated from the one who lived and walked among men.[116] He is the same Christ who died on the Cross, rose again, and ascended on high. Such a Christ could not be localized. The expression "right hand of the Father," so often quoted in the writings of the Zwinglians, Luther understood to mean the transcendent, all-embracing presence with which He now rules the universe.[117] The fact that Christ became man that we poor humans might better understand Him in the realm of our experience also made Him a part of the larger realm of grace through which He still offers Himself to sinful man.[118] In his book *The Christology of Luther in the Communion Controversy*, P. W. Gennrich has shown the role Luther's conception of Christ played in his view of the Lord's Supper:

> The Christology of Luther is not a result of the struggle over the Lord's Supper. Rather his position in the battle grows fundamentally from his Christology. True, in the struggle over the Lord's Supper, Luther was forced to stress and bring to the fore certain aspects of his Christology, but what he now develops is already fundamentally a part of the conception of Christ in his theology.[119]

Luther further believed that the Christ who appeared in the Holy Eucharist was not limited to time and space like mortal man. Nor was His flesh like human flesh, for it was sinless and vitally connected with divinity.[120] How all this was possible Luther did not attempt to explain; it was enough for him to believe, on the basis of the text, that the God of heaven and earth could be there, as He had promised in the words of institution.[121] When man partook of this bread, he received a part of Christ and of eternity. Its blessing to the sinner he well summarized in the tract of 1527:

> Thus the words (of institution) hold first the bread and cup for the sacrament, the bread and the cup hold the body and blood of Christ, the body and blood hold the New Testament, the New Testament holds forgiveness of sins, and forgiveness of sins holds life eternal and salvation.[122]

In Luther's Christology, God cannot be rationalized by mere human reason as though he were resting on one place and could be examined by man. Though God orders the destiny of the human race and of the world, yet He permitted Himself to be revealed in Christ and offered to the sinner at the Lord's Table.[123] The divinity and humanity are inseparable in the God-Man. Christ's human form did not affect this divine relationship. Luther called it *Gottesfleisch*, the flesh of God, and *Geistesfleisch*, a spiritual flesh, which had been penetrated through and through with divinity.[124] The two natures, divine and human, are united in Christ and form the new person. In his tract of 1528 Luther wrote on this relationship:

> If you can say: Here is God, then you must also grant that the Man Christ is likewise present. And, if you were to point to a place where God is present and not the man, then the person would already be divided, for then I could really make the assertion: Here is God who is not man and never was man and not my God. . . . No, my dear fellow, where you place God, there you must likewise put the humanity of Christ, for they cannot be separated in that they have become one person.[125]

God is not limited to space, yet He revealed Himself in space.[126] He can be where he wishes and can be everywhere present.[127] To define this presence, Luther used the terms *in, with,* and *under,* implying "real presence," yet not in the physical sense of space. The same Christ who could pass through stone walls, bolted doors, and disappear in a moment, could for Luther also be in the bread and wine through this quality of ubiquity, even though Communion was celebrated in ten thousand places at the same time.[128]

Zwingli's theology had an entirely different orientation. He had had no formal training in theology, but had grown up in the Erasmian tradition and was a Biblical Humanist of the rationalistic type.[129] He was also influenced by Augustine and by the tract of Honius.[130] By 1524 he believed in the symbolic view of the Lord's

Supper, considering John 6, the "flesh profiteth nothing," as his
sedes doctrinae.[131] Being a child of the Renaissance, he was individualistic, overly self-confident, and anxious to be independent
of the German Reformers, even though at Marburg he confessed
with tears in his eyes that he would have wished the good will and
brotherhood of no one more than that of Luther and Melanchthon.[132]

Zwingli's theology of the Lord's Supper was simple. He held
that in Communion the individual receives only bread and wine,
but that by reflecting on the Lord's death the individual received
a spiritual blessing from this symbolical eating and drinking.[133]
In the symbolic view a commemorative feast, it was all-important
what the individual did, for the more sincerely he reflected on the
Lord's death, the greater its benefits. Thus in the Zwinglian sense
man would have to lift himself in faith to God's right hand instead
of Christ lowering Himself to sinful man. The bread and the wine
became mere symbols of an historic reality, Christ's suffering and
death for mankind. The *est* in the words of institution he interpreted with Honius to mean *significat,* and therefore he gave the
words of institution a figurative interpretation.[134] This explanation
satisfied his human reasoning, for he believed that Christ was now
at the right hand of God and could not, therefore, be present in the
Supper, except contemplatively through the meditation of the
recipient. Communion for Zwingli and his followers became, then,
a spiritual exercise. In his conception of Christ, Zwingli always
distinguished between Christ's divine and human natures. If God
were present in the bread and the wine according to His divine
nature, He could not be present as the God-Man of Luther. With
Zwingli, as with Erasmus, religion was something to be made simple
and understandable for the common man. Revelation did not provide its own interpretation. Human reason by itself could determine what God had meant. Should the message contradict reason,
then reason had to explain the Scriptural language figuratively.[135]

The conflict between the Zwinglians and the Lutherans was
not, then, solely a clash of personalities, although that was a factor,
but rather a conflict between opposing ideologies. As with Erasmus, it was again a matter of primary assumptions which separated

them. In their interpretation of the Lord's Supper these basic differences were most sharply drawn.

For information on the actual events of the Marburg Colloquy the student is indebted to Walther Koehler for his reconstruction of the main conversations of October 2 and 3, based on the reports of some half dozen eyewitnesses. For the first and fourth days only the reports of the participants and general accounts are available. A combination of all these materials with those of the *Weimar Edition,* 30, III, provides a rather complete account of what transpired.[136] The preliminary discussions took place on Friday morning, October 1, at 6 A. M., when Melanchthon and Zwingli, Luther and Oecolampadius were paired off to discuss various aspects of the teachings of the two groups.[137] Bucer states that the prince realized that both Luther and Zwingli were hot-tempered and hoped that by pairing the gentle Melanchthon with Zwingli and the more even-tempered Oecolampadius with Luther the meeting might have a more favorable beginning. Bucer has given a rather detailed account of the conversation between Melanchthon and Zwingli, stating that they discussed the divinity of Christ, original sin, the Scriptures, and the Lord's Supper, adding that Melanchthon had been instructed to determine the purity of the Zwinglian teaching on the Trinity, as Wittenberg had received some disturbing reports about the Reformed doctrines on this point.[138]

In a letter to Elector John written early in October, Melanchthon reported that he found Zwingli poorly informed as a theologian and in error in many points.[139] He seemed to deny the existence of original sin, claiming only outward transgression was sinful; did not hold that the Holy Spirit was given to sinful man in the Word and the Sacraments; did not sufficiently emphasize justification in the plan of redemption, but was inclined to credit human effort. Melanchthon added, however, that on these points Zwingli concurred after some discussion.[140] In a report to Duke Henry of Saxony, Melanchthon related the conversations similarly but added a few details not in the Elector's letter.[141] He stated that there was disagreement on the Lord's Supper as well as on the ministry of the Word and the Sacraments. He made no mention of having acquiesced to Zwingli on the word *signifies* as the latter claimed in his conversation with Luther, nor do the accounts of the eye-

witnesses warrant such a conclusion.[142] Perhaps Zwingli misconstrued Philip's lack of aggressiveness for admission of persuasion.

Of the conversation which took place between Luther and
Oecolampadius very little is known except that Luther mentioned
the discussion in a letter to Agricola and that Melanchthon wrote
Duke Henry that "Doctor Luther presented many articles to
Oecolampadius, on some of which he had written incorrectly." [143]
Some of the general reports stated that these discussions were of
little avail, which opinion seems to have been confirmed by the
general discussions of October 2 and 3.[144] It is worthy of note that
the entire discussions were maintained on a very high academic
plane with but little of the sarcasm and personal references which
had sullied the earlier correspondence and publications. Luther
displayed admirable self-control, and the other disputants followed
his example.[145]

At 6 A. M. on Saturday morning, October 2, Chancellor Feige
of Hesse as the presiding officer opened the official colloquy.[146]
Reports do not quite agree on those present in addition to the
official delegations; possibly not more than fifty were admitted to
audit the discussions from among the considerable number who
had hopefully made the journey.[147] Carlstadt is mentioned as being
denied admission, but Philip of Hesse, Duke Ulrich of Wuerttemberg, a number of the court lawyers, some local preachers, and a
few others were allowed to join the select group.[148] Philip of Hesse
attended all of the sessions and took a special interest in the discussions.[149] After a brief word of welcome and explanation the
Chancellor asked Luther to present the opening address.[150]

Before addressing the audience, Luther had written on the
table before him *Hoc est corpus meum* and covered it with a
cloth.[151] This was to be the lodestar in moments of conflict, the
basic text on which he wished to anchor his whole faith. In a calm
and quiet manner Luther explained why the Wittenberg delegation
was at Marburg.[152] Recalling his three major tracts and Zwingli's
replies and the years of strife that lay in the background, he pointed
out that it was very doubtful whether any new arguments could be
presented. As for himself, he was certain that the views he now
held would be retained to the end of his days. In view of the
Speyer situation, however, the Wittenberg group had made the

journey at the request of Philip of Hesse and their own Elector of Saxony.

When the discussion opened, Oecolampadius and Zwingli both mentioned their willingness to consider the problem of doctrinal unity, but pointed out that their views were also already in print.[153] Zwingli suggested that they discuss the problem which seemed most acute, the Lord's Supper. Beginning with John 6, "the flesh profiteth nothing," they challenged Luther to prove from the words of institution that Christ was really present in the Holy Eucharist, since He was now at the right hand of God.[154] Luther seemed to feel that the burden of proof did not rest with him, but with those who had challenged his position.[155] He did not bother to explain the meaning of the Scripture with reference to the expression "the right hand of God" nor to reiterate his former arguments which he had already set forth in his tracts. As the discussion progressed, it became ever clearer that the issue was not so much whether the word *est* meant *significat*, but in the understanding of the location of Christ.[156] Luther's Christ was not in a specific place, but could be wherever He chose to be as the risen Lord of heaven and earth. When Zwingli claimed that Luther was prejudiced on the words of institution, Luther replied that God was speaking these words, not mere man; faith demanded that there be no tampering with the words or with their meaning.[157] To this Zwingli replied that God did not ask anything of us in the Bible that we could not comprehend. When he cited the Fathers to prove that Christ's body could be in only one place, Luther rejected such testimony. When Luther continued to insist on the words of institution, Zwingli accused him of begging the point and added: "You will have to sing a different song to me."[158] Luther suggested that Zwingli was resorting to sarcasm because his dialectics was poor. Zwingli retorted that what hurt Luther was that John 6 was breaking his neck.[159] Luther reminded Zwingli that he was in Hesse, where necks did not break that easily.[160] Zwingli recovered his poise and excused himself, explaining that it was a national custom so to address people. The Landgrave of Hesse accepted the apology and invited the delegations to lunch.

The afternoon session pursued much the same course. Luther enlarged upon his meaning, explaining that he, too, held that there

is a spiritual eating in the Lord's Supper as well as a real one.[161]
He mentioned the "eternal food" of which Jesus speaks and thought
that something of eternity entered into the life of the communicant.
He also pointed out that even unbelievers are affected by the Lord's
Supper according to the Scripture, which indicated that it was
more than a mere memorial feast.[162] Again his opponents came
back to the location of Christ and how He could not be present in
both places. Oecolampadius cited John 16:28, claiming that Christ
had come from the Father and returned, and John 16:7, asserting
that it was essential for Christ to depart that the Comforter might
come.[163] Luther admitted that he did not know much about heaven
or how God could be in many places at the same time, but that did
not change the texts of the Bible.

By late afternoon the lines of demarcation were clearly drawn,
as shown in the following conversation, which marked the climax
of the day's discussion.

> *Zwingli:* Oecolampadius and I gladly admit: Certainly God can
> make it possible for one body to be in different places at once, but
> that He does this in the Lord's Supper demands proof. The Holy
> Scriptures always place Christ in a specific place, such as, in the
> crib, the Temple, in the desert, on the Cross, in the grave, on the
> right hand of the Father.
>
> *Osiander:* With such passages one cannot prove anything except
> that Christ at certain times was in a specific place; that, however,
> He is eternally and always in a specific place and limited, yes, and
> never exists without a place or could not be in many places in a
> natural or supernatural manner, as you claim, this can never be
> proved on the basis of these passages.
>
> *Zwingli:* I have proved that Christ was in one place. You prove,
> on the contrary, that He exists without space or in many places
> simultaneously.
>
> *Luther:* In the beginning you set out to prove that it were impos-
> sible and that our reasoning was false. You are obligated to prove
> this and not demand proof from us, for we do not have to prove
> our position.
>
> *Zwingli:* It would be a shame to believe in such an important doc-
> trine, teach, and defend it, and yet be unable or unwilling to cite
> a single Scripture passage to prove it.
>
> *Luther* (taking the cover from the inscription on the table): "This
> is My body!" Here is our Scripture passage. You have not yet
> taken it from us, as you set out to do; we need no other. My

dearest lords, since the words of my Lord Jesus Christ stand there, *Hoc est corpus meum,* I cannot truthfully pass over them, but must confess and believe that the body of Christ is there.

Zwingli (leaping to his feet): Dear Doctor, you admit Christ's body is spatially in the Lord's Supper. You just said: "The body of Christ must be there." There, there, there, that is an adverb of space. *Luther:* I simply repeated the words of Christ and was not looking for a snare. If you seek to deal with me so craftily, then I must confess once more as earlier, that I have no interest in mathematical approaches and that I shall forthwith exclude and throw out the adverb of space from the Lord's Supper. The words read: "This," not "There is My body." Whether He be there in space or outside of space, I do not wish to question. I am not interested in that, for God has not revealed anything with reference to that, and no mortal can prove it one way or the other.[164]

The discussion then ended for that day to be resumed on Sunday morning.

No new arguments were set forth the following day. Zwingli and Oecolampadius continued to alternate for their group, while Osiander and Brenz added an occasional word to Luther's stand. Melanchthon took little part in the entire colloquy, although Luther twice requested that Philip relieve him.[165] By Sunday afternoon it became clear that no progress was being made. Luther made one final effort when he said:

I would know of no teacher who could bring you around to agree with us, for no one can understand your approach. We wonder, however, why we should fuss over the idea [of "place"] when it is certain and accepted by the whole Christian world that God can exist outside of space or of a specific place. Let us think of ways to get together that the people may not become aroused and that this ugly division may be put out of the world. Over the Trinity we are agreed. There are symbols given by angels and symbols given by men. Augustine states in one place: "I saw our Lord God," as one speaks concerning the Sacrament with reference to the words "This is My body." I do not object to calling this the symbol of Christ's body; I grant that the Sacraments are holy symbols and that they are there to point to something further and used for the sake of comprehension. It is childish for someone to look at the host and exclaim: "I have seen the Lord!" Reason must be directed above that. But to speak only of a mere symbol, in that I could agree only with great reluctance. Natural symbols and those instituted by God are two different things. On that we are agreed.[166]

Oecolampadius admitted in reply that he, too, agreed that there was more to the Lord's Supper than a mere symbol, but the ensuing discussion revealed that basically the groups were still far apart.[167] In spite of the fact that both sides desired to find a common ground, the two theological approaches made it impossible.

Seeing that it was useless to continue, Luther turned to Oecolampadius and thanked him for so faithfully presenting his views without bitterness or rancor.[168] Then he also turned to Zwingli, who had been somewhat sharper in his remarks, and thanked him, adding: "Pardon me, please, for now and then speaking rather harsh words against you, for I am after all flesh and blood." [169] Realizing that this meant the end, Oecolampadius exclaimed: "I beg you for the Lord's sake, give heed to the poor Church." [170] Zwingli, too, then excused himself for his occasional asperity and with tears in his eyes added: "I have always had the great desire to remain on friendly terms and still wish this. There are no men in Italy or France with whom I would rather be friendly than you." [171]

Although the participants considered the colloquy ended, Chancellor Feige called another private session for the evening of October 3, and it was at this meeting that Luther made what Reu has called "far-reaching concessions." [172] Oecolampadius kept careful notes of the meeting, which were published by von Schubert in 1928 and again by Koehler in 1929.[173] Reu gives the following version of Luther's proposition:

> We confess that by virtue of the words "This is My body. This is My blood" the body and the blood of Christ are truly . . . present and distributed in the Holy Supper. Now inasmuch as until now we were of the opinion that our dear sirs and brethren Oecolampadius, Zwinglius, and their adherents totally rejected the true presence of the body and the blood, but in this friendly colloquy have found it to be otherwise, therefore we herewith declare and state that the *argumenta* and reasons found in our books concerning the Sacrament are not directed against Oecolampadius, Zwinglius, and their adherents, but against those who totally reject the presence of the body in the Supper.[174]

Zwingli and Oecolampadius rejected this proposition, says Reu, because they could not interpret it in the sense of spiritual manducation, which they alone granted.[175]

The colloquy was not entirely fruitless, however, for it did formulate the fourteen points signed by all present which set forth the points of agreement and which formed the basis for further co-operation in the Wittenberg Concord.[176] That Zwingli did not subscribe unreservedly to the fourteen points, later known as the *Marburg Articles*, was revealed by his *Fidei ratio*, sent to Augsburg.[177] Of the fifteenth point, on which they could not agree, the *Articles* read as follows:

> We all believe and hold concerning the Supper of our dear Lord Jesus Christ, that both forms should be used according to the institution; also that the mass is not a work, whereby one obtains grace for another, dead and living; also, that the sacrament of the altar is a sacrament of the true Body and Blood of Jesus Christ and that the spiritual partaking of this Body and Blood is specially necessary to every true Christian. In like manner, as to the use of the sacrament, that like the Word of God Almighty, it has been given and ordained, in order that weak consciences might be excited by the Holy Ghost to faith and love.
>
> And although we are not at this time agreed, as to whether the true Body and Blood of Christ are bodily present in the bread and wine, nevertheless the one party should show to the other Christian love, so far as conscience can permit, and both should fervently pray God Almighty, that, by His Spirit, He would confirm us in the true understanding.[178]

This document was signed by all of the delegates present.

Some misunderstanding has arisen around a remark supposedly made by Luther to Zwingli: "You have a different spirit." The various accounts of the discussions make no mention of this incident, and it may be concluded that Luther in speaking of it later confused the incident with a meeting with Bucer.[179] In order to clarify fully the circumstances surrounding the episode, it is necessary to examine the relationship between Luther and Bucer. Bucer first met Luther at the Augustinian meeting at Heidelberg in 1518 and was much impressed by Luther's "New Theology." [180] From then on he was a devoted follower of the Wittenberg group and was received unreservedly by them. When he offered his services in translating some of the leading Wittenberg publications, a field in which he was singularly gifted, he was accorded a free hand and did the work so well that he enjoyed the complete confidence of the theological faculty of the University of Wittenberg.[181]

When the controversy over the "real presence" developed, he was engaged in translating Bugenhagen's *Commentary on the*

Psalms.[182] Since he was completely trusted in Wittenberg, he had
been given full permission to omit, correct, and improve the work
in the process of translation, in short, the full rights of an editor.
When he came upon a section treating the Lord's Supper, however,
he could not bring himself to further the Wittenberg position and
took the unusual liberty of introducing the symbolical view in place
of the author's original. In the eyes of the reader, therefore, Bugenhagen appeared to be teaching the Reformed doctrine.[813] Some
even believed that Bugenhagen was in league with the Reformed
group. Bugenhagen did not learn what had been done until the
work had been published for six months. When challenged, Bucer
excused himself on the grounds that he had been given full permission to make changes, but admitted that Zwingli and Capito
had advised against it. Bugenhagen immediately published a second edition in which he disclaimed the whole Bucer work and told
the world how he had been betrayed.[184]

Bucer apparently did not profit by his first mistake and became
more deeply involved this time with Luther himself, whose *Postils*
he was translating. Again he encountered a section in the last
volume in which Luther set forth his views on the Holy Supper in
clear and unmistakable language. Mindful of his former error, he
reproduced Luther's thoughts in the text with his former fidelity,
but he added a prefatory warning to the reader, pointing out Luther's error and citing the *Apologia* of Oecolampadius as the source
for a true understanding of the Sacrament.[185]

As was to be expected, Luther was terribly angry at the audacity of the former friend. In a scathing denunciation he wrote:

> The earlier volumes were faithfully and correctly rendered, but in
> the fourth volume that spirit, which pants with eagerness and in-
> credible rage to spread its own opinions, could not restrain itself,
> and crucified my work with an awful and sacrilegious preface and
> virulent notes. These miserable men are not content to spread their
> virus in their own books, already infinite in number, but spoil other
> men's books by smearing them with that poison.[186]

In rebuttal, Bucer published his account of the episode under the
title *Preface by M. Bucer to the Fourth Volume of Luther's
Postils.*[187] Presenting himself as having been unjustly accused, he
attacked Luther for false interpretations, lack of Christian charity,

and the tendency to insist on his own interpretations as the only correct viewpoint.[188]

From then on, feeling between the two groups continued to grow worse until the publication of Luther's *Confession* and its resultant change in Bucer's attitude. He made no public or private retraction or apology for his earlier acts, however, and when the two met at Marburg, Luther shook his finger at Bucer and said laughingly: "You are a rogue." [189] Several of their fellow delegates sought to effect some reconciliation between them, but Luther apparently could not forget the earlier perfidy of his former friend and could not bring himself to trust him fully. Bucer outlined the teachings of the Strassburgers on the Trinity and the Lord's Supper and asked for Luther's comments, to which he replied that he was neither their judge nor teacher. Rather abruptly Luther implied that he could not be certain they actually taught as Bucer claimed. If his words seem harsh, one must recall the background of bitter controversy which had raged, much of it at Bucer's instigation.

> I am not your lord, nor your judge, nor your teacher; for it is quite apparent that we do not have the same spirit. For, how can it be the same spirit to believe the words of the Lord in one part of the Bible in all simplicity, yet in another part censure the faith and picture it as false and attack it with all kinds of outrageous blasphemy? . . . Therefore, as I have said earlier, I commend you to God's judgment. Teach as you can answer to God.[190]

Although the delegates had ceased to hope for any agreement, the prince was reluctant to abandon his project and called further meetings for the following Monday.[191] Again from Osiander's notes may be gathered that the discussions continued much along previous lines. He stated that Luther made a real effort to achieve a common viewpoint.[192] When all realized that further attempt was futile, the Zwinglians asked that they might be considered as brothers and receive Communion from the Lutherans, but, in Osiander's words, "this was denied them for important Christian reasons." [193] Brenz made the following report:

> Finally the Zwinglians asked that the Lutherans might accept them as brethren and members of the Church. This the Lutherans entirely rejected. The final decision was that the Zwinglians be regarded as our friends (as one is obligated to love even an enemy), but not as brethren and members of the Church.[194]

Since the two groups had apparently reached external agreement on all issues but one, this decision might appear unduly rigorous until it is recalled that the Wittenberg delegation had been instructed to achieve complete doctrinal unity before considering political union.[195] The colloquy had succeeded, however, in eliminating much of the former personal enmity and discord existing between the opposing parties and made future co-operation much more likely.

THE AUGSBURG CONFESSION

The next attempt to achieve harmony and unification within the Church, and far eclipsing all others in importance, occurred at the Diet of Augsburg in 1530. As a result of the researches of Kolde, Brieger, von Schubert, Gussmann, Kuehn, Ficker, and Reu, the famous Diet can now be viewed in much clearer perspective.[196] Some scholars regard it as the climax of the Luther story which began October 31, 1517, with the nailing of the *Ninety-Five Theses* on the door of the Castle Church in Wittenberg.[197] In the interim the movement had gathered enormous momentum. Where at Worms Charles V had faced a single monk whose conscience would not permit him to recant, at the second Diet of Speyer and at the Diet of Augsburg it was plainly evident that Luther no longer stood alone. Here a number of evangelical princes and representatives from many cities risked their lives in their support of the views of a heretic who could not even be present, as he was still under the condemnation of the Edict of Worms.[198] Viewed in its relationship to the entire Reformation, the Diet of Augsburg was the final clash in the conflict between two irreconcilable ecclesiastical systems.

There can be little doubt that Charles V was a conscientious Roman Catholic, but he was not of the orthodox Italian type. During his youth in the Netherlands he had absorbed much of the pious spirit of the Brethren of the Common Life.[199] He was sincere in his efforts to be just and fair to all his subjects, but as Emperor of such widely diverse elements as were found in his empire he was caught in the crosscurrents of political expediency.[200] The Turkish menace made imperative a common front in Christendom, and the imperial chancellor Balthasar Merklin strongly advised a friendly compromise with the Lutherans, promising them a national council to deal with the problem of reforms.[201] Nor was Charles allowed to forget the promises made in his coronation oath which had not been fulfilled. Typical of the counsel received on every hand was the advice of his former father-confessor Garcia di Loaysa, who had accompanied him from Spain and now become the Cardinal of Osma:

> Now one must use flattery, then forceful threats; next presents and worldly goods; in this way you must take God from the Cross.[202]

Charles, however, even though he may have been influenced to practice greater patience and moderation in the problem of the Reformation by this advice from his court, regarded himself as entirely capable of making his own decisions once he had examined the Lutheran problem. The conqueror of Italy and Spain was no longer the young, inarticulate boy who had faced Luther at Worms in 1521.[203] He instructed his Catholic theologians to catalog the heresies in Luther's teachings and writings and believed that on the basis of this evidence he could solve the problem which had been neglected because of his extended absence from Germany. For the basic premises of Lutheranism or Zwinglianism he, unfortunately, had no theological background and was simply unable to grasp the reasoning which presented the Protestants as the apostles of the original Catholic Church.[204] He was aware, however, as Duke George and other princes kept reminding him, that certain of the *Gravamina* required reform, and for this aspect of the Reformation he had some sympathy and understanding.

Charles had finally concluded his conquests in Italy after nine years' absence from the German lands. Having made his peace with the Pope in the treaty of Barcelona and with Francis I at Cambrai, he turned next to the solution of the Lutheran problem, after which he hoped to join his brother, Ferdinand, in expelling the forces of Suleiman II threatening Vienna.[205] The following report by the Venetian envoy Tiepolo of a conversation with Charles seems indicative of the trend of his thinking:

> The sad state of affairs which characterizes the life of all members of society, spiritual and lay, had caused him since his early childhood to have in mind, should it be possible in his day, to summon

a general council that would put aside the great irregularities. Such a council it seemed to him would more likely come about in a day when the Turk lifted his head, for only in that way could it be hoped that all Christians would be united and take up arms against the invader. On no other basis could he hope to accomplish his purpose. Even though he and his brother had always done their duty, yet they recognized quite well that by themselves they had not sufficient means to enter upon such an undertaking.[206]

Accordingly, the announcement was issued on January 21, 1530, that Charles would be in Augsburg to preside personally over that august assembly on April 8.[207] On all sides the belief prevailed that now the issue would be settled one way or another. The Catholics hoped that he would crush the revolt and force the heretics to return to the fold. The Protestants hoped for a fair and impartial hearing of their case. Both were to be disappointed. The imperial summons was couched in an unusually friendly tone. In the copy sent to Saxony, Charles addressed the Elector as "Dear Uncle," expressing his regret that he had been prevented from returning to Germany for so many years and that his unremitting efforts toward German unity had not been too successful.[208] He hoped that his presence would insure a solution to all the troublesome problems, adding that he had discussed the subject with the Pope and implying that all were agreed upon a fair hearing.

The summons was received by the German princes with varying reactions.[209] The Elector of Saxony was certain that Charles had experienced a change of heart and that the forthcoming meeting would be a National Assembly. He sent enthusiastic letters to his fellow princes, but not all of them shared his enthusiasm. Some of them recalled too vividly how Charles had imprisoned the "Protest" delegation after Speyer.[210] Philip of Hesse was convinced that Charles was far from sincere and further questioned his jurisdiction in ecclesiastical problems.[211] Strassburg and Ulm supported the Landgrave in his conviction that only by presenting a united front could the Protestants hope to force the Emperor to summon a general council.[212] The town council of Nuernberg was also doubtful that Charles could heal the religious schism in the Roman Church, but they felt it expedient to support the Saxon program.[213]

Before the Diet convened, the leadership of the Evangelicals was sharply divided between Saxony and Hesse, and there seemed little hope of a uniform stand. As noted in connection with the Marburg Colloquy, the Elector of Saxony and George of Brandenburg-Ansbach thought it necessary to achieve confessional unity before forming a political league. Various meetings had been held by some of the princes and lawyers of the two groups at Rotach, Saalfeld, and Schleiss, resulting finally in a series of articles drawn up by the Wittenberg theologians and known as the *Schwabach Articles,* because they were first officially announced at Schwabach on October 16.[214] It is now known that they were completed in the summer of 1529 and that Luther must have had a copy at Marburg.[215] These seventeen articles formed the basis upon which complete agreement seemed essential before a league of princes and cities might be formed.

At the meeting at Schmalkalden on November 29 Strassburg and Ulm could not agree with some of the doctrines and refused to join the Saxons and Brandenburgers on such a basis.[216] The Zwinglians were not even present. Another meeting was held in Nuernberg, to which only Lutherans were invited.[217] Attempts at union had reached this stage when the imperial summons calling the Diet of Augsburg was issued. On the one hand was Philip of Hesse keenly aware of the political implications of the situation and not deeply concerned with the religious or spiritual aspects; on the other was the Elector of Saxony advised by Luther. Still, consistent with the stand he had taken on the occasions of the knights' uprising and the Peasants' Revolt, Luther insisted that as long as the Emperor occupied the imperial throne, he could demand obedience in all worldly affairs.[218] Only if he should insist that they renounce their faith, could the princes justifiably refuse to obey him. In the face of considerable pressure from court circles, Luther maintained his position that it would be sinful to place faith in a human league and to rebel against their divinely appointed overlord, and in no case could Christians take up the sword. He doubted that Charles meant to attack the Lutheran princes, but if he should, they could then decide what course to pursue.

The Emperor had completely ignored the "Protest" of the previous Diet and stated that he intended to treat the case of each

city and territory separately.[219] In such an event the Elector of
Saxony would be obliged to explain and to justify the confiscation
of church property and the deviations from established church
practices throughout his lands. His court lawyers feared that no
theologians would be permitted to attend the sessions of the Diet
and that the Saxon case would have to be presented by lay delegates.[220] The Elector, therefore, requested the Wittenberg theological faculty to compose a second set of articles treating the abuses
within the Church, which could be presented in addition to the
Schwabach Articles, which set forth the fundamental doctrines and
teachings then practiced in Saxon lands.[221]

In spite of the careful researches on this subject many details
of the request and its reply are still vague. Melanchthon, Luther,
and Jonas all worked on the document now referred to as the
Torgau Articles, but it is not certain just what or how much material
was forwarded to the Elector on March 27, probably much more
than was used by Melanchthon in preparing the second part of
the Augsburg Confession.[222] In harmony with their consistent belief that they were not advocating a separate Church, but merely
a revival of the original Christian Church, the Saxons hopefully
believed that a clear presentation of their views explaining their
return to Early-Church practices would be sufficient to convince
Charles of the rightness of their stand and would even convert him
to their point of view.[223] This did not mean that the Wittenberg
theologians were willing to grant that the "true" Christian Church
of Jesus Christ could grow and flourish in the atmosphere of the
Roman hierarchy nor to accept the misguided interpretations of the
Anabaptists, Sacramentarians, and Zwinglians, although some members of these bodies undoubtedly belonged to the Invisible Church
of Christ.[224] They proposed to set forth those basic Lutheran teachings which they believed to be in harmony with the Bible and
the Apostolic Church but which needed to be reconciled with pre-
vailing Catholic practices. To the Reformers there seemed to be
some hope, therefore, that Charles might examine the ground of
their belief and discover that the reforms they had made were not
new, but in keeping with the original Christian Church, to which
he, too, should return. They thought, what Kuehn has shown to

be true, that the decision of the second Diet of Speyer, reversing the action of the previous Diet with regard to the evangelical princes, did not come from the Emperor, but from the more aggressive Ferdinand.[225] They believed the situation which had grown out of the "Protest" was not of Charles' will or making.[226] Charles did not see eye to eye with the papal court on the policy to be pursued in dealing with the Lutheran heresy, but he did feel obligated to support his brother until the subject could be given a further hearing.

After his coronation at Bologna, Charles proceeded by leisurely stages from Italy to Germany, accompanied and preceded by the usual hangers-on and court dalliers, each with his own cause to further or favor to seek.[227] The papal legate, Campegio, especially assigned to the Diet, had gone ahead to lay the desired groundwork for the Catholic cause. His specific assignment was "to inform the Emperor in matters of heresy, faith, and other subjects." [228] He did his work well. His dispatches provide an interesting and detailed account of the intrigues, plots, and machinations by which each faction sought to gain the advantage.[229] Charles tarried for some time at Innsbruck, and it was there that the first attempt was made to present the Saxon case.[230]

As early as February the Counts of Nassau and Neuenahr had advised Elector John to send preliminary emissaries to the Emperor's court to influence him toward a favorable reception of the Lutherans. They had some personal motives for their proposal, but they succeeded in convincing the Elector of the importance of the matter and requested that he send his court chancellor with them. He agreed, instead, to send his lawyer, Hans von Dolzig, who would join the counts late in March for the proposed journey.[231] After receiving the Emperor's summons and noting its conciliatory tone, the Elector was not so convinced of the necessity for the preliminary groundwork but, nevertheless, upon the insistence of the counts, sent Dolzig to Dillenburg, as he had promised. Dolzig carried a copy of the *Schwabach Articles* and another document, which may have been the *Instruction to the Visitors* of 1528, showing the teachings and practices of the Saxon lands.[232] The Elector was not moved entirely by religious considerations,

but had some matters of political importance which needed settlement. Among others, there was his own confirmation as Elector
of Saxony succeeding Frederick the Wise, and he hoped, also, for
the Emperor's favor in legalizing the right of his son John Frederick to the succession of his father-in-law, the Duke of Juelich.[233]
The messengers were carefully instructed as to the matters they
were to present in the Elector's behalf, and they were specifically
warned to make no concessions whatever in religious matters.[234]

The Elector hesitated for some time as to whether he would
personally attend the Diet, but upon the strong advice of his counselors he decided to go. On April 3 the Wittenberg delegation,
consisting of Luther, Melanchthon, Jonas, and Dietrich, joined the
Elector's party at Torgau, from where the entire retinue set out
the next day.[235] Along the route they were joined by Spalatin,
Agricola, and Aquila.[236] Upon arriving at Weimar, they learned
that the Emperor was delayed. After resting briefly, they continued
to the Coburg, where they arrived on Good Friday, April 15.[237]
Here they celebrated Easter and awaited word of the Emperor and
the date of the Diet. The Elector had hoped to take Luther as far
as Nuernberg to have him near by if his counsel would be needed.
However, for perfectly valid reasons, which the Elector fully accepted, the Nuernberg authorities felt it advisable for Luther to
remain at the Coburg.[238] Luther was deeply disappointed but continued to hope he might be summoned later. When it was decided
that Luther would not be available, the burden of preparing the
Saxon defense fell on the shoulders of the gentle, easy-going Melanchthon, who at once began the labor of preparing a document
which would explain and defend the Saxon position.[239]

From Coburg the Elector dispatched a fast messenger with
further instructions for the delegation, which had left earlier. Since
this messenger had better information as to the Emperor's route,
he arrived at the court ahead of the representatives and delivered
the Elector's message to the imperial vice-chancellor and to the
court chamberlain, Henry of Nassau, through whom the Elector
had hoped his delegates could arrange an interview with Charles.[240]
Both sent friendly replies, which further raised the hopes of the
Elector. He thereupon wrote to Hans of Minckwitz, who was also
in Innsbruck, to announce his arrival in Augsburg to the Emperor.

Before Minckwitz could comply with this request, Dolzig arrived at Innsbruck and delivered his messages to the Emperor.[241] At first they believed they were favorably received and began arrangements for the Elector to journey to Innsbruck for a personal interview. In the meantime the crafty Campegio was succeeding in swaying the Emperor from his impartial viewpoint. The further information that the Elector had arranged for evangelical preaching in Augsburg greatly disturbed the Emperor.[242] On April 23 the Electoral party left the Coburg and arrived in Augsburg on May 2, the first prince to reach the imperial city.[243] On May 8 Dolzig reported that Charles had refused permission for the Elector to come to Innsbruck, had postponed his decision in all other matters, and that an official request would be forthcoming to stop the Augsburg preaching.[244] Unknown to the Elector, the Emperor had obtained a poor Latin translation of the *Schwabach Articles* about that time, for Campegio reported the fact in his dispatches on May 9. The Emperor was much displeased and asked Campegio's advice in dealing with the situation. As might have been expected, it was to "exterminate these stiff-necked heretics with fire and sword." [245] On May 12 the Bavarian dukes and Duke George of Saxony arrived at Innsbruck and soon joined forces with Campegio.[246] Thus the hopes for an impartial hearing of the Saxon case grew dimmer as the days passed.

The change in their fortunes was not unknown to the Saxon delegation, and they labored mightily to prepare a fitting presentation of their case. At Augsburg a new factor entered into the situation. Complying with a request issued by Ferdinand, the faculties of Vienna and other Catholic universities gathered materials from Luther's writings, listing the innovations and errors in doctrine.[247] To John Eck of Ingolstadt fell the task of synthesizing this vast body of materials, a task which he joyfully undertook and completed within a month. Copies of the work were available in Augsburg titled *Four Hundred and Four Articles for the Diet in Augsburg,* and Melanchthon procured a copy.[248] A copy also reached Emperor Charles at about the same time as the *Schwabach Articles.*[249] Eck's document not only reflected great industry in its compilation, but also considerable ability in asserting that there

was little difference between the heresies of the Anabaptists, Lutherans, and Sacramentarians and that all were but revivals of
earlier heresies already condemned by the church councils. Its
preface was a masterpiece of flattery dedicated to Charles and intended to stir him to action in defense of the pure faith of the
Catholic Church.

Melanchthon fully realized the deadly effect this document
would have upon the Lutheran cause and turned even more
furiously to the revision of his earlier efforts to meet this new
threat.[250] That he was also thoroughly frightened and dismayed
by the enormity of his task is indicated by the fact that he was
often discovered at his desk in tears.[251] The Saxon delegation had
originally intended to present merely the Torgau materials, but in
the face of the new developments they thought it advisable to
include a doctrinal section, which made a new preface necessary.
Reu summarizes their intention as follows:

> A writing was necessary *which on the one hand would make clear
> the connection of the Lutheran Church with the old faith and the
> doctrines accepted at the ancient general synods, and on the other
> hand would most emphatically stress the differences between them
> and the Sacramentarians, Anabaptists, and fanatics.* Only in this
> way would Eck's attack be sucessfully [sic] halted and the danger
> to the Lutherans routed or at least the influence of Eck's articles on
> the Emperor and his council paralyzed.[252]

The new document consisted of a preface, a section of "Articles on Faith and Teaching," a section of "Articles on Which
There is Division, in Which are Enumerated the Abuses Which
have been Altered," and a conclusion.[253] For the first section the
Schwabach Articles, which stressed the differences between the
Lutherans and the Zwinglians, Sacramentarians, and Anabaptists,
were used rather than the *Marburg Articles*, which stressed the
likenesses.[254] The first draft, containing the preface, the Articles
of Faith, and the Articles on Abuses, was sent to Luther on May 11
by the Elector with the following letter:

> After you and our other learned men at Wittenberg had, at our
> gracious thought and desire, made a draught of the Articles of Re-
> ligion concerning which there is now strife, it is our wish to let you
> know that Melanchthon has further revised the same and drawn
> them up into a form, which we are sending you herewith. And it is

our gracious desire that you would feel free to further consider and revise the same Articles; and where you deem it wise and well to take away or add anything, please do so on the margin. Send back the same carefully secured and sealed without delay, that we may be ready and prepared for the arrival of his Imperial Majesty whom we expect in a short time.[255]

Melanchthon also wrote Luther explaining the necessity for the changes which he had made:

Our "Apology" is being sent you, but in truth it is rather a confession! For the Emperor has not time to listen to lengthy disputations. Yet I have succinctly given nearly all the Articles of Faith, since Eck has circulated the most Satanic slanders against us. Over against these I wished to oppose a remedy. Please give judgment on the whole writing according to your spirit.[256]

Luther returned the document on May 15 with the following comment:

I have read the Apology of M. Philip. It pleases me right well, and I do not know what to improve or change in it; neither would it be proper, for I cannot tread so gently and quietly. Christ our Lord help that it bear much and great fruit, as we hope and pray. Amen.[257]

This original draft of the Augsburg Confession has been lost, and it is not known whether Luther made any marginal changes.[258] The oldest available manuscript is a copy dated May 31 and sent home by the Nuernberg delegation with the comment, "It still lacks an article or two at the end and also a conclusion, on which the Saxon theologians are still working." [259] This copy contained some deviations as to text from the one seen by Luther, but it had the three parts. At this time the Saxons were still hopeful that the Emperor would give the Lutheran cause a favorable hearing; therefore this draft was still strictly Saxon in character. Melanchthon placed great hope in the ability of Mercurinus· to influence the Emperor in favor of their cause, but the imperial chancellor, already ill, died on June 4, leaving a clear field to Campegio and Valdes, one of the imperial secretaries.[260]

Between May 31 and June 15 a third draft of the Augsburg Confession was prepared, in which Melanchthon made some very sweeping changes.[261] It was during this period that the Augustana,

as the document is often called, was changed in character from a
Saxon to a general Lutheran confession.[262] The reasons for this
shift are not fully clear, but Johannes von Walter has added new
information on the basis of hitherto unknown Italian sources, especially the dispatches of Tiepolo.[263] He concluded that the discouraging report by the preliminary delegation sent to the Emperor
greatly influenced the Elector's decision. John now realized that
Philip of Hesse had been right and that he had misinterpreted the
courteous invitation to the Diet. Now he thought it advisable to
broaden the Confession to include the Lutherans of other lands.[264]
Accordingly, Melanchthon made still another draft, now known
as the Nuernberg text and published by Johannes Ficker.[265] German historians have pointed out that for this draft Melanchthon
had before him the opinions of a number of Protestant states and
drew freely from the materials gathered by George of Brandenburg-Ansbach from his clergy, the reports from some of the southern
cities, and other materials.[266] There is also evidence that Philip
of Hesse had some influence in the drafting of this document.[267]
By June 15 it was completed except for the new preface and a
satisfactory conclusion.[268] This Nuernberg text of June 15 forms
the connecting link between the draft of May 31 and the one read
before the Diet on June 25, with the exception of the preface and
conclusion, which in the final copy were drawn up by Chancellor
Brueck and the princes.[269]

The long-awaited arrival of the Emperor at Augsburg found
the entire city prepared for the royal reception.[270] The Electors,
princes, nobles and estates, and a large crowd of citizens awaited
the arrival of His Imperial Majesty at the bridge of the Lech
River, and as the dust clouds rose in the distance, cannons began
to boom in greeting. Charles dismounted and graciously shook
hands and greeted each prince. Campegio seized upon this moment
to bless the group, whereupon all knelt except the Elector John and
Landgrave Philip.[271] The procession then formed in order of rank,
led by soldiery of the six Electors, the Electors and the princes,
and, immediately preceding the Emperor, Elector John of Saxony,
bearing the gleaming sword as *Erzmarschall*. The way led to the
Cathedral, where an impressive service was held, but it was noted

that Elector John and Landgrave Philip again remained standing and failed to remove their head coverings during the blessing.

That same evening the Protestant princes were summoned to a meeting with the Emperor, where Ferdinand, in the name of his brother, demanded that the Gospel preaching in the city be stopped.[272] His vehemence left Elector John speechless, but Margrave George and Landgrave Philip boldly stated that it was not within the Emperor's province to dictate to their consciences.[273] George pointed out that the preaching was not heretical, but the same Word of God as that heard by the Fathers. The Emperor was furious, but the men stood their ground; in fact, Margrave George stepped forward and, looking the Emperor in the eyes, said:

> Before I would deny my God and His Gospel, I would rather kneel down here before Your Imperial Majesty and let you cut off my head.[274]

It was then Charles' turn to be shocked and surprised, and he stammered in his broken German: "Not cut off head! Not cut off head!"[275] He then dismissed the princes, giving them time until the following morning to consider the request and asking them to join in the Corpus Christi procession. Through the night Spalatin labored on a statement of their position which declared:

> The Sacrament was not instituted to be worshipped [sic] like the brazen serpent of the Jews. We are here to confess the truth and not to confirm abuses.[276]

The question of preaching was delayed until Luther could be consulted. He advised that the Emperor could order whatever he wished in his own imperial city, just as the Elector could determine the religious practices of his Saxon lands.

In spite of considerable pressure and an appeal to personal loyalty to the Emperor the dissenting princes remained firm in their refusal to participate in the religious ceremony. Charles marched behind the Host, accompanied by the few Catholic princes and scarcely a hundred citizens of Augsburg.[277] He was so angry that he would have sent the Lutherans home at once had not the other princes convinced him that such action would result in civil war. All of these events confirmed the Elector's growing conviction that the dissenting princes were to be considered as a group and would not be treated as individual cases.

There now followed a series of private negotiations between Melanchthon on the one hand and Campegio, Valdes, and Schepper, another secretary, on the other.[278] Details of these conferences are vague. Kolde has placed the whole responsibility upon Melanchthon for instigating the conferences because he feared the anger of the Emperor and a definite rupture of the Church. Again the dispatches of Tiepolo seem to place Melanchthon in a much more favorable position and reveal the following sequence of events.[279] On the morning of June 18 the Emperor summoned the Catholic princes for a private conference.[280] Charles had apparently been much impressed with the sincerity and steadfast determination of the Lutheran princes and was anxious to find some moderate means of dealing with the situation. In the discussion Valdes revealed some acquaintance with the Confession being drawn up by Melanchthon, particularly the four points which required conciliation, namely, the marriage of priests, both forms in the Sacrament, the Mass, and the property of the Church. Ensuing discussions seemed to indicate a hope of finding agreement. Charles met next with the Protestant princes and finally with both groups jointly.[281] He urged them all to attend Mass on June 20, after which they would seek a solution to their problems. The Emperor still gave an impression of neutrality and even ordered that Catholic preaching also be stopped and only Scripture reading permitted.[282]

The hopes for a peaceful settlement were severely rocked when the Protestant princes attended the Mass as requested but refused to enter into the service.[283] Perhaps they were irked by the sermon delivered by Pimpinella, one of the papal nuncios, which did not lack criticism of the Protestants, or they may have been offended by the opening address delivered in the name of the Emperor by the Elector of the Palatinate, Frederick, who likewise could not refrain from injecting some of his personal feelings into his remarks.[284] If there had been any disposition on the part of the Protestants to discard their Confession in favor of a brief summary of their views on the four points, they now returned to their former position and in a meeting on June 21 hastened the composition of the preface and conclusion in conformity with the new aspect of the document as a Protestant rather than a Saxon confession.[285]

The Diet was now officially in session, and after considerable discussion as to order of procedure the Protestants were successful in separating the confessional question from that of the Turkish War and the previous *Gravamina* remaining from other diets.[286] They also insisted that the Catholics prepare a statement of their position comparable to the Protestant Confession, to which the Catholics replied that since they were the "true" Church, it was not necessary for them to state their beliefs.[287] The Evangelicals replied that from that viewpoint only a general council could solve their problems.[288] Their opponents then proposed that a committee of twelve be selected to examine the Augsburg Confession and report to the Emperor as the final judge.[289] Campegio believed he could privately arrange for the committee membership to be two-thirds Catholic.[290] The Protestant princes saw clearly the shape of things to come and knew that after an outward semblance of a hearing the whole matter would die in the committee. They insisted upon reading the document publicly.[291]

Accordingly, between June 20 and 24, when the Confession was scheduled to be presented to the Emperor, the Protestant princes held a number of meetings. In the session of June 23 the Elector, the Margrave, the Landgrave, Duke Ernest of Lueneburg, their lawyers, and about a dozen theologians worked tirelessly on the preface and the conclusion, while Melanchthon edited the main text.[292] The Landgrave insisted upon further changes before he was willing to sign, and the final form was due in no small degree to his influence. The article on the Lord's Supper remained, but Articles 20 and 21 were added.[293] The new preface omitted all mention of the Zwinglians or Sacramentarians. The article on Justification received its final form.[294] So rushed were the writers for time that the Latin text had not been recopied, but was still in Melanchthon's handwriting.[295] The intrepid signers now affixed their names to the document: Elector John of Saxony, Margrave George of Brandenburg-Ansbach, Duke Ernest of Brunswick-

Lueneburg, Landgrave Philip of Hesse, Prince Wolfgang of Anhalt, and the cities of Nuernberg and Reutlingen.[296] It may also
have been signed by Prince John Frederick of Saxony and Duke
Francis of Lueneburg.

That much was wanting in the Confession is readily admitted.
It made no mention of Luther's statements of the "priesthood of
believers," of the Lutheran view of the Sacrament, and it certainly
passed lightly over many of the distinctive differences between the
"New Theology" and that of Rome.[297] These defects are understandable in the atmosphere of strain and uncertainty and the
constantly shifting tides of political circumstance which surrounded its composers. Nor should Melanchthon be too severely
censured for his seeming compromise, for without Luther's strength
to draw upon he was continually buffeted about by the streams
of conflicting counsel poured upon him from all directions.

When the afternoon of June 24 arrived, the Evangelicals were
ready. Chancellor Brueck had the Latin translation, and his colleague Dr. Christian Beyer carried the German.[298] They were
firm in their determination to insist upon a public hearing, and
they were wary of any new subterfuge which would seek to
disarm or dissuade them from their purpose. They were suspicious
of the long harangues delivered upon the Turkish menace and a
lengthy negotiation with the papal legate.[299] They wondered if
Charles had deliberately arranged for the time to be consumed
thus so that he might use the lateness of the hour as an excuse to
omit the public reading and thereby limit the knowledge of the
contents of the Confession. The hour was late when Dr. Brueck
was finally recognized, too late for the reading of a two-hour
document, and the Emperor suggested that the Confession be
handed to him without being read.[300] But Chancellor Brueck, able
statesman, astute lawyer, and clever diplomat, reminded the Emperor that permission for the reading had already been given and
made the further request that it be done in German.[301] This proposal the Emperor did not favor, for more of the audience would
understand German than Latin. Ferdinand, too, tried to prevent
the German reading on the ground that the audience was mixed
and could not all follow the language. Elector John reminded

them that they were on German soil and it would be most fitting that the reading be in German. The point was won, but the day was now spent, and so the Emperor had no choice but to assign the reading to the calendar of the next day's business.[302] The place was changed, however, from the customary *Rathaus* to the "lower large room" of the Episcopal Palace, probably to prevent a large audience from gathering.[303] Jonas estimated that the latter place held not over 200 people.

On the following afternoon the room was filled to capacity, and other persons crowded the corridors and the courtyard.[304] The Emperor and princes entered about three o'clock, and the session was opened.[305] When Dr. Brueck and Dr. Beyer stepped to the front, all of the Protestant delegates rose to their feet.[306] The historic moment which followed has been described by J. S. Mueller in his *Annales* of 1700, taken from the official acts of the Saxon court.

> At the Diet of Augsburg the Evangelical Confession prepared by Philip Melanchthon and approved by Elector John and other princes and estates alike, written in both Latin and German, was read in German by the Chancellor of Electoral Saxony, Doctor Christian Beyer, in the so-called Bishop's Court so loudly and distinctly that not only the assembled Emperor, Electors, and estates, before which he spoke, could hear it, but also outside in front of the room and even in the Palatinate and the Castle Court they could understand every word. The reading took two hours. After the reading Doctor Gregorius Pontanus took from Doctor Beyer the German text, which had been read, and gave it with the Latin copy, which he already had, to the imperial secretary, Alexander Schweiss, from whom the Kaiser took the Latin copy.[307]

These acts have been variously reported, and the details are not clear. Some reports state that the Emperor kept the Latin copy, requesting his secretary, Schweiss, to translate it into French, and that the German copy was given to the Elector of Mainz for safe-keeping. Both copies have been lost.[308] Some credence may be given to the latter account, since the oldest copy extant is now called the Mainz Manuscript and seems to be a carefully prepared copy of the original.[309] This copy, as well as a copy of the Latin text, was discovered and published by Johannes Ficker.[310]

The general reception accorded the Augsburg Confession is difficult to establish. As might be expected, many stories grew out of the dramatic event. Justus Jonas wrote Luther that the Emperor listened to the reading with sufficient interest; Brenz and Heller both reported that he fell asleep.[311] Reaction was also varied among the audience. Some Catholic princes objected to the Protestant tone of the document; others thought it quite mild and conciliatory.[312] William of Bavaria realized that this was a different theology from the one reported to him as Lutheran and asked Eck how it might be refuted. Eck is supposed to have replied that he could refute it from the Fathers, but not on the basis of Scripture, to which the discerning Duke replied, "Do I understand that the Lutherans are sitting in the Scriptures and we outside?"[313] More to be considered was the action of those free cities, Heilbronn, Kempten, Windsheim, Weissenburg, and Frankfurt am Main, which immediately added their names to the document.[314] Others, deeply impressed, later joined the Protestant ranks.

Although Luther rejoiced that the Confession had been made before the Emperor and the German estates, he made it clear that it contained considerable *Leisetreterei*, a "lightly stepping-over" of points of difference.[315] The instructions to his fellow Reformers reveal that Luther was not interested in reducing the teachings of the Lutheran *Landeskirche* to a set of dogmas, and it was probably for this reason that he never supplanted the Augsburg Confession with a more comprehensive statement of Lutheran belief, as requested by the Emperor toward the close of the Diet. Not until 1537 did he correct the weaknesses in the Melanchthonian document, when he published the Schmalkald Articles.[316] Those who seek a comprehensive understanding of Luther's teachings must obtain it from his exegetical writings and not from any well-formulated system, such as Calvin's *Institutes of Christianity*.

After the delivery of the Confession to Charles, his next problem was what action to take. Again historians are indebted to Theodor Brieger and Johannes Ficker for a reconstruction of the story following the session of June 25.[317] For two days there were closed sessions, in which the Emperor sought the advice of the Catholic princes and theologians, including Campegio, as to the best method of procedure. The papal legate replied in a surprisingly balanced statement, suggesting that the Confession be carefully analyzed by a group of qualified theologians in the light of the Gospels and Scripture in general and that errors be singled out, together with the information as to what church councils had already condemned these heresies. The result should be presented to the Lutherans and an opportunity be given them to recant, but under no conditions would they be given further opportunity to reply, as that would only waste time and effort. Should they refuse, the Emperor should extirpate this heresy with his "temporal arm," aided by the Catholic estates.[318]

Upon Campegio's advice, the Confession was divided into two parts. The "Articles of Faith" were to be examined and refuted; the section on Abuses was to be studied and suggestions for their correction made to the Emperor.[319] The work was at first divided among Cochlaeus, Usingen, Wimpina, Fabri, and Eck.[320] Much of their material may be seen in manuscript form in the Court Library at Vienna.[321] Since John Eck had already gathered the 404 articles and other materials against Luther, he seemed the logical person to formulate the final draft of the document in reply to the Confession. He worked with amazing speed, and by July 8 the document of 351 pages was done.[322] When the first draft was read to the Emperor, he was deeply disappointed, for he felt that the theologians had allowed their bitter feelings to vent themselves in too much sarcasm and scorn. He still hoped to conciliate the Lutherans, as he needed their support in having his brother Ferdinand crowned King of the Romans. He was also concerned with the growing sympathy among the various Protestant princes. Zwingli and Bucer had sent their own confessions to the Diet, and Philip of Hesse was quietly strengthening the movement for a political league among the princes and cities.[323] Guided by these factors, Charles ordered that the preface and the conclusion be discarded entirely and nothing included but answers based on the Gospels and Scripture.[324]

After much further revision on the part of Eck, Granvella, Valdes, and others, the document was finally ready on August 3.[325] The assembly again gathered in the same room where the Confession had been read to hear Alexander Schweiss read the *Confutatio*

Pontifica, as it came to be known.[326] All bitterness had been eliminated, and the style and content were mild and conciliatory. It was
replete with Scripture passages and was a scholarly attempt to
point out the many possibilities of agreement between the Lutherans and the Mother Church. It expressed the hope that a
mutually satisfactory solution would be reached at the Diet. Only
in the final phrases was there an implied threat that, if the Lutherans failed to heed this last fatherly attempt to bring them to
the light, Charles would know what action to take.[327] The Lutherans naturally expected to be provided with a copy of the document but, in accordance with Campegio's advice, they were to
receive a copy only on condition that they would not prepare or
publish a reply and would accept its provisions.[328] These conditions the Lutherans refused, as Campegio knew they would. Fortunately for their cause, Camerarius had taken some notes during
the reading, and on the basis of these and his own memory Melanchthon undertook to reply.[329]

Immediately after these events the outlook for the Protestant
cause seemed rather dark. Melanchthon now reached his lowest
ebb in concessions, compromise, and almost childish weakness.[330]
Fortunately, the princes did not share his fearful agitation and in
the moment of crisis were more firm in their convictions. The Emperor employed every strategy to win over the evangelical princes
and induce them to forsake the Augsburg Confession.[331] He brought
particular pressure upon the Elector of Saxony, threatening to withhold his investiture, whereupon Elector John informed His Imperial
Majesty that, though it was his lawful right, he would forego that
right rather than deny his God.[332] Added threats by the Margrave
Joachim of Brandenburg as to the consequences of his willful opposition to the Emperor, including the confiscation of his lands and
exile from the country, did not weaken the determined prince in
his stand.[333]

Still hoping to resolve the differences between the two groups,
the Emperor next appointed a commission of fourteen with equal
representation from both sides, later reduced to six.[334] This opportunity was welcomed by the Lutherans, as only in that way could
they hope to show the Catholic representatives the instances in
which the Roman Church was out of harmony with the faith of

the Fathers.[335] Luther was consulted and wrote a series of letters to the Elector, Melanchthon, Jonas, and others in which he once more stated the basic principle that the Scriptures could be the only ground for refusal or consent to agreement:

> We will suffer everything and yield where it is in our power to do so. But what is not in our power, we ask that it be not required of us. And what is God's Word is not in our power.[336]

It soon became evident that even the small sessions were making little progress toward understanding and union. A letter from Baumgartner to Spengler at Nuernberg on September 13, 1530, painted the picture as dark and practically hopeless.[337] In fact, he feared that in the face of the clever Roman manipulations the Evangelicals might finally lose everything. Luther wrote Melanchthon his views of the negotiations as early as August 26:

> In short, I am thoroughly displeased with this negotiating concerning union in doctrine, since it is utterly impossible, except the Pope wishes to put away his power. It was enough to give account of our faith and to ask for peace. Why do we hope to convert them to the truth? We have come, to hear whether or not they will assent to our Confession, and they be free to remain where they are. And we ask whether they reject our side, or acknowledge it as right. If they reject it, of what use is it to try to enter into harmony with enemies? If they acknowledge it as right, why should we retain the old abuses? And since it is certain that our side will be condemned by them, as they are not repenting, and are striving to retain their side, why do we not see through the matter and recognize that all their concessions are a lie? . . .[338]

Finally, since little or no progress was being made, on September 22 the Emperor gave his verdict on the unsuccessful negotiations with the Protestant princes in the form of an imperial recess.[339] In cleverly written, polite, yet forceful language His Imperial Majesty pointed out that whereas he had summoned the Diet to give each group a fair hearing and had heard the Protestant Electors, princes, and other estates of the Holy Roman Empire, had considered their views together with those of his fellow Catholic princes, prelates, counts, and estates of the said empire, and had looked carefully and devotedly into the matter and found the Protestant declarations thoroughly refuted "by means of the Gospel and other writings," he, therefore, made the following reply:

Therefore His Imperial Majesty, for the benefit and prosperity of the Holy Empire, for the restoration of peace and unity, and for the purpose of manifesting His Majesty's leniency and special grace, has granted to the Elector of Saxony, the five Princes, and the six Cities a time of grace from now until the 15th day of April next year in which to consider whether or not they will confess the other articles together with the Christian Church, His Holiness the Pope, His Imperial Majesty, the other Electors, Princes, and Estates of the Holy Roman Empire, and other Christian rulers and the members of universal Christendom until a general council shall be convoked. . . .[340]

In the interim, while the recalcitrants were making up their minds, they were to prohibit the printing and selling of new books on religion in their lands and endeavor to promote peace and unity.[341] Nor were they to force or induce any of the subjects of His Majesty to join their sects or to interfere with the Catholic worship of those in their lands who did not accept their views. They were to aid the Catholic Church in opposing the Anabaptists and others who "reject the holy and blessed Sacrament." [342] Finally, it was promised by the Emperor that he would try to influence the Pope to summon a Christian council within the six months following the Diet, said council to meet within a year after that date.[343] As far as the Emperor and his Catholic supporters were concerned, the subject was closed.

Melanchthon had begun his reply immediately after the reading of the *Confutation*, but when rumors of the Emperor's intended recess reached the Lutherans, he redoubled his efforts to produce a response now known as the Apology.[344] It was ready on the day the recess was announced, and the Protestants tried to present it to the Emperor, but upon the whispered advice of Ferdinand he refused to accept it.[345] Its content reveals a much stronger stand than Melanchthon had shown up to this time. Either Luther's counsel had strengthened his attitude regarding a compromise with the Catholics, or Brueck and the Elector had taken a hand in its composition. On September 23, the day of the recess, the Elector decided to leave the Diet and to go home, without his investiture, but with a clear conscience.[346] The Diet of Augsburg ended for the Lutheran delegation with the future still uncertain.

After his return from Augsburg, Melanchthon procured and studied a copy of the *Confutation*, which he probably obtained through his Nuernberg friends.[347] He decided to rewrite his Apology and enlarge upon his former points. Early in 1531 he was still deeply involved in writing an able presentation of the doctrine of "justification by faith," and by early spring the work was completed and published together with the Augsburg Confession.[348] The document emphasized the assertion that the *Confutation* had not refuted the Lutheran position. In this final form his work later appeared in the *Symbolical Books* and bore little resemblance to the document which Brueck had tried to present to the Emperor.[349] By the time of the Schweinfurt meeting in 1532 the revised Apology had been accepted in Lutheran circles as a component part of the Augsburg Confession and passed into the *Credo* of Lutheranism.[350] At Schmalkalden in 1537 it was again included as one of the confessional documents of the Lutheran *Landeskirche* along with the Confession.[351]

In spite of its apparent failure to solve the religious differences, the Diet of Augsburg was a milestone in the German Reformation. For the Protestants it proved to be a great disappointment. Posing as a neutral judge in the religious controversy, the Emperor had conducted only nine plenary sessions.[352] After the first his mind had been made up. In his decision he had declared the Evangelicals refuted, and in a decree of November 19 he revived the Edict of Worms and ordered all church property reinstated. Through these methods of coercion the Protestants were driven closer together, and in February, 1531, they formed the League of Schmalkalden.[353] Ferdinand was finally elected King of the Romans without the vote of the Elector of Saxony, but the *Holy Roman Empire of the German Nation* had really come to an end.[354] Germany had broken up into a *corpus evangelicorum* and a *corpus catholicorum*, two political unions formed on the basis of two different faiths. When the time arrived for a reply to the recess, none was made, and the following year the Emperor signed the Peace of Nuernberg, July, 1532, in which he agreed to postpone the day of reckoning.[355] The Turk in eastern Europe and in the Mediterranean kept Charles too preoccupied to deal with the Lutheran heresy, and in the interim the Reformation grew to full stature.

THE WITTENBERG CONCORD

After the disappointing failure of the Diet to heal the schism the Evangelicals made new attempts to achieve confessional as well as military unity among themselves. The two leaders in this movement were Bucer and Melanchthon. Bucer had attended the Diet of Augsburg and had made great efforts to come to an understanding with Melanchthon.[356] Like Luther, Melanchthon was suspicious of Bucer's professed conversion, but by the close of the Diet, Bucer had convinced Melanchthon that his change of heart was genuine.[357] The Elector, too, hoped that an avenue for agreement had finally opened and arranged for Bucer to visit Luther at the Coburg as a "prophet of concord," where he was received by Luther in a friendly spirit. The Reformer was still doubtful of Bucer's sincerity and during the conversation turned to him and said: "Martin, are you in earnest? It is better to have us as enemies than to form a false alliance."[358] Persuaded by Bucer's apparent earnestness and changed attitude, Luther consented to his plan to visit the Swiss leaders in an attempt to draw up a tentative formula for peace, provided he did not use Luther's name nor print the document prematurely. Bucer's reception by Zwingli was not too friendly, and Swiss opposition to the Lutherans continued even though their leader was killed in the battle of Cappel in October, 1531.[359] In November of the same year Oecolampadius also died, a great blow to the cause of peace, as he had begun to favor closer union with the Lutherans. Bucer, however, was not discouraged. In the early thirties he continued his efforts toward union both in person and through his writings.

When Bucer learned in 1533 that the Emperor had succeeded in inducing the Pope to summon a general council, he published a dialog called *In Preparation for Union*, by which he hoped to bring the Protestants and the Catholics into a new corporate body.[360] His labor impressed the Wittenberg group very much, for Melanchthon wrote him: "I love you sincerely and wholeheartedly."[361] In March, 1534, Bucer published a polemic against the Anabaptists, known as the *Report*, in which he further expressed his views on the Lord's Supper and tried to show that the Lutherans and the Zwinglians were fundamentally agreed. Although not wholly accepted, this work furthered the prospect of union between the two evangelical groups and resulted in a meeting at Cassel late in December, 1534, where Melanchthon was completely won to Bucer's plan for concord between the rival factions within the ranks of the Protestants.[362] In time even Luther also began to accept Bucer's sincerity, especially when he learned that the extreme Zwinglians were turning against Bucer. A delegation consisting of Gereon Sailer and Caspar Huber of Augsburg visited Wittenberg in July, 1535, and met with the Wittenberg leaders.[363] They had brought Bucer's *Simple Report,* a combination of the former *Report* against the Anabaptists and the *Ten Articles* which he had drawn up in May, 1535, to satisfy some of the Reformed cities of south-western Germany.[364] Luther was so impressed by its content that he wept tears of joy at the peace about to be realized. Out of these beginnings grew the famous *Wittenberg Concord* of 1536.

On April 11, 1536, Bucer received a letter from Luther inviting him and other Reformed theologians to a meeting at Eisenach on May 14.[365] Although the Swiss could not send a representative, a number of the southwestern cities did send delegates. The envoys arrived in Eisenach only to learn that Luther was not there. After waiting a few days, they continued their journey toward Wittenberg. At Gotha they learned that Luther had become ill, and at Grimma they were met by Melanchthon and Cruciger with the further discouraging news that Luther had been much offended by a recent publication of the letters of Zwingli and Oecolampadius containing a prefatory letter by Bucer.[366] Undaunted, the party continued and arrived in Wittenberg on Sunday evening, May 21, 1536.[367] While Luther was eating his evening meal, Bucer explained that the offensive preface had been a letter which he had written several years earlier and which the publisher had used without his consent. The discussions continued until midnight, while Luther sat in an armchair, still too ill to move about freely.[368]

The next morning Bucer and Capito called on Luther in his home and delivered the letters and documents which they had brought. It was agreed that the Lutherans should first decide among themselves the doctrines on which agreement should be sought and that Bucer and his party would present a written state-

ment of their present position on them.[369] Luther's first reaction to
the documents and the sincerity of the Zwinglians was rather
dubious. When he addressed the entire group at three in the afternoon, his apparent lack of confidence in their sincerity considerably
shocked the delegates to the conference.[370] Bucer, taken aback,
tried to collect himself and expressed his surprise at Luther's sus-
picions of their motives. He explained still further the recent
Zwinglian publication, and gradually Luther began to believe that
perhaps Bucer was not so much involved as had been thought.[371]

The next day they gathered again in Luther's study and found
the Reformer in a more receptive mood. Bucer was prepared to
make a definite proposition which he hoped would further clear
the air. He admitted that he had formerly been in error about the
Lutheran teachings and that he had changed his views on the partaking of the Holy Eucharist by the "wicked." These he divided
into the "unworthy," of whom Paul speaks, and the "unbelievers."
The former partake of the Lord's Supper to their damnation, while
the latter "received no more than a worm." He added that he did
not believe the reception of Christ's body and blood depended
upon man's belief or disbelief.[372] His statement impressed Luther,
but he was not sure that the entire group shared that belief. Upon
questioning each member individually, Luther learned that they
had been teaching this viewpoint in their home communities for
over a year.[373] They also accepted the Augsburg Confession and
the Apology.[374] The Lutheran theologians withdrew to another
room for a private conference in which they agreed that the worst
obstacle had been removed. It was decided that Luther should
ask them one more question: Was it true that the bread of Christ
when given to the unworthy was still the body of Christ? The
Zwinglians readily granted this point.[375] Their declaration was followed by great exultation. Each gave the other the hand of Christian fellowship, while Bucer and Capito wept tears of joy.[376]

On the following day Baptism, absolution, and the educational
system were discussed.[377] On Thursday Luther's illness became
worse, and the conferences were temporarily discontinued, but on
Friday the forms of the church service, images, vestments, the
elevation of the host, and other outward practices were discussed.[378]

Many of the southwestern cities had progressed more rapidly in eliminating these non-essentials than had Wittenberg. On Saturday there were further discussions on the Basel Confession and the approach to be used to win the Swiss.

Now that all obstacles toward Christian fellowship had been removed, a joint service was arranged at which Matthew Alber of Reutlingen preached in the morning and Bucer in the afternoon. On this occasion Holy Communion was also celebrated in all simplicity.[379] Indeed, it seemed as though the day of a unified Protestantism had dawned. Melanchthon was selected to prepare a report of the discussions between the Lutherans and the Zwinglians, the document which was later known as the *Wittenberg Concord*.[380] It contained a rather detailed explanation of their common belief on the Lord's Supper in phraseology both sides could accept, even though the words were differently interpreted by each group. This document was not meant to supplant the Augsburg Confession, but rather to explain in more detail the points in question between the Zwinglians and the Lutherans.[381] While the *Wittenberg Concord* did not result in an organic union of the Protestants, it did end the strife and bitterness between the Lutherans and the Zwinglians of southwestern Germany and prepared the way for a formula that outwardly satisfied both groups. It also divided the Zwinglians into two groups, those who followed Bucer and the Strassburgers and those ultra-Zwinglians who still retained the extreme symbolical view of the Lord's Supper. The latter group continued to draw farther away from the Wittenberg theologians, while Bucer and his group became more Lutheran.[382]

In the middle thirties Charles V seemed to be successful in his attempt to persuade the new pope, Paul III, to summon a general council. The meeting place was to be Mantua and the date June 2, 1536.[383] The Protestants were invited to send delegates. By this time the Lutheran *Landeskirche* had progressed in its organization to a point where not too much could be expected from a general church council. Yet, to be prepared for any and every emergency, the young Elector John Frederick called the Lutheran princes together at Schmalkalden to draw up the necessary articles for presentation on such an occasion.

The Schmalkald Articles

Although Charles V had been busy with secular problems after the Diet of Augsburg, he had not forgotten his promise to the German princes of a Christian council to settle finally the problem of reform, nor had he abandoned hope that the Lutherans at last might be brought back into the fold.[384] There was agitation for such a council in France and England as well as in the German lands. Paul III also realized that the Lutheran movement could be arrested only by some much-needed reforms in the Roman Church.[385] In February, 1536, the Pope sent his able and somewhat liberal-minded nuncio Paolo Vergerio to prepare the way for a council by visiting Wittenberg itself.[386] With Bugenhagen he was invited to Luther's home for dinner, the first time he had met the Saxon leader. As Luther himself admitted, he was far from servile and apologetic with the papal legate, in fact, he was almost condescending.[387] When Vergerio brought up the subject of the Christian council, Luther's answer took him greatly by surprise. Instead of excusing the reforms that had been made in Saxon lands, Luther replied:

> Our group does not need a council, for we already have the firm evangelical teaching and order of service; but Christendom needs it, that that part which is still held captive may discover error and truth.[388]

When Vergerio raised his voice in angry reply, Luther became equally vehement, but he agreed to attend such a council.[389] Later he told the Elector he doubted that such a council would aid their difficulties. When the legate later met Elector John Frederick in Prague, he discovered that the prince was in complete agreement with his Wittenberg theologians.[390] If the Pope had thought the Lutheran princes would easily be brought back into line, he was to be deeply disappointed, for at Schmalkalden they replied to the papal invitation with the following conditions: (1) It would have to be a free Christian council, not a papal one in which everything was settled beforehand; (2) it would have to be a council in which all the estates were represented on equal terms, not regarding the Protestants as heretics; (3) the basis of judgment would have to be the Bible rather than human decision of the Papacy; (4) unless it was absolutely impossible, such a council should meet in German lands.[391]

Elector John Frederick and Chancellor Brueck visited Wittenberg to discuss the problem of preparing for the council with the theological faculty of the University. Several documents were prepared during the summer, none of which quite satisfied the Elector. Finally, Luther turned his attention to the problem and, according to a letter from Brueck to the court, began work early in September. Luther no longer had any hope of reconciling the Lutheran and Roman faiths through a Christian council. However, should the Elector require some articles of faith, he would prepare a Lutheran confession which would serve a double purpose.[392] On the one hand, he had never been quite satisfied with the Augsburg Confession or the Apology, as he felt Melanchthon had tried to minimize the differences between the Roman and the Protestant teachings. His articles for the Elector would bring out in much sharper relief the distinctive features of Lutheranism and could be used at the council to show in what ways the Gospel ministry differed from the Roman priesthood. On the other hand, Luther believed that he would not live much longer. Should the Lutheran princes never have an opportunity to present these articles of faith, they would still serve as a last testament to the faith and teachings of Martin Luther, so that posterity could know exactly what his position had been.[393] The Schmalkald Articles are a declaration of independence on the part of Luther from the compromising *Leisetreterei* of Melanchthon at the Diet of Augsburg.[394] They also mark the final establishment of the Lutheran *Landeskirche* as a distinct outward body completely separated from the Roman Church.

Again many details of the drafting of the Schmalkald Articles are lacking. Luther seems to have consulted Agricola and Spalatin on December 15, and according to Spalatin's *Annales* the document was ready for presentation to a group of theologians by Christmas.

> 1537. During the beginning of this year, from Christmas [1536] on, we were together at Wittenberg upon the order of Duke John, the Elector of Saxony, namely, Doctor Martin Luther, Doctor Justus Jonas, the Propst, Doctor Caspar Creutziger, Doctor Johannes Bugenhagen, Pommer, Licentiate Nicholas Amsdorf, Philip Melanchthon, Johannes Agricola of Eisleben, and I, George Spalatin. And

we all agreed and signed the twenty-one most important articles of Christian doctrine, which the Honorable Learned Mister Doctor Martin Luther has prepared in all purity and Christian piety and which were then read, considered consecutively, weighed, and treated. These were also signed by the following Christian and evangelical princes, estates, and theologians on the evangelical day of Schmalkalden, except for Hesse, Wuerttemberg, Strassburg, etc.[395]

On January 3, 1537, these twenty-one articles were carried to the Elector by Spalatin.[396] By January 7 Elector John Frederick wrote to Luther, expressing his real joy over the new articles of faith. After reading them twice, he declared them to be Christian and right, and he was ready to defend them before the proposed council. He next asked Brueck to arrange for the leading theologians in his lands to sign the articles also so that, should Luther be called from this life, they would be committed to this confession.[397]

To make further preparations for a general council, the Elector summoned a group of princes and theologians to Schmalkalden early in 1537. On January 31 Luther, Melanchthon, and Bugenhagen began the journey to Schmalkalden.[398] They arrived on February 7 and found that in addition to the princes about forty theologians had gathered for the meeting. The Elector requested Luther to prepare a directive for his conduct in relationship to the summons to the council. Brueck requested all the theologians present to acquaint themselves with the Schmalkald Articles so that they would know their content should they be presented to the proposed council.[399] Unfortunately, Luther became very ill, and Melanchthon again had to take his place in the discussions which followed. Almost at once he fell under the influence of Philip of Hesse and began to belittle Luther's accomplishment.[400] He explained that the Lord's Supper received more emphasis than in the *Wittenberg Concord* because of Luther and Bugenhagen. He also pointed out the difference between the treatment of the Lord's Supper in Luther's articles and in the Augsburg Confession and Apology, which they had already accepted.[401] Under his leadership it was decided to use the two documents he had drawn up previously and merely to fortify them still more with Scripture.

In neither of the two confessions of Melanchthon was there a clear-cut statement about the primacy of the Papacy. Melanchthon was now assigned the task of remedying the defect. By February 17 he had completed *A Tract on the Power and Primacy of the Papacy,* to which he later added a second part, *On the Power and Jurisdiction of Bishops.*[402] The delegation accepted and signed these statements on a plane with the Augsburg Confession and the Apology.[403] It was further decided that the Protestants would not attend the Council of Mantua, as the purpose of the Council was to "exterminate the Lutheran heresy." [404] By February 23, 1537, the deliberations had been concluded, and the meeting dissolved.

In one sense the Schmalkald Articles have been misnamed, for due to Luther's illness and the opposition of the southwestern German cities they were never presented at this conference. Spalatin, however, apparently prepared a copy of them under the title *Reflections on Faith and the Position on Which a Stand is to be Taken at a Future Council,*[405] which was signed by most of the theologians present. The eight principal theologians had signed previously in Wittenberg on New Year's. Owing to his grievous illness, Luther did not know what had happened to his articles of faith at Schmalkalden. He still wished them to stand as his testament to Lutheranism and thought they might still be used as the basis of doctrinal consideration at a future council. In the spring of 1538 he carefully re-edited the Schmalkald Articles and permitted their publication.[406] Before his death they had begun to displace the importance of the Augsburg Confession and the Apology as the official Lutheran position on many doubtful points. In the strife between Jena and Wittenberg in the confused years following Luther's death, Luther's testament became all the more important, for it distinguished between the compromises of Melanchthon and the stand of Luther, who in this document declared his position on the points that his fellow professor had tried to minimize because of his fear. The Schmalkald Articles, therefore, became the official declaration of Lutheran independence from the Roman Church.[407]

Since 1523 Martin Luther had faced the problem of determining the position of the Evangelicals in the larger body of Christendom. As noted earlier, Luther clearly distinguished between the Christian Church as the invisible body of Jesus Christ and the Lutheran *Landeskirche,* composed of congregations scattered throughout Germany.[408] In earlier years he still hoped that those Christians who had accepted the Reformation would in time win over all the remainder. As he expressed his view to Vergerio in 1535, he was convinced that only those parts of Christendom still in darkness needed a Christian council.[409] Luther's conception of the Christian Church was a contributing factor to his lack of interest in outward organic union. After he had rejected the Roman concept of the Christian Church as an outward organization, he never returned to this view which identified the Church with a corporate body.[410] The key to the "true" Church was "justification by faith," by which the believer became a member of that great invisible body which Christ had joined unto Himself through faith. Luther never dignified the Lutheran *Landeskirche,* made up of individual congregations, with the title "Church" and further claimed that, when so used, the title was a misnomer.[411] He stood firm in his conviction that he had not started a new organization, as he pointed out in his tract *On Councils and Churches* in 1539,[412] but merely re-established those conditions under which the original Christian Church had flourished, the same Church which had lived on through the centuries, although the Roman Church in its corporate conception and human innovations had departed from the faith.

The many attempts to achieve unity can be examined in their proper perspective only when it is recalled that prior to the Council of Trent (1545–1563) there was no single accepted body of Christian dogma that might be dignified as solely orthodox, but rather there were many schools of thought flourishing under the Catholic canopy.[413] Not until 1563 was Thomism officially recognized.[414] Since the Evangelicals believed that they had returned to the Gospel preaching and pristine purity of early Christianity, they hoped for a general council which would examine the bases of each group with equal impartiality and determine whether they or the traditionalists were right. There was as yet no thought that the Lutherans and the Reformed groups had started new church bodies. In its embryonic form this concept can first be found in the Melanchthonian document, the Augsburg Confession, the Apology, and the *Loci of 1543,*[415] but it does not come to its full realization until several decades after Luther's death. The Reformer died in the belief that he had restored the Gospel and the Sacraments of early Christianity.[416]

The Close of Life

THE AGING LUTHER

THE YEARS OF LUTHER'S LIFE from 1537 on are noted for a strange contradiction. His home life, the table companions, his work on the Bible translation, the many visitors who sought his counsel, the growth of his beloved Lutheran university, all contributed to make these the happiest years of his life.[1] Although he was frequently ill, the *Table Talks* and other sources indicate that he had not lost the humor and congeniality which made him so popular with his friends.

Yet these closing years of Luthers' life are marred with several unfortunate incidents and marked by bitter polemics. One of the incidents was the "Turkish marriage," in which the already married Landgrave Philip of Hesse secretly married Margaret von der Saale on March 4, 1540. This episode has been treated in detail by Heinrich Boehmer.[2] Judged by present-day standards, Luther made a grievous error in judgment in giving his consent. In his defense Boehmer points out that Philip withheld some of the facts from Luther and that there were many instances of similar cases which had established precedent for his action.[3] His enjoinder to secrecy was a remnant from his Catholic background which maintained that the confidences given and advice received in the confessional were to be held inviolable by both parties.[4] When Luther later learned the whole truth, he was furious, claiming that not even an angel from heaven could have won this concession from him.[5] Naturally his Catholic enemies seized upon and misrepresented his role in the unfortunate affair.

745

Also unfortunate was Luther's apparent sanction of the persecution of the Anabaptists by the evangelical princes.[6] Against the
background of the Inquisition and the general intolerance of the
age this is understandable, but the Evangelicals were claiming to
preach the Gospel of peace. In this light the intolerance of Luther,
Calvin, Zwingli, and many of the lesser lights toward those who
did not agree with their interpretation of the Bible is difficult to
rationalize.[7] Into this same category fall the wars with the Anti-
nomians, extreme Zwinglians, and other radical groups.[8]

With his increasing disappointment with the refusal of Christendom to accept his reforms, Luther's bitterness toward those who
constantly were attacking him likewise increased. No better example of this bitterness and violent language can be found than
in his final tracts against Rome.[9] In 1537 he published a translation
of the so-called *Donation of Constantine*,[10] which he described as
a "shameful, desperate, and wicked lie" which all these years had
supported a despicable system. Even more bitter invective was
directed against three of his Catholic enemies in Germany, Duke
George of Albertine Saxony, Duke Henry of Brunswick, and the
Archbishop Albert of Mainz. In fairness to Luther it must be
pointed out that his tracts are but half of the story. Too often the
attacks launched against him are overlooked, and only his more
famous replies come under scrutiny. His enemies were equally
violent and abusive.[11] Luther's tract *On Councils and Churches*
(1539)[12] and *Against Jack Sausage* (1541)[13] were both written in
support of his view that the Reformation had not introduced a new
Church into Christendom, but had really restored the Church of
the Apostolic Fathers. "Jack Sausage" was Henry of Brunswick,
who had seized upon the Hesse marriage to attack both his personal enemy, Philip, and the Reformation, of which Philip was a
part. In Henry's case the pot was calling the kettle black, for his
own life was anything but an exemplary example.[14] Far the most
bitter of all of Luther's polemics was *Against the Papacy of Rome,
Founded by the Devil*, written in 1545, the year before he died.[15]
In speaking of the "hellish Roman Church," Luther wrote:

> One would like to curse them, so that thunder and lightning would
> strike them, hell-fire burn them, the plague, syphilis, epilepsy,
> scurvy, leprosy, carbuncles, and all diseases attack them.[16]

Bullinger, the Swiss Reformer, claimed he had never read anything more "savage or imprudent." [17] Such violent attacks not only nullified any good they might have accomplished, but also reflected unfavorably on the Reformer and his work.[18]

With all of his faults, the verdict of history has found in Martin Luther a man lovable in his human frailty, ever true to his convictions, imbued with indomitable courage, and unswerving in devotion to that which he believed. In the words of that most able neutral historian Preserved Smith:

> Measured by the work that he accomplished and by the impression that his personality made both on contemporaries and on posterity, there are few men like him in history. Dogmatic, superstitious, intolerant, overbearing, and violent as he was, he yet had that inscrutable prerogative of genius of transforming what he touched into new values. His contemporaries bore his invective because of his earnestness; they bowed to "the almost disgraceful servitude" which, says Melanchthon, he imposed upon his followers, because they knew that he was leading them to victory in a great and worthy cause. Even so, now, many men overlook his narrowness and bigotry because of his genius and bravery.
>
> His grandest quality was sincerity. Priest and public man as he was, there was not a line of hypocrisy or cant in his whole being. A sham was to him intolerable, the abomination of desolation standing where it ought not. Reckless of consequences, of danger, of his popularity, and of his life, he blurted out the whole truth, as he saw it, "despite all cardinals, popes, kings, and emperors, together with all devils and hell." Whether his ideal is ours or not, his courage in daring and his strength to labor for it must command our respect.[19]

LUTHER'S DEATH

Of no event in history are more details known than of the death of Martin Luther.[20] His contemporaries and companions must have realized the importance of an accurate account for future generations, for the fourteen eyewitnesses present at his bedside prepared a certified document which appeared in print a few months after his death. On the basis of this document and other accounts the closing days of Luther's life can be reviewed with accuracy.[21]

During the twenty years in which Luther was a monk he exposed his body to many hardships. The many fastings, wakings, prayers, and penances took their toll of even his robust frame. Added to this rigorous physical self-discipline were his constant labors as a professor, preacher, and author, and the strain of the controversy which raged over and around him during his last twenty years. Until his forty-second year he was thin and under-nourished, owing to his utter disregard of his bodily needs. Luther was one of those exacting individuals who would stay at their desk night and day until they had completed an undertaking. Often he dashed off material for publication comprising over a hundred pages in print in the unbelievably short time of a few days or a week, but during that time he worked almost unceasingly. He seldom gave his body proper rest. When one considers the combina-tion of prodigious labor, nervous tension, and undernourishment, it is not strange that Martin Luther was a sick man for much of his life-time and that he died at the relatively early age of sixty-two.[22]

Luther suffered many illnesses throughout his lifetime. Boeh-mer says he was a sick man from his fortieth year on and believes that this condition contributed greatly to his increasing im-patience and irascibility.[23] Jonas described an illness in July, 1527, which began with "a loud and troublesome roaring in the left ear, which the physicians said was a precursor of a fainting spell." [24] References to attacks of "the stone" are frequent in Luther's cor-respondence. A particularly violent attack occurred at Schmal-kalden in 1537, and another in 1545 caused his friends and family to fear for his life.[25] In a letter to Melanchthon in 1541 he men-tioned a painful and wearing infection of the ear.[26] Added to the sufferings of his many illnesses, and perhaps abetted by them, was an increasingly pessimistic view of the success of the Gospel move-ment. Many times Luther expressed the wish that God would call him to his heavenly rest.[27] His faith in God and his conviction that he was God's instrument on earth never left him, but the note of world-weariness became increasingly frequent in his letters and conversation.[28]

Late in 1545 the princes of Mansfeld engaged in a bitter family quarrel, which Luther was finally asked to arbitrate.[29] Old and ill as he was, he was not eager to undertake a journey from Witten-berg to Eisleben, a distance of some eighty miles, in the midst of winter; but his strong sense of duty and consideration for the welfare of his home country finally persuaded him to attempt the task. Accompanied by his sons Martin and Paul, the party set out for Mansfeld on January 23, 1546.[30] Jonas joined the party at Halle, where they were delayed several days because of the flooded condition of the Saale River, which they finally crossed by boat.[31] At the border of the domain of the Prince of Mansfeld they were met by an escort of 113 horsemen.[32] The journey proved even more arduous than had been anticipated, and Luther was extremely fatigued when he arrived at the prince's quarters in Eisleben on the evening of January 28. After a hot bath and massage he felt considerably refreshed and dined with the family in jovial mood.[33]

The following three weeks proved very trying. The tangled affairs of the princes and the incessant wrangling of their lawyers taxed Luther's patience exceedingly. In addition to these labors he was asked to preach four times and participated in the distribution of Communion and the ordination of two clergymen.[34] He seemed to be feeling fairly well, however, and apparently enjoyed participating in lively conversations with the princes, his fellow professor Jonas, the neighboring minister Coelius, Aurifaber, and others.[35] His friends noted that frequent references to death and the hereafter crept into his conversation, and several times he was observed standing before his bedroom window deeply lost in prayer.

The dispute was finally settled amicably on February 17. During the day Luther's sons and close friends detected his apparent fatigue and urged him to rest.[36] After the evening meal his sons followed their father to his rooms, for they did not wish him to be left alone.[37] Later Jonas, Aurifaber, and Coelius joined them. Luther complained of a sharp pain in his chest in the neighborhood of the heart.[38] Hot baths and massage were given to improve his circulation, and the prince recommended his own medicine. About nine o'clock he fell asleep and slept quietly for nearly an hour.[39] When he wakened, he seemed surprised that the others had not retired and expressed his desire to do so. He went into the adjoining bedroom and again fell asleep.[40]

An uneasiness pervaded the little group of companions, and they kept the rooms warm and lamps lighted for any emergency.

About two o'clock Luther suffered another sharp seizure of pains around the heart.[41] He returned to the couch in the living room where the former hot-towel treatment was repeated.[42] Pillows were heated and placed around his body in an attempt to stimulate the circulation. The attack passed, and the patient once more fell into a light sleep which was of short duration. The third attack was much more severe, and the physicians who were quickly summoned knew the end was near.[43] It was clearly evident that he, too, realized that this was the long-awaited release. In spite of his weakness he recited several passages of Scriptures and repeatedly commended his soul to God. The doctors tried to strengthen him by injecting a stimulant into his veins, but he grew steadily weaker.[44] Finally, Jonas asked in a penetrating voice: "Reverend Father, are you willing to die in the name of the Christ and the doctrine which you have preached?" Luther rallied his last strength and replied "Yes" so distinctly that the whole group heard it.[45] Shortly thereafter the anxious watchers thought he had again fallen asleep, but the doctors informed them that it was the sleep from which there would be no awaking in this world. Although they continued their attempts to revive him, their efforts were futile, and the doctors declared him officially dead.[46]

By daybreak many prominent citizens of the town and neighboring princes had received the news of Luther's death and hastened to the bedside where his body rested until the tin coffin could be prepared.[47] Later in the day his body was removed to Doctor Trachstet's house to await the funeral service, held at two o'clock on February 19 in St. Andrew's Church just across the street from the house where Luther had died.[48] Here in the church, where he had last preached and not more than a few blocks from where he was born, his friend Professor Jonas delivered a stirring funeral sermon.[49] While waiting for official instructions as to interment, the body rested in the choir of this church, guarded by the citizens.

In the forenoon of February 20 a second memorial service was held in the church, conducted by the Reverend Coelius.[50] By this time the local prince had received the request from Luther's prince, John Frederick, that the body be returned to Wittenberg, there to be buried with distinction in the Castle Church, so intimately associated with Luther in life.[51] Between twelve and one o'clock of the same day the funeral procession started from Eisleben under the escort of the prince's officials, who were to continue as far as Bitterfeld, where they would be relieved by the Elector's officials, who would provide the escort to Wittenberg.

So began the long and mournful homeward journey.[52] All along the route crowds of sorrowing people gathered from the neighboring countryside, some having traveled several miles to honor one of Germany's leading citizens.[53] Bells tolled as the procession passed through the villages. In Halle a reception party waited several miles outside the city. The city pastors, the town council, teachers, and school children singing hymns joined the procession as it entered the city gates. The streets of the town were so overcrowded with vehicles and people that the funeral party could scarcely make its way to one of the churches, where the body rested overnight.[54]

Early the next morning at six o'clock the procession continued from the Church of Our Dear Lady. About noon of that day, which happened to be Sunday, the party reached Bitterfeld on the border of Electoral Saxony.[55] Here the change of escort was effected, and by evening the town of Kemberg just outside Wittenberg was reached.[56] Here the body rested in the same church where Luther had first introduced the "Lutheran" church service before substituting it for the Catholic liturgy in Wittenberg. On Monday, February 22, Luther's body finally returned to Wittenberg by way of the Elster Gate near the University. Here the university faculty, the leading city officials, and numerous citizens joined the final procession down the long, narrow college avenue leading to the Castle Church.[57] Near the town square they were joined by the student body, led by the pastor of the Town Church, Johannes Bugenhagen, who was also a professor of the theological faculty.

Leading the procession were two mounted knights, accompanied by sixty horsemen preceding the hearse.[58] In a carriage immediately behind the hearse rode Luther's wife, Kathie, accompanied by several distinguished ladies and followed by a carriage in which rode the three sons, Johannes, Martin, and Paul, and

their uncle Jacob, a burgher from Mansfeld.[59] These were followed
by several other carriages filled with relatives. Next came the
faculty of the University, led by the Rector, then the students, the
town council, many distinguished citizens, and several thousand
people.[60]

The large Castle Church was filled to capacity. The body entered the church by the north door, the same door on which had
been nailed the *Ninety-Five Theses,* and was placed near the pulpit
on the south side.[61] The moving addresses delivered by Bugenhagen and Melanchthon made the vast audience deeply aware
of the fact that one of the great leaders of history had been taken
from their midst.[62] Bugenhagen eulogized Luther as one of the
leading citizens of Germany, a national hero. Melanchthon compared him to Moses, who had also been reluctant to undertake
God's command to lead His people from the wilderness. Melanchthon further called him one of the greatest theologians since
St. Paul, pointing out his great courage, his indomitable will, and
his unflagging zeal for the cause of the Gospel.[63] He called attention to the fact that Luther's anger had never been unloosed for
personal gain or satisfaction, but only when he felt the Gospel was
being hindered or the faith maligned.[64] After the service the body
was lowered into the grave prepared beneath the floor of the
church directly in front of the pulpit. A special stone tablet was
ordered to be placed over the final resting place.[65]

Among the many unsupported tales circulated concerning the
death and burial of Luther was one which claimed that the troops
of Charles V had desecrated the grave and destroyed the remains
during their sack of Wittenberg in the Schmalkaldic War. Professor H. Heubner, keeper of the town archives, was present at the
restoration of the Castle Church in 1892 and saw the coffin at
that time. It was well preserved and still contained the mortal
remains of the great Reformer slowly turning to dust.[66]

Bibliographical Notes

Abbreviations of Titles Frequently Cited

KEY	TITLE
Album	*Album Academiae Vitebergensis,* C. E. Foerstemann (Leipzig, 1841 ff.), 3 Vols.
Allen, *Opus Erasmi*	*Opus epistolarum Des. Erasmi Roterdami,* ed., P. S. Allen (Oxonii, 1906 ff.), 5 Vols.
A. R.	*Archiv fuer Reformationsgeschichte,* ed., Walter Friedensburg (Berlin, 1904–1943), 40 Vols.
Barge, *Karlstadt*	Hermann Barge, *Andreas Bodenstein von Karlstadt* (Leipzig, 1905), 2 Vols.
Boedler	K. E. F. Boedler, *Die Gewalt der askanischen Herzoege in Westfalen und Engern bis zum Ausgang des 14. Jahrhunderts* (Halle a. S., 1912).
Boehmer, *Luthers erste Vorlesung*	Heinrich Boehmer, *Luthers erste Vorlesung* (Leipzig, 1924).
Boehmer, *L. L. R. R.*	Heinrich Boehmer, *Luther in Light of Recent Research* (New York, 1916).
Boehmer, *Romfahrt*	Heinrich Boehmer, *Luthers Romfahrt* (Leipzig, 1914).
Borcherdt, *Werke*	*Martin Luther, Ausgewaehlte Werke,* ed., Hans Heinrich Borcherdt (Muenchen, 1922 ff.), 8 Vols.
Brandi, *Deutsche Reformation*	Karl Brandi, *Deutsche Reformation und Gegenreformation* (Leipzig, 1927).
Brieger, "Die Torgauer Artikel"	Theodor Brieger, "Die Torgauer Artikel, Ein Beitrag zur Entstehungsgeschichte der Augsburgischen Confession," · *Kirchengeschichtliche Studien* (Leipzig, 1888).
Bruchmann, *Luthers Bibelverdeutschung*	Gerhard Bruchmann, "Luthers Bibelverdeutschung auf der Wartburg in ihrem Verhaeltnis zu den mittelalterlichen Uebersetzungen," *Luther-Jahrbuch,* XVIII (1936).
Burkhardt, *G. K. S.*	C. A. H. Burkhardt, *Geschichte der saechsischen Kirchen und Schulvisitationen von 1524 bis 1545* (Leipzig, 1879).

753

KEY	TITLE
Charitius	M. D. Andreas Charitius, *Chronik des Wittenberger Archidiakonus* (c. 1740). Unpublished in Max Senf Collection, Wittenberg, Germany.
Clark, *Libraries*	J. W. Clark, *Libraries in the Medieval and Renaissance Periods* (Cambridge, 1894).
Colloquia	*D. Martini Lutheri Colloquia, Meditationes, Consolationes, iudicia* etc., ed., H. E. Bindseil (1863–1866), 3 Vols.
C. R.	*Philippi Melanchthonis Opera, Corpus Reformatorum*, ed., C. G. Bretschneider und H. E. Bindseil (Halis Saxonium, 1834 ff.), 28 Vols.
Cyprian	Wilhelm Ernst Tentzel, *Historischer Bericht vom Anfang und ersten Fortgang der Reformation Lutheri*, ed., Ernst Salomon Cyprian (Leipzig, 1718), Third Edition.
De Jongh, *Louvain*	H. de Jongh, *L'Ancienne Faculté de Théologie de Louvain au Premier Siecle de son Existence* (1911).
Deutsche Reichstagsakten	*Deutsche Reichstagsakten unter Karl V* (Gotha, 1896), 4 Vols. Eds., A. Kluckholm und A. Wrede.
De Wette	*Martin Luthers Briefe*, ed., Wilhelm Martin Leberecht de Wette (Berlin, 1825–1828), 5 Vols.
Dialogus of 1507	*Dialogus illustrate ac augustissime urbis Albiorenae, vulge Wittenberg dicte, situm, amenitatem ac illustrationem docens tirocinia nobilium artium jacientibus editus*, Andreas Meinhardi (Leipzig, 1508).
Die Wartburg	*Die Wartburg*, ed., Max Baumgaertel (Berlin, 1907).
Dilichs, *Federzeichnungen*	Wilhelm Dilichs, *Federzeichnungen Kursaechsischer und Meissnischer Ortschaften aus den Jahren 1626–1629*, eds., Paul E. Richter und Christian Krollmann (Dresden, 1907).
Drews, *Der evangelische Geistliche*	Paul Drews, *Der evangelische Geistliche in der deutschen Vergangenheit* (Jena, 1905). In *Monographien zur deutschen Kulturgeschichte*, ed., Georg Steinhausen.
Drews, *Spalatiniana*	D. Drews, "Spalatiniana," *Z. K. G.*, XIX (1899).

KEY	TITLE
E. A.	*Dr. Martin Luthers saemmtliche Werke* (Erlangen, 1826 ff.), 65 Vols. First Edition.
Eells, *Martin Bucer*	H. Eells, *Martin Bucer* (New Haven, 1931).
Eger, *Luthers Gottesdienstreform*	Karl Eger, "Luthers Gottesdienstreform 1523– 1526," *Luther-Mitteilungen der Luthergesellschaft*, VII (1925).
Enders	*Dr. Martin Luthers Briefwechsel*, eds., E. L. Enders und G. Kawerau (Stuttgart und Leipzig, 1884 ff.), 19 Vols.
Eschenhagen, "Wittenberger Studien"	Edith Eschenhagen, "Wittenberger Studien," *Luther-Jahrbuch*, IX (1927).
Faber, *Historische Nachricht*	Matthaeus Faber, *Kurtzgefasste Historische Nachricht von der Schlosz und Academischen Stiffts Kirche zu Aller-Heiligen* etc. (Wittenberg, 1717).
Ferguson, *Opuscula Erasmi*	W. Ferguson, *Opuscula Erasmi Quae in Operibus a Clerico Editis Desiderantur* (Haag, 1927). Thesis.
Ficker, *Die Konfutation*	Johannes Ficker, *Die Konfutation des Augsburgischen Bekenntnisses, Ihre Gestalt und ihre Geschichte* (Leipzig, 1891).
Ficker, *Exposition of Luther's Pictures*	Johannes Ficker, *Ansprache zur Eroeffnung der Lutherbildnis-Ausstellung im Provinzialmuseum zu Halle, Luther, Vierteljahrsschrift der Luthergesellschaft*, XIII (Muenchen, 1931).
Ficker, *Roemerbrief*	*Luthers Vorlesung ueber den Roemerbrief, 1515–1516*, ed., Johannes Ficker (Leipzig, 1908), 2 Vols.
Foerstemann, *Urkundenbuch*	*Neues Urkundenbuch zur Geschichte der evangelischen Kirchen Reformation*, ed., Carl Foerstemann (Hamburg, 1842), I.
Friedensburg, *Urkundenbuch*	*Urkundenbuch der Universitaet Wittenberg*, ed., Walter Friedensburg (Magdeburg, 1926 to 1927), 2 Vols.
Friedensburg, *G. U. W.*	Walter Friedensburg, *Geschichte der Universitaet Wittenberg* (Halle, 1917).
Geffcken, *Bilderkatechismus*	*Der Bilderkatechismus des 15. Jahrhunderts*, ed., Joh. Geffcken (1855).

Key	Title
Gess, *Akten und Briefe*	*Akten und Briefe zur Kirchenpolitik Herzog Georgs von Sachsen,* ed., G. Gess (Leipzig, 1905 ff.), 2 Vols.
Goulet, *Compendium*	Robert Goulet, *Compendium Universitatis Parisiensis,* 1517, tr., R. B. Burke (1928).
Greving, *Corpus Catholicorum*	J. Greving, *Corpus Catholicorum,* I (1919).
Grisar, *Luther zu Worms*	Hartmann Grisar, *Luther zu Worms und die juengsten drei Jahrhundertfeste der Reformation* (Freiburg, 1921).
Grohmann, *Annalen*	*Annalen der Universitaet Wittenberg,* ed., J. C. A. Grohmann (Meissen, 1801), 2 Vols.
Gussmann, *Quellen*	*Quellen und Forschungen zur Geschichte des Augsburgischen Glaubensbekenntnisses,* ed., Wilhelm Gussmann (Leipzig und Berlin, 1911), 2 Vols.
Hauszleiter, *D. U. W.*	Johannes Hauszleiter, *Die Universitaet Wittenberg vor dem Eintritt Luthers, Nach der Schilderung des Mag. Andreas Meinhardi vom Jahre 1507* (Leipzig, 1903).
Heeren und Ukert	A. H. L. Heeren und F. A. Ukert, *Geschichte der Europaeischen Staaten, Geschichte des Kurstaates und Koenigreiches Sachsens,* ed., C. W. Boettiger (Hamburg, 1830).
Heubner, *Schlosz*	H. Heubner, *Der Bau des kurfuerstlichen Schloszes* (Wittenberg, 1937).
Hirschfeld	G. von Hirschfeld, *Geschichte der Saechsisch-Askanischen Kurfuersten.*
Holborn, *Ulrich von Hutten*	Hajo Holborn, *Ulrich von Hutten and the German Reformation,* tr., Roland Bainton (New Haven, 1937).
Holl, *G. A.*	Karl Holl, *Gesammelte Aufsaetze zur Kirchengeschichte* (Tuebingen, 1921 ff.), 3 Vols.
Holman, *W. M. L.*	*Works of Martin Luther,* tr., C. M. Jacobs *et al.* (Philadelphia, 1915), 6 Vols.
Huizinga, "Das Problem der Renaissance"	J. Huizinga, "Das Problem der Renaissance," *Wege der Kulturgeschichte* (Muenchen, 1930).
Hutten, *Opera*	*Ulrichi Hutteri, equitis Germani, opera,* etc., ed., Eduard Boecking (Leipzig, 1859 ff), 7 Vols.

KEY	TITLE
H. V.	*Historische Vierteljahrschrift,* ed., G. Seeliger (Leipzig, 1898 ff.).
H. Z.	*Historische Zeitschrift,* eds., H. von Sybel *et al.* (Muenchen, 1859 ff.).
I. M. R.	*Im Morgenrot der Reformation,* ed., Julius von Pflugk-Harttung (Hersfeld, 1915).
Joachimsen, "Humanismus"	Paul Joachimsen, "Der Humanismus und die Entwicklung des deutschen Geistes," *Deutsche Vierteljahrschrift fuer Literaturwissenschaft und Geistesgeschichte* (Halle, 1930).
Kalkoff, *Depeschen*	*Die Depeschen des Nuntius Aleander vom Wormser Reichstage 1521,* tr. and ed., Paul Kalkoff, S. V. R. G., XVII (1886). First Edition.
Kalkoff, *Forschungen*	Paul Kalkoff, *Forschungen zu Luthers roemischem Process* (Rom, 1905).
Kalkoff, *Entstehung des Wormser Edikts*	Paul Kalkoff, *Die Entstehung des Wormser Edikts, Eine Geschichte des Wormser Reichstags vom Standpunkt der lutherischen Frage* (Leipzig, 1913).
Kalkoff, *Entscheidungsjahre*	Paul Kalkoff, *Luther und die Entscheidungsjahre der Reformation, Von den Ablassthesen bis zum Wormser Edikt* (Muenchen und Leipzig, 1917).
Kalkoff, *Erasmus, Luther und Friedrich der Weise*	Paul Kalkoff, *Erasmus, Luther und Friedrich der Weise, Eine reformationsgeschichtliche Studie* (Leipzig, 1919).
Kalkoff, *Hutten*	Paul Kalkoff, *Ulrich von Hutten und die Reformation* (Leipzig, 1920).
Kalkoff, *Der grosse Wormser Reichstag*	Paul Kalkoff, *Der grosse Wormser Reichstag von 1521* (Darmstadt, 1921).
Kalkoff, *Huttens Vagantenzeit*	Paul Kalkoff, *Huttens Vagantenzeit und Untergang* (Weimar, 1925).
Kessler, *Sabbata*	*Johannes Kesslers Sabbata mit kleineren Schriften und Briefen,* eds., Emil Egli und Rudolf Schoch (St. Gallen, 1902).
Kirn, *Friedrich der Weise*	Paul Kirn, *Friedrich der Weise und die Kirche* (Leipzig-Berlin, 1926).
Koehler, *Zwingli und Luther*	W. Koehler, *Zwingli und Luther* (Leipzig, 1924).

Key	Title
Koehler, *Religionsgespraech*	"Das Marburger Religionsgespraech 1529, Versuch einer Rekonstruktion," ed., Walther Koehler, *S. V. R. G.*, XLVIII (1929), no. 148.
Koehler, *Erasmus Briefe*	*Erasmus von Rotterdam, Briefe,* tr. and ed., Walther Koehler (Wiesbaden, 1947).
Koehler, *Ablass-Streit*	Walther Koehler, *Documente zum Ablass-Streit von 1517* (Tuebingen, 1902).
Kohlschmidt	R. Kohlschmidt, "Luther im Kloster der Augustiner-Eremiten zu Erfurt 1505–1511," *Luther, Vierteljahrsschrift,* XIII (1931).
Kolde, *Analecta*	Theodor Kolde, *Analecta Lutherana* (Gotha, 1883).
Kolde, *Augustiner-Kongregation*	Theodor Kolde, *Die deutsche Augustinerkongregation und Johann Staupitz, Ein Beitrag zur Ordens- und Reformationsgeschichte nach meistens ungedruckten Quellen* (Gotha, 1879).
Kroker	Ernst Kroker, *Katharina von Bora, Martin Luthers Frau* (Zwickau, 1925). Second Edition.
Krueger, *Wittenberg*	Gottfried Krueger, "Wie sah die Stadt Wittenberg zu Luthers Lebzeiten aus?" *Luther, Vierteljahrsschrift der Luthergesellschaft,* XV (1933).
Kuehn, *Wormser Reichstag*	Johannes Kuehn, *Luther und der Wormser Reichstag 1521, Voigtlaender Quellenbuecher* (Leipzig, 1914), LXXIII.
Lauterbach, *Tagebuch*	*M. Anton Lauterbach's, Diaconi zu Wittenberg, Tagebuch auf das Jahr 1538, die Hauptquelle der Tischreden Luthers,* ed., Johann Karl Seidemann (Dresden, 1872).
Liber Decanorum	*Liber Decanorum Facultatis Theologicae Academiae Vitebergensis,* ed., C. E. Foerstemann (Leipzig, 1838).
Loofs, *Leitfaden*	Friedrich Loofs, *Leitfaden zum Studium der Dogmengeschichte* (Halle a. S., 1906).
Luther-Jahrbuch	*Jahrbuch der Luthergesellschaft,* eds., D. Jordan und Th. Knolle (Wittenberg und Muenchen, 1919 ff.).
Mackinnon, *Martin Luther*	James Mackinnon, *Luther and the Reformation* (New York, 1928), 4 Vols.

KEY	TITLE
Martin Luther (Berlin, 1933)	*Martin Luther,* s. a. (Berlin, Atlantis Verlag, 1933).
Meissinger, *Luthers Exegese*	K. A. Meissinger, *Luthers Exegese in der Fruehzeit* (Leipzig, 1910).
Mentz, *Johann Friedrich*	G. Mentz, *Johann Friedrich der Grossmuetige, Beitraege zur neueren Geschichte Thueringens* (Jena, 1908), I, Dritter Teil.
Mentzius, *Syntagma*	*Syntagma Epitaphio Rem quae in inclyta* etc., Balthasar Mentzius. Saxone. (Magdeburgi, Anno MDCIV.), 2 Vols.
Merian, *Topographia Saxoniae*	Matthaeus Merian, *Topographia Superioris Saxoniae, Thuringiae, Misniae, Lusatiae,* etc. (Franckfurt, 1650).
Merriman, *Spanish Empire*	Roger B. Merriman, *The Rise of the Spanish Empire* (New York, 1925), 4 Vols.
Mirbt, *Quellen*	C. Mirbt, *Quellen zur Geschichte des Papsttums und des roemischen Katholizismus* (Tuebingen, 1924).
Mueller, *Werdegang*	A. V. Mueller, *Luthers Werdegang bis zum Turmerlebnis* (Gotha, 1920).
Mueller, *Luther und Karlstadt*	Karl Mueller, *Luther und Karlstadt* (Tuebingen, 1907).
Mueller, *Die Wittenberger Bewegung*	Nikolaus Mueller, *Die Wittenberger Bewegung 1521 und 1522* (Leipzig, 1911). Second Edition.
Mueller, *D. L.*	Nikolaus Mueller, "Ein Urteil der Theologen zu Paris ueber die Lehre D. Luthers etc.," *Neudrucke deutscher Literaturwerke des 16. und 17. Jahrhunderts,* CIII. (Original, Halle a. S., 1892).
Mueller, *Annalen*	J. S. Mueller, *Des Chur- und Fuerstlichen Hauses Sachsen Ernestin- und Albertinischer Linien Annales, von Anno 1400. bis 1700.* (Leipzig, 1701).
M. V. G. A. E.	*Mitteilungen des Vereins fuer Geschichte und Altertumskunde zu Erfurt* (1865 ff.).
Myconius, *Historia Reformationis*	*Historia Reformationis vom Jahr Christi 1517 bis 1542,* F. Myconius. Ed., E. S. Cyprian (Leipzig, 1718).

Key	Title
Mylius, *Memorabilia*	M. J. C. Mylius, *Memorabilia Bibliothecae Academicae Jenensis* (Jenae et Weissenfelsae, 1746).
Nebe, *Die Lutherstube*	Hermann Nebe, "Die Lutherstube auf der Wartburg," *Vierteljahrsschrift der Luthergesellschaft,* XI (1929).
Negwer, *Wimpina*	Joseph Negwer, *Konrad Wimpina, Ein katholischer Theologe aus der Reformationszeit* (Breslau, 1909).
Nuntiaturberichte	*Nuntiaturberichte aus Deutschland nebst ergaenzenden Aktenstuecken,* ed., Walter Friedensburg, *Das k. preuss. Hist. Institut zu Rom* (Gotha, 1892), I.
Opera Lutheri	*D. Martini Lutheri Opera Latina varii argumenti ad reformationis historiam imprimis pertinentia,* ed., H. Schmidt (Frankfurt a. M. und Erlangen, 1865 ff.), 7 Vols. Second Edition.
Paulsen, *Geschichte*	Friedrich Paulsen, *Geschichte des gelehrten Unterrichts* (Berlin, 1919).
Paulus, *Ablass*	Nikolaus Paulus, *Geschichte des Ablasses am Ausgange des Mittelalters* (Paderborn, 1923), 3 Vols.
Paulus, *Johann Tetzel*	Nikolaus Paulus, *Johann Tetzel der Ablassprediger* (Mainz, 1899).
Paulus, *Usingen*	Nikolaus Paulus, *Der Augustiner Bartholomaeus Arnoldi von Usingen, Luthers Lehrer und Gegner* (Freiburg, 1893).
Plitt, *Trutvetter*	G. Plitt, *Jodokus Trutvetter von Eisenach der Lehrer Luthers* (Erlangen, 1876).
Pressel, *Spengler*	Th. Pressel, *Lazarus Spengler, Leben und ausgewaehlte Schriften der Vaeter und Begruender der lutherischen Kirche* (Elberfeld, 1862), VIII.
Prutz, *Weltgeschichte*	Hans Prutz, "Mittelalter," *Allgemeine Weltgeschichte,* ed., F. Flathe (Berlin, 1890), IX.
Ratzeberger	*Die handschriftliche Geschichte Ratzebergers ueber Luther und seine Zeit mit literarischen, kritischen und historischen Anmerkungen zum ersten Male herausgegeben,* ed., C. G. Neudecker (Jena, 1850).

Key	Title
R. E.	*Realencyklopaedie fuer protestantische Theologie und Kirche*, ed., D. A. Hauck (1896 to 1913), 24 Vols.
Reu, *Luther's German Bible*	M. Reu, *Luther's German Bible* (Columbus, Ohio, 1934).
Reu, *Augsburg Confession*	M. Reu, *Augsburg Confession* (Chicago, 1930).
Richter, *Kirchenordnungen*	*Die Evangelischen Kirchenordnungen des sechzehnten Jahrhunderts*, ed., A. L. Richter (Weimar, 1846), 2 Vols.
Rietschel, *Luther und die Ordination*	Georg Rietschel, *Luther und die Ordination* (Wittenberg, 1883).
Rommel, *Randbemerkungen*	Herbert Rommel, *Ueber Luthers Randbemerkungen von 1509 bis 10* (Kiel, 1931). Thesis.
Roth, *Augsburger Reformationsgeschichte*	Friedrich Roth, *Augsburger Reformationsgeschichte, 1517—1555* (Muenchen, 1901—1911), 4 Vols.
Schaefer	Ernst Schaefer, *Luther als Kirchenhistoriker, Ein Beitrag zur Geschichte der Wissenschaft* (Guetersloh, 1897).
Schalscheleth	P. Schalscheleth, nom de plume (Name, P. Heynig), *Historisch-geographische Beschreibung Wittenbergs und seiner Universitaet* (Frankfurt und Leipzig, 1795).
Scheel, *Documente*	Otto Scheel, *Documente zu Luthers Entwicklung (bis 1519)* (Tuebingen, 1911). A second edition (1929).
Scheel, *Martin Luther*	Otto Scheel, *Martin Luther, Vom Katholizismus zur Reformation* (Tuebingen, 1917), 2 Vols.
Scheurl, *Briefbuch*	*Christoph Scheurls Briefbuch*, J. K. F. Knaake (Potsdam, 1867), 2 Vols.
Schramm, *Luther und die Bibel*	Albert Schramm, *Luther und die Bibel* (Leipzig, 1923).
Schreckenbach and Neubert	Paul Schreckenbach and Franz Neubert, *Martin Luther* (Leipzig, 1921).
Schubert, *Galaterbrief*	*Luthers Vorlesung ueber den Galaterbrief 1516/17*, ed., Hans von Schubert (Heidelberg, 1918).

KEY	TITLE
Schubert, *Der Reichstag von Augsburg*	Hans von Schubert, "Der Reichstag von Augsburg im Zusammenhang der Reformationsgeschichte," *Schriften des Vereins fuer Reformationsgeschichte*, XLV, Pt. III (1930).
Schulte, *Die Fugger*	Aloys Schulte, *Die Fugger in Rom, 1495–1523* (Leipzig, 1904).
Schwiebert, *Thesis*	E. G. Schwiebert, *The University of Wittenberg and Some Other Universities in Their Relation to the German Reformation* (Cornell University, 1930). Unprinted.
Seeberg, *Greifswalder Studien*	R. Seeberg, "Die religioesen Grundgedanken des jungen Luther und ihr Verhaeltnis zu dem Ockamismus und der deutschen Mystik," *Greifswalder Studien zur Lutherforschung und neuzeitlichen Geistesgeschichte* (Berlin und Leipzig, 1931).
Seeberg, *Lehrbuch*	Reinhold Seeberg, *Lehrbuch der Dogmengeschichte* (Leipzig, 1930 ff.), Vols. III and IV.
Sehling, *Kirchenordnungen*	*Die evangelischen Kirchenordnungen des XVI. Jahrhunderts*, ed., E. Sehling (Leipzig, 1902 ff.), 5 Vols.
Seitz, *Leipziger Text*	*Der authentische Text der Leipziger Disputation*, ed., Otto Seitz (Berlin, 1903).
Smith, *Correspondence*	*Luther's Correspondence and Other Contemporary Letters*, tr. and ed., Preserved Smith and C. M. Jacobs (Philadelphia, 1913 ff.), 2 Vols.
Sohm, *Kirchenrecht*	Rudolf Sohm, *Kirchenrecht, Systematisches Handbuch der Deutschen Rechtswissenschaft* (Leipzig, 1892).
Spalatin, *Annales*	Georgii Spalatini, *Annales Reformationis, oder, Jahrbuecher von der Reformation Lutheri aus dessen Autographo ans Licht gestellet*, ed., E. S. Cyprian (Leipzig, 1718).
Spalatin, *Annales*, ed., Mencke	"Chronicon et annales 1463 bis 1525," *Scriptores Rerum Germanicarum, praecipue Saxonicarum*, ed., Johannes B. Mencke, II (1728).
Spalatin, *Chronik*	*Spalatins Chronik fuer die Jahre 1513 bis 1520*, ed., Alfred Kleeberg (Borna-Leipzig, 1919).

KEY	TITLE
Spalatin, *Ephemerides*	G. Berbig, "Georgii Spalatini Ephemerides, inchoatae anno MCCCCLXXX," *Quellen und Darstellungen aus der Geschichte des Reformationsjahrhunderts* (Leipzig, 1908), V.
Spalatin, *Friedrichs des Weisen Leben*	Georg Spalatin, *Friedrichs des Weisen Leben und Zeitgeschichte*, eds., Neudecker und Preller (Jena, 1851).
S. V. B. K.	*Leben und ausgewaehlte Schriften der Vaeter und Begruender der lutherischen Kirche*, ed., Karl I. Nitzsch *et al.* (Elberfeld, 1861 ff.), 8 Vols.
Stein, *Lutherhaus*	Hermann Stein, *Geschichte des Lutherhauses* (Wittenberg, 1883).
Stracke, *Luthers Selbstzeugnis*	Ernst Stracke, "Luthers groszes Selbstzeugnis 1545," *S. V. R. G.* (1926) CXL.
Strohl	Henri Strohl, *L'Evolution Religieuse de Luther jusqu'en 1515, Etudes d'Histoire et Philosophie Religieuses* (Strasbourg, 1922).
Stutz, *Eigenkirche*	Ulrich Stutz, "Die Eigenkirche als Element des mittelalterlich - germanischen Kirchenrechtes," tr., G. Barraclough, *Studies in Mediaeval History, Mediaeval Germany 911–1250* (Oxford, 1938), II.
S. V. R. G.	*Schriften des Vereins fuer Reformationsgeschichte* (Leipzig, 1882 ff.).
Thulin, *Die Lutherhalle*	Oskar Thulin, *Die Lutherhalle in der Lutherstadt Wittenberg* (Wittenberg, 1930).
T. S. K.	*Theologische Studien und Kritiken*, ed., E. Ullmann *et al.* (Hamburg, 1828 ff.).
Uhrig, "Der Bauer"	Kurt Uhrig, "Der Bauer," *Archiv fuer Reformationsgeschichte*, ed., Walter Friedensburg (Berlin, 1904 ff.), XXXIII.
Ullmann, *Reformatoren*	C. Ullmann, *Reformatoren vor der Reformation, vornehmlich in Deutschland und den Niederlanden* (Gotha, 1866), 2 Vols. Second Edition.
Vierordt, *Badische Reformationsgeschichte*	Karl F. Vierordt, *Geschichte der evangelischen Kirche in dem Grossherzogthum Baden* (Karlsruhe, 1847–1856), 2 Vols.
Vogt, *Bugenhagen*	*Dr. Johannes Bugenhagens Briefwechsel*, ed., Otto Vogt (Stettin, 1888).

Key	Title
W. A.	D. Martin Luthers Werke, kritische Gesammt-ausgabe, eds., J. K. F. Knaake et al. (Weimar, 1883 ff.), 57 Vols.
W. A., "Deutsche Bibel"	Die Deutsche Bibel, D. Martin Luthers Werke, kritische Gesamtausgabe, eds., Karl Drescher et al. (Weimar, 1906 ff.), 9 Vols.
W. A., "Briefe"	D. Martin Luthers Briefwechsel, D. Martin Luthers Werke, kritische Gesamtausgabe, eds., Konrad Burdach et al. (Weimar, 1930 ff.), 11 Vols.
W. A., T. R.	Tischreden, D. Martin Luthers Werke, kritische Gesamtausgabe, ed., Karl Drescher (Weimar, 1912 ff.), 6 Vols.
Wace and Buchheim	Wace and Buchheim, The First Principles of the Reformation (London, 1883).
Walch	D. Martin Luthers Saemtliche Schriften, tr. and ed., Johann Georg Walch (Halle, 1740 ff.), 24 Vols.
Walter, De Libero Arbitrio	Desiderius Erasmus: De libero arbitrio Diatribe sive Collatio, ed., Johannes von Walter, Quellen und Schriften zur Geschichte des Protestantismus, VIII (Leipzig, 1910).
Walter, "Der Reichstag zu Augsburg 1530"	Johannes von Walter, "Der Reichstag zu Augsburg 1530," Luther-Jahrbuch, XII (1930).
Walther, Luthers Deutsche Bibel	Wilhelm Walther, Luthers Deutsche Bibel (Berlin, 1917).
Weissenborn, Akten der Erfurter Universitaet	J. C. Hermann Weissenborn, Akten der Erfurter Universitaet, Historische Commission der Provinz Sachsen (Halle, 1881–1889), 3 Vols.
Weissenborn, Statuten	H. Weissenborn, Statuten und Ordnungen des amplonianischen Collegiums, M. V. G. A. E. (Erfurt, 1880).
Wernle, Die Renaissance	Paul Wernle, Die Renaissance des Christentums im 16. Jahrhundert (Tuebingen, 1904).
Zeumer, "Die Goldene Bulle"	Karl Zeumer, "Die Goldene Bulle Kaiser Karls V," Quellen und Studien zur Verfassungsgeschichte des Deutschen Reiches im Mittelalter und Neuzeit, II (1908).
Z. K. G.	Zeitschrift fuer Kirchengeschichte, ed., Th. Brieger et al. (Gotha, 1877 ff.).
Zwingli, Opera	Huldrici Zuinglii opera, eds., Schuler und Schulthess (1828 ff.), 8 Vols.

Notes

CHAPTER ONE

1. For titles, see abbreviations for Holl, Scheel, and Strohl.
2. Cf. text, p. 254 ff., especially 293 ff., *passim.*
3. *Album,* III, 804 ff. Cf. E. G. Schwiebert, "The Reformation from a New Perspective," *Church History,* XVII (1948), 14 ff.
4. Louise W. Holborn, "Printing and the Growth of a Protestant Movement in Germany from 1517 to 1524," *Church History,* XI (1942), 129—30.
5. Kalkoff, *Depeschen,* p. 43, "Tod dem roemischen Hofe!"
6. J. Huizinga, "Das Problem der Renaissance," *Wege der Kulturgeschichte* (Muenchen, 1930), pp. 123—125.
7. *W. A.,* L, 488—653; *E. A.,* XXV, 219—338; tr., Holman, *W. M. L.,* V, 131—300.
8. L. R. Loomis, *The Book of the Popes, Records of Civilization: Sources and Studies* (New York, 1916), p. 4.
9. C. B. Coleman, *The Treatise of Lorenzo Valla on the Donation of Constantine* (New Haven, 1922), pp. i—viii.
10. Carl Mirbt, *Quellen zur Geschichte des Papsttums und des Roemischen Katholizismus* (Tuebingen, 1924), p. 146.
11. Hans Prutz, *Weltgeschichte* (1905), IX, 191.
12. A. Harnack, *History of Dogma* (Boston, 1907), VI, 19 ff.; 118 ff.; Schaefer, 193 ff.
13. Schaefer, pp. 29 and 199. Cf. also n. 2, p. 29.
14. Schaefer, p. 200; Enders, III, 18; *E. A.,* LX, 372 ff. Cf. text, p. 486 ff.
15. See text, "History of Indulgences," p. 303 ff.
16. Prutz, *Weltgeschichte,* IX, 143—144.
17. Prutz, *Weltgeschichte,* IX, 160. Cf. *I. M. R.,* p. 6.
18. Prutz, *Weltgeschichte,* IX, 184 ff.
19. Gustav Krueger, *The Papacy; the Idea and Its Exponent* (London, 1909), p. 140.
20. J. A. Froude, *Life and Letters of Erasmus* (New York, 1896), pp. 149—168, for a translation of the play.
21. Gustav Krueger, *The Papacy,* p. 165.
22. Ludwig Pastor, *The History of the Popes* (St. Louis, 1923), VII, 5—6.

CHAPTER TWO

1. E. G. Schwiebert, "The Medieval Pattern in Luther's Views of the State," *Church History,* XII (1943), 98—117.
2. A good account of Emperor Maximilian is found in Joh. Haller, "Auswaertige Politik und Krieg," *I. M. R.,* pp. 58—118.
3. Sir Charles Oman, *The Sixteenth Century* (New York, 1937), p. 173 ff.
4. Louis Batiffol, *The Century of the Renaissance in France* (New York, 1916), p. 10 ff.

5. Edward Armstrong, *The Emperor Charles V* (London, 1902), 2 Vols., is slightly out of date, but still useful; Roger B. Merriman, *The Rise of the Spanish Empire* (New York, 1925), III, contains the standard views of Charles V; Karl Brandi, *The Emperor Charles V* (New York, 1939), interesting but slightly too favorable.

6. Marino Sanuto, *Diarii* (Venice), XX, 20, c. 422, cited by Merriman, *Spanish Empire*, III, 10–11.

7. Armstrong, *The Emperor Charles V*, I, 31.

8. See text, p. 379 ff.; also James Mackinnon, *Martin Luther*, II, 182 ff.; Wilhelm Pauck's historiographical article in *Church History*, IX (1940), 325–326.

9. Hajo Holborn, *Ulrich von Hutten and the German Reformation* (New Haven, 1937), pp. 109–110.

10. Brandi, *The Emperor Charles V*, pp. 110–111.

11. Brandi, *The Emperor Charles V*, p. 111; Spalatin, *Friedrichs des Weisen Leben*, pp. 40–41; cf. p. 162.

12. Kalkoff, *Depeschen*, p. 153. See text, p. 381.

13. The claim is made by Paul Kalkoff, *Die Kaiserwahl Friedrichs IV und Karls V* (Leipzig, 1925), but Gustav Wolf, Z. K. G., XLV (1926), 22–26, refutes the statement. Cf. Karl Brandi, "Die Wahl Karls V," *Nachrichten der Gesellschaft der Wissenschaften zu Goettingen* (1925) for similar view.

14. Merriman, *Spanish Empire*, III, 43; Brandi, *The Emperor Charles V*, pp. 111–112.

15. Armstrong, *The Emperor Charles V*, I, 38–39; Merriman, *Spanish Empire*, III, 50.

16. Brandi, *The Emperor Charles V*, p. 123.

17. Spalatin, *Annales*, pp. 11–12, 27–30.

18. Holborn, *Ulrich von Hutten*, pp. 67–71.

19. Georg v. Below, "Die Reichsreform," *I. M. R.*, pp. 142–143.

20. Kalkoff, *Depeschen*, pp. 135–139 for report on April 17; pp. 140–145 for report on April 18; for details see text, p. 501 ff.

21. Merriman, *Spanish Empire*, III, 67.

22. Joh. Haller, "Auswaertige Politik und Krieg," *I. M. R.*, pp. 60–61.

23. Oman, *The Sixteenth Century*, p. 182 ff.

24. Oman, *The Sixteenth Century*, p. 188 ff.

25. Brandi, *The Emperor Charles V*, p. 236.

26. W. Friedensburg, "Die Reformation und der Speierer Reichstag," *Luther-Jahrbuch*, VIII (1926), 145.

27. Schwiebert, *Church History*, XII (1943), 105–106.

28. Merriman, *Spanish Empire*, III, 246.

29. Friedensburg, *Luther-Jahrbuch*, VIII, 127–130.

30. See text, p. 716 ff.

31. For bibliography see L. J. Paetow, *A Guide to the Study of Medieval History*, pp. 176–180. Cf. H. Pirenne, *Mohammed and Charlemagne* (1939), Part II.

32. J. W. Thompson and E. N. Johnson, *An Introduction to Medieval Europe, 300–1500* (New York, 1937), pp. 943–944; Oman, *The Sixteenth Century*, p. 146 ff.

33. Oman, *The Sixteenth Century*, pp. 162–163; Merriman, *Spanish Empire*, III, 290.

34. Oman, *The Sixteenth Century*, pp. 163–164.

35. Oman, *The Sixteenth Century*, pp. 165–166.

36. Brandi, *The Emperor Charles V*, pp. 633–645.

CHAPTER THREE

1. A good, brief introduction to this region is in A. K. Lobeck, *Physiographic Diagram of Europe*, The Geographical Press, Columbia University, 1930. For a more extensive study see Alfred Hettner, *Grundzuege der Laenderkunde* (Leipzig, 1927). For early aspects of the region consult Matthaeus Merian, *Topographia Saxoniae*.

2. For a discussion of "Old Saxony" see J. W. Thompson, *Feudal Germany* (Chicago, 1928), pp. 167–184. For sources consult *Adami Gesta Hammaburgensis Ecclesiae Pontificum ex Recensione Lappenbergii, Scriptores Rerum Germanicarum* (Hanoverae, 1876), p. 3, sec. 1; Francis J. Tschan, *The Chronicle of the Slavs by Helmold, Priest of Bosau* (New York, 1935), p. 7. For German institutions see Geoffrey Barraclough, *Mediaeval Germany, 911 to 1250* (Oxford, 1938), I, 7–46, 81–112. On "New Saxony" see text, p. 70 ff.

3. J. W. Thompson, *The Middle Ages* (New York, 1931), I, 375, 386, 422.

4. K. G. Hugelmann, "Die deutsche Nation und der deutsche Nationalstaat im Mittelalter," *Historisches Jahrbuch*, LI (1931), 6–7. On the "Flaeming" see E. G. Schwiebert, "The Electoral Town of Wittenberg," *Medievalia et Humanistica*, III (1945), 99, and n. 3.

5. Barraclough, *Mediaeval Germany*, I, 7–8, 32, 49–55.

6. Thompson, *The Middle Ages*, I, 473–517. See also *Church History*, XII (1943), 104–106.

7. The name of this document is derived from the Castle at Gelnhausen, where Emperor Frederick Barbarossa deposed his ducal rival, Henry the Lion. Two excellent studies of this important historic event are: Ferdinand Gueterbock, *Die Gelnhauser Urkunde und der Prozesz Heinrichs des Loewen, Quellen und Darstellungen zur Geschichte Niedersachsens* (Hildesheim u. Leipzig, 1920), XXXII, 1–2; and Johannes Haller, "Der Sturz Heinrichs des Loewen," *Archiv fuer Urkundenforschung*, III (1911), 443 ff.

8. Karl E. F. Boedler, *Die Gewalt der askanischen Herzoege in Westfalen und Engern bis zum Ausgang des 14. Jahrhunderts* (Halle a. S., 1912), p. 3 ff.

9. Boedler, *Die Gewalt der askanischen Herzoege*, etc., p. 4 ff., especially p. 36.

10. Schalscheleth, p. 3 ff.

11. Wolfgang Ebert *et al.*, *Kulturraeume und Kulturstroemungen im mittel-deutschen Osten* (Halle, Saale, 1936), pp. 323–324, supplement No. 7.

12. Ebert, *Kulturraeume und Kulturstroemungen*, etc., p. 52 ff. Cf. map, text, p. 73.

13. A. H. L. Heeren und F. A. Ukert, *Geschichte der Europaeischen Staaten, Geschichte des Kurstaates und Koenigreiches Sachsen*, ed., C. W. Boettiger (Hamburg, 1830), claims Agnes built the monastery, but Charitius, p. 144, says that Helena built it. He was a careful worker and the better authority.

14. Schalscheleth, pp. 16–18; G. von Hirschfeld, *Geschichte der Saechsisch-Askanischen Kurfuersten*, pp. 281–282. Cf. Boedler, pp. 65–66; Heeren und Ukert, pp. 304 and 309.

15. F. Berendt, *Die Beziehungen Anhalts zu Kur-Sachsen von 1212 bis 1485* (Halle, 1907), pp. 42–43; Boedler, p. 66.

16. Berendt, *Die Beziehungen Anhalts zu Kur-Sachsen*, etc., pp. 66–67.

17. Heeren und Ukert, pp. 306–307.

18. Boedler, p. 68. Karl Zeumer, "Die Goldene Bulle Kaiser Karls V," *Quellen und Studien zur Verfassungsgeschichte des Deutschen Reiches im Mittelalter und Neuzeit*, II (1908), 67 ff., note 20.

19. Boedler, pp. 71–72.

20. Boedler, pp. 71–72. Zeumer, "Die Goldene Bulle," pp. 152–164.

21. See note 14, Chapter Three; also Charitius, p. 125.

22. Schalscheleth, pp. 21–22; Hirschfeld, pp. 285–286.

23. Ebert *et al.*, *Kulturraeume und Kulturstroemungen*, etc., pp. 41–47.

24. Ebert *et al.*, *Kulturraeume und Kulturstroemungen*, etc., pp. 49–50 and 56–57.

25. Ebert *et al.*, p. 58; Heeren und Ukert, pp. 339–343.

26. For the story of Frederick the Wise see text, p. 358 ff.

27. Mentz, *Johann Friedrich*, I, 103 ff. Cf. Mylius, *Memorabilia*, p. 27.

28. For his biography see *R. E.*, VI, 529–533. See text, p. 384 ff.

29. See text, p. 616; Burkhardt, *G. K. S.*, p. 231; *R. E.*, VI, 533.

30. See *R. E.*, IX, 210–213.

31. Wilhelm Dilichs, *Federzeichnungen Kursaechsischer und Meissnischer Ortschaften aus den Jahren 1626–1629* (Dresden, 1907), ed., Paul E. Richter and Christian Krollmann, is in Harper Memorial Library, University of Chicago; Matthaeus Merian, *Topographia Saxoniae*, p. 4 ff.

32. Erasmus, *Opera* (Leyden Ed.), I, 715–718, translation by Albert Hyma, "Erasmus and the Humanists," *Landmarks in History* (New York, 1930), pp. 48–55.

33. Fynes Moryson, *Itinerary* (London, 1617), *passim*.

34. Richard Erfurth, *Fuehrer durch die Lutherstadt Wittenberg und ihre Umgebung* (Wittenberg, 1927), p. 48. Cf. Oskar Thulin, *Lutherstadt Wittenberg und Torgau* (Berlin, 1932), p. 28.

35. Albert Hyma, *The Youth of Erasmus* (Ann Arbor, 1930), pp. 67–69.

36. Hyma, "The Inns," *Landmarks in History,* p. 50.
37. Hyma, "The Inns," p. 51.
38. Edith Eschenhagen, "Wittenberger Studien," *Luther-Jahrbuch* IX, (1927), 20 ff.
39. Eschenhagen, "Wittenberger Studien," p. 21.
40. Eschenhagen, "Wittenberger Studien," p. 23.

CHAPTER FOUR

1. *W. A., T. R.,* is the definitive edition of the Table Talks; for a good introduction see Preserved Smith, *Luther's Table Talk: A Critical Study* (New York, 1907), which discusses the reliability of the conversational-ists. Borcherdt, *Werke,* also contains a good evaluation.
2. *Martin Luther* (Berlin, 1933), pp. 289–315.
3. *Opera Lutheri,* I, 15–24. Cf. Stracke, *Luthers Selbstzeugnis,* CXL, 5–136.
4. *Opera Lutheri,* I, 3–14.
5. This "Praefatio" was for volume II of Luther's works in 1546, *Opera Lutheri,* which is reprinted in *C. R.,* VI, 155–170. For a German trans-lation see *Martin Luther* (Berlin, 1933), pp. 44–64, made by D. Fr. Th. Zimmermann, 1813.
6. *Martin Luther* (Berlin, 1933), p. 121 ff.; M. Johann Mathesius, *Dr. Mar-tin Luthers Leben* (St. Louis, 1883), pp. 1–337.
7. Myconius, *Historia Reformationis,* p. 1 ff.
8. See E. G. Schwiebert, *Reformation Lectures* (Valparaiso, 1937), p. 229 ff.
9. Scheel, *Martin Luther,* I, 1; Boehmer, *Der Junge Luther* (Gotha, 1925), p. 386 on *Stammhaus,* family, pp. 13–17; Koehler, *I. M. R.,* pp. 335 and 338.
10. Boehmer, *Der Junge Luther,* p. 21.
11. Scheel, *Martin Luther,* I, 1.
12. Boehmer, *Der Junge Luther,* p. 22; Koehler, *I. M. R.,* p. 335.
13. Scheel, *Martin Luther,* I, 1; *Christian Friederich Junii kurzgefaszte Re-formations-Geschichte, aus des Hrn. Veit Ludwigs von Seckendorf Historia Lutheranismi,* ed., A. Schlitt (Baltimore, Md., 1865), I, 35.
14. Boehmer, *Der Junge Luther,* p. 22.
15. Boehmer, *Der Junge Luther,* p. 386; Scheel, *Martin Luther,* I, 3.
16. *C. R.,* VI, 156; tr., *Martin Luther* (Berlin, 1933), p. 45.
17. *Liber Decanorum,* p. 33.
18. For details on different views, see Scheel, *Martin Luther,* I, 263, n. 4. Cf. E. Kroker, *Archiv fuer Reformationsgeschichte,* V (1907–1908), 337 ff., 372, and Georg Oergel, *Vom Jungen Luther* (Erfurt, 1899), p. 1 ff.
19. Francke, *Historie der Grafschaft Mansfeld,* p. 10, cited by Scheel, *Martin Luther,* I, 264, n. 11.
20. Scheel, *Martin Luther,* I, 5. Scheel gives this town plan on which no. 24, next to no. 17, is the Ratsschule, now Lutherschule.

21. Scheel, *Martin Luther,* I, 6 ff.; Boehmer, *Der Junge Luther,* p. 23.

22. *C. R.,* VI, 156–157. Cf. Scheel, *Martin Luther,* I, 8 and 265, n. 41; Strohl, p. 43.

23. Scheel, *Martin Luther,* I, 6.

24. Scheel, *Martin Luther,* I, 7.

25. Scheel, *Martin Luther,* I, 264–265, n. 25. Cf. *W. A., T. R.,* I, 500–503, and *W. A.,* XLIX, 322.

26. *Martin Luther* (Berlin, 1933), p. 122.

27. Scheel, *Martin Luther,* I, 148 and 299, sec. 12, 7, "in habendo" from Weissenborn, *Akten der Erfurter Universitaet,* I, 12, Rubr. 4, 3.

28. Boehmer, *Der Junge Luther,* p. 23, mentions that the amount was 1,250 Gulden when it was divided in 1534 among the heirs. See text, p. 257 ff., for value of sixteenth-century money.

29. *Colloquia,* II, 76. First edition.

30. *Colloquia,* II, 129.

31. *W. A., T. R.,* IV, 636; *W. A.,* XXXVIII, 338.

32. Strohl, p. 46; Scheel, *Martin Luther,* I, 34–36; and Boehmer, *Der Junge Luther,* pp. 25–26.

33. Otto Scheel, "Luther und die Schule seiner Zeit," *Luther-Jahrbuch,* VII (1925), 158–160.

34. "An die Ratherren aller Staedte deutsches Lands, dasz sie christliche Schulen aufrichten und halten sollen," *W. A.,* XV, 9–53. Cf. Scheel, *Luther-Jahrbuch,* VII, 141–146; Scheel, *Martin Luther,* I, 44–52; and *W. A., T. R.,* III, 353–355. M. Reu, *Luther's German Bible,* p. 75, also agrees with Scheel.

35. Scheel, *Luther-Jahrbuch,* VII, 159 ff.

36. *C. R.,* VI, 156–157. Cf. de Wette, V, 709.

37. Scheel, *Martin Luther,* I, 44 ff.; Reu, *Luther's German Bible,* p. 76; 319–320, n. 4.

38. Scheel, *Luther-Jahrbuch,* VII, 162.

39. Scheel, *Martin Luther,* I, 44.

40. Scheel, *Martin Luther,* I, 48–49. Cf. 274, n. 92. Wittenberg College has a reproduction of *Ein bet-buechlin mit eym Calender und Passional huebsch zu gericht.* Marti. Luther. Wittemberg, M. D. XXIX, which contains the later *Cisio Janus.*

41. Scheel, *Luther-Jahrbuch,* VII, 151–152. Cf. Walter E. Buszin, "Luther on Music," *The Musical Quarterly,* XXXII (1946), 80 ff.

42. J. Warncke, *Mittelalterliche Schulgeraete im Museum zu Luebeck,* cited by Scheel, *Martin Luther,* I, 274, n. 95.

43. *W. A., T. R.,* III, 353–355.

44. Scheel, *Martin Luther,* I, 34; *Luther-Jahrbuch,* VII, 160.

45. Scheel, *Martin Luther,* I, 34.

46. Scheel, *Martin Luther,* I, 35. Cf. n. 21 on p. 271.

47. See *Album*, I, for those years signed *ex Mansfelde*.

48. W. A., XV, 31. Cf. Boehmer, *Der Junge Luther*, p. 26.

49. See text, p. 293 ff.

50. W. A., T. R., I, 44, n. 116. Cf. Reu, *Luther's German Bible*, pp. 79—83.

51. C. R., VI, 157; Scheel, *Martin Luther*, I, 60, claims he was in his fourteenth year. See W. A., XXXVIII, 105, and a letter by Luther to Spalatin, January 14, 1520, Enders, II, 294, where he states he was fourteen. Cf. Scheel, *Martin Luther*, I, 275, n. 1, for a detailed criticism and bibliography.

52. G. Sello, "Domaltertuemer," *Geschichtsblaetter fuer Stadt und Land Magdeburg* (1891), p. 108 ff.; Scheel, *Martin Luther*, I, 66—67.

53. W. A., XXXVIII, 105. Cf. T. R., III, 103, and Beckmann, *Historie des Fuerstentums Anhalt*, V, 103—105, who states that he died Sept. 2, 1504. Cochlaeus questioned his early death, W. A., XXXVI, 490, 12.

54. Scheel, *Martin Luther*, I, 67—70.

55. E. A., XXIX, 370; Enders, III, 402, n. 3; Scheel, *Martin Luther*, I, 78—82, 277, n. 50, for further references.

56. Preserved Smith, *Luther's Table Talk: A Critical Study* (New York, 1907).

57. Reu, *Luther's German Bible*, pp. 79—80. Cf. *Martin Luther* (Berlin, 1933), p. 124.

58. Reu, *Luther's German Bible*, p. 81. Cf. W. A., T. R., III, 599, n. 3767.

59. Reu, *Luther's German Bible*, p. 81.

60. Scheel, *Martin Luther*, I, 91—92, based on Weissenborn, *Akten der Erfurter Universitaet*, II, 148.

61. Strohl, pp. 47—49; Scheel, *Martin Luther*, I, 92; W. A., I, 44, n. 116.

62. Reu, *Luther's German Bible*, p. 323, n. 12. Cf. Friedensburg, *Urkundenbuch*, I, 186; J. W. Thompson, *The Medieval Library* (Chicago, 1939), p. 624; J. W. Clark, *Libraries in the Medieval and Renaissance Periods* (Cambridge, 1894), pp. 44—45.

63. Friedensburg, *Urkundenbuch*, I, 186. Cf. Reu, *Luther's German Bible*, p. 323; Gottfried Zedler, *Geschichte der Universitaetsbibliothek zu Marburg von 1527 bis 1887* (Marburg, 1896), pp. 14—15.

64. See text, p. 527 ff. and 643 ff.

65. Ratzeberger, p. 43, "bey Cuntz Kotten sein herberge und unterhalt gehabt." Cf. Melanchthon, C. R., VI, 157, and *Martin Luther* (Berlin, 1933), p. 123 adds, "da er seiner Mutter Freundschaft hatte."

66. Scheel, *Martin Luther*, I, 104 ff.

67. W. A., XXX, II, 576. Cf. translation F. V. N. Painter, *Luther on Education* (1928), pp. 260—261.

68. Scheel, *Martin Luther*, I, 101.

69. Scheel, *Martin Luther*, I, 117, based on Paullinus, *Syntagma*, p. 245.

70. Ratzeberger, p. 43. Cf. C. R., VI, 157.

71. *C. R.*, VI, 157.

72. Scheel, *Martin Luther*, I, 118–119. Cf. *Luther-Jahrbuch* VII, 149–151.

73. *Martin Luther* (Berlin, 1933), 122–123.

74. From Painter, *Luther on Education* (St. Louis, 1928), pp. 260–261.

75. Scheel, *Martin Luther*, I, 104 ff. Cf. Boehmer, *Der Junge Luther*, pp. 34–35.

76. Mattheus Dresser, *De festis diebus christianorum et ethnicorum liber* (Leipzig, 1590), pp. 179–180. Cf. Nikolaus Rebhan, *historia ecclesiae Isenacensis*, p. 109. For a critical evaluation of the two men, Scheel, *Martin Luther*, I, 104–107.

77. See *A. R.* (1908), V, 365; *E. A.*, LXI, 212. Cf. *W. A.*, "*Briefe*," I, 13, n. 11; *W. A.*, XXX, Pt. III, 491; and *W. A.*, *T. R.*, V, 5362. Boehmer, *Der Junge Luther*, p. 35; Scheel, *Martin Luther*, I, 109 ff.

78. *Martin Luther* (Berlin, 1933), p. 123.

79. See n. 77, Chapter Four.

80. *W. A.*, "*Briefe*," I, 10–13 and n. 11; Scheel, *Martin Luther*, I, 108–109.

81. Paul Schreckenbach und Franz Neubert, *Martin Luther* (Leipzig, 1921), p. 49, has a photostatic reproduction of that part of the *Erfurter Universitaetsmatrikel*. Cf. Weissenborn, *Akten der Erfurter Universitaet*, II, 219, and Scheel, *Martin Luther*, I, 147. On the purchase of the *Corpus Juris* see *W. A.*, *T. R.*, I, 44, n. 116. His father no doubt gave him the money, for Scheel, *Martin Luther*, I, 240, states, "dank der Freigebigkeit seines Vaters" he already had a copy. Cf. Schaefer, p. 199.

82. Scheel, *Martin Luther*, I, 121 ff. Cf. *W. A.*, *T. R.*, IV, 177, n. 4170.

83. *W. A.*, *T. R.*, III, 3517. Cf. Scheel, *Martin Luther*, I, 126–127 for bibliography and discussion.

84. *W. A.*, *T. R.*, II, 614, n. 2719b. Cf. Koehler, *I. M. R.*, pp. 348–349, and Scheel, *Martin Luther*, I, 123–124 for description. Also see E. G. Schwiebert, "The Electoral Town of Wittenberg," *Medievalia et Humanistica*, III (1945), 114–115; E. Eschenhagen, "Wittenberger Studien," p. 25; H. Werdermann, *Luthers Wittenberger Gemeinde* (Guetersloh, 1929), p. 10, n. 2.

85. "Hierographia Erfordensis," *Mitteilungen des Vereins fuer Geschichte und Altertuemer zu Erfurt*, III (1867), 146. Cf. K. Herrmann, *Bibliotheka Erfurtina*, p. 3, and Koehler, *I. M. R.*, p. 348.

86. Scheel, *Martin Luther*, I, 130–132. Cf. *W. A.*, *T. R.*, II, 660, 2788a and 2788b.

87. Strohl, p. 53.

88. Strohl, p. 13; Scheel, *Martin Luther*, I, 132–133; Boehmer, *Der Junge Luther*, pp. 37–38. Cf. also Strohl, pp. 54–55.

89. Strohl, pp. 54–55; Koehler, *I. M. R.*, p. 350. Cf. Weissenborn, *Akten der Erfurter Universitaet* (Halle, 1881), II, 145.

90. Strohl, p. 54; Scheel, *Martin Luther*, I, 139–147.

91. Scheel, *Martin Luther*, I, 140 ff.

92. For a discussion of this controversy see Scheel, *Martin Luther*, I, 144, n. 54, and *W. A., "Briefe,"* I, 1–7 on "viropolitanus." For *Collegium Majus* statutes of 1427 see G. Oergel, *Urkunden zur Geschichte des Collegium Majus in Erfurt* (Erfurt, 1894); for Himmelspforte, Weissenborn, *Statuten* in *M. V. G. A. E.*

93. Weissenborn, *Statuten*, n. 2.

94. Weissenborn, *Akten der Erfurter Universitaet*, I, 24, Rubr. 11, 4. Cf. Weissenborn, *Statuten*, sec. 32; Scheel, *Martin Luther*, I, 145.

95. Weissenborn, *Akten der Erfurter Universitaet*, I, 21, Rubr. 10, 6.

96. Weissenborn, *Akten der Erfurter Universitaet*, I, 24, Rubr. 11, 7; 18, Rubr. 8, 18; 20, Rubr. 8, 18.

97. Enders, II, 391. Cf. Strohl, p. 55; Scheel, *Martin Luther*, I, 152.

98. *W. A., T. R.*, II, 613–614, nos. 2719a and 2719b. Cf. 669.

99. *C. R.*, VI, 157.

100. Koehler, *I. M. R.*, p. 354 ff., presents former view. For the accepted view see Holborn, *Ulrich von Hutten*, pp. 30–31; Scheel, *Martin Luther*, II, 223 ff.; Rommel, *Randbemerkungen*, pp. 1–10; G. Ritter, "Die geschichtliche Bedeutung des deutschen Humanismus," *H. Z.*, CXXVII (1923), 393 ff.; Hans von Schubert, "Reformation und Humanismus," *Luther-Jahrbuch*, VIII (1926), 7 ff.; and Paul Joachimsen, "Der Humanismus und die Entwicklung des deutschen Geistes," *Deutsche Vierteljahrschrift fuer Literaturwissenschaft und Geistesgeschichte*, VIII, 456 ff.

101. Schubert, *Luther-Jahrbuch*, VIII (1926), 9. Cf. Rommel, *Randbemerkungen*, pp. 4–10.

102. Rommel, *Randbemerkungen*, pp. 4–10; Schubert, *Luther-Jahrbuch*, VIII, 11. Cf. G. Plitt, *Jodokus Trutvetter von Eisenach der Lehrer Luthers* (Erlangen, 1876), p. 14 and p. 29; Boehmer, *Der Junge Luther*, pp. 39–40.

103. Rommel, *Randbemerkungen*, pp. 5–6; Plitt, *Trutvetter*, p. 31 ff. Cf. Nicolaus Paulus, *Der Augustiner Bartholomaeus Arnoldi von Usingen* (Freiburg, 1893), p. 8 ff.

104. Paulus, *Usingen*, p. 8. Cf. *W. A.*, IX, 31, 35, 37.

105. Boehmer, *Der Junge Luther*, p. 39; Mackinnon, *Martin Luther*, I, 23 ff.

106. J. Huizinga, "Das Problem der Renaissance," p. 134. Cf. C. J. H. Hayes, *A Political and Cultural History of Modern Europe* (New York, 1932), I, 123–125.

107. A good summary may be found in Strohl, pp. 56–64. Cf. Scheel, *Martin Luther*, I, 241–248; and Enders, II, 208, in which Crotus Rubeanus calls him an "alterum Paulum ante oppidum Erffurdianum."

108. Scheel, *Dokumente*, p. 30. (In second edition, p. 151.)

109. Scheel, *Dokumente*, p. 30.

110. *W. A., T. R.*, IV, 440, n. 4707; Scheel, *Dokumente* (Second Edition), pp. 154–155.

111. See text, p. 132; also n. 92, Chapter IV.

112. Strohl, pp. 11–12.

113. Strohl, p. 9 ff. Cf. Schwiebert, *Reformation Lectures* (Valparaiso, 1937), pp. 232–233.

114. *W. A.*, VIII, 573–574, "De Votis Monasticis." Cf. Walther Koehler, *Luther und die Deutsche Reformation* (1917); Mueller, *Werdegang;* Scheel, *Martin Luther*, I, all of which express the conviction that the step was not premeditated.

115. Enders, II, 208; *W. A.*, *"Briefe,"* I, 540–544.

116. Scheel, *Martin Luther*, I, 249–250; Koehler, *I. M. R.*, p. 357. Cf. Enders, III, 225; *W. A.*, *T. R.*, IV, 440, n. 4707; and for Scheel's arguments in favor of a sudden decision see pp. 243–248 and n. 9, pp. 319–320.

117. Strohl, p. 59.

118. *W. A.*, XXXVII, 661. Cf. Strohl, pp. 59–61; Scheel, *Martin Luther*, I, 242–244.

119. *W. A.*, XXXVII, 274. Cf. Strohl, p. 61.

120. *W. A.*, *"Briefe,"* I, 10–13; Enders, I, 1–6.

121. *W. A.*, *T. R.*, I, 46, n. 119. "Cum vellet proficisci in patriam et esset in itinere, forti impegit crure in gladium (Another reading: Das messer schuss aus, und er stiss sich drein), et cephalicam perrupit, etc." The cephalic vein is really in the arm, but the writer may not have been too familiar with anatomy. Cf. Strohl, p. 63.

122. *W. A.*, *T. R.*, I, 46, n. 3.

123. *C. R.*, VI, 158.

124. Strohl, p. 61.

125. Boehmer, *Der Junge Luther*, pp. 46–48.

CHAPTER FIVE

1. Scheel, *Martin Luther*, II, 125–154; Strohl, pp. 72–73.

2. An excellent introduction may be found in Kohlschmidt. See also *Constitutiones Fratrum Heremitarum sancti Augustini ad apostolicorum privilegiorum formam pro reformatione Alemanie* (Nuernberg, 1504); and Kolde, *Augustinerkongregation;* E. Wolff, *Staupitz und Luther* (Leipzig, 1927); and Karl Bauer, *Die Wittenberger Universitaetstheologie und die Anfaenge der Deutschen Reformation* (Tuebingen, 1928).

3. Mackinnon, *Martin Luther*, I, 92 ff. Kohlschmidt, p. 8 ff.

4. Kohlschmidt, pp. 55–56, points out that Luther must have occupied several rooms: one as *Novize*, another as *Professor*, and a final one as *Subregens*.

5. Kohlschmidt, pp. 33–34; Strohl, pp. 69–70. For a detailed description of Luther's reception as a *Novitiate* see Kohlschmidt, p. 37 ff.

6. *W. A.*, *"Briefe,"* I, 10–13. Cf. Otto Scheel, "Luthers Primiz," *Studien zur Reformationsgeschichte und zur Praktischen Theologie* (1917), 1 ff., and his *Martin Luther*, II, 29–58, especially, 44; Kohlschmidt, p. 42; and *W. A.*, *"Briefe,"* I, 12, n. 6.

7. *W. A.*, *T. R.*, II, 133–134, n. 1558. Cf. *W. A.*, *"Briefe,"* I, 12, n. 6.

8. Strohl, p. 85.

9. *W. A.*, VIII, 574.

10. Kohlschmidt, pp. 44–45. Usingen was not Luther's teacher in the monastery. For what Luther studied see Kohlschmidt, p. 46.

11. Reu, *Luther's German Bible*, p. 94. Kohlschmidt, p. 47, points out that Nathin was alone, as Professor Pfalz had left. Luther was promoted to *Sententiarius* so he could serve as *Subregens* under Nathin and lived in the *Zelle* now shown.

12. Luther had preached privately to the monks at Erfurt, but he did not preach before any congregation until he went to Wittenberg. Kohlschmidt, p. 48. The Elector could not have heard Luther preach before his promotion to the doctorate.

13. Strohl, p. 80.

14. *E. A.*, XLIX, 27.

15. *W. A.*, XXXIII, 574–575.

16. Kohlschmidt, p. 45: "ym iuneckfrawen closter zu muhlhausen in der visitation des selbigen als eyn andern Paulum, der durch Christum wunderbarlichen bekerth."

17. Strohl, p. 72 ff.

18. *W. A., "Briefe,"* I, 37–38.

19. *W. A.*, XLV, 86.

20. Strohl, pp. 76–77.

21. Strohl, p. 19.

22. *E. A.*, XXXI, 279.

23. *E. A.*, III, 20.

24. Text, p. 137, n. 108.

25. *E. A.*, XLV, 156.

26. *E. A.*, XLV, 156.

27. *E. A.*, XLIX, 27.

28. Strohl, p. 83.

29. Strohl, p. 82: "docuit aliquid omittere crimen esse."

30. Cited by Seeberg, *Lehrbuch*, IV, 1, 2.

31. Jakob Wille, "Humanismus und Renaissance," *I. M. R.*, pp. 210–211.

32. Seeberg, *Greifswalder Studien*, VI, 3 ff.

33. Rommel, *Randbemerkungen*, pp. 15–16. Cf. *W. A.*, IX, 31.

34. Seeberg, *Lehrbuch*, IV, 1, 204.

35. *C. R.*, VI, 159. Melanchthon is in error, for Luther did not read Augustine's book before 1515.

36. M. Reu, *Luther and the Scriptures* (Columbus, 1944), p. 13 ff.

37. R. Seeberg, *Lehrbuch*, III, 325 ff.; Loofs, *Leitfaden*, p. 348 ff., p. 393 ff.

38. Mackinnon, *Martin Luther*, I, 63 ff. Cf. Rommel, *Randbemerkungen*, pp. 70–72; *W. A.*, IX, 56, 69, 71, and 72.

39. Mackinnon, *Martin Luther*, I, 73.

40. Seeberg, *Lehrbuch*, I, 272–273.

41. Mackinnon, *Martin Luther*, I, 58.

42. Loofs, *Leitfaden*, p. 386 ff., for Augustine's views on justification. Cf. Adolf von Harnack, *History of Dogma* (Boston, 1903), V, 207–210; Seeberg, *Lehrbuch*, I, 276–278.

43. Harnack, *History of Dogma*, VI, 200 ff.

44. Harnack, *History of Dogma*, VI, 200.

45. Harnack, *History of Dogma*, VI, 200—201.

46. Seeberg, *Lehrbuch*, III, 507. Cf. Harnack, *History of Dogma*, VI, 203—204.

47. Harnack, *History of Dogma*, VI, 276.

48. Stutz, *Eigenkirche*, II, 35—70. Cf. E. G. Schwiebert, "The Medieval Pattern in Luther's Views of the State," *Church History*, XII (June, 1943), 101—103.

49. H. O. Taylor, *The Mediaeval Mind* (New York, 1919), I, 66; 42 ff.; 55 ff.

50. H. O. Taylor, *The Mediaeval Mind*, I, 13.

51. H. O. Taylor, *The Mediaeval Mind*, II, 421, relates how Greek writers were later translated for St. Thomas by the Dominican William of Moerbeke. Cf. Seeberg, *Lehrbuch*, III, 336; J. W. Thompson, *The Middle Ages*, II, 770 ff. For further study, see C. H. Haskins, *Studies in the History of Medieval Science* (Cambridge, 1927), pp. 1—19; F. Wuestenfeld, "Die Uebersetzungen arabischer Werke in das Lateinische," *Abhandlungen der Goettinger Academie*, XXII (1877); M. Steinschneider, *Die arabischen Uebersetzungen aus dem Griechischen* (Leipzig, 1897).

52. Taylor, *The Mediaeval Mind*, I, 278, from *Cur Deus homo*, I, 2.

53. Seeberg, *Lehrbuch*, III, 377 ff.: "auctor sacrae scripturae est deus . . . auctor principalis . . . est spiritus sanctus, homo autem est auctor instrumentalis."

54. Charles G. Shaw, *Trends of Civilization and Culture* (New York, 1932), p. 244.

55. For a good introduction see Thompson, *The Middle Ages*, II, 752 ff. Also Henry Adams, *Mont-Saint-Michel and Chartres* (Boston, 1904), p. 285 ff.; Taylor, *The Mediaeval Mind*, II, 368—554; Shaw, *Trends of Civilization and Culture*, p. 242 ff.; and Seeberg, *Lehrbuch*, III, 368 ff.

56. Boehmer, *Der Junge Luther*, pp. 39—40; Adams, *Mont-Saint-Michel and Chartres*, p. 352; Koehler, *I. M. R.*, pp. 351—352; Seeberg, *Greifswalder Studien*, VI, 7.

57. Seeberg, *Greifswalder Studien*, VI, 5.

58. Mackinnon, *Martin Luther*, I, 69. Cf. Denifle, *Luther und Lutherthum*, I, 577, 578.

59. Mackinnon, *Martin Luther*, I, 71—72.

60. Seeberg, *Greifswalder Studien*, VI, 7; Rommel, *Randbemerkungen*, p. 70. Cf. also Scotus, in Harnack, *History of Dogma*, VI, 306 ff.

61. Seeberg, *Greifswalder Studien*, VI, 9—12.

62. Loofs, *Leitfaden*, p. 615. Tr. by Mackinnon, *Martin Luther*, I, 75—76.

63. Mackinnon, *Martin Luther*, I, n. 1, for free rendition by author.

64. *E. A.*, XLIX, 27, in exegesis of Gospel of St. John.

65. *C. R.*, VI, 158. Cf. Kohlschmidt, p. 45 ff.

66. *W. A., T. R.*, I, 44, n. 116: "Ibi monarchi ei dederunt bibliam rubro corio tectam," writes Veit Dietrich. Cf. Mathesius in *Martin Luther* (Berlin, 1933), p. 125. This was doubtless from the same source as that of Nicolaus Selnecker in his *historica narratio et oratio*, where he wrote (1575): "Now that Luther had become a priest he was required in obedience to his vow to lay aside the Holy Books and to read the Scholastics and Sophistic writings." Cf. Reu, *Luther's German Bible*, p. 88 ff.

67. *C. R.*, VI, 159. Cf. *Martin Luther* (Berlin, 1933), p. 125. See also Mueller, *Werdegang*, p. 83 ff., and Loofs, *Leitfaden*, pp. 523–524.

68. On February 23, 1542, Luther wrote Graf Albrecht von Mansfeld, Enders, XIV, 189: "And in case Doctor Staupitz, or rather God through Doctor Staupitz, had not rescued me, I would long have drowned (in sea of confusion) and been in hell." For a more detailed study of this problem see Wilhelm Pauck, "The Historiography of the German Reformation during the Past Twenty Years," *Church History*, IX (1940), 324–325.

69. *C. R.*, VI, 159.

70. For a discussion of the Mystics consult Seeberg, *Greifswalder Studien*, VI, 27 ff.; Mackinnon, *Martin Luther*, I, 212–235; *W. A.*, IX, 95; I, 137; I, 557; Boehmer, *L. L. R. R.*, p. 102 ff.

71. For an excellent thesis on these, see Rommel, *Randbemerkungen*, p. 5 ff. Cf. Pauck, "Historiography," *Church History*, IX, 325; Loofs, *Leitfaden*, p. 691 ff.

72. Rommel, *Randbemerkungen*, pp. 21–22.

73. *W. A.*, IX, 69, 74, 81. Rommel, *Randbemerkungen*, pp. 44–45, also pp. 53–54 for four kinds of sins.

74. Rommel, *Randbemerkungen*, pp. 62–63. Cf. *W. A.*, IX, 72, Dist. 27, 7.

75. *W. A.*, IX, 10, 16, 24, 25, 26, 31, 62, and 68.

76. Rommel, *Randbemerkungen*, pp. 28–29; Schubert, *Luther-Jahrbuch*, VIII, 9. For an opposing view see Karl Bauer, *Die Wittenberger Universitaetstheologie und die Anfaenge der Deutschen Reformation* (Tuebingen, 1928).

77. Enders, I, 187; *W. A.*, "*Briefe*," I, 171: "ex te primo omnium didici, solis canonicis libris deberi fidem, caeteris omnibus iudicium, ut B. Augustinus, imo Paulus et Johannes praecipiunt."

78. Boehmer, *L. L. R. R.*, pp. 79–80 and 107–108.

79. *C. R.*, VI, 159. Cf. *W. A., T. R.*, I, 146, n. 352: "Ich hab mein theologiam nit auff ein mal gelernt, sonder hab ymmer tieffer und tieffer grubeln mussen, da haben mich meine tentationes hin bracht, quia sine usu non potest disci." Cf. Reu, *Luther's German Bible*, pp. 93–97, and *W. A.*, IX, 35, 46, 65.

80. The best introduction to this journey is still Boehmer, *Romfahrt*, pp. 1–177. There is also a detailed discussion in Scheel, *Martin Luther*, II, 248–297.

81. According to Boehmer, *Romfahrt*, p. 5, n. 3, Paul Luther died March 8, 1593, and Dresser, who knew him well, preached the funeral sermon. Cf. Scheel, *Dokumente*, pp. 2 and 6; Matthaeus Dresser, "Narratio de profectione M. Lutheri in Urbem," *Historiae Lutheri Lipsiae* (1598); Georg Mylius, *Epistola ad Romanos* (Jena, 1595). This source is copiously quoted on the Rome journey.

82. "Luthers Aufruf an den Adel, die Kirche zu reformieren," *A. R.*, XXXII (1935), 167 ff.

83. The best edition is *Epistolae Obscurorum Virorum*, tr., F. G. Stokes (1909), with Latin text.

84. At the time he was only a graduate student. For a comparison with the journey of Erasmus, who went as a scholar with an established European reputation, see Schubert, *Luther-Jahrbuch*, VIII, 11—12.

85. Cochlaeus wrote many bitter tracts against Luther, three of which discuss the journey to Rome. For a discussion of these and of other sources see Boehmer, *Romfahrt*, pp. 8—9 and 10—25.

86. *C. R.*, VI, 159—160. Cf. text, p. 282 ff.

87. M. Johann Mathesius, *Dr. Martin Luthers Leben* (St. Louis, 1883), p. 9. Cf. Roerer, *A. R.*, V, 347: "1510 fui Romae."

88. *E. A.*, XXV, 2, 147: "That you are the Pope's greatest enemy is common knowledge, and only because, while you were in Rome he would not free you from your monastic vow and permit you to take a public woman as a wife; and secondly, in that he did not immediately make you a cardinal or a bishop; and thirdly, because Pope Leo X checked and restricted the ordinary process of conviction on account of your devilish teachings, disobedience and heresy; for these reasons, you as all the damned are plagued day and night by your conscience and in your heart and innermost being can never be happy."

89. Boehmer, *Romfahrt*, p. 10 ff.

90. *W. A., T. R.*, II, 49, n. 1327.

91. Boehmer, *Romfahrt*, p. 37 ff.

92. Boehmer, *Romfahrt*, p. 56, n. 3, cites the members.

93. Boehmer, *Der Junge Luther*, p. 69.

94. Scheel, *Martin Luther*, II, 255 ff.; see map, p. 257.

95. Lauterbach, *Tagebuch*, p. 43.

96. Boehmer, *Der Junge Luther*, p. 71.

97. *Colloquia*, I, 134. Cf. Boehmer, *Romfahrt*, p. 82.

98. Boehmer, *Romfahrt*, pp. 82—83.

99. *W. A.*, XLIII, 330; *Colloquia*, I, 373. Cf. Boehmer, *Romfahrt*, p. 84 f.

100. Boehmer, *Romfahrt*, pp. 118—119. Cf. p. 80, n. 6, p. 81, n. 2.

101. Boehmer, *Romfahrt*, p. 88. Cf. Pastor, *Geschichte der Paepste*, III, 653 ff.

102. Boehmer, *Der Junge Luther*, p. 83.

103. Schulte, *Die Fugger*, I, 8 ff. Cf. Georg von Graevenitz, *Deutsche in Rom* (Leipzig, 1902); Friedrich Noack, *Das Deutsche Rom* (Rom, 1912).

104. Boehmer, *Romfahrt,* p. 111, cf. n. 1.

105. S. *Agostino* always had forty members, while S. *Maria del Popolo* was larger, Boehmer, *Romfahrt,* p. 113, n. 4, says forty-nine members. The papal houses of Riario and Rovere had blessed these houses, according to Pastor, *The History of the Popes,* II, 677 f.

106. Boehmer, *Romfahrt,* pp. 119–121.

107. Boehmer, *Romfahrt,* p. 121. Cf. Z. K., XXXII, 606 f.; Mackinnon, *Martin Luther,* I, 144, n. 78.

108. Scheel, *Theologische Rundschau,* XV (1912), 88 ff.

109. W. A., XXXI, I, 226; Mathesius, T. R., p. 566; *Colloquia,* III, 249.

110. Scheel, *Dokumente,* p. 43; W. A., XXXI, I, 226.

111. W. A., II, 72; XIV, 394; XLV, 28; *Colloquia,* I, 163; III, 107, 230, 249. For all the places visited by Luther see Boehmer, *Romfahrt,* p. 123 ff. Luther spoke of the German national church, S. *Maria dell' Anima* behind *Piazza Navona* in a sermon delivered on April 2, 1538, W. A., XLVII, 425.

112. Karl Bauer, A. R., XXXII (1935), 197.

113. E. A., 20, 2, 484. Cf. W. A., XLVII, 394, 816 f.; *Opera Lutheri,* VII, 569.

114. Boehmer, *Romfahrt,* pp. 125–127.

115. W. A., XLVII, 816–817; Cf. W. A., XXXI, I, 226; E. A., XXVI, 2, 193.

116. Pastor, *The History of the Popes,* III, 320. Cf. Mathesius, T. R., p. 742; *Colloquia,* III, 232 ff.

117. Schulte, *Die Fugger,* I, 208, says 10,000 rh. florin; Boehmer, *Romfahrt,* pp. 132–133. Cf. E. A., LVII, 330.

118. Boehmer, *Romfahrt,* pp. 142–147, gives Luther's impressions of Rome. W. A., T. R., IV, 193, n. 4195; Lauterbach, *Tagebuch,* p. 193; *Colloquia,* I, 165; III, 249; Ficker, *Roemerbrief,* 272, 301, 310, 319; W. A., IV, 637, 651; II, 72 ff.; 600; VI, 437; XXXVIII, 211; XLIII, 57; XLV, 421.

119. Karl Bauer, A. R., XXXII, 197; Enders, II, 432–433, and n. 4. Cf. *Colloquia,* II, 331; Lauterbach, *Tagebuch,* p. 100; and *Erasmi Opera,* I, 106 f.

120. *Colloquia,* III, 102; Boehmer, *Romfahrt,* p. 83. Cf. Boehmer, *Der Junge Luther,* p. 80.

121. Mathesius, T. R., "De Diabolo," n. 68. Cf. Foerstemann, T. R., IV, 435 f., and Boehmer, *Romfahrt,* p. 83.

122. Boehmer, *Der Junge Luther,* pp. 85–86, suggests that the two men may have been asked to leave Erfurt and that they then appealed to Staupitz. Luther did invite the Erfurt Prior and the Convent to attend his promotion to the doctorate, Enders, I, 7; W. A., "*Briefe,*" I, 18–19. He had received the degree of *Biblicus* while at Wittenberg, March 9, 1509, the degree of *Sententiarius* at Erfurt in October, 1509, after his recall. Nathin, whom he had assisted as instructor, accused Luther of having broken an earlier promise by accepting his doctorate from Wittenberg rather than Erfurt. For Luther's reply see Enders, I, 16–20; W. A., "*Briefe,*" I, 24–27. Cf. Steinlein, *Neue kirchliche Zeitschrift,* XXIII, 767 ff. For further information on Nathin see W. A., "*Briefe,*" I, 26, n. 2.

123. Boehmer, *Der Junge Luther*, p. 89. Cf. *W. A., T. R.*, III, 187—188, for Staupitz's reply; also II, 379; IV, 13, 129—130; Mathesius, *Dr. Martin Luthers Leben*, p. 9; Melanchthon, *C. R.*, "*Vita*," VI, 160; Enders, I, 7—8.

124. Mathesius, *Dr. Martin Luthers Leben*, p. 9; *C. R.*, VI, 160, for Melanchthon's account.

125. Scheel, *Martin Luther*, II, 311. For notation in books of the exchequer see Reu, *Luther's German Bible*, p. 331, n. 51.

126. See n. 122, Chapter Five.

127. See text, p. 287; notes 37, 38, and 39, Chapter Nine.

128. Boehmer, *Der Junge Luther*, p. 92. For picture of ring see Schreckenbach and Neubert, p. 57; for the bells, Charitius, p. 156; for doctor's oath see Reu, *Luther's German Bible*, pp. 98—99, and Mathesius, *Dr. Martin Luthers Leben*, pp. 10—13.

129. Friedensburg, *Urkundenbuch*, I, 34—36, treats the subject of promotions in the theological faculty. The complete statutes of this faculty are given on pages 31—38.

130. *W. A.*, XLV, 86: "Iterum acquisivimus lucem. Sed ego, cum Doctor fierem, nescivi."

CHAPTER SIX

1. H. Heubner, *Der Bau des kurfuerstlichen Schloszes* (Wittenberg, 1937), p. 5, speaks of a Roman depot on this site. For the author's study of the town see "The Electoral Town of Wittenberg," *Medievalia et Humanistica*, III (1945), p. 99 ff.

2. See text, p. 72 ff.

3. Schalscheleth, pp. 25—41.

4. Gottfried Krueger, "Wie sah die Stadt Wittenberg zu Luthers Lebzeiten aus?" *Vierteljahrsschrift der Luthergesellschaft*, XV (1933), 15.

5. *Dialogus of 1507*, sec. 16, a dialogue written by a Wittenberg professor as a "Lockschrift" to draw students. It contains much valuable information on the old Luther city. In 1936 there were only three copies in Germany. See also D. Dr. Johannes Hauszleiter, *Die Universitaet Wittenberg vor dem Eintritt Luthers* (Leipzig, 1903), p. 27 ff.; Thulin, *Lutherstadt Wittenberg und Torgau* (Berlin, 1932), pp. 12—18; Charitius, pp. 130—137; Krueger, *Wittenberg*, pp. 22—23.

6. Friedensburg, *G. U. W.*, p. 1 ff. gives a rather detailed description of this university on the Elbe. No.19 is also called *Das Alte Friederici Collegium*, named for Frederick the Wise, the founder. No. 20 is also called *Das Neue Collegium* or *Neue Friederici Collegium*. The best account on the Black Cloister is Hermann Stein, *Geschichte des Lutherhauses* (Wittenberg, 1883), p. 3 ff.; Thulin, *Lutherstadt Wittenberg und Torgau*, p. 28 ff.

7. See n. 5, Chapter Six; full title in abbreviations.

8. See *Plan of Wittenberg in 1623*, p. 202 in text.

9. Koehler, *I. M. R.*, p. 379.

10. Balthasar Mentzius, *Syntagma Epitaphio Rem quae in inclyta,* etc. (Saxone. Magdeburgi, Anno MDCIV), II, 2—3, for a description of church. Text is reproduced in *Medievalia et Humanistica,* III, 104—105, n. 25, also the statement by Melanchthon from the document placed in the church tower in 1556. Cf. picture in Max Senf, *Die Reformationsfeier zu Wittenberg 1917* (Wittenberg, 1918), p. 26. The drawings by A. Spitzer on pp. 62—63 are very good, except that "Stadttuerme seit 1558" should be dated 1556.

11. Thulin, *Lutherstadt Wittenberg und Torgau,* pp. 7—10.

12. The author examined both copies but based most of his observations on the Halle copy. Cf. illustration, p. 263; *Medievalia et Humanistica,* III, 101, n. 11.

13. See note 31, Chapter Three.

14. *Medievalia et Humanistica,* III, 106, n. 29; or note 1, Chapter Three.

15. The original manuscript, written in Melanchthon's own hand, is well preserved in the Lutherhalle, Wittenberg. Cf. Max Senf, *Die Reformationsfeier zu Wittenberg 1917* (Wittenberg, 1918), pp. 62—63, also 82, 88, 104, and 105.

16. Grohmann, *Annalen,* I, 70 ff.; Schreckenbach and Neubert, p. 58; Thulin, *Lutherstadt Wittenberg und Torgau,* plate 41.

17. *Album,* I, for 1644—45. For copy, Krueger, *Wittenberg,* pp. 16—17.

18. Heubner, *Schlosz,* pp. 5—8, 32 ff. *passim.*

19. Sec. 16.

20. Boehmer, *Der Junge Luther,* p. 60, cites Scheurl: "roh, versoffen und gefraeszig." Cf. *W. A., T. R.,* II, 669.

21. Myconius, *Historia Reformationis,* pp. 26—27.

22. Boehmer, *Der Junge Luther,* p. 59.

23. Schreckenbach and Neubert, p. 89.

24. Schalscheleth, p. 47.

25. *W. A., T. R.,* II, 669, n. 2800b.

26. Schalscheleth, p. 47.

27. Krueger, *Wittenberg,* p. 13.

28. Sec. 16; Hauszleiter, *D. U. W.,* p. 5 ff.; Friedensburg, *G. U. W.,* pp. 43—44.

29. Charitius. The manuscript is now owned by the son of Max Senf, who declined its publication, but very generously permitted quotations.

30. *Medievalia et Humanistica,* III, 99—100, n. 3.

31. Krueger, *Wittenberg,* p. 5.

32. *Luther-Jahrbuch,* IX (1927), 9—118.

33. Note 1, Chapter Six.

34. Eschenhagen, "Wittenberger Studien," pp. 40—42.

35. Eschenhagen, "Wittenberger Studien," pp. 40—42. See also "Die Einwohnerzahl," pp. 28—42.

36. This is calculated on the basis of the 1623 plan. See note 8, Chapter Six.

37. The aged Oberbuergermeister Schirmer took the author to the outskirts of the old city and pointed out remnants of the *Bedeckter Weg.* See Eschenhagen, "Wittenberger Studien," p. 16 and n. 13 for the watchmen on the walls.

38. Krueger, *Wittenberg,* p. 16. A mill operates on the same spot today, using power supplied by these streams; but it is not the three-story structure seen in the Halle and Dresden woodcuts of 1611 enlarged by Bossoegel in 1744, I. M. R., 360.

39. Eschenhagen, "Wittenberger Studien," p. 14 ff.; Krueger, *Wittenberg,* pp. 17—19.

40. *Dialogus of 1507,* sec. 16. The conversation was as follows: "How did the name of this street originate?" "It is called Jewish Street after the Jews who formerly lived in this section." "Have you now really driven them out?" "Completely."

41. Krueger, *Wittenberg,* pp. 16—17, and 23. For a description of the Castle Church see Charitius, pp. 125—136, 202—209; also Heubner, *Schlosz,* pp. 8—29, for a recent description.

42. Cranach was very intimate with Luther, and no doubt most of the portraits made in the 1520's were done in this house. Cf. *Medievalia et Humanistica,* III, 105, n. 27.

43. Dr. Krueger could no longer locate the building with certainty. Mellerstadt was so favored because he was an authority on "morbo Franco." See Grohmann, *Annalen,* I, 8.

44. *Dialogus of 1507,* sec. 16.

45. Richard Erfurth, *Die Lutherstadt Wittenberg und ihre Umgebung* (Wittenberg, 1927), pp. 82—83. For details G. Mentz, *Johann Friedrich der Grossmuetige* (Jena, 1908), I, Dritter Teil, 103 ff.; Mylius, *Memorabilia,* p. 26 ff.

46. Eschenhagen, "Wittenberger Studien," p. 19, n. 25; also p. 20, n. 29.

47. Eschenhagen, "Wittenberger Studien," p. 20, n. 34.

48. *Medievalia et Humanistica,* III, 102, n. 14. Cf. notes 62, 64, 67, 68, and 69.

49. Eschenhagen, "Wittenberger Studien," p. 22, n. 42.

50. *Medievalia et Humanistica,* III, 111—112. Cf. Krueger, *Wittenberg,* pp. 25—26.

51. Thulin, *Lutherstadt Wittenberg und Torgau,* plate 27; Schreckenbach and Neubert, p. 59.

52. Mentzius, *Syntagma,* II, 7; Charitius, pp. 155—156.

53. Charitius, pp. 155—159.

54. The author visited the tower rooms and read the Charitius account to the elderly woman then living there. She confirmed the authenticity of the account and still observed many of the ancient customs.

55. Charitius, pp. 113—121. Cf. Krueger, *Wittenberg,* p. 26.

56. Krueger, *Wittenberg,* pp. 26—27. See text, p. 679 ff.

57. The author visited the two homes with Dr. Krueger, who explained the reasons for his conclusion.

58. Eschenhagen, "Wittenberger Studien," p. 25, cites Kersten's story. Hermann Werdermann, *Luthers Wittenberger Gemeinde* (Guetersloh, 1929), pp. 9–10.

59. Werdermann, *Luthers Wittenberger Gemeinde*, p. 10.

60. Charitius, pp. 109–110. Cf. *E. A.*, LIII, 402. The wooden coffins were still there in 1936.

61. *Dialogus of 1507*, sec. 16.

62. See text, pp. 617 ff. and 634 ff. The role of the Augsburg Confession has been overemphasized. It was used in the Wittenberg Theological Faculty, but in the lands of most of the Protestant princes the Catechism was sufficient. See text, p. 740 ff.

63. See text, p. 496. *W. A.*, *"Briefe,"* II, 306; Mueller, *Die Wittenberger Bewegung*, p. 126, n. 4.

64. Eschenhagen, "Wittenberger Studien," p. 26, n. 73.

65. *Dialogus of 1507*, sec. 16.

66. *Dialogus of 1507*, sec. 16. Eschenhagen, "Wittenberger Studien," p. 25, n. 59.

67. Cited by Krueger, *Wittenberg*, p. 27. Also *Dialogus of 1507*, sec. 16, which uses the spelling given.

68. Krueger, *Wittenberg*, p. 28.

CHAPTER SEVEN

1. This reproduction by W. Seidel first appeared as the frontispiece of E. G. Schwiebert, *Reformation Lectures* (Valparaiso, 1937). Text, p. 222.

2. This work was executed for the author by the Wittenberg artist O. H. Heubner in 1936, son of the H. Heubner cited in note 1, Chapter Six. This drawing was later enlarged and slightly changed under the author's direction by Miss Renata Ludwig, student at Valparaiso University. See text, plate 19. Numbers in text refer to buildings on woodcut.

3. Discussed in detail in Friedensburg, *G. U. W.*, first part; also briefly in Krueger, *Wittenberg*, pp. 28–29.

4. *Dialogus of 1507*, sec. 16. Cf. Hauszleiter, *D. U. W.*, p. 27 ff.

5. Hauszleiter, *D. U. W.*, pp. 27–28. Cf. Eschenhagen, "Wittenberger Studien," p. 18, for later location of the law school.

6. Notes 67 and 68, Chapter Six.

7. For original order by Elector John Frederick see Friedensburg, *Urkundenbuch*, I, 165–166. Cf. Erfurth, *Die Lutherstadt Wittenberg und ihre Umgebung*, p. 44.

8. Myconius, *Historia Reformationis*, p. 24.

9. Charitius, p. 97; Krueger, *Wittenberg*, p. 29.

10. Krueger, *Wittenberg*, p. 29; Stein, *Lutherhaus*, p. 5.

11. Stein, *Lutherhaus*, p. 8.

12. Stein, *Lutherhaus*, p. 8; cf. note 8.

13. Stein, *Lutherhaus*, pp. 8–9.

14. Stein, *Lutherhaus*, p. 12.

15. *Epistolae Obscurorum Virorum*, ed. F. G. Stokes (1909).

16. See text, p. 536. Stein, *Lutherhaus*, p. 16.

17. Stein, *Lutherhaus*, p. 17.

18. Stein, *Lutherhaus*, p. 17.

19. Stein, *Lutherhaus*, p. 18.

20. W. A., *"Briefe,"* VI, 257—258.

21. Friedensburg, *Urkundenbuch*, I, 348—349. For the value of the gulden see Schwiebert, *Reformation Lectures*, p. 207 ff.

22. Enders, XIV, 15—17. According to the *Kaufbrief* it was bought for 430 gulden June 29, 1541. Cf. note 1, Chapter Seven.

23. Text, p. 589.

24. Grohmann, *Annalen*, I, 67 ff.

25. Text, p. 287. Cf. Stein, *Lutherhaus*, p. 27; Enders, VI, 117; W. A., T. R., III, 228, n. 3232.

26. Erfurth, *Die Lutherstadt Wittenberg und ihre Umgebung*, pp. 37—42.

27. Grohmann, *Annalen*, I, 85—86; Merian, *Topographia Saxoniae*, p. 195.

28. *Luther-Jahrbuch*, III (1921), 109—135.

29. *Luther-Jahrbuch*, III, 117 ff.

30. *Luther-Jahrbuch*, IV (1922), 101—104. Cf. Enders, VI, 117.

31. Grohmann, *Annalen*, I, 78.

32. Grohmann, *Annalen*, I, 88—89; Merian, *Topographia Saxoniae*, p. 195.

33. S. *Oratio Secularis in Academia Vitebergensi* a Joanne Zangero, 1602, is Grohmann's source in *Annalen*, I, 85 ff. Cf. also Friedensburg, *G. U. W.*, p. 81; Merian, *Topographia Saxoniae*, pp. 195—196.

34. Friedensburg, *G. U. W.*, p. 81; Scheurl, *Briefbuch*, I, 58.

35. Friedensburg, *Urkundenbuch*, I, 28.

36. Erfurth, *Die Lutherstadt Wittenberg und ihre Umgebung*, p. 44. Friedensburg, *Urkundenbuch*, I, 165—166, n. 2.

37. Schalscheleth, p. 42; Heubner, *Schlosz*, p. 6.

38. *Wittemberger Heiligthumsbuch*, illustrated by Lucas Cranach the Elder (Wittemberg, 1509), p. 1 of introduction. Faber, *Historische Nachricht*, p. 11, for the story of Rudolf's gift.

39. Charitius, pp. 124—125. Cf. Faber, *Historische Nachricht*, p. 8.

40. Cornelius Gurlitt, *Die Lutherstadt Wittenberg*, p. 38. The picture of the old Castle Church, dated by author as 1499, is the tower of 1558, p. 64. The tower of the Pflueger church was Gothic as the Cranach source shows, n. 38. Cf. Krueger, *Wittenberg*, p. 28.

41. Gurlitt, *Die Lutherstadt Wittenberg*, pp. 38—39. Heubner, *Schlosz*, pp. 12—14, points out that it was not completed.

42. Dilichs, *Federzeichnungen*, I, 37.

43. Charitius, pp. 130—131.

44. Krueger, *Wittenberg*, p. 22.

45. Melanchthon document in Lutherhalle, Germany, tells the story. Mentzius, *Syntagma,* II, 2–3, also tells this story. The text is reproduced in *Medievalia et Humanistica,* III (1945), 104–105, n. 25.

46. Sec. 16; Charitius, pp. 130–137.

47. Dilichs, *Federzeichnungen,* 1, 4, 5, 36, and 37. There is an excellent reproduction of the original in Harper Memorial Library at the University of Chicago.

48. Charitius, p. 132.

49. *Dialogus of 1507,* sec. 7 ff., *passim;* Hauszleiter, *D. U. W.,* pp. 22–27; Andrea Sennerto, *Athenae Itemque Inscriptiones Wittebergensis* (Wittenberg, 1655), Libri II; Wernsdorf wrote the introduction to Faber, *Historische Nachricht;* Charitius, 130 ff., also has a good description.

50. Cornelius Gurlitt, *Die Lutherstadt Wittenberg,* p. 39.

51. Schreckenbach and Neubert, p. 64; Thulin, *Lutherstadt Wittenberg und Torgau,* "Bildernachweis," no. 4.

52. *Dialogus of 1507,* sec. 7 ff.

53. Gurlitt, *Die Lutherstadt Wittenberg,* p. 49.

54. Hauszleiter, *D. U. W.,* pp. 22–23, has an analysis of chapter 7 of the *Dialogus of 1507.*

55. Hauszleiter, *D. U. W.,* p. 26, and n. 2.

56. *Wittemberger Heiligthumsbuch,* introduction pp. 1–4; Cf. Faber, *Historische Nachricht,* p. 67.

57. Hauszleiter, *D. U. W.,* p. 26, n. 2. Cf. *Dialogus of 1507,* sec. 8.

58. Georg Hirth of Munich reproduced a facsimile of the original Lucas Cranach, *Wittemberger Heiligthumsbuch* in *Liebhaber-Bibliothek Alter Illustratoren* (Muenchen, 1884), copies of which are now extremely rare. An original Cranach guide is in the Lutherhalle, Wittenberg, Germany.

59. Hauszleiter, *D. U. W.,* p. 27.

60. *Dialogus of 1507,* sec. 8; Hauszleiter, *D. U. W.,* pp. 27–28.

61. *Dialogus of 1507,* sec. 8; Hauszleiter, *D. U. W.,* p. 28.

62. *Dialogus of 1507,* sec. 8; Hauszleiter, *D. U. W.,* p. 30.

63. *Dialogus of 1507,* sec. 8; Hauszleiter, *D. U. W.,* p. 31.

64. Heubner, *Schlosz,* pp. 14–18.

65. Mylius, *Memorabilia,* p. 26.

66. *Annalen des Chur-Fuerstlichen Hauses Sachsen Ernestin- und Albertinischer Linien, von Anno 1400 bis 1700* (Weimar, 1700), p. 68.

67. Mylius, *Memorabilia,* p. 2, n. (aaa).

68. Spalatin, *Ephemerides,* V, 53.

69. Buchwald, *Archiv fuer die Geschichte des deutschen Buchhandels,* XVIII (1896), 10.

70. Scheurl, *Briefbuch,* I, 105. Cf. also letters nos. 45 and 63.

71. Ernst Hildebrandt, "Die kurfuerstliche Schlosz und Universitaetsbibliothek zu Wittenberg 1512–1547," *Zeitschrift fuer Buchkunde,* II (1925), 40, claims there were 163 volumes. The above figures are quoted by Friedensburg, *G. U. W.,* p. 154. The total was 202 gulden. For value of gulden see Schwiebert, *Reformation Lectures,* pp. 207–209.

72. J. W. Thompson, *The Medieval Library* (Chicago, 1939), p. 61. Cf. Clark, *Libraries*, p. 25; also, Thompson, pp. 597, 613, and 623.

73. Friedensburg, *G. U. W.*, p. 238. For the use of wall bookcases see Clark, *Libraries*, pp. 43–45; Clark, *The Care of Books*, p. 265 ff.; and Thompson, *The Medieval Library*, p. 624.

74. Friedensburg, *Urkundenbuch*, I, 181.

75. Heubner, *Schlosz*, p. 21.

76. Mylius, *Memorabilia*, pp. 36–37.

77. Friedensburg, *Urkundenbuch*, I, 186.

78. Clark, *Libraries*, pp. 27–28.

79. Clark, *Libraries*, p. 29.

80. See I. M. L., p. 360.

81. Friedensburg, *Urkundenbuch*, I, 68, n. 46.

82. *Der Briefwechsel des Conradus Mutianus*, ed., Gillert (Halle, 1890), I, 374.

83. Kolde, *Analecta*, p. 310.

84. Friedensburg, *Urkundenbuch*, I, 234–235, n. 243.

85. Friedensburg, *Urkundenbuch*, I, 186.

86. Schwiebert, "Remnants of a Reformation Library," *The Library Quarterly*, X (1940), 494–495.

87. Schwiebert, "Remnants of a Reformation Library," *The Library Quarterly*, X (1940), 499–500.

88. Mentz, *Johann Friedrich*, I, Pt. III, 108–111; Mylius, *Memorabilia*, p. 27; cf. Friedensburg, *Urkundenbuch*, I, 297–300; Mentz, *Johann Friedrich*, I, Pt. III, 256; Grohmann, *Annalen*, I, 97 f.

89. Friedensburg, *Urkundenbuch*, I, 181.

90. Mylius, *Memorabilia*, p. 2.

91. *C. R.*, II, 625, n. 1089.

92. Schwiebert, *The Library Quarterly*, X, 504.

93. Schwiebert, *The Library Quarterly*, X, n. 61.

94. Friedensburg, *G. U. W.*, p. 154.

95. Gillert, *Der Briefwechsel des Conradus Mutianus*, I, 374.

96. Scheurl, *Briefbuch*, I, 105.

97. Drews, *Spalatiniana*, pp. 69–70, letter of January 13, 1514.

98. Drews, *Spalatiniana*, p. 88.

99. Friedensburg, *Urkundenbuch*, I, 187–188.

100. Friedensburg, *Urkundenbuch*, I, 188, n. 203.

101. Schwiebert, *The Library Quarterly*, X, 524–525.

102. Friedensburg, *Urkundenbuch*, I, 234–235; cf. 297–301 for the moving of the library to Jena.

CHAPTER EIGHT

1. Friedensburg, *Urkundenbuch*, I, 1–6; Grohmann, *Annalen*, I, 1 ff., *passim*, for documents and early history.

2. Friedensburg, *G. U. W.*, p. 1. Erfurt was really under the Archbishop of Mainz. In the north were Rostock and Greifswald. Cologne was in the northwest.

3. Friedensburg, *Urkundenbuch*, I, 3.

4. *Album*, III, 803–804. For enrollments and actual student matriculations see I, 1502 ff.

5. *Album*, III, 803–804.

6. *Album*, I, 86–108; III, 804.

7. Friedensburg, *Urkundenbuch*, I, 109.

8. Friedensburg, *Urkundenbuch*, I, 17 ff., has statutes of 1508. For names of Rectors consult *Album*, III, 803 ff.

9. *Liber Decanorum*, pp. 30–33.

10. Friedensburg, *Urkundenbuch*, I, 14–17.

11. Friedensburg, *Urkundenbuch*, I, 167–169. For salaries see Schwiebert, *Reformation Lectures*, pp. 215–224.

12. Grohmann, *Annalen*, I, 116–117.

13. Grohmann, *Annalen*, I, 116–117. Cf. Friedensburg, *Urkundenbuch*, I, 491–499.

14. Grohmann, *Annalen*, I, 116–118.

15. Friedensburg, *Urkundenbuch*, I, 17, 147, 167–187. Cf. Friedrich Israël, "Das Wittenberger Universitaetsarchiv, seine Geschichte und seine Bestaende," *Forschungen zur Thueringisch-Saechsischen Geschichte*, IV (Halle, 1913), 66–67 and 112–113.

16. Friedensburg, *Urkundenbuch*, I, 458 ff.

17. Friedensburg, *Urkundenbuch*, I, 461.

18. Friedensburg, *Urkundenbuch*, I, 472.

19. Friedensburg, *Urkundenbuch*, I, 16.

20. Smith, *The Age of the Reformation*, p. 463. Cf. Schwiebert, *Reformation Lectures*, p. 207 ff.

21. Schwiebert, *Reformation Lectures*, p. 209. Grohmann, *Annalen*, I, 165–166.

22. See text, p. 268, for Luther's will. Enders, XIV, 217.

23. Grohmann, *Annalen*, I, 45–55. Cf. Schwiebert, *Reformation Lectures*, pp. 207–214.

24. Grohmann, *Annalen*, I, 46 ff.

25. Grohmann, *Annalen*, I, 46 ff.

26. Schwiebert, *Reformation Lectures*, p. 210. Cf. Grohmann, *Annalen*, I, 46 ff.

27. Grohmann, *Annalen*, I, 46 ff.

28. Grohmann, *Annalen*, I, 46 ff.

29. Friedensburg, *Urkundenbuch*, I, 179–180.

30. Friedensburg, *Urkundenbuch*, I, 179–180.
31. Grohmann, *Annalen*, I, 46–51.
32. Grohmann, *Annalen*, I, 46–51; Friedenbsurg, *Urkundenbuch*, I, 179–183.
33. Grohmann, *Annalen*, I, 46–51; Friedensburg, *Urkundenbuch*, I, 179–183.
34. Grohmann, *Annalen*, I, 52–53.
35. Grohmann, *Annalen*, I, 52–53.
36. Grohmann, *Annalen*, I, 62 ff., sep. 70.
37. Grohmann, *Annalen*, I, 52–53.
38. Friedensburg, *Urkundenbuch*, I, 371–373; Grohmann, *Annalen*, I, 52–53.
39. Friedensburg, *Urkundenbuch*, I, 174–178.
40. Grohmann, *Annalen*, I, 27.
41. Grohmann, *Annalen*, I, 41.
42. Grohmann, *Annalen*, I, 33.
43. Enders, XIV, 214–218; for the text of the letter see "Anlage II" to Eschenhagen, "Wittenberger Studien," p. 106.
44. Eschenhagen, "Wittenberger Studien," p. 88.
45. Friedensburg, *Urkundenbuch*, I, 348–349.
46. Enders, XIV, 217.
47. Enders, XIII, 107 and 108, n. 2.
48. Enders, X, 294–295. Cf. *E. A.*, 55, 121, for text of Luther's letter to the Elector of January 25, 1536; also *W. A.*, *"Briefe,"* VII, 352–354.
49. Friedensburg, *Urkundenbuch*, I, 171–172; cf. 202, n. 211, for Luther's income from debates.
50. Grohmann, *Annalen*, I, 111. Cf. Friedensburg, *Urkundenbuch*, I, 21–22, for Rector's fees; 25–27 for promotions in theology, law, and medicine.
51. Grohmann, *Annalen*, I, 111, says that Luther really saved 16 gulden as he did not have to become *Formatus* and *Sententiarius;* but this is a doubtful deduction. See note 122, Chapter Five.
52. Grohmann, *Annalen*, I, 114–115.
53. Schwiebert, *Reformation Lectures*, p. 222.
54. Enders, XIV, 294–295.
55. Schwiebert, *Reformation Lectures*, p. 222. Cf. Enders, X, 294, n. 2, and *E. A.*, LV, 121, n. 519.
56. Schwiebert, *Reformation Lectures*, pp. 222–223.
57. Enders, XIV, 217.
58. Enders, XIV, 149.
59. Based upon a gulden value of $13.40. Schwiebert, *Reformation Lectures*, pp. 207–209; Eschenhagen, "Wittenberger Studien," pp. 72–103.
60. Enders, XIV, 217, n. 3119.
61. In the older western part of Germany, Catholicism had become much more deeply rooted. The two sections might be compared to the conservative East in the United States and the more open-minded new West.
62. Friedensburg, *Urkundenbuch*, I, 14–15.

63. Friedensburg, *G. U. W.*, p. 49.
64. Grohmann, *Annalen*, I, 7–8. Mellerstadt had published S. *Pollichii declaratio defensiva de morbo Franco*, etc. (Leipzig, 1500).
65. Friedensburg, *G. U. W.*, pp. 45–46.
66. Friedensburg, *G. U. W.*, pp. 54–57 and 68–72.
67. Hauszleiter, *D. U. W.*, p. 9. Cf. Friedensburg, *G. U. W.*, p. 40.
68. Friedensburg, *G. U. W.*, pp. 50–53. Cf. Scheurl, *Briefbuch*, I, 124.
69. Friedensburg, *G. U. W.*, pp. 52–53 and 64–68.
70. Scheurl, *Briefbuch*, I, 124.
71. See text, p. 294 ff. Friedensburg, *G. U. W.*, pp. 47–48.
72. Friedensburg, *G. U. W.*, pp. 52–57.
73. Friedensburg, *G. U. W.*, pp. 53–54. He was the first dean of Canon Law and became Rector in the fall of 1519. *Album*, III, 804.
74. Friedensburg, *G. U. W.*, p. 58.
75. Friedensburg, *G. U. W.*, pp. 58–61. Author of the two-volume *Briefbuch*, important source for the period.
76. Friedensburg, *Urkundenbuch*, I, 14–17.
77. A copy of the photostatic reproduction is in the Valparaiso University Library. Cf. Friedensburg, *G. U. W.*, pp. 58–61.
78. Friedensburg, *G. U. W.*, p. 61.
79. Friedensburg, *Urkundenbuch*, I, 15; Friedensburg, *G. U. W.*, pp. 62–64.
80. Friedensburg, *G. U. W.*, pp. 64–68.
81. Friedensburg, *G. U. W.*, pp. 68–72.
82. Friedensburg, *G. U. W.*, p. 75.
83. Friedensburg, *G. U. W.*, pp. 82–83.
84. Friedensburg, *G. U. W.*, p. 83.
85. Friedensburg, *G. U. W.*, p. 82 ff.
86. Friedensburg, *G. U. W.*, pp. 75–77.
87. Friedensburg, *G. U. W.*, pp. 66–68.
88. Friedensburg, *G. U. W.*, p. 74.

CHAPTER NINE

1. Joachimsen, "Humanismus," VIII, 437 ff. Cf. J. Huizinga, "Das Problem der Renaissance," pp. 126–128.
2. Huizinga, "Das Problem der Renaissance," p. 128.
3. Joachimsen, "Humanismus," for an evaluation of Erasmus, p. 449 ff.
4. Wernle, *Die Renaissance*, p. 19; Mackinnon, *Martin Luther*, I, 157, n. 2, says the 1513 was already a second edition. Cf. *W. A.*, IV, 466 ff., for Luther's notes; Reu, *Luther's German Bible*, p. 101.
5. Meissinger, *Luthers Exegese*, pp. 1–2; Reu, *Luther's German Bible*, p. 101; Stein, *Lutherhaus*, p. 11; *W. A.*, III, 4 ff.
6. Wernle, *Die Renaissance*, p. 18 ff., 20–22. Cf. P. Smith, *Erasmus* (New York, 1923), p. 159 ff.; Reu, *Luther's German Bible*, p. 344.

7. Reu, *Luther's German Bible*, p. 120. Published by the Froben Press in February, 1516, Luther had a copy by August, 1516. Ficker cites first evidence of its use, *Roemerbrief*, I, 84, 22; Smith, *Erasmus*, p. 182 ff.

8. Text, p. 529.

9. Wernle, *Die Renaissance*, p. 26.

10. Reu, *Luther's German Bible*, pp. 115, 339—340. Cf. Meissinger, *Luthers Exegese*, pp. 38—39; Smith, *The Age of the Reformation*, p. 54; Rommel, *Randbemerkungen*, pp. 29—30.

11. Hans von Schubert, "Reformation und Humanismus," *Luther-Jahrbuch*, VIII (1926), 9. Cf. Rommel, *Randbemerkungen*, pp. 29—30; Meissinger, *Luthers Exegese*, pp. 22—26; W. A., III and IV, for the sources.

12. Theodosius Harnack, *Luthers Theologie* (Muenchen, 1927), II, 326; *Opera Lutheri*, I, 15 ff.; Holl, *Luther*, I, 111 ff.

13. Text, pp. 193—196.

14. Rommel, *Randbemerkungen*, pp. 5—6, 8; N. Paulus, *Usingen*, p. 8; Wernle, *Die Renaissance*, p. 17.

15. A. Hamel, *Der Junge Luther und Augustin* (Guetersloh, 1935), treats the influence on the young Luther. W. A., L, 624 ff., expresses the mature Luther's evaluation of Augustine.

16. Rommel, *Randbemerkungen*, p. 30 ff.; Enders, I, 187—190.

17. Meissinger, *Luthers Exegese*, pp. 38—39; Rommel, *Randbemerkungen*, pp. 28—30; W. A., IX, 10, 24, 25, 26, 31, 62, and 68, for evidence of knowledge of Greek.

18. Friedensburg, *G. U. W.*, pp. 97—98; Enders, III, 379—383, indicates that Lang also assisted in Hebrew. Cf. W. A., "Briefe," II, 548, n. 6; G. Bauch, *Monatsschrift fuer Geschichte und Wissenschaft des Judentums*, XLVIII (1904), 147. For further bibliography see Reu, *Luther's German Bible*, pp. 340—341.

19. Text, p. 527 ff.

20. Text, p. 384 ff.

21. Text, p. 695 ff.

22. H. Boehmer, *Luthers erste Vorlesung* (Leipzig, 1924), p. 3, says Luther began his first series of lectures on Genesis on October 25, 1512. See W. A., L, 519, 26, for the famous tract "Von den Konziliis und Kirchen." Cf. J. Ficker, "Luthers erste Vorlesung — welche?" *T. S. K. Lutherana*, V (1928). Luther did not lecture on Hebrews again until 1535, Boehmer, *Der Junge Luther*, p. 117.

23. Boehmer, *Der Junge Luther*, p. 117.

24. Boehmer, *Der Junge Luther*, p. 118; Stein, *Lutherhaus*, p. 12.

25. Hans Schmidt, *Luther und das Buch der Psalmen* (Tuebingen, 1933), p. 6, expresses the view that Luther preferred poetry to prose, hence the change. Cf. Reu, *Luther's German Bible*, p. 333, n. 56.

26. Reu, *Luther's German Bible*, p. 115. Cf. Boehmer, *Der Junge Luther*, pp. 121—122; W. A., III, 4 ff., for the text; Meissinger, *Luthers Exegese*, pp. 5—6.

27. Boehmer, *Luthers erste Vorlesung;* E. Vogelsang, *Die Anfaenge von Luthers Christologie nach der ersten Psalmenvorlesung* (Berlin, 1929). For further literature see Pauck, *Church History,* IX, 325.

28. *Luthers Exegese,* p. 6 ff. Ellwein, *Roemerbrief,* p. vii.

29. Reu, *Luther's German Bible,* pp. 333—334, notes 57—61. For example, Psalm 64 contains a *scholia* referring to *glosse* of Psalm 92. Cf. *W. A.,* III, 368. For a recent study see H. Wendorf, "Der Durchbruch der neuen Erkenntnis Luthers im Lichte der handschriftlichen Ueberlieferung," *H. V.,* XXVII (1932), 124—144, 285—327.

30. Meissinger, *Luthers Exegese,* pp. 39—49; Boehmer, *Der Junge Luther,* pp. 121—122.

31. Boehmer, *Der Junge Luther,* p. 124. The study of Romans was greatly facilitated for the modern student by Ficker's discovery of the original lecture notes in the Berlin Library. Cf. Ellwein, *Roemerbrief,* pp. v-vi.

32. Boehmer, *Der Junge Luther,* p. 124.

33. Boehmer, *Der Junge Luther,* p. 125. For text see Schubert, *Galaterbrief.*

34. E. Hirsch und H. Rueckert, *Luthers Vorlesung ueber den Hebraeerbrief* (Berlin, 1929), translated by E. Vogelsang and G. Helbig. Cf. Reu, "Source Material," *Luther's German Bible,* p. 148 ff., for translation of portions; H. Borcherdt, *Martin Luther, Ausgewaehlte Werke* (Muenchen, 1922), I, 11—12.

35. *Opera Lutheri,* I, 22—23; Borcherdt, *Werke,* I, 11—12; Th. Harnack, *Luthers Theologie* (Muenchen, 1927), II, 326—327; Stracke, *Luthers Selbstzeugnis,* CXL, 112, 128.

36. Schubert, *Galaterbrief,* p. 42. For his 1519 statement *W. A.,* II, 503.

37. Stein, *Lutherhaus,* pp. 27—28.

38. These evidences were clearly discernible in 1936 and were being pointed out to tourists.

39. Enders, VI, 117, "in meo hypocausto." Cf. *W. A., T. R.,* III, 228, n. 3232c, "in hac turri et hypocausto."

40. Boehmer, *Der Junge Luther,* pp. 110—112.

41. Vogelsang, *Anfaenge von Luthers Christologie,* p. 59; Reu, *Luther's German Bible,* p. 109 ff., cites Psalm 32 in *W. A.,* III, 174, as evidence of little change, and Psalm 50, *W. A.,* III, 283. In Psalm 71, *W. A.,* III, 457 ff., and Psalm 72, *W. A.,* III, 465 ff., he finds evidence of real change. See also Reu, "Source Material," *Luther's German Bible,* p. 95 ff.

42. *W. A., T. R.,* II, 177; III, 228; IV, 72—73; V, 26.

43. Vogelsang, *Anfaenge von Luthers Christologie,* p. 59. This is still a very controversial question. For Reu's evaluation see *Luther's German Bible,* pp. 109—114. For an emphasis of the importance of the actual *Turmerlebnis* and its dating somewhat earlier see Scheel, *Martin Luther* (Tuebingen, 1930, Fourth Edition), II, 567 ff., and 665—667, n. 2. A still different analysis of the whole situation, which places less emphasis on the *Turmerlebnis* and more on the influence of John Staupitz, is found in Johannes von Walter, *Die Theologie Luthers* (Guetersloh, 1940), p. 66 ff. Cf. also Werndorf, *H. V.,* XXVI, 124—144, 285, 327. For additional literature see Pauck, *Church History,* IX, 325.

44. *W. A., T. R.,* V, 168, n. 5468, dated February 16, 1546, according to Kaspar Heydenreich's notes.

45. Holl, *G. A.,* I, 2, "den Gottesgedanken selbst neu erbaut."

46. Holl, *G. A.,* I, 3. Luther was greatly frightened by the *Corpus Christi* procession, *W. A.,* XV, 496. Cf. Enders, VIII, 159, Luther confessed such thoughts to John Staupitz. Also *E. A.,* XXXI, 280, for the reply to Duke George in 1533.

47. Holl, *G. A.,* I, 3.

48. Holl, *G. A.,* I, 4. Cf. Harnack, *History of Dogma,* VI, 200 ff.; Seeberg, *Lehrbuch,* III, 507 ff.

49. Holl, *G. A.,* I, 25—27. Cf. Seeberg, "Der Gottesbegriff Luthers," *Lehrbuch,* IV, 173 ff.; also *W. A., T. R.,* II, 468.

50. Holl, *G. A.,* I, 28.

51. Holl, *G. A.,* I, 30.

52. Boehmer, *Der Junge Luther,* pp. 125—126. Cf. Holl, *G. A.,* I, 155 ff.

53. Holl, *G. A.,* I, 249 ff., traces this growth clear back to the Psalms. Cf. *W. A.,* IV, 239, and Boehmer, *Der Junge Luther,* pp. 127—128.

54. Boehmer, *Der Junge Luther,* p. 131; Seeberg, *Lehrbuch,* IV, 329.

55. Holl, *G. A.,* I, 245 ff.

56. Boehmer, *Der Junge Luther,* p. 148.

57. This was Gregor Heyns, the former Buergermeister of Brueck and father of the town pastor Simon Heyns.

58. Koehler, *I. M. R.,* p. 378.

59. Friedensburg, *G. U. W.,* pp. 97—98; cf. Enders, III, 379. By May 29, 1516, Lang had returned to Erfurt. For the contact between Luther and Spalatin see G. Berbig, *Georg Spalatin, Sein Verhaeltnis zu Martin Luther auf Grund ihres Briefwechsels bis zum Jahre 1525* (Halle, 1906).

60. Friedensburg, *G. U. W.,* pp. 64—68. Cf. pp. 50—53 on Trutvetter. Also Friedensburg, *Urkundenbuch,* I, 14—17.

61. Friedensburg, *G. U. W.,* pp. 64—68.

62. *W. A.,* "Briefe," I, 64—69, contains the letter which Luther wrote to Lang about this occasion. See especially n. 5, p. 68. For degree see *Liber Decanorum,* p. 19. For Theses, *W. A.,* I, 142. Bernhardi was from Feldkirch and was later prior at Kemberg. Enders, I, 58, n. 3; XVII, n. 1.

63. Barge, *Karlstadt,* I, 73—74. Cf. n. 20, p. 75, for 1517 Theses.

64. The Theses against scholastic theology debated under Luther's chairmanship for the degree of *Baccalaureus ad Biblia,* printed *W. A.,* I, 224—228. Cf. *Liber Decanorum,* p. 20; Luther's letter to Lang Sept. 4, 1517, *W. A.,* "Briefe," I, 103—104, and n. 2.

65. Friedensburg, *G. U. W.,* p. 100.

66. Friedensburg, *G. U. W.,* p. 100. Cf. Luther's letter to Trutvetter about law professors May 9, 1518, Enders, I, 187—191, and especially, 188; also Friedensburg, *Urkundenbuch,* I, 15, 77, 81, and 83; for Wolfgang Staehelin's biographical sketch, *W. A.,* "Briefe," I, 171, n. 3. On Philymnus see Friedensburg, *G. U. W.,* p. 98.

67. G. Bauch, "Die Einfuehrung des Hebraeischen in Wittenberg," *Monatsschrift fuer Geschichte und Wissenschaft des Judentums,* Neue Folge, XLVIII (1904), 147.

68. W. A., *"Briefe,"* I, 88—89. In this letter to Lang, Luther tried to turn his old teachers Trutvetter and Usingen from Aristotle. Cf. Enders, I, 86; also G. Plitt, *Jodocus Trutfetter von Eisenach* (Erlangen, 1876), p. 57.

69. This is a free translation of Theses 40 to 45 inclusive, W. A., I, 226.

70. W. A., *"Briefe,"* I, 98—99; Enders, I, 100—101.

71. Friedensburg, *Urkundenbuch,* I, 76 ff., *passim.*

72. W. A., *"Briefe,"* I, 153—154. Cf. Enders, I, 168.

73. Enders, I, 170—171. Cf. W. A., *"Briefe,"* I, 156, notes 9—11.

74. Friedensburg, *Urkundenbuch,* I, 86.

75. W. A., *"Briefe,"* I, 154—156. Cf. Friedensburg, *G. U. W.,* pp. 43—44, for the story of Conrad Wimpina's founding of the University of Frankfurt an der Oder. Also Grohmann, *Annalen,* I, 7—8, and Joseph Negwer, *Wimpina* (Breslau, 1909), p. 147.

76. Friedensburg, *G. U. W.,* p. 111 ff. Cf. *Urkundenbuch,* I, 85—86, n. 1.

77. W. A., *"Briefe,"* I, 175, n. 17 shows that Reuchlin received the letter from Frederick the Wise April 25, 1518, and replied May 7, 1518, proposing Melanchthon. Spalatin's letter to the Elector of June 9, 1518, *T. S. K.,* p. 519 f., indicates that Petrus Mosellanus of Leipzig was also considered. Cf. W. A., *"Briefe,"* I, 180, n. 2; Friedensburg, *G. U. W.,* pp. 115—116. For Luther's interest in the matter see his letter to Spalatin, May 18, 1518, W. A., *"Briefe,"* I, 172—175.

78. Friedensburg, *G. U. W.,* pp. 115—116. In early August, 1518, Melanchthon met Frederick the Wise in Augsburg and agreed to teach at Wittenberg. Cf. W. A., *"Briefe,"* I, 193.

79. Myconius, *Historia Reformationis,* p. 27. On his arrival in Wittenberg and his address see W. A., *"Briefe,"* I, 193, n. 3, and the Grunenberg "Druck," *Supplementa Melanchthoniana,* VI, 1, 49. In Leipzig he had also been met with a great reception August 20, 1518, W. A., *"Briefe,"* I, 193, n. 4.

80. Enders, I, 220, dated October 31.

81. Enders, I, 237, dated September 16. Cf. Melanchthon's letter to Scheurl in Nuernberg, September 24, 1518, *C. R.,* I, 48.

82. Friedensburg, *G. U. W.,* p. 118.

83. Enders, I, 227.

84. Friedensburg, *G. U. W.,* pp. 126—127.

85. On December 10, 1518, Spalatin wrote to Veit Bild in Augsburg: "Philip Melanchthon is here teaching the Greek language, and he has no less than four hundred auditors." On the number of students in Melanchthon's and Luther's classes in 1520 see Friedensburg, *Urkundenbuch,* I, 109.

86. Schiesz, *Briefwechsel der Brueder Ambrosius und Thomas Blaurer* (1908), I, 29 f.; cf. 30—32 and 34; Friedensburg, *G. U. W.,* p. 152.

87. Friedensburg, *G. U. W.*, p. 152. Cf. Hartfelder, *Melanchthoniana paedagogica*, pp. 112—114.

88. Text, pp. 365—366.

89. *W. A., Deutsche Bibel*, IV, 583—584.

CHAPTER TEN

1. A. Gottlob, *Kreuzablasz und Almosenablasz* (1906); see also his work *Aus der Camera Apostolica des 15. Jahrhunderts* (Innsbruck, 1889). Cf. W. Koehler, *Ablass-Streit*, pp. 5—7; Moeller, *History of the Christian Church* (1910), II, 117—118; and Boehmer, *L. L. R. R.*, p. 121 ff.

2. Koehler, *Ablass-Streit*, pp. 7, 10, and 11; Boehmer, *L. L. R. R.*, p. 124.

3. Moeller, *History of the Christian Church*, II, 343—344.

4. Koehler, *Ablass-Streit*, pp. 7, 8, 9, 10, and 11; Boehmer, *Der Junge Luther*, p. 160.

5. Koehler, *Ablass-Streit*, pp. 18—19; Boehmer, *Der Junge Luther*, p. 162. For more detailed study see A. W. Dieckhoff, *Der Ablass-Streit dogmengeschichtlich dargestellt* (Gotha, 1886); Th. Brieger, *Das Wesen des Ablasses am Ausgange des Mittelalters* (Leipzig, 1887); and Paulus, *Ablass*, III, 374 ff.

6. Koehler, *Ablass-Streit*, pp. 19—24 and 32; Hefele, *Conciliengeschichte*, VII, 341; Brieger, *Das Wesen des Ablasses*, p. 48 ff.; Creighton, *A History of the Papacy*, I, 113; Seeberg, *Lehrbuch*, III, 621—623.

7. Seeberg, *Lehrbuch*, III, 549. Cf. Paulus, *Ablass*, I, 268 ff.; and Koehler, *Ablass-Streit*, pp. 17 and 20.

8. Koehler, *Ablass-Streit*, p. 37; H. C. Lea, *A History of Auricular Confession and Indulgences* (1896), III, 345 ff.; Paulus, *Ablass*, III, 380, states that Calixtus III granted one to the king of Castile in 1457. Cf. Boehmer, *L. L. R. R.*, p. 127; also Seeberg, *Lehrbuch*, III, 549 and 625 for part of Sixtus IV.

9. Boehmer, *Der Junge Luther*, pp. 163—164.

10. Ullmann, *Reformers Before the Reformation*, I, 260; Boehmer, *Der Junge Luther*, p. 165; Koehler, *Ablass-Streit*, pp. 30—34. Cf. the Catholic historians Pastor, *The History of the Popes*, VII, 336—338, and Grisar, *Luther*, I, 35 and 55, who have tried to compare the indulgence traffic with popular missions today; but Boehmer, *L. L. R. R.*, p. 130, believes "the comparison limps." Pastor did realize its bad effects, pp. 340—341.

11. Schulte, *Die Fugger*, pp. 97—98: "Toward the end of 1504 Berthold von Henneberg died; in September, 1508, Jakob von Liebenstein; in February, 1514, Uriel von Gemmingen." Uriel had paid 17,143 ducats for his election.

12. Schulte, *Die Fugger*, p. 104, points out that a ducat was worth 1.4 gulden. In buying power it was worth about $25. See pp. 103 and 106 ff. for Dr. Blankenfeld's activities, and Boehmer, *L. L. R. R.*, p. 132.

13. Schulte, *Die Fugger*, p. 107. Cf. Boehmer, *Romfahrt*, p. 96, for the account of Johannes Zink.

14. For story of finances see Schulte, *Die Fugger*, pp. 98–104. There is much disagreement on the sums paid for these appointments. Th. Seelmann, *Jacob Fugger* (Stuttgart, 1909), p. 140, says a figure of 44,710 gulden was agreed upon; Schulte says 17,143; and Kalkoff, *Entscheidungsjahre*, pp. 16–18, claims the additional fees were 21,000 ducats. Cf. Grisar, *Luther*, I, 347–350; Boehmer, *Der Junge Luther*, pp. 165–166; and his earlier account in *L. L. R. R.*, pp. 130–134. For Luther's view see Holman, *W. M. L.*, I, 342–343.

15. Seelmann, *Jacob Fugger*, p. 142.

16. Text, p. 311.

17. Boehmer, *L. L. R. R.*, p. 134.

18. Mackinnon, *Martin Luther*, I, 291. Boehmer, *L. L. R. R.*, p. 133.

19. Mackinnon, *Martin Luther*, I, 291–292; Koehler, *Ablass-Streit*, p. 83 f.

20. For the full title of the archbishop's instructions see *W. A.*, *"Briefe,"* I, 112–113. There are copies extant in Wernigerode and Koenigsberg. Paulus, *Historisches Jahrbuch*, XLI, 81, says the *Instructio* was drawn up in the chancellory of Albert of Mainz without the aid of Tetzel. Cf. Koehler, *Ablass-Streit*, p. 104 ff. and Boehmer, *Der Junge Luther*, p. 170.

21. Myconius, *Historia Reformationis*, pp. 14–23. The Catholic historian Paulus, *Johann Tetzel*, p. 89 ff., gives much valuable information. Tetzel was not permitted in the lands of the Elector of Saxony, but Wittenbergers went to the neighboring regions to hear him. Jueterbock was politically under the Erzstift Magdeburg, Zerbst under Anhalt; but both were under the ecclesiastical dominance of Magdeburg, *W. A.*, *"Briefe,"* I, 112, n. 2. On April 10, 1517, Tetzel was in Jueterbock and by fall in Mark Brandenburg, on October 5, in Berlin, Paulus, *Johann Tetzel*, p. 40 ff.

22. Myconius, *Historia Reformationis*, pp. 17–20. Cf. Boehmer, *Der Junge Luther*, pp. 170–173.

23. Boehmer, *Der Junge Luther*, pp. 172–173.

24. Myconius, *Historia Reformationis*, p. 22.

25. Myconius, *Historia Reformationis*, p. 15.

26. Myconius, *Historia Reformationis*, pp. 14–15. Cf. Paulus, *Johann Tetzel*, p. 139, states that, even though he did not use these exact words, there can be little doubt that he said something similar. See also *W. A.*, *"Briefe,"* I, 112, n. 4.

27. A good illustration of Tetzel's methods is given in Myconius, *Historia Reformationis*, p. 14 ff. See also Th. Brieger, *Die Reformation* (Berlin, 1914), pp. 63–64; Hoffmann, *Geschichte der Stadt Magdeburg* (Magdeburg, 1847), II, 1 ff.; P. Wernle, *Der Evangelische Glaube nach den Hauptschriften der Reformation, Luther* (Tuebingen, 1918), I, 1 ff.

28. Seelmann, *Jacob Fugger*, pp. 140–141.

29. Hoffmann, *Geschichte der Stadt Magdeburg*, II, 9.

30. Seeberg, *Lehrbuch*, III, 548–550, for an interesting discussion of indulgences. Cf. Boehmer, *L. L. R. R.*, pp. 129–130.

31. Myconius, *Historia Reformationis*, p. 17, tells of the deplorable state of affairs. For the exclamation of Luther, Koehler, *I. M. R.*, p. 387. Cf. also Stracke, *Luthers Selbstzeugnis*, CXL, 20 ff.; and Koehler, *Ablass-Streit*, p. 83 ff.; for Luther's reaction, *W. A.*, LI, 539.

32. Myconius, *Historia Reformationis*, p. 22. Cf. *W. A.*, *"Briefe,"* I, 138–140, and n. 3.

33. Mathesius in *Martin Luther* (Berlin, 1933), pp. 133–134. Cf. also Myconius, *Historia Reformationis*, p. 22.

34. Matthaeus Faber, *Schlosz Kirche*, pp. 33–34; and Charitius, pp. 124–125.

35. Matthaeus Faber, *Schlosz Kirche*, pp. 48 ff. and 67 ff.

36. *Wittemberger Heiligthumsbuch*, illustrated by Lucas Cranach the Elder. According to P. Kalkoff, *Ablasz- und Reliquienverehrung an der Schlosz Kirche zu Wittenberg unter Friedrich dem Weisen* (Gotha, 1907), one of the relic gatherers was Jacob Vogt. See *W. A.*, *"Briefe,"* I, 79–80, n. 2.

37. Hauszleiter, *D. U. W.*, p. 26, n. 2. Cf. *Z. K. G.*, XVIII, 409.

38. Boehmer, *Der Junge Luther*, p. 167.

39. Ernst Stracke, *Luthers Selbstzeugnis*, CXL, 18, says Luther attacked indulgences in a sermon preached in the "Wittenberger Pfarrkirche," July 27, 1516. Bauer, *Z. K. G.*, XLIII (1924), 1, 174 ff., dates this sermon October 31, 1517. Cf. Stracke, n. 1. Apparently, the first sermon was preached in the Town Church July 27, 1516, the second in the Castle Church October 31, 1516, and the third when Tetzel was in the neighboring lands, February 24, 1517. *W. A.*, I, 65 ff.; IX, 764, LI, 539; Paulus, *Johann Tetzel*, p. 41.

40. For an exposition see Holl, *G. A.*, I, 35 ff.; also Seeberg, *Lehrbuch*, IV, 158 ff.; and Th. Brieger, *Das Wesen des Ablasses*, p. 1: "Die 95 Thesen sind nicht das eitle Spiel haarspaltenden scholastischen Scharfsinnes, nicht das Erzeugnis gelehrten Muessigganges, sondern herausgeboren aus dem Gewissen."

41. According to Melanchthon, it was noon October 31, 1517. See *W. A.*, I, 229.

42. On *famulus*, Boehmer, *Der Junge Luther*, p. 174.

43. *W. A.*, *"Briefe,"* I, 141, n. 6.

44. See *W. A.*, I, 233 ff., for text of Theses. Schreckenbach and Neubert, p. 75, reproduces a facsimile of the first twenty Theses. See *W. A.*, *"Briefe,"* I, 139 and 141, n. 6, for evidence of the purpose of the debate.

45. For the story of the rapid spread of the news about the Theses see text, p. 321 ff., and especially note 67, Chapter Ten.

46. *W. A.*, *"Briefe,"* I, 108–113; Enders, I, 113–120. Janssen, *History of the German People* (1910), III, 91, holds that the real cause of Luther's attack on Tetzel was the doctrine of justification by faith; but Pastor, *The History of the Popes*, VII, 351–352, and Paulus, *Johann Tetzel*, pp. 168–169, hold that abuses in Rome's fiscal program were the deep-seated cause.

47. Koehler, *I. M. R.*, pp. 387–389. Cf. Paulus, *Johann Tetzel*, pp. 168–169.

48. Koehler, *I. M. R.*, pp. 387–389. Cf. Theses, 1–4.

49. *W. A.*, I, 522–628.

50. Translation Holman, *W. M. L.*, I, 170–171.

51. Theses, 5–8.

52. Theses, 9, 10, 17, and 32.
53. Theses, 11.
54. Theses, 9–32.
55. Theses, 24.
56. Theses, 50, 51, 77, 78, 82, and 86.
57. Theses, 54, 55, 56, and especially 62.
58. See Paul Wernle, *Der evangelische Glaube nach den Hauptschriften der Reformation* (Tuebingen, 1918), I, 1–22, for a good analysis. Cf. also Brieger, *Die Reformation*, pp. 61–62.
59. *Der Christliche Lutheraner* (1717), p. 154, has the "Traum zu Schweinitz den 31. October 1517."
60. Spalatin, *Annales*, pp. 28–29.
61. Koehler, *I. M. R.*, p. 390. Cf. Mackinnon, *Martin Luther*, I, 303–305, and Enders, I, 168–172.
62. *W. A.*, "*Briefe*," I, 108–115. Editor Knaake, *W. A.*, I, 238–246, claims that Luther wanted word from Albert of Mainz before circulating the Theses in print. Th. Brieger, *Z. K. G.*, XI, 172, has proved that Luther's *Sermon on Indulgences and Grace* could not have been sent to Albert at this time, for it contains reference to Wimpina's counter theses.
63. *W. A.*, "*Briefe*," I, 113–114. The editors feel that the same letter may have been sent to both Albert and Schulze. Cf. *W. A.*, LI, 540; LIV, 180; *W. A.*, *T. R.*, IV, 4446; VI, 6861.
64. Myconius, *Historia Reformationis*, p. 20. Cf. *W. A.*, "*Briefe*," I, 112, n. 2; and Smith, *Correspondence*, I, 63, n. 3.
65. Smith, *Correspondence*, I, 63–64. Cf. Boehmer, *Der Junge Luther*, p. 178, on how this was misunderstood; and Stracke, *Luthers Selbstzeugnis*, CXL, 21–22, claims Luther published the *Sermon on Indulgences and Grace* to counteract the rapid spread of the Theses.
66. Boehmer, *Der Junge Luther*, p. 180. Kaspar Nuetzel in Nuernberg translated the Theses and helped to spread them. See Scheurl, *Briefbuch*, II, 42–43.
67. Myconius, *Historia Reformationis*, p. 23.
68. *E. A.*, XXVI, 53: "liefen schier in vierzehn Tagen durch ganz Deutschland." Cf. *W. A.*, LI, 540, "Wider Hans Worst."
69. *Z. K. G.*, XXIII, 267–268.
70. *Z. K. G.*, XXIII, 267–268. Cf. Mackinnon, *Martin Luther*, II, 14.
71. *Z. K. G.*, XXIII, 265. Cf. Schwiebert, *Thesis*, p. 140:
72. *Z. K. G.*, XXIII, 267–268. Cf. Th. Brieger, *Ueber den Process des Erzbischofs Albrechts gegen Luther* (Leipzig, 1894), p. 191, stresses the influence of Mainz. See also Schwiebert, *Thesis*, pp. 142–143; for further literature consult Mackinnon, *Martin Luther*, II, 14, n. 43.
73. Koehler, *I. M. R.*, p. 391.
74. Boehmer, *Der Junge Luther*, p. 190. For the authorship of the Theses see *W. A.*, "*Briefe*," I, 156, n. 8. Dr. Koch was the dean of the theological faculty who presided at the disputation. Cf. Negwer, *Wimpina*, p. 147; and Mackinnon, *Martin Luther*, II, 18 ff.

75. Smith, *Correspondence*, I, 75.

76. Boehmer, *Der Junge Luther*, p. 186.

77. See note 62, Chapter Ten, on sermon.

78. Boehmer, *Der Junge Luther*, p. 180.

79. Kalkoff, *Entscheidungsjahre*, p. 25.

80. On Cardinal Cajetan see *R. E.*, III, 632—634. He was a distinguished Thomist, but did not believe the Theses were sufficient ground to condemn Luther of heresy. Cf. *W. A., T. R.*, II, 567, n. 2635a and 2635b, for the Pope's reaction when he first heard of Luther's Theses.

81. Kolde, *Augustiner-Kongregation*, p. 312. See also Walch, XV, 518—521, Leo X's letter of January 23, 1518, to Gabriel della Volta informing him he will be the successor of Egidio. Cf. Boehmer, *Der Junge Luther*, p. 190.

82. Enders, I, 175. Translation in Smith, *Correspondence*, I, 78.

83. *W. A.*, "Briefe," I, 161, n. 5, for brief discussion. Cf. Joh. Staupitii, *opera*, I, 90, and *Zentralblatt fuer Bibliothekswesen*, VII, 197 ff. Gruenenberg was the printer.

84. *W. A.*, "Briefe," I, 155, n. 6, and n. 4.

85. Enders, I, 183—185; cf. *W. A.*, "Briefe," I, 167, n. 1 and n. 4, on Pfeffinger and the cost of the meal.

86. *W. A.*, "Briefe," I, 168—169; and Enders, I, 185—186. Translation, Smith, *Correspondence*, I, 79—80. Lawrence von Bibra, the Bishop, was Luther's friend and admirer who later asked the Elector to protect Luther.

87. Kolde, *Augustiner-Kongregation*, pp. 313—314.

88. On Francis Guenther see text, p. 295; and *W. A.*, I, 221—228. Cf. Scheurl, *Briefbuch*, II, 25—27. This debate had attacked Scholasticism at its very foundations. For the Theses debated at Heidelberg see *W. A.*, I, 353—374; also Kolde, *Augustiner-Kongregation*, p. 313 ff.; Bauer, "Die Heidelberger Disputation Luthers," *Z. K. G.*, XXI (1901); and Koestlin's reply, p. 577 ff.; Stracke, *Luthers Selbstzeugnis*, CXL, 131—136.

89. On Georg Niger von Loewenstein, who had recently received the doctorate, *W. A.*, "Briefe," I, 174, n. 8, and p. 173 for quotation. Translation in Smith, *Correspondence*, I, 85.

90. Smith, *Correspondence*, I, 83. Source, Walch, XV, 517.

91. *Briefwechsel des Beatus Rhenanus, gesammelt und herausgegeben* von A. Horawitz und K. Hartfelder (Leipzig, 1886), p. 106 ff.; translated by Smith, *Correspondence*, I, 80—82. For those present see Eduard Winkelmann, *Urkundenbuch der Universitaet Heidelberg* (Heidelberg, 1886), II, no. 671. Cf. J. W. Baum, *Capito und Butzer* (Eberfeld, 1860), p. 96.

92. Smith, *Correspondence*, I, 81—82.

93. Pfalzgraf Wolfgang was a brother of the Elector Ludwig V. He matriculated at Wittenberg in March, 1515. See *W. A.*, "Briefe," I, 174, n. 2; also *Album*, I, matriculation list of 1515; and Vierordt, *Badische Reformationsgeschichte*, p. 110.

94. Enders, I, 212. Translation in Smith, *Correspondence*, I, 98, n. 2. Cf. Koehler, *I. M. R.*, p. 394.

95. Kalkoff, *Z. K. G.*, XXVII, 322–323. Cf. Boehmer, *Der Junge Luther*, p. 194.

96. *W. A.*, *"Briefe,"* I, 172–175; Enders, I, 191.

97. *W. A.*, *"Briefe,"* I, 172–175.

98. *W. A.*, *"Briefe,"* I, 175, n. 12. Cf. p. 186, n. 23.

99. *W. A.*, *"Briefe,"* I, 415, and n. 1. Cf. p. 407, n. 7, for further sources.

100. Holl, *G. A.*, I, 382 ff.; also p. 383, n. 1; *W. A.*, VIII, 411; XXIII, 421; *W. A.*, *T. R.*, I, 61; II, 13. Roland Bainton also presented an excellent treatment of this subject in *Church History*, XVII (1948), 193–206.

101. Boehmer, *Der Junge Luther*, p. 196.

102. *W. A.*, *"Briefe,"* I, 173–174; Enders, I, 191–193; translation in Smith, *Correspondence*, I, 84–85.

CHAPTER ELEVEN

1. Schulte, *Die Fugger*, I, 1 ff.

2. *W. A.*, *"Briefe,"* I, 185, n. 6, states that Luther was warned not to go to Dresden; cf. Enders, I, 210. The Weimar editors advance seemingly valid reasons for their position. Translation in Smith, *Correspondence*, I, 97.

3. For original title and text see *W. A.*, I, 634–643. Luther wrote Wenzel Link that he had wished to debate this material in public, but the Bishop of Brandenburg objected. Some of his friends, however, formulated a set of theses from some of the materials; and, likewise, some of his enemies compiled a number of theses greatly misrepresenting his position. These actions forced Luther to publish the sermon between August 21 and August 31.

4. *W. A.*, I, 643.

5. *W. A.*, I, 278. Greving, "Johannes Eck, Defensio contra Carolstatini Invectiones," *Corpus Catholicorum*, I, 8, for the *Obelisks*. Cf. also Luther's letter to John Sylvius Egranus, Enders, I, 172–173; and *W. A.*, *"Briefe,"* I, 156–159.

6. *W. A.*, I, 278; translation in Smith, *Correspondence*, I, 76–77.

7. *W. A.*, I, 279, 281–314; for a critical examination *W. A.*, IX, 770 ff.; and Greving, *Corpus Catholicorum*, I, 8–9. See also the letter of Luther and Carlstadt to Frederick the Wise, *W. A.*, *"Briefe,"* I, 458–501, and a letter from Eck to Frederick the Wise, *W. A.*, I, 279, in which he claims to have only a handwritten copy of the *Asterisks*. W. Reindell, *Doktor Wenzeslaus Linck aus Colditz 1483–1547* (Marburg, 1892), p. 257, states that Link showed the *Asterisks* to Pirckheimer, but asked him not to show them to anyone else.

8. Smith, *Correspondence*, I, 85–86, translated from Enders, V, 1–2.

9. Enders, I, 174, n. 5. Cf. Greving, *Corpus Catholicorum*, 9–10, 36–37, who strongly defends Eck; and Kalkoff, *Z. K. G.* (1925), pp. 220–222. See also Barge, *Karlstadt*, I, 125 ff.

10. Mackinnon, *Martin Luther*, II, 33; Greving, *Corpus Catholicorum*, I, 10. Cf. Luther's letter to Staupitz, March 31, 1518, Enders, I, 175–177, in which he stated that Eck's attack was due to his prejudice against the Bible and the Fathers.

11. Smith, *Correspondence*, I, 90, translated from J. G. Olearius, *Scrinium Antiquarium* (Halle, 1671), p. 30.

12. Smith, *Correspondence*, I, 94.

13. This was reworked lecture material delivered between 1516 and 1517, see *W. A.*, I, 394–521. On the German Theology see *W. A.*, I, 375 ff. Franz Pfeiffer counted 70 editions in 1854, but missed some; see Franz Pfeiffer, *Theologia deutsch* (Stuttgart, 1855), Second Edition; C. Ullmann, *Reformatoren vor der Reformation* (Gotha, 1866), II, 193 ff.; W. Dress, *Die Theologie Gersons* (Guetersloh, 1931), pp. 166–175, 193—204; and "Gerson und Luther," *Z. K. G.* (1933), pp. 122–161.

14. *W. A.*, I, 522–643. These were submitted to Bishop Schulze of Brandenburg early in February. He advised Luther to wait. After the Heidelberg meeting, Luther prepared the Resolutions in final form and on May 30 sent them to Staupitz, who forwarded them to Rome, where they arrived the latter part of June. By August 21, 1518, they were published in Wittenberg. Smith, *Correspondence*, I, 87–88. For Luther's letter to Staupitz of May 30, 1518, see *W. A.*, I, 525–527; Enders, I, 196–199; for the letter to Leo X which was included, *W. A.*, I, 527–529; Enders, I, 200–203; cf. also *W. A.*, IX, 173–175; and Enders, XVII, 101.

15. Enders, I, 196–199; translation in Smith, *Correspondence*, I, 91–93.

16. *W. A.*, I, 527–529; Borcherdt, *Werke*, I, 87.

17. *W. A.*, I, 582–583, 606; Borcherdt, *Werke*, I, 87, 99, 143, 170.

18. Borcherdt, *Werke*, I, 190.

19. Borcherdt, *Werke*, I, 243–244.

20. Mackinnon, *Martin Luther*, II, 56. Original in Enders, I, 200–203.

21. Rab had attended the Dominican Chapter at Frankfurt an der Oder on January 20, 1518, when Tetzel was promoted. The group had gone on record as opposed to Luther. Stracke, *Luthers Selbstzeugnis*, CXL, 28–29 and n. 1; Boehmer, *Der Junge Luther*, p. 203; cf. also K. Mueller, "Luthers Roemischer Process," *Z. K. G.*, XXIV, 51; and Kalkoff, *Forschungen*, p. 28 ff.

22. Boehmer, *L. L. R. R.*, p. 136. Cf. Kalkoff, *Entscheidungsjahre*, p. 25, tells how Rab used the Dominican Nicholas von Schoenberg, secretary to Giulio di Medici, the papal vice-chancellor, to gain his ends.

23. The Pope later remarked it would have been better if he had taken three months, *W. A.*, I, 644–646. For a brief biography of Prierias see *R. E.*, XVI, 32–34; also Enders, I, 164, n. 1. Prierias titled his tract *Dialogus in praesumptuosas M. Lutheri Conclusiones de potestate Papae*, written at the request of Pope Leo X. For further details see *Opera Lutheri*, I, 341 f.; Enders, I, 163–165; and the translation in Smith, *Correspondence*, I, 95–96, noting his foreword about the dating of the letter. It must have appeared in June, when the *Dialogus* was published.

24. Enders, I, 164; Smith, *Correspondence*, I, 96; *W. A.*, I, 685. For the Dares reference see Virgil, *Aeneid*, V, 369 ff.

25. Boehmer, *Der Junge Luther*, p. 204.

26. Boehmer, *Der Junge Luther*, p. 204. Cf. *W. A.*, II, 1; also, Mueller, *Z. K. G.*, XXIV, 59—60.

27. *W. A.*, I, 647, 686; Boehmer, *Der Junge Luther*, p. 205.

28. Enders, I, 216—217; translation in Smith, *Correspondence*, I, 101.

29. Holl, *G. A.*, I, 306 ff.; *W. A.*, I, 618 ff., 642; Seeberg, *Lehrbuch*, IV, 344 ff.

30. Boehmer, *Der Junge Luther*, p. 209 ff.

31. According to G. Fabricius, *Saxonia illustrata*, cited in *W. A.*, *"Briefe,"* I, 301, Luther was sent to Dresden to satisfy Duke George; but the editors believe he and John Lang went there on business for the order. For the account to Spalatin, Enders, I, 349—355, 353, n. 1; and *W. A.*, *"Briefe,"* I, 300, "Vorbemerkungen."

32. *W. A.*, *"Briefe,"* I, 303, n. 2; *W. A.*, *T. R.*, V, 462—463. On Emser see Smith, *Correspondence*, I, 149, n. 6.

33. On Johannes Kuszwerth de Weysbenstadt see *W. A.*, *"Briefe,"* I, 303, n. 2. Cf. *Colloquia*, I, 152; and *Z. K. G.*, XXIII, 36; *W. A.*, *"Briefe,"* I, 301—303; Smith, *Correspondence*, I, 149—152.

34. Smith, *Correspondence*, I, 150—151; Kalkoff, *Z. K. G.*, XXIII, 37; Gess, *Akten und Briefe*, I, 254 f., 268. On later interview see *W. A.*, *"Briefe,"* I, 304, n. 2, and G. Kawerau, *Hieronymus Emser Ein Lebensbild* (Halle a. S., 1898), p. 28 ff.

35. *W. A.*, I, 635.

36. Text, p. 332 ff.; note 3, Chapter Eleven. Cf. *Opera Lutheri*, II, 349, for letter of Emperor Maximilian to the Pope, translation in Smith, *Correspondence*, I, 98—100.

37. Smith, *Correspondence*, I, 100.

38. *W. A.*, *"Briefe,"* I, 188—189.

39. *W. A.*, II, 23. For translation see Smith, *Correspondence*, I, 101—104. Frederick the Wise secured a copy of this letter and forwarded it to Luther late in October, *W. A.*, *"Briefe,"* I, 225, n. 7.

40. *Opera Lutheri*, II, 352, translated by Smith, *Correspondence*, I, 105.

41. *Z. K. G.*, II, 476. See Smith, *Correspondence*, I, 106 ff., for a translation of Volta's letter to Gerard Hecker.

42. *Z. K. G.*, II, 472 ff.; Mackinnon, *Martin Luther*, II, 74, n. 47.

43. Smith, *Correspondence*, I, 107—108. On the legality of such action see Mueller, *Z. K. G.*, XXIV, 63 ff.

44. Enders, I, 210—213, translated by Smith, *Correspondence*, I, 96—98.

45. Enders, I, 210—213.

46. Mackinnon, *Martin Luther*, II, 75—76, and n. 51; Boehmer, *Der Junge Luther*, pp. 242—246.

47. The best account is by Kirn, *Friedrich der Weise*, pp. 11—16, 165 ff. Cf. Th. Kolde, *Friedrich der Weise und die Anfaenge der Reformation* (Erlangen, 1881), p. 7 ff.

48. Text, p. 77.

49. *W. A., "Briefe,"* I, 200–202. Cf. Mackinnon, *Martin Luther,* II, 76–77.

50. Kalkoff, *Forschungen,* p. 153. Cf. *Opera Lutheri,* I, 17.

51. Kalkoff, *Forschungen,* p. 56; Z. K. G., XXV, 279 ff. For the "Golden Rose" in a later connection see text, p. 361 ff.

52. Kalkoff, *Forschungen,* pp. 57–58, contains the papal brief. This did not mean that the Curia had dropped the brief of August 23, but had merely temporarily set it aside.

53. Mackinnon, *Martin Luther,* II, 79. Cf. Boehmer, *Der Junge Luther,* p. 216, who thinks he left September 25. On his companion see Enders, I, 243, n. 18. According to *W. A., T. R.,* V, 78, the two men did not get a ride on the way until within three miles of Augsburg.

54. Kalkoff, *Forschungen,* p. 64, claims Luther picked up the safe-conduct for the Saxon lands and other documents in Weimar. The imperial safe-conduct was sent October 11, *W. A., "Briefe,"* I, 210, n. 7. Cf. *W. A., T. R.,* II, 595, for the precautions taken by the Elector in his lands. On papers written by the Wittenberg faculty *Opera Lutheri,* II, 361 ff.

55. *W. A., T. R.,* II, 595–596.

56. *W. A., T. R.,* II, 596.

57. Myconius, *Historia Reformationis,* p. 28. The words are those of Mackinnon, *Martin Luther,* II, 80, but this writer is wrong when, on the basis of Enders, I, 234–235, he claims that Staupitz offered Luther a refuge in Salzburg, for the Weimar editors have shown this letter to be misdated. Staupitz could not have written from Salzburg September 14 as he was already in Nuernberg. He did visit Salzburg in December while on a preaching trip and at that time wrote to Luther. See *W. A., "Briefe,"* I, 264 ff.

58. Enders, I, 238, translated by Mackinnon, *Martin Luther,* II, 81. Cf. *W. A., T. R.,* V, 78, about demons which vexed him.

59. Enders, I, 239. On date see *W. A., "Briefe,"* I, 209, n. 2. Cf. Scheurl, *Briefbuch,* II, 50, on Spalatin's recent return.

60. *W. A., "Briefe,"* I, 224, n. 3. Based on Roth, *Augsburger Reformationsgeschichte,* I, 51. Cf. *W. A., T. R.,* V, 79, n. 2.

61. Enders, I, 239–240; *W. A., "Briefe,"* I, 209–210, and n. 7; *W. A., T. R.,* V, 79.

62. *W. A., T. R.,* V, 79. On Serralonga, Smith, *Correspondence,* I, 116, n. 5. Cf. Kalkoff, *Z. K. G.,* XXV, 568, 2.

63. Enders, I, 240–241. Cf. Smith, *Correspondence,* I, 117.

64. *W. A., T. R.,* II, 596–597; V, 79; *Opera Lutheri,* I, 18; Stracke, *Luthers Selbstzeugnis,* CXL, 56 ff.

65. *W. A., "Briefe,"* I, 210, n. 7.

66. Enders, I, 244–245.

67. *W. A., T. R.,* V, 79. Told by Mathesius, summer of 1540.

68. Enders, I, 285.

69. Walch, XV, 732, translated by Smith, *Correspondence,* I, 123.

70. *W. A.,* II, 7.

71. *W. A.,* II, 7, and Enders, I, 246.

72. Holl, *G. A.*, I, 551 ff., shows how mature Luther was by this time and why those who clung to the old scholastic approach could not understand him.

73. Smith, *Correspondence*, I, 119, from De Wette, I, 159.

74. *W. A.*, II, 7.

75. Mirbt, *Quellen*, pp. 224—225; Mackinnon, *Martin Luther*, II, 84 ff.; Koehler, *Ablass-Streit* (1934), no. 10.

76. Enders, I, 286. Luther wrote Carlstadt, October 14, 1518, *W. A.*, "*Briefe*," I, 215—217: "Er ist vielleicht ein namhaftiger Thomist, aber ein undeutlicher, verborgener, unverstaendlicher Theologus oder Christ, und derhalb diese Sach zu richten, erkennen und urteilen eben so geschickt als ein Esel zu der Harfen." Cf. *Erasmi adagia*, I, 4, 35, and other references cited in *W. A.*, "*Briefe*," I, 217, n. 5.

77. Enders, I, 287. Cf. Mackinnon, *Martin Luther*, II, 85—86, and *Church History*, XVI (1947), 174.

78. Luther was quite familiar with the contents of the Bull of Clement VI, as shown by *W. A.*, II, 7.

79. *W. A.*, II, 8; Enders, I, 287—288, 290. Roland Bainton states that Cajetan was clever and had Luther in a corner over this bull, *Church History*, XVI, 174; but does this refute the main point? True, Luther was quibbling over the language of the bull in making a distinction between the Treasure of the Church and the winning of a treasure for the Church; but he still claimed that Cajetan was not qualified to judge his New Theology (n. 76, Chapter Eleven). Luther was willing to grant that Cajetan was a master of Thomist theology, but he was not capable of grasping the Biblical Humanism of Wittenberg. If one grants Cajetan's fundamental assumptions, the burden of proof rested on Luther, and it was not difficult to place him in an embarrassing position.

80. Enders, I, 287.

81. Enders, I, 291.

82. *W. A.*, II, 8—9.

83. Myconius, *Historia Reformationis*, p. 33. Cf. *Acta Augustana*, *W. A.*, II, 9.

84. Enders, I, 270, 292.

85. Enders, I, 270—271.

86. *Opera Lutheri*, II, 365—366. Cf. Enders, I, 246—247.

87. *W. A.*, II, 16; Enders, I, 261.

88. *W. A.*, II, 16; Enders, I, 247, 292; *W. A.*, *T. R.*, V, 79—80. Cf. Cajetan's later claim of maintaining a fatherly composure, Enders, I, 270.

89. Myconius, *Historia Reformationis*, p. 33.

90. Myconius, *Historia Reformationis*, p. 33. "Ego nolo amplius cum hac bestia loqui. Habet enim profundos oculos, et mirabiles speculationes in capite suo."

91. *W. A.*, "*Briefe*," I, 220—222, and 222, n. 1.

92. *W. A.*, II, 19; Enders, I, 293, on danger. For absolving from monastic vow see Boehmer, *Der Junge Luther*, p. 224.

93. Boehmer, *Der Junge Luther*, p. 224.

94. *W. A., T. R.,* V, 80, 102.

95. Enders, I, 277–278. On the drafting of the Appeal to the Pope see *W. A.,* "*Briefe,*" I, 225, n. 3; for its text see *W. A.,* II, 28 ff.

96. *W. A., T. R.,* V, 78, tells us that he took the Coburg, Leipzig, Kemberg route. Cf. *W. A.,* "*Briefe,*" I, 225, n. 1; Scheurl, *Briefbuch,* II, 57; Enders I, 272.

97. Enders, I, 273.

98. Enders, I, 274; translation in Smith, *Correspondence,* I, 129.

99. *W. A.,* "*Briefe,*" I, 225, n. 4; Smith, *Correspondence,* I, 135, n. 2; *W. A.,* II, 36–38, contains text; on p. 34 the editor makes date of publication December 10. *C. R.,* I, 56; Mueller, *Z. K. G.,* XXIV, 74; Creighton, *A History of the Papacy,* III, 239–240. The printer distributed copies of the appeal without Luther's knowledge or permission. Enders, I, 323–325.

100. Mirbt, *Quellen,* p. 256.

101. Cornell University has a copy of this 1518 edition.

102. Smith, *Correspondence,* I, 129–130.

103. Smith, *Correspondence,* I, 137–138.

CHAPTER TWELVE

1. Enders, I, 269–272, for Aleander's complaint to the Elector of Saxony; *W. A.,* "*Briefe,*" I, 233–251, contains Luther's answer.

2. Enders, I, 268 ff.; Smith, *Correspondence,* I, 124 ff.

3. Enders, I, 271; *W. A.,* "*Briefe,*" I, 234.

4. Schwiebert, *Thesis,* p. 163 ff. Cf. Kolde, *Friedrich der Weise und die Anfaenge der Reformation* (Erlangen, 1881), p. 16 ff.; and Kirn, *Friedrich der Weise,* p. 164 ff.; cf. also pp. 130–164.

5. See "Vorbemerkungen," *W. A.,* "*Briefe,*" I, 232.

6. The Weimar editors question the date, *W. A.,* "*Briefe,*" I, 232 ff.; Walch, XV, 772, gives November 29. See note 5, Chapter Twelve.

7. *W. A.,* "*Briefe,*" I, 236–246; translated into German in Walch, XV, 772 ff.

8. *W. A.,* "*Briefe,*" I, 238.

9. *W. A.,* "*Briefe,*" I, 241.

10. *W. A.,* "*Briefe,*" I, 241.

11. See Wolfgang Capito's "Preface" to the Froben edition of Luther's works in 1518, Smith, *Correspondence,* I, 129–130. The preface appeared anonymously.

12. *Opera Lutheri,* II, 362.

13. *Opera Lutheri,* II, 363, dated September 25, 1518.

14. Boehmer, *Der Junge Luther,* p. 230 ff. On his rank and commission see Kalkoff, *Z. K. G.* (1925), p. 215; also Walch, XV, 811–812.

15. Gess, *Akten und Briefe,* I, 45. There is a good biography of Duke George in *R. E.,* VI, 529–533.

16. *Opera Lutheri,* II, 448; translation in Smith, *Correspondence,* I, 127.

17. Walch, XV, 812–815; translation in Smith, *Correspondence,* I, 126.

18. Walch, XV, 812; translation in Smith, *Correspondence,* I, 126.

19. Walch, XV, 815–816.
20. Walch, XV, 820–823.
21. Enders, I, 307–310; translation in Smith, *Correspondence,* I, 134–135.
22. *W. A., "Deutsche Bibel,"* IV, 583 ff.
23. *W. A., "Deutsche Bibel,"* IV, 583 ff.; *Opera Lutheri,* II, 426 ff.
24. For H. Degering's introduction, *W. A., "Deutsche Bibel,"* IV, 583–584.
25. The *Lichtdruck* of Luther's lecture notes on Romans, delivered between 1515 and 1516, reveals the same handwriting, *W. A., "Deutsche Bibel,"* IV, 583. Luther speaks of this letter in a letter to Spalatin, *W. A., "Briefe,"* I, 253–254, n. 3.
26. *W. A., "Deutsche Bibel,"* IV, 584.
27. Boehmer, *Der Junge Luther,* p. 227.
28. Boehmer, *Der Junge Luther,* p. 227. See also Enders, I, 313–315, translation in Smith, *Correspondence,* I, 137.
29. *W. A., "Briefe,"* I, 261, n. 1. Enders claims the letter of December 2, referred to by Luther, has been lost. In this letter Luther stated that had Spalatin's letter of the previous day not arrived, he would have been gone and that he was still prepared to go or stay. See also *W. A., T. R.,* I, 1203, and V, 5375c; Enders, I, 309, n. 1. The editor suggests that after 18 years Luther did not recall the details too clearly and that this resulted in some confusion.
30. Enders, I, 309, n. 1, based on Cyprian, *Nuetzliche Urkunden,* I, 384 f., where this excerpt is quoted.
31. *W. A., "Briefe,"* I, 261, n. 1. Cf. Boehmer, *Der Junge Luther,* pp. 227–228, based on this source.
32. *W. A., "Briefe,"* I, 264 ff. Because of the correction in date by the Weimar editors, this letter of Staupitz inviting Luther to come to Salzburg to stay with him awhile assumes special significance, especially when he adds: "Id ipsum et Principi complacitum est." The Weimar editor points out in n. 5, "dem Kurfuersten," that Frederick was in agreement with this plan.
33. *W. A.,* II, 2.
34. *W. A.,* II, 34; Enders, I, 314 and n. 4.
35. See note 99, Chapter Eleven. Also Mirbt, *Quellen,* p. 242; Pastor, *The History of the Popes,* II, 70.
36. The two best biographies are Kolde, *Friedrich der Weise und die Anfaenge der Reformation* and Kirn, *Friedrich der Weise.* See especially the latter, pp. 11–12.
37. Kalkoff, *Ablasz und Reliquienverehrung an der Schlosz Kirche zu Wittenberg unter Friedrich dem Weisen,* tried to prove this, but Kirn, *Friedrich der Weise,* p. 166 ff., has refuted the claim.
38. *E. A.,* XVII, 174. Kirn, *Friedrich der Weise,* pp. 176–177, "Langsam, sehr langsam folgte er dem Reformator, der die Fackel so kuehn vorantrug."
39. Kirn, *Friedrich der Weise,* p. 174. Cf. Pauck, *Church History,* IX (1940), 326, who agrees with Kirn and calls Frederick's attitude, at best, but that of a "conscientious spectator."

40. Enders, I, 310–312. Frederick also included Luther's letter of November 21; W. A., "Briefe," I, 232 ff. See "Vorbemerkungen," and Kalkoff, Z. K. G., XXVII, 324.

41. Boehmer, Der Junge Luther, p. 229.

42. On the original assignment of the mission to Germany, September 10, 1518, see W. A., "Briefe," I, 212, n. 23. For information on Miltitz see Smith, Correspondence, I, 125, n. 1; further details H. A. Creutzberg, Karl von Miltitz (Freiburg, 1907); P. Kalkoff, Die Miltitziade (Leipzig, 1911); and Pastor, The History of the Popes, VIII.

43. A. R., IX, 150; Creutzberg, Karl von Miltitz, p. 10.

44. Kalkoff, Z. K. G. (1925), p. 215; and Walch, XV, 811–812.

45. Boehmer, Der Junge Luther, pp. 230–231.

46. Text, p. 346, note 51, Chapter Eleven.

47. W. A., "Briefe," I, 276, n. 8. Cf. Enders, I, 407; 430–431. Also, Kalkoff, A. R., IX, 152 ff.; and G. Spalatin, Friedrichs des Weisen Leben, pp. 38, 51.

48. W. A., "Briefe," I, 276, n. 8.

49. Boehmer, Der Junge Luther, p. 232.

50. W. A., "Briefe," I, 263, and n. 2. Cf. Scheurl, Briefbuch, II, 63, had written to Staupitz about Miltitz's journey and pictured the situation as grave.

51. Scheurl, Briefbuch, II, 70. On the date of the visit see W. A., "Briefe," I, 272.

52. Enders, I, 335; translation in Smith, Correspondence, I, 142–143.

53. Enders, I, 335; translation in Smith, Correspondence, I, 142–143. W. A., "Briefe," I, 278, dates this letter December 20.

54. Enders, I, 335; translation in Smith, Correspondence, I, 142–143.

55. W. A., "Briefe," I, 278, n. 40 and n. 49, based on Cyprian, II, 105: "ob malam corporis disposicionem" he remained while Pfeffinger went on to Altenburg.

56. W. A., "Briefe," I, 278, n. 49.

57. Enders, I, 408, 430–432.

58. Boehmer, Der Junge Luther, pp. 232–233.

59. Boehmer, Der Junge Luther, pp. 232–233.

60. Boehmer, Der Junge Luther, p. 233. Cf. Walch, XV, 853–855; Kalkoff, Entscheidungsjahre, p. 99; Kalkoff, Forschungen, pp. 168–169.

61. Enders, I, 348–349; W. A., "Briefe," I, 300, n. 1; Enders, I, 407–409.

62. W. A., "Briefe," I, 289–291; Walch, XV, 840–842; E. A., LIII, 5–7.

63. W. A., "Briefe," I, 290 and 291, n. 8. For text W. A., II, 66.

64. W. A., "Briefe," I, 290 and 291, n. 9.

65. Enders, I, "Luthers Niederschrift fuer die Verhandlung mit Miltitz," 341–342.

66. W. A., "Briefe," I, 291: "Denn ausz der Reuocation wirt nichts." Cf. E. A., LIII, 7.

67. *W. A., "Briefe,"* I, 291–292, "Vorbemerkungen." On the wrong date of this letter in the *Wittenbergische Ausgabe* see Th. Brieger, *Z. K. G.,* XV, 209. This error was copied in later editions, even Enders, I, 442.

68. Mackinnon, *Martin Luther,* II, 112–113. For a typical Roman Catholic reaction see Pastor, *The History of the Popes,* VII, 383–384.

69. Luther did not repeat in the first point what he had written the Elector, "hynfurter still zcu steen und die sach sich selb laszen zcu todt bluetenn," *W. A., "Briefe,"* I, 290; but it is implied in the second report, *W. A., "Briefe,"* I, 293–294. On "a learned German bishop," Brieger, "Lutherstudien," *Z. K. G.,* XV, 204 ff.

70. *W. A., T. R.,* I, 74; III, 308.

71. *W. A., "Briefe,"* I, 344. This ratio was variously reported. In the *Preface* to Luther's Latin works, 1545, it is three for Luther to one for Rome, *Opera Lutheri,* I, 21. This source also mentioned the 25,000 soldiers; but in *W. A., T. R.,* I, 73, it is "trigenta milia." Cf. Boehmer, *Der Junge Luther,* p. 234.

72. Enders, I, 408; translation in Smith, *Correspondence,* I, 160.

73. Walch, XV, 862–863.

74. Paulus, *Johann Tetzel,* pp. 81–82.

75. Enders, I, 492–493; translation in Smith, *Correspondence,* I, 172–173.

76. Text, pp. 39–43.

77. Enders, I, 492–493; translation in Smith, *Correspondence,* I, 173.

78. Enders, II, 18–21. On Cajetan's part see *W. A., "Briefe,"* I, 375, n. 4.

79. *W. A., "Briefe,"* I, 401–403. Enders, I, 56, n. 1, states this is the only letter which Luther wrote to Miltitz which has been preserved. Another missive was lost, see Cyprian, *Nuetzliche Urkunden,* I, 381.

80. Luther wrote Spalatin that he was not such a fool as to walk into a trap like that, Enders, II, 46; see also the letter to Lang, p. 51. Cf. "Beilage" to the Spalatin letter, *W. A., "Briefe,"* I, 395.

81. Boehmer, *Der Junge Luther,* p. 236.

82. Kalkoff, *Depeschen,* p. 34. As in the case of most political "deals," much is left to inference and innuendo. All parties were most careful to omit specific names. The official source, *Deutsche Reichstagsakten,* I, 823–824, gives a different version, claiming that Orsini made Frederick the offer that, were the King of France elected, "his Excellency" could make any of his friends a cardinal. Kalkoff, *Entscheidungsjahre,* pp. 111–112, has overdone the story. Luther must have also heard this report, for in a letter to Spalatin, July 9, 1520, he wrote: "Non peto Galerum, non aurum, non, quicquid Roma hodie in precio habet." *W. A., "Briefe,"* II, 135. For an evaluation of the situation see Bainton, *Church History,* XVI (1947), 176. Stracke, *Luthers Selbstzeugnis,* CXL, 64, n. 1, repeats the Orsini story, but does not go so far as to assert, as does Kalkoff, that the Pope had Luther in mind. It is difficult to determine what else the Pope could have meant. He needed Frederick's support; and, at the moment, the Luther problem offered his only opportunity to make a "deal" with Frederick. The fact that Frederick and Luther both drew this conclusion adds considerable support to this interpretation, though the fact remains that the Pope did not specifically mention Luther.

83. Kalkoff, *Entscheidungsjahre*, pp. 111–112. The language is rather vague, but Boehmer, *Der Junge Luther*, p. 236, concluded that eventually he would also have been given a "groszartiges Erzbistum." Perhaps this is too strong a deduction; but the language has strange implications: "The Pope has also sent a communication to the Bishop of Cologne that, in case the King of France is elected, we will send him the cardinal's hat and also other great exemptions of his Stift," etc., *Deutsche Reichstags- akten*, I, 824.

84. *Deutsche Reichstagsakten*, I, 832–833. On the Elector's attitude toward papal willingness to evade the Golden Bull of 1356, Walch, XV, 887–889. He wished to follow honorable and Christian practice, *Deutsche Reichs- tagsakten*, I, 766.

85. The claim of Paul Kalkoff, *Z. K. G.*, XXV, 415–416, that the Elector of Saxony received four imperial votes and was Emperor for three hours, is not supported by the facts. For a refutation see Gustav Wolf, "Zur Frage des Kaisertums Friedrichs des Weisen," *Z. K. G.*, XLV (1926), 22 ff.; also Kirn, *Friedrich der Weise*, p. 132. The three ecclesiastical Electors of Mainz, Cologne, and Trier would have voted for him, but Frederick the Wise declined the honor.

86. Boehmer, *Der Junge Luther*, p. 237. Cf. W. A., II, 66.

87. *W. A., "Briefe,"* I, 291.

88. *W. A.*, II, 66–73.

CHAPTER THIRTEEN

1. *Opera Lutheri*, III, 476.

2. Text, p. 333 ff. and n. 5, Chapter Eleven. Koehler, *I. M. R.*, pp. 391—392; Smith, *Correspondence*, I, 234.

3. *Opera Lutheri*, III, 476. Cf. Walch, XV, 1453–1455. Hochstraten was to use his influence at Paris in behalf of Eck as he was acquainted there.

4. E. Reinhardt, *Jacob Fugger der Reiche aus Augsburg* (Berlin, 1926), p. 143.

5. *Corpus Catholicorum*, I, 81–82.

6. Gess, *Akten und Briefe*, I, 48—49, claims that Eck's first letter to Leipzig was lost, for he refers to it in a later letter of December 4. According to Mackinnon, *Martin Luther*, II, 120, Eck had proposed Rome or Cologne and, when those were denied, chose Leipzig because the *Via Antiqua* was still very strong there. Schwiebert, *Thesis*, pp. 177–180. Otto Kirn, *Die Leipziger Theologische Fakultaet in fuenf Jahrhunderten* (Leipzig, 1809), I, 31 ff.

7. For this correspondence between the Leipzig faculty and Duke George, and also from the Bishop of Merseburg, see Gess, *Akten und Briefe*, I, 47–73. For Duke George's pressure on the faculty see Gess, *Akten und Briefe*, I, 59–64, and for their acquiescence, pp. 69–70. A personal visit by Eck to Leipzig may have had additional influence.

8. W. A., II, 250.

9. Boehmer, *Der Junge Luther*, p. 247. For text W. A., IX, 208–209. Cf. also Thesis No. 22, "Resolutions," W. A., I, 571, and Enders, I, 401.

10. Schaefer, p. 46, n. 2, quotes text. *Opera Lutheri*, III, 11.

11. *W. A.*, I, 571. Schaefer, pp. 46–47.

12. *W. A.*, II, 20, gives the Augustana text. For Eck's counter thesis 12 see *Opera Lutheri*, III, 11. Cf. *I. M. R.*, p. 404.

13. Enders, I, 402–405; *W. A.*, "Briefe," I, 415–419.

14. Luther's counter theses are given in *W. A.*, II, 160–161, of which no. 13 is here quoted. Originally Eck had but 12 theses, but on March 14 he added a new thesis, no. 7, on "Free Will," directed principally against Carlstadt. This moved the original thesis no. 12 to no. 13. Cf. Schaefer, p. 47.

15. Enders, I, 402 ff. Cf. *W. A.*, II, 155.

16. *W. A.*, II, 155 ff. For letter *W. A.*, "Briefe," I, 325.

17. *W. A.*, II, 155; *Corpus Catholicorum*, VI, 52, 9; "Beilage," *W. A.*, "Briefe," I, 319, which suggests that Eck added thesis no. 7 on the freedom of the will to refute the charge that he had directed his whole attack against Luther. Cf. also Walch, XV, 969–974, XVIII, 861–863.

18. *W. A.*, II, 157 a., has the Gruenenberg *Urdruck*; text, pp. 158–161. Cf. *W. A.*, "Briefe," I, 319.

19. Gess, *Akten und Briefe*, I, 69–70. On Luther's mistake see *W. A.*, "Briefe," I, 315–319. For Eck's admission that Luther was the principal opponent, Enders, I, 428–430.

20. Gess, *Akten und Briefe*, I, 77.

21. For the correspondence between Luther and Duke George see Gess, *Akten und Briefe*, I, 72, 76, 81, 84, and 85.

22. *W. A.*, II, 250–251. Cf. Luther's letter to Spalatin, *W. A.*, "Briefe," I, 420 ff., reporting debate. For details of safe-conduct, Gess, *Akten und Briefe*, I, 81 and 86.

23. *I. M. R.*, p. 409.

24. On Luther's preparation for the debate, see Schaefer, p. 45 ff.; the text of the "Resolutions," *W. A.*, II, 181–183. These were printed by June 27, and in an enlarged edition on August 18.

25. Schaefer, p. 53 ff. Cf. Melanchthon, *C. R.*, I, 96.

26. Schaefer, pp. 40–55, 193–205.

27. Froude, *Life and Letters of Erasmus* (New York, 1896), pp. 149–188, gives a translation of this play. For a critical evaluation see W. Ferguson, *Opuscola Erasmi Quae in Operibus a Clerico Editis Desiderantur* (1927); cf. B. Pineau, *Erasme et la papaute! Étude critique du Iulius Exclusus* (Paris, 1924), especially, chapter two; and Durand de Laur and Allen, *Z. K. G.*, XLV, 294 ff. On Luther's first contact see *W. A.*, "Briefe," I, 346 and n. 1.

28. Enders, I, 450.

29. *W. A.*, II, 250. Cf. Smith, *Correspondence*, I, 258; Boehmer, *Der Junge Luther*, p. 252; Walch, XV, 1428; Enders, II, 85; and *W. A.*, "Briefe," I, 426, n. 32, on Eck's reception in Leipzig.

30. Froeschel's report, Walch, XV, 1428; Peifer's report, p. 1435; Eck's report, p. 1457. Cf. *W. A.*, "Briefe," I, 40, on Barnim XI of Pomerania.

31. W. A., "Briefe," I, 425, n. 5. Cf. Walch, XV, 1435; and Boehmer, *Der Junge Luther*, p. 253.

32. W. A., "Briefe," I, 425, n. 10; "Beilage," W. A., "Briefe," I, 428–30. For German text of agreement W. A., II, 250.

33. W. A., II, 251. Cf. W. A., "Briefe," I, 429–430, and n. 7. On advice of friends, W. A., "Briefe," I, 421, and 425, n. 18.

34. W. A., II, 251. Froeschel's report, Walch, XV, 1429; on Simon Pistoris, W. A., "Briefe," I, 427, n. 35; Mosellanus' description, Smith, *Correspondence*, I, 258–259.

35. Wiedemann, *Dr. Johann Eck* (Regensburg, 1865), pp. 98–99. The original was printed by Melchior Lotther in Leipzig, 1519, W. A., II, 251, n. 1. For text in German, Walch, XV, 998–1015.

36. Smith, *Correspondence*, I, 257–262.

37. Text, p. 571 ff. Melanchthon's impressions, C. R., I, 96; Mosellanus' descriptions, Smith, *Correspondence*, I, 261. Cf. Walch, XV, 1458–1459.

38. Walch, XV, 1496, 1422–1424; Stracke, *Luthers Selbstzeugnis*, CXL, 83–84; Smith, *Correspondence*, I, 261–262.

39. Boehmer, *Der Junge Luther*, p. 257; C. R., I, 91–96.

40. Mackinnon, *Martin Luther*, II, 131–132, feels that Mosellanus was prejudiced in his judgment. Cf. Walch, XV, 1461.

41. On the official opening see Froeschel's report, Walch, XV, 1430; W. A., II, 251. For an authentic text of the debate see Otto Seitz, *Der authentische Text der Leipziger Disputation* (Berlin, 1903). The Latin text may be found in W. A., II, 254–383. The Walch text, XV, 1015–1340, must be used with great care.

42. Walch, XV, 1430–1431. On the Wittenberg student demonstration, Walch, XV, 1460–1461. Eck was provided with thirty-four guards. Cf. also Luther's letter to the Elector, Walch, XV, 1382 ff.

43. Boehmer, *Der Junge Luther*, p. 258. W. A., "Briefe," I, 425, n. 19.

44. Seitz, *Leipziger Text*, p. 54. Smith, *Correspondence*, I, 260; C. R., I, 92; Barge, *Karlstadt*, I, 159 ff.

45. W. A., "Briefe," I, 428–430 and n. 7. In spite of repeated requests to Duke George, W. A., "Briefe," I, 341, 373, 400, Luther wrote Lang on June 6 that he had not received permission to debate, W. A., "Briefe," I, 415.

46. W. A., "Briefe," I, 423, 427, notes 39–44. Cf. Boehmer, *Der Junge Luther*, p. 254.

47. Walch, XV, 1427, for Froeschel's report; on Katheder see Schreckenbach and Neubert, p. 57. For further story, Walch, XV, 1429 ff.; Smith, *Correspondence*, I, 175, n. 5. On Tetzel's death, Boehmer, *Der Junge Luther*, p. 259.

48. Walch, XV, 1461.

49. Enders, II, 103 ff.

50. Enders, II, 105–106.

51. W. A., "Briefe," I, 428 ff.

52. *W. A.*, II, 255; *"Briefe,"* I, 571.
53. *W. A.*, II, 255 ff., "ad me nihil pertinet."
54. *W. A.*, II, 256—257. Of course, Luther had not granted this point.
55. *W. A.*, II, 257. The text here is Walch, XV, 1073 ff.
56. *W. A.*, II, 257.
57. *W. A.*, II, 258.
58. *W. A.*, II, 258.
59. *W. A.*, II, 258—259.
60. *W. A.*, II, 259.
61. *W. A.*, II, 259—260. He refers to Luther's tract, *W. A.*, II, 183 ff.
62. *W. A.*, II, 261—262. Cf. Melanchthon's reactions, *C. R.*, I, 87 ff.
63. *W. A.*, II, 263.
64. *W. A.*, II, 263 ff.
65. *W. A.*, II, 269.
66. *W. A.*, II, 272.
67. *W. A.*, II, 274, 277—278.
68. *W. A.*, II, 276—278, 280. Cf. Enders, II, 78; translation in Smith, *Correspondence*, I, 197—199.
69. *W. A.*, II, 275 f.
70. *W. A.*, II, 278—280.
71. Walch, XV, 1430. On this account see Sebastian Froeschel, *Vom Koenigreich Christi Jesu* (Wittenberg, 1566). Cf. *Beitraege zur saechsischen Kirchengeschichte* XIV, 10; "He wrote from a living memory, therefore his report, although written later, is quite reliable."
72. Walch, XV, 1430.
73. *W. A.*, II, 279.
74. *W. A.*, II, 280—285.
75. *W. A.*, II, 280, 283.
76. *W. A.*, II, 285: "Quod ecclesia Christi 20 annos ad minus fuit, antequam Romana ecclesia nasceretur," etc.
77. *W. A.*, II, 286.
78. *W. A.*, II, 286.
79. *W. A.*, II, 288—289.
80. Mackinnon, *Martin Luther*, II, 140.
81. *W. A.*, II, 296.
82. *W. A.*, II, 298—299.
83. *W. A.*, II, 319 ff.
84. *W. A.*, II, 344 ff. *W. A.*, *"Briefe,"* I, 422 and n. 27; Enders, II, 88, n. 15.
85. Enders, II, 111; translated in Mackinnon, *Martin Luther*, II, 142.
86. *W. A.*, II, 359 ff.
87. *W. A.*, II, 382.
88. *W. A.*, II, 382; translated in Mackinnon, *Martin Luther*, II, 143.

89. Walch, XV, 1305 ff.; 1431–1432.

90. Enders, II, 103–121. Cf. Walch, XV, 1364–1365.

91. Holl, G. A., I, 551 ff.; Schaefer, pp. 55–68. Cf. Melanchthon, C. R., I, 96.

92. Schaefer, pp. 53–55.

93. Schaefer, pp. 53–55.

94. Smith, *Correspondence*, I, 262.

95. Smith, *Correspondence*, I, 210.

96. C. R., I, 87 ff.; Walch, XV, 1443–1451.

97. Walch, XV, 1442.

98. Walch, XV, 1442; as recorded in *Album*, I, 87, "Johannes grauman Naustadt Herbipo dioc. Magister Lipzen."

99. Boehmer, *Der Junge Luther*, p. 265.

100. W. A., *"Briefe,"* I, 427, n. 34.

101. W. A., *"Briefe,"* I, 427, n. 35.

102. Smith, *Correspondence*, I, 261.

103. C. R., I, 87 ff.; Walch, XV, 1404–1407.

104. Luther wrote Spalatin March 13, 1519, Enders, I, 450: "Verso et decreta Pontificum pro mea disputatione, et (in aurem tibi loquor) nescio, an papa sit Antichristus ipse vel apostolus ejus." Cf. n. 10.

105. Gess, *Akten und Briefe*, I, 91, n. 123; W. A., *"Briefe,"* I, 428–431.

106. Gess, *Akten und Briefe*, I, 92, n. 124; W. A., *"Briefe,"* I, 430.

107. Gess, *Akten und Briefe*, I, 93; W. A., *"Briefe,"* I, 430.

108. W. A., *"Briefe,"* I, 430–431. Luther's statement is very brief, a single page, with a note pasted on "To Mr. Caesar Pflug," etc. Eck's statement is much longer, Seidemann, *Disputation*, p. 149 f. *"Beilage,"* p. 33b; Gess, *Akten und Briefe*, I, 93, 1. It is full of charges against Luther. Cf. W. A., XLVIII, 317, 692; and W. A., T. R., VI, 7030.

109. W. A., *"Briefe,"* I, 431; Gess, *Akten und Briefe*, 94, no. 125; Enders, II, 74.

110. W. A., *"Briefe,"* I, 426, n. 32, which also gives source.

111. W. A., *"Briefe,"* I, 423; Enders, II, 89, n. 19. Walch, XV, 1385–1386.

112. W. A., *"Briefe,"* I, 426–427, n. 32 and n. 36. The latter source is *Briefmappe*, II, 90, from which they quote. See Boehmer, *Der Junge Luther*, pp. 262–263.

113. W. A., II, 622 f.; *"Briefe,"* I, 387–393, especially the historical introduction; 426, n. 32; Enders, II, 130 and 139.

114. W. A., II, 621 ff.

115. Boehmer, *Der Junge Luther*, p. 263. For the role played by Luther and Carlstadt in this, W. A., *"Briefe,"* I, 458–501, which includes Eck's letter to the Elector of July 22, pp. 459–461; the Elector's reply to Eck of July 24, p. 463; Carlstadt's letter to the Elector of July 31, pp. 463–464; Luther's and Carlstadt's defense against Eck, pp. 465–478; the Elector's short letter to Eck enclosing the letter of Luther and Carlstadt, p. 478; and Eck's long reply, p. 479 ff.

116. W. A., "Briefe," I, 463 ff. Boehmer, Der Junge Luther, p. 263.

117. W. A., "Briefe," I, 432, n. 6.

118. W. A., II, 388. For Melanchthon's reactions C. R., I, 104; 107—108.

119. Enders, II, 111; Walch, XV, 1366—1367. Consult notes 84 and 85, Chapter Thirteen.

120. Enders, II, 139.

121. C. R., I, 97 f.; Luther's account, Walch, XV, 1377—1379; the original Latin, Enders, II, 120—121.

122. C. R., I, 108—118.

123. Boehmer, Der Junge Luther, p. 264.

124. For full title, W. A., II, 388.

125. Reu, Luther's German Bible, pp. 170—171, quoting the "Preface" to the New Testament.

126. Reu, Luther's German Bible, pp. 172—175, 227, 355, n. 53. W. A., "Deutsche Bibel," II, 480 f., VII, 386.

127. Mackinnon, Martin Luther, II, 151—152, De Primatu Petri adversus Ludderum, in Ms. form.

128. Mackinnon, Martin Luther, II, 151.

129. Mackinnon, Martin Luther, II, 151. Perhaps this was a Froben reprint.

130. Boehmer, Der Junge Luther, p. 264.

131. W. A., II, 623 ff.

132. W. A., "Briefe," II, 37, n. 6, and, especially, p. 59, n. 3. On "Jeck" see Smith, Correspondence, I, 220, n. 2. For claim that Gerbel wrote this, see Mackinnon, Martin Luther, II, 152, n. 24.

133. W. A., "Briefe," II, 36—37, n. 3; 56—57.

134. It was sent October 4, 1519; Gess, Akten und Briefe, I, 100; W. A., VIII, 256. When it was sent to Erfurt is not known. Cf. W. A., "Briefe," I, 506, Luther's letter to Lang, and n. 1. He no doubt sent it earlier to Erfurt, but it was December 29 before they announced their refusal to give a verdict, Gess, Akten und Briefe, I, 113.

135. Opera Lutheri, III, 476; Walch, XV, 1451—1456; Smith, Correspondence, I, 205—207. Eck did not know anyone on the Paris faculty, W. A., VIII, 256. See also Nikolas Paulus, Die deutschen Dominikaner im Kampfe gegen Luther (Freiburg, 1903), p. 87 ff.

136. W. A., VIII, 256.

137. W. A., "Briefe," I, 429: "auch dasz die Acta dieser Disputation nicht in paepistlichen Hof, aus Ursachen ihne bewegend, darubir zu erkennen, sollen geschickt werden."

138. For this letter see Société de L'Histoire du Protestantisme Français, LXVI, 38—42. Cf. Schwiebert, Thesis, p. 223, and n. 5.

139. W. A., "Briefe," I, 545 ff. For translation see Smith, Correspondence, I, 236—237; based on Enders, II, 211.

140. Smith, Correspondence, I, 237.

141. For a good description of the Paris faculties at that time see Robert Goulet, *Compendium Universitatis Parisiensis* (1517), translated by R. B. Burke, 1928.

142. Smith, *The Age of the Reformation* (New York, 1920), p. 42.

143. On the conciliar position of Paris see L'Abbé P. Feret, *La Faculté de Théologie de Paris, Ép. Moderne*, I, 98; and M. Crevier, *Histoire de L'Université de Paris*, V, 35 ff. For material on the period of Louis XII see *Church History*, XVII, 5, and n. 12. Schwiebert, *Thesis*, p. 226.

144. Crevier, *Histoire de L'Université de Paris*, V, 35; Schwiebert, *Thesis*, p. 226, n. 4.

145. Goulet, *Compendium*, p. 74. On processions, Schwiebert, *Thesis*, p. 226 ff.

146. Goulet, *Compendium*, pp. 78—80.

147. Feret, *La Faculté de Théologie de Paris, Ép. Moderne*, I, 99; Schwiebert, *Thesis*, p. 227 ff. Cf. also, Mueller, *D. L., CIII*, 101—109.

148. Schwiebert, *Thesis*, p. 227. *W. A.*, VIII, 257.

149. Mueller, *D. L., CIII*, 101—109; Feret, *La Faculté de Théologie de Paris, Ép. Moderne*, I, 99; Crevier, *Histoire de L'Université de Paris*, V, 137. The faculty decided on March 2, 1520, to answer no letters prior to the official verdict.

150. Gess, *Akten und Briefe*, I, 113; note 134, Chapter Thirteen.

151. Schwiebert, *Thesis*, 229, n. 1. Cf. *W. A.*, VIII, 256; Crevier, *Histoire de L'Université de Paris*, V, 137; and Feret, *La Faculté de Théologie de Paris, Ép. Moderne*, I, 98.

152. The original owner of the Cornell University copy was Bonifaz Amerbach, who later gave it to Basel University. In 1904 Professor G. L. Burr purchased it for the Cornell Library. On various editions see Schwiebert, *Thesis*, p. 232.

153. Schwiebert, *Thesis*, p. 232; Enders, I, 420—422.

154. Schwiebert, *Thesis*, p. 232, n. 5. Cf. *C. R.*, I, 75, Melanchthon to Spalatin. See also *W. A.*, "*Briefe*," I, 331, n. 1.

155. Burr's note in Cornell copy, Schwiebert, *Thesis*, p. 135.

156. Schwiebert, *Thesis*, p. 233, n. 2. Cf. Baum, *Capito und Butzer*, p. 32. For text, pp. 7—11 of the Cornell copy. For a translation, Smith, *Correspondence*, I, 129.

157. For an analysis of the two editions see Schwiebert, *Thesis*, p. 235 ff. Cf. problem of Guenther theses, p. 237, n. 2.

158. For a scholarly study see H. de Jongh, "Les Membres de la Faculté de Théologie au moment de la lutte contre Erasmus et Luther," *L'Ancienne Faculté de Théologie de Louvain au Premier Siècle de son Existence* (1911), p. 148 ff. Cf. Schwiebert, *Thesis*, p. 239 ff.

159. H. de Jongh, *Louvain*, pp. 149, 168—169, 173—186.

160. De Jongh, *Louvain*, p. 219.

161. The author was doubtless Erasmus; Smith, *Erasmus*, pp. 231—232. Cf. Ferguson, *Opuscula Erasmi*, p. 174 ff.

162. De Jongh, *Louvain*, p. 194.

163. De Longh, *Louvain*, pp. 208—209.
164. The Latin text of the Cologne articles is in *Opera Lutheri*, IV, 182—185. For translation see Schwiebert, *Thesis*, pp. 245—248.
165. De Jongh, *Louvain*, p. 208.
166. De Jongh, *Louvain*, pp. 217—218.
167. De Jongh, *Louvain*, pp. 208, 212—213. On the meeting in St. Peter's see Schwiebert, *Thesis*, p. 250, and n. 1.
168. For text of Louvain articles see *Opera Lutheri*, IV, 178—182. For translation and discussion, Schwiebert, *Thesis*, pp. 251—256.
169. De Jongh, *Louvain*, pp. 213—214. On Adrian's reply to the Louvain faculty, *Opera Lutheri*, IV, 176; translation in Smith, *Correspondence*, I, 256—257.
170. Kalkoff, *Forschungen*, p. 188 ff.; De Jongh, *Louvain*, p. 222.
171. Kalkoff, *Forschungen*, pp. 188—203; De Jongh, *Louvain*, p. 222 ff. On 1544 Louvain articles see Schwiebert, *Thesis*, p. 256, n. 3. Text, *W. A.*, LIV, 412 ff.
172. *W. A.*, LIV, 412 ff.
173. De Jongh, *Louvain*, pp. 264—265. Cf. Schwiebert, *Thesis*, p. 256, n. 3; *Opera Lutheri*, IV, 412 ff.
174. Mueller, *D. L.*, CIII, 1 ff.
175. Mueller, *D. L.*, CIII, 12.
176. *Opera Lutheri*, VI, 34—38; and *W. A.*, VIII, 255 ff. For a discussion, Schwiebert, *Thesis*, p. 257 ff.
177. *W. A.*, VIII, 258. Cf. Mueller, *D. L.*, CIII, 12.
178. *Ulrich Zwingli opera*, eds. Schueler und Schulthess, VII, 151.
179. Mueller, *D. L.*, CIII, 12; *W. A.*, VIII, 258, date April 15, 1521. On Noel Beda, Smith, *The Age of the Reformation*, p. 161; Schwiebert, *Thesis*, p. 259 and n. 5.
180. *W. A.*, VIII, 258. See n. 1 on other sources.
181. *W. A.*, VIII, 258.
182. *Opera Lutheri*, VI, 37.
183. *W. A.*, VIII, 271, 273. Cf. *Opera Lutheri*, VI, 37.
184. *W. A.*, VIII, 272; *Opera Lutheri*, VI, 38. On cited articles see *W. A.*, VIII, 272 ff.
185. *W. A.*, VIII, 272—280, *passim; Opera Lutheri*, VI, 43—48.
186. *W. A.*, VIII, 290.
187. *W. A.*, VIII, 259.
188. *W. A.*, VIII, 259. Cf. Mueller, *D. L.*, CIII, 13.
189. Mueller, *D. L.*, CIII, 13.
190. Mueller, *D. L.*, CIII, 14.
191. *W. A.*, VIII, 291.
192. *W. A.*, VIII, 291—293.
193. *W. A.*, VIII, 295 ff.; Schwiebert, *Thesis*, p. 282, n. 1.

194. *Opera Lutheri*, VI, 58 ff.; *W. A.*, VIII, 295.
195. Schwiebert, *Thesis*, p. 287, n. 1. Cf. *Opera Lutheri*, VI, 71.
196. Mueller, *D. L.*, CIII, 12.
197. *Opera Lutheri*, VI, 78—83.
198. Schwiebert, *Thesis*, p. 284, n. 1 and 2. On Melanchthon, *Opera Lutheri*, VI, 87 ff.; Walch, XVIII, 1183—1184.
199. *Opera Lutheri*, VI, 89.
200. *Opera Lutheri*, VI, 90—91. Cf. for a slightly different reading of the text, Walch, XVIII, 1185 ff.
201. *W. A.*, LIV, 141 ff.
202. Those who would explore Luther's advanced exegetical skill should see Holl, *G. A.*, I, 544 ff.

CHAPTER FOURTEEN

1. *W. A.*, "*Briefe*," II, 128—129.
2. *W. A.*, IX, 314 ff.
3. Georg Buchwald, *Doctor Martin Luther* (Leipzig, 1914), p. 159.
4. Boehmer, *Der Junge Luther*, p. 270.
5. Quoted from Boehmer, *Road to Reformation*, p. 299.
6. Louise W. Holborn, "Printing and the Growth of a Protestant Movement in Germany from 1517 to 1524," *Church History*, XI (1942), 129—130.
7. Boehmer, *Der Junge Luther*, p. 276.
8. *W. A.*, II, 443—620. On the beginning of Luther's work, *W. A.*, "*Briefe*," I, 73.
9. *W. A.*, II, 437.
10. *W. A.*, VI, 196—197. Cf. *W. A.*, "*Briefe*," I, 550, n. 4; *W. A.*, II, 685—699, 727—737, and 742—758.
11. Mueller, *Annalen*, p. 72. Cf. *W. A.*, VI, 99; Boehmer, *Der Junge Luther*, p. 269.
12. For original title, *W. A.*, VI, 101; for text, 104 ff.
13. *W. A.*, VI, 104—119.
14. *W. A.*, VI, 119 ff.
15. By February 5, 1520, the Latin text was completed, and by February 11, the German reading was finished. See I. B. Menckenius (ed.) *Annales G. Spalatini, Scriptores rerum Germanicarum*, II, 598; and Spalatin, *Friedrichs des Weisen Leben*, p. 36.
16. Buchwald, *Doctor Martin Luther*, p. 163.
17. *W. A.*, "*Briefe*," II, 41, places the date February 14. Cf. *W. A.*, IX, 321 f.
18. Text, p. 519 ff.
19. *Opera Lutheri*, I, 22.
20. *W. A.*, V, 2. Cf. G. Loesche, *Analecta Lutherana et Melanchthoniana* (Gotha, 1892), no. 52.

21. *C. R.*, I, 76; Enders, II, 68.
22. *C. R.*, I, 76; *W. A.*, V, 4.
23. *W. A.*, V, 6; Enders, III, 172 f., n. 7, 93, 150, 154, 171.
24. *W. A.*, II, 712 ff. Cf. Enders, I, 331, n. 10; *W. A.*, II, 727 ff.; 742 ff. For background, *W. A.*, *"Briefe,"* I, 550, n. 1; Smith, *Correspondence*, I, 227–228.
25. *W. A.*, II, 680 ff. He died in Hesse in 1529, De Wette, III, 432. Cf. *W. A.*, *"Briefe,"* I, 549, n. 1 and n. 4.
26. For a good introduction see Albert Hyma, *Christianity, Capitalism and Communism* (Ann Arbor, 1937), p. 41 ff., especially p. 45 on this sermon. Sources, *W. A.*, VI, 1–8; 34–60; XV, 279–322.
27. Reinhardt, *Jacob Fugger der Reiche*, pp. 142–144; Schulte, *Die Fugger in Rom*, p. 162.
28. *W. A.*, I, 499–505.
29. *W. A.*, VI, 3–8. Cf. Theodor Wiedemann, *Dr. Johann Eck* (Regensburg, 1865), p. 53 ff.; and Kolde, *Martin Luther* (Gotha, 1884), p. 217 ff.
30. *W. A.*, VI, 36–60, has original text.
31. *W. A.*, VI, 293–322, contains original text.
32. *W. A.*, LI, 331–424.
33. *W. A.*, VII, 194–195, 204–229; XXX, 434.
34. *W. A.*, VI, 63–75.
35. Luther had become deeply involved over the "Stolpen Zettel," which had grown out of Duke George's taking exception to parts of Luther's *Sermon on the Holy Eucharist* in 1519. *W. A.*, VI, 196.
36. *W. A.*, *"Briefe,"* II, 49, n. 3, 55; VI, 196, 202–276, *Von den guten werckenn D. M. L.*
37. *W. A.*, VI, 196–197.
38. *W. A.*, VI, 197; *C. R.*, I, 160.
39. Seeberg, *Lehrbuch*, III, 761 ff., 793 f.; IV, 158 ff.
40. Seeberg, *Lehrbuch*, III, 538 f.; IV, 159.
41. *W. A.*, II, 754, Baptism and the Lord's Supper the two main Sacraments; yet, even later, he often spoke of three, including Penance. *W. A.*, VI, 501; IX, 313. See also Seeberg, *Lehrbuch*, IV, 386–387.
42. *W. A.*, II, 742 ff.
43. *W. A.*, I, 539; II, 715; VI, 501.
44. *W. A.*, II, 716; Seeberg, *Lehrbuch*, IV, 163–164. Cf. *W. A.*, VI, 544–545.
45. *W. A.*, I, 534; II, 714.
46. *W. A.*, II, 719.
47. *W. A.*, *"Briefe,"* I, 595, has the first reference to the later principle of the "Priesthood of Believers." It is more clearly set forth in *W. A.*, VI, 407–411. See also Boehmer, *Der Junge Luther*, p. 273.
48. Seeberg, *Lehrbuch*, IV, 163–164.
49. *W. A.*, I, 446; VII, 116.
50. Seeberg, *Lehrbuch*, IV, 165. Cf. *W. A.*, I, 576.

51. Seeberg, *Lehrbuch*, IV, 390–391. Cf. *W. A.*, II, 728.
52. *W. A.*, XLVI, 687; XLVII, 11. Cf. XIX, 496; XXXVII, 648 and 650.
53. *W. A.*, XXX, 1, 220; XXXVII, 670.
54. Seeberg, *Lehrbuch*, IV, 395–396. Cf. *W. A.*, II, 447; XXVI, 154.
55. *W. A.*, XXX, Pt. 1, 219. Cf. XI, 453.
56. *W. A.*, XXVI, 159–160; XLVI, 687; and XLVII, 328.
57. *W. A.*, II, 749.
58. This viewpoint can be traced back to Rupert v. Deutz in the Middle Ages; Seeberg, *Lehrbuch*, III, 214. Cf. *W. A.*, II, 522 f., 789 ff. On Luther, *W. A.*, VI, 508; VII, 131; X, Pt. 2, 245 ff.; Holman, *W. M. L.*, II, 188.
59. *W. A.*, II, 749–750, translation from Holman, *W. M. L.*, II, 20.
60. *E. A.*, XIV, 188; XI, 131; XII, 300; *W. A.*, XXXIII, 279; and XLVI, 57. Cf. also Holman, *W. M. L.*, II, 191; *W. A.*, VI, 510; X, Pt. 1, 207; XVIII, 186.
61. *W. A.*, VI, 360. Cf. Seeberg, *Lehrbuch*, IV, 400.
62. *W. A.*, VI, 355, 360, 363, 373 f., 515, 517 f.; X, Pt. 2, 29.
63. Seeberg, *Lehrbuch*, IV, 405. Luther's own plan had been to make the change very gradually. *W. A.*, X, Pt. 2, 25, 30.
64. *W. A.*, X, Pt. 2, 14, 20 ff. Cf. also his later position. *W. A.*, XXVI, 565; XLVI, 780.
65. Text, p. 665.
66. For a discussion of Luther's "social ethics" see Holl, *G. A.*, I, 155–287, "Der Neubau der Sittlichkeit."
67. Holl, *G. A.*, I, 155 ff.; III, 189–219, especially, 215 ff.
68. *W. A.*, "*Briefe*," I, 595; Boehmer, *Der Junge Luther*, p. 273.
69. Holl, *G. A.*, III, 215 ff. *W. A.*, XXII, 208–209; *E. A.*, XLV, 260 ff.; XLIII, 14–17.
70. *W. A.*, *T. R.*, IV, 523–525, n. 4805.
71. Hyma, *Christianity, Capitalism and Communism* (Ann Arbor, 1937), p. 63.
72. Hyma, *Christianity, Capitalism and Communism*, pp. 89–90.
73. Text, p. 550 ff.
74. For Luther's views on "Ordnung eines gemeinen Kastens," see *W. A.*, XXII, 105 ff. For a description of the monastery, Charitius, pp. 108–111.
75. *W. A.*, VI, 206–276.
76. *W. A.*, VI, 205–206; Boehmer, *Der Junge Luther*, p. 278.
77. *W. A.*, VI, 205.
78. *W. A.*, VI, 246, 257–258.
79. *W. A.*, VI, 205–206, and 250 ff.
80. Holl, *G. A.*, I, 288 ff.; Boehmer, *Der Junge Luther*, p. 292 ff.
81. Seeberg, *Lehrbuch*, IV, 346–352.
82. Holl, *G. A.*, I, 289; Seeberg, *Lehrbuch*, IV, 344–345.
83. Text, p. 743 f.
84. Seeberg, *Lehrbuch*, IV, 360. Cf. Holl, *G. A.*, I, 294 ff.
85. Holl, *G. A.*, I, 382. Cf. *W. A.*, XXIII, 421.

86. *W. A.*, VIII, 482–483.

87. Boehmer, *Der Junge Luther*, pp. 288–290.

88. Alveld tried to prove through canon law that the apostolic chair rested on divine right, *W. A.*, VI, 277–279.

89. For text of Luther's reply, *W. A.*, VI, 285 ff. On the nature of the Church see pp. 296–297.

90. Sohm, *Weltliches und Geistliches Recht*, p. 12.

91. Rietschel, "Das Problem der unsichtbar-sichtbaren Kirche bei Luther," *S. V. R. G.*, CLIV (1932), 1–109.

92. *W. A.*, VI, 293. Rietschel, "Das Problem der unsichtbar-sichtbaren Kirche bei Luther," *S. V. R. G.*, CLIV, 28; *W. A.*, VII, 710.

93. *W. A.*, VI, 296; translation Holman, *W. M. L.*, I, 353–354.

94. For a discussion of this question see Holl, *G. A.*, I, 326–380.

95. Rietschel, "Das Problem der unsichtbar-sichtbaren Kirche bei Luther," *S. V. R. G.*, CLIV, 3 ff.

96. Rietschel, "Das Problem der unsichtbar-sichtbaren Kirche bei Luther," *S. V. R. G.*, CLIV, 3–5.

97. Rietschel, "Das Problem der unsichtbar-sichtbaren Kirche bei Luther," *S. V. R. G.*, CLIV, 2–3. For an opposite viewpoint see Ferdinand Kattenbusch, *Die Doppelschichtigkeit in Luthers Kirchenbegriff* (Gotha, 1928), p. 3 ff., especially, 68 ff. and 117 ff. For further literature, Schwiebert, "The Reformation from a New Perspective," *Church History*, XVII, 24, n. 11.

98. Kattenbusch, *Die Doppelschichtigkeit in Luthers Kirchenbegriff*, p. 68 ff.

99. *W. A.*, VI, 297.

100. Rietschel, "Das Problem der unsichtbar-sichtbaren Kirche bei Luther," *S. V. R. G.*, CLIV, 28.

101. Rietschel, "Das Problem der unsichtbar-sichtbaren Kirche bei Luther," *S. V. R. G.*, CLIV, 28.

102. Seeberg, *Lehrbuch*, IV, 354 ff.

103. *W. A.*, XLIII, 610; XLIV, 713; on faith as the "Trennungsseil," V, 455.

104. Sohm, *Weltliches und Geistliches Recht*, p. 46.

105. Rietschel, "Das Problem der unsichtbar-sichtbaren Kirche bei Luther," *S. V. R. G.*, CLIV, 19–20. *W. A.*, VII, 683.

106. Holl, *G. A.*, I, 289.

107. *W. A.*, VIII, 685.

108. Karl Rieker, *Die rechtliche Stellung der evangelischen Kirche in ihrer geschichtlichen Entwickelung bis zur Gegenwart* (Leipzig, 1893), pp. 46–49. *C. R.*, XXI, 506 ff.; 825 ff.; and *Z. K. G.*, I, 51 ff.

109. *W. A.*, II, 742 ff. *W. A.*, "Briefe," I, 563–564.

110. *W. A.*, VI, 135; *Opera Lutheri*, IV, 139; Gess, *Akten und Briefe*, I, 147, 150.

111. *W. A.*, VI, 135; Smith, *Correspondence*, I, 288.

112. *W. A.*, VI, 112; *W. A.*, "Briefe," II, 40, n. 3.

113. *W. A.*, VI, 136.

114. *W. A.*, *"Briefe,"* II, 40, n. 3. Cf. Gess, *Akten und Briefe*, I, no. 155.

115. Enders, II, 322; translation in Smith, *Correspondence*, I, 285. See also *W. A.*, VI, 135, n. 1.

116. *W. A.*, *"Briefe,"* II, 39, and n. 2. For text see *W. A.*, VI, 137—141. *W. A.*, *"Briefe,"* II, 24, n. 1; 24—29.

117. Enders, II, 327; translation in Smith, *Correspondence*, I, 286.

118. Enders, II, 327; Smith, *Correspondence*, I, 287.

119. Enders, II, 324—325; Smith, *Correspondence*, I, 289.

120. *W. A.*, *"Briefe,"* II, 24—29; Enders, II, 324—343. See also *W. A.*, *"Briefe,"* II, 48—49, for letter to Spalatin, and 52—55, for replies.

121. Enders, II, 336—339; *W. A.*, *"Briefe,"* II, 53—55. Though dated February 26, it had not yet reached Luther by February 29, *W. A.*, *"Briefe,"* II, 57.

122. Enders, II, 336; Smith, *Correspondence*, I, 292—293.

123. De Wette, II, 112; translation, Smith, *Correspondence*, II, 27.

124. Enders, II, 242—243; *W. A.*, *"Briefe,"* II, 57—58.

125. *W. A.*, *"Briefe,"* II, 48—49, especially, 49, n. 2.

126. Holman, *W. M. L.*, I, 337 ff.

127. *W. A.*, *"Briefe,"* II, 98—99, and n. 10.

128. Luther received the Italian original of Prierias' *Epitome* on June 7, 1520, *W. A.*, *"Briefe,"* II, 119, n. 6. At first he did not consider it worthy of reply, *W. A.*, VI, 326. For a detailed discussion see Boehmer, *Der Junge Luther*, p. 287 ff.

129. Hans Preuss, *Die Vorstellungen vom Antichrist im spaeteren Mittelalter bei Luther und der konfessionellen Polemik* (Leipzig, 1906), p. 110 ff. Cf. Boehmer, *Der Junge Luther*, pp. 288—289. For text, *W. A.*, VI, 328—348.

130. See *W. A.*, *"Briefe,"* II, 51, notes 13 and 14; also Kalkoff, *Huttens Vagantenzeit*, p. 223, n. 1; and Paul Joachimsen, *H. Z.*, 136, 339.

131. Mackinnon, *Martin Luther*, II, 172 ff., 173, n. 99.

132. Boehmer, *Der Junge Luther*, pp. 288—289.

133. *Martin Luther* (Berlin, 1933), p. 302 ff., especially 310. This address was delivered in the Castle Church at the time of Luther's burial.

134. *W. A.*, VI, 347, 585, 620.

135. Mackinnon, *Martin Luther*, II, 173. The best that can be said of this unfortunate outburst is that it was not typical of Luther.

136. Enders, III, 73; translation in Smith, *Correspondence*, I, 442.

137. *W. A.*, *"Briefe,"* V, 208 ff., *passim*. Schwiebert, "The Medieval Pattern in Luther's Views of the State," *Church History*, XII (1943), 114 ff.

138. Walther Koehler, *Das katholische Lutherbild der Gegenwart* (Bern, 1922), pp. 33—34. Cf. Boehmer, *Der Junge Luther*, p. 290, note at bottom. He also cites *W. A.*, VI, 585, 620; VII, 645 f., as typical of Luther.

139. *W. A.*, II, 447–449; Enders, II, 139, 156. Cf. *W. A.*, *"Briefe,"* I, 509, n. 2.

140. Enders, II, 331, 340. Mackinnon, *Martin Luther*, II, 174

141. Mackinnon, *Martin Luther*, II, 222.

142. *Luthers Werke fuer das christliche Haus*, I, 202.

143. *Luthers Werke in Auswahl* (Bonn, 1912), I, 362.

144. Walther Koehler, "Zu Luthers Schrift 'An den christlichen Adel deutscher Nation,'" *Zeitschrift fuer Savigny-Stiftung fuer Rechtsgeschichte*, XIV, 1–17; Ernst Kohlmeyer, "Noch ein Wort zu Luthers Schrift an den christlichen Adel," *Z. K. G.*, XLIV, 582 ff.; Karl Bauer, "Luthers Aufruf an den Adel, die Kirche zu reformieren," *A. R.*, XXXII (1935), 167 ff. On Luther as court fool, *W. A.*, VI, 404.

145. *C. R.*, I, 211. Bauer, "Luthers Aufruf an den Adel, die Kirche zu reformieren," *A. R.*, XXXII, 200; On Johann von der Wieck, Enders, II, 432, 443.

146. *W. A.*, VI, 405–406, appeal to Charles V; Bauer, "Luthers Aufruf an den Adel, die Kirche zu reformieren," *A. R.*, XXXII, 202, on the participation of Frederick and the Court; 210–211, on the appeal to the General Council.

147. *C. R.*, I, 211; Bauer, "Luthers Aufruf an den Adel, die Kirche zu reformieren," *A. R.*, XXXII, 174 ff.

148. Bauer, "Luthers Aufruf an den Adel, die Kirche zu reformieren," *A. R.*, XXXII, 196 ff.; Koestlin, *Martin Luther* (1875), I, 791, Anm. 2, 336; Enders, II, 432.

149. Enders, II, 406, n. 2.

150. Lauterbach, *Tagebuch*, p. 12; Bauer, "Luthers Aufruf an den Adel, die Kirche zu reformieren," *A. R.*, XXXII, 199–200.

151. *"Noster libellus"* in a letter to Link, July 20, 1520, Enders, II, 444.

152. *W. A.*, VI, 396.

153. *W. A.*, VI, 396.

154. Carl Foerstemann, *Neues Urkundenbuch zur Geschichte der evangelischen Kirchenordnungen* (Hamburg, 1842), p. 2, n. 2: "ffyl selczams dynges fynden."

155. Bauer, "Luthers Aufruf an den Adel, die Kirche zu reformieren," *A. R.*, XXXII, 178.

156. *W. A.*, *"Briefe,"* II, 121–122, for Silvester von Schaumberg's letter to Luther offering the protection of 100 fellow knights, June 11, 1520. On Hutten see Hajo Holborn, *Ulrich von Hutten*, pp. 137–173.

157. Lauterbach, *Tagebuch*, p. 19. Bruno Gebhardt, *Die Gravamina der deutschen Nation gegen den roemischen Hof* (Breslau, 1884); *Deutsche Reichstagsakten*, II, 661 ff.

158. On *Julius Exclusus*, *W. A.*, VI, 393; the *Donation of Constantine*, published by Hutten in 1519, first came to Luther's desk through Dominic Schleupner of Breslau. Enders, II, 331, and n. 11, gives its history. Translation in Smith, *Correspondence*, I, 290–291, and n. 2.

159. Bauer, "Luthers Aufruf an den Adel, die Kirche zu reformieren," *A. R.*, XXXII, 216.
160. *W. A.*, VI, 405—469; translation in Holman, *W. M. L.*, II, 63—164.
161. Schwiebert, *Church History*, XII, 99 ff.; *W. A.*, VI, 408—410.
162. *W. A.*, VI, 408.
163. *W. A.*, VI, 407—408.
164. *W. A.*, VI, 407—408.
165. *W. A.*, VI, 409. Bauer, "Luthers Aufruf an den Adel, die Kirche zu reformieren," *A. R.*, XXXII, 210—214.
166. Stutz, *Eigenkirche*, II, 35—70. For a shorter account see Schwiebert, *Church History*, XII, 101 ff.
167. Schwiebert, *Church History*, XII, 104—106.
168. *W. A.*, VI, 411.
169. Text, pp. 619 ff. Holl, *G. A.*, I, 544—582.
170. Holman, *W. M. L.*, II, 76—80.
171. Mirbt, Quellen, p. 146.
172. For literature see Schwiebert, "The Reformation from a New Perspective," *Church History*, XVII (1948), 5, n. 12.
173. *W. A.*, VI, 414; Schaefer, p. 291 ff., treats Nicaea.
174. *W. A.*, VI, 415.
175. *W. A.*, VI, 425 f.; translation in Mackinnon, *Martin Luther*, II, 234—235.
176. Mackinnon, *Martin Luther*, II, 236, n. 46: "Consilium de emendanda Ecclesia," 1537; Luther's translation, *W. A.*, L, 288 ff.
177. *W. A.*, VI, 415—418.
178. *W. A.*, VI, 453.
179. *W. A.*, VI, 429—431.
180. *W. A.*, VI, 462—465. Cf. Bauer, "Luthers Aufruf an den Adel, die Kirche zu reformieren," *A. R.*, XXXII, 200—201.
181. *W. A.*, XI, 229—230.
182. On "Beruf" see Holl, *G. A.*, III, 189—219.
183. *W. A.*, VI, 497—573, text of tract. Luther used the term "Babylonian Captivity" earlier, see *W. A.*, VI, 484, in his "Resolutio" of 1519 and the tract against Alveld, June, 1520, p. 485.
184. *W. A.*, VI, 485; II, 709 ff., 724 ff., and 738 ff.
185. *W. A.*, "*Briefe*," I, 595.
186. Enders, II, 279, 446; *W. A.*, "*Briefe*," II, 148, n. 6; *E. A.*, XXVII, 163.
187. Mackinnon, *Martin Luther*, II, 250.
188. *W. A.*, VI, 497.
189. *W. A.*, VI, 498; Wace and Buchheim, p. 142.
190. *W. A.*, VI, 502.
191. Enders, II, 414, 461. *C. R.*, I, 211.
192. *W. A.*, VI, 487.

193. Wace and Buchheim, pp. 147–149; Holman, *W. M. L.*, II, 178–180.

194. Holman, *W. M. L.*, II, 186 ff., 194 ff.

195. Holman, *W. M. L.*, II, 188. Schwiebert, *Church History*, XVII, 6, n. 17.

196. Wace and Buchheim, p. 160; Holman, *W. M. L.*, II, 193–194, based on *W. A.*, VI, 511.

197. Wace and Buchheim, p. 162.

198. *W. A.*, VI, 513.

199. *W. A.*, VI, 536; translation by Mackinnon, *Martin Luther*, II, 257.

200. *W. A.*, VI, 543–549.

201. *W. A.*, VI, 549–561. Cf. Boehmer, *Der Junge Luther*, pp. 292–294.

202. Miltitz wrote Luther about it August 29, 1520, *W. A.*, "*Briefe*," II, 171; Enders, II, 466–467; *W. A.*, "*Briefe*," II, 180, and n. 2.

203. Enders, II, 478; Walch, XV, 929.

204. For Staupitz's report of the Wittenberg interview see *W. A.*, "*Briefe*," II, 186, n. 2, 190–193.

205. *W. A.*, "*Briefe*," II, 197. Cf. Cyprian, I, 444 f., 449; Smith, *Correspondence*, I, 367, translated from Walch, XV, 947.

206. *W. A.*, VII, 13, for date, text, pp. 3–11; translation in Holman, *W. M. L.*, II, 301–311. For letter to Hermann Muehlpfort, *W. A.*, "*Briefe*," II, 198. (Spelling as found in *W. A.*, VII, 121.)

207. *W. A.*, VII, 39.

208. *W. A.*, VII, 49 ff., for original Latin text. For a Catholic reaction see Grisar, *Luther*, I, 351.

209. Holman, *W. M. L.*, II, 328 ff., especially 338 ff.

210. Holl, *G. A.*, I, 216 ff.

211. The studies of Holl have caused the rejection of the earlier Troeltsch thesis. Luther's fundamental views on business have been well set forth by Hyma, *Christianity, Capitalism and Communism*, pp. 41–65. Cf. Holl, *G. A.*, III, 189 ff.

212. *W. A.*, VII, 64; translation by Mackinnon, *Martin Luther*, II, 269.

213. Text, p. 381, notes 82 and 83, Chapter Twelve.

214. Walch, XV, 894; Enders, II, 139, 187–188.

215. The Elector received conflicting reports of the Liebenwerda meeting. Enders, II, 187–189; *W. A.*, "*Briefe*," I, 524–528; Enders, II, 189–200.

216. *Opera Lutheri*, IV, 256. Kalkoff, *Forschungen*, p. 70; *Z. K. G.*, XXV, 436.

217. Walch, XV, 910–919; Kalkoff, *Z. K. G.*, XXV, 437–441.

218. Mackinnon, *Martin Luther*, II, 190, n. 26.

219. Kalkoff, "Die Bulle 'Exsurge,' " *Z. K. G.*, XXXV (1914), 174.

220. Kalkoff, *Z. K. G.*, XXXV, 171 ff.

221. Pastor, *The History of the Popes*, VII, 394, claims that Accolti drafted the bull, but that Cardinal Giulio de' Medici was the guiding spirit.

222. *Opera Lutheri,* IV, 257. Mackinnon, *Martin Luther,* II, 190, names Prierias and Rhadino as members of the second commission.

223. Kalkoff, *Forschungen,* p. 188; Pastor, *The History of the Popes,* VII, 394. Cf. Kalkoff, *Z. K. G.,* XXV, 104 ff.

224. *Opera Lutheri,* IV, 257; Pastor, *The History of the Popes,* VII, 395; Kalkoff, *Forschungen,* p. 110 ff.

225. Kalkoff, "Die Bulle 'Exsurge,'" *Z. K. G.,* XXXV, 167; Cf. Pastor, *The History of the Popes,* VII, 396—398.

226. Kalkoff, *Entscheidungsjahre,* p. 128 ff.; *Z. K. G.,* XXV, 129.

227. Pastor, *The History of the Popes,* VII, 404. On Aleander's reports see Kalkoff, *Depeschen,* p. 10 ff., *passim.*

228. Pastor, *The History of the Popes,* VII, 405—406, tells of Eck's qualifications. Cf. Mackinnon, *Martin Luther,* II, 198—199.

229. Pastor, *The History of the Popes,* VII, 402; Mackinnon, *Martin Luther,* II, 196. Pastor claims the bull applied to Luther the "monitio evangelica," which always preceded the sentence of excommunication, p. 403. In heresy, the moment of obstinacy had first to be determined.

230. Pastor, *The History of the Popes,* VII, 400, cites Ps. 73:22, as the source of this phrase and points out that much of the language of the bull was Biblical. Papal bulls are always identified by the opening words or phrase. Pastor, of course, quotes from the Latin Vulgate. Cf. Kalkoff, *Forschungen,* 129, 2.

231. Mirbt, *Quellen,* pp. 257—258; Pastor, *The History of the Popes,* VII, 401.

232. Mirbt, *Quellen,* p. 257.

233. Enders, II, 358.

234. Enders, II, 409; *W. A.,* "Briefe," II, 117, notes 1 and 2; *C. R.,* I, 201.

235. Enders, II, 365, 404—407, 419—421. Luther wrote to Spalatin, "Dominus regnat ut palpare possimus."

236. *W. A.,* VI, 171—195, Luther's reply to Louvain and Cologne. On Erasmus, *W. A.,* "Briefe," II, 90—93, n. 53, 115—117; Boecking, *Opera Hutteni,* I, 355; Enders, II, 386 ff., 408 ff.

237. *W. A.,* "Briefe," II, 121—122.

238. *C. R.,* I, 201, Melanchthon to John Hesz, June 8, 1520.

239. Holborn, *Ulrich von Hutten,* p. 125 ff.

240. Smith, *Correspondence,* I, 321, Luther expressed his basic attitude in a letter to Spalatin. For Hutten's lack of understanding of Luther's cause, Holborn, *Ulrich von Hutten,* pp. 130 ff. and 141.

241. Enders, II, 443; translation in Mackinnon, *Martin Luther,* II, 203.

242. Enders, II, 430—431; *W. A.,* "Briefe," II, 134—136, n. 1. Cf. Spalatin, *Chronik,* p. 32.

243. *W. A.,* "Briefe," II, 136.

244. Enders, II, 432–433; translation in Mackinnon, *Martin Luther*, II, 205–206. Cf. *W. A.*, "Briefe," II, 138, n. 7, which cites Enders, II, 371, n. 3, that this expression "A me quidem, iacta mihi alea" was taken from Hutten.

245. Enders, II, 432–433; *W. A.*, "Briefe," II, 137–138.

246. *Opera Lutheri*, II, 351–352, is misdated August 5, 1518. Cf. Kalkoff, *Z. K. G.*, XXV, 508–509, 587 ff., 589 for Riario's writing.

247. Kalkoff, *Depeschen*, pp. 10–11; Boecking, *Opera Hutteni*, I, 429.

248. Spalatin, *Annales*, p. 29.

249. Spalatin, *Annales*, p. 30.

250. Enders, II, 486–489, and n. 6, which cites Cyprian, I, 438, for the story of Eck's flight to St. Paul's Monastery and, finally, to Freiburg.

251. *W. A.*, "Briefe," II, 215, n. 5; *Z. K. G.*, II, 119; Gess, *Akten und Briefe*, I, 143 f.; Enders, II, 503, 511; III, 104, 106.

252. *Opera Lutheri*, V, 245; Kalkoff, *Z. K. G.*, XXV, 531–532.

253. *W. A.*, "Briefe," II, 213–216, and n. 3; *Opera Lutheri*, IV, 305–306; Barge, *Karlstadt*, I, 219, n. 101; Pastor, *The History of the Popes*, VII, 407–408.

254. *W. A.*, VI, 579–593, 597–612, for the texts of the two tracts. Enders, II, 490 ff. and 510.

255. *W. A.*, VI, 604; translation in Mackinnon, *Martin Luther*, II, 218.

256. *W. A.*, VII, 74–82, gives title and text in Latin; 85–90, in German. Enders, II, 510; *E. A.*, LIII, 54.

257. *W. A.*, VII, 153, general account; *W. A.*, "Briefe," II, 234–235, n. 1.

258. *W. A.*, "Briefe," II, 234–235, and, especially, n. 2; Spalatin's report, *Z. K. G.*, II, 122; *W. A.*, *T. R.*, V, 6471; Dietterle, *Z. K. G.*, XXVII, 296 ff.

259. On the *Corpus iuris canonici*, Schaefer, pp. 193–205, especially, p. 200; *E. A.*, LX, 372 ff. For Melanchthon text of the announcement see *W. A.*, VII, 183–186.

260. *W. A.*, VII, 183 ff.; Clemen, *T. S. K.*, LXXXI (1908), 461; Boehmer, *Der Junge Luther*, pp. 332–333, for full account.

261. Grisar, *Luther zu Worms*, p. 6, supports this view; but the editors of the *W. A.*, "Briefe," II, 235, n. 2, question this point on the basis of Spalatin's report to the Elector of December 3, 1520, *Z. K. G.*, II, 122; *W. A.*, VI, 161–182.

262. Grisar, *Luther zu Worms*, p. 10; Boehmer, *Der Junge Luther*, pp. 333–334.

263. Grisar, *Luther zu Worms*, p. 10.

264. *W. A.*, VII, 186.

265. Grisar, *Luther zu Worms*, p. 9.

266. Pastor, *The History of the Popes*, VII, 415–416. The original bull, which mentioned Luther, Hutten, Pirckheimer, and Spengler, was lost. There exists only an altered form, at Aleander's request, which named only Luther. Pastor based his conclusions on Kalkoff, *Depeschen*, p. 135 ff.

267. *Deutsche Reichstagsakten unter Karl V*, II, 670 ff.; Mirbt, *Quellen*, pp. 259–260.

CHAPTER FIFTEEN

1. Holborn, *Ulrich von Hutten*, p. 163 ff. Text, p. 43 ff.

2. Spalatin, *Annales*, p. 11. Kalkoff, *Depeschen*, p. 1 ff.

3. *Deutsche Reichstagsakten*, I, 871, 873. The constitution of the Holy Roman Empire permitted Luther's appeal to a General Council and specifically stated that no German subject could be condemned by an imperial mandate. Even though urged to do so by Aleander, Charles V refused to issue a mandate against Luther at Aachen, but assured Frederick the Wise that Luther would receive a fair hearing, Kalkoff, *Depeschen*, p. 33; *Entscheidungsjahre*, pp. 187—192; Kalkoff, *Erasmus, Luther und Friedrich der Weise*, p. 86 ff.

4. Spalatin, *Annales*, pp. 27—30; Kalkoff, *Depeschen*, pp. 35, 49—50; *I. M. R.*, p. 429.

5. Kalkoff, *Depeschen*, p. 5.

6. Kalkoff, *Depeschen*, pp. 7—8.

7. Kalkoff, *Depeschen*, pp. 35—36.

8. Koehler, *I. M. R.*, p. 428.

9. Kalkoff, *Depeschen*, p. 35 ff., *passim*, shows that Rome would have preferred the first choice, pp. 64—66.

10. Koehler, *I. M. R.*, p. 428.

11. *Deutsche Reichstagsakten*, II, 462—466.

12. The date of Frederick's interview with the Kaiser was November 1, 1520, in Cologne; Kalkoff, *Entscheidungsjahre*, pp. 191—192; Kalkoff, *Erasmus, Luther und Friedrich der Weise*, p. 86 ff.; *I. M. R.*, p. 431.

13. Kalkoff, *Entscheidungsjahre*, pp. 191—192.

14. *W. A.*, "Briefe," II, 250, n. 1, claims he arrived in Worms January 5, 1521; Spalatin, *Annales*, ed., Mencke, II, 605. *W. A.*, "Briefe," II, 219, n. 1, and 247, n. 9; *Deutsche Reichstagsakten*, II, 473.

15. *I. M. R.*, p. 431. Kalkoff, *Depeschen*, pp. 52—53.

16. Kalkoff, *Depeschen*, p. 43.

17. This request was issued from Oppenheim, November 28, 1520; Walch, XV, 2018—2022; *I. M. R.*, p. 431; Boehmer, *Der Junge Luther*, p. 341.

18. *W. A.*, "Briefe," II, 246, n. 9; *Deutsche Reichstagsakten*, II, 468, 473; *I. M. R.*, pp. 432—433. Kalkoff, *Entscheidungsjahre*, p. 202; *Depeschen*, p. 36.

19. Kalkoff, *Entscheidungsjahre*, p. 202; *Deutsche Reichstagsakten*, II, 473.

20. *I. M. R.*, p. 432 ff.

21. Kalkoff, *Depeschen*, pp. 55—59; *I. M. R.*, pp. 433—434.

22. Boehmer, *Der Junge Luther*, p. 346 ff.; *I. M. R.*, pp. 433—434.

23. *I. M. R.*, p. 434.

24. *I. M. R.*, pp. 434—435.

25. *I. M. R.*, p. 435, for reproduction of the *Geleitsbrief* of Charles V.

26. Holborn, *Ulrich von Hutten*, p. 169; *I. M. R.*, p. 436.

27. *I. M. R.*, p. 436; *W. A.*, *"Briefe,"* II, 294, n. 2.

28. *W. A.*, *"Briefe,"* II, 293—294.

29. *Z. K. G.*, XVIII, 408; Boehmer, *Der Junge Luther*, p. 357. He also seems to have received "Geld zur Zehrung" from Duke John in Weimar, *W. A.*, *T. R.*, V, 68; and one gulden from John Lang as a gift, *W. A.*, *"Briefe,"* II, 294, n. 6. On the student Peter Suaven, *W. A.*, *"Briefe,"* II, 352, n. 54.

30. *W. A.*, *"Briefe,"* II, 306, n. 9; Mueller, *Die Wittenberg Bewegung*, p. 126, n. 4. On the route followed see *W. A.*, *"Briefe,"* II, 296, n. 2; Kalkoff, *Depeschen*, pp. 130—131.

31. *W. A.*, *T. R.*, V, 65, 68; III, 282; Walch, XV, 2184; *W. A.*, VII, 803—804; Kalkòff, *Depeschen*, pp. 130—131.

32. Myconius, *Historia Reformationis*, p. 38. *W. A.*, *"Briefe,"* II, 298, notes 1 and 2.

33. *W. A.*, *T. R.*, V, 5342a; Spalatin, *Annales*, p. 38; *W. A.*, *"Briefe,"* II, 298, n. 4.

34. *W. A.*, *"Briefe,"* II, 296—297, n. 3.

35. *W. A.*, *"Briefe,"* II, 454—457. Translation in Smith, *Correspondence*, II, 94, from De Wette, II, 137.

36. *W. A.*, *T. R.*, III, 282, 285; V, 69, n. 1; *W. A.*, VII, 826; Kalkoff, *Depeschen*, pp. 123—125, 146 ff., 157—158; *Z. K. G.*, II, 126—127; Kalkoff, *Hutten*, p. 358 ff.; Holborn, *Ulrich von Hutten*, pp. 170—171.

37. Kalkoff, *Depeschen*, p. 133 ff.; Walch, XV, 2182 ff.; Smith, *Correspondence*, I, 521.

38. *W. A.*, VII, 826; Smith, *Correspondence*, I, 521; *W. A.*, *T. R.*, V, 69; *Deutsche Reichstagsakten*, II, 850—851. This was near the "Swan Inn," where the Elector of the Palatinate was staying. Glapion had wanted Luther brought into Worms very quietly.

39. Kalkoff, *Depeschen*, p. 133.

40. Spalatin, *Annales*, p. 39: "Pfaltz oder des Bischofs hof, do Kaeys Mat lagen." Myconius, *Historia Reformationis*, p. 39; Smith, *Correspondence*, I, 525; Kuehn, *Wormser Reichstag*, pp. 64—68.

41. Myconius, *Historia Reformationis*, pp. 39—40; Spalatin, *Annales*, p. 39; *I. M. R.*, pp. 439—440; Kuehn, *Wormser Reichstag*, p. 65.

42. Kuehn, *Wormser Reichstag*, p. 64; Kalkoff, *Der Grosse Wormser Reichstag*, p. 77, says that this session took place in "der' niedrigen Hofstube." See also *Deutsche Reichstagsakten*, II, 547, 862; *W. A.*, VII, 825; *Opera Lutheri*, VI, 5 f.

43. Text, pp. 51 and 55. *Deutsche Reichstagsakten*, II, 549; *I. M. R.*, p. 439.

44. Spalatin, *Annales*, pp. 39—40, implies that it was late, "nu vertzog es sich, bisz es gar Abend wardt." Of the crowd he says, "in einem groszen gedreng und Volk." Myconius, *Historia Reformationis*, p. 39, "unzehlich Volck." For descriptions, Kuehn, *Wormser Reichstag*, pp. 67—76; and Kalkoff, *Der Grosse Wormser Reichstag*, p. 78 ff.; Kalkoff, *Depeschen*, p. 136.

45. Kalkoff, *Depeschen*, p. 136; Kuehn, *Wormser Reichstag*, pp. 65, 67–76. For a detailed Latin account, W. A., VII, 825 ff.

46. W. A., VII, 828; Myconius, *Historia Reformationis*, p. 40; Kalkoff, *Depeschen*, pp. 136–139.

47. Kalkoff, *Depeschen*, p. 136, says the books had been gathered at the request of the Kaiser; W. A., VII, 828; *Deutsche Reichstagsakten*, II, 633; Kuehn, *Wormser Reichstag*, pp. 65–66.

48. Myconius, *Historia Reformationis*, p. 40; Kalkoff, *Depeschen*, p. 137; W. A., VII, 829–830; Kuehn, *Wormser Reichstag*, p. 66; Spalatin, *Annales*, pp. 40–41.

49. W. A., VII, 815. It was at this time that Hutten wrote his famous letter to Luther: "Be strong and courageous. You must realize what is staked on you, what a crisis this is. You must never doubt me as long as you are constant; I will cling to you to my last breath," etc. W. A., *"Briefe,"* II, 301–302.

50. *Deutsche Reichstagsakten*, II, 549; Kalkoff, *Depeschen*, p. 140 ff.; Kalkoff, *Der Grosse Wormser Reichstag*, p. 78; Kuehn, *Wormser Reichstag*, p. 68; Kalkoff, *Entscheidungsjahre*, p. 236.

51. *Deutsche Reichstagsakten*, II, 510; Kalkoff, *Depeschen*, p. 141; W. A., VII, 829–831; Spalatin, *Annales*, p. 41.

52. A good introduction to this session may be found in Kuehn, *Wormser Reichstag*, pp. 68–76; *Acta et Res Gestae*, D. Martini Lutheri, W. A., VII, 825 ff., especially, 832 ff., for Luther's famous speech on April 18, 1521.

53. W. A., VII, 832 ff.; Kalkoff, *Depeschen*, pp. 141–142; *Entscheidungsjahre*, p. 238, relates that Glapion acted as interpreter for the Emperor, who understood no Latin.

54. *Deutsche Reichstagsakten*, II, 551–554; Kalkoff, *Depeschen*, pp. 142–143; *Entscheidungsjahre*, pp. 237–238; Kuehn, *Wormser Reichstag*, pp. 73–74.

55. W. A., VII, 838; *Deutsche Reichstagsakten*, II, 555 f.; Kuehn, *Wormser Reichstag*, pp. 74–75, n. 1.

56. W. A., VII, 838; Kuehn, *Wormser Reichstag*, p. 75, n. 2; W. A., VII, 838, n. 1; *Deutsche Reichstagsakten*, II, 555 f. Anm.

57. Kuehn, *Wormser Reichstag*, p. 75, n. 4.

58. Kalkoff, *Depeschen*, p. 176; *Entscheidungsjahre*, p. 240.

59. *Deutsche Reichstagsakten*, II, 558, 638; Kalkoff, *Depeschen*, pp. 142–143; *Entscheidungsjahre*, p. 240.

60. Spalatin, *Annales*, pp. 49–50; W. A., T. R., III, 285; V, 81, on Philip of Hesse.

61. This story cannot be supported by historical facts, though related by Selnecker, *Vita Lutheri* in 1590. Boehmer, *Der Junge Luther*, p. 371.

62. W. A., VII, 841; Spalatin, *Annales*, p. 42; Kuehn, *Wormser Reichstag*, pp. 76–77.

63. Kalkoff, *Depeschen*, pp. 146–147; W. A., *"Briefe,"* II, 351, n. 42; W. A., VII, 842.

64. Kalkoff, *Depeschen*, pp. 147–148; *Deutsche Reichstagsakten*, II, 601.

65. *Deutsche Reichstagsakten*, II, 563–564. Cf. Luther's own report to Graf Albrecht von Mansfeld, *W. A.*, "*Briefe*," II, 319–329; *W. A.*, VII, 843 ff.; Kalkoff, *Depeschen*, p. 149.

66. *W. A.*, VII, 849.

67. *W. A.*, VII, 849; Kalkoff, *Depeschen*, p. 150.

68. *W. A.*, VII, 851.

69. *W. A.*, VII, 851.

70. *W. A.*, VII, 851.

71. *W. A.*, VII, 853–855.

72. *W. A.*, VII, 854–855.

73. *W. A.*, VII, 855; Spalatin, *Annales*, p. 46; *W. A.*, "*Briefe*," II, 327.

74. *W. A.*, VII, 855–856; Spalatin, *Annales*, pp. 47–48; *Deutsche Reichstagsakten*, II, 568.

75. *W. A.*, VII, 856; Spalatin, *Annales*, pp. 47–48; Kalkoff, *Depeschen*, p. 153 f.; Kuehn, *Wormser Reichstag*, p. 92.

76. *W. A.*, VII, 856; Spalatin, *Annales*, pp. 47–48.

77. *W. A.*, VII, 857; two reports say he left for Oppenheim between nine and ten a. m. Luther's letter to Cranach, April 28, 1521, *W. A.*, "*Briefe*," II, 305–306, and n. 1; Kalkoff, *Depeschen*, pp. 154–155; Spalatin, *Annales*, pp. 150–151.

78. Kuehn, *Wormser Reichstag*, pp. 102–103. *Deutsche Reichstagsakten*, II, 893 and 898.

79. Kalkoff, *Entstehung des Wormser Edikts*, p. 195, on Archbishop of Salzburg; Kuehn, *Wormser Reichstag*, p. 103; *Deutsche Reichstagsakten*, II, 638.

80. Kuehn, *Wormser Reichstag*, p. 103; Kalkoff, *Entstehung des Wormser Edikts*, pp. 196–197.

81. Kuehn, *Wormser Reichstag*, p. 103; Kalkoff, *Depeschen*, p. 230.

82. *Deutsche Reichstagsakten*, II, 640; Kalkoff, *Depeschen*, p. 156 ff., *passim*; *Deutsche Reichstagsakten*, II, 931.

83. Spalatin, *Annales*, p. 51 on confusion at Worms; *Z. K. G.*, XVIII, 112, indicates Cochlaeus knew Luther was captured near Eisenach, *W. A.*, "*Briefe*," II, 338–339, n. 4.

84. *Deutsche Reichstagsakten*, II, 937 ff.; Kuehn, *Wormser Reichstag*, pp. 104–105.

85. Kuehn, *Wormser Reichstag*, pp. 104–105.

86. *Deutsche Reichstagsakten*, II, 937.

87. Kuehn, *Wormser Reichstag*, pp. 104–105; Kalkoff, *Entscheidungsjahre*, p. 266.

88. Kuehn, *Wormser Reichstag*, pp. 105 and 111, n. 1; *Deutsche Reichstagsakten*, II, 947.

89. *Deutsche Reichstagsakten*, II, 947; Mirbt, *Quellen*, pp. 260–261.

90. For Edict, Schreckenbach and Neubert, *Martin Luther*, p. 106; *Deutsche Reichstagsakten*, II, 640 ff., for text; Mirbt, *Quellen*, pp. 260–261, for short form and bibliography.

91. Kuehn, *Wormser Reichstag*, pp. 116–117. The Elector of Brandenburg, Joachim I, immediately published the Edict in his lands. John the Constant did not even receive a copy. Capito blocked enforcement in the lands of Albert of Mainz.

92. Enders, III, 80; Paulus, *Historisches Jahrbuch*, XXXIX (1919), 273 ff., doubts that it was Aleander's fault; but Kalkoff makes a strong case against him. Scheurl, *Briefbuch*, II, 123–124; Enders, III, 80, n. 6.

CHAPTER SIXTEEN

1. Spalatin, *Annales*, p. 50; *W. A.*, "*Briefe*," II, 306, n. 3, relates that the Elector discussed the plan for Luther's custody with Philip von Feilitzsch and Frederick von Thun, who were to work out the details. Cf. *W. A.*, *T. R.*, V, 82.

2. *W. A.*, "*Briefe*," II, 338; translation in Smith, *Correspondence*, II, 28–29, from Enders, III, 152.

3. *W. A.*, "*Briefe*," II, 340, n. 29.

4. *W. A.*, "*Briefe*," II, 314–317.

5. *W. A.*, "*Briefe*," II, 305–306, and notes 1 and 9; 318–319.

6. *W. A.*, "*Briefe*," 306 ff. The original is now in the Lutherhalle of Wittenberg, Germany. John Pierpont Morgan purchased it through an agent for 102,000 marks and then presented it to the German Kaiser as a present. For a facsimile see Schreckenbach and Neubert, pp. 97–99; for the text, *W. A.*, "*Briefe*," II, 307–310, and 318 for Otto Clemen's criticism. *Deutsche Reichstagsakten*, II, 893; Johannes Kessler, *Sabbata*, p. 75.

7. *W. A.*, "*Briefe*," II, 314–317.

8. *W. A.*, "*Briefe*," II, 318–319, Luther to Spalatin.

9. Boehmer, *Der Junge Luther*, p. 383.

10. *W. A.*, "*Briefe*," II, 296–297, and n. 9; *Z. K. G.*, XXI, 138; Enders, III, 158, 20, on Petzensteiner. Boehmer, *Der Junge Luther*, p. 384.

11. Luther probably stayed with his uncle Heinz, in whose interest he had written the Elector in 1527, Enders, VI, 64. For other details see Burkhardt, *Neues Archiv fuer Saechsische Geschichte*, X, 330 ff.; *W. A.*, "*Briefe*," II, 340, n. 28.

12. *W. A.*, *T. R.*, V, 82, n. 5353, Mathesius report; *Martin Luther* (Berlin, 1933), p. 156; Myconius, *Historia Reformationis*, pp. 41–42.

13. *W. A.*, *T. R.*, V, 82.

14. *W. A.*, *T. R.*, V, 82; Enders, III, 150.

15. Myconius, *Historia Reformationis*, p. 42.

16. Schreckenbach and Neubert, p. 108. Luther was supplied with servants and was fully instructed in the knights' habits; Foerstemann, *T. R.*, III, 37; Enders, III, 155; *W. A.*, "*Briefe*," II, 336–338; 347–349.

17. *W. A.*, *T. R.*, VI, 209–210, n. 6816, Aurifaber's report.

18. *Luther, Vierteljahrsschrift der Luthergesellschaft,* XI (1929), 34 ff.; cf. the marvelous publication by a number of German scholars edited by Max Baumgaertel, *Die Wartburg* (Berlin, 1907) for its illustrations and details, especially, Wilhelm Oncken, "Martin Luther auf der Wartburg," p. 267 ff.

19. Nebe, *Die Lutherstube,* p. 35.

20. Nebe, *Die Lutherstube,* p. 35.

21. The plan is by Baumeister F. W. Saeltzer, Nebe, *Die Lutherstube,* pp. 40—41.

22. The ruler Karl Alexander had the stairs built in the 19th century. They do not appear in the Saeltzer plan. Nebe, *Die Lutherstube,* p. 38.

23. Nebe, *Die Lutherstube,* p. 38.

24. Nebe, *Die Lutherstube,* p. 37, 40—41.

25. Nebe, *Die Lutherstube,* p. 42.

26. Nebe, *Die Lutherstube,* p. 42.

27. Boehmer, *Der Junge Luther,* pp. 386—387. Boehmer revised this section in a second edition (Gotha, 1929), which has not been as yet available to the author.

28. Nebe, *Die Lutherstube,* p. 42.

29. Nebe, *Die Lutherstube,* p. 44; Boehmer, *Der Junge Luther,* p. 386.

30. Nebe, *Die Lutherstube,* p. 37.

31. Boehmer, *Der Junge Luther,* p. 386.

32. *Luther-Jahrbuch,* III (1921—1922), 117, 132, n. 42.

33. Nebe, *Die Lutherstube,* p. 45, tells of many other references to ink spots. Merian referred to the one at the Wartburg already in his day (1650—1690).

34. Nebe, *Die Lutherstube,* p. 45. When the author visited the Wartburg, a husky Swedish tourist was struggling valiantly to tear a stone from the wall at the spot. The guides claim it has been periodically replastered and re-inked.

35. Nebe, *Die Lutherstube,* p. 45.

36. Enders, III, 147, 148—149, 151—152.

37. Smith, *Correspondence,* II, 53—54.

38. Enders, III, 164; W. A., "Briefe," II, 347—349, 330—331, and n. 1.

39. W. A., VIII, 205 ff. It was sent to Melanchthon May 26, 1521, and came from the press August 12, but was not widely circulated before November 11, 1521. W. A., VIII, 210—240.

40. Enders, III, 171, 189, 199, 204, 214, 216, 236.

41. Enders, III, 154; Oncken, "Martin Luther auf der Wartburg," *Die Wartburg,* p. 267 ff.

42. W. A., "Briefe," II, 355, n. 9; 340, n. 19. It was later called the *Wartburgpostille.* Cf. W. A., X, Pt. 1, xlvi ff. On January 25, 1522, Melanchthon sent the whole *Wartburgpostille* to Spalatin, C. R., I, 203—204. Luther had completed the four Advent Sundays before going to Worms; see W. A., VII, 458 ff.

43. Reu, *Luther's German Bible*, p. 146. W. A., VII, 538–539; W. A., "*Briefe*," II, 354–356.
44. Oncken, "Martin Luther auf der Wartburg," *Die Wartburg*, p. 267 ff.
45. Text, p. 484 ff.; note 231, Chapter Fourteen.
46. For background of the Latomus attack, W. A., VIII, 36–37. Latomus was one of the agitators against Erasmus on the Louvain faculty and now decided to reply to Luther's earlier tract on the Leipzig Debate, W. A., II, 388 ff. The Latomus tract appeared May 8, 1521, and Luther had received a copy by May 26, W. A., "*Briefe*," II, 347, and n. 2. For Luther's reply, W. A., VIII, 43–128.
47. Text, p. 434 ff.; n. 179, Chapter Thirteen. W. A., "*Briefe*," II, 356–361, 360, n. 8; W. A., VIII, 255–312.
48. W. A., VIII, 267–294.
49. W. A., VII, 705–778; W. A., "*Briefe*," II, 414–416, n. 2, cf. 295; Enders, III, 119.
50. W. A., VII, 722 ff.; Boehmer, *Der Junge Luther*, p. 354.
51. W. A., VIII, 129–130. Cf. E. A. (2d Ed.), XXIV, 204.
52. For Fourth Lateran Council see Mirbt, *Quellen*, p. 179; Mackinnon, *Martin Luther*, III, 15; W. A., VIII, 164 ff.
53. W. A., "*Briefe*," II, 337, and n. 17; text in W. A., VIII, 138–185.
54. W. A., VIII, 149 ff.
55. W. A., VIII, 164–185, "Das dritte teyll," on proper attitude in confession.
56. W. A., "*Briefe*," II, 395, n. 3; 402–404.
57. W. A., "*Briefe*," II, 405–409, and introduction.
58. Smith, *Correspondence*, II, 73–74.
59. On Spalatin's withholding of the tract sent December 21, 1521, see W. A., "*Briefe*," II, 405–406, introduction. Cf. C. R., I, 492, and W. A., "*Briefe*," II, 413, n. 3.
60. Smith, *Correspondence*, II, 80–81.
61. W. A., "*Briefe*," II, 420, introduction. Cf. C. R., I, 462–465, Melanchthon's letter to Spalatin.
62. The tract had, however, accomplished the desired result; Mackinnon, *Martin Luther*, III, 50–51. In March, 1522, Capito and Luther were reconciled, Z. K. G., V, 333.
63. Barge, *Karlstadt*, I, 265 ff.
64. Barge, *Karlstadt*, I, 265 ff.
65. W. A., "*Briefe*," II, 377–379.
66. W. A., "*Briefe*," II, 370–372, 373–376, 376, n. 1. On the passage, "Esto peccator et pecca fortiter," see W. A., "*Briefe*," II, 373, n. 14.
67. W. A., "*Briefe*," II, 370–372, 373–376, 376, n. 1.
68. W. A., VIII, 313–317; 323–329; 330–335; *De votis monasticis*, 597.
69. W. A., VIII, 597 and 573.
70. W. A., "*Briefe*," II, 382–391.
71. W. A., VIII, 317.

72. *W. A.*, VIII, 317.

73. *W. A.*, *"Briefe,"* II, 404; *W. A.*, VIII, 573–576, for the letter; text of *De votis monasticis*, VIII, 577–669. There ıs a translation of the letter by Jonas in Walch, XIX, 1808–1816.

74. Enders, III, 227; *W. A.*, *"Briefe,"* II, 385–386.

75. *W. A.*, VIII, 565, 569, 577, 593–594.

76. *W. A.*, VIII, 595.

77. *W. A.*, VIII, 606, on Christian Liberty.

78. *W. A.*, *"Briefe,"* II, 404–415, for letters to Spalatin and Link. Luther was most indignant because the Court had withheld his tracts from publication for fear of political repercussions. *W. A.*, *"Briefe,"* II, 402 ff., *passim.* For date of publication see *W. A.*, VIII, 565–566.

79. *W. A.*, VIII, 566.

80. Luther issued detailed instructions to the German Vicar Link for conducting the Wittenberg Chapter held in January, 1522, that the situation might be kept in control, *W. A.*, *"Briefe,"* II, 414–416. See also the letter to Lang, 413–414, and, especially, n. 1. Cf. Stein, *Lutherhaus*, p. 16.

81. Stein, *Lutherhaus*, pp. 15–16.

82. Enders, III, 258; translation by Mackinnon, *Martin Luther*, III, 33.

83. Bruchmann, *Luthers Bibelverdeutschung*, p. 47 ff.; Paul Althaus, "Der Geist der Lutherbibel," *Luther-Jahrbuch*, XVI (1934), 1 ff. Cf. Reu, *Luther's German Bible*, p. 136 ff.; and *W. A.*, *Deutsche Bibel*, IV, xi.

84. G. L. Kraft, *Sacram Memoriam Dr. Martini Lutheri Germaniae Reformatoris* (Bonn), pp. 3–7; and Oskar Thulin, "Die Gestalt der Lutherbibel in Druck und Bild," *Vierteljahrsschrift der Luthergesellschaft*, XVI (1934), 60–61.

85. W. Walther, *Die ersten Konkurrenten des Bibeluebersetzers Luther* (Leipzig, 1917); and *Luthers Deutsche Bibel* (Festschrift, 1917). Pietsch and Freytag were very active in gathering the materials for the *W. A.*, *Deutsche Bibel*, which is invaluable for this study. For a more complete bibliography see Reu, *Luther's German Bible*, p. 352, n. 19.

86. Bruchmann, *Luthers Bibelverdeutschung*, pp. 49–50.

87. Bruchmann, *Luthers Bibelverdeutschung*, pp. 49–50; Freytag, *W. A.*, *Deutsche Bibel*, VI.

88. Bruchmann, *Luthers Bibelverdeutschung*, pp. 51–52; 53–54; Walther, *Luthers Deutsche Bibel*, p. 57.

89. Th. Knolle, "Deutsche ueber Luthers Deutsche Bibel," *Luther, Vierteljahrsschrift der Luthergesellschaft*, XVI (1934), 72.

90. Th. Knolle, "Deutsche ueber Luthers Deutsche Bibel," *Luther, Vierteljahrsschrift der Luthergesellschaft*, XVI, 74.

91. Th. Knolle, "Deutsche ueber Luthers Deutsche Bibel," *Luther, Vierteljahrsschrift der Luthergesellschaft*, XVI, 74.

92. Mackinnon, *Martin Luther*, III, 66. Cf. Enders, III, 256; *W. A.*, *T. R.*, I, 487.

93. *W. A.*, *"Briefe,"* II, 413.

94. Kraft, *Sacram Memoriam Dr. Martini Lutheri Germaniae Reformatoris,* pp. 8–9; *W. A.,* VIII, 1–35; 205–240; 538–542; 546–604.

95. *W. A., "Briefe,"* II, 422–424; translation from Reu, *Luther's German Bible,* p. 148.

96. *W. A., "Briefe,"* II, 423, "secretum cubile apud vestrum."

97. Paul H. Andreen, *Martin Luther, Humanist, The Intellectual Contribution of the Italian Renaissance to the German Reformation* (St. Paul, s. d.), p. 13 ff. Text, pp. 275–302.

98. Freytag, "Luthers Deutsche Bibel," *W. A.,* VII, 546; Reu, *Luther's German Bible,* p. 149 ff.; Smith, *Erasmus,* p. 159 ff.

99. Hort, *Introduction to the New Testament,* in rare book collection at U. of Chicago, p. 91.

100. Reu, *Luther's German Bible,* pp. 149 ff., 351–352, notes 9–14; *W. A., "Briefe,"* II, 396–398, and n. 27.

101. *W. A., Deutsche Bibel,* VI, 599 ff.

102. Reu, *Luther's German Bible,* p. 151.

103. Reu, *Luther's German Bible,* pp. 150–154.

104. Luther arrived in Wittenberg on March 6, 1522, with the manuscript of the New Testament translation. See "Die Bibelrevisionen Luthers, ihre Entstehung und ihre Bedeutung," *W. A., Deutsche Bibel,* IV, xi. Cf. *C. R.,* I, 567.

105. *W. A., Deutsche Bibel,* IV, xi.

106. *W. A., "Briefe,"* II, 602, n. 8; *W. A., Deutsche Bibel,* VI, xlvii.

107. Reu, *Luther's German Bible,* appendix, facsimile.

108. Erich Zimmermann, "Die Verbreitung der Lutherbibel zur Reformationszeit," *Luther, Vierteljahrsschrift der Luthergesellschaft,* XVI (1934), 83.

CHAPTER SEVENTEEN

1. It would be more correct to regard Luther as a liberal Catholic who was rapidly changing from his former Roman point of view to what has been called Lutheran. Luther was not entirely clear on many points of Scriptural teaching until the late 1520's.

2. *W. A.,* VIII, 685.

3. *W. A., "Briefe,"* II, 339, n. 9, gives a detailed discussion and much bibliographical material on the Erfurt disturbances. Cf. Enders, III, 156, n. 4; *Z. K. G.,* XVI, 496 f.

4. *W. A., "Briefe,"* II, 370–372; Barge, *Karlstadt,* I, 265, 290.

5. Barge, *Karlstadt,* I, 291. Cf. Holman, *W. M. L.,* II, 387 ff.

6. Barge, *Karlstadt,* I, 290–291; Enders, III, 207–208; Smith, *Correspondence,* II, 47–51.

7. Gabriel Zwilling was a native of Bohemia, a member of the Augustinian Hermits, and a fiery, eloquent preacher. *T. S. K.* (1885), pp. 132–135; Mueller, *Die Wittenberger Bewegung,* p. 15 ff.; Barge, *Karlstadt,* I, 312; *W. A.,* VIII, 398–409; Theodor Kolde, *Martin Luther* (Gotha, 1884 to 1889), II, 567.

8. Note 80, Chapter Sixteen. Z. K. G., V, 332; Mueller, *Die Wittenberger Bewegung*, pp. 169, 212; Enders, III, 256—258. W. A., *"Briefe,"* II, 471—473, 478—479.

9. Barge, *Karlstadt*, I, 386 ff., on Wittenberg excesses; Z. K. G., V, 331; Holman, W. M. L., II, 388—389; Richter, *Kirchenordnungen*, II, 484—485; and C. R., I, 540—541.

10. For defense of Carlstadt see Barge, *Karlstadt*,· I, 407; for reply see Mueller, *Luther und Karlstadt*, p. 168 ff.; cf. also C. R., I, 544—547.

11. Barge, *Karlstadt*, I, 558—559; C. R., I, 512; Mueller, *Die Wittenberger Bewegung*, p. 131 f.; Z. K. G., V, 330.

12. Heinrich Boehmer, *Neues Archiv fuer Saechsische Geschichte*, XXXVI (1915), 1—38; Smith, *Correspondence*, II, 81, and n. 3.

13. Smith, *Correspondence*, II, 82; A. R., VI, 385.

14. A. R., VI, 390; translation from Smith, *Correspondence*, II, 82—83.

15. Enders, III, 229—232; translation in Smith, *Correspondence*, II, 58.

16. W. A., *"Briefe,"* II, 409—411.

17. W. A., VIII, 670 ff.; E. A., XXII, 43; C. R., I, 484—485, 488—489, 504 and 506. Cf. Kolde, *Martin Luther*, II, 28 ff.

18. Smith, *Correspondence*, II, 90—93, from Enders, III, 292 ff. Cf. W. A., *"Briefe,"* II, 448—449, 452, n. 6, and "Nachgeschichte," 449.

19. The Diet of Nuernberg was about to meet; W. A., *"Briefe,"* II, 453, n. 19.

20. For story of the correspondence with the court see W. A., *"Briefe,"* II, 453—470.

21. Smith, *Correspondence*, II, 95; translated from De Wette, II, 137.

22. Smith, *Correspondence*, II, 94.

23. W. A., X, Pt. III, xlvi; A. R., VI (1909), 467 ff.; translation from Smith, *Correspondence*, II, 115.

24. W. A., X, Pt. III, liv; translation in Holman, W. M. L., II, 391 ff. For original text, W. A., X, Pt. III, 1 ff.

25. From sermon, W. A., X, Pt. III, 13—21. Translation in Holman, W. M. L., II, 391—392.

26. W. A., X, Pt. III, 21—30; Holman, W. M. L., II, 405—406. Cf. W. A., *"Briefe,"* II, 474—475, 491.

27. W. A.,˙ X, Pt. III, 40—47; 48—54.

28. W. A., X, Pt. III, 55—58, 58—64.

29. Smith, *Correspondence*, II, 102, from Enders, III, 307. Cf. W. A., X, Pt. III, li-lii.

30. Smith, *Correspondence*, II, 115, from A. R., VI (1909), 467 ff.

31. W. A., *"Briefe,"* II, 478—480. Cf. Mackinnon, *Martin Luther*, III, 99—100; C. R., III, 328, 331; W. A., *"Briefe,"* II, 492—494.

32. W. A., X, Pt. II, 1—41, for introduction and text. W. A., *"Briefe,"* II, 482, 489—490, 502—505.

33. W. A., *"Briefe,"* II, 496—497, and n. 4. Cf. Barge, *Karlstadt*, I, 451. For trip and bibliography, W. A., *"Briefe,"* II, 516, n. 1.

34. *W. A.,* *"Briefe,"* II, 478.

35. Enders, III, 353–435, *passim; W. A., "Briefe,"* II, 517 ff., *passim.*

36. Mackinnon, *Martin Luther,* III, 105 ff.

37. *W. A.,* X, Pt. II, 159–168, introduction and text. The title is from Mackinnon, *Martin Luther,* III, 106.

38. Enders, III, 403–405.

39. *W. A.,* X, Pt. III, 352 ff.; Enders, IV, 27, and n. 2. For Luther's sermon at the court, *W. A.,* X, Pt. III, 371 ff.

40. Hauszleiter, *D. U. W.,* p. 26, names 17,443 relics by 1518. *Z. K. G.,* XVIII (1898), 409.

41. *W. A.,* *"Briefe,"* II, 573–574. The Elector did not change the All-Saints-Church situation until 1524; Mackinnon, *Martin Luther,* III, 107–108.

42. Enders, IV, 89; *E. A.,* LIII, 178–180.

43. Enders, IV, 89 ff.; for sermon of August 2, 1523, *W. A.,* XII, 645 ff.

44. *W. A.,* XV, 764 ff.

45. Enders, V, 80; *T. S. K.* (1884), p. 754 ff.

46. For bibliographical references see Franklin Littell, "The Anabaptists and Christian Tradition," *The Journal of Religious Thought,* IV, 2 (1947), 167 ff.; Roland Bainton, "The Left Wing of the Reformation," *The Journal of Religion,* XXI (1941), 2, 124–134; Pauck, *Church History,* IX (1940), 336–339.

47. Littell, "The Anabaptists and Christian Tradition," *The Journal of Religious Thought,* IV, 2, 168–171.

48. The Enders edition is full of these official acts. Often the Elector presented the case to the University of Wittenberg for their official opinion, *Gutachten,* and then acted according to the advice of the Theological Faculty.

49. Mackinnon, *Martin Luther,* III, 181, and n. 44.

50. Mackinnon, *Martin Luther,* III, 181, and n. 44.

51. Borcherdt, *Werke,* IV, xlii.

52. Borcherdt, *Werke,* IV, xliii ff.; Mackinnon, *Martin Luther,* III, 181 ff.; *W. A., "Briefe,"* II, 549–551, on dogma of Zwickau prophets.

53. Borcherdt, *Werke,* IV, xli; *W. A.,* XV, 210 ff.

54. Borcherdt, *Werke,* IV, xliii.

55. Enders, II, 404–405; *W. A., "Briefe,"* II, 139–141. Cf. P. Wappler, *Thomas Muenzer in Zwickau und die "Zwickauer Propheten"* (Zwickau, 1908), p. 9 ff.

56. Mackinnon, *Martin Luther,* III, 182–183.

57. *W. A.,* XV, 210 ff., especially, 218–219.

58. *W. A.,* XV, 230 ff., and "Ein Sendbrief," 238–240.

59. Text, pp. 294–295.

60. *W. A.,* X, Pt. III, 1–64. Cf. Enders, V, 37–38; translated in Smith, *Correspondence,* II, 272–274.

61. On his marriage to Anna von Mochau, daughter of an impoverished nobleman, Z. K. G., V, 331; XXII, 125; and C. R., I, 538. For Carlstadt's new theology, Borcherdt, Werke, IV, liv–lx.

62. Text, 536 ff. Borcherdt, Werke, IV, xlix–liv.

63. Smith, Correspondence, II, 272–273.

64. Borcherdt, Werke, IV, lii.

65. "Acta Jenensia," August 24, 1524, were printed by a Carlstadt sympathizer, Martin Reinhard of Jena. E. A., LXIV, 385 ff.; Walch (2d edition), XV, 2028 ff.; Enders, V, 32; W. A., XV, 323 ff.

66. Mackinnon, Martin Luther, III, 198; Borcherdt, Werke, IV, liii–liv; W. A., XV, 323–347, and bibliography, 330.

67. W. A., XV, 328, based on the tract Against the Heavenly Prophets and relating interview with Duke John Frederick at Weimar.

68. Borcherdt, Werke, IV, xlii f. Smith, Correspondence, II, 273.

69. Borcherdt, Werke, IV, xliii.

70. Eells, Martin Bucer, pp. 71–72.

71. W. A., XVIII, 62 ff. Cf. W. A., "Briefe," II, 418–420; 421–422; 424–425, and n. 6; 429, n. 12; 441–443.

72. Althaus, "Luthers Abendmahlslehre," Luther-Jahrbuch, X (1929), 8–9; W. A., XVIII, 204–205.

73. C. R., I, 794, cited by Oskar Thulin, Luther und Melanchthonworte (Lutherstadt, Wittenberg, 1947), p. 2: "Oh, that Luther would keep quiet. I had hoped that with so much opposition, that with age he would become milder. I notice, however, that so much opposition stirs him up and makes him more violent." C. R., III, 291. Before Luther is criticized too severely, one should examine the language utilized by some of his opponents, such as Latomus, Emser, and even Sir Thomas More, who called Luther "this apostate, this open incestuous lecher, this plain limb of the devil and manifest messenger from hell." See Latomus' tract in Walch, XVIII, 1262 ff. That Luther could return such compliments in kind is evidenced by his calling Henry VIII "a damnable and rotten worm, a sniveling, driveling swine of a sophist." Erasmus Alber, Martin Luther (Berlin, 1933), p. 104, writes of Luther: "One could detect in him no wrath except on the field of battle against the Papists and the Anabaptists; and there one observed the wrath of the Holy Ghost, and not that of a human being." Urbanus Rhegius wrote: "He is a special instrument of the Holy Spirit and has an apostolic spirit," Martin Luther (Berlin, 1933), pp. 103–104. W. A., III, 529 ff., passim. Melanchthon's opinion of Luther was expressed, C. R., I, 417, thus: "There is nothing more godly on earth now than he."

74. S. B. Clough and C. W. Cole, Economic History of Europe (Boston, 1941), p. 97; Friedrich von Bezold, Geschichte der deutschen Reformation (Berlin, 1890), p. 24 ff.

75. S. B. Clough and C. W. Cole, Economic History of Europe, pp. 86–87, 140.

76. S. B. Clough and C. W. Cole, Economic History of Europe, p. 74 ff.

77. S. B. Clough and C. W. Cole, *Economic History of Europe*, pp. 129–130.
78. S. B. Clough and C. W. Cole, *Economic History of Europe*, pp. 126–127.
79. Walter Friedensburg, "Franz von Sickingen," *I. M. R.*, pp. 654–655.
80. Holborn, *Ulrich von Hutten*, p. 177 ff.
81. Karl Brandi, *Die deutsche Reformation* (Leipzig, 1927), pp. 166–167; Mackinnon, *Martin Luther*, III, 165–166.
82. Holborn, *Ulrich von Hutten*, pp. 181–184.
83. *I. M. R.*, pp. 654–655, 142 ff.
84. Holborn, *Ulrich von Hutten*, p. 178; Kalkoff, *Depeschen*, p. 43.
85. Luther dedicated his tract *On Confessions*, June 1, 1521, to the knight Franz von Sickingen, *W. A.*, VIII, 138 ff.
86. *I. M. R.*, pp. 657–658; cf. 643–649.
87. *I. M. R.*, pp. 657–666.
88. *I. M. R.*, p. 666.
89. Mackinnon, *Martin Luther*, III, 170; Brandi, *Die deutsche Reformation*, p. 169.
90. Hutten died August 29, 1523, on the island of Ufenau on Lake Zurich, Holborn, *Ulrich von Hutten*, p. 202; cf. n. 24.
91. Enders, IV, 40 and 143, "Deus iustus, sed mirabilis iudex."
92. Josef Kulischer, *Allgemeine Wirtschaftsgeschichte des Mittelalters und der Neuzeit* (Muenchen, 1929), II, 87–92; Uhrig, "Der Bauer," p. 74 ff., 165 ff.; Bezold, *Geschichte der deutschen Reformation*, pp. 24–25.
93. Borcherdt, *Werke*, IV, lxii–lxiii. Cf. Kulischer, *Allgemeine Wirtschaftsgeschichte des Mittelalters und der Neuzeit*, II, 90–92.
94. Kulischer, *Allgemeine Wirtschaftsgeschichte des Mittelalters und der Neuzeit*, II, 87 ff., *passim*. Uhrig, "Der Bauer," pp. 78–80.
95. Uhrig, "Der Bauer," pp. 79–81, 196, 199–200.
96. Uhrig, "Der Bauer," p. 198.
97. Adolf Bartels, *Der Bauer in der deutschen Vergangenheit* (Leipzig, 1900), pp. 96–97. Cf. Uhrig, "Der Bauer," p. 196 ff.
98. Uhrig, "Der Bauer," pp. 106–107.
99. Uhrig, "Der Bauer," pp. 98–99, 216–217.
100. Uhrig, "Der Bauer," p. 99. Cf. *W. A.*, XII, 317; VI, 409, 467; X, Pt. I, 371, 534; X, Pt. III, 229.
101. Uhrig, "Der Bauer," p. 103. Cf. *W. A.*, X, Pt. III, 263.
102. Uhrig, "Der Bauer," pp. 122–125.
103. Uhrig, "Der Bauer," p. 100; *W. A.*, XI, 285; X, Pt. I, 413.
104. Uhrig, "Der Bauer," pp. 213–214, 215, 217–224.
105. Borcherdt, *Werke*, IV, lxii.
106. *W. A.*, X, Pt. I, 63; Pt. III, 263; Uhrig, "Der Bauer," pp. 102–103.
107. Borcherdt, *Werke*, IV, lxiii–lxiv.

108. Mackinnon, *Martin Luther,* III, 188—189.
109. Friedensburg, *I. M. R.,* p. 643; Mackinnon, *Martin Luther,* III, 189.
110. Paul Althaus, "Luthers Haltung im Bauernkriege," *Luther-Jahrbuch,* VII (1925), 14 ff.; Borcherdt, *Werke,* IV, lxiv.
111. Paul Althaus, "Luthers Haltung im Bauernkriege," *Luther-Jahrbuch,* VII (1925), p. 6; Mackinnon, *Martin Luther,* III, 190—194; Borcherdt, *Werke,* IV, lxiii—lxiv.
112. Borcherdt, *Werke,* IV, lxiv.
113. *E. A.,* XXIV, 260 ff.; *W. A.,* XVIII, 279 ff.
114. Borcherdt, *Werke,* IV, lxiv.
115. Althaus, "Luthers Haltung im Bauernkriege," *Luther-Jahrbuch,* VII, 9; *W. A.,* XVIII, 326 ff.; *E. A.,* XXIV, 264—266.
116. Althaus, "Luthers Haltung im Bauernkriege," *Luther-Jahrbuch,* VII, 10—12; *E. A.,* XXIV, 265—266.
117. *E. A.,* XXIV, 267—268.
118. *E. A.,* XXIV, 274—275; *W. A.,* XVIII, 310.
119. Schwiebert, "The Medieval Pattern in Luther's Views of the State," *Church History,* XII (1943), 13 ff.; *W. A.,* VI, 408, 410.
120. *W. A.,* XI, 229 ff.; Schwiebert, *Church History,* XII, 16.
121. *W. A.,* XI, 268.
122. *W. A.,* XI, 276—277.
123. *E. A.,* XXIV, 264—265. Cf. Borcherdt, *Werke,* IV, lxv.
124. Althaus, "Luthers Haltung im Bauernkriege," *Luther-Jahrbuch,* VII, 12—14; Borcherdt, *Werke,* IV, lxv—lxvi; Albert Clos, *A. R.,* XXXIII, 126 ff.
125. Enders, V, 157; Althaus, "Luthers Haltung im Bauernkriege," *Luther-Jahrbuch,* VII, 14—15; *W. A.,* XVII, I, 195 ff. Cf. Smith, *Correspondence,* II, 305.
126. Borcherdt, *Werke,* IV, lxvii—lxviii; *W. A.,* XVII, I, 195 f.
127. The situation at this time looked grave indeed. Frederick the Wise was on his deathbed and died May 5, 1525. It was reported that 35,000 peasants were ready to strike in Thuringia, and the princes were totally unprepared to meet the emergency. Borcherdt, *Werke,* IV, lxvii—lxix; Althaus, "Luthers Haltung im Bauernkriege," *Luther-Jahrbuch,* VII, 16; Clos, *A. R.,* XXXIII, 130 ff.; *W. A.,* XIX, 224.
128. Borcherdt, *Werke,* IV, lxvii—lxviii.
129. Althaus, "Luthers Haltung im Bauernkriege," *Luther-Jahrbuch,* VII, 18 ff.; *W. A.,* XVII, I, 237.
130. *W. A.,* XVII, I, 237.
131. *E. A.,* XXIV, 290—291; Borcherdt, *Werke,* IV, lxviii; Althaus, "Luthers Haltung im Bauernkriege," *Luther-Jahrbuch,* VII, 16—17.
132. *E. A.,* XXIV, 292—293.
133. Althaus, "Luthers Haltung im Bauernkriege," *Luther-Jahrbuch,* VII, 19—20.

134. This text was one of his *sedes doctrinae* which Luther quoted frequently on government.
135. Althaus, "Luthers Haltung im Bauernkriege," *Luther-Jahrbuch*, VII, 22—23; Borcherdt, *Werke*, IV, lxix.
136. Borcherdt, *Werke*, IV, lxx.
137. Borcherdt, *Werke*, IV, lxiv—lxix.
138. Althaus, "Luthers Haltung im Bauernkriege," *Luther-Jahrbuch*, VII, 24—28; Clos, *A. R.*, XXXIII, 128—130.
139. Borcherdt, *Werke*, IV, lxxi; Althaus, "Luthers Haltung im Bauernkriege," *Luther-Jahrbuch*, VII, 28—30.
140. Althaus, "Luthers Haltung im Bauernkriege," *Luther-Jahrbuch*, VII, 28 ff.; Borcherdt, *Werke*, IV, lxxi—lxxii.
141. *E. A.*, XXIV, 310.
142. Borcherdt, *Werke*, IV, lxx—lxxiii; Althaus, "Luthers Haltung im Bauernkriege," *Luther-Jahrbuch*, VII, 33—34.
143. Althaus, "Luthers Haltung im Bauernkriege," *Luther-Jahrbuch*, VII, 27—30.
144. Althaus, "Luthers Haltung im Bauernkriege," *Luther-Jahrbuch*, VII, 30—33.
145. Text, p. 613 ff.
146. The *Gutachten* printed in the Enders collection of correspondence after 1525 bear ample testimony to this fact.

CHAPTER EIGHTEEN

1. Oskar Thulin, "Das Antlitz des Reformators," *Die Lutherstadt Wittenberg und Torgau* (Berlin, 1932), p. 38; Boehmer, *L. L. R. R.*, pp. 5—6, also note p. 3. A former curator of the Lutherhalle, Julius Jordan, writes in "Luthers Bild," *Luther-Mitteilungen der Luther-Gesellschaft* (1919), I, 67: "Nothing is so certain as the fact that neither Holbein d. J. nor Albrecht Duerer came in contact with Luther." For a more recent review of the problem see Oskar Thulin, "Das Lutherbild der Gegenwart" (Sonderdruck), *Luther-Jahrbuch*, XXIII (1941), 123 ff.
2. Ficker, Exposition of Luther's Pictures, p. 69.
3. Ficker, Exposition of Luther's Pictures, p. 65 ff.
4. Schreckenbach and Neubert, p. 108; Ficker, Exposition of Luther's Pictures, p. 66 ff.
5. Schreckenbach and Neubert, p. 158; Ficker, Exposition of Luther's Pictures, p. 66; H. Hahne, "Luthers Totenmaske," *Luther, Vierteljahrsschrift*, XIII (1931), 74 ff.
6. *Martin Luther* (Berlin, 1933), pp. 81—104; Myconius, *Historia Reformationis*, p. 33.
7. *Martin Luther* (Berlin, 1933), p. 81.
8. Schreckenbach and Neubert, p. 100.
9. Boehmer, *L. L. R. R.*, p. 205.

10. *Nuntiaturberichte,* I, 539 f.

11. Kessler, *Sabbata,* p. 65; *Martin Luther* (Berlin, 1933), pp. 93—97.

12. *Martin Luther* (Berlin, 1933), p. 102 ff.

13. Z. K. G., IV, 326. Cf. Jordan, "Luthers Bild," *Luther, Mitteilungen,* I, 66.

14. Kessler, *Sabbata,* p. 65.

15. Jordan, "Luthers Bild," *Luther-Mitteilungen,* 1, 66.

16. Jordan, "Luthers Bild," *Luther-Mitteilungen,* 1, 66.

17. Jordan, "Luthers Bild," *Luther-Mitteilungen,* I, 66.

18. Myconius, *Historia Reformationis,* p. 33.

19. Kalkoff, *Depeschen,* p. 133.

20. *Martin Luther* (Berlin, 1933), p. 101.

21. *Martin Luther* (Berlin, 1933), p. 104; cf. Mosellanus, *Martin Luther* (Berlin, 1933), p. 81.

22. *Martin Luther* (Berlin, 1933), p. 104.

23. Friedensburg, *Urkundenbuch,* I, 109. No doubt this was just an estimate, for the lectures were held in the "Grosse Hoersaal," and the present curator estimates its capacity, including the "Kleine Hoersaal," at 300, Thulin, *Die Lutherhalle,* p. 6.

24. Myconius, *Historia Reformationis,* p. 26.

25. Friedensburg, *G. U. W.,* p. 118.

26. Friedensburg, *G. U. W.,* p. 118.

27. Friedensburg, *G. U. W.,* p. 152.

28. Friedensburg, *G. U. W.,* p. 152.

29. Text, p. 389 ff.

30. Text, p. 278 ff.

31. Seeberg, *Greifswalder Studien,* p. 1 ff.

32. Seeberg, *Greifswalder Studien,* pp. 20, 35—36.

33. Wernle, *Die Renaissance,* pp. 26, 30—31.

34. Hans von Schubert, *Luther-Jahrbuch,* VIII (1926), 22.

35. *De servo arbitrio, W. A.,* XVIII, 600 ff.

36. *C. R.,* I, 285.

37. Adams, *The March of Democracy* (New York, 1932), I, 70, for description of Whitefield's art of public speaking.

38. *Martin Luther* (Berlin, 1933), pp. 103—104.

39. *Martin Luther* (Berlin, 1933), pp. 103—104.

40. Text, p. 367; note 27, Chapter Twelve.

41. *Martin Luther* (Berlin, 1933), p. 104.

42. Boehmer, *L. L. R. R.,* pp. 203—204.

43. Text, p. 742.

44. Boehmer, *L. L. R. R.,* p. 244 ff. Melanchthon compared him to a Herakles, *C. R.,* I, 318, cited by Oskar Thulin, *Luther und Melanchthonworte* (Lutherstadt-Wittenberg, 1947).

45. Note 73, Chapter Seventeen; text, p. 550.
46. W. A., XV, 28 ff., is a good case in point.
47. *Martin Luther* (Berlin, 1933), p. 104.
48. W. A., II, 170–171.
49. Text, p. 524 ff.; W. A., VIII, 314.
50. Text, p. 525; W. A., VIII, 593–594, 606 ff.
51. "Vom ehelichen Leben," W. A., X, Pt. II, 275–304; cf. Sermons, W. A., X, Pt. II, 108, 265.
52. Smith, *Correspondence*, II, 35, and n. 4.
53. W. A., "*Briefe*," II, 408–409, n. 20. On Albert's mistresses, W. A., XXX, Pt. II, 338, n. 3; Fritz Herrmann, *Die evangelische Bewegung im Reformationszeitalter* (Mainz, 1907), p. 96. On priests in trouble, W. A., "*Briefe*," II, 408, n. 16. Cf. Smith, *Correspondence*, II, 51, n. 4; Enders, III, 279–284.
54. Note 61, Chapter Seventeen; text, p. 548.
55. W. A., "*Briefe*," II, 605, and n. 9; 606, n. 4; Kroker, p. 248.
56. W. A., "*Briefe*," III, 53–54, and notes 1 and 2. Cf. Enders, IV, 126, n. 7.
57. W. A., "*Briefe*," III, 298–301, dated May 25, 1524.
58. He was probably influenced by Luther's writings as were so many of the monks and secular clergymen.
59. Th. Knolle, "Luthers Heirat nach seinen und seiner Zeitgenossen Aussagen," *Luther, Vierteljahrsschrift*, VI (1925), 25.
60. Th. Knolle, "Luthers Heirat nach seinen und seiner Zeitgenossen Aussagen," *Luther, Vierteljahrsschrift*, VI, 27.
61. Th. Knolle, "Luthers Heirat nach seinen und seiner Zeitgenossen Aussagen," *Luther, Vierteljahrsschrift*, VI, 27.
62. W. A., "*Briefe*," III, 54–55, also n. 2, on Koppe. Remaining notes contain valuable material on nuns. Smith, *Correspondence*, II, 179–181, translated from Enders, IV, 127.
63. W. A., "*Briefe*," III, 56, n. 5. Cf. Kolde, *Analecta*, p. 442.
64. Kroker, p. 3.
65. Enders, XIII, 106–108, and especially n. 2.
66. Kroker, p. 4.
67. Kroker, p. 10.
68. Kroker, pp. 7–8.
69. Kroker, p. 8.
70. Kroker, p. 12.
71. Kroker, p. 14.
72. Kroker, p. 31.
73. Kroker, p. 32.
74. Kroker, pp. 31–32.
75. Kroker, pp. 32–33.
76. W. A., "*Briefe*," III, 56, n. 2.

77. W. A., "Briefe," III, 56, n. 3. This story comes from the Torgau chronicler, who was still living in 1600, but he does not mention the empty barrels. Nine nuns would about fill such a wagon to capacity.

78. Kroker, p. 38.

79. W. A., "Briefe," III, 54—55, 56—57, notes.

80. For those nuns from lands which had embraced the new Gospel there was no problem in returning home; but those whose former homes were in lands hostile to the Reformation faced a very real threat.

81. For a treatment of the many implications of Luther's marriage and a discussion of Saxon marriage customs see Boehmer, "Luthers Ehe," Luther-Jahrbuch, VII (1925), 40—70. Also see W. A., T. R., IV, 503—505, n. 4786; Kroker, p. 46, on Ave Schoenfeld.

82. Kroker, p. 53.

83. Boehmer, L. L. R. R., pp. 244—245.

84. Wilhelm Beste, Die Geschichte Catharina's von Bora (Halle, 1843), p. 43; Kroker, pp. 55—56; Koehler, Erasmus von Rotterdam, Briefe (Wiesbaden, 1947), pp. 358—361, p. 359, n. 1, and letter to Franz Sylvius, p. 369.

85. W. A., "Briefe," III, 57, n. 8. Note 81, Chapter Eighteen.

86. Joachim Camerarius was of Bamberg extraction. He had studied at Leipzig and Erfurt before matriculating at Wittenberg in 1521. He lived in Melanchthon's home and was one of his best classical students.

87. Kroker, p. 56. They were not formally engaged, Smith, Correspondence, II, 257. For a detailed biographical sketch of Baumgaertner see W. A., "Briefe," III, 358; on Glatz see Boehmer, "Luthers Ehe," Luther-Jahrbuch, VII, 58 ff.

88. W. A., "Briefe," III, 358.

89. W. A., "Briefe," III, 358, n. 1; Smith, Correspondence, II, 258, n. 1. Album, III, 804.

90. W. A., "Briefe," III, 358, n. 1; Kroker, p. 59. Baumgaertner was married January 23, 1526.

91. Enders, III, 215; W. A., "Briefe," II, 377.

92. Enders, V, 76; translation from Smith, Correspondence, II, 264.

93. Enders, V, 204—205, cf. 157; W. A., "Briefe," III, 476, n. 7.

94. W. A., "Briefe," III, 531, n. 7, 541, for letter to Amsdorf.

95. Knolle, "Luthers Heirat nach seinen und seiner Zeitgenossen Aussagen," Luther, Vierteljahrsschrift, VI, 21—22; W. A., T. R., I, 47 ff., notes 121 and 122.

96. Arthur C. McGiffert, Martin Luther, The Man and His Work (New York, 1919), pp. 284—285.

97. Kroker, pp. 66—67. On the Reichenbach tradition see Boehmer, "Luthers Ehe," Luther-Jahrbuch, VII, 42 ff.; Spalatin, Annales, ed., Mencke, II, 645; Smith, Correspondence, II, 322.

98. Smith, Correspondence, II, 322.

99. Smith, Correspondence, II, 324. Cf. Z. K. G., XXI, 596.

100. Smith, Correspondence, II, 325—326.

101. *C. R.*, I, 750, n. 340; cf. *W. A.*, *"Briefe,"* III, 537, n. 4; Boehmer, "Luthers Ehe," *Luther-Jahrbuch*, VII, 52.

102. McGiffert, *Martin Luther, The Man and His Work*, p. 279.

103. Enders, V, 195, notes 1–5; translation from Smith, *Correspondence*, II, 323, from De Wette, III, 1, German text; cf. *E. A.*, LIII, 314, n. 136.

104. Enders, V, 200; *W. A.*, *"Briefe,"* III, 536–537.

105. *W. A.*, *"Briefe,"* III, 537–538, 540.

106. *W. A.*, *"Briefe,"* III, 538–539.

107. Kroker, p. 70.

108. Boehmer, "Luthers Ehe," *Luther-Jahrbuch*, VII, 40, 48–52.

109. Boehmer, "Luthers Ehe," *Luther-Jahrbuch*, VII, 41.

110. *W. A.*, *"Briefe,"* III, 541.

111. McGiffert, *Martin Luther, The Man and His Work*, pp. 286–287.

112. Enders, XIV, 221; XIII, 108, n. 2.

113. For the history of the old "Black Cloister" see Hermann Stein, *Geschichte des Lutherhauses* (Wittenberg, 1883); J. C. A. Grohmann, *Annalen*, I, 65 ff.; and for a specific study of "Die Lutherstube," *Luther-Jahrbuch*, III (1921), 109–135.

114. Stein, *Lutherhaus*, p. 7; Th. Knolle, "Luther ueber seinen Garten," *Luther, Mitteilungen der Luthergesellschaft*, II (1920), 59–63.

115. Myconius, *Historia Reformationis*, p. 24.

116. Stein, *Lutherhaus*, p. 25, based on *Urbarium der Stadt Wittenberg*, Part III, now in the castle at Wittenberg.

117. Stein, *Lutherhaus*, p. 27.

118. Stein, *Lutherhaus*, p. 8 ff.

119. *W. A.*, *"Briefe,"* IV, 87; cf. Spalatin, *Annales*, ed., Mencke, II, 657, which gives the date as June 8.

120. *W. A.*, *"Briefe,"* IV, 87, n. 4.

121. *W. A.*, *"Briefe,"* IV, 88, n. 4; cf. *W. A.*, *T. R.*, II, 90; III, 641.

122. Kroker, p. 127.

123. Enders, VI, 314; Smith, *Correspondence*, II, 451; Kroker, p. 126.

124. *W. A.*, *"Briefe,"* IV, 511, and n. 2; cf. Kroker, p. 127; *W. A.*, *"Briefe,"* IV, 294–295, and 296, n. 1.

125. Enders, VII, 93; *W. A.*, *"Briefe,"* V, 61, 63–65; Kroker, p. 127.

126. *W. A.*, *T. R.*, I, 521, n. 1032.

127. *W. A.*, *"Briefe,"* VI, 425.

128. *W. A.*, *"Briefe,"* VII, 128–132, and 132, n. 1.

129. *W. A.*, *"Briefe,"* V, 377–378, and n. 3.

130. *W. A.*, *T. R.*, V, 489, n. 6102.

131. Kroker, pp. 147–148, 156 ff., 185 ff.

132. Kroker, p. 156 ff.

133. Kroker, pp. 130–131.

134. The best evaluation of the Table Talks is Preserved Smith, *Luther's Table Talk: A Critical Study* (New York, 1907), which was Smith's doctoral dissertation.
135. Text, p. 634 f.
136. Georg Rietschel, "Luther und sein Haus," *Schriften fuer das deutsche Volk* (Leipzig, 1909), p. 43, cited from Ratzeberger, *Die handschriftliche Geschichte ueber Luther und seine Zeit,* ed., Neudecker (Jena, 1850).
137. Paul Nettl, *Luther and Music* (Philadelphia, 1948), p. 12 ff.
138. *W. A., T. R.,* I, 490, n. 968.
139. Enders, VII, 120.
140. Text, p. 649.
141. *W. A., "Briefe,"* IV, 221, n. 3; *W. A., T. R.,* III, 81, 2922b; *W. A., "Briefe,"* IV, 226; *C. R.,* I, 883.
142. Note 124, Chapter Eighteen.
143. Kroker, p. 133.
144. *W. A., "Briefe,"* VIII, 41, n. 14.
145. Kroker, p. 145.
146. Text, p. 747 ff.
147. Kroker, p. 136.
148. Kroker, pp. 237—238. The Elector paid 2,000 gulden, the Vormunde 100 gulden, and Amsdorf the remaining 100 gulden.
149. Kroker, pp. 138—141.
150. Smith, *The Age of the Reformation,* pp. 127—128.
151. Smith, *The Age of the Reformation,* pp. 128—130; Kroker, p. 244.
152. Kroker, pp. 245—246.
153. G. Mentz, *Johann Friedrich,* pp. 100—111; Mylius, *Memorabilia,* p. 27.
154. Mentz, *Johann Friedrich,* pp. 100—105.
155. Kroker, p. 248.
156. Kroker, p. 246 ff.
157. Mentz, *Johann Friedrich,* pp. 109—111; Kroker, p. 249.
158. Kroker, pp. 250—251.
159. Kroker, p. 254.
160. Kroker, pp. 254—255.
161. Kroker, p. 257.
162. Also known as the "Marienkirche." Her dying words are supposed to have been: "Ich will an meinem Herrn Christus kleben bleiben wie die Klette am Kleide." Kroker, pp. 257—258.
163. Kroker, pp. 261—262.
164. Kroker, pp. 261—262.
165. Kroker, pp. 261—262.
166. Kroker, pp. 261—262.
167. Kroker, pp. 261—262.
168. Kroker, pp. 262—263.

CHAPTER NINETEEN

1. For full title of *Album* see abbreviations.
2. *Album*, I, 1–99, lists the students each year, divided into fall and summer semesters, giving both the name of the student and his home city.
3. Schwiebert, "The Reformation from a New Perspective." *Church History*, XVII (1948), 20.
4. The original "Matrikel" is in the Halle-Wittenberg Library in Halle, Germany. It is beautifully illustrated and much more attractive than the printed copy.
5. *Album*, III, 803–806, for the total enrollment from 1502–1560. By actual count there were 16,292 students enrolled in the halls of Wittenberg during those years when the Reformation came to German lands.
6. *Album*, III, 804–806; Schwiebert, *Church History*, XVII, 30–31.
7. Schwiebert, *Thesis*, p. 71 ff., *passim*.
8. Schwiebert, *Thesis*, p. 68 ff.
9. *Album*, III, 804.
10. This was 38.7% of the total enrollment.
11. *Album*, I, 137–140. This was 4% of the total enrollment.
12. *Album*, I, 250–261.
13. Schreckenbach and Neubert, pp. 86–87.
14. Burkhardt, *G. K. S.*, p. 225 ff.
15. *W. A.*, XV, 27 ff.
16. *W. A.*, XXX, Pt. II, 508–588.
17. Painter, *Luther on Education* (St. Louis, 1928), p. 238.
18. *Album*, III, 804–805.
19. Text, p. 676 ff.
20. Friedensburg, *Urkundenbuch*, I, 154–158, for the Melanchthonian *Statutes* of 1533; 162–186, for further changes made in the University from 1535 to 1536.
21. Friedensburg, *Urkundenbuch*, I, 128–130.
22. Friedensburg, *Urkundenbuch*, I, 154.
23. Friedensburg, *Urkundenbuch*, I, 155.
24. Friedensburg, *Urkundenbuch*, I, 155.
25. Friedensburg, *Urkundenbuch*, I, 155.
26. Friedensburg, *Urkundenbuch*, I, 155.
27. Friedensburg, *Urkundenbuch*, I, 155–156.
28. Friedensburg, *Urkundenbuch*, I, 156.
29. Friedensburg, *Urkundenbuch*, I, 156.
30. Friedensburg, *Urkundenbuch*, I, 156.
31. Friedensburg, *Urkundenbuch*, I, 156.
32. Friedensburg, *Urkundenbuch*, I, 172 ff.
33. *Album*, III, 803–806, lists their names by semesters. This practice is still followed by German universities.

34. Friedensburg, *Urkundenbuch*, I, 17 ff.

35. Friedensburg, *Urkundenbuch*, I, 167; "Rotulus of 1507," *Urkundenbuch*, I, 17.

36. Friedensburg, *Urkundenbuch*, I, 174—175.

37. Friedensburgh, *Urkundenbuch*, I, 175—176.

38. Ferdinand Cohrs, *Philipp Melanchthon Deutschlands Lehrer* (Halle, 1897), pp. 44—46, cf. pp. 6—8, 12, 23, 38—40.

39. Cohrs, *Philipp Melanchthon Deutschlands Lehrer*, p. 44.

40. *Briefwechsel des Justus Jonas*, ed., G. Kawerau (Halle, 1885), II, xxxiii ff.; R. E., IX, 343.

41. Text, p. 262 ff.

42. Text, p. 244 ff.

43. Friedensburg, *Urkundenbuch*, I, 378 ff.

44. Friedensburg, *Urkundenbuch*, I, 234—236.

45. Ferdinand Cohrs, *Philipp Melanchthon Deutschlands Lehrer* (Halle, 1897), p. 44, states that Melanchthon permitted Rhaticus to come to Wittenberg even though he taught the Copernican theory of astronomy. An evaluation of the problem may be found in Carleton J. H. Hayes, *Political and Cultural History of Modern Europe* (New York, 1932), I, 122—125.

46. Preserved Smith, *A History of Modern Culture*, I, pp. 22, 34; W. T. Sedgwick and H. W. Tyler, *A Short History of Science* (New York, 1927), pp. 196, 206, 218.

CHAPTER TWENTY

1. For a study of the differences between the ecclesiastical organization of the Church in the Mediterranean lands and in the North see Stutz, *Eigenkirche*, p. 35 ff.

2. Stutz, *Eigenkirche*, p. 35 ff.

3. Stutz, *Eigenkirche*, p. 35 ff.

4. Stutz, *Eigenkirche*, pp. 56—57.

5. Schwiebert, *Church History*, XII, 104 ff., notes 15—20.

6. Schwiebert, *Church History*, XII, 104, n. 16.

7. Schwiebert, *Church History*, XII, 104, n. 16.

8. Paul Werminghoff, "Neuere Arbeiten ueber das Verhaeltnis von Staat und Kirche in Deutschland waehrend des spaeteren Mittelalters, *H. V.*, XI (1908), 153.

9. *Deutsche Reichstagsakten*, III, 383 ff., 645 ff., 911; IV, 603—605.

10. The Gospel was preached during the meeting of the Diet, and the Town Council refused to take any action. *Deutsche Reichstagsakten*, III, 410 ff.

11. *Deutsche Reichstagsakten*, III, 419 ff.; 447, for the imperial mandate.

12. Friedensburg, "Die Reformation und der Speierer Reichstag," *Luther-Jahrbuch*, VIII (1926), 127 ff.

13. Schwiebert, *Church History*, XII, 106.

14. Text, pp. 546—550.

15. Sehling, *Kirchenordnungen*, I, 31—35.

16. Burkhardt, *G. K. S.*, 3—8; Sehling, *Kirchenordnungen*, I, 35.

17. Sehling, *Kirchenordnungen*, p. 33; Sohm, *Kirchenrecht*, p. 484, claims Luther hesitated as he did not believe in force in matters of religion.

18. Sehling, *Kirchenordnungen*, I, 35.

19. Sehling, *Kirchenordnungen*, I, 35; Burkhardt, *G. K. S.*, pp. 14—15.

20. Sehling, *Kirchenordnungen*, I, 142 ff.

21. Sehling, *Kirchenordnungen*, I, 40.

22. Burkhardt, *G. K. S.*, pp. 9—10.

23. Sehling, *Kirchenordnungen*, I, 50 ff.; Burkhardt, *G. K. S.*, p. 36 ff.

24. Georg Mertz, *Das Schulwesen der deutschen Reformation im 16. Jahrhundert* (Heidelberg, 1902), pp. 14 ff., 179 ff., 244 ff. Richter, *Kirchenordnungen*, I, 358; II, 116, 169. The Catechism became a model for instruction of both the children and the adults. *W. A.*, XXX, 461—464; Hans von Schubert, *Bekenntnisbildung und Religionspolitik 1529—30* (Gotha, 1910), found the Catechism was already stressed in the earlier visitations.

25. Duke George died April 17, 1539, Burkhardt, *G. K. S.*, pp. 231—233.

26. Burkhardt, *G. K. S.*, p. 225 ff.

27. Schwiebert, *Church History*, XVII, 25 ff., *passim*.

28. Schwiebert, *Church History*, XVII, 26, n. 119.

29. Schwiebert, *Church History*, XVII, 26, n. 118.

30. Sehling, *Kirchenordnungen*, I, 32—33.

31. Sehling, *Kirchenordnungen*, I, 56.

32. Sehling, *Kirchenordnungen*, I, 58; Burkhardt, *G. K. S.*, pp. 201—204.

33. Sehling, *Kirchenordnungen*, I, 57, 49, 202—203; cf. *Z. K. G.*, XIII, 38 ff.

34. Burkhardt, *G. K. S.*, p. 204.

35. Burkhardt, *G. K. S.*, p. 3 ff.; Sehling, *Kirchenordnungen*, I, 31 ff., *passim*.

36. Drews, *Der evangelische Geistliche*, pp. 13—16.

37. Drews, *Der evangelische Geistliche*, pp. 14—15.

38. The early examination was a mere "Scheinexamina," Drews, *Der evangelische Geistliche*, pp. 41—42; *W. A.*, XXXVIII, 406—407.

39. Drews, *Der evangelische Geistliche*, p. 30.

40. Drews, *Der evangelische Geistliche*, pp. 33 and 36.

41. Drews, *Der evangelische Geistliche*, p. 30.

42. Drews, *Der evangelische Geistliche*, p. 30.

43. Drews, *Der evangelische Geistliche*, p. 19.

44. Several of the *Kirchenordnungen* have these provisions. See, for example, Sehling, *Kirchenordnungen*, I, 55—61, 202—203.

45. Sehling, *Kirchenordnungen*, I, 55—61.

46. Reu, *Luther and the Scriptures*, p. 13 ff., well illustrates Luther's basic approach.

47. Drews, *Der evangelische Geistliche,* pp. 14–15; Burkhardt, *G. K. S.,* pp. 29 ff., 149 ff., 294 ff.

48. Burkhardt, *G. K. S.,* pp. 294–296.

49. Drews, *Der evangelische Geistliche,* p. 15.

50. Burkhardt, *G. K. S.,* pp. 250–251.

51. Drews, *Der evangelische Geistliche,* pp. 15–19, 25–26.

52. Burkhardt, *G. K. S.,* p. 36 ff.

53. Text, p. 622 ff.

54. Text, p. 633 ff.; note 124, Chapter Twenty.

55. *W. A.,* VI, 407–408.

56. *W. A.,* VI, 407–408.

57. *W. A.,* VI, 407–408.

58. *W. A.,* VI, 408.

59. Harnack, *History of Dogma,* pp. 270–272; Loofs, *Leitfaden,* pp. 589–590.

60. *W. A.,* XXXVIII, 401.

61. *W. A.,* XXXVIII, 401.

62. *W. A.,* XXXVIII, 401.

63. *W. A.,* XXXVIII, 401–402; XVII, 511.

64. *W. A.,* XVII, 511.

65. *W. A.,* XV, 721; XXXVIII, 402 ff.

66. Roerer was called by the congregation on May 3, 1525; *W. A.,* XVI, 226; XVII, xvii, xxxviii, 243; *W. A.,* XXXVIII, 403.

67. *W. A.,* XXXVIII, 409.

68. *W. A.,* XXXVIII, 403.

69. *W. A.,* XXXVIII, 403.

70. Holman, *W. M. L.,* VI, 233–234; Drews, *Der evangelische Geistliche,* p. 42.

71. *W. A.,* XXXVIII, 406–407; Richter, *Kirchenordnungen,* I, 99; Sehling *Kirchenordnungen,* II, 171.

72. *W. A.,* XXXVIII, 406–408.

73. Enders, VIII, 332–333.

74. *Nuntiaturberichte,* I, 544.

75. Georg Rietschel, *Luther und die Ordination* (Wittenberg, 1883), p. 69; Rietschel, *Lehrbuch der Liturgik* (Berlin, 1908), II, 422.

76. *W. A.,* XXXVIII, 409; Drews, *Der evangelische Geistliche,* p. 42.

77. *W. A.,* XXXVIII, 410; Richter, *Kirchenordnungen,* II, 118–119; Rietschel, *Luther und die Ordination,* p. 22 ff. For a translation of the Rietschel text see Holman, *W. M. L.,* VI, 235 ff. For an example of ordination in 1535 see Luther's letter to Friedrich Myconius of October 20, 1535, *W. A.,* "*Briefe,*" VII, 302–303.

78. Georg Buchwald, *Wittenberger Ordiniertenbuch* (Leipzig, 1894), I, 1–10; Drews, *Der evangelische Geistliche,* pp. 10–23, for a discussion of the type of clergymen who filled the pulpits.

79. Buchwald, *Wittenberger Ordiniertenbuch*, pp. 3–10.

80. Buchwald, *Wittenberger Ordiniertenbuch*, pp. 23–49, for the years 1542 to 1546.

81. *W. A.*, XXXVIII, 406–407; Richter, *Kirchenordnungen*, I, 99; Sehling, *Kirchenordnungen*, II, 171.

82. Burkhardt, *G. K. S.*, p. 36.

83. Burkhardt, *G. K. S.*, pp. 47–48.

84. Burkhardt, *G. K. S.*, pp. 87–88.

85. Burkhardt, *G. K. S.*, p. 100. Drews, *Der evangelische Geistliche*, p. 15 ff., cites Justus Menius' complaint about the "groben Gesellen."

86. Drews, *Der evangelische Geistliche*, p. 41.

87. Drews, *Der evangelische Geistliche*, pp. 41–44. Luther on ordaining openly, *W. A.*, XLI, 240; Holman, *W. M. L.*, VI, 235; *W. A.*, XXXVIII, 407; *Z. K. G.* (1905), 288 ff.; Mentz, *Johann Friedrich* (Jena, 1908), III, 240.

88. Drews, *Der evangelische Geistliche*, p. 41.

89. Drews, *Der evangelische Geistliche*, pp. 41–42.

90. Drews, *Der evangelische Geistliche*, pp. 41–42.

91. Drews, *Der evangelische Geistliche*, pp. 41–42.

92. *W. A.*, XXXVIII, 404.

93. Drews, *Der evangelische Geistliche*, pp. 41–42; *W. A.*, XXXVIII, 404, 409–410.

94. *W. A.*, XXXVIII, 410.

95. *W. A.*, XXXVIII, 404; Holman, *W. M. L.*, VI, 235 ff.

96. Drews, *Der evangelische Geistliche*, pp. 7, 10–13.

97. Drews, *Der evangelische Geistliche*, p. 10.

98. Drews, *Der evangelische Geistliche*, pp. 20–22.

99. Drews, *Der evangelische Geistliche*, pp. 10–13.

100. Drews, *Der evangelische Geistliche*, pp. 25–30.

101. Drews, *Der evangelische Geistliche*, p. 25.

102. Drews, *Der evangelische Geistliche*, p. 26.

103. Drews, *Der evangelische Geistliche*, p. 26.

104. Drews, *Der evangelische Geistliche*, p. 27.

105. Drews, *Der evangelische Geistliche*, pp. 27–28.

106. Drews, *Der evangelische Geistliche*, p. 20.

107. Drews, *Der evangelische Geistliche*, pp. 25–28.

108. Drews, *Der evangelische Geistliche*, pp. 20–22, 28–30.

109. Drews, *Der evangelische Geistliche*, pp. 20–22.

110. Drews, *Der evangelische Geistliche*, p. 22.

111. Drews, *Der evangelische Geistliche*, pp. 23–24.

112. They wore "Pluderhosen, Schnabel-Schuhen und Bunten Rocken," Drews, *Der evangelische Geistliche*, p. 37.

113. Drews, *Der evangelische Geistliche*, p. 38.

114. Drews, *Der evangelische Geistliche*, p. 38.

115. Drews, *Der evangelische Geistliche*, p. 38.

116. Stein, *Lutherhaus*, p. 17, says Luther put away his "schwarze Augustiner kutte" and substituted "einen schwarzen Predigerrok" from cloth supplied by the Elector. Cf. Drews, *Der evangelische Geistliche*, p. 38.

117. Drews, *Der evangelische Geistliche*, pp. 37—39.

118. Hermann Werdermann, *Luthers Wittenberger Gemeinde*, p. 8, speaks of three "Diakons" in 1528. Drews, *Der evangelische Geistliche*, p. 33, mentions three "diakonen" to 1533, after which there were four, the additional one being a "Dorf Kaplan." He was provided with a horse to enable him to make his circuit of the "Doerfer."

119. Drews, *Der evangelische Geistliche*, p. 33. Melanchthon thought the amount of preaching was overdone for maximum efficiency.

120. Werdermann, *Luthers Wittenberger Gemeinde*, p. 24; Drews, *Der evangelische Geistliche*, pp. 33 and 36.

121. Schwiebert, *Thesis*, section on student matriculations between 1520 and 1560, *passim;* Drews, *Der evangelische Geistliche*, pp. 14 and 16.

122. Drews, *Der evangelische Geistliche*, p. 14 ff.

123. Drews, *Der evangelische Geistliche*, pp. 17—19.

124. W. A., XXX, Pt. I, 265—267.

125. On Luther's basic principle of Sola Scriptura see Reu, *Luther and the Scriptures* (Columbus, 1944), pp. 49 ff. and 13 ff.

126. Text, p. 573 ff.

127. W. A., X, Pt. I, lxi—lxii, lxix.

128. W. A., XIX, 95.

129. W. A., X, Pt. I, lxxi; E. A., LXIII, 371.

130. W. A., VII, 458 ff.; W. A., X, Pt. I, xlvi, lxii, lviii; Enders, III, 461; C. R., I, 203—204.

131. W. A., X, Pt. I, lxii, lviii; C. R., I, 203—204.

132. W. A., XVII, Pt. II, xviii.

133. W. A., X, Pt. I, v; XVII, Pt. II, xviii.

134. W. A., X, Pt. I, v.

135. W. A., XVII, Pt. II, x; X, Pt. I, v.

136. W. A., XVII, Pt. II, x.

137. W. A., XVII, Pt. II, x—xii.

138. W. A., XVII, Pt. II, x—xii.

139. W. A., XVII, Pt. II, x—xii.

140. W. A., XVII, Pt. II, xx.

141. W. A., XVII, Pt. II, xx.

142. G. Buchwald, "Zur Postillen Melanchthoniana," A. R. (1924), p. 21.

143. W. A., X, Pt. I, lxxiv—lxxv.

144. W. A., X, Pt. I, lxxix.

145. W. A., X, Pt. I, lxiv—lxv; Enders, III, 171; C. R., I, no. 127.

146. P. Drews, *R. E.* (3d Edition), XV, 486.

147. *W. A.*, X, Pt. I, lxix.

148. *W. A.*, X, Pt. I, lxix.

149. Zwingli, *Opera*, II, 2, 157.

150. Emanuel Hirsch, *Die Theologie des Andreas Osiander* (Goettingen, 1919), p. 70; *T. S. K.* (1897), p. 374 ff.

151. *W. A.*, *"Briefe,"* VIII, 99—100, July 9, 1537; VII, 433, June 13, 1536; *W. A., T. R.*, III, 3797; *W. A.*, XXXVIII, 133; L, 657.

152. *W. A.*, I, 450, 494; XXX, Pt. I, 440—441, 458—460.

153. *W. A.*, XXX, Pt. I, 436.

154. *W. A.*, XXX, Pt. I, 437.

155. *W. A.*, XXX, Pt. I, 430—431.

156. *W. A.*, XXX, Pt. I, 427, 455—456; Buchwald, *Die Entstehung der Kate-chismen Luthers und die Grundlage des Groszen Katechismus* (Leipzig, 1894); Ferdinand Cohrs, "Luthers Katechismen," *R. E.*, X (1901), 130—135; *Monumenta Germaniae Paedagogica* (1900—1907), XX, XXI, XXII, XXIII, and for a detailed discussion of earlier Catechisms before Luther's time, XXXIX.

157. *W. A.*, XXX, Pt. I, 432.

158. *W. A.*, XXX, Pt. I, 444—449; VII, 204 ff.

159. *W. A.*, XXX, Pt. I, 435—436.

160. *W. A.*, XXX, Pt. I, 445—449.

161. *W. A.*, XXX, Pt. I, 444—445.

162. *W. A.*, XXX, Pt. I, 444—445.

163. *W. A.*, XXX, Pt. I, 448—449.

164. *W. A.*, XXX, Pt. I, 435; Geffcken, *Der Bilderkatechismus des 15. Jahr-hunderts* etc. (1855), 26 ff.

165. Reu, *Luther's German Bible* (1934), pp. 76—77, and 319—322 for additional bibliography.

166. Karl Knoke, *D. Martin Luthers Kleiner Katechismus nach den aeltesten Ausgaben* etc. (Halle a. S., 1904), p. 6.

167. *W. A.*, XXX, Pt. I, 436—437.

168. *W. A.*, XXX, Pt. I, 445.

169. Richter, *Kirchenordnungen*, I, 16b; Sehling, *Kirchenordnungen*, I, 1, 700 ff.; *W. A.*, XXVI, 230; XXX, Pt. I, 438—439, 475 ff.

170. *W. A.*, XXX, Pt. I, 438—439, 451.

171. *W. A.*, XXX, Pt. I, 449; G. Kawerau, *Zwei aelteste Katechismen der lutherischen Reformation* (Halle a. S., 1890), p. 5.

172. *W. A.*, XXX, Pt. I, 437—438.

173. *W. A.*, XXVI, 147; XXX, Pt. I, 464—465.

174. *W. A.*, VII, 204 ff.; XXX, Pt. I, 434, 437—438; XIX, 75—79.

175. *W. A.*, XXX, Pt. I, 449—450.

176. *W. A.*, XXX, Pt. I, 449—450.

177. *W. A.*, XXX, Pt. I, 451; *E. A.*, XXVI, 383.
178. Text, p. 636.
179. *W. A.*, XXX, Pt. I, 438–441.
180. *W. A.*, XXX, Pt. I, 440–441.
181. *W. A.*, XXX, Pt. I, 441–444.
182. *E. A.*, XXVI, 383 f.
183. *W. A.*, XXX, Pt. I, 126: "I still recite it daily as a little child which is being instructed in the Catechism, and I likewise recite it word for word every morning; and, when I have time, I recite the Lord's Prayer, the Ten Commandments, the Creed, Psalms, etc., for I must remain a child and a student of the Catechism, which I do gladly."
184. Kroker, pp. 118–119.
185. *W. A.*, VIII, 684; *E. A.*, XXIII, 239.
186. "Die Gestalt der Lutherbibel in Druck und Bild," *Luther, Vierteljahrsschrift der Luthergesellschaft*, XVI (1934), 60.
187. "Die Gestalt der Lutherbibel in Druck und Bild," *Luther, Vierteljahrsschrift der Luthergesellschaft*, XVI, 60–61, cites 14 High and 4 Low German Bibles.
188. Paul Althaus, "Der Geist der Lutherbibel," *Luther-Jahrbuch*, XVI, 1.
189. Luther speaks of the difficulty with the "stili grandissimi grandiatem," Enders, IV, 300.
190. Althaus, "Der Geist der Lutherbibel," *Luther-Jahrbuch*, XVI, 1–2.
191. *W. A.*, "*Deutsche Bibel*," IV, xi.
192. See "Einleitung," by Pietsch and Thiele, *W. A.*, "*Deutsche Bibel*," I, xiii ff.; Reichert, "Die Bibelrevisionen Luthers" etc., *W. A.*, IV, xi ff.; and especially *W. A.*, III, xiii.
193. *W. A.*, "*Briefe*," II, 490, n. 5; *C. R.*, I, 567: "Recognescimus una D. Martinus et ego novum testamentum, quod ille totum vertit in nostram linguam." Cf. *W. A.*, "*Deutsche Bibel*," IV, xii.
194. *C. R.*, I, 567, 570, 571, 574.
195. Enders, III, 271.
196. Johannes Eger, "Martin Luther: Die heilige Schrift deutsch," *Luther, Vierteljahrsschrift der Luthergesellschaft*, XVI (1934), 50; Bauch, "Die Einfuehrung des Hebraeischen in Wittenberg," *Monatschrift fuer Geschichte und Wissenschaft des Judentums*, XLVIII (1904), 22 ff., 469 ff.; *W. A.*, "*Deutsche Bibel*," IV, xiii–xiv.
197. *W. A.*, "*Deutsche Bibel*," IV, xii–xiii.
198. *W. A.*, "*Deutsche Bibel*," I, xiii ff. See Enders, IV, 23, 33, and 40, for letters to Spalatin, Stein, and Link.
199. Enders, IV, 261, a letter of December 4, 1523, from Luther to Hausmann shows that the work on "Das Ander Teyl" had been started. Cf. *W. A.*, "*Deutsche Bibel*," II, 217; and Albert Schramm, *Luther und die Bibel* (Leipzig, 1923), p. 6, table p. 27 ff.
200. *W. A.*, "*Deutsche Bibel*," I, xiii. Cf. Reu, *Luther's German Bible*, p. 195.
201. Schramm, *Luther und die Bibel*, p. 121.

202. Reu, *Luther's German Bible*, p. 195.

203. Enders, IV, 300; translation by Reu, *Luther's German Bible*, p. 197.

204. Reu, *Luther's German Bible*, pp. 201–202.

205. W. A., *"Deutsche Bibel,"* I, xiv.

206. Reu, *Luther's German Bible*, p. 204.

207. Text, p. 695 ff.

208. W. A., *"Briefe,"* III, 433, 437, 439; W. A., XIV, 407–744. Cf. Reu, *Luther's German Bible*, p. 205; W. A., *"Deutsche Bibel,"* IV, 198, says May, 1527.

209. W. A., *"Deutsche Bibel,"* II, 392, 394, 439. Cf. W. A., *"Briefe,"* IV, 110, says Luther was also lecturing in Ecclesiastes in 1526. By February, 1527, he had begun the Prophets, Enders, VI, 20. Jesaias gave him trouble, Enders, VI, 276, 291. See also C. R., I, 986.

210. Translation by Reu, *Luther's German Bible*, p. 205.

211. Enders, VI, 291; VII, 101.

212. Enders, VII, 303.

213. W. A., XXX, Pt. II, 220 f. According to Enders, VIII, 163, 191, Luther was working on the Minor Prophets by August 15, 1530.

214. Enders, IX, 155; Reu, *Luther's German Bible*, p. 208.

215. W. A., *"Deutsche Bibel,"* II, 528 and 531; IV, xviii; and Reu, *Luther's German Bible*, p. 211.

216. W. A., *"Deutsche Bibel,"* IV, xv–xviii. The Protokols of Roerer indicate the very careful checking of Luther's translations of the various books of the Bible. The value in the use of his fellow professors was already learned in the 1531 publication of the Psalter. The 1534 Bible states that it was published "Begnadet mit Kuerfurstlicher zu Sachsen freiheit."

217. Reu, *Luther's German Bible*, pp. 212–213.

218. W. A., *"Deutsche Bibel,"* III, vi–vii, xviii. Cf. T. S. K. (1894), p. 391, and Z. K. G., XIV, 603.

219. W. A., *"Deutsche Bibel,"* II, xx–xxviii; III, v–vii, xv–xxv.

220. W. A., XXX, Pt. II, 636 f.

221. W. A., *"Deutsche Bibel,"* IV, xiii–xiv, lii–liv.

222. W. A., *"Deutsche Bibel,"* IV, xiii–xiv, lii–liv.

223. W. A., *"Deutsche Bibel,"* IV, lii–liv.

224. W. A., *"Deutsche Bibel,"* IV, xiv.

225. W. A., *"Deutsche Bibel,"* IV, xv; cf. III, v, xvi–xvii.

226. W. A., *"Deutsche Bibel,"* IV, xx–xxi; DeWette, IV, 214; Enders, VIII, 345; W. A., XXXVIII, 9. On Roerer, W. A., *"Deutsche Bibel,"* III, xvii.

227. W. A., *"Deutsche Bibel,"* III, xviii–xx; IV, 16–19.

228. W. A., *"Deutsche Bibel,"* III, vi–vii.

229. W. A., *"Deutsche Bibel,"* IV, xvi, xliii–xliv; cf. II, 438.

230. W. A., *"Deutsche Bibel,"* IV, xliii–xliv.

231. W. A., "Deutsche Bibel," IV, xliii–lii.
232. W. A., "Deutsche Bibel," IV, xix, xxiv.
233. W. A., "Deutsche Bibel," IV, xviii.
234. W. A., "Deutsche Bibel," IV, xviii–xix.
235. W. A., "Deutsche Bibel," IV, xix, xx–xxi.
236. W. A., "Deutsche Bibel," IV, xxiv.
237. W. A., "Deutsche Bibel," III, v; cf. IV, xxiv.
238. Enders, IX, 381 ff., and n. 2.
239. Enders, X, 21; cf. W. A., "Deutsche Bibel," IV, xxiv.
240. W. A., "Deutsche Bibel," IV, xxv.
241. W. A., "Deutsche Bibel," IV, xxiv–xxv. Enders, X, 27 and Anm. 36; Koestlin-Kawerau, Martin Luther, II, 294.
242. W. A., "Deutsche Bibel," IV, xxv.
243. W. A., "Deutsche Bibel," III, vii, called the 1539/38 Old Testament by the editor. Cf. also W. A., "Deutsche Bibel," IV, xxv–xxvi. In the Jena Appendix Manuscriptorum, No. 24, it is called J. A.
244. W. A., "Deutsche Bibel," IV, xxxi–xxxii.
245. W. A., "Deutsche Bibel," IV, xxxii. In the process of binding some of the marginal notes were lost.
246. W. A., "Deutsche Bibel," IV, xxvii–xxviii, xxxi–xxxii.
247. W. A., "Deutsche Bibel," III, xv f.
248. W. A., "Deutsche Bibel," III, 167–IV, 418.
249. W. A., "Deutsche Bibel," IV, xxvii–xxviii.
250. W. A., "Deutsche Bibel," IV, xxvi–xxix.
251. W. A., "Deutsche Bibel," IV, xxviii.
252. W. A., "Deutsche Bibel," IV, xxx.
253. W. A., "Deutsche Bibel," IV, xxx.
254. W. A., "Deutsche Bibel," IV, xxxi; cf. Holl, G. A., I, 544 ff.
255. Reu, Luther's German Bible, pp. 235–236.
256. W. A., "Deutsche Bibel," IV, xxxviii–xxxix.
257. W. A., "Deutsche Bibel," IV, xl. This was called the Bible "G," printed in September, 1541, which fully utilized Luther's J. A. for the first time.
258. W. A., "Deutsche Bibel," IV, xxxv–xl.
259. W. A., "Deutsche Bibel," IV, xxxiv.
260. W. A., "Deutsche Bibel," IV, xl.
261. W. A., "Deutsche Bibel," IV, xxxv.
262. W. A., "Deutsche Bibel," IV, xxxviii, on the revision of the New Testament. Luther's New Testament, J. N., the parallel to the J. A., is Appendix Manuscriptorum, No. 25, still in the Jena Library, called "Jena Neues." W. A., "Deutsche Bibel," IV, xliv–xlv.
263. W. A., "Deutsche Bibel," IV, xliv.
264. W. A., "Deutsche Bibel," IV, xlv–xlvi.
265. W. A., "Deutsche Bibel," IV, xlv–xlvi.

266. *C. R.*, IV, 638.

267. Enders, XIII, 352; *W. A.*, *"Deutsche Bibel,"* IV, xlv ff.; *T. S. K.* (1913), p. 298.

268. *W. A.*, *"Deutsche Bibel,"* IV, xlix and li.

269. *W. A.*, *"Deutsche Bibel,"* IV, l–li.

270. *W. A.*, *"Deutsche Bibel,"* IV, l–lii, xx–xxi.

271. *W. A.*, *"Deutsche Bibel,"* IV, xx–xxii; O. Albrecht, "Das lutherische Handexemplar des deutschen Neuen Testaments," *T. S. K.*, LXXXVII (1914), 153–208; Otto Reichert, "Wert und Bedeutung der Bibel 1546," *T. S. K.*, XCI (1918), 193 ff.

272. Schwiebert, *Reformation Lectures,* p. 229 ff.

273. *W. A.*, *"Deutsche Bibel,"* IV, xix–xx, l–li.

274. *W. A.*, *"Deutsche Bibel,"* IV, xl–xliii, li–lii.

275. *W. A.*, *"Deutsche Bibel,"* IV, xlii.

276. *W. A.*, *"Deutsche Bibel,"* IV, l–li.

277. *W. A.*, *"Deutsche Bibel,"* IV, xl, xlix–l.

278. *W. A.*, *"Deutsche Bibel,"* IV, xxxv, xliii, xlix–lxii.

279. Althaus, "Der Geist der Lutherbibel," *Luther-Jahrbuch,* XVI (1934), 8.

280. Althaus, "Der Geist der Lutherbibel," *Luther-Jahrbuch,* XVI, 12–14. Cf. *W. A.*, *T. R.*, III, 3043a; *E. A.*, LXIII, 22 f.

281. Althaus, "Der Geist der Lutherbibel," *Luther-Jahrbuch,* XVI, 25 ff. Cf. *W. A.*, *T. R.*, V, 5533.

282. Johannes Eger, "Martin Luther: Die heilige Schrift deutsch," *Luther, Vierteljahrsschrift der Luthergesellschaft,* XVI, 49 ff.; *W. A.*, XV, 37–38; XXX, Pt. II, 639; *W. A.*, *"Deutsche Bibel,"* IV, xiii; *W. A.*, *T. R.*, V, 5324.

283. Johannes Eger, "Martin Luther: Die heilige Schrift deutsch," *Luther, Vierteljahrsschrift der Luthergesellschaft,* XVI, 49 ff., 54–56; *W. A.*, *T. R.*, II, 2771b: "One must use the language of the people in the market place."

284. *W. A.*, *T. R.*, I, 312; IV, 5002.

285. Zimmermann, "Die Verbreitung der Lutherbibel zur Reformationszeit," *Luther, Vierteljahrsschrift der Luthergesellschaft,* XVI (1934), 82 ff.; *W. A.*, *"Deutsche Bibel,"* II, xxiv–xxviii.

286. Zimmermann, "Die Verbreitung der Lutherbibel zur Reformationszeit," *Luther, Vierteljahrsschrift der Luthergesellschaft,* XVI, 83.

287. Zimmermann, "Die Verbreitung der Lutherbibel zur Reformationszeit," *Luther, Vierteljahrsschrift der Luthergesellschaft,* XVI, 84–85.

288. *W. A.*, *"Deutsche Bibel,"* II, xxviii.

289. Zimmermann, "Die Verbreitung der Lutherbibel zur Reformationszeit," *Luther, Vierteljahrsschrift der Luthergesellschaft,* XVI, 86–87.

290. Zimmermann, "Die Verbreitung der Lutherbibel zur Reformationszeit," *Luther, Vierteljahrsschrift der Luthergesellschaft,* XVI, 83. *W. A.*, *"Deutsche Bibel,"* II, xxiv, makes the statement that 100,000 Lufft Bibles were sold between 1534 and 1584. It would appear that nearly 1,000,000 Luther Bibles were in circulation during the time of the Reformation.

291. Thulin, *Luther, Vierteljahrsschrift der Luthergesellschaft,* XVI (1934), 62. W. A., *"Deutsche Bibel,"* II, xxviii.

292. W. A., T. R., II, 2628b.

293. An able discussion of Luther's contribution to sixteenth-century music is found in W. A., XXXV, 79 ff.

294. W. A., XXXV, 80—81; Ratzeberger, p. 58 ff.

295. Otto Scheel, "Luther und die Schule seiner Zeit," *Luther-Jahrbuch,* VII (1925), 149—151.

296. Paul H. Lang, *Music in Western Civilization* (New York, 1941), pp. 207 to 208.

297. Walter E. Buszin, "Luther on Music," *The Musical Quarterly,* XXXII (1946), 95—96.

298. Lang, *Music in Western Civilization,* p. 209.

299. Buszin, "Luther on Music," *The Musical Quarterly,* XXXII, 88.

300. Buszin, "Luther on Music," *The Musical Quarterly,* XXXII, 91.

301. Lang, *Music in Western Civilization,* p. 209.

302. Lang, *Music in Western Civilization,* p. 207.

303. W. A., XII, 35—37; E. A., XXII, 151. See also Karl Eger, "Luthers Gottesdienstreform 1523—1526," *Luther-Mitteilungen der Luther-Gesellschaft,* VII (1925), 2—4; Sehling, *Kirchenordnungen,* I, 10 f.; W. A., XIX, 44.

304. W. A., XIX, 44—45; Holman, W. M. L., VI, 67 ff.

305. Eger, *Luthers Gottesdienstreform,* p. 5; Holman, W. M. L., VI, 77.

306. Holman, W. M. L., VI, 77.

307. W. A., XII, 197; Eger, *Luthers Gottesdienstreform,* p. 5.

308. Eger, *Luthers Gottesdienstreform,* p. 3.

309. Eger, *Luthers Gottesdienstreform,* p. 6; W. A., XIX, 80, 99, n. 7, states that the elevation of the host was not dropped in Wittenberg until 1542.

310. Sehling, *Kirchenordnungen,* I, 2; W. A., XIX, 44 ff.

311. The author visited Kemberg in 1936, and the Buergermeister produced an old town record which established the fact that Luther had worked out his reforms in collaboration with his former student.

312. W. A., XIX, 44 ff.; Holman, W. M. L., VI, 67 ff.

313. Holman, W. M. L., VI, 84—85.

314. Holman, W. M. L., VI, 71.

315. W. A., XII, 197; De Wette, II, 430; Holman, W. M. L., VI, 70; Eger, *Luthers Gottesdienstreform,* p. 6.

316. W. A., XII, 197; Holman, W. M. L., VI, 77.

317. Holman, W. M. L., VI, 79—80.

318. Holman, W. M. L., VI, 79—80.

319. Holman, W. M. L., VI, 79—80.

320. W. A., XII, 199.

321. W. A., XIX, 45—46.

322. *W. A.*, XII, 198; *W. A.*, *"Briefe,"* III, 199, and n. 1; cf. *W. A.*, XIX, 51; and *E. A.* (2d Ed.), XIV, 278.

323. *W. A.*, XIX, 46.

324. *W. A.*, XIX, 46—47.

325. *W. A.*, XIX, 48 ff.; Enders, V, 363, 395; 'Hugo Holstein, "Der Lieder- und Tondichter Johann Walther," *Archiv fuer Literaturgeschichte*, XII, 185—218.

326. *W. A.*, XIX, 50—51.

327. *W. A.*, XIX, 51.

328. *W. A.*, XIX, 75—76, 80; Paul Graff, *Geschichte der Aufloesung der alten gottesdienstlichen Formen in der evangelischen Kirche Deutschlands bis zum Eintritt der Aufklaerung und des Rationalismus* (Goettingen, 1921), p. 2.

329. *W. A.*, XIX, 51.

330. *W. A.*, XIX, 81 ff.; Sehling, *Kirchenordnungen*, I, 14 ff.

331. *W. A.*, XXX, Pt. I, 441—444; Richter, *Kirchenordnungen*, I, 30, points out that in Prussia such announcements were usually received by the minister on Friday. If on any other day, an assistant served as the examiner.

332. *W. A.*, XXX, Pt. I, 439—444, *passim;* Drews, *Der evangelische Geistliche*, pp. 30, 33—35.

333. *W. A.*, XIX, 81 ff., 86; Eger, *Luthers Gottesdienstreform*, p. 5.

334. *W. A.*, XIX, 86—90.

335. *W. A.*, XIX, 90—95.

336. *W. A.*, XIX, 95.

337. *W. A.*, XIX, 95—96.

338. *W. A.*, XIX, 97.

339. *W. A.*, XIX, 99; cf. n. 6.

340. Richter, *Kirchenordnungen*, I, 201.

341. Richter, *Kirchenordnungen*, I, 31; Drews, *Der evangelische Geistliche*, pp. 30—35.

342. *R. E.*, III, 792—793, on John Hesz, relates how carefully the changes were introduced.

343. Graff, *Geschichte der Aufloesung der alten gottesdienstlichen Formen in der evangelischen Kirche Deutschlands bis zum Eintritt der Aufklaerung und des Rationalismus*, p. 3. Cf. G. Kawerau, *Monatschrift fuer die evangelische-lutherische Kirche Preuszens*, XXVI (1873), 287.

344. *W. A.*, XIX, 99, n. 7.

345. *W. A.*, XXXV, 70 ff.

346. *W. A.*, XXXV, 70—71; Achelis Marburger, *Die Entstehungszeit von Luthers geistlichen Liedern* (1883); F. Spitta, *Ein' feste Burg ist unser Gott, Die Lieder Luthers in ihrer Bedeutung fuer das evangelische Kirchenlied* (Goettingen, 1905).

347. *W. A.*, XXXV, 71–72, and n. 2; Johannes Bachmann, "Zur Entstehungs-geschichte der geistlichen Lieder Luthers," *Zeitschrift fuer kirchliche Wissenschaft und kirchliches Leben*, V (1884), 151–168, 294–312; W. Nelle, *Geschichte des deutschen evangelischen Kirchenliedes* (Hamburg, 1909), p. 24; *W. A.*, XII, 73–80; XXXV, 74–75.

348. *W. A.*, XXXV, 8–10.

349. Nelle, *Geschichte des deutschen evangelischen Kirchenliedes*, p. 24; *W. A.*, XXXV, 5, 75.

350. Wackernagel, *A. R.*, VIII, 24 ff.; Bachmann, "Zur Entstehungsgeschichte der geistlichen Lieder Luthers," *Zeitschrift fuer kirchliche Wissenschaft und kirchliches Leben*, V, 162; *W. A.*, XXXV, 18–19.

351. *W. A.*, XXXV, 22.

352. *W. A.*, XXXV, 25.

353. *W. A.*, XXXV, 14.

354. *W. A.*, XXXV, 15–17.

355. *W. A.*, XXXV, 28–29.

356. "Luthers Lied 'Ein' feste Burg' etc.," *Zeitschrift fuer kirchliche Wissenschaft und kirchliches Leben*, II (1881), 39 ff.; *W. A.*, XXXV, 26.

357. *W. A.*, XXXV, 26.

358. *W. A.*, XXXV, 27–28.

359. *W. A.*, XXXV, 42, also tables, 38–42.

360. *W. A.*, XXXV, 55.

361. Enders, VII, 53, 70; *W. A.*, XXXV, 53–54; XXX, Pt. III, 1–3, 20–21, 22–40.

362. *W. A.*, XXXV, 54–55.

363. The wide variation in opinions is shown by the following persons and the date which they believed covered the composition of *A Mighty Fortress:* Achelis, 1521; Spitta, 1513–1521; Linke, 1525; Bachmann, 1526; Schneider, 1527; Biltz, Hausrath, and Tschackert, 1528–1529; Sleidan, 1530; Wackernagel, 1529; Koestlin, 1527. The Weimar editors seem to favor the years 1527–1528.

364. *W. A.*, XXXV, 70 ff. For the Pack story, *W. A.*, *"Briefe,"* IV, 421 ff., especially, "Nachgeschichte," 424 ff., 430 ff., 433 ff., 430, n. 1, 474–475, notes 5 and 6; *W. A.*, XII, 73–80; XXXV, 226, for Luther's first reference to the hymn in 1531. On Leonhard Kaiser, who died August 16, 1527, *W. A.*, XXXV, 197; Luther's letter to Michael Stifel, October 22, 1527, Enders, VI, 108; *W. A.*, XXXV, 199–200; for evaluation of the entire story, *W. A.*, XXXV, 228–229.

365. *W. A.*, XXXV, 227–229.

366. *W. A.*, XXXV, 227–229. Cf. 197 ff. for Schneider and his followers.

367. *W. A.*, XXXV, 80. C. v. Winterfeld, *Der evangelische Kirchengesang und sein Verhaeltnis zur Kunst des Tonsatzes* (Leipzig, 1843), I, 162.

368. *W. A.*, XXXV, 80, n. 3, cites Baeumker's chief sources.

369. W. Baeumker, "Das deutsche Sanctus von Luther," *Monatshefte fuer Musik-Geschichte*, XII (1880), 14–15, 20–22.

370. *W. A.*, XXXV, 83–84.

371. *W. A.*, XXXV, 83.
372. *W. A.*, XXXV, 84.
373. *W. A.*, XXXV, 84.
374. Lang, *Music in Western Civilization*, pp. 208–210.
375. Lang, *Music in Western Civilization*, pp. 208–210.
376. *W. A.*, XXXV, 85.
377. Lang, *Music in Western Civilization*, p. 209.
378. *W. A.*, XXXV, 322.
379. *W. A.*, XXXV, 385–386.
380. *W. A.*, XXXV, 325.
381. *W. A.*, XXXV, 331–333.
382. Text, p. 659 ff.
383. As the student matriculations of the University of Wittenberg reveal, during Luther's lifetime almost as many students came from southern as from northern Germany; but after 1560 these regions were lost. The same applies to many sections of the country to the east.
384. Text, pp. 110, 116; Scheel, *Luther-Jahrbuch*, VII, 144–145.
385. *W. A.*, XV, 28 ff.; Scheel, *Luther-Jahrbuch*, VII, 141 ff.; Paulsen, *Geschichte*, I, 204–207.
386. Paulsen, *Geschichte*, I, 209–210; for text, *W. A.*, XXX, Pt. I, 508–588; Schwiebert, "The Reformation from a New Perspective," *Church History*, XVII (1948), 23–24, n. 108.
387. Drews, *Der evangelische Geistliche*, pp. 6 ff., 17–19; and Burkhardt, *G. K. S.*, p. 40 ff.
388. Richter, *Kirchenordnungen*, I, 48–49.
389. Sehling, *Kirchenordnungen*, I, 172–174.
390. *R. E.*, III, 528–529; Richter, *Kirchenordnungen*, I, 106 ff., for the text. For Bugenhagen's letter of July 22, 1528, to Luther see *W. A.*, "Briefe," IV, 502–503.
391. Bugenhagen had received a call to Hamburg in 1524, *W. A.*, "Briefe," III, 339, n. 7; *R. E.*, III, 528–529; K. A. T. Vogt, "Johannes Bugenhagen Pommeranus," *Leben und ausgewaehlte Schriften der Vaeter und Begruender der lutherischen Kirche* (Elberfeld, 1867), IV, 308–322. On Bugenhagen's temporary call to the Nikolaigemeinde in Hamburg see Vogt, *Bugenhagen*, p. 18 ff.; *C. R.*, I, 673, 676; C. W. Sillem, *Die Einfuehrung der Reformation in Hamburg* (Halle, 1886), p. 43 ff.; Hermann Hering, *Doctor Pommeranus Johannes Bugenhagen* (Halle, 1888), p. 33 ff. Bugenhagen arrived in Hamburg on October 9, 1528.
392. On Amsdorf's call to Magdeburg see Enders, V, 106, n. 9; *C. R.*, I, 674, Suppl. Mel. VI, 1, 258; Friedrich Huelsze, *Die Einfuehrung der Reformation in der Stadt Magdeburg* (Magdeburg, 1883), p. 104 ff. On the early reforms in Magdeburg see F. W. Hoffmann, *Geschichte der Stadt Magdeburg* (Magdeburg, 1847), II, 9 ff.; and the school founded there, Paulsen, *Geschichte*, I, 276; on the Eisleben school, Paulsen, *Geschichte*, I, 276—277; *W. A.*, "Briefe," III, 474, 475, n. 2; cf. Kawerau, *Agricola*, p. 59; *C. R.*, I, 739.

393. Sehling, *Kirchenordnungen*, I, 151 ff. Cf. *W. A.*, "*Briefe*," V, 33–34; and Sehling, *Kirchenordnungen*, V, 488–540.

394. On Bugenhagen's wide activity in the northern lands, *R. E.*, III, 528–529; Julius Rost, *Die Paedagogische Bedeutung Bugenhagens* (Leipzig, 1890); p. 10 ff.; Vogt, *Bugenhagen*, p. 303 ff.

395. Rost, *Die Paedagogische Bedeutung Bugenhagens*, pp. 24–51, speaks of "Deutsche Schulen," "Knaben Schulen," "Maedchen Schulen," "Dorf-schulen," "Volksschulen," and "Lateinschulen."

396. On Hesz, see *R. E.*, III, 741, 789–792. This great clergyman had studied in Wittenberg under Luther and Melanchthon and later completed his doctorate in Italy. He always remained a close friend of the Wittenberg faculty and organized a cluster of flourishing Lutheran congregations in the Breslau region.

397. Schwiebert, *Church History*, XVII, n. 118; *Thesis*, p. 94, n. 6.

398. Schwiebert, *Reformation Lectures*, p. 288. This is based on 1913 values with a Rhenish gulden being considered worth $13.40 in buying power.

399. Schwiebert, *Thesis*, p. 94, n. 7; Pressel, *Spengler*, p. 51.

400. Scheel, *Luther-Jahrbuch*, VII, 141–175; Paulsen, *Geschichte*, I, 280 ff. Rost, *Die Paedagogische Bedeutung Bugenhagens*, p. 51; Paulsen, *Geschichte*, I, 276–277; Friedensburg, *G. U. W.*, p. 174, for the curricula of these schools.

401. Paulsen, *Geschichte*, I, 280 ff.; and, especially, Scheel, *Luther-Jahrbuch*, VII, 153–158.

402. Krueger, *Vierteljahrsschrift der Luthergesellschaft*, XV, 26–27.

403. Krueger, *Vierteljahrsschrift der Luthergesellschaft*, XV, 27; Scheel, *Luther-Jahrbuch*, VII, 149–151.

404. Scheel, *Luther-Jahrbuch*, VII, 158–161. Text, pp. 114–115.

405. Scheel, *Luther-Jahrbuch*, VII, 158.

406. Charitius, p. 153; Mentzius, *Syntagma*, II, 3.

407. Paulsen, *Geschichte*, I, 280–281; Scheel, *Luther-Jahrbuch*, VII, 149–151, 162–163, 166.

408. Scheel, *Luther-Jahrbuch*, VII, 149–150, 153, 160–163.

409. Scheel, *Luther-Jahrbuch*, VII, 166; Paulsen, *Geschichte*, I, 281.

410. Paulsen, *Geschichte*, I, 281.

411. Paulsen, *Geschichte*, I, 281; Scheel, *Luther-Jahrbuch*, VII, 166.

412. Paulsen, *Geschichte*, I, 281 ff.; Scheel, *Martin Luther*, I, 48–49, and n. 92; Boehmer, *Der Junge Luther*, p. 25.

413. Scheel, *Luther-Jahrbuch*, VII, 174–175.

414. Painter, *Luther on Education*, pp. 138–139.

415. Krueger, *Wittenberg*, p. 27.

416. Rost, *Die Paedagogische Bedeutung Bugenhagens*, p. 61 ff.

417. Rost, *Die Paedagogische Bedeutung Bugenhagens*, p. 66.

418. Scheel, *Luther-Jahrbuch*, VII, 166, 169–175.

419. It must be said to the credit of Luther and Melanchthon that when they revised the school system of Germany they effected an integration of the Gospel with the most modern techniques known to Europe in the first half of the sixteenth century. Even Erasmus had not caught the full impact of this new progressive movement in Lutheran education at all levels.

420. *Album*, III, 804—806.

CHAPTER TWENTY-ONE

1. Text, pp. 275—289.
2. Paul Wernle, *Die Renaissance des Christentums im 16. Jahrhundert* (Tuebingen, 1904), pp. 14—17.
3. Note 46, Chapter Seventeen; especially, Franklin Littell's article in *The Journal of Religious Thought*, IV, 2 (1947), 167 ff.
4. Text, p. 289 ff.
5. Note 3, Chapter Twenty-one.
6. The Enders edition of Luther's correspondence should be consulted for these *Gutachten*, which begin to appear after the middle twenties, *passim*.
7. Smith, *Correspondence*, I, 122; also *Erasmus von Rotterdam, Briefe*, tr. and ed., W. Koehler (Wiesbaden, 1947), 219—220.
8. Text, p. 423.
9. For evidences of Luther's misgivings see Enders, I, 62; the quotation from Lang's letter is from Smith, *Correspondence*, I, 54.
10. Smith, *Erasmus*, pp. 324—325. Cf. Enders, II, 64; Allen, *Opus Erasmi*, III, 605.
11. Allen, *Opus Erasmi*, III, 513; Smith, *Correspondence*, I, 235.
12. Allen, *Opus Erasmi*, III, 587; translation from Mackinnon, *Martin Luther*, III, 236.
13. *Erasmi opera*, III (1703), 1695.
14. *Erasmi opera*, III (1703), 585, 607.
15. Smith, *Correspondence*, I, 402.
16. *Erasmi opera*, III (1703), 1695.
17. Smith, *Erasmus*, p. 327.
18. Smith, *Erasmus*, p. 327. Cf. Smith, *Correspondence*, II, 248—250.
19. Hutten, *Opera*, II, 247. Cf. Holborn, *Ulrich von Hutten*, p. 194.
20. Smith, *Erasmus*, p. 333.
21. Zwingli, *Werke*, VIII, 119. See also Smith, *Erasmus*, p. 335; and Holborn, *Ulrich von Hutten*, p. 195.
22. Allen, *Opus Erasmi*, IV, 311; Hutten, *Opera*, II, 256; *Erasmus von Rotterdam, Briefe*, tr., Walter Koehler, pp. 319—320 and n. 2; Holborn, *Ulrich von Hutten*, pp. 195—198.
23. Smith, *Erasmus*, p. 335 ff.
24. Smith, *Erasmus*, p. 335 ff. Cf. Enders, IV, 234, for Luther's reaction; also III, 360.
25. Smith, *Correspondence*, II, 190—191.

26. Smith, *Correspondence*, II, 196–198. Cf. Allen, *Opus Erasmi*, V, 329 to 330.

27. Smith, *Correspondence*, II, 228–230.

28. Allen, *Opus Erasmi*, V, 451–453; Mackinnon, *Martin Luther*, III, 241 to 242.

29. Mackinnon, *Martin Luther*, III, 241–242. On the tract of Erasmus see Johannes von Walter, "De Libero Arbitrio," *Quellen und Schriften zur Geschichte des Protestantismus*, VIII (Leipzig, 1910), Introduction, 11–12.

30. Mackinnon, *Martin Luther*, III, 242.

31. *W. A.*, XVIII, 786.

32. Mackinnon, *Martin Luther*, III, 242–243.

33. Mackinnon, *Martin Luther*, III, 242–243.

34. Mackinnon, *Martin Luther*, III, 244.

35. Seeberg, *Lehrbuch*, IV, 1 (1933), 173 ff.; *W. A.*, VII, "Assertio omnium articulorum," 1520; "Galatians," *W. A.*, XL, Pt. 1 and Pt. 2; "Genesis," *W. A.*, XLII–XLIV, delivered between 1535 and 1545.

36. Mackinnon, *Martin Luther*, III, 249–251.

37. *Erasmi opera*, IX, 1002; Walter, *De Libero Arbitrio*, p. 19.

38. Walter, *De Libero Arbitrio*, p. 25.

39. Gess, *Akten und Briefe*, I, 734, 745, 753, 777; Smith, *Correspondence*, II, 250–251.

40. Smith, *Correspondence*, II, 249, 254; *C. R.*, I, 667.

41. There are occasional brief references in the correspondence with his friends, but by September, 1525, Luther had begun his famous reply, Enders, V, 245, 247.

42. *C. R.*, I, 674; Smith, *Correspondence*, II, 254.

43. The tract appeared in December, 1525, *W. A.*, XVIII, 600 ff.

44. *W. A.*, XVIII, 600–601.

45. Luther to Capito, July 9, 1537, Enders, XI, 247; *W. A.*, "Briefe," VIII, 99–100; and *W. A.*, *T. R.*, III, 3797, March 29, 1538.

46. Smith, *Erasmus*, pp. 353–354.

47. *W. A.*, XVIII, 605; also Mackinnon, *Martin Luther*, III, 254.

48. Mackinnon, *Martin Luther*, III, 254.

49. *W. A.*, XVIII, 611 ff.

50. *W. A.*, XVIII, 606–607, 614.

51. *W. A.*, XVIII, 644.

52. *W. A.*, XVIII, 625 ff.

53. *W. A.*, XVIII, 634–635.

54. *W. A.*, XVIII, 634–635.

55. Seeberg, *Lehrbuch*, IV, 1 (1933), 173 ff.

56. Holl, *G. A.*, I, 1–110, "Was verstand Luther unter Religion?" Cf. also "Galatians," *W. A.*, XL, Pt. 1 and Pt. 2, *passim;* "Genesis," *W. A.*, ✗LII to XLIV, *passim*.

57. Holl, *G. A.*, I, 179–181. Cf. *W. A.*, XVIII, 684 ff.

58. *W. A.*, XVIII, 684–685, 689; XLII, 295.

59. *W. A.*, XVIII, 615, 707, 719; XLIII, 643; XLIV, 65, 67.

60. *W. A.*, XVIII, 709.

61. Seeberg, *Lehrbuch*, IV, 1, 174–175. Cf. *W. A.*, XVIII, 712.

62. *W. A.*, XVIII, 684 f., 689; XLII, 295.

63. Seeberg, *Lehrbuch*, IV, 1, 178.

64. *W. A.*, XVIII, 394.

65. *W. A.*, XVIII, 709.

66. Mackinnon, *Martin Luther*, III, 272. Cf. Enders, V, 335–336.

67. Smith, *Erasmus*, pp. 354–355.

68. For text, *Erasmi opera*, IX; Smith, *The Age of the Reformation*, pp. 105–106.

69. *W. A.*, XXX, Pt. III, 93–94.

70. Seeberg, *Lehrbuch*, IV, 1, 458–462. Cf. *W. A.*, XXIII, 123, 127, 161, 199; *C. R.*, IV, 970, 2.

71. The references in Luther's writings are numerous. See, for example, *W. A.*, XX, 541; XXIII, 141, 185, 243; XXVI, 324, 332, 340, 346, 387; XXX, Pt. III, 137–138; Seeberg, *Lehrbuch*, IV, 1, 460–463, 464–465, 469–477. Paul Althaus, "Luthers Abendmahlslehre," *Luther-Jahrbuch*, XI (1929), 11, cites the key to Luther's doctrine of the "real presence" as 1 Cor. 10:16, and points to *W. A.*, XVIII, 166.

72. Especially during the period of "pamphlet warfare" preceding the Marburg Colloquy. *W. A.*, XIX, 474 ff.; XXIII, 38 ff.; XXVI, 241 ff.; Hastings Eells, *Martin Bucer* (New Haven, 1931), p. 70 ff. For a complete picture the reader should read the tracts of Zwingli, Oecolampadius, and their supporters to which Luther was replying.

73. Text, pp. 524, 536, 538, 542, 548 ff.

74. Eells, *Martin Bucer*, p. 71.

75. *W. A.*, XVIII, 62 ff. Althaus, *Luther-Jahrbuch*, XI, 8–10.

76. Eells, *Martin Bucer*, pp. 71–72; Seeberg, *Lehrbuch*, IV, 1, 463–464; Mackinnon, *Martin Luther*, III, 306–307; Enders, III, 423–425; Clemen, *Z. K. G.*, XVIII, 353 ff.; Enders, III, 412–421.

77. For Luther's reply to Hoen, *W. A.*, XI, 431 ff.

78. Eells, *Martin Bucer*, p. 72.

79. Seeberg, *Lehrbuch*, IV, 1, 458. After 1524 John 6 became the *sedes doctrinae* for the Reformed group, which insisted that "est" meant "significat."

80. Eells, *Martin Bucer*, p. 73.

81. Eells, *Martin Bucer*, p. 75; Luther's reply, *W. A.*, XXIII, 38 ff.

82. Eells, *Martin Bucer*, pp. 75–76.

83. Eells, *Martin Bucer*, pp. 75–76.

84. Althaus, *Luther-Jahrbuch*, XI, 8–10. For Luther's mature view see "Vom Abendmahl Christi, Bekenntnis, 1528," *W. A.*, XXVI, 241 ff.

85. Text, p. 445 ff.
86. Althaus, *Luther-Jahrbuch*, XI, 5–10.
87. Althaus, *Luther-Jahrbuch*, XI, 5–10; W. A., XXIII, 141, 242, 251; XXVI, 324, 332, 340; XXXIII, 224, 262.
88. W. A., XIX, 474 ff.; XXIII, 38 ff.; XXVI, 261 ff.
89. These were preached between March 28 and 29, 1526, W. A., XIX, 474–475.
90. W. A., XIX, 475–477. By October, 1526, a copy was in the hands of Oecolampadius.
91. W. A., XXIII, 38–44; Enders, VI, 124.
92. W. A., XXIII, 44; XXVI, 241.
93. W. A., XXIII, 38 ff., 44.
94. W. A., XXIII, 44 ff.; XXVI, 241–242; C. R., I, 865; Enders, VI, 108, 116.
95. On Luther's illness, Enders, VI, 77, 111; W. A., XXVI, 244. For his wife's illness, W. A., XXVI, 244 ff.
96. Luther had begun his reply by December 31, 1527, W. A., XXVI, 244 ff.; Enders, VI, 168. He wrote only once more on the Lord's Supper, *Kurz Bekenntnis vom heiligen Sacrament*, in 1544, W. A., XXVI, 248.
97. Enders, VI, 200, 204, 233, 265.
98. Capito wrote Zwingli, April 15, 1528, that the tract contained much "Galle," Zwingli, *Opera*, VIII, 160, 166; W. A., XXVI, 247–248.
99. W. A., XXVI, 248; Zwingli, *Opera*, VIII, 165, 191.
100. Eells, *Martin Bucer*, p. 85 ff.
101. Eells, *Martin Bucer*, p. 85 ff.
102. W. A., XXX, Pt. III, 82.
103. Johannes von Walter, "Der Reichstag zu Augsburg 1530," pp. 6–7. W. A., XXX, Pt. III, 82; Kattenbusch, "Protestantismus," R. E., XVI (1905), 135 ff.; and for the modern significance to Germany, Kurt Leese, *Die Religion des Protestantischen Menschen* (Munich, 1948), pp. 16–21.
104. W. A., XXX, Pt. III, 82–85; Th. Kolde, *Der Tag von Schleiz und die Entstehung der Schwabacher Artikel, Beitraege zur Reformationsgeschichte* (Gotha, 1896), pp. 98–99. Reu believes they were written sometime between the Saalfeld and Marburg meetings of July 8 and September 14, *Augsburg Confession*, pp. 22–29.
105. For a good background of the Marburg Colloquy see Hans von Schubert, "Beitraege zur Geschichte der evangelischen Bekenntnis- und Buendnisbildung," Z. K. G., VII (1908), 323 ff.
106. W. A., "Briefe," V, 161, n. 4; Koehler, *Religionsgespraech*, p. 1 ff.; W. A., XXX, Pt. III, 97 ff.
107. C. R., I, 1095; Koehler, *Religionsgespraech*, p. 1 ff., for the Lutherans who participated; T. S. K., p. 513.
108. W. A., "Briefe," V, 161, n. 4.
109. W. A., XXX, Pt. III, 144, for Osiander's report.
110. Althaus, *Luther-Jahrbuch*, XI, 11; W. A., XVIII, 166.

111. *W. A.*, XXVI, 487.

112. Althaus, *Luther-Jahrbuch*, XI, 13; *W. A.*, XXVI, 446.

113. Seeberg, *Lehrbuch*, IV, 1, 464—475, *passim;* Althaus, *Luther-Jahrbuch*, XI, 20 ff.

114. Althaus, *Luther-Jahrbuch*, XI, 20—22.

115. *W. A.*, XXIII, 201, 243, 253; XXVI, 351; Seeberg, *Lehrbuch*, IV, 475 to 477.

116. *W. A.*, XXIII, 141, 181; XXV, 64.

117. Seeberg, *Lehrbuch*, IV, 1, 469—470.

118. Althaus, *Luther-Jahrbuch*, XI, 20—21.

119. Gennrich, *Die Christologie Luthers im Abendmahlsstreit 1524—1529* (Berlin, 1929), p. 129; Althaus, *Luther-Jahrbuch*, XI, 25, n. 76.

120. *W. A.*, XXIII, 243, 251; XXXIII, 224, 262; XXVI, 321; XXXIII, 154; XLIII, 581; XLVII, 86, 199; L, 587.

121. *W. A.*, XVIII, 87: "How all this is possible, or how He can appear in the bread, we do not know, nor are we able to comprehend it; we are to believe God's Word rather than order standards or ways for God."

122. *W. A.*, XXVI, 479.

123. *W. A.*, XIX, 507; XXIII, 179, 211, 261, 279; XXXIII, 219; Althaus, *Luther-Jahrbuch*, XI, 20—21.

124. Note 120, Chapter Twenty-one.

125. *W. A.*, XXVI, 332.

126. Seeberg, *Lehrbuch*, IV, 469—472.

127. *W. A.*, XIX, 492; XXIII, 151.

128. *W. A.*, XXVI, 330, 336—337; XIX, 387, 500.

129. *W. A.*, XXVI, 405; Enders, VI, 124, 233.

130. Seeberg, *Lehrbuch*, IV, 1, 458—459.

131. Koehler, *Zwingli und Luther* (Leipzig, 1924), I, 257.

132. *C. R.*, I, 865; Koehler, *Religionsgespraech*, pp. 36—37; *W. A.*, XXVI, 242.

133. Seeberg, *Lehrbuch*, IV, 1, 460—461.

134. Seeberg, *Lehrbuch*, IV, 1, 458—459.

135. *W. A.*, XXX, Pt. III, 94.

136. *W. A.*, "*Briefe*," V, 161, n. 4; Koehler, *Religionsgespraech*, p. 1 ff.; *W. A.*, XXX, Pt. III, 97 ff.

137. Koehler, *Religionsgespraech*, p. 5 ff.; *W. A.*, XXX, Pt. III, 93, n. 1, 152; *W. A.*, "*Briefe*," V, 160; *C. R.*, I, 1099—1102.

138. *W. A.*, XXX, Pt. III, 92 ff.

139. *C. R.*, I, 1099—1102.

140. *C. R.*, I, 1099—1102.

141. *C. R.*, I, 1102—1106.

142. Koehler, *Religionsgespraech*, pp. 16, 22.

143. *C. R.*, I, 1103; Enders, VII, 168; *W. A.*, "*Briefe*," V, 160—161.

144. Osiander wrote: "Nichts fruchtpars aussgericht," *W. A.*, XXX, Pt. III, 144; Brenz: "illa collatione nihil effectum est," p. 152. Cf. p. 110 ff.

145. Koehler, *Religionsgespraech*, p. 17 ff.

146. *W. A.*, XXX, Pt. III, 110: "Hora sexta die secunda octobris." Koehler, *Religionsgespraech*, p. 5 ff.

147. Brenz reported: "The number of those present at the colloquy was between 50 and 60." *W. A.*, XXX, Pt. III, 152.

148. *W. A.*, XXX, Pt. III, 152.

149. Osiander observed: "Fuerst in aigner person vom anfanng bisz an das enndt" was present, *W. A.*, XXX, Pt. III, 144.

150. *W. A.*, XXX, Pt. III, 110.

151. *W. A.*, XXX, Pt. III, 110. Text, p. 708.

152. Koehler, *Religionsgespraech*, pp. 7—8.

153. Koehler, *Religionsgespraech*, p. 8 ff.; *W. A.*, XXX, Pt. III, 111 f.

154. Koehler, *Religionsgespraech*, pp. 8 ff., 14—15, 19—20.

155. Koehler, *Religionsgespraech*, pp. 17—20, 28, 31.

156. Text, p. 703.

157. Koehler, *Religionsgespraech*, pp. 13—14, 17—19.

158. Koehler, *Religionsgespraech*, p. 19.

159. Koehler, *Religionsgespraech*, p. 19.

160. Koehler, *Religionsgespraech*, p. 19.

161. Koehler, *Religionsgespraech*, p. 21 ff.

162. Koehler, *Religionsgespraech*, p. 23.

163. Koehler, *Religionsgespraech*, p. 25.

164. Koehler, *Religionsgespraech*, pp. 30—31.

165. Koehler, *Religionsgespraech*, p. 22 ff.

166. Koehler, *Religionsgespraech*, pp. 35—36.

167. Koehler, *Religionsgespraech*, p. 37.

168. Koehler, *Religionsgespraech*, p. 37; *W. A.*, XXX, Pt. III, 143.

169. Koehler, *Religionsgespraech*, p. 37.

170. Koehler, *Religionsgespraech*, p. 37.

171. Koehler, *Religionsgespraech*, p. 37.

172. Reu, *Augsburg Confession*, Pt. I, p. 32.

173. Reu, *Augsburg Confession*, Pt. II, p. 44.

174. Reu, *Augsburg Confession*, Pt. II, p. 44.

175. Reu, *Augsburg Confession*, Pt. I, p. 32.

176. Reu, *Augsburg Confession*, Pt. I, p. 32, n. 44; Pt. II, pp. 44—47.

177. Reu, *Augsburg Confession*, Pt. I, p. 32, n. 44; Pt. II, pp. 44—47.

178. Reu, *Augsburg Confession*, Pt. II, pp. 46—47.

179. Koehler, *Religionsgespraech*, pp. 38, 129—130.

180. Smith, *Correspondence*, I, 80—83.

181. Eells, *Martin Bucer*, p. 77 ff.

182. Eells, *Martin Bucer*, pp. 77—78.

183. Eells, *Martin Bucer*, pp. 77—78.

184. Eells, *Martin Bucer*, p. 78.

185. Eells, *Martin Bucer*, pp. 78—80.

186. Smith, *Correspondence*, II, 378.

187. Eells, *Martin Bucer*, pp. 81—82.

188. Eells, *Martin Bucer*, pp. 81—82.

189. Koehler, *Religionsgespraech*, p. 39.

190. Koehler, *Religionsgespraech*, p. 38.

191. W. A., XXX, Pt. III, 150.

192. W. A., XXX, Pt. III, 150; Koehler, *Religionsgespraech*, pp. 139—140.

193. W. A., XXX, Pt. III, 151.

194. Koehler, *Religionsgespraech*, pp. 140—141.

195. W. A., XXX, Pt. III, 92, 96; Reu, *Augsburg Confession*, Pt. II, pp. 44—47.

196. Schubert, *Der Reichstag von Augsburg;* Kuehn, *Luther-Jahrbuch*, XI
   (1929); Walter, "Der Reichstag zu Augsburg 1530"; Reu, *Augsburg
   Confession;* and Johannes Ficker, "Die Augsburgische Konfession in ihrer
   ersten Gestalt als gemeinsames Bekenntnis deutscher Reichsstaende,"
   Schriften der Gesellschaft der Freunde der Universitaet Halle-Wittenberg
   (Halle, 1930).

197. Schubert, *Der Reichstag von Augsburg*, p. 3.

198. Walter, "Der Reichstag zu Augsburg 1530," p. 1.

199. Schubert, *Der Reichstag von Augsburg*, pp. 7—8; *Deutsche Reichstagsakten*, J. F., II, 189—191.

200. Schubert, *Der Reichstag von Augsburg*, pp. 18, 20.

201. Reu, *Augsburg Confession*, p. 39; Walter, "Der Reichstag zu Augsburg
   1530," pp. 1—2.

202. Schubert, *Der Reichstag von Augsburg*, pp. 19—20.

203. Walter, "Der Reichstag zu Augsburg 1530," pp. 5—6; Reu, *Augsburg
   Confession*, p. 39.

204. Walter, "Der Reichstag zu Augsburg 1530," pp. 5—7, 17—18.

205. Walter, "Der Reichstag zu Augsburg 1530," pp. 3—4.

206. Walter, "Der Reichstag zu Augsburg 1530," p. 5.

207. Walter, "Der Reichstag zu Augsburg 1530," p. 7; Reu, *Augsburg Confession*, pp. 69—72.

208. Schubert, *Der Reichstag von Augsburg*, pp. 19—20; Reu, *Augsburg Confession*, pp. 69—72, for the text.

209. Walter, "Der Reichstag zu Augsburg 1530," pp. 8—11; Reu, *Augsburg
   Confession*, pp. 43—44; W. A., XXX, Pt. II, 269; Wilhelm Gussmann,
   *Quellen und Forschungen zur Geschichte des Augsburgischen Glaubens-
   bekenntnisses* (Leipzig und Berlin, 1911), I, 1, 327.

210. Walter, "Der Reichstag zu Augsburg 1530," pp. 10—11.

211. Walter, "Der Reichstag zu Augsburg 1530," pp. 10—11.
212. Walter, "Der Reichstag zu Augsburg 1530," p. 12.
213. Walter, "Der Reichstag zu Augsburg 1530," p. 12.
214. Reu, *Augsburg Confession*, pp. 21—29, for a discussion of the background of these articles; Schubert, *Der Reichstag von Augsburg*, pp. 20—21.
215. These articles were written between July 26 and September 14, 1529, Reu, *Augsburg Confession*, pp. 28—29.
216. Reu, *Augsburg Confession*, pp. 34—35.
217. Reu, *Augsburg Confession*, p. 36.
218. W. A., "*Briefe*," V and VI, for the years from 1529 to 1531, which consistently show Luther's passive attitude.
219. Walter, "Der Reichstag zu Augsburg 1530," pp. 6—7, 8; C. R., II, 167.
220. Walter, "Der Reichstag zu Augsburg 1530," pp. 23—25.
221. Walter, "Der Reichstag zu Augsburg 1530," pp. 23—25; Brieger, "Die Torgauer Artikel," p. 272 ff.; Schubert, *Der Reichstag von Augsburg*, pp. 21—22.
222. Brieger, "Die Torgauer Artikel," p. 272 ff.
223. Schubert, *Der Reichstag von Augsburg*, pp. 20—21.
224. See Luther's tract of 1539, *Von Konzilien und Kirchen*, W. A., L, 509—553.
225. Kuehn, *Luther-Jahrbuch*, XI (1929), 59 ff.; Schubert, *Der Reichstag von Augsburg*, pp. 16—17.
226. Kuehn, *Luther-Jahrbuch*, XI, 59 ff.; Schubert, *Der Reichstag von Augsburg*, pp. 19—20; Foerstemann, *Urkundenbuch*, I, 4 ff.
227. Walter, "Der Reichstag zu Augsburg 1530," p. 12 ff.; Gussmann, *Quellen*, p. 249 ff.
228. Walter, "Der Reichstag zu Augsburg 1530," pp. 13—16.
229. Walter, "Der Reichstag zu Augsburg 1530," pp. 16, 20—22.
230. Gussmann, *Quellen*, p. 257; Walter, "Der Reichstag zu Augsburg 1530," pp. 27—28.
231. Walter, "Der Reichstag zu Augsburg 1530," pp. 27—28.
232. Reu, *Augsburg Confession*, p. 47.
233. Gussmann, *Quellen*, p. 257.
234. Gussmann, *Quellen*, p. 257; Walter, "Der Reichstag zu Augsburg 1530," pp. 27—28.
235. Reu, *Augsburg Confession*, pp. 52—54; Walter, "Der Reichstag zu Augsburg 1530," pp. 25—26.
236. Walter, "Der Reichstag zu Augsburg 1530," pp. 25—26.
237. Walter, "Der Reichstag zu Augsburg 1530," pp. 25—26.
238. Walter, "Der Reichstag zu Augsburg 1530," pp. 25—26.
239. C. R., II, 39 ff.; Walter, "Der Reichstag zu Augsburg 1530," pp. 26—27; Reu, *Augsburg Confession*, p. 54.
240. Walter, "Der Reichstag zu Augsburg 1530," pp. 15—16, 27—28; Schubert, *Der Reichstag von Augsburg*, pp. 21—22.

241. Walter, "Der Reichstag zu Augsburg 1530," pp. 27—28.

242. Walter, "Der Reichstag zu Augsburg 1530," p. 28.

243. Reu, *Augsburg Confession*, p. 54.

244. Walter, "Der Reichstag zu Augsburg 1530," pp. 27—29, cf. 15—16.

245. Reu, *Augsburg Confession*, p. 80.

246. Walter, "Der Reichstag zu Augsburg 1530," pp. 17—18.

247. Reu, *Augsburg Confession*, pp. 57—58.

248. Reu, *Augsburg Confession*, p. 58 ff.; Schubert, *Der Reichstag von Augsburg*, p. 22.

249. Reu, *Augsburg Confession*, pp. 80—82.

250. Reu, *Augsburg Confession*, pp. 63—65; *C. R.*, II, 45.

251. Enders, VIII, 20 ff., 190, 191, 220—222, 258—259.

252. Reu, *Augsburg Confession*, p. 63.

253. Reu, *Augsburg Confession*, p. 64.

254. Reu, *Augsburg Confession*, p. 64 ff. Schubert, *Der Reichstag von Augsburg*, pp. 22—23.

255. *C. R.*, II, 47; translated by Reu, *Augsburg Confession*, p. 68.

256. *C. R.*, II, 45; translated by Reu, *Augsburg Confession*, p. 64.

257. Reu, *Augsburg Confession*, p. 68.

258. *C. R.*, II, 47; *E. A.*, LIV, 145; Reu, *Augsburg Confession*, pp. 68—69; Schubert, *Der Reichstag von Augsburg*, pp. 22—23.

259. *C. R.*, II, 56—61; Reu, *Augsburg Confession*, p. 68—72.

260. *C. R.*, II, 59 f.; Reu, *Augsburg Confession*, p. 84.

261. Reu, *Augsburg Confession*, pp. 84—90.

262. Reu, *Augsburg Confession*, pp. 84—90; Ficker, "Die Augsburgische Confession, etc.," *Schriften der Gesellschaft der Freunde der Universitaet Halle-Wittenberg*, p. 12 ff.

263. Walter, "Der Reichstag zu Augsburg 1530," p. 41 ff.; Reu, *Augsburg Confession*, pp. 97—101.

264. Reu, *Augsburg Confession*, pp. 103—105.

265. Reu, *Augsburg Confession*, p. 105.

266. Reu, *Augsburg Confession*, pp. 86—89.

267. Reu, *Augsburg Confession*, pp. 86—89.

268. Reu, *Augsburg Confession*, p. 103.

269. Reu, *Augsburg Confession*, p. 107; Ficker, "Die Augsburgische Confession, etc.," *Schriften der Gesellschaft der Freunde der Universitaet Halle-Wittenberg*, pp. 13—15.

270. Walter, "Der Reichstag zu Augsburg 1530," p. 37 ff.; Reu, *Augsburg Confession*, pp. 90—94.

271. Walter, "Der Reichstag zu Augsburg 1530," p. 38.

272. Walter, "Der Reichstag zu Augsburg 1530," pp. 38—39; Schubert, *Der Reichstag von Augsburg*, pp. 25—26.

273. Walter, "Der Reichstag zu Augsburg 1530," pp. 38—39.

274. Walter, "Der Reichstag zu Augsburg 1530," p. 39.

275. Walter, "Der Reichstag zu Augsburg 1530," p. 39.

276. Reu, *Augsburg Confession*, p. 93.

277. Reu, *Augsburg Confession*, pp. 93–95.

278. Walter, "Der Reichstag zu Augsburg 1530," p. 40 ff.; Reu, *Augsburg Confession*, pp. 96–101; Enders, VII, 324.

279. Reu, *Augsburg Confession*, pp. 97–99; Walter, "Der Reichstag zu Augsburg 1530," p. 41 ff.

280. Reu, *Augsburg Confession*, pp. 97–99.

281. Walter, "Der Reichstag zu Augsburg 1530, " pp. 44–45.

282. *C. R.*, II, 116 ff.

283. Walter, "Der Reichstag zu Augsburg 1530," p. 45.

284. Walter, "Der Reichstag zu Augsburg 1530," pp. 45–46.

285. Reu, *Augsburg Confession*, pp. 103–104, 105–107.

286. Walter, "Der Reichstag zu Augsburg 1530," p. 46.

287. Walter, "Der Reichstag zu Augsburg 1530," pp. 46–47.

288. Walter, "Der Reichstag zu Augsburg 1530," pp. 46–47.

289. Walter, "Der Reichstag zu Augsburg 1530," p. 47.

290. Walter, "Der Reichstag zu Augsburg 1530," p. 47.

291. Walter, "Der Reichstag zu Augsburg 1530," p. 48.

292. *C. R.*, II, 127; Reu, *Augsburg Confession*, pp. 107–108.

293. Ficker, "Die Augsburgische Confession, etc.," *Schriften der Gesellschaft der Freunde der Universitaet Halle-Wittenberg*, p. 12; Walter, "Der Reichstag zu Augsburg 1530," p. 48.

294. Reu, *Augsburg Confession*, Pt. II, p. 36 ff., Pt. I, p. 107.

295. Reu, *Augsburg Confession*, Pt. I, p. 109.

296. Walter, "Der Reichstag zu Augsburg 1530," p. 48.

297. Walter, "Der Reichstag zu Augsburg 1530," p. 48 ff.

298. *C. R.*, II, 128; Enders, VIII, 31; Reu, *Augsburg Confession,* p. 110.

299. Walter, "Der Reichstag zu Augsburg 1530," pp. 50–51.

300. Walter, "Der Reichstag zu Augsburg 1530," pp. 51–52.

301. Walter, "Der Reichstag zu Augsburg 1530," pp. 51–52.

302. *C. R.*, II, 128 ff.

303. *C. R.*, II, 128 ff.

304. Reu, *Augsburg Confession*, p. 110.

305. Walter, "Der Reichstag zu Augsburg 1530," p. 52.

306. Reu, *Augsburg Confession*, p. 110.

307. Mueller, *Annalen*, p. 84; 1. 40–50.

308. Ficker, "Die Augsburgische Confession, etc.," *Schriften der Gesellschaft der Freunde der Universitaet Halle-Wittenberg*, pp. 13–15.

309. Reu, *Augsburg Confession,* p. 105.

310. Reu, *Augsburg Confession,* p. 105.

311. W. A., *"Briefe,"* V, 427—429, and n. 5; Brenz, C. R., II, 245—246.

312. Reu, *Augsburg Confession,* pp. 112—113; Walter, "Der Reichstag zu Augsburg 1530," pp. 52—53.

313. Reu, *Augsburg Confession,* pp. 112—113.

314. W. A., *"Briefe,"* V, 440—441, and n. 3; Walter, "Der Reichstag zu Augsburg 1530," pp. 64—65.

315. W. A., L, 161, and n. 2. For Luther's reaction, W. A., *"Briefe,"* V, 435—436, and n. 4, 581, 587—597, 622—628; C. R., II, 363—364: "Philip has become more childish than a child."

316. W. A., L, 160 ff., 192—254.

317. Reu, *Augsburg Confession,* pp. 114—115.

318. Walter, "Der Reichstag zu Augsburg 1530," p. 56 ff.

319. Reu, *Augsburg Confession,* p. 115.

320. Reu, *Augsburg Confession,* pp. 118—120.

321. Reu, *Augsburg Confession,* p. 119.

322. Reu, *Augsburg Confession,* pp. 120—122; Walter, "Der Reichstag zu Augsburg 1530," pp. 71—72; Johannes Ficker, *Die Konfutation des Augsburgischen Bekenntnisses, ihre Gestalt und ihre Geschichte* (Leipzig, 1891), pp. lviii—lxxv; W. A., *"Briefe,"* V, 509, n. 2.

323. Eells, *Martin Bucer,* pp. 99—102; Walter, "Der Reichstag zu Augsburg 1530," pp. 62—66, *passim;* W. A., *"Briefe,"* V, 513—514, n. 9, 566—572.

324. Reu, *Augsburg Confession,* p. 124; Ficker, *Die Konfutation,* p. lviii ff.

325. Walter, "Der Reichstag zu Augsburg 1530," pp. 72—73; Reu, *Augsburg Confession,* pp. 124—126; Ficker, *Die Konfutation,* p. lxxxviii; W. A., *"Briefe,"* V, 533—538; C. R., II, 245, 250—252.

326. Walter, "Der Reichstag zu Augsburg 1530," pp. 72—73.

327. The words were really those of the Roman legate Campegio, who hoped to intimidate the Lutherans with an implied threat, but they had been revised by the Emperor's officials. Walter, "Der Reichstag zu Augsburg 1530," pp. 71—72.

328. Walter, "Der Reichstag zu Augsburg 1530," p. 73; Ficker, *Die Konfutation,* p. lxxxvii ff.; W. A., *"Briefe,"* V, 533—538.

329. C. R., II, 250.

330. Baumgartner, C. R., II, 363—364, 268—270, 227, 243—244; Reu, *Augsburg Confession,* p. 129.

331. Reu, *Augsburg Confession,* pp. 128—129.

332. Reu, *Augsburg Confession,* pp. 128—131.

333. W. A., *"Briefe,"* V, 490, n. 4; Reu, *Augsburg Confession,* pp. 128—129.

334. Reu, *Augsburg Confession,* pp. 130—132.

335. Reu, *Augsburg Confession,* pp. 130—132.

336. Reu, *Augsburg Confession,* p. 132.

337. *C. R.,* II, 363–364.

338. W. A., *"Briefe,"* V, 578; Enders, VIII, 218; translation from Reu, *Augsburg Confession,* Pt. II, p. 387.

339. Walter, "Der Reichstag zu Augsburg 1530," pp. 85–86; Schubert, *Der Reichstag von Augsburg,* p. 31.

340. Reu, *Augsburg Confession,* Pt. II, p. 391, Pt. I, pp. 15–25.

341. Walter, "Der Reichstag zu Augsburg 1530," pp. 85–86.

342. Walter, "Der Reichstag zu Augsburg 1530," pp. 85–86.

343. Schubert, *Der Reichstag von Augsburg,* p. 31. Reu, *Augsburg Confession,* Pt. II, p. 51.

344. Walter, "Der Reichstag zu Augsburg 1530," pp. 85–86; Schubert, *Der Reichstag von Augsburg,* p. 31.

345. Walter, "Der Reichstag zu Augsburg 1530," pp. 85–86.

346. W. A., *"Briefe,"* V, 631–632, and n. 8; Reu, *Augsburg Confession,* pp. 128–129, 138.

347. Reu, *Augsburg Confession,* p. 138.

348. Reu, *Augsburg Confession,* p. 139.

349. Reu, *Augsburg Confession,* p. 140.

350. Reu, *Augsburg Confession,* p. 141.

351. W. A., L, 175 ff.

352. Schubert, *Der Reichstag von Augsburg,* p. 32, n. 2.

353. Schubert, *Der Reichstag von Augsburg,* p. 34, believes the League was already in existence before the close of 1530.

354. Schubert, *Der Reichstag von Augsburg,* p. 32.

355. Schubert, *Der Reichstag von Augsburg,* p. 36.

356. Eells, *Martin Bucer,* pp. 103–108; W. A., *"Briefe,"* V, 467, n. 3.

357. Eells, *Martin Bucer,* pp. 103–108; W. A., *"Briefe,"* V, 562–564, 566 to 572.

358. Eells, *Martin Bucer,* p. 109.

359. The Battle of Cappel took place October 11, 1531, Karl Brandi, *Deutsche Reformation und Gegenreformation* (Leipzig, 1927), I, 242; Koehler, *Das Buch der Reformation Huldrych Zwinglis von ihm selbst und gleichzeitigen Quellen erzaehlt* (Muenchen, 1926), pp. 346–352.

360. W. A., *"Briefe,"* V, 658, n. 2; VI, 18–21, 24–26; *C. R.,* II, 470.

361. Eells, *Martin Bucer,* p. 160; *C. R.,* II, 675.

362. W. A., *"Briefe,"* VII, 145–146, n. 2; W. A., XXXVIII, 297 ff.; Baum, *Capito und Butzer,* p. 498 ff.; Roth, *Augsburger Reformationsgeschichte,* II, 184 ff.; Hausrath, *Luthers Leben,* II, 252–253.

363. W. A., *"Briefe,"* VII, 195–196; Roth, *Augsburger Reformationsgeschichte,* II, 181 ff., 241 ff.; W. A., *"Briefe,"* VII, 210–212.

364. W. A., *"Briefe,"* VII, 195–196, 198, n. 3: "Ain kurtzer einfeltiger bericht, etc."; 199, "Beilage"; cf. 220—221, 234, 247–248, 252–254, 256–266, 272–273, 287–289.

365. The exchange of letters was begun by Bucer and Capito, who had written Luther on February 4, 1536, *W. A.*, VII, 357–359, to which Luther replied March 25, 1536, 378–379, but the letter did not reach Augsburg until April 11. Cf. Roth, *Augsburger Reformationsgeschichte*, II, 256 f.

366. *W. A.*, *"Briefe,"* VII, 409, 413; Enders, X, 336, *Bemerkungen*. There is a conflict in the sources as to whether the delegations met at Torgau or Grimma.

367. Enders, X, 333, n. 1.

368. Eells, *Martin Bucer*, p. 200.

369. Eells, *Martin Bucer*, p. 198: Adolf Hausrath, *Luthers Leben* (Berlin, 1904), II, 356. *W. A.*, *"Briefe,"* VII, 411–413, "Beilage"; *Z. K. G.*, XXXIV, 98; Enders, XI, 271; *A. R.*, XIII, 31, 3.

370. Eells, *Martin Bucer*, p. 198 ff.; Hausrath, *Luthers Leben*, II, 356–357; A. E. Berger, *Martin Luther* (Berlin, 1921), III, 160–161.

371. Eells, *Martin Bucer*, p. 199.

372. Hausrath, *Luthers Leben*, II, 357–358; Eells, *Martin Bucer*, p. 200.

373. Eells, *Martin Bucer*, p. 200; Walch, XVII, 2037, 2110, 2111.

374. Luther wrote to Margrave George of Brandenburg in a letter of May 30, 1536: "They freely accepted our Confession and Apology and promised to teach and practice it." *W. A.*, *"Briefe,"* VII, 425.

375. Eells, *Martin Bucer*, p. 201; Hausrath, *Luthers Leben*, II, 358; Georg Buchwald, *Doctor Martin Luther* (Leipzig, 1917), pp. 459–460.

376. Berger, *Martin Luther*, III, 161; Hausrath, *Luthers Leben*, II, 358.

377. Buchwald, *Doctor Martin Luther*, p. 460.

378. Buchwald, *Doctor Martin Luther*, p. 460; Berger, *Martin Luther*, III, 161.

379. Berger, *Martin Luther*, III, 162; *Kirchliches Handlexikon*, ed., Carl Mensel *et al.* (Leipzig, 1902), VII, 286–287.

380. *W. A.*, *"Briefe,"* VII, 420–422, "Beilage." Cf. *C. R.*, III, 224.

381. Eells, *Martin Bucer*, p. 202 ff.

382. Enders, X, 341–342; *Z. K. G.*, XIII, 333; *E. A.*, LV, 136—137, all indicate Luther's attempts toward peace; cf. *E. A.*, LV, 138, n. 530.

383. Hausrath, *Luthers Leben*, II, 363. The bull of Paul III appeared June 2, 1536, summoning a Council at Mantua for May 23, 1537. *W. A.*, L, 165, and n. 1.

384. *W. A.*, L, 163 ff., *passim*.

385. Paul III was really a much better Pope than his predecessor Clement VII, *W. A.*, L, 163.

386. *W. A.*, L., 164; *W. A.*, *"Briefe,"* VII, 317–318, "Beilage"; cf. *W. A.*, *T. R.*, V, 6384, 6388; *R. E.*, XX, 546 ff.; Enders X, 267.

387. Enders, X, 267; *W. A.*, L, 164; Berger, *Martin Luther*, III, 23.

388. *W. A.*, L, 164; cf. *C. R.*, II, 962 f., 982 f., 987; Friedensburg, *Nuntiaturberichte*, I, 539 ff., 553.

389. *W. A.*, L, 164.

390. *W. A.*, L, 164.

391. *W. A.*, L, 164—165.

392. *W. A.*, L, 161; *C. R.*, III, 156 f.; *W. A.*, *"Briefe,"* VII, 605, 614, n. 1; *A. R.*, XX, 81.

393. *W. A.*, L, 161; *W. A.*, *"Briefe,"* VII, 614, n. 4.

394. *W. A.*, L, 161: "The Schmalkald Articles are, therefore, Luther's emancipation from Melanchthon's 'Leisetreterei' of 1530."

395. Spalatin, *Annales*, p. 307; *W. A.*, L, 173, n. 4; *W. A.*, *"Briefe,"* VIII, 2—3.

396. *W. A.*, L, 174; *W. A.*, *"Briefe,"* VIII, 2—3.

397. *W. A.*, L, 174; *W. A.*, *"Briefe,"* VIII, 4—6, for the Elector's appreciation.

398. *W. A.*, *"Briefe,"* VII, 613—614, 620—621; *W. A.*, L, 175.

399. *W. A.*, L, 175, states that some forty theologians attended; Kolde, *T. S. K.* (1894), p. 157 ff., asserts that later changes in the text altered the original Luther reading which more closely resembled the Wittenberg Concord agreement.

400. *W. A.*, L, 175.

401. *W. A.*, L, 175—176; *C. R.*, III, 270 f., 292; Kolde, *Analecta Lutherana*, p. 293.

402. *W. A.*, L, 176. Melanchthon's original tract read: *Tractatus de potestate de primatu Papae.* Cf. *C. R.*, III, 271, 286—288.

403. *C. R.*, III, 271, 286—288; *W. A.*, L, 176.

404. *W. A.*, L, 176.

405. *W. A.*, L, 177.

406. *W. A.*, L, 177.

407. *W. A.*, L, 177—178; *R. E.*, IV, 293 ff.

408. Text, p. 691.

409. *W. A.*, L, 164.

410. Schwiebert, *Church History*, XVII (1948), 24, n. 111.

411. Quotations on the Church are numerous in Luther's writings; a few of the more typical are *W. A.*, VI, 296—297; VII, 683 ff., 710; *E. A.*, XXV, 412; Ernst Rietschel, *S. V. R. G.*, CLIV (1932), 1—109.

412. *W. A.*, L, 509—553.

413. Schwiebert, *Church History*, XVII, 3—8.

414. Smith, *The Age of the Reformation*, p. 163. The Council of Trent, 1545—1563, established the official position of the Roman Catholic Church in matters of doctrine. Thomism was made the official theological position, and the *Index*, controlling Roman Catholic thought from the days of Pope Gregory VII's *Dictatus*, had now fully matured.

415. Melanchthon's "De Ecclesia" states in his *Loci* of 1543: "The Evangelical is the true Catholic Church," *C. R.*, XXI, 506, 825 ff.; Karl Rieker, *Die rechtliche Stellung der evangelischen Kirche in ihrer geschichtlichen Entwicklung bis zur Gegenwart* (Leipzig, 1893), pp. 46—49.

416. Walch, XXI, 288—289; *W. A.*, L, 509—553.

CHAPTER TWENTY-TWO

1. Bainton, *Church History*, XVII (1948), 193 ff., for new evaluation.

2. Boehmer, *L. L. R. R.*, p. 227 ff.; Mackinnon, *Martin Luther*, IV, 265–272; *C. R.*, III, 855–856; Enders, XIII, 80; XIV, 152; and "Fuenf Lutherbriefe," *T. S. K.* (1913), p. 299.

3. Boehmer, *L. L. R. R.*, p. 180; Enders, XIII, 80; Mackinnon, *Martin Luther*, IV, 269, and n. 10.

4. Mackinnon, *Martin Luther*, IV, 269; Boehmer, *L. L. R. R.*, p. 227 ff.

5. Enders, XIII, 80, letter of June 10, 1540, to the Elector.

6. Enders' correspondence from the middle twenties on contains many instances of cases which were presented to the theological faculty of the University of Wittenberg for *Gutachten*. Modern tolerance is not much in evidence in Western Europe until after the Thirty Years' War.

7. Mackinnon, *Martin Luther*, IV, 161–179.

8. Mackinnon, *Martin Luther*, IV, 179–192; *W. A.*, XIII, 153 ff.; *Z. K. G.*, IV, 301 ff.; *C. R.*, III, 454; Enders, XI, 290, 323–324; *W. A.*, XXXIX, Pt. I, 345 ff.

9. *W. A.*, L, 69 ff.; *E. A.*, XXV, 176 ff.

10. Mackinnon, *Martin Luther*, IV, 128.

11. In the earlier collections of Luther's works these attacks and Luther's replies were often printed together. Walch, XV and XVIII, contain many of the writings of Luther's enemies to which his tracts were in reply. A thorough study of the use of the *Flugschriften* is necessary for a complete understanding of this period. See note 4, Chapter One.

12. *W. A.*, L, 509 ff.; Holman, *W. M. L.*, V, 131–300.

13. *W. A.*, LI, 469–572.

14. Smith, *The Age of the Reformation*, p. 120.

15. *W. A.*, XXVI, 109 ff.; *E. A.*, LIV, 206 ff.

16. Smith, *The Age of the Reformation*, p. 123.

17. Smith, *The Age of the Reformation*, p. 123.

18. Mackinnon, *Martin Luther*, IV, 142; *W. A.*, XXVI, 200.

19. Smith, *The Age of the Reformation*, p. 124.

20. The story is told in considerable detail in Walch, XXI, 279 ff. It is interesting to note that Luther's enemies assumed he had died a natural death until several decades after he had passed away. The account of the Roman Catholic apothecary Landau must be subjected to severe scrutiny in the light of the eyewitness accounts. For an evaluation of the official report see Walther, *Zur Wertung der deutschen Reformation* (Leipzig, 1909), p. 174 ff.; Christof Schubert, *Die Berichte ueber Luthers Tod und Begraebnis Texte und Untersuchungen* (Weimar, 1917); O. Albrecht, "Berichte ueber Luthers Tod," *Theologische Studien und Kritiken* (1919), pp. 335–353; Mackinnon, *Martin Luther*, IV, 210, n. 20. For other literature consult Karl Schottenloher, *Bibliographie zur deutschen Geschichte im Zeitalter der Glaubensspaltung 1517–1585* (Leipzig, 1933), I, 554–556.

21. Walch, XXI, 279–296.
22. Luther was 62 years, three months, and eight days of age when he died if the traditional date of his birth is accepted.
23. Boehmer, *L. L. R. R.*, pp. 203–204.
24. *W. A., "Briefe,"* IV, 221, n. 3.
25. Enders, XI, 197 ff.; *W. A., T. R.*, VI, 301–302; *W. A., "Briefe,"* VIII, 41, n. 14; see text, p. 599.
26. Enders, XIII, 318.
27. *W. A., T. R.*, IV, 416; Enders, XIII, 328, 351; XIV, 203, 218; XVI, 196, 249, 270–271. He even considered retiring to Zulsdorf, Enders, XVI, 270–271, 278 ff.
28. *W. A., T. R.*, IV, 416; Enders, XIII, 328, 351; XIV, 203, 218; XVI, 196, 249, 270–271, 278.
29. *Martin Luther* (Berlin, 1933), p. 264.
30. *Martin Luther* (Berlin, 1933), p. 264; Walch, XXI, 280–281, speaks of Luther's three sons, but the actual story of Luther's death indicates that only Martin and Paul accompanied their father.
31. Walch, XXI, 281; *W. A.*, LIV, 478–496.
32. Walch, XXI, 281; *Martin Luther* (Berlin, 1933), p. 266.
33. Walch, XXI, 281.
34. *Martin Luther* (Berlin, 1933), p. 266; Walch, XXI, 282.
35. Walch, XXI, 282.
36. *Martin Luther* (Berlin, 1933), p. 267; Walch, XXI, 275.
37. Walch, XXI, 284–285.
38. Walch, XXI, 276.
39. Walch, XXI, 276, 285. This was on the cot in the living room between nine and ten o'clock. Coelius, Jonas, Wirth, Martin, and Paul were at his side. The date was February 15, 1546.
40. Mathesius calls this room "seine Kammer," *Martin Luther* (Berlin, 1933), p. 268; Walch, XXI, 277.
41. Walch, XXI, 277.
42. Walch, XXI, 286.
43. Walch, XXI, 277.
44. Walch, XXI, 278.
45. Walch, XXI, 288–289.
46. Walch, XXI, 278–279, 290.
47. Walch, XXI, 290.
46. *Martin Luther* (Berlin, 1933), p. 270; Walch, XXI, 291.
49. *Martin Luther* (Berlin, 1933), pp. 289–295, contains Jonas' funeral address.
50. Walch, XXI, 291; *Martin Luther* (Berlin, 1933), p. 270.
51. Walch, XXI, 291.
52. Walch, XXI, 291–292.

53. Walch, XXI, 291–292: "Da sind auch weit ueber den Steinweg Buerger und Buergerinen entgegen kommen."

54. Walch, XXI, 292, 293; *Martin Luther* (Berlin, 1933), p. 270. The body rested in the church of Our Dear Lady in Halle, watched over by an honor guard.

55. *Martin Luther* (Berlin, 1933), p. 270; Walch, XXI, 293.

56. *Martin Luther* (Berlin, 1933), p. 270.

57. *Martin Luther* (Berlin, 1933), p. 270.

58. Walch, XXI, 293–294.

59. *Martin Luther* (Berlin, 1933), p. 272, also mentions Ciliax Kaufmann from Mansfeld.

60. Walch, XXI, 295, "etliche Tausend menschen."

61. Walch, XXI, 295, "gegen den Predigtstuhl niedergesetzt."

62. Walch, XXI, 295; *Martin Luther* (Berlin, 1933), pp. 296–301.

63. *Martin Luther* (Berlin, 1933), pp. 302–317, for Melanchthon's funeral address.

64. *Martin Luther* (Berlin, 1933), pp. 309–311.

65. Walch, XXI, 295.

66. Professor Heubner related this story to the author in 1936. He stated that the coffin was well preserved and the bones plainly discernible.

Index

A *Mighty Fortress*, 663, 672–675
Aachen, 39, 42–43, 242
Abelard, Peter, 163, 165–167, 306
Acta Augustana, 349, 368, 387
Address to the German Nobility, An,
    5, 43, 175, 443, 445, 447, 466–475,
    535, 558, 581, 619, 681
Adrian of Utrecht, 38–39, 47–48,
    430–431, 686
*Against Jack Sausage (Wider Hans
    Worst)*, 322, 746
Against the Heavenly Prophets, 550,
    697
Against the Idol of Halle, 523–524
*Against the Malicious Judgment of
    Eck*, 423
*Against the Murderous and Plunder-
    ing Bands Among the Peasants*,
    565–567
*Against the Papacy of Rome, Founded
    by the Devil*, 746
Agricola, 265, 490, 543, 564, 706,
    720, 741
Alber, Erasmus, 573–576, 579
Albert the Bear, 72, 74, 199–200
Albert of Mainz, 178, 185, 325, 378,
    379, 460–462, 488, 507, 510–511,
    582, 583, 746, election of, 306–308,
    indulgences, 308–322, 522–524
Albert of Mansfeld, 331, 354, 564
Albert I, Duke of Saxony, 75–76, 218
Albert II, 76, 200, 235
Albertus Magnus, 163, 263
*Album Academiae Vitebergensis (Ma-
    trikel)*, 3, 115, 205, 232, 255, 603,
    604
Aleander, 6, 7, 9, 42, 44–45, 152,
    429, 434, 484, 488, 489, 493–496,
    501–505, 508–512, 513, 573, 576,
    635, 685, 686
Alexander of Hales, 23, 304–305
Alexander V, 25
Alexander VI, 29, 180, 190, 307
Alexandria, 12, 403
Altes Friederici Collegium, 88, 201,
    205, 212, 221, 222, 232, 235
Althamer, 638
Althaus, Paul, 457, 568, 701
Alveld, Augustin von, 152, 423, 456,
    457, 463, 470, 473, 474

Ambrose, 357, 407, 410, 427
Amsdorf, Nicholas von, 5, 100–101,
    271, 294, 295, 398, 414, 416, 496,
    507, 508, 513–515, 528, 544,
    587–588, 592, 603, 607, 627, 630,
    632, 644, 654, 678, 741
Anabaptists, 449, 471, 617, 621, 642,
    677, 683, 684, 718, 722, 734, 736,
    737, 746
Anhalt, Prince William of, 118, 142
Anselm, 164, 167
Appeal to a General Council, 369
Aquinas, St. Thomas, 9, 135–136,
    157, 161, 163, 164, 166, 167, 168,
    338, 339, 341, 353, 357, 427, 639
Aristotle, 135, 136, 156, 163, 165,
    166, 167, 172, 176, 251, 272, 280,
    296, 298, 299, 328, 341, 357, 427
Ascanier, 75–78, 106, 200, 214, 218,
    240
Asterisks, 334–335
Athanasius, 163, 357, 393
Augsburg, 64, 67, 183, 184, 192, 334,
    371, 422, 677, 716, 720, 721
Augsburg Confession, 101, 219, 282,
    459, 616, 618, 646, 714–735, 738,
    739, 741–744
Augsburg, Diet of (1518), 339–342,
    345
Augsburg, Diet of (1530), 36, 58, 63,
    84, 714–735, 736, 740, 741
Augsburg, Peace of (1555), 54, 65,
    468
August, Elector of Saxony, 85, 214,
    221, 228, 229, 257, 260, 261–262,
    659
Augusteum (Augustinian College),
    85, 88, 221, 222, 227, 231–232,
    261, 262
Augustine, 17, 33, 152, 157, 158–163,
    167, 172–173, 176, 280, 285, 295,
    296, 329, 357, 393, 402, 403, 407,
    409, 427, 578, 609, 635, 642, 703
Augustinian Order of Hermits, 128,
    145–149, 155, 179, 224, 225
Aurifaber, 154, 656, 749
Aurogallus, 253, 598, 644, 649, 651
Avignon, 22, 24

Babylonian Captivity, 22, 614
Babylonian Captivity of the Church, The, 5, 316, 432–433, 445, 449, 473–477, 495, 535
Baccalaureus Biblicus, 149
Baptism, Sacrament of, 18, 160, 161, 331, 442, 446–449, 474, 476, 618, 619, 625, 629, 638, 640, 641, 738
Barbarossa, Khaireddin, 62, 64–65
Barnim, Duke of Pomerania, 391, 398, 408
Basel, 278, 322, 357, 427, 636, 640, 667, 686, 697
Basel, University of, 254, 360
Basil the Great, 393, 408
Bauer, Karl, 175, 466, 468
Baumgaertner, Jerome, 587–589
Beckmann, Otto, 271, 272, 442
Beier, Leonhard, 327, 346, 354
Bernard of Clairveaux, 161, 167, 170, 171, 174, 405, 406, 409, 524, 579, 584
Bernhard, Duke of Saxony, 72–75, 79, 199–200
Bernhardi, Bartholomaeus, 256, 294 –296, 301, 366–367, 581–582, 666
Beyer, Dr. Christian, 728–729
Bible, Discovery of, 119–123
Biblicus (lector), 149, 265, 609
Biel, Gabriel, 135, 136, 148, 156, 157, 168–169, 172–173, 290, 295
Bienna of Navarre, 17
Black Cloister (Erfurt), 136, 147
Black Cloister (Wittenberg), 85, 88, 95, 131, 193–196, 221–232, 264, 267, 258, 277, 282, 287, 314, 323, 324, 330, 367, 439, 526, 589, 592, 594
Blaurer, Thomas, 300, 573, 577
Boehmer, Heinrich, 1, 102, 131, 142, 144, 178–179, 287, 369, 395, 439, 465, 491, 515–516, 586, 745, 748
Boethius, 162, 165
Bologna, 178, 182, 192, 443
Bologna, University of, 16, 370
Bondage of the Will, The (De servo arbitrio), 578, 690–694
Boniface VIII, 22, 304
Boniface IX, 304, 312

Bora, Katharine von, 217, 226–227, 232, 264, 266–268, 573, 577, 581–601, 643, 751
Bossoegel, John William, 203
Brahe, Tycho, 136, 612
Bramante, 28, 184
Brandenburg, Bishop Jerome Schulze of, 321, 324, 419, 423
Brandi, Karl, 41, 43, 55
Brenz, Johannes, 57, 607, 616, 627, 630, 667, 678, 698, 700, 709, 713, 730
Brethren of the Common Life (Nullbrueder), 9, 119, 122, 714
Brieger, Theodor, 714, 730
Brisger, Eberhard, 226–227, 582
Brueck, Chancellor, 217, 253, 293, 494, 496, 600, 724, 728–729, 734, 735, 741, 742
Bucer, Martin, 328, 423, 486, 499, 550, 552, 646, 671, 683, 684, 695–714, 731, 736–739
Bugenhagen, Johannes, 5, 57, 99, 150, 217, 234, 262, 265, 525, 527, 582, 589, 592, 594, 598, 599, 600, 603, 607, 610, 616, 621, 622, 624, 627, 649, 671, 678, 679, 711–712, 740–742, 751–752
Busche, Herman von, 134, 269, 271–272, 506, 510

Caesarea, 12
Cajetan, 301, 325, 339–357, 358–370, 371–373, 378–380, 398, 463, 481–484, 573
Calvin, John, 218, 452, 529, 664, 683, 691, 730, 746
Cambrai, Peace of (1529), 53, 57–58, 63, 715
Camerarius, 207, 234, 582, 586, 590, 679, 732
Campegio, 719, 721, 723–724, 726–727, 730–732
Canon Law, 8, 19–20, 225, 256, 285, 299, 304–306, 316, 323, 333, 342, 350, 352, 360–361, 369, 374, 382, 390, 409, 414, 416, 443, 467, 482, 486, 490–491, 495, 501, 504, 585
Canossa, 15, 162

Capito, Wolfgang, 357, 423, 427, 486, 523, 538, 582, 638, 697, 699, 700, 712, 737–738
Carlstadt, Bodenstein von, 195, 225, 271, 272, 285, 294–295, 326, 336, 350, 357, 385–389, 391–399, 404, 413, 419, 440, 471, 489, 524, 536–546, 548–550, 560, 580, 582, 604, 615, 617, 634, 667, 684, 690, 695–698, 706
Castle Church (Schlosskirche), Wittenberg, 2, 30, 76, 78, 88, 195, 200–203, 208, 212, 217–220, 223, 235–244, 252, 259–261, 263, 298, 300, 311–321, 346, 445, 481, 522, 538, 543, 548, 584, 603, 714, 751–752
Catacombs, 187–188, 191
Cateau-Cambrésis, Treaty of, 35, 65
Catechism, 101, 444, 597, 616–619, 629, 631, 638–643, 662, 681, 691
Celtis, Conrad, 134, 275, 276
Charitius, M. D. Andreas, 208, 235, 237, 238
Charlemagne, 33, 43, 69, 470, 473, 613
Charles IV (Emperor), 76–77
Charles V (Emperor), 5, 32–66, 85, 203, 213, 216, 281, 307, 345, 379–381, 419, 432, 436, 466, 470, 488, 493–496, 501–507, 509–512, 600, 608, 612, 714–735, 736, 739, 740, 752
Chièvres, 37–39, 44, 47, 494
Chrysostom, 357, 393, 407
Church and State, 5, 446, 473, 563
Churstadt Wittenberg A. D. 1546, 203, 210, 221
Cisio Janus, 112, 681
Clemen, Otto, 101, 466
Clement VI, 304, 350, 351
Clement VII, 24, 27, 53, 55–57, 364, 688
Coburg, 67, 81–83, 327, 571, 595, 599, 647, 651, 674, 720–721, 736
Cochlaeus, Johann, 152, 175–177, 181, 206–208, 506, 508, 567, 690, 694, 731
Coelius, 749–750
Cognac, Alliance of, 53–56
Cologne, 43, 242, 320, 494

Cologne, University of, 298, 370, 384, 419, 423, 427–430, 432, 435, 481, 483–484, 486, 685
Communio sanctorum, 7, 11
Concerning the Abrogation of the Private Mass, 540
Concerning Confession, Whether the Pope has Power to Order It, 522
Concerning Government, to What Extent One is Obligated to Obey It, 5, 473, 563
Concerning the Lord's Supper, a Confession, 699
Concerning Married Life, 581
Concerning the Papacy in Rome, 456
Concerning the Validity of Excommunication, 332
Concordat of Worms, 613
Consistorium (Konsistorium), 219, 223, 617, 618
Constantine, 13, 406, 471
Constantinople, 12–13, 59–63, 403
Copernicus, 136, 612
Corpus iuris canonici, 20, 121, 128, 390, 406, 490
Corunna, 39, 42
Council of Basel, 27, 352
Council of Chalcedon, 12
Council of Constance, 26–27, 78, 318, 410, 419, 506, 511
Council of Constantinople, 12
Council of Florence, 161, 411
Council of Nicea, 12, 387, 403, 422, 471–472
Council of Pisa, 25, 382
Council of Trent, 9, 186, 431, 512, 677, 744
Cranach, Lucas, the Elder, 94, 106, 203–204, 212–213, 216, 235–237, 239–244, 295, 312, 314, 515, 518, 571–572, 582, 586, 589, 595, 645, 670
Cranach, Lucas, the Younger, 203
Croy, Guillaume de (Chièvres), 37–39, 44, 47, 494
Cruciger, 118, 262, 598, 600–601, 610, 649, 658, 700, 737
Cuius regio eius religio, 54, 470, 612, 615, 700
Cyprian, 357, 401–403, 405, 407

De Jongh, H., 428, 430
De servo arbitrio, 638
De viris illustribus, 12
De votis monasticis (On Monastic
  Vows), 141, 146, 148, 525, 540,
  581
Decet Romanum pontificem (Bull of
  Excommunication), 492, 495
Degering, H., 301, 367
Denifle, 131, 145, 152, 153, 155, 177
Denmark, King of, 265, 586, 600–601
Dessau, League of (1525), 57, 615
Deutsche Messe (1526), 633, 638,
  667, 668–669, 674, 675
Deventer, 90–92
Dialogus of 1507, 201, 205, 208, 211,
  213, 219, 220, 237, 242–244, 246,
Dictatus, 14
Die Deutsche Bibel, 301, 365–367,
  529, 651, 655
Dietrich, Veit, 121, 143, 634, 651,
  654, 720
Dilich, Wilhelm, 87–90, 204, 236–
  237
Dionysius of Corinth, 11
Dionysius the Areopagite, 401–402,
  405, 422
Dobeneck, Dr. (Cochlaeus), 152, 175
  –177, 181, 206–208, 506, 508, 567,
  690, 694, 731
Dolzig, Hans von, 592, 719, 721
Don Juan of Spain, 34, 37
Donation of Constantine, 13, 746
Drescher, 123, 127
Dresden, 67, 83, 86–87, 90, 94, 209–
  210, 261
Dresden banquet, 340–341, 399
Dresden Psalter, 283
Dresser, Matthaeus, 175, 178
Duerer, Albrecht, 32, 236, 240, 424,
  557, 571
Dungersheim, Hieronymus, 398, 423,
  439

Ebernburg, 44, 499, 554–555
Eck, John, 9, 84, 152, 193, 333–336,
  378, 380, 384–427, 443, 461, 463,
  474, 477–478, 482–485, 489, 490,
  492, 721–723, 731

Edict of Worms, 2, 43, 45, 54, 493,
  509–512, 536, 552, 604, 612, 614,
  685, 714
Egidio, 179–183
Egranus, John Sylvius, 334, 377, 489
Eigenkirche, 162, 470, 613
Eisenach, 33, 67, 69, 86, 102–103,
  110, 113, 115–116, 122–128, 140,
  143, 497, 510, 513–514, 663, 737
Eisleben, 67, 86, 99, 104–106, 123,
  209, 330, 477, 516, 564, 599, 678,
  748–749, 751
Eleanor of Portugal, 58
Elert, Dr. Werner, 457
Emser, Jerome, 9, 134, 152, 341, 399,
  423, 439, 461, 463, 474, 490, 567,
  690
Erasmus, Desiderus, 7, 9–11, 29, 32,
  44, 89–90, 92–93, 116, 185, 191,
  251, 275, 277–278, 280–281, 285,
  288, 294, 298, 320, 328–329, 390,
  442, 467, 486, 488–489, 493–494,
  529, 550, 558, 571, 578–579, 586,
  635, 682–695, 704
Erbzinsleute, 102
Erfurt, 33, 67–69, 81, 83, 86, 90,
  93–95, 129–131, 184, 192, 200,
  210, 272, 326, 329–330, 420, 496–
  497, 514, 543, 607, 662
Erfurt monastery, 10, 25, 107, 122,
  128, 136–144, 145–155, 169–170,
  181, 193, 289, 416
Erfurt, University of, 20, 107, 121,
  126, 128–136, 147, 166, 169, 172,
  254, 269–270, 280, 361, 385, 390,
  418, 420–421, 425–427, 437, 497
Erzmarschall, 77, 254, 724
Eugubium, 403
Ex cathedra, 15
Excommunication, 18, 332–333, 341,
  444, 485–486, 491–492, 495, 618
Excommunication, Bull of (Decet
  Romanum pontificem), 492, 495
Execrabilis (Bull of Pius II), 369
Exsurge, Domine, 20, 207, 429, 431–
  432, 444, 446, 478, 481–492, 494,
  520
Extreme Unction, 18, 331, 536
Exultate Deo, 161

Faber, Matthaeus, 240, 312
Faithful Exhortation for All Christians to Shun Riot and Rebellion, A, 540
Feilitzsch, Fabian von, 297, 352, 374 –375, 478
Ferdinand of Austria, 37–38, 50, 54, 57, 63, 65–66, 600, 612, 715, 719, 721, 725, 728, 731, 734–735
Ferdinand of Spain, 34, 36–38, 46, 59
Ficker, Dr. Johannes, 134, 141, 176, 209, 270, 714, 724, 729–730
Flacius, 151, 659–660
"Flaeming," 70, 200
Florence, 182, 192
Flugschrift, 6
Formatus, 149, 265, 609
Formula of Concord, 101
Fourth Lateran Council, 17–18, 30, 522
Francis I of France, 34, 40, 42, 49, 51–53, 55–58, 62–63, 381, 424– 426, 715
Frankfurt am Main, 42, 250, 252, 372, 381, 419, 440, 481, 495, 497, 513, 699, 730
Frankfurt an der Oder, 269, 323, 325, 546
Frau Cotta, 127–128
Frauenhaeuser, 130, 218
Frederick Barbarossa, 71–74
Frederick the Wise, 32, 54, 70–71, 82, 194, 201, 212, 217, 224, 226, 235, 238, 240, 242, 244–245, 254, 256, 259–261, 264–267, 269–270, 286, 296, 298, 312, 318–320, 325– 328, 342–346, 357, 358–383, 384, 419–420, 426, 436, 441, 460–461, 466–467, 481–482, 484, 487–488, 513, 538–540, 542–544, 546, 579, 585, 593, 606, 608, 633, 663, 720, Diet of Worms, 44, 493–497, 503– 510, Dream, 318–320, election of Charles V, 41–42, 440, faculty letter, 301–302, 364–367, indulgences, 321, 324
Freedom of the Christian, The, 292, 445, 477–481, 535, 558, 560
Freiberg, 69, 209, 489
Freiburg, University of, 254, 352, 360, 384

Friedensburg, Walter, 251, 258, 270
Froben, John, 278, 357, 360, 427, 430, 688
Froeschel, Sebastian, 398, 408, 642
Frundsberg, 55–56, 502
Fugger Banking House, 6, 40–41, 185, 191, 307–311, 320, 339, 371, 378, 385, 443, 452, 551
Fundationsurkunde fuer die Universitaet, 249, 609

Galatians, Commentary on, 286, 439, 440, 465
Galatians, Luther's Lectures on, 283, 285, 441, 692
Gattinara, 44, 47, 509, 511
Gelnhauser Urkunde, 72
Genesis, Luther's lectures on, 282
George, Duke of Albertine Saxony, 7, 70, 84–85, 152–153, 176–177, 206, 235, 239, 253, 363, 385–386, 388–389, 397–398, 400, 408, 410 –411, 415, 418–419, 423–424, 426–427, 432, 437, 450, 459–461, 472, 489, 507, 512, 540, 567, 582, 584, 606, 614, 616, 619, 686, 688, 690, 715, 721, 746
George of Brandenburg-Ansbach, 700, 717, 724–728
Gerson, Jean, 9, 25, 292, 409, 468
Ghinucci, 338–339, 342
Glapion, 44, 494–495, 499
Glatz, Dr. Kasper, 587
Goede, Henning, 20, 271
Golden Bull of 1356, 40, 76–77, 81
Golden Rose, 41, 346, 361–363, 371, 373, 481
Good Works, Sermon on, 439, 444– 445, 453, 463, 465
Gratian's Decretum, 20, 390
Gratius, Ortwin, 225
Graumann, John (Poliander), 415, 439, 442
Gravamina, 7, 45, 54, 157, 467, 469, 473, 715, 727
Gregorovius, 472
Gregory the Great, 13–14, 157, 162, 391, 405
Gregory VII, 14–16, 24, 162, 471, 613

Gregory IX, 20
Gregory XI, 24
Gregory XII, 26
Gresemund, Dietrich, 134
Grisar, 131, 145, 152, 154, 177
Grohmann, 257, 259, 263
Gruenenberg, John, 225, 272, 277, 315, 478, 634
Grundherrschaft, 556
Guenther, Francis, 295—296, 328, 419, 423, 428
Gutachten, 219, 564, 684
Gutsherrschaft, 556

Halle, University of, 361, 604
Hamlet House, 220
Harnack, 141, 160—161
Hausleiter, 312
Hausmann, Nicholas, 615, 627, 630, 634, 667, 673, 699
Hausrath, 141
Heavenly Prophets (Zwickau Prophets), 225, 449, 538, 542, 604, 615
Hebrews, Luther's lectures on, 283, 285, 441
Hecker, Gerard, 343—344
Heidelberg Meeting, 326—330, 332, 337, 385
Heidelberg, University of, 221, 254, 298, 328, 384
Helena, wife of Albert I, Duke of Saxony, 75—76, 218
Henry of Albertine Saxony, 85, 253, 606, 616, 705, 706
Henry of Brunswick, 746
Henry the Fowler, 70
Henry, Graf von Ascanien, 75
Henry the Lion, 71—75
Henry I of France, 65
Henry IV, 15, 69, 79, 87, 162
Henry VII, 34
Henry VIII, 16, 40—42, 49—54, 265, 571, 686, 688
Hesz, Johann, 607, 627, 630, 671, 678
Hettner, Alfred, 86—87
Heubner, H., 205, 209, 244, 246, 752
Heynig, P. (Schalscheleth), 75, 208—209, 229
Hitzschold von Posa, 399, 422
Hochstraten, Jacob, 175, 423—424, 428—430, 487, 685

Holbein, the Younger, 571, 662
Holborn, 487, 552, 555
Holl, Karl, 1, 102, 142, 289, 340, 454, 457, 459, 692
Holy Eucharist, 17—18, 161, 166, 187, 430, 433, 442, 444, 446, 449—450, 462—463, 474—477, 485, 538, 542, 550, 629, 640, 646, 668—672, 698—711, 736, 738—739, 742
Holy Roman Empire, 32—33, 40
Honius, Christopher, 697—698, 703
Hove, Jodocus van den, 429, 431
Hugo of St. Victor, 157, 161
Huizinga, 275
Humanism, 7, 116, 173, 275, 277, 333, 423, 528, 683
Humanism, Biblical, 116, 252, 270, 275, 277—278, 280, 294—295, 297, 300, 302, 328, 330, 548, 608, 679, 683, 703
Hus, John, 6, 9, 11, 25—26, 78, 200, 318, 400, 407, 408, 410, 504, 509, 581
Hutten, Ulrich von, 5—6, 32, 44, 90, 423, 425, 465—467, 486—489, 494, 498—499, 521, 552—553, 555, 563, 684, 686
Hyma, Albert, 90—92, 452

Indulgences, 5—6, 8, 177—178, 224—225, 297, 300—301, 328—329, 332, 334, 336, 353, 356, 360, 375, 377—378, 382—383, 385, 386, 411—412, 420, 430, 474, 485, 522, 541, Albert of Mainz and, 306—311, Castle Church and, 242—243, 312, churches, 239, history of, 23, 303—306, Luther and, 311—320, 327, 383
Ingolstadt, University of, 254, 333—334, 336, 384, 721
Innocent III, 14—22, 304
Innsbrueck, 183, 192, 719, 720—721
Inquisition, 28
Interdict, 18, 21
Interregnum, 40, 77, 380
Investiture Controversy, 162
Isabella of Spain, 34, 37, 46
Isidore of Seville, 13, 162

Janissaries (Yeni Cheri), 60, 63
Jena, 192, 200, 249, 623
Jena Ausgabe, 101, 635
Jena, University of, 84, 221, 654, 659, 743
Jerome of Prague, 318
Joachim of Brandenburg, 306, 419
Joanna the Mad, 34, 38, 48
John, son of Albert I, 76
John the Constant, 54, 57, 82, 226, 240, 244, 252, 445, 467, 497, 595, 615, 663, 705, 707, 716–736
John Frederick, 82, 84–85, 203, 211– 213, 218, 248–249, 252–253, 255, 261, 265, 267, 599–600, 602, 608– 609, 615, 617, 622–623, 626, 654, 658–670, 720, 728, 739–742, 750– 751
John XXII, 23, 25
John XXIII, 25–26
Jonas, Justus, 5, 99, 101, 137–138, 142, 154, 234, 262, 265, 287, 442, 486, 497, 507, 514, 527, 544, 582, 589, 595, 598, 601, 603, 607, 610, 620, 627, 649, 678, 700–701, 718, 720, 729–730, 733, 741, 748–752
Julius II, 28–29, 180, 182, 186, 190– 191, 217, 381, 485
"Junker Georg," 295, 515, 518, 520, 541, 552, 573
Justification by Faith, 2, 5, 131, 134, 171, 175, 178, 195, 205, 227, 280, 283, 286, 287–289, 291, 293, 352, 451, 454, 459, 485, 525, 545, 578, 608, 617, 665, 687–689, 692, 727, 735, 744

Kalkoff, Paul, 371, 431, 482–483, 512
Katharinen-portal, 228, 233
Kattenbusch, 142, 457, 458
Kawerau, 122, 283, 641, 673
Kemberg, 87, 89, 355, 443, 582, 666, 751
Kessler, 573–576
Khaireddin Barbarossa, 62, 64–65
Knights of the Golden Fleece, 43, 66
Knights of St. John, 62, 501
Knights' Uprising, 550–556, 686, 690, 717
Knoke, 640

Koehler, Walther, 102, 115, 141, 293, 316, 465–466, 635–636, 705, 710,
Koenigsberg, University of, 601
Koestlin, 122, 141
Kolde, 141, 248, 467, 622, 714, 726
Konsistorium (Consistorium), 219, 223, 617–618
Koppe, Leonard, 583, 585, 592
Kresz, Anton, 177, 181–183
Kroker, 584, 586
Krueger, Dr. Gottfried, 209, 217, 236
Krueger, Gustav, 27, 30
Kurkreis, 72, 75–78, 81–82, 84, 87, 89, 95, 207, 254

Lamenit, Anna, 192
Landeskirche (Territorial Church), 457, 459, 468, 570, 615–617, 621, 624, 627, 629, 635, 730, 735, 739, 741, 743–744
Landessteuer, 264
Landstuhl, Castle of, 554–555
Lang, John, 193, 225, 281, 294, 296– 299, 324, 326–327, 329–330, 399, 421, 442, 486, 496, 528, 543, 684
Lang, Paul Henry, 664
Lange, Paul, 293, 300
Langen, Rudolf von, 134, 271
Latomus, 9, 423, 428, 431, 439, 520
Lauenburg line, 76–78
Lauterbach, 150, 467
Lautrec, 56–57
Lectura in Biblia, 149, 194, 201, 245
Lefèvre d'Etaples, 277, 280, 282, 285, 288, 635, 685
Leipzig, 69, 83, 86–87, 90, 93–94, 175, 195, 209–210, 250, 252–253, 272, 295, 309, 322, 327, 373, 378, 380, 388, 391, 399, 407–410, 417, 419, 422, 443, 489, 497, 546, 602, 607, 662
Leipzig Debate, 20, 84, 193, 282, 384–437, 438–440, 454–455, 463, 467, 481, 484, 489, 502, 520, 547, 573, 578
Leipzig Settlement, 79–84
Leipzig, University of, 128, 131, 221, 254, 361, 385–389, 396, 400, 489, 520
Leo the Great, 13–14

Leo X, 6, 29–31, 40, 44, 50, 179–
180, 185, 306–308, 320, 325, 341–
344, 352, 354–355, 362–364, 366,
372–373, 376, 378–383, 425, 427
464, 478, 482–483, 485, 489, 491
*Letter on the Harsh Booklet Against
the Peasants, A,* 568–569
Letters of Obscure Men, 175, 225,
277, 298, 423, 526
Liber Decanorum, 104, 256, 270
Licentiatus, 149, 195, 265
Lindemann, Margarethe, Luther's
grandmother, 103
Link, Wenceslaus, 225–226, 269, 333
–334, 336, 344, 348, 353, 358, 478,
526, 543, 582, 591–592, 647
Loesser, Thomas, 244–246
Lombard, Peter, 149, 157, 161, 172–
173, 176, 192, 281, 285, 296, 609,
689
Lorenzo the Magnificent, 28–29, 182
Lotther, Melchor, 339, 392, 521, 529,
634, 645–646
Louis the Great of Hungary, 60, 63
Louis XII of France, 34, 382, 426
Louvain, University of, 38, 352, 360,
419, 423, 427–432, 435, 481–484,
486, 494, 520, 685
Luder, Heine, Luther's grandfather,
103, 187
Luder, Peter, 134
Lufft, Hans, 217, 634, 647, 654, 656,
658–659, 673–674
Lupinus, 294–295, 440
Luther, Elizabeth, Luther's daughter,
595
Luther, Gross-Hans, Luther's father,
103–110, 115, 122, 126, 128, 138,
146, 148, 592, 599
Luther, Hans, Luther's son, 594–602,
751
Luther, Heinz, Luther's uncle 103,
514
Luther, Jacob, Luther's brother, 104,
752
Luther, Klein-Hans, Luther's uncle,
102–103
Luther, Magdalena, Luther's daughter, 595, 599

Luther, Margarethe, Luther's daughter, 595, 601–602
Luther, Martin, appearance, 573–575,
birth, 104, and Cajetan, 344–354,
childhood, 109, education, 110–
119, 122–136, 147–149, 193–196,
and faculty, 293–302, income, 262
–268, at Marburg, 700–714, sermon
on ban, 332–333, 341, 444, on indulgences and grace, 324, on the
institution of marriage, 581, on the
duty of sending children to school,
126, 607, 677, 678, on the Ten
Commandments, 336, and students,
300, journey to Rome, 149, 173–
192, 196; knowledge of Greek and
Hebrew, 173, 252, 281, 416, 528;
promotion to the Doctorate, 193–
196, 216, 223, 245, 265–266, 269;
translation of New Testament, 122,
228, 278, 281, 422, 441, 527–531,
643–644
Luther, Martin, Luther's son, 595, 601
–602, 749, 751
Luther, Paul, Luther's son, 175, 178,
595, 601–602, 749, 751
Luther, Veit, Luther's uncle, 103
Lutherhaus (Lutherhalle), 140, 195,
203–204, 208–209, 212, 216, 222,
229, 240, 264, 287, 597–598, 662
Lutherstube, 228–229
Lyra, Nicolaus of, 283, 288, 635

Madrid, Treaty of, 52–53, 55, 62–63
Magdeburg, 78, 110, 113, 115, 117–
122, 124, 126, 140, 142, 210–211,
322, 600, 627, 644, 671–672, 678
Magdeburg, University of, 361
Mainz, University of, 254, 322
Mansfeld, 33, 67, 104, 106–117, 140,
749
Manucius, Aldus, 245, 248, 251
Marburg, 696, 704, 706, 713, 717
Marburg Articles, 711, 722
Marburg Castle, 700–701
Marburg Colloquy, 282, 449, 646,
695–714, 717
Marburg, University of, 122
Margaret of Austria, 34, 37, 42, 57

Margarete von der Saale, 584, 745
Marienburg, Castle, 327
Marienthron cloister, 583–585
Marignano, Battle of, 49, 51
Marriage, Sacrament of, 18
Marschalk, Nicolaus, 269, 271–272
Mary of Burgundy, 34, 49
Mathesius, Johann, 100–101, 107, 111, 115, 117, 118, 120, 123, 126–127, 143–144, 170, 175–176, 293, 649, 654, 656
Matrikel (Album of Wittenberg), 3, 115, 205, 232, 255, 603–604
Maximilian I, 7, 33–35, 39–40, 49, 181, 191, 254, 276, 307, 342, 345, 379, 382, 444, 481, 614
Meinhardus, 208, 213, 218, 219–220, 237–238, 242–243
Meissen, 78–83, 87, 89–90, 95, 209–210, 235, 260, 282, 425, 623
Meissinger, Karl, 134, 281, 283
Melanchthon, Philip, 5, 7, 90, 99, 101, 109, 115, 120, 141, 206–207, 213, 217, 248, 250, 253, 275, 348–349, 356, 391, 397–398, 415–416, 421, 437, 442, 445, 459, 466, 473–474, 486, 499, 518, 523–525, 527–528, 538, 540, 543, 564, 571, 577, 582, 586, 600–601, 603–604, 610, 624, 632, 635, 643–660, 680, 690, 718, 736–739, 741, 747–748; Apology, 459, 734–735, 738, 741–744; Augsburg Confession, 720–734; Bible translation, 598, 643–660; income, 262, 265; Loci, 459, 744; Luther's biography, 100, 103–104, 111, 117 118, 123–125, 134, 143, 157, 170–171, 174–179, 293, 573–575; Luther's funeral sermon, 464, 752; Luther's marriage, 589–591; Marburg Colloquy, 700–709; Paris verdict, 435–436; Schmalkald Articles, 742—744; school organization, 3, 112, 119, 564, 607, 677–679; University of Wittenberg, 255, 271, 298–300, 357, 608; Wittenberg Concord, 736–739
Melanchthon School, 217

Melanchthonhaus, 222–223, 233–234, 264
Mellerstadt, Polich von, 194, 208, 212, 251, 264, 269, 271, 293, 314
Mellerstadt, Valentin von, 206
Merian, 87, 89, 90, 204, 232–233, 518
Meritum de condigno, 167–169, 689
Meritum de congruo, 167–170, 173–174, 689
Merriman, Roger B., 47, 55
Michelangelo, 28–29, 184
Miltitz, Charles von, 41, 301, 346, 356, 361–364, 370–384, 387, 398, 460, 477–478, 481–482
Moehra, 102–103, 107, 185, 514, 518
Moritz, Duke of Saxony, 65, 84–85, 203, 257, 261, 600–601, 659
Moryson, Fynes, 89, 93
Mosellanus, 393, 397, 414, 416, 573
Muehlberg, Battle of, 84, 213, 249, 600, 658
Muehlhausen, 209–210
Muenzer, Thomas, 546–548, 560, 562, 564, 567, 580, 615, 617, 690
Mutian, 251, 644
Myconius, Friedrich, 101, 206, 223–224, 309–310, 315, 322, 347, 353, 515, 700
Mylius, 175, 178, 245, 247, 249–250, 252
·Mysticism, 171, 546, 550

Nathin, 148–149, 151, 181, 330
Nazianzen, Gregor of, 401–402, 407–408
Nebe, Herman, 516, 518
Neo-Platonists, 158, 162
Neues Friederici Collegium, 88, 201, 205, 212, 221–222, 230, 232–233
Nicolaus of Lyra, 283, 288, 635
Ninety-five Theses, 2, 30, 300, 311, 313–324, 329, 333–338, 354, 359–360, 365, 387, 416, 428, 430, 445, 481, 603, 684, 714, 752
Nogaret, 21–22
Nominalists, 165–166
Nullbruedern (Brethren of the Common Life), 9, 119, 122, 714

Nuernberg, 44, 54, 89, 95, 106, 110, 116, 129, 180–182, 184, 192, 205, 240, 248–249, 251–253, 256, 269, 271, 329, 333, 336, 344, 347, 354, 372, 420, 478, 547, 560, 587, 614, 616, 662, 667, 677–678, 701, 716, 717, 720, 723, 728, 733

Nuernberg, Diets of, 544, 614

Nuernberg, School, 679, 682

Nuernberg, Truce of, 64, 735

Occam, William, 9, 135–136, 156–157, 166, 168–169, 172, 290, 295, 449, 578

Oecolampadius, John, 421, 423, 636, 646, 667, 683–684, 687, 695, 697 –700, 705–712, 736–737

Oldecop, Johann, 175–178, 293

On Councils and Churches, 8, 744, 746

On Monastic Vows (De Votis Monasticis), 141, 146, 148, 525, 540, 581

Origen of Alexandria, 12, 334, 393

Osiander, Andreas, 636, 700–701, 708 –709, 713

O to the Great, 70, 74, 235

Oxford, University of, 25

Pace, Richard, 37, 685

Padua, University of, 179

Paris, University of, 9, 16, 25, 122, 131, 161, 163, 254, 256, 351–352, 360, 418–421, 423–427, 432–437, 471, 520–521

Pastor, Ludwig, 30, 177, 472

Paul III, 56, 472, 739–740

Paullinus, 123, 127

Pavia, Battle of, 51–52, 62, 502

Peasants' Revolt, 54, 548, 550, 556–570, 583, 593, 615, 646, 690, 697, 717

Penance, 23, 166, 304, 311, 316–318, 327, 350, 352, 386, 411–412, 429, 442, 445–447, 453, 474, 476, 485, 522, 638, 641

Petrus of Ravenna, 269, 270, 272

Petzensteiner, 496, 514

Peutinger, Conrad, 348, 502, 505, 507 –508

Pfeffinger, Degenhard, 327, 364, 368, 371–373, 378

Pflueger, Konrad, 232, 235–236

Pflug, Caesar, 409–410, 417–418

Philip Augustus of France, 16–17

Philip the Fair, 21–22

Philip of Hesse, 57, 505, 510, 554, 584, 616, 700–701, 706–707, 716–717, 724–728, 731, 742, 745

Philip II, 65–66

Piazza Navona, 484, 492

Piccolomini, Aeneas Silvius (Pius II), 27–28, 369, 485, 614

Pierre d'Ailly, 9, 25, 136, 156–157, 168, 295, 449, 467

Pirckheimer, Willibald, 354, 423–424, 478, 489, 684

Pistoris, Simon, 393, 416

Pius II (Piccolomini), 27–28, 369, 485, 614

Plan of Wittenberg in 1623, 201–202, 211

Planitz, Hans von der, 399, 409

Plato, 165, 179

Pleissenburg, 393–394

Poliander (Johann Graumann), 415, 439, 442

Postils, 441, 520, 528, 619, 627, 631–636, 662

Prague, University of, 25, 131, 254, 400

Prierias, Sylvester, 337–340, 381, 418, 424, 463–466, 470, 473–474

Priesthood of Believers, 5, 157, 447, 451, 469–470, 473, 477, 535, 558, 560, 619–621, 728

Processus Inhibitorius, 322, 345, 362, 384, 481

Psalms, Luther's lectures on, 134, 151, 173, 176, 280–283, 285, 290–291, 441–442, 478, 520

Purgatory, 382, 383, 386, 411, 429, 433, 485

Raphael, 28, 184

Ratzeberger, Matthaeus, 100, 123–125, 127, 519

Realists, 166

Reformation, definition, 7–8

Reformation Festival, 229

Reichenbach, Widow, 217, 586, 589

Reichsregiment, 44, 53–54, 510, 512, 552

Reichsvikar, 77, 81, 254, 345
Resolutio Lutheriana super propositione sua decima tertia de potestate papae, 389, 521
Resolutions Concerning the Virtue of Indulgences, 316, 324, 329, 337– 338, 387, 401, 420, 422
Reu, M., 656, 710, 714, 722
Reuchlin, John, 173, 175, 206, 225, 251, 275, 278, 279, 283, 285, 298, 338, 344, 428, 430, 487, 526, 529, 635
Reutlingen, 728, 739
Rhau, George, 393, 413, 415, 637, 673
Rhegium, 403
Rhegius, Urbanus, 579
Rhenanus, Beatus, 328, 542
Rietschel, 102, 457, 458, 622, 624
Roerer, Georg, 104, 121, 142–143, 150, 176, 594, 621, 624, 634–635, 649, 652, 655–660, 700
Roman Curia, 19, 23, 27, 181, 191, 302–308, 316, 323, 325, 331–332, 337–338, 341–342, 346, 348, 355, 362, 371–379, 384–385, 420, 422, 426, 467, 471–472, 484, 494, 504, 520–521, 685
Romans, Luther's lectures on, 134, 140, 151, 176–178, 278, 281, 283– 285, 290, 441, 478, 692
Rome, 12, 180–192, 318, 403, 471
Rome, Sack of, 55–56
Rommel, Herbert, 134–135, 172, 281
Roth, Stephan, 634, 673
Rotolus of 1507, 256, 269–271
Rubeanus, Crotus, 133, 137, 141, 225, 420, 423, 425, 486, 684
Rudolf of Hapsburg, 76–77
Rudolf I of Saxony, 76–78, 235, 238, 240, 242, 259
Rudolf II, 78, 224, 259
Ruehel, Dr. John, 352, 399, 564–565, 583, 592

Sacerdotalism, 160
Sachs, Hans, 32, 560
Sachsenspiegel, 70
Sachsen-Wittenberg line, 76–78
Sacramental system, 17–19

San Benedetto Po, 182
Santa Maria dell'Anima, 188, 190– 191
Santa Maria del Popolo, 182–183, 185–186
Saxony, Albertine, 81–85, 129
Saxony Electoral, 67, 71–85, 87, 199 –200, 266, 584, 623, 658, 677, 751
Saxony, Ernestine, 81–84, 260, 615– 616
Saxony, New, 69–81, 95
Saxony, Old, 69–81
Scala Sancta, 175, 187–188
Schalbe, Henry, 124, 127–128, 143
Schalscheleth (P. Heynig), 75, 208– 209, 229
Schaumburg, silvester von, 467, 486, 488
Scheel, Otto, 1, 102–103, 115, 131, 141, 172, 187, 677
Scheurl, Christopher, 89, 205, 245, 251, 256, 269–272, 372
Schism (Babylonian Captivity), 22, 24, 26–27, 30, 614
Schlosskirche (Castle Church), 2, 30, 76, 78, 88, 195, 200–203, 208, 212, 217–220, 223, 235–244, 252, 259– 261, 263, 298, 300, 311–321, 346, 445, 481, 522, 538, 543, 548, 603, 714, 751–752
Schmalkald Articles, 730, 735, 740– 743
Schmalkaldic League, 57, 616, 735
Schmalkaldic War, 65, 82, 84–85, 203, 212, 216, 234, 600, 658–659, 752
Scholasticism, 8, 116, 135, 164–174, 277–278, 294, 335, 421, 428, 433, 436, 477, 508, 548, 608
Schubert, Hans von, 134, 142, 173, 280, 710, 714
Schulte, Aloys, 191
Schultze, Bishop of Brandenburg, 321, 324, 419, 423
Schurff, Augustin, 298
Schurff, Jerome, 262, 270, 296, 298, 467, 501–502, 507–508, 514, 542, 582, 592, 610
Schwabach Articles (Torgau Articles), 700, 717–719, 721–722

Schwaermer, 546, 633, 642, 684, 698
  −699, 701
Schweinitz Castle, 76−78, 90, 200
Schwenckfeld, Caspar, 155, 636
Scotus, Duns, 157, 166, 168, 172, 295,
  329, 357, 427, 449
Seeberg, Reinhold, 156−157, 166,
  445, 457−458, 692, 701
Selnecker, Nicholas, 101, 576
Senf, Max, 203, 208
Sennert, 216, 238
Sententiarius, 149, 265, 294, 609
September Bibel, 529
Sermon on the Ban, 332−333, 341,
  444
Sermon on Indulgences and Grace,
  324
*Sermon on the Duty of Sending Chil-
  dren to School,* 126, 607, 677−678
*Sermon on the Institution of Mar-
  riage,* 581
Sermons on the Ten Commandments,
  336
Sickingen, Franz von, 41, 44, 90, 466,
  487−489, 494, 499, 506, 510, 546,
  552, 554−556, 563
Sieberger, Wolf, 267, 601
Sievershausen, Battle of, 85, 261
Sigismund, Emperor, 25−26, 78, 81
Sistine Chapel, 28−29, 184
Sixtus IV, 28, 305, 337
Smith, Preserved, 257−258, 691, 747
Sola Scriptura, 9, 122, 135, 156, 158,
  172, 174, 280, 416, 617−618, 632,
  683, 695
Spalatin, George, 20, 41, 82, 230, 236,
  246, 248, 250−253, 255, 266, 294,
  296−300, 321, 324−325, 327, 341,
  345−349, 355−357, 363, 367−368,
  372−374, 391, 412, 415, 440−442,
  444, 460−463, 474, 482, 486−487,
  489−490, 497, 501, 503, 505, 508,
  513, 514, 526, 538, 577, 583, 586,
  588−589, 592, 644−645, 647, 720,
  725, 741−743; *Annalen,* 104, 245,
  488, 499, 741; *Diary,* 245; *Ephemerides,* 245
Spangenberg, 106
Spengler, 423, 489, 607, 616, 678−
  679, 733

Speyer, Diets of, 54, 57, 82, 253, 470,
  612, 615, 700, 714, 716, 719
Spitzer, A., 204−205, 215, 236
Stadtkirche (Town Church), 75, 88,
  154, 200, 203−204, 214−217, 224,
  236, 282, 300, 332, 439, 450, 536,
  538, 541, 592, 594, 622, 624, 627,
  629, 632, 666, 668, 673−674, 679
  −680, 698
Stammhaus, 102
Statutes of 1508, 231
Statutes of 1523, 608
Statutes of 1533, 608−609
Statutes of 1536, 231, 260, 262, 608−
  609
Statutes of 1548, 231, 261
Statutes of 1555, 231, 261−262
Statutes of 1569, 231, 233, 262
Staupitz, John, 121, 138, 148−149,
  170−171, 177−178, 180−181, 183,
  192−194, 205, 223−225, 269−270,
  282, 294, 325−327, 329, 337, 343,
  351, 353−354, 358, 368, 447, 477,
  582−583
Stein, Hermann, 224, 226, 228, 594
Stotternheim, 137−138, 144, 148
Strassburg, 716−717
Strohl, Henri, 1, 102, 131, 142, 151,
  155
St. Francis, 167
St. Jerome, 173, 329, 357, 393, 402,
  405−407, 427, 661
St. Peter's in Rome, 11, 22, 28−29,
  184, 189, 304, 308
St. Thomas Aquinas, 9, 135−136, 157,
  161, 163−164, 166−168, 338−339,
  341, 353, 357, 427, 640
Stueblein (Tower Room), 195, 230,
  287
Sturm, Kaspar (*Reichsherold*), 496,
  501, 509, 513−514
Suaven, Peter, 496, 514, 525
Suleiman the Magnificent, 55, 60, 62
  −65, 715
Sum of Theology, 166
Swabian League, 41, 562
Sylvester, 14, 386, 401

Table Talks (Tischreden), 104, 109,
  119−121, 143, 148, 175, 266, 287
  −288, 347−348, 377, 519, 568, 745

Taubenheim, Hans von, 297, 467
Tauler, 174, 292, 326, 480, 578
Territorial Church (Landeskirche), 457, 459, 468, 570, 615–617, 621, 624, 627, 629, 635, 730, 735, 739, 741, 743–744
Territorialism, 157, 613–614
Tessaradecas consolatoria, 441
Tetzel, John, 6, 138, 177, 185, 224–225, 297, 301, 306, 309–324, 328, 332–333, 337–338, 340, 345, 348, 355–356, 359–360, 372–373, 378 –379, 382, 398, 401, 523
Thulin, Oskar, 209, 643, 662
Thuringia, 30, 67, 69–70, 78–83, 87, 89, 95, 103, 123, 260, 282, 425, 540, 547, 562, 564, 626
Thuringian Basin, 69, 81, 129
Tischreden (Table Talks), 104, 109, 119–121, 143, 148, 175, 266, 287, 288, 347–348, 377, 519, 568, 745
To the Councilors of all German Cities, 110
Torgau, 87, 90, 200, 209–211, 248, 261, 543, 585, 601, 663, 677, 720
Torgau Articles (Schwabach Articles), 700, 717–719, 721–722
Toszen Haus, 85, 221–222, 231
Tower Discovery, 134, 173, 227, 282 –289, 455
Tower Room (Stueblein), 195, 230, 287
Town Church (Stadtkirche), 75, 88, 154, 200, 203–204, 214–217, 224, 236, 282, 300, 332, 439, 450, 536, 538, 541, 592, 594, 622, 624, 627, 629, 632, 666, 668, 673–674, 679–680, 698
Transubstantiation, 9, 17, 166, 449, 475
Trebonius, 124–125
Trivialschule, 111–113, 115–116, 125, 128
Troeltsch, Ernst, 452
Trutvetter, Jodocus, 128, 135–136, 173, 269, 272, 294, 330
Tuebingen, University of, 148, 169, 254, 270, 298, 384
Tuerkensteuer, 62, 264, 267–268
Turmerlebnis (Tower Discovery), 134, 173, 227, 282–289, 455

Uhrig, Kurt, 558
Ulm, 116, 182, 677, 716–717
Ulrich, Duke of Wuerttemberg, 701, 706
Ulscenius, Felix, 577
Unigenitus, 350, 356
University of Wittenberg in 1586, The, 221–222
Urkundenbuch, 227, 247, 258, 265, 297, 300
Usingen, Bartholomaeus von, 135, 151, 328, 330, 543, 731
Usury, 308, 443, 446, 451, 568

Valla, Lorenzo, 14, 277, 464, 467
Vehus, Chancellor of Baden, 507–508
Venice, 250–251, 253, 471
Vergerio, 622, 740, 744
Via Antiqua, 135, 166, 268–269, 271 272, 294–295, 300, 349
Via Moderna, 135, 156, 166, 171, 269, 294, 300, 328, 330
Vienna, 443, 677, 715, 731
Vienna, Siege of, 63–64
Vienna, University of, 131, 721
Vischer, Hans, 240
Vischer, Hermann, the Elder, 216, 595
Vischer, Peter, the Younger, 240
Volta, Gabriel della (Venetus), 325–326, 329, 343

Walch, 123, 482, 635
Walther, Johann, 663–676
Warning Toward Peace Based on the Twelve Articles of the Peasants in Swabia, 562, 564
Wartburg, 45, 67, 69, 79, 82–83, 103, 123–124, 141, 225, 278, 281, 295, 435, 441–442, 462, 499, 512–531, 535, 552, 573–574, 579, 588, 615, 634, 643, 672, 695
Weckruf of 1524, 113, 606, 677–678
Weimar, 69, 84, 90, 203, 213, 249, 347, 381, 497, 547, 549, 564, 720
Weimar Ausgabe 140, 172, 283, 301, 442, 673–674, 705
Wenceslaus, 217, 259
Wends, 70, 199–200
Wernle, Paul, 278
Wettin, House of, 78–85, 200

Wider Hans Worst (Against Jack Sausage), 322, 746
Wieck, Johann von der, 175, 188, 466
William, Prince of Anhalt, 118, 142
Wimpina (Dr. Konrad Koch), 269, 271, 297, 323–324, 731
Wittenberg, 67, 72, 75, 77–78, 81, 83, 86–95, 130, 140, 171, 196, 199 –220, 286, 293, 295, 311, 331– 332, 514, 571, 601, 617, 629, 667, 671, 714, 748, 750–751
Wittenberg Capitulation, 249, 600, 752
Wittenberg Concord, 695, 711, 736– 739
Wittenberg Latin School, 679–681
Wittenberg, University of, 87, 99, 110, 116, 122, 133, 135, 149, 151, 177, 254–272, 323, 328, 329, 333, 335, 357, 364, 414, 436, 520, 570, 601, 603–612, 622, 631, 654, 659, 677 –679, 695, 711, 743, 751; and August, 85, 257, 261; and John Frederick, 84, 255, 608–612, 622, 659; and Luther, 158, 176, 192, 194–195, 201, 282–302; enrollment 3, 110, 25, 603–607, 677, 682; faculty and Luther, 2, 293– 302; finances, 78, 235, 257–262; founding, 82, 194, 201, 224, 249– 250, 254; library, 223, 244–253
Wittenberger Ordiniertenbuch, 622
Wittenbergische Ausgabe, 100–101, 635
Wolfenbuettel Handschrift, 154

Wolsey, Cardinal, 34, 41–42, 50, 52, 427, 688
Worms, 6, 45, 62, 67, 86, 103, 219, 295, 372, 432, 434, 442, 484, 495 –501, 521, 541, 576, 633, 635, 672, 674, 685, 714; Diet of, 6, 7, 33, 36, 42, 43, 44–45, 49–50, 53–54, 66, 84, 110, 225, 252, 254–255, 281, 438, 482, 493–513, 515, 535, 552; Edict of, 2, 43, 45, 54, 493, 509– 512, 536, 552, 604, 612, 614, 685, 714
Wuerzburg, 327, 329, 639
Wyclif, John, 9, 24–25, 306, 407

Ximenes, Cardinal of Spain, 36, 38, 47, 278

Yeni Cheri (Janissaries), 60, 63

Ziegler, Margarethe, Luther's mother, 103–110, 122, 592, 599
Zink, Johannes, 185, 307
Zulsdorf farm, 264, 267–268, 583, 593
Zurich, 667, 686, 697
Zwickau, 69, 94, 334, 377, 538, 543, 547, 615, 617, 627, 634, 667
Zwickau Prophets (Heavenly Prophets), 225, 449, 538, 542, 604, 615
Zwilling, Gabriel, 526, 536, 542–543, 585
Zwingli, Ulrich, 50, 57, 218, 449, 529, 550, 555, 629, 636, 646, 667, 683, 686, 687, 695–714, 731, 736, 737 746